R00788 19821

THE CHICAGO PUBLIC LIBRARY

BUSINESS/SCIENCE/TECHNOLOGY
DIVISION

FORM 19

REPAIR MANUAL

JEEP WAGONEER COMANCHE/CHEROKEE 1984-89

All U.S. and Canadian models of JEEP WAGONEER • JEEP COMANCHE • JEEP CHEROKEE

President GARY R. INGERSOLL
Senior Vice President, Book Publishing and Research RONALD A. HOXTER
Vice President and General Manager JOHN P. KUSHNERICK
Editor-in-Chief KERRY A. FREEMAN, S.A.E.
Managing Editor DEAN F. MORGANTINI, S.A.E.
Senior Editor RICHARD J. RIVELE, S.A.E.
Senior Editor W. CALVIN SETTLE, JR., S.A.E.
Editor RICHARD J. RIVELE, S.A.E.

CHILTON BOOK COMPANY
Radnor, Pennsylvania
19089

CONTENTS

1 GENERAL INFORMATION and MAINTENANCE

- **1** How to use this book
- **2** Tools and Equipment
- **10** Routine Maintenance

TL
215
.W25
C45
1989

2 ENGINE PERFORMANCE and TUNE-UP

- **60** Tune-Up Procedures
- **60** Tune-Up Specifications

3 ENGINE and ENGINE OVERHAUL

- **79** Engine Specificaitons
- **81** Engine Electrical System
- **95** Engine Service
- **96** Engine Troubleshooting

4 EMISSION CONTROLS

- **164** Emission Controls System and Service

5 FUEL SYSTEM

- **181** Fuel System Service

6 CHASSIS ELECTRICAL

- **241** Heating and Air Conditioning
- **245** Accessory Service
- **247** Instruments and Switches
- **250** Lights, Fuses and Flashers
- **252** Trailer Wiring

7 DRIVE TRAIN

258 Manual Transmission
300 Clutch
304 Automatic Transmission
362 Driveline
367 Rear Axle

8 SUSPENSION and STEERING

377 Front Suspension
380 Rear Suspension
384 Steering

9 BRAKES

403 Specifications
410 Front Disc Brakes
417 Rear Drum Brakes

10 BODY

435 Exterior
447 Interior

11 MECHANIC'S DATA

452 Mechanic's Data
454 Glossary
460 Abbreviations
462 Index

216 Chilton's Fuel Economy and Tune-Up Tips

440 Chilton's Body Repair Tips

SAFETY NOTICE
Proper service and repair procedures are vital to the safe, reliable operation of all motor vehicles, as well as the personal safety of those performing repairs. This book outlines procedures for servicing and repairing vehicles using safe, effective methods. The procedures contain many NOTES, CAUTIONS and WARNINGS which should be followed along with standard safety procedures to eliminate the possibility of personal injury or improper service which could damage the vehicle or compromise its safety.

It is important to note that repair procedures and techniques, tools and parts for servicing motor vehicles, as well as the skill and experience of the individual performing the work vary widely. It is not possible to anticipate all of the conceivable ways or conditions under which vehicles may be serviced, or to provide cautions as to all of the possible hazards that may result. Standard and accepted safety precautions and equipment should be used during cutting, grinding, chiseling, prying, or any other process that can cause material removal or projectiles.

Some procedures require the use of tools specially designed for a specific purpose. Before substituting another tool or procedure, you must be completely satisfied that neither your personal safety, nor the performance of the vehicle will be endangered.

Although the information in this guide is based on industry sources and is as complete as possible at the time of publication, the possibility exists that the manufacturer made later changes which could not be included here. While striving for total accuracy, Chilton Book Company cannot assume responsibility for any errors, changes, or omissions that may occur in the compilation of this data.

PART NUMBERS
Part numbers listed in this reference are not recommendations by Chilton for any product by brand name. They are references that can be used with interchange manuals and aftermarket supplier catalogs to locate each brand supplier's discrete part number.

SPECIAL TOOLS
Special tools are recommended by the vehicle manufacturer to perform their specific job. Use has been kept to a minimum, but where absolutely necessary, they are referred to in the text by the part number of the tool manufacturer. These tools can be purchased, under the appropriate part number, from your Jeep dealer or regional distributor or an equivalent tool can be purchased locally from a tool supplier or parts outlet. Before substituting any tool for the one recommended, read the SAFETY NOTICE at the top of this page.

ACKNOWLEDGMENTS
Chilton Book Company expresses appreciation to the Jeep/Eagle Division of Chrysler Corporation for their generous assistance.

Copyright © 1989 by Chilton Book Company
All Rights Reserved
Published in Radnor, Pennsylvania 19089, by Chilton Book Company

Manufactured in the United States of America
234567890   876543210

Chilton's Repair Manual: Jeep Wagoneer/Comanche/Cherokee 1984–89
ISBN 0-8019-7939-0 pbk.
Library of Congress Catalog Card No. 88-43183

General Information and Maintenance

HOW TO USE THIS BOOK

This book covers all Wagoneer, Cherokee, and Comanche models from 1984 through 1989.

The first two chapters will be the most used, since they contain maintenance and tune-up information and procedures. Studies have shown that a properly tuned and maintained truck can get at least 10% better gas mileage (which translates into lower operating costs) and periodic maintenance will catch minor problems before they turn into major repair bills. The other chapters deal with the more complex systems of your truck. Operating systems from engine through brakes are covered to the extent that the average do-it-yourselfer becomes mechanically involved. This book will not explain such things as rebuilding the differential for the simple reason that the expertise required and the investment in special tools make this task impractical and uneconomical. It will give you the detailed instructions to help you change your own brake pads and shoes, tune-up the engine, replace spark plugs and filters, and do many more jobs that will save you money, give you personal satisfaction and help you avoid expensive problems.

A secondary purpose of this book is a reference guide for owners who want to understand their truck and/or their mechanics better. In this case, no tools at all are required. Knowing just what a particular repair job requires in parts and labor time will allow you to evaluate whether or not you're getting a fair price quote and help decipher itemized bills from a repair shop.

Before attempting any repairs or service on your truck, read through the entire procedure outlined in the appropriate chapter. This will give you the overall view of what tools and supplies will be required. There is nothing more frustrating than having to walk to the bus stop on Monday morning because you were short one gasket on Sunday afternoon. So read ahead and plan ahead. Each operation should be approached logically and all procedures thoroughly understood before attempting any work. Some special tools that may be required can often be rented from local automotive jobbers or places specializing in renting tools and equipment. Check the yellow pages of your phone book.

All chapters contain adjustments, maintenance, removal and installation procedures, and overhaul procedures. When overhaul is not considered practical, we tell you how to remove the failed part and then how to install the new or rebuilt replacement. In this way, you at least save the labor costs. Backyard overhaul of some components (such as the alternator or water pump) is just not practical, but the removal and installation procedure is often simple and well within the capabilities of the average truck owner.

Two basic mechanic's rules should be mentioned here. First, whenever the LEFT side of the truck or engine is referred to, it is meant to specify the DRIVER'S side of the truck. Conversely, the RIGHT side of the truck means the PASSENGER'S side. Second, all screws and bolts are removed by turning counterclockwise, and tightened by turning clockwise, unless otherwise noted.

Safety is always the most important rule. Constantly be aware of the dangers involved in working on or around an automobile and take proper precautions to avoid the risk of personal injury or damage to the vehicle. See the section in this chapter, Servicing Your Vehicle Safely, and the SAFETY NOTICE on the acknowledgment page before attempting any service procedures and pay attention to the instructions provided. There are 3 common mistakes in mechanical work:

1. Incorrect order of assembly, disassembly

or adjustment. When taking something apart or putting it together, doing things in the wrong order usually just costs you extra time; however it CAN break something. Read the entire procedure before beginning disassembly. Do everything in the order in which the instructions say you should do it, even if you can't immediately see a reason for it. When you're taking apart something that is very intricate (for example, a carburetor), you might want to draw a picture of how it looks when assembled at one point in order to make sure you get everything back in its proper position. We will supply exploded views whenever possible, but sometimes the job requires more attention to detail than an illustration provides. When making adjustments (especially tune-up adjustments), do them in order. One adjustment often affects another and you cannot expect satisfactory results unless each adjustment is made only when it cannot be changed by any other.

2. Overtorquing (or undertorquing) nuts and bolts. While it is more common for overtorquing to cause damage, undertorquing can cause a fastener to vibrate loose and cause serious damage, especially when dealing with aluminum parts. Pay attention to torque specifications and utilize a torque wrench in assembly. If a torque figure is not available remember that, if you are using the right tool to do the job, you will probably not have to strain yourself to get a fastener tight enough. The pitch of most threads is so slight that the tension you put on the wrench will be multiplied many times in actual force on what you are tightening. A good example of how critical torque is can be seen in the case of spark plug installation, especially where you are putting the plug into an aluminum cylinder head. Too little torque can fail to crush the gasket, causing leakage of combustion gases and consequent overheating of the plug and engine parts. Too much torque can damage the threads or distort the plug, which changes the spark gap at the electrode. Since more and more manufacturers are using aluminum in their engine and chassis parts to save weight, a torque wrench should be in any serious do-it-yourselfer's tool box.

There are many commercial chemical products available for ensuring that fasteners won't come loose, even if they are not torqued just right (a very common brand is Loctite®). If you're worried about getting something together tight enough to hold, but loose enough to avoid mechanical damage during assembly, one of these products might offer substantial insurance. Read the label on the package and make sure the product is compatible with the materials, fluids, etc. involved before choosing one.

3. Crossthreading. This occurs when a part such as a bolt is screwed into a nut or casting at the wrong angle and forced, causing the threads to become damaged. Crossthreading is more likely to occur if access is difficult. It helps to clean and lubricate fasteners, and to start threading with the part to be installed going straight in, using your fingers. If you encounter resistance, unscrew the part and start over again at a different angle until it can be inserted and turned several times without much effort. Keep in mind that many parts, especially spark plugs, use tapered threads so that gentle turning will automatically bring the part you're threading to the proper angle if you don't force it or resist a change in angle. Don't put a wrench on the part until it's been turned in a couple of times by hand. If you suddenly encounter resistance and the part has not seated fully, don't force it. Pull it back out and make sure it's clean and threading properly.

Always take your time and be patient; once you have some experience, working on your truck will become an enjoyable hobby.

TOOLS AND EQUIPMENT

Naturally, without the proper tools and equipment it is impossible to properly service your vehicle. It would be impossible to catalog each tool that you would need to perform each or every operation in this book. It would also be unwise for the amateur to rush out and buy an expensive set of tools an the theory that he may need one or more of them at sometime.

The best approach is to proceed slowly, gathering together a good quality set of those tools that are used most frequently. Don't be misled by the low cost of bargain tools. It is far better to spend a little more for better quality. Forged wrenches, 10 or 12 point sockets and fine tooth ratchets are by far preferable to their less expensive counterparts. As any good mechanic can tell you, there are few worse experiences than trying to work on a truck with bad tools. Your monetary savings will be far outweighed by frustration and mangled knuckles.

Certain tools, plus a basic ability to handle tools, are required to get started. A basic mechanics tool set, a torque wrench, and, for 1976 and later models, a Torx bits set. Torx bits are hexlobular drivers which fit both inside and outside on special Torx head fasteners used in various places on Jeep vehicles.

A special wheel bearing nut socket would be helpful when removing the front wheel bearings on 4x4 models.

Begin accumulating those tools that are used most frequently; those associated with routine maintenance and tune-up.

GENERAL INFORMATION AND MAINTENANCE 3

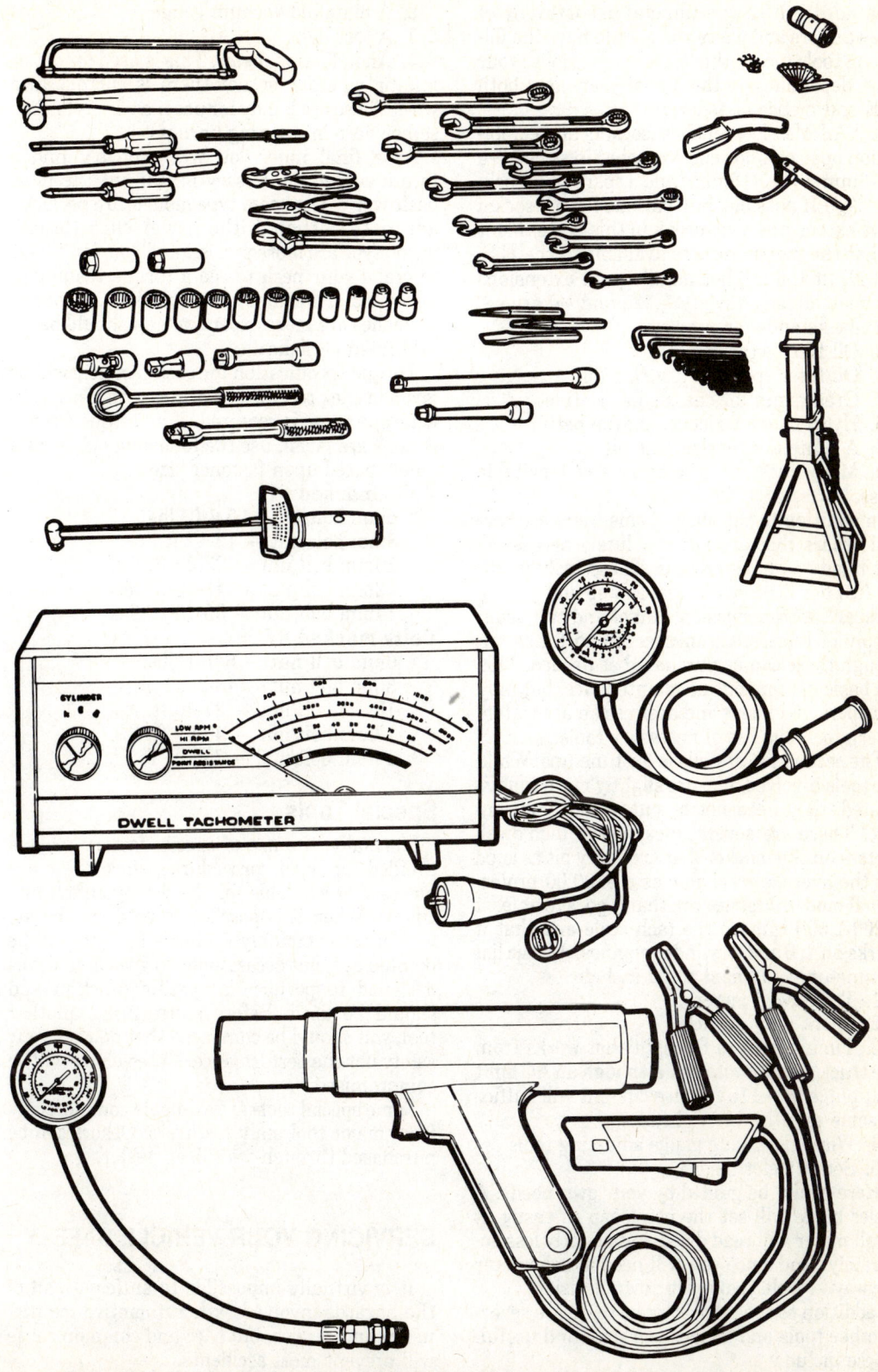

You need only a basic assortment of hand tools for most maintenance and repair jobs

GENERAL INFORMATION AND MAINTENANCE

In addition to the normal assortment of screwdrivers and pliers you should have the following tools for routine maintenance jobs (your Jeep, depending on the model year, uses both SAE and metric fasteners):

1. SAE/Metric wrenches, sockets and combination open end/box end wrenches in sizes from ⅛" (3mm) to ¾" (19mm); and a spark plug socket ($^{13}/_{16}$") If possible, buy various length socket drive extensions. One break in this department is that the metric sockets available in the U.S. will all fit the ratchet handles and extensions you may already have (¼", ⅜", and ½" drive).
2. Jackstands for support
3. Oil filter wrench
4. Oil filter spout for pouring oil
5. Grease gun for chassis lubrication
6. Hydrometer for checking the battery
7. A container for draining oil
8. Many rags for wiping up the inevitable mess.

In addition to the above items there are several others that are not absolutely necessary, but handy to have around. These include oil-dry (cat box litter works just as well and may be cheaper), a transmission funnel and the usual supply of lubricants, antifreeze and fluids, although these can be purchased as needed. This is a basic list for routine maintenance, but only your personal needs and desires can accurately determine your list of necessary tools.

The second list of tools is for tune-ups. While the tools involved here are slightly more sophisticated, they need not be outrageously expensive. There are several inexpensive tach/dwell meters on the market that are every bit as good for the average mechanic as a $100.00 professional model. Just be sure that it goes to at least 1,200-1,500 rpm on the tach scale and that it works on 4, 6 and 8 cylinder engines. A basic list of tune-up equipment could include:

1. Tach-dwell meter
2. Spark plug wrench
3. Timing light (a DC light that works from the truck's battery is best, although an AC light that plugs into 110V house current will suffice at some sacrifice in brightness)
4. Wire spark plug gauge/adjusting tools
5. Set of feeler blades.

Here again, be guided by your own needs. A feeler blade will set the point gap as easily as dwell meter will read dwell, but slightly less accurately. And since you will need a tachometer anyway ... well, make your own decision.
In addition to these basic tools, there are several other tools and gauges you may find useful. These include:

1. A compression gauge. The screw-in type is slower to use, but eliminates the possibility of a faulty reading due to escaping pressure

2. A manifold vacuum gauge
3. A test light
4. An induction meter. This is used for determining whether or not there is current in a wire. These are handy for use if a wire is broken somewhere in a wiring harness.

As a final note, you will probably find a torque wrench necessary for all but the most basic work. The beam type models are perfectly adequate, although the newer click (breakaway) type are more precise, and you don't have to crane your neck to see a torque reading in awkward situations. The breakaway torque wrenches are more expensive and should be recalibrated periodically.

Torque specification for each fastener will be given in the procedure in any case that a specific torque value is required. If no torque specifications are given, use the following values as a guide, based upon fastener size:

Bolts marked 6T
6mm bolt/nut — 5-7 ft. lbs.
8mm bolt/nut — 12-17 ft. lbs.
10mm bolt/nut — 23-34 ft. lbs.
12mm bolt/nut — 41-59 ft. lbs.
14mm bolt/nut — 56-76 ft. lbs.

Bolts marked 8T
6mm bolt/nut — 6-9 ft. lbs.
8mm bolt/nut — 13-20 ft. lbs.
10mm bolt/nut — 27-40 ft. lbs.
12mm bolt/nut — 46-69 ft. lbs.
14mm bolt/nut — 75-101 ft. lbs.

Special Tools

Normally, the use of special factory tools is avoided for repair procedures, since these are not readily available for the do-it-yourself mechanic. When it is possible to perform the job with more commonly available tools, it will be pointed out, but occasionally, a special tool was designed to perform a specific function and should be used. Before substituting another tool, you should be convinced that neither your safety nor the performance of the vehicle will be compromised.

Some special tools are available commercially from major tool manufacturers. Others can be purchased through your Jeep dealer.

SERVICING YOUR VEHICLE SAFELY

It is virtually impossible to anticipate all of the hazards involved with automotive maintenance and service, but care and common sense will prevent most accidents.

The rules of safety for mechanics range from "don't smoke around gasoline," to "use the proper tool for the job." The trick to avoiding injuries is to develop safe work habits and take every possible precaution.

Dos

• Do keep a fire extinguisher and first aid kit within easy reach.

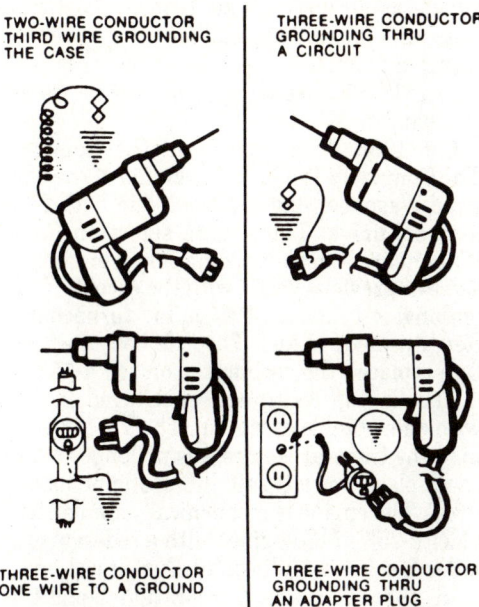

When using electric tools make sure they are properly grounded

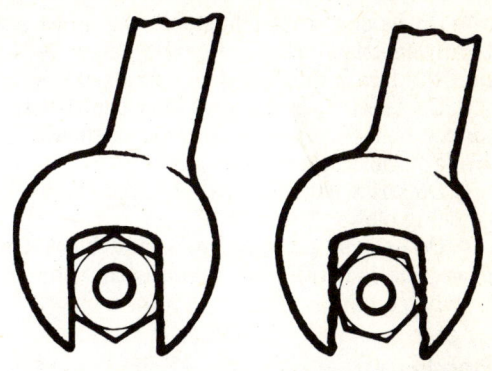

If you're using an open end wrench, use the correct size, and position it properly on the nut or bolt

• Do wear safety glasses or goggles when cutting, drilling or prying, even if you have 20-20 vision. If you wear glasses for the sake of vision, they should be made of hardened glass that can also serve as safety glasses, or wear safety goggles over your regular glasses.

• Do shield your eyes whenever you work around the battery. Batteries contain sulphuric acid; in case of contact with the eyes or skin, flush the area with water or a mixture of water and baking soda and get medical attention immediately.

• Do use safety stands for any undertruck service. Jacks are for raising vehicles; safety stands are for making sure the vehicle stays raised until you want it to come down. Whenever the vehicle is raised, block the wheels remaining on the ground and set the parking brake.

• Do use adequate ventilation when working with any chemicals. Like carbon monoxide, the asbestos dust resulting from brake lining wear can be poisonous in sufficient quantities.

• Do disconnect the negative battery cable when working on the electrical system. The primary ignition system can contain up to 40,000 volts.

• Do follow manufacturer's directions whenever working with potentially hazardous materials. Both brake fluid and antifreeze are poisonous if taken internally.

• Do properly maintain your tools. Loose hammerheads, mushroomed punches and chisels, frayed or poorly grounded electrical cords, excessively worn screwdrivers, spread wrenches (open end), cracked sockets, slipping ratchets, or faulty droplight sockets can cause accidents.

• Do use the proper size and type of tool for the job being done.

• Do when possible, pull on a wrench handle rather than push on it, and adjust your stance to prevent a fall.

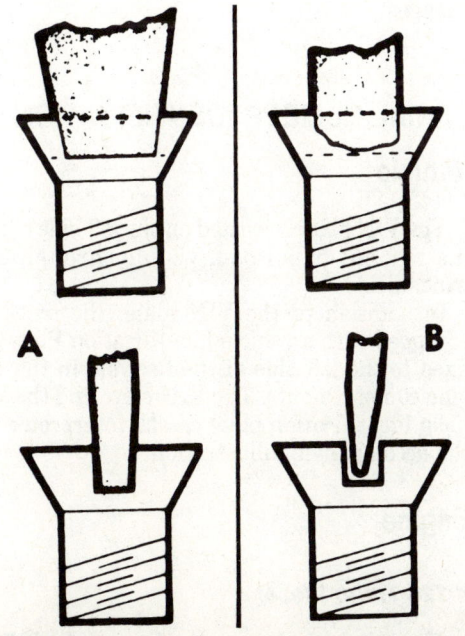

Keep screwdriver tips in good shape. They should fit the slot as shown in "A". If they look like those in "B", they need grinding or replacing

6 GENERAL INFORMATION AND MAINTENANCE

- Do be sure that adjustable wrenches are tightly adjusted on the nut or bolt and pulled so that the face is on the side of the fixed jaw.
- Do select a wrench or socket that fits the nut or bolt. The wrench or socket should sit straight, not cocked.
- Do strike squarely with a hammer – avoid glancing blows.
- Do set the parking brake and block the drive wheels if the work requires that the engine be running.

Don'ts

- Don't run an engine in a garage or anywhere else without proper ventilation – EVER! Carbon monoxide is poisonous; it takes a long time to leave the human body and you can build up a deadly supply of it in your system by simply breathing in a little every day. You may not realize you are slowly poisoning yourself. Always use power vents, windows, fans or open the garage doors.
- Don't work around moving parts while wearing a necktie or other loose clothing. Short sleeves are much safer than long, loose sleeves and hard-toed shoes with neoprene soles protect your toes and give a better grip on slippery surfaces. Jewelry such as watches, fancy belt buckles, beads or body adornment of any kind is not safe working around a truck. Long hair should be hidden under a hat or cap.
- Don't use pockets for toolboxes. A fall or bump can drive a screwdriver deep into you body. Even a wiping cloth hanging from the back pocket can wrap around a spinning shaft or fan.
- Don't smoke when working around gasoline, cleaning solvent or other flammable material.
- Don't smoke when working around the battery. When the battery is being charged, it gives off explosive hydrogen gas.
- Don't use gasoline to wash your hands; there are excellent soaps available. Gasoline may contain lead, and lead can enter the body through a cut, accumulating in the body until you are very ill. Gasoline also removes all the natural oils from the skin so that bone dry hands will suck up oil and grease.
- Don't service the air conditioning system unless you are equipped with the necessary tools and training. The refrigerant, R-12, is extremely cold and when exposed to the air, will instantly freeze any surface it comes in contact with, including your eyes. Although the refrigerant is normally non-toxic, R-12 becomes a deadly poisonous gas in the presence of an open flame. One good whiff of the vapors from burning refrigerant can be fatal.

HISTORY AND MODEL IDENTIFICATION

In 1984 a new, redesigned, downsized version of the Wagoneer/Cherokee line was introduced. These smaller, fuel efficient models incorporated features such as a standard 4-cylinder, 150 cu.in. engine, with a V6-173 cu.in. engine as an option, new transfer case/transmission combinations, and for the first time, integrated frames.

For 1985, the Jeep line-up remained unchanged.

For 1986, Jeep introduced the Comanche. The Comanche is a pick-up version of the downsized Wagoneer and is available in both 2- and 4-wheel drive. The engine selection for the Wagoneer/Cherokee/Comanche remains the same as previous years, with the exception of an optional 4-cylinder, 126 cu.in. turbocharged, Renault-made Diesel. Throttle body fuel injection replaced the carburetor on the 4-150.

The line-up continued unchanged in 1987, with one, notable exception. The V6-173 engine made by General Motors was no longer offered. In its place was a 6-243, inline engine made by AMC. The engine is mechanically similar to the older 6-258 AMC engines with a redesigned cylinder head and Multi-point Fuel Injection.

In 1988 Chrysler Corporation bought the Jeep division from AMC. The model line-up remained unchanged but the diesel engine was discontinued.

For 1989 there were no significant model changes.

SERIAL NUMBER IDENTIFICATION

Vehicle

The VIN plate is located on the left side of the instrument panel pad, visible through the windshield.

In addition to the VIN plate, the truck is equipped with a vehicle Identification Plate affixed to the left side of the firewall, in the engine compartments. The VIN plate and the Vehicle Identification plate can be interpreted by the accompanying illustration.

Engine

4-126 Turbo Diesel

The serial number for the Renault built Diesel is found on a machined pad located at the front of the block.

GENERAL INFORMATION AND MAINTENANCE

4-150

The engine serial number for the American Motors built 4-150 is located on a machined pad at the rear right side of the block, just below the head.

Also on the block, just above the oil filter, is the oversized/undersized component code. The codes are explained as follows:

B: cylinder bores 0.010″ over
C: camshaft bearing bores 0.010″ over
M: main bearing journals 0.010″ under
P: connecting rod journals 0.010″ under

6-173

The engine serial number for the Chevrolet built V6-173 is located on an upward facing,

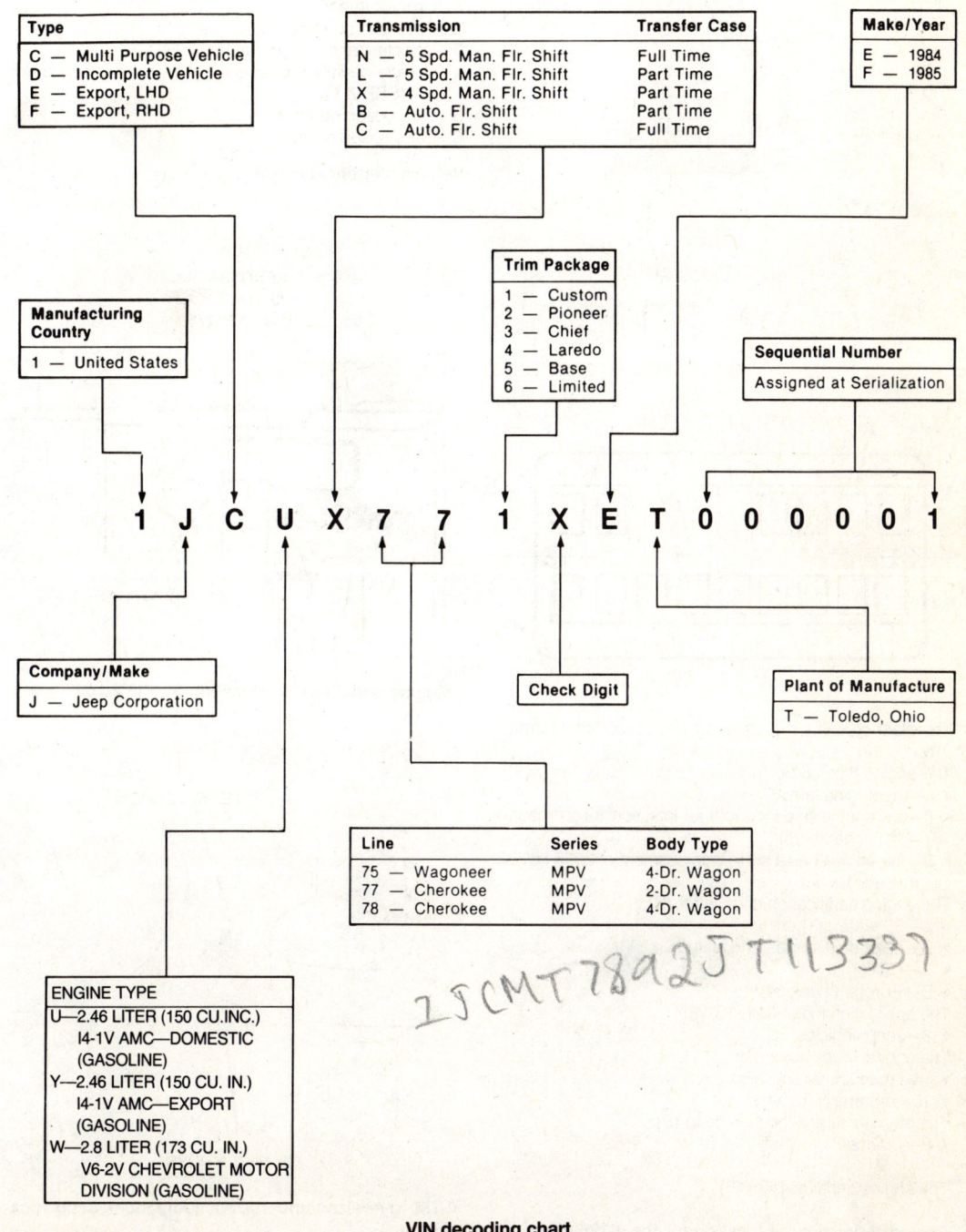

VIN decoding chart

8 GENERAL INFORMATION AND MAINTENANCE

machined surface on the right side of the block, just below the head and above the water pump.

6-243

The engine code is, of course, found in the identification plate on the firewall. The second

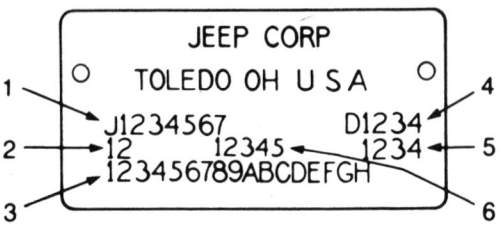

A metal identification plate is riveted to the driver side of the dash panel in the engine compartment.
1. Order number
2. Paint gun number
3. Vehicle identification number (VIN)
4. Vehicle deviation or special sales request and order (SSR & O)
5. Trim option number
6. Paint option number

Vehicle identification plate

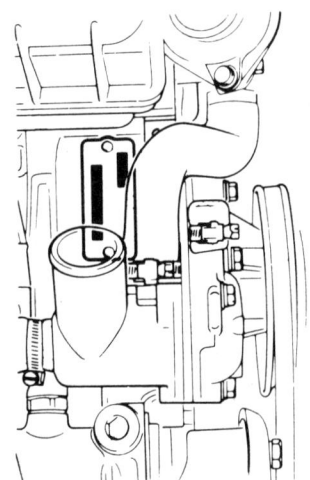

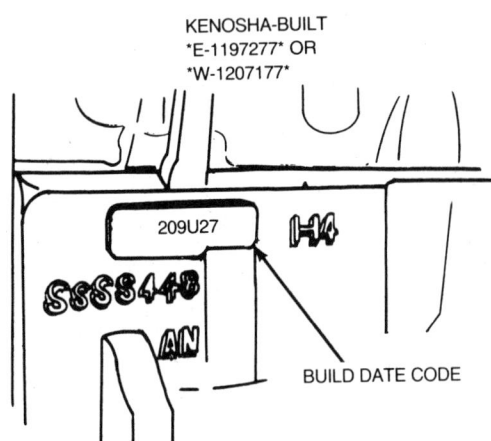

Engine serial number location for the 4-150

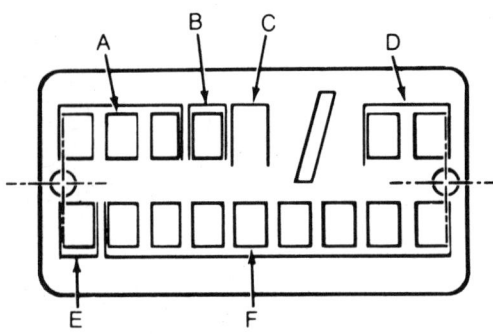

The plate contains the following engine coded information.
The engine type code (A):
- J—the engine family
- 8—the engine has indirect fuel injection (precombustion chambers)
- S—the engine has a cubic displacement of 2068 cc/2.1 liters/126 in^3

The engine certification code letter (B):
- A—50-state
- B—49-state, Canada and altitude
- C—California
- D—Europe (if unique)

The application index code (C):
- 8—Jeep vehicles

The engine index code (D):
- 14—manual transmission
- 15—automatic transmission

The manufacturer's location code (E):
- F—France

The engine serial number (F).

Engine serial number location for the 4-126 diesel

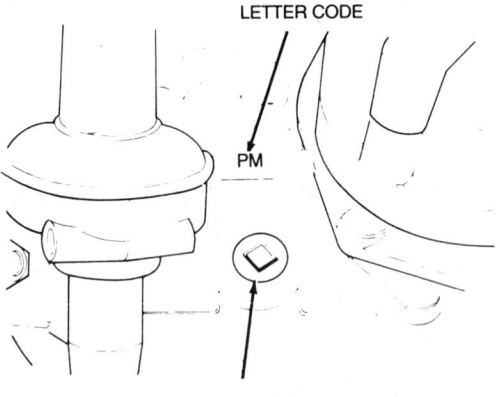

4-150 oversized/undersized component code location

GENERAL INFORMATION AND MAINTENANCE

Engine Identification Chart

No. of Cylinders and Cu. In. Displacement	Actual Displacement			Fuel System	Engine Type	Built by	Years
	Cu. In.	cc	Liters				
4-126	126.09	2066.36	2.1	Diesel	OHC	Renault	1986–87
4-150	150.46	2465.67	2.5	1-bbl	OHV	AMC	1984–85
				TBI	OHV	AMC/Chrysler	1986–89
6-173	172.60	2828.45	2.8	2-bbl	OHV	Chevrolet	1984–86
6-243	243.35	3987.89	4.0	MFI	OHV	Chrysler	1987–89

TBI: Throttle Body Fuel Injection
MFI: Multi-point Fuel Injection
OHV: Overhead Valve
OHC: Overhead Camshaft

location is on a machined surface of the block between number 2 and 3 spark plugs. For further identification, the displacement is cast into the side of the block. The letter in the code identifies the engine by displacement (cu in.), carburetor type and compression ratio.

All of the engines have the undersize/oversize letter codes, located on the boss directly above the oil filter. The parts size code is as follows:

Letter B indicates 0.010" oversized cylinder bore.

Letter M indicates 0.010" undersized main bearings.

Letter P indicates 0.010" undersized connecting rod bearings.

Letter C indicates 0.010" oversized camshaft block bores.

Transfer Case

The New Process transfer cases have a build date tag attached to the front of the case.

Manual Transmissions

The transmission identification number is located on a tag secured by 2 bolts to the case.

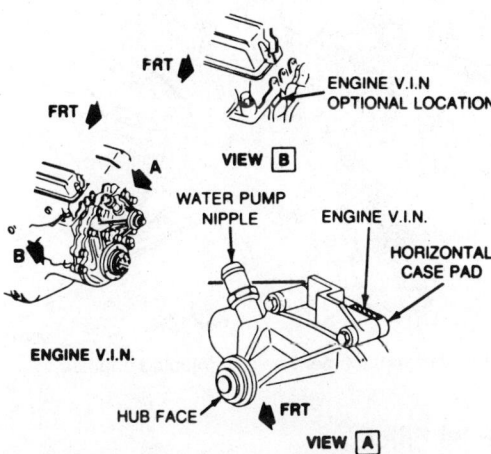

Engine serial number location on the 6-173

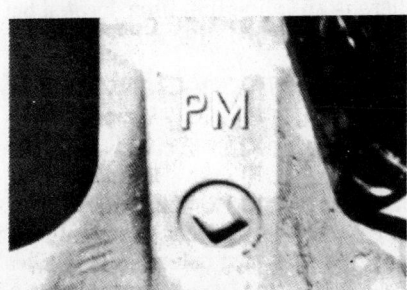

6-243 parts letter size code

Transfer Case Application Chart

Transfer Case Types	Years
New Process 207	1984–87 all
New Process 228	1985–87 w/auto trans.
New Process 229	1984 w/auto. trans.
New Process 231	1988–89 all
New Process 242	1988–89 Wagoneer and Cherokee

Manual Transmission Application Chart

Transmission Types	Years
Warner T4 4-speed	1984 w/4-150
Warner T5 5-speed	1984 all
AISIN AX4 4-speed	1984–87 w/4-150
AISIN AX5 5-speed	1984–89 all
BA 10/5 5-speed	1988–89 all

NOTE: The T4 and T5 were used in 1984 only, as substitutes for the AX4 and AX5 during a production shortage

10 GENERAL INFORMATION AND MAINTENANCE

Automatic Transmission Application Chart

Transmission	Years
Chrysler 903 3-speed	1984–86
AISIN/Warner AW4 4-speed	1986–89

Front Drive Axle Application Chart

Axle	Model	Years
Dana 30	All	1984–89

Rear Drive Axle Application Chart

Axle	Model	Years
AMC 7 9/16 in.	All	1984–86
Dana 35	All	1987–89

Axles

The drive axle code is found stamped on a flat surface on the axle tube, next to the differential housing, or, on a tag secured by one of the differential housing cover bolts.

ROUTINE MAINTENANCE

Air Cleaner
SERVICING

Engines with the dry paper type filter should have the filter replaced every 12,000 miles. Under dusty conditions, the element should be checked weekly, or more often if conditions warrant, and should be replaced at the first signs of clogging.

On engines using a dry paper filter with the polyurethane wrap, the wrap should be carefully removed every 6,000 miles. Shake the dirt from the wrap, DO NOT WASH IT, squeeze the old oil out by pressing it flat between two rags, then liberally soak it with SAE 10W-30 engine oil. Squeeze it flat to remove excess oil. At the same time, direct compressed air at the inside of the paper element to remove dirt. Replace the paper element every 15,000 miles, or sooner if necessary.

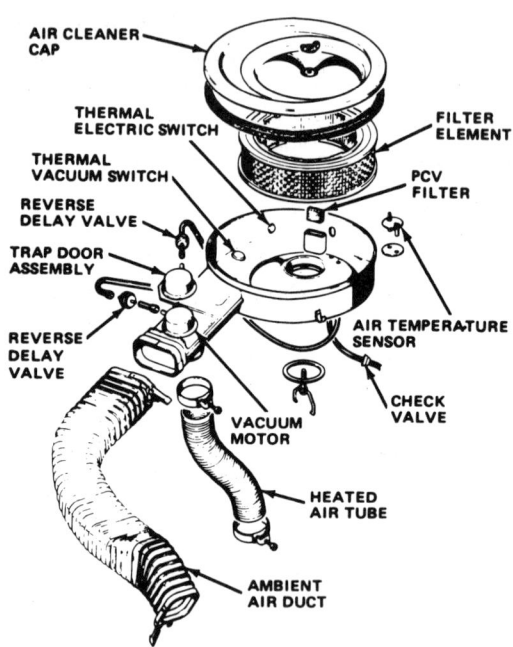

Typical carbureted engine air cleaner

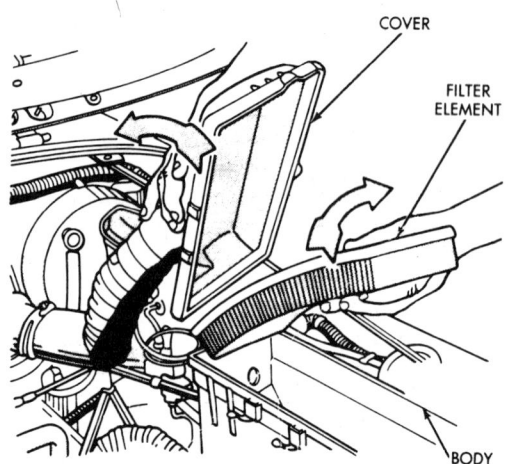

Air filter replacement on fuel injected engines

Fuel Filter
CARBURETED ENGINES

There is an inline fuel filter located between the fuel pump and the carburetor on most models.

On the 6-173, the filter is in the carburetor, behind the inlet nut.

The inline fuel filter should be cleaned or replaced every 15,000 miles. If the vehicle is driven in abnormally dirty conditions or if contaminated gasoline was put in the gas tank, the filter could become clogged before 15,000 miles. The fuel sediment bowl type filter need not be serviced unless there is evidence of foreign matter

GENERAL INFORMATION AND MAINTENANCE 11

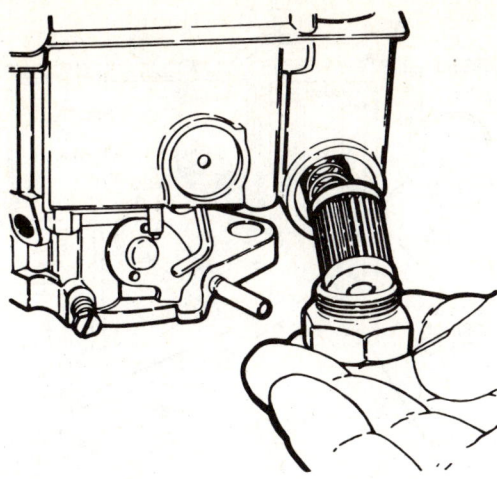

Fuel filter for the 6-173

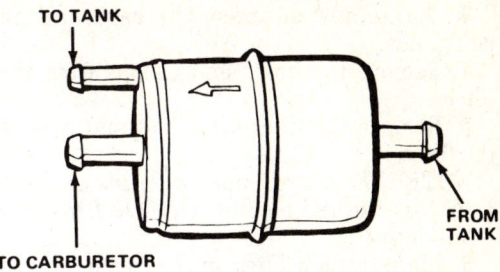

Fuel filter for the carbureted 4-150

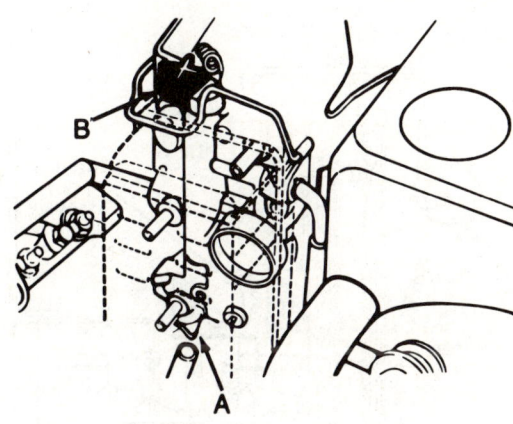

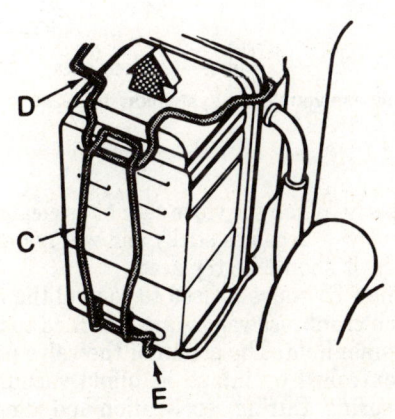

A. Draincock
B. Vent valve
C. Primary retaining clip
D. Top retaining clip
E. Bottom retaining clip

Diesel fuel filter replacement. A is the draincock, B is the vent, C, D, and E are the retaining clips

(e.g., water, dirt) visible in the bowl. If there is, remove and empty the bowl, wipe it dry with a clean cloth and replace it.

On the 6-173, when replacing the filter, hold the large nut with a wrench and unscrew the fuel line fitting. Pull the fuel pipe from the carburetor and catch any fuel with a clean rag. Next, unscrew the large nut. There is a spring behind the nut, so be careful. Remove the spring and the old filter. Install the new filter and, if you are at all in doubt about its condition, a new gasket behind the inlet nut. Tighten the inlet nut carefully, because the carburetor is made of very soft metal and the threads could EASILY strip with disastrous results! Hold the inlet nut securely while tightening the fuel line fitting.

GASOLINE FUEL INJECTION

The filter on both the 4-150 and 6-243 is located under the truck, mounted on the frame rail on the driver's side.

4-150

1. Disconnect the battery ground cable.
2. Remove the fuel tank filler cap.

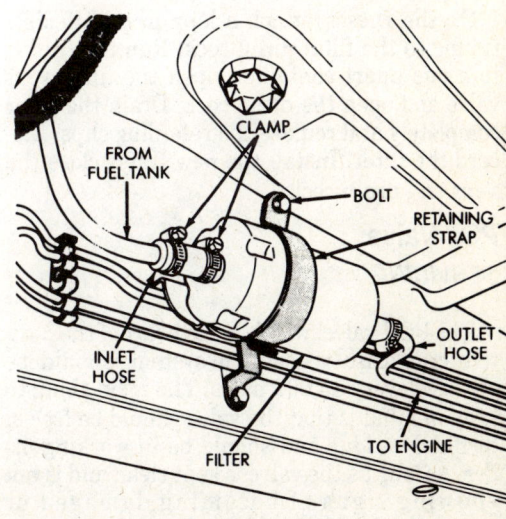

Fuel filter with fuel injection

12 GENERAL INFORMATION AND MAINTENANCE

3. Raise and support the rear end on jackstands.
4. Remove the hoses and clamps from the filter.
5. Remove the filter strap bolt and remove the filter.
NOTE: *The filter is marked for installation. IN goes towards the fuel tank; OUT towards the engine.*
6. Place the new filter on the frame rail and tighten the strap bolt to 106 in. lbs.
7. Install and securely clamp the hoses.

6-243

1. Disconnect the battery ground cable.
2. Remove the fuel tank filler cap.
3. Remove the cap from the pressure test port on the fuel rail in the engine compartment.
CAUTION: *DON'T ALLOW FUEL TO SPRAY OR SPILL ON THE ENGINE OR EXHAUST MANIFOLD! PLACE HEAVY SHOP TOWELS UNDER THE PRESSURE PORT TO ABSORB ANY ESCAPED FUEL!*
4. Using a small pin punch, push the test port valve inward to relieve fuel system pressure.
5. Install the test port cap.
6. Raise and support the rear end on jackstands.
7. Remove the hoses and clamps from the filter.
8. Remove the filter strap bolt and remove the filter.
NOTE: *The filter is marked for installation. IN goes towards the fuel tank; OUT towards the engine.*
9. Place the new filter on the frame rail and tighten the strap bolt to 106 in. lbs.
10. Install and securely clamp the hoses.

DIESEL ENGINES

On the Diesel, attach a long pice of flexible tubing to the filter drain cock. Run the tubing to a one quart container, open the filter vent valve and open the drain cock. Drain the filter completely and remove the retaining clips. Discard the filter. Install the new filter, close the vent and drain cock.

PCV Valve

SERVICING

The PCV valve, which is the heart of the positive crankcase ventilation system, should be changed every 15,000 miles. The main thing to keep in mind is that the valve should be free of dirt and residue and should be in working order. As long as the valve is kept clean and is not showing signs of becoming damaged or gummed up, it should perform its function

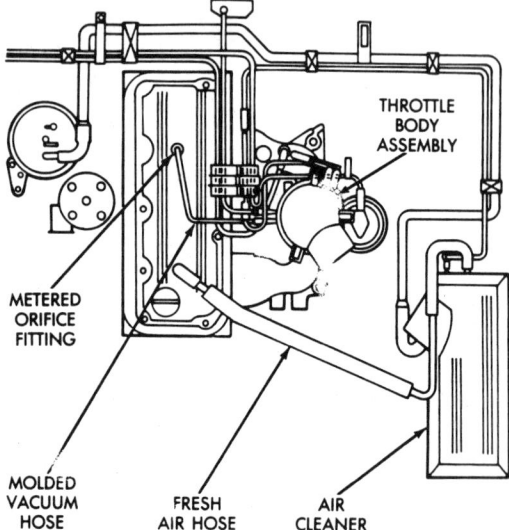
Crankcase ventilation system on the fuel injected 4-150

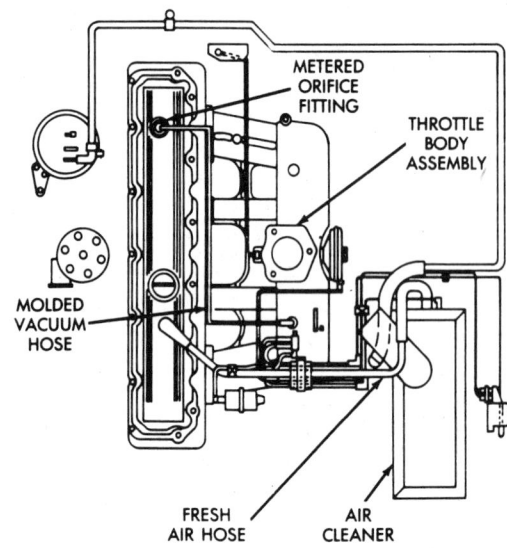
Crankcase ventilation system on the 6-243

properly. When the valve cannot be cleaned sufficiently or becomes sticky and will not operate freely, it should be replaced.

The PCV valve is used to control the rate at which crankcase vapors are returned to the intake manifold. The action of the valve plunger is controlled by intake manifold vacuum and the spring. During deceleration and idle, when manifold vacuum is high, it overcomes the tension of the valve spring and the plunger bottoms in the manifold end of the valve housing. Because of the valve construction, it reduces, but dies not stop, the passage of vapors to the intake manifold. When the engine is lightly ac-

GENERAL INFORMATION AND MAINTENANCE

celerated or operated at constant speed, spring tension matches intake manifold vacuum pull and the plunger takes a mid-position in the valve body, allowing more vapors to flow into the manifold.

SERVICE

An inoperative PCV system will cause rough idling, sludge and oil dilution. In the event erratic idle, never attempt to compensate by disconnecting the PCV system. Disconnecting the PCV system will adversely affect engine ventilation. It could also shorten engine life through the buildup of sludge.

To inspect the PCV valve, proceed as follows:

1. With the engine idling, remove the PCV valve from the rocker cover. If the valve is not plugged, a hissing sound will be heard. A strong vacuum should be felt when you place your finger over the valve.
2. Reinstall the PCV valve and allow about a minute for pressure to drop.
3. Remove the crankcase intake air cleaner. Cover the opening in the rocker cover with a piece of stiff paper. The paper should be sucked against the opening with noticeable force.
4. With the engine stopped, remove the PCV valve and shake it. A rattle or clicking should be heard to indicate that the valve is free.
5. If the system meets the tests in Steps 1, 2, 3, and 4 (above), no further service is required, unless replacement is specified in the Maintenance Intervals Chart. If the system does not meet the tests, the valve should be replaced with a new one.
   NOTE: *Do not attempt to clean a PCV valve.*
6. With a new PCV valve installed, if the paper is not sucked against the crankcase air intake opening (see Step 2), it will be necessary to clean the PCV valve hose and the passage in the lower part of the carburetor.
7. Clean the line with Combustion Chamber Conditioner or similar solvent. Do not leave the hoses in solvent for more than ½ hour. Allow the line to air dry.
8. Remove the carburetor and HAND turn a ¼" drill through the passages to dislodge solid particles and blow clean.
   NOTE: *It is not necessary to disassembly the carburetor for this operation. If necessary, use a smaller drill, so that no metal is removed.*
9. After checking and/or servicing the Crankcase Ventilation System, any components that do not allow passage or air to the intake manifold should be replaced.

The PCV valve is located in the left valve cover on the 6-173 and on the valve rocker cover on the 4-150, and 6-243.

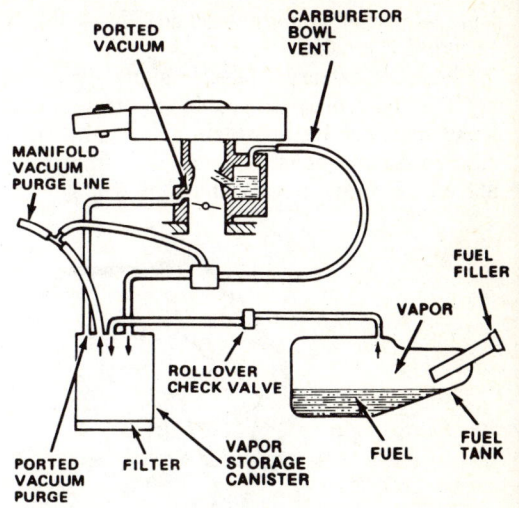

Typical fuel vapor control system

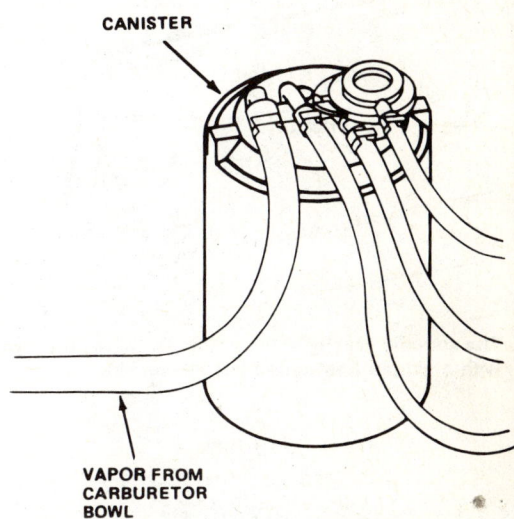

Fuel vapor storage canister and hoses

Evaporative Canister

All models have fuel evaporative emission control systems which include an evaporative storage canister. The purpose of this charcoal canister is to store gasoline vapors until they can be drawn into the engine and burned along with the air/fuel mixture. The air filter in the bottom of the canister should be replaced every 15,000 miles.

Battery

Loose, dirty, or corroded battery terminals are a major cause of "no-start." Every 3 months or so, remove the battery terminals and clean them, giving them a light coating of petro-

14 GENERAL INFORMATION AND MAINTENANCE

leum jelly when you are finished. This will help to retard corrosion.

Check the battery cables for signs of wear or chafing and replace any cable or terminal that looks marginal. Battery terminals can be easily cleaned and inexpensive terminal cleaning tools are an excellent investment that will pay for themselves many times over. They can usually be purchased from any well-equipped auto store or parts department. Side terminal batteries require a different tool to clean the threads in the battery case. The accumulated white powder and corrosion can be cleaned from the top of the battery with an old tooth-

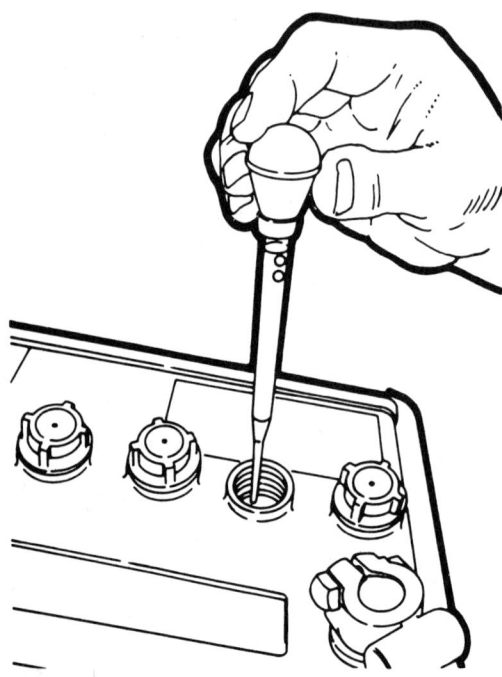

The specific gravity of the battery can be checked with a simple float-type hydrometer

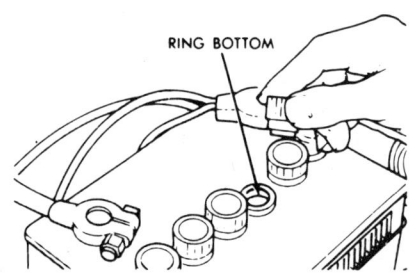

Fill each battery cell to the bottom of the split ring with distilled water

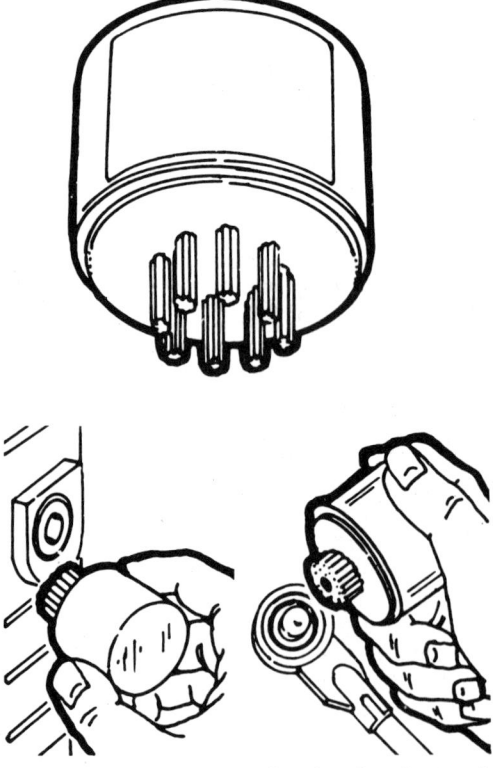

Special tools are available for cleaning the terminals and cable clamps on side terminal batteries

Battery State of Charge at Room Temperature

Specific Gravity Reading	Charged Condition
1.260–1.280	Fully Charged
1.230–1.250	¾ Charged
1.200–1.220	½ Charged
1.170–1.190	¼ Charged
1.140–1.160	Almost no Charge
1.110–1.130	No Charge

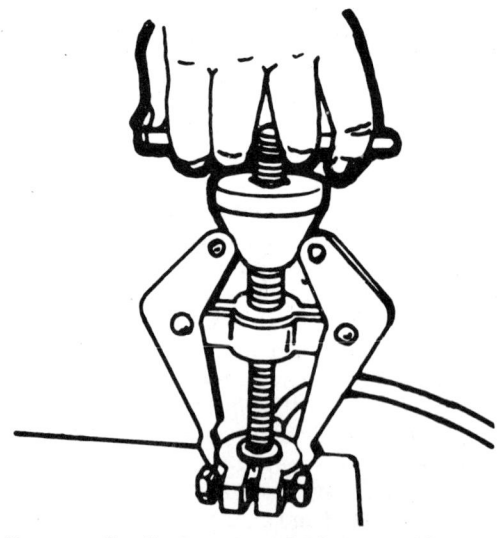

Use a small puller to remove the battery cables

GENERAL INFORMATION AND MAINTENANCE

Cleaning the inside of the cable end

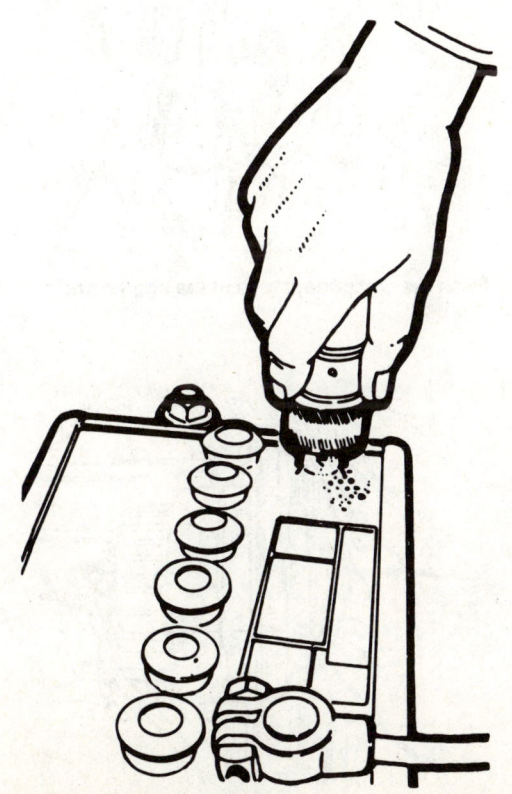

Cleaning the battery terminal

brush and a solution of baking soda and water.

Unless you have a maintenance-free battery, check the electrolyte level (see Battery under Fluid Level Checks in this chapter) and check the specific gravity of each cell. Be sure that the vent holes in each cell cap are not blocked by grease or dirt. The vent holes allow hydrogen gas, formed by the chemical reaction in the battery, to escape safely.

REPLACEMENT BATTERIES

The cold power rating of a battery measures battery starting performance and provides an approximate relationship between battery size and engine size. The cold power rating of a replacement battery should match or exceed your engine size in cubic inches.

FLUID LEVEL (EXCEPT MAINTENANCE FREE BATTERIES)

Check the battery electrolyte level at least once a month, or more often in hot weather or during periods of extended truck operation. The level can be checked through the case on translucent polypropylene batteries; the cell caps must be removed on other models. The electrolyte level in each cell should be kept filled to the split ring inside, or the line marked on the outside of the case.

If the level is low, add only distilled water, or colorless, odorless drinking water, through the opening until the level is correct. Each cell is completely separate from the others, so each must be checked and filled individually.

If water is added in freezing weather, the truck should be driven several miles to allow the water to mix with the electrolyte. Otherwise, the battery could freeze.

SPECIFIC GRAVITY (EXCEPT MAINTENANCE FREE BATTERIES)

At least once a year, check the specific gravity of the battery. It should be between 1.20 in.Hg and 1.26 in.Hg at room temperature.

The specific gravity can be check with the use of an hydrometer, an inexpensive instrument available from many sources, including auto parts stores. The hydrometer has a squeeze bulb at one end and a nozzle at the other. Battery electrolyte is sucked into the hydrometer until the float is lifted from its seat. The specific gravity is then read by noting the position of the float. Generally, if after charging, the specific gravity between any two cells varies more than 50 points (0.50), the battery is bad and should be replaced.

It is not possible to check the specific gravity in this manner on sealed (maintenance free) batteries. Instead, the indicator built into the

16 GENERAL INFORMATION AND MAINTENANCE

top of the case must be relied on to display any signs of battery deterioration. If the indicator is dark, the battery can be assumed to be OK. If the indicator is light, the specific gravity is low, and the battery should be charged or replaced.

CABLES AND CLAMPS

Once a year, the battery terminals and the cable clamps should be cleaned. Loosen the clamps and remove the cables, negative cable first. On batteries with posts on top, the use of a puller specially made for the purpose is recommended. These are inexpensive, and available in auto parts stores. Side terminal battery cables are secured with a bolt.

Clean the cable lamps and the battery terminal with a wire brush, until all corrosion, grease, etc., is removed and the metal is shiny. It is especially important to clean the inside of the clamp thoroughly, since a small deposit of foreign material or oxidation there will prevent a sound electrical connection and inhibit either starting or charging. Special tools are available for cleaning these parts, one type for conventional batteries and another type for side terminal batteries.

Before installing the cables, loosen the battery holddown clamp or strap, remove the battery and check the battery tray. Clear it of any debris, and check it for soundness. Rust should be wire brushed away, and the metal given a coat of anti-rust paint. Replace the battery and tighten the holddown clamp or strap securely, but be careful not to overtighten, which will crack the battery case.

After the clamps and terminals are clean, reinstall the cables, negative cable last; do not hammer on the clamps to install. Tighten the clamps securely, but do not distort them. Give the clamps and terminals a thin external coat of grease after installation, to retard corrosion.

Check the cables at the same time that the terminals are cleaned. If the cable insulation is cracked or broken, or if the ends are frayed, the cable should be replaced with a new cable of the same length and gauge.

CAUTION: *Keep flame or sparks away from the battery; it gives off explosive hydrogen gas. Battery electrolyte contains sulphuric acid. If you should splash any on your skin or in your eyes, flush the affected area with plenty of clear water. If it lands in your eyes, get medical help immediately.*

Belts

Once a year or at 12,000 mile intervals, the tension (and condition) of the alternator, power steering (if so equipped), air conditioning (if so equipped), and Thermactor air pump drive belts should be checked, and, if necessary, adjusted. Loose accessory drive belts can lead to poor engine cooling and diminish alternator, power steering pump, air conditioning compressor or air pump output. A belt that is too

To adjust belt tension or to replace belts, first loosen the component's mounting and adjusting bolts slightly

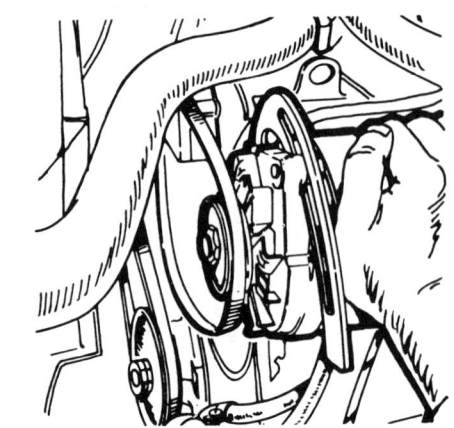

Push the component toward the engine and slip off the belt

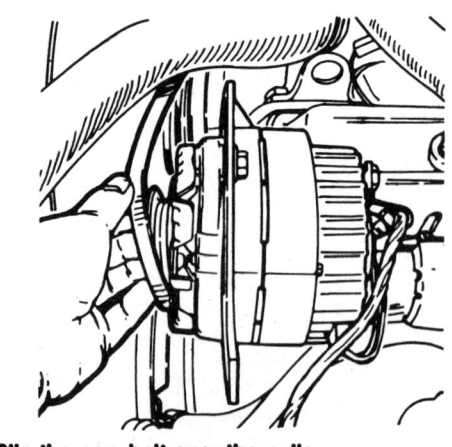

Slip the new belt over the pulley

GENERAL INFORMATION AND MAINTENANCE

tight places a severe strain on the water pump, alternator, power steering pump, compressor or air pump bearings.

Replace any belt that is so glazed, worn or stretched that it cannot be tightened sufficiently.

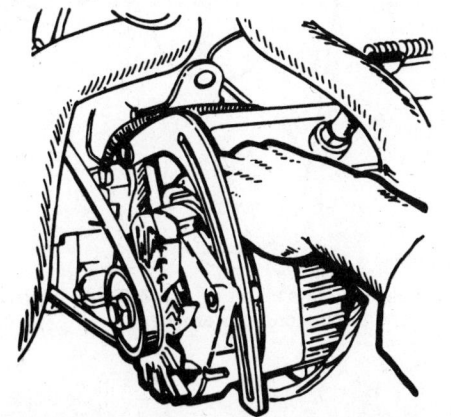

Pull outward on the component and tighten the mounting bolts

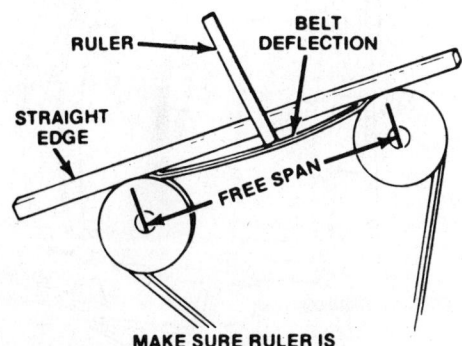

Measuring belt deflection

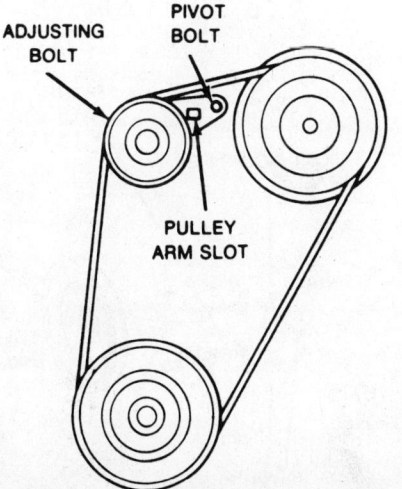

Some pulleys have a rectangular slot to aid in moving the accessories to be tightened

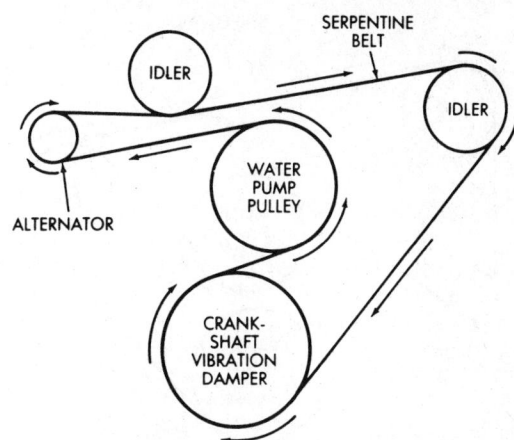

Serpentine belt installation on a 4-150 with an alternator only

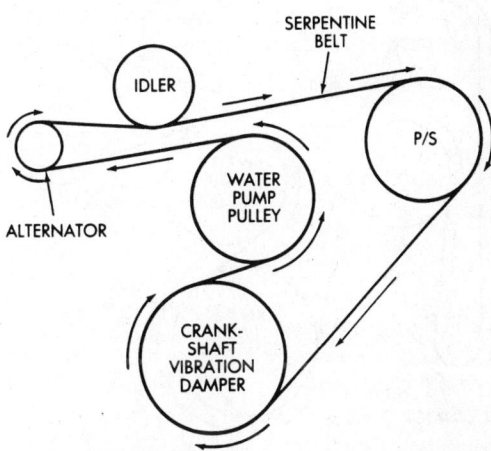

Serpentine belt installation on a 4-150 with alternator and power steering

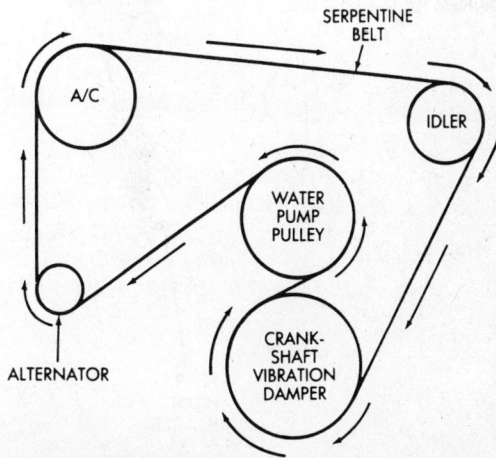

Serpentine belt installation on a 4-150 with alternator and air conditioning

18 GENERAL INFORMATION AND MAINTENANCE

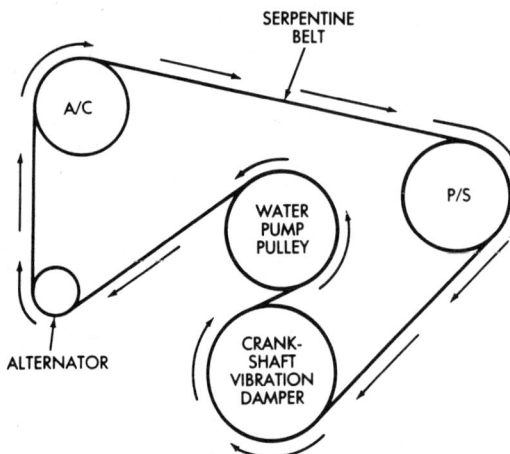

Serpentine belt installation on a 4-150 with alternator, air conditioning and power steering

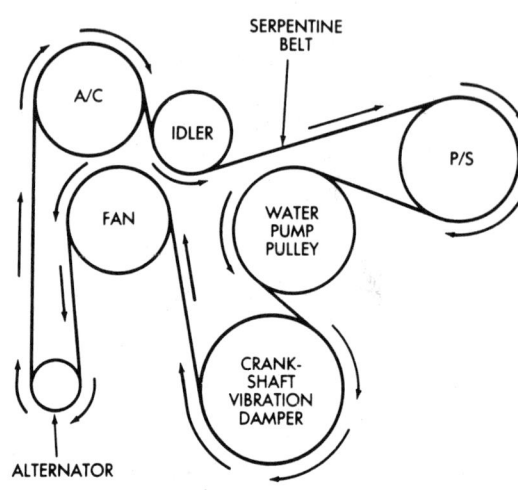

Serpentine belt installation on a 6-243 with alternator, air conditioning and power steering

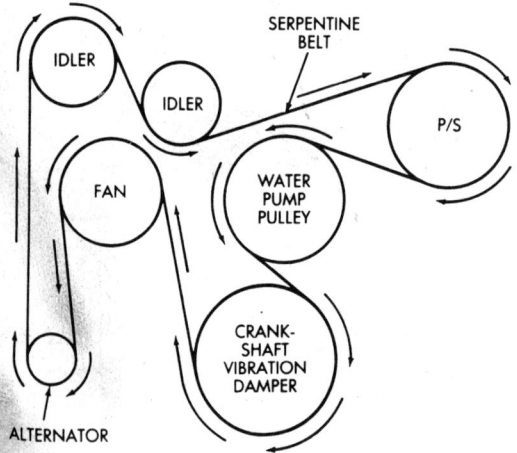

Serpentine belt installation on a 6-243 with alternator and power steering

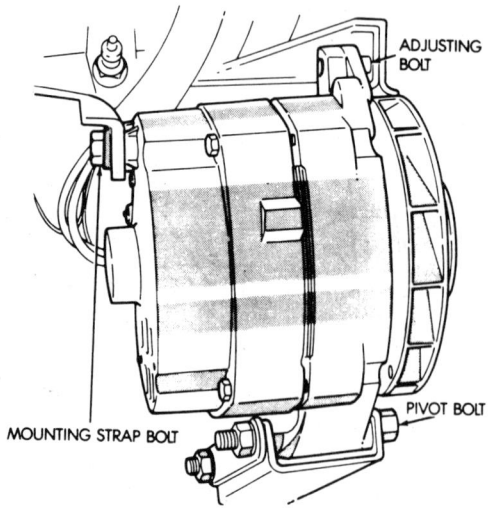

Alternator adjustment points on a 4-150 with a V-belt

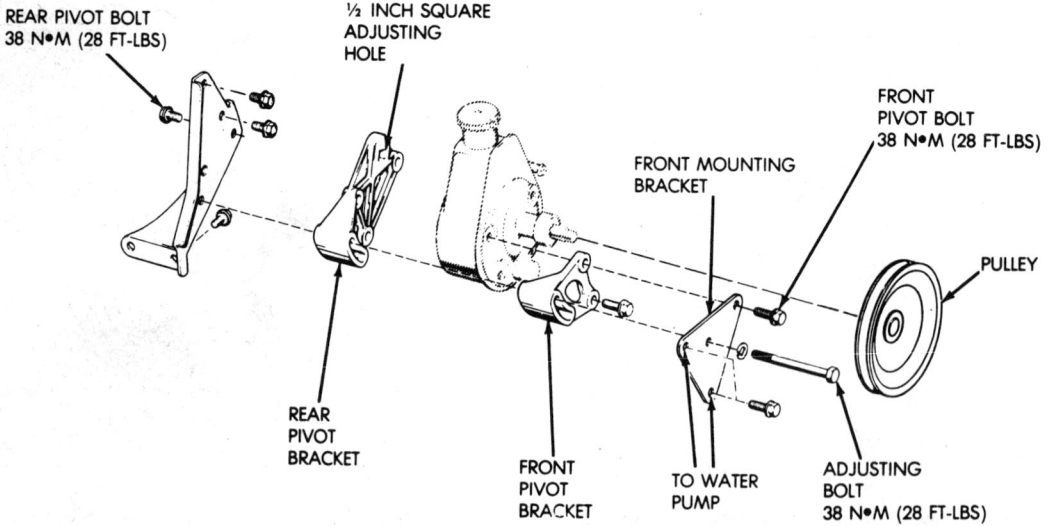

Power steering pump adjustment points on a 4-150 with a V-belt

GENERAL INFORMATION AND MAINTENANCE

NOTE: *The material used in late model drive belts is such that the belts do not show wear. Replace belts at least every three years.*

On vehicles with matched belts, replace both belts. New ½", ⅜" and ¹⁵⁄₃₂" wide belts are to be adjusted to a tension of 140 lbs.; ¼" wide belts are adjusted to 80 lbs., measured on a belt tension gauge. Any belt that has been operating for a minimum of 10 minutes is considered a used belt. In the first 10 minutes, the belt should stretch to its maximum extent. After 10 minutes, stop the engine and recheck the belt tension. Belt tension for a used belt should be maintained at 110 lbs. (all except ¼" wide belts) or 60 lbs. (¼" wide belts). If a belt tension gauge is not available, the following procedures may be used.

ADJUSTMENTS FOR ALL V-BELTS

On models equipped with an electric cooling fan, disconnect the negative battery cable or fan motor wiring harness connector before replacing or adjusting drive belts. The fan may come on, under certain circumstances, even though the ignition is off.

Alternator (Fan Drive) Belt

1. Position the ruler perpendicular to the drive belt at its longest straight run. Test the tightness of the belt by pressing it firmly with your thumb. The deflection should not exceed ¼".

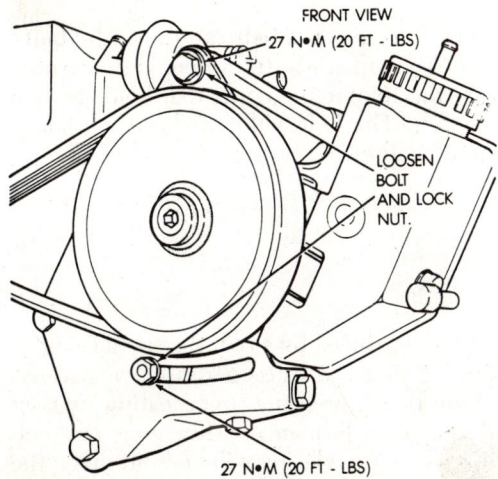

Power steering pump adjustment points on all engines with a serpentine belt—front view

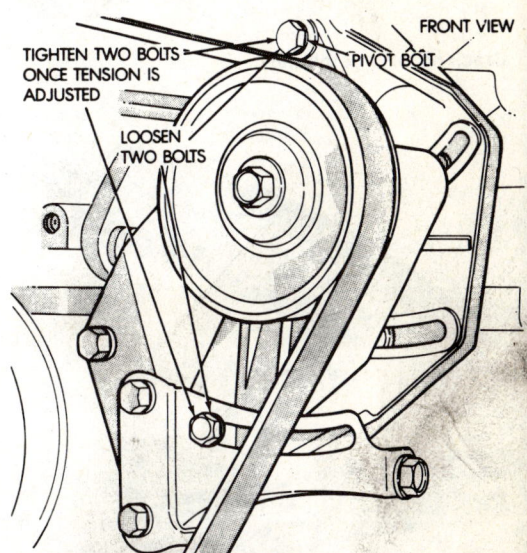

Serpentine belt adjustment points on 4-150 engines without power steering—front view

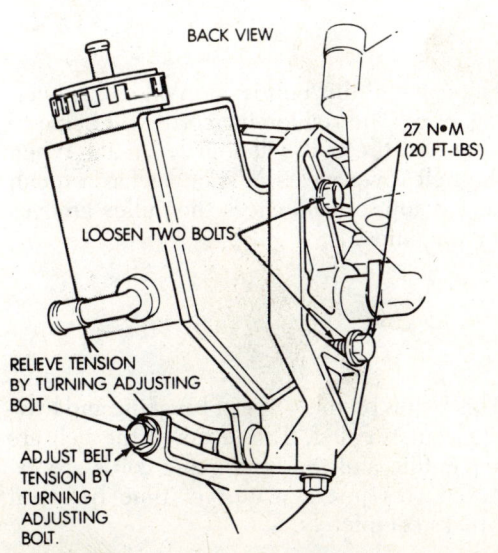

Power steering pump adjustment points on all engines with a serpentine belt—rear view

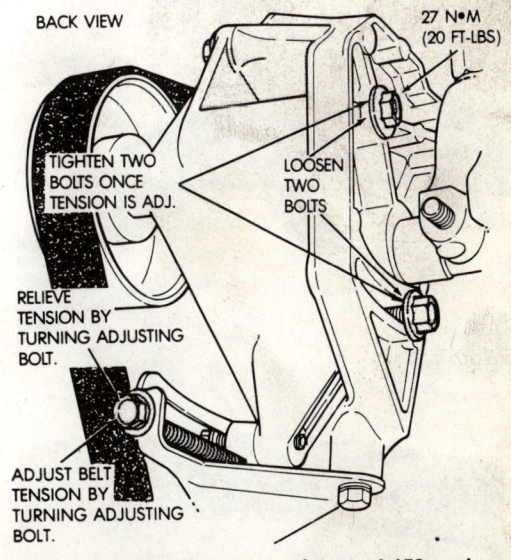

Serpentine belt adjustment points on 4-150 engines without power steering—rear view

20 GENERAL INFORMATION AND MAINTENANCE

HOW TO SPOT WORN V-BELTS

V-Belts are vital to efficient engine operation—they drive the fan, water pump and other accessories. They require little maintenance (occasional tightening) but they will not last forever. Slipping or failure of the V-belt will lead to overheating. If your V-belt looks like any of these, it should be replaced.

Cracking or weathering

This belt has deep cracks, which cause it to flex. Too much flexing leads to heat build-up and premature failure. These cracks can be caused by using the belt on a pulley that is too small. Notched belts are available for small diameter pulleys.

Softening (grease and oil)

Oil and grease on a belt can cause the belt's rubber compounds to soften and separate from the reinforcing cords that hold the belt together. The belt will first slip, then finally fail altogether.

Glazing

Glazing is caused by a belt that is slipping. A slipping belt can cause a run-down battery, erratic power steering, overheating or poor accessory performance. The more the belt slips, the more glazing will be built up on the surface of the belt. The more the belt is glazed, the more it will slip. If the glazing is light, tighten the belt.

Worn cover

The cover of this belt is worn off and is peeling away. The reinforcing cords will begin to wear and the belt will shortly break. When the belt cover wears in spots or has a rough jagged appearance, check the pulley grooves for roughness.

Separation

This belt is on the verge of breaking and leaving you stranded. The layers of the belt are separating and the reinforcing cords are exposed. It's just a matter of time before it breaks completely.

GENERAL INFORMATION AND MAINTENANCE

2. If the deflection exceeds ¼", loosen the alternator mounting and adjusting arm bolts.

3. Place a 1" open-end or adjustable wrench on the adjusting ridge cast on the body, and pull on the wrench until the proper tension is achieved.

4. Holding the alternator in place to maintain tension, tighten the adjusting arm bolt. Recheck the belt tension. When the belt is properly tensioned, tighten the alternator mounting bolt.

Power Steering Drive Belt

1. Hold a ruler perpendicularly to the drive belt at its longest run, test the tightness of the belt by pressing it firmly with your thumb. The deflection should not exceed ¼".

2. To adjust the belt tension, loosen the adjusting and mounting bolts on the front face of the steering pump cover plate (hub side).

3. Using a pry bar or broom handle on the pump hub, move the power steering pump toward or away from the engine until the proper tension is reached. Do not pry against the reservoir as it is relatively soft and easily deformed.

4. Holding the pump in place, tighten the adjusting arm bolt and then recheck the belt tension. When the belt is properly tensioned tighten the mounting bolts.

Air Conditioning Compressor Drive Belt

1. Position a ruler perpendicular to the drive belt at its longest run. Test the tightness of the belt by pressing it firmly with your thumb. The deflection should not exceed ¼".

2. If the engine is equipped with an idler pulley, loosen the idler pulley adjusting bolt, insert a pry bar between the pulley and the engine (or in the idler pulley adjusting slot), and adjust the tension accordingly. If the engine is not equipped with an idler pulley, the alternator must be moved to accomplish this adjustment, as outlined under Alternator (Fan Drive) Belt.

3. When the proper tension is reached, tighten the idler pulley adjusting bolt (if so equipped) or the alternator adjusting and mounting bolts.

Air Pump Drive Belt

1. Position a ruler perpendicular to the drive belt at its longest run. Test the tightness of the belt by pressing it firmly with your thumb. The deflection should be about ¼".

2. To adjust the belt tension, loosen the adjusting arm bolt slightly. If necessary, also loosen the mounting belt slightly.

3. Using a pry bar or broom handle, pry against the pump rear cover to move the pump toward or away from the engine as necessary.

CAUTION: *Do not pry against the pump housing itself, as damage to the housing may result.*

4. Holding the pump in place, tighten the adjusting arm bolt and recheck the tension. When the belt is properly tensioned, tighten the mounting bolt.

SERPENTINE (SINGLE) DRIVE BELT MODELS

Some models feature a single, wide, ribbed V-belt that drives the water pump, alternator, and (on some models) the air conditioner compressor. To install a new belt, loosen the bracket lock bolt, retract the belt tensioner with a pry bar and slide the old belt off of the pulleys. Slip on a new belt and release the tensioner and tighten the lock bolt. The spring powered tensioner eliminates the need for periodic adjustments.

WARNING: *Check to make sure that the V-ribbed belt is located properly in all drive pulleys before applying tensioner pressure.*

Hoses

REMOVAL AND INSTALLATION

Radiator hoses are generally of two constructions, the preformed (molded) type, which is custom made for a particular application, and the spring-loaded type, which is made to fit several different applications. Heater hoses are all of the same general construction.

REPLACEMENT

Inspect the condition of the radiator and heater hoses periodically. Early spring and at the beginning of the fall or winter, when you are performing other maintenance, are good times. Make sure the engine and cooling system are cold. Visually inspect for cracking, rotting or collapsed hoses, replace as necessary. Run your hand along the length of the hose. If a weak or swollen spot is noted when squeezing the hose wall, replace the hose.

1. Drain the cooling system into a suitable container (if the coolant is to be reused).

CAUTION: *When draining the coolant, keep in mind that cats and dogs are attracted by the ethylene glycol antifreeze, and are quite likely to drink any that is left in an uncovered container or in puddles on the ground. This will prove fatal in sufficient quantity. Always drain the coolant into a sealable container. Coolant should be reused unless it is contaminated or several years old.*

2. Loosen the hose clamps at each end of the hose that requires replacement.

3. Twist, pull and slide the hose off the radia-

22 GENERAL INFORMATION AND MAINTENANCE

HOW TO SPOT BAD HOSES

Both the upper and lower radiator hoses are called upon to perform difficult jobs in an inhospitable environment. They are subject to nearly 18 psi at under hood temperatures often over 280°F., and must circulate nearly 7500 gallons of coolant an hour—3 good reasons to have good hoses.

Swollen hose

A good test for any hose is to feel it for soft or spongy spots. Frequently these will appear as swollen areas of the hose. The most likely cause is oil soaking. This hose could burst at any time, when hot or under pressure.

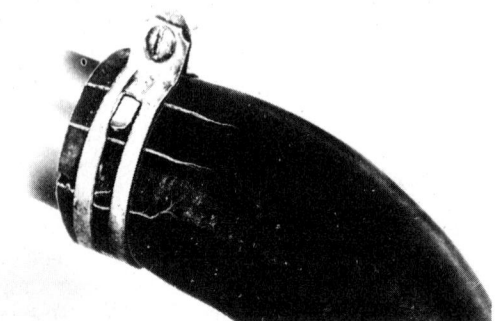

Cracked hose

Cracked hoses can usually be seen but feel the hoses to be sure they have not hardened; a prime cause of cracking. This hose has cracked down to the reinforcing cords and could split at any of the cracks.

Frayed hose end (due to weak clamp)

Weakened clamps frequently are the cause of hose and cooling system failure. The connection between the pipe and hose has deteriorated enough to allow coolant to escape when the engine is hot.

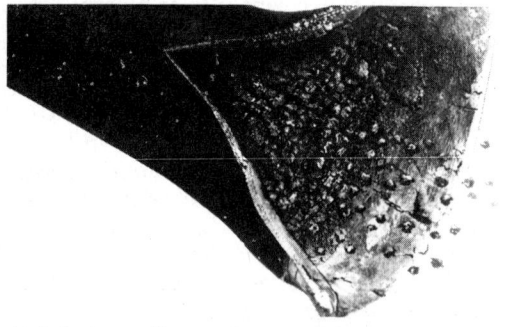

Debris in cooling system

Debris, rust and scale in the cooling system can cause the inside of a hose to weaken. This can usually be felt on the outside of the hose as soft or thinner areas.

GENERAL INFORMATION AND MAINTENANCE

tor, water pump, thermostat or heater connection.

4. Clean the hose mounting connections. Position the hose clamps on the new hose.

5. Coat the connection surfaces with a water resistant sealer and slide the hose into position. Make sure the hose clamps are located beyond the raised bead of the connector (if equipped) and centered in the clamping area of the connection.

6. Tighten the clamps to 20-30 in. lbs. Do not overtighten.

7. Fill the cooling system.

8. Start the engine and allow it to reach normal operating temperature. Check for leaks.

Air Conditioning System

GENERAL SERVICING PROCEDURES

The most important aspect of air conditioning service is the maintenance of pure and adequate charge of refrigerant in the system. A refrigeration system cannot function properly if a significant percentage of the charge is lost. Leaks are common because the severe vibration encountered in an automobile can easily cause a sufficient cracking or loosening of the air conditioning fittings. As a result, the extreme operating pressures of the system force refrigerant out.

The problem can be understood by considering what happens to the system as it is operated with a continuous leak. Because the expansion valve regulates the flow of refrigerant to the evaporator, the level of refrigerant there is fairly constant. The receiver/drier stores any excess of refrigerant, and so a loss will first appear there as a reduction in the level of liquid. As this level nears the bottom of the vessel, some refrigerant vapor bubbles will begin to appear in the stream of liquid supplied to the expansion valve. This vapor decreases the capacity of the expansion valve very little as the valve opens to compensate for its presence. As the quantity of liquid in the condenser decreases, the operating pressure will drop there and throughout the high side of the system. As the R-12 continues to be expelled, the pressure available to force the liquid through the expansion valve will continue to decrease, and, eventually, the valve's orifice will prove to be too much of a restriction for adequate flow even with the needle fully withdrawn.

At this point, low side pressure will start to drop, and severe reduction in cooling capacity, marked by freeze-up of the evaporator coil, will result. Eventually, the operating pressure of the evaporator will be lower than the pressure of the atmosphere surrounding it, and air will be drawn into the system wherever there are leaks in the low side.

Because all atmospheric air contains at least some moisture, water will enter the system and mix with the R-12 and the oil. Trace amounts of moisture will cause sludging of the oil, and cor-

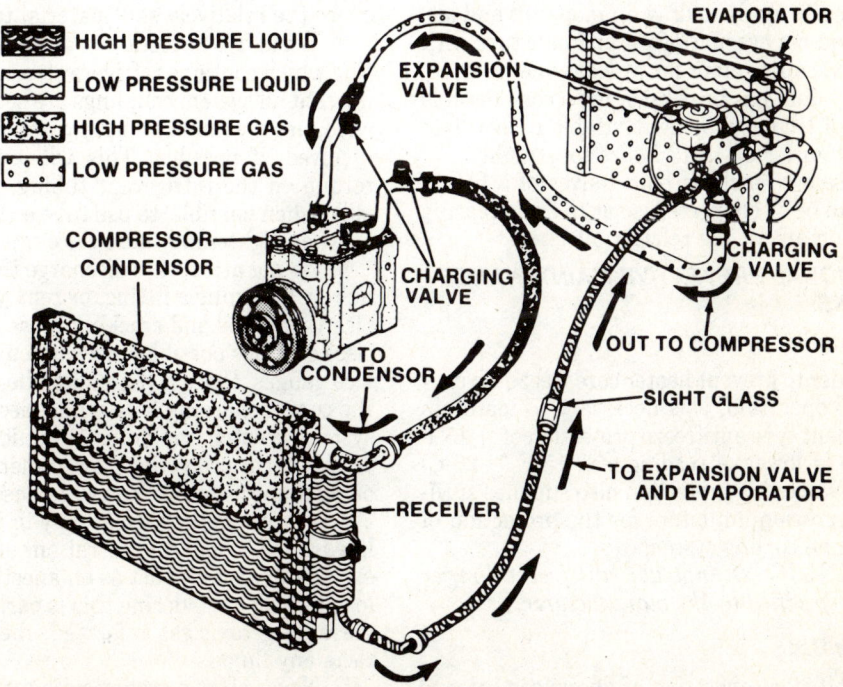

Basic components of an air conditioning system and the flow of refrigerant.

GENERAL INFORMATION AND MAINTENANCE

rosion of the system. Saturation and clogging of the filter/drier, and freezing of the expansion valve orifice will eventually result. As air fills the system to a greater and greater extend, it will interfere more and more with the normal flows of refrigerant and heat.

A list of general precautions that should be observed while doing this follows:

1. Keep all tools as clean and dry as possible.
2. Thoroughly purge the service gauges and hoses of air and moisture before connecting them to the system. Keep them capped when not in use.
3. Thoroughly clean any refrigerant fitting before disconnecting it, in order to minimize the entrance of dirt into the system.
4. Plan any operation that requires opening the system beforehand in order to minimize the length of time it will be exposed to open air. Cap or seal the open ends to minimize the entrance of foreign material.
5. When adding oil, pour it through an extremely clean and dry tube or funnel. Keep the oil capped whenever possible. Do not use oil that has not been kept tightly sealed.
6. Use only refrigerant 12. Purchase refrigerant intended for use in only automotive air conditioning system. Avoid the use of refrigerant 12 that may be packaged for another use, such as cleaning, or powering a horn, as it is impure.
7. Completely evacuate any system that has been opened to replace a component, other than when isolating the compressor, or that has leaked sufficiently to draw in moisture and air. This requires evacuating air and moisture with a good vacuum pump for at least one hour.

If a system has been open for a considerable length of time it may be advisable to evacuate the system for up to 12 hours (overnight).

8. Use a wrench on both halves of a fitting that is to be disconnected, so as to avoid placing torque on any of the refrigerant lines.

ADDITIONAL PREVENTIVE MAINTENANCE CHECKS

Antifreeze

In order to prevent heater core freeze-up during A/C operation, it is necessary to maintain permanent type antifreeze protection of +15°F (−9°C) or lower. A reading of −15°F (−26°C) is ideal since this protection also supplies sufficient corrosion inhibitors for the protection of the engine cooling system.

WARNING: *Do not use antifreeze longer than specified by the manufacturer.*

Radiator Cap

For efficient operation of an air conditioned truck's cooling system, the radiator cap should have a holding pressure which meets manufacturer's specifications. A cap which fails to hold these pressure should be replaced.

Condenser

Any obstruction of or damage to the condenser configuration will restrict the air flow which is essential to its efficient operation. It is therefore, a good rule to keep this unit clean and in proper physical shape.

NOTE: *Bug screens are regarded as obstructions.*

Condensation Drain Tube

This single molded drain tube expels the condensation, which accumulates on the bottom of the evaporator housing, into the engine compartment.

If this tube is obstructed, the air conditioning performance can be restricted and condensation buildup can spill over onto the vehicle's floor.

SAFETY PRECAUTIONS

Because of the importance of the necessary safety precautions that must be exercised when working with air conditioning systems and R-12 refrigerant, a recap of the safety precautions are outlined.

1. Avoid contact with a charged refrigeration system, even when working on another part of the air conditioning system or vehicle. If a heavy tool comes into contact with a section of copper tubing or a heat exchanger, it can easily cause the relatively soft material to rupture.
2. When it is necessary to apply force to a fitting which contains refrigerant, as when checking that all system couplings are securely tightened, use a wrench on both parts of the fitting involved, if possible. This will avoid putting torque on the refrigerant tubing. (It is advisable, when possible, to use tube or line wrenches when tightening these flare nut fittings.)
3. Do not attempt to discharge the system by merely loosening a fitting, or removing the service valve caps and cracking these valves. Precise control is possibly only when using the service gauges. Place a rag under the open end of the center charging hose while discharging the system to catch any drops of liquid that might escape. Wear protective gloves when connecting or disconnecting service gauge hoses.
4. Discharge the system only in a well ventilated area, as high concentrations of the gas can exclude oxygen and act as an anesthetic. When leak testing or soldering this is particularly important, as toxic gas is formed when R-12 contacts any flame.
5. Never start a system without first verifying that both service valves are backseated, if

GENERAL INFORMATION AND MAINTENANCE

equipped, and that all fittings are throughout the system are snugly connected.

6. Avoid applying heat to any refrigerant line or storage vessel. Charging may be aided by using water heated to less than 125°F (52°C) to warm the refrigerant container. Never allow a refrigerant storage container to sit out in the sun, or near any other source of heat, such as a radiator.

7. Always wear goggles when working on a system to protect the eyes. If refrigerant contacts the eye, it is advisable in all cases to see a physician as soon as possible.

8. Frostbite from liquid refrigerant should be treated by first gradually warming the area with cool water, and then gently applying petroleum jelly. A physician should be consulted.

9. Always keep refrigerant can fittings capped when not in use. Avoid sudden shock to the can which might occur from dropping it, or from banging a heavy tool against it. Never carry a refrigerant can in the passenger compartment of a truck.

10. Always completely discharge the system before painting the vehicle (if the paint is to be baked on), or before welding anywhere near the refrigerant lines.

TEST GAUGES

Most of the service work performed in air conditioning requires the use of a set of two gauges, one for the high (head) pressure side of the system, the other for the low (suction) side.

The low side gauge records both pressure and vacuum. Vacuum readings are calibrated from 0 to 30 inches Hg and the pressure graduations read from 0 to no less than 60 psi.

The high side gauge measures pressure from 0 to at last 600 psi.

Both gauges are threaded into a manifold that contains two hand shut-off valves. Proper manipulation of these valves and the use of the attached test hoses allow the user to perform the following services:

1. Test high and low side pressures.
2. Remove air, moisture, and contaminated refrigerant.
3. Purge the system (of refrigerant).
4. Charge the system (with refrigerant).

The manifold valves are designed so that they have no direct effect on gauge readings, but serve only to provide for, or cut off, flow of refrigerant through the manifold. During all testing and hook-up operations, the valves are kept in a close position to avoid disturbing the refrigeration system. The valves are opened only to purge the system or refrigerant or to charge it.

INSPECTION

CAUTION: *The compressed refrigerant used in the air conditioning system expands into the atmosphere at a temperature of −21.7°F (−30°C) or lower. This will freeze any surface, including your eyes, that it contacts. In addition, the refrigerant decomposes into a poisonous gas in the presence of a flame. Do not open or disconnect any part of the air conditioning system.*

Sight Glass Check

You can safely make a few simple checks to determine if your air conditioning system needs

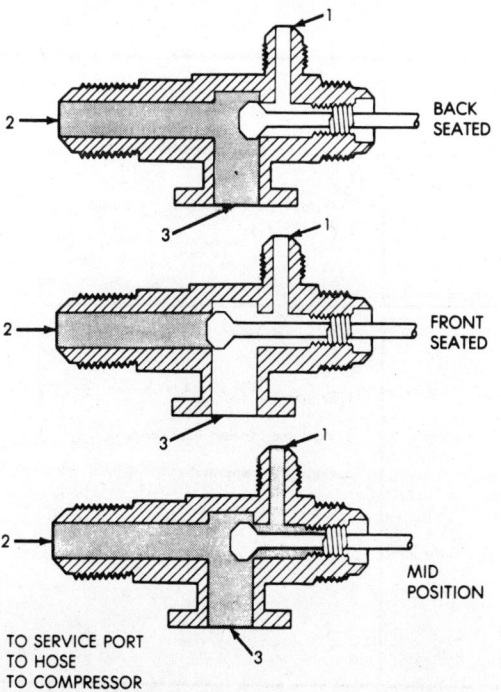

1. TO SERVICE PORT
2. TO HOSE
3. TO COMPRESSOR

Service valve positions

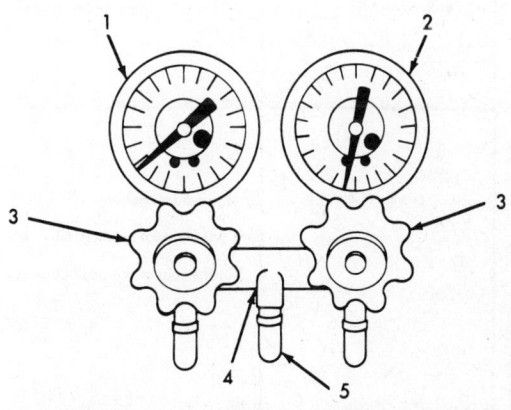

1. Compound gauge (suction)
2. High side gauge (discharge)
3. Hand valves
4. Manifold
5. Center service fitting

Manifold and gauge set

GENERAL INFORMATION AND MAINTENANCE

service. The tests work best if the temperature is warm (about 70°F [21.1°C]).

NOTE: *If your vehicle is equipped with an aftermarket air conditioner, the following system check may not apply. You should contact the manufacturer of the unit for instructions on systems checks.*

1. Place the automatic transmission in Park or the manual transmission in Neutral. Set the parking brake.
2. Run the engine at a fast idle (about 1,500 rpm) either with the help of a friend or by temporarily readjusting the idle speed screw.
3. Set the controls for maximum cold with the blower on High.
4. Locate the sight glass in one of the system

Condition	Possible Cause	Correction
COMPRESSOR NOISE	(1) Broken valves. (2) Overcharged. (3) Incorrect oil level. (4) Piston slap. (5) Broken rings. (6) Drive belt pulley bolts are loose.	(1) Replace the valve plate. (2) Discharge, evacuate and install the correct charge. (3) Isolate the compressor and check the oil level. Correct as necessary. (4) Replace the compressor. (5) Replace the compressor. (6) Tighten with the correct torque specification.
EXCESSIVE VIBRATION	(1) Incorrect belt tension. (2) Clutch loose. (3) Overcharged. (4) Pulley is misaligned.	(1) Adjust the belt tension. (2) Tighten the clutch. (3) Discharge, evacuate and install the correct charge. (4) Align the pulley.
CONDENSATION DRIPPING IN THE PASSENGER COMPARTMENT	(1) Drain hose plugged or improperly positioned. (2) Insulation removed or improperly installed.	(1) Clean the drain hose and check for proper installation. (2) Replace the insulation on the expansion valve and hoses.
FROZEN EVAPORATOR COIL	(1) Faulty thermostat. (2) Thermostat capillary tube improperly installed. (3) Thermostat not adjusted properly.	(1) Replace the thermostat. (2) Install the capillary tube correctly. (3) Adjust the thermostat.

Performance diagnosis chart

GENERAL INFORMATION AND MAINTENANCE

lines. Usually it is on the left alongside the top of the radiator.

5. If you see bubbles, the system must be recharged. Very likely there is a leak at some point.

6. If there are no bubbles, there is either no refrigerant at all or the system is fully charged. Feel the two hoses going to the belt driven compressor. If they are both at the same temperature, the system is empty and must be recharged.

7. If one hose (high pressure) is warm and the other (low pressure) is cold, the system may be all right. However, you are probably making these tests because you think there is something wrong, so proceed to the next step.

Condition	Possible Cause	Correction
LOW SIDE LOW – HIGH SIDE LOW	(1) System refrigerant is low. (2) Expansion valve is restricted.	(1) Evacuate, leak test and charge the system. (2) Replace the expansion valve.
LOW SIDE HIGH – HIGH SIDE LOW	(1) Internal leak in the compressor – worn. (2) Cylinder head gasket is leaking. (3) Expansion valve is defective. (4) Drive belt slipping.	(1) Remove the compressor cylinder head and inspect the compressor. Replace the valve plate assembly if necessary. If the compressor pistons, rings or cylinders are excessively worn or scored, replace the compressor. (2) Install a replacement cylinder head gasket. (3) Replace the expansion valve. (4) Adjust the belt tension.
LOW SIDE HIGH – HIGH SIDE HIGH	(1) Condenser fins obstructed. (2) Air in the system. (3) Expansion valve is defective. (4) Loose or worn fan belts.	(1) Clean the condenser fins. (2) Evacuate, leak test and charge the system. (3) Replace the expansion valve. (4) Adjust or replace the belts as necessary.
LOW SIDE LOW – HIGH SIDE HIGH	(1) Expansion valve is defective. (2) Restriction in the refrigerant hose. (3) Restriction in the receiver/drier. (4) Restriction in the condenser.	(1) Replace the expansion valve. (2) Check the hose for kinks – replace if necessary. (3) Replace the receiver/drier. (4) Replace the condenser.
LOW SIDE AND HIGH SIDE NORMAL (INADEQUATE COOLING)	(1) Air in the system. (2) Moisture in the system.	(1) Evacuate, leak test and charge the system. (2) Evacuate, leak test and charge the system.

Performance diagnosis chart (cont.)

GENERAL INFORMATION AND MAINTENANCE

8. Have an assistant in the truck turn the fan control on and off to operate the compressor clutch. Watch the sight glass.

9. If bubbles appear when the clutch is disengaged and disappear when it is engaged, the system is properly charged.

10. If the refrigerant takes more than 45 seconds to bubble when the clutch is disengaged, the system is overcharged. This usually causes poor cooling at low speeds.

WARNING: *If it is determined that the system has a leak, it should be corrected as soon as possible. Leaks may allow moisture to enter and cause a very expensive rust problem.*

Exercise the air conditioner for a few minutes, every two weeks or so, during the cold months. This avoids the possibility of the compressor seals drying out from lack of lubrication.

Temp. °F	Press. PSI	Temp. °F	Press. PSI	Temp. °F	Press. PSI	Temp. °F	Press. PSI	Temp. °F	Press. PSI
0	9.1	35	32.5	60	57.7	85	91.7	110	136.0
2	10.1	36	33.4	61	58.9	86	93.2	111	138.0
4	11.2	37	34.3	62	60.0	87	94.8	112	140.1
6	12.3	38	35.1	63	61.3	88	96.4	113	142.1
8	13.4	39	36.0	64	62.5	89	98.0	114	144.2
10	14.6	40	36.9	65	63.7	90	99.6	115	146.3
12	15.8	41	37.9	66	64.9	91	101.3	116	148.4
14	17.1	42	38.8	67	66.2	92	103.0	117	151.2
16	18.3	43	39.7	68	67.5	93	104.6	118	152.7
18	19.7	44	40.7	69	68.8	94	106.3	119	154.9
20	21.0	45	41.7	70	70.1	95	108.1	120	157.1
21	21.7	46	42.6	71	71.4	96	109.8	121	159.3
22	22.4	47	43.6	72	72.8	97	111.5	122	161.5
23	23.1	48	44.6	73	74.2	98	113.3	123	163.8
24	23.8	49	45.6	74	75.5	99	115.1	124	166.1
25	24.6	50	46.6	75	76.9	100	116.9	125	168.4
26	25.3	51	47.6	76	78.3	101	118.8	126	170.7
27	26.1	52	48.7	77	79.2	102	120.6	127	173.1
28	26.8	53	49.8	78	81.1	103	122.4	128	175.4
29	27.6	54	50.9	79	82.5	104	124.3	129	177.8
30	28.4	55	52.0	80	84.0	105	126.2	130	182.2
31	29.2	56	53.1	81	85.5	106	128.1	131	182.6
32	30.0	57	55.4	82	87.0	107	130.0	132	185.1
33	30.9	58	56.6	83	88.5	108	132.1	133	187.6
34	31.7	59	57.1	84	90.1	109	135.1	134	190.1

Temperature/pressure relationship chart

Refrigerant	Vaporizes °C (°F)[1]	Approximate Closed Container Pressure[1] kPa (psi)[2]					Adaptability
		15.57°C (60°)	21.13°C (70°)	26.69°C (80°)	32.25°C (90°)	37.81°C (100°)	
R-12	-29.80 (-21.6)	393 (57)	483 (70)	579 (84)	689 (100)	807 (117)	Self Propelling
R-11[3]	23.74 (74.7)	27 (8 in Hg)	10 (3 in Hg)	7 (1)	34 (5)	62 (9)	

[1]At sea level atmospheric pressure.
[2]kPa (psi) unless otherwise noted.

Refrigerant flushing chart

GENERAL INFORMATION AND MAINTENANCE

TESTING THE SYSTEM

1. Connect a gauge set.
2. Close (clockwise) both gauge set valves.
3. Park the truck in the shade, at least 5 feet from any walls. Start the engine, set the parking brake, place the transmission in NEUTRAL and establish an idle of 1,100-1,300 rpm.
4. Run the air conditioning system for full cooling, in the MAX or COLD mode.
5. The low pressure gauge should read 5-20 psi; the high pressure gauge should indicate 120-180 psi.

WARNING: *These pressures are the norm for an ambient temperature of 70-80°F (21-27°C). Higher air temperatures along with high humidity will cause higher syustem pressures. At idle speed and an ambient temperature of 110°F (43°C), the high pressure reading can exceed 300 psi.*

Under these extreme conditions, you can keep the pressures down by directing a large electric floor fan through the condenser.

ISOLATING THE COMPRESSOR

It is not necessary to discharge the system for compressor removal. The compressor can be isolated from the rest of the system, thus eliminating the need for evacuating and recharging the system after compressor removal.

1. Coonect the gauge set and manifold.
2. Close both gauge hand valves.
3. Mid-position both service valves.

CAUTION: *Be very careful of the engine fan! Your work will take you in close proximity to the moving fan blades!*

4. Start the engine and turn the system on.
5. Turn the suction service valve slowly clockwise to the front-seated position.
6. When the pressure drops to zero, stop the engine and quickle finish frontr-seating the suction service valve.
7. Front-seat the discharge service valve.
8. Loosen the oil level check plug slowly to release any internal pressure in the compressor.
9. The compressor is now isolated from the system. The service valves may be removed from the compressor.

DISCHARGING THE SYSTEM

1. Remove the caps from the high and low pressure charging valves in the high and low pressure lines.
2. Turn both manifold gauge set hand valves to the fully closed (clockwise) position.
3. Connect the manifold gauge set.
4. If the gauge set hoses do not have the gauge port actuating pins, install fitting adapters on the manifold gauge set hoses. If the truck does not have a service access gauge port valve, connect the gauge set low pressure hose to the evaporator service access gauge port valve.
5. Place the end of the center hose away from you and the truck.
6. Open the low pressure gauge valve slightly and allow the system pressure to bleed off.
7. When the system is just about empty, open the high pressure valve very slowly to avoid losing an excessive amount of refrigerant oil. Allow any remaining refrigerant to escape.

EVACUATING THE SYSTEM

NOTE: *This procedure requires the use of a vacuum pump.*

1. Connect the manifold gauge set.
2. Discharge the system.
3. Make sure that the low pressure gauge set hose is connected to the low pressure service gauge port on the top center of the accumulator/drier assembly and the high pressure hose connected to the high pressure service gauge port on the compressor discharge line.
4. Connect the center service hose to the inlet fitting of the vacuum pump.
5. Turn both gauge set valves to the wide open position.
6. Start the pump and note the low side gauge reading.
7. Operate the pump until the low pressure gauge reads 25-30 in.Hg. Continue running the vacuum pump for 10 minutes more. If you've replaced some component in the system, run the pump for an additional 20-30 minutes.
8. Leak test the system. Close both gauge set valves. Turn off the pump. The needle should remain stationary at the point at which the pump was turned off. If the needle drops to zero rapidly, there is a leak in the system which must be repaired.

LEAK TESTING

Some leak tests can be performed with a soapy water solution. There must be at least a ½ lb. charge in the system for a leak to be detected. The most extensive leak tests are performed with either a Halide flame type leak tester or the more preferable electronic leak tester.

In either case, the equipment is expensive, and, the use of a Halide detector can be **extremely** hazardous!

CHARGING THE SYSTEM

CAUTION: *NEVER OPEN THE HIGH PRESSURE SIDE WITH A CAN OF REFRIGERANT CONNECTED TO THE SYSTEM! OPENING THE HIGH PRESSURE SIDE WILL OVERPRESSURIZE THE CAN, CAUSING IT TO EXPLODE!*

GENERAL INFORMATION AND MAINTENANCE

Troubleshooting Basic Air Conditioning Problems

Problem	Cause	Solution
There's little or no air coming from the vents (and you're sure it's on)	• The A/C fuse is blown • Broken or loose wires or connections • The on/off switch is defective	• Check and/or replace fuse • Check and/or repair connections • Replace switch
The air coming from the vents is not cool enough	• Windows and air vent wings open • The compressor belt is slipping • Heater is on • Condenser is clogged with debris • Refrigerant has escaped through a leak in the system • Receiver/drier is plugged	• Close windows and vent wings • Tighten or replace compressor belt • Shut heater off • Clean the condenser • Check system • Service system
The air has an odor	• Vacuum system is disrupted • Odor producing substances on the evaporator case • Condensation has collected in the bottom of the evaporator housing	• Have the system checked/repaired • Clean the evaporator case • Clean the evaporator housing drains
System is noisy or vibrating	• Compressor belt or mountings loose • Air in the system	• Tighten or replace belt; tighten mounting bolts • Have the system serviced

Sight glass condition
  Constant bubbles, foam or oil streaks
  Clear sight glass, but no cold air
  Clear sight glass, but air is cold
  Clouded with milky fluid
	• Undercharged system
	
	• No refrigerant at all
	• System is OK
	• Receiver drier is leaking dessicant
		• Charge the system
		
		• Check and charge the system
		
		• Have system checked

Large difference in temperature of lines	• System undercharged	• Charge and leak test the system
Compressor noise	• Broken valves • Overcharged • Incorrect oil level • Piston slap • Broken rings • Drive belt pulley bolts are loose	• Replace the valve plate • Discharge, evacuate and install the correct charge • Isolate the compressor and check the oil level. Correct as necessary. • Replace the compressor • Replace the compressor • Tighten with the correct torque specification
Excessive vibration	• Incorrect belt tension • Clutch loose • Overcharged • Pulley is misaligned	• Adjust the belt tension • Tighten the clutch • Discharge, evacuate and install the correct charge • Align the pulley
Condensation dripping in the passenger compartment	• Drain hose plugged or improperly positioned • Insulation removed or improperly installed	• Clean the drain hose and check for proper installation • Replace the insulation on the expansion valve and hoses
Frozen evaporator coil	• Faulty thermostat • Thermostat capillary tube improperly installed • Thermostat not adjusted properly	• Replace the thermostat • Install the capillary tube correctly • Adjust the thermostat
Low side low—high side low	• System refrigerant is low • Expansion valve is restricted	• Evacuate, leak test and charge the system • Replace the expansion valve
Low side high—high side low	• Internal leak in the compressor—worn	• Remove the compressor cylinder head and inspect the compressor. Replace the valve plate assembly if necessary. If the compressor pistons, rings or

GENERAL INFORMATION AND MAINTENANCE

Troubleshooting Basic Air Conditioning Problems (cont.)

Problem	Cause	Solution
Low side high—high side low (cont.)		cylinders are excessively worn or scored replace the compressor
	• Cylinder head gasket is leaking	• Install a replacement cylinder head gasket
	• Expansion valve is defective	• Replace the expansion valve
	• Drive belt slipping	• Adjust the belt tension
Low side high—high side high	• Condenser fins obstructed	• Clean the condenser fins
	• Air in the system	• Evacuate, leak test and charge the system
	• Expansion valve is defective	• Replace the expansion valve
	• Loose or worn fan belts	• Adjust or replace the belts as necessary
Low side low—high side high	• Expansion valve is defective	• Replace the expansion valve
	• Restriction in the refrigerant hose	• Check the hose for kinks—replace if necessary
	• Restriction in the receiver/drier	• Replace the receiver/drier
	• Restriction in the condenser	• Replace the condenser
Low side and high side normal (inadequate cooling)	• Air in the system	• Evacuate, leak test and charge the system
	• Moisture in the system	• Evacuate, leak test and charge the system

Systems With Sight Glass

In this procedure the refrigerant enters the suction side of the system as a vapor while the compressor is running. Before proceeding, the system should be in a partial vacuum after adequate evacuation. Both hand valves on the gauge manifold should be closed.

1. Attach both test hoses to their respective service valve ports. Mid-position manually operated service valves, if present.
2. Install the dispensing valve (closed position) on the refrigerant container. (Single and multiple refrigerant manifolds are available to accommodate one to four 15 oz. cans.)
3. Attach the center charging hose to the refrigerant container valve.
4. Open dispensing valve on the refrigerant valve.
5. Loosen the center charging hose coupler where it connect to the gauge manifold to allow the escaping refrigerant to purge the hose of contaminants.
6. Tighten the center charging hose connector.
7. Purge the low pressure test hose at the gauge manifold.
8. Start the truck engine, roll down the truck windows and adjust the air conditioner to maximum cooling. The truck engine should be at normal operating temperature before proceeding. The heated environment helps the liquid vaporize more efficiently.
9. Crack open the low side hand valve on the manifold. Manipulate the valve so that the refrigerant that enters the system does not cause the low side pressure to exceed 40 psi. Too sudden a surge may permit the entrance of unwanted liquid to the compressor. Since liquids cannot be compressed, the compressor will suffer damage if compelled to attempt it. If the suction side of the system remains in a vacuum the system is blocked. Locate and correct the condition before proceeding any further.

NOTE: *Placing the refrigerant can in a container of warm water (no hotter than +125°F [+51.6°C]) will speed the charging process. Slight agitation of the can is helpful too, but be careful not to turn the can upside down.*

Systems Without Sight Glass

1. Connect the gauge set.
2. Close (clockwise) both gauge set valves.
3. Connect the center hose to the refrigerant can opener valve.
4. Make sure the can opener valve is closed, that is, the needle is raised, and connect the valve to the can. Open the valve, puncturing the can with the needle.
5. Loosen the center hose fitting at the pressure gauge, allowing refrigerant to purge the hose of air. When the air is bled, tighten the fitting.

CAUTION: *IF THE LOW PRESSURE GAUGE SET HOSE IS NOT CONNECTED TO THE ACCUMULATOR/DRIER, KEEP THE CAN IN AN UPRIGHT POSITION!*

6. Disconnect the wire harness snap-lock connector from the clutch cycling pressure

32 GENERAL INFORMATION AND MAINTENANCE

switch and install a jumper wire across the two terminals of the connector.

7. Open the low side gauge set valve and the can valve.

8. Allow refrigerant to be drawn into the system.

9. When no more refrigerant is drawn into the system, start the engine and run it at about 1,500 rpm. Turn on the system and operate it at the full high position. The compressor will operate and pull refrigerant gas into the system.

NOTE: *To help speed the process, the can may be placed, upright, in a pan of warm water, not exceeding 125°F (52°C).*

10. If more than one can of refrigerant is needed, close the can valve and gauge set low side valve when the can is empty and connect a new can to the opener. Repeat the charging process until no more refirgerant is drawn into the system. The frost line on the outside of the can will indicate what portion of the can has been used.

CAUTION: *NEVER ALLOW THE HIGH PRESSURE SIDE READING TO EXCEED 240 psi.*

11. When the charging process has been completed, close the gauge set valve and can valve. Remove the jumper wire and reconnect the cycling clutch wire. Run the system for at least five minutes to allow it to normalize. Low pressure side reading should be 4-25 psi; high pressure reading should be 120-210 psi at an ambient temperature of 70-90°F (21-32°C).

12. Loosen both service hoses at the gauges to allow any refrigerant to escape. Remove the gauge set and install the dust caps on the service valves.

NOTE: *Multi-can dispensers are available which allow a simultaneous hook-up of up to four 1 lb. cans of R-12.*

CAUTION: *Never exceed the recommended maximum charge for the system. The maximum charge for systems is 2 lbs.*

Windshield Wipers

Intense heat from the sun, snow, and ice, road oils and the chemicals used in windshield washer solvent combine to deteriorate the rubber wiper refills. The refills should be replaced about twice a year or whenever the blades begin to streak or chatter.

WIPER REFILL REPLACEMENT

Normally, if the wipers are not cleaning the windshield properly, only the refill has to be replaced. The blade and arm usually require replacement only in the event of damage. It is not necessary (except on new Tridon® refills) to remove the arm or the blade to replace the refill (rubber part), though you may have to position the arm higher on the glass. You can do this turning the ignition switch on and operating the wipers. When they are positioned where they are accessible, turn the ignition switch off.

There are several types of refills and your vehicle could have any kind, since aftermarket blades and arms may not use exactly the same type refill as the original equipment.

Most Anco® styles use a release button that is pushed down to allow the refill to slide out of the yoke jaws. The new refill slides in and locks in place.

Some Trico® refills are removed by locating where the metal backing strip or the refill is wider. Insert a small screwdriver blade between the frame and metal backing strip. Press down to release the refill from the retaining tab.

Other Trico® blades are unlocked at one end by squeezing 2 metal tabs, and the refill is slid out of the frame jaws. When the new refill is installed, the tabs will click into place, locking the refill.

The polycarbonate type is held in place by a locking lever that is pushed downward out of the groove in the arm to free the refill. When the new refill is installed, it will lock in place automatically.

The Tridon® refill has a plastic backing strip with a notch about 1" (25mm) from the end. Hold the blade (frame) on a hard surface so that the frame is tightly bowed. Grip the tip of the backing strip and pull up while twisting counterclockwise. The backing strip will snap out of the retaining tab. Do this for the remaining tabs until the refill is free of the arm. The length of these refills is molded into the end and they should be replaced with identical types.

No matter which type of refill you use, be sure that all of the frame claws engage the refill. Before operating the wipers, be sure that no part of the metal frame is contacting the windshield.

Tires and Wheels

The tires should be rotated as specified in the Maintenance Intervals Chart. Refer to the accompanying illustrations for the recommended rotation patterns.

The tires on your truck should have built-in tread wear indicators, which appear as $\frac{1}{2}$" (12.7mm) bands when the tread depth gets as low as $\frac{1}{16}$" (1.6mm). When the indicators appear in 2 or more adjacent grooves, it's time for new tires.

For optimum tire life, you should keep the tires properly inflated, rotate them often and

GENERAL INFORMATION AND MAINTENANCE

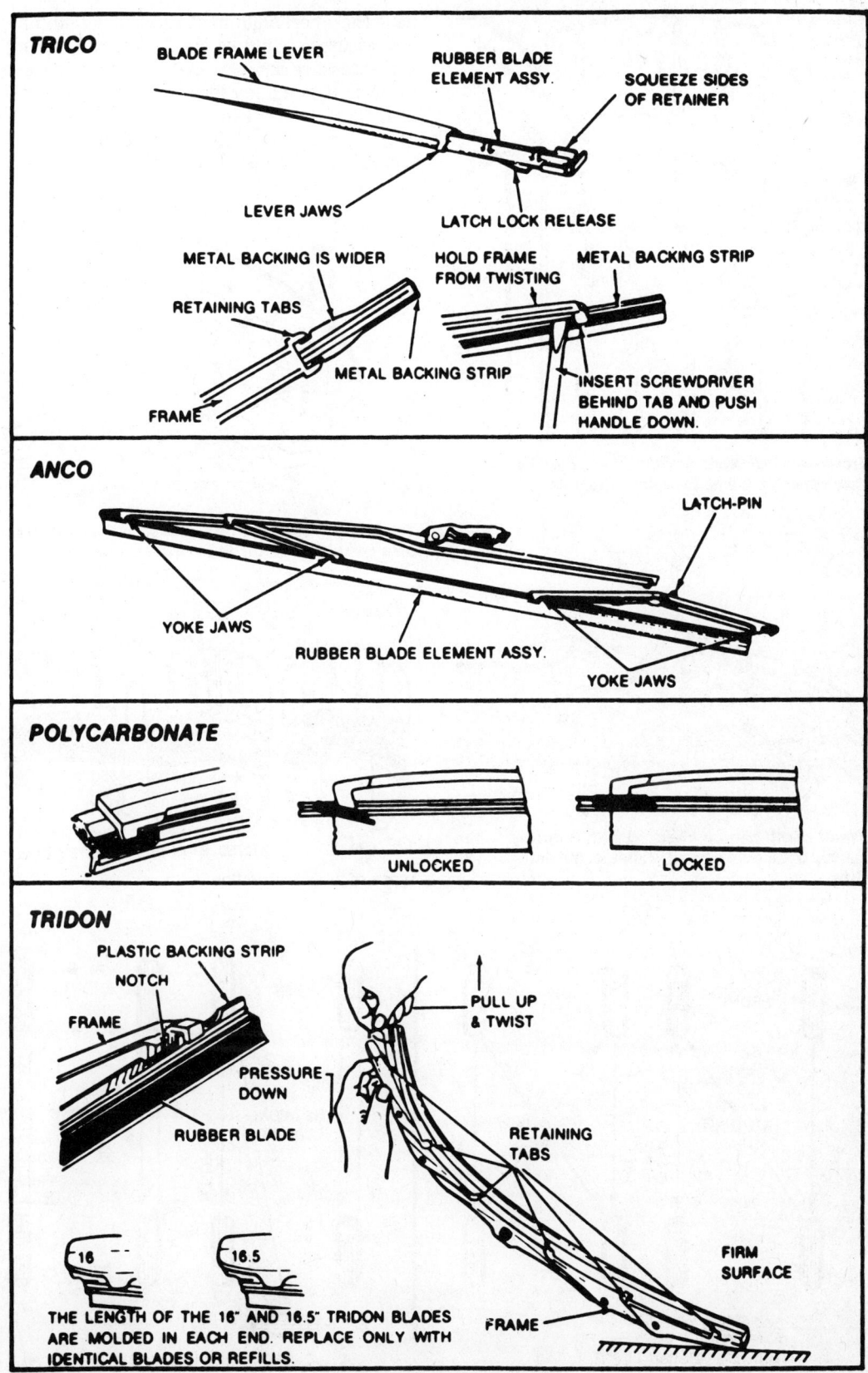

Popular styles of wiper refills

34 GENERAL INFORMATION AND MAINTENANCE

have the wheel alignment checked periodically.

Pressures should be checked before driving, since pressure can increase as much as 6 psi due to heat. It is a good idea to have an accurate gauge and to check pressures weekly. Not all gauges on service station air pumps are to be trusted. In general, truck type tires require

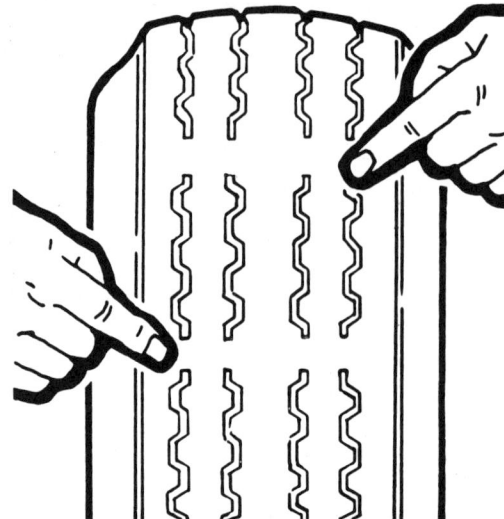

Tread wear indicators are built into all new tires. When they appear, it's time to replace the tires

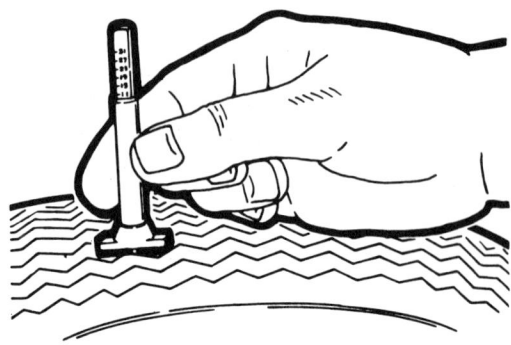

Tread depth can also be checked with an inexpensive gauge made for the purpose

Tread depth can be checked with a penny; when the top of Lincoln's head is visible, it's time for new tires

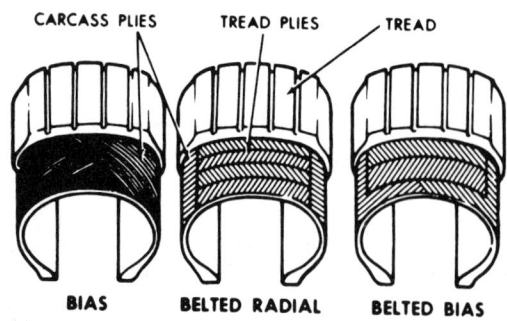

Types of tire construction

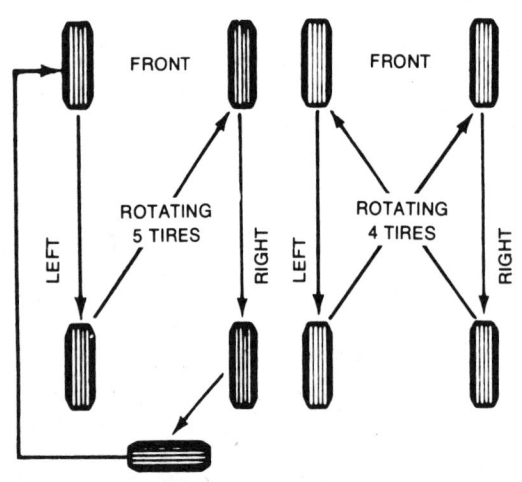

Bias/Bias-Belted Tire Rotation

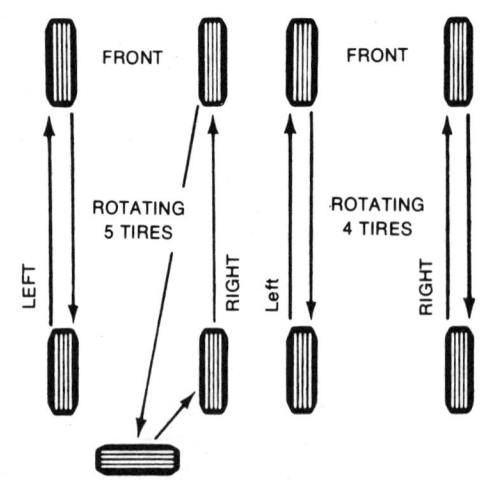

Radial Tire Rotation

Tire rotation

GENERAL INFORMATION AND MAINTENANCE

higher pressures and flotation type tires, lower pressures.

TIRE ROTATION

It is recommended that you have the tires rotated and the balance checked every 6,000 miles. There is no way to give a tire rotation diagram for every combination of tires and vehicles, but the accompanying diagrams are a general rule to follow. Radial tires should not be cross-switched; they last longer if their direction of rotation is not changed. Some truck tires and some high-performance tires sometimes have directional tread, indicated by arrows on the sidewalls; the arrow shows the direction of rotation. They will wear very rapidly if reversed. Studded snow tires will lose their studs if their direction of rotation is reversed.

NOTE: *Mark the wheel position or direction of rotation on radial tires or studded snow tires before removing them.*

If your truck is equipped with tires having

Troubleshooting Basic Wheel Problems

Problem	Cause	Solution
The car's front end vibrates at high speed	• The wheels are out of balance • Wheels are out of alignment	• Have wheels balanced • Have wheel alignment checked/adjusted
Car pulls to either side	• Wheels are out of alignment • Unequal tire pressure • Different size tires or wheels	• Have wheel alignment checked/adjusted • Check/adjust tire pressure • Change tires or wheels to same size
The car's wheel(s) wobbles	• Loose wheel lug nuts • Wheels out of balance • Damaged wheel • Wheels are out of alignment • Worn or damaged ball joint • Excessive play in the steering linkage (usually due to worn parts) • Defective shock absorber	• Tighten wheel lug nuts • Have tires balanced • Raise car and spin the wheel. If the wheel is bent, it should be replaced • Have wheel alignment checked/adjusted • Check ball joints • Check steering linkage • Check shock absorbers
Tires wear unevenly or prematurely	• Incorrect wheel size • Wheels are out of balance • Wheels are out of alignment	• Check if wheel and tire size are compatible • Have wheels balanced • Have wheel alignment checked/adjusted

Troubleshooting Basic Tire Problems

Problem	Cause	Solution
The car's front end vibrates at high speeds and the steering wheel shakes	• Wheels out of balance • Front end needs aligning	• Have wheels balanced • Have front end alignment checked
The car pulls to one side while cruising	• Unequal tire pressure (car will usually pull to the low side) • Mismatched tires • Front end needs aligning	• Check/adjust tire pressure • Be sure tires are of the same type and size • Have front end alignment checked
Abnormal, excessive or uneven tire wear See "How to Read Tire Wear"	• Infrequent tire rotation • Improper tire pressure • Sudden stops/starts or high speed on curves	• Rotate tires more frequently to equalize wear • Check/adjust pressure • Correct driving habits
Tire squeals	• Improper tire pressure • Front end needs aligning	• Check/adjust tire pressure • Have front end alignment checked

GENERAL INFORMATION AND MAINTENANCE

different load ratings on the front and the rear, the tires should not be rotated front to rear. Rotating these tires could affect tire life (the tires with the lower rating will wear faster, and could become overloaded), and upset the handling of the truck.

TIRE USAGE

The tires on your truck were selected to provide the best all around performance for normal operation when inflated as specified. Oversize tires will not increase the maximum carrying capacity of the vehicle, although they will provide an extra margin of tread life. Be sure to check overall height before using larger size tires which may cause interference with suspension components or wheel wells. When replacing conventional tire sizes with other tire size designations, be sure to check the manufacturer's recommendations. Interchangeability is not always possible because of differences in load ratings, tire dimensions, wheel well clearances, and rim size. Also due to differences in handling characteristics, 70 Series and 60 Series tires should be used only in pairs on the same axle; radial tires should be used only in sets of four.

NOTE: *Many states have vehicle height restrictions; some states prohibit the lifting of vehicles beyond their design limits.*

The wheels must be the correct width for the tire. Tire dealers have charts of tire and rim compatibility. A mismatch can cause sloppy handling and rapid tread wear. The old rule of thumb is that the tread width should match the rim width (inside bead to inside bead) within an

Tire Size Comparison Chart

"Letter" sizes			Inch Sizes	Metric-inch Sizes		
"60 Series"	"70 Series"	"78 Series"	1965–77	"60 Series"	"70 Series"	"80 Series"
			5.50-12, 5.60-12	165/60-12	165/70-12	155-12
		Y78-12	6.00-12			
		W78-13	5.20-13	165/60-13	145/70-13	135-13
		Y78-13	5.60-13	175/60-13	155/70-13	145-13
			6.15-13	185/60-13	165/70-13	155-13, P155/80-13
A60-13	A70-13	A78-13	6.40-13	195/60-13	175/70-13	165-13
B60-13	B70-13	B78-13	6.70-13	205/60-13	185/70-13	175-13
			6.90-13			
C60-13	C70-13	C78-13	7.00-13	215/60-13	195/70-13	185-13
D60-13	D70-13	D78-13	7.25-13			
E60-13	E70-13	E78-13	7.75-13			195-13
			5.20-14	165/60-14	145/70-14	135-14
			5.60-14	175/60-14	155/70-14	145-14
			5.90-14			
A60-14	A70-14	A78-14	6.15-14	185/60-14	165/70-14	155-14
	B70-14	B78-14	6.45-14	195/60-14	175/70-14	165-14
	C70-14	C78-14	6.95-14	205/60-14	185/70-14	175-14
D60-14	D70-14	D78-14				
E60-14	E70-14	E78-14	7.35-14	215/60-14	195/70-14	185-14
F60-14	F70-14	F78-14, F83-14	7.75-14	225/60-14	200/70-14	195-14
G60-14	G70-14	G77-14, G78-14	8.25-14	235/60-14	205/70-14	205-14
H60-14	H70-14	H78-14	8.55-14	245/60-14	215/70-14	215-14
J60-14	J70-14	J78-14	8.85-14	255/60-14	225/70-14	225-14
L60-14	L70-14		9.15-14	265/60-14	235/70-14	
	A70-15	A78-15	5.60-15	185/60-15	165/70-15	155-15
B60-15	B70-15	B78-15	6.35-15	195/60-15	175/70-15	165-15
C60-15	C70-15	C78-15	6.85-15	205/60-15	185/70-15	175-15
	D70-15	D78-15				
E60-15	E70-15	E78-15	7.35-15	215/60-15	195/70-15	185-15
F60-15	F70-15	F78-15	7.75-15	225/60-15	205/70-15	195-15
G60-15	G70-15	G78-15	8.15-15/8.25-15	235/60-15	215/70-15	205-15
H60-15	H70-15	H78-15	8.45-15/8.55-15	245/60-15	225/70-15	215-15
J60-15	J70-15	J78-15	8.85-15/8.90-15	255/60-15	235/70-15	225-15
	K70-15		9.00-15	265/60-15	245/70-15	230-15
L60-15	L70-15	L78-15, L84-15	9.15-15			235-15
	M70-15	M78-15				255-15
		N78-15				

Note: Every size tire is not listed and many size comparisons are approximate, based on load ratings. Wider tires than those supplied new with the vehicle, should always be checked for clearance.

inch. For radial tires, the rim width should be 80% or less of the tire (not tread) width.

The height (mounted diameter) of the new tires can greatly change speedometer accuracy, engine speed at a given road speed, fuel mileage, acceleration, and ground clearance. Tire manufacturers furnish full measurement specifications. Speedometer drive gears are available for correction.

NOTE: *Dimensions of tires marked the same size may vary significantly, even among tires from the same manufacturer.*

The spare tire should be of the same size, construction and design as the tires on the vehicle. It's not a good idea to carry a spare of a different contstruction.

TIRE DESIGN

For maximum satisfaction, tires should be used in sets of five. Mixing or different types (radial, bias-belted, fiberglass belted) should be avoided. Conventional bias tires are constructed so that the cords run bead-to-bead at an angle. Alternate plies run at an opposite angle. This type of construction gives rigidity to both tread and sidewall. Bias-belted tires are similar in construction to conventional bias ply tires. Belts run at an angle and also at a 90° angle to the bead, as in the radial tire. Tread life is improved considerably over the conventional bias tire. The radial tire differs in construction, but instead of the carcass plies running at an angle of 90° to each other, they run at an angle of 90° to the bead. This gives the tread a great deal of rigidity and the sidewall a great deal of flexibility and accounts for the characteristic bulge associated with radial tires.

When radial tires are used, tire sizes and wheel diameters should be selected to maintain ground clearance and tire load capacity equivalent to the minimum specified tire. Radial tires should always be used in sets of five, but in an emergency, radial tires can be used with caution on the rear axle only. If this is done, both tires on the rear should be of radial design.

WARNING: *Radial tires should never be used on only the front axle!*

FLUIDS AND LUBRICANTS

Oil and Fuel Recommendations

All gasoline engines are designed to run on unleaded gasoline.

The Diesel engine in you Jeep is designed to run on No.2 Diesel fuel with a cetane rating of 40. For operation when the outdoor air temperature is consistently below freezing, the use of No.1 Diesel fuel or the addition of a cold weather additive, is recommended.

Fuel makers produce two grades of diesel fuel, No. 1 and No. 2, for use in automotive diesel engines. Generally speaking, No. 2 fuel is recommended over No. 1 for driving in temperatures above 20°F (−7°C). In fact, in many areas, No. 2 diesel is the only fuel available. By comparison, No. 2 diesel fuel is less volatile than No. 1 fuel, and gives better fuel economy. No. 2 fuel is also a better injection pump lubricant.

Two important characteristics of diesel fuel are its cetane number and its viscosity.

The cetane number of a diesel fuel refers to the ease with which a diesel fuel ignites. High cetane numbers mean that the fuel will ignite with relative ease or that it ignites well at low temperatures. Naturally, the lower the cetane number, the higher the temperature must be to ignite the fuel. Most commercial fuels have cetane numbers that range from 35 to 65. No. 1 diesel fuel generally has a higher cetane rating than No. 2 fuel.

Viscosity is the ability of a liquid, in this case diesel fuel, to flow. Using straight No. 2 diesel fuel below 20°F (−7°C) can cause problems, because this fuel tends to become cloudy, meaning wax crystals begin forming in the fuel. 20°F (−7°C) is often call the cloud point for No. 2 fuel. In extremely cold weather, No. 2 fuel can stop flowing altogether. In either case, fuel flow is restricted, which can result in no start condition or poor engine performance. Fuel manufacturers often winterize No. 2 diesel fuel by using various fuel additives and blends (no. 1 diesel fuel, kerosene, etc.) to lower its winter time viscosity. Generally speaking, though, No. 1 diesel fuel is more satisfactory in extremely cold weather.

NOTE: *No. 1 and No. 2 diesel fuels will mix and burn with no ill effects, although the engine manufacturer will undoubtedly recommend on or the other. Consult the owner's manual for information.*

Depending on local climate, most fuel manufacturers make winterized No. 2 fuel available seasonally.

Many automobile manufacturers publish pamphlets giving the locations of diesel fuel stations nationwide. Contact the local dealer for information.

Do not substitute home heating oil for automotive diesel fuel. While in some cases, home heating oil refinement levels equal those of diesel fuel, many times they are far below diesel engine requirements. The result of using dirty home heating oil will be a clogged fuel system, in which case the entire system may have to be dismantled and cleaned.

38 GENERAL INFORMATION AND MAINTENANCE

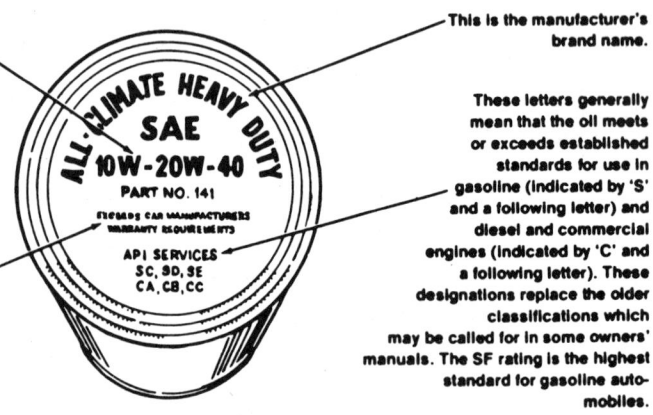

This is the oil's SAE viscosity grade. The numbers followed by a 'W' indicate an oil with low temperature performance characteristics and the 'non-W' numbers describe an oil with high temperature characteristics. If there is one number, it is a single grade. Two or more numbers indicate a 'multi-viscosity' oil which has both low and high temperature characteristics.

This means that the oil will protect expensive engine components. Even if your car is no longer under warranty, it indicates that the oil is of good quality.

This is the manufacturer's brand name.

These letters generally mean that the oil meets or exceeds established standards for use in gasoline (indicated by 'S' and a following letter) and diesel and commercial engines (indicated by 'C' and a following letter). These designations replace the older classifications which may be called for in some owners' manuals. The SF rating is the highest standard for gasoline automobiles.

The top of the oil can will tell you all you need to know about the oil

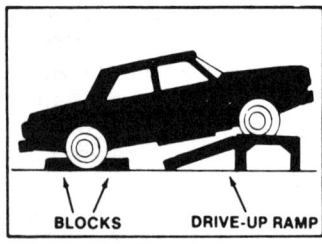

1. Warm the car up before changing your oil. Raise the front end of the car and support it on drive-on ramps or jackstands.

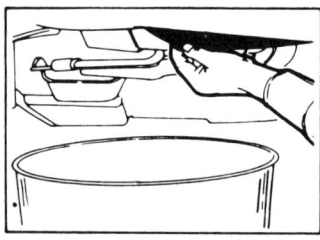

2. Locate the drain plug on the bottom of the oil pan and slide a low flat pan of sufficient capacity under the engine to catch the oil. Loosen the plug with a wrench and turn it out the last few turns by hand. Keep a steady inward pressure on the plug to avoid hot oil from running down your arm.

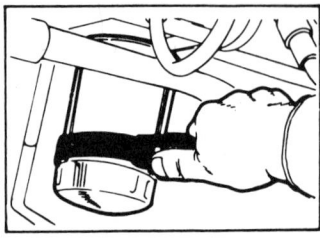

3. Remove the oil filter with a filter wrench. The filter can hold more than a quart of oil, which will be hot. Be sure the gasket comes off with the filter and clean the mounting base on the engine.

4. Lubricate the gasket on the new filter with clean engine oil. A dry gasket may not make a good seal and will allow the filter to leak.

5. Position a new filter on the mounting base and spin it on by hand. Do not use a wrench. When the gasket contacts the engine, tighten it another ½-1 turn by hand.

6. Using a rag, clean the drain plug and the area around the drain hole in the oil pan.

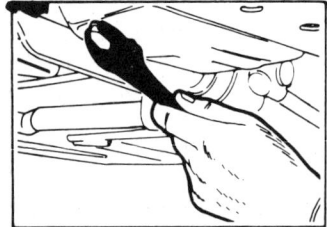

7. Install the drain plug and tighten it finger-tight. If you feel resistance, stop and be sure you are not cross-threading the plug. Finally, tighten the plug with a wrench.

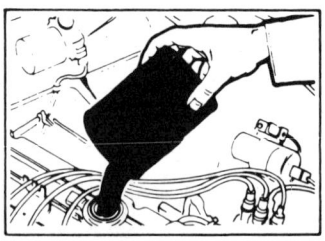

8. Locate the oil cap on the valve cover. An oil spout is the easiest way to add oil, but a funnel will do just as well.

9. Start the engine and check for leaks. The oil pressure warning light will remain on for a few seconds; when it goes out, stop the engine and check the level on the dipstick.

GENERAL INFORMATION AND MAINTENANCE

One more word on diesel fuels. Don't thin diesel fuel with gasoline in cold weather. The lighter gasoline, which is more explosive, will cause rough running at the very least, and may cause extensive damage to the fuel system if enough is used.

Many factors help to determine the proper oil for your Jeep. The big question is what viscosity to use and when. The whole question of viscosity revolves around the lowest anticipated ambient temperature to be encountered before your next oil change. The recommended viscosity ratings for temperatures ranging from below 0°F to above 32°F are listed in the accompanying chart. They are broken down into multiviscosities and single viscosities. Multiviscosity oils are recommended because of their wider range of acceptable temperatures and driving conditions.

Oil viscosities should be chosen from those oils recommended for the lowest anticipated temperatures during the oil change interval. Due to the need for an oil that embodies both good lubrication at high temperatures and easy cranking in cold weather, multigrade oils have been developed. Basically, a multigrade oil is thinner at low temperatures and thicker at high temperatures. For example, a 10W-40 oil (the W stands for winter) exhibits the characteristics of a 10 weight (SAE 10) oil when the truck is first started and the oil is cold. Its lighter weight allows it to travel to the lubricating surfaces quicker and offer less resistance to starter motor cranking than, say, a straight 30 weight (SAE 30) oil. But after the engine reaches operating temperature, the 10W-40 oil begins acting like straight 40 weight (SAE 40) oil, its heavier weight providing greater lubrication with less chance of foaming than a straight 30 weight oil.

The SAE grade number indicates the viscosity of the engine oil, or its ability to lubricate under a given temperature. The lower the SAE grade number, the lighter the oil; the lower the viscosity, the easier it is to crank the engine in cold weather.

The API (American Petroleum Institute) designation indicates the classification of engine oil for use under given operating conditions. For gasoline engines, only oils designated for Service SE/SF, or just SF, should be used. For Diesel engines, use only those oils designated Service SF/CD. These oils provide maximum engine protection. Both the SAE grade number and the API designation can be found on the top of a can of oil.

NOTE: *Non-detergent or straight mineral oils should not be used.*

Oil viscosities should be chosen from those oils recommended for the lowest anticipated temperatures during the oil change interval.

Engine Oil

OIL LEVEL CHECK

First, it is necessary to make sure that your vehicle is on a level surface to ensure an accurate reading. Then, raise the hood, position the hold-up rod, if so equipped, and measure the oil with the dipstick which is on the right side of 4-cylinder engines and on the left of 6-cylinder engines. Add oil through valve cover filler hole.

If the oil is below the half mark, add a quart of oil, then recheck the level. If the level is still not reading full, add only ½ quart at a time, until the dipstick reads full. Do not overfill the engine. When you check the oil in any engine, make sure that you allow sufficient time for all the oil to drain back into the crankcase after stopping the engine or else you will only mea-

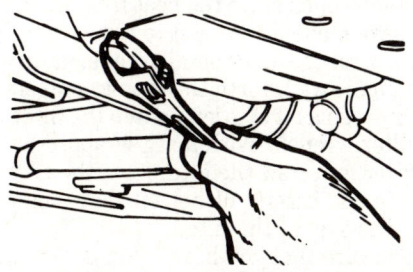

The oil drain plug is located at the lowest point of the pan

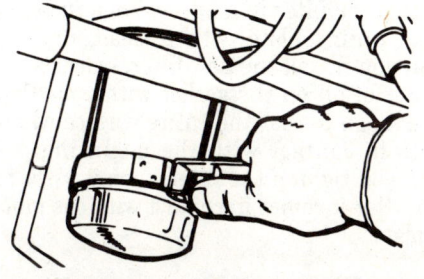

Use an oil filter strap wrench to remove the old filter; install the new filter by hand

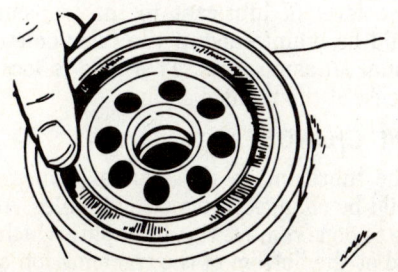

Apply a thin film of clean oil to the gasket to prevent its distortion during tightening

sure a fraction of the actual amount. A minute or so should be enough time.

OIL AND FILTER CHANGE

CAUTION: *The EPA warns that prolonged contact with used engine oil may cause a number of skin disorders, including cancer! You should make every effort to minimize your exposure to used engine oil. Protective gloves should be worn when changing the oil. Wash your hands and any other exposed skin areas as soon as possible after exposure to used engine oil. Soap and water, or waterless hand cleaner should be used.*

The engine oil is to be changed every 4,000 miles. The oil should be changed more frequently, however, under conditions such as:
- Driving in dusty conditions
- Continuous trailer pulling or RV use
- Extensive or prolonged idling
- Extensive short trip operation in freezing temperatures (when the engine is not thoroughly warmed up)
- Frequent long runs at high speeds and high ambient temperatures
- Stop-and-go service, such as delivery trucks,

the oil change interval and filter replacement interval should be cut in half. Operation of the engine in severe conditions, such as a dust storm, volcanic ash or deep water, may require an immediate oil and filter change.

Before draining the oil, make sure that the engine is at operating temperature. Hot oil will hold more impurities in suspension and will flow better, allowing it to remove more oil and dirt.

Drain the oil into a suitable receptacle. After the drain plug is loosened, unscrew the plug with your fingers, using a rag to shield your fingers from the heat. Push in on the plug as you unscrew it so you can feel when all of the screw threads are out of the hole. You can then remove the plug quickly with the minimum amount of oil running down your arm and you will also have the plug in your hand and not in the bottom of a pan of hot oil. Be careful of the oil. If it is at operating temperatures, it is hot enough to burn you or at least make you uncomfortable.

The engine should be at operating temperatures when the filter and oil are changed.

On the 4-150 engines, the filter is located on the right hand side of the engine.

On the 4-126 Turbo Diesel, the filter is remotely mounted, inline with the oil cooler.

On the 6-173, the filter is on the left side at the front.

On the 6-243, the filter is located on the lower, center right side of the engine.

To remove a spin-on filter, you will need an oil filter wrench since the heat from the engine may have made it too tight to remove by hand. A filter wrench can be obtained at an auto parts store and is well worth the investment, since it will save you a lot of grief. Loosen the filter with the filter wrench. With a rag wrapped around the filter, unscrew the filter from the oil pump housing. Be careful of hot oil that might run down the side of the filter.

Make sure that you have a pan under the filter before you start to remove it from the engine to avoid a mess and, if some of the hot oil does happen to get on you, you will have place to dump the filter in a hurry. Wipe the base of the mounting plate with a clean, dry cloth. When you install the new filter, smear a small amount of oil on the gasket with your finger, just enough to coat the entire surface where it comes in contact with the mounting plate. When you tighten the filter, turn it ¼-¾ turn more after it comes in contact with the mounting plate.

Manual Transmissions

FLUID LEVEL CHECK

The level of lubricant in the transmission should be maintained at the filler hole on all manual transmissions. This hole is locate on the side of the transmission.

FLUID CHANGE

The lubricant in the manual transmission should be changed every 30,000 miles. All you have to do is remove the drain plug which is located at the bottom of the transmission or else on the side near the bottom. Allow all the lubricant to run out before replacing the plug. Re-

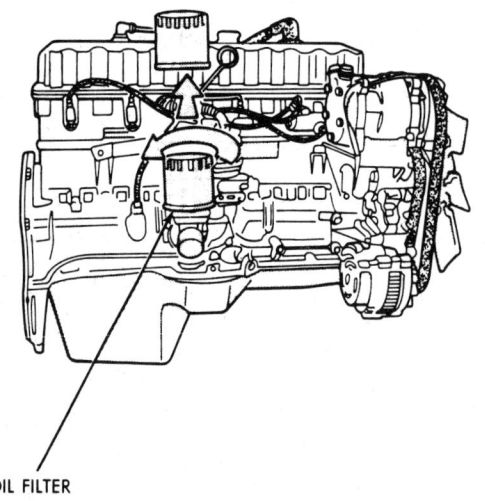

OIL FILTER

6-243 oil filter

GENERAL INFORMATION AND MAINTENANCE

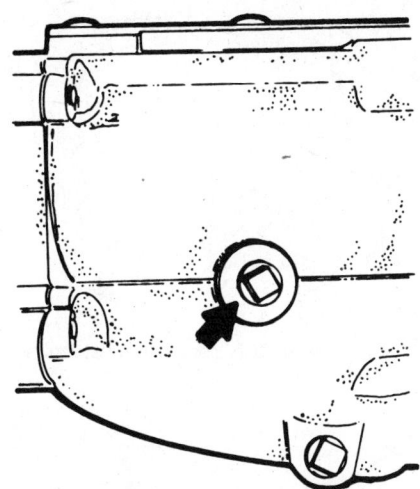

Manual transmission fill and drain plugs with the drain plug at the bottom center

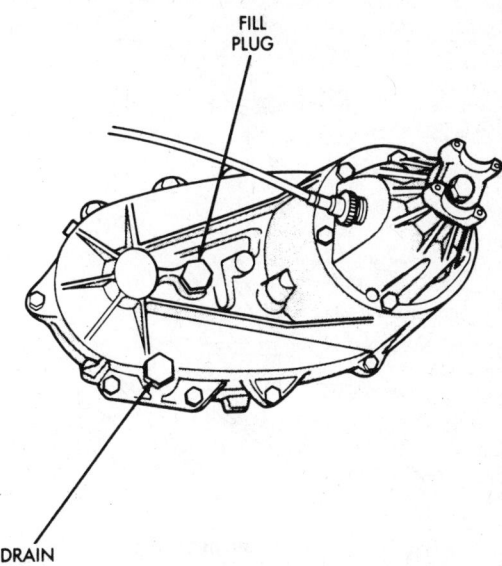

Transfer case drain and fill plugs

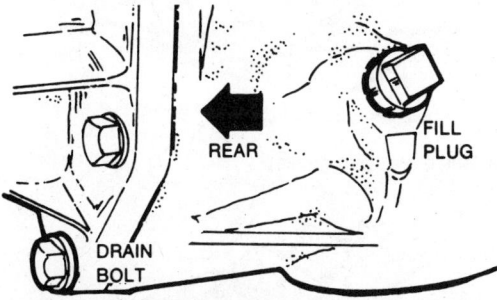

Manual transmission fill and drain plugs, using a tailshaft bolt as the drain plug

place the oil with the correct oil. All manual transmissions, except the T4 & T5, use SAE 80W-90 gear oil. The T4 & T5 use DEXRON®II automatic transmission fluid. Many brands of 80 and 90 weight now come in handy squeeze bottles which make filling easy and clean.

Transfer Case
FLUID LEVEL CHECK

Fluid should be maintained at the level of the filler plug hole. When you check the level, make sure that the vehicle is level so that you get a true reading. When you remove the filler plug, the lubricant should run out of the hole. If there is lubricant present at the hole, you know that the case is filled to the proper level. Replace the plug quickly for a minimum loss of lubricant. If lubricant does not run out of the hole when the plug is removed, lubricant should be added until it does. Replace the plug as soon as the lubricant reaches the level of the hole.

FLUID CHANGE

All transfer cases are to be serviced at the same time and in the same manner as the manual transmissions. The transfer case has its own drain plug which should be opened; do not rely on the transmission drain plug to completely drain the transfer case, even if they are interconnected. Once the transfer case has been drained, replace the drain plug, remove the fill plug and fill the transfer case. All transfer cases use Dexron®II automatic transmission fluid.

Automatic Transmission
FLUID LEVEL CHECK

The fluid level in automatic transmissions is checked with a dipstick which is located in the filler pipe at the right rear of the engine. The fluid level should be maintained between the ADD and FULL marks on the end of the dipstick with the automatic transmission fluid at normal operating temperatures. To raise the level from the ADD mark to the FULL mark, requires the addition of one pint of fluid. The fluid level with the fluid at room temperature (75°F [24°C]) should be approximately ¼" below the ADD mark.

NOTE: *In checking the automatic transmission fluid, insert the dipstick in the filler tube with the markings toward the center of the truck. Also, remember that the FULL mark on the dipstick is the indication of the level of the automatic transmission fluid when it is at operating temperature. This temperature is only obtained after at least 15 miles of ex-*

42 GENERAL INFORMATION AND MAINTENANCE

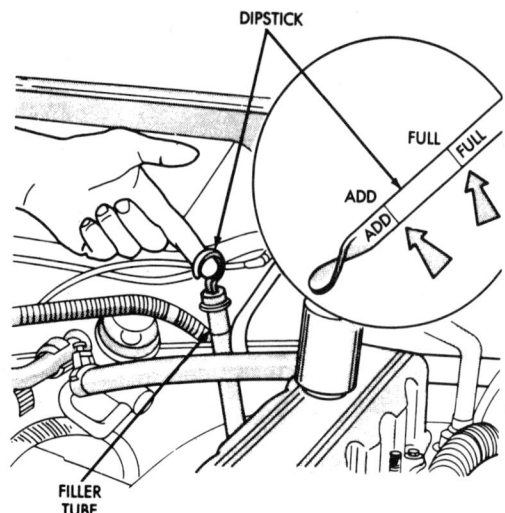

Checking the automatic transmission fluid level

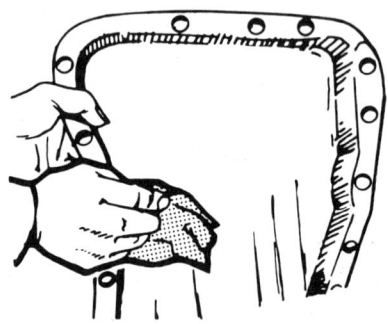

Clean the pan thoroughly with a safe solvent and allow it to air dry

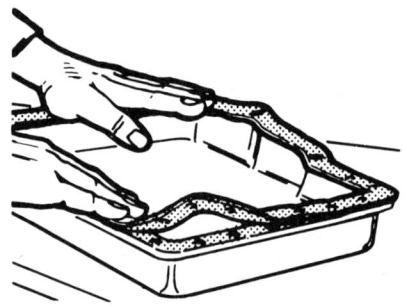

Install a new pan gasket

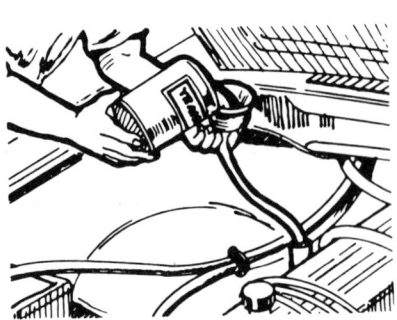

Fill the transmission with the required amount of fluid. Do not overfill. Start the engine and run the selector through all the shift points. Check the fluid and add as necessary

pressway driving or the equivalent of city driving.

To check the automatic transmission fluid level, follow the procedure given below. This procedure is applicable either when the fluid is at room temperature or at operating temperature.

1. With the transmission in Park, the engine running at idle speed, the foot brake applied and the vehicle resting on level ground, move the transmission gear selector through each of the gear positions, including Reverse, allowing time for the transmission to engage. Return the shift selector to the Park position and apply the parking brake. Do not turn the engine off, but leave it running at idle speed.

2. Clean all dirt from around the transmission dipstick cap and the end of the filler tube.

3. Pull the dipstick out of the tube, wipe it off with a clean cloth, and push it back into the tube all the way, making sure that it seats completely.

4. Pull the dipstick out of the tube again and

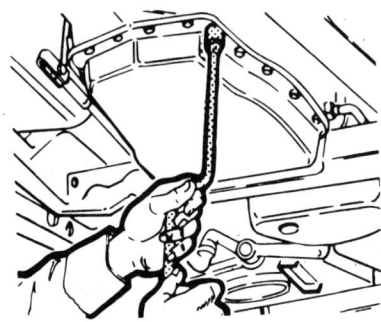

Many late model vehicles have no drain plug. Loosen the pan bolts and allow one corner of the pan to hang, so that the fluid will drain out

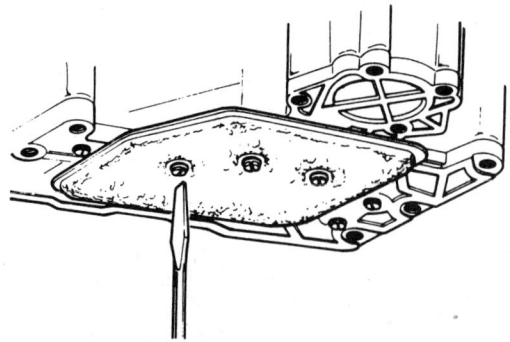

Removing automatic transmission filter

GENERAL INFORMATION AND MAINTENANCE

read the level of the fluid on the stick. The level should be between the ADD and FULL marks. Do not overfill the transmission because this will cause foaming and loss of fluid through the vent and malfunctioning of the transmission. Use only DEXRON® II transmission fluid.

FLUID AND FILTER CHANGE

The transmission fluid in an automatic transmission should be changed every 24,000 miles of normal driving or every 12,000 miles of driving under abnormal or severe conditions. All models use Dexron®II fluid. The fluid should be drained immediately after the vehicle has been driven for at least 20 minutes at expressway speeds or the equivalent of city driving, before it has had the chance to cool. Follow the procedure given below:

1. Drain the automatic transmission fluid from the transmission into an appropriate container, by removing the transmission bottom pan screws, pan and gasket.
2. Remove the oil strainer and discard it.
3. Remove the O-ring seal from the pickup pipe and discard it.
4. Install a new O-ring seal on the pickup pipe and install the new oil strainer and pipe assembly.
5. Thoroughly clean the bottom pan and position a new gasket on the pan mating surface. Install the bottom pan and secure it with the attaching screws, torqued to 10-13 ft. lbs.
6. Pour about 4 quarts of automatic transmission fluid in the filler pipe. Make sure that the funnel, container, hose or any other item used to assist in filling the transmission is clean.
7. Start the engine. DO NOT race it. Allow the engine to idle for a few minutes.
8. Place the selector lever in Park and apply the parking brake. With the transmission fluid at operating temperatures, check the fluid level; add fluid to bring the level to the FULL mark.

Front and Rear Axle

FLUID LEVEL CHECK

The standard front and rear axle differentials use SAE 80W/90 gear oil. Either is acceptable for use in the differential housing. Powr-Lok® differentials use only Jeep Powr-Lok® Lubricant or its equivalent. In Trac-Lok® axles, use any limited slip gear oil meeting SAE 75W/90, 80W/90 or 85W/90 specifications. Jeep recommends the use of 80W/140 gear oil when towing trailers on a regular basis. Check the level of the oil in the differential housing every 5,000 miles under normal driving conditions and every 3,000 miles if the vehicle is used in severe driving conditions. The level should be up to the filler hole. When you remove the filler plug, the oil should start to run out. If it does not, replenish the supply until it does.

The lubricant should be changed every 30,000 miles. If running in deep water, change the lubricant daily.

FLUID CHANGE

The lubricant in the front and rear axle differentials should be checked about every 5,000 miles or sooner, if the vehicle is operated under severe conditions, and should be changed every 12,000 miles. Follow the procedure given below for changing the lubricant in the front and rear axle differentials:

1. Remove the axle differential housing cov-

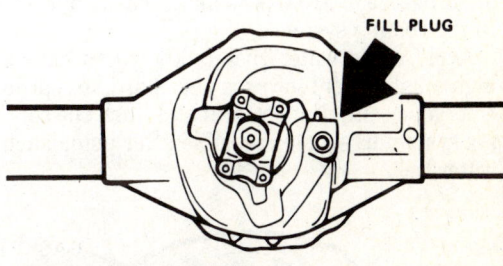

AMC axle fill plug location

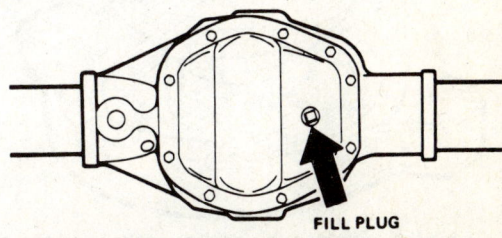

Dana/Spicer axle fill plug location

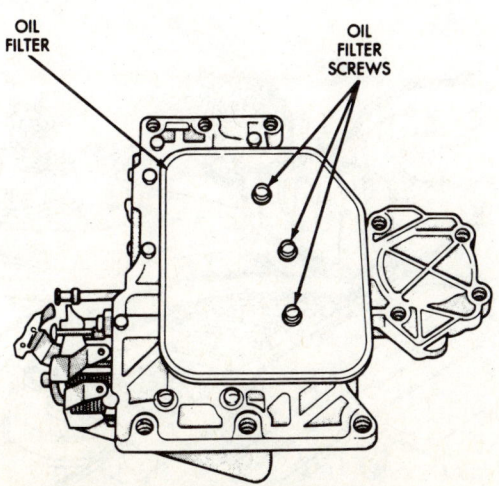

Automatic transmission fluid filter service

44 GENERAL INFORMATION AND MAINTENANCE

er and allow the lubricant to drain out into a proper container.

2. Install the differential housing cover and a new gasket.

3. Tighten the cover attaching bolts to 15-25 ft. lbs.

4. Remove the fill plug and add new lubricant to the fill hole level.

5. Replace the fill plug.

NOTE: *Trac-Lok® (limited-slip) differentials may be cleaned only by disassembling the unit and wiping with clean, lint-free rags.*

Coolant

CAUTION: *When draining the coolant, keep in mind that cats and dogs are attracted by the ethylene glycol antifreeze, and are quite likely to drink any that is left in an uncovered container or in puddles on the ground. This will prove fatal in sufficient quantity. Always drain the coolant into a sealable container. Coolant should be reused unless it is contaminated or several years old.*

COOLANT CHECK AND CHANGE

On systems without a coolant recovery tank, the engine coolant level should be maintained 1-2" below the bottom of the radiator filler neck when the engine is at air temperature and 1" below the bottom of the filler neck when the engine is hot.

On systems with a coolant recovery tank, maintain the coolant level at the level marks on the recovery bottle.

For best protection against freezing and overheating, maintain an approximate 50% water and 50% ethylene glycol antifreeze mixture in the cooling system. Do not mix different brands of antifreeze to avoid possible chemical damage to the cooling system.

Avoid using water that is known to have a high alkaline content or is very hard, except in emergency situations. Drain and flush the cooling system as soon as possible after using such water.

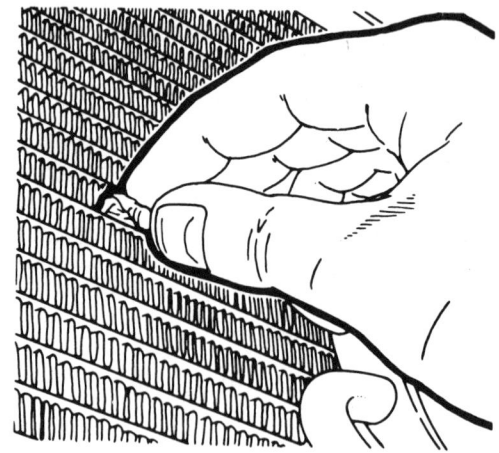
Keep the radiator fins clear for maximum cooling

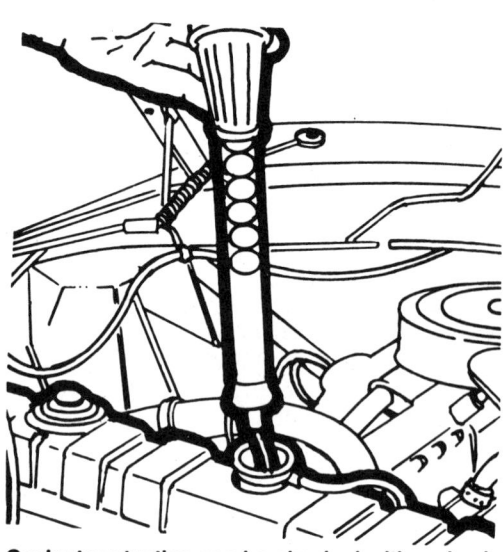
Coolant protection can be checked with a simple float-type tester

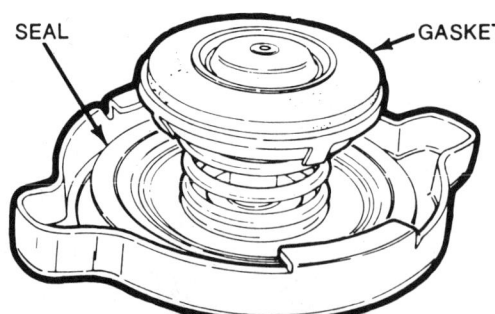
Check the radiator cap's rubber gasket and metal seal for deterioration at least once a year

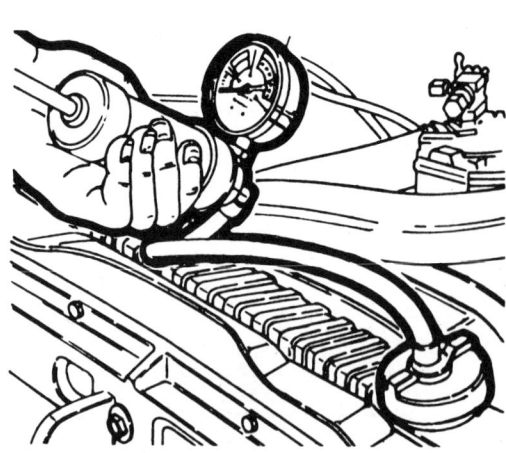
The system should be pressure tested once a year

GENERAL INFORMATION AND MAINTENANCE

CAUTION: *Cover the radiator cap with a thick cloth before removing it from a radiator in a vehicle that is hot. Turn the cap counterclockwise slowly until pressure can be heard escaping. Allow all pressure to escape from the radiator before completely removing the radiator cap. It is best to allow the engine to cool if possible, before removing the radiator cap.*

NOTE: *Never add cold water to an overheated engine while the engine is not running.*

After filling the radiator, run the engine until it reaches normal operating temperature, to make sure that the thermostat has opened and all the air is bled from the system.

DRAINING, FLUSHING AND REFILLING

CAUTION: *When draining the coolant, keep in mind that cats and dogs are attracted by the ethylene glycol antifreeze, and are quite likely to drink any that is left in an uncovered container or in puddles on the ground. This will prove fatal in sufficient quantity. Always drain the coolant into a sealable container. Coolant should be reused unless it is contaminated or several years old.*

To drain the cooling system, allow the engine to cool down **BEFORE ATTEMPTING TO REMOVE THE RADIATOR CAP**. Then turn the cap until it hisses. Wait until all pressure is off the cap before removing it completely.

CAUTION: *To avoid burns and scalding, always handle a warm radiator cap with a heavy rag.*

1. At the dash, set the heater TEMP control lever to the fully HOT position.
2. With the radiator cap removed, drain the radiator by loosening the petcock at the bottom of the radiator. Locate any drain plugs in the block and remove them. Flush the radiator with water until the fluid runs clear.
3. Close the petcock and replace the plug(s), then refill the system with a 50/50 mix of ethylene glycol antifreeze. Fill the system to 3/4-1 1/4" from the bottom of the filler neck. Reinstall the radiator cap.

NOTE: *If equipped with a fluid reservoir tank, fill it up to the MAX level.*

4. Operate the engine at 2,000 rpm for a few minutes and check the system for signs of leaks.

RADIATOR CAP INSPECTION

Allow the engine to cool sufficiently before attempting to remove the radiator cap. Use a rag to cover the cap, then remove by pressing down and turning counterclockwise to the first stop. If any hissing is noted (indicating the release of pressure), wait until the hissing stops completely, then press down again and turn counterclockwise until the cap can be removed.

CAUTION: *DO NOT attempt to remove the radiator cap while the engine is hot. Severe personal injury from steam burns can result.*

Check the condition of the radiator cap gasket and seal inside of the cap. The radiator cap is designed to seal the cooling system under normal operating conditions which allows the build up of a certain amount of pressure (this pressure rating is stamped or printed on the cap). The pressure in the system raises the boiling point of the coolant to help prevent overheating. If the radiator cap does not seal, the boiling point of the coolant is lowered and overheating will occur. If the cap must be replaced, purchase the new cap according to the pressure rating which is specified for your vehicle.

Prior to installing the radiator cap, inspect and clean the filler neck. If you are reusing the old cap, clean it thoroughly with clear water. After turning the cap on, make sure the arrows align with the overflow hose.

Brake and/or Clutch Master Cylinder

FLUID LEVEL CHECK

The master cylinder reservoir is located under the hood, on the left side of the firewall. Before removing the master cylinder reservoir cap, make sure the vehicle is resting on level ground and clean all dirt away from the top of the master cylinder. Pry off the retaining clip or unscrew the holddown bolt and remove the cap. The fluid level should be within 1/4" of the top of the reservoir on both single and dual master cylinders.

If the level of the fluid is less than half the volume of the reservoir, it is advised that you check the brake system for leaks. Leaks in a hy-

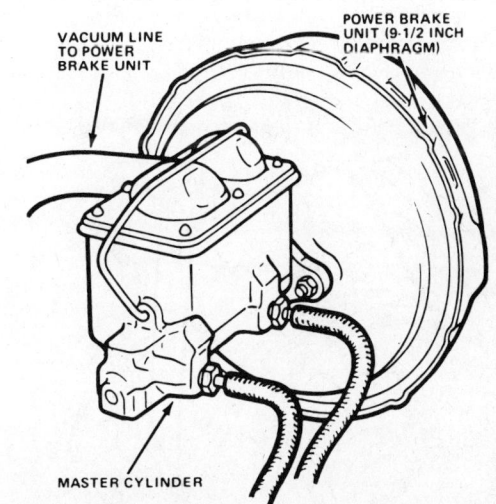

Typical master cylinder

46 GENERAL INFORMATION AND MAINTENANCE

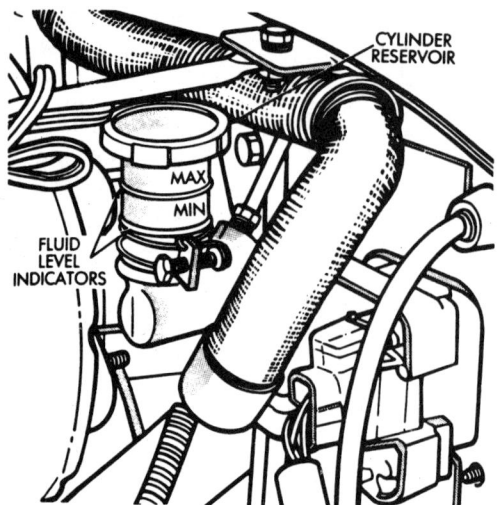

Clutch master cylinder fluid level

draulic brake system most commonly occur at the wheel cylinders.

There is a rubber diaphragm in the top of the master cylinder cap. As the fluid level lowers in the reservoir due to normal brake shoe wear or leakage, the diaphragm takes up the space. This acts to prevent the loss of brake fluid out of the vented cap and to prevent contamination of the brake fluid by dirt. After filling the master cylinder to the proper level with brake fluid, but before replacing the cap, fold the rubber diaphragm up into the cap, then replace the cap on the reservoir and tighten the retaining bolt or snap the retaining clip into place.

Power Steering Reservoir

FLUID CHECK

On models with power steering, check the fluid in the power steering pump every 1,000

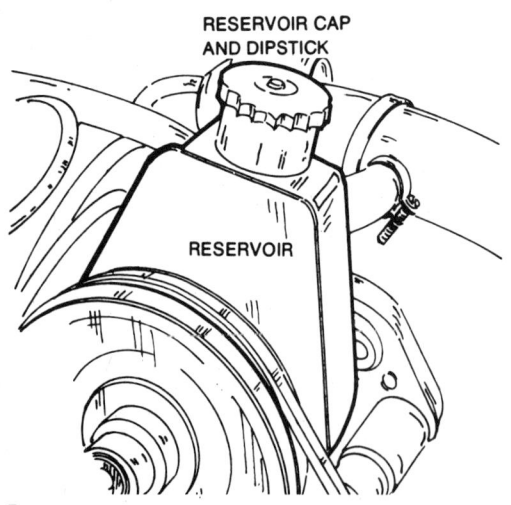

Power steering pump dipstick location

miles. The level of the fluid should be at the correct point on the dipstick attached to the inside of the lid of the power steering pump. Fill the unit with DEXRON®II automatic transmission fluid. If the pump is abnormally low on fluid, check all the power steering hoses and connections, and the hydraulic cylinder for possible leaks.

Chassis Greasing

The lubrication chart indicates where the grease fittings are located. The vehicle should be greased according to the intervals in the Preventive Maintenance Schedule at the end of this chapter.

Water resistant EP chassis lubricant (grease) should be used for all chassis grease points.

Every year or 7,500 miles the front suspension ball points, both upper and lower on each side of the truck, must be greased. Most trucks covered in this guide should be equipped with grease nipples on the ball joints, although some may have plugs which must be removed and nipples fitted.

WARNING: *Do not pump so much grease into the ball joint that excess grease squeezes out of the rubber boot. This destroys the watertight seal.*

Jack up the front end of the truck and safely support it with jackstands. Block the rear wheels and firmly apply the parking brake. If the truck has been parked in temperatures below 20°F for any length of time, park it in a heated garage for an hour or so until the ball joints loosen up enough to accept the grease.

Depending on which front wheel you work on first, turn the wheel and tire outward, either full-lock right or full-lock left. You now have the ends of the upper and lower suspension control arms in front of you; the grease nipples are visible pointing up (top ball joint) and down (lower ball joint) through the end of each control arm. If the nipples are not accessible enough, remove the wheel and tire. Wipe all dirt and crud from the nipples or from around the plugs (if installed). If plugs are on the truck, remove them and install grease nipples in the holes (nipples are available in various thread sizes at most auto parts stores). Using a hand operated, low pressure grease gun loaded with a quality chassis grease, grease the ball joint only until the rubber joint boot begins to swell out.

Steering Linkage

The steering linkage should be greased at the same interval as the ball joints. Grease nipples are installed on the steering tie rod ends on most models. Wipe all dirt and crud from around the nipples at each tie rod end. Using a

GENERAL INFORMATION AND MAINTENANCE

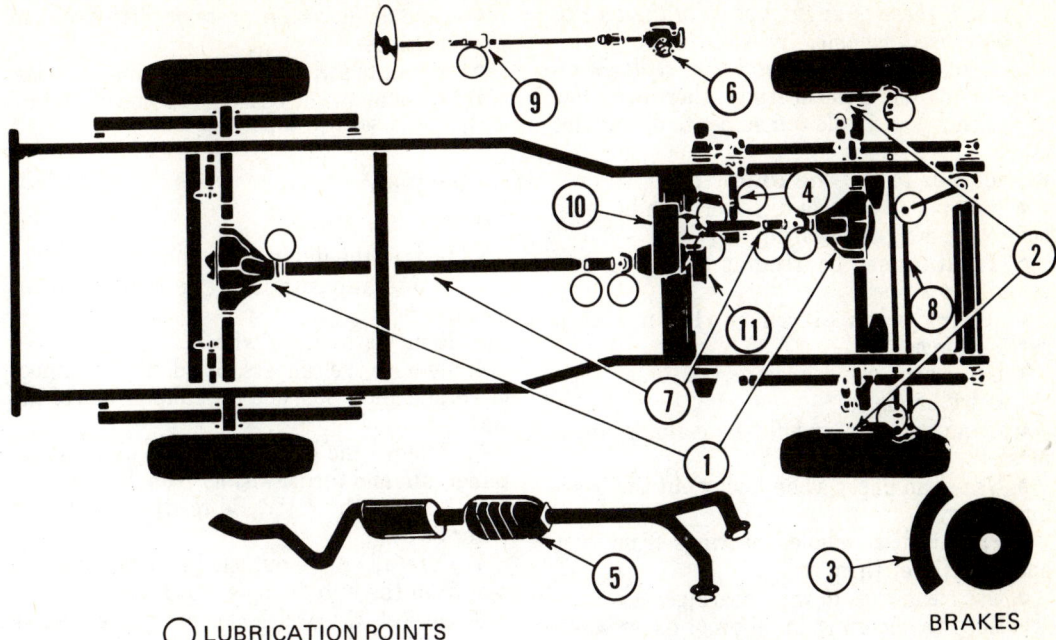

○ LUBRICATION POINTS   BRAKES

See the Preventive Maintenance Charts for recommended intervals and lubricants:
1. Differentials
2. Front wheel bearings: Clean and repack
3. Brakes: Check ling wear, master cylinder fluid level, brake lines and hoses
4. Clutch cross-shaft grease fitting
5. Inspect the exhaust system
6. Manual steering gear
7. Driveshaft U-joints and splines
8. Steering linkage grease fittings
9. Steering column coupling
10. Transfer case
11. Manual transmission fluid or automatic transmission fluid and filter

1970–86 Wagoneer, Cherokee, Comanche and J-Series truck chassis maintenance points

hand operated, low pressure grease gun loaded with a suitable chassis grease, grease the linkage until the old grease begins to squeeze out around the tie rod ends. Wipe off the nipples and any excess grease. Also grease the nipples on the steering idler arms.

Parking Brake Linkage

Use chassis grease on the parking brake cable where it contacts the cable guides, levers and linkage.

Automatic Transmission Linkage

Apply a small amount of clean engine oil to the kickdown and shift linkage points at 7,500 mile intervals.

OUTSIDE VEHICLE MAINTENANCE

Lock Cylinders

Apply graphite lubricant sparingly thought the key slot. Insert the key and operate the lock several times to be sure that the lubricant is worked into the lock cylinder.

Door Hinges and Hinge Checks

Spray a silicone lubricant on the hinge pivot points to eliminate any binding conditions. Open and close the door several times to be sure that the lubricant is evenly and thoroughly distributed.

Tailgate

Spray a silicone lubricant on all of the pivot and friction surfaces to eliminate any squeaks or binds. Work the tailgate to distribute the lubricant

Body Drain Holes

Be sure that the drain holes in the doors and rocker panels are cleared of obstruction. A small screwdriver can be used to clear them of any debris.

Front Wheel Bearings

PACKING AND ADJUSTMENT

NOTE: *Sodium-based grease is not compatible with lithium-based grease. Read the package labels and be careful not to mix the two*

48 GENERAL INFORMATION AND MAINTENANCE

types. *If there is any doubt as to the type of grease used, completely clean the old grease from the bearing and hub before replacing.*

Before handling the bearings, there are a few things that you should remember to do and not to do.

Remember to DO the following:
- Remove all outside dirt from the housing before exposing the bearing.
- Treat a used bearing as gently as you would a new one.
- Work with clean tools in clean surroundings.
- Use clean, dry canvas gloves, or at least clean, dry hands.
- Clean solvents and flushing fluids are a must.
- Use clean paper when laying out the bearings to dry.
- Protect disassembled bearings from rust and dirt. Cover them up.
- Use clean rags to wipe bearings.
- Keep the bearings in oil-proof paper when they are to be stored or are not in use.
- Clean the inside of the housing before replacing the bearing.

Do NOT do the following:
- Don't work in dirty surroundings.
- Don't use dirty, chipped or damaged tools.
- Try not to work on wooden work benches or use wooden mallets.
- Don't handle bearings with dirty or moist hands.
- Do not use gasoline for cleaning; use a safe solvent.
- Do not spin-dry bearings with compressed air. They will be damaged.
- Do not spin dirty bearings.
- Avoid using cotton waste or dirty cloths to wipe bearings.
- Try not to scratch or nick bearing surfaces.
- Do not allow the bearing to come in contact with dirt or rust at any time.

2-Wheel Drive

TYPE ONE

1. Loosen the lug nuts on the front wheels.
2. Raise and support the front end on jackstands.
3. Remove the front wheels.
4. Remove the calipers, but don't disconnect the brake lines. Suspend the calipers out of the way.
5. Remove the dust cap, cotter pin, nut retainer, nut and thrust washer from the spindle.
6. Remove the rotor. Be ready to catch the outer bearing.
7. Carefully drive out the inner bearing and seal from the hub, using a wood block.
8. Inspect the bearing races for excessive wear, pitting or grooves. If they are cracked or grooved, or if pitting and excess wear is present, drive them out with a drift or punch.
9. Check the bearing for excess wear, pitting or cracks, or excess looseness.

NOTE: *If it is necessary to replace either the bearing or the race, replace both. Never replace just a bearing or a race. These parts wear in a mating pattern. If just one is replaced, premature failure of the new part will result.*

10. If the old parts are retained, thoroughly clean them in a safe solvent and allow them to dry on a clean towel. Never spin dry them with compressed air.
11. Thoroughly clean the spindle.

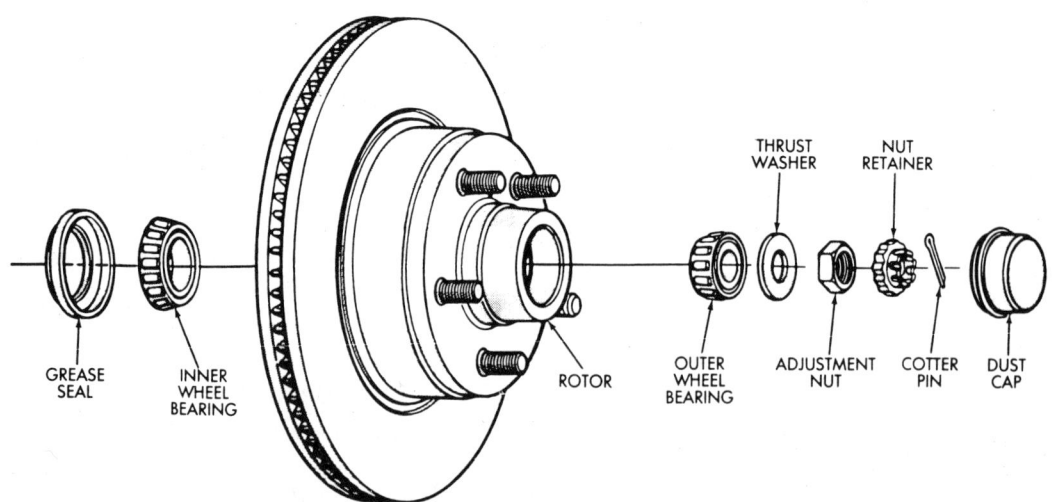

2wd front wheel bearings

GENERAL INFORMATION AND MAINTENANCE

12. Thoroughly clean the inside of the hub.
13. Pack the inside of the hub with EP wheel bearing grease. Add grease to the hub until it is flush with the inside diameter of the bearing cup.
14. Pack the bearing with the same grease. A needle-shaped wheel bearing packer is best for this operation. If one is not available, place a large amount of grease in the palm of your hand and slide the edge of the bearing cage through the grease to pick up as much as possible, then work the grease in as best you can with your fingers.
15. If a new race is being installed, very carefully drive it into position until it bottoms all around, using a brass drift. Be careful to avoid scratching the surface.
16. Place the inner bearing in the race and install a new grease seal.
17. Position the hub and rotor on the spindle and install the outer bearing.
18. Install the washer and nut.
19. While turning the rotor, torque the nut to 25 ft. lbs. to seat the bearings.
20. Back off the nut ½ turn, and, while turning the rotor, torque the nut to 19 in. lbs.
21. Install the nut cap and a new cotter pin. Install the grease cap.
22. Install the caliper.
23. Install the wheels.

TYPE 2

1. Raise and support the front end on jackstands.
2. Remove the wheels.
3. Remove the caliper without disconnecting the brake line. Suspend it out of the way.
4. Remove the grease cap, cotter pin, nut cap, nut, and washer from the spindle.
5. Pull slowly on the hub and catch the outer bearing as it falls.
6. Remove the hub and rotor. The inner bearing and seal can be removed by prying out and discarding the inner seal.
7. Carefully drive out the inner bearing and seal from the hub, using a wood block.
8. Inspect the bearing races for excessive wear, pitting or grooves. If they are cracked or grooved, or if pitting and excess wear is present, drive them out with a drift or punch.
9. Check the bearing for excess wear, pitting or cracks, or excess looseness.

NOTE: *If it is necessary to replace either the bearing or the race, replace both. Never replace just a bearing or a race. These parts wear in a mating pattern. If just one is replaced, premature failure of the new part will result.*

10. If the old parts are retained, thoroughly clean them in a safe solvent and allow them to dry on a clean towel. Never spin dry them with compressed air.
11. On vehicles with drum brakes, cover the spindle with a cloth and thoroughly brush all dirt from the brakes. Never blow the dirt off the brakes, due to the presence of asbestos in the dirt, which is harmful to your health when inhaled.
12. Remove the cloth and thoroughly clean the spindle.
13. Thoroughly clean the inside of the hub.
14. Pack the inside of the hub with EP wheel bearing grease. Add grease to the hub until it is flush with the inside diameter of the bearing cup.
15. Pack the bearing with the same grease. A needle-shaped wheel bearing packer is best for this operation. If one is not available, place a large amount of grease in the palm of your hand and slide the edge of the bearing cage through the grease to pick up as much as possible, then work the grease in as best you can with your fingers.
16. If a new race is being installed, very carefully drive it into position until it bottoms all around, using a brass drift. Be careful to avoid scratching the surface.
17. Place the inner bearing in the race and install a new grease seal.
18. Clean and repack the hub and bearings, install the inner bearing and a new seal.
19. Position the hub and rotor on the spindle and install the outer bearing.
20. Install the washer and nut.
21. While turning the rotor, torque the nut to 25 ft. lbs. to seat the bearings.
22. Back off the nut ½ turn, and, while turning the rotor, torque the nut to 19 in. lbs.
23. Install the nut cap and a new cotter pin. Install the grease cap.
24. Install the caliper.
25. Install the wheels.

4-Wheel Drive

WARNING: *The following procedure requires the use of an arbor press. Chrysler Corp. notes that only the special press tools listed below should be used or damage to the internal machined shoulder of the bearing carrier is probable!*

1. Raise and support the front end on jackstands.
2. Remove the wheels.
3. Remove, but do not disconnect, the caliper. Suspend it out of the way.
4. Remove the rotor. See Chapter 9.
5. Remove the cotter pin, nut retainer, axle nut and washer.
6. Remove the 3 bearing carrier bolts.

50 GENERAL INFORMATION AND MAINTENANCE

7. Remove the hub/bearing carrier and the rotor shield.
8. Using an arbor press, press the hub out of the bearing carrier. Special tools 5073 and 5074 are available for this job. Secure the carrier to the press plate with M12 × 1.75mm × 40mm bolts.
9. Cut and remove the plastic cage from the hub inner bearing. Using diagonal pliers or tin snips, cut the bearing cage. Discard the rollers after removing the cage.
10. Remove what remians of the inner bearing by:
    a. Install a bearing separator tool on the inner bearing.
    b. Position the separator tool and hub in an arbor press.
    c. Force the hub out of the inner bearing with press pin tool 5074.
11. Remove the bearing carrier outer seal and discard it.
12. Drive the inner bearing seal out and discard it. If you're using tool 5078, make sure that the word JEEP faces downward.
13. Attach press plate tool 5073 to the rear of the carrier. Secure it in the press using M12 × 1.75mm × 40mm bolts.
14. Position bearing race remover 5076 in the carrier bore between the inner and outer bearing races.
15. Position the press pin tool 5074 on tool 5076.
16. Place the bearing carrier in the press and force the inner bearing race from the carrier

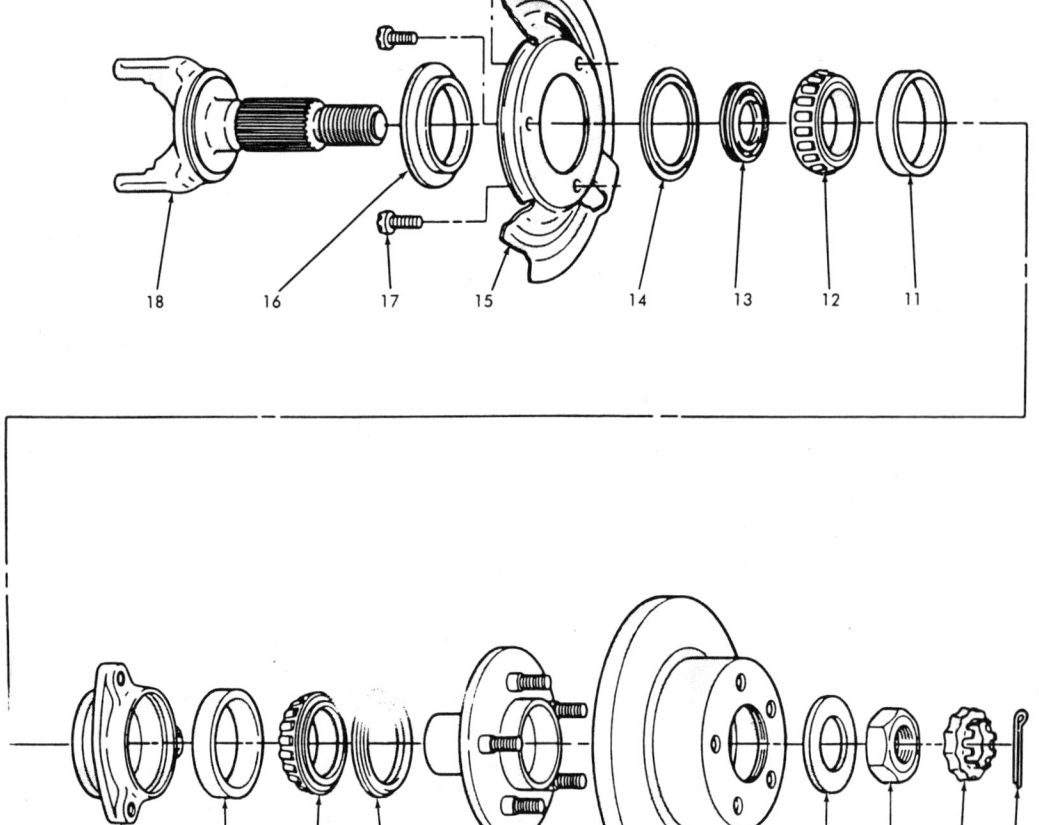

1. Cotter pin
2. Nut retainer
3. Nut
4. Washer
5. Brake rotor
6. Hub
7. Outer bearing seal
8. Outer bearing
9. Outer bearing race
10. Bearing carrier
11. Inner bearing race
12. Inner bearing
13. Inner bearing seal
14. Carrier seal
15. Rotor shield
16. Axle shaft dust slinger
17. Bearing carrier bolts
18. Axle shaft

4wd front wheel bearings

GENERAL INFORMATION AND MAINTENANCE 51

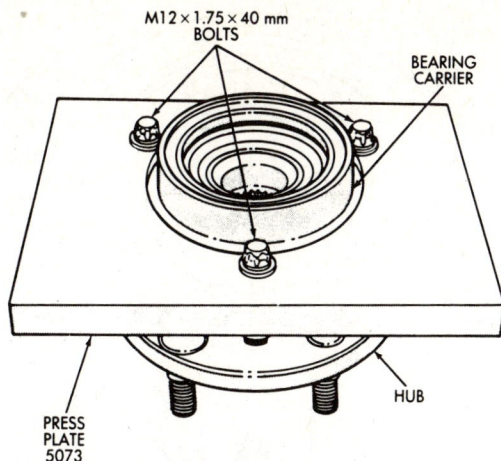

Hub and bearing carrier in a press plate

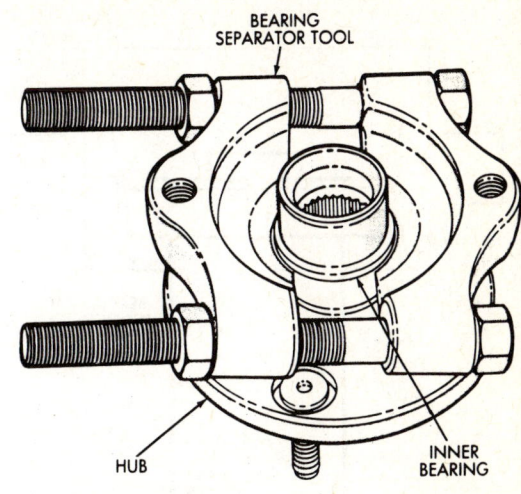

Bearing separator tool

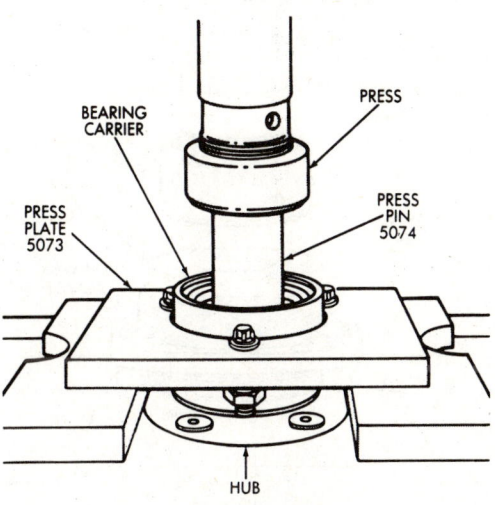

Hub and bearing carrier separation

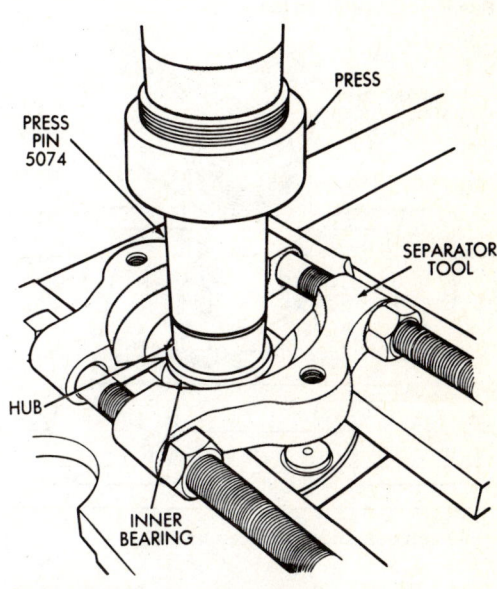

Hub and inner bearing separation

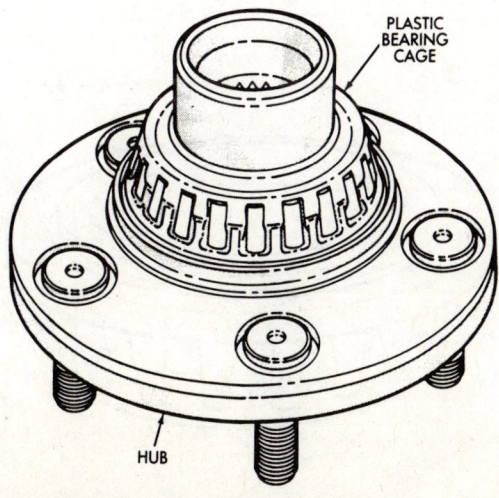

Inner bearing cage removal

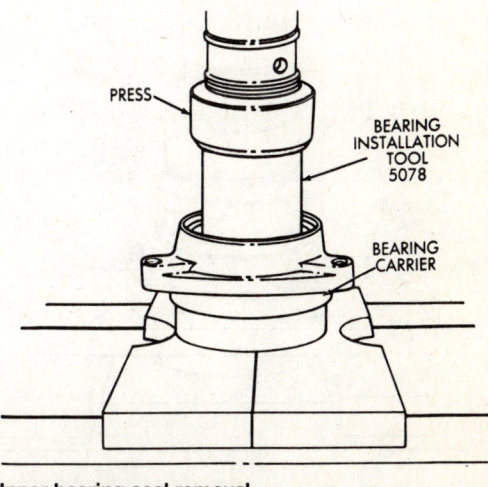

Inner bearing seal removal

52 GENERAL INFORMATION AND MAINTENANCE

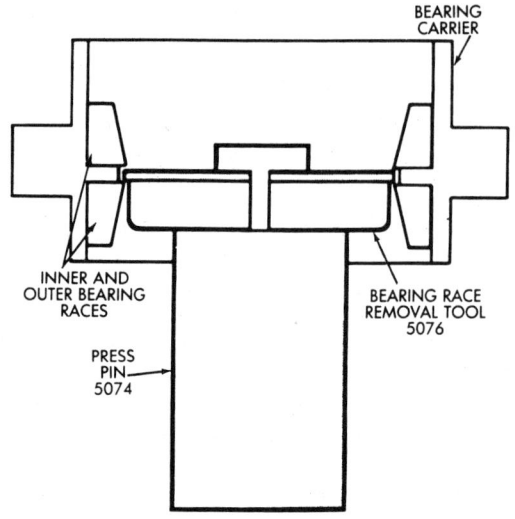

Bearing race removal tools

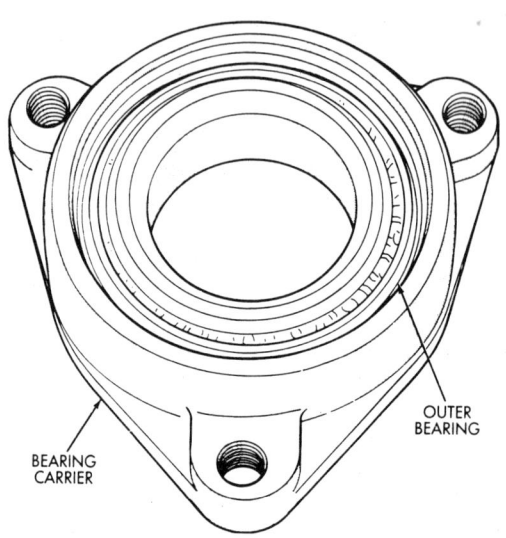

Outer bearing installation

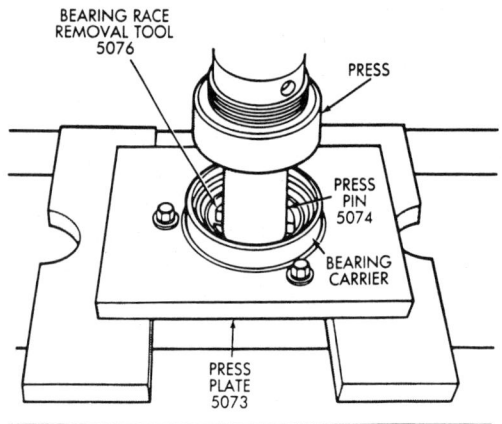

Inner and outer bearing race removal

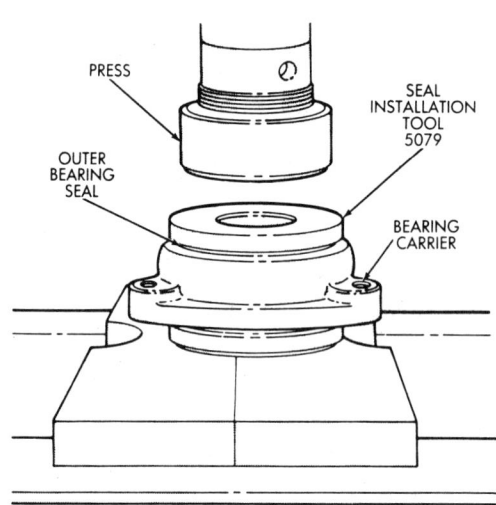

Outer bearing seal installation

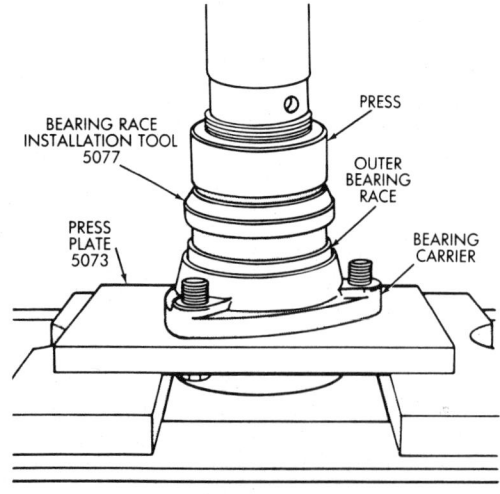

Outer bearing race installation

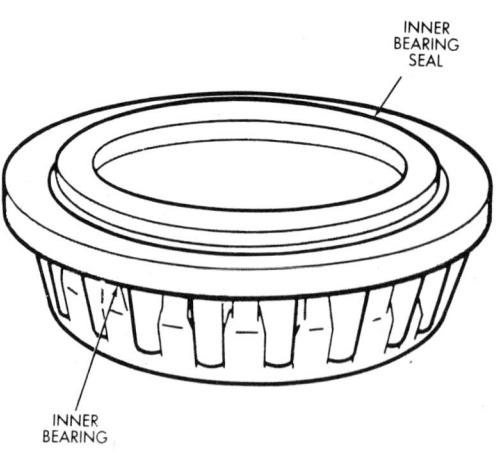

Inner bearing and seal

GENERAL INFORMATION AND MAINTENANCE 53

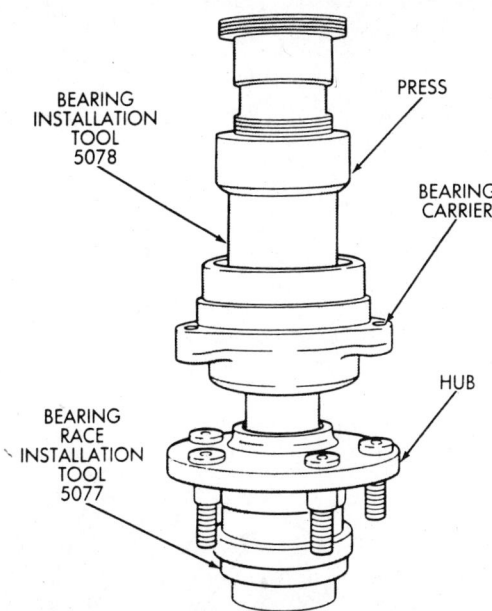

Joining the hub and bearing carrier

bore. Reverse the position of the carrier and tools and force the outer bearing race from the bore.

To assemble and install

17. Thoroughly clean all reusable parts with a safe solvent. Discard any parts that appear worn or damaged.
18. Attach press plate tool 5073 on the bearing carrier. Secure it in the press using M12 × 1.75mm × 40mm bolts.
19. Position the new outer bearing race in the bore.
20. Position bearing race installation tool 5077 on the race. Make sure that the word JEEP faces the downward. Press the race into the bore. The race should be flush with the machined shoulder of the carrier.
21. Position the new inner bearing race in the carrier bore. Reverse the position of the carrier and tools and force the inner race into the bore.
22. Thoroughly pack the new outer bearing with wheel bearing grease. Make sure that the bearing is fully packed.
23. Coat the race with wheel bearing grease and place the bearing in the bore.
24. Place the new outer seal on the bearing and position bearing installation tool 5079 on the seal. Place the carrier in the press and force the seal into the bore. Apply wheel bearing grease to the seal ip.
25. Insert the hub through the seal and outer bearing and into the bearing carrier bore.
26. Install bearing installation tool 5078 into the rear of the bearing carrier bore and place the race installation tool 5077 on the front of the hub. Make sure that the word JEEP on 5077 is facing the hub.
27. Place the assembly in the press and force the hub shaft into the carrier bore.
28. Pack the new inner bearing with wheel bearing grease. Make sure that the bearing is thoroughly packed.
29. Coat the inner seal lip with wheel bearing grease and place it on the inner bearing.
30. Coat the inner bearing race with wheel bearing grease.
31. Place the carrier in a press along with tool 5077. The word JEEP on 5077 must face the hub. Position the bearing and seal in the carrier. Place seal installation tool 5080 on the seal.
32. Force the bearing and seal into the bore and onto the hub shaft.

> **WARNING:** *Use extreme care when forcing the assembly into position! The acrrier must rotate freely after installation of the bearing! Do not attempt to eliminate bearing lash with the press. Final bearing preload is attained by tightening the drive axle nut.*

33. Install the new outer seal on the carrier.
34. Thoroughly clean the axle shaft and apply a thin coating of lithium-based grease to the splines and seal contact surfaces.
35. Install the slinger, rotor shield and hub/bearing assembly on the axle shaft.
36. Coat the carrier bolt threads with Loctite®, install them and torque them to 75 ft. lbs.
37. Install the rotor and caliper. See Chapter 9.
38. Install the washer and axle shaft nut. Torque the nut to 175 ft. lbs.
39. Install the nut retainer and cotter pin. NEVER back off the nut to install the cotter pin! ALWAYS advance it!
40. Install the wheel.

JUMP STARTING A DUAL-BATTERY DIESEL

Trucks equipped with the diesel engine utilize two 12 volt batteries, one on either side of the engine compartment. The batteries are connected in a parallel circuit (positive terminal to positive terminal, negative terminal to negative terminal). Hooking the batteries up in parallel circuit increases battery cranking power without increasing total battery voltage output. Output remains at 12 volts. On the other hand, hooking two 12 volt batteries up in a series circuit (positive terminal to negative terminal, positive terminal to negative terminal) increases total battery output to 24 volts (12 volts plus 12 volts).

GENERAL INFORMATION AND MAINTENANCE

JUMP STARTING A DEAD BATTERY

The chemical reaction in a battery produces explosive hydrogen gas. This is the safe way to jump start a dead battery, reducing the chances of an accidental spark that could cause an explosion.

Jump Starting Precautions

1. Be sure both batteries are of the same voltage.
2. Be sure both batteries are of the same polarity (have the same grounded terminal).
3. Be sure the vehicles are not touching.
4. Be sure the vent cap holes are not obstructed.
5. Do not smoke or allow sparks around the battery.
6. In cold weather, check for frozen electrolyte in the battery. Do not jump start a frozen battery.
7. Do not allow electrolyte on your skin or clothing.
8. Be sure the electrolyte is not frozen.

CAUTION: *Make certain that the ignition key, in the vehicle with the dead battery, is in the OFF position. Connecting cables to vehicles with on-board computers will result in computer destruction if the key is not in the OFF position.*

Jump Starting Procedure

1. Determine voltages of the two batteries; they must be the same.
2. Bring the starting vehicle close (they must not touch) so that the batteries can be reached easily.
3. Turn off all accessories and both engines. Put both cars in Neutral or Park and set the handbrake.
4. Cover the cell caps with a rag—do not cover terminals.
5. If the terminals on the run-down battery are heavily corroded, clean them.
6. Identify the positive and negative posts on both batteries and connect the cables in the order shown.
7. Start the engine of the starting vehicle and run it at fast idle. Try to start the car with the dead battery. Crank it for no more than 10 seconds at a time and let it cool off for 20 seconds in between tries.
8. If it doesn't start in 3 tries, there is something else wrong.
9. Disconnect the cables in the reverse order.
10. Replace the cell covers and dispose of the rags.

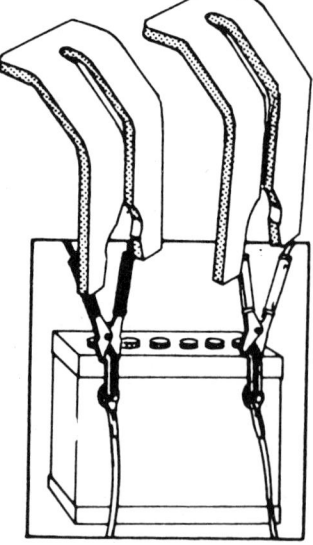

Side terminal batteries occasionally pose a problem when connecting jumper cables. There frequently isn't enough room to clamp the cables without touching sheet metal. Side terminal adaptors are available to alleviate this problem and should be removed after use.

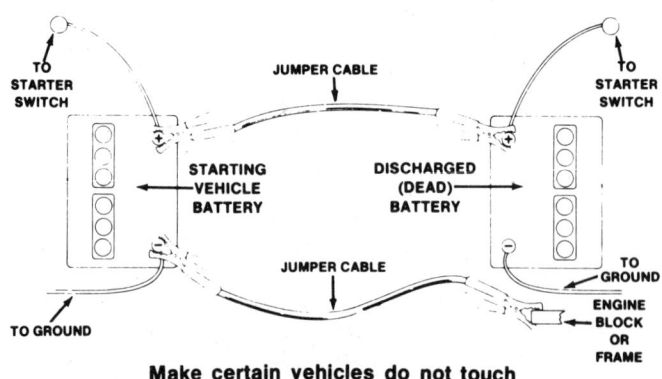

Make certain vehicles do not touch

This hook-up for negative ground cars only

GENERAL INFORMATION AND MAINTENANCE

CAUTION: *NEVER hook the batteries up in a series circuit or the entire electrical system will go up in smoke, especially the starter.*

In the event that a diesel pickup needs to be jump started, use the following procedure.

1. Turn all lights off.
2. Turn on the heater blower motor to remove transient voltage.
3. Connect one jumper cable to the passenger side battery positive (+) terminal and the other cable clamp to the positive (+) terminal to the booster (good) battery.
4. Connect one end of the other jumper cable to the negative (−) terminal of the booster (good) battery and the other cable clamp to an engine bolt head, alternator bracket or other solid, metallic point on the diesel engine. DO NOT connect this clamp to the negative (−) terminal of the bad battery.

CAUTION: *Be very careful to keep the jumper cables away from moving parts (cooling fan, belts, etc.) on both engines.*

5. Start the engine of the donor truck and run it at moderate speed.
6. Start the engine of the diesel.
7. When the diesel starts, remove the cable from the engine block before disconnecting the positive terminal.

JACKING AND HOISTING

Scissors jacks or hydraulic jacks are recommended for all Jeep vehicles. To change a tire, place the jack beneath the spring plate, below the axle, near the wheel to be changed.

Make sure that you are on level ground, that the transmission is in Reverse or with automatic transmissions, Park; the parking brake is set, and the tire diagonally opposite to the one to be changed is blocked so that it will not roll. Loosen the lug nuts before you jack the wheel to be changed completely free of the ground.

If you use a hoist, make sure that the pads of the hoist are located in such a way as to lift on the Jeep frame and not on a shock absorber mount, floor boards, oil pan, or any other part

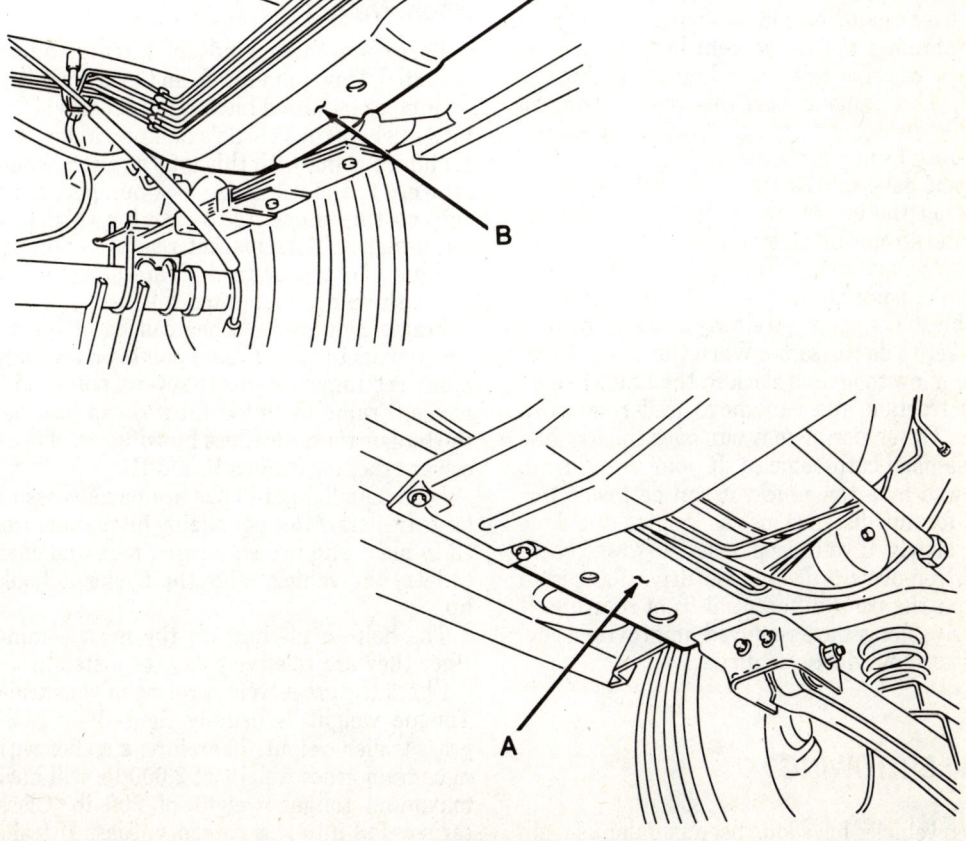

Jacking points

PUSHING AND TOWING

To push-start your vehicle (manual transmissions only), follow the procedures below. Check to make sure that the bumpers of both vehicles are aligned so neither will be damaged. Be sure that all electrical system components are turned off (headlights, heater, blower, etc.). Turn on the ignition switch. Place the shift lever in first or second and push in the clutch pedal. At about 15 mph, signal the driver of the pushing vehicle to fall back, depress the accelerator pedal, and release the clutch pedal slowly. The engine should start.

When you are doing the pushing or pulling, make sure that the two bumpers match so you won't damage the vehicle you are to push. Another good idea is to put an old tire in between the two vehicles. If the bumpers don't match, perhaps you should tow the other vehicle. If the other vehicle is just stuck, use first gear to slowly push it out. Tell the driver of the other vehicle to go slowly, too. Try to keep your Jeep right up against the other vehicle while you are pushing. If the two vehicles do separate, stop and start over again instead of trying to catch up and ramming the other vehicle. Also try, as much as possible, to avoid riding or slipping the clutch. Low range makes this easy. When the other vehicle gains enough traction, it should pull away from your vehicle.

If you have to tow the other vehicle, make sure that the tow chain or rope is sufficiently long and strong, and that it is attached securely to both vehicles at a strong place. Attach the chain at a point on the frame or as close to it as possible. Once again, go slowly and tell the other driver to do the same. Warn the other driver not to allow too much slack in the line when he gains traction and can move under his own power. Otherwise he may run over the tow line and damage both vehicles. If your Jeep has to be towed by a tow truck, it can be towed forward for any distance just as long as it is done fairly slowly. If your Jeep has to be towed backward, remove the front axle drive flanges to prevent the front differential from rotating. If the drive flanges are removed, improvise a cover to keep out dust and dirt.

TRAILER TOWING

Jeep vehicles have long been popular as trailer towing vehicles. Their strong construction, 4-wheel drive and wide range of engine/transmission combinations make them ideal for towing campers, boat trailers and utility trailers. Factory trailer towing packages are available on most Jeep vehicles. However, if you are installing a trailer hitch and wiring on your Jeep, there are a few thing that you ought to know.

Trailer Weight

Trailer weight is the first, and most important, factor in determining whether or not your vehicle is suitable for towing the trailer you have in mind. The horsepower-to-weight ratio should be calculated. The basic standard is a ratio of 35:1. That is, 35 pounds of GVW for every horsepower.

To calculate this ratio, multiply you engine's rated horsepower by 35, then subtract the weight of the vehicle, including passengers and luggage. The resulting figure is the ideal maximum trailer weight that you can tow. One point to consider: a numerically higher axle ratio can offset what appears to be a low trailer weight. If the weight of the trailer that you have in mind is somewhat higher than the weight you just calculated, you might consider changing your rear axle ratio to compensate.

Hitch Weight

There are three kinds of hitches: bumper mounted, frame mounted, and load equalizing.

Bumper mounted hitches are those which attach solely to the vehicle's bumper. Many states prohibit towing with this type of hitch, when it attaches to the vehicle's stock bumper, since it subjects the bumper to stresses for which it was not designed. Aftermarket rear step bumpers, designed for trailer towing, are acceptable for use with bumper mounted hitches.

Frame mounted hitches can be of the type which bolts to two or more points on the frame, plus the bumper, or just to several points on the frame. Frame mounted hitches can also be of the tongue type, for Class I towing, or, of the receiver type, for classes II and III.

Load equalizing hitches are usually used for large trailers. Most equalizing hitches are welded in place and use equalizing bars and chains to level the vehicle after the trailer is hooked up.

The bolt-on hitches are the most common, since they are relatively easy to install.

Check the gross weight rating of your trailer. Tongue weight is usually figured as 10% of gross trailer weight. Therefore, a trailer with a maximum gross weight of 2,000 lb. will have a maximum tongue weight of 200 lb. Class I tarilers fall into this category. Class II trailers are those with a gross weight rating of 2,000-

GENERAL INFORMATION AND MAINTENANCE

3,500 lb., while Class III trailers fall into the 3,500-6,000 lb. category. Class IV trailers are those over 6,000 lb. and are for use with fifth wheel trucks, only.

When you've determined the hitch that you'll need, follow the manufacturer's installation instructions, exactly, especially when it comes to fastener torques. The hitch will subjected to a lot of stress and good hitches come with hardened bolts. Never substitute an inferior bolt for a hardened bolt.

Wiring

Wiring the car for towing is fairly easy. There are a number of good wiring kits available and these should be used, rather than trying to design your own. All trailers will need brake lights and turn signals as well as tail lights and side marker lights. Most states require extra marker lights for overwide trailers. Also, most states have recently required back-up lights for trailers, and most trailer manufacturers have been building trailers with back-up lights for several years.

Additionally, some Class I, most Class II and just about all Class III trailers will have electric brakes.

Add to this number an accessories wire, to operate trailer internal equipment or to charge the trailer's battery, and you can have as many as seven wires in the harness.

Determine the equipment on your trailer and buy the wiring kit necessary. The kit will contain all the wires needed, plus a plug adapter set which included the female plug, mounted on the bumper or hitch, and the male plug, wired into, or plugged into the trailer harness.

When installing the kit, follow the manufacturer's instructions. The color coding of the wires is standard throughout the industry.

One point to note: some domestic vehicles, and most imported vehicles, have separate turn signals. On most domestic vehicles, the brake lights and rear turn signals operate with the same bulb. For those vehicles with separate turn signals, you can purchase an isolation unit so that the brake lights won't blink whenever the turn signals are operated, or, you can go to your local electronics supply house and buy four diodes to wire in series with the brake and

Recommended Equipment Checklist

Equipment	Class I Trailers Under 2,000 pounds	Class II Trailers 2,000-3,500 pounds	Class III Trailers 3,500-6,000 pounds	Class IV Trailers 6,000 pounds and up
Hitch	Frame or Equalizing	Equalizing	Equalizing	Fifth wheel Pick-up truck only
Tongue Load Limit**	Up to 200 pounds	200-350 pounds	350-600 pounds	600 pounds and up
Trailer Brakes	Not Required	Required	Required	Required
Safety Chain	3/16" diameter links	1/4" diameter links	5/16" diameter links	—
Fender Mounted Mirrors	Useful, but not necessary	Recommended	Recommended	Recommended
Turn Signal Flasher	Standard	Constant Rate or heavy duty	Constant Rate or heavy duty	Constant Rate or heavy duty
Coolant Recovery System	Recommended	Required	Required	Required
Transmission Oil Cooler	Recommended	Recommended	Recommended	Recommended
Engine Oil Cooler	Recommended	Recommended	Recommended	Recommended
Air Adjustable Shock Absorbers	Recommended	Recommended	Recommended	Recommended
Flex or Clutch Fan	Recommended	Recommended	Recommended	Recommended
Tires	***	***	***	***

NOTE: The information in this chart is a guide. Check the manufacturer's recommendations for your car if in doubt.
* Local laws may require specific equipment such as trailer brakes or fender mounted mirrors. Check your local laws. Hitch weight is usually 10-15% of trailer gross weight and should be measured with trailer loaded.
** Most manufacturer's do not recommend towing trailers of over 1,000 pounds with compacts. Some intermediates cannot tow Class III trailers.
*** Check manufacturer's recommendations for your specific car/ trailer combination.
—Does not apply

GENERAL INFORMATION AND MAINTENANCE

Capacities Chart

Engine	Crank-case Incl. Filter (qt)	Transmission (pt.)			Transfer Case		Drive Axle (pt.)		Fuel Tank (gal.)	Cooling System (qt)	
		4-sp	5-sp	Auto.	Man.	Auto.	Front	Rear		w/AC	wo/AC
4-126	5.5	—	7.0	—	4.5	7.0	2.5	2.5	①	9.0	9.0
4-150	4.0	②	③	15.8	4.5	6.0	④	2.5	①	10.0	10.0
6-173	5.0	②	③	15.8	4.5	6.0	④	2.5	①	12.0	12.0
6-243	6.0	②	③	17.0	⑤	⑤	2.5	⑥	⑦	12.0	12.0

① Standard: 13.5
  Optional: 20.2
② AX4 w/4WD: 7.4
    w/2WD: 7.8
  T4: 3.9
③ T5: 4.5
  AX5 w/4WD: 7.0
    w/2WD: 7.4
  BA 10/5 w/4WD: 4.9
    w/2WD: 5.2
④ Without Selec Trac: 3.0
  With Selec Trac: 4.5
  Add 5 oz. for Selec Trac disconnect housing
⑤ NP-208: 6.0
  NP-231: 2.2
  NP-242: 3.0
⑥ Standard Axle: 2.5
  Heavy duty: 3.0
⑦ Comanche short bed: 18.5
  Comanche long bed: 23.5
  Wagoneer/Cherokee: 20.2

Preventive Maintenance Chart

Interval	Item	Service
Every 5,000 miles	Engine oil and filter Steering gear Power steering reservoir Differentials Manual transmission Transfer case Automatic transmission Air cleaner Drive belts	Change Check level Check level Check level Check level Check level Check level Change filter Check
Every 15,000 miles	All chassis lube fittings U-joints Fuel filter PCV valve Oil filler cap Spark plugs	EP chassis lube EP chassis lube Replace Replace Clean Replace
Every 30,000 miles	Spark plug wires Front wheel bearings	Change Clean and repack
Every 48,000 miles	Manual transmission Differentials Automatic transmission Transfer case	Change fluid Change fluid Change fluid and filter Change fluid

GENERAL INFORMATION AND MAINTENANCE

turn signal bulbs. Diodes will isolate the brake and turn signals. The choice is yours. The isolation units are simple and quick to install, but far more expensive than the diodes. The diodes, however, require more work to install properly, since they require the cutting of each bulb's wire and soldering in place of the diode.

One, final point, the best kits are those with a spring loaded cover on the vehicle mounted socket. This cover prevent dirt and moisture from corroding the terminals. Never let the vehicle socket hang loosely; always mount it securely to the bumper or hitch.

Cooling
ENGINE

One of the most common, if not THE most common, problems associated with trailer towing is engine overheating.

With factory installed trailer towing packages, a heavy duty cooling system is usually included. Heavy duty cooling systems are available as optional equipment on most Jeep vehicles, with or without a trailer package. If you have one of these extra-capacity systems, you shouldn't have any overheating problems.

If you have a standard cooling system, without an expansion tank, you'll definitely need to get an aftermarket expansion tank kit, preferably one with at least a 2 quart capacity. These kits are easily installed on the radiator's overflow hose, and come with a pressure cap designed for expansion tanks.

Another helpful accessory is a Flex Fan. These fan are large diameter units are designed to provide more airflow at low speeds, with blades that have deeply cupped surfaces. The blades then flex, or flatten out, at high speed, when less cooling air is needed. These fans are far lighter in weight than stock fans, requiring less horsepower to drive them. Also, they are far quieter than stock fans.

If you do decide to replace your stock fan with a flex fan, note that if your Jeep has a fan clutch, a spacer between the flex fan and water pump hub will be needed.

Aftermarket engine oil coolers are helpful for prolonging engine oil life and reducing overall engine temperatures. Both of these factors increase engine life.

While not absolutely necessary in towing Class I and some Class II trailers, they are recommended for heavier Class II and all Class III towing.

Engine oil cooler systems consist of an adapter, screwed on in place of the oil filter, a remote filter mounting and a multi-tube, finned heat exchanger, which is mounted in front of the radiator or air conditioning condenser.

TRANSMISSION

An automatic transmission is usually recommended for trailer towing. Modern automatics have proven reliable and, of course, easy to operate, in trailer towing.

The increased load of a trailer, however, causes an increase in the temperature of the automatic transmission fluid. Heat is the worst enemy of an automatic transmission. As the temperature of the fluid increases, the life of the fluid decreases.

It is essential, therefore, that you install an automatic transmission cooler.

The cooler, which consists of a multi-tube, finned heat exchanger, is usually installed in front of the radiator or air conditioning compressor, and hooked inline with the transmission cooler tank inlet line. Follow the cooler manufacturer's installation instructions.

Select a cooler of at least adequate capacity, based upon the combined gross weights of the Jeep and trailer.

Cooler manufacturers recommend that you use an aftermarket cooler in addition to, and not instead of, the present cooling tank in your Jeep radiator. If you do want to use it in place of the radiator cooling tank, get a cooler at least two sizes larger than normally necessary.

One note: the transmission cooler can, sometimes, cause slow or harsh shifting in the transmission during cold weather, until the fluid has a chance to come up to normal operating temperature. Some coolers can be purchased with or retrofitted with a temperature bypass valve which will allow fluid flow through the cooler only when the fluid has reached operating temperature, or above.

Engine Performance and Tune-Up

Tune-up Specifications Gasoline Engines

Years	Engines	Spark Plugs Type	Spark Plugs Gap (in.)	Ignition Timing (deg.) Man. Trans.	Ignition Timing (deg.) Auto. Trans.	Valve* Clearance In.	Valve* Clearance Exh.	Idle Speed Man. Trans.	Idle Speed Auto. Trans.
1984–85	4-150	RFN-12LY	0.035	12B	12B	Hyd.	Hyd.	750	750
	6-173	RN-12YC	0.041	10B	10B	Hyd.	Hyd.	750	750
1986	4-150	RC-12LYC	0.035	①	①	Hyd.	Hyd.	①	①
	6-173	RV-12YC	0.041	12B	10B	Hyd.	Hyd.	700	700
1987–89	4-150	RC-12LYC	0.035	①	①	Hyd.	Hyd.	①	①
	6-243	RC-9YC	0.035	①	①	Hyd.	Hyd.	①	①

① Not adjustable

Tune-up Specifications Diesel Engines

Engine	Injection Timing (deg)	(mm)	Nozzle Opening Pressure (psi)	Idle Speed (rpm) wo/sol.	Idle Speed (rpm) w/sol.	Valve Clearance Cold (in.) Int.	Valve Clearance Cold (in.) Exh.
4-126	8B	0.82±0.02	1,885	800	1,100	0.008	0.010

TUNE-UP PROCEDURES

In order to extract the full measure of performance and economy from your engine it is essential that it be properly tuned at regular intervals. A regular tune-up will keep your vehicle's engine running smoothly and will prevent the annoying minor breakdowns and poor performance associated with an untuned engine.

A complete tune-up should be performed every 12,000 miles or twelve months, whichever comes first. This interval should be halved if the vehicle is operated under severe conditions, such as trailer towing, prolonged idling, continual stop and start driving, or if starting or running problems are noticed. It is assumed that the routine maintenance described in Chapter 1 has been kept up, as this will have a decided effect on the results of a tune-up. All of the applicable steps of a tune-up should be followed in order, as the result is a cumulative one.

If the specifications on the tune-up sticker in the engine compartment disagree with the Tune-Up Specifications chart in this chapter, the figures on the sticker must be used. The sticker often reflects changes made during the production run.

Spark Plugs

A typical spark plug consists of a metal shell surrounding a ceramic insulator. A metal elec-

ENGINE PERFORMANCE AND TUNE-UP 61

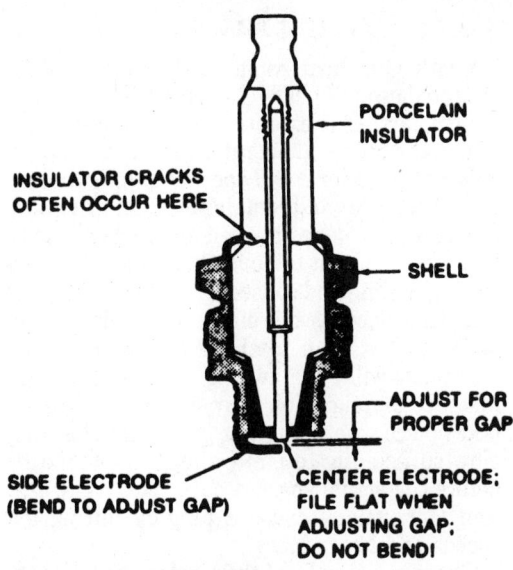

Cross section of a spark plug

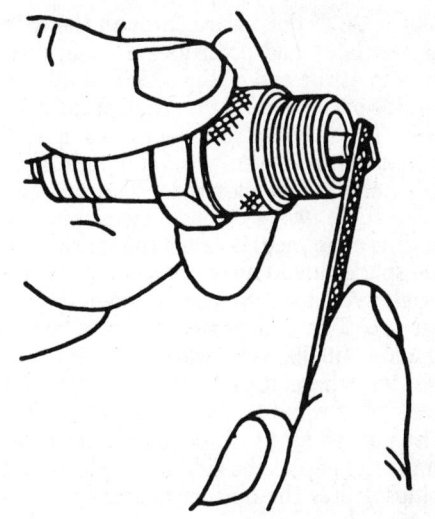

Plugs that are in good condition can be filed and re-used

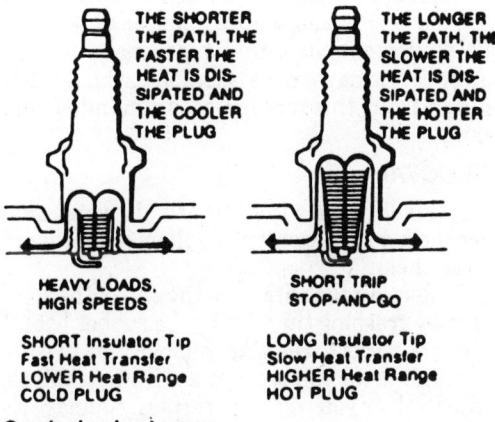

Spark plug heat range

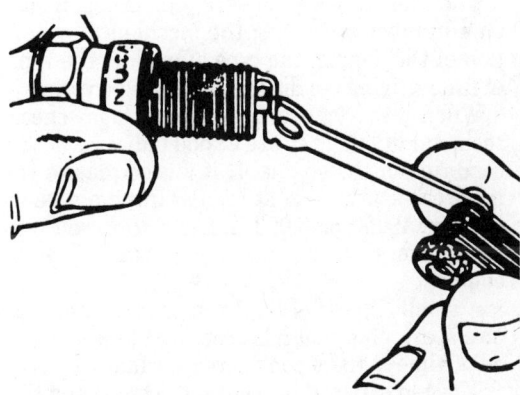

Adjust the electrode gap by bending the side electrode

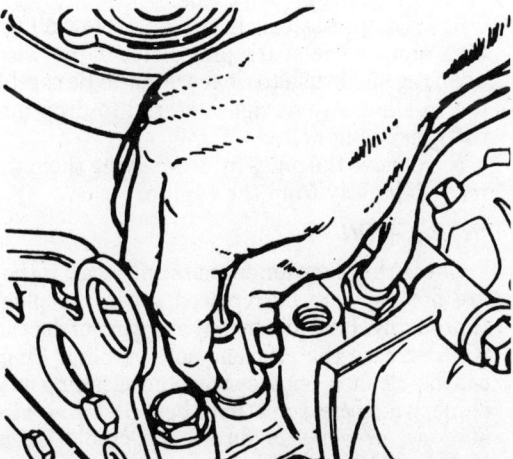

Twist and pull on the rubber boot to remove the spark plug wires; never pull on the wire itself

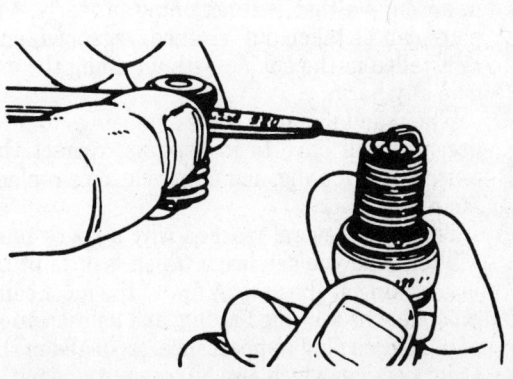

Always use a wire gauge to check the electrode gap

trode extends downward through the center of the insulator and protrudes a small distance. Located at the end of the plug and attached to the side of the outer metal shell is the side electrode. The side electrode bends in at a 90° angle so that its tip is even with, and parallel to, the tip of the center electrode. The distance between these two electrodes (measured in thousandths of an inch) is called the spark plug gap. The spark plug in no way produces a spark but merely provides a gap across which the current can arc. The coil produces anywhere from 20,000 to 40,000 volts which travels to the distributor where it is distributed through the spark plug wires to the spark plugs. The current passes along the center electrode and jumps the gap to the side electrode, and, in do doing, ignites the air/fuel mixture in the combustion chamber.

Spark plugs ignite the air and fuel mixture in the cylinder as the piston reaches the top of the compression stroke. The controlled explosion that results forces the piston down, turning the crankshaft and the rest of the drive train.

The average life of a spark plug is dependent on a number of factors: the mechanical condition of the engine; the type of engine; the type of fuel; driving conditions; and the driver.

When you remove the spark plugs, check their condition. They are a good indicator of the condition of the engine. It it a good idea to remove the spark plugs at regular intervals, such as every 2,000 or 3,000 miles, just so you can keep an eye on the mechanical state of your engine.

A small deposit of light tan or gray material on a spark plug that has been used for any period of time is to be considered normal.

The gap between the center electrode and the side or ground electrode can be expected to increase not more than 0.001" every 1,000 miles under normal conditions.

When a spark plug is functioning normally or, more accurately, when the plug is installed in an engine that is functioning properly, the plugs can be taken out, cleaned, regapped, and reinstalled in the engine without doing the engine any harm.

When, and if, a plug fouls and beings to misfire, you will have to investigate, correct the cause of the fouling, and either clean or replace the plug.

There are several reasons why a spark plug will foul and you can learn which is at fault by just looking at the plug. A few of the most common reasons for plug fouling, and a description of the fouled plug's appearance, are listed in the Color Section, which also offers solutions to the problems.

SPARK PLUG HEAT RANGE

Spark plug heat range is the ability of the plug to dissipate heat. The longer the insulator (or the farther it extends into the engine), the hotter the plug will operate; the shorter the insulator the cooler it will operate. A plug that absorbs little heat and remains too cool will quickly accumulate deposits of oil and carbon since it is not hot enough to burn them off. This leads to plug fouling and consequently to misfiring. A plug that absorbs too much heat will have no deposits, but, due to the excessive heat, the electrodes will burn away quickly and in some instances, preignition may result. Preignition takes place when plug tips get so hot that they glow sufficiently to ignite the fuel/air mixture before the actual spark occurs. This early ignition will usually cause a pinging during low speeds and heavy loads.

The general rule of thumb for choosing the correct heat range when picking a spark plug is: if most of your driving is long distance, high speed travel, use a colder plug; if most of your driving is stop and to, use a hotter plug. Original equipment plugs are compromise plugs, but most people never have occasion to change their plugs from the factory-recommended heat range.

REMOVAL

1. Remove the wires one at a time and number them so you won't cross them when you replace them.
2. Remove the wire from the end of the spark plug by grasping the wire by the rubber boot. If the boot sticks to the plug, remove it by twisting and pulling at the same time. Do not pull the wire itself or you will most certainly damage the core, or tear the connector.
3. Use a $^{13}/_{16}$" spark plug socket to loosen all of the plugs about two turns.
4. If compressed air is available, blow off the area around the spark plug holes. Otherwise, use a rag or a brush to clean the area. Be careful not to allow any foreign material to drop into the spark plug holes.
5. Remove the plugs by unscrewing them the rest of the way from the engine.

INSPECTION

Check the plugs for deposits and wear. If they are not going to be replaced, clean the plugs thoroughly. Remember that any kind of deposit will decrease the efficiency of the plug. Plugs can be cleaned on a spark plug cleaning machine, which can sometimes be found in service stations, or you can do an acceptable job of cleaning with a stiff brush.

Check spark plug gap before installation. The ground electrode must be aligned with the cen-

ENGINE PERFORMANCE AND TUNE-UP

ter electrode and the specified size wire gauge should pass through the gap with a slight drag. If the electrodes are worn, it is possible to file them level.

INSTALLATION

1. Insert the plugs in the spark plug hole and tighten them hand tight. Take care not to crossthread them.
2. Tighten the plugs to the torque figure specified in the Tune-Up section at the end of this chapter.
3. Install the spark plug wires on their plugs. Make sure that each wire is firmly connected to each plug.

CHECKING AND REPLACING SPARK PLUG CABLES

Visually inspect the spark plug cables for burns, cuts, or breaks in the insulation. Check the spark plug boots and the nipples on the distributor cap and coil. Replace any damages wiring. If no physical damage is obvious, the wires can be checked with an ohmmeter for excessive resistance. (See the tune-up and troubleshooting section).

When installing a new set of spark plug cables, replace the cables one at a time so there will be no mixup. Start by replacing the longest cable first. Install the boot firmly over the spark plug. Route the wire exactly the same as the original. Insert the nipple firmly into the tower on the distributor cap.

FIRING ORDERS

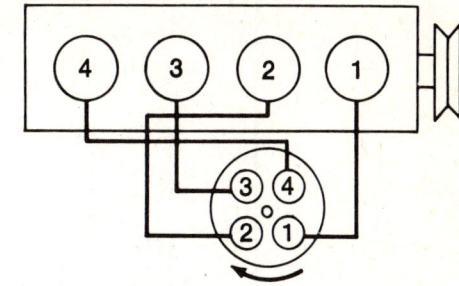
Distributor wiring and firing order: 4-150

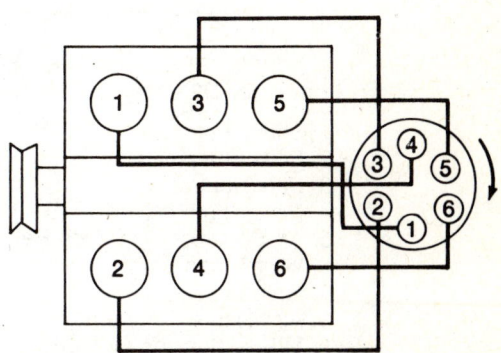
Distributor wiring and firing order: 6-173

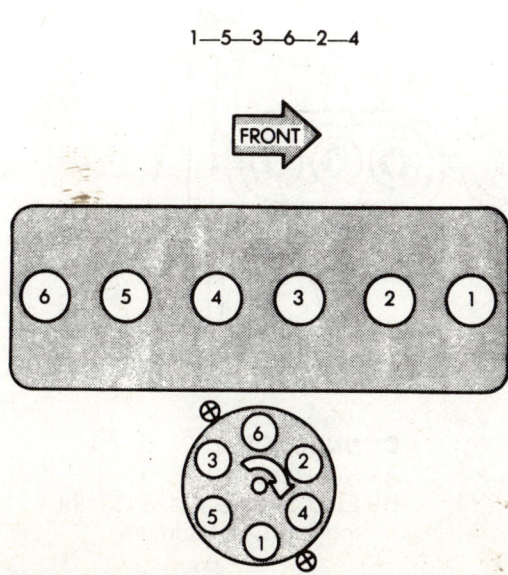
6-243 engine firing order

ELECTRONIC IGNITION SYSTEMS

American Motors Solid State Ignition (SSI) System

The SSI system is standard equipment on all 1984-85 American Motors built engines.

The system consists of a sensor and toothed trigger wheel inside the distributor, and a permanently sealed electronic control unit which determines dwell, in addition to the coil, ignition wires, and spark plugs.

The trigger wheel rotates on the distributor shaft. As one of its teeth nears the sensor magnet, the magnetic field shifts toward the tooth. When the tooth and sensor are aligned, the magnetic field is shifted to its maximum, signaling the electronic control unit to switch off the coil primary current. This starts an electronic timer inside the control unit, which allows the primary current to remain off only long enough for the spark plug to fire. The timer adjusts the amount of time primary current is off according to conditions, thus automatically adjusting dwell. There is also a special circuit within the control unit to detect and ignore spurious signals. Spark timing is adjusted by

64 ENGINE PERFORMANCE AND TUNE-UP

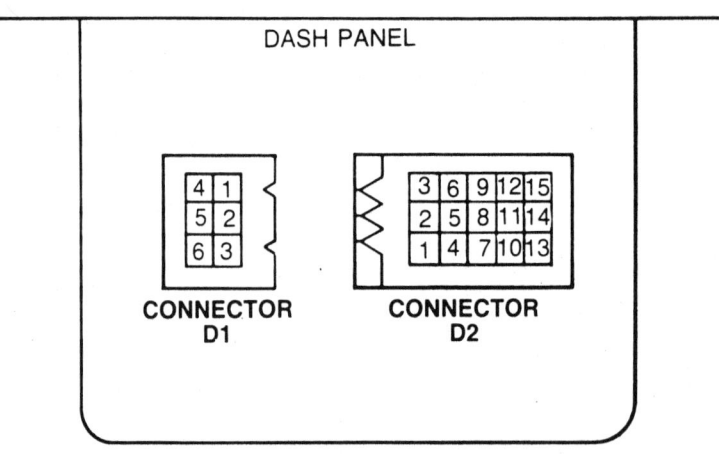

Connector D2
1. Shift Lamp
2. Power Latch Relay
3. Park/Neutral
4. Power Latched Relay (B+)
5. Air Conditioning Clutch Relay
6. Wide-Open Throttle Switch
7. Ground
8. Air Mixture Temperature
9. M.P.A. (Ignition Output)
10. EGR/Canister Purge Solenoid
11. Idle Speed Control Motor Forward
12. Coolant Temperature Sensor
13. Closed Throttle Switch
14. Idle Speed Control Motor Reverse
15. Not Used

Connector D1
1. Tach Input
2. Ignition
3. Ground
4. Start Solenoid
5. Battery
6. Fuel Pump

4-150 w/TBI diagnostic connector

CONNECTOR 1:
A - Ignition (+)
B - Ground (−)
C - Tach Signal Diagnostic Connector
    D1 - Pin 1

CONNECTOR 2:
A - Not Used
B - ECU Square Wave Output
    Ignition Coil Interface

4-150 ignition control module

ENGINE PERFORMANCE AND TUNE-UP

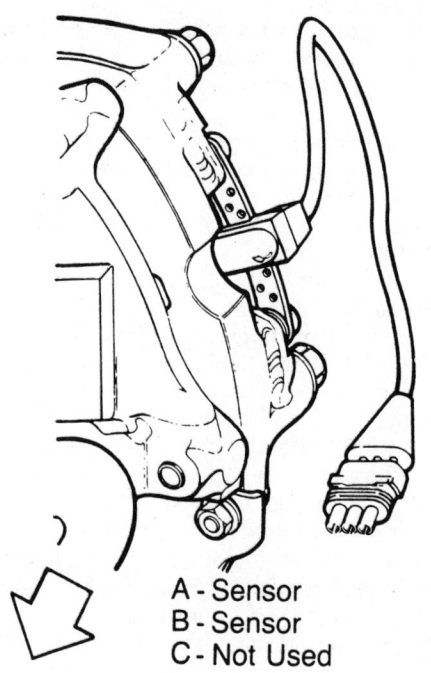

A - Sensor
B - Sensor
C - Not Used

4-150 w/TBI TDC sensor

both mechanical (centrifugal) and vacuum advance.

A wire of 1.35Ω resistance is spliced into the ignition feed to reduce voltage to the coil during running conditions. The resistance wire is bypassed when the engine is being started so that full battery voltage may be supplied to the coil. Bypass is accomplished by the I-terminal on the solenoid.

SECONDARY CIRCUIT TEST

1. Disconnect the coil wire from the center of the distributor cap.
NOTE: *Twist the rubber boot slightly in either direction, then grasp the boot and pull straight up. Do not pull on the wire, and do not use pliers.*
2. Hold the wire ½" from a ground with a pair of insulated pliers and a heavy glove. As the engine is cranked, watch for a spark.
3. If a spark appears, reconnect the coil wire. Remove the wire from one spark plug, and test for a spark as above.

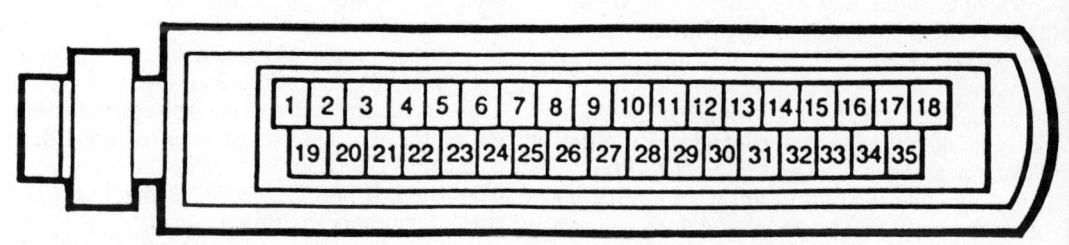

1. Ground
2. Ground
3. Ignition switch
4. Battery
5. EGR valve/canister purge
6. Fuel pump relay
7. System power relay (latch relay)
8. WOT switch
9. Not used
10. System ground
11. Speed sensor
12. Park/neutral switch (A/T only)
13. Throttle position sensor (TPS) ground
14. Manifold air/fuel temperature sensor
15. Coolant temperature sensor
16. Manifold absolute pressure (supply voltage)
17. Manifold absolute pressure (ground)
18. Shift lamp
19. System power (B+)
20. Not used
21. Injector
22. A/C compressor clutch
23. ISA motor retract (reverse)
24. ISA motor extend (forward)
25. Closed throttle (idle) switch
26. Not used
27. Ignition (output)
28. Speed sensor
29. Start
30. A/C select
31. Throttle position sensor (TPS)
32. Sensor ground
33. Manifold absolute pressure (output voltage)
34. A/C temperature control (request)
35. Oxygen sensor

4-150 w/TBI ECU connector

ENGINE PERFORMANCE AND TUNE-UP

CAUTION: *Do not remove the spark plug wires from cylinder 3 on the 4-150.*

3. If a spark occurs, the problem is in the fuel system or ignition timing. If no spark occurs, check for a defective rotor, cap, or spark plug wires.

4. If no spark occurs from the coil wire in Step 2, test the coil wire resistance with an ohmmeter. It should be 7,700-9,300Ω at 75°F or 12,000Ω maximum at 93°F.

COIL PRIMARY CIRCUIT TEST

1. Turn the ignition On. Connect a multitester to the coil positive (+) terminal and a ground. If the voltage is 5.5-6.5 volts, go to Step 2. If above 7 volts, go to Step 4. If below 5.5 volts, disconnect the condenser lead and measure. If the voltage is now 5.5-6.5 volts, replace the condenser. If not, go to Step 6.

2. With the multitester connected as in Step 1, read the voltage with the engine cranking. If battery voltage is indicated, the circuit is okay. If not, go to Step 3.

3. Check for a short or open in the starter solenoid I-terminal wire. Check the solenoid for proper operation.

4. Disconnect the wire from the starter solenoid I-terminal, with the ignition On and the multitester connected as in Step 1. If the voltage drops to 5.5-6.5 volts, replace the solenoid. If not, connect a jumper between the coil negative (−) terminal and a ground. If the voltage drops to 5.5-6.5 volts, go to Step 5. If not, repair the resistance wire.

5. Check for continuity between the coil (−) terminal and D4, and D1 to ground. If the continuity is okay, replace the control unit. If not, check for an open wire and go back to Step 2.

6. Turn ignition Off. Connect an ohmmeter between the + coil terminal and dash connector AV. If above 1.40Ω, repair the resistance wire.

7. With the ignition Off, connect the ohmmeter between connector AV and ignition switch terminal 11. If less than 0.1 ohm, replace the ignition switch or repair the wire, whichever is the cause. If above 0.1 ohm, check connections, and check for defective wiring.

COIL TEST

1. Check the coil for cracks, carbon tracks, etc., and replace as necessary.

2. Connect an ohmmeter across the coil + and − terminals, with the coil connector removed. If 1.13-1.23Ω @ 75°F, the coil is okay. If not, replace it.

CONTROL UNIT AND SENSOR TEST

1. With the ignition On, remove the coil high tension wire from the distributor cap and hold ½" from ground with insulated pliers. Disconnect the 4-wire connector at the control unit. If a spark occurs (normal), go to Step 2. If not, go to Step 5.

2. Connect an ohmmeter to D2 and D3. If the resistance is 400-800Ω (normal), go to Step 6. If not, go to Step 3.

3. Disconnect and reconnect the 3-wire connector at distributor. If the reading is now 400-800Ω, go to Step 6. If not, disconnect the 3-wire connector and go to Step 4.

4. Connect the ohmmeter across B2 and B3. If 300-800Ω, repair the harness between the 3-wire and 4-wire connectors. If not, replace the sensor.

5. Connect the ohmmeter between D1 and the battery negative terminal. If the reading is 0 (0.002 or less), go to Step 2. If above 0.002Ω, there is a bad ground in the cable or at the distributor. Repair the ground and retest.

6. Connect a multitester across D2 and D3. Crank the engine. If the needle fluctuates, the system is okay. If not, either the trigger wheel is defective, or the distributor is not turning. Repair or replace as required.

IGNITION FEED TO CONTROL UNIT TEST

NOTE: *Do not perform this test without first performing the Coil Primary Circuit Test.*

1. With the ignition On, unplug the 2-wire connector at the module. Connect a multitester between F2 and ground. If the reading is battery voltage, replace the control unit and go to Step 3. If not, go to Step 2.

2. Repair the cause of the voltage reduction: either the ignition switch or a corroded dash connector. Check for a spark at the coil wire. If okay, stop. If not, replace the control unit and check for proper operation.

3. Reconnect the 2-wire connector at the control unit, and unplug the 4-wire connector at the control unit. Connect an ammeter between C1 and ground. If it reads 0.9-1.1 amps, the system is okay. If not, replace the module.

American Motors Solid State Ignition System for 1986-89 4-150 and 6-243 Engines

These engines are equipped with electronically controlled fuel injection. Therefore, the electronic ignition system is different from that used on carbureted engines.

The system consists of:
- a solid state ignition control module (ICM)
- an electronic control module (ECU)
- a forty tooth rotor in the distributor
- TDC sensor mounted at the rear of the engine on the flywheel housing

ENGINE PERFORMANCE AND TUNE-UP 67

The control module consists of a solid state ignition circuit and an integrated ignition coil each of which can be removed and serviced separately. Spark timing control is determined by the ignition control module. Signals fromn the ECU relay information about engine load and other driving conditions to both the ICM and fuel injection system electronic control components.

Electrical feed to the ICM is through terminal A of connector 1 (see illustration). Electrical feed ocurs only when the ignition switch is in the START and RUN positions. Terminal B of connector 1 is grounded at the engine oil dipstick bracket, along with the ECU ground wire and the O_2 sensor ground.

DIAGNOSIS

Primary System

Primary system diagnosis is made through the diagnostic connector, using the appropiate diagnostic computer. Primary circuit tests are made at (D1-2) B+ after ignition; tachometer voltage is at D1-1; vehicle ground is at D1-3.

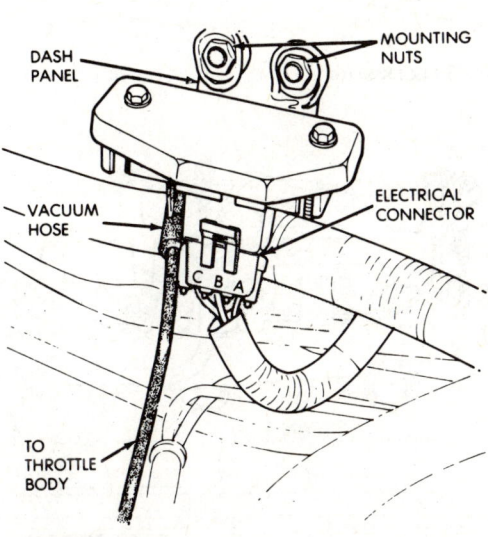

6-243 MAP sensor

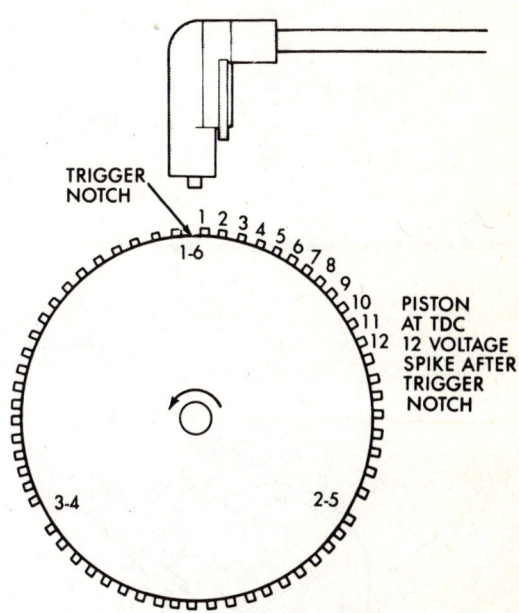

6-243 engine speed sensor-to-flywheel TDC position

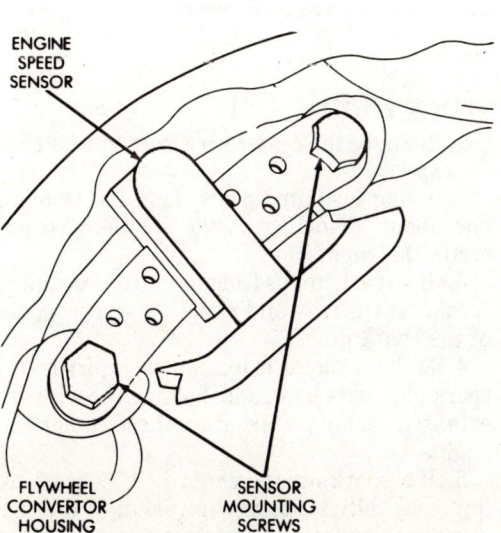

6-243 engine speed sensor

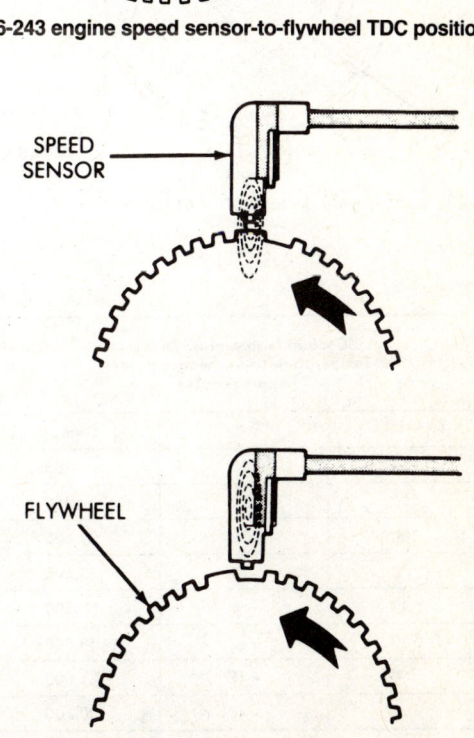

6-243 engine speed sensor operation

68 ENGINE PERFORMANCE AND TUNE-UP

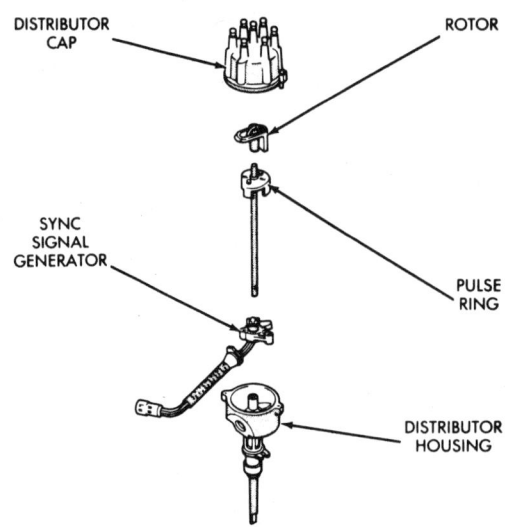

6-243 sync signal generator and pulse ring

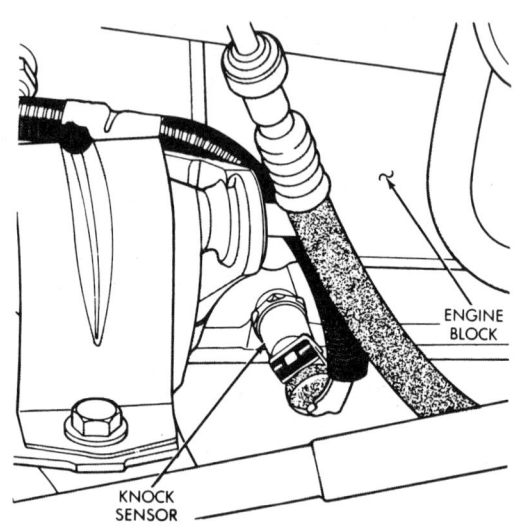

6-243 knock sensor

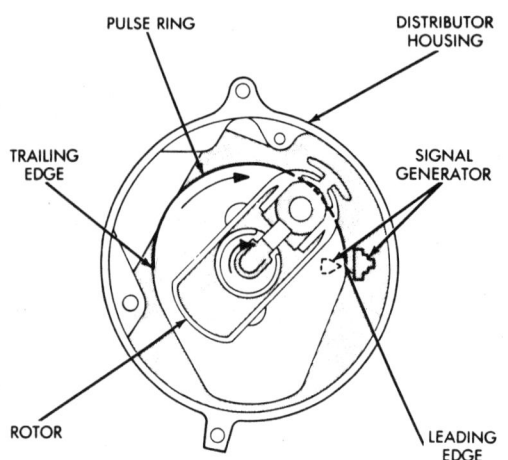

6-243 sync signal generator operation

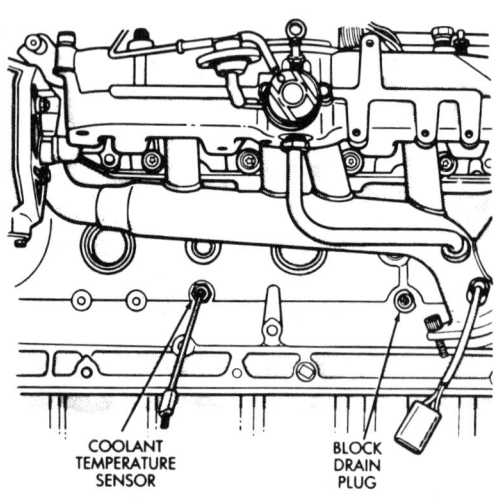

6-243 coolant temperature sensor

Coolant Temperature Sensor Temperature-to-Resistance Values (Approximate)		
°F	°C	Ohms
212	100	185
160	70	450
100	38	1,600
70	20	3,400
40	4	7,500
20	-7	13,500
0	-18	25,000
-40	-40	100,700

6-243 coolant temperature sensor resistance chart

Secondary System

1. Remove the center wire from the distributor cap.
2. Using insulated pliers, hold the terminal end about ½ inch from the engine head and crank the engine.
3. If a spark jumps from the wire to the head, reconnect the wire and remove a wire from one of the spark plugs.
4. Make a metal extension to insert in the spark plug wire boot, and, holding the wire and extension about ½" from the head, crank the engine.
5. If a spark occurs, check ECU sensors using tester MS 1700, or equivalent. If the sensors check out okay, the problem is probably in the fuel system.

ENGINE PERFORMANCE AND TUNE-UP

6. If no spark occurs, The rotor, distributor cap or spark plug wires are defective.

Delco High Energy Ignition (HEI) System — 6-173

The General Motors HEI system is a pulse triggered, transistor controlled, inductive discharge ignition system. The entire HEI system is contained within the distributor cap.

The distributor, in addition to housing the mechanical and vacuum advance mechanisms, contains the ignition coil (except on some inline six engines), the electronic control module, and the magnetic triggering device. The magnetic pick-up assembly contains a permanent magnet, a pole piece with internal teeth, and a pick-up coil (not to be confused with the ignition coil).

In the HEI system, as in other electronic ignition systems, the breaker points have been replaced with an electronic switch—a transistor, which is located within the control module. This switching transistor performs the same function the points did in a conventional ignition system; it simply turns coil primary current on and off at the correct time. Essentially then, electronic and conventional ignition systems operate on the same principle.

The module which houses the switching transistor is controlled (turned on and off) by a magnetically generated impulse induced in the pick-up coil. When the teeth of the rotating timer align with the teeth of the pole piece, the induced voltage in the pick-up coil signals the electronic module to open the coil primary circuit. The primary current then decreases, and a high voltage is induced in the ignition coil secondary windings, which is then directed through the rotor and spark plug wires to fire the spark plugs.

In essence, then, the pick-up coil module system simply replaces the conventional breaker points and condenser. The condenser found within the distributor is for radio suppression purposes only and has nothing to do with the ignition process. The module automatically con-

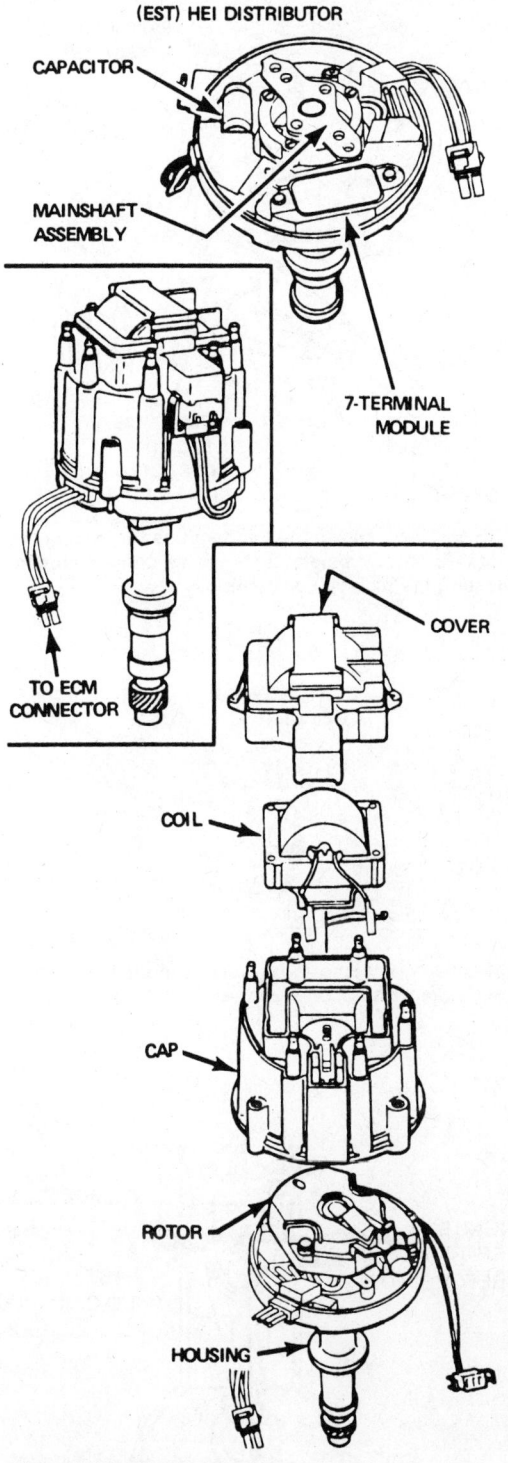

H.E.I. (EST) distributor

HEI Plug Wire Resistance Chart

Wire Length (inches)	Minimum Ohms	Maximum Ohms
Up to 15	3,000	10,000
15–25	4,000	15,000
25–35	6,000	20,000
Over 35		25,000

Distributor Components Testing

trols the dwell period, increasing it with increasing engine speed. Since dwell is automatically controlled, it cannot be adjusted. The module itself is non-adjustable and non-repairable and must be replaced if found defective.

70 ENGINE PERFORMANCE AND TUNE-UP

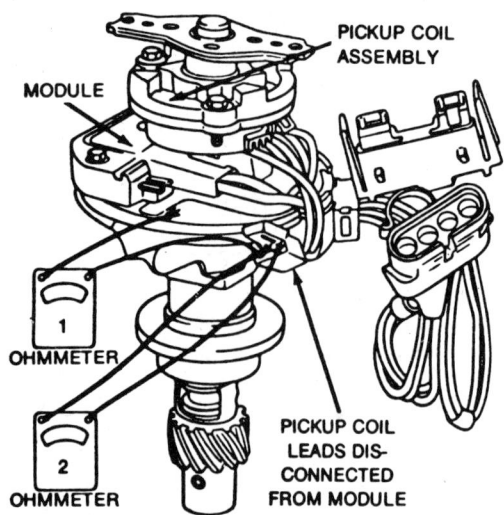

Ohmmeter 1 shows the connections for testing the pick-up coil. Ohmmeter 2 shows the connections for testing the pick-up coil continuity

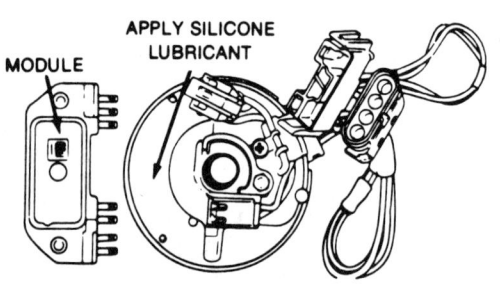

Module replacement; be sure to coat the mating surfaces with silicone lubricant

HEI SYSTEM PRECAUTIONS

Before going on to troubleshooting, it might be a good idea to take note of the following precautions.

Timing Light Use

Inductive pick-up timing lights are the best kind to use with HEI. Timing lights which connect between the spark plug and the spark plug wire occasionally (not always) give false readings.

Spark Plug Wires

The plug wires used with HEI systems are of a different construction than conventional wires. When replacing them, make sure you get the correct wires, since conventional wires won't carry the voltage. Also handle them carefully to avoid cracking or splitting them and never pierce them.

Tachometer Use

Not all tachometers will operate or indicate correctly when used on an HEI system. While some tachometers may give a reading, this does not necessarily mean the reading is correct. In addition, some tachometers hook up differently from others. If you can't figure out whether or not your tachometer will work on your truck, check with the tachometer manufacturer. Dwell readings have no significance at all.

HEI System Testers

Instruments designed specifically for testing HEI systems are available from several tool

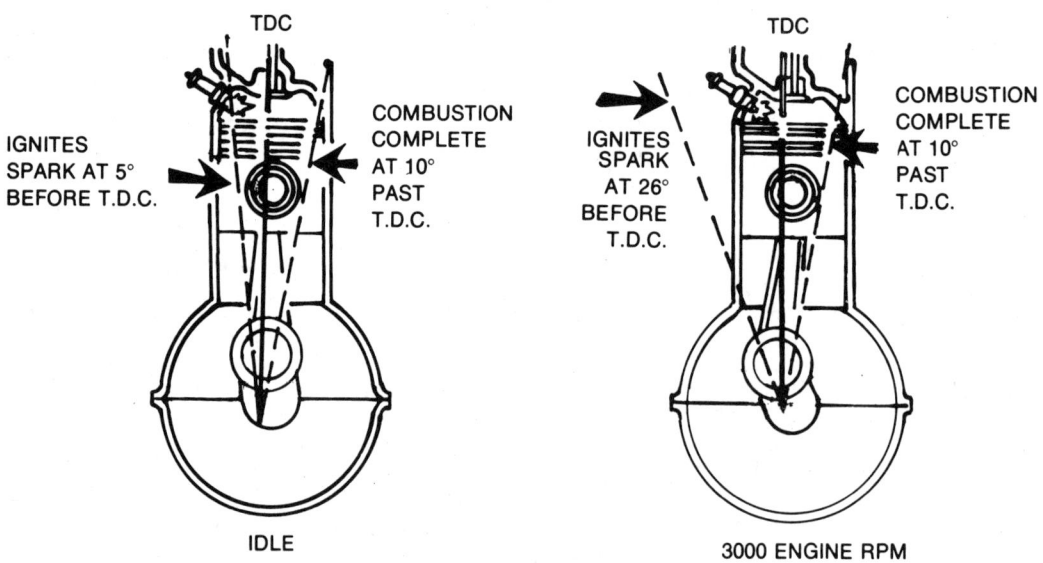

Ignition timing at idle and at 3,000 rpm

ENGINE PERFORMANCE AND TUNE-UP

manufacturers. Some of these will even test the module itself. However, the test given in the following section will require only a multitester with volt and ohm scales.

TROUBLESHOOTING THE HEI SYSTEM

The symptoms of a defective component within the HEI system are exactly the same as those you would encounter in a conventional system. Some of these symptoms are:
Hard or no starting
Rough idle
Poor fuel economy
Engine misses under load or while accelerating

If you suspect a problem in the ignition system, there are certain preliminary checks which you should carry out before you begin to check the electronic portions of the system.

First, it is extremely important to make sure that the vehicle's battery is in good condition. A defective or poorly charged battery will cause the various components of the ignition system to read incorrectly when tested.

Second, make sure all of the wiring connections are clean and tight, not only at the battery, but also at the distributor cap, coil and module.

Since the major difference between electronic and point type ignition systems is in the distributor area, it is imperative to check the secondary ignition wires first. If the secondary system checks out okay, then the problem is probably not in the ignition system. To check the secondary system, perform a simple spark test. Remove on of the spark plug wires from the plug and insert a makeshift extension made of conductive metal, in the wire boot. Hold the wire and extension about ¼" away from the block and crank the engine. If a normal spark occurs, then the problem is most likely not in the ignition system. Check for fuel system problems, or fouled spark plugs.

If, however, there is no spark or a weak spark, then further ignition system testing will have to be done. Troubleshooting techniques fall into two categories, depending on the nature of the problem. The categories are (1) Engine cranks, but won't start, and (2) Engine runs, but runs rough or cuts out.

Engine Fails to Start

If the engine won't start, perform a spark test as described earlier. If no spark occurs, check for the presence of normal battery voltage at the battery (BAT) terminal in the distributor cap. The ignition switch must be in the on position for this test. Either a multitester or a test light may be used for this test. Connect the test light wire to ground and the probe end to the BAT terminal at the distributor. If the light comes on, you have voltage to the distributor. If the light fails to come on, this indicates an open circuit in the ignition primary wiring leading to the distributor. In this case, you will have to check wiring continuity back to the ignition switch using test light. If there is battery voltage at the BAT terminal, but no spark at the plugs, then the problem lies within the distributor assembly. Go on to the distributor components test section.

Engine Runs, but Runs Roughly or Cuts Out

1. Make sure the plug wires are in good shape first. There should be no obvious cracks or breaks. You can check the plug wires with an ohmmeter, but do not pierce the wires with a probe. Check the chart for the correct plug wire resistance.

2. If the plug wires are okay, remove the cap assembly, and check for moisture, cracks, chips, or carbon tracks, or any other high voltage leaks or failures. Replace the cap if you find any defects. Make sure the timer wheel rotates when the engine is cranked. If everything is all right so far, go on to the distributor components test section.

Distributor Components Testing

If the trouble has been narrowed down to the units within the distributor, the following tests can help pinpoint the defective component. An ohmmeter with both high and low ranges should be used. These tests are made with the cap assembly removed and the battery wire disconnected.

1. Connect an ohmmeter between the TACH and BAT terminals in the distributor cap. The primary coil resistance should be less than one ohm (zero or nearly zero).

2. To check the coil secondary resistance, connect an ohmmeter between the rotor button and the BAT terminal. Then connect the ohmmeter between the ground terminal and the rotor button. The resistance in both cases should be between 6,000 and 30,000Ω.

3. Replace the coil only if the readings in steps 1 and 2 are infinite.

NOTE: *These resistance checks will not disclose shorted coil windings. This condition can be detected only with scope analysis or a suitably designed coil tester. If these instruments are unavailable, replace the coil with a known good coil as a final coil test.*

4. To test the pick-up coil, first disconnect the white and green module leads. Set the ohmmeter on the high scale and connect it between a ground and either the white or green lead. Any resistance measurement less than infinity requires replacement of the pick-up coil.

72 ENGINE PERFORMANCE AND TUNE-UP

5. Pick-up coil continuity is tested by connecting the ohmmeter (on low range) between the white and green leads. Normal resistance is between 500 and 1500Ω. Move the vacuum advance arm while performing this test. This will detect any break in coil continuity. Such a condition can cause intermittent misfiring. Replace the pick-up coil if the reading is outside the specific limits.

6. If no defects have been found at this time, and you still have a problem, then the module will have to be checked. If you do not have access to a module tester, the only possible alternative is a substitution test. If the module fails the substitution test, replace it.

COMPONENT REPLACEMENT

Integral Ignition Coil

1. Disconnect the feed and module wire terminal connectors from the distributor cap.
2. Remove the ignition set retainer.
3. Remove the 4 coil cover-to-distributor cap screws and coil cover.
4. Remove the 4 coil-to-distributor cap screws.
5. Using a blunt drift, press the coil wire spade terminals up out of distributor cap.
6. Lift the coil up out of the distributor cap.
7. Remove and clean the coil spring, rubber seal washer and coil cavity of the distributor cap.
8. Coat the rubber seal with a dielectric lubricant furnished in the replacement ignition coil package.
9. Reverse the above procedures to install.

Distributor Cap

1. Remove the feed and module wire terminal connectors from the distributor cap.
2. Remove the retainer and spark plug wires from the cap.
3. Depress and release the 4 distributor cap-to-housing retainers and lift off the cap assembly.
4. Remove the 4 coil cover screws and cover.
5. Using a finger or a blunt drift, push the spade terminals up out of the distributor cap.
6. Remove all 4 coil screws and lift the coil, coil spring, and rubber seal washer out of the cap coil cavity.
7. Using a new distributor cap, reverse the above procedures to assembly, being sure to clean and lubricate the rubber seal washer with dielectric lubricant.

Rotor

1. Disconnect the feed and module wire connectors from the distributor.
2. Depress and release the 4 distributor cap to housing retainers and lift off the cap assembly.
3. Remove the two rotor attaching screws and rotor.
4. Reverse the above procedure to install.

Vacuum Advance

1. Remove the distributor cap and rotor as previously described.
2. Disconnect the vacuum hose from the vacuum advance unit.
3. Remove the two vacuum advance retaining screws, pull the advance unit outward, rotate, and disengage the operating rod from its tang.
4. Reverse the above procedure to install.

Module

1. Remove the distributor cap and rotor as previously described.
2. Disconnect the harness connector and pick-up coil spade connectors from the module. Be careful not to damage the wires when removing the connector.
3. Remove the two screws and module from the distributor housing.
4. Coat the bottom of the new module with dielectric lubricant supplied with the new module. Reverse the above procedure to install.

Ignition Timing

Ignition timing is the measurement, in degrees of crankshaft rotation, of the point at which the spark plugs fire in each of the cylinders. It is measured in degrees before or after Top Dead Center (TDC) of the compression stroke. Ignition timing is controlled by turning the distributor body in the engine.

Ideally, the air/fuel mixture in the cylinder will be ignited by the spark plug just as the piston passes TDC of the compression stroke. If this happens, the piston will be beginning its downward motion of the power stroke just as the compressed and ignited air/fuel mixture starts to expand. The expansion of the air/fuel mixture then forces the piston down on the power stroke and turns the crankshaft.

Because it takes a fraction of a second for the spark plug to ignite the mixture in the cylinder, the spark plug must fire a little before the piston reaches TDC. Otherwise, the mixture will not be completely ignited as the piston passes TDC and the full power of the explosion will not be used by the engine.

The timing measurement is given in degrees of crankshaft rotation before the piston reaches TDC (BTDC). If the setting for the ignition timing is 5° BTDC, the spark plug must fire 5° be-

ENGINE PERFORMANCE AND TUNE-UP

fore each piston reaches TDC. This only holds true, however, when the engine is at idle speed.

As the engine speed increases, the pistons go faster. The spark plugs have to ignite the fuel even sooner if it is to be completely ignited when the piston reaches TDC. To do this, the distributor has a means to advance the timing of the spark as the engine speed increases. This

6-173 timing marks

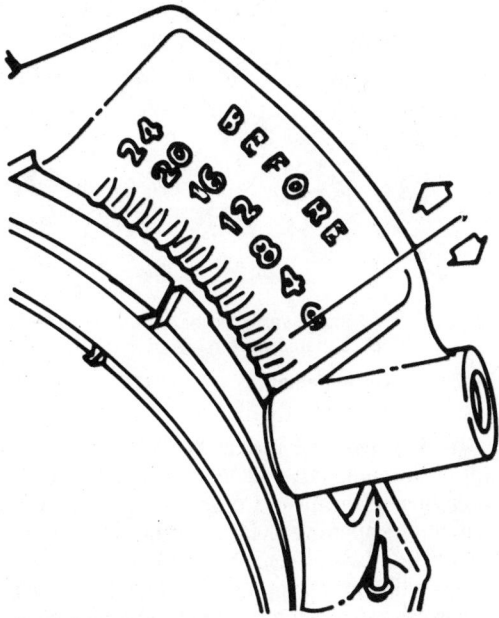

4-150 timing marks

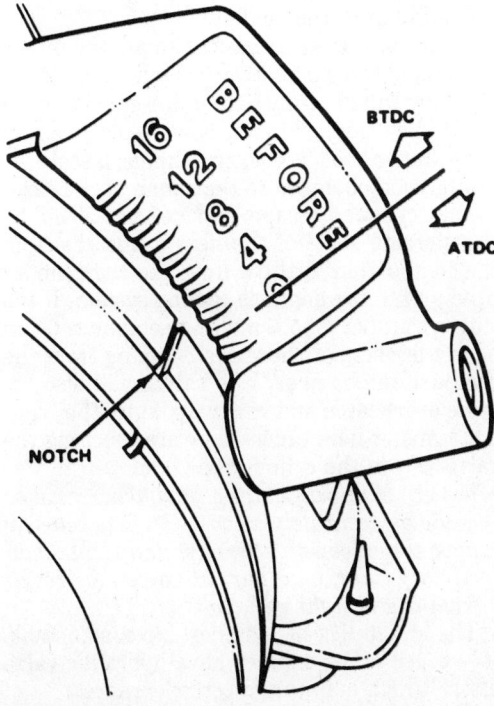

6-243 timing marks

is accomplished by input from the electronic ignition control module and other computer sources. If the distributor is equipped with a vacuum advance unit, it is necessary to disconnect the vacuum line from the diaphragm when the ignition timing is being set.

If the ignition is set too far advanced (BTDC), the ignition and expansion of the fuel in the cylinder will occur too soon and tend to force the piston down while it is still traveling up. This causes engine ping. If the ignition spark is set too far retarded, after TDC (ATDC), the piston will have already passed TDC and started on its way down when the fuel is ignited. This will cause the piston to be forced down for only a portion of its travel. This will result in poor engine performance and lack of power.

The timing is best checked with a timing light. This device is connected in series with the No. 1 spark plug. The current that fires the spark plug also causes the timing light to flash. When the engine is running, the timing light is aimed at the timing marks on the engine and crankshaft pulley.

IGNITION TIMING ADJUSTMENT

Timing should be checked at each tune-up and any time the points are adjusted or replaced. The timing marks consist of a notch on the rim of the crankshaft pulley and a graduated scale attached to the engine front (timing) cover. A stroboscopic flash (dynamic) timing light must be used, as a static light is too inaccurate for emission controlled engines.

There are three basic types of timing lights available. The first is a simple neon bulb with two wire connections. One wire connects to the spark plug terminal and the other plugs into the end of the spark plug wire for the No. 1 cylinder, thus connecting the light in series with the spark plug. This type of light is pretty dim and must be held very close to the timing marks to be seen. Sometimes a dark corner has to be sought out to see the flash at all. This type of light is very inexpensive. The second type operates from the car battery—two alligator clips connect to the battery terminals, while an adapter enables a third clip to be connected to the No. 1 spark plug and wire. This type is a bit

74 ENGINE PERFORMANCE AND TUNE-UP

more expensive, but it provides a nice bright flash that you can see even in bright sunlight. It is the type most often seen in professional shops. The third type replaces the battery power source with 110 volt current.

NOTE: *Connect a tachometer to the SSI ignition system in the conventional way; to the negative (distributor) side of the coil and to a ground. HEI distributor caps have a* **Tach** *terminal. Some tachometers may not work with a SSI or HEI ignition system and there is a possibility that some could be damaged. Check with the manufacturer of the tachometer to make sure it can be used.*

To check and adjust the timing:

1. Warm up the engine to normal operating temperature. Stop the engine and connect the timing light to the No. 1 spark plug wire. Clean off the timing marks and mark the pulley notch and timing scale with white chalk.

2. Disconnect and plug the vacuum line at the distributor. This is done to prevent any distributor vacuum advance.

3. Start the engine and adjust the idle to the idle speed to the figure shown on the underhood sticker. This is done to prevent any distributor centrifugal advance. If there is a throttle stop solenoid, disconnect it electrically.

4. Aim the timing light at the pointer marks. Be careful not to touch the fan, because it may appear to be standing still. If the pulley notch isn't aligned with the proper timing mark (refer to the Tune-Up Specifications chart), the timing will have to be adjusted.

NOTE: *TDC or Top Dead Center corresponds to 0 degrees. B, or BTDC, or Before Top Dead Center, may be shown as A for Advanced on a V8 timing scale. R on a V8 timing scale means Retarded, corresponding to ATDC, or After Top Dead Center.*

5. Loosen the distributor clamp locknut. You can buy trick wrenches that make this task a lot easier. Turn the distributor slowly to adjust the timing, holding it by the base and not the cap. Turn counterclockwise to advance timing (toward BTDC), and clockwise to retard (toward TDC or ATDC).

6. Tighten the locknut. Check the timing again, in case the distributor moved slightly as you tightened it.

7. Replace the distributor vacuum line and correct the idle speed to that specified in the Tune-Up Specifications chart.

8. Stop the engine and disconnect the timing light.

Valve Lash

Valve adjustment determines how far the valves enter the cylinder and how long they stay open and closed.

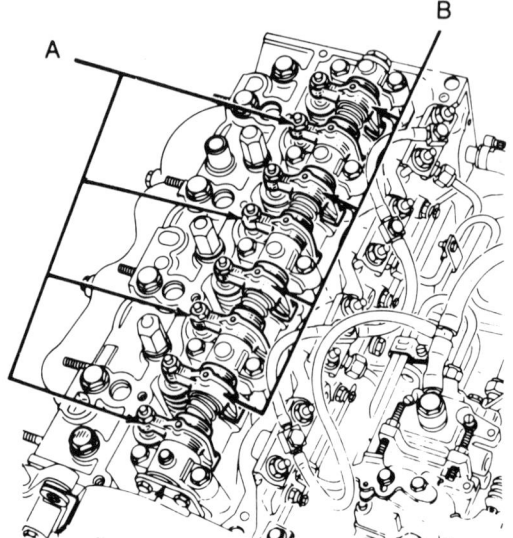

A. Intake valve rocker arms
B. Exhaust valve rocker arms

4-126 valve arrangement

If the valve clearance is too large, part of the lift of the camshaft will be used in removing the excessive clearance. Consequently, the valve will not be opening as far as it should. This condition has two effects: the valve train components will emit a tapping sound as they take up the excessive clearance and the engine will perform poorly because the valves don't open fully and allow the proper amount of gases to flow into and out of the engine.

If the valve clearance is too small, the intake valves and the exhaust valves will open too far and they will not fully seat on the cylinder head when they close. When a valve seats itself on the cylinder head, it does two things: it seals the combustion chamber so that none of the gases in the cylinder escape and it cools itself by transferring some of the heat it absorbs from the combustion in the cylinder to the cylinder head and to the engine's cooling system. If the valve clearance is too small, the engine will run poorly because of the gases escaping from the combustion chamber. The valves will also become overheated and will warp, since they cannot transfer heat unless they are touching the valve seat in the cylinder head.

NOTE: *While all valve adjustments must be made as accurately as possible, it is better to have the valve adjustment slightly loose than slightly tight, as a burned valve may result from overly tight adjustments.*

The 4-126 Diesel engines have adjustable valves. All other engines have hydraulic valve lifters which maintain a zero clearance. These hydraulic lifters are set after overhaul,

ENGINE PERFORMANCE AND TUNE-UP

by bringing the piston to TDC compression and turning the nut until the rocker arm just touches the valve stem, then ½ turn more.

ADJUSTMENT

4-126 Diesel Engine

1. Be sure that the engine is cold before adjusting the valves. Remove the valve cover.
2. Set the no.1 cylinder to TDC on the compression stroke and check the valve clearance of number one and number two intake and number one and number three exhaust valves. Adjust as required.

NOTE: *The no.1 cylinder is located at the flywheel end of the engine.*

3. Rotate the crankshaft 360 degrees and check the clearance of the number three and number four intake and number two and number four exhaust valves. Adjust as required.
4. To adjust, loosen locknut and turn adjustment screw as necessary. As each adjustment screw is tightened, be sure that the bottom of the screw is aligned with the valve stem. If the adjustment screw is not aligned with the stem when tightened, the stem could bend. Tighten locknut.
5. The exhaust valve adjustment specification is 0.010″. The intake valve adjustment specification is 0.008″.

Fuel System

This section contains only tune-up adjustment procedures for fuel systems. Descriptions, adjustments, and overhaul procedures for fuel system components can be found in Chapter 5.

IDLE SPEED AND MIXTURE ADJUSTMENTS

1984

4-150

1. Fully warm up the engine.
2. Check the choke fast idle adjustment: Disconnect and plug the EGR valve vacuum hose. Position the fast idle adjustment screw on the second step of the fast idle cam with the transmission in neutral. Adjust the fast idle speed to 2,000 rpm for manual transmission and 2,300 rpm for automatic transmission. Allow the throttle to return to normal curb idle and reconnect the EGR vacuum hose.
3. To adjust the Sol-Vac Vacuum Actuator: Remove the vacuum hose from the vacuum actuator and plug the hose. Connect an external vacuum source to the actuator and apply 10-15 inches Hg. of vacuum to the actuator. Shift the transmission to Neutral. Adjust the idle speed to the following rpm using the vacuum actuator adjustment screw on the throttle lever: 850 rpm for automatic transmission 950 rpm for

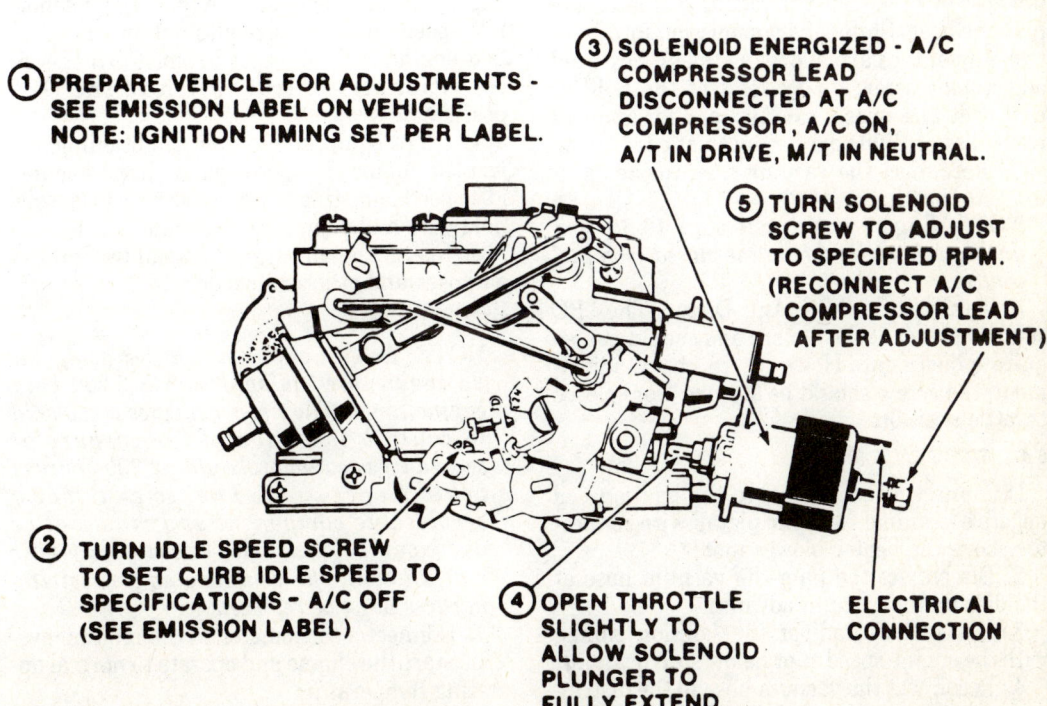

Idle Speed Adjustment—without A/C—E2SE

76 ENGINE PERFORMANCE AND TUNE-UP

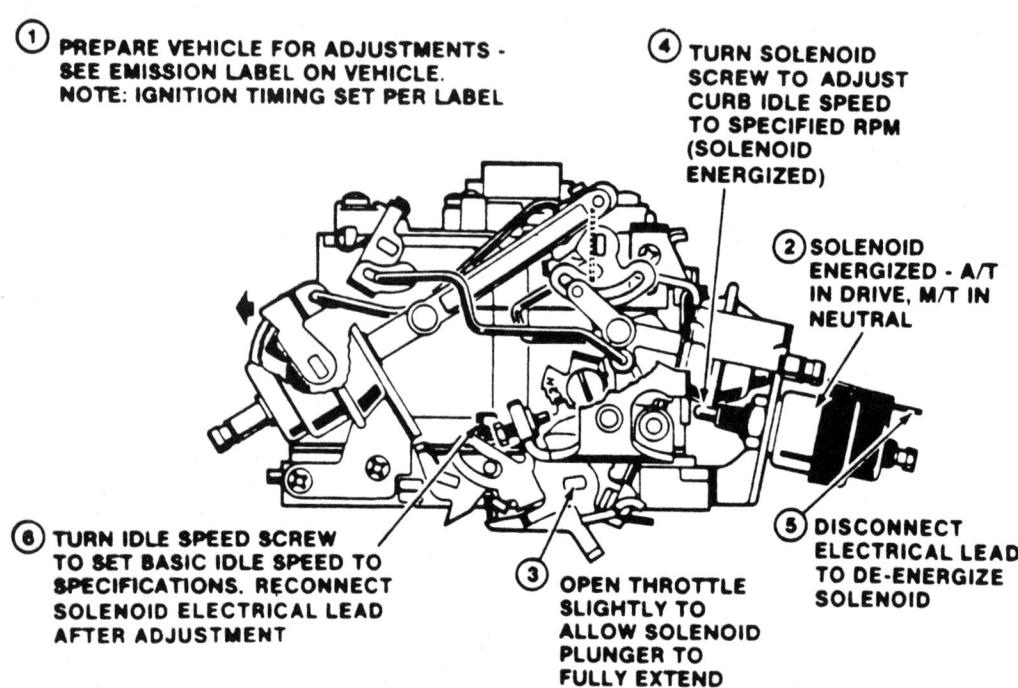

Idle Speed Adjustment—with A/C—E2SE

manual transmission. The adjustment is made with all accessories turned off.

NOTE: *The curb idle should always be adjusted after vacuum actuator adjustment.*

4. To adjust the curb idle: Remove the vacuum hose from the Sol-Vac vacuum actuator and plug the hose. Shift the transmission into Neutral. Adjust the curb idle using the ¼" hex-head adjustment screw on the end of the Sol-Vac unit. Set the speed to 750 rpm for manual transmission, 700 rpm for automatic transmission. Reconnect the vacuum hose to the vacuum actuator.

NOTE: *Engine speed will vary 10-30 rpm during this mode due to the closed loop fuel control.*

5. To adjust the TRC (Anti-Diesel): The TRC screw is preset at the factory and should not require adjustment. However, to check adjustment, the screw should be ¾ turn from closed throttle position.

6-173, EXCEPT CALIFORNIA

1. Connect a tachometer to the ignition coil negative terminal or to the pigtail wire connector above the heater blower motor.
2. Disconnect the plug the vacuum hose at the distributor vacuum advance.
3. If necessary, adjust the ignition timing with the engine speed at or below specifications.
4. Reconnect the vacuum hose to the distributor vacuum advance unit.
5. Disconnect the deceleration valve hose and canister purge hose. Plug the hose and remove the air cleaner assembly.
6. If equipped with air conditioning, turn the control switch to the ON position and open the throttle momentarily to insure the solenoid armature is fully extended. Adjust the solenoid idle speed adjusting screw to obtain the specified engine curb idle speed rpm. Turn the air conditioning control switch to the OFF position.
7. If not equipped with air conditioning, adjust the engine idle speed rpm with the solenoid idle speed adjusting screw. Disconnect the solenoid wire and adjust the curb idle.
8. Install the air cleaner assembly. Connect all hoses and other connections.

6-173, CALIFORNIA

NOTE: *Some California vehicles using the V6 engine, are equipped with a 2,200 hour engine timer. The timer activates a solenoid to control operation of the carburetor secondary vacuum brake after 2,200 hours of vehicle operation. The timer is not a serviceable component and must not be disassembled. In the event of a timer malfunction, the complete engine wiring harness must be replaced.*

1. Connect a tachometer to the ignition system. Start the engine and operate to normal operating temperature.
2. Turn off all accessories including the air conditioning system.

ENGINE PERFORMANCE AND TUNE-UP

3. Put the manual transmission equipped vehicles in NEUTRAL and the automatic trasnmission equipped vehicles in DRIVE with the parking brake locked and the wheels chocked.

4. Adjust the curb idle speed adjusting screw to obtain the specified rpm of 700 for both manual and automatic transmission equipped vehicles.

5. Disconnect the vacuum hose from the idle kick actuator and connect an outside vacuum source to the actuator. Apply 15 in.Hg of vacuum to the actuator.

6. Adjust the actuator hexhead adjustment screw for the specified 1,200 rpm with both types of transmissions in the NEUTRAL position.

7. Stop the engine, remove the tachometer and vacuum pump. Install the vacuum hose to the actuator.

1985-87

4-126 DIESEL

1. The idle speed is adjusted on the injection pump linkage.

2. Loosen the screw locknut, adjust the idle speed to 800 ± 50 rpm with the adjusting screw and tighten the locknut.

4-150 W/YFA CARBURETOR

1. The TRC (anti-Diesel) adjustment screw is statically set at ¾ of turn from the throttle valve closed position during factory assembly and does not normally require readjustment. Should this adjustment be required, turn the adjustment screw counterclockwise to the throttle plate closed position and then turn the screw clockwise ¾ turn.

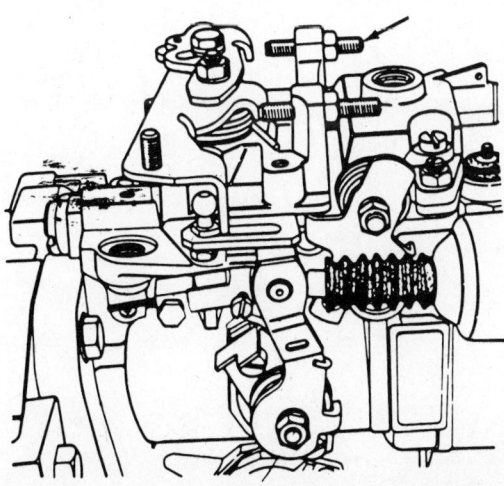

The arrow indicates the diesel idle speed adjusting screw

2. Connect a tachometer to the ignition coil TACH wire connector.

3. Place the transmission in NEUTRAL and lock the parking brake.

4. Start the engine and allow it to reach normal operating temperature.

5. Connect an external vacuum source to the Sol-Vac vacuum actuator and apply 10-15 in.Hg of vacuum. Plug the engine vacuum hose.

6. Adjust the vacuum actuator until an engine speed of approximately 1,000 rpm is achieved.

NOTE: *Refer to the Vehicle Emission Control Information Label for the latest specifications for the particular engine being adjusted.*

7. Remove the vacuum source from the vacuum actuator and retain the plug in the vacuum hose from the engine.

8. Turn the hex-head curb idle speed adjustment screw until the speed of 500 rpm is obtained.

NOTE: *Refer to the Vehicle Emission Control Label for the latest specifications for the particular engine being adjusted.*

9. Stop the engine and connect the engine vacuum hose to the vacuum actuator.

10. Remove the tachometer from the engine.

4-150 W/THROTTLE BODY FUEL INJECTION

Adjustments are not possible on this unit, as all functions are computer controlled.

6-173, EXCEPT CALIFORNIA

1. Connect a tachometer to the ignition coil negative terminal or to the pigtail wire connector above the heater blower motor.

2. Disconnect the plug the vacuum hose at the distributor vacuum advance.

3. If necessary, adjust the ignition timing with the engine speed at or below specifications.

4. Reconnect the vacuum hose to the distributor vacuum advance unit.

5. Disconnect the deceleration valve hose and canister purge hose. Plug the hose and remove the air cleaner assembly.

6. If equipped with air conditioning, turn the control switch to the ON position and open the throttle momentarily to insure the solenoid armature is fully extended. Adjust the solenoid idle speed adjusting screw to obtain the specified engine curb idle speed rpm. Turn the air conditioning control switch to the OFF position.

7. If not equipped with air conditioning, adjust the engine idle speed rpm with the solenoid idle speed adjusting screw. Disconnect the solenoid wire and adjust the curb idle.

8. Install the air cleaner assembly. Connect all hoses and other connections.

ENGINE PERFORMANCE AND TUNE-UP

6-173, CALIFORNIA

NOTE: *Some California vehicles using the V6 engine, are equipped with a 2,200 hour engine timer. The timer activates a solenoid to control operation of the carburetor secondary vacuum brake after 2,200 hours of vehicle operation. The timer is not a serviceable component and must not be disassembled. In the event of a timer malfunction, the complete engine wiring harness must be replaced.*

1. Connect a tachometer to the ignition system. Start the engine and operate to normal operating temperature.
2. Turn off all accessories including the air conditioning system.
3. Put the manual transmission equipped vehicles in NEUTRAL and the automatic trasnmission equipped vehicles in DRIVE with the parking brake locked and the wheels chocked.
4. Adjust the curb idle speed adjusting screw to obtain the specified rpm of 700 for both manual and automatic transmission equipped vehicles.
5. Disconnect the vacuum hose from the idle kick actuator and connect an outside vacuum source to the actuator. Apply 15 in.Hg of vacuum to the actuator.
6. Adjust the actuator hexhead adjustment screw for the specified 1,200 rpm with both types of transmissions in the NEUTRAL position.
7. Stop the engine, remove the tachometer and vacuum pump. Install the vacuum hose to the actuator.

1988-89

Both the 4-150 and 6-243 are fuel injected and all routine adjustments are computer controlled. No routine idle speed adjustments are possible.

Engine and Engine Overhaul

3

Camshaft Specifications
(All specifications in inches)

Engine	Journal Diameter					Bearing Clearance	Lobe Lift		End Play
	1	2	3	4	5		Int.	Exh.	
4-126	NA	NA	NA	NA	NA	NA	NA	NA	0.001–0.005
4-150	2.0300–2.0290	2.0200–2.0190	2.0100–2.0009	2.0000–1.9990	—	0.0010–0.0030	0.2650	0.2650	0
6-173	1.8690–1.8670	1.8690–1.8670	1.8690–1.8670	—	—	0.0010–0.0039	0.2311	0.2625	0
6-243	2.0300–2.0290	2.0200–2.0190	2.0100–2.009	2.0000–1.9990	—	0.0010–0.0030	0.2530	0.2530	0

Crankshaft and Connecting Rod Specifications
(All specifications in inches)

Engines	Crankshaft				Connecting Rod		
	Main Bearing Journal Dia.	Main Bearing Oil Clearance	Shaft End Play	Thrust on No.	Journal Dia.	Oil Clearance	Side Clearance
4-126	2.4750	0.0098	0.0050–0.0090	3	2.2163	0.0098	0.012–0.019
4-150	2.4996–2.5001	0.0010–0.0025	0.0015–0.0065	2	2.0934–2.0955	③	0.010–0.019
6-173	①	②	0.0020–0.0060	3	1.9980–1.9990	0.0010–0.0030	0.006–0.017
6-243	2.4996–2.5001	0.0010–0.0025	0.0015–0.0065	3	2.0934–2.0955	0.0010–0.0030	0.010–0.019

① Nos. 1, 2, 4: 2.4930–2.4940
   No. 3: 2.4920–2.4930
② Nos. 1, 2, 4: 0.0016–0.0030
   No. 3: 0.0020–0.0030
③ 1984–85: 0.0010–0.0030
   1986–89: 0.0010–0.0025

ENGINE AND ENGINE OVERHAUL

General Engine Specifications

Engine	Years	Fuel System Type	SAE net Horsepower @ rpm	SAE net Torque ft. lb. @ rpm	Bore × Stroke (in.)	Comp. Ratio	Oil Press. (psi.) @ 2000 rpm
4-126	1986–87	Diesel	85 @ 3750	132 @ 2750	3.385 × 3.503	21.5:1	43
4-150	1984–85	1-bbl	83 @ 4200	116 @ 2600	3.876 × 3.188	9.2:1	40
	1986–89	TBI	117 @ 5000	135 @ 3000	3.976 × 3.188	9.2:1	40
6-173	1984–85	2-bbl	115 @ 4800	150 @ 3500	3.500 × 2.990	8.5:1	45
6-243	1987–89	MFI	150 @ 4300	210 @ 2100	3.874 × 3.441	8.8:1	40

Valve Specifications

Engines	Seat Angle (deg)	Face Angle (deg)	Spring Test Pressure (lbs. @ in.)	Spring Installed Height (in.)	Stem-to-Guide Clearance (in.)		Stem Diameter (in.)	
					Intake	Exhaust	Intake	Exhaust
4-126	45	45	135 @ 1.173	1.547	0.0010–0.0030	0.0010–0.0030	0.3140	0.3140
4-150	44.5	①	②	③	0.0010–0.0030	0.0010–0.0030	0.3110–0.3120	0.3110–0.3120
6-173	46	45	195 @ 1.180	1.570	0.0010–0.0027	0.0010–0.0027	0.3410–0.3416	0.3410–0.3416
6-243	44.5	45	210 @ 1.200	1.625	0.0010–0.0030	0.0010–0.0030	0.3120	0.3120

① 1984–85: 44
   1986–89: 45
② 1984–85: 212 @ 1.203
   1986–89: 200 @ 1.216
③ 1984–85: 1.625
   1986–89: 1.640

Piston and Ring Specifications
(All specifications in inches)

Engines	Ring Gap			Ring Side Clearance			Piston-to-Bore* Clearance
	#1 Compr.	#2 Compr.	Oil Control	#1 Compr.	#2 Compr.	Oil Control	
4-150	0.0100–0.0200	0.0100–0.0200	①	②	②	③	④
6-173	0.0098–0.0196	0.0098–0.0196	0.0200–0.0550	0.0010–0.0027	0.0015–0.0037	0.0078 max.	0.0006–0.0016
6-243	0.0100–0.0200	0.0100–0.0200	0.0100–0.0250	0.0017–0.0032	0.0017–0.0032	0.0010–0.0080	0.0009–0.0017

*Measured at the skirt
NOTE: For the 4-126 Turbo Diesel, pistons, rings and cylinder liners are installed as a matched set. Specifications for individual parts are not applicable.
① 1984–85: 0.0100–0.0250
   1986–89: 0.0150–0.0550
② 1984–85: 0.0017–0.0032
   1986–89: 0.0010–0.0032
③ 1984–85: 0.0010–0.0080
   1986–89: 0.0010–0.0085
④ 1984–85: 0.0009–0.0017
   1986–89: 0.0013–0.0021

ENGINE AND ENGINE OVERHAUL

Torque Specifications
(All specifications in ft. lbs.)

Engines	Cyl. Head	Conn. Rod	Main Bearing	Crankshaft Damper	Flywheel	Manifold Intake	Manifold Exhaust
4-126	70–77	48	69	96	44	15–20	15–20
4-150	80–90⑤	30–35	75–85	75–85	50①	20–25	20–25④
6-173	65–75	34–40	63–74	66–84	45–55	20–25	22–28
6-243	②	30–35	80	80	100–110	20–25	③

① Plus a 60 degree turn
② See the illustration accompanying the text.
   Bolt #11: 100 ft. lbs.
   All other bolts: 110 ft. lbs.
③ Middle nuts: 30 ft. lbs.
   Outside nuts: 23 ft. lbs.
④ 1988–89: 30 ft. lbs.
⑤ See the illustration accompanying the text.
   Fuel Injected Engines
   Bolt #8: 100 ft. lbs.
   All other bolts: 110 ft. lbs.

ENGINE ELECTRICAL

Understanding the Engine Electrical System

The engine electrical system can be broken down into three separate and distinct systems:
1. The starting system.
2. The charging system.
3. The ignition system.

BATTERY AND STARTING SYSTEM

Basic Operating Principles

The battery is the first link in the chain of mechanisms which work together to provide cranking of the automobile engine. In most modern cars, the battery is a lead/acid electrochemical device consisting of six 2v subsections connected in series so the unit is capable of producing approximately 12v of electrical pressure. Each subsection, or cell, consists of a series of positive and negative plates held a short distance apart in a solution of sulfuric acid and water. The two types of plates are of dissimilar metals. This causes a chemical reaction to be set up, and it is this reaction which produces current flow from the battery when its positive and negative terminals are connected to an electrical appliance such as a lamp or motor. The continued transfer of electrons would eventually convert the sulfuric acid in the electrolyte to water, and make the two plates identical in chemical composition. As electrical energy is removed from the battery, its voltage output tends to drop. Thus, measuring battery voltage and battery electrolyte composition are two ways of checking the ability of the unit to supply power. During the starting of the engine, electrical energy is removed from the battery. However, if the charging circuit is in good condition and the operating conditions are normal, the power removed from the battery will be replaced by the generator (or alternator) which will force electrons back through the battery, reversing the normal flow, and restoring the battery to its original chemical state.

The battery and starting motor are linked by very heavy electrical cables designed to minimize resistance to the flow of current. Generally, the major power supply cable that leaves the battery goes directly to the starter, while other electrical system needs are supplied by a smaller cable. During starter operation, power flows from the battery to the starter and is grounded through the car's frame and the battery's negative ground strap.

The starting motor is a specially designed, direct current electric motor capable of producing a very great amount of power for its size. One thing that allows the motor to produce a great deal of power is its tremendous rotating speed. It drives the engine through a tiny pinion gear (attached to the starter's armature), which drives the very large flywheel ring gear at a greatly reduced speed. Another factor allowing it to produce so much power is that only intermittent operation is required of it. This, little allowance for air circulation is required, and the windings can be built into a very small space.

The starter solenoid is a magnetic device which employs the small current supplied by the starting switch circuit of the ignition switch. This magnetic action moves a plunger which mechanically engages the starter and electrically closes the heavy switch which con-

ENGINE AND ENGINE OVERHAUL

nects it to the battery. The starting switch circuit consists of the starting switch contained within the ignition switch, a transmission neutral safety switch or clutch pedal switch, and the wiring necessary to connect these in series with the starter solenoid or relay.

A pinion, which is a small gear, is mounted to a one-way drive clutch. This clutch is splined to the starter armature shaft. When the ignition switch is moved to the **start** position, the solenoid plunger slides the pinion toward the flywheel ring gear via a collar and spring. If the teeth on the pinion and flywheel match properly, the pinion will engage the flywheel immediately. If the gear teeth butt one another, the spring will be compressed and will force the gears to mesh as soon as the starter turns far enough to allow them to do so. As the solenoid plunger reaches the end of its travel, it closes the contacts that connect the battery and starter and then the engine is cranked.

As soon as the engine starts, the flywheel ring gear begins turning fast enough to drive the pinion at an extremely high rate of speed. At this point, the one-way clutch begins allowing the pinion to spin faster than the starter shaft so that the starter will not operate at excessive speed. When the ignition switch is released from the starter position, the solenoid is de-energized, and a spring contained within the solenoid assembly pulls the gear out of mesh and interrupts the current flow to the starter.

Some starter employ a separate relay, mounted away from the starter, to switch the motor and solenoid current on and off. The relay thus replaces the solenoid electrical switch, buy does not eliminate the need for a solenoid mounted on the starter used to mechanically engage the starter drive gears. The relay is used to reduce the amount of current the starting switch must carry.

THE CHARGING SYSTEM

Basic Operating Principles

The automobile charging system provides electrical power for operation of the vehicle's ignition and starting systems and all the electrical accessories. The battery services as an electrical surge or storage tank, storing (in chemical form) the energy originally produced by the engine driven generator. The system also provides a means of regulating generator output to protect the battery from being overcharged and to avoid excessive voltage to the accessories.

The storage battery is a chemical device incorporating parallel lead plates in a tank containing a sulfuric acid/water solution. Adjacent plates are slightly dissimilar, and the chemical reaction of the two dissimilar plates produces electrical energy when the battery is connected to a load such as the starter motor. The chemical reaction is reversible, so that when the generator is producing a voltage (electrical pressure) greater than that produced by the battery, electricity is forced into the battery, and the battery is returned to its fully charged state.

The vehicle's generator is driven mechanically, through V-belts, by the engine crankshaft. It consists of two coils of fine wire, one stationary (the stator), and one movable (the rotor). The rotor may also be known as the armature, and consists of fine wire wrapped around an iron core which is mounted on a shaft. The electricity which flows through the two coils of wire (provided initially by the battery in some cases) creates an intense magnetic field around both rotor and stator, and the interaction between the two fields creates voltage, allowing the generator to power the accessories and charge the battery.

There are two types of generators: the earlier is the direct current (DC) type. The current produced by the DC generator is generated in the armature and carried off the spinning armature by stationary brushes contacting the commutator. The commutator is a series of smooth metal contact plates on the end of the armature. The commutator is a series of smooth metal contact plates on the end of the armature. The commutator plates, which are separated from one another by a very short gap, are connected to the armature circuits so that current will flow in one directions only in the wires carrying the generator output. The generator stator consists of two stationary coils of wire which draw some of the output current of the generator to form a powerful magnetic field and create the interaction of fields which generates the voltage. The generator field is wired in series with the regulator.

Newer automobiles use alternating current generators or alternators, because they are more efficient, can be rotated at higher speeds, and have fewer brush problems. In an alternator, the field rotates while all the current produced passes only through the stator winding. The brushes bear against continuous slip rings rather than a commutator. This causes the current produced to periodically reverse the direction of its flow. Diodes (electrical one-way switches) block the flow of current from traveling in the wrong direction. A series of diodes is wired together to permit the alternating flow of the stator to be converted to a pulsating, but unidirectional flow at the alternator output. The alternator's field is wired in series with the voltage regulator.

The regulator consists of several circuits.

Each circuit has a core, or magnetic coil of wire, which operates a switch. Each switch is connected to ground through one or more resistors. The coil of wire responds directly to system voltage. When the voltage reaches the required level, the magnetic field created by the winding of wire closes the switch and inserts a resistance into the generator field circuit, thus reducing the output. The contacts of the switch cycle open and close many times each second to precisely control voltage.

While alternators are self-limiting as far as maximum current is concerned, DC generators employ a current regulating circuit which responds directly to the total amount of current flowing through the generator circuit rather than to the output voltage. The current regulator is similar to the voltage regulator except that all system current must flow through the energizing coil on its way to the various accessories.

ENGINE ELECTRICAL

Ignition Coil

REMOVAL AND INSTALLATION

1. Disconnect the battery ground.
2. Disconnect the 3 wires from the coil.
3. Disconnect the condenser connector from the coil, if equipped.
4. Unbolt and remove the coil.
5. Installation is the reverse of removal.

Ignition Control Module

REMOVAL AND INSTALLATION

4-150

The module is located on the right shock tower sheet metal. To replace it, simply unplug the wiring and remove the mounting screws.

6-173

1. Remove the distributor cap and rotor.
2. Remove the 2 control module screws and lift up on the module.
3. Disconnect the pick-up coli wire connector from the module. Note the color coding of the wires. Disconnect the wiring harness connector.

NOTE: *If you're going to reuse the module, don't wipe the grease from the module base. If a new module is being installed, a package of silicone grease should come with the new module. Spread the grease on the metal face of the module and on the distributor base where the module seats. The grease is necessary for module cooling.*

4. Installation is the reverse of removal.

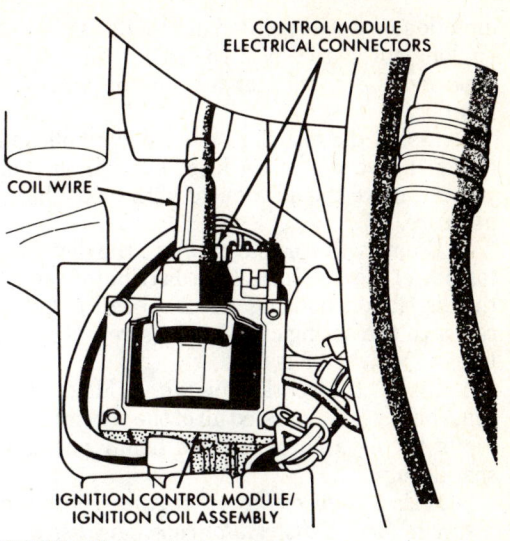

6-243 ignition control module

6-243

The ignition control module is mounted on the ignition coil. To replace it, simply disconnect the wiring connectors and remove the fasteners.

Distributor

REMOVAL

All

1. Remove the high-tension wires from the distributor cap terminal towers, noting their positions to assure correct reassembly. For diagrams of firing orders and distributor wiring, refer to the tune-up and troubleshooting section.
2. Remove the primary lead from the terminal post at the side of the distributor.
3. Disconnect the vacuum line if there is one.
4. Remove the two distributor cap retaining hooks or screws and remove the distributor cap.
5. Note the position of the rotor in relation to the base. Scribe a mark on the base of the distributor and on the engine to facilitate reinstallation. Align the marks with the direction the metal tip of the rotor is pointing.
6. Remove the bolt that holds the distributor to the engine.
7. Lift the distributor assembly from the engine.

INSTALLATION

6-173

1. Insert the distributor shaft and assembly into the engine. Line up the mark on the distributor and the one on the engine with the metal tip of the rotor. Make sure that the vacuum advance diaphragm is pointed in the same

direction as it was pointed originally. This will be done automatically if the marks on the engine and the distributor are line up with the rotor.

2. Install the distributor holddown bolt and clamp. Leave the screw loose enough so that you can move the distributor with heavy hand pressure.

3. Connect the primary wire to the distributor side of the coil. Install the distributor cap on the distributor housing. Secure the distributor cap with the spring clips or the screw type retainers, whichever is used.

4. Install the spark plug wires. Make sure that the wires are pressed all of the way into the top of the distributor cap and firmly onto the spark plugs.

NOTE: *Design of the V6 engine requires a special form of distributor cam. The distributor may be serviced in the regular way and should cause no more problems than any other distributor, if the firing plan is thoroughly understood. The distributor cam is not ground to standard six-cylinder indexing intervals. This particular form requires that the original pattern of spark plug wiring be used. The engine will not run in balance if No. 1 spark plug wire is inserted into No. 6 distributor cap tower, even though each wire in the firing sequence is advanced to the next distributor tower. There is a difference between the firing intervals of each succeeding cylinder through the 720° engine cycle.*

5. Set the ignition timing. Refer to the tune-up section.

If the engine has been turned while the distributor has been removed, or if the marks were not drawn, it will be necessary to initially time the engine. Follow the procedure below.

INSTALLATION, ENGINE ROTATED

6-173

1. If the engine has been rotated while the distributor was out, you'll have to first put the engine on No. 1 cylinder at Top Dead Center firing position. You can either remove the valve cover or No. 1 spark plug to determine engine position. Rotate the engine with a socket wrench on the nut at the center of the front pulley in the normal direction of rotation. Either feel for air being expelled forcefully through the spark plug hole or watch for the engine to rotate up to the Top Center mark without the valves moving (both valves will be closed). If the valves are moving as you approach TDC or there is no air being expelled through the plug hole, turn the engine another full turn until you get the appropriate indication as the engine approaches TDC position.

2. Start the distributor into the engine with the matchmarks between the distributor body and the engine lined up. Turn the rotor slightly until the matchmarks on the bottom of the distributor body and the bottom of the distributor shaft near the gear are aligned.

Then, insert the distributor all the way into the engine. If you have trouble getting the distributor and camshaft gears to mesh, turn the rotor back and forth very slightly until the distributor can be inserted easily. If the rotor is not now lined up with the position of No. 1 plug terminal, you'll have to pull the distributor back out slightly, shift the position of the rotor appropriately, and then reinstall it.

3. Align the matchmarks between the distributor and engine. Install the distributor mounting bolt and tighten it finger tight. Reconnect the vacuum advance line and distributor wiring connector, and reinstall the cap. Reconnect the negative battery cable. Adjust the ignition timing as described in Chapter 2. Then, tighten the distributor mounting bolt securely.

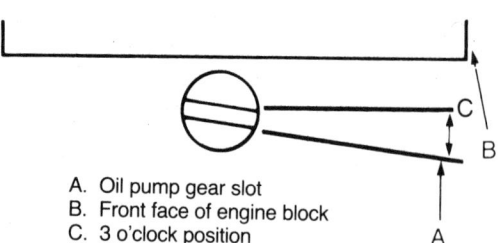

A. Oil pump gear slot
B. Front face of engine block
C. 3 o'clock position

Positioning the oil pump shaft for distributor installation on the 4-150

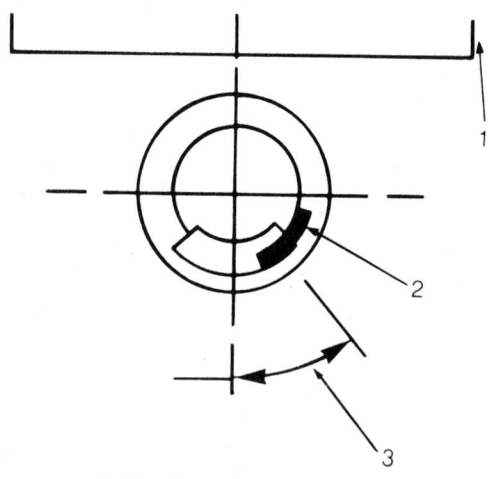

1. Front face of engine block
2. Rotor pre-positioned
3. 5 o'clock position (approx.)

Positioning the distributor rotor and shaft for installation, on the 4-150

ENGINE AND ENGINE OVERHAUL   85

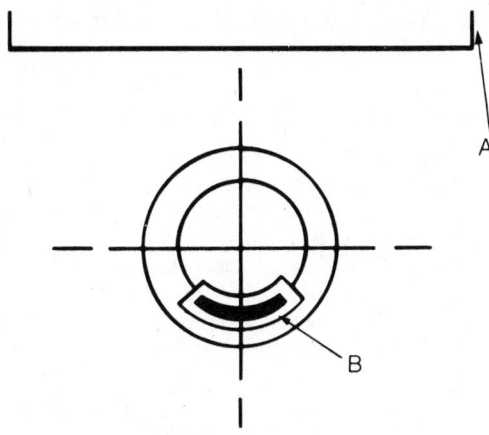

A. Front face of engine block
B. Rotor position when properly installed

Rotor position with the distributor properly installed on the 4-150

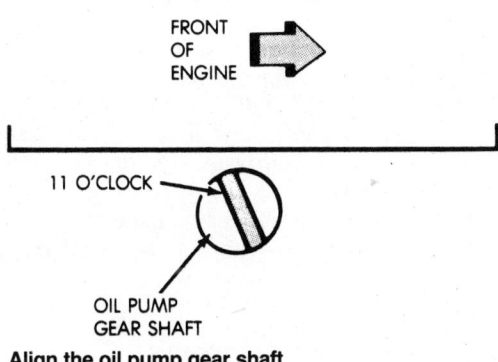

Align the oil pump gear shaft

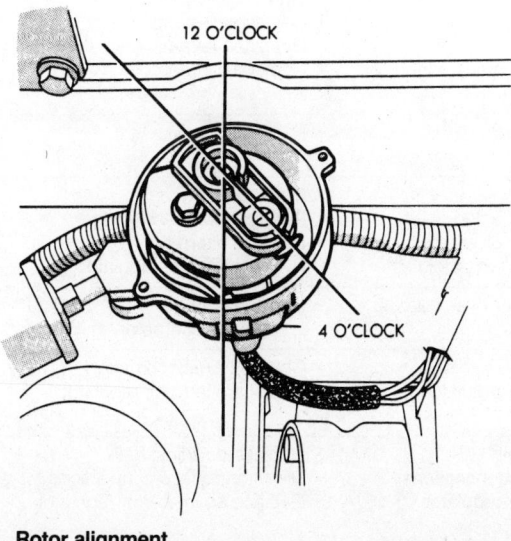

Rotor alignment

INSTALLATION
4-150 and 6-243

1. Rotate the engine until the No.1 piston is at TDC compression.
2. Using a flat bladed screwdriver, in the distributor hole, rotate the oil pump gear so that the slot in the oil pump shaft is slightly past the 3:00 o'clock position, relative to the length of the engine block.
3. With the distributor cap removed, install the distributor with the rotor at the 5:00 o'clock position, relative to the oil pump gear shaft slot. When the distributor is comnpletely in place, the rotor should be at the 6:00 o'clock position. If not, remove the distributor and perform the entire procedure again.
4. Tighten the lockbolt.

Alternator

The alternator charging system is a negative (−) ground system which consists of an alternator, a regulator, a charge indicator, a storage battery and wiring connecting the components, and fuse link wire.

The alternator is belt-driven from the engine. Energy is supplied from the alternator/regulator system to the rotating field through two brushes to two slip-rings. The slip-rings are mounted on the rotor shaft and are connected to the field coil. This energy supplied to the rotating field from the battery is called excitation current and is used to initially energize the field to begin the generation of electricity. Once the alternator starts to generate electricity, the excitation current comes from its own output rather than the battery.

The alternator produces power in the form of alternating current. The alternating current is rectified by 6 diodes into direct current. The direct current is used to charge the battery and power the rest of the electrical system.

When the ignition key is turned on, current flows from the battery, through the charging system indicator light on the instrument panel, to the voltage regulator, and to the alternator. Since the alternator is not producing any current, the alternator warning light comes on. When the engine is started, the alternator begins to produce current and turns the alternator light off. As the alternator turns and produces current, the current is divided in two ways: part to the battery to charge the battery and power the electrical components of the vehicle, and part is returned to the alternator to enable it to increase its output. In this situation, the alternator is receiving current from the battery and from itself. A voltage regulator is wired into the current supply to the alternator to prevent it from receiving too much current which would cause it to put out too much current. Conversely, if the voltage regulator does not allow the alternator to receive enough current, the battery will not be fully charged and will eventually go dead.

The battery is connected to the alternator at all times, whether the ignition key is turned on or not. If the battery were shorted to ground, the alternator would also be shorted. This would damage the alternator. To prevent this, a fuse link is installed in the wiring between the battery and the alternator. If the battery is shorted, the fuse link is melted, protecting the alternator.

ALTERNATOR PRECAUTIONS

Some precautions should be taken when working on this, or any other, AC charging system.
1. Never switch battery polarity.
2. When installing a battery, always connect the grounded terminal first.
3. Never disconnect the battery while the engine is running.
4. If the molded connector is disconnected from the alternator, never ground the hot wire.
5. Never run the alternator with the main output cable disconnected.
6. Never electric weld around the truck without disconnecting the alternator.
7. Never apply any voltage in excess of battery voltage while testing.
8. Never jump a battery for starting purposes with more than 12v.

CHARGING SYSTEM TROUBLESHOOTING

There are many possible ways in which the charging system can malfunction. Often the source of a problem is difficult to diagnose, requiring special equipment and a good deal of experience. This is usually not the case, however, where the charging system fails completely and causes the dash board warning light to come on or the battery to become dead. To troubleshoot a complete system failure only two pieces of equipment are needed: a test light, to determine that current is reaching a certain point; and a current indicator (ammeter), to determine the direction of the current flow and its measurement in amps.

This test works under three assumptions:
1. The battery is known to be good and fully charged.
2. The alternator belt is in good condition and adjusted to the proper tension.
3. All connections in the system are clean and tight.

NOTE: *In order for the current indicator to give a valid reading, the car must be equipped with battery cables which are of the same gauge size and quality as original equipment battery cables.*

1. Turn off all electrical components on the car. Make sure the doors of the car are closed. If

Troubleshooting Basic Charging System Problems

Problem	Cause	Solution
Noisy alternator	• Loose mountings • Loose drive pulley • Worn bearings • Brush noise • Internal circuits shorted (High pitched whine)	• Tighten mounting bolts • Tighten pulley • Replace alternator • Replace alternator • Replace alternator
Squeal when starting engine or accelerating	• Glazed or loose belt	• Replace or adjust belt
Indicator light remains on or ammeter indicates discharge (engine running)	• Broken fan belt • Broken or disconnected wires • Internal alternator problems • Defective voltage regulator	• Install belt • Repair or connect wiring • Replace alternator • Replace voltage regulator
Car light bulbs continually burn out—battery needs water continually	• Alternator/regulator overcharging	• Replace voltage regulator/alternator
Car lights flare on acceleration	• Battery low • Internal alternator/regulator problems	• Charge or replace battery • Replace alternator/regulator
Low voltage output (alternator light flickers continually or ammeter needle wanders)	• Loose or worn belt • Dirty or corroded connections • Internal alternator/regulator problems	• Replace or adjust belt • Clean or replace connections • Replace alternator or regulator

ENGINE AND ENGINE OVERHAUL

the car is equipped with a clock, disconnect the clock by removing the lead wire from the rear of the clock. Disconnect the positive battery cable from the battery and connect the ground wire on a test light to the disconnected positive battery cable. Touch the probe end of the test light to the positive battery post. The test light should not light. If the test light does light, there is a short or open circuit on the car.

2. Disconnect the voltage regulator wiring harness connector at the voltage regulator. Turn on the ignition key. Connect the wire on a test light to a good ground (engine bolt). Touch the probe end of a test light to the ignition wire connector into the voltage regulator wiring connector. This wire corresponds to the **I** terminal on the regulator. If the test light goes on, the charging system warning light circuit is complete. If the test light does not come on and the warning light on the instrument panel is on, either the resistor wire, which is parallel with the warning light, or the wiring to the voltage regulator, is defective. If the test light does not come on and the warning light is not on, either the bulb is defective or the power supply wire form the battery through the ignition switch to the bulb has an open circuit. Connect the wiring harness to the regulator.

3. Examine the fuse link wire in the wiring harness from the starter relay to the alternator. If the insulation on the wire is cracked or split, the fuse link may be melted. Connect a test light to the fuse link by attaching the ground wire on the test light to an engine bolt and touching the probe end of the light to the bottom of the fuse link wire where it splices into the alternator output wire. If the bulb in the test light does not light, the fuse link is melted.

4. Start the engine and place a current indicator on the positive battery cable. Turn off all electrical accessories and make sure the doors are closed. If the charging system is working properly, the gauge will show a draw of less than 5 amps. If the system is not working properly, the gauge will show a draw of more than 5 amps. A charge moves the needle toward the battery, a draw moves the needle away from the battery. Turn the engine off.

5. Disconnect the wiring harness from the voltage regulator at the regulator at the regulator connector. Connect a male spade terminal (solderless connector) to each end of a jumper wire. Insert one end of the wire into the wiring harness connector which corresponds to the **A** terminal on the regulator. Insert the other end of the wire into the wiring harness connector which corresponds to the **F** terminal on the regulator. Position the connector with the jumper wire installed so that it cannot contact any metal surface under the hood. Position a current indicator gauge on the positive battery cable. Have an assistant start the engine. Observe the reading on the current indicator. Have your assistant slowly raise the speed of the engine to about 2,000 rpm or until the current indicator needle stops moving, whichever comes first. Do not run the engine for more than a short period of time in this condition. If the wiring harness connector or jumper wire becomes excessively hot during this test, turn off the engine and check for a grounded wire in the regulator wiring harness. If the current indicator shows a charge of about three amps less than the output of the alternator, the alternator is working properly. If the previous tests showed a draw, the voltage regulator is defective. If the gauge does not show the proper charging rate, the alternator is defective.

REMOVAL AND INSTALLATION

1. Disconnect the battery ground.
2. Remove and tag all alternator wiring.
3. Remove the adjusting bolt, loosen the mounting bolts and remove the belt.
4. Support the alternator with your hand and remove the mounting bolts. Lift the alternator out.
5. Installation is the reverse of removal. Make sure that the belt is properly tensioned. A ½" deflection of the belt at the mid-point of its longest straight run indicates proper belt tension. NEVER PRY ON THE ALTERNATOR HOUSING TO APPLY BELT TENSION! THE HOUSING IS ALUMINUM AND WILL EASILY BE DAMAGED!

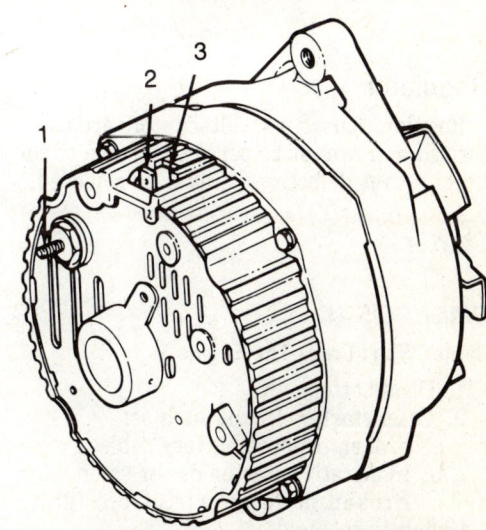

- Alternator "BAT" terminal to ground (1).
- Alternator No. 1 terminal to ground (2).
- Alternator No. 2 terminal to ground (3).

Typical Delco alternator

88 ENGINE AND ENGINE OVERHAUL

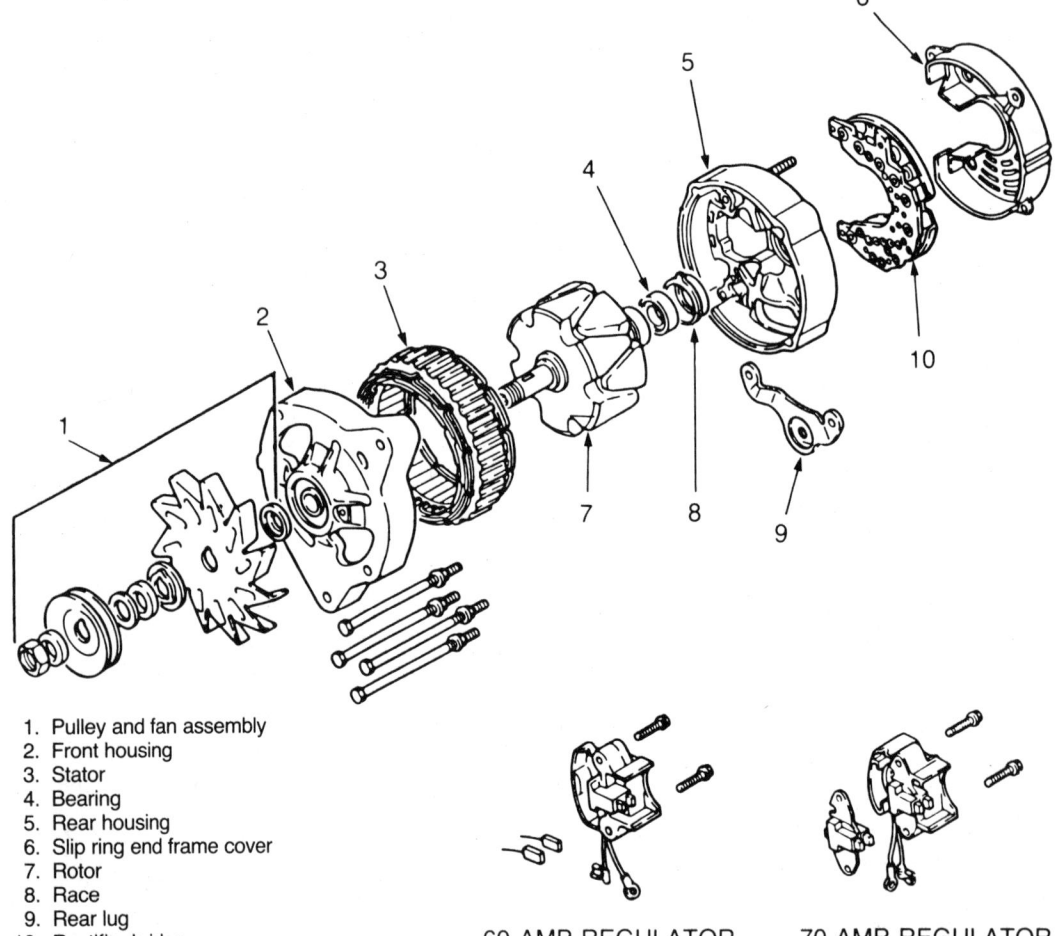

1. Pulley and fan assembly
2. Front housing
3. Stator
4. Bearing
5. Rear housing
6. Slip ring end frame cover
7. Rotor
8. Race
9. Rear lug
10. Rectifier bridge

60 AMP REGULATOR   **70 AMP REGULATOR**

Paris-Rhone alternator used on the diesel

Regulator

Regulators used with alternators are transistorized and cannot be serviced. If one of these units proves defective, it must be replaced.

Starter

DIAGNOSIS

Starter Won't Crank The Engine

1. Dead battery.
2. Open starter circuit, such as:
    a. Broken or loose battery cables.
    b. Inoperative starter motor solenoid.
    c. Broken or loose wire from ignition switch to solenoid.
    d. Poor solenoid or starter ground.
    e. Bad ignition switch.
3. Defective starter internal circuit, such as:
    a. Dirty or burnt commutator.
    b. Stuck, worn or broken brushes.
    c. Open or shorted armature.
    d. Open or grounded fields.
4. Starter motor mechanical faults, such as:
    a. Jammed armature end bearings.
    b. Bad bearings, allowing armature to rub fields.
    c. Bent shaft.
    d. Broken starter housing.
    e. Bad starter drive mechanism.
    f. Bad starter drive or flywheel-driven gear.
5. Engine hard or impossible to crank, such as:
    a. Hydrostatic lock, water in combustion chamber.
    b. Crankshaft seizing in bearings.
    c. Piston or ring seizing.
    d. Bent or broken connecting rod.
    e. Seizing of connecting rod bearings.
    f. Flywheel jammed or broken.

ENGINE AND ENGINE OVERHAUL

Starter Spins Freely, Won't Engage

1. Sticking or broken drive mechanism.
2. Damaged ring gear.

REMOVAL AND INSTALLATION

All Except the 4-126 Diesel

1. Disconnect the battery ground.
2. Raise and support the vehicle on jackstands.
3. Remove all wires from the starter and tag them for installation.
4. Remove all but one upper attaching bolt, support the starter (it's heavier than it looks) and remove the last bolt.
5. Pull the starter from the engine.
6. Installation is the reverse of removal. Torque the mounting bolts to:

- 6-243: 25 ft. lbs.
- 4-150, 6-173: 17 ft. lbs.

4-126 Diesel

1. Disconnect the battery ground.
2. Remove all wires from the starter and tag them for installation.
3. Raise and support the vehicle on jackstands.
4. Remove the starter upper bracket.
5. Take up the weight of the engine with a floor jack and remove the left side engine mount.
6. Remove the starter lower support bracket.
7. Support the starter (it's heavier than it looks) and remove the attaching bolts. Remove the starter.

Troubleshooting Basic Starting System Problems

Problem	Cause	Solution
Starter motor rotates engine slowly	• Battery charge low or battery defective • Defective circuit between battery and starter motor • Low load current • High load current	• Charge or replace battery • Clean and tighten, or replace cables • Bench-test starter motor. Inspect for worn brushes and weak brush springs. • Bench-test starter motor. Check engine for friction, drag or coolant in cylinders. Check ring gear-to-pinion gear clearance.
Starter motor will not rotate engine	• Battery charge low or battery defective • Faulty solenoid • Damage drive pinion gear or ring gear • Starter motor engagement weak • Starter motor rotates slowly with high load current • Engine seized	• Charge or replace battery • Check solenoid ground. Repair or replace as necessary. • Replace damaged gear(s) • Bench-test starter motor • Inspect drive yoke pull-down and point gap, check for worn end bushings, check ring gear clearance • Repair engine
Starter motor drive will not engage (solenoid known to be good)	• Defective contact point assembly • Inadequate contact point assembly ground • Defective hold-in coil	• Repair or replace contact point assembly • Repair connection at ground screw • Replace field winding assembly
Starter motor drive will not disengage	• Starter motor loose on flywheel housing • Worn drive end busing • Damaged ring gear teeth • Drive yoke return spring broken or missing	• Tighten mounting bolts • Replace bushing • Replace ring gear or driveplate • Replace spring
Starter motor drive disengages prematurely	• Weak drive assembly thrust spring • Hold-in coil defective	• Replace drive mechanism • Replace field winding assembly
Low load current	• Worn brushes • Weak brush springs	• Replace brushes • Replace springs

ENGINE AND ENGINE OVERHAUL

8. Install the starter and HAND TIGHTEN ONLY, the attaching bolts.
9. Install the upper support bracket, hand tighten only.
10. Install the lower support bracket, hand tighten only.
11. Torque the starter attaching bolts to 37 ft. lbs., then, tighten the upper bracket bolts to 37 ft. lbs. and then the lower bracket bolts, also to 37 ft. lbs.
12. Install the engine mount. Torque the engine mount-to-block bolt to 40 ft. lbs.; the engine mount-to-frame bolt to 48 ft. lbs.; the engine mount-to-bell housing bolt to 35 ft. lbs.
13. Remove the jack, connect the wires and lower the vehicle.

STARTER OVERHAUL
Motorcraft
DISASSEMBLY

1. Remove the cover screw, the cover thru-bolts, the starter drive end housing and the starter drive plunger lever return spring.
2. Remove the starter gear plunger lever pivot pin, the lever and the armature. Remove the stop ring retainer and the stop ring from the armature shaft (discard the ring), then the starter drive gear assembly.
3. Remove the brush end plate, the insulator assembly and the brushes from the plastic holder, then lift out the brush holder. For reassembly, note the position of the brush holder with respect to the end terminal.

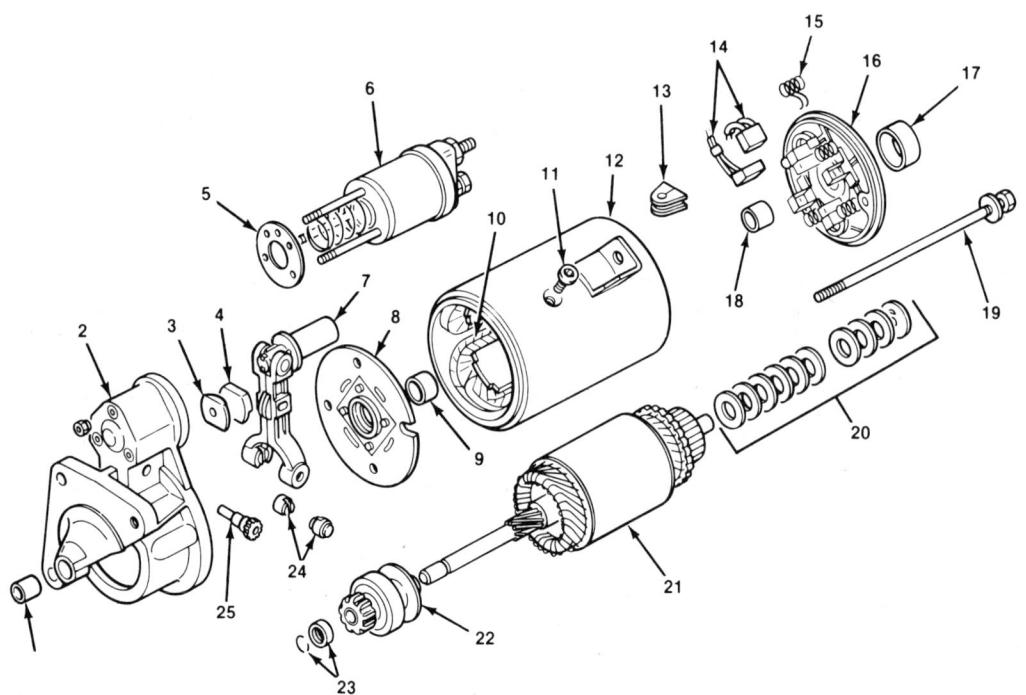

1. End housing bushing
2. Drive-end housing
3. Spacer
4. Pad
5. Solenoid plate
6. Solenoid
7. Pinion shift yoke
8. Support plate
9. Support plate bushing
10. Field winding and pole shoe sets (4)
11. Pole shoe screw (4)
12. Armature housing
13. Grommet
14. Brush set (4)
15. Brush spring (4)
16. Brush holder
17. Cap
18. Brush holder bushing
19. Through bolts (4)
20. Armature brake assembly
21. Armature
22. Starter drive pinion
23. Drive pinion stop
24. Shift yoke pivot pins
25. Shift yoke axle

Delco starter used on the 6-173

ENGINE AND ENGINE OVERHAUL

4. Remove the two ground brush-to-frame screws.
5. Bend up the sleeve's edges which are inserted in the frame's rectangular hole, then remove the sleeve and the retainer. Detach the field coil ground wire from the copper tab.
6. Remove the three coil retaining screws. Cut the field coil connection at the switch post lead, then remove the pole shoes and the coils from the frame.
7. Cut the positive brush leads from the field coils (as close to the field connection point as possible).
8. Check the armature and the armature windings for broken or burned insulation, open circuits or grounds.
9. Check the commutator for runout; if it is rough, has flat spots or is more than 0.005" out of round, reface the commutator face.
10. Inspect the armature shaft and the two bearings for scoring and excessive wear, then replace (if necessary).

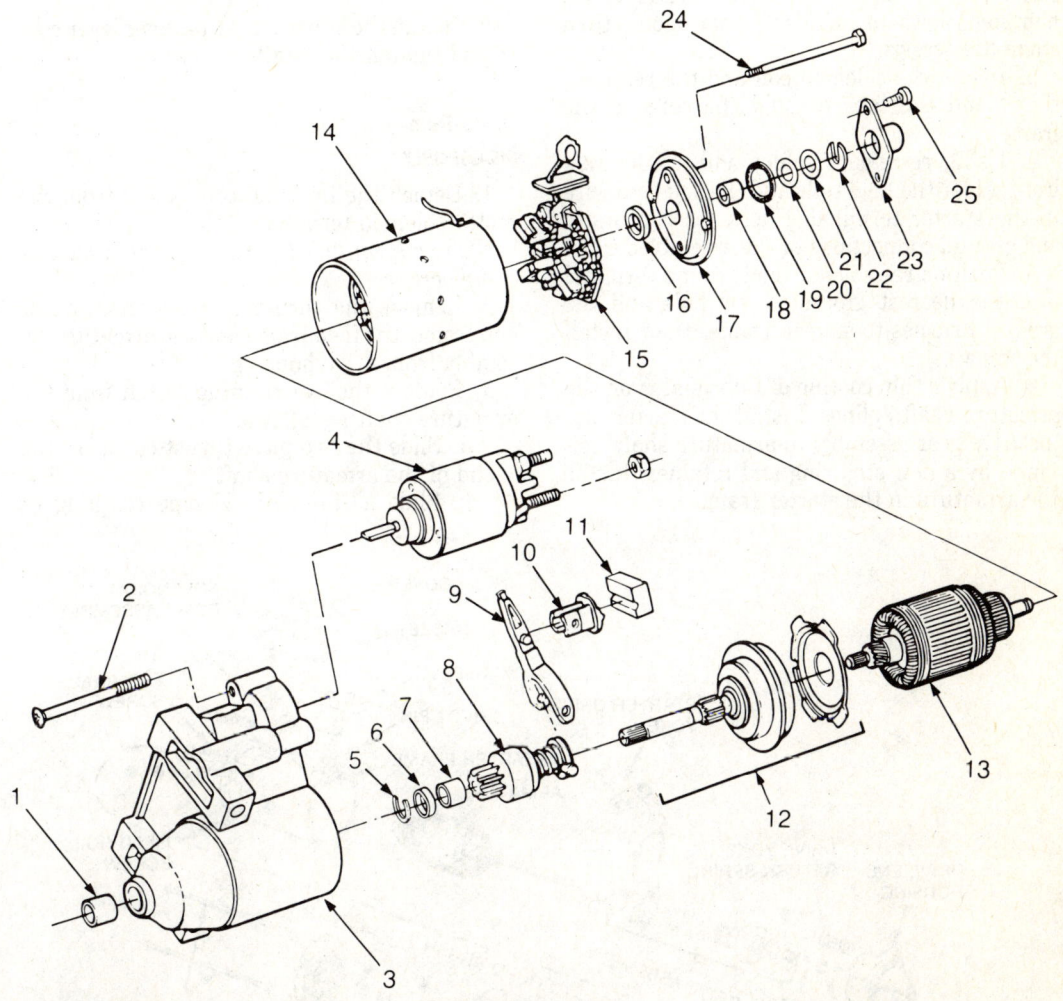

1. Bushing
2. Screw
3. Shield
4. Solenoid switch
5. Retainer
6. Stop ring
7. Bushing
8. Overrunning clutch drive
9. Fork
10. Bearing pedestal
11. Sealing rubber
12. Planetary gear system
13. Armature
14. Stator frame
15. Brush holder
16. Gasket
17. Commutator end shield
18. Bushing
19. Seal ring
20. Shim
21. Shim
22. Retaining washer
23. Closure cap
24. Hexagon screw
25. Screw

Bosch starter used on the 1986–89 4-150

92 ENGINE AND ENGINE OVERHAUL

11. Inspect the starter drive; if the gear teeth are pitted, broken or excessively worn, replace the starter drive.

NOTE: *The factory brush length is ½"; the wear limit is ¼".*

ASSEMBLY

1. Install the starter terminal, the insulator, the washers and the nut in the frame.

NOTE: *Be sure to position the screw slot perpendicular to the frame end surface.*

2. Position the coils and the pole pieces, with the coil leads in the terminal screw slot, then install the screws. When tightening the pole screws, strike the frame with several sharp hammer blows to align the pole shoes, then stake the screws.

3. Install the solenoid coil and the retainer, then bend the tabs to hold the coils to the frame.

4. Using resin-core solder and a 300 watt iron, solder the field coils and the solenoid wire to the starter terminal. Check for continuity and ground connections of the assembled coils.

5. Position the solenoid coil ground terminal over the nearest ground screw hole and the ground brushes-to-starter frame, then install the screws.

6. Apply a thin coating of Lubriplate® on the armature shaft splines. Install the starter motor drive gear assembly-to-armature shaft, followed by a new stop ring and retainer. Install the armature in the starter frame.

7. Position the starter drive gear plunger lever to the frame and the starter drive assembly, then install the pivot pin. Place some grease into the end housing bore; fill it about ¼ full, then position the drive end housing to the frame.

8. Install the brush holder and the brush springs; the positive brush leads should be positioned in their respective brush holder slots, to prevent grounding problems.

9. Install the brush end plate; be certain that the end plate insulator is in the proper position on the end plate. Install the two starter frame through-bolts and torque them to 55-75 inch lbs.

10. Install the starter drive plunger lever cover and tighten the retaining screw.

Delco-Remy

DISASSEMBLY

1. Detach the field coil connectors from the motor solenoid terminal.

NOTE: *If equipped, remove solenoid mounting screws.*

2. Remove the thru-bolts, the commutator end frame, the field frame and the armature assembly from drive housing.

3. Remove the overrunning clutch from the armature shaft as follows:
   a. Slide the two piece thrust collar off the end of the armature shaft.
   b. Slide a standard ½" pipe coupling or

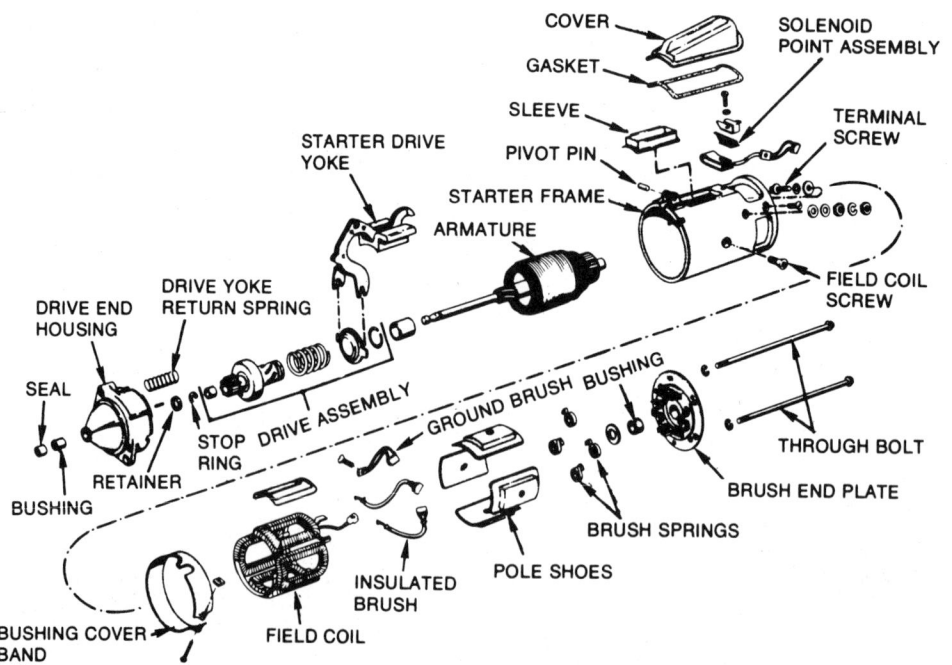

American motors starter motor

ENGINE AND ENGINE OVERHAUL

other spacer onto the shaft, so that the coupling end butts against the retainer edge.

c. Using a hammer, tap the coupling end, driving the retainer towards the armature end of the snapring.

d. Using snapring pliers, remove the snapring from its groove in the shaft, then slide the retainer and the clutch from the shaft.

4. Disassemble the field frame brush assembly by releasing the V-spring and removing the support pin. The brush holders, the brushes and the springs can now be pulled out as a unit and the leads disconnected.

NOTE: *On the integral frame units, remove the brush holder from the brush support and the brush screw.*

5. If equipped, separate the solenoid from the lever housing.

CLEANING AND INSPECTION

1. Clean the parts with a rag; do not immerse the parts in a solvent.

CAUTION: *Immersion in a solvent will dissolve the grease that is packed in the clutch mechanism; it will damage the armature and the field coil insulation.*

2. Test the overrunning clutch action; the pinion should turn freely in the overrunning direction but must not slip in the cranking direction. Check that the pinion teeth have not been chipped, cracked or excessively worn; replace the unit (if necessary).

3. Inspect the armature commutator; if the commutator is rough or out of round, it should be machined and undercut.

NOTE: *Undercut the insulation between the commutator bars by $1/32$". The undercut must be the full width of the insulation and flat at*

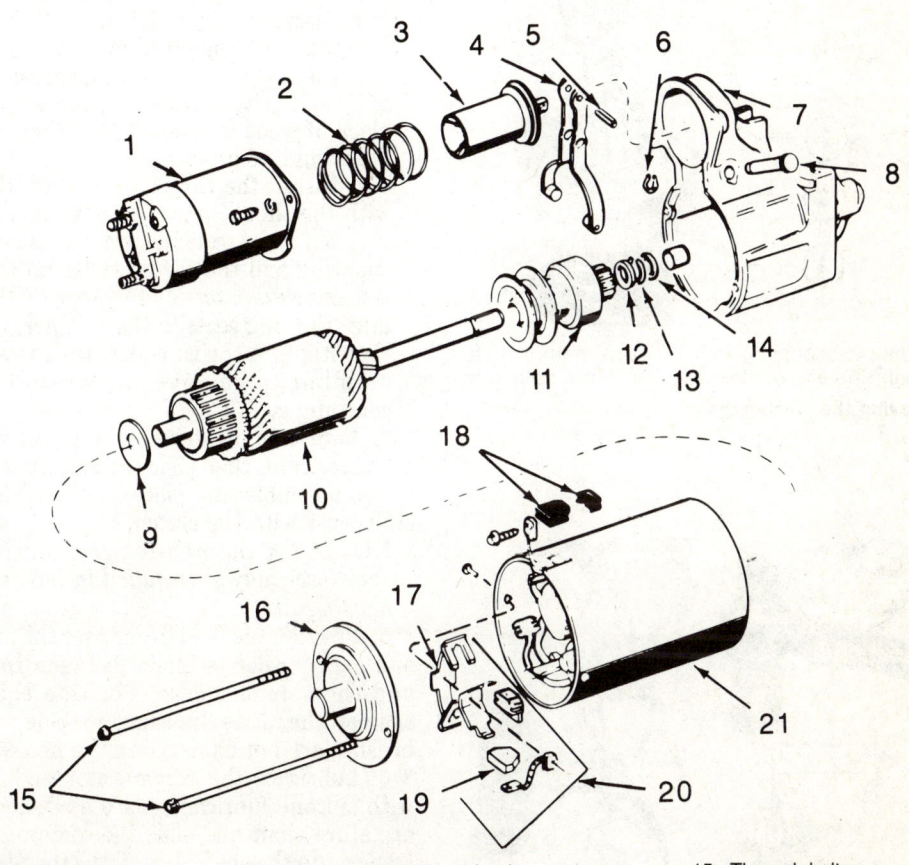

1. Solenoid switch
2. Plunger return spring
3. Plunger
4. Shift lever
5. Plunger pin
6. Lever shaft retaining ring
7. Drive end housing
8. Shift lever shank
9. Washer
10. Armature
11. Drive
12. Pinion collar stop
13. Pinion stop retaining ring
14. Thrust collar
15. Through bolts
16. Commutator end frame
17. Brush holder
18. Grommet
19. Brush
20. Brush and holder assembly
21. Frame and field winding

Paris-Rhone starter used on the 4-126 Turbo diesel

94 ENGINE AND ENGINE OVERHAUL

the bottom; a triangular groove will not be satisfactory. Most late model starter motor use a molded armature commutator design; no attempt to undercut the insulation should be made or serious damage may result to the commutator.

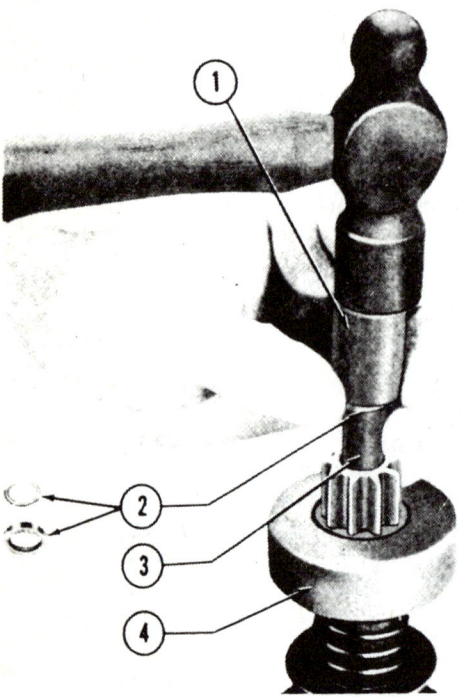

1. ½ in. pipe coupling
2. Snap-ring and retainer
3. Armature shaft
4. Drive assembly

Removing the starter drive

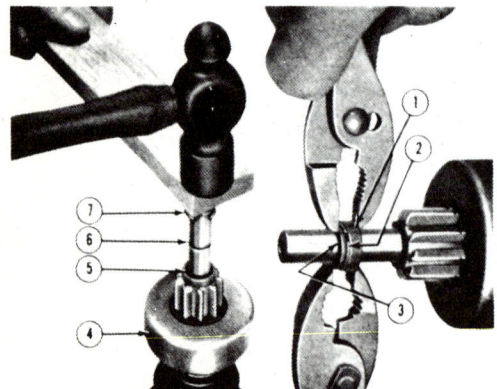

1. Retainer
2. Snap-ring
3. Thrust collar
4. Drive assembly
5. Retainer
6. Groove in the armature shaft
7. Snap-ring

Installing the pinion stop retainer and thrust collar

ASSEMBLY

1. Install the brushes into the holders, then install solenoid (if equipped).
2. Assemble the insulated and the grounded holder together. Using the V-spring, position and assemble the unit on the support pin. Push the holders and the spring to bottom of the support, then rotate the spring to engage the slot in the support. Attach the ground wire to the grounded brush and the field lead wire to the insulated brush, then repeat this procedure for other brush sets.
3. Assemble the overrunning clutch to the armature shaft as follows:
   a. Lubricate the drive end of the shaft with silicone lubricant.
   b. Slide the clutch assembly onto the shaft with the pinion outward.
   c. Slide the retainer onto the shaft with the cupped surface facing away from the pinion.
   d. Stand the armature up on a wood surface with the commutator downward. Position the snapring on the upper end of the shaft and drive it onto the shaft with a small block of wood and a hammer, then slide the snapring into groove.
   e. Install the thrust collar onto the shaft with the shoulder next to snapring.
   f. With the retainer on one side of the snapring and the thrust collar on the other side, squeeze two sets together (with pliers) until the ring seats in the retainer. On models without a thrust collar use a washer; remember to remove the washer before continuing.
4. Lubricate the drive end bushing with silicone lubricant, then slide the armature and the clutch assembly into place, while engaging the shift lever with the clutch.
   NOTE: *On the non-integral starters, the shift lever may be installed in the drive gear housing first.*
5. Position the field frame over the armature and apply sealer (silicone) between the frame and the solenoid case. Position the frame against the drive housing, making sure the brushes are not damaged in the process.
6. Lubricate the commutator end bushing with silicone lubricant, place a washer on the armature shaft and slide the commutator end frame onto the shaft. Install the thru-bolts and tighten.
7. Reconnect the field coil connections to the solenoid motor terminal. Install the solenoid mounting screws (if equipped).
8. Check the pinion clearance; it should be 0.25-3.55mm with the pinion in the cranking position, on all models.

ENGINE AND ENGINE OVERHAUL

Bosch

DISASSEMBLY

1. Disconnect the field coil wire from the solenoid terminal.
2. Remove the solenoid and work the plunger off the shift fork.
3. Remove the two end shield bearing cap screws, the cap and the washers.
4. Remove the two commutator end frame cover thru-bolts, the cover, the two brushes and the brush plate.
5. Slide the field frame off over the armature. Remove the shift lever pivot bolt, the rubber gasket and the metal plate.
6. Remove the armature assembly and the shift lever from the drive end housing. Press the stop collar off the snapring, then remove the snapring, the clutch assembly, the clutch assembly and the drive end housing from the armature.

INSPECTION AND SERVICE

1. The brushes that are worn more than ½ the length of new brushes or are oil-soaked, should be replaced; the new brushes are 18mm long.
2. Do not immerse the starter clutch unit in cleaning solvent; solvent will wash the lubricant from the clutch.
3. Place the drive unit on the armature shaft, then, while holding the armature, rotate the pinion.
   NOTE: *The drive pinion should rotate smoothly in one direction only. The pinion may not rotate easily but as long as it rotates smoothly it is in good condition. If the clutch unit does not function properly or if the pinion is worn, chipped or burred, replace the unit.*

ASSEMBLY

1. Lubricate the armature shaft and the splines with SAE 10W or 30W oil.
2. Fit the drive end housing onto the armature, then install the clutch, the stop collar and the snapring onto the armature.
3. Install the shift fork pivot bolt, the rubber gasket and the metal plate. Slide the field frame into position and install the brush holder and the brushes.
4. Position the commutator end frame cover and the thru-bolts.
5. Install the shim and the armature shaft lock. Check the endplay (0.050-0.300mm), then install the bearing cover.
6. Assemble the plunger to the shift fork, then install the solenoid with its mounting bolts. Connect the field wire to the solenoid.

ENGINE MECHANICAL

Design

4-126 Diesel

The Renault-built 4-cylinder turbocharged diesel engine was introduced for use in the 1986 Wagoneer, Cherokee and Comanche models. The engine is of an inline, overhead camshaft configuration, with the rocker arms riding directly on the camshaft lobes. The camshaft is belt driven. A cast iron head and block with removable liners, are used. The crankshaft is supported by five main bearings.

4-150

This AMC-built engine was first introduced for use in the 1984 Wagoneer/Cherokee line and is a new design, developed from the technology existing in the 6-258 engine. It is a 4-cylinder, inline, overhead valve configuration, with cast iron head and block. The crankshaft is supported by five main bearings.

6-173

This Chevrolet-built engine was first introduced for use in the 1984 Wagoneer/Cherokee line. The engine is a 60° V, overhead valve configuration, with cast iron head and block. The crankshaft is supported by four main bearings. The intake manifold is aluminum.

6-243

The AMC-built inline 6-cylinder engines are of conventional overhead valve configuration and cast iron construction. These engines mount the rocker arms on a common shaft. The crankshaft is supported by four main bearings.

Engine Overhaul Tips

Most engine overhaul procedures are fairly standard. In addition to specific parts replacement procedures and complete specifications for your individual engine, this chapter also is a guide to accept rebuilding procedures. Examples of standard rebuilding practice are shown and should be used along with specific details concerning your particular engine.

Competent and accurate machine shop services will ensure maximum performance, reliability and engine life.

In most instances it is more profitable for the do-it-yourself mechanic to remove, clean and inspect the component, buy the necessary parts and deliver these to a shop for actual machine work.

On the other hand, much of the rebuilding

ENGINE AND ENGINE OVERHAUL

Troubleshooting Engine Mechanical Problems

Problem	Cause	Solution
External oil leaks	• Fuel pump gasket broken or improperly seated	• Replace gasket
	• Cylinder head cover RTV sealant broken or improperly seated	• Replace sealant; inspect cylinder head cover sealant flange and cylinder head sealant surface for distortion and cracks
	• Oil filler cap leaking or missing	• Replace cap
	• Oil filter gasket broken or improperly seated	• Replace oil filter
	• Oil pan side gasket broken, improperly seated or opening in RTV sealant	• Replace gasket or repair opening in sealant; inspect oil pan gasket flange for distortion
	• Oil pan front oil seal broken or improperly seated	• Replace seal; inspect timing case cover and oil pan seal flange for distortion
	• Oil pan rear oil seal broken or improperly seated	• Replace seal; inspect oil pan rear oil seal flange; inspect rear main bearing cap for cracks, plugged oil return channels, or distortion in seal groove
	• Timing case cover oil seal broken or improperly seated	• Replace seal
	• Excess oil pressure because of restricted PCV valve	• Replace PCV valve
	• Oil pan drain plug loose or has stripped threads	• Repair as necessary and tighten
	• Rear oil gallery plug loose	• Use appropriate sealant on gallery plug and tighten
	• Rear camshaft plug loose or improperly seated	• Seat camshaft plug or replace and seal, as necessary
	• Distributor base gasket damaged	• Replace gasket
Excessive oil consumption	• Oil level too high	• Drain oil to specified level
	• Oil with wrong viscosity being used	• Replace with specified oil
	• PCV valve stuck closed	• Replace PCV valve
	• Valve stem oil deflectors (or seals) are damaged, missing, or incorrect type	• Replace valve stem oil deflectors
	• Valve stems or valve guides worn	• Measure stem-to-guide clearance and repair as necessary
	• Poorly fitted or missing valve cover baffles	• Replace valve cover
	• Piston rings broken or missing	• Replace broken or missing rings
	• Scuffed piston	• Replace piston
	• Incorrect piston ring gap	• Measure ring gap, repair as necessary
	• Piston rings sticking or excessively loose in grooves	• Measure ring side clearance, repair as necessary
	• Compression rings installed upside down	• Repair as necessary
	• Cylinder walls worn, scored, or glazed	• Repair as necessary
	• Piston ring gaps not properly staggered	• Repair as necessary
	• Excessive main or connecting rod bearing clearance	• Measure bearing clearance, repair as necessary
No oil pressure	• Low oil level	• Add oil to correct level
	• Oil pressure gauge, warning lamp or sending unit inaccurate	• Replace oil pressure gauge or warning lamp
	• Oil pump malfunction	• Replace oil pump
	• Oil pressure relief valve sticking	• Remove and inspect oil pressure relief valve assembly
	• Oil passages on pressure side of pump obstructed	• Inspect oil passages for obstruction

ENGINE AND ENGINE OVERHAUL

Troubleshooting Engine Mechanical Problems (cont.)

Problem	Cause	Solution
No oil pressure (cont.)	• Oil pickup screen or tube obstructed	• Inspect oil pickup for obstruction
	• Loose oil inlet tube	• Tighten or seal inlet tube
Low oil pressure	• Low oil level	• Add oil to correct level
	• Inaccurate gauge, warning lamp or sending unit	• Replace oil pressure gauge or warning lamp
	• Oil excessively thin because of dilution, poor quality, or improper grade	• Drain and refill crankcase with recommended oil
	• Excessive oil temperature	• Correct cause of overheating engine
	• Oil pressure relief spring weak or sticking	• Remove and inspect oil pressure relief valve assembly
	• Oil inlet tube and screen assembly has restriction or air leak	• Remove and inspect oil inlet tube and screen assembly. (Fill inlet tube with lacquer thinner to locate leaks.)
	• Excessive oil pump clearance	• Measure clearances
	• Excessive main, rod, or camshaft bearing clearance	• Measure bearing clearances, repair as necessary
High oil pressure	• Improper oil viscosity	• Drain and refill crankcase with correct viscosity oil
	• Oil pressure gauge or sending unit inaccurate	• Replace oil pressure gauge
	• Oil pressure relief valve sticking closed	• Remove and inspect oil pressure relief valve assembly
Main bearing noise	• Insufficient oil supply	• Inspect for low oil level and low oil pressure
	• Main bearing clearance excessive	• Measure main bearing clearance, repair as necessary
	• Bearing insert missing	• Replace missing insert
	• Crankshaft end play excessive	• Measure end play, repair as necessary
	• Improperly tightened main bearing cap bolts	• Tighten bolts with specified torque
	• Loose flywheel or drive plate	• Tighten flywheel or drive plate attaching bolts
	• Loose or damaged vibration damper	• Repair as necessary
Connecting rod bearing noise	• Insufficient oil supply	• Inspect for low oil level and low oil pressure
	• Carbon build-up on piston	• Remove carbon from piston crown
	• Bearing clearance excessive or bearing missing	• Measure clearance, repair as necessary
	• Crankshaft connecting rod journal out-of-round	• Measure journal dimensions, repair or replace as necessary
	• Misaligned connecting rod or cap	• Repair as necessary
	• Connecting rod bolts tightened improperly	• Tighten bolts with specified torque
Piston noise	• Piston-to-cylinder wall clearance excessive (scuffed piston)	• Measure clearance and examine piston
	• Cylinder walls excessively tapered or out-of-round	• Measure cylinder wall dimensions, rebore cylinder
	• Piston ring broken	• Replace all rings on piston
	• Loose or seized piston pin	• Measure piston-to-pin clearance, repair as necessary
	• Connecting rods misaligned	• Measure rod alignment, straighten or replace
	• Piston ring side clearance excessively loose or tight	• Measure ring side clearance, repair as necessary
	• Carbon build-up on piston is excessive	• Remove carbon from piston

Troubleshooting Engine Mechanical Problems (cont.)

Problem	Cause	Solution
Valve actuating component noise	• Insufficient oil supply	• Check for: (a) Low oil level (b) Low oil pressure (c) Plugged push rods (d) Wrong hydraulic tappets (e) Restricted oil gallery (f) Excessive tappet to bore clearance
	• Push rods worn or bent	• Replace worn or bent push rods
	• Rocker arms or pivots worn	• Replace worn rocker arms or pivots
	• Foreign objects or chips in hydraulic tappets	• Clean tappets
	• Excessive tappet leak-down	• Replace valve tappet
	• Tappet face worn	• Replace tappet; inspect corresponding cam lobe for wear
	• Broken or cocked valve springs	• Properly seat cocked springs; replace broken springs
	• Stem-to-guide clearance excessive	• Measure stem-to-guide clearance, repair as required
	• Valve bent	• Replace valve
	• Loose rocker arms	• Tighten bolts with specified torque
	• Valve seat runout excessive	• Regrind valve seat/valves
	• Missing valve lock	• Install valve lock
	• Push rod rubbing or contacting cylinder head	• Remove cylinder head and remove obstruction in head
	• Excessive engine oil (four-cylinder engine)	• Correct oil level

Troubleshooting the Cooling System

Problem	Cause	Solution
High temperature gauge indication—overheating	• Coolant level low	• Replenish coolant
	• Fan belt loose	• Adjust fan belt tension
	• Radiator hose(s) collapsed	• Replace hose(s)
	• Radiator airflow blocked	• Remove restriction (bug screen, fog lamps, etc.)
	• Faulty radiator cap	• Replace radiator cap
	• Ignition timing incorrect	• Adjust ignition timing
	• Idle speed low	• Adjust idle speed
	• Air trapped in cooling system	• Purge air
	• Heavy traffic driving	• Operate at fast idle in neutral intermittently to cool engine
	• Incorrect cooling system component(s) installed	• Install proper component(s)
	• Faulty thermostat	• Replace thermostat
	• Water pump shaft broken or impeller loose	• Replace water pump
	• Radiator tubes clogged	• Flush radiator
	• Cooling system clogged	• Flush system
	• Casting flash in cooling passages	• Repair or replace as necessary. Flash may be visible by removing cooling system components or removing core plugs.
	• Brakes dragging	• Repair brakes
	• Excessive engine friction	• Repair engine
	• Antifreeze concentration over 68%	• Lower antifreeze concentration percentage
	• Missing air seals	• Replace air seals
	• Faulty gauge or sending unit	• Repair or replace faulty component
	• Loss of coolant flow caused by leakage or foaming	• Repair or replace leaking component, replace coolant
	• Viscous fan drive failed	• Replace unit

ENGINE AND ENGINE OVERHAUL

Troubleshooting the Cooling System (cont.)

Problem	Cause	Solution
Low temperature indication—undercooling	• Thermostat stuck open • Faulty gauge or sending unit	• Replace thermostat • Repair or replace faulty component
Coolant loss—boilover	• Overfilled cooling system • Quick shutdown after hard (hot) run • Air in system resulting in occasional "burping" of coolant • Insufficient antifreeze allowing coolant boiling point to be too low • Antifreeze deteriorated because of age or contamination • Leaks due to loose hose clamps, loose nuts, bolts, drain plugs, faulty hoses, or defective radiator • Faulty head gasket • Cracked head, manifold, or block • Faulty radiator cap	• Reduce coolant level to proper specification • Allow engine to run at fast idle prior to shutdown • Purge system • Add antifreeze to raise boiling point • Replace coolant • Pressure test system to locate source of leak(s) then repair as necessary • Replace head gasket • Replace as necessary • Replace cap
Coolant entry into crankcase or cylinder(s)	• Faulty head gasket • Crack in head, manifold or block	• Replace head gasket • Replace as necessary
Coolant recovery system inoperative	• Coolant level low • Leak in system • Pressure cap not tight or seal missing, or leaking • Pressure cap defective • Overflow tube clogged or leaking • Recovery bottle vent restricted	• Replenish coolant to FULL mark • Pressure test to isolate leak and repair as necessary • Repair as necessary • Replace cap • Repair as necessary • Remove restriction
Noise	• Fan contacting shroud • Loose water pump impeller • Glazed fan belt • Loose fan belt • Rough surface on drive pulley • Water pump bearing worn • Belt alignment	• Reposition shroud and inspect engine mounts • Replace pump • Apply silicone or replace belt • Adjust fan belt tension • Replace pulley • Remove belt to isolate. Replace pump. • Check pulley alignment. Repair as necessary.
No coolant flow through heater core	• Restricted return inlet in water pump • Heater hose collapsed or restricted • Restricted heater core • Restricted outlet in thermostat housing • Intake manifold bypass hole in cylinder head restricted • Faulty heater control valve • Intake manifold coolant passage restricted	• Remove restriction • Remove restriction or replace hose • Remove restriction or replace core • Remove flash or restriction • Remove restriction • Replace valve • Remove restriction or replace intake manifold

NOTE: *Immediately after shutdown, the engine enters a condition known as heat soak. This is caused by the cooling system being inoperative while engine temperature is still high. If coolant temperature rises above boiling point, expansion and pressure may push some coolant out of the radiator overflow tube. If this does not occur frequently it is considered normal.*

ENGINE AND ENGINE OVERHAUL

Troubleshooting the Serpentine Drive Belt

Problem	Cause	Solution
Tension sheeting fabric failure (woven fabric on outside circumference of belt has cracked or separated from body of belt)	• Grooved or backside idler pulley diameters are less than minimum recommended • Tension sheeting contacting (rubbing) stationary object • Excessive heat causing woven fabric to age • Tension sheeting splice has fractured	• Replace pulley(s) not conforming to specification • Correct rubbing condition • Replace belt • Replace belt
Noise (objectional squeal, squeak, or rumble is heard or felt while drive belt is in operation)	• Belt slippage • Bearing noise • Belt misalignment • Belt-to-pulley mismatch • Driven component inducing vibration • System resonant frequency inducing vibration	• Adjust belt • Locate and repair • Align belt/pulley(s) • Install correct belt • Locate defective driven component and repair • Vary belt tension within specifications. Replace belt.
Rib chunking (one or more ribs has separated from belt body)	• Foreign objects imbedded in pulley grooves • Installation damage • Drive loads in excess of design specifications • Insufficient internal belt adhesion	• Remove foreign objects from pulley grooves • Replace belt • Adjust belt tension • Replace belt
Rib or belt wear (belt ribs contact bottom of pulley grooves)	• Pulley(s) misaligned • Mismatch of belt and pulley groove widths • Abrasive environment • Rusted pulley(s) • Sharp or jagged pulley groove tips • Rubber deteriorated	• Align pulley(s) • Replace belt • Replace belt • Clean rust from pulley(s) • Replace pulley • Replace belt
Longitudinal belt cracking (cracks between two ribs)	• Belt has mistracked from pulley groove • Pulley groove tip has worn away rubber-to-tensile member	• Replace belt • Replace belt
Belt slips	• Belt slipping because of insufficient tension • Belt or pulley subjected to substance (belt dressing, oil, ethylene glycol) that has reduced friction • Driven component bearing failure • Belt glazed and hardened from heat and excessive slippage	• Adjust tension • Replace belt and clean pulleys • Replace faulty component bearing • Replace belt
"Groove jumping" (belt does not maintain correct position on pulley, or turns over and/or runs off pulleys)	• Insufficient belt tension • Pulley(s) not within design tolerance • Foreign object(s) in grooves • Excessive belt speed • Pulley misalignment • Belt-to-pulley profile mismatched • Belt cordline is distorted	• Adjust belt tension • Replace pulley(s) • Remove foreign objects from grooves • Avoid excessive engine acceleration • Align pulley(s) • Install correct belt • Replace belt
Belt broken (Note: identify and correct problem before replacement belt is installed)	• Excessive tension • Tensile members damaged during belt installation • Belt turnover • Severe pulley misalignment • Bracket, pulley, or bearing failure	• Replace belt and adjust tension to specification • Replace belt • Replace belt • Align pulley(s) • Replace defective component and belt

ENGINE AND ENGINE OVERHAUL

Troubleshooting the Serpentine Drive Belt (cont.)

Problem	Cause	Solution
Cord edge failure (tensile member exposed at edges of belt or separated from belt body)	• Excessive tension • Drive pulley misalignment • Belt contacting stationary object • Pulley irregularities • Improper pulley construction • Insufficient adhesion between tensile member and rubber matrix	• Adjust belt tension • Align pulley • Correct as necessary • Replace pulley • Replace pulley • Replace belt and adjust tension to specifications
Sporadic rib cracking (multiple cracks in belt ribs at random intervals)	• Ribbed pulley(s) diameter less than minimum specification • Backside bend flat pulley(s) diameter less than minimum • Excessive heat condition causing rubber to harden • Excessive belt thickness • Belt overcured • Excessive tension	• Replace pulley(s) • Replace pulley(s) • Correct heat condition as necessary • Replace belt • Replace belt • Adjust belt tension

work (crankshaft, block, bearings, piston rods, and other components) is well within the scope of the do-it-yourself mechanic.

TOOLS

The tools required for an engine overhaul or parts replacement will depend on the depth of your involvement. With a few exceptions, they will be the tools found in a mechanic's tool kit (see Chapter 1). More in-depth work will require any or all of the following:
• A dial indicator (reading in thousandths) mounted on a universal base
• Micrometers and telescope gauges
• Jaw and screw-type pullers
• Scraper
• Valve spring compressor
• Ring groove cleaner
• Piston ring expander and compressor
• Ridge reamer
• Cylinder hone or glaze breaker
• Plastigage®
• Engine stand

The use of most of these tools is illustrated in this chapter. Many can be rented for a one-time use from a local parts jobber or tool supply house specializing in automotive work.

Occasionally, the use of special tools is called for. See the information on Special Tools and Safety Notice in the front of this book before substituting another tool.

INSPECTION TECHNIQUES

Procedures and specifications are given in this chapter for inspecting, cleaning and assessing the wear limits of most major components. Other procedures such as Magnaflux® and Zyglo® can be used to locate material flaws and stress cracks. Magnaflux® is a magnetic process applicable only to ferrous materials. The Zyglo® process coats the material with a fluorescent dye penetrant and can be used on any material Check for suspected surface cracks can be more readily made using spot check dye. The dye is sprayed onto the suspected area, wiped off and the area sprayed with a developer. Cracks will show up brightly.

OVERHAUL TIPS

Aluminum has become extremely popular for use in engines, due to its low weight. Observe the following precautions when handling aluminum parts:
• Never hot tank aluminum parts (the caustic hot tank solution will eat the aluminum.
• Remove all aluminum parts (identification tag, etc.) from engine parts prior to the tanking.
• Always coat threads lightly with engine oil or anti-seize compounds before installation, to prevent seizure.
• Never over-torque bolts or spark plugs especially in aluminum threads.

Stripped threads in any component can be repaired using any of several commercial repair kits (Heli-Coil®, Microdot®, Keenserts®, etc.).

When assembling the engine, any parts that will be frictional contact must be prelubed to provide lubrication at initial start-up. Any product specifically formulated for this purpose can be used, but engine oil is not recommended as a prelube.

When semi-permanent (locked, but removable) installation of bolts or nuts is desired, threads should be cleaned and coated with Loctite® or other similar, commercial non-hardening sealant.

REPAIRING DAMAGED THREADS

Several methods of repairing damaged threads are available. Heli-Coil® (shown here),

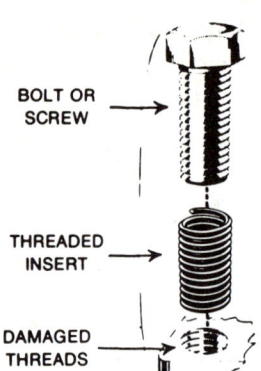

Damaged bolt holes can be repaired with thread repair inserts

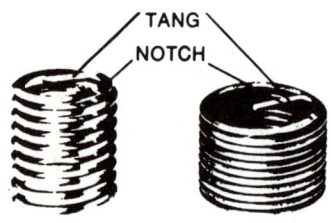

Standard thread repair insert (left) and spark plug thread insert (right)

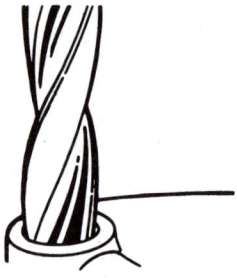

Drill out the damaged threads with specified drill. Drill completely through the hole or to the bottom of a blind hole

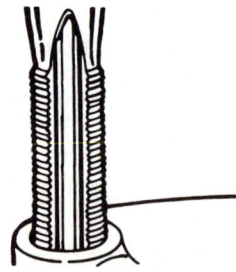

With the tap supplied, tap the hole to receive the thread insert. Keep the tap well oiled and back it out frequently to avoid clogging the threads

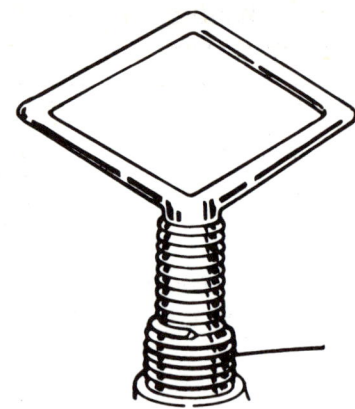

Screw the threaded insert onto the installation tool until the tang engages the slot. Screw the insert into the tapped hole until it is ¼–½ turn below the top surface. After installation break off the tang with a hammer and punch

Keenserts® and Microdot® are among the most widely used. All involve basically the same principle—drilling out stripped threads, tapping the hole and installing a prewound insert—making welding, plugging and oversize fasteners unnecessary.

Two types of thread repair inserts are usually supplied: a standard type for most Inch Coarse, Inch Fine, Metric Course and Metric Fine thread sizes and a spark lug type to fit most spark plug port sizes. Consult the individual manufacturer's catalog to determine exact applications. Typical thread repair kits will contain a selection of prewound threaded inserts, a tap (corresponding to the outside diameter threads of the insert) and an installation tool. Spark plug inserts usually differ because they require a tap equipped with pilot threads and a combined reamer/tap section. Most manufacturers also supply blister-packed thread repair inserts separately in addition to a master kit containing a variety of taps and inserts plus installation tools.

Before effecting a repair to a threaded hole, remove any snapped, broken or damaged bolts or studs. Penetrating oil can be used to free frozen threads; the offending item can be removed with locking pliers or with a screw or stud extractor. After the hole is clear, the thread can be repaired, as follows:

Checking Engine Compression

A noticeable lack of engine power, excessive oil consumption and/or poor fuel mileage measured over an extended period are all indicators of internal engine war. Worn piston rings, scored or worn cylinder bores, blown head gaskets, sticking or burnt valves and worn valve

ENGINE AND ENGINE OVERHAUL

seats are all possible culprits here. A check of each cylinder's compression will help you locate the problems.

As mentioned in the Tools and Equipment section of Chapter 1, a screw-in type compression gauge is more accurate that the type you simply hold against the spark plug hole, although it takes slightly longer to use. It's worth it to obtain a more accurate reading. Follow the procedures below for gasoline and diesel engined trucks.

GASOLINE ENGINES

1. Warm up the engine to normal operating temperature.
2. Remove all spark plugs.
3. Disconnect the high tension lead from the ignition coil.
4. On fully open the throttle either by operating the carburetor throttle linkage by hand or by having an assistant floor the accelerator pedal.
5. Screw the compression gauge into the no.1 spark plug hole until the fitting is snug.

NOTE: *Be careful not to crossthread the plug hole. On aluminum cylinder heads use extra care, as the threads in these heads are easily ruined.*

6. Ask an assistant to depress the accelerator pedal fully on both carbureted and fuel injected trucks. Then, while you read the compression gauge, ask the assistant to crank the engine two or three times in short bursts using the ignition switch.
7. Read the compression gauge at the end of each series of cranks, and record the highest of these readings. Repeat this procedure for each of the engine's cylinders. Compare the highest reading of each cylinder to the compression pressure specification in the Tune-Up Specifications chart in Chapter 2. The specs in this chart are maximum values.

A cylinder's compression pressure is usually acceptable if it is not less than 80% of maximum. The difference between each cylinder should be no more than 12-14 pounds.

8. If a cylinder is unusually low, pour a tablespoon of clean engine oil into the cylinder through the spark plug hole and repeat the compression test. If the compression comes up after adding the oil, it appears that the cylinder's piston rings or bore are damaged or worn. If the pressure remains low, the valves may not be seating properly (a valve job is needed), or the head gasket may be blown near that cylinder. If compression in any two adjacent cylinders is low, and if the addition of oil doesn't help the compression, there is leakage past the head gasket. Oil and coolant water in the combustion chamber can result from this problem. There may be evidence of water droplets on the engine dipstick when a head gasket has blown.

DIESEL ENGINES

Checking cylinder compression on diesel engines is basically the same procedure as on gasoline engines except for the following:

1. A special compression gauge adaptor suitable for diesel engines (because these engines have much greater compression pressures) must be used.
2. Remove the injector tubes and remove the injectors from each cylinder.

NOTE: *Don't forget to remove the washer underneath each injector; otherwise, it may get lost when the engine is cranked.*

3. When fitting the compression gauge adaptor to the cylinder head, make sure the bleeder of the gauge (if equipped) is closed.
4. When reinstalling the injector assemblies, install new washers underneath each injector.

Engine
REMOVAL AND INSTALLATION
4-126 Diesel

CAUTION: *The following procedure requires the discharge of the air conditioning*

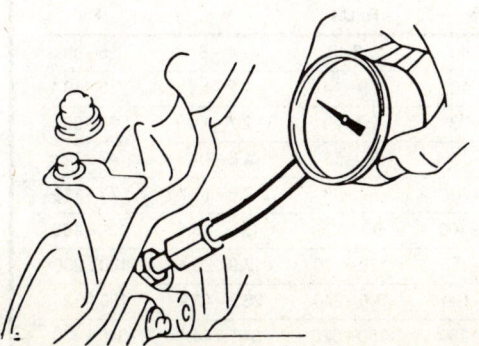
The screw-in type compression gauge is more accurate

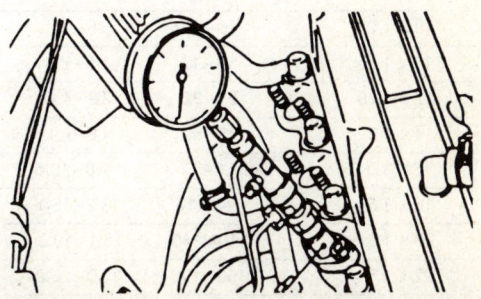
Diesel engines require a special compression gauge adaptor

Standard Torque Specifications and Fastener Markings

In the absence of specific torques, the following chart can be used as a guide to the maximum safe torque of a particular size/grade of fastener.
- There is no torque difference for fine or coarse threads.
- Torque values are based on clean, dry threads. Reduce the value by 10% if threads are oiled prior to assembly.
- The torque required for aluminum components or fasteners is considerably less.

U.S. Bolts

SAE Grade Number Number of lines always 2 less than the grade number.	1 or 2			5			6 or 7		
	Maximum Torque			Maximum Torque			Maximum Torque		
Bolt Size (Inches)—(Thread)	Ft./Lbs.	Kgm	Nm	Ft./Lbs.	Kgm	Nm	Ft./Lbs.	Kgm	Nm
¼—20 —28	5 6	0.7 0.8	6.8 8.1	8 10	1.1 1.4	10.8 13.6	10	1.4	13.5
5/16—18 —24	11 13	1.5 1.8	14.9 17.6	17 19	2.3 2.6	23.0 25.7	19	2.6	25.8
3/8—16 —24	18 20	2.5 2.75	24.4 27.1	31 35	4.3 4.8	42.0 47.5	34	4.7	46.0
7/16—14 —20	28 30	3.8 4.2	37.0 40.7	49 55	6.8 7.6	66.4 74.5	55	7.6	74.5
½—13 —20	39 41	5.4 5.7	52.8 55.6	75 85	10.4 11.7	101.7 115.2	85	11.75	115.2
9/16—12 —18	51 55	7.0 7.6	69.2 74.5	110 120	15.2 16.6	149.1 162.7	120	16.6	162.7
5/8—11 —18	83 95	11.5 13.1	112.5 128.8	150 170	20.7 23.5	203.3 230.5	167	23.0	226.5
¾—10 —16	105 115	14.5 15.9	142.3 155.9	270 295	37.3 40.8	366.0 400.0	280	38.7	379.6
7/8—9 —14	160 175	22.1 24.2	216.9 237.2	395 435	54.6 60.1	535.5 589.7	440	60.9	596.5
1—8 —14	236 250	32.5 34.6	318.6 338.9	590 660	81.6 91.3	799.9 849.8	660	91.3	894.8

Metric Bolts

Relative Strength Marking	4.6, 4.8			8.8		
Bolt Markings						
	Maximum Torque			Maximum Torque		
Bolt Size Thread Size x Pitch (mm)	Ft./Lbs.	Kgm	Nm	Ft./Lbs.	Kgm	Nm
6 x 1.0	2–3	.2–.4	3–4	3–6	.4–.8	5–8
8 x 1.25	6–8	.8–1	8–12	9–14	1.2–1.9	13–19
10 x 1.25	12–17	1.5–2.3	16–23	20–29	2.7–4.0	27–39
12 x 1.25	21–32	2.9–4.4	29–43	35–53	4.8–7.3	47–72
14 x 1.5	35–52	4.8–7.1	48–70	57–85	7.8–11.7	77–110
16 x 1.5	51–77	7.0–10.6	67–100	90–120	12.4–16.5	130–160
18 x 1.5	74–110	10.2–15.1	100–150	130–170	17.9–23.4	180–230
20 x 1.5	110–140	15.1–19.3	150–190	190–240	26.2–46.9	160–320
22 x 1.5	150–190	22.0–26.2	200–260	250–320	34.5–44.1	340–430
24 x 1.5	190–240	26.2–46.9	260–320	310–410	42.7–56.5	420–550

ENGINE AND ENGINE OVERHAUL

refrigerant. See Chapter 1. If you are not thoroughly familiar with the handling of refrigerant, leave this to someone who is. Severe personal injury will result from accidental contact with refrigerant.

1. Disconnect the battery cables and remove the battery. Remove the hood.
2. If equipped, remove the skid plate.
3. Drain the radiator. Remove the air cleaner assembly.

CAUTION: *When draining the coolant, keep in mind that cats and dogs are attracted by the ethylene glycol antifreeze, and are quite likely to drink any that is left in an uncovered container or in puddles on the ground. This will prove fatal in sufficient quantity. Always drain the coolant into a sealable container. Coolant should be reused unless it is contaminated or several years old.*

4. If equipped, discharge the air conditioning compressor. Be sure to observe all safety precautions.
5. Disconnect the radiator hoses and remove the E-clip from the bottom of the radiator.
6. Raise and support the vehicle safely. If the vehicle is equipped with automatic transmis-

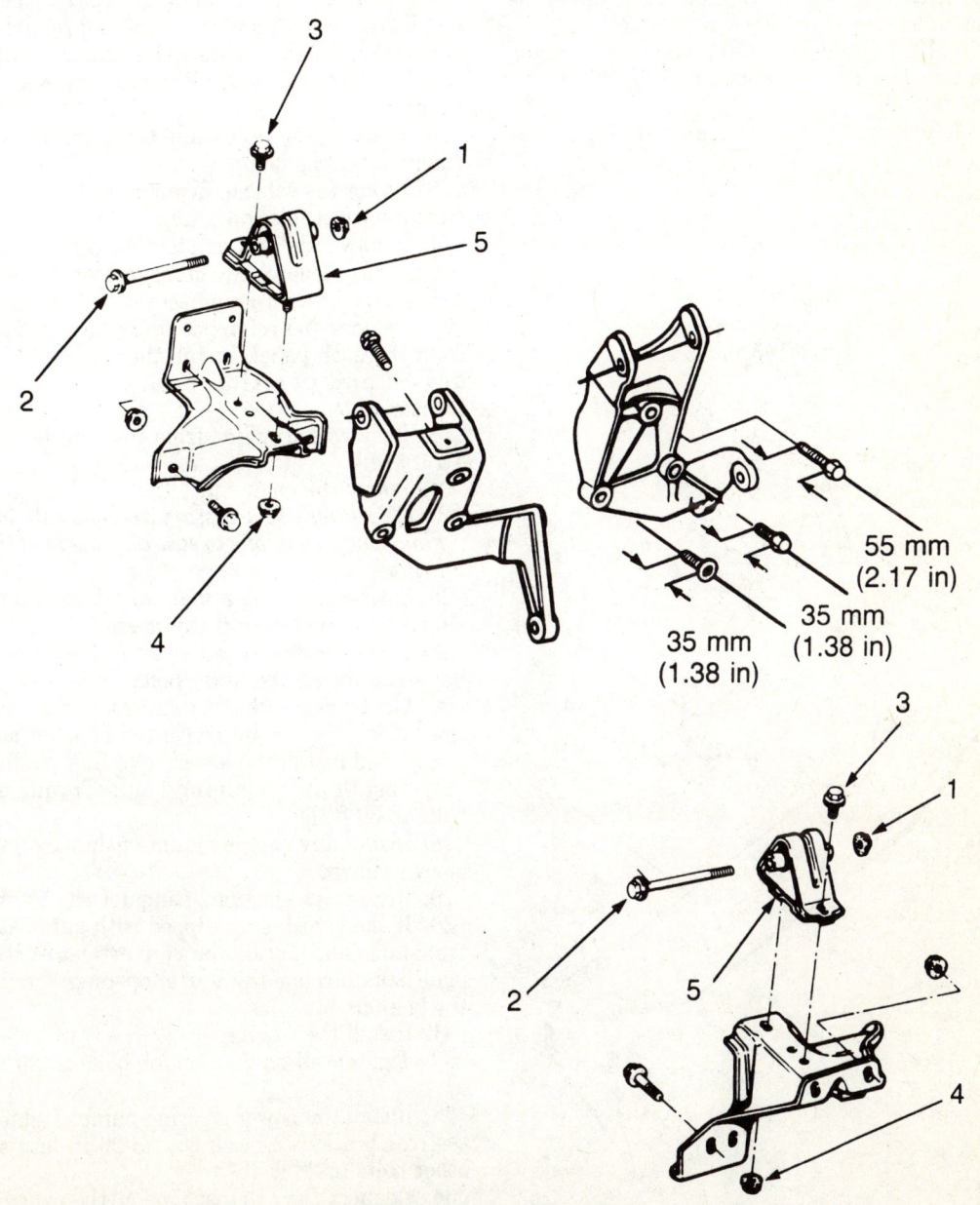

Front engine mounts for the diesel

106 ENGINE AND ENGINE OVERHAUL

sion disconnect the oil cooler lines at the radiator.
7. Remove the splash shield from the oil pan. Lower the vehicle.
8. Loosen the radiator shroud and remove the radiator fan assembly. Remove the shroud and the splash shield.
9. Remove the radiator and the condenser assembly from the vehicle. Remove the inner cooler.
10. Remove the exhaust shield from the manifold. Disconnect the hoses at the remote oil filter. Remove the oil filter.
11. Tag and disconnect all vacuum hoses and electrical connections. Disconnect and plug the fuel inlet and outlet lines at the fuel pump.
12. If equipped with automatic transmission, remove the left motor mount through bolt retaining nut.
13. Remove the motor mount retaining bolts.

Disconnect the accelerator cable. Raise and support the vehicle safely.
14. Disconnect and drain the power steering hoses at the power steering pump.
15. Disconnect the exhaust pipe at the exhaust manifold. Remove the motor mount retaining nuts.
16. Support the engine. Remove the left motor mount bolts. On automatic transmission equipped vehicles, remove the left motor mount.
17. Remove the starter.
18. If the vehicle is equipped with automatic transmission, mark and remove the converter-to-drive plate bolts through the starter opening. Install the left motor mount and retaining bolts finger tight. Install the motor mount cushion through bolt. Remove the engine support.
19. Remove the accessible transmission-to-engine retaining bolts.
20. Lower the vehicle. Remove the remaining engine-to-transmission retaining bolts.
21. Remove the power steering pump from the engine. Remove the oil separator and disconnect the hoses. Disconnect the heater hoses.
22. Remove the reference pressure regulator from the dash panel. Install the engine lifting device and position a jack under the transmission.
23. Remove the engine from the vehicle.

To install:
24. Lower the engine into the vehicle.
   NOTE: *It may be necessary to remove the engine mount cushions to ease alignment of the engine.*
25. On trucks with a manual transmission, slide the transmission input shaft into the clutch splines, align the flywheel housing bolt holes and install the lower bolts finger tight.
26. On trucks with an automatic transmission, align the torque converter housing and engine and install the lower bolts finger tight.
27. Install all remaining bolts. Torque all bolts to 30 ft. lbs.
28. Install any engine mount cushions previously removed.
29. Remove the engine lifting device.
30. If the vehicle is equipped with automatic transmission, install the converter-to-drive plate bolts through the starter opening. Torque the bolts to 40 ft. lbs.
31. Install the starter.
32. Tighten all engine mount bolts to 30 ft. lbs.
33. Install the power steering pump. Tighten the rear bracket-to-block bolt to 20 ft. lbs.; all other bolts to 28 ft. lbs.
34. Connect the exhaust pipe at the exhaust manifold.

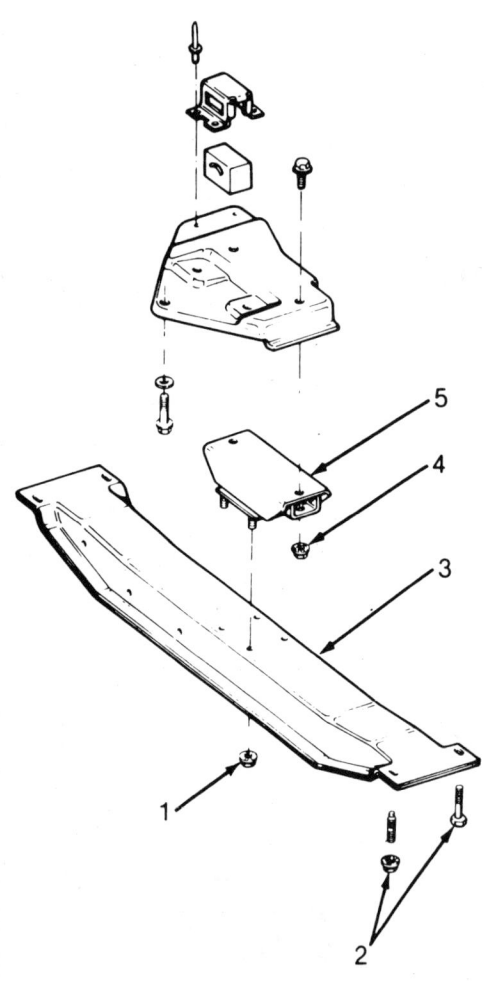

Rear engine mount for the diesel

ENGINE AND ENGINE OVERHAUL

35. Install the oil filter and lines.
36. Install the oil separator and connect the hoses.
37. Connect the heater hoses.
38. Connect all vacuum hoses and electrical connections.
39. Connect the fuel inlet and outlet lines at the fuel pump.
40. Install the reference pressure regulator from the dash panel.
41. Connect the accelerator cable.
42. Install the exhaust shield at the manifold.
43. Install the radiator and the condenser assembly from the vehicle.
44. Install the inner cooler.
45. Install the radiator fan assembly.
46. Install the shroud and the splash shield.
47. Install the splash shield on the oil pan.
48. If the vehicle is equipped with automatic transmission connect the oil cooler lines at the radiator.
49. Connect the radiator hoses and install the E-clip at the bottom of the radiator.
50. Install the air conditioning compressor.
51. Evacuate, charge and leak test the air conditioning system. Be sure to observe all safety precautions. See Chapter 1.
52. Fill the cooling system.
53. Install the air cleaner assembly.
54. If equipped, install the skid plate.
55. Install the battery.
56. Install the hood.

4-150

CAUTION: *This procedure requires that on vehicles with air conditioning, the refrigerant system be discharged. See Chapter 1. This is a dangerous procedure. Anyone who is not thoroughly familiar with the handling of refrigerant systems should not attempt this procedure. Serious personal injury could result from the mishandling of refrigerant.*

1. Disconnect the battery.
2. Matchmark the hood and hinges, and remove the hood.
3. Remove the air cleaner.
4. Drain the coolant and engine oil.

CAUTION: *When draining the coolant, keep in mind that cats and dogs are attracted by the ethylene glycol antifreeze, and are quite likely to drink any that is left in an uncovered container or in puddles on the ground. This will prove fatal in sufficient quantity. Always drain the coolant into a sealable container. Coolant should be reused unless it is contaminated or several years old.*

5. Remove the radiator hoses.
6. Remove the fan shroud and transmission cooler lines.
7. Discharge the refrigerant.
8. Remove the condenser and radiator.
9. Remove the fan and install a $5/16'' \times 1/2''$ capscrew through the pulley and into the water pump flange to maintain pulley alignment.
10. Disconnect the heater hoses.

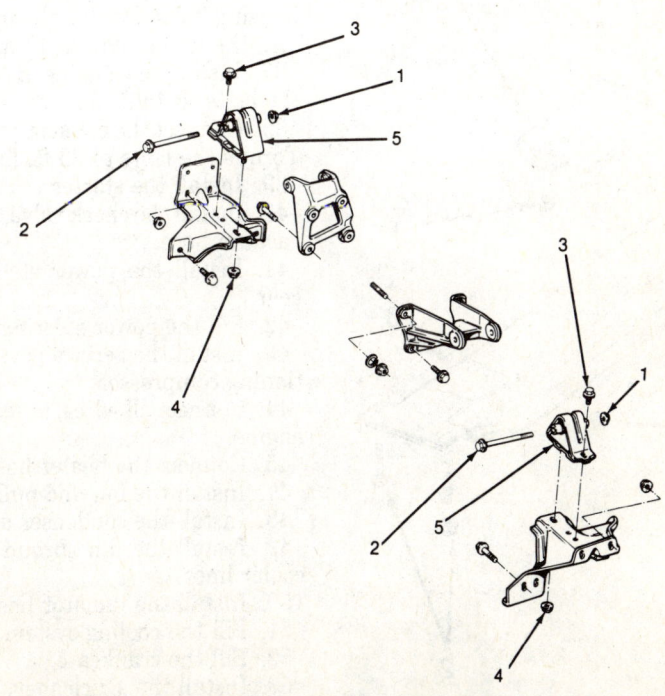

Front engine mount for the 4-150

108 ENGINE AND ENGINE OVERHAUL

11. Disconnect and tag all wires, hoses, and cables connected to the engine.
12. Remove the service ports from the air conditioning compressor and cap the openings.
13. Drain the power steering reservoir.
14. Remove the power steering hoses at the gear.
15. Remove the check valve from the power brake vacuum hose.
16. Raise and support the front end on jackstands.
17. Remove the starter.
18. Disconnect the exhaust pipe at the manifold.
19. Remove the bell housing access plate.
20. On trucks equipped with automatic transmission, matchmark the torque converter and flywheel. Remove the attaching bolts.
21. Remove the upper flywheel housing-to-engine bolts; loosen the lower ones.
22. Take up the weight of the engine with a shop crane.
23. Remove the engine mount bolts.
24. Raise the engine off the mounts.
25. Support the transmission with a floor jack.
26. Remove the remaining engine-to-flywheel housing bolts.
27. Move the engine forward to clear the transmission, and lift it from the vehicle.

To install:
28. Lower the engine into the vehicle.
NOTE: *It may be easier to align the engine and transmission if you remove the engine mount cushions from the brackets.*
29. On trucks with a manual trasnmission, engage the transmission input shaft with the clutch splines. Align the flywheel housing bolt holes and install the lower engine-to-transmission bolts finger tight.
30. On trucks with an automatic transmission, align the torque converter housing and engine. Loosely install the 4 lower transmission-to-engine bolts.
31. Install the engine mount cushions.
32. Lower the engine onto the mounts.
33. Remove the shop crane.
34. On trucks equipped with automatic transmission, install the torque converter-to-flywheel bolts. Torque the bolts to 40 ft. lbs.
35. Install the converter housing access plate.
36. Install the remaining engine-to-flywheel housing bolts. Torque the upper bolts to 27 ft. lbs.; the lower bolts to 43 ft. lbs.
37. Install the engine mount bolts. Torque the bolts to 48 ft. lbs.
38. Connect the exhaust pipe at the manifold. Torque the bolts to 23 ft. lbs.
39. Install the starter.
40. Install the check valve on the power brake vacuum hose.
41. Install the power steering hoses at the gear.
42. Fill the power steering reservoir.
43. Install the service ports on the air conditioning compressor.
44. Connect all wires, hoses, and cables to the engine.
45. Connect the heater hoses.
47. Install the fan and pulley.
48. Install the condenser and radiator.
49. Install the fan shroud and transmission cooler lines.
50. Install the radiator hoses.
51. Fill the cooling system.
52. Fill the crankcase.
53. Install the air cleaner.
54. Install the hood.

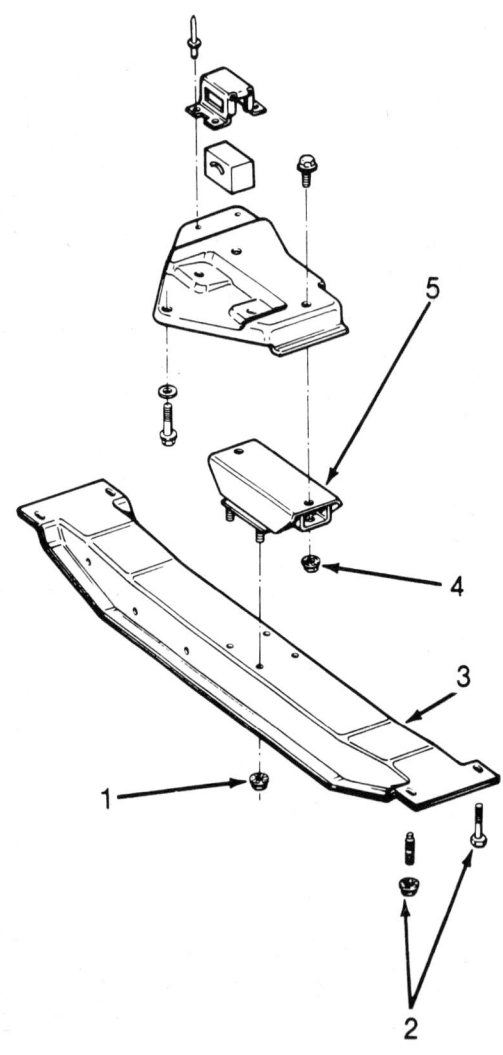

Rear engine mount for the 4-150

ENGINE AND ENGINE OVERHAUL

55. Connect the battery.
56. Evacuate, charge and leak test the refrigerant system.

6-173

CAUTION: *This procedure requires that on vehicles with air conditioning, the refrigerant system be discharged. See Chapter 1. This is a dangerous procedure. Anyone who is not thoroughly familiar with the handling of refrigerant systems should not attempt this procedure. Serious personal injury could result from the mishandling of refrigerant.*

1. Remove the battery cables.
2. Remove the air cleaner.
3. Remove the hood.
4. Drain the cooling system.

CAUTION: *When draining the coolant, keep in mind that cats and dogs are attracted by the ethylene glycol antifreeze, and are quite likely to drink any that is left in an uncovered container or in puddles on the ground. This will prove fatal in sufficient quantity. Always drain the coolant into a sealable container. Coolant should be reused unless it is contaminated or several years old.*

5. Remove the upper and lower radiator hoses.
6. Remove the fan shroud.
7. Disconnect the automatic transmission cooler lines.
8. Discharge the air conditioning refrigerant.
9. Remove the radiator/condenser assembly.
10. Remove the fan. If equipped with a fan clutch, do not lay the fan on its back or front. This will cause the clutch to leak and be irreversibly damaged.
11. Remove the heater hoses.
12. Disconnect and tag all remaining hoses attached to the engine.
13. Disconnect and tag all cables attached to the engine.
14. Disconnect and tag all wires attached to the engine.
15. Remove the power steering pump.
16. Disconnect the fuel pipe at the pump.
17. Disconnect the refrigerant hoses at the compressor and cap the openings.
18. Raise and support the truck on jackstands.
19. Disconnect the exhaust pipe at the converter flange.
20. Remove the flywheel housing access plate.
21. On vehicles equipped with automatic transmission, matchmark the converter-to-flywheel and remove the bolts.
22. Remove the flywheel housing-to-engine bolts.
23. Lower the vehicle.

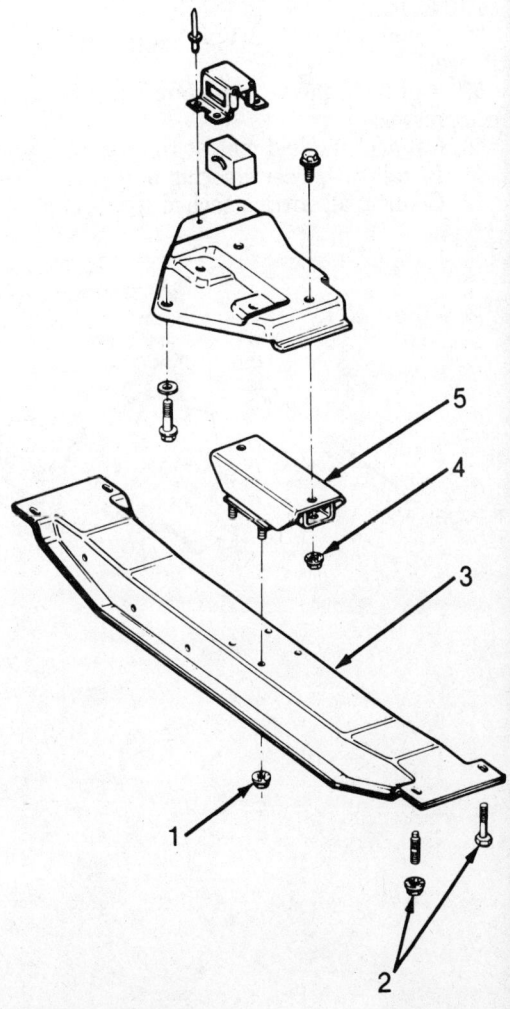

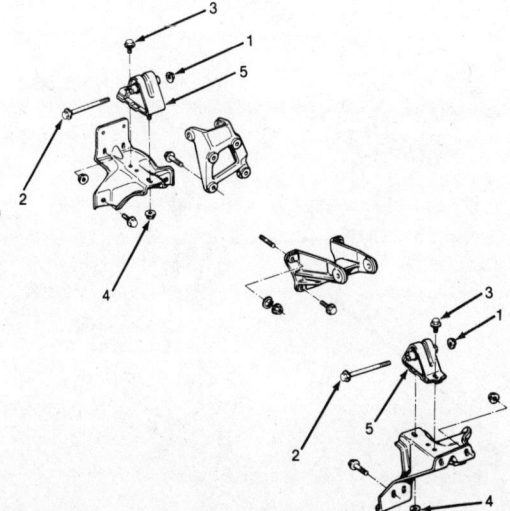

6-173 front engine mounts　　　6-173 rear engine mount

110 ENGINE AND ENGINE OVERHAUL

24. Place a floor jack under the transmission.
25. Attach a shop crane to the engine lifting eyes.
26. Remove the engine mount bolts.
27. Lift the engine from the truck.

To install:
28. Lift the engine from the truck.
NOTE: *It will be easier to align the engine if you remove the engine support cushions.*
29. Install the flywheel housing-to-engine bolts. Finger tight.
30. Install the support cushions and lower the engine onto the mounts.
31. Install the engine mount bolts. Torque the through-bolts to 92 ft. lbs.
32. Remove the shop crane.
34. Remove the floor jack under the transmission.
35. On vehicles equipped with automatic transmission, install the converter-to-flywheel bolts. Torque the bolts to 25 ft. lbs.
36. Install the flywheel housing access plate.
37. Torque the engine-to-transmission bolts to 40 ft. lbs.
38. Connect the exhaust pipe at the converter flange.
39. Connect the refrigerant hoses at the compressor.
40. Connect the fuel pipe at the pump.
41. Install the power steering pump.
42. Connect all wires attached to the engine.
43. Connect all cables attached to the engine.
44. Connect all remaining hoses attached to the engine.
45. Install the heater hoses.
46. Install the fan.
47. Install the radiator/condenser assembly.
48. Connect the automatic transmission cooler lines.
49. Install the fan shroud.
50. Install the upper and lower radiator hoses.
51. Fill the cooling system.
52. Install the hood.
53. Install the air cleaner.
54. Install the battery cables.
55. Evacuate, charge and leak test the refrigerant system.

6-243

CAUTION: *This procedure requires that on vehicles with air conditioning, the refrigerant system be discharged. See Chapter 1. This is a dangerous procedure. Anyone who is not thoroughly familiar with the handling of refrigerant systems should not attempt this procedure. Serious personal injury could result from the mishandling of refrigerant.*

1. Matchmark the hood and hinges and remove the hood.
2. Drain the engine oil.
3. Drain the cooling system.

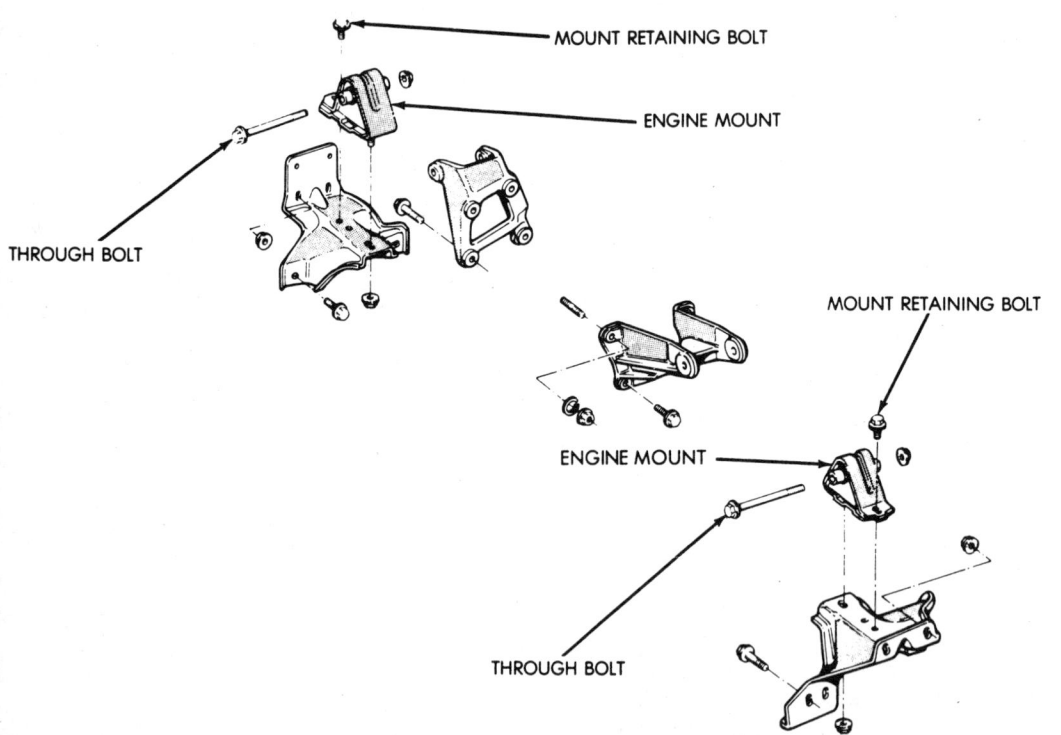

6-243 front engine mounts

ENGINE AND ENGINE OVERHAUL

CAUTION: *When draining the coolant, keep in mind that cats and dogs are attracted by the ethylene glycol antifreeze, and are quite likely to drink any that is left in an uncovered container or in puddles on the ground. This will prove fatal in sufficient quantity. Always drain the coolant into a sealable container. Coolant should be reused unless it is contaminated or several years old.*

4. Remove the battery.
5. Remove the air cleaner.
6. Remove the upper and lower radiator hoses.
7. Disconnect and cap the automatic transmission cooler lines.
8. Remove the fan shroud.
9. Remove the radiator.
10. Remove the electric cooling fan.
11. Disconnect the vacuum harness connector at the intake manifold.
12. Disconnect the electric fan switch.
13. On trucks with air conditioning, discharge the system, remove the compressor service valves and cap the ports at once!
14. Remove the radiator or radiator/condenser assembly.
15. Disconnect the accelerator linkage.
16. Disconnect the heater hoses at the engine.
17. Disconnect the cruise control cable.
18. Disconnect and tag all wires, hoses, cables, vacuum lines, etc., connected to the engine or in the way of engine removal.
19. Disconnect the injection system wiring harness at the firewall.
20. Relieve fuel system pressure. See Chapter 5.
21. Disconnect the quick-connect fuel lines at the fuel rail and return line by squeezing the 2 tabs against the tube. Pull the fuel tube and retainer from the quick-connect fitting.
22. Remove the power brake vacuum check valve from the booster.
23. Disconnect the power steering hoses from the gear, drain the pump reservoir, and cap all openings.
24. Raise and support the front end on jackstands.
25. Remove the starter.
26. Disconnect the exhaust pipe at the support bracket and the manifold.
27. Disconnect the engine speed sensor wiring (2 screws).
28. Remove the exhaust pipe support bracket.
29. On engines, equipped with automatic transmission, remove the inspection cover. Matchmark the torque converter and flex plate. Turning the engine by hand, remove each torque converter-to-flex plate bolt.
30. Remove the upper flywheel housing-to-engine bolts and loosen the bottom bolts.
31. Remove the engine front support-to-frame nuts.
32. Lower the truck.
33. Take up the weight of the engine with a shop crane.
34. Support the transmission with a floor jack.
35. Remove the lower engine-to-bellhousing bolts.
36. Raise the engine, while guiding it forward and out of the vehicle.

To install:
37. Lower the engine into the vehicle. It may make it easier to align the engine and transmission if you remove the engine mount cushions.

WARNING: *Be very careful to avoid damaging the trigger wheel on the flywheel on trucks with an automatic transmission!*

38. On trucks with a manual transmission, insert the input shaft into the clutch splines, align the flywheel housing with the engine and install the lower bolts finger tight.
39. On trucks with an automatic transmission, align the engine and converter housing and install the 4 lower bolts finger tight.
40. Install the engine mount cushions.
41. Lower the engine onto the mounts.
42. Install the mount bolts finger tight.
43. Remove the floor jack.
44. Remove the shop crane.
45. Install the remaining flywheel housing-to-engine bolts and tighten all bolts to 28 ft. lbs..
46. On engines equipped with automatic transmission, turning the engine by hand, install each torque converter-to-flex plate bolt. Torque the bolts to 40 ft. lbs.
47. Install the access cover.
48. Remove the exhaust pipe support bracket and connect the exhaust pipe.
49. Connect the engine speed sensor wiring (2 screws).
50. Install the starter.
51. Connect the power steering hoses at the gear and fill the pump reservoir.
52. Install the power brake vacuum check valve at the booster.
53. Connect the quick-connect fuel lines at the fuel rail and return line.
54. Connect the injection system wiring harness at the firewall.
55. Connect all wires, hoses, cables, vacuum lines, etc.
56. Connect the cruise control cable.
57. Connect the heater hoses at the engine.
58. Connect the accelerator linkage.
59. Install the radiator or radiator/condenser assembly.
60. On trucks with air conditioning, install the compressor service valves.

112 ENGINE AND ENGINE OVERHAUL

61. Install the electric cooling fan.
62. Connect the electric fan switch.
63. Connect the vacuum harness connector at the intake manifold.
64. Install the fan shroud.
65. Connect the automatic transmission cooler lines.
66. Install the upper and lower radiator hoses.
67. Install the air cleaner.
68. Install the battery.
69. Fill the cooling system.
70. Fill the crankcase.
71. Install the hood.
72. Evacuate, charge and leak test the refrigerant system.

Rocker Shafts and Rocker Studs
REMOVAL AND INSTALLATION
4-126 Diesel

1. Disconnect the negative battery cable. Remove the cylinder head cover and gasket.
2. Remove the valve cover.
3. Remove the rocker shaft retaining bolts. Remove the rocker arm shaft assembly from the vehicle.
4. Installation is the reverse of the removal procedure. Be sure to use new gaskets and adjust the valves as required. Torque the bolts to 20 ft. lbs.
5. Be sure that the engine is cold before adjusting the valves.
6. Set number one cylinder to TDC on the compression stroke and check the valve clearance of No.1 and No.2 intake and No.1 and No.3 exhaust valves. Adjust as required.
7. Rotate the crankshaft 360° and check the clearance of the No.3 and No.4 intake and No.2 and No.4 exhaust valves. Adjust as required.
NOTE: *The No.1 cylinder is located at the flywheel end of the engine.*
8. To adjust, loosen the locknut and turn the adjustment screw as necessary. As each adjustment screw is tightened, be sure that the bottom of the screw is aligned with the valve stem. If the adjustment screw is not aligned with the stem when tightened, the stem could bend. Tighten the locknut.
9. The exhaust valve adjustment specification is 0.25mm. The intake valve adjustment specification is 0.20mm.

4-150

1. Remove the rocker arm cover. The cover seal is RTV sealer. Break the seal with a clean putty knife or razor blade. Don't attempt to remove the cover until the seal is broken. To remove the cover, pry where indicated at the bolt holes.

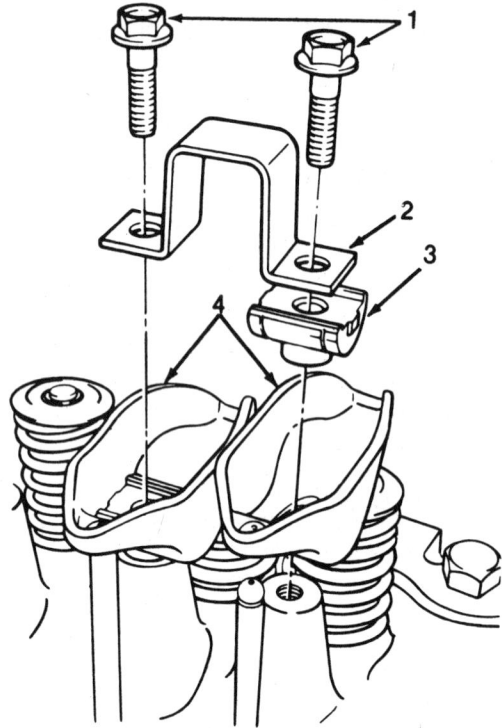

Rocker arm removal for the 4-150 and 6-243

2. Remove the two capscrews at each bridge and pivot assembly. It's best to remove the capscrews alternately, a little at a time each to avoid damage to the bridge.
3. Remove the bridges, pivots and rocker arms. Keep them in order.
4. Installation is the reverse of removal. Tighten the capscrews to 19 ft. lbs. Thoroughly clean the mating surfaces of the head and cover. Run a ⅛" bead of RTV sealer along the length of the sealing surface of the head. Position the cover on the head within 10 minutes of applying the sealer. Torque the cover bolts, in a crisscross pattern, to 55 in. lbs.

6-173

1. Remove the rocker arm cover.
2. Remove the rocker arm holddown nuts, pivots and rocker arms. Keep them in order.
3. Installation is the reverse of removal. Apply a thin coat of Molykote®, or equivalent, to the bearing surfaces of the rocker arms and pivots. Tighten the rocker arm nut until it just touches the valve stem. Rotate the engine until the No. 1 piston is at TDC of the compression stroke. The 0 mark on the timing scale should be aligned with the timing pointer and the rotor should be at the No. 1 spark plug tower of the distributor cap. The following valves can be adjusted:
Exhaust — 1, 2, 3

ENGINE AND ENGINE OVERHAUL 113

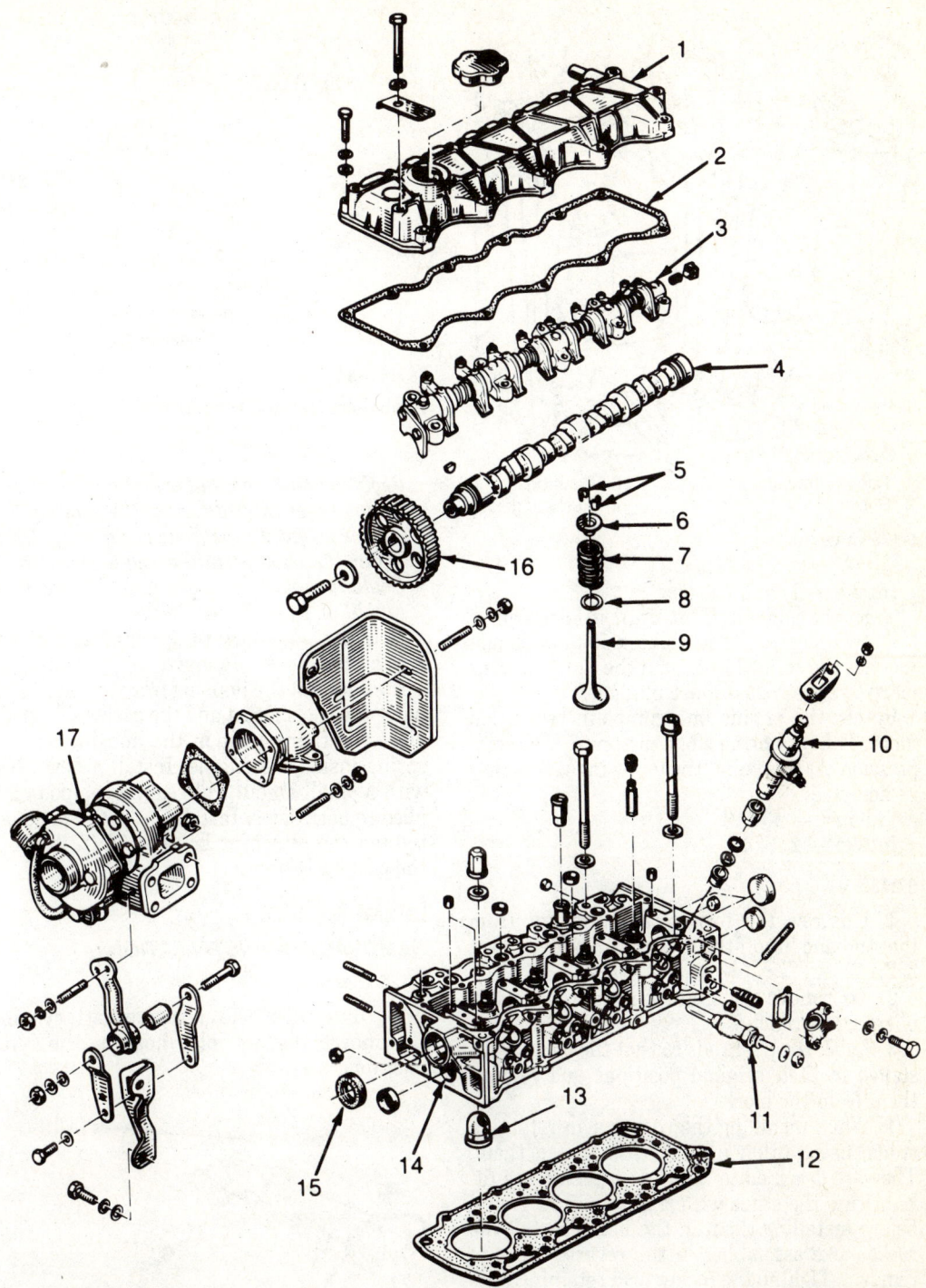

1. Cylinder head cover
2. Cylinder head cover gasket
3. Rocker arm and shaft assembly
4. Camshaft
5. Valve spring locks
6. Valve spring retainer
7. Valve spring
8. Valve spring washer
9. Valve
10. Injector
11. Glow plug
12. Cylinder head gasket
13. Pre-combustion chamber
14. Cylinder head
15. Camshaft oil seal
16. Camshaft sprocket
17. Turbocharger

Exploded view of the 4-126 diesel cylinder head

114 ENGINE AND ENGINE OVERHAUL

1. Rocker arm nuts
2. Rocker arms
3. Pushrods
4. Pushrod guides

6-173 valve train

Intake — 1, 5, 6
Turn the adjusting nut until it backs off of the stem slightly, then tighten it until it just touches the stem. Then, turn the nut 1½ turns more to center the tappet plunger.
Rotate the engine one complete revolution more. This will bring No. 4 piston to TDC compression. At this point, the following valves may be adjusted:
Exhaust — 4, 5, 6
Intake — 2, 3, 4

6-243

1. Unscrew the rocker retaining nut from the stud and lift off the rocker arm and its pivot ball.
2. To remove the stud from the block use a pliers and wrench.
3. Label the pushrods to that they can be installed in their original positions and remove them from the block.
4. When installing the rocker arm retaining studs, use caution not to cross thread them. They are designed to cause an interference fit. Lubricate the studs with high pressure grease before installing them in the head. Install the rocker arm assemblies in the reverse order of removal. Tighten the rocker arm retaining nuts to 23 ft. lbs.

Thermostat

REMOVAL AND INSTALLATION

To remove the thermostats from all of these engines, first drain the cooling system.
CAUTION: *When draining the coolant, keep in mind that cats and dogs are attracted by the ethylene glycol antifreeze, and are quite*

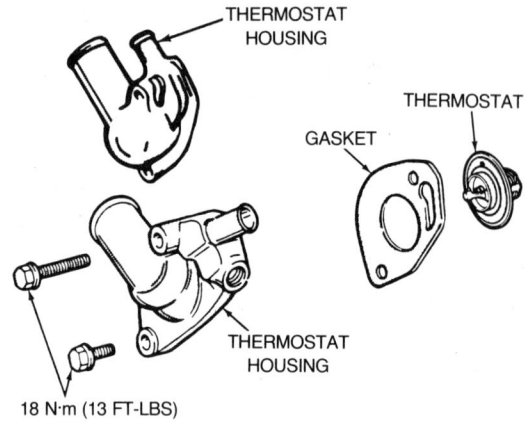

Thermostat for the 4-150 and 6-243

likely to drink any that is left in an uncovered container or in puddles on the ground. This will prove fatal in sufficient quantity. Always drain the coolant into a sealable container. Coolant should be reused unless it is contaminated or several years old.

It is not necessary to disconnect or remove any of the hoses. Remove the two attaching screws and lift the housing from the engine. Remove the thermostat and the gasket. To install, place the thermostat in the housing with the spring inside the engine. Install a new gasket with a small amount of sealing compound applied to both sides. Install the water outlet and tighten the attaching bolts to 30 ft. lbs. Refill the cooling system.

Intake Manifold

REMOVAL AND INSTALLATION

4-126 Diesel

1. Disconnect the negative battery cable. Disconnect the air inlet hose at the intake manifold.

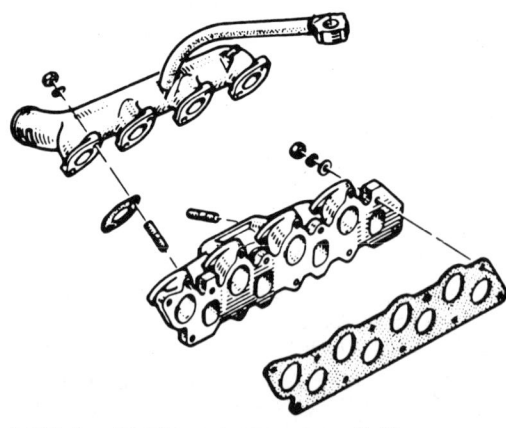

4-126 diesel intake and exhaust manifolds

ENGINE AND ENGINE OVERHAUL

2. Tag and remove all hoses and/or wires as necessary in order to gain access to the intake manifold retaining bolts.
3. Tag and remove all vacuum hoses and electrical connections that are attached to the intake manifold.
4. Remove the intake manifold retaining bolts. Remove the assembly from the vehicle. Discard the intake manifold gaskets.
5. Installation is the reverse of removal.

4-150

NOTE: *It may be necessary to remove the carburetor or the throttle body from the intake manifold before the manifold is removed.*

1. Disconnect the negative battery cable. Drain the radiator.

CAUTION: *When draining the coolant, keep in mind that cats and dogs are attracted by the ethylene glycol antifreeze, and are quite likely to drink any that is left in an uncovered container or in puddles on the ground. This will prove fatal in sufficient quantity. Always drain the coolant into a sealable container. Coolant should be reused unless it is contaminated or several years old.*

2. Remove the air cleaner. Disconnect the fuel pipe. Remove the carburetor or the throttle body, as required.
3. Disconnect the coolant hoses from the intake manifold.
4. Disconnect the throttle cable from the bellcrank.
5. Disconnect the PCV valve vacuum hose from the intake manifold.
6. If equipped, remove the vacuum advance CTO valve vacuum hoses.

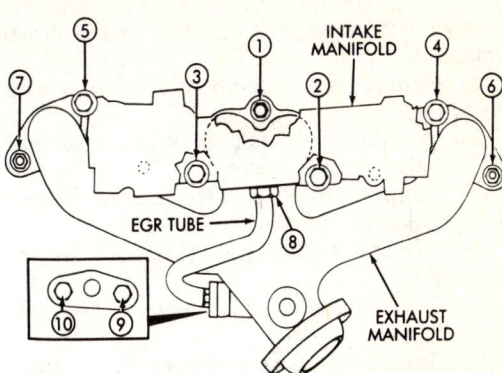

Fuel injected 4-150 intake and exhaust manifold installation

7. Disconnect the system coolant temperature sender wire connector (located on the intake manifold). Disconnect the air temperature sensor wire, if equipped.
8. Disconnect the vacuum hose from the EGR valve.
9. On vehicles equipped with power steering remove the power steering pump and its mounting bracket. Do not detach the power steering pump hoses.
10. Disconnect the intake manifold electric heater wire connector, as required.
11. Disconnect the throttle valve linkage, if equipped with automatic transmission.
12. Disconnect the EGR valve tube from the intake manifold.
13. Remove the intake manifold attaching screws, nuts and clamps. Remove the intake manifold. Discard the gasket.
14. Clean the mating surfaces of the manifold and cylinder head.

NOTE: *If the manifold is being replaced, ensure all fittings, etc., are transferred to the replacement manifold.*

To install:

15. Clean the mating surfaces of the manifold and cylinder head.
16. Install the intake manifold, with a new gasket. Install the intake manifold attaching screws, nuts and clamps. Torque the nuts to 23 ft. lbs..
17. Connect the EGR valve tube.
18. Connect the throttle valve linkage, if equipped with automatic transmission.
19. Connect the intake manifold electric heater wire connector, as required.
20. On vehicles equipped with power steering install the power steering pump and its mounting bracket.
21. Connect the vacuum hose to the EGR valve.
22. Connect the system coolant temperature

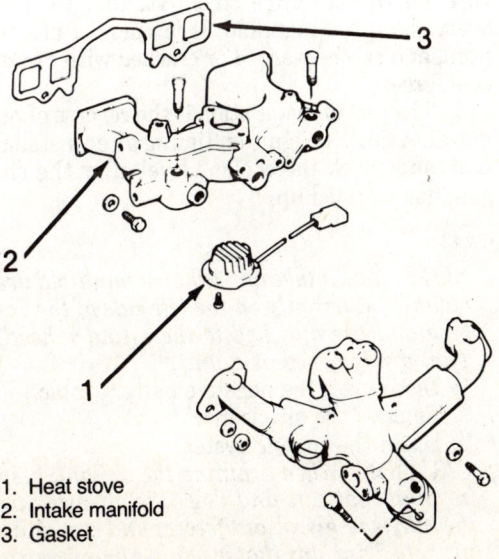

1. Heat stove
2. Intake manifold
3. Gasket

Carbureted 4-150 manifolds

116 ENGINE AND ENGINE OVERHAUL

sender wire connector (located on the intake manifold).
23. Connect the air temperature sensor wire, if equipped.
24. If equipped, install the vacuum advance CTO valve vacuum hoses.
25. Connect the PCV valve vacuum hose at the intake manifold.
26. Connect the throttle cable at the bellcrank.
27. Connect the coolant hoses at the intake manifold.
28. Install the carburetor or the throttle body, as required. Torque the nuts to 14 ft. lbs.
29. Connect the fuel pipe.
30. Install the air cleaner.
31. Connect the negative battery cable.
32. Fill the cooling system.

6-173

NOTE: *It may be necessary to remove the carburetor from the intake manifold before the manifold is removed.*

1. Disconnect the negative battery cable. Remove the rocker covers. Drain the radiator.
CAUTION: *When draining the coolant, keep in mind that cats and dogs are attracted by the ethylene glycol antifreeze, and are quite likely to drink any that is left in an uncovered container or in puddles on the ground. This will prove fatal in sufficient quantity. Always drain the coolant into a sealable container. Coolant should be reused unless it is contaminated or several years old.*
2. If equipped with air conditioning disconnect the compressor and move it to one side. Disconnect the spark plugs wires at the spark plugs. Disconnect the wires at the ignition coil.
3. If equipped, remove the air pump and bracket.

4. Remove the distributor cap. Mark the position of the ignition rotor in relation to the distributor body, and remove the distributor. Do not crank the engine with the distributor removed.
5. Remove the EGR valve. Remove the air hose. Disconnect the charcoal canister hoses. Remove the pipe bracket from the left cylinder head, if equipped.
6. Remove the diverter valve. Remove the power brake vacuum hose. Remove the heater and radiator hoses from the intake manifold.
7. Disconnect and label the vacuum hoses. If equipped, remove the EFE pipe from the rear of the manifold. Disconnect the coolant temperature switches.
8. Remove the carburetor linkage. Disconnect and plug the fuel line.
9. Remove the manifold retaining bolts and nuts.
10. Remove the intake manifold. Remove and discard the gaskets, and scrape off the old silicone seal from the front and rear ridges.
11. The gaskets are marked for right and left side installation; do not interchange them. Clean the sealing surface of the engine block, and apply a 5mm wide bead of silicone sealer to each ridge.
12. Install the new gaskets onto the heads. The gaskets will have to be cut slightly to fit past the center pushrods. Do not cut any more material than necessary. Hold the gaskets in place by extending the ridge bead of sealer ¼" onto the gasket ends.
13. Install the intake manifold. The area between the ridges and the manifold should be completely sealed.
14. Install the retaining bolts and nuts, and tighten in sequence to 23 ft. lbs. Do not overtighten the manifold. It is made of aluminum, and can be warped or cracked with excessive force.
15. The rest of installation is the reverse of removal. Adjust the ignition timing after installation, and check the coolant level after the engine has warmed up.

6-243

NOTE: *The intake and exhaust manifold are mounted externally on the left side of the engine and are attached to the cylinder head. They are removed as a unit.*

1. Disconnect the negative battery cable.
2. Remove the air cleaner.
3. Drain the cooling system.
CAUTION: *When draining the coolant, keep in mind that cats and dogs are attracted by the ethylene glycol antifreeze, and are quite likely to drink any that is left in an uncovered container or in puddles on the ground. This*

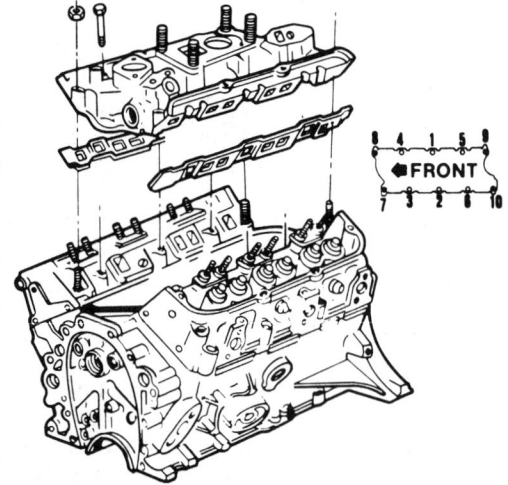

6-173 intake manifold

ENGINE AND ENGINE OVERHAUL 117

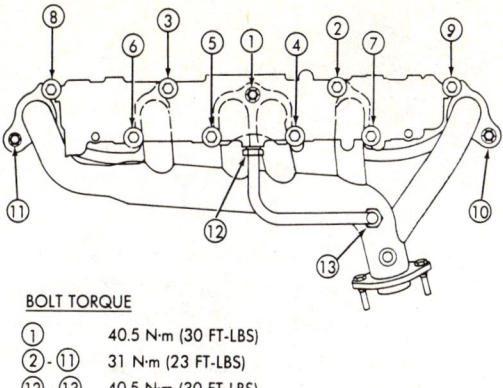

BOLT TORQUE
① 40.5 N·m (30 FT-LBS)
②-⑪ 31 N·m (23 FT-LBS)
⑫-⑬ 40.5 N·m (30 FT-LBS)

6-243 intake and exhaust manifold installation

will prove fatal in sufficient quantity. Always drain the coolant into a sealable container. Coolant should be reused unless it is contaminated or several years old.

4. Disconnect the EGR tube nuts at the intake manifold and exhaust manifold.
5. Disconnect the accelerator cable, cruise control cable and transmission line pressure cable.
6. Disconnect the vacuum multiconnector at the intake manifold.
7. Disconnect all wiring connectors at the manifold.
8. Disconnect the fuel supply and return lines from the fuel rail.
9. Loosen the serpentine belt tensioner.
10. Unbolt the power steering pump and bracket and set it aside. Don't disconnect the hoses.
11. Remove the fuel rail and injectors.
12. Remove the intake manifold heat shield.
13. Raise and support the front end on jackstands.
14. Disconnect the exhaust pipe at the exhaust manifold.
15. Disconnect the oxygen sensor wiring at the sensor.
16. Lower the truck.
17. Remove the manifold attaching bolts, nuts and clamps.
18. Separate the intake manifold and exhaust manifold from the engine as an assembly, and discard the gasket.
19. If either manifold is to be replaced, they should be separated.
20. Clean the mating surface of the manifolds and the cylinder head before replacing the manifolds.

To install:
21. If the manifolds were separated, install the EGR tube loosely. Don't tighten it until the manifold assembly is installed.
22. Install a new gasket over the alignment dowels on the head.
23. Position the manifold assemblies and loosely install the bolts. See the illustration and tighten the bolts as follows:
- No.1: 30 ft. lbs.
- Nos. 2 through 11: 23 ft. lbs.
- Nos. 12 & 13 (EGR tube): 30 ft. lbs.
24. Connect the oxygen sensor wiring at the sensor.
25. Connect the exhaust pipe at the exhaust manifold.
26. Install the intake manifold heat shield.
27. Install the fuel rail and injectors.
28. Install the power steering pump and bracket and set it aside.
29. Adjust the serpentine belt tensioner.
30. Connect the fuel supply and return lines at the fuel rail. Use new O-rings at the quick-connect fittings.
31. Connect all wiring connectors at the manifold.
32. Connect the vacuum multiconnector at the intake manifold.
33. Connect the accelerator cable, cruise control cable and transmission line pressure cable.
34. Connect the EGR tube nuts at the intake manifold and exhaust manifold.
35. Drain the cooling system.
36. Install the air cleaner.
37. Connect the negative battery cable.

Exhaust Manifold
REMOVAL AND INSTALLATION
4-126 Diesel

1. Disconnect the negative battery. Remove the intake manifold.
2. Disconnect the exhaust pipe from the adapter.
3. Remove the oil supply pipe and the oil return hose from the turbocharger assembly.
4. Disconnect the turbocharger air inlet and outlet hoses.
5. Remove the turbocharger retaining bolts. Remove the turbocharger from the vehicle.
6. Remove the exhaust manifold retaining bolts. Remove the exhaust manifold and gasket. Discard the gasket.
7. Installation is the reverse of removal. Torque the bolts to the specification shown in the Torque Specifications Chart.

4-150

1. Remove the intake manifold.
2. Disconnect the EGR tube.
3. Disconnect the exhaust pipe at the manifold.
4. Disconnect the oxygen sensor wire.

118 ENGINE AND ENGINE OVERHAUL

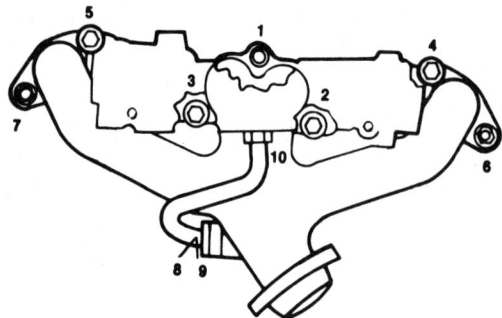

4-150 exhaust valve installation

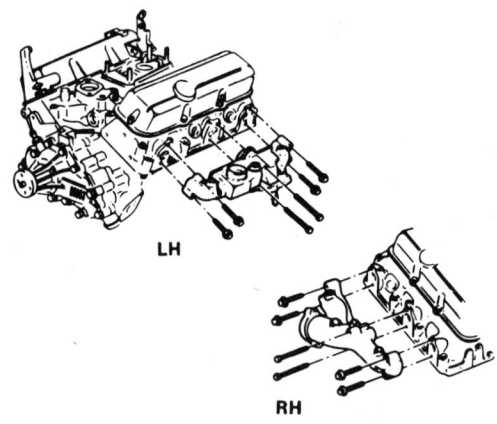

6-173 exhaust manifolds

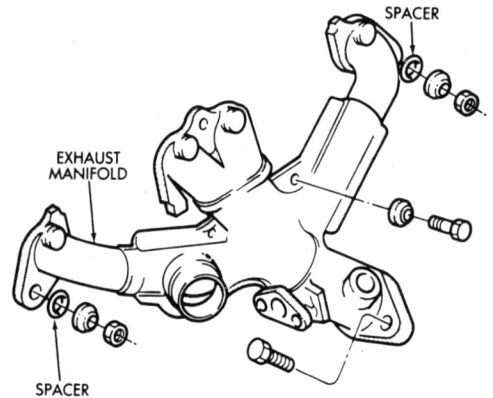

Exhaust manifold spacers

5. Support the manifold and remove the nuts from the studs.
6. If a new manifold is being installed, transfer the oxygen sensor. Torque the sensor to 35 ft. lbs.
7. Installation is the reverse of removal. Torque the nuts to 23 ft. lbs.

6-173

LEFT SIDE

1. Disconnect the negative battery cable. Remove the air cleaner. Remove the carburetor heat stove pipe.
2. Remove the air supply plumbing from the exhaust manifold.
3. Raise and support the vehicle safely. Unbolt and remove the exhaust pipe at the manifold.
4. Unbolt and remove the manifold.
5. Clean the mating surfaces of the cylinder head and manifold. Install the manifold onto the head, and install the retaining bolts finger tight.
6. Tighten the manifold bolts in a circular pattern, working from the center to the ends, to 25 ft. lbs. in two stages.
7. Connect the exhaust pipe to the manifold.
8. The remainder of installation is the reverse of removal.

RIGHT SIDE

1. Disconnect the negative battery cable. Raise and support the vehicle safely.
2. Disconnect the exhaust pipe from the exhaust manifold.
3. Lower the vehicle. Remove the spark plug wires from the plugs. Number them first if they are not already labeled. Remove the cruise control servo from the right inner fender panel, if equipped.
4. Remove the air supply pipes from the manifold. Remove the Pulsair bracket bolt from the rocker cover, on models so equipped, then remove the pipe assembly.
5. Remove the manifold retaining bolts and remove the manifold.
6. Clean the mating surfaces of the cylinder head and manifold. Position the manifold against the head and install the retaining bolts finger tight.
7. Tighten the bolts in a circular pattern, working from the center to the ends, to 25 ft. lbs. in two stages.
8. Install the air supply system. Install the spark plug wires. If equipped install the cruise control servo.
9. Raise and support the vehicle safely. Connect the exhaust pipe to the manifold.

6-243

The intake and exhaust manifolds of the 6-243 must be removed together. See the procedure for removing and installing the intake manifold.

Turbocharger

REMOVAL AND INSTALLATION

4-126 Diesel

1. Disconnect the negative battery cable.
2. Remove all the necessary components in

ENGINE AND ENGINE OVERHAUL

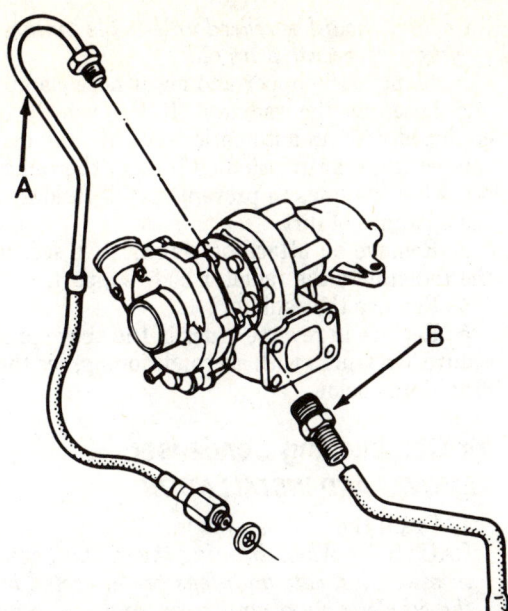

4-126 turbocharger oil supply line (A) and oil return line (B) connections

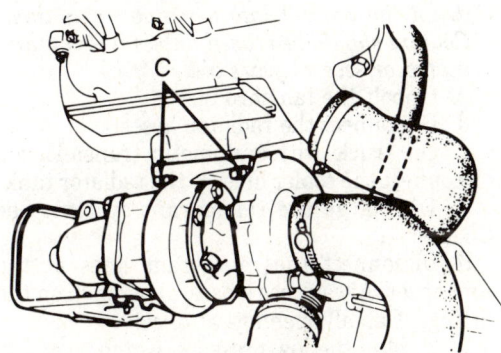

4-126 turbocharger mounting bolts (C)

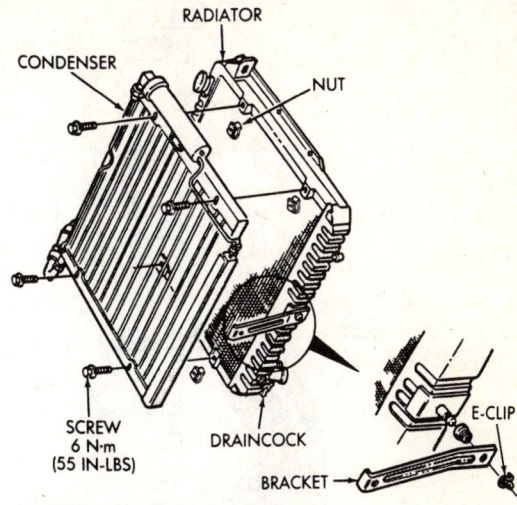

Radiator installation on the 4-150

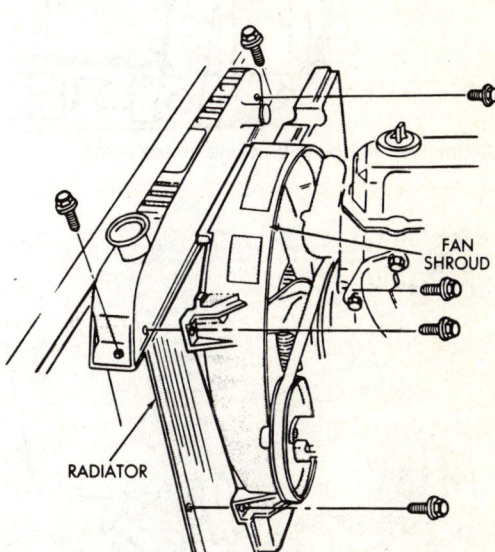

Fan shroud removal on the 4-150

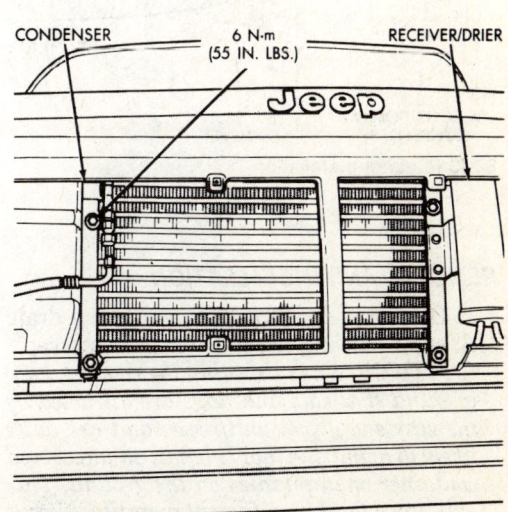

Condenser mounting screws on the 4-150

order to gain access to the turbocharger retaining bolts.

3. Disconnect the exhaust pipe flange. Remove the oil supply pipe. Remove the oil return hose.

4. Remove the turbocharger retaining bolts. Remove the turbocharger from the vehicle.

5. Installation is the reverse of removal. Torque the turbocharger support bracket bolts to 30 ft. lbs.

Radiator

NOTE: *The air conditioning condenser must be removed with the radiator. This involves purging the refrigerant. See Chapter 1 and the Condenser procedure below. Be sure to use the proper precautions as Freon® can be dangerous if proper safety conditions are not taken.*

ENGINE AND ENGINE OVERHAUL

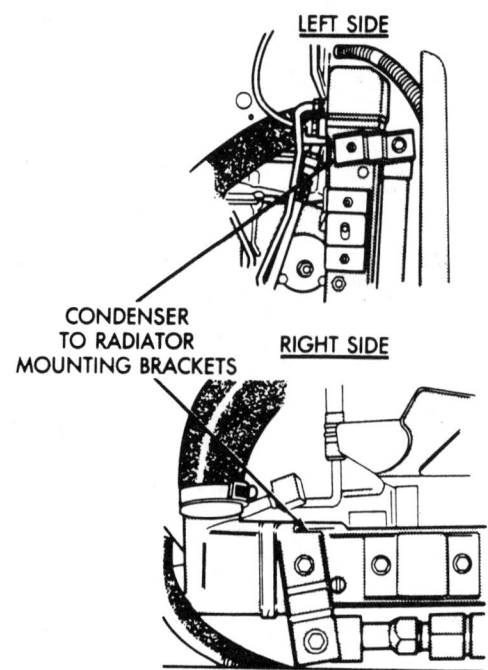

Condenser mounting brackets for the 6-243

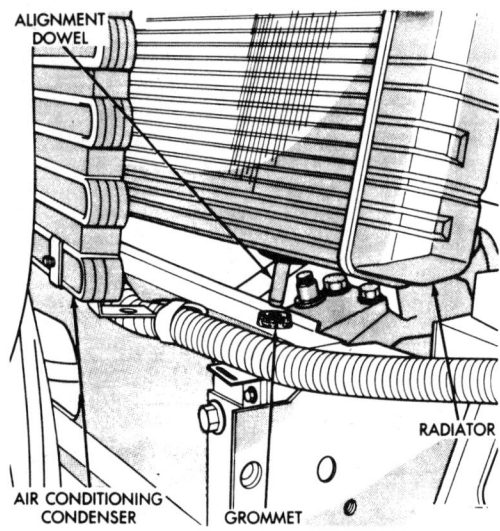

6-243 Radiator installation

REMOVAL AND INSTALLATION

1. Drain the radiator by opening the drain cock and removing the radiator pressure cap.
    CAUTION: *When draining the coolant, keep in mind that cats and dogs are attracted by the ethylene glycol antifreeze, and are quite likely to drink any that is left in an uncovered container or in puddles on the ground. This will prove fatal in sufficient quantity. Always drain the coolant into a sealable container.* Coolant should be reused unless it is contaminated or several years old.
2. Remove the upper and lower hose clamps and hoses at the radiator. If the vehicle is equipped with an automatic transmission, disconnect the transmission oil lines at the radiator. Plug the lines to prevent loss of fluid and the entrance of dirt.
3. Remove all attaching screws that secure the radiator to the radiator body support.
4. Remove the radiator.
5. Replace in reverse order of the above procedure. On trucks with air conditioning, see the procedures below.

Air Conditioning Condenser
REMOVAL AND INSTALLATION

1. Drain the cooling system.
    CAUTION: *When draining the coolant, keep in mind that cats and dogs are attracted by the ethylene glycol antifreeze, and are quite likely to drink any that is left in an uncovered container or in puddles on the ground. This will prove fatal in sufficient quantity. Always drain the coolant into a sealable container.* Coolant should be reused unless it is contaminated or several years old.
2. Unbolt the fan shroud.
3. Disconnect the radiator hoses.
4. On truck with automatic transmission, disconnect the cooler lines at the radiator tank.
5. Discharge the refrigerant system. See Chapter 1.
6. Disconnect the refrigerant lines at the condenser. Always use a back-up wrench on the fittings. Cap all openings at once!
7. Unplug the low pressure switch.
8. Unbolt and remove the radiator and condenser as an assembly.
9. Remove the retaining bolts and separate the radiator and condenser.
10. Installation is the reverse of removal. Add 1 oz. of refrigerant oil to the condenser before installation.
11. Fill the cooling system.
12. Evacuate, charge and leak test the refrigerant system.

Water Pump
REMOVAL AND INSTALLATION
4-126 Diesel

1. Disconnect the negative battery cable. Drain the engine coolant.
    CAUTION: *When draining the coolant, keep in mind that cats and dogs are attracted by the ethylene glycol antifreeze, and are quite likely to drink any that is left in an uncovered container or in puddles on the ground. This*

ENGINE AND ENGINE OVERHAUL

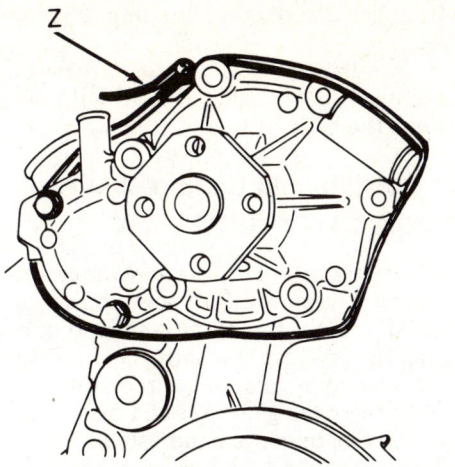

Using a strap and clip to retain the 4-126 timing belt tensioner

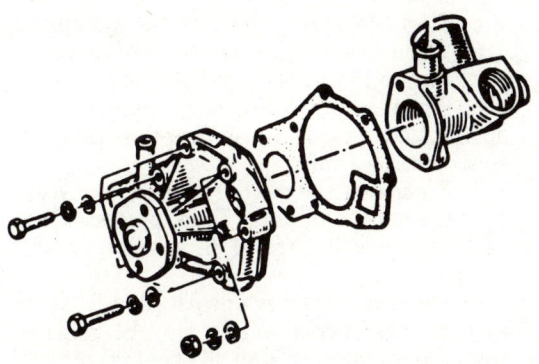

4-126 water pump mounting

13. Fill the cooling system.
14. Connect the battery.

4-150, 6-173

NOTE: *Some 4-150 engines with air conditioning are equipped with a serpentine drive belt and have a reverse rotating water pump coupled with a viscous fan drive assembly. The components are identified by the words REVERSE stamped on the cover of the viscous drive and on the inner side of the fan. The word REV is also cast into the body of the water pump.*

1. Drain the cooling system.

CAUTION: *When draining the coolant, keep in mind that cats and dogs are attracted by the ethylene glycol antifreeze, and are quite likely to drink any that is left in an uncovered will prove fatal in sufficient quantity. Always drain the coolant into a sealable container. Coolant should be reused unless it is contaminated or several years old.*

2. Remove the coolant hose from the water pump.
3. Remove the drive belts.
4. Remove the fan and hub assembly.
5. It is not necessary to remove the timing belt tensioner. Use a long strap and clip in order to retain the timing belt tensioner plunger in place.
6. Remove the water pump retaining bolts. Remove the water pump assembly from the vehicle.
7. Clean the mating surfaces of all gasket material.
8. Do not use sealer on the new gasket. Position the gasket and pump on the engine and install the bolts. Torque the bolts to 15 ft. lbs.
9. Retension the timing belt.
10. Install the fan and hub.
11. Install the drive belts.
12. Install the coolant hoses.

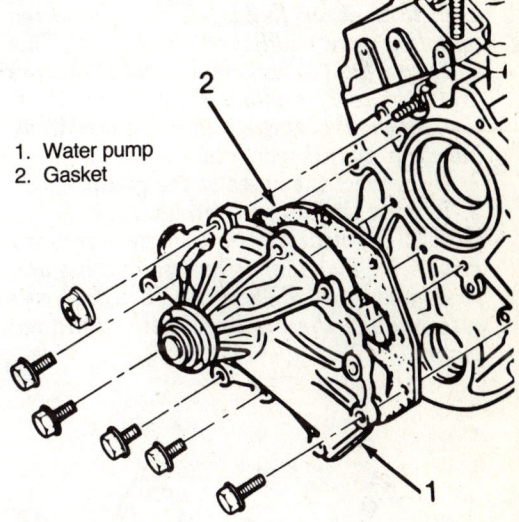

1. Water pump
2. Gasket

4-150 water pump

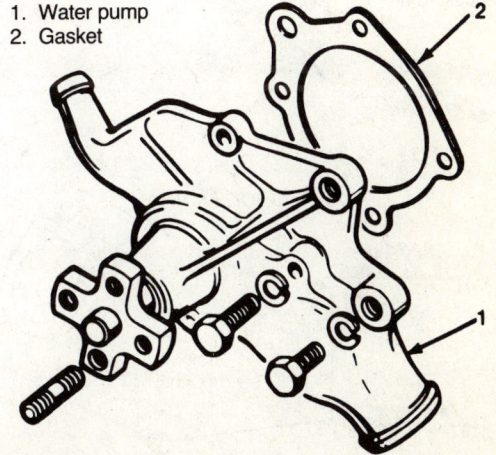

1. Water pump
2. Gasket

6-173 water pump

ENGINE AND ENGINE OVERHAUL

container or in puddles on the ground. This will prove fatal in sufficient quantity. Always drain the coolant into a sealable container. Coolant should be reused unless it is contaminated or several years old.
2. Disconnect the hoses at the pump.
3. Remove the drive belts.
4. Remove the power steering pump bracket.
5. Remove the fan and shroud.
6. Unbolt and remove the pump.
7. Clean the mating surfaces thoroughly.
8. Using a new gasket, install the pump and torque the bolts to 13 ft. lbs.
9. Install all other parts in reverse order of removal.

6-243

1. Drain the cooling system.
CAUTION: *When draining the coolant, keep in mind that cats and dogs are attracted by the ethylene glycol antifreeze, and are quite likely to drink any that is left in an uncovered container or in puddles on the ground. This will prove fatal in sufficient quantity. Always drain the coolant into a sealable container. Coolant should be reused unless it is contaminated or several years old.*
2. Disconnect the hoses at the pump.
3. Remove the fan and shroud.
NOTE: *On models with a single serpentine drive belts, the pump is reverse rotating and is stamped with REV or REVERSE. Never interchange these pumps with standard pumps.*

4. Unbolt and remove the pump. Discard the gasket.
5. Installation is the reverse of removal. Always use a new gasket coated with sealer. Torque the bolts to 13-18 ft. lbs.

Air Conditioning Compressor
REMOVAL AND INSTALLATION

It is not necessary to discharge the system for compressor removal. The compressor can be isolated from the rest of the system, thus eliminating the need for evacuating and recharging the system after compressor removal.
1. Coonect the gauge set and manifold.
2. Close both gauge hand valves.
3. Mid-position both service valves.
CAUTION: *Be very careful of the engine fan! Your work will take you in close proximity to the moving fan blades!*
4. Start the engine and turn the system on.
5. Turn the suction service valve slowly clockwise to the front-seated position.
6. When the pressure drops to zero, stop the engine and quickle finish frontr-seating the suction service valve.
7. Front-seat the discharge service valve.
8. Loosen the oil level check plug slowly to release any internal pressure in the compressor.
9. The compressor is now isolated from the system. The service valves may be removed from the compressor. Cap all openings at once!
10. Remove the compressor drive belt
11. Unbolt and remove the compressor from the mounting bracket.
12. If a new compressor is being installed, drain the oil from the old compressor into a graduated beaker. The new compressor should have 1 fl.oz. more oil than the old compressor. Add or delete oil as necessary.
13. Mount the compressor on the bracket. Torque the M8 bolts to 20 ft. lbs.; the M10 bolts to 30 ft. lbs.
14. Install and tension the drive belt.
15. Install the service valves. Torque them to 35 ft. lbs. Use new O-rings coated with clean refrigerant oil.
16. Connect the battery ground and check the refrigerant charge. See Chapter 1.

Cylinder Head
REMOVAL AND INSTALLATION

NOTE: *It is important to note that each engine has its own head bolt tightening sequence and torque. Incorrect tightening procedure may cause head warpage and compression loss. Correct sequence and torque for each engine model is shown in this chapter.*

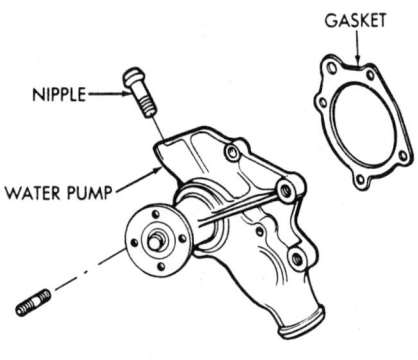

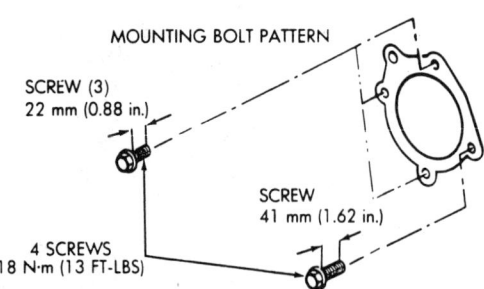

6-243 water pump

ENGINE AND ENGINE OVERHAUL

4-126 Diesel

NOTE: *Special tools are needed for this job.*

1. Disconnect the negative battery cable.
2. Remove the intake manifold. Remove the exhaust manifold.
3. Remove the valve cover. Drain the engine coolant. Remove the timing belt cover.

CAUTION: *When draining the coolant, keep in mind that cats and dogs are attracted by the ethylene glycol antifreeze, and are quite likely to drink any that is left in an uncovered container or in puddles on the ground. This will prove fatal in sufficient quantity. Always drain the coolant into a sealable container. Coolant should be reused unless it is contaminated or several years old.*

4. Install sprocket holding tool MOT-854 or equivalent and remove the camshaft sprocket retaining bolt. Remove the special tool.
5. Loosen the bolts and move the tensioner away from the timing belt. Retighten the tensioner bolts.
6. Remove the timing belt from the sprockets.

NOTE: *If it is necessary to remove the fuel injection pump sprocket use special tool BVI-28-01 or BVI-859 to accomplish this procedure.*

7. Disconnect the fuel pipe fittings from the injectors. Plug them in order to prevent dirt from entering the system.
8. Disconnect the fuel pipe fittings from the fuel injection pump. Plug them in order to prevent dirt from entering the system.
9. Remove the fuel pipes from there mountings on the engine. Remove all hoses and connectors from the fuel injection pump.
10. Remove the injection pump retaining bolts. Remove the fuel injection pump and its

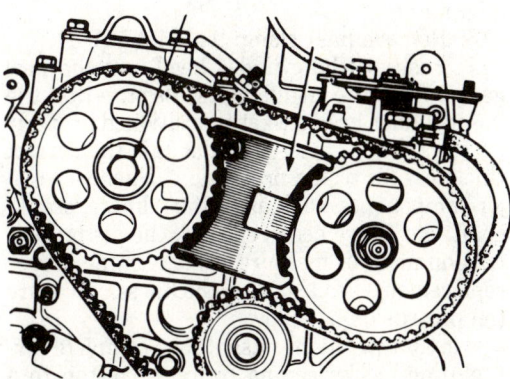

Using a special tool to hold the sprockets for removal of the camshaft sprocket bolt

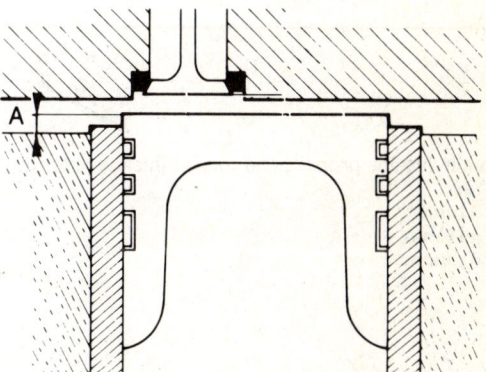

Piston protrusion measured at A on the 4-126

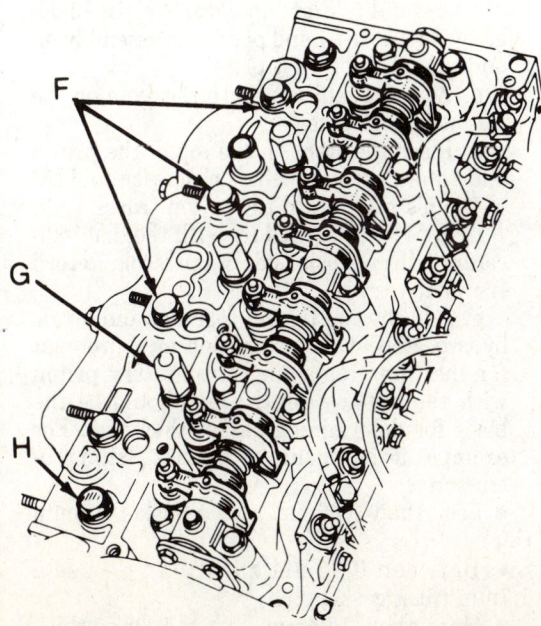

4-126 head bolts (F), nuts (G) and pivot bolt (H)

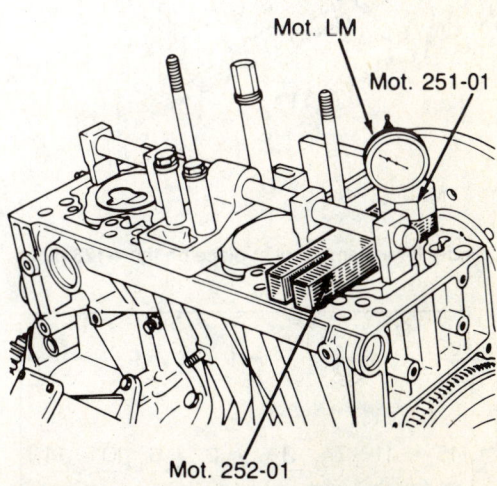

Piston protrusion measurement tools in place on the 4-126

mounting brackets, as an assembly, from the vehicle.

11. Remove the the retaining bolts and nuts from the cylinder head. Loosen pivot bolt but do not remove it. Remove the remaining cylinder head bolts.

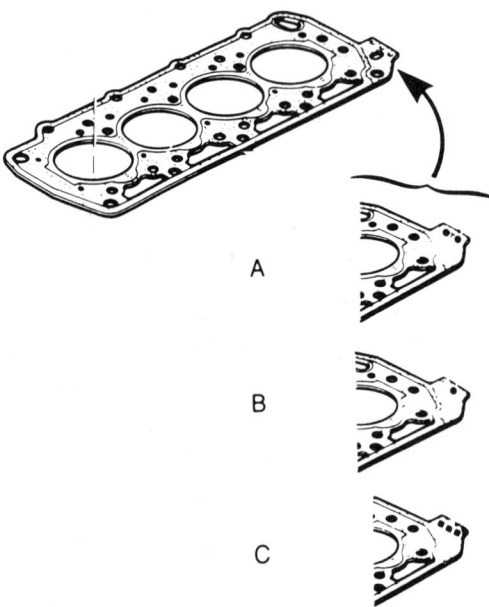

Identifying the proper head gasket thickness for the 4-126:
A = 1.6mm
B = 1.7mm
C = 1.8mm

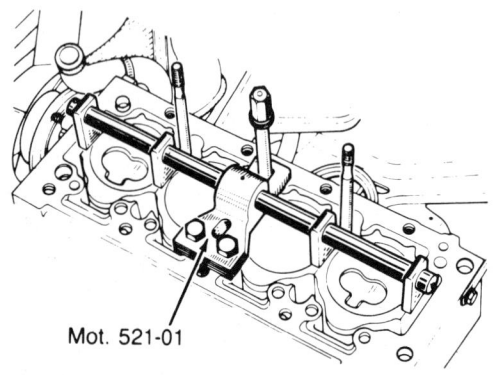

Mot. 521-01

Cylinder liner clamp tool in place on the 4-126 block

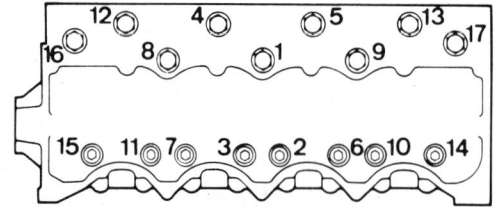

4-126 diesel head bolt torque

12. Place a block of wood against the cylinder head and tap it with a hammer in order to loosen the cylinder head gasket. The pivot movement will be minimal due to the small clearance between the studs and the cylinder head. Remove the pivot bolt from the cylinder head.

13. Remove the retaining bolts and the rocker arm shaft assembly from the cylinder head.

NOTE: *Do not lift the cylinder head from the cylinder block until the gasket is completely loosened from the cylinder liners. Otherwise, the liner seals could be broken.*

14. Remove the cylinder head and the gasket from the engine block. While the head is off, install liner clamp tool Mot.521-01 to hold the liners in place in the block.

To install:

15. Position cylinder head locating tool Mot.720 on the block to insure proper alignment.

16. Remove liner clamp tool Mot.521-01.

17. Position the cylinder head and the new gasket from the engine block. Be sure that the new cylinder head gasket is positioned properly on the cylinder head and that it is the correct thickness for piston protrusion. Whenever major components, such as pistons, liners, crankshaft, etc., have been replaced, the piston protrusion must be measured to determine proper replacement head gasket thickness. Measure the protrusion as follows:

 a. Rotate the crankshaft one complete revolution clockwise and bring #1 piston to a point just below and before TDC.

 b. Place thrust plate tool Mot.252-01 on top of the piston.

 c. Assemble dial indicator LM in block gauge Mot.251-01 and place this assembly on one side of the thrust plate.

 d. Zero the indicator with the stem on the cylinder block face.

 e. Place the stem on the top of the piston and rotate the crankshaft clockwise to TDC of the piston. Record the psiton travel.

 f. Repeat the procedure with the dial indicator on the opposite side of the block. Record the piston travel.

 g. Add the two figures together and divide by two. Repeat the protrusion measurement for the three remaining pistons. The piston with the greatest protrusion should be the basis for determining gasket thickness. For example, if the amount of greatest piston protrusion is:

• Less than 0.96mm, use a gasket 1.6mm thick

• Between 0.96mm and 1.04mm, use a 1.7mm thick gasket

• More than 1.04mm, use a 1.8mm thick gasket

ENGINE AND ENGINE OVERHAUL

18. Install the head bolts. Torque the cylinder head retaining bolts to 22 ft. lbs., then to 37 ft. lbs., then to 70-77 ft. lbs. Once all the bolts are tightened, recheck the torque.

NOTE: *The cylinder head bolts must be retightened after the cylinder head is installed in the vehicle. Operate the engine for a minimum of twenty minutes. Allow the engine to cool for a minimum of two and one half hours. Loosen each cylinder head bolt in sequence about one-half turn. Then retighten in the proper sequence and torque to 70-77 ft. lbs. For the final tightening, tighten the bolts again, in sequence, without loosening them to 70-77 ft. lbs.*

19. Remove tool Mot.720.
20. Install the rocker arm shaft assembly.
21. Install the fuel injection pump and its mounting brackets, as an assembly. See Chapter 5.
22. Install the fuel pipes on their mountings on the engine. Install all hoses and connectors on the fuel injection pump.
23. Connect the fuel pipe fittings to the fuel injection pump.
24. Connect the fuel pipe fittings from the injectors.
25. Install the timing belt.
26. Retension the timing belt.
27. Install the camshaft sprocket retaining bolt.
28. Install the valve cover.
29. Install the timing belt cover.
30. Install the intake manifold.
31. Install the exhaust manifold.
32. Fill the cooling system.
33. Connect the negative battery cable.

4-150

1. Disconnect the battery ground.
2. Drain the cooling system.

CAUTION: *When draining the coolant, keep in mind that cats and dogs are attracted by the ethylene glycol antifreeze, and are quite likely to drink any that is left in an uncovered container or in puddles on the ground. This will prove fatal in sufficient quantity. Always drain the coolant into a sealable container. Coolant should be reused unless it is contaminated or several years old.*

3. Disconnect the hoses at the thermostat housing.
4. Remove the air cleaner.
5. Remove the rocker arm cover. The cover seal is RTV sealer. Break the seal with a clean putty knife or razor blade. Don't attempt to remove the cover until the seal is broken. To remove the cover, pry where indicated at the bolt holes.

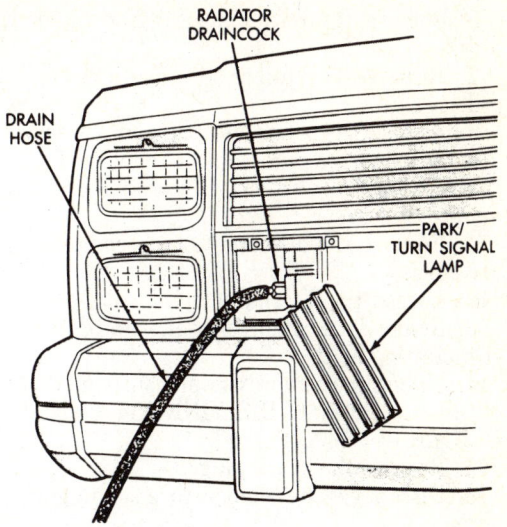

Draining the Wagoneer radiator

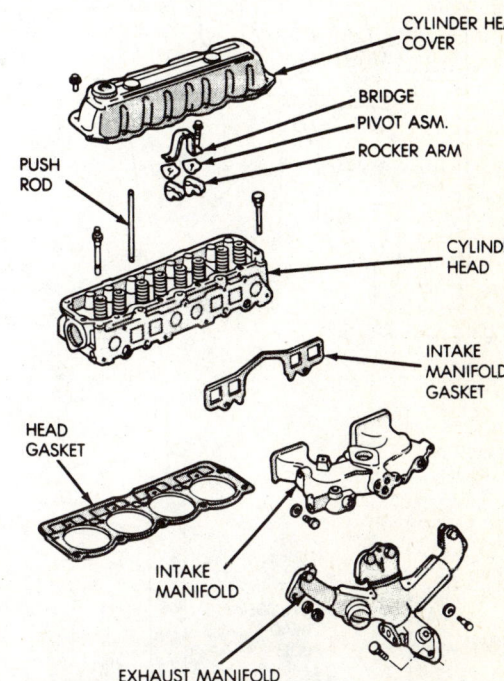

4-150 cylinder head components

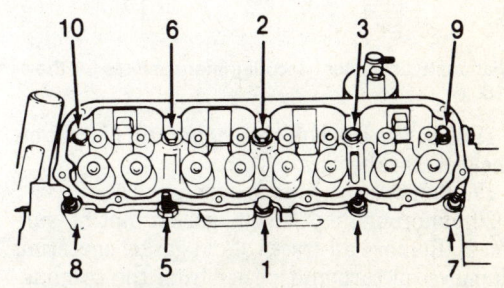

4-150 head bolt torque sequence

126 ENGINE AND ENGINE OVERHAUL

6. Remove the rocker arms. Keep them in order!
7. Remove the pushrods. Keep them in order!
8. Remove the power steering pump bracket.
9. Suspend the pump out of the way.
10. Remove the intake and exhaust manifolds.
11. Remove the air conditioning compressor drive belt.
12. Loosen the alternator drive belt.
13. Remove the compressor/alternator bracket mounting bolt.
14. Unbolt the compressor and suspend it out of the way. DO NOT DISCONNECT THE REFRIGERANT LINES!
15. Remove the spark plugs.
16. Disconnect the temperature sending unit wire.
17. Remove the head bolts.

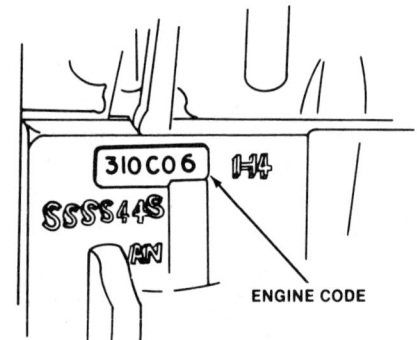

Engine code location

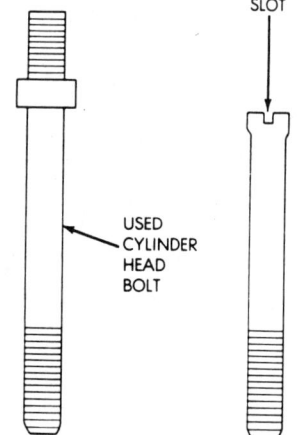

Fabricated cylinder head alignment dowels for the 4-150

18. Lift the head off the engine and place it on a clean workbench.
19. Remove the head gasket.
20. Thoroughly clean the gasket mating surfaces. Remove all traces of old gasket material. Remove all carbon deposits from the combustion chambers. Lay a straightedge across the head and check for flatness. Total deviation should not exceed 0.025mm.

To install:
21. Install the head gasket. Apply sealer to both sides of the new gasket; never to the head or block surfaces!
22. Place the head on the engine.
23a. For carbureted engines:
Using the acompanying illustration, coat No.8 head bolt threads with Permatex No.2 sealant. Install the head bolts. Torque all the head bolts in sequence, in three even steps. The final step should be 85 ft. lbs. for all bolts except No.8. That bolt is torqued to 75 ft. lbs.
23b. For fuel injected engines:
Using the acompanying illustration, coat No.8 head bolt threads with Permatex No.2 sealant. Install the head bolts. Torque all the head bolts in sequence, in three even steps. The final step should be 110 ft. lbs. for all bolts except No.8. That bolt is torqued to 100 ft. lbs.

NOTE: *Some head bolts used on the spark plug side of the 1984 4-150 were improperly hardened and may break under the head during service or at head installation while torquing the bolts. Engines with the defective bolts are serial numbers 310U06 through 310U14. Whenever a broken bolt is found, replace all bolts on the spark plug side of the head with bolt #400 6593.*

24. Connect the temperature sending unit wire.
25. Install the spark plugs.
26. Install the compressor/alternator bracket mounting bolt.
27. Loosen the alternator drive belt.
28. Install the air conditioning compressor drive belt.
29. Install the intake and exhaust manifolds.
30. Install the power steering pump bracket.
31. Install the pushrods. Keep them in order!
32. Install the rocker arms. Keep them in order!
33. Install the rocker arm cover. The cover gasket is RTV sealer. Thoroughly clean the mating surfaces of the head and rocker cover. Run a 1/8 inch bead of RTV sealer along the length of the sealing surface of the head. Position the cover on the head within 10 minutes of applying the sealer. Torque the cover bolts, in a crisscross pattern, to 55 in. lbs.
34. Install the air cleaner.
35. Connect the hoses at the thermostat housing.
36. Fill the cooling system.
37. Connect the battery ground.

6-173
LEFT SIDE
1. Disconnect the negative battery cable. Raise and support the vehicle safely. Discon-

ENGINE AND ENGINE OVERHAUL

nect the exhaust pipe from the exhaust manifold.
2. Drain the coolant from the block and lower the vehicle.
CAUTION: *When draining the coolant, keep in mind that cats and dogs are attracted by the ethylene glycol antifreeze, and are quite likely to drink any that is left in an uncovered container or in puddles on the ground. This will prove fatal in sufficient quantity. Always drain the coolant into a sealable container. Coolant should be reused unless it is contaminated or several years old.*
3. Remove the intake manifold.
4. Remove the exhaust manifold.
5. If equipped, remove the power steering pump and bracket.
6. Remove the dipstick tube.
7. Loosen the rocker arm bolts and remove the pushrods. Keep the pushrods in the same order as removed.
8. Remove the cylinder head bolts in stages and in the reverse order of the tightening sequence.
9. Remove the cylinder head. Do not pry on the head to loosen it.
To install:
10. Thoroughly clean the head and block mating surfaces. All bolt holes must be free of foreign material.
11. Place a new head gasket on the block with the words **This Side Up**, up.
12. Position the cylinder head on the block.
13. Coat the cylinder head bolts with RTV silicone sealant and install them. Torque the bolts, in sequence, in three equal stages. The final stage should be 70 ft. lbs.
14. Install the pushrods, keeping them in the same order as removed.
15. Install the rocker arms.
16. Remove the dipstick tube.
17. Install the power steering pump and bracket.
18. Install the exhaust manifold.
19. Install the intake manifold.
20. Connect the exhaust pipe from the exhaust manifold.
21. Fill the cooling system.
22. Connect the negative battery cable.
23. Adjust the valves.

RIGHT SIDE
1. Disconnect the negative battery cable. Raise and support the vehicle safely. Drain the coolant from the block.
CAUTION: *When draining the coolant, keep in mind that cats and dogs are attracted by the ethylene glycol antifreeze, and are quite likely to drink any that is left in an uncovered container or in puddles on the ground. This will prove fatal in sufficient quantity. Always drain the coolant into a sealable container. Coolant should be reused unless it is contaminated or several years old.*
2. Disconnect the exhaust pipe and lower the vehicle.
3. If equipped, remove the cruise control servo bracket.
4. Remove the alternator and air pump bracket assembly.
5. Remove the intake manifold.
6. Loosen the rocker arm nuts and remove the pushrods. Keep the pushrods in the order in which they were removed.
7. Remove the cylinder head bolts in stages and in the reverse order of the tightening sequence.
8. Remove the cylinder head. Do not pry on the cylinder head to loosen it.
To install:
9. Thoroughly clean the head and block mating surfaces. All bolt holes must be free of foreign material.
10. Place a new head gasket on the block with the words **This Side Up**, up.
11. Position the cylinder head on the block.
12. Coat the cylinder head bolts with RTV silicone sealant and install them. Torque the bolts, in sequence, in three equal stages. The final stage should be 70 ft. lbs.
13. Install the pushrods, keeping them in the same order as removed.
14. Install the rocker arms.
15. Install the exhaust manifold.
16. Install the intake manifold.
17. Connect the exhaust pipe from the exhaust manifold.
18. Fill the cooling system.
19. Connect the negative battery cable.
20. Adjust the valves.

6-243

1. Drain the cooling system and disconnect the hoses at the thermostat housing.
CAUTION: *When draining the coolant, keep in mind that cats and dogs are attracted by the ethylene glycol antifreeze, and are quite likely to drink any that is left in an uncovered container or in puddles on the ground. This will prove fatal in sufficient quantity. Always*

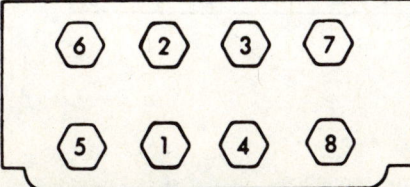

6-173 head bolt torque sequence

128 ENGINE AND ENGINE OVERHAUL

drain the coolant into a sealable container. Coolant should be reused unless it is contaminated or several years old.

2. Remove the cylinder head cover (valve cover), the gasket, the rocker arm assembly, and the pushrods.

NOTE: *The pushrods must be replaced in their original positions.*

3. Remove the intake and exhaust manifold from the cylinder head.
4. Disconnect the spark plug wires and the spark plugs to avoid damaging them.
5. Disconnect the temperature sending unit wire, ignition coil and bracket assembly from the engine.
6. Unbolt and set aside the power steering pump and bracket. Do not disconnect the hoses.
7. Remove the intake and exhaust manifold assembly.
8. Remove the air conditioning compressor drive belt pulley.
9. Loosen the serpentine belt tension.
10. Remove the alternator.
11. Unbolt the air conditioning compressor and set it aside. Don't disconnect the refrigerant lines.
12. Remove the ignition coil.
13. Remove the cylinder head bolts, the cylinder head and gasket from the block.
14. Discard the gasket. Thoroughly clean the head and block mating surfaces. Check them for warpage with a straightedge. Deviation should not exceed 0.002" in a 6" span.

To install:

15. Coat a new head gasket with sealer and place it on the block. Most replacement gaskets will have the word TOP stamped on them.
16. Install the cylinder head and bolts. The threads of bolt No.11 must be coated with Loctite®592 sealant before installation. Tighten the bolts in sequence, using the accompanying illustration to 22 ft. lbs. Then, torque them to 45 ft. lbs. in sequence. When that's done, check the torque at 45 ft. lbs. on all bolts in sequence. Then, torque all the bolts in sequence to 110 ft. lbs., except for No.11. That one is torqued to 100 ft. lbs.
17. Install the ignition coil.
18. Install the air conditioning compressor.
19. Install the alternator.
20. Adjust the serpentine belt tension.
21. Install the air conditioning compressor drive belt pulley.
22. Install the intake and exhaust manifold assembly.
23. Install the power steering pump and bracket.
24. Connect the temperature sending unit wire, ignition coil and bracket.
25. Connect the spark plug wires.
26. Install the pushrods, rocker arm assembly, gasket, and cylinder head cover.
27. Connect the hoses at the thermostat housing.
28. Fill the cooling system.

CLEANING AND INSPECTION

1. With the valves installed to protect the valve seats, remove deposits from the combustion chambers and valve heads with a scraper and a wire brush. Be careful not to damage the cylinder head gasket surface. After the valves are removed, clean the valve guide bores with a valve guide cleaning tool. Using cleaning solvent to remove dirt, grease and other deposits, clean all bolts holes; be sure the oil passage is clean (V6 engines).
2. Remove all deposits from the valves with a fine wire brush or buffing wheel.
3. Inspect the cylinder heads for cracks or ex-

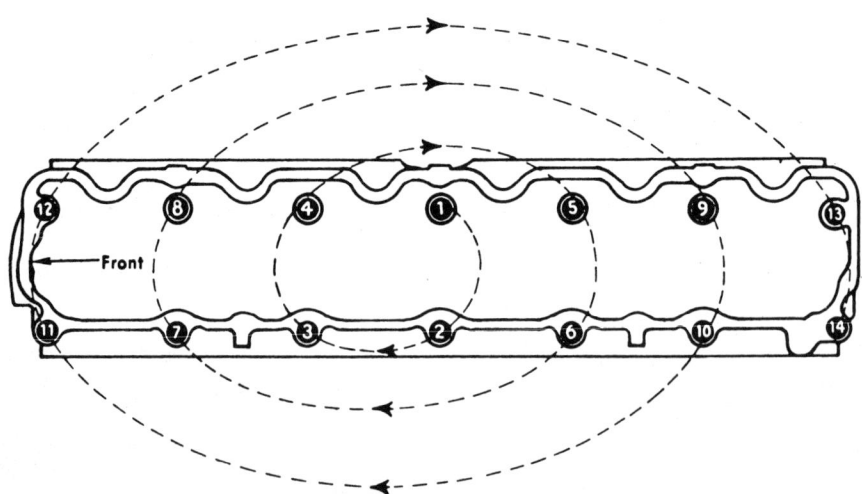

6-243 cylinder head bolt torque sequence

cessively burned areas in the exhaust outlet ports.

4. Check the cylinder head for cracks and inspect the gasket surface for burrs and nicks. Replace the head if it is cracked.

5. On cylinder heads that incorporate valve seat inserts, check the inserts for excessive wear, cracks, or looseness.

RESURFACING

Cylinder Head Flatness

When the cylinder head is removed, check the flatness of the cylinder head gasket surfaces.

1. Place a straightedge across the gasket surface of the cylinder head. Using feeler gauges, determine the clearance at the center of the straightedge.

2. If warpage exceeds 0.003" in a 6" span, or 0.006" (0.008" for the diesel) over the total length, the cylinder head must be resurfaced.

3. If necessary to refinish the cylinder head gasket surface, do not plane or grind off more than 0.010" (0.002" for the diesel) from the original gasket surface.

NOTE: *When milling the cylinder heads of V6 engines, the intake manifold mounting position is altered, and must be corrected by milling the manifold flange a proportionate amount. Consult an experienced machinist about this.*

Valves and Springs

NOTE: *Fabricate a valve arrangement board to use when you remove the valves, which will indicate the port in which each valve was originally installed (and which cylinder head on V6 models). Also note that the valve keys, rotators, caps, etc. should be arranged in a manner which will allow you to install them on the valve on which they were originally used.*

REMOVAL

1. Remove the cylinder head.
2. Remove the rocker arm assemblies.
3. Using a spring compressor, compress the valve springs and remove the keepers (locks). Relax the compressor and remove the washers or rotators, the springs and the lower washers (on some engines). Keep all parts in order.
4. Slide the valve seals from the stems and slide the valves from the head, keeping them in order for installation.

INSPECTION AND REFACING

1. Clean the valves with a wire wheel.
2. Inspect the valves for warping, cracks or wear.

3. The valves may be refaced if not worn or pitted excessively.

4. Using a valve guide cleaner chucked into a drill, clean all of the valve guides. Check the valve stem diameter and the guide diameter with micrometers. Valve guides on the 4-126 diesel are replaceable. On the other engines, the guides must be reamed and inserts pressed in, or they may be knurled to bring up interior metal, restoring their diameter. Oversized valve stems are available to compensate for wear.

5. Install each valve into its respective port (guide) of the cylinder head.

6. Mount a dial indicator so that the stem is at 90° to the valve stem, as close to the valve guide as possible.

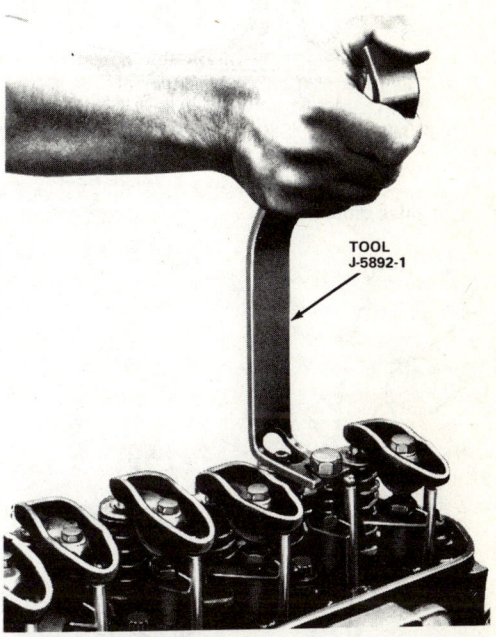

Using a valve spring compressor

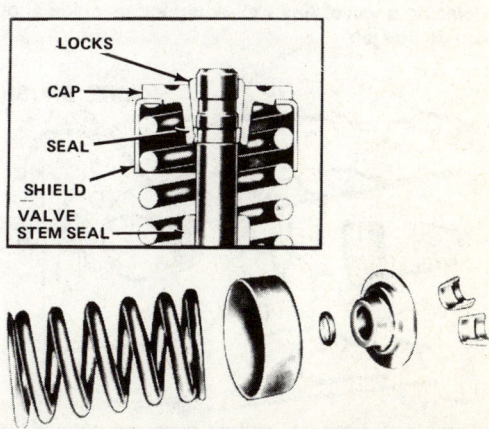

Typical upper valve train components

ENGINE AND ENGINE OVERHAUL

7. Move the valve off its seat, and measure the valve guide-to-stem clearance by rocking the stem back and forth to actuate the dial indicator.

8. The valve guide, if worn, must be repaired before the valve seats can be resurfaced. Ford supplies valves with oversize stems to fit valve guides that are reamed to oversize for repair. The machine shop will be able to handle the guide reaming for you. In some cases, if the guide is not too badly worn, knurling may be all that is required.

9. Reface, or have the valves and valve seats refaced. The valve seats should be a true 45° angle. Remove only enough material to clean up any pits or grooves. Be sure the valve seat is not too wide or narrow. Use a 60° grinding wheel to remove material from the bottom of the seat for raising and a 30° grinding wheel to remove material from the top of the seat to narrow.

10. After the valves are refaced by machine, hand lap them to the valve seat. Clean the grinding compound off and check the position of face-to-seat contact. Contact should be close

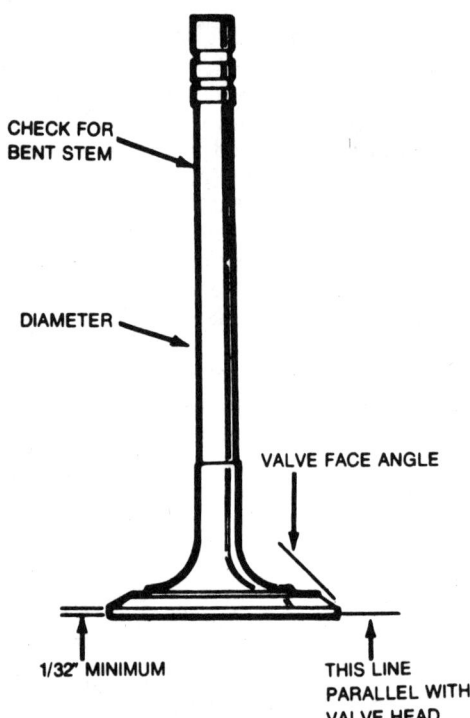

Critical valve dimensions

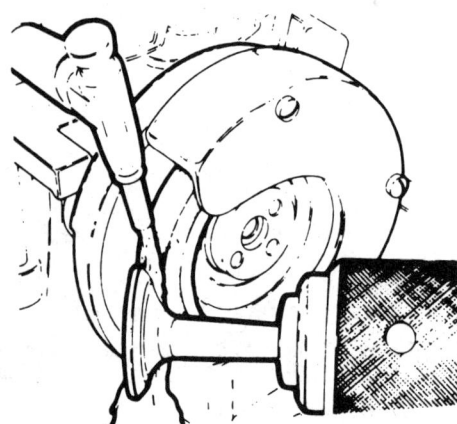

Refacing a valve. Any well equipped machine shop can do this job

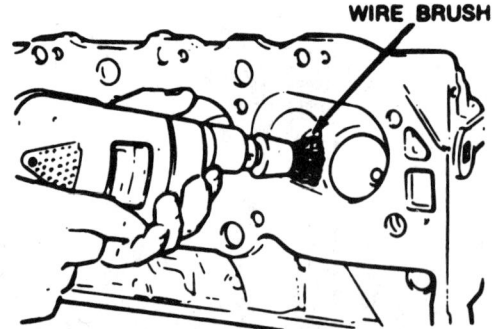

Remove all traces of carbon from the combustion chambers with a drill-mounted wire brush

Checking valve seat concentricity with a dial gauge

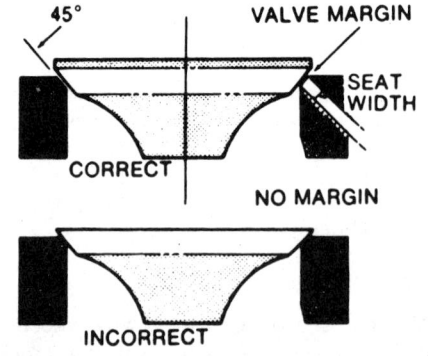

Valve seat width and centering after proper reaming

ENGINE AND ENGINE OVERHAUL 131

to the center of the valve face. If contact is close to the top edge of the valve, narrow the seat; if too close to the bottom edge, raise the seat.

11. Valves should be refaced to a true angle of 45°. Remove only enough metal to clean up the valve face or to correct runout. If the edge of a valve head, after machining, is $\frac{1}{32}''$ (0.8mm) or less replace the valve. The tip of the valve stem should also be dressed on the valve grinding machine, however, do not remove more than 0.010″ (0.254mm).

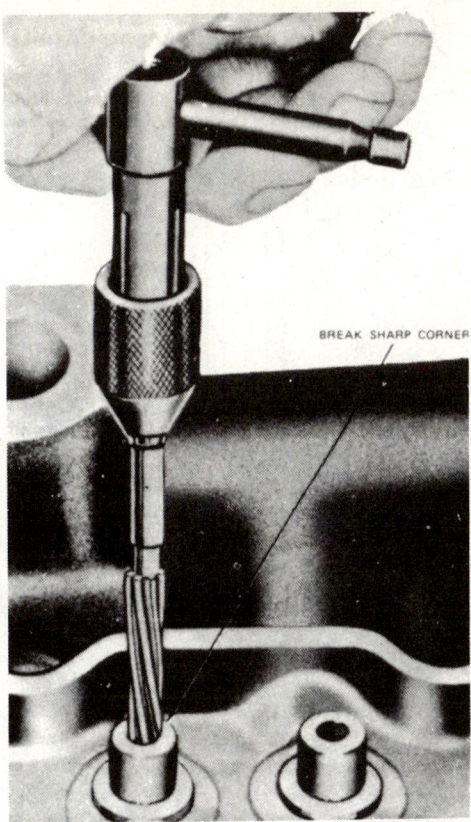

Close-up of a hand reamer

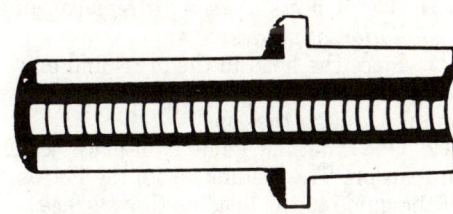

Cross section of a knurled valve guide

Lapping the valves by hand. The finish should be smooth; shiny and uniform

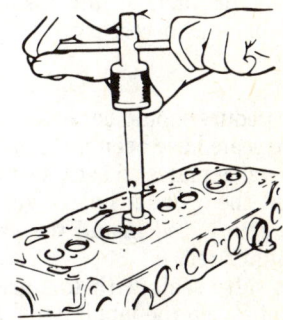

Reaming a valve seat with a hand reamer

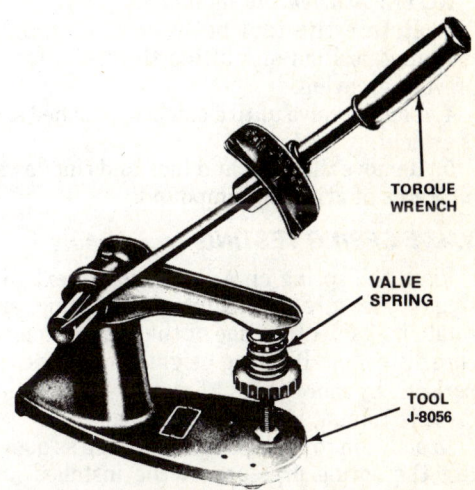

Testing a valve spring

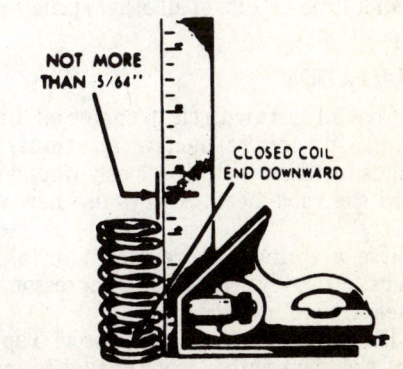

Check the valve spring free length and squareness

132 ENGINE AND ENGINE OVERHAUL

12. After all valve and valve seats have been machined, check the remaining valve train parts (springs, retainers, keepers, etc.) for wear. Check the valve springs for straightness and tension.
13. Install the valves in the cylinder head and metal caps.
14. Install new valve stem oil seals.
15. Install the valve keepers, retainer, spring shield and valve spring using a valve spring compressor (the locking C-clamp type is the easiest kind to use).
16. Check the valve spring installed height, shim or replace as necessary.

LAPPING

This procedure should be performed after the valves and seats have been machined, to insure that each valve mates to each seat precisely.

1. Invert the cylinder head, lightly lubricate the valve stems, and install the valves in the head as numbered.
2. Coat valve seats with fine grinding compound, and attach the lapping tool suction cup to a valve head.

NOTE: *Moisten the suction cup.*

3. Rotate the tool between your palms, changing position and lifting the tool often to prevent grooving.
4. Lap the valve until a smooth, polished seat is evident.
5. Remove the valve and tool, and rinse away all traces of grinding compound.

VALVE SPRING TESTING

Place the spring on a flat surface next to a square. Measure the height of the spring, and rotate it against the edge of the square to measure distortion. If spring height varies (by comparison) by more than 1.5mm or if distortion exceeds 1.5mm, replace the spring.

In addition to evaluating the spring as above, test the spring pressure at the installed and compressed (installed height minus valve lift) height using a valve spring tester. Spring pressure should be ± 1 lb. of all other springs in either position.

INSTALLATION

1. Coat all parts with clean engine oil. Install all parts in their respective locations. The spring is installed with the closely wound coils toward the valve head. Always use new valve seals.
2. Use a spring compressor to install the keepers and slowly release the compressor after the keepers are in place.
3. Release the spring compressor. Tap the end of the stem with a wood mallet to insure that the keepers are securely in place.

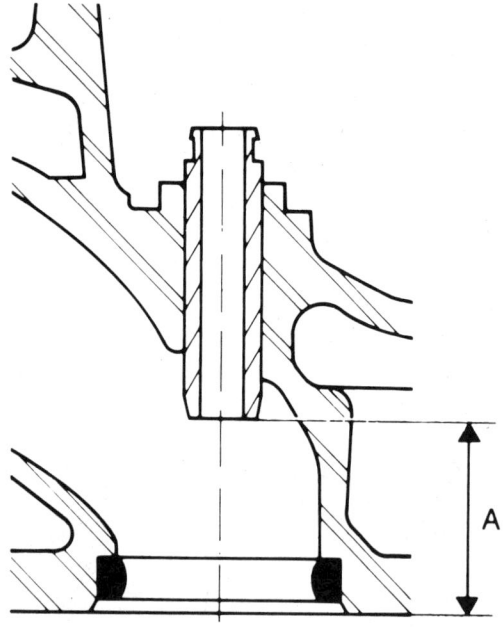

Measuring valve guide protrusion on the 4-126 diesel

4. Install all other parts in reverse order of removal.

Valve Guides

REMOVAL AND INSTALLATION

4-126 diesel

NOTE: *A press is used for removal and installation of guides.*

1. Place the head in the press and press the old guide out through the bottom and the new one in through the top.
2. Once the new guide is in place, check its protrusion. The distance from the bottom end of the guide to the head mating surface should be 32.5mm.
3. On all three engines, after the guides are in place, they must be reamed to 8mm.

Valve Seats

INSPECTION AND REFACING

All engines have integral seats. Check the condition of the seats for excessive wear, pitting or cracks. Remove all traces of deposits from the seats. The seats may be refaced with a special grinding tool, to the dimensions shown in the Valve Specifications Charts.

Valve Stem Oil Seal

REPLACEMENT WITH THE CYLINDER HEAD INSTALLED

Gasoline Engines

If valve stem oil seals are found to be the cause of excessive oil consumption, they may be replaced without removing the cylinder block.

ENGINE AND ENGINE OVERHAUL

1. Remove the air cleaner.
2. Remove rocker arm covers and spark plugs.
3. Detach the coil wire from the distributor.
4. Turn the engine so that no. 1 cylinder is at Top Dead Center on the compression stroke. Both Valves for no. 1 cylinder should be fully closed and the crankshaft damper timing mark at TDC. The distributor rotor will point at the no. 1 spark plug wire location in the cap.
5. Remove the rocker shaft and install a dummy shaft.
6. Apply 90 - 100 psi air pressure to no. 1 cylinder, using a spark plug hole air hose adaptor.
7. Use a valve spring compressor to compress each no. 1 cylinder valve spring and remove the retainer locks and the spring. Remove the old seals.
8. Install a cup shield on the exhaust valve stem. Position it down against the valve guide.
9. Push the intake valve stem seal firmly and squarely over the valve guide.
10. Compress the valve spring only enough to install the lock.
11. Repeat the operation on each successive cylinder in the firing order, making sure that the crankshaft is exactly on TDC for each cylinder. See the Firing Order and Distributor Rotation illustrations in the Specifications section of this chapter for cylinder numbering.
12. Replace the rocker arms, covers, spark plugs and coil wire.

Crankshaft Pulley (Vibration Damper)

REMOVAL AND INSTALLATION

1. Remove the fan shroud, as required.
2. On those engines with a separate pulley, remove the retaining bolts and separate the pulley from the vibration damper.
3. Remove the vibration damper/pulley retaining bolt from the crankshaft end.
4. Using a puller, remove the damper/pulley from the crankshaft.
5. Upon installation, align the key slot of the pulley hub to the crankshaft key. Complete the assembly in the reverse order of removal. Torque the retaining bolts to specifications.

Oil Pan

REMOVAL AND INSTALLATION

4-126 Diesel

1. Disconnect the negative battery cable. Raise and support the vehicle safely. Remove the converter housing shield, as required.
2. Drain the engine oil. This engine has two oil drain plugs, both must be opened.
3. Remove all the necessary components in order to gain access to the oil pan retaining bolts.

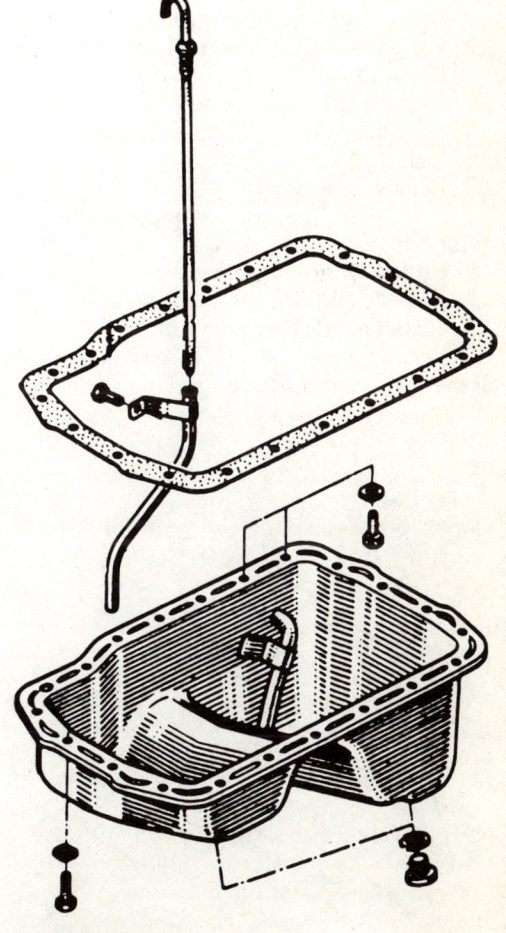

4-126 oil pan

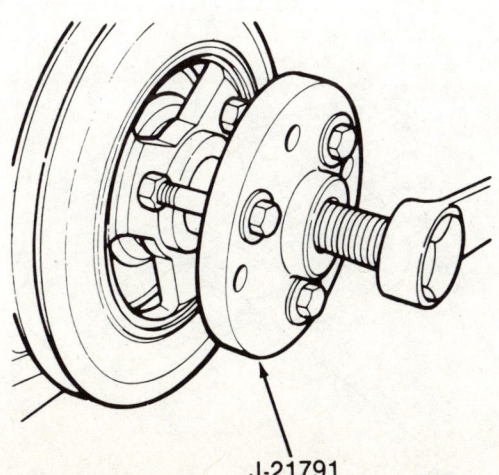

J-21791

Using a puller to remove the crankshaft damper

134 ENGINE AND ENGINE OVERHAUL

4. Remove the oil pan retaining bolts. Remove the oil pan from the engine.
5. Installation is the reverse of removal. Torque the bolts to 79 in. lbs.

4-150

1. Disconnect the battery ground.
2. Raise and support the truck on jackstands.
3. Drain the oil.
4. Disconnect the exhaust pipe at the manifold.
5. Remove the starter.
6. Remove the bellhousing access plate.
7. Unbolt and remove the oil pan.
8. Clean the gasket surfaces thoroughly.
9. Install a replacement seal at the bottom of the timing case cover and at the rear bearing cap.
10. Using new gaskets coated with sealer, install the pan and torque the ¼-20 bolts to 84 in. lbs.; the ⁵⁄₁₆-18 bolts to 11 ft. lbs.
11. Install all other parts in reverse order of removal.

6-173

1. Disconnect the battery ground.
2. Raise the support the truck on jackstands.
3. Drain the oil.
4. Remove the bellhousing access cover.
5. Disconnect the left exhaust pipe at the manifold.
6. Remove the starter.
7. Disconnect the exhaust pipe at the converter flange.
8. Unbolt and remove the pan.
9. Remove all RTV gasket material.
10. Install a new rear pan seal.
11. Apply a 3mm bead of RTV gasket material all the way around the pan sealing surface.

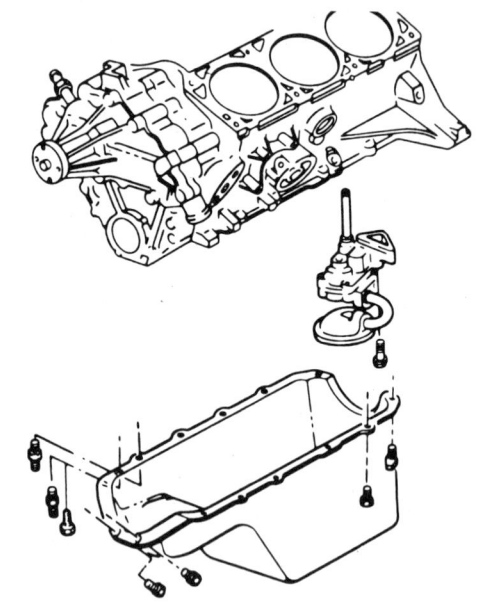

6-173 oil pan

12. Install the pan and torque the bolts to 12 ft. lbs.
13. Install all other parts in reverse order of removal.

6-243

1. Raise and support the front end on jackstands placed under the frame rails Allow the suspension to hang.
2. Drain the engine oil.
3. Remove the starter motor.
4. Remove all of the oil pan attaching bolts and remove the oil pan.
5. Remove the oil pan front and rear oil seals and side gaskets. Thoroughly clean the gasket

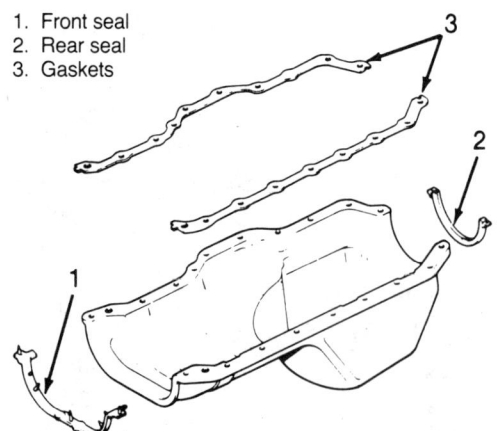

1. Front seal
2. Rear seal
3. Gaskets

4-150 oil pan gasket and seal positioning

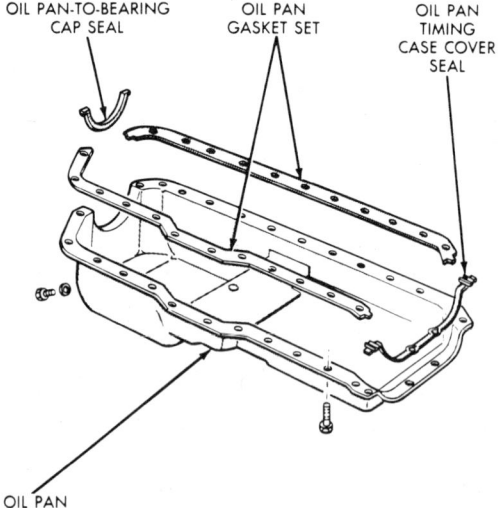

6-243 oil pan

ENGINE AND ENGINE OVERHAUL

surfaces of the oil pan and engine block. Remove all sludge and dirt from the oil pan sump.

6. When installing the front oil pan seal to the timing chain cover, apply a generous amount of Permatex® No. 2 to the end tabs. Also, cement the oil pan side gaskets to the mating surface on the bottom of the engine block. Coat the inside curved surface of the new oil pan rear seal with soap and apply a generous amount of Permatex® No. 2 to the gasket contacting surface of the seal end tabs.

7. Install the seal in the recess of the rear main bearing cap, making certain that it is fully seated.

8. Apply engine oil to the oil pan contacting surface of the front and rear oil pan seals.

9. Install the oil pan. Torque the ¼-20 bolts to 80 in. lbs.; the $^{5}/_{16}$-18 bolts to 11 ft. lbs.

10. Install the starter motor.

11. Fill the crankcase with oil.

Oil Pump

REMOVAL AND INSTALLATION

4-126 Diesel

NOTE: *Special tools are needed for this job.*

1. Disconnect the negative battery cable.
2. Remove the vacuum pump along with the oil pump drive gear.
3. Remove the timing belt cover. Loosen the intermediate shaft drive sprocket using tool MOT-855 or equivalent.
4. Remove the intermediate shaft bolt, sprocket, cover, clamp plate and intermediate shaft.
5. Raise and support the vehicle safely. Drain the engine oil. Remove the oil pan.
6. Remove the piston skirt cooling oil jet assembly to oil pump pipe.
7. Remove the oil pump retaining bolts. Remove the oil pump.
8. Be sure that the oil pump locating dowels are in place on the pump.
9. Inspect the gears for abnormal wear, chips, looseness on the shafts, galling, and scoring.
10. Inspect the cover and cavity for breaks, cracks, distortion, and abnormal wear.
11. Install the gears into the pump cavity, and with the use of a straight edge and feeler gauge, check the gear to housing clearance.
12. Repair or replace defective components as required.
13. Installation is the reverse of the removal procedure. Be sure to use new gaskets and seals as required. Torque the pump mounting bolts to 33 ft. lbs.

4-150

1. Remove the oil pan.
2. Unbolt and remove the pump assembly from the block. Discard the gasket.
3. Using a new gasket, install the pump on the block. Torque the short bolt to 10 ft. lbs. and the long bolt to 17 ft. lbs.
4. Install the pan.

6-173

1. Remove the oil pan.
2. Unbolt and remove the pump from the extension housing.
3. Installation is the reverse of removal. Torque the bolts to 25-30 ft. lbs.

6-243

1. Drain the oil and remove the oil pan.
2. Remove the oil pump retaining screws and separate the oil pump and gasket from the engine block.

NOTE: *Do not disturb the position of the oil pick-up tube and screen assembly in the*

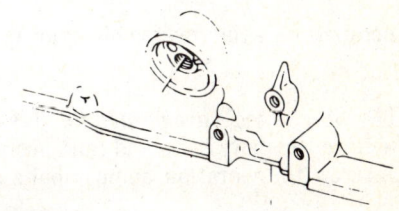

1. Bolts
2. Pump body
3. Gasket

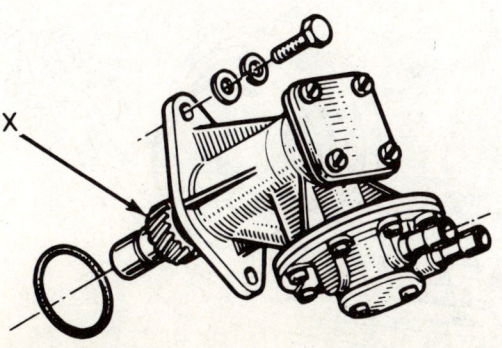

4-126 oil pump/vacuum pump combination. X is the drive gear

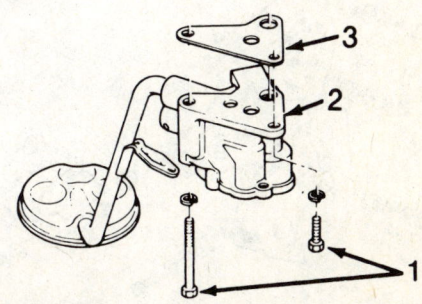

4-150 oil pump

136 ENGINE AND ENGINE OVERHAUL

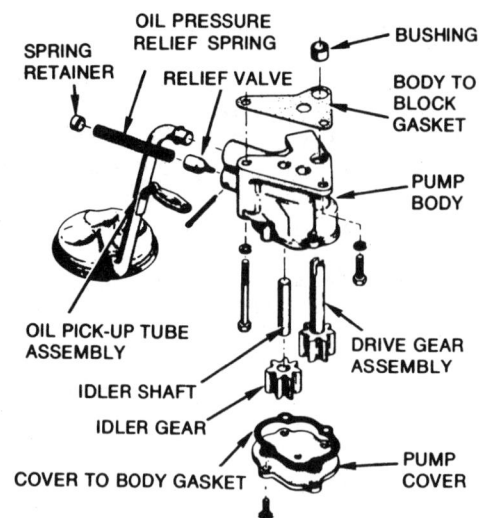

6-243 oil pump

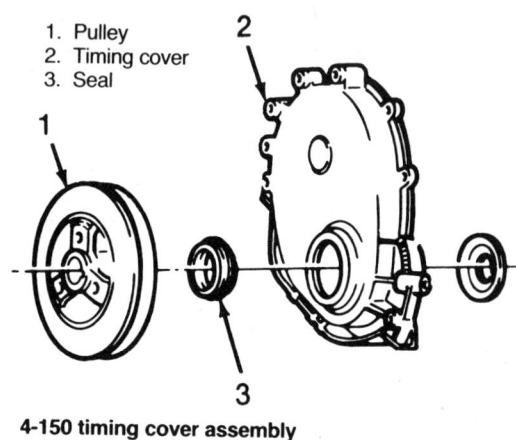

4-150 timing cover assembly

pump body. If the tube is moved within the pump body, a new assembly must be installed to assure an airtight seal.

3. Installation is the reverse of removal. Torque the short bolts to 10 ft. lbs.; the long bolts to 17 ft. lbs.

Timing Cover and Seal
REPLACEMENT
4-126 Diesel

1. Disconnect the negative battery cable.
2. Remove all necessary components in order to gain access to the timing belt cover bolts.
3. Remove the timing belt cover retaining bolts. Remove the timing belt cover from the engine.
4. Installation is the reverse of removal.

4-150

NOTE: *Special tools are needed for this job.*
1. Remove the drive belts and fan shroud.
2. Unscrew the vibration damper bolts and washer.

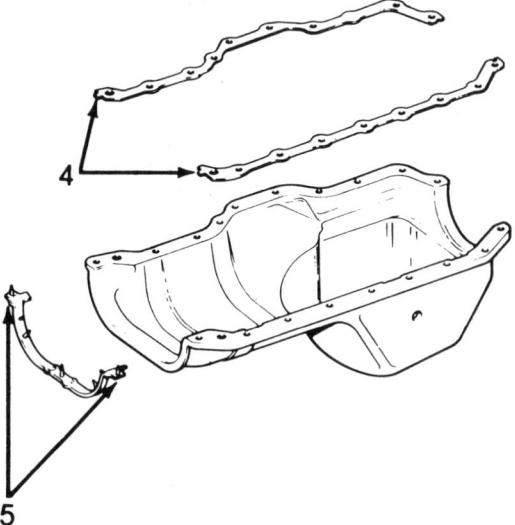

4-150 oil pan and gaskets

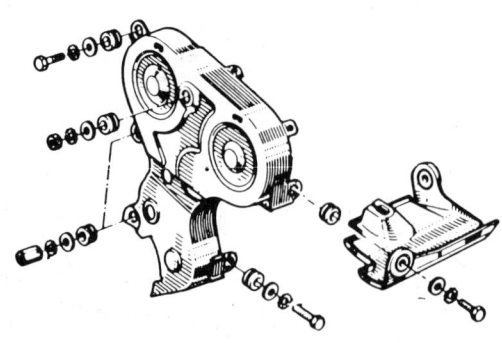

4-126 diesel timing belt cover

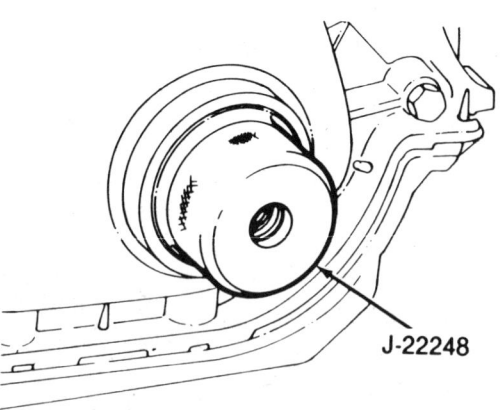

Timing cover centering tool for the 4-150/6-243

ENGINE AND ENGINE OVERHAUL 137

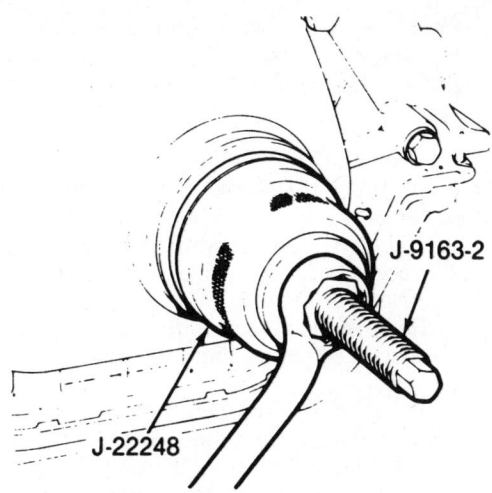

Oil seal installation tool for the 4-150/6-243

3. Using a puller, remove the vibration damper.
4. Remove the fan assembly. If the fan is equipped with a fan clutch DO NOT LAY IT DOWN! If you lay it down, the fluid will leak out of the clutch and irreversibly damage the fan.
5. Disconnect the battery ground.
6. Remove the air conditioning compressor/alternator bracket assembly and lay it out of the way. DO NOT DISCONNECT THE REFRIGERANT LINES!
7. Unbolt the cover from the block and oil pan. Remove the cover and front seal.
8. Cut off the oil pan side gasket end tabs and oil pan front seal tabs.
9. Clean all gasket mating surfaces thoroughly.
10. Remove the seal from the cover.
11. Apply sealer to both sides of the new case cover gasket and position it on the block.
12. Cut the end tabs off the new oil pan side gaskets corresponding to those cut off the original gasket and attach the tabs to the oil pan with gasket cement.
13. Coat the front cover seal end tab recesses generously with RTV sealant and position the side seal in the cover.
14. Apply engine oil to the seal-to-pan contact surface.
15. Position the cover on the block.
16. Insert alignment tool J-22248 into the crankshaft opening in the cover.
17. Install the cover bolts. Tighten the cover-to-block bolts to 5 ft. lbs.; the cover-to-pan bolts to 11 ft. lbs.
18. Remove the alignment tool and position the new front seal on the tool with the seal lip facing outward. Apply a light film of sealer to the outside diameter of the seal. Lightly coat the crankshaft with clean engine oil.
19. Position the tool and seal over the end of the crankshaft and insert the Draw Screw J-9163-2 into the installation tool.
20. Tighten the nut until the tool just contacts the cover.
21. Remove the tools and apply a light film of engine oil on the vibration damper hub contact surface of the seal.
22. With the key inserted in the keyway in the crankshaft, install the vibration damper, washer and bolt. Lubricate the bolt and tighten it to 108 ft. lbs.
23. Install all other parts in reverse order of removal.

6-173

1. Disconnect the battery ground.
2. Remove the drive belts.
3. Remove the fan shroud.
4. Remove the fan and pulley. If the fan is equipped with a fan clutch, DO NOT LAY IT ON ITS SIDE! If you do, the fluid will leak out and the fan clutch will have to be replaced.
5. Drain the cooling system.
CAUTION: *When draining the coolant, keep in mind that cats and dogs are attracted by the ethylene glycol antifreeze, and are quite likely to drink any that is left in an uncovered container or in puddles on the ground. This will prove fatal in sufficient quantity. Always drain the coolant into a sealable container. Coolant should be reused unless it is contaminated or several years old.*
6. Remove the air conditioning compressor and mounting bracket and position them out of the way. DO NOT DISCONNECT THE REFRIGERANT LINES!
7. Remove the water pump.
8. Remove the vibration damper retaining bolt and, using a puller, remove the damper.
NOTE: *On some vehicles the outer ring (weight) of the harmonic balancer is bonded to the hub with rubber. The balancer must be removed with a puller which acts on the inner hub only. Pulling on the outer portion of the balancer will break the rubber bond or destroy the tuning of the torsional damper.*
9. Disconnect the lower radiator hose.
10. Unbolt and remove the cover. Pry out the seal.
11. Thoroughly remove all traces of gasket material from the mating surfaces.
12. Position a new seal in the cover with the open end of the seal facing outward.
13. Apply a $3/32''$ bead of RTV silicone gasket material to the mating surfaces of the cover and block. Place the cover on the block and install the bolts. Torque the M8 x 1.25 bolts to 18 ft.

138 ENGINE AND ENGINE OVERHAUL

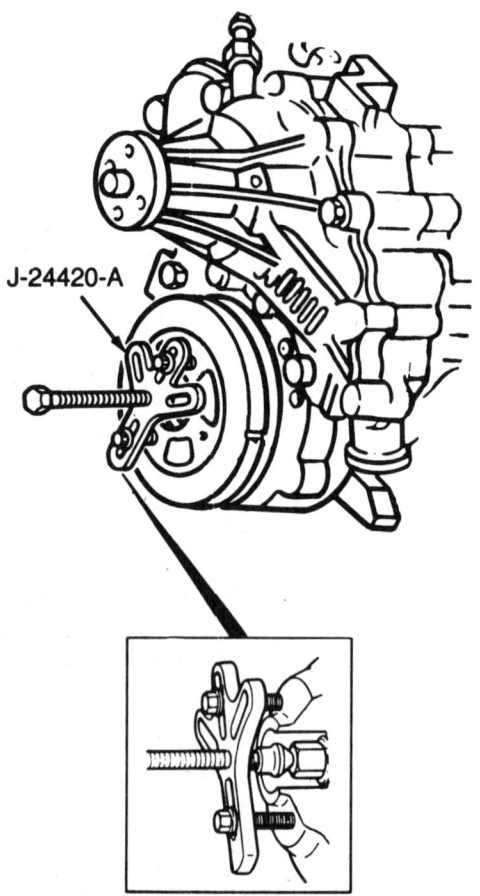

Using a puller to remove the vibration damper from a 6-173

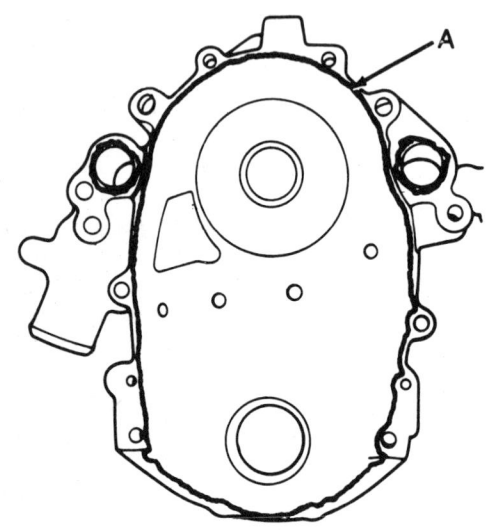

Sealer application on the 6-173 timing cover

NOTE: *Breakage may occur if the balancer is hammered back onto the crankshaft. A press or special installation tool is necessary.*

6-243

1. Remove the drive belts, engine fan and hub assembly, the accessory pulley and vibration damper.
2. Unbolt the air conditioning compressor and bracket and set it aside. Don't disconnect the refrigerant lines.
3. Remove the oil pan to timing chain cover screws and the screws that attach the cover to the block.
4. Raise the timing chain cover just high enough to detach the retaining nibs of the oil pan neoprene seal from the bottom side of the cover. This must be done to prevent pulling the seal end tabs away from the tongues of the oil pan gaskets, which would cause a leak.
5. Remove the timing chain cover and gasket from the engine.
6. Use a razor blade to cut off the oil pan seal end tabs flush with the front face of the cylinder block and remove the seal. Clean the timing chain cover, oil pan, and cylinder block surfaces.
7. Remove the crankshaft oil seal from the timing chain cover. Thoroughly clean the mating surfaces.

To install:

8. Apply RTV gasket material to both sides of the new gasket and position the gasket on the block.
9. Cut the end tabs off of the replacement oil pan side gaskets, corresponding to those cut off of the original gasket. Cement the end tabs to the oil pan.
10. Coat the front cover end tab recesses with a generous amount of RTV gasket sealant and position the seal on the timing case cover. Apply a coat of clean engine oil to the seal-to-pan contact surfaces.
11. Position the case cover on the block.

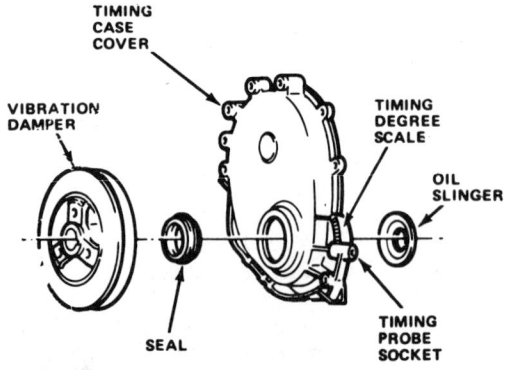

6-243 timing cover and seal

lbs.; the M10 x 1.5 bolts to 30 ft. lbs. Tighten the bolts within five minutes, as the sealer will begin to set.

14. Install all other parts in reverse order of removal.

ENGINE AND ENGINE OVERHAUL 139

12. Place cover alignment tool in the crankshaft opening of the cover.
13. Install the cover-to-block bolts and the oil pan-to-cover bolts. Torque the cover-to-block bolts to 62 in. lbs.; the cover-to-pan bolts to 11 ft. lbs.
14. Remove the alignment tool and position the seal on the tool with the lip facing outward.
15. Apply a light coat of sealer on the outside diameter of the seal.
16. Lightly coat the crankshaft with clean engine oil.
17. Position the tool and seal over the end of the crankshaft and insert a screw tool into the seal installation tool.
18. Tighten the nut against the tool until it contacts the cover.
19. Remove the tools and apply a light coating of engine oil on the vibration damper hub contact surface of the seal.
20. Install the damper.
21. Install all other parts in reverse order of removal.

Timing Belt

REMOVAL AND INSTALLATION

4-126 Diesel

NOTE: *Special tools are needed for this job.*

1. Disconnect the negative battery cable.
2. Remove the timing belt cover.
3. Install sprocket holding tool MOT-854 or equivalent and remove the camshaft sprocket retaining bolt. Remove the special tool.
4. Loosen the bolts and move the chain tensioner away from the timing belt. Tighten the tensioner bolts.

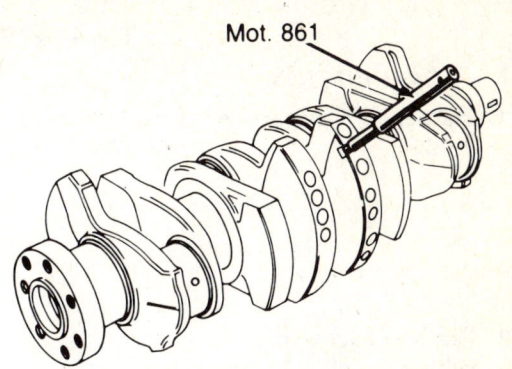

TDC locating tool in the crankshaft TDC locating slot

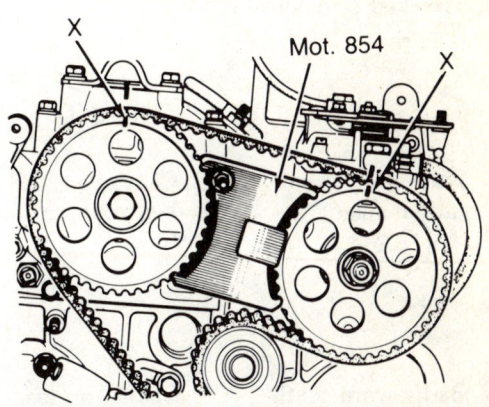

Camshaft and injection pump timing marks aligned on the 4-126 diesel

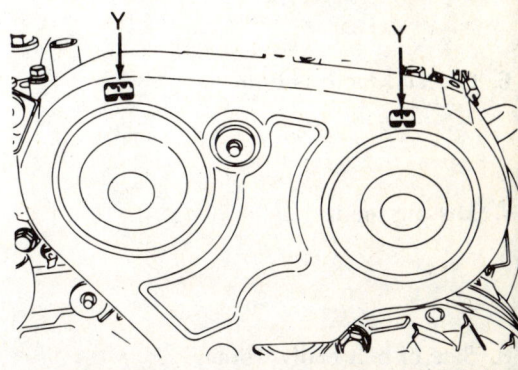

Indexing the timing cover slots and sprocket timing marks on the 4-126 diesel

5. Remove the timing belt from the sprockets. Inspect the belt, using the accompanying diagnosis chart.
6. If it is necessary to remove the fuel injection pump sprocket, use tools BVI-28-01 and BVI-859, or equivalent.

NOTE: *The following installation steps must be followed, exactly!*

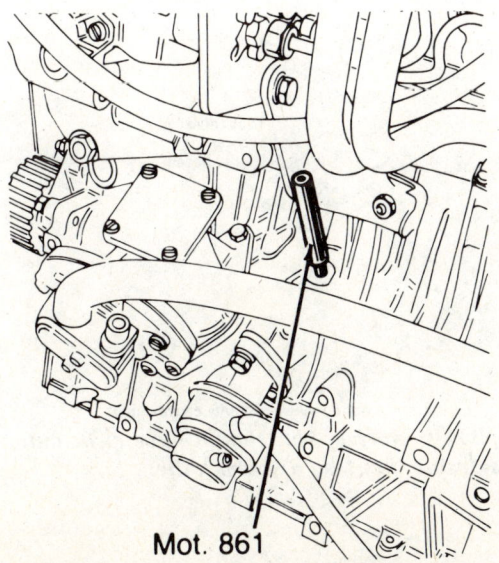

4-126 diesel TDC locating tool installed in the block

140 ENGINE AND ENGINE OVERHAUL

Timing Belt Wear

DESCRIPTION	FLAW CONDITIONS
1. Hardened back surface rubber	Back surface glossy. Non-elastic and so hard that even if a finger nail is forced into it, no mark is produced.

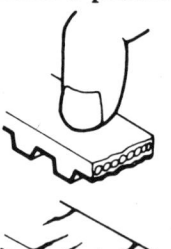

2. Cracked back surface rubber

3. Cracked or exfoliated canvas

4. Badly worn teeth (initial stage) — Canvas on load side tooth flank worn (Fluffy canvas fibers, rubber gone and color changed to white, and unclear canvas texture)

5. Badly worn teeth (last stage) — Canvas on load side tooth flank worn down and rubber exposed (tooth width reduced)

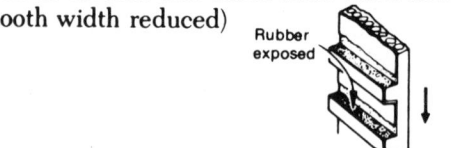

6. Cracked tooth bottom

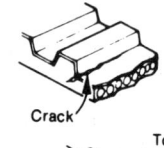

7. Missing tooth

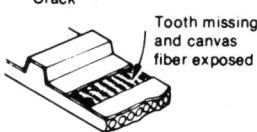

8. Side of belt badly worn

Abnormal wear (Fluffy canvas fiber)

NOTE: *Normal belt should have clear-cut sides as if cut by a sharp knife.*

9. Side of belt cracked

Timing belt wear diagnosis

ENGINE AND ENGINE OVERHAUL

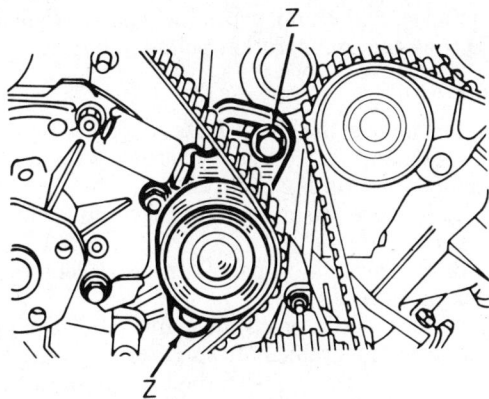

Timing belt tensioner adjusting bolts (Z) on the 4-126 diesel

7. Remove the access plug in the block, on the left side, and install the holding tool, Mot.861 in the hole. Rotate the crankshaft slowly, clockwise, until the tool drops into the TDC locating slot in the crankshaft counterweight.

NOTE: *Don't use this tool as a crankshaft holding tool. When tightening or loosening gear train fasteners, use a flywheel holding tool, such as tool Mot.582.*

8. Install sprocket holding tool, Mot.854 to retain the camshaft and injection pump sprockets. Make sure that the timing marks are positioned as shown.
9. Install the timing belt. There should be a total of 19 belt teeth between the camshaft and injection pump timing marks.
10. Temporarily position the timing cover over the sprockets. The camshaft and injection pump timing marks must index with the pointers in the cover's timing slots.
11. Remove the cover.
12. Remove the holding tool, Mot.854.
13. Make sure that the timing belt tensioner bolts are ½ turn loose, maximum.
14. The tensioner should, automatically, bear against the belt, giving the proper belt tension. Tighten the tensioner bolts.
15. Remove the TDC locating tool and install the plug.
16. Rotate the crankshaft, slowly, CLOCKWISE, two complete revolutions.

NOTE: *NEVER rotate the crankshaft counterclockwise while adjusting belt tension.*

17. Loosen the tensioner bolts ½ turn, maximum, then tighten them again.
18. Check the belt deflection at a point midway between the camshaft and injection pump sprockets. The belt should deflect 3-5mm.
19. Install the timing belt cover.

Timing Chain and Gears
REMOVAL AND INSTALLATION
4-150

1. Remove the timing case cover.
2. Rotate the crankshaft so that the timing marks on the cam and crank sprockets align next to each other, as illustrated.
3. Remove the oil slinger from the crankshaft.
4. Remove the cam sprocket retaining bolt and remove the sprocket and chain. The crank sprocket may also be removed at this time. If the tensioner is to be removed, the oil pan must be removed. first.
5. Prior to installation, turn the tensioner lever to the unlock (down) position.
6. Pull the tensioner block toward the tensioner to compress the spring. Hold the block and turn the tensioner lever to the lock (up) position. The camshaft sprocket bolt should be torqued to 50 ft. lbs.
7. Install the sprockets and chain together,

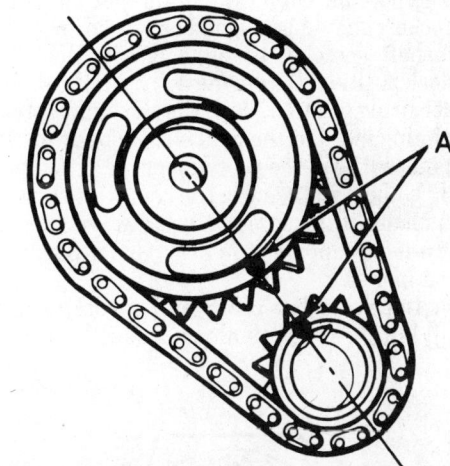

4-150 valve timing mark alignment

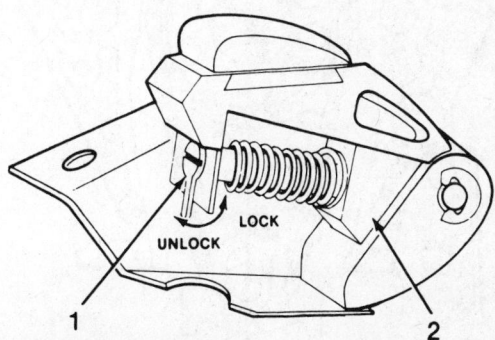

4-150 timing chain tensioner. 1 is the tensioner lever, 2 is the block

142 ENGINE AND ENGINE OVERHAUL

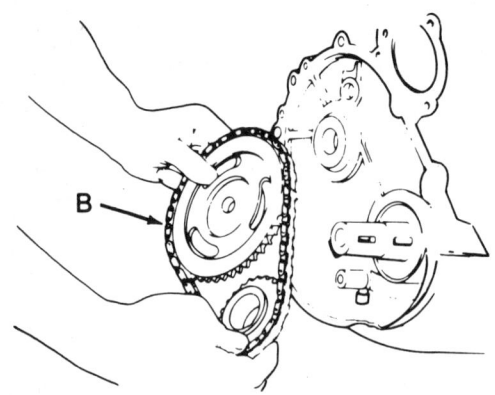

Installing the timing chain and sprockets on the 4-150

sprocket and chain, with the marks aligned. Torque the cam sprocket bolts to 20 ft. lbs.

6-243

1. Remove the drive belts, engine fan and hub assembly, accessory pulley, vibration damper and timing chain cover.
2. Remove the oil seal from the timing chain cover.
3. Remove the camshaft sprocket retaining bolt and washer.
4. Rotate the crankshaft until the timing mark on the crankshaft sprocket is closest to and in a center line with the timing pointer of the camshaft sprocket.
5. Remove the crankshaft sprocket, camshaft sprocket, and timing chain as an assembly. Disassemble the chain and sprockets.
6. Assemble the timing chain, crankshaft

as a unit. Make sure the timing marks are aligned.

8. Install the oil pan, slinger and timing cover.

6-173

1. Remove the timing cover.
2. Turn the crankshaft to bring the #1 piston to TDC of its compression stroke. The timing marks on the crankshaft and camshaft sprockets should be aligned as shown. With the camshaft sprocket timing mark at the 12:00 o'clock position, the engine will be in the #1 cylinder firing position. With the camshaft sprocket timing mark at the 6:00 o'clock position, the engine will be in the #4 cylinder firing position.
3. Unbolt and remove the camshaft sprocket and chain. If the sprocket is stuck, you can remove it by tapping it lightly with a plastic or wood mallet.
4. Lubricate the chain and sprockets with Molykote®, or equivalent. Install the cam

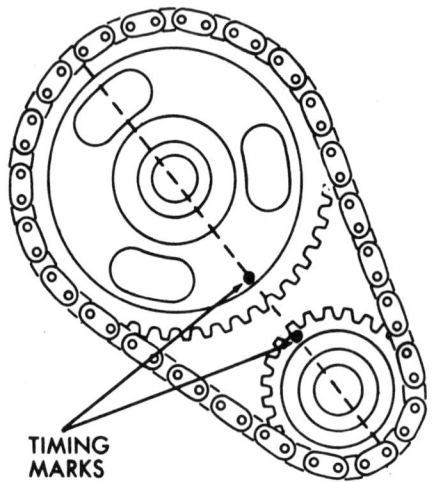

6-243 timing mark alignment

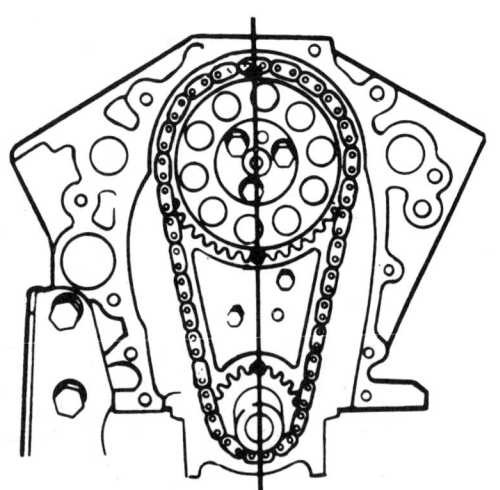

6-173 timing mark alignment

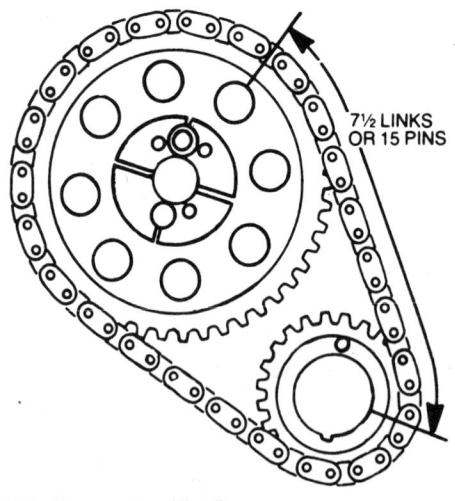

6-243 alignment verification

ENGINE AND ENGINE OVERHAUL

sprocket and camshaft sprocket with the timing marks aligned.

7. Install the assembly to the crankshaft and the camshaft. Double check the alignment by counting the number of links or pins with the sprockets positioned as illustrated. There must be 15 pins between the timing marks on both sprockets.

8. Install the camshaft sprocket retaining bolt and washer and tighten to 80 ft. lbs.

9. Install the timing chain cover and a new oil seal.

10. Install the vibration damper, accessory pulley, engine fan and hub assembly and drive belts. Tighten the belts to the proper tension.

Camshaft

REMOVAL AND INSTALLATION

NOTE: *Caution must be taken when performing this procedure. Camshaft bearings are coated with babbit material, which can be damaged by scraping the cam lobes across the bearing.*

4-126 Diesel

1. Disconnect the negative battery cable.
2. Drain the cooling system. Remove the valve cover. Remove the timing belt cover.

CAUTION: *When draining the coolant, keep in mind that cats and dogs are attracted by the ethylene glycol antifreeze, and are quite likely to drink any that is left in an uncovered container or in puddles on the ground. This will prove fatal in sufficient quantity. Always drain the coolant into a sealable container. Coolant should be reused unless it is contaminated or several years old.*

3. Remove the cylinder head. Remove the rocker arm shaft. Remove the camshaft gear. Remove the oil seal from the cylinder head by prying it out using a suitable tool. Remove the camshaft from the cylinder head.

4. Installation is the reverse of removal. Always use a new front seal. Hold the sprocket with holding tool Mot.855, or equivalent, while tightening the nut. Torque the nut to 37 ft. lbs.

4-150

CAUTION: *To remove perform this procedure the air conditioning system must be discharged. Mishandling of refrigerant gas can cause severe personal injury. If you are not completely familiar with the handling of refrigerant systems, have the system discharged by someone who is.*

1. Disconnect the battery ground.
2. Drain the cooling system.

CAUTION: *When draining the coolant, keep in mind that cats and dogs are attracted by the ethylene glycol antifreeze, and are quite likely to drink any that is left in an uncovered container or in puddles on the ground. This will prove fatal in sufficient quantity. Always drain the coolant into a sealable container. Coolant should be reused unless it is contaminated or several years old.*

3. Remove the radiator and condenser.
4. Remove the fuel pump.
5. Matchmark the distributor and engine for installation. Note the rotor position by marking it on the distributor body. Unbolt and remove the distributor and wires.
6. Remove the rocker arm cover.
7. Remove the rocker arm assemblies.
8. Remove the pushrods.

NOTE: *Keep everything in order for installation.*

9. Using a tool J-21884, or equivalent, remove the hydraulic lifters.

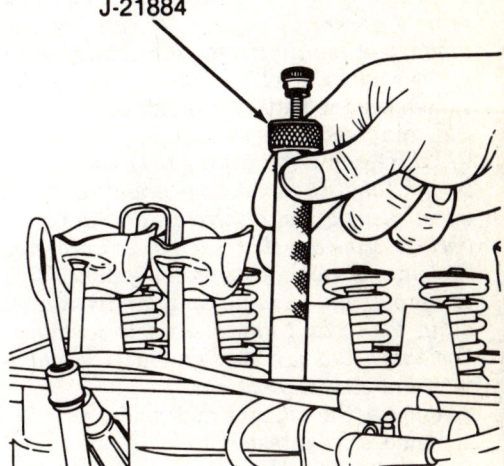

Using a special tool to remove the lifters from a 4-150/6-243

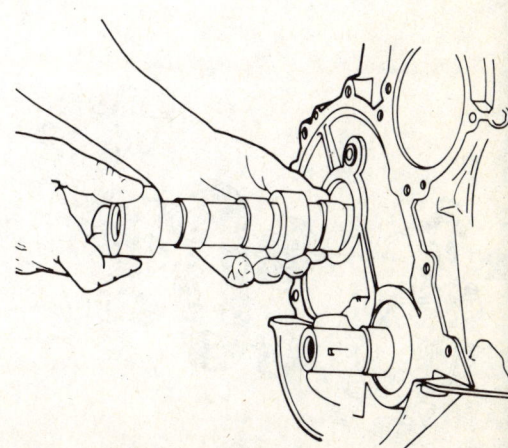

Removing the camshaft from a 4-150/6-243

ENGINE AND ENGINE OVERHAUL

10. Remove the timing case cover.
NOTE: *If the camshaft sprocket appears to have been rubbing against the cover, check the oil pressure relief holes in the rear cam journal for debris.*
11. Remove the timing chain and sprockets.
12. Slide the camshaft from the engine.
13. Installation is the reverse of removal. Inspect the camshaft for wear and damage. Lubricate all moving parts with engine oil supplement. When installing the distributor, make sure that all matchmarks align. Make sure that all camshaft timing marks align. It may be necessary to rotate the oil pump drive tang with a long-bladed screwdriver to facilitate installation of the distributor. Torque the camshaft sprocket bolt to 50 ft. lbs.

6-173

CAUTION: *This procedure requires discharge of the refrigerant gas. Mishandling of refrigerant gas can cause severe personal injury. If you are not completely familiar with air conditioning systems, give the job to someone who is.*
1. Remove the battery ground.
2. Drain the cooling system.
CAUTION: *When draining the coolant, keep in mind that cats and dogs are attracted by the ethylene glycol antifreeze, and are quite likely to drink any that is left in an uncovered container or in puddles on the ground. This will prove fatal in sufficient quantity. Always drain the coolant into a sealable container. Coolant should be reused unless it is contaminated or several years old.*
3. Remove the radiator and condenser.
4. Remove the intake manifold.
5. Remove the fuel pump.
6. Remove the pushrods.
7. Remove the tappets.
8. Remove the timing case cover.

Camshaft removal for the 6-173

9. Remove the timing chain and sprockets.
10. Carefully slide the camshaft from the block.
11. Inspect the camshaft for wear or damage. If any journal is more than 0.025mm out of round, replace the camshaft.
12. Installation is the reverse of removal. Coat all parts with engine oil supplement, prior to installation. Whenever a new camshaft is installed, replace the oil filter and all the tappets. Torque the camshaft sprocket bolts to 20 ft. lbs.

6-243

CAUTION: *This procedure requires discharge of the refrigerant gas on those trucks not equipped with quick-disconnect couplings. Mishandling of refrigerant gas can cause severe personal injury. If you are not completely familiar with air conditioning systems, give the job to someone who is.*
1. Drain the cooling system and remove the radiator.
CAUTION: *When draining the coolant, keep in mind that cats and dogs are attracted by the ethylene glycol antifreeze, and are quite likely to drink any that is left in an uncovered container or in puddles on the ground. This will prove fatal in sufficient quantity. Always drain the coolant into a sealable container. Coolant should be reused unless it is contaminated or several years old*
2. Remove the condenser and receiver/drier as a charged unit.
3. Remove the valve cover and gasket, the rocker assemblies, pushrods, cylinder head and gasket and the lifters.
NOTE: *The pushrods must be replaced in their original locations.*
4. Remove the drive belts, cooling fan, fan hub assembly, vibration damper and the timing chain cover.
5. Remove the distributor assembly, including the spark plug wires.
6. Remove the cylinder head.
7. Remove the valve lifters. Keep them in order for installation.
8. Rotate the crankshaft until the timing mark of the crankshaft sprocket is adjacent to, and on a center line with, the timing mark of the camshaft sprocket.
9. Remove the crankshaft sprocket, camshaft sprocket, and the timing chain as an assembly.
10. Remove the front bumper or grille as required and carefully slide out the camshaft.
To install:
11. Lubricate the camshaft with an engine oil supplement.
12. Slide the camshaft into the block carefully to avoid damage to the bearings.

ENGINE AND ENGINE OVERHAUL

13. Install the crankshaft sprocket, camshaft sprocket, and the timing chain as an assembly.
14. Make sure the timing mark of the crankshaft sprocket is adjacent to, and on a center line with, the timing mark of the camshaft sprocket. Torque the camshaft sprocket bolt to 80 ft. lbs.
15. Install the valve lifters.
16. Install the cylinder head.
17. Install the distributor assembly.
18. Install the timing chain cover, vibration damper, fan hub, cooling fan and the drive belts.
19. Install the pushrods, the rocker assemblies, valve cover and gasket.
20. Install the condenser and receiver/drier as a charged unit.
21. Install the radiator.
22. Fill the cooling system.

CHECKING CAMSHAFT

Camshaft Lobe Lift

Check the lift of each lobe in consecutive order and make a note of the reading.

1. Remove the fresh air inlet tube and the air cleaner. Remove the heater hose and crankcase ventilation hoses. Remove valve rocker arm cover(s).
2. Remove the rocker arm stud nut or fulcrum bolts, fulcrum seat and rocker arm.
3. Make sure the pushrod is in the valve tappet socket. Install a dial indicator so that the actuating point of the indicator is in the pushrod socket (or the indicator ball socket adaptor is on the end of the pushrod) and in the same plane as the push rod movement.
4. Install an auxiliary starter switch Crank the engine with the ignition switch off. Turn the crankshaft over until the tappet is on the base circle of the camshaft lobe. At this position, the pushrod will be in its lowest position.
5. Zero the dial indicator. Continue to rotate the crankshaft slowly until the pushrod is in the fully raised position.
6. Compare the total lift recorded on the dial indicator with the specification shown on the Camshaft Specification chart.

To check the accuracy of the original indicator reading, continue to rotate the crankshaft until the indicator reads zero. If the left on any lobe is below specified wear limits listed, the camshaft and the valve tappet operating on the worn lobe(s) must be replaced.

7. Install the dial indicator and auxiliary starter switch.
8. Install the rocker arm, fulcrum seat and stud nut or fulcrum bolts. Check the valve clearance. Adjust if required (refer to procedure in this chapter).

9. Install the valve rocker arm cover(s) and the air cleaner.

Camshaft End Play

NOTE: *On engines with an aluminum or nylon camshaft sprocket, prying against the sprocket, with the valve train load on the camshaft, can break or damage the sprocket. Therefore, the rocker arm adjusting nuts must be backed off, or the rocker arm and shaft assembly must be loosened sufficiently to free the camshaft. After checking the camshaft end play, check the valve clearance. Adjust if required (refer to procedure in this chapter).*

1. Push the camshaft toward the rear of the engine. Install a dial indicator so that the indicator point is on the camshaft sprocket attaching screw.
2. Zero the dial indicator. Position a prybar between the camshaft gear and the block. Pull the camshaft forward and release it. Compare

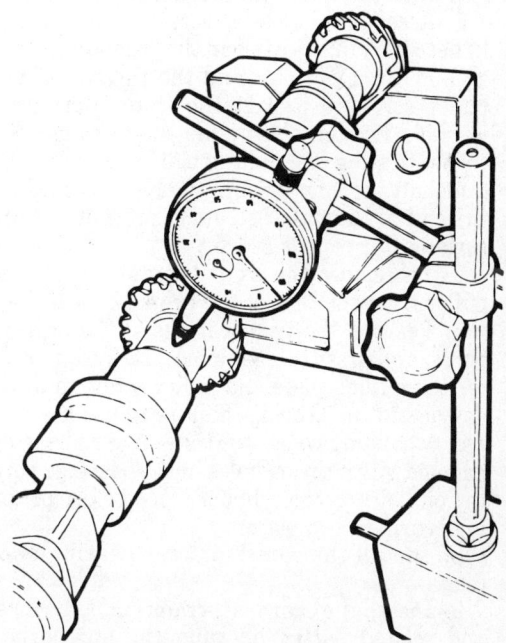

Check the camshaft for straightness

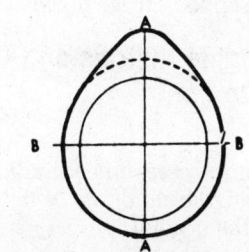

Camshaft lobe measurement

146 ENGINE AND ENGINE OVERHAUL

the dial indicator reading with the specifications.

3. If the end play is excessive, check the spacer for correct installation before it is removed. If the spacer is correctly installed, replace the thrust plate.

4. Remove the dial indicator.

CAMSHAFT BEARING REPLACEMENT

1. Remove the engine following the procedures in this chapter and install it on a work stand.

2. Remove the camshaft, flywheel and crankshaft, following the appropriate procedures. Push the pistons to the top of the cylinder.

3. Remove the camshaft rear bearing bore plug. Remove the camshaft bearings with a bearing removal tool.

4. Select the proper size expanding collet and back-up nut and assemble on the mandrel. With the expanding collet collapsed, install the collet assembly in the camshaft bearing and tighten the back-up nut on the expanding mandrel until the collet fits the camshaft bearing.

5. Assemble the puller screw and extension (if necessary) and install on the expanding mandrel. Wrap a cloth around the threads of the puller screw to protect the front bearing or journal. Tighten the pulling nut against the thrust bearing and pulling plate to remove the camshaft bearing. Be sure to hold a wrench on the end of the puller screw to prevent it from turning.

6. To remove the front bearing, install the puller from the rear of the cylinder block.

7. Position the new bearings at the bearing bores, and press them in place. Be sure to center the pulling plate and puller screw to avoid damage to the bearing. Failure to use the correct expanding collet can cause severe bearing damage. Align the oil holes in the bearings with the oil holes in the cylinder block before pressing bearings into place.

8. Install the camshaft rear bearing bore plug.

9. Install the camshaft, crankshaft, flywheel and related parts, following the appropriate procedures.

10. Install the engine in the truck, following procedures described earlier in this chapter.

Gasoline Engine Pistons and Connecting Rods

REMOVAL

NOTE: *In most cases, this procedure is easier with the engine out of the vehicle.*

1. Remove the head(s).
2. Remove the oil pan.
3. Rotate the engine to bring each piston, in

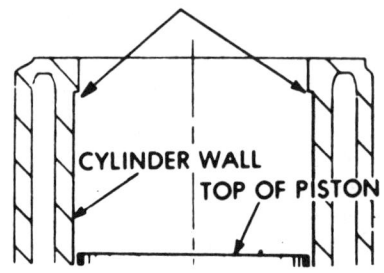
Ridge caused by cylinder wear

Push the piston and rod assembly out with a hammer handle

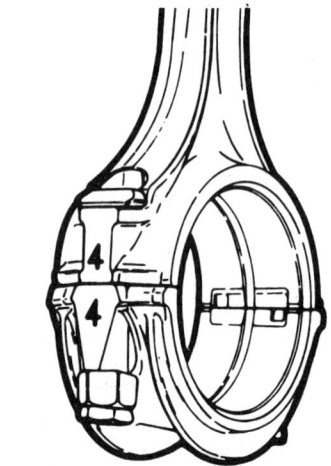
Number each rod and cap accordingly

Use needle-nosed pliers to remove the piston pin clips

ENGINE AND ENGINE OVERHAUL 147

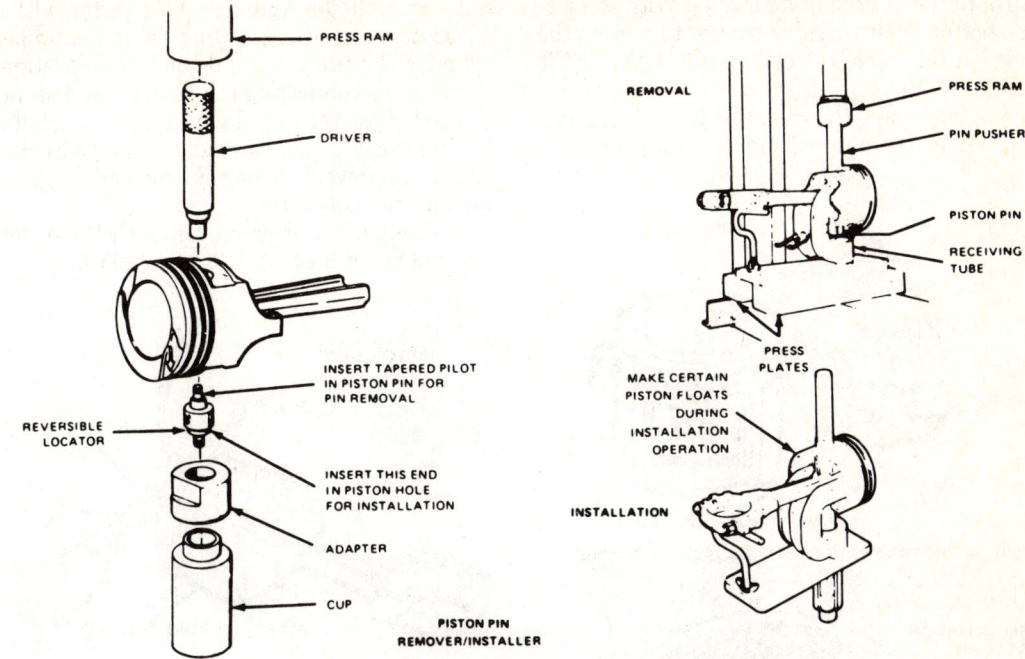

Piston pins must be pressed in with an arbor press

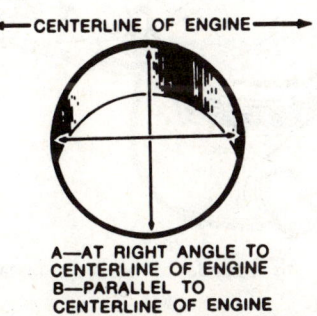

Cylinder bore measuring points. Take the top measurement ½ inch below the top; the bottom measurement ½ inch above the top of the piston at BDC

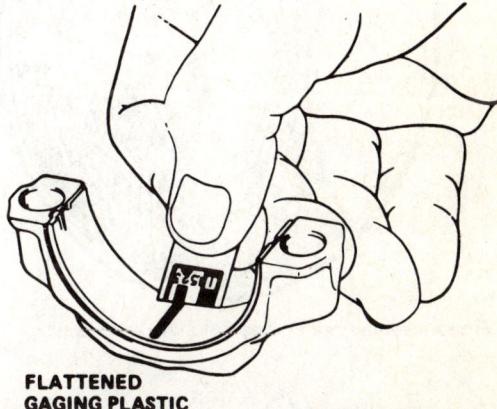

Checking the connecting rod bearing clearance with Plastigage®

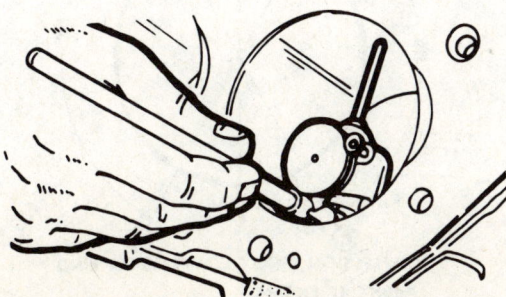

Measuring the cylinder bore with a dial gauge

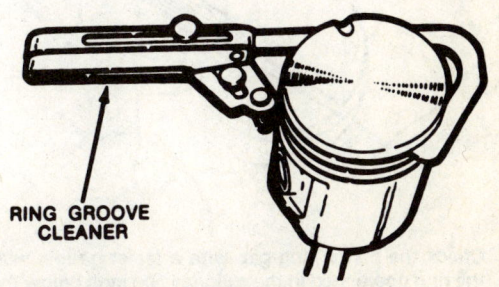

Using a ring groove cleaner

148   ENGINE AND ENGINE OVERHAUL

turn, to the bottom of its stroke. With the piston bottomed, use a ridge reamer to remove the ridge at the top of the cylinder. DO NOT CUT TOO DEEPLY!

4. Matchmark the rods and caps. If the pistons are to be removed from the connecting rod, mark the cylinder number on the piston with a silver pencil or quick drying paint for proper cylinder identification and cap-to-rod location. Remove the connecting rod capnuts and lift off the rod caps, keeping them in order. Install a guide hose over the threads of the rod bolts. This is to prevent damage to the bearing journal and rod bolt threads.

5. Using a hammer handle, push the piston and rod assemblies up out of the block.

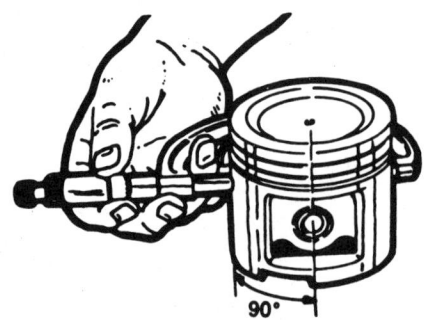
Using a micrometer to check the piston diameter

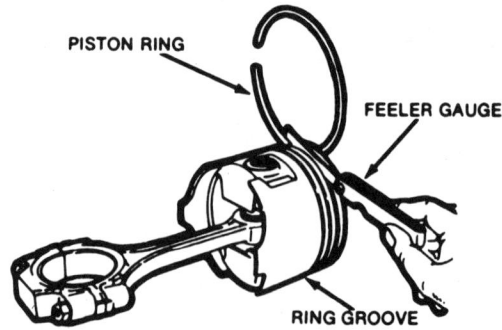
Checking ring side clearance

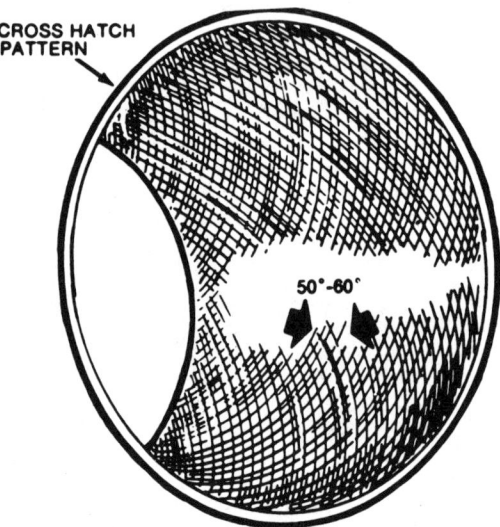
Proper cylinder bore cross-hatching after honing

Using a ring expander to remove or install the rings

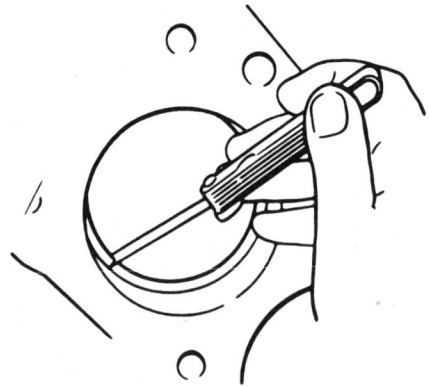
Check the piston ring gap with a feeler gauge, with the ring positioned in the cylinder one inch below the deck of the block

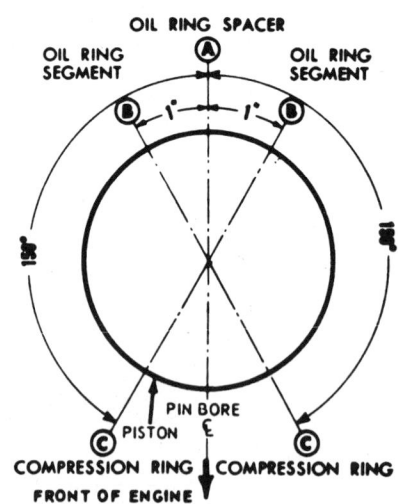
Proper ring gap spacing

ENGINE AND ENGINE OVERHAUL 149

PISTON PIN REMOVAL AND INSTALLATION

Use care at all times when handling and servicing connecting rods and pistons. To prevent possible damage to these units, do not clamp the rod or piston in a vise since they may become distorted. Do not allow the pistons to strike against one another, against hard objects or bench surfaces, since distortion of the piston contour or nicks in the soft aluminum material may result.

1. Remove the piston rings using a suitable piston ring remover.
2. Remove the piston pin lockring, if used. Install the guide bushing of the piston pin removing and installing tool.
3. Install the piston and connecting rod assembly on a support, and place the assembly in an arbor press. Press the pin out of the connecting rod, using the appropriate piston pin tool.
4. Assembly is the reverse of disassembly. Use new lockrings where needed.

INSPECTION

Cylinder Block

Check the cylinder walls for evidence of rust, which would indicate a cracked block. Check the block face for distortion with a straightedge. Maximum distortion variance is 0.13mm The block cannot be planed, so it will have to be

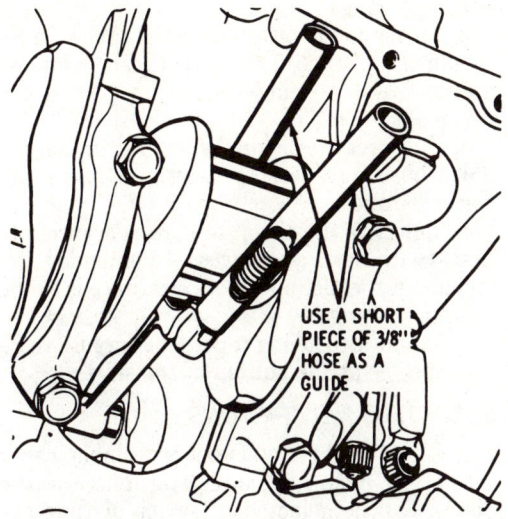

Make connecting rod bolt guides out of rubber tubing. These will protect the cylinder walls and crankshaft journals

Using a ring compressor and hammer handle to install the pistons

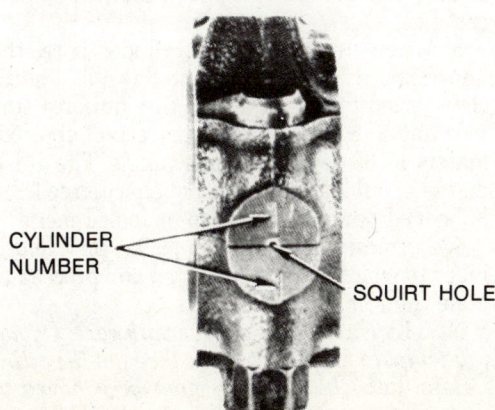

6-243 connecting rod and cap

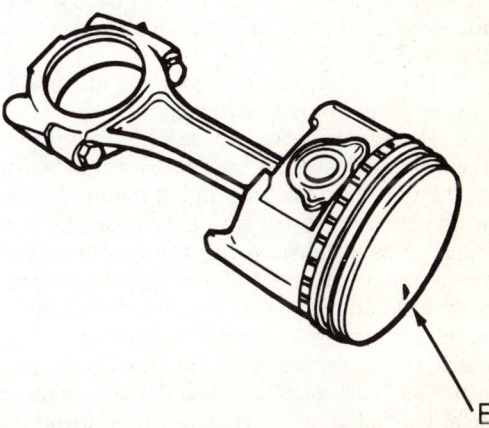

On the 6-173, the notch (E) on the piston crown faces front

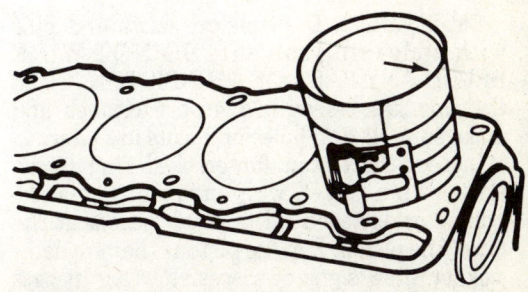

On the 4-150/6-243 the arrow on the piston crown faces front

ENGINE AND ENGINE OVERHAUL

replaced if too distorted. Using a micrometer, check the cylinders for out-of-roundness.

Connecting Rods and Bearings

Wash connecting rods in cleaning solvent and dry with compressed air. Check for twisted or bent rods and inspect for nicks or cracks. Replace connecting rods that are damaged.

Inspect journals for roughness and wear. Slight roughness may be removed with a fine grit polishing cloth saturated with engine oil. Burrs may be removed with a fine oil stone by moving the stone on the journal circumference. Do not move the stone back and forth across the journal. If the journals are scored or ridged, the crankshaft must be replaced.

The connecting rod journals should be checked for out-of-round and correct size with a micrometer.

NOTE: *Crankshaft rod journals will normally be standard size. If any undersized bearings are used, the size will be stamped on a counterweight.*

If plastic gauging material is to be used:

1. Clean oil from the journal bearing cap, connecting rod and outer and inner surfaces of the bearing inserts. Position the insert so that the tang is properly aligned with the notch in the rod and cap.
2. Place a piece of plastic gauging material in the center of lower bearing shell.
3. Remove the bearing cap and determine the bearing clearances by comparing the width of the flattened plastic gauging material at its widest point with the graduation on the container. The number within the graduation on the envelope indicates the clearance in thousandths of an inch or millimeters. If this clearance is excessive, replace the bearing and recheck the clearance with the plastic gauging material. Lubricate the bearing with engine oil before installation. Repeat the procedure on the remaining connecting rod bearings. All rods must be connected to their journals when rotating the crankshaft, to prevent engine damage.

Pistons

Clean varnish from piston skirts and pins with a cleaning solvent. DO NOT WIRE BRUSH ANY PART OF THE PISTON. Clean the ring grooves with a groove cleaner and make sure oil ring holes and slots are clean.

Inspect the piston for cracked ring lands, skirts or pin bosses, wavy or worn ring lands, scuffed or damaged skirts, eroded areas at the top of the piston. Replace pistons that are damaged or show signs of excessive wear. Inspect the grooves for nicks or burrs that might cause the rings to hang up.

Measure piston skirt (across center line of piston pin) and check piston clearance.

MEASURING THE OLD PISTONS

Check used piston-to-cylinder bore clearance as follows:

1. Measure the cylinder bore diameter with a telescope gauge.
2. Measure the piston diameter. When measuring the pistons for size or taper, measurements must be made with the piston pin removed.
3. Subtract the piston diameter from the cylinder bore diameter to determine piston-to-bore clearance.
4. Compare the piston-to-bore clearances obtained with those clearances recommended. Determine if the piston-to-bore clearance is in the acceptable range.
5. When measuring taper, the largest reading must be at the bottom of the skirt.

SELECTING NEW PISTONS

1. If the used piston is not acceptable, check the service piston size and determine if a new piston can be selected. (Service pistons are available in standard, high limit and standard oversize.
2. If the cylinder bore must be reconditioned, measure the new piston diameter, then hone the cylinder bore to obtain the preferred clearance.
3. Select a new piston and mark the piston to identify the cylinder for which it was fitted. (On some vehicles, oversize pistons may be found. These pistons will be 0.254mm oversize.

CYLINDER HONING

1. When cylinders are being honed, follow the manufacturer's recommendations for the use of the hone.
2. Occasionally, during the honing operation, the cylinder bore should be thoroughly cleaned and the selected piston checked for correct fit.
3. When finish-honing a cylinder bore, the hone should be moved up and down at a sufficient speed to obtain a very fine uniform surface finish in a cross-hatch pattern of approximately 45-65 degrees included angle. The finish marks should be clean but not sharp, free from imbedded particles and torn or folded metal.
4. Permanently mark the piston for the cylinder to which it has been fitted and proceed to hone the remaining cylinders.

NOTE: *Handle the pistons with care. Do not attempt to force the pistons through the cylinders until the cylinders have been honed to the correct size. Pistons can be distorted through careless handling.*

ENGINE AND ENGINE OVERHAUL 151

5. Thoroughly clean the bores with hot water and detergent. Scrub well with a stiff bristle brush and rinse thoroughly with hot water. It is extremely essential that a good cleaning operation be performed. If any of the abrasive material is allowed to remain in the cylinder bores, it will rapidly wear the new rings and cylinder bores. The bores should be swabbed several times with light engine oil and a clean cloth and then wiped with a clean dry cloth. CYLINDERS SHOULD NOT BE CLEANED WITH KEROSENE OR GASOLINE. Clean the remainder of the cylinder block to remove the excess material spread during the honing operation.

CHECKING CYLINDER BORE

Cylinder bore size can be measured with inside micrometers or a cylinder gauge. The most wear will occur at the top of the ring travel.

Reconditioned cylinder bores should be held to not more than 0.025mm taper.

If the cylinder bores are smooth, the cylinder walls should not be deglazed. If the cylinder walls are scored, the walls may have to be honed before installing new rings. It is important that reconditioned cylinder bores be thoroughly washed with a soap and water solution to remove all traces of abrasive material to eliminate premature wear.

RING TOLERANCES

When installing new rings, ring gap and side clearance should be checked as follows:

Piston Ring and Rail Gap

Each ring and rail gap must be measured with the ring or rail positioned squarely and at the bottom of the ring-travel area of the bore.

Side Clearance

Each ring must be checked for side clearance in its respective piston groove by inserting a feeler gauge between the ring and its upper land. The piston grooves must be cleaned before checking the ring for side clearance specifications. To check oil ring side clearance, the oil rings must be installed on the piston.

RING INSTALLATION

For service ring specifications and detailed installation productions, refer to the instructions furnished with the parts package.

PISTON ASSEMBLY AND INSTALLATION

1. Using a ring expander, install new rings in the grooves, with their gaps staggered to be 270° apart.
2. Using a straightedge, check the rods for straightness. Check, also, for cracks. Before assembling the block, it's a good idea to have the block checked for cracks with Magnaflux® or its equivalent.
3. Install the pins and retainers.
4. Coat the pistons with clean engine oil and apply a ring compressor. Position the assembly over the cylinder bore and slide the piston into the cylinder slowly, taking care to avoid nicking the walls. The pistons will have a mark on the crown, such as a groove or notch or stamped symbol. This mark indicates the side of the piston which should face front. Lower the piston slowly, until it bottoms on the crankshaft. A good idea is to cover the rod studs with length of rubber hose to avoid nicking the crank journals. Assemble the rod caps at this time. Check the rod bearing clearances using Plastigage®, going by the instructions on the package.
5. Install the bearing caps with the stamped numbers matched. Torque the caps to the figure shown in the Torque Specifications Chart. See the accompanying illustrations for proper piston and rod installation.

Diesel Engine Pistons and Connecting Rods

REMOVAL AND INSTALLATION

Mark the connecting rods and rod bearing caps on the intermediate shaft side of the cylinder block with the number of the corresponding cylinder. Number one cylinder is located at the flywheel/drive plate end of the engine block. When removing, remove each connecting rod, cylinder liner and piston as a complete assembly. Each piston and cylinder liner are matched as a set, so, be sure that they are marked properly for installation. Install the assembly according to the marks made during the removal stage of the overhaul.

Cylinder Liners

REMOVAL AND INSTALLATION

4-126 Diesel

NOTE: *Special tools are needed for this job.*
1. Remove the engine from the vehicle.
2. Remove the cylinder head.
3. Remove the oil pan.
4. Number the connecting rod caps and remove them, keeping them in order.

NOTE: *Number 1 cylinder is at the flywheel end.*

5. Remove the cylinder liner along with the piston and connecting rod assembly.
6. Separate the piston assembly from the cylinder liner. Remove the O-ring seal and the plastic ring from the cylinder liner.
7. If the liner is going to be replaced, be sure to also replace the piston assembly, as they are a matched set.

152 ENGINE AND ENGINE OVERHAUL

8. Upon installation, install the piston assembly into the cylinder liner with tool MOT-851 or equivalent.

NOTE: *The cylinder liners require a rubber O-ring seal and a plastic ring to provide a seal between the liner and the cylinder block, as each liner is supported by the cylinder block. The correct liner protrusion, X in the accompanying illustration, which is above the cylinder block, is achieved by close matching tolerances when the cylinder liner and block are manufactured. If replacement liners are required, the liner protrusions above the cylinder block must be measured and all the cylinder liners rearranged according to the results of the measurements.*

CYLINDER LINER PROTRUSION MEASUREMENT

NOTE: *Special tools are needed for this job.*

1. Insert each reusable cylinder liner in its original position in the cylinder block. If applicable, insert the replacement liner in the cylinder block.

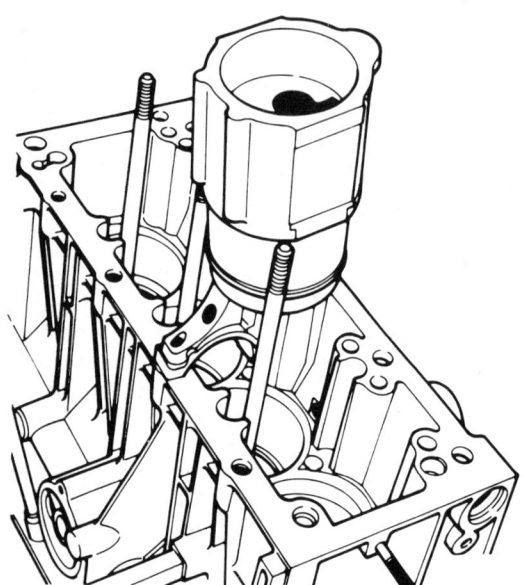
Removing the liner, piston and rod assembly

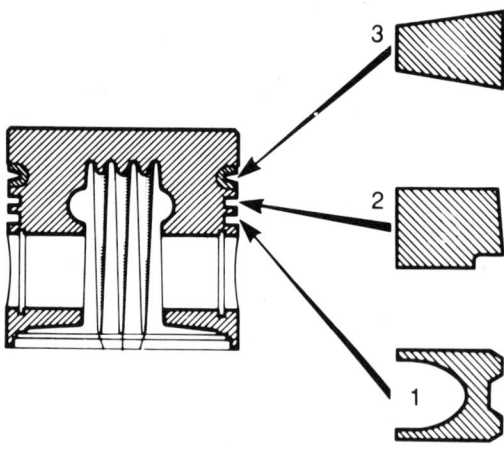
Ring installation on the diesel piston

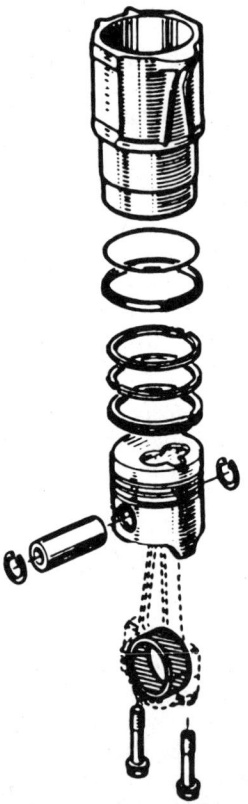
Exploded view of the piston and liner assembly

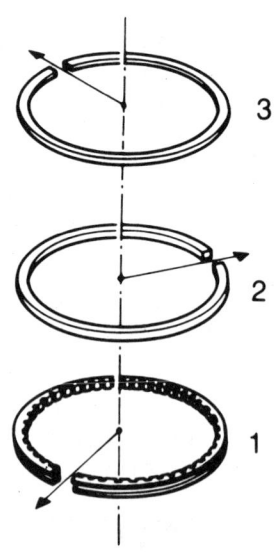
Ring gap positioning on the diesel engine

ENGINE AND ENGINE OVERHAUL 153

2. Install tool MOT-LM and MOT-251-01 or equivalent, on the engine block and tighten the screw clamp. Position tool MOT-252-01 or equivalent, across each cylinder liner, in turn, and secure it with tool MOT-853 or equivalent. Tighten the tool retaining bolts gradually and torque them to 37 ft. lbs. This will assure that each cylinder liner will be firmly in contact with the cylinder block.

3. Measure the protrusion, X, of each cylinder liner above the cylinder block using the dial indicator and block gauge. The correct specification is 0.050-0.120mm.

4. If an out of specification cylinder liner protrusion is measured, install a replacement liner. Measure the protrusion to determine if the cylinder block or the cylinder liner is defective.

5. With all cylinder liner protrusions within specification arrange them so that the difference in protrusion between any two adjacent liners does not exceed 0.040mm.

6. The protrusions are stepped down from the number one cylinder to the number four cylinder or from the number four cylinder to the number one cylinder.

7. When the correct cylinder liner protrusion arrangement has been determined, match each piston and connecting rod assembly with its original liner and remark each according to the new position in the cylinder block.

Rear Main Oil Seal

REPLACEMENT

4-150

1. Remove the transmission.
2. Remove the flywheel.
3. Pry out the seal from around the crankshaft flange.
4. Coat the inner lip of the new seal with clean engine oil.
5. Gently tap the new seal into place, flush with the block, using a rubber or plastic mallet.
6. Install all parts in reverse order of removal.

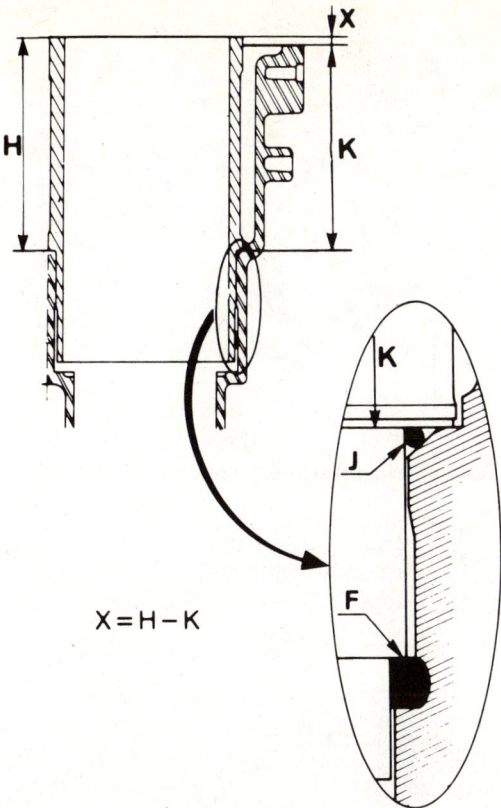

Diesel cylinder liner installation. X is the liner protrusion; J is the rubber O-ring; F is the plastic O-ring

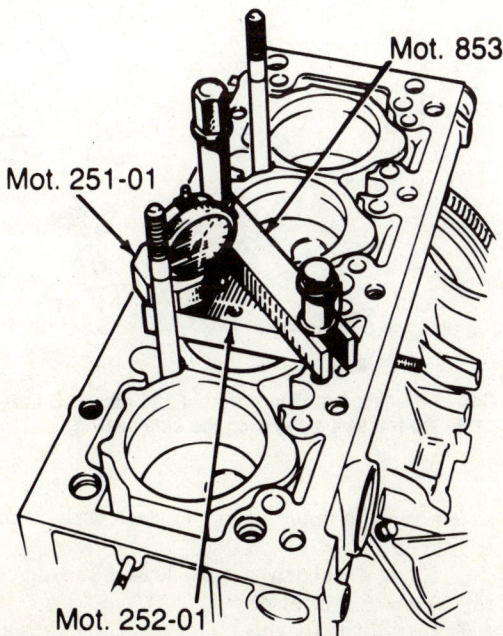

Special tools in place to measure liner protrusion

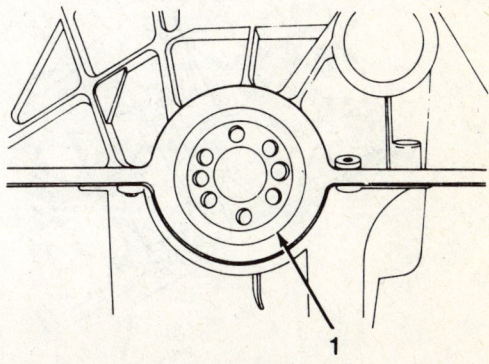

4-150 rear main seal. 1 is the actual seal surface

154 ENGINE AND ENGINE OVERHAUL

4-126 Diesel

NOTE: *Replacement front and rear main side seals are available in 2 different thicknesses: 5.4mm and 5.1mm. There are identical main seals in both the front (#5) and rear (#1) main bearing positions. They are replaced in an identical manner. Both ends are sealed with identical, but not interchangeable, one piece round seals.*

If the end seals are being replaced, remove the engine and place it on a work stand. If just the side seals are being replaced, just remove the oil pan. It might be a good idea, however, to replace the end seals if the side seal are leaking.

FRONT END MAIN SEAL

1. Remove the engine.
2. Remove the timing chain and sprockets as described above.
3. Using a sharp awl, punch a hole in the seal and pry it out of its bore.
4. Thoroughly clean the bore.
5. Coat the outer edge of the new seal with sealer and the inner sealing surface with clean engine oil.
6. Using a seal driver, such as Mot.789, drive the new seal into place.
7. Install the timing chain and sprockets, and all other related parts.
8. Install the engine.

REAR END MAIN SEAL

1. Remove the engine.
2. Remove the flywheel.
3. Using a sharp awl, punch a hole in the seal and pry it out of its bore.
4. Thoroughly clean the bore.
5. Coat the outer edge of the new seal with

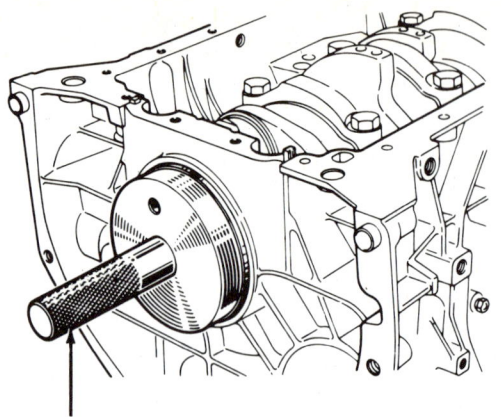

Rear end main seal installation on the 4-126 diesel

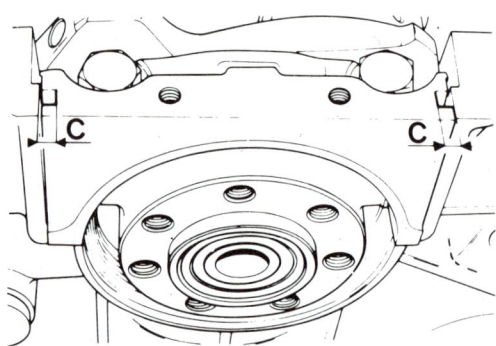

Measuring the side seal bore (C) on the 4-126 diesel

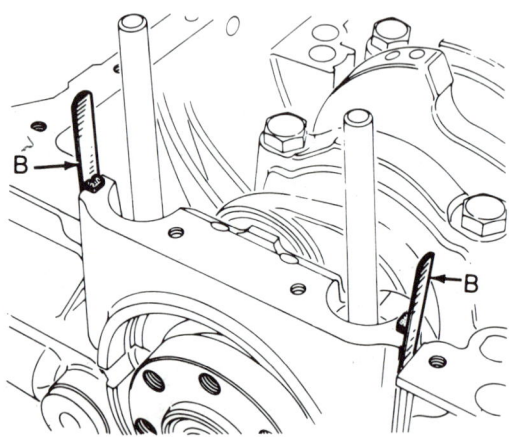

Cap and seals installed on the 4-126 diesel. B indicates the foil strips covering the side seals

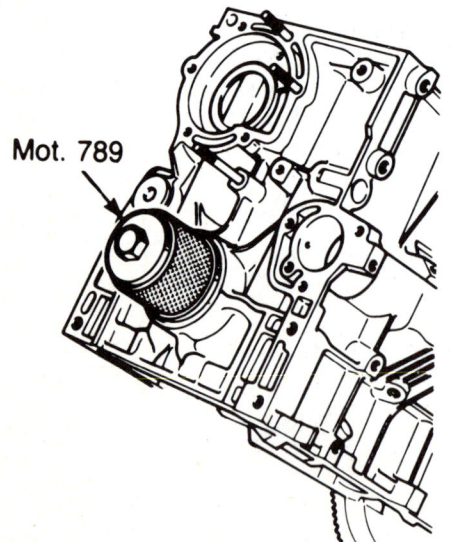

Front end main seal installation on the 4-126 diesel

sealer and the inner sealing surface with clean engine oil.
6. Using a seal driver, such as Mot.788, drive the new seal into place.
7. Install the flywheel.
8. Install the engine.

ENGINE AND ENGINE OVERHAUL 155

FRONT END AND/OR REAR END MAIN SIDE SEALS

NOTE: *Depending on working clearance, it may be necessary to remove the engine.*

1. Remove the oil pan.
2. Remove the main bearing cap.
3. Remove the side seals.
4. Thoroughly clean the seal surfaces in the block and cap.
5. Replace the cap.
6. Measure the width of the seal bore.
7. If the seal bore is 5mm or less, use a 5.1mm thick seal; if it is more than 5mm, use a 5.4mm thick seal.
8. Remove the bearing cap.
9. Insert the proper side seals in the cap grooves with the grooves in the seals facing outward. Each seal should stick out from the cap about 0.2mm.
10. Lightly coat the seals with clean engine oil.
11. Cover the length of each seal with a strip of aluminum foil and install the cap and seals in the block. Don't install the cap bolts. Remove the foil.
12. Measure the side seal protrusion above the cap. Protrusion should be greater than 0.7mm.
13. Torque the bearing cap bolts to 72 ft. lbs.
14. Cut the side seals to within 0.5-0.7mm protrusion.
15. Install the oil pan.

6-173

1. Remove the oil pan and pump.
2. Remove the rear main bearing cap.
3. Gently pack the upper seal into the groove approximately ¼" on each side.
4. Measure the amount the seal was driven in on one side and add $\frac{1}{16}$". Cut this length from the old lower cap seal. Be sure to get a sharp cut. Repeat for the other side.
5. Place the piece of cut seal into the groove and pack the seal into the block. Do this for each side.

NOTE: *GM makes a guide tool (J-29114-1) which bolts to the block via an oil pan bolt hole, and a packing tool (J-29114-2) which are machined to provide a built-in stop for the installation of the short cut pieces. Using the packing tool, work the short pieces of seal onto the guide tool, then pack them into the block with the packing tool.*

6. Install a new lower seal in the rear main cap.
7. Install a piece of Plastigage® or the equivalent on the bearing journal. Install the rear cap and tighten to 70 ft.lbs. Remove the cap and check the gauge for bearing clearance. If out of specification, the ends of the seal may be frayed

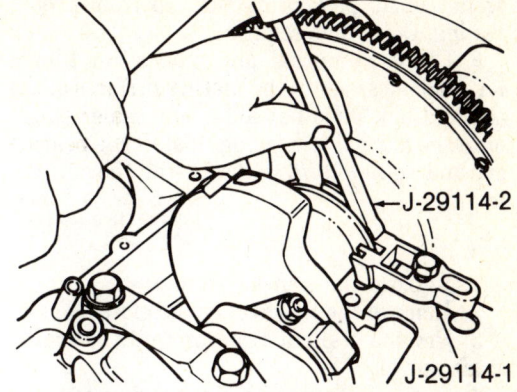
Installing the upper rear main seal in the 6-173

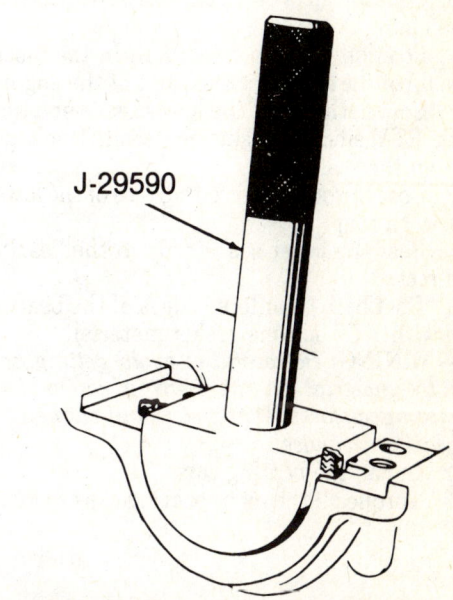
Installing the lower rear main seal in the cap

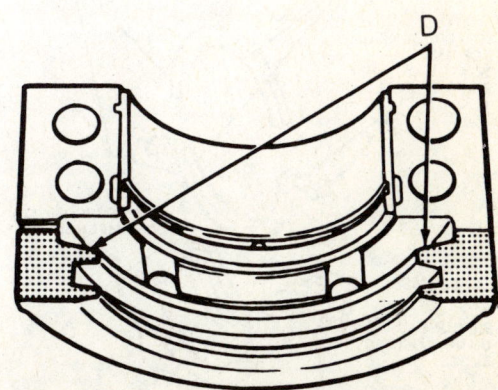
On the 6-173 rear main seal cap, D shows the shaded areas for RTV sealer application

156 ENGINE AND ENGINE OVERHAUL

or not flush, preventing the cap from proper sealing. Correct as required.

8. Clean the journal, and apply a thin film of RTV silicone sealer to the mating surfaces of the cap and block. Do not allow any sealer to get onto the journal or bearing. Install the bearing cap and tighten to 70 ft. lbs. Install the pan and pump.

6-243

1. Remove the transmission.
2. Remove the flywheel or flexplate.
3. Pry the seal out from around the crankshaft flange.
4. Remove the rear main bearing cap and wipe clean the cpa and crankshaft seal surfaces.
5. Apply a thin coat of engine oil to the seal surfaces of the cap and crankshaft.
6. Coat the lip of each seal half with clean engine oil.
7. Position the upper seal half in the block. The lip of the seal faces the front of the engine.
8. Coat both side of the lower seal's end tabs with RTV silicone gasket material. Don't get any on the seal lip.
9. Coat the outer, curved surface of the lower seal with soap.
10. Seat the lower seal firmly in the bearing cap recess.
11. Coat both chamfered edges of the bearing cap with RTV silicone gasket material.
    WARNING: *Be careful to avoid getting and RTV material on the bearing cao-to-block mating surfaces! Doing so would change the bearing cleanace!*
12. Install the bearing cap.
13. Torque all the main bearing caps to 80 ft. lbs.

Crankshaft and Main Bearings
REMOVAL AND INSTALLATION

Engine Removed

1. With the engine removed from the vehicle and placed in a work stand, disconnect the spark plug wires from the spark plugs and remove the wires and bracket assembly from the attaching stud on the valve rocker arm cover(s) if so equipped. Disconnect the coil to distributor high tension lead at the coil. Remove the distributor cap and spark plug wires as an assembly. Remove the spark plugs to allow easy rotation of the crankshaft.
2. Remove the fuel pump and oil filter. Slide the water pump by-pass hose clamp (if so equipped) toward the water pump. Remove the alternator and mounting brackets.
3. Remove the crankshaft pulley from the crankshaft vibration damper. Remove the capscrew and washer from the end of the crankshaft. Install a universal puller on the crankshaft vibration damper and remove the damper.
4. Remove the cylinder front cover and crankshaft gear, refer to Cylinder Front Cover and Timing Chain in this chapter.
5. Invert the engine on the work stand. Remove the clutch pressure plate and disc (manual shift transmission). Remove the flywheel and engine rear cover plate. Remove the oil pan and gasket. Remove the oil pump.
6. Make sure all bearing caps (main and connecting rod) are marked so that they can be installed in their original locations. Turn the crankshaft until the connecting rod from which the cap is being removed is down, and remove the bearing cap. Push the connecting rod and piston assembly up into the cylinder. Repeat this procedure until all the connecting rod bearing caps are removed.
7. Remove the main bearings caps.

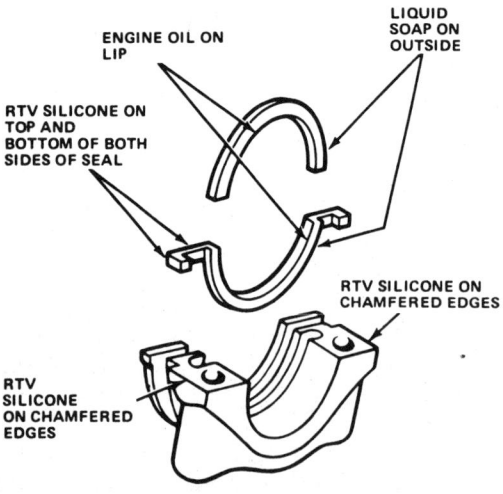

Rear main seal installation for the 6-243

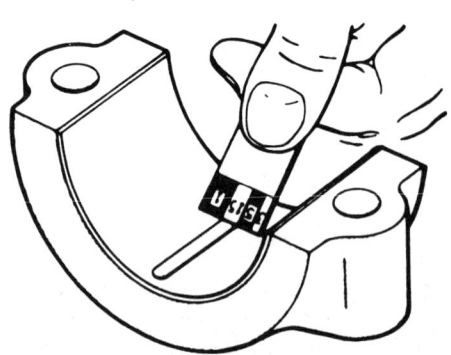

Checking main bearing oil clearance with Plastigage®

ENGINE AND ENGINE OVERHAUL

8. Carefully lift the crankshaft out of the block so that the thrust bearing surfaces are not damaged. Handle the crankshaft with care to avoid possible fracture to the finished surfaces.

9. Remove the rear journal seal from the block and rear main bearing cap.

10. Remove the main bearing inserts from the block and bearing caps.

11. Remove the connecting rod bearing inserts from the connecting rods and caps.

12. If the crankshaft main bearing journals have been refinished to a definite undersize, install the correct undersize bearings. Be sure the bearing inserts and bearing bores are clean. Foreign material under the inserts will distort the bearing and cause a failure.

13. Place the upper main bearing inserts in position in the bores with the tang fitting in the slot. Be sure the oil holes in the bearing inserts are aligned with the oil holes in the cylinder block.

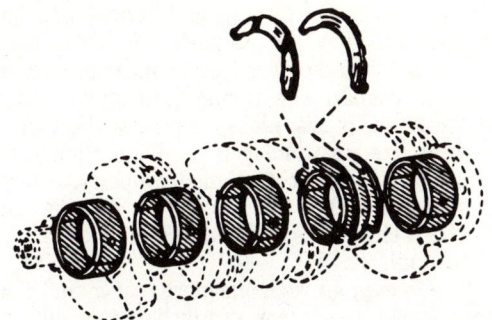

Main bearing positioning on the 4-126 diesel. The thrust washers are shown

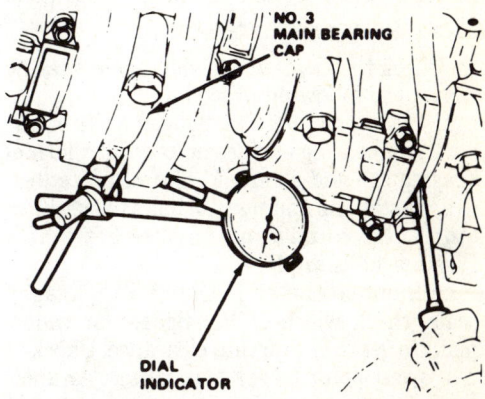

Checking crankshaft endplay with a dial indicator

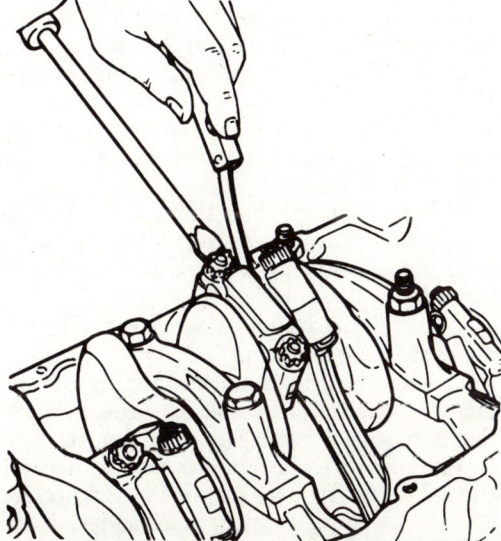

Checking rod side clearance with a flat feeler gauge. Use a small prybar to spread the rods

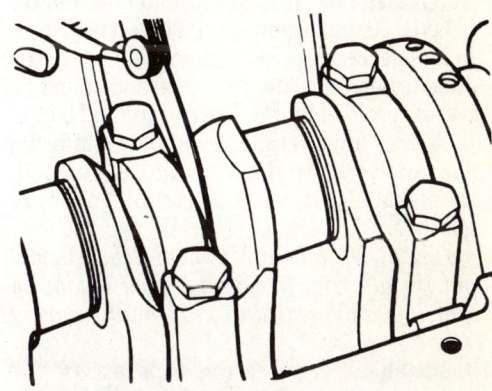

Checking crankshaft endplay with a feeler gauge

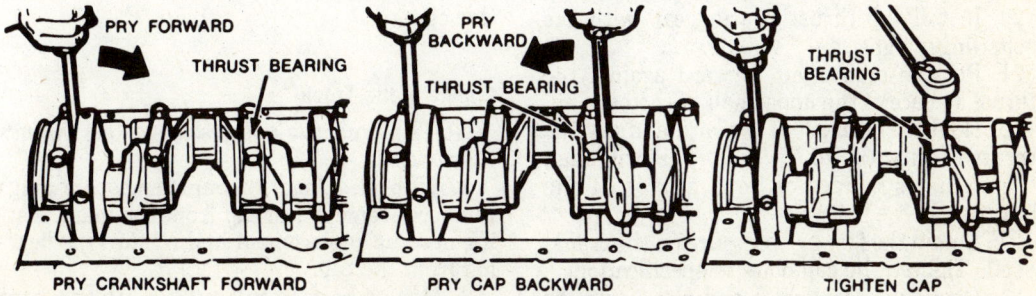

Crankshaft thrust bearing alignment

ENGINE AND ENGINE OVERHAUL

14. Install the lower main bearing inserts in the bearing caps.
15. Clean the rear journal oil seal groove and the mating surfaces of the block and rear main bearing cap.
16. Dip the lip-type seal halves in clean engine oil. Install the seals in the bearing cap and block with the undercut side of the seal toward the front of the engine.

NOTE: *This procedure applies only to engines with two piece rear main bearing oil seals. those having one piece seals will be installed after the crankshaft is in place.*

17. Carefully lower the crankshaft into place. Be careful not to damage the bearing surfaces.

CHECKING MAIN BEARING CLEARANCES

18. Check the clearance of each main bearing by using the following procedure:
    a. Place a piece of Plastigage® or its equivalent, on bearing surface across full width of bearing cap and about ¼" (6mm) off center.
    b. Install cap and tighten bolts to specifications. Do not turn crankshaft while Plastigage® is in place.
    c. Remove the cap. Using Plastigage® scale, check width of Plastigage® at widest point to get the minimum clearance. Check at narrowest point to get maximum clearance. Difference between readings is taper of journal.
    d. If clearance exceeds specified limits, try a 0.001" (0.0254mm) or 0.002" (0.051mm) undersize bearing in combination with the standard bearing. Bearing clearance must be within specified limits. If standard and 0.002" (0.051mm) undersize bearing does not bring clearance within desired limits, refinish crankshaft journal, then install undersize bearings.

NOTE: *Refer to Rear Main Oil Seal removal and installation, for special instructions in applying RTV sealer to rear main bearing cup.*

19. Install all the bearing caps except the thrust bearing cap. Be sure the main bearing caps are installed in their original locations. Tighten the bearing cap bolts to specifications.
20. Install the thrust bearing cap with the bolts finger tight.
21. Pry the crankshaft forward against the thrust surface of the upper half of the bearing.
22. Hold the crankshaft forward and pry the thrust bearing cap to the rear. This will align the thrust surfaces of both halves of the bearing.
23. Retain the forward pressure on the crankshaft. Tighten the cap bolts to specifications.
24. Check the crankshaft end play using the following procedures:
    a. Force the crankshaft toward the rear of the engine.
    b. Install a dial indicator so that the contact point rests against the crankshaft flange and the indicator axis is parallel to the crankshaft axis.
    c. Zero the dial indicator. Push the crankshaft forward and note the reading on the dial.
    d. If the end play exceeds the wear limit listed in the Crankshaft and Connecting Rod Specifications chart, replace the thrust bearing. If the end play is less than the minimum limit, inspect the thrust bearing faces for scratches, burrs, nicks, or dirt. If the thrust faces are not damaged or dirty, then they probably were not aligned properly. Lubricate and install the new thrust bearing and align the faces following procedures 21 through 24.
25. On engines with one piece rear main bearing oil seal, coat a new crankshaft rear oil seal with oil and install using a seal driver. Inspect the seal to be sure it was not damaged during installation.
26. Install new bearing inserts in the connecting rods and caps. Check the clearance of each bearing, following the procedure (18a through 18d).
27. After the connecting rod bearings have been fitted, apply a light coat of engine oil to the journals and bearings.
28. Turn the crankshaft throw to the bottom of its stroke. Push the piston all the way down until the rod bearing seats on the crankshaft journal.
29. Install the connecting rod cap. Tighten the nuts to specification.
30. After the piston and connecting rod assemblies have been installed, check the side clearance with a feeler gauge between the connecting rods on each connecting rod crankshaft journal. Refer to Crankshaft and Connecting Rod specifications chart in this chapter.
31. Install the timing chain and sprockets or gears, cylinder front cover and crankshaft pulley and adapter, following steps under Cylinder Front Cover and Timing Chain Installation in this chapter.

Engine in the Truck

NOTE: *This won't be possible on all engines or trucks.*

1. With the oil pan, oil pump and spark plugs removed, remove the cap from the main bearing needing replacement and remove the bearing from the cap.
2. Make a bearing roll-out pin, using a bent cotter pin as shown in the illustration. Install

ENGINE AND ENGINE OVERHAUL 159

the end of the pin in the oil hole in the crankshaft journal.

3. Rotate the crankshaft clockwise as viewed from the front of the engine. This will roll the upper bearing out of the block.

4. Lube the new upper bearing with clean engine oil and insert the plain (unnotch) end between the crankshaft and the indented or notched side of the block. Roll the bearing into place, making sure that the oil holes are aligned. Remove the roll pin from the oil hole.

5. Lube the new lower bearing and install it in the main bearing cap. Install the main bearing cap onto the block, making sure it is positioned in proper direction with the matchmarks in alignment.

6. Torque the main bearing cap to specification.

NOTE: *See Crankshaft Installation for thrust bearing alignment.*

CRANKSHAFT CLEANING AND INSPECTION

NOTE: *handle the crankshaft carefully to avoid damage to the finish surfaces.*

1. Clean the crankshaft with solvent, and blow out all oil passages with compressed air.

2. Use crocus cloth to remove any sharp edges, burrs or other imperfections which might damage the oil seal during installation or cause premature seal wear.

NOTE: *Do not use crocus cloth to polish the seal surfaces. A finely polished surface may produce poor sealing or cause premature seal wear.*

3. Inspect the main and connecting rod journals for cracks, scratches, grooves or scores.

4. Measure the diameter of each journal at least four places to determine out-of-round, taper or undersize condition.

5. On an engine with a manual transmission, check the fit of the clutch pilot bearing in the bore of the crankshaft. A needle roller bearing and adapter assembly is used as a clutch pilot bearing. It is inserted directly into the engine crank shaft. The bearing and adapter assembly cannot be serviced separately. A new bearing must be installed whenever a bearing is removed.

6. Inspect the pilot bearing, when used, for roughness, evidence of overheating or loss of lubricant. Replace if any of these conditions are found.

Main Bearings

1. Clean the bearing inserts and caps thoroughly in solvent, and dry them with compressed air.

NOTE: *Do not scrape varnish or gum deposits from the bearing shells.*

2. Inspect each bearing carefully. Bearings that have a scored, chipped, or worn surface should be replaced.

3. The copper-lead bearing base may be visible through the bearing overlay in small localized areas. This may not mean that the bearing is excessively worn. It is not necessary to replace the bearing if the bearing clearance is within recommended specifications.

4. Check the clearance of bearings that appear to be satisfactory with Plastigage® or its equivalent. Fit the new bearings following the procedure Crankshaft and Main Bearings removal and installation, they should be reground to size for the next undersize bearing.

5. Regrind the journals to give the proper clearance with the next undersize bearing. If the journal will not clean up to maximum undersize bearing available, replace the crankshaft.

6. Always reproduce the same journal shoulder radius that existed originally. Too small a radius will result in fatigue failure of the crankshaft. Too large a radius will result in bearing failure due to radius ride of the bearing.

7. After regrinding the journals, chamfer the oil holes, then polish the journals with a #320 grit polishing cloth and engine oil. Crocus cloth may also be used as a polishing agent.

COMPLETING THE REBUILDING PROCESS

Fill the oil pump with oil, to prevent cavitating (sucking air) on initial engine start up. Install the oil pump and the pickup tube on the engine. Coat the oil pan gasket as necessary, and install the gasket and the oil pan. Mount the flywheel and the crankshaft vibration damper or pulley on the crankshaft.

NOTE: *Always use new bolts when installing the flywheel. Inspect the clutch shaft pilot bushing in the crankshaft. If the bushing is excessively worn, remove it with an expanding puller and a slide hammer, and tap a new bushing into place.*

Position the engine, cylinder head side up. Lubricate the lifters, and install them into their bores. Install the cylinder head, and torque it as specified. Insert the pushrods (where applicable), and install the rocker shaft(s) (if so equipped) or position the rocker.

Install the intake and exhaust manifolds, the carburetor(s), the distributor and spark plugs. Mount all accessories and install the engine in the car. Fill the radiator with coolant, and the crankcase with high quality engine oil.

BREAK-IN PROCEDURE

Start the engine, and allow it to run at low speed for a few minutes, while checking for leaks. Stop the engine, check the oil level, and

ENGINE AND ENGINE OVERHAUL

fill as necessary. Restart the engine, and fill the cooling system to capacity. Check and adjust the ignition timing. Run the engine at low to medium speed (800-2,500 rpm) for approximately ½ hour, and retorque the cylinder head bolts. Road test the car, and check again for leaks.

NOTE: *Some gasket manufacturers recommend not retorquing the cylinder head(s) due to the composition of the head gasket. Follow the directions in the gasket set.*

Flywheel/Flexplate and Ring Gear

NOTE: *Flexplate is the term for a flywheel mated with an automatic transmission.*

REMOVAL AND INSTALLATION
All Engines

NOTE: *The ring gear is replaceable only on engines mated with a manual transmission. Engine with automatic transmissions have ring gears which are welded to the flex plate.*

1. Remove the transmission and transfer case.
2. Remove the clutch, if equipped, or torque converter from the flywheel. The flywheel bolts should be loosened a little at a time in a cross pattern to avoid warping the flywheel. On trucks with manual transmission, replace the pilot bearing in the end of the crankshaft if removing the flywheel.
3. The flywheel should be checked for cracks and glazing. It can be resurfaced by a machine shop.
4. If the ring gear is to be replaced, drill a hole in the gear between two teeth, being careful not to contact the flywheel surface. Using a cold chisel at this point, crack the ring gear and remove it.
5. Polish the inner surface of the new ring gear and heat it in an oven to about 600°F. Quickly place the ring gear on the flywheel and tap it into place, making sure that it is fully seated.

NOTE: *Never heat the ring gear past 800°F, or the tempering will be destroyed.*

6. Installation is the reverse of removal. Torque the bolts a little at a time in a cross pattern, to the torque figure shown in the Torque Specifications Chart.

EXHAUST SYSTEM

Safety Precautions

For a number of reasons, exhaust system work can be the most dangerous type of work you can do on your car. Always observe the following precautions:

- Support the car extra securely. Not only will you often be working directly under it, but you'll frequently be using a lot of force, say, heavy hammer blows, to dislodge rusted parts. This can cause a car that's improperly supported to shift and possibly fall.
- Wear goggles. Exhaust system parts are always rusty. Metal chips can be dislodged, even when you're only turning rusted bolts. Attempting to pry pipes apart with a chisel makes the chips fly even more frequently.
- If you're using a cutting torch, keep it a great distance from either the fuel tank or lines. Stop what you're doing and feel the temperature of the fuel bearing pipes on the tank frequently. Even slight heat can expand and/or vaporize fuel, resulting in accumulated vapor, or even a liquid leak, near your torch.
- Watch where your hammer blows fall and make sure you hit squarely. You could easily tap a brake or fuel line when you hit an exhaust system part with a glancing blow. Inspect all lines and hoses in the area where you've been working.

CAUTION: *Be very careful when working on or near the catalytic converter. External temperatures can reach 1,500°F (816°C) and more, causing severe burns. Removal or installation should be performed only on a cold exhaust system.*

Special Tools

A number of special exhaust system tools can be rented from auto supply houses or local stores that rent special equipment. A common one is a tail pipe expander, designed to enable you to join pipes of identical diameter.

It may also be quite helpful to use solvents designed to loosen rusted bolts or flanges. Soaking rusted parts the night before you do the job can speed the work of freeing rusted parts considerably. Remember that these solvents are often flammable. Apply only to parts after they are cool!

COMPONENT REPLACEMENT
Exhaust Downpipe

1. Raise and truck on jackstands.
2. Saturate all bolts and nuts with penetrating lubricant.
3. Disconnect the downpipe from the manifold and discard the seal.
4. Support the transmission with a floor jack and remove the rear crossmember.
5. Remove the pipe-to-flyweek housing bracket.
6. Support the catalytic converter and disconnect the downpipe. Discard the gasket.
7. Installation is the reverse of removal. Use

ENGINE AND ENGINE OVERHAUL 161

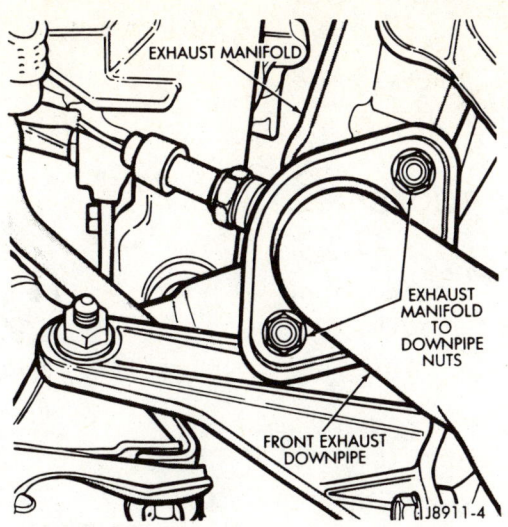

Exhaust pipe-to-manifold nuts

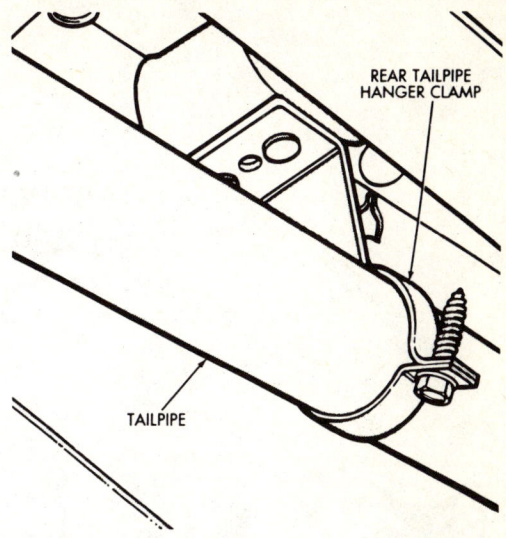

Rear tailpipe hanger

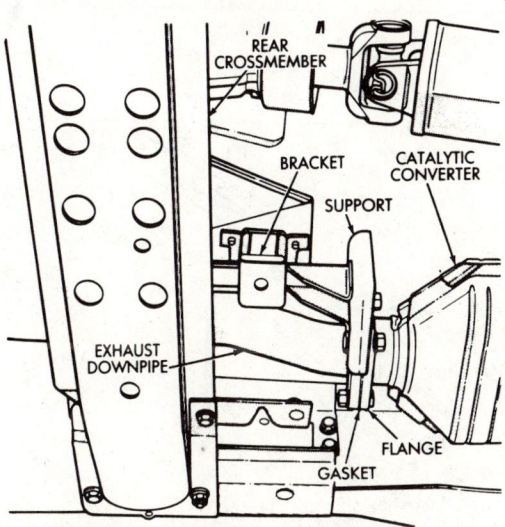

Exhaust pipe-to-converter connection

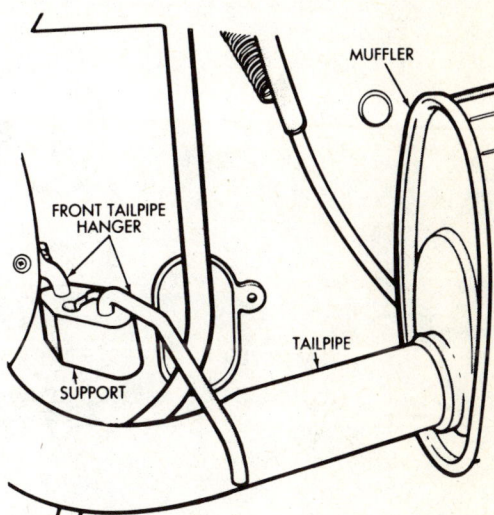

Front tailpipe hanger

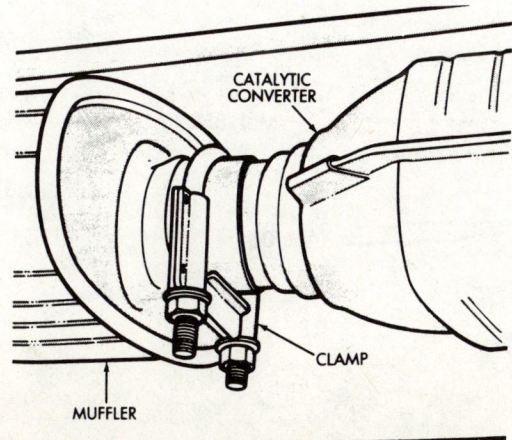

Converter-to-muffler connection

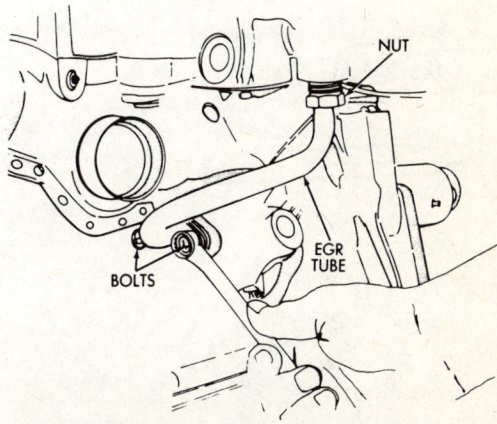

4-150 EGR tube

162 ENGINE AND ENGINE OVERHAUL

SPECIAL TOOLS

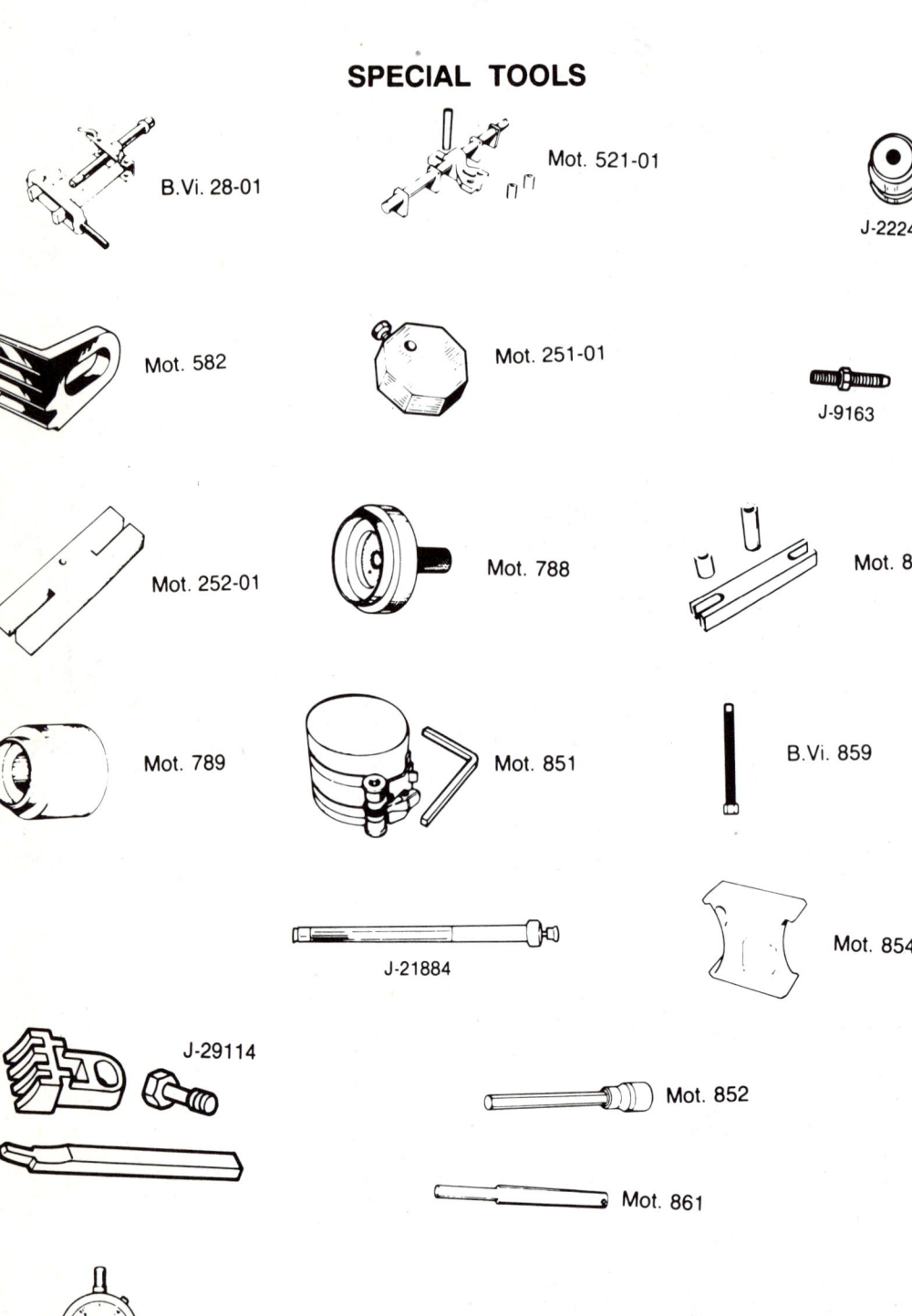

ENGINE AND ENGINE OVERHAUL 163

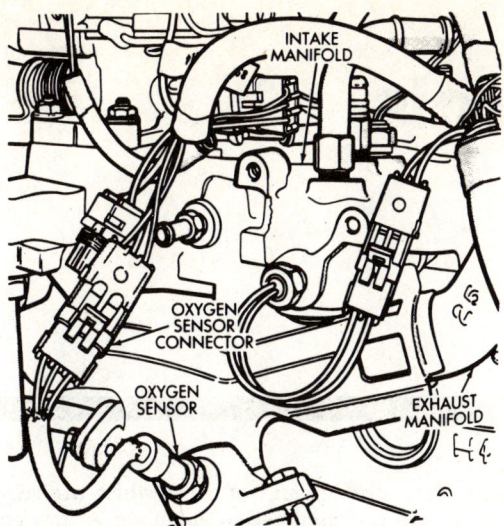

Oxygen sensor and connector

new gaskets and seals. Tighten all fasteners to 23 ft. lbs.

Catalytic Converter

1. Raise and truck on jackstands.
2. Saturate all bolts and nuts with penetrating lubricant.
3. Remove the converter-to-muffler clamp.
4. Heat the converter-to-muffler connection with a torch until it becomes cherry red.
5. Remove all muffler hangers and twist the muffler back-and-forth to free it from the converter.
6. Disconnect the downpipe from the converter. Discard the gasket.
7. Installation is the reverse of removal. Use new gaskets. Torque the downpipe connection to 23 ft. lbs.; the muffler clamp to 45 ft. lbs.

Muffler and Tailpipe

1. Raise and truck on jackstands.
2. Saturate all bolts and nuts with penetrating lubricant.
3. Remove the converter-to-muffler clamp.
4. Heat the converter-to-muffler connection with a torch until it becomes cherry red.
5. Remove all muffler hangers and twist the muffler back-and-forth to free it from the converter.

NOTE: *Original equipment mufflers are welded to the tailpipe. Replacement mufflers and tailpipes clamp together.*

6. Installation is the reverse of removal. Torque the muffler-to-converter clamp bolt to 45 ft. lbs.

Emission Controls

EMISSION CONTROLS

There are three types of automotive pollutants: crankcase fumes, exhaust gases and gasoline evaporation. The equipment that is used to limit these pollutants is commonly called emission control equipment.

Crankcase Emission Controls

The crankcase emission control equipment consists of a positive crankcase ventilation valve (PCV), a closed or open oil filler cap and hoses to connect this equipment.

When the engine is running, a small portion of the gases which are formed in the combustion chamber during combustion leak by the piston rings and enter the crankcase. Since these gases are under pressure, they tend to escape from the crankcase and enter into the atmosphere. If these gases were allowed to remain the the crankcase for any length of time, they would contaminate the engine oil and cause sludge to build up. If the gases are allowed to escape into the atmosphere, they would pollute the air, as they contain unburned hydrocarbons. The crankcase emission control equipment recycles these gases back into the engine combustion chamber where they are burned.

Crankcase gases are recycled in the following manner: while the engine is running, clean filtered air is drawn into the crankcase either directly through the oil filler cap, or through the carburetor air filter and then through a hose leading to the oil filler cap. As the air passes through the crankcase, it picks up the combustion gases and carries them out of the crankcase, up through the PCV valve and into the intake manifold. After they enter the intake manifold, they are drawn into the combustion chamber and burned.

The most critical component in the system is the PCV valve. This vacuum controlled valve regulates the amount of gases which are recycled into the combustion chamber. At low engine speeds, the valve is partially closed, limiting the flow of gases into the intake manifold. As engine speed increases, the valve opens to admit greater quantities of the gases into the intake manifold. If the valve should become blocked or plugged, the gases will be prevented from escaping from the crankcases by the normal route. Since these gases are under pressure, they will find their own way out of the crankcase. This alternate route is usually a weak oil seal or gasket in the engine. As the gas escapes by the gasket, it also creates an oil leak. Besides causing oil leaks, a clogged PCV valve also allows these gases to remain in the crankcase for an extended period of time, promoting the formation of sludge in the engine.

The above explanation and the troubleshooting procedure which follows applies to all engines with PCV systems.

TROUBLESHOOTING

With the engine running, pull the PCV valve and hose from the engine. Block off the end of the valve with your finger. The engine speed should drop at least 50 rpm when the end of the valve is blocked. If the engine speed does not drop at least 50 rpm, then the valve is defective and should be replaced.

REMOVAL AND INSTALLATION

1. Pull the PCV valve and hose from the engine.
2. Remove the PCV valve from the hose. Inspect the inside of the PCV valve from the hose. If it is dirty, disconnect if from the intake manifold and clean it.
3. If the PCV valve hose was removed, connect it to the intake manifold.
4. Connect the PCV valve to its hose.
5. Install the PCV valve on the engine.

EMISSION CONTROLS

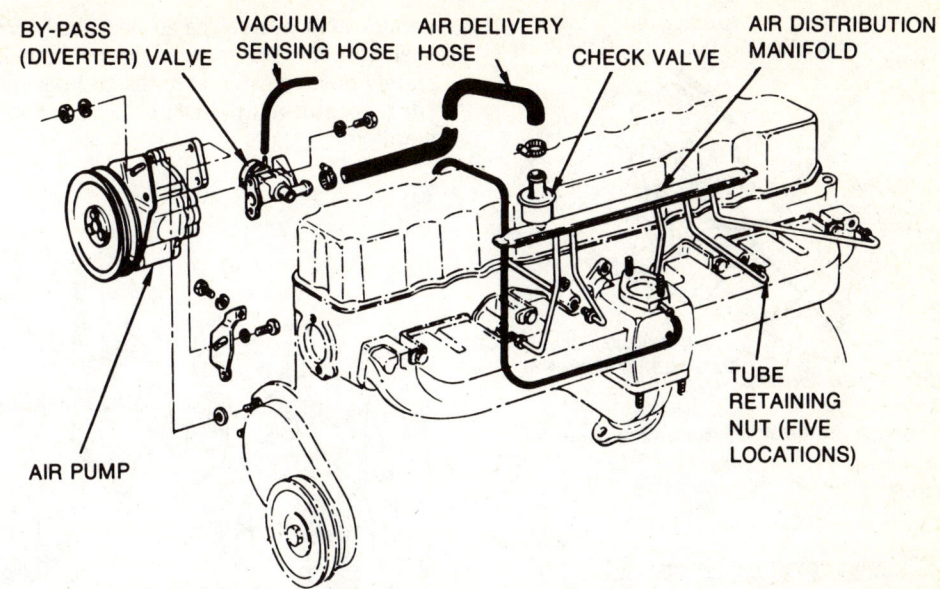

Air injection system, in-line six

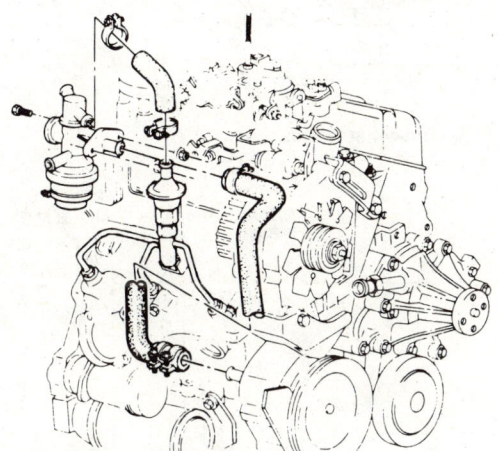

4-150 AIR diverter valve and manifold

4-150 AIR pump mounting

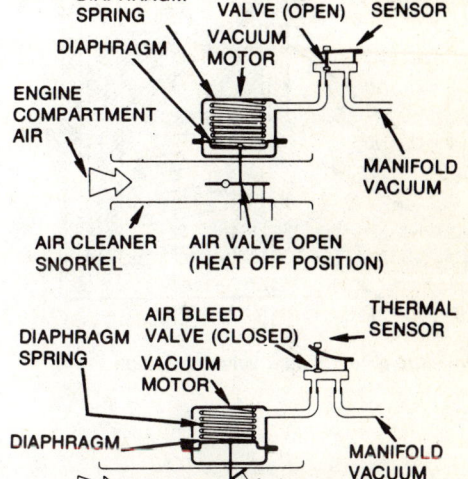

Thermostatically controlled air cleaner (upper open, lower closed)

Exhaust Emission Controls

All of the gasoline engines used in Jeep vehicles incorporate the air injection system for controlling the emission of exhaust gases into the atmosphere.

The exhaust emission air injection system consists of a belt driven air pump which directs compressed air through connecting hoses to a steel distribution manifold into stainless steel injection tubes in the exhaust port adjacent to

166 EMISSION CONTROLS

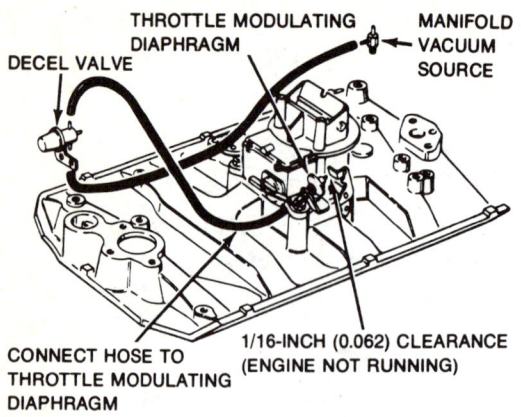
Typical vacuum throttle modulating system

each exhaust valve. The air, with its normal oxygen content, reacts with the hot, but incompletely burned exhaust gases and permits further combustion in the exhaust port or manifold.

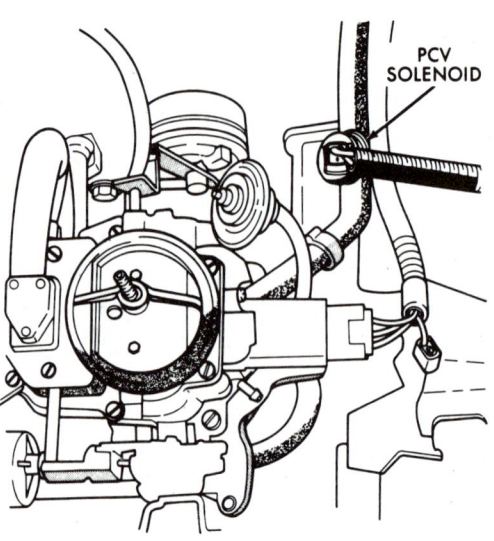
PCV shut-off solenoid

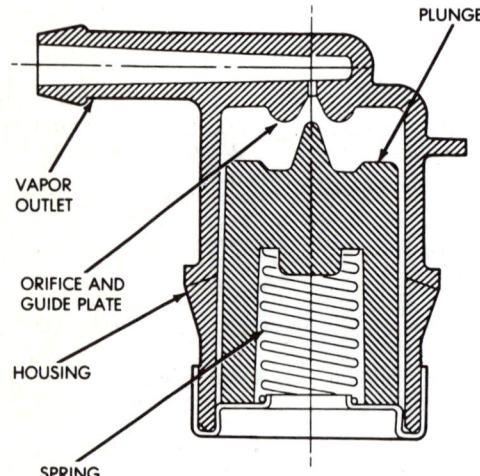
Pressure relief/rollover valve operation

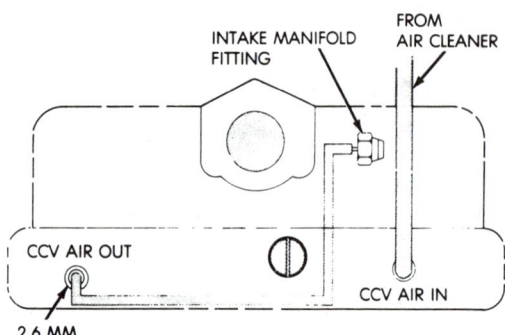
CCV system for the 6-243

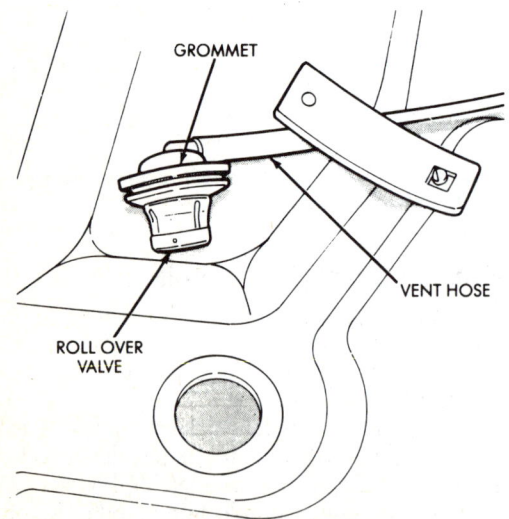
Pressure relief/rollover valve installation

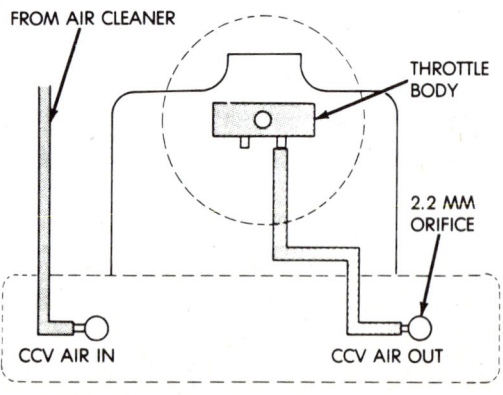
CCV system for the 4-150

EMISSION CONTROLS 167

AIR PUMP

The air injection pump is a positive displacement vane type which is permanently lubricated and requires little periodic maintenance. The only serviceable parts on the air pump are the filter, exhaust tube, and relief valve. The relief valve relieves the air flow when the pump pressure reaches a preset level. This occurs at high engine rpm. This serves to prevent damage to the pump and to limit maximum exhaust manifold temperatures.

Pump Air Filter

The air filter attached to the pump is a replaceable element type. The filter should be replaced every 12,000 miles under normal conditions and sooner under off-road use. Some models draw their air supply through the carburetor air filter.

Air Delivery Manifold

The air delivery manifold distributes the air from the pump to each of the air delivery tubes in a uniform manner. A check valve is integral with the air delivery manifold. Its function is to prevent the reverse flow of exhaust gases to the pump should the pump fail. This reverse flow would damage the air pump and connecting hose.

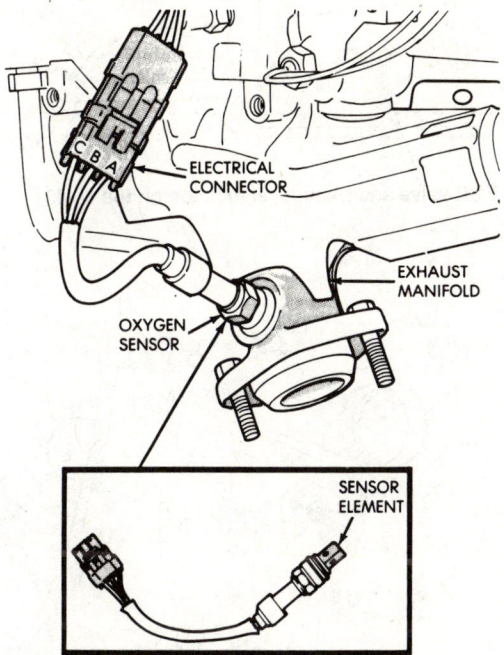

6-243 heated oxygen sensor

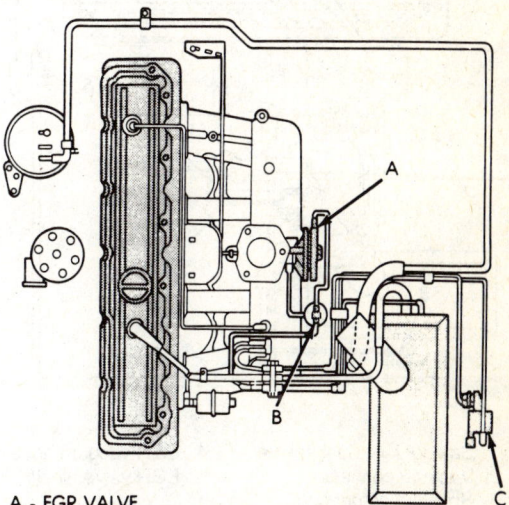

A - EGR VALVE
B - VACUUM TRANSDUCER
C - EGR SOLENOID

6-243 EGR system

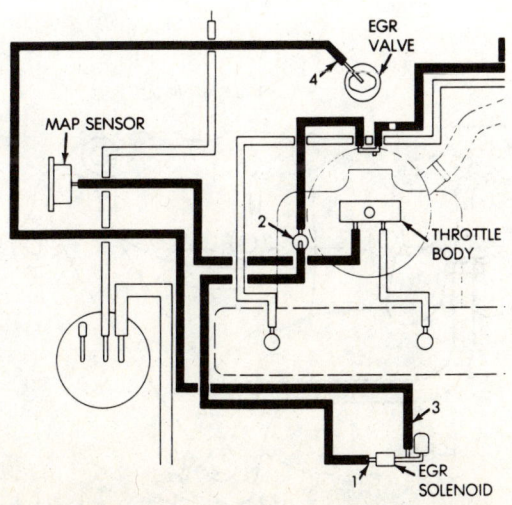

1. Solenoid vacuum source
2. Manifold fitting
3. Solenoid output port
4. EGR vacuum hose

4-150 w/TBI EGR system test points

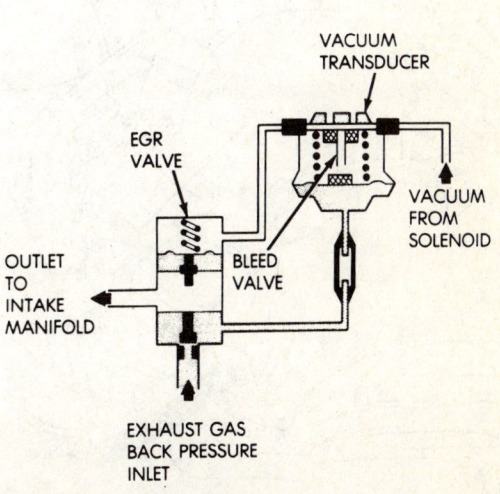

6-243 EGR valve operation

168 EMISSION CONTROLS

Air Injection Tubes

The air injection tubes are inserted into the exhaust ports. The tubes project into the exhaust ports, directing air into the vicinity of the exhaust valve.

Anti-Backfire Valve

The anti-backfire diverter valve prevents engine backfire by briefly interrupting the air being injected into the exhaust manifold during periods of deceleration or rapid throttle closure. The valve opens when a sudden increase in manifold vacuum overcomes the diaphragm spring tension. With the valve in the open posi-

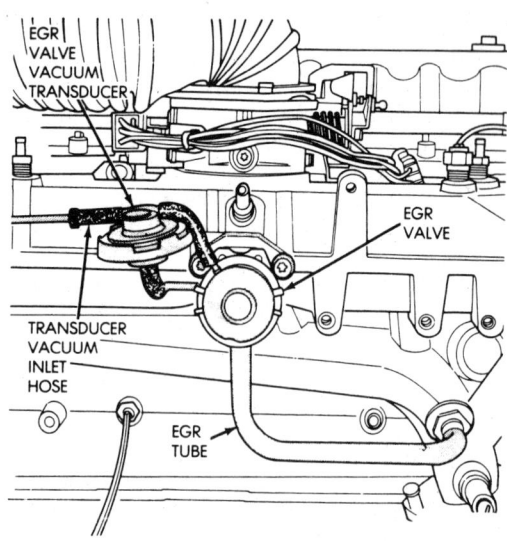

EGR valve and transducer location on the 6-243

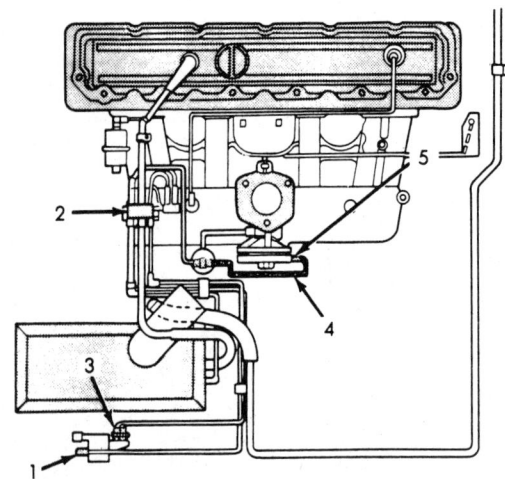

1. Solenoid vacuum source
2. Vacuum connector
3. Solenoid output port
4. EGR vacuum hose
5. EGR valve nipple

6-243 EGR system test points

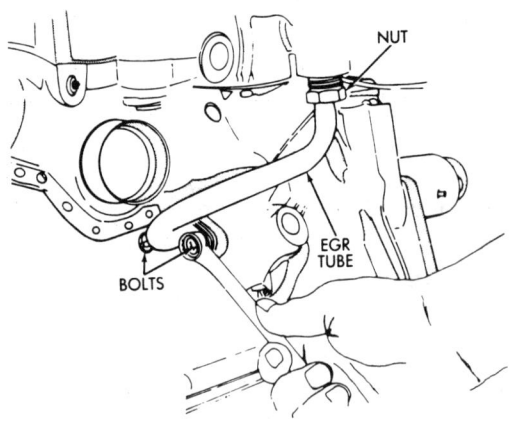

4-150 EGR tube removal

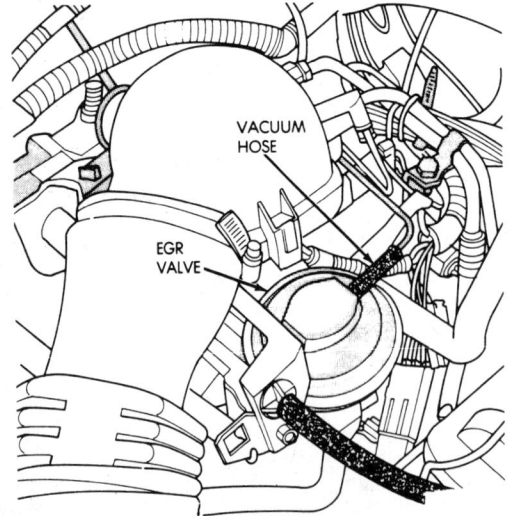

EGR valve location on the 4-150

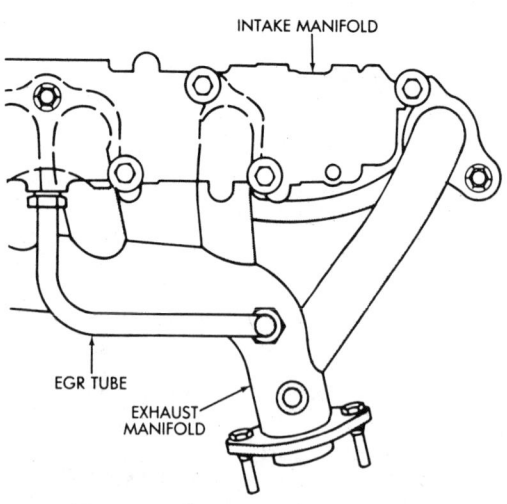

6-243 EGR tube removal

EMISSION CONTROLS

tion, the air flow from the air pump is directed to the atmosphere.

Carburetor

The carburetors used on engines equipped with emission controls have specific flow characteristics that differ from the carburetors used on vehicles not equipped with emission control devices. The carburetors are identified by number. The correct carburetor should be used when replacement is necessary.

Thermostatically Controlled Air Cleaner System (TAC)

This system consists of a heat shroud which is integral with the right side exhaust manifold, a hot air hose and a special air cleaner assembly equipped with a thermal sensor and a vacuum motor and air valve assembly.

The thermal sensor incorporates an air bleed valve which regulates the amount of vacuum applied to the vacuum motor, controlling the air valve position to supply either heated air from the exhaust manifold or air from the engine compartment.

During the warm-up period when underhood temperatures are low, the air bleed valve is closed and sufficient vacuum is applied to the vacuum motor to hold the air valve in the closed (heat on) position.

As the temperature of the air entering the air cleaner approaches approximately 115°F, the air bleed valve opens to decrease the amount of vacuum applied to the vacuum motor. The diaphragm spring in the vacuum motor then moves the air valve into the open (heat off) position, allowing only underhood air to enter the air cleaner.

The air valve in the air cleaner will also open, regardless of air temperature, during heavy acceleration to obtain maximum air flow through the air cleaner.

AMBIENT TEMPERATURE OVERRIDE SWITCH

This switch, located at the firewall, senses ambient temperatures and completes the electrical circuit from the battery to the solenoid vacuum valve when the ambient temperatures are above 63°F.

SOLENOID VACUUM VALVE

This valve is attached to the ignition coil bracket at the right side of the engine (V6 engines) or to a bracket at the rear of the intake manifold (inline engines). When the valve is energized, carburetor vacuum is blocked off and the distributor vacuum line is vented to the atmosphere through a port in the valve, resulting in no vacuum advance. When the valve is deenergized, vacuum is applied to the distributor resulting in normal vacuum advance.

SOLENOID CONTROL SWITCH

This switch is located at the transmission valve body. It opens or closes in relation to car speed and gear range. When the transmission is in high gear, the switch opens and breaks the ground circuit to the solenoid vacuum valve. In lower gear ranges the switch closes and completes the ground circuit to the solenoid vacuum valve. With a manual transmission, the switch is operated by the transmission shifter shaft. With automatic transmissions, the switch is controlled by the speedometer gear speed. Under speeds of 25 mph, the switch is activated.

MAINTENANCE AND SERVICE

Efficient performance of the exhaust emission control system is dependent upon precise maintenance.

Carburetor

Proper idle mixture adjustment is imperative for best exhaust emission control. The idle adjustment should be made with the engine at normal operating temperature and the air cleaner in place. All lights and accessories must be turned off and the transmission must be in neutral. See Chapter 2 for adjustment procedures.

Check Valve

The check valve in the air distribution manifold prevents the reverse flow of exhaust gases to the pump in the event the pump should become inoperative or should exhaust pressure ever exceed the pump pressure.

To check this valve for proper operation, remove the air supply hose from the pump at the distribution manifold. With the engine running, listen for exhaust leakage where the check valve is connected to the distribution manifold. If leakage is audible, the valve is not operating correctly.

Air Pump

Check for the proper drive belt tension and adjust as necessary. Do not pry on the die cast pump housing. Check to see if the pump is discharging air. Remove the air outlet hose at the pump. With the engine running, air should be felt at the pump outlet opening.

REMOVAL AND INSTALLATION

Air Pump

1. Loosen the air pump adjusting bracket bolts.

2. Remove the drive belt.
3. Remove the air pump intake and discharge hoses.
4. Remove the air pump from the engine.
5. To install, reverse the above procedure.

Anti-Backfire Valve

To remove the anti-backfire valve, disconnect the hoses and bracket-to-engine attaching screws. Install in the reverse order of removal.

Air Distribution Manifold and Air Injection Tubes

1. Disconnect the air delivery hose from the air injection manifold.
2. Unscrew the air injection tube from the exhaust manifold or the head. Some resistance may be encountered because of the normal buildup of carbon. The application of heat may be helpful in removing the air injection tubes.
3. Install in the reverse order of removal.

Exhaust Gas Recirculation (EGR) System

The EGR system consists of a diaphragm actuated flow control valve (EGR valve), coolant temperature override switch, low temperature vacuum signal modulator, high temperature vacuum signal modulator.

All California units have a back pressure sensor which modulates EGR signal vacuum according to the rise or fall of exhaust pressure in the manifold. A restrictor plate is not used in these applications.

The purpose of the EGR system is to limit the formation of nitrogen oxides by diluting the fresh air intake charge with a metered amount of exhaust gas, thereby reducing the peak temperatures of the burning gases in the combustion chambers.

EGR VALVE

The EGR valve is mounted on a machined surface at the rear of the intake manifold on the V8s and on the side of the intake manifold on the sixes.

The valve is held in a normally closed position by a coil spring located above the diaphragm. A special fitting is provided at the carburetor to route ported (above the throttle plates) vacuum through hose connections to a fitting located above the diaphragm on the valve. A passage in the intake manifold directs exhaust gas from the exhaust crossover passage (V6) or from below the riser area (inline engines) to the EGR valve. When the diaphragm is actuated by vacuum, the valve opens and meters exhaust gas through another passage in the intake manifold to the floor of the intake manifold below the carburetor.

COOLANT TEMPERATURE OVERRIDE SWITCH

This switch is located at the left side of the engine block on the 6-243. The outer port of the switch is open and not used. The inner port is connected by a host to the EGR fitting at the carburetor. The center port is connected to the EGR valve. When coolant temperature is below 115°F, the center port of the switch is closed and no vacuum signal is applied to the EGR valve; therefore, no exhaust gas will flow through the valve. When the coolant temperature reaches 115°F, both the center port and the inner port of the switch are open and a vacuum signal is applied to the EGR valve. This vacuum signal is, however, subject to regulation by the low and high temperature signal modulators.

LOW TEMPERATURE VACUUM SIGNAL MODULATOR

This unit is located just to the right of the radiator behind the grill opening. The low temperature vacuum signal modulator vacuum hose is connected by a plastic T-fitting to the EGR vacuum signal hose. The modulator is open when ambient temperatures are below 60°F. This causes a weakened vacuum signal to the EGR valve and a resultant decrease in the amount of exhaust gas being recirculated.

HIGH TEMPERATURE VACUUM SIGNAL MODULATOR

This unit is located at the right front fender inner panel on the Wagoneer and Cherokee. The high temperature vacuum signal modulator is connected to the EGR vacuum signal hose by a plastic T-fitting. The modulator opens when the underhood air temperatures reach 115°F and it causes a weakened vacuum signal to the EGR valve, thus reducing the amount of exhaust gases being recirculated.

Electric Assist Choke

An electric assist choke is used to more accurately match the choke operation to engine requirements. It provides extra heat to the choke bimetal spring to speed up the choke valve opening after the underhood air temperature reaches 95°F ± 15°F. Its purpose is to reduce the emission of carbon monoxide (CO) during the engine's warmup period.

A special AC terminal is provided at the alternator to supply a 7 volt power source for the electric choke. A thermostatic switch within the choke cover closes when the underhood air temperature reaches 95°F ± 15°F and allows current to flow to a ceramic heating element. The circuit is completed through the choke cover ground strap and choke housing to the engine. As the heating element warms up, heat is absorbed by an attached metal plate which in turn heats the coke bimetal spring.

After the engine is turned off, the thermostatic switch remains closed until the underhood temperature drops below approximately 65°F. Therefore, the heating element will immediately begin warming up when the engine is restarted, if the underhood temperature is above 65°F.

Fuel Tank Vapor Emission Control System

A closed fuel tank system is used on all models to route raw fuel vapor from the fuel tank into the PCV system, where it is burned along with the fuel-air mixture. The system prevents raw fuel vapors from entering the atmosphere.

The fuel vapor system consists of internal fuel tank venting, a vacuum-pressure fuel tank filler cap, an expansion tank or charcoal filled canister, liquid limit fill valve, and internal carburetor venting.

Fuel vapor pressure in the fuel tank forces the vapor through vent lines to the expansion tank or charcoal filled storage canister. The vapor then travels through a single vent line to the limit fill valve, which regulates the vapor flow to the valve cover or air cleaner.

LIMIT FILL VALVE

This valve is essentially a combination vapor flow regulator and pressure relief valve. It regulates vapor flow from the fuel tank vent line into the valve cover. The valve consists of a housing, a spring-loaded diaphragm and a diaphragm cover. As tank vent pressure increases, the diaphragm lifts, permitting vapor to flow through. The pressure at which this occurs is 4-6 in. of water column. This action regulates the flow of vapors under severe conditions, but generally prohibits the flow of vapor during normal temperature operation, thus minimizing driveability problems.

Catalytic Converter

All gasoline engines are equipped with a catalytic converter. Most models use a single pellet-filled unit, while some California models use a single monolithic type unit.

The pellet type contains beads of alumina coated with platinum and palladium, contained in a stainless steel canister. A plug is provided in the unit for replacement of the beads if they become fouled. The monolithic unit uses an extruded core resembling a honeycomb. The core layers are coated with platinum and palladium. This unit is not serviceable.

Oxygen Sensor
REMOVAL AND INSTALLATION

1. Raise the vehicle and support it safely. Allow the exhaust system to cool sufficiently to permit servicing.
2. Disconnect the wire connector from the oxygen sensor.
3. Remove the oxygen sensor from the exhaust manifold.
4. If not already done, coat the threads of the replacement sensor with anti-seize compound. Be careful not to contaminate the oxygen sensor probe with the anti-seize.
5. Install the oxygen sensor into the exhaust manifold and tighten to 35 ft. lbs. (48 Nm). Reconnect the wire connector.

AMC/JEEP COMPUTERIZED EMISSION CONTROL (CEC) SYSTEM

General Information

The Computerized Emission Control System (CEC) is used on all gasoline engines. There are two primary modes of operation for the CEC feedback system, open loop and closed loop. The system will be in the open loop mode of operation (or a variation of it) whenever the engine operating conditions do not meet the programmed criteria for closed loop operation. During open loop operation, the air/fuel mixture is maintained at a programmed ratio that is dependent on the type of engine operation involved. The oxygen sensor data is not accepted by the system during this mode of operation. The following conditions involve open loop operation.
- Engine start-up
- Coolant temperature too low
- Oxygen sensor temperature too low
- Engine idling
- Wide open throttle (WOT)
- Battery voltage too low

When all input data meets the programmed criteria for closed loop operation, the exhaust gas oxygen content signal from the oxygen sensor is accepted by the computer. This results in an air/fuel mixture that will be optimum for the engine operating condition and also will correct any pre-existing mixture condition which is too lean or too rich.

NOTE: *A high oxygen content in the exhaust gas indicates a lean air/fuel mixture. A low oxygen content indicates a rich air/fuel mixture. The optimum air/fuel mixture ratio is 14.7:1.*

EMISSION CONTROLS

Micro Computer Unit (MCU)

The micro computer unit, or MCU, is the heart of the CEC system. The MCU receives signals from various engine sensors to constantly monitor the engine operating conditions, then it uses this information to make adjustments in order to achieve the optimum performance and economy with a minimum of engine emissions. The MCU monitors the oxygen sensor voltage and, based upon the mode of operation, generates an output control signal for the carburetor stepper motor or mixture control solenoid. If the system is in the closed loop mode of operation, the air/fuel mixture will vary according to the oxygen content in the exhaust gas and engine operating conditions. If the system is in the open loop mode of operation, the air/fuel mixture will be based on a predetermined ratio that is dependent on engine rpm. In addition, the MCU generates output signals to control ignition timing and engine idle speed, PCV flow and Pulse Air System operation.

Mixture Control Solenoid

On engines with the Carter YFA or Rochester E2SE carburetors, a mixture control (MC) solenoid is used to regulate the air/fuel mixture. During open loop operation, the MC solenoid supplies a preprogrammed amount of air to the carburetor idle circuit and main metering circuit where it mixes with the fuel. During closed loop operation, the MCU operates the MC solenoid to provide additional or less air to the fuel mixture, depending on the engine operating conditions as monitored by the various engine sensors.

Idle Relay and Solenoid

The idle relay is energized by the MCU to control the vacuum actuator portion of the Sole-Vac throttle positioner by providing a ground for the idle relay. The relay energizes the idle solenoid, which allows vacuum to operate the Sole-Vac vacuum actuator. This, in turn, opens the throttle and increases engine speed. The idle solenoid is located on a bracket on the left front inner fender panel and can be identified by the red connecting wires.

Sole-Vac Throttle Positioner

The Sole-Vac throttle positioner is attached to the carburetor. The unit consists of a closed throttle switch, a holding solenoid and a vacuum actuator. The holding solenoid maintains the throttle position, while the vacuum actuator provides additional engine idle speed when accessories such as the air conditioner or rear window defogger are in use. The vacuum actuator is also activated during deceleration and if the steering wheel is turned to the full stop position on vehicles equipped with power steering.

Upstream and Downstream Air Switch Solenoids

The upstream and downstream solenoids of the pulse air system distribute air to the exhaust pipe and catalytic converter. Both solenoids are energized by the MCU to route air into the the exhaust pipe at a point after the oxygen sensor. When energized, the downstream solenoid routes air into the second bed of the dual-bed catalytic converter. This additional air reacts with the exhaust gases to reduce engine emissions.

The solenoids are located on a bracket attached to the left inner front fender panel. The idle solenoid is also located on this same bracket.

PCV Shutoff Solenoid

The positive crankcse ventilation shutoff solenoid is installed in the PCV valve hose and is energized by the MCU to turn off the crankcase ventilation system when the engine is at idle speed. An anti-diesel relay system on 4 cylinder engines, consisting of an anti-diesel relay and a delay relay, prevents engine run-on when the ignition is switched off by momentarily energizing the PCV valve solenoid when the ignition is switched off to prevent air entering below the throttle plate.

Bowl Vent Solenoid

The bowl vent solenoid is located in the hose between the carburetor bowl vent and the canister. The bowl vent solenoid is closed and allows no fuel vapor to flow when the engine is operating. When the engine is not operating, the solenoid is open and allows vapor to flow to the charcoal canister to control hydrocarbon emissions from the carburetor float bowl. The bowl vent solenoid is electrically energized when the ignition is switched ON and is not controlled by the MCU.

Intake Manifold Heater Switch

The intake manifold heater switch is located in the intake manifold and is controlled by the temperature of the engine coolant. Below 160°F (71°C) the manifold heater switch activates the intake manifold heater to improve fuel vaporization. The switch is not controlled by the MCU and does not provide input information to it.

Oxygen Sensor

This component of the system provides a variable voltage (millivolts) for the micro computer unit (MCU) that is proportional to the oxygen content in the exhaust gas. In addition to

EMISSION CONTROLS

the oxygen sensor, the following data senders are used to supply the MCU with engine operation data.

Knock Sensor

The knock sensor is a tuned piezoelectric crystal transducer that is located in the cylinder head. The knock sensor provides the MCU with an electrical signal that is created by vibrations that correspond to its center frequency (5550 Hz). Vibrations from engine knock (detonation) cause the crystal inside the sensor to vibrate and produce an electrical signal that is used by the MCU to selectively retard the ignition timing of any single cylinder or combination of cylinders to eliminate the knock condition.

Vacuum Switches

Two vacuum-operated electrical switches (ported and manifold) are used to detect and send throttle position data to the MCU for idle (closed), partial and wide open throttle (WOT). These switches are located together in a bracket attached to the dash panel in the engine compartment. The 4 in. Hg vacuum switch can be identified by its natural (beige) color, while the 10 in. Hg vacuum switch is green in color. The 4 in. Hg switch is controlled by ported vacuum and its electrical contact is normally in the open position when the vacuum level is less than 4 in. Hg. When the vacuum exceeds 4 in. Hg, the switch closes. The 4 in. Hg vacuum switch tells the MCU when either a closed or deep throttle condition exists.

The 10 in. Hg vacuum switch is controlled by manifold vacuum. Its electrical contact is normally closed when the vacuum level is less than 10 in. Hg; if the vacuum level exceeds 10 in. Hg, the switch opens. This switch tells the MCU that either a partial or medium throttle condition exists.

Engine RPM Voltage

This voltage is supplied from a terminal on the distributor. Until a voltage equivalent to a predetermined rpm is received by the MCU, the system remains in the open loop mode of operation. The result is a fixed rich air/fuel mixture for starting purposes.

Coolant Temperature Switch

The temperature switch supplies engine coolant temperature data to the MCU. Until the engine is sufficiently warmed (above 135°F/57°C), the system remains in the open loop mode of operation (i.e., a fixed air/fuel mixture based upon engine rpm).

Thermal Electric Switch

The thermal electric switch is located inside the air cleaner to sense the incoming air temperature and indicate a cold weather start-up condition to the MCU when the air temperature is below 50°F (10°C). Above 65°F (18°C), the switch opens to indicate a normal engine start-up condition to the MCU.

Wide Open Throttle (WOT) Switch

The wide open throttle switch is attached to the base of the carburetor by a mounting bracket. It is a mechanically operated electrical switch that is controlled by the position of the throttle. When the throttle is placed in the wide open position, a cam on the throttle shaft actuates the switch about 15° before wide open position to indicate a full-throttle demand to the MCU.

Altitude Jumper Wire

The altitude jumper wire connector is located next to the MCU. The jumper wire provides the MCU with an indication of whether the vehicle is being operated above or below a 4000 ft. elevation (high altitude operation). The connector normally has no jumper wire installed. If a vehicle is to be operated in a designated high altitude area, a jumper wire must be installed.

CEC SYSTEM OPERATION – 4-150

The open loop mode of operation occurs when:

1. Starting engine, engine is cold or air cleaner air is cold.
2. Engine is at idle speed, accelerating to partial throttle or decelerating from partial throttle to idle speed.
3. Carburetor is either at or near wide open throttle (WOT).

When any of these conditions occur, the mixture control (MC) solenoid provides a predetermined air/fuel mixture ratio for each condition. Because the air/fuel ratios are predetermined and no feedback relative to the results is accepted, this type of operation is referred to as open loop operation. All open loop operations are characterized by predetermined air/fuel mixture ratios. Each operation (except closed loop) has a specific air/fuel ratio and because more than one of the engine operational selection conditions can be present at one time, the MCU is programmed with a priority ranking for the operations. It complies with the conditions that pertain to the operation having the highest priority. The priorities are as described below.

Cold Weather Engine Start-Up and Operation

If the air cleaner air temperature is below the calibrated value (55°F or 13°C) of the thermal electric switch (TES), the air/fuel mixture is at a "rich" ratio. Lean air/fuel mixtures are not

174 EMISSION CONTROLS

permitted for a preset period following a cold weather start-up.

At or Near Wide Open Throttle (WOT) Operation (Cold Engine)

This open loop operation occurs whenever the coolant temperature is below the calibrated switching value (95°F or 35°C) of the open loop coolant temperature switch and the WOT vacuum switch (cold) has been closed because of the decrease in manifold vacuum (less than 5 in. Hg or 17 kPa). When this open loop condition occurs the MC solenoid provides a rich air/fuel mixture for cold engine operation at wide open throttle.

NOTE: *Temperature and switching vacuum levels are nominal values. The actual switching temperature or vacuum level will vary slightly from switch to switch.*

At or Near Wide Open Throttle (WOT) Operation (Warm Engine)

This open loop operation occurs whenever the coolant temperature is above the calibrated switching temperature (135°F or 57°C) of the enrichment coolant temperature switch and the WOT vacuum switch (warm) has been opened because of the decrease in manifold vacuum (less than 3 in. Hg or 10 kPa). When this open loop condition occurs the MC solenoid provides a rich air/fuel mixture for warm engine operation at wide open throttle.

Adaptive Mode of Operation

This open loop operation occurs when the engine is either at idle speed, accelerating from idle speed or decelerating to idle speed. If the engine rpm (tach) voltage is less than the calibrated value and manifold vacuum is above the calibrated switching level for the adaptive vacuum switch (i.e., switch closed), an engine idle condition is assumed to exist. If the engine rpm (tach) voltage is greater than the calibrated value and manifold vacuum is above the calibrated switching level of the adaptive vacuum switch (i.e., switch closed), an engine-deceleration-to-idle speed condition is assumed to exist. During the adaptive mode of operation the MC solenoid provides a predetermined air/fuel mixture.

Closed Loop Operation

Closed loop operation occurs whenever none of the open loop engine operating conditions exist. The MCU causes the MC solenoid to vary the air/fuel mixture in reaction to the voltage input from the oxygen sensor located in the exhaust manifold. The oxygen sensor voltage varies in reaction to changes in oxygen content present in the exhaust gas. Because the content of oxygen in the exhaust gas indicates the completeness of the combustion process, it is a reliable indicator of the air/fuel mixture that is entering the combustion chamber.

Because the oxygen sensor only reacts to oxygen, manifold air leak or malfunction between the carburetor and sensor may cause the sensor to provide an erroneous voltage output. The engine operation characteristics never quite permit the MCU to compute a single air/fuel mixture ratio that constantly provides the optimum air/fuel mixture. Therefore, closed loop operation is characterized by constant variation of the air/fuel mixture because the MCU is forced constantly to make small corrections in an attempt to create an optimum air/fuel mixture ratio.

DIAGNOSIS AND TESTING

The CEC System should be considered as a possible source of trouble for engine performance, fuel economy and exhaust emission complaints only after normal tests and inspections that would apply to an automobile without the system have been performed. The steps in each test will provide a systematic evaluation of each component that could cause an operational malfunction.

To determine if fault exists with the system, a system operational test is necessary. This test should be performed when the CEC System is suspected because no other reason can be determined for a specific complaint. A dwell meter, digital volt-ohmmeter, tachometer, vacuum gauge and jumper wires are required to diagnose system problems. Although most dwell meters should be acceptable, if one causes a change in engine operation when it is connected to the mixture control (MC) solenoid dwell pigtail wire test connector, it should not be used.

The dwell meter, set for the six-cylinder engine scale and connected to a pigtail wire test connector leading from the mixture control (MC) solenoid, is used to determine the air/fuel mixture dwell. When the dwell meter is connected, do not allow the connector terminal to contact any engine component that is connected to engine ground. This includes hoses because they may be electrically conductive. With a normally operating engine, the dwell at both idle speed and partial throttle will be between 10 degrees and 50 degrees and will be varying. Varying means the pointer continually moves back and forth across the scale. The amount it varies is not important, only the fact that is does vary. This indicates closed loop operation, indicating the mixture is being varied according to the input voltage to the MCU from the oxygen sensor. With wide open throttle (WOT) and/or cold engine operation, the air/fuel mixture ratio will be predetermined and the pointer will only vary slightly. This is open loop operation, indicating the oxygen sensor output has no effect on the air/fuel mixture. If there is a question whether or not the system is in closed loop operation, richening or leaning the air/fuel mixture will cause the dwell to vary more if the system is in closed loop operation.

Test Equipment

The equipment required to perform the checks and tests includes a tachometer, a hand vacuum pump and a digital volt-ohmmeter (DVOM) with a minimum ohms per volt of 10 mega-ohms.

CAUTION: *The use of a voltmeter with less than 10 mega-ohms per volt input impedance can destroy the oxygen sensor. Since it is necessary to look inside the carburetor with the engine running, observe the following precautions.*

1. Shape a sheet of clear acrylic plastic at least 0.250" thick and 15" × 15".

2. Secure the acrylic sheet with an air cleaner wing nut after the top of the air cleaner has been removed.

3. Wear eye protection whenever performing checks and tests.

4. When engine is operating, keep hands and arms clear of fan, drive pulleys and belts. Do not wear loose clothing. Do not stand in line with fan blades.

5. Do not stand in front of running car.

CEC SYSTEM OPERATION–6 CYLINDER ENGINE

The open loop mode of operation occurs when:
1. Starting the engine, engine is cold or air cleaner air is cold.
2. Engine is at idle speed.
3. Carburetor is either at or near wide open throttle (WOT).

When any of these conditions occur, the metering pins are driven to a predetermined (programmed) position for each condition. Because the positions are predetermined and no feedback relative to the results is accepted, this type of operation is referred to as open loop operation. The five open loop operations are characterized by the metering pins being driven to a position where they are stopped and remain stationary.

Each operation (except closed loop) has a specific metering pin position and because more than one of the operation selection conditions can be present at one time, the MCU is programmed with a priority ranking for the operations. It complies with conditions that pertain to the operation having the highest priority. The priorities are as described below.

Cold Weather Engine Start-Up and Operation

If the air cleaner air temperature is below the calibrated value of the thermal electric switch (TES), the stepper motor is positioned a predetermined number of steps rich of the initialization position and air injection is diverted upstream. Lean air/fuel mixtures are not permitted for a preset period following a cold weather start-up.

Open Loop 1

Open Loop 1 will be selected if the air cleaner air temperature is above a calibrated value and open loop 2, 3, or 4 is not selected, and if the engine coolant temperature is below the calibrated value. The OL1 mode operates in lieu of normal closed loop operation during a cold engine operating condition. If OL1 operation is selected, one of two predetermined stepper motor positions are chosen, dependent if the altitude circuit (lean limit) jumper wire is installed. With each engine start-up, a start-up timer is activated. During this interval, if the engine operating condition would otherwise trigger normal closed loop operation, OL1 operation is selected.

Open Loop 2, Wide Open Throttle (WOT)

Open Loop 2 is selected whenever the air cleaner air temperature is above the calibrated value of the thermal electric switch (TES) and the WOT switch has been engaged. When the Open Loop 2 mode is selected, the stepper motor is driven to a calibrated number of steps rich of initialization and the air control valve switches air "downstream". However, if the "lean limit" circuit (with altitude jumper wire) is being used, the air is instead directed "upstream". The WOT timer is activated whenever OL2 is selected and remains active for a preset period of time. The WOT timer remains inoperative if the "lean limit" circuit is being used.

Open Loop 3

Open Loop 3 is selected when the ignition advance vacuum level falls below a predetermined level. When the OL3 mode is selected, the engine rpm is also determined. If the rpm (tach) voltage is greater than the calibrated value, an engine deceleration condition is assumed to exist. If the rpm (tach) voltage is less than the calibrated value, an engine idle speed condition is assumed to exist.

Open Loop 4

Open Loop 4 is selected whenever manifold vacuum falls below a predetermined level. During OL4 operation, the stepper motor is positioned at the initialization position. Air injection is switched "upstream" during OL4 operation. However, air is switch "downstream" if the extended OL4 timer is activated and if the "lean limit" circuit is not being used (without altitude jumper wire). Air is also switch "downstream" if the WOT timer is activated.

Closed Loop

Closed loop operation is selected after either OL1, OL2, OL3 or OL4 modes have been selected and the start-up timer has timed out. Air injection is routed "downstream" during closed loop operation. The predetermined "lean" air/fuel mixture ceiling is selected for a preset length of time at the onset of closed loop operation.

High Altitude Adjustment

An additional function of the MCU is to correct for a change in ambient conditions (e.g., high altitude). During closed loop operation the MCU stores the number of steps and direction that the metering pins are driven to correct the oxygen content of the exhaust. If the movements are consistently to the same position, the MCU will vary all open loop operation predetermined metering pin positions a corresponding amount. This function allows the open loop air/fuel mixture ratios to be "tailored" to the existing ambient conditions during each uninterrupted use of the system. This optimizes emission control and engine performance.

Closed Loop Operation

The CEC system controls the air/fuel ratio with movable air metering pins, visible from the top of the carburetor air horn, that are driven by the stepper motor. The stepper motor moves the metering pins in increments or small steps via electrical impulses generated by the MCU. The MCU causes the stepper motor to drive the metering pins to a "richer" or "leaner" position in reaction to the voltage input from the oxygen content present in the exhaust gas. Because the content of oxygen in the exhaust gas indicates the completeness of the combustion process, it is a reliable indicator of the air/fuel mixture that is entering the combustion chamber.

Because the oxygen sensor only reacts to oxygen, any air leak or malfunction between the carburetor and sensor may cause the sensor to provide an erroneous voltage output. This could be caused by a manifold air leak or malfunctioning secondary air check value. The engine operation characteristics never quite permit the MCU to compute a single metering pin position that constantly provides the optimum air/fuel mixture. Therefore, closed loop operation is characterized by constant movement of the metering pins because the MCU is forced constantly to make small corrections in the air/fuel mixture in an attempt to create an optimum air/fuel mixture ratio.

DIAGNOSIS AND TESTING

The idle speed control system is interrelated with the CEC system and must be diagnosed in conjunction with the CEC System. Refer to Diagnostic Tests 9, 10 and 11, if a malfunction occurs.

The electronic ignition retard function of the ignition control module is interrelated with CEC System and must be diagnosed in conjunction with CEC System. Refer to Diagnostic Test 4 if a malfunction occurs.

The air injection system is interrelated with the CEC System and must be diagnosed in conjunction with the CEC System. Refer to Diagnostic Test 6, 7 and 8 if a malfunction occurs.

Preliminary Tests

Before performing the Diagnostic Tests, other engine associated systems that can affect air/fuel mixture, combustion efficiency or exhaust gas composition should be tested for faults. These systems include:

1. Basic carburetor adjustments.
2. Mechanical engine operation (spark plugs, valves, rings, etc.).
3. Ignition system components and operation.
4. Gaskets (intake manifold, carburetor or base plate); loose vacuum hoses or fittings, or loose electrical connections.

Initialization

When the ignition system is turned off, the MCU is also turned off. It has no long term memory circuit for prior operation. As a result, it has an initialization function that is activated when the ignition switch is turned ON.

The MCU initialization function moves the metering pins to the predetermined starting position by first driving them all the way to the rich end stop and then driving them in the lean direction by a predetermined number of steps. No matter where they were before initialization, they will be at the correct position at the end of every initialization period. Because each open loop operation metering pin position is dependent on the initialization function, this function is the first test in the diagnostic procedure.

NOTE: *The CEC System should be considered as a possible source of trouble for engine performance, fuel economy and exhaust emission complaints only after normal tests that would apply to an automobile without the system have been performed.*

EMISSION CONTROLS

Jeep Self-Diagnostic System

Late model Jeep vehicles equipped with a six cylinder engine and California emissions package have a self-diagnostic system with a CHECK ENGINE light mounted in the instrument panel. The self-diagnostic system is designed to detect problems most likely to occur within the various system components.

When a jumper wire is connected between the trouble code test terminals 6 and 7 of the 15-terminal diagnostic connector (D2), the CHECK ENGINE light will flash a trouble code or codes that indicate a problem area. For a bulb and system check, the CHECK ENGINE light will illuminate when the ignition switch is ON and the engine not started. If the test terminals are then grounded, the light will flash a code 12 that indicates the self-diagnostic system is operational. A code 12 consists of one flash, followed by a short pause, then two more flashes in quick succession. After a longer pause, the code will repeat two more times.

When the engine is started, the CHECK ENGINE light will remain ON momentarily and then be turned off. If the CHECK ENGINE light remains on, the self-diagnostic system has detected a problem. If the trouble code test terminals are then grounded, the trouble code will be flashed three times; if more than one trouble code is stored, each will be flashed three more times in numerical order, from the lowest to the highest numbered code. This trouble code series will repeat as long as the test terminals are grounded.

A trouble code indicates a problem in a particular circuit or component. Trouble code 14, for example, indicates a problem in the coolant sensor circuit. It should be noted that the self-diagnostic system doesn't pinpoint where the problem is in the coolant sensor circuit, which includes the coolant sensor, connector, wire harness and the electronic control unit itself. The following diagnostic charts contain procedures for isolating the problem to a particular point in the circuit to avoid the unnecessary replacement of working components. A diagnosis chart is provided for each trouble code.

Because the self-diagnostic system does not detect all possible problems, the absence of a trouble code does not necessarily mean the system is functioning normally. The System Performance Test should be performed when the self-diagnostic system does not indicate a problem, but the system operation is suspect.

All system connectors in the engine compartment are sealed against debris and moisture. Because the system operates on low voltage and low current, corrosion on the connectors can cause problems. Before repairing or replacing any component, disconnect the appropriate connector(s) and check for proper installation, bent, broken or dirty terminals or mating tabs. Clean, straighten or replace the connectors as required, then reconnect everything and recheck the system operation to see if the problem has been corrected. The system should be considered as a possible cause of trouble only after normal engine diagnosis for ignition timing, carburetor and idle speed adjustments has been performed. The electronic control module (ECM) is located in the passenger compartment at the right side of the steering column below the instrument panel.

TROUBLE CODE MEMORY

When a problem develops in the feedback system, the CHECK ENGINE light will illuminate and a trouble code will be stored in the on-board computer memory. If the fault is intermittent, the CHECK ENGINE light will be turned off 10 seconds after the problem disappears. The trouble code will be retained in the memory until the battery voltage to the control unit is removed. Disconnecting the battery for 10 seconds will erase all stored trouble codes.

The CHECK ENIGNE light will be illuminated only if a problem exists that pertains to the conditions listed below. It takes up to 5 seconds minimum for the light to come on when a problem occurs. Code 12 is not stored in memory and any codes stored will be cleared if the problem does not reoccur within 50 engine starts. The trouble codes indicate problems as follows:

CODE 12: No distributor reference pulses to the ECM. This code is not stored in memory and will only flash while the trouble exists. This code is normal when the igition is switched ON with the engine not running.

CODE 13: Oxygen sensor circuit. The engine must operate for up to 5 minutes at part throttle, under road load, before this code will be set.

CODE 14: Shorted coolant sensor circuit. The engine must operate for up to 5 minutes before this code will be set.

CODE 15: Open coolant sensor circuit. The engine must operate for up to 5 minutes before this code will be set.

CODE 21: Throttle position sensor circuit. The engine must operate for at least 25 seconds at curb idle speed before this code will be set.

CODE 23: Mixture control solenoid circuit is shorted or open.

CODE 34: Vacuum sensor circuit. The engine must operate for up to 5 minutes at curb idle speed before this code will be set.

CODE 41: No distributor reference pulses to the ECM at the specified engine manifold vacuum. This code will be stored in memory.

178 EMISSION CONTROLS

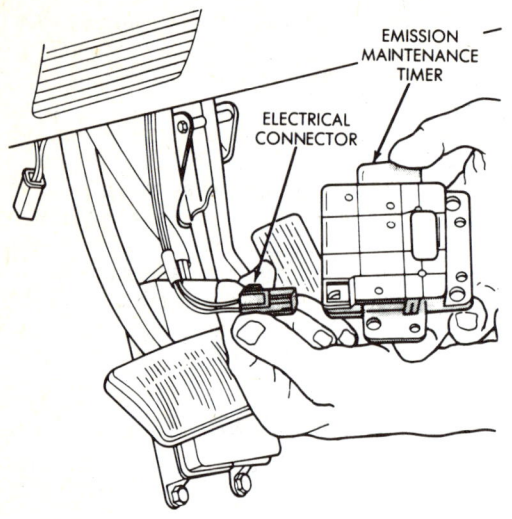

Emission timer

CODE 42: Electronic spark timing (EST) bypass circuit or EST circuit has short circuit to ground or an open circuit.

CODE 44: Lean exhaust indication. The engine must operate for up to 5 minutes, be in closed loop operation and at part throttle before this code will be set.

CODE 44 & 45: If these two codes appear at the same time, it indicates a problem in the oxygen sensor circuit.

CODE 45: Rich exhaust indication. The engine must operate for up to 5 minutes, be in closed loop and at part throttle before this code will be set.

CODE 51: Faulty calibration unit (PROM) or installation. It requires up to 30 seconds for this code to be set.

CODE 54: Mixture control (MC) solenoid circuit is shorted or the ECM is faulty.

CODE 55: Voltage reference has short circuit to ground (terminal 21), faulty oxygen sensor or faulty ECM.

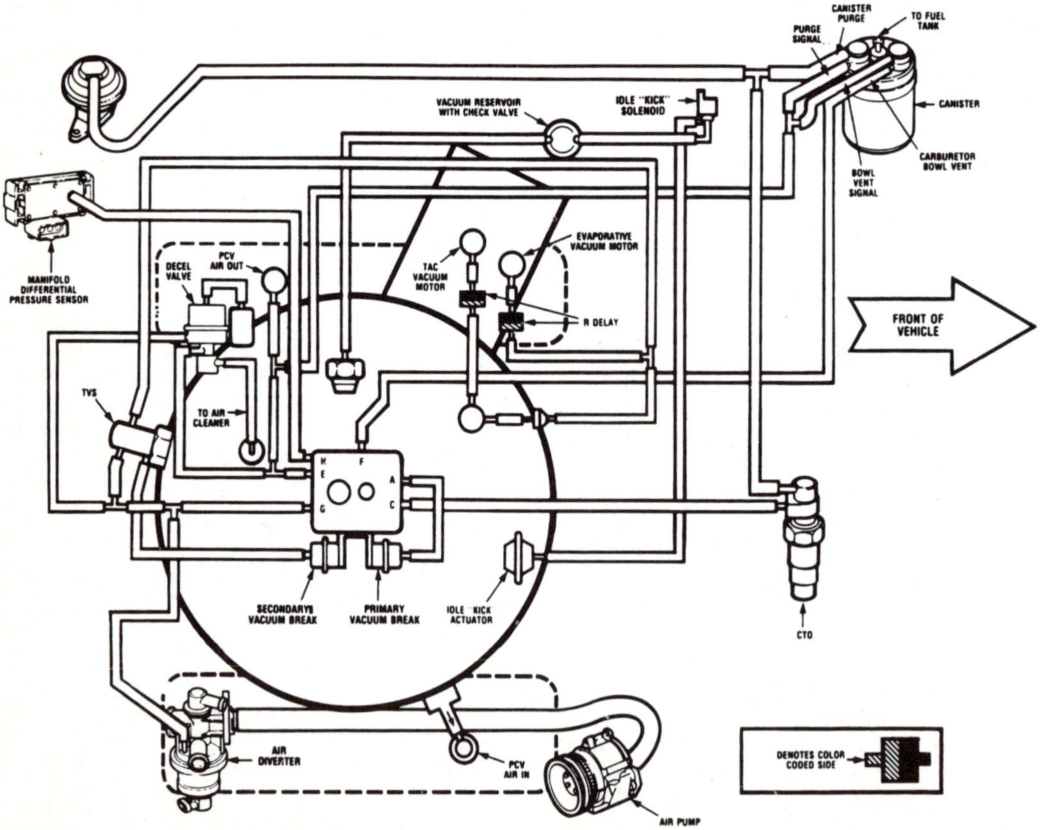

Emission control schematic for California 6-173 engines

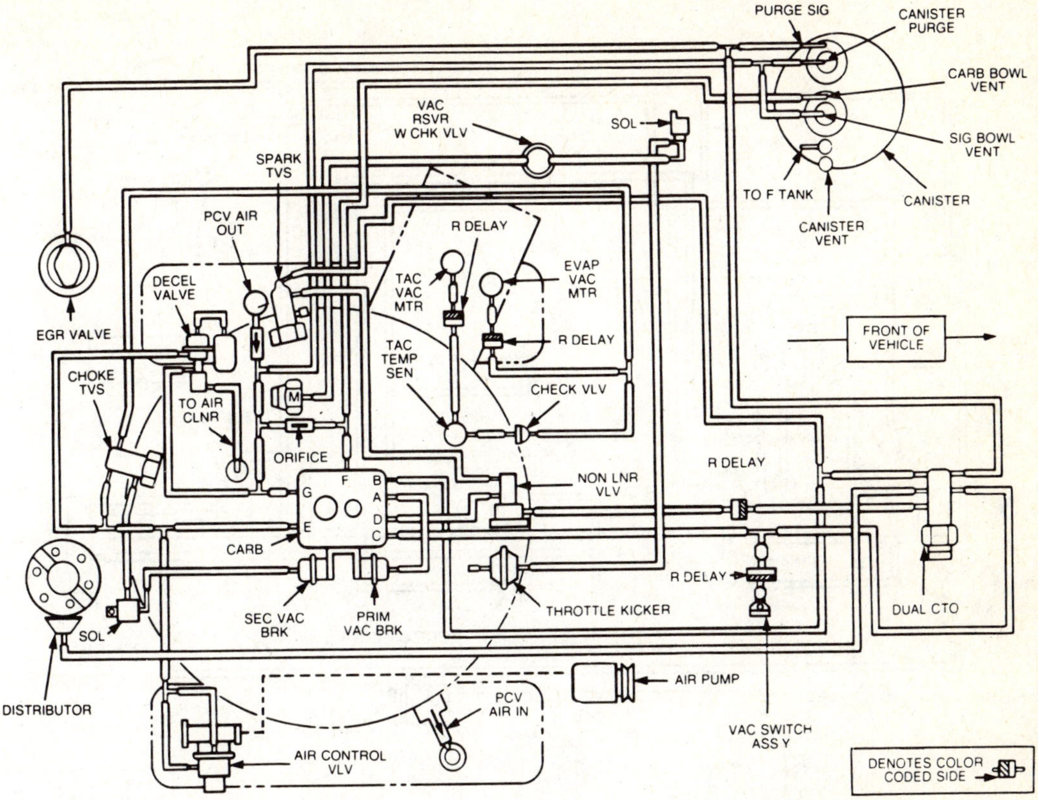

EMISSION CONTROLS 179

Emission control schematic for the U.S. 6-173 w/man. trans., except California

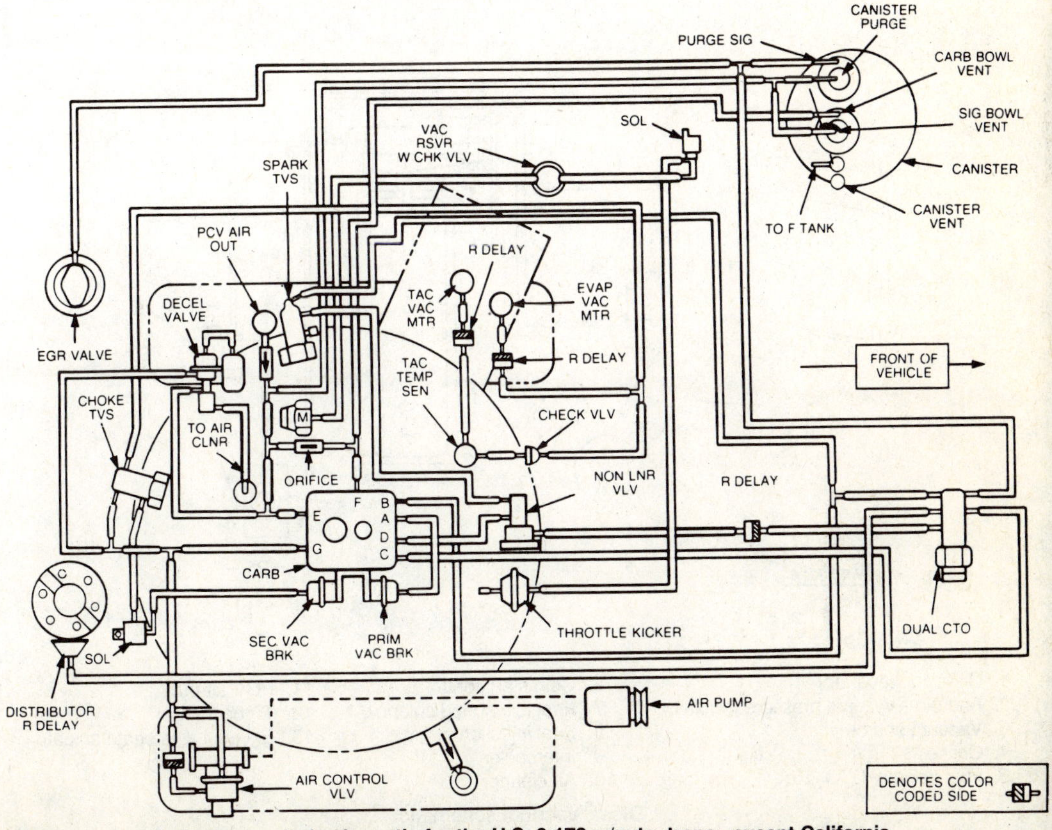

Emission control schematic for the U.S. 6-173 w/auto. trans., except California

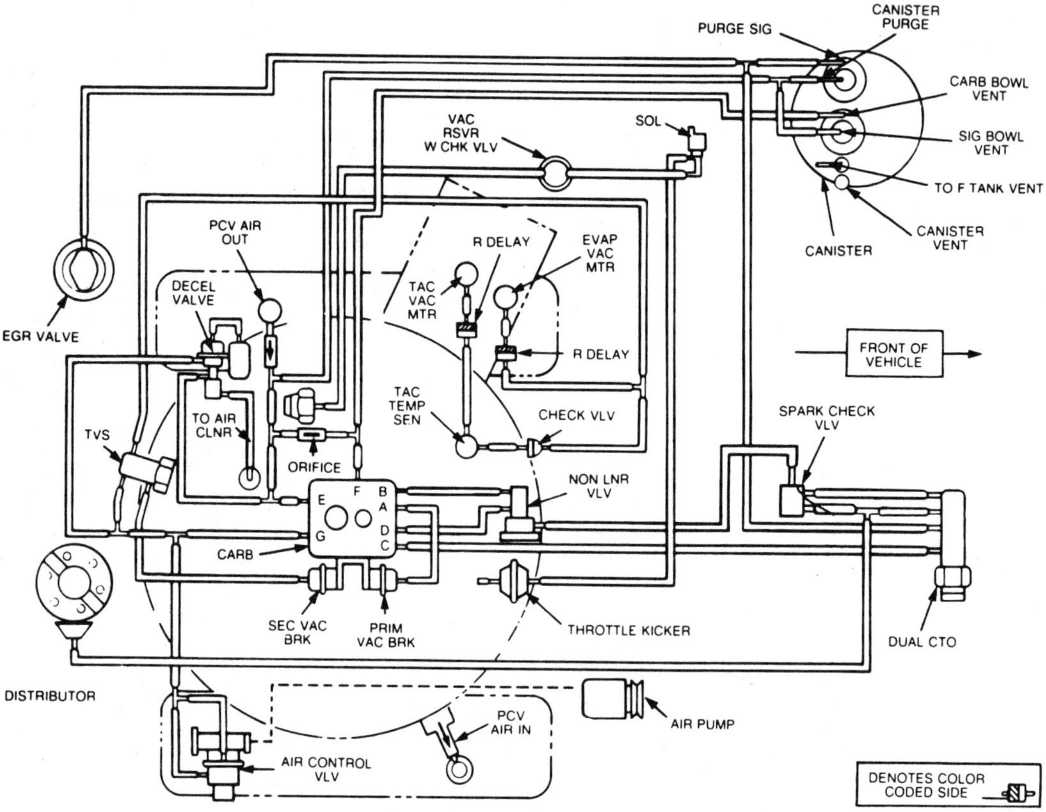

180 EMISSION CONTROLS

Emission control schematic for the Canadian 6-173

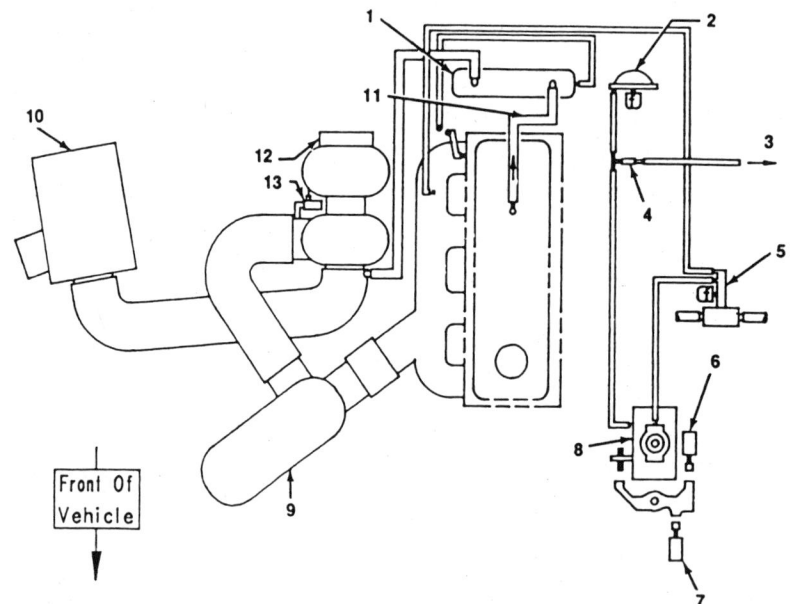

1. Oil/vapor separator
2. Aneroid—vacuum pressure regulator
3. Vacuum source
4. Orifice
5. Fuel delivery CTO
6. Cold start control
7. Fast idle speed solenoid
8. Fuel injection pump
9. Intercooler
10. Air cleaner
11. PCV air out
12. Turbocharger
13. Exhaust wastegate actuator

Diesel vacuum schematic

Fuel System
5

CARBURETED FUEL SYSTEM

Mechanical Fuel Pump
REMOVAL AND INSTALLATION
All Engines

1. Disconnect the inlet and outlet fuel lines and, on the 6-173, the fuel return line.
2. Remove the fuel pump body attaching nuts and lockwashers.
3. Pull the pump and gasket or O-ring free of the engine. On the 6-173, the actuating rod may fall from the engine. Make sure that the mating surfaces of the fuel pump and the engine are clean.
4. Cement a new gasket to the mounting flange of the fuel pump.
5. Position the fuel pump on the engine block so that the lever of the fuel pump rests on the fuel pump cam of the camshaft.
6. Secure the fuel pump to the block with the capscrews and lockwashers.
7. Connect the fuel lines to the fuel pump.

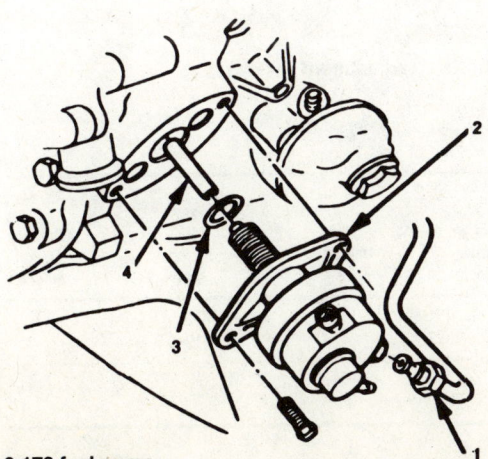

6-173 fuel pump

FUEL PUMP TESTING
Volume Check

Disconnect the fuel line from the carburetor. Place the open end in a one quart metal can. Start the engine and operate it at a normal idle speed. The pump should deliver at least one quart in one minute.

Pressure Check

Disconnect the fuel line at the carburetor. Install a T-fitting on the open end of the fuel line and refit the line to the carburetor. Plug a pressure gauge into the remaining opening of the T-fitting. The hose leading to the pressure gauge should not be any longer than 6". On pumps with a fuel return line, the line must be plugged. Start the engine. Fuel pressures are as follows:
4-150: 4.00-5.00 psi @ idle
6-173: 6.00-7.50 psi @ idle

Carter Model YFA Feedback Carburetor
4-150 Engine

DESCRIPTION

The Carter/Weber YFA carburetor consists of three main assemblies. The air horn contains the choke, vacuum break, choke plate, duty cycle solenoid, float and assembly. The main body contains the pump diaphragm assembly, metering jet, low-speed jet, accelerator pump check ball and weight, pump bleed valve and wide open throttle switch. The throttle body contains the throttle plate, throttle shaft and lever, idle mixture screw with O-ring and a tamper-proof plug.

The duty cycle solenoid is an integral part of the YFA carburetor. The control unit operates the duty cycle solenoid to provide the proper air/fuel ratio by controlling the air flow. In open

182 FUEL SYSTEM

loop operation, the air supplied by the duty cycle solenoid is preprogrammed. In closed loop operation, the control unit signals the duty cycle solenoid to provide additional air to the air/fuel mixture depending upon the sensor inputs to the control unit. Air from the duty cycle solenoid is then distributed to the carburetor idle circuit and main metering circuit where it mixes with the fuel.

ADJUSTMENTS

Fast Idle Speed Adjustment

1. Disconnect and plug the EGR valve vacuum hose at the valve.
2. Connect a tachometer to the ignition coil TACH terminal.
3. Place the automatic transmission in Park, or the manual transmission in Neutral, then start the engine and allow it to reach normal operating temperature.
4. Position the fast idle speed adjustment screw on the second step of the fast idle cam.
5. Turn the fast idle adjustment screw to obtain a fast idle speed of approximately 1500 rpm. The exact fast idle speed specification should be listed on the underhood emission sticker.
6. Allow the throttle to return to curb idle speed, then reconnect the EGR valve vacuum hose. Turn the ignition OFF and disconnect the tachometer.

Sole-Vac Vacuum Actuator Adjustment

1. Connect a tachometer to the ignition coil TACH terminal.
2. Place the automatic transmission in Park, or the manual transmission in Neutral.
3. Start the engine and allow it to reach normal operating temperature.
4. Connect an external vacuum source and apply 10-15 in. Hg (34-51 kPa) of vacuum to the Sole-Vac vacuum actuator.
5. Adjust the vacuum actuator to achieve an engine speed of approximately 1000 rpm. Check the underhood emission sticker for Sole-Vac rpm specification.
6. Turn the ignition OFF and disconnect the tachometer and vacuum pump. The Sole-Vac curb idle speed should be adjusted following this procedure.

Sole-Vac Curb Idle Speed Adjustment

1. Connect a tachometer to the ignition coil TACH terminal.

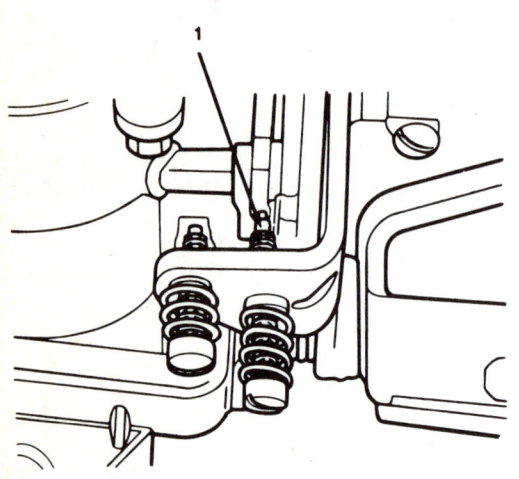

Carter YFA fast idle adjustment

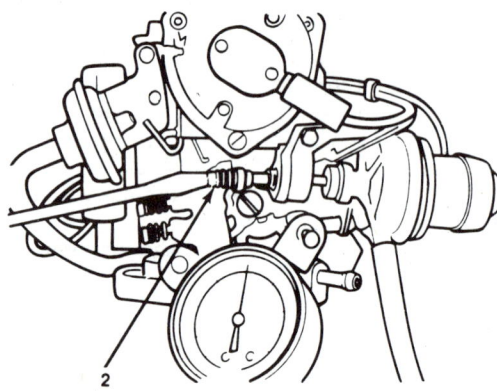

Sole-Vac adjustment screw (2)

Carter YFA

Engine	Years	Float Level (in.)	Initial Choke Valve Clearance (in.)	Fast Idle Cam Setting (in.)	Choke Unloader (in.)	Fast Idle Speed rpm	Automatic Choke Setting
4-150	1984	39/64	15/64	11/64	15/64	2,000 MT 2,300 AT	TR
	1985–86	39/64	9/32	11/64	15/64	2,000 MT 2,300 AT	TR

MT: Manual Transmission
AT: Automatic Transmission
TR: Tamper Resistant

FUEL SYSTEM 183

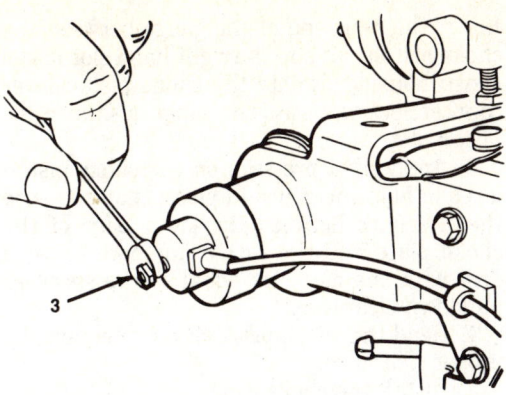

Curb idle speed adjustment screw (3)

2. Place the automatic transmission in Park, or the manual transmission in Neutral.
3. Start the engine and allow it to reach normal operating temperature.
4. Disconnect and plug the vacuum actuator vacuum hose.
5. Turn the hex head curb idle speed adjustment screw to achieve the curb idle speed specification listed on the underhood emission sticker.
6. Turn the ignition switch OFF, then disconnect the tachometer and reconnect the vacuum actuator hose.

Float Adjustment

Remove and invert the air horn assembly and check the clearance from the top of the float to the surface of the air horn with a T-scale. The air horn should be held at eye level when gauging and the float arm should be resting on the needle pin. Do not exert pressure on the needle valve when measuring or adjusting the float. Bend the float arm as necessary to adjust the float level.

CAUTION: *Do not bend the tab at the end of the float arm as it prevents the float from striking the bottom of the fuel bowl when empty and keeps the needle in place.*

Float Drop Adjustment

Hold the air horn upright and let the float hang freely. Measure the maximum clearance from the toe end of the float to the casting surface. Hold the air horn at eye level when measuring. To adjust, bend the tab at the end of the float arm.

Metering Rod Adjustment

1. Remove the air horn. Back out the idle speed adjusting screw until the throttle plate is seated fully in its bore.
2. Press down on the upper end of the diaphragm shaft until the diaphragm bottoms in the vacuum chamber.
3. The metering rod should contact the bottom of the metering rod well. The lifter link at the outer end nearest the springs and at the supporting link should be bottomed.
4. Turn the rod adjusting screw until the metering rod just bottoms in the body casting. For

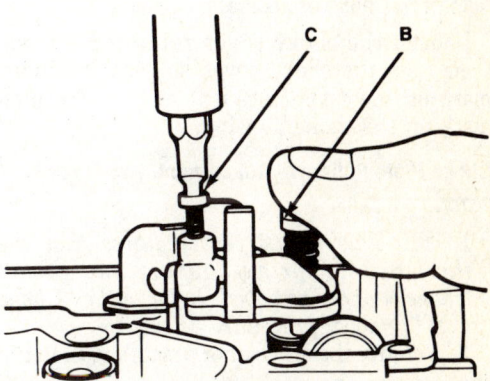

Metering rod adjustment. (B) is the pump diaphragm shaft; (C) is the adjusting screw

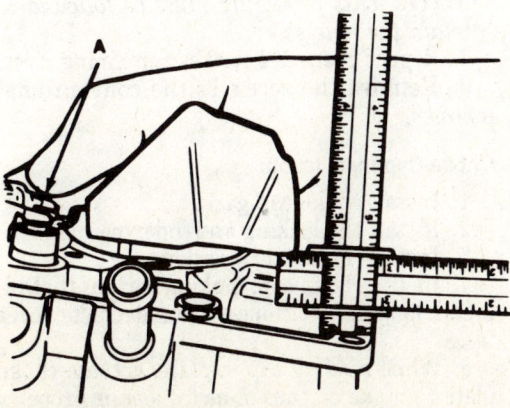

Measuring float clearance on the 4-150

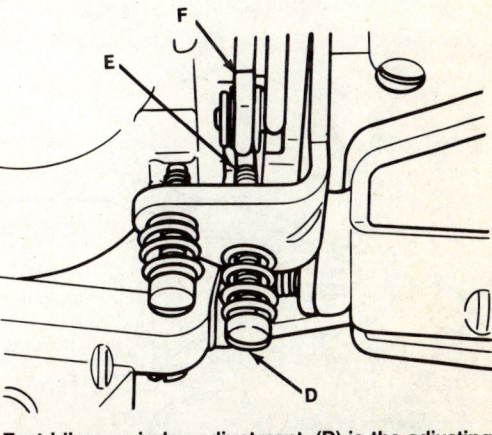

Fast idle cam index adjustment. (D) is the adjusting screw; (E) is the second step of the cam (F)

184 FUEL SYSTEM

final adjustment, turn the screw one additional turn clockwise.

5. Install the carburetor air horn and replacement gasket on the carburetor, then set the curb idle speed to specifications.

Fast Idle Cam Adjustment

Put the fast idle screw on the second highest step of the fast idle cam, against the shoulder of the high step. Measure the clearance between the lower edge of the choke valve and the air horn wall. It is not necessary to remove the air cleaner bracket when measuring clearance between the choke valve and air horn wall; position the gauge next to the bracket. Adjust by bending the choke plate connecting rod to obtain the specified clearance between the lower edge of the choke plate and the air horn wall.

Choke Unloader Adjustment

With the throttle valve held wide open and the choke valve held in the closed position, bend the unloader tang on the throttle lever to obtain the specified clearance between the lower edge of the choke valve and their air horn wall.

Automatic Choke Adjustment

Loosen the choke cover retaining screws, then turn the choke cover so that the index mark on the cover lines up with the specified mark on the choke housing.

Choke Plate Pulldown Adjustment

PISTON TYPE CHOKE

NOTE: *This adjustment requires that the thermostatic spring housing and gasket (choke cap) are removed. Refer to the "Choke Cap" removal procedure below.*

1. Remove the air cleaner assembly, then the choke cap.
2. Bend a 0.026" diameter wire gauge at a 90 degree angle approximately 1/8" from one end.

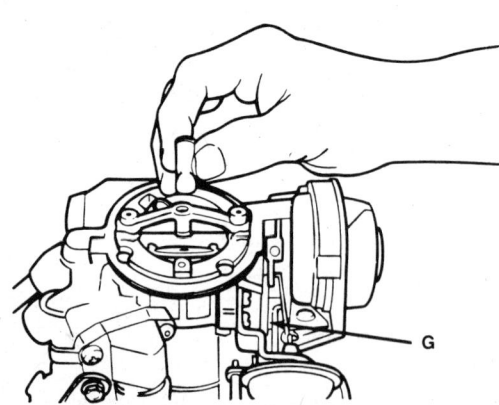

Bending the link (G)

Insert the bent end of the gauge between the choke piston slot and the right hand slot in the choke housing. Rotate the choke piston lever counterclockwise until the gauge is shut in the piston slot.

3. Apply light pressure on the choke piston lever to hold the gauge in place, then measure the clearance between the lower edge of the choke plate and the carburetor bore using a drill with the diameter equal to the specified pulldown clearance.
4. Bend the choke piston lever to obtain the proper clearance.
5. Install the choke cap.

DIAPHRAGM TYPE CHOKE

1. Activate the pulldown motor by applying an external vacuum source.
2. Close the choke plate as far as possible without forcing it.
3. Using a drill of the specified size, measure the clearance between the lower edge of the choke plate and the air horn wall.
4. If adjustment is necessary, bend the choke diaphragm link as required.

Choke Cap Removal

NOTE: *The automatic choke has two rivets and a screw, retaining the choke cap in place. There is a locking and indexing plate to prevent misadjustment.*

1. Remove the air cleaner assembly from the carburetor.
2. Check choke cap retaining ring rivets to determine if mandrel is well below the rivet head. If mandrel appears to be at or within the rivet head thickness, drive it down or out with a 1/16" diameter punch.
3. Use a 1/8" diameter drill for drilling the rivet heads. Drill into the rivet head until the rivet head comes loose from the rivet body.
4. After the rivet head is removed, drive the remaining portion of the rivet out of the hole with a 1/8" diameter punch.

NOTE: *This procedure must be followed to retain the hole size.*

5. Repeat Steps 1-4 for the remaining rivet.
6. Remove the screw in the conventional manner.

Choke Cap Installation

1. Install choke cap gasket.
2. Install the locking and indexing plate.
3. Install the notched gasket.
4. Install choke cap, making certain that bi-metal loop is positioned around choke lever tang.
5. While holding cap in place, actuate choke plate to make certain bi-metal loop is properly engaged with lever tang. Set retaining clamp

FUEL SYSTEM 185

over choke cap and orient clamp to match holes in casting (holes are not equally spaced). Make sure retaining clamp is not upside down.

6. Place rivet in rivet gun and trigger lightly to retain rivet (⅛" diameter ½" long ¼" diameter head).

7. Press rivet fully into casting after passing through retaining clamp and pop rivet (mandrel breaks off).

8. Repeat this step for the remaining rivet.

9. Install screw in conventional manner. Tighten to 17-20 in. lbs.

Choke Plate Clearance (Dechoke) Adjustment

1. Remove the air cleaner assembly.

2. Hold the throttle plate fully open and close the choke plate as far as possible without forcing it. Use a drill of the proper diameter to check the clearance between the choke plate and air horn.

3. If the clearance is not within specification, adjust by bending the arm on the choke lever of the throttle lever. Bending the arm downward will decrease the clearance, and bending it upward will increase the clearance. Always recheck the clearance after making any adjustment.

Mechanical Fuel Bowl Vent Adjustment

1. Start the engine and wait until it has reached normal operating temperature before proceeding.

2. Check engine idle rpm and set to specifications.

3. Check DC motor operation by opening throttle off idle. The DC motor should extend. Release the throttle, and the DC motor should retract when in contact with the throttle lever.

4. Disconnect the idle speed motor in the idle position.

5. Turn engine Off.

6. Open the throttle lever so that the throttle lever actuating lever does not touch the fuel bowl vent rod.

7. Close the throttle lever to the idle set position and measure the travel of the fuel bowl vent rod at point A. The distance measured represents the travel of the vent rod from where there is no contact with the actuating lever to where the actuating lever moves the vent rod to the idle set position. The travel of the vent rod at point A should be 0.100-0.150".

8. If adjustment is required, bend the throttle actuating lever at notch shown.

9. Reconnect the idle speed control motor.

Secondary Throttle Stop Screw Adjustment

Back off the screw until it does not touch the lever. Turn the screw in until it touches the lever, then turn it an additional ¼ turn.

CARBURETOR REMOVAL AND INSTALLATION

1. Remove the air cleaner.

2. Tag and disconnect all hoses leading to the carburetor.

3. Disconnect the control shaft from the throttle lever.

4. Disconnect the in-line fuel filter, pullback spring and all electrical connectors.

5. Remove the carburetor mounting nuts and lift off the carburetor.

6. Remove the carburetor mounting gasket from the spacer.

7. Clean all gasket mating surfaces on the spacer and carburetor.

8. Install a new gasket on the spacer, then install the carburetor and secure it with the mounting nuts.

9. Reconnect all vacuum hoses, fuel lines and electrical connectors. Connect the control shaft and pullback spring.

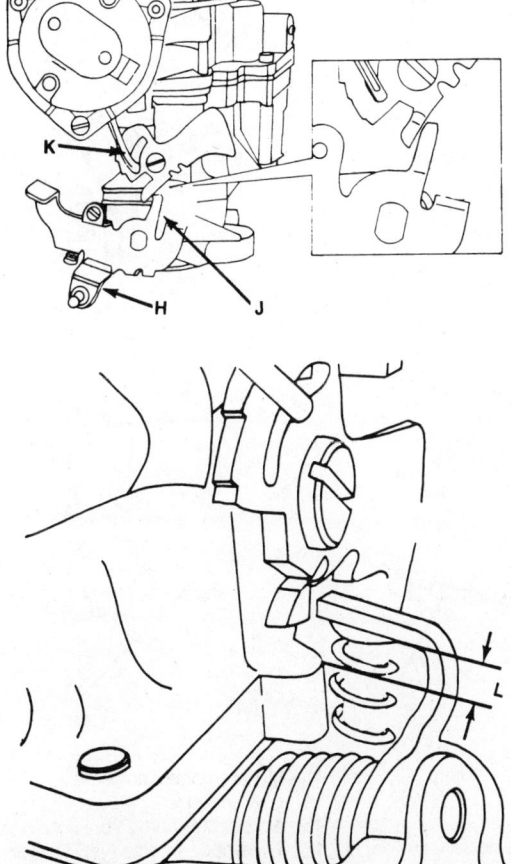

Choke unloader adjustment. (H) is the throttle lever; (J) is the unloader tang; (K) is the cam; (L) is the gap

186 FUEL SYSTEM

10. Install the air cleaner and adjust the curb and fast idle speed as previously described.

CARBURETOR OVERHAUL

The following procedure applies to complete overhaul with the carburetor removed from the engine. A complete disassembly is not necessary when performing adjustments. In most cases, service adjustments of individual systems may be completed without removing the carburetor from the engine. A complete carburetor overhaul includes disassembly, thorough cleaning, inspection and replacement of gaskets and worn or damaged parts. When using an overhaul kit, use all parts in the kit.

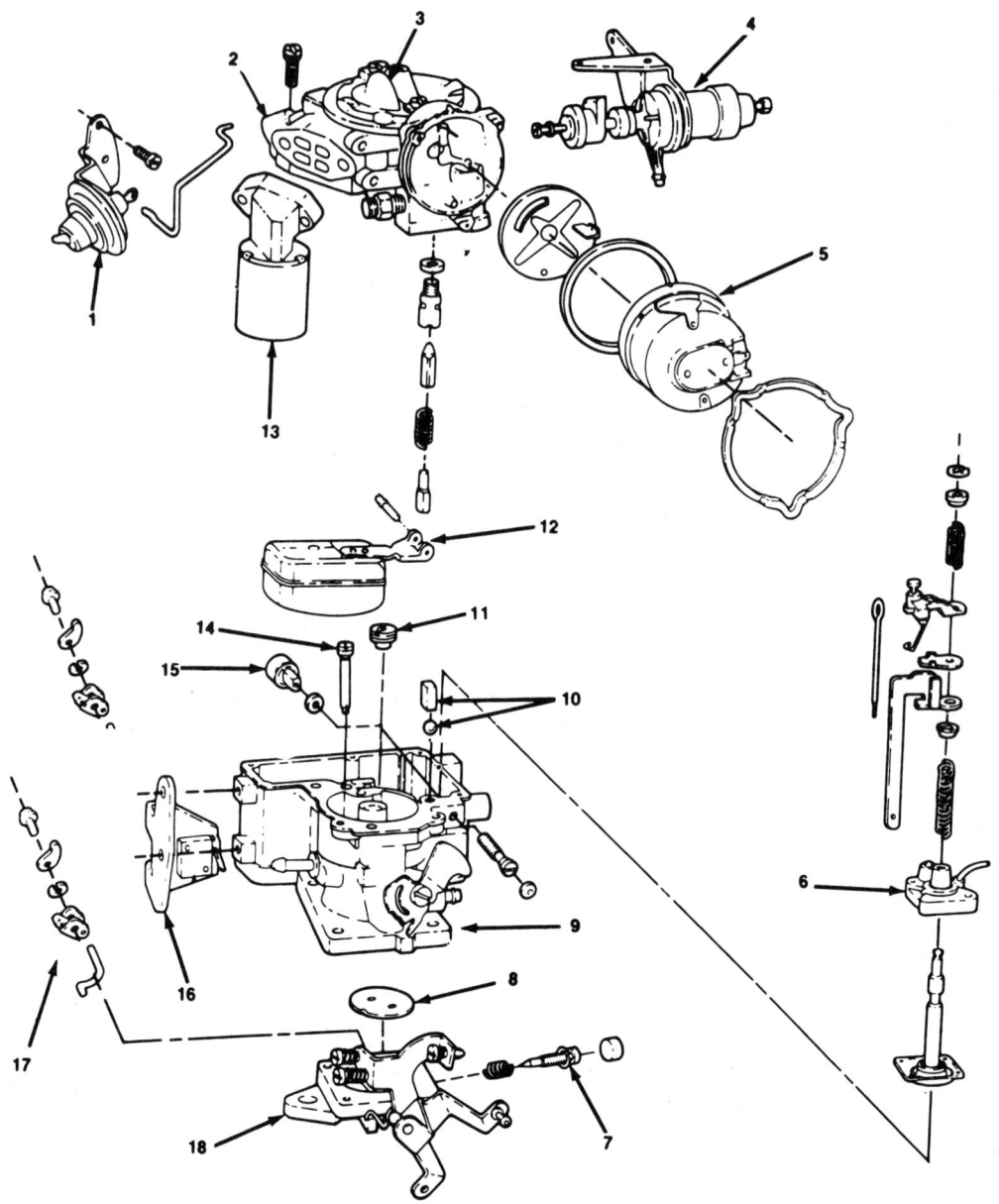

1. Vacuum break
2. Air horn
3. Choke plate
4. Sole-vac throttle positioner
5. Choke assembly
6. Accelerator pump assembly
7. Idle mixture screw with O-ring
8. Throttle plate
9. Main body
10. Accelerator pump check ball and weight
11. Main metering jet
12. Float assembly
13. Mixture control solenoid
14. Low speed jet
15. Accelerator pump vent valve
16. Wide open throttle (WOT) switch
17. Throttle shaft and lever
18. Throttle body

Carter YFA

FUEL SYSTEM

NOTE: *Flooding, stumble on acceleration and other performance problems are in many instances caused by the presence of dirt, water or other foreign material in the carburetor. To help in diagnosing the problem, carefully remove the carburetor from the engine without removing the fuel from the float bowl. Examine the bowl contents for contamination as the carburetor is disassembled.*

1. Drill out the choke retainer rivet heads using a No. 30 (⅛″) drill bit. After the rivet heads are removed, drive out the remaining portion of the rivets with a ⅛″ punch. This procedure must be followed exactly to retain the hole sizes.
2. Remove the screw holding the retainer.
3. Remove the retainer, thermostatic spring housing assembly, spring housing gasket and the locking/indexing plate.
4. Remove the vacuum break.
5. Disengage and remove the vacuum break connector link from the choke shaft lever.
6. Remove the sole-vac and the mounting bracket.
7. Remove the duty cycle solenoid from the air horn.
8. Remove the air horn attaching screws.
9. Remove the fast idle cam link.
10. Remove the air horn and gasket from the carburetor main body.
11. To remove the float from the air horn, hold the air horn bottom side up and remove the float pin and float.
12. Invert the air horn and catch the needle pin, spring and needle.
13. Remove the needle seat and gasket.
14. To remove the pump check ball and weight, turn the main body casting upside down and catch the accelerator pump check ball and weight.
15. Loosen the throttle shaft arm screw and remove the arm and pump connector link.
16. Remove the retaining screws and separate the throttle body from the main body.
17. Remove the wide open throttle switch and mounting bracket.
18. Remove the accelerator pump housing screws from the main body.
19. Lift out the pump assembly, pump lifter link and metering rod as a unit.
20. Disassemble the pump as follows:
    a. Disengage the metering rod arm spring from the metering rod.
    b. Remove the metering rod from the metering rod assembly.
    c. Compress the upper pump spring and remove the spring retainer cup.
    d. Remove the upper spring, metering rod arm assembly and pump lifter link from the pump diaphragm shaft.
    e. Compress the pump diaphragm spring and remove the pump diaphragm spring retainer, spring and pump diaphragm assembly from the pump diaphragm housing.
21. Remove the low speed jet and the main metering jet.
22. Using a sharp punch, remove the accelerator pump bleed valve plug from outside the main body casting. Loosen the bleed valve screw and remove the valve.
23. Drill out and remove the tamperproof plug. After removing the plug, count the number of turns required to seat the idle mixture screw lightly. Remove the idle mixture screw and O-ring.
24. Thoroughly clean and inspect all components and replace any that are damaged, worn or malfunctioning. Check the idle mixture screw needle for scoring or damage and replace it if any grooves are noted.
25. Install the throttle body to the main body with the retaining srews, then install the idle mixture screw.
26. Install the low speed jet and main metering jet.
27. Install the pump bleed valve and spring.
28. Install the accelerator pump assembly.
29. Install the pump passage tube.
30. Install the throttle shaft arm and pump connector link and retaining screw.
31. Install the wide open throttle switch actuator.
32. Install the throttle shaft retaining bolt.
33. Install the wide open throttle switch and bracket.
34. To adjust the metering rod:
    a. Make sure the idle speed adjusting screw allows the throttle plate to close tightly in the throttle bore.
    b. Press down on top of the pump diaphragm shaft until the assembly bottoms.
    c. While holding the pump diaphragm down, adjust the metering rod by turning the metering rod adjusting screw counterclockwise until the metering rod just bottoms in the main metering jet.
    d. Turn the metering rod adjusting screw clockwise one turn for final adjustment.
35. Install the needle pin, spring, needle, seat, gasket and strainer.
36. Install the float and pin.
37. Invert the air horn assembly and check the clearance from the top of the float to the bottom of the air horn with the gauge. The float arm should be resting on the needle pin. Bend the float arm as necessary to adjust the float level.
38. Install the accelerator pump check ball and weight, then install the air horn and gasket to the main body.

39. Install the fast idle cam link.
40. Install the sole-vac and mounting bracket, then install the duty cycle solenoid and gasket.
41. Install the locking and indexing plate, spring housing gasket, thermostatic spring housing assembly, choke cover retainer and attaching screws.
42. Position the fast idle cam screw on the second step of the fast idle cam and against the shoulder of the high step. Adjust by bending the fast idle cam link to obtain the specified clearance between the lower edge of the choke plate and the carburetor air horn.
43. Position the fast idle screw on the top step of the fast idle cam.
44. Seat the vacuum break using a hand vacuum pump.
45. Apply a light closing pressure to the choke plate to position the plate as far closed as possible without forcing it. Measure the distance between the choke plate and the air horn. To adjust, bend the vacuum break connector link.
46. Adjust the sole-vac for curb idle speed. Refer to the Sole-Vac Adjustment procedure.
47. Set the idle mixture screw to the same number of turns as noted during disassembly. The idle mixture screw must be set to the **exact** number of turns as noted during disassembly. Install a new tamperproof plug.
48. Install the carburetor. To adjust the fast idle, turn the fast idle adjusting screw to contact the fast idle cam until the desired engine rpm is achieved. See the underhood emission control sticker for rpm specifications.

NOTE: *Make sure the curb idle speed and mixture are adjusted to specifications before attempting the fast idle adjustment.*

Rochester E2SE Carburetor
6-173

DESCRIPTION

The Rochester Model E2SE Varajet is a two barrel, two stage down-draft carburetor used with the Computer Command Control system of fuel control. It has three major assemblies; air horn, float bowl and throttle body; and has the following six basic operating systems:
  a. FLOAT
  b. IDLE
  c. MAIN METERING
  d. POWER
  e. PUMP
  f. CHOKE

A single float chamber supplies fuel to both bores. a float, a float needle seat, a float needle with pull clip and float bowl inserts, help control the level of fuel in the float chamber. On some models, a float stabilizing spring adds further control of fuel level for vehicles used in rugged terrain.

An electrically operated mixture control solenoid, mounted in the air horn and extending into the float bowl, controls the air/fuel mixture in the primary bore. A plunger, at the end of the solenoid, is submerged in the fuel chamber of the float bowl, and is controlled (or pulsed) by signals from the Electronic Control Module (ECM).

In the secondary bore, an air valve, and a tapered metering rod operating in a fixed jet, controlled the air/fuel mixture during increased engine air flow at wide open throttle.

NOTE: *The carburetor part number is stamped vertically on the float bowl in the float. Refer to this part number when servicing the carburetor.*

Before checking or resetting the carburetor as the cause of poor engine performance or rough idle; check the ignition system including the distributor, timing, spark plugs and wire. Check the air cleaner, evaporative emission system, EFE system, PCV system, EGR valve and engine compression. Also inspect the intake manifold vacuum hose and connections for leaks and check the torque of the carburetor mounting bolts or nuts.

Make all adjustments with the engine at normal operating temperature, choke plate fully opened, air cleaner removed, thermac vacuum source plugged and A/C off (except if needed for

Rochester 2SE/E2SE

Engine	Years	Float Level (in.)	Choke Coil Lever (in.)	Fast Idle Cam Clearance (in.)	Choke Vacuum Break (in.) Primary	Secondary	Choke Unloader (in.)	Air Valve Rod (deg.)
6-173	1984–86	①	5/64	1/8	9/64	②	17/64	1

① Carb. part #17084384 & 17085384: 1/8
  All other part numbers: 5/32
② Carb. part #17084384 & 17085384: 11/64
  All other part numbers: 13/64

FUEL SYSTEM 189

a certain adjustment). Set the idle speeds only when the emission control system is in closed loop mode.

SERVICE AND ADJUSTMENTS

Float and Fuel Level Adjustment

NOTE: *Special tools are needed for this procedure.*

1. Run the engine to normal operating temperature.
2. Remove the vent stack screws and the vent stack.
3. Remove the air horn screw adjacent to the vent stack.
4. With the engine idling and the choke fully opened, carefully insert float gauge J-9789-136 for E2SE carbs or J-9789-138 for 2SE carbs, into the air horn screw hole and vent hole. Allow the gauge to rest freely on the float. DO NOT PRESS DOWN ON THE FLOAT!
5. With the gauge at eye level, observe the mark that aligns with the top of the casting at the vent hole. The float level should be within 0.06" of the specification listed in the chart. If not, remove the air horn and adjust as follows:
   a. Hold the retainer pin firmly in place and push the float down, lightly, against the inlet needle.
   b. Using an adjustable T-scale, at a point $3/16"$ from the end of the float, at the toe, measure the distance from the float bowl top surface (gasket removed) to the top of the float at the toe. If the distance isn't as specified in the Chart, remove the float and bend the float arm as necessary.

Throttle Position Sensor (TPS) Adjustment

A tamper-resistant plug covers the TPS adjustment screw. This plug should not be removed unless diagnosis indicates the TPS sensor is not adjusted properly or it is necessary to replace the air horn assembly, float bowl, TPS sensor or TPS adjustment screw. This is a critical adjustment that must be performed accurately and carefully to ensure proper engine performance and emission control. If TPS adjustment is indicated, proceed as follows:

1. Use a $5/64"$ (0.078") drill bit to drill a hole in the steel cup plug covering the TPS adjustment screw. Use care in drilling to prevent damage to the adjustment screw head.
2. Use a small slide hammer to remove the steel plug from the air horn.
3. Disconnect the TPS connector and use jumper wires to connect all three terminals.
4. Connect a digital voltmeter between the

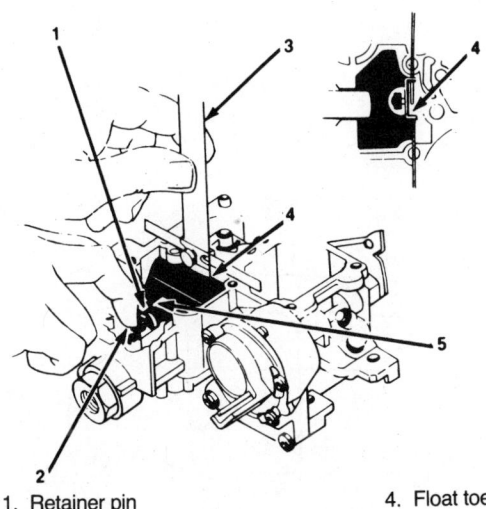

1. Retainer pin
2. Needle
3. T-scale
4. Float toe
5. Float arm

Float adjustment on the 6-173

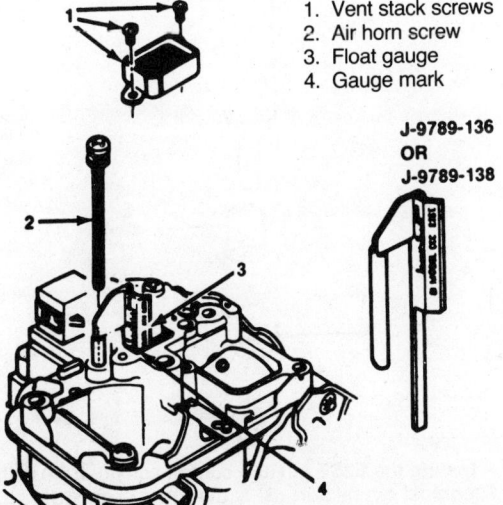

1. Vent stack screws
2. Air horn screw
3. Float gauge
4. Gauge mark

J-9789-136 OR J-9789-138

Measuring float clearance on the 6-173

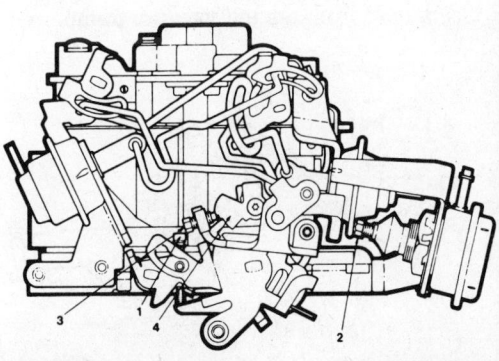

1. Idle speed screw
2. Vacuum diaphagm
3. Fast idle screw
4. Fast idle cam

2SE adjustment points

190 FUEL SYSTEM

TPS connector center terminal **B** and the bottom terminal **C** (ground).

5. With the ignition ON (engine OFF), turn the TPS adjustment screw to obtain 0.26 volts (260 mv) at the curb idle throttle position with the A/C off.

6. After all adjustments are complete, a new tamper-proof plug (supplied in service kits) or silicone RTV rubber sealant must be inserted into the TPS adjustment screw hole to seal the adjustment. If a plug is used, it should be installed with the cup facing outward and flush with the top of the casting.

Fast Idle Speed Adjustment

1. Place the fast idle screw on the high step of the fast idle cam.
2. Disconnect and plug the EGR valve hose and the canister purge line at the canister.
3. Set the parking brake firmly and start the engine. Place the transmission in Neutral (manual) or Park (automatic).
4. Turn the fast idle screw in or out to obtain the specified fast idle speed. Refer to the underhood emission sticker for fast idle speed specifications.
5. Once all adjustments are complete, reconnect the EGR valve hose and the canister purge line at the canister.

Testing Mixture Control (MC) Solenoid

If the mixture control solenoid is suspected of either sticking, binding or leaking, test it using the following procedure:

1. Connect one end of a jumper wire to either terminal of the solenoid wire connector and the other end to the positive (+) terminal of a 12 volt battery.
2. Connect one end of another jumper wire to the other terminal of the solenoid wire connector and the other end to the negative (-) terminal of the battery.
3. With the rubber seal, retainer and spacer removed from the end of the solenoid stem, attach a hose from a hand vacuum pump.

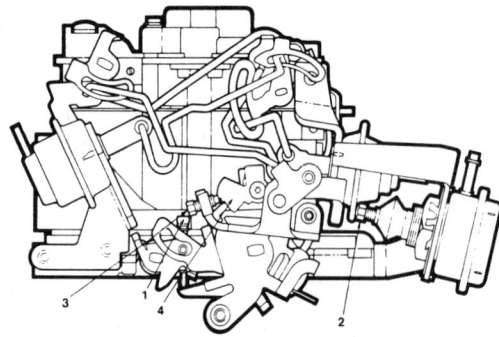

Fast idle speed adjustment points

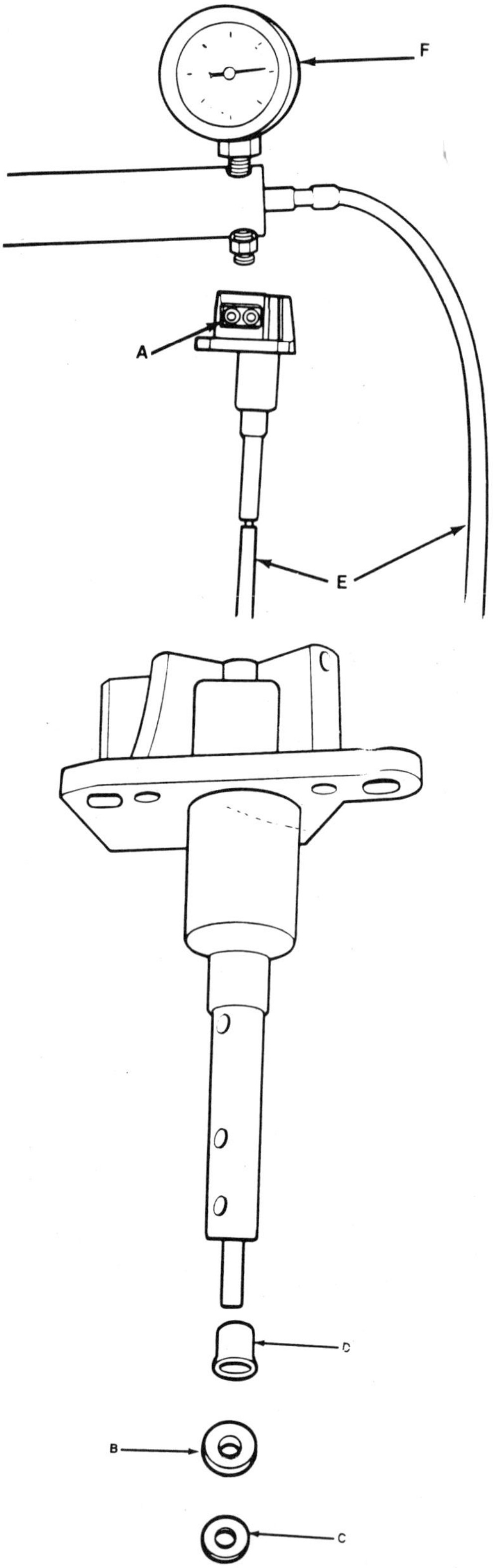

Testing the E2SE mixture control solenoid: (A) is the terminal connector; (B) is the rubber seal; (C) is the retainer; (D) is the spacer; (E) is the hose; (F) is the vacuum gauge

FUEL SYSTEM

4. With the solenoid fully energized (lean position), apply at least 25 in. Hg of vacuum and time the leak-down rate from 20 to 15 in. Hg. The leak-down rate should not exceed 5 in. Hg in 5 seconds. If the leak-down rate exceeds that amount, replace the solenoid.

5. To test the solenoid for sticking in the down (de-energized) position, remove the jumper wire to the 12 volt battery and observe the hand vacuum pump gauge. It should move to zero in less than one second.

Electric Choke Test

1. Check voltage at the choke heater connection with the engine running. If voltage is between 12 and 15 volts, replace the electric choke unit.

2. If the voltage is low or zero, check all wires and connections.

3. If Steps 1 and 2 pass the test properly, check and see if the connection on the oil pressure switch is faulty, the temperature pressure warning light will be off with the key in the ON position and the engine not running. Repair wires as required.

4. If the choke is still inoperarative, replace the oil pressure switch.

Choke Coil Replacement

1. Remove air cleaner and disconnect the choke electrical connector.

2. Align a $5/32''$ (4mm) drill on the retainer rivet head and drill only enough to remove rivet head. After removing rivet heads and retainers, use a drift and small hammer to drive the remainder of the rivet from the choke housing. Use care in drilling to prevent damage to the choke cover or housing. Remove the three rivets and choke cover assembly from choke housing.

3. Remove choke coil from housing.

4. Install the choke cover and coil assembly in choke housing as follows:

   a. Install the choke cover and coil assembly in the choke housing, aligning notch in cover with raised casting projection on housing cover flange. Make sure coil pickup tank engages the inside choke coil lever.

   b. A choke cover retainer kit is required to attach the choke cover to the choke housing. Install a suitable blind rivet installing tool.

5. Connect choke electrical connector.

6. Start engine, check operation of choke and then install air cleaner.

Choke Coil Lever Adjustment

1. Remove the three retaining screws and remove the choke cover and coil. On models with a riveted choke cover, drill out the three rivets and remove the cover and choke coil.

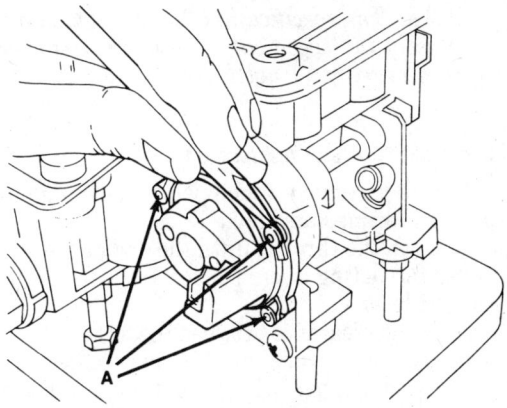

(A) shows the choke coil cap rivets

NOTE: *A choke stat cover retainer kit is required for reassembly.*

2. Place the fast idle screw on the high step of the dam.

3. Close the choke by pushing in on the intermediate choke lever. On front wheel drive models, the intermediate choke lever is behind the choke vacuum diaphragm.

4. Insert a drill or gauge of the specified size into the hole in the choke housing. The choke lever in the housing should be up against the side of the gauge.

5. If the lever does not just touch the gauge, bend the intermediate choke rod to adjust.

Electric Choke Setting

This procedure is only for those carburetors with choke covers retained by screws. Riveted choke covers are preset and non-adjustable.

1. Loosen the three retaining screws.

2. Place the fast idle screw on the high step of the cam.

3. Rotate the choke cover to align the cover mark with the specified housing mark.

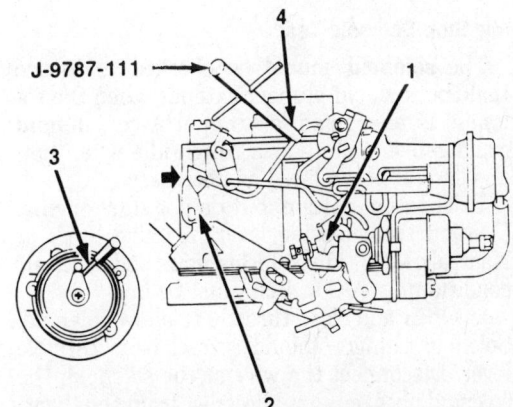

Choke coil lever adjustment points: (1) is the fast idle screw; (2) is the intermediate choke lever; (3) is the gauge; (4) is the bending point on the rod

192 FUEL SYSTEM

NOTE: *The specification "index" which appears in the specification table refers to the mark between "1 notch lean" and "1 notch rich".*

Secondary Lockout Adjustment

1. Pull the choke wide open by pushing out on the intermediate choke lever.
2. Open the throttle until the end of the secondary actuating lever is opposite the toe of the lockout lever.
3. Gauge clearance between the lockout lever and secondary lever should be as specified.
4. To adjust, bend the lockout lever where it contacts the fast idle cam.

Secondary Vacuum Break TVS Test

The secondary vacuum break TVS (thermal vacuum switch), located in the air cleaner, improves cold starting and cold driveability by sensing carburetor air inlet temperature to control the carburetor secondary vacuum break.

1. With engine at normal operating temperature, the Thermal Vacuum Switch (TVS) must be open (air cleaner cover on).
2. Apply either engine or auxiliary vacuum to the TVS inlet port and check for vacuum at the outlet port (outlet port connects to secondary vacuum break).
3. If there is no vacuum, check air cleaner assembly for leaks, thermostatic air cleaner vacuum hoses and/or replace the TVS.

Secondary Vacuum Break Replacement

1. Remove air cleaner cover and element.
2. Disconnect vacuum hoses.
3. Remove clip from TVS and remove TVS.
4. Install new TVS and replace clip.
5. Reconnect vacuum hoses (refer to Vehicle Emission Control Information Label).
6. Install air cleaner cover and element.

Idle Stop Solenoid Test

The solenoid should be checked to assure that the solenoid plunger extends when the solenoid is energized. an inoperative solenoid could cause stalling or a rough idle when hot, and should be replaced as necessary.

1. Turn on ignition, but do not start engine. Position transmission lever in Drive (A/T) or Neutral (M/T). On vehicles equipped with air conditioning, A/C switch must be on.
2. Open and close throttle to allow solenoid. Solenoid plunger should retract from throttle lever. Disconnect the wire at the solenoid, the solenoid plunger should retract from the throttle lever.
3. Connect solenoid wire. Plunger should move out and contact the throttle lever. Solenoid may not be strong enough to open the throttle, but the plunger should move.
4. If the plunger does not move in and out as the wire is disconnected and connected, check the voltage feed wire:
   a. If voltage is 12-15 volts, replace the solenoid.
   b. If voltage is low or zero, locate the cause of the open circuit in the solenoid feed wire and repair.

Idle Stop Solenoid Replacement

1. Remove carburetor air cleaner.
2. Disconnect electrical connector at solenoid.
3. Remove large retaining nut, tabbed lock washer, and remove solenoid.
4. To install, install the solenoid and retaining nut, bending the lock tabs against nut flats.
5. Connect electrical connector.
6. Install air cleaner and adjust idle speed as necessary.

Carburetor Pre-set Procedure

1. Remove the carburetor from the engine following normal service procedures to gain access to the plug covering the idle mixture needle.
2. To remove the plug, make two parallel cuts in the throttle body, one on each side of the plug, with a hacksaw. There is a locator point marking the casting at the plug. The cuts should extend down to the steel plug, but should not extend more than 1/8" (3mm) beyond the locator point.
3. Place a flat punch at a point near the ends of the saw cuts in the throttle body. Hold the punch at a 45° angle and drive it into the throttle body until the casting breaks away and exposes the steel plug. Hold a center punch in the vertical position and drive it into the the plug, then hold the punch at a 45° angle and drive the plug out of the housing. The hardened steel plug will shatter rather than remain intact. It is not necessary to remove the plug completely; instead, remove the loose pieces, then turn the idle mixture needle in until lightly seated and back out 4 turns.
4. If the plug in air horn covering the idle air has been removed, replace air horn. If plug is still in place, do not remove plug.
5. Remove vent stack screen assembly to gain access to lean mixture screw. (Be sure to reinstall vent stack screen assembly after adjustment).
6. Using tool J-28696-10 BT 7928 or equivalent, turn lean mixture screw in until lightly bottomed and back out 2½ turns.
7. Reinstall the carburetor on the engine and perform the following:

a. Do not install air cleaner and gasket.
b. Disconnect the bowl vent line at carburetor.
c. Disconnect the EGR valve hose and canister purge hose at the carburetor and cap the carburetor ports.
d. Refer to Vehicle Emission control Information Label and observe hose from sensor and secondary vacuum break TVS. Disconnect hose at temperature sensor on air cleaner and plug open hose.
e. Connect the positive lead of a dwell meter to the mixture control solenoid test lead (green connector). Connect the other meter lead to ground. Set dwell meter to 6 cylinder position. Connect a tachometer to distributor lead (brown connector). Tachometer should be connected to the distributor side of the tach filter if vehicle is equipped with a tachometer.
f. Block the drive wheels.
g. Place the transmission in Park (automatic transmission) or Neurtal (manual transmission) and set the parking brake.

8. Proceed to Mixture Adjustment Procedure.

MIXTURE ADJUSTMENT PROCEDURE

1. Perform carburetor pre-set procedure.
2. Run engine on high step of fast idle cam until engine cooling fan starts to cycle (at least three minutes and until in closed loop).
3. Run the engine at 3000 rpm and adjust the lean mixture screw slowly in small increments allowing time for the dwell to stabilize after turning the screw to obtain an average dwell of 35°.
4. If dwell is too low, back screw out; if too high, turn it in. If unable to adjust to specifications, inspect main metering circuit for leaks, restrictions, etc.
5. The dwell reading of the M/C solenoid is used to determine calibration and is sensitive to changes in fuel mixture caused by heat, air leaks, etc. While idling, it is normal for the dwell to increase and decrease fairly constantly over a relatively narrow range, such as 5°. However, it may occasionally vary be as much as 10-15° momentarily due to temporary mixture changes.
6. The dwell reading specified is the average of the most consistent variation. The engine must be allowed a few moments to stabilize at idle or 3000 rpm as applicable before taking a dwell reading. Return to idle.
7. Adjust idle mixture screw to obtain an average dwell of 25° with cooling fan in off cycle. If reading is too low, back screw out. If too high, turn it in. Allow time for reading to stabilize after each adjustment. Adjustment is very sensitive. Make final check with adjusting tool removed.
8. If unable to adjust to specifications, inspect idle system for leaks, restrictions, etc.
9. Disconnect mixture control solenoid when cooling fan is in off cycle and check for an rpm change of at least 50 rpm. If rpm does not change enough, inspect idle air bleed circuit for restrictions, leaks, etc.
10. Run engine at 3000 rpm for a few moments and note dwell reading. Dwell should be varying with an average reading of 35°. If not at 35° average dwell: Reset lean mixture screw per Step 3. Then reset idle mixture screw to obtain 25° dwell per Step 5.
11. If at 35° average dwell: Reconnect systems disconnected earlier (purge and vent hoses, EGR valve, etc.), reinstall vent screen and set idle speed to specifications. It is not necessary to repeat the System Performance Check after proper adjustment of the carburetor.

Mixture Control Solenoid Removal and Installation

1. Remove three (3) mixture control solenoid screws in the horn, then using a slight twisting motion, carefully lift solenoid out of air horn. Remove and discard solenoid gasket.
2. Remove seal retainer and rubber seal from end of solenoid stem being careful not to damage or nick end of solenoid stem. Discard seal and retainer.
3. Install spacer and new rubber seal on new mixture control solenoid stem making sure seal is up against the spacer. Then, using a suitable socket and hammer, carefully drive retainer on stem. Drive retainer on stem only far enough to retain rubber seal on stem leaving a slight clearance between the retainer and seal to allow for seal expansion.
4. Prior to installing a replacement mixture control solenoid, lightly coat the rubber seal on the end of the solenoid stem with a automatic transmission fluid or light engine oil.
5. Using a new mounting gasket, install mixture control solenoid on air horn, carefully aligning solenoid stem with recess in bottom of bowl.
6. Use a slight twisting motion of the solenoid during installation to ensure rubber seal on stem is guided into recess in the bottom of the bowl to prevent distortion or damage to the rubber seal. Install three (3) solenoid attaching screws and tighten securely.
7. Install mixture control solenoid connector, and check for proper latching. The latch may require filing. Check colors of wires in connector for proper position. Pink wire must be on right hand terminal of connector, as viewed from harness end. If incorrect, use Tool J-28742, BT 8234-A or equivalent to remove

FUEL SYSTEM

wires from connector and replace. The System Performance Check should be performed after any repairs to the CCC system have been made.

CARBURETOR REMOVAL AND INSTALLATION

Always replace all internal gaskets that are removed. Base gasket should be inspected and replaced only if damaged. Flooding, stumble on acceleration and other performance complaints are in many instances, caused by presence of dirt, water, or other foreign matter in carburetor. To aid in diagnosis, carburetor should be carefully removed from engine without draining fuel from bowl. Contents of fuel bowl may then be examined for contamination as carburetor is disassembled. Check fuel filter.

1. Remove air cleaner and gasket.
2. Disconnect fuel pipe and vacuum lines.
3. Disconnect electrical connectors.
4. Disconnect accelerator linkage.
5. If equipped with automatic transmission, disconnect downshift cable.
6. If equipped with cruise control, disconnect linkage.
7. Remove carburetor attaching bolts.
8. Remove carburetor and EFE heater/insulator (if used).
9. Fill carburetor bowl before installing carburetor. A small supply of no-lead fuel will enable the carburetor to be filled and the operation of the float and inlet needle and seat to be checked. Operate throttle lever several times and check discharge from pump jets before installing carburetor.
10. Inspect EFE heater/insulator for damage. Be certain throttle body and EFE heater/insulator surfaces are clean.
11. Install EFE heater; insulator.
12. Install carburetor and tighten nuts alternately to the correct torque.
13. Connect downshift cable as required.
14. Connect cruise control cable as required.
15. Connect accelerator linkage.
16. Connect electrical connections.
17. Connect fuel pipe sand vacuum hoses.
18. Check base (slow) and fast idle.
19. Install air cleaner.

CARBURETOR OVERHAUL

Air Horn

1. Invert the carburetor, then remove the plug covering the idle mixture needle as previously described.
2. Install the carburetor in a suitable holding stand.
3. Remove the primary and secondary vacuum break assemblies. Be sure to take note of the linkage positions for installation.
4. Remove the three screws from the mixture control solenoid. Remove the mixture control solenoid with gasket and discard the gasket.
5. Remove the two screws from the vent stack and remove the vent stack. Remove the intermidiate choke shaft link retainer at the choke lever and discard it.
6. Remove the choke link and bushing from choke lever and save the bushing.
7. Remove the retainer and bushing from the fast idle cam link and discard the retainer.

NOTE: *Do not remove fast idle cam screw and cam from the float bowl. If removed, the cam might not operate properly when reassembled. If needed, a replacement float bowl will include a secondary locknut lever, fast idle cam, and cam screw.*

8. Remove the retainer from the pump link. Do not remove the screw attaching the pump lever to the air horn assembly. When reassembled, the screw might not hold properly.
9. Remove the seven screw assemblies of various length that retain the air horn to the carburetor and remove the air horn assembly. Tilt the air horn to disconnect fast idle cam link from the slot in fast idle cam and the pump link from the hole in the pump lever.
10. Remove the cam link from the choke lever. Be sure to line up the "squirt" on link with slot in lever.
11. Invert the air horn and remove the TPS actuator plunger. The TPS adjusting screw and plug should not be removed.
12. Remove the stakings that holds the TPS plunger seal retainer and pump stem seal retainer.
13. Remove the retainers and seals and discard them.
14. Further disassembly of the air horn is not required for cleaning purposes. The choke valve and choke valve screws, the air valve and air valve shaft should not be removed.

NOTE: *Do not turn the secondary metering rod adjusting screw. The rod could come out of jet and possibly cause damage.*

Float Bowl

1. Remove the accelerator pump, air horn gasket and pump return spring.
2. Remove the Throttle Position Sensor (TPS) assembly and spring. Inspect the TPS connector wires for broken insulation, which could cause grounding of the TPS.
3. Remove the upper insert and the hinge pin. Remove the float and lever assembly with the float stabilizing spring if used. Remove the float needle and pull clip.
4. Remove the lower insert, if used.

FUEL SYSTEM 195

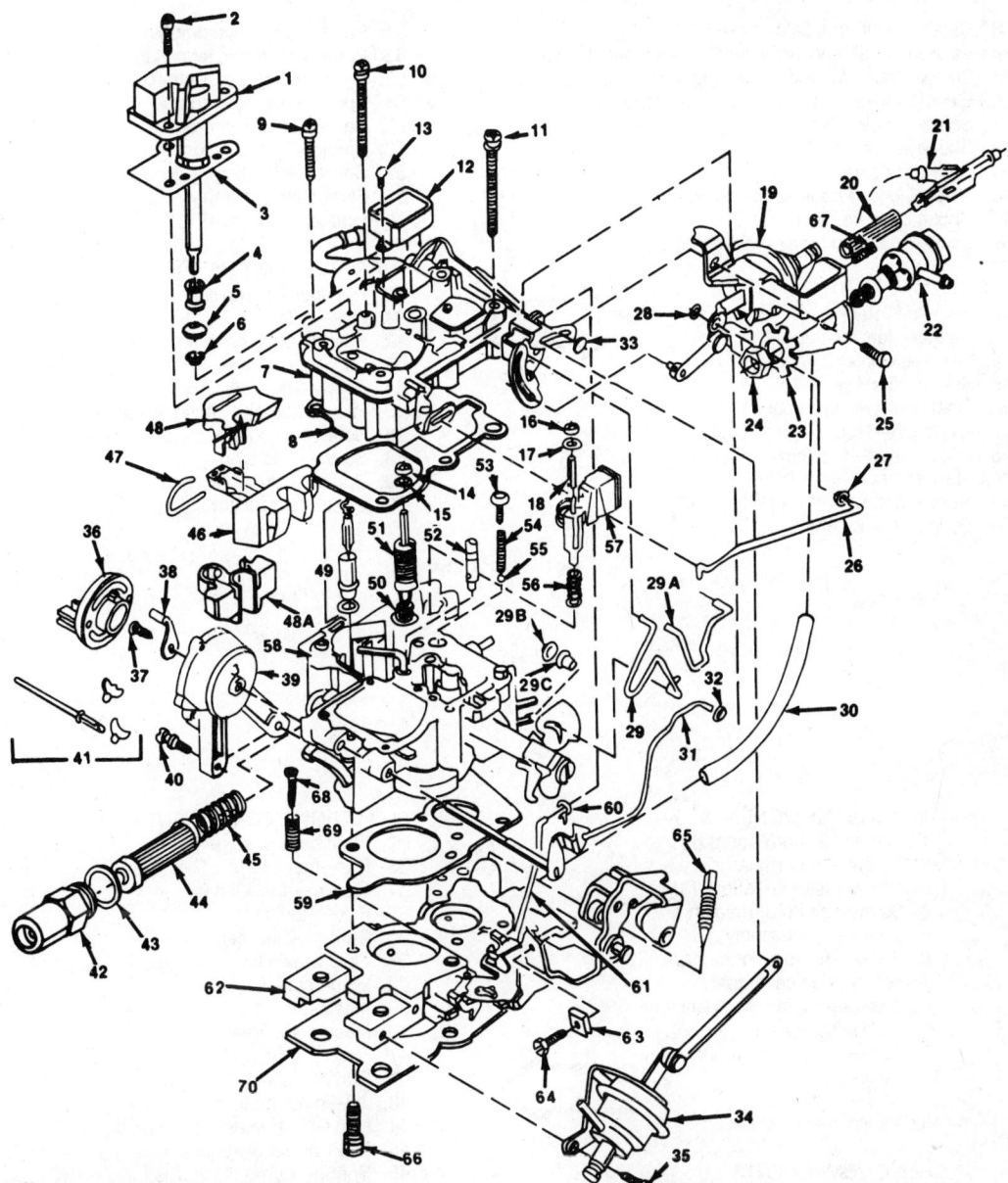

AIR HORN PARTS
1. Mixture control (M/C) solenoid
2. Screw assembly—solenoid attaching
3. Gasket—M/C solenoid to air horn
4. Spacer—M/C solenoid
5. Seal—M/C solenoid to float bowl
6. Retainer—M/C solenoid seal
7. Air horn assembly
8. Gasket—air horn to float bowl
9. Screw—air horn to float bowl (short)
10. Screw—air horn to float bowl (long)
11. Screw—air horn to float bowl (large)
12. Vent stack and screen assembly
13. Screw—vent stack attaching
14. Seal—pump stem
15. Retainer—pump stem seal
16. Seal—T.P.S. plunger
17. Retainer—T.P.S. actuator

CHOKE PARTS
19. Vacuum break and bracket assembly—primary
20. Hose—vacuum break primary
21. Tee–vacuum break
22. Solenoid—idle speed
23. Retainer—idle speed solenoid
24. Nut—idle speed solenoid attaching
25. Screw—vacuum break bracket attaching
26. Link—air valve
27. Bushing—air valve link
28. Retainer—air valve link
29. Link—fast idle cam
29A. Link—fast idle cam
29B. Link—fast idle cam
29C. Bushing—link
30. Hose—vacuum break
31. Intermediate choke shaft/lever/link assembly
32. Bushing—intermediate choke link

Rochester E2SE

196 FUEL SYSTEM

33. Retainer—intermediate choke link
34. Vacuum break and link assembly—secondary
35. Screw—vacuum break attaching
36. Electric choke—cover and coil assembly
37. Screw—choke lever attaching
38. Choke coil lever assembly
39. Choke housing
40. Screw—choke housing attaching
41. Choke cover retainer kit
67. Screw—vacuum break bracket attaching

FLOAT BOWL PARTS
42. Nut—fuel inlet
43. Gasket—fuel inlet nut
44. Filter—fuel inlet
45. Spring—fuel filter
46. Float and lever assembly
47. Hinge pin—float
48. Upper insert—float bowl
48A. Lower insert—float bowl
49. Needle and seat assembly
50. Spring—pump return

51. Pump plunger assembly
52. Primary metering jet assembly
53. Retainer—pump discharge ball
54. Spring—pump discharge
55. Ball—pump discharge
56. Spring—T.P.S. adjusting
57. Sensor—throttle position (TPS)
58. Float bowl assembly
59. Gasket—float bowl

THROTTLE BODY PARTS
60. Retainer—pump link
61. Link—pump
62. Throttle body assembly
63. Clip—cam screw
64. Screw—fast idle cam
65. Idle needle and spring assembly
66. Screw—throttle body to float bowl
68. Screw—idle stop
69. Spring—idle stop screw
70. Gasket—insulator flange

Rochester E2SE

AIR HORN COMPONENTS
1. Screw—air horn (long) (2)
2. Screw—air horn (large)
3. Screw—air horn (short) (3)
4. Screw—air horn (medium)
5. Vent stack assembly
6. Screw—hot idle compensator (2)
7. Hot idle compensator
8. Gasket—hot idle compensator
9. Air horn assembly
10. Gasket—air horn
11. Retainer—pump
12. Seal—pump stem
13. Retainer—stem seal

CHOKE COMPONENTS
14. Vacuum break and bracket assembly—primary
15. Screw—vacuum break attaching
16. Bushing—air valve—rod
17. Retainer—air valve rod
18. Hose—vacuum break—primary
19. Rod—air valve
20. Rod—fast idle cam
21. Intermediate choke shaft/lever/rod assembly
22. Bushing—intermediate choke shaft rod
23. Retainer—intermediate choke shaft rod
24. Vacuum break and bracket assembly—secondary
25. Choke cover and coil assembly
26. Screw—choke lever
27. Choke lever and contact assembly
28. Choke h ousing
29. Screw—choke housing (2)
30. Stat cover retainer kit
31. Screw—vacuum break attaching (2)

FLOAT BOWL COMPONENTS
32. Float bowl assembly
33. Nut—fuel inlet
34. Gasket—fuel inlet nut
35. Filter—fuel inlet
36. Spring—fuel filter
37. Float assembly
38. Hinge pin—float
39. Insert—float bowl
40. Needle and seat assembly
41. Spring—pump return
42. Pump—assembly
43. Jet—main metering
44. Rod—main metering assembly
45. Ball—pump discharge
46. Spring—pump discharge
47. Retainer—pump discharge spring
48. Power piston assembly
49. Spring—power piston

THROTTLE BODY COMPONENTS
50. Gasket—throttle body
51. Throttle body assembly
52. Pump rod
53. Clip—cam screw
54. Screw—cam
55. Spring—throttle stop screw
56. Screw—throttle stop
57. Idle needle and spring
58. Screw—throttle body attaching (4)
59. Nut—idle speed kick actuator
60. Retainer—idle speed kick actuator
61. Idle speed kick actuator

Rochester 2SE

FUEL SYSTEM 197

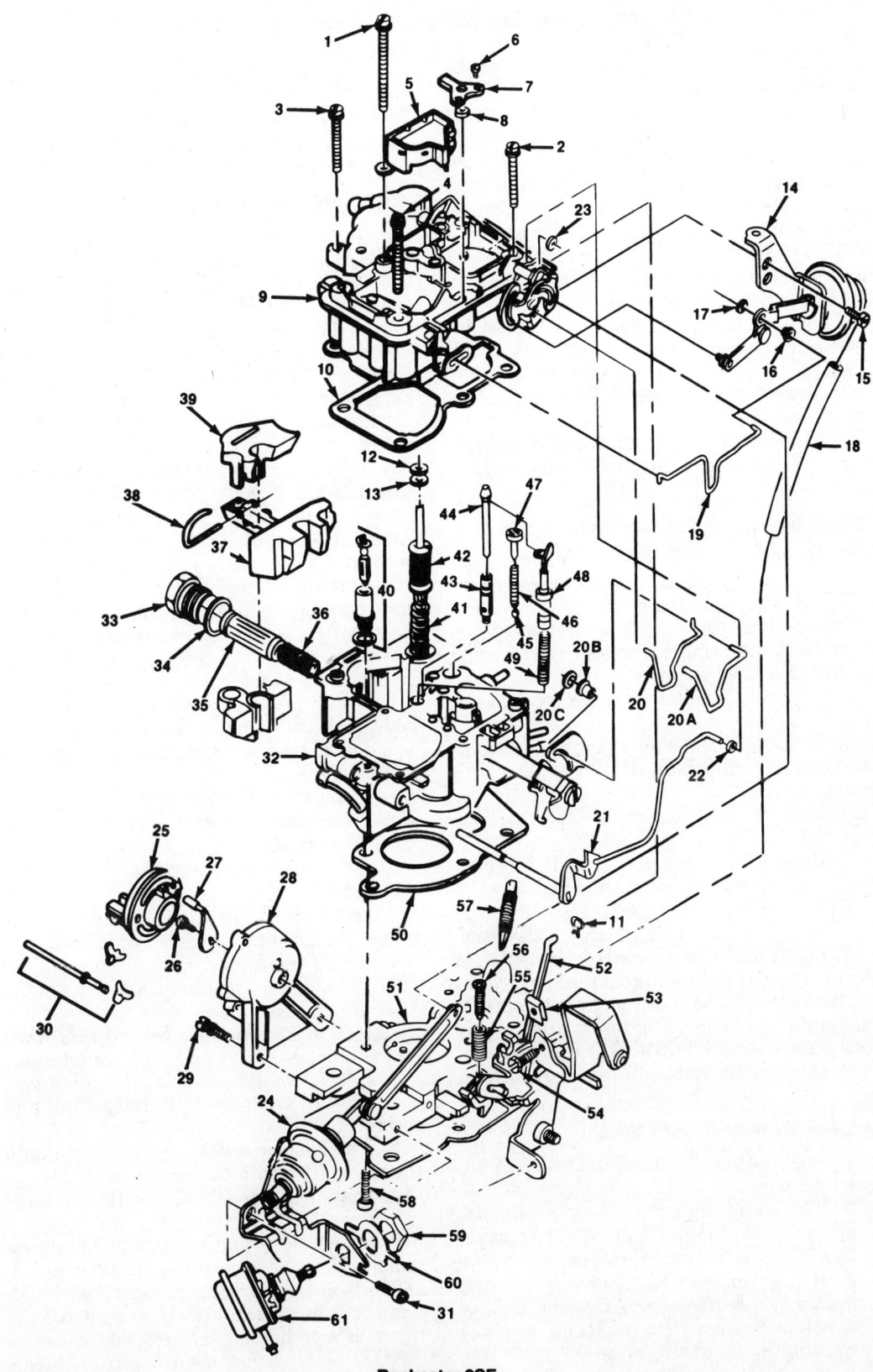

Rochester 2SE

5. Remove the float needle seat and seat gasket.

6. Remove the jet and lean mixture needle assembly.

NOTE: *Do not remove or change the preset adjustment of calibration needle in the metering jet unless the Computer Command Control system performance check requires it.*

7. Remove the pump discharge spring guide, using a suitable slide hammer puller only.

NOTE: *Do not pry the guide. Damage could occur to the sealing surfaces, and could require replacement of the float bowl.*

8. Remove the spring and check ball, by inverting the bowl and catching them as they fall out.

9. Remove the fuel inlet nut and the fuel filter spring.

10. Remove the fuel filter assembly and discard it. Remove the filter gasket and discard it.

Choke Assembly and Throttle Body

1. Remove the choke cover as follows:
   a. Use a $5/32"$ (4mm) drill bit to remove the heads (only) from the rivets.
   b. Remove the choke cover retainers. Remove the remaining pieces of rivets, using drift and small hammer.
   c. Remove the electric choke cover and stat assembly.

2. Remove the stat lever screw, Stat lever, intermediate choke shaft, lever and link assembly.

3. Remove the two screws and the choke housing.

4. Remove the four screws, and the throttle body assembly from the inverted float bowl.

5. Remove the gasket, pump link and line up the "squirt" on link with the slot in the lever.

6. Count and make a record of the number of turns needed to lightly bottom the idle mixture needle (69), then back out and remove needle and spring assembly using Idle mixture socket tool J-29030-B or BT-7610-B or equivalent.

7. Do not disassemble throttle body further.

INSPECTION AND CLEANING

1. Place the metal parts in immersion carburetor cleaner.

NOTE: *Do not immerse idle stop solenoid, mixture control solenoid, throttle lever actuator, TPS, electric choke, rubber and plastic parts, diaphragms, and pump in the cleaner, as they may be damaged. Plastic bushing in throttle lever will withstand normal cleaning.*

2. Blow dry the parts with shop air. Be sure all fuel and air passages are free of burrs and dirt. Do not pass drill bits or wires through jets and passages.

3. Be sure to check the mating surfaces of casting for damage. Replace if necessary. Check for holes in levers for wear or out-of-round conditions. Check the bushings for damage and excessive wear. Replace if necessary.

CARBURETOR REASSEMBLY

1. Install the mixture needle and spring assembly using Idle mixture socket tool J-29030-B or BT-7610-B or equivalent. Lightly bottom the needle and back it out the number of turns recorded during removal, as a preliminary adjustment. Refer to idle mixture adjustment procedure in this section for the final idle mixture adjustment.

2. Install the pump link and a new gasket on the inverted float bowl.

3. Install the throttle body to the float bowl assembly and finger tighten the four retaining screws. If the secondary actuating lever engages the lockout lever, and linkage moves without binding, tighten retaining screws.

4. If the float bowl assembly was replaced, stamp or engrave the model number on the new float bowl in same location as on old bowl.

5. Place the throttle body and float bowl together on a suitable carburetor holding stand.

6. Install the choke housing on the throttle body, with the retaining screws.

7. Install the intermediate choke shaft, lever and link assembly.

8. Install the choke stat lever on the intermediate choke shaft. The intermediate choke lever must be upright.

9. Install the choke lever attaching screw in the shaft.

10. Install the gasket on the fuel inlet nut and install the new filter assembly in the nut.

11. Install the filter spring and then install the fuel inlet nut. Tighten the fuel inlet nut to 18 ft. lbs. (24 Nm).

CAUTION: *Tightening beyond this limit may damage gasket and could cause a fuel leak, which might result in personal injury.*

12. Install the pump discharge ball and spring.

13. Install a new spring guide and tap it until the top is flush with the bowl casting.

14. Install the needle seat with gasket. If used, lower the insert.

15. Install the jet and lean mixture needle assembly. Using lean mixture adjusting tool J-28696-10 or BT-7928 or equivalent, lightly bottom the lean mixture needle. Back it out 2½ turns, as a preliminary adjustment.

NOTE: *Only adjust the lean mixture needle screw if it was removed or touched during disassembly or if the Computer Command*

Control system performance check, made before disassembly, indicated an incorrect lean mixture needle setting:

16. Bend the float lever upward slightly at the notch.
17. If used, install the float stabilizing spring on float. Install the hinge pin in float lever, with ends toward the pump well.
18. Install the needle with pull clip assembly on the edge of the float lever. Install the float and lever assembly in float bowl.

NOTE: *Adjust the float level using Float Level T-Scale J-9789-90 or BT-8037 or equivalent.*

19. Install the upper insert over the hinge pin, with the top flush with the bowl. Install the TPS spring and the TPS assembly. The parts must be below the surface of the bowl.
20. Install the gasket over the dowels. Install the spring and pump assembly.
21. Install a new pump stem seal with the lip facing outside of carburetor and install the retainer. Be sure to stake it at new locations.
22. Install a new TPS actuator plunger seal with the lip facing outside of carburetor and install the retainer. Be sure to stake it at new locations.
23. Install the TPS plunger through the seal in the air horn. Use lithium base grease, liberally to pin, if used, where contacted by spring.
24. Install the fast idle cam link in the choke lever. Be sure to line-up the "squirt" on link with slot in lever.
25. Rotate the cam to the highest position. The lower end of the fast idle cam link goes in cam slot, and the pump link end goes into the hole in the lever.
26. Hold the pump down, and than lower the air horn assembly onto the float bowl. Be sure to guide the pump stem through the seal.
27. Install the one of the air horn retaining screws, finger tight to hold the air horn in place.
28. Install the cam link in the slot of the cam. Install a new bushing and retainer to the link, with the large end of bushing facing the retainer. Check for freedom of movement.
29. Install the rest of the air horn retaining screws.
30. Install the spacer and a new seal, lightly coat the seal with automatic transmission fluid. Assemble the seal on the solenoid stem, touching the spacer.
31. Install a new retainer and a new gasket on the air horn. Install the mixture control solenoid lining up the stem with the recess in the bowl.
32. Install the solenoid retaining screws. Install the vent stack, with two retaining screws, (unless lean mixture needle requires on-vehicle adjustment).
33. Install a new retainer on the pump link. Adjust the air valve spring, if adjustable.
34. Install the bushing on the choke link. With the intermediate choke lever upright, install the link in the choke lever hole. Install the new link retainer.
35. The following procedures is for reassembly of any small components that have been removed from the carburetor, if part replacement is necessary or for any other reason.

   a. Install the idle stop solenoid, retainer and nut to the secondary side vacuum break bracket. Bend the retainer tab to secure nut.
   b. Install the bushing to the link and the link to the vacuum break plunger. Install the retainer to the link.
   c. Rotate the assembly, insert the end of the link in the upper slot of the choke lever. Install the bracket screws.
   d. Install the idle speed device, retainer and nut to the primary side vacuum break bracket. Bend the retainer tab to secure the nut.
   e. Install the bushing to the vacuum break link. Install the link to vacuum break plunger. Install the retainer to the link and the bushing to the air valve link. Install the link to the plunger and the retainer to the link.

36. Rotate the vacuum break assembly (primary side) and insert the end of the air valve link into the air valve lever and the vacuum break link into the lower slot of the choke lever.
37. Install the bracket screws, vacuum hose between the throttle body tube and the vacuum break assembly.
38. Install the choke thermostat lever. Install the choke cover and thermostat assembly in the choke housing.
39. If the thermostat has a "trap" (box-shaped pick-up tang), the trap surrounds the lever.
40. Line up the notch in the cover with projection on the housing flange. Install the retainers and rivets with rivet tool. If necessary, use an adapter. Adjust the choke as previously described.

4-150 THROTTLE BODY INJECTION FUEL SYSTEM

Components and Operation

The Renix throttle body fuel injection is a "pulse time" system that uses a single solenoid-type injector to meter fuel into the throttle body above the throttle blade. Fuel is metered to the engine by an electronic control unit (ECU), which controls the amount of fuel delivery according to input from various engine sensors that monitor exhaust gas oxygen content, coolant temperature, manifold absolute pressure, crankshaft position and throttle position. These sensors provide an electronic signal by varying resistance within the sensor itself. By reading the difference in resistance, the ECU can determine engine operating conditions and calculate the correct air/fuel mixture, and ignition timing under varying engine loads and temperatures. In addition, the ECU controls idle speed, emission control and fuel pump operation, the upshift indicator lamp and the A/C compressor clutch.

Renix TBI fuel injection has two main subsystems; a fuel subsystem and a control subsystem. The fuel subsystem consists of an electric fuel pump (mounted in the fuel tank), a fuel filter, a pressure regulator and the fuel injector. The control subsystem consists of a manifold air/fuel mixture temperature sensor (MAT), a coolant temperature sensor (CTS), a manifold absolute pressure sensor (MAP), a knock sensor, an exhaust gas oxygen (O_2) sensor, an electronic control unit (ECU), a gear position indicator (automatic transmission only), a throttle position sensor and power steering pressure switch with a load swap relay. In addition to these sensors which send signals to the ECU, there are various devices which receive signals from the ECU to control different functions such as exhaust gas recirculation, idle speed control, air conditioner operation, etc.

Electronic Control Unit (ECU)

The electronic control unit (ECU) is a sealed microprocessor unit located above the accelerator pedal under the instrument panel or below the glove box, next to the fuse panel, and is the heart of the electronic engine control system. The throttle position sensor (or wide open throttle switch) is mounted on the throttle body assembly and provides the ECU with an input signal of up to 5 volts to indicate throttle position. At minimum throttle opening (idle speed), a signal input of approximately one volt is transmitted to the ECU. As the throttle opening increases, the signal voltage to the ECU increases.

Manifold Absolute Pressure (MAP) Sensor

The manifold absolute pressure (MAP) sensor is attached to the plenum chamber near the hood latch. It reacts to absolute pressure in the intake manifold and provides an input voltage to the ECU. Manifold pressure is used to supply mixture density information and ambient barometric pressure information that is necessary for computing the air/fuel mixture. A vacuum line from the throttle body attaches to the MAP sensor to provide its input pressure. The mani-

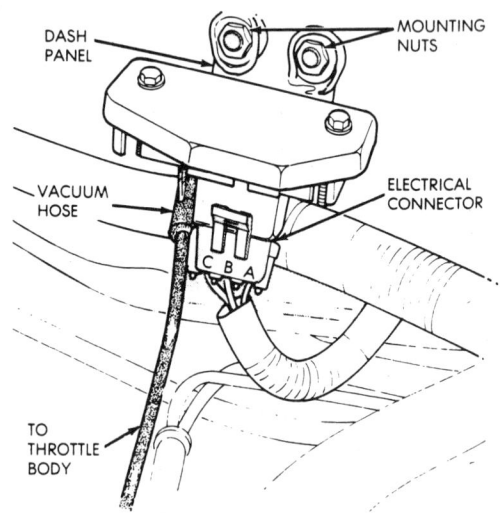

MAP sensor w/TBI

fold air temperature (MAT) sensor is located in the intake manifold and measures the air/fuel mixture temperature to allow the ECU to compensate for air density changes during high temperature operation.

Coolant Temperature Sensor

The coolant temperature sensor (CTS) is located in the intake manifold coolant jacket and provides an engine coolant temperature signal to the ECU. The ECU uses the coolant temperature signal to enrich the air fuel mixture when the engine is cold, compensate for fuel condensation in the intake manifold, control engine warm-up speed, increase the ignition advance when the engine is cold and to cut off the EGR system when the engine is cold.

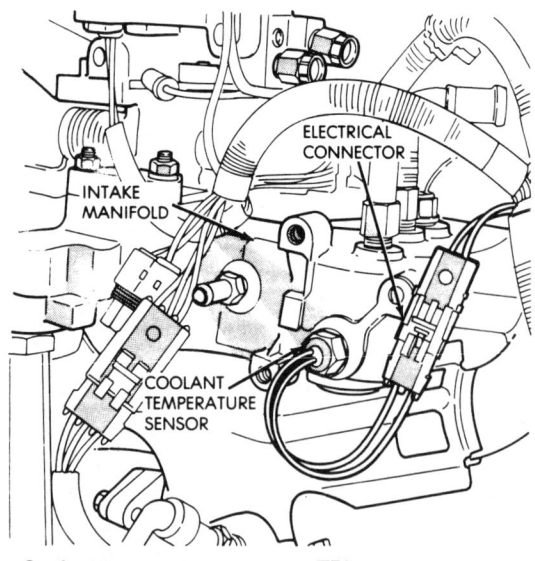

Coolant temperature sensor w/TBI

FUEL SYSTEM 201

Knock Sensor

The knock sensor is located in the cylinder head and provides a signal to the ECU to detect detonation (spark knock) during engine operation. When detonation occurs, the ECU retards the ignition timing to elimintate it. On automatic transmission models, a transmission gear position indicator provides an input to the ECU to determine whether the transaxle is in a driving gear and not in Park or Neutral.

Pressure Sensing Switch

A pressure sensing switch is included in the power steering system to increase the idle speed during periods of high pump load and low engine rpm. Input signals from the pressure switch to the ECU are routed through the A/C request and A/C select input circuits. When pump pressure exceeds 250-300 psi, the switch contacts close and transmit an input signal to the ECU. The ECU raises engine idle speed immediately after receiving the pressure switch input signal.

Load Swap Relay

The load swap relay is used on models with air conditioning and power steering. The relay works in conjunction with the power steering pressure switch to disengage the A/C compressor clutch. If the A/C compressor clutch is engaged when the power steering pressure switch contacts close, the input signal from the switch to the ECU also activates the load swap relay. The relay contacts then open, cutting off electrical feed to the compressor clutch. The clutch remains disengaged until the pressure switch contacts open and the engine returns to normal idle speed. The load swap relay does not reengage the compressor clutch immediately. The relay has a timer that delays energizing the clutch for 0.5 seconds to permit smooth engagement.

System Power Relay

The system power relay is located on the right strut tower and is initially energized when starting the engine. The relay remains energized for 3-5 seconds after the engine stops to enable the ECU to extend the idle speed actuator (ISA) for the next start-up. The fuel pump control relay is also located on the front of the right strut tower. Battery voltage is applied to the fuel pump control relay through the ignition switch and is energized when a ground is provided by the ECU. In this manner, the ECU controls fuel pump operation.

EGR/Canister Purge Solenoid

The vacuum for both the EGR valve and the vapor canister purge function is controlled by the EGR/Canister Purge Solenoid. When energized by the ECU, it cuts off vacuum to the EGR valve and canister. The solenoid is engergized during engine warm-up, closed throttle (idle), wide open throttle (WOT) and rapid acceleration/deceleraton. If the solenoid wire connector is disconnected, the EGR valve and canister purge function will be operational at all times.

Idle Speed Actuator

The idle speed actuator (ISA) is mounted on the throttle body and controls idle speed and engine deceleration throttle stop angle. The actuator changes the throttle stop angle by being a movable throttle stop. The ECU controls the ISA motor by providing the appropriate voltage outputs to produce the idle speed or throttle stop angle required for the particular engine operating condition. There is no idle speed adjustment.

Speed Sensor

The speed sensor is attached to the flywheel drive plate housing. This sensor detects the flywheel/drive plate teeth as they pass during engine operation and provides engine speed and crankshaft angle information to the ECU. The flywheel/drive plate has a large trigger tooth and notch located every 90 degrees and 12 smaller teeth before each top dead center (TDC) position. When a small tooth and notch pass the magnet core in the sensor, the concentration and then collapse of the magnetic flux induces a small voltage spike into the sensor pickup coil winding. The higher voltage spike indicates to the ECU that a piston will be at TDC position 12 teeth later. The ignition timing for the cylinder is either advanced or retarded as necessary by the ECU according to the sensor inputs.

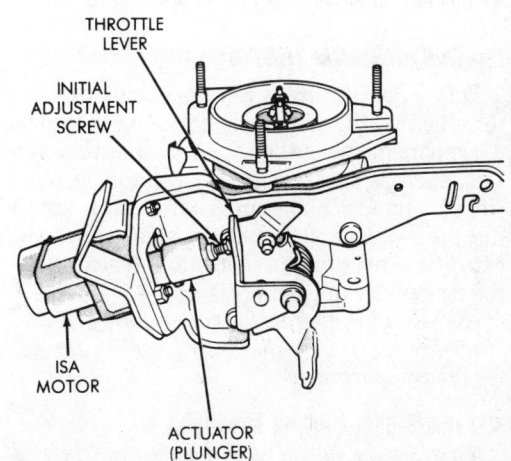

ISA motor w/TBI

202 FUEL SYSTEM

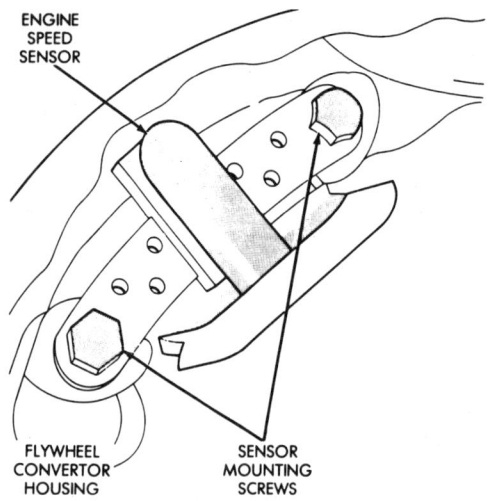

Engine speed sensor attaching bolts w/TBI

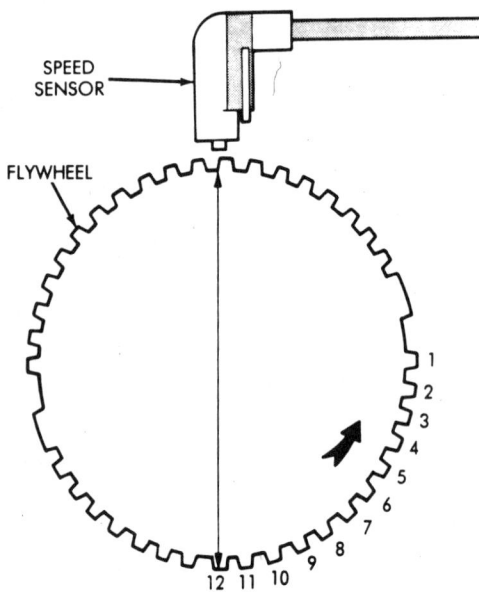

Engine speed sensor-to-flywheel position w/TBI

DIAGNOSIS AND TESTING

Before performing any system tests, first determine that the problem is not being caused by a component other than the fuel injection system, such as spark plugs, distributor, ignition timing, etc. Also make sure that no air is entering the intake and exhaust system above the catalytic converter and that fuel is reaching the injector under normal pressure.

NOTE: *The diagnostic connectors D1 and D2 are located on the dash panel in the engine compartment.*

Oxygen Sensor Heating Element

The oxygen sensor heating element can be tested by connecting an ohmmeter test leads to terminals **A** and **B** of the sensor connector. Resistance should be between 5-7 ohms. Replace the sensor if an infinite reading is obtained.

Fuel Pump Pressure Test

Fuel pump operating pressure is 14.5 psi. The fuel pressure regulator is adjustable by means of a torx head screw on the bottom of the pressure regulator.

1. Remove the air cleaner assembly. Remove the screw plug on the throttle body and install a fuel pressure test fitting (No. 8983 501 572).
2. Connect an accurate pressure test gauge to the test fitting.
3. Connect a tachometer to diagnostic connector terminals D1-1 and D1-3, then start the engine and accelerate it to 2000 rpm.
4. Read the fuel pressure on the gauge. If necessary, turn the adjustment screw on the bottom of the fuel pressure regulator to obtain 14.5 psi (1 bar) of fuel pressure. Turning the screw inward increases the pressure and turning the screw outward decreases the pressure.
5. Once all adjustments are complete, install a lead seal ball to cover the regulator adjusting screw. Turn the ignition OFF, then disconnect the tachometer and remove the fuel pressure gauge. Install the original plug screw into the throttle body, then install the air cleaner assembly.

Throttle Position Sensor Adjustment

1. Turn the ignition key ON.
2. Check the sensor input voltage. Connect the negative lead of a voltmeter to sensor terminal **B**, then connect the voltmeter positive lead to sensor terminal **C**.

NOTE: *Do not disconnect the sensor wire harness connector. Insert the voltmeter test*

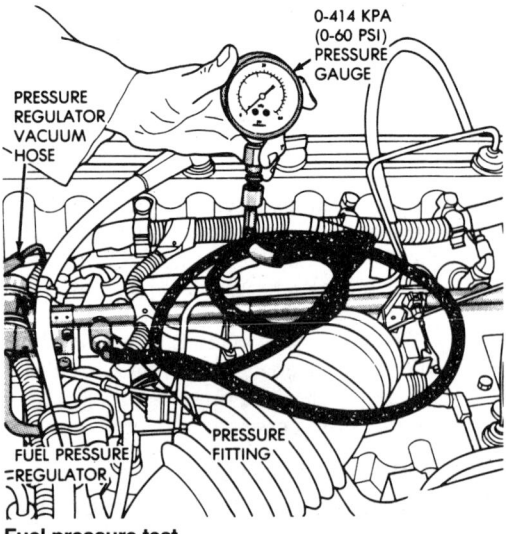

Fuel pressure test

FUEL SYSTEM 203

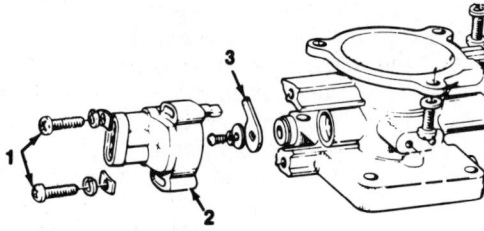

1. Retaining screws
2. TPS
3. Throttle shaft lever

Throttle position sensor mounting

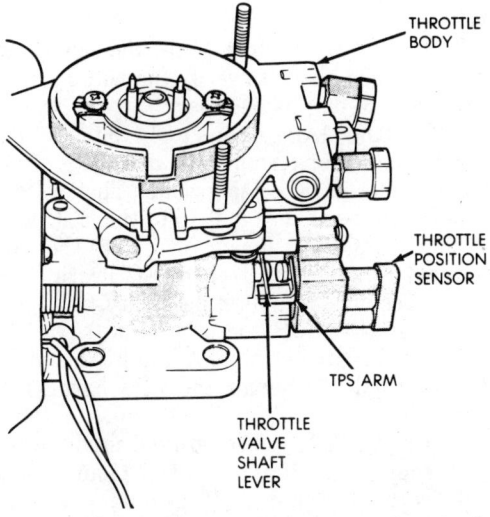

Throttle position sensor, TBI with manual transmission

leads through the back of the wire harness connector to make contact with the sensor terminals during testing. It may be necessary to remove the throttle body from the intake manifold to gain access to the wire harness connector.

3. Move and hold the throttle plate in the wide open position. Make sure the throttle linkage contacts the stop.
4. Note the voltmeter reading. Input voltage at terminals **B** and **C** should be 5.0 volts at wide open throttle.
5. Return the throttle plate to the closed position.
6. Check the sensor output voltage. Disconnect the voltmeter positive lead from sensor terminal **C** and connect it to terminal **A**.
7. Move and hold the throttle plate in the wide open position. Make sure the throttle linkage contacts the stop.
8. Note the voltmeter reading. Output voltage should be 4.6-4.7 volts. Adjust the output voltage by loosening the lower sensor retaining screw and pivoting the sensor in the adjustment slot for coarse adjustment. Loosen the other retaining screw and pivot the sensor for fine adjustment.
9. Remove the voltmeter and return the throttle plate to the closed position. Make sure the sensor retaining screws are tightened securely.

Wide-Open Throttle (WOT) Switch Test

1. Disconnect the harness terminal connector from the WOT switch.
2. Test the on-off operation of the switch with a digital volt-ohmmeter while operating the switch manually.
3. The resistance should be infinite when the

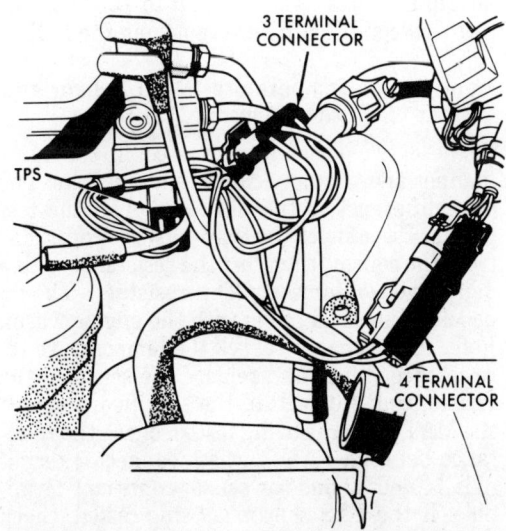

Throttle position sensor, TBI with automatic transmission

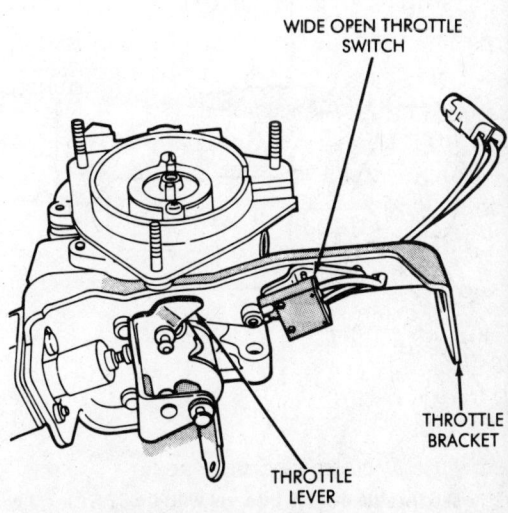

Wide open throttle switch w/TBI

throttle is closed and a low resistance should be indicated when the throttle is wide open. Test the switch operation several times and replace the WOT switch is defective.

4. Connect the wire harness connector. With the ignition switch ON, test the WOT switch voltage at the diagnostic connector terminals D2-6 (+) and D2-7 (−). The voltage should be zero at the WOT position and greater than 2 volts if not at the WOT position.

5. If the voltage is always zero, test for a short circuit to ground in the wire harness or switch, or an open circuit between terminal 8 of the ECU connector and the switch connector. Repair or replace the wire harness as necessary.

6. If the voltage is always greater than 2 volts, test for an open circuit in the wire or connector between the switch and ground. Repair as necessary.

Closed Throttle (Idle) Switch Test

NOTE: *It is important that all testing be done with the idle speed actuator (ISA) motor plunger in the fully extended position, as it would be after normal engine shutdown. If it is necessary to extend the ISA motor plunger to test the switch, an ISA motor failure can be suspected.*

1. With the ignition switch ON, test the switch voltage at the diagnostic connector terminals D2-13 (+) and D2-7 (−). The voltage should be close to zero at closed throttle and greater than 2 volts when off the closed throttle position.

2. If the voltage is always zero, test for a short circuit to ground in the wire harness or switch, or for an open circuit between ECU connector terminal 25 and the switch.

3. If the voltage is always more than 2 volts, test for an open circuit in the wire harness between the ECU and the switch connector, and between the switch connector and ground. Repair or replace the wire harness as necessary.

Manifold Absolute Pressure (MAP) Sensor Test

1. Inspect the MAP sensor vacuum hose connections at the throttle body and sensor and repair as necessary.

2. Test the MAP sensor output voltage at the MAP sensor connector terminal **B** as marked on the sensor body, with the ignition switch ON (engine OFF). The output voltage should be 4-5 volts.

3. Test ECU terminal 33 for the same voltage described above to verify the wire harness condition. Repair as necessary.

4. Test the MAP sensor supply voltage at the sensor connector terminal **C** with the ignition ON. It should be 4.5-5.5 volts. This voltage should also be at terminal 16 of the ECU wire harness connector. Repair or replace the wire harness as necessary. Test the ECU with Diagnostic Tester MS 1700, if necessary.

5. Test the MAP sensor ground circuit at sensor connector terminal **A** and ECU connector terminal 17. Repair the wire harness, if necessary.

6. Test the MAP sensor ground circuit at the ECU connector between terminal 17 and terminal 2 with an ohmmeter. If the ohmmeter indicates an open circuit, inspect for a defective sensor ground connection on the flywheel/drive plate housing near the starter motor. If the ground connection is good, replace the ECU. If terminal 17 has a short circuit to 12 volts, correct this condition before replacing the ECU.

Manifold Air Temperature (MAT) Sensor and Coolant Temperature Sensor (CTS) Test

These two sensors are tested in the same manner and should yield the same results. The only difference is the pin number of the test points. Disconnect the wire harness connector from the sensor, then test the resistance with a digital volt-ohmmeter. The resistance should be less than 1000 ohms with the engine warm. Refer to the chart to check the temperature-to-resistance values and replace the sensor if the resistance is not within the specified range. If the MAT sensor is being tested, check the resistance between ECU harness connector terminals 14 and 32 and the sensor connector terminals. If the CTS sensor is being tested, check the resistance between ECU harness connector terminals 15 and 32 and the sensor terminals.

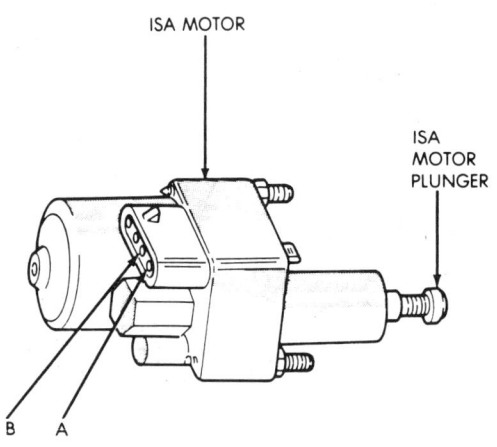

A - GROUND (−)
B - CLOSED THROTTLE SWITCH

Closed throttle switch, integral with the ISA motor w/ TBI

FUEL SYSTEM

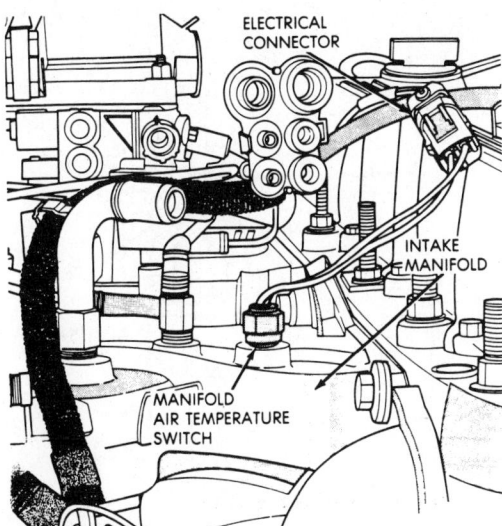

Manifold air temperature sensor w/TBI

In either case, repair the wire harness if an open circuit is indicated.

Component Service

FUEL PUMP
REMOVAL AND INSTALLATION

1. Disconnect the negative battery cable.
2. Remove the fuel tank filler cap.
3. Drain the fuel from the fuel tank.
4. Raise and support the rear end on jackstands.
5. Remove the fuel inlet and outlet hoses from the sending unit. Be ready to catch any spilled fuel.
6. Remove the sending unit wires.
7. Using a brass punch and hammer, remove the sending unit retaining lock ring by tapping it counterclockwise.
8. Remove the sending unit, which incorporates the electric fuel pump, along with the O-ring seal from the fuel tank. Discard the O-ring.
9. Remove and discard the pump inlet filter.
10. Disconnect the fuel pump terminal wires.
11. Remove the pump outlet hose and clamp.
12. Remove the pump top mounting bracket nut and remove the pump.

To install:
13. Install a new inlet filter on the pump.
14. Assemble the pump and bracket. Connect the hose and wiring.
15. Install the unit and new O-ring in the tank. The rubber stopper on the end of the fuel return tube must be inserted into the cup in the fuel tank reservoir.
16. Install the lock ring. Carefully tap it into place until it seats against the stop on the tank.
17. Connect the hoses.
18. Connect the wiring.
19. Lower the truck, fill the tank, run the engine and check for leaks.

THROTTLE BODY
REMOVAL AND INSTALLATION

1. Disconnect the negative battery cable. Remove the upper air cleaner assembly.
2. Remove the lower air cleaner assembly retaining bolts. Remove the lower air cleaner assembly.
3. Remove the throttle cable and the return spring. Disconnect the wire harness connector from the injector.
4. Disconnect the wire harness connector from the wide open throttle switch. Disconnect the wire harness connector from the ISC motor.
5. Disconnect the fuel supply pipe from the

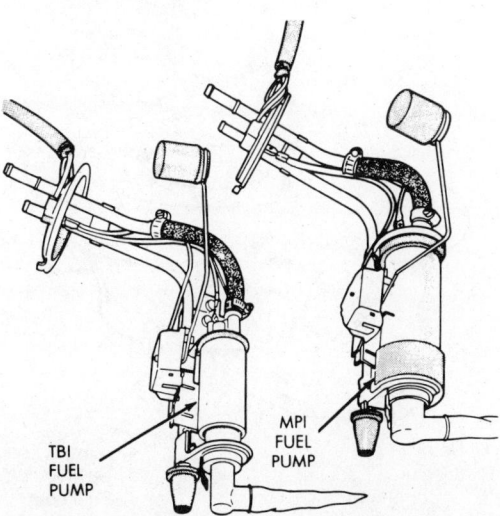

Electric fuel pumps

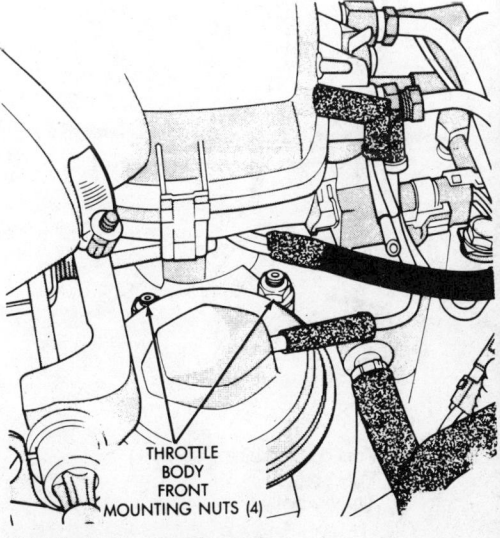

Throttle body attaching nuts

206 FUEL SYSTEM

throttle body. Disconnect the fuel return pipe from the throttle body.

6. Disconnect the vacuum hoses from the throttle body assembly. Disconnect the potentiometer wire connector.

7. Remove the throttle body to manifold retaining bolts. Remove the throttle body assembly from the intake manifold.

8. Installation is the reverse of removal. Be sure to use a new gasket between the throttle body assembly and the intake manifold. Torque the mounting nuts to 16 ft. lbs.

FUEL BODY ASSEMBLY REMOVAL AND INSTALLATION

1. Remove the throttle body assembly from the vehicle.

2. Remove the Torx® head screws that retain the fuel body to the throttle body. Remove and discard the gasket.

3. Installation is the reverse of removal. Be sure to use a new gasket.

FUEL PRESSURE REGULATOR REMOVAL AND INSTALLATION

1. Remove the throttle body assembly from the vehicle.

WARNING: *To prevent spring pressure release, hold the regulator housing against the throttle body while removing the mounting screws.*

2. Remove the three retaining screws that hold the pressure regulator to the fuel body.

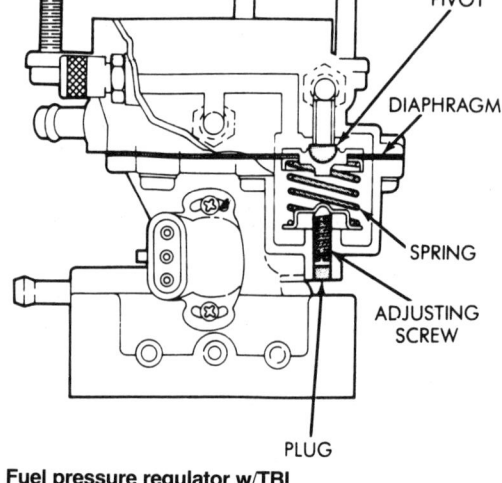

Fuel pressure regulator w/TBI

3. Remove the pressure regulator assembly. Note the location of the components for reassembly. Discard the gasket.

4. Installation is the reverse of the removal procedure. Be sure to use a new gasket.

WARNING: *The pressure regulator diaphragm MUST be installed with the vent hole aligned with the vent holes in the throttle body and regulator housing!*

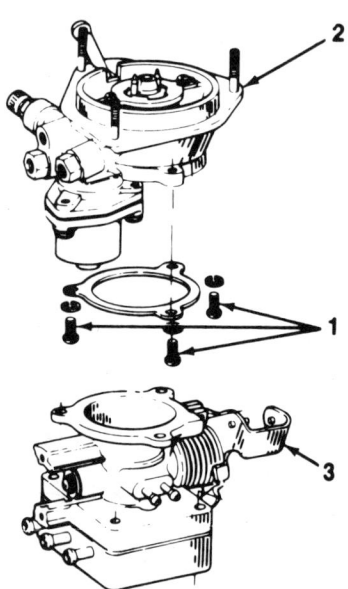

1. Fuel body retaining screws
2. Fuel body
3. Throttly body

Fuel body assembly removal

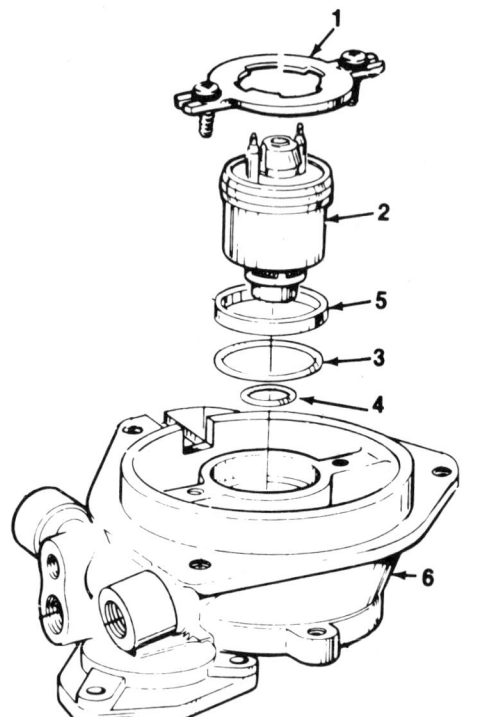

1. Retainer clip
2. Injector
3. Upper O-ring
4. Lower O-ring
5. Backup ring
6. Fuel body

Injector removal

FUEL SYSTEM

FUEL INJECTOR
REMOVAL AND INSTALLATION

1. Remove the air cleaner and hose assembly.
2. Remove the throttle body upper and lower covers.
3. Remove the fuel injector wire by compressing the tabs and pulling it upwards.
4. Remove the fuel injector retainer clip screws. Remove the fuel injector retainer clip.
   NOTE: *The injector has a small locating tab that fits into a slot in the bottom of the injector bore of the throttle body. DO NOT twist the injector during removal!*
5. Using a small pair of pliers, gently grasp the center collar of the injector, between the electrical terminals, and carefully remove the injector using a lifting-rocking motion.
6. Discard the centering ring and the upper and lower O-rings. Never reuse these rings!
7. Installation is the reverse of the removal procedure. Lubricate both O-rings with light oil before installation. Align the tab on the injector with the slot in the throttle body.

THROTTLE POSITION SENSOR
REMOVAL AND INSTALLATION

1. Remove the upper and lower air cleaner assemblies.
2. Remove the throttle body assembly from the vehicle.
3. Remove the two Torx® head retaining screws holding the TPS assembly to the throttle body.
4. Remove the throttle position sensor from the throttle shaft lever.
5. Installation is the reverse of removal.
   WARNING: *Make sure that the sensor arm is installed UNDERNEATH the arm of the throttle valve shaft!*

IDLE SPEED ACTUATOR MOTOR
REMOVAL AND INSTALLATION

NOTE: *The closed throttle switch is integral with the motor.*
1. Disconnect the throttle return spring. Disconnect the wire harness connector from the motor.
2. Remove the motor to bracket retaining nuts. **Be sure to use a back-up wrench** as not to remove the motor studs which hold the motor together.
3. Remove the motor from the bracket.
4. Installation is the reverse of removal.

WIDE OPEN THROTTLE (WOT) SWITCH
REMOVAL AND INSTALLATION

1. Remove the air cleaner assembly.
2. Disconnect the throttle return spring.

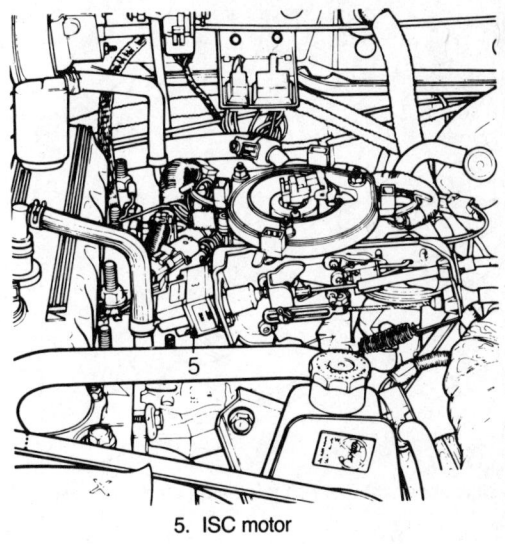

5. ISC motor

ISC motor location

3. Disconnect the throttle cable.
4. Disconnector the wire harness connector to the WOT switch.
5. Remove the two WOT switch-to-bracket mounting screws.
6. Remove the WOT switch.
7. Installation is the reverse of removal.

Quick-Connect Fuel Line
O-RING REPLACEMENT

1. Release the fuel system pressure, then separate the quick-connect fuel line tubes at the inner fender panel by squeezing the two retaining tabs against the fuel line, then pulling the tube and retainer from the fitting.
2. Remove the two O-rings and the spacer from the fitting. This can be accomplished by

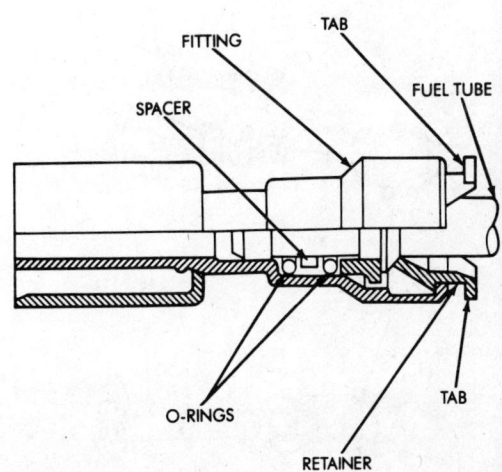

Quick-connect fuel fitting

208 FUEL SYSTEM

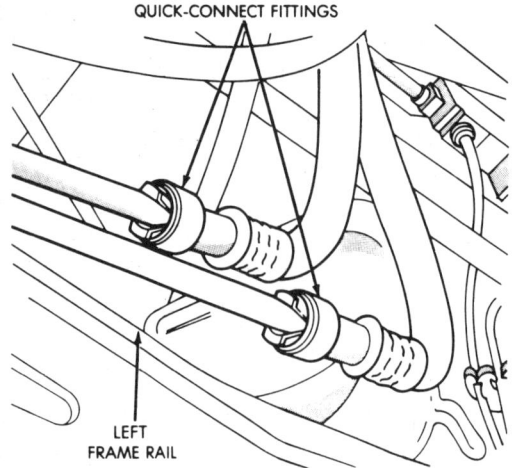

Quick-connect fuel fitting location on models with TBI

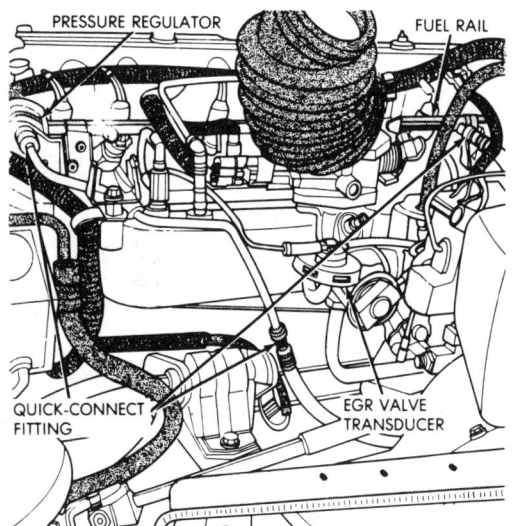

Quick-connect fuel fitting location on models with MFI

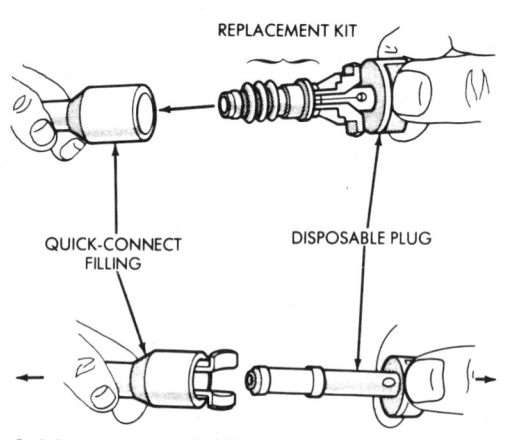

Quick-connect repair kit

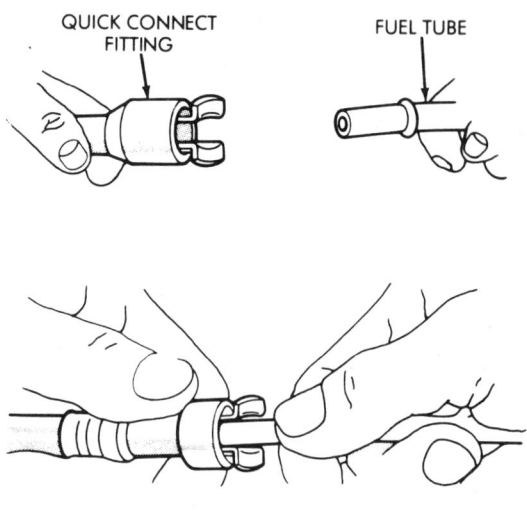

Fuel tube-to-fitting connection

using a paper clip or piece of heavy wire bent into an L-shape.

3. Remove the retainer from the fuel tube and discard the O-rings, spacer and retainer.

4. Install the new retainer assembly by pushing it into the quick-connect fitting until it clicks.

5. Grasp the disposable plastic plug and remove it from the replacement fitting. By removing only the plastic plug, the O-rings, spacer and retainer will remain in the fitting.

6. Push the fuel line into the fitting until a click is heard and the connection is complete. Give the fuel line connection a firm tug to verify that it is seated and locked properly.

6-243 MULTI-POINT FUEL INJECTION SYSTEM

The Renix multi-point fuel injection system is controlled by a digital microprocessor called the electronic control unit, or ECU. The ECU receives information from various input sensors. Based on this information, the ECU is programmed to provide a precise amount of fuel and the correct ignition timing to meet existing engine speed and load conditions.

The ECU also calculates ignition timing and operates the ignition power module. The ignition timing is modified by the ECU to meet any engine operating condition. Information such as air temperature, engine coolant temperature, engine speed, absolute pressure in the intake manifold, or the presense of spark knock is used by the ECU when calculating the correct ignition timing.

FUEL SYSTEM 209

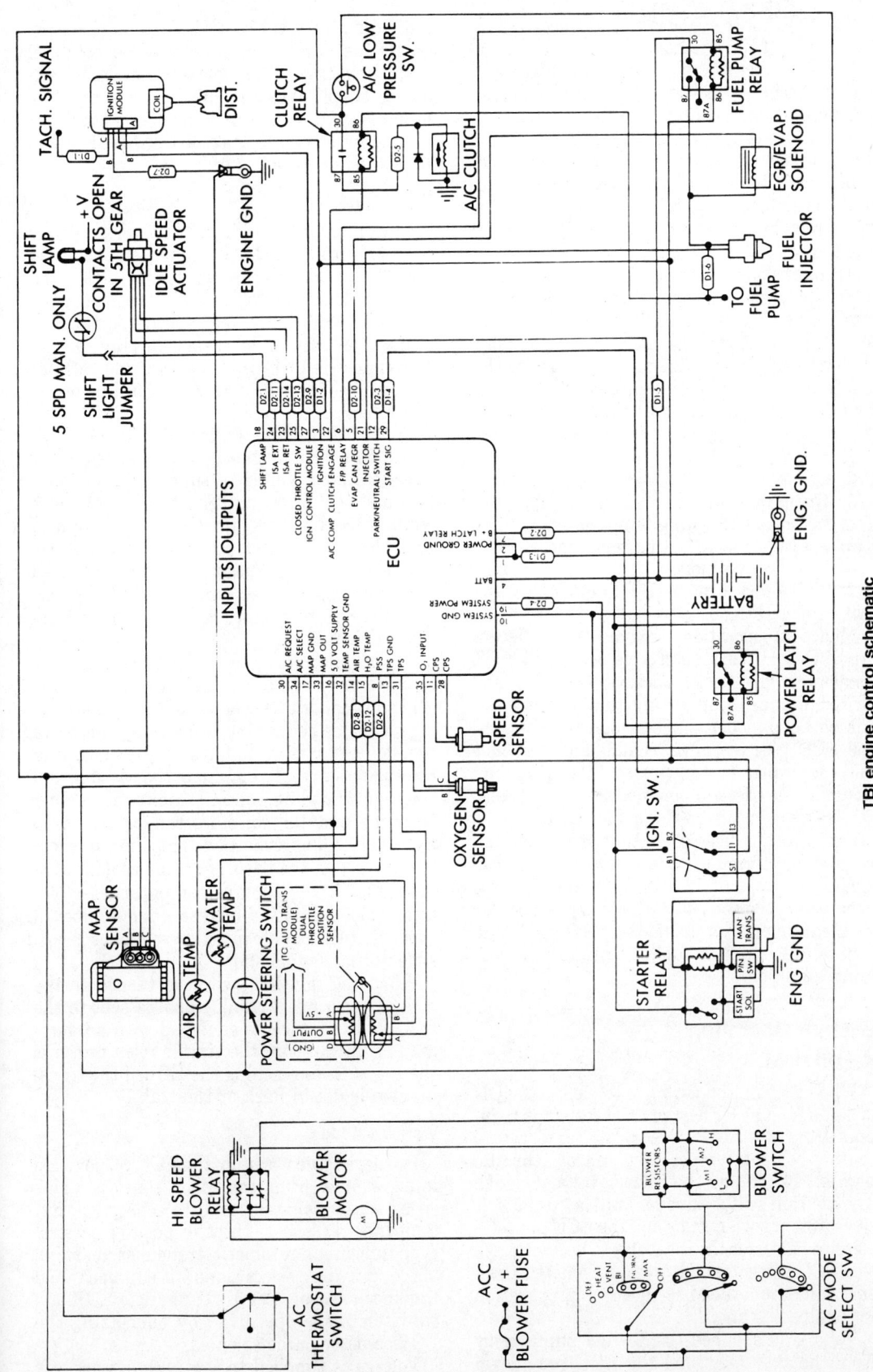

TBI engine control schematic

FUEL SYSTEM

The ECU controls the engine by receiving input signals from the manifold absolute pressure (MAP) sensor, the engine speed sensor, knock sensor, exhaust oxygen sensor, throttle position switch, coolant temperature sensor, air temperature sensor and battery voltage. Based on the information received from the input sensors, the ECU then sends control (output) signals to the fuel pump relay, fuel injectors, idle speed regulator, ignition power module and the EGR valve.

As input signals to the ECU change, the ECU adjusts its signals to the output devices. For example, the ECU must calculate a different injector pulse width and ignition timing for idle than it calculates for wide open throttle (WOT). There are eight different modes of operation that determine how and why the ECU responds to various input signals. The modes are:

1. Key ON mode
2. Crank mode
3. Warmup mode
4. Idle mode-operating temperature
5. Cruise mode-operating temperature
6. Deceleration mode
7. Wide open throttle (WOT) mode
8. Key OFF mode

Modes of operation exist as two different types. Crank, Warmup, Deceleration and WOT modes are Open Loop modes, while the Idle and Cruise modes at operating temperature are Closed Loop modes. In the Open Loop modes, the ECU receives input signals and responds only according to the preset ECU programming. In the Closed Loop modes, the ECU also receives a signal from the exhaust gas oxygen sensor which indicates whether or not the calculated injector pulse width results in the ideal air/fuel mixture of 14.7:1. By monitoring the exhaust oxygen content with the O_2 sensor, the ECU can fine tune the injector pulse width and achieve the optimum fuel mixture for all operating conditions.

System Operation

Key ON Mode

When the ignition switch is turned to the ON position (engine OFF), the ECU responds to inputs from the MAP sensor, air temperature sensor, coolant temperature sensor, throttle position switch and the battery voltage signal. The ignition switch supplies voltage to the B+ (fuel system power) relay and the ECU provides a ground path for the B+ relay to be energized. The ECU receives and stores a barometric pressure value from the MAP sensor in preparation for engine starting.

Voltage is supplied to the fuel pump relay from the B+ relay and the ECU provides a ground path for 1-3 seconds. During this period, the fuel pump relay is energized and the fuel pump pressurizes the fuel supply system. Voltage is supplied to the injectors via the fuel pump relay, but the ECU does not provide a ground path for the injector circuits. The idle regulating valve opens fully.

Crank Mode

During engine cranking, the ECU responds to inputs from the MAP sensor, engine speed sensor, air temperature sensor, throttle position switch, starter relay (automatic transmission only) and the battery voltage signal. The ballast resistor is bypassed during engine cranking. The ECU provides a ground path for the fuel pump relay and the fuel pump is energized.

The ECU restricts EGR and canister purge operation by energizing the EGR/canister purge solenoid. Voltage is supplied to the injectors and the ECU controls the injector pulse width (ON time) by controlling the length of time that the injector circuit ground path remains completed. Based on signals received from the engine speed sensor, the ECU determines the correct ignition timing and triggers the ignition coil.

All fuel injectors are energized simultaneously, once per engine revolution, except during cold start conditions when the injectors are energized twice per engine revolution. This extra fuel delivery continues for a few seconds after the engine starts. To eliminate the possibility of the engine flooding, the ECU limits the number of times that the injectors can be energized twice per engine revolution. This limit is calculated solely on the basis of engine coolant temperature. If the coolant temperature is extremely low, the ECU increases the number of times that the double injection sequence is possible during engine start.

When the ignition switch is turned to the START position, a crank signal is sent to the ECU. If the vehicle is equipped with an automatic transmission, the starter relay prevents the signal from reaching the ECU if the transmission is not in Park or Neutral.

Warmup Mode

During engine warmup, the ECU responds to input signals from the MAP sensor, engine speed sensor, air temperature sensor, coolant temperature sensor, throttle position switch, gear indicator (automatic transmission only), air conditioning select signal (if equipped) and the knock sensor. The ECU restricts EGR and canister purge operation by energizing the EGR/canister purge solenoid.

Voltage is supplied to the injectors and the

ECU controls the injector pulse width by controlling the length of time that the injector circuit ground path remains closed. All fuel injectors are energized simultaneously once per engine revolution. The ECU also establishes the correct idle speed by providing the ground to the idle regulating valve. If necessary, the idle speed is also adjusted to compensate for increased engine load during the A/C compressor operation, if equipped.

In addition to the above, the ECU determines the correct ignition timing and triggers the ignition power module. The shift indicator light is actuated if the engine speed and load conditions warrant a change to a higher gear.

Idle Mode

During engine idle, the ECU responds to input signals from the MAP sensor, engine speed sensor, air temperature sensor, coolant temperature sensor, throttle position switch, battery voltage signal, oxygen sensor, knock sensor and air conditioning select signal (if equipped). The ECU restricts EGR and canister purge operation by energizing the EGR/canister purge solenoid.

Voltage is supplied to the injectors and the ECU controls the injector pulse width by controlling the length of time that the injector circuit ground path remains closed. All fuel injectors are energized simultaneously once per engine revolution. The ECU also establishes the correct idle speed by providing the ground to the idle regulating valve. If necessary, the idle speed is also adjusted to compensate for increased engine load during the A/C compressor operation, if equipped.

In addition to the above, the ECU determines the correct ignition timing and triggers the ignition power module. By monitoring the oxygen sensor signal, the ECU can fine tune the fuel delivery by adjusting the injector pulse width (ON time), until the ideal 14.7:1 air/fuel mixture is achieved.

Cruise Mode

When the vehicle is moving at road speed, the ECU responds to input signals from the MAP sensor, engine speed sensor, air temperature sensor, coolant temperature sensor, throttle position switch, battery voltage signal, oxygen sensor, knock sensor and air contitioner select signal (if equipped). The ECU opens the ground path for the EGR/canister purge solenoid, allowing the EGR transducer and the evaporative vapor canister to receive manifold vacuum. Fuel delivery and timing control are as described under the Idle Mode.

Wide Open Throttle (WOT) Mode

During WOT operation, the ECU responds to input signals from the MAP sensor, engine speed sensor, air temperature sensor, coolant temperature sensor, battery voltage signal and the knock sensor. The barometric pressure is also updated in the computer. The ECU restricts EGR and canister purge operation by energizing the EGR/canister purge solenoid. The ECU controls fuel injector pulse width by controlling the time that the injector circuit ground remains closed.

The ECU also determines the correct ignition timing and triggers the ignition power module. If spark knock is detected, the ECU retards the ignition timing at the cylinder which is knocking until the knock is eliminated, with ignition timing progressively returning to its value prior to when the knock was detected.

Deceleration Mode

During engine deceleration, the ECU responds to input signals from the MAP sensor, engine speed sensor, air temperature sensor, coolant temperature sensor, throttle position switch and air conditioner select signal (if equipped). The ECU restricts EGR and canister purge operation by energizing the EGR/canister purge solenoid. The ECU controls fuel injector pulse width by controlling the time that the injector circuit ground remains closed, and determines correct ignition timing and triggers the ignition power module.

If the ECU receives a closed throttle signal and engine speed is over 1500 rpm, the ECU determines that the engine is in a hard deceleration condition and responds by completely shutting off fuel injection. Injection is resumed when the engine speed decreases to 1500 rpm.

Key OFF Mode

When the ignition switch is moved to the OFF position, the ECU breaks the injector ground circuit and all fuel injection stops. The ignition power module is deactivated and the ECU opens the ground circuit for the B + relay, cutting off the voltage supply to the fuel injection circuitry.

SPECIAL OPERATING CONDITIONS

Full Load Altitude Correction

When the pressure in the intake manifold is around atmospheric pressure, the computer will modify the mixture fed to the engine to pass gradually from the minimum specific consumption point to the power point. The atmospheric pressure is stored in the ECU. It is measured each time the key is turned to the ON position and brought up to date each time the

FUEL SYSTEM

throttle is fully opened or each time the pressure noted is higher than atmospheric pressure. At higher altitude, the air is less dense and therefore has less oxygen per unit volume. To maintain a constant manifold pressure, the fuel mixture must be leaner at low load and when idling. The atmospheric pressure reading provides a basis for altitude correction.

Operation In Defect Mode

The injection system can remain operative when some of its sensors are defective. The ECU diagnoses its sensors by comparing their values to preset limits. If the value sensed does not lie between these limits, the sensor is treated as defective and the system operates in a defect mode.

If the coolant sensor is inoperative, air temperature is used in determining injection pulse width and ignition timing values. The air temperature value is then increased as a function of engine rpm to simulate coolant sensor output. If the oxygen sensor fails, open loop operation is forced.

Component Operation
ECU INPUTS
Coolant Temperature Sensor (CTS)

The coolant temperature sensor is located on the left side of the cylinder block, just below the exhaust manifold. The CTS provides an engine coolant temperature input to the ECU, which will then enrich the air/fuel mixture delivered by the injectors when the engine coolant is cold. Based on the CTS signal, the ECU will also control engine warmup idle speed, increase ignition advance and inhibit EGR operation when the coolant is cold.

Manifold Air Temperature (MAT) Sensor

The manifold air temperature sensor is located in the intake manifold. The MAT sensor reacts to the temperature of the air in the intake manifold and provides an input to the ECU to allow it to compensate for air density changes during high temperature operation.

Manifold Absolute Pressure (MAP) Sensor

The manifold absolute pressure sensor is mounted on the dash panel behind the engine. The MAP sensor reacts to absolute pressure in the intake manifold and provides an input voltage to the ECU. Manifold pressure is used to supply mixture density information and ambient barometric pressure information to the ECU. A hose from the intake manifold provides the input pressure.

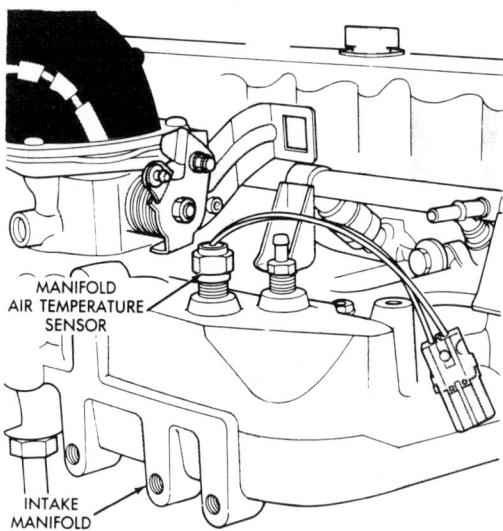

Manifold air temperature sensor w/MFI

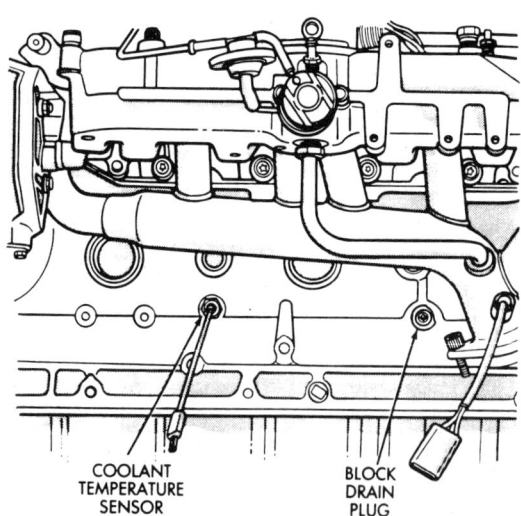

Coolant temperature sensor w/MFI

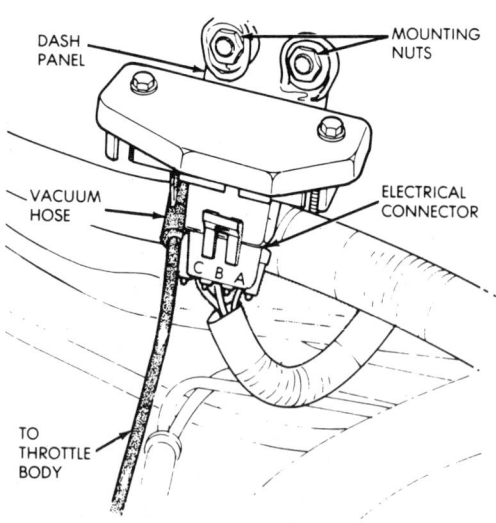

MAP sensor w/MFI

FUEL SYSTEM 213

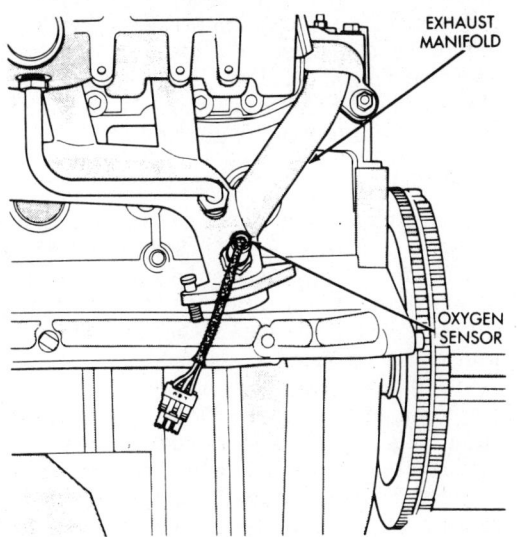

Heated oxygen sensor w/MFI

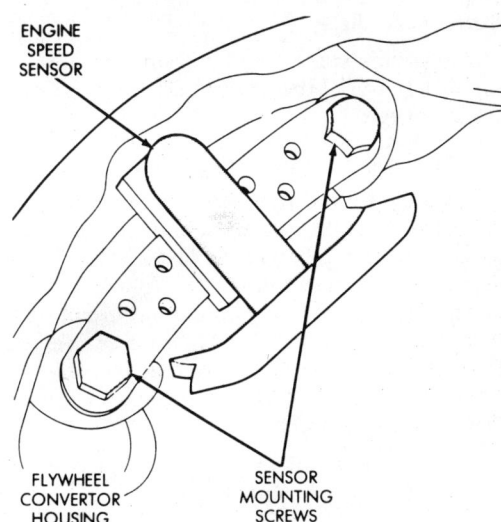

Engine speed sensor attaching bolts w/MFI

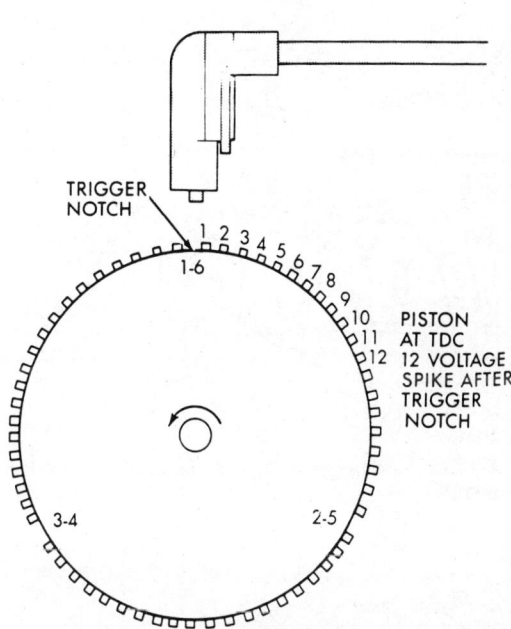

Engine speed sensor-to-flywheel positioning w/MFI

Oxygen (O₂) Sensor

The oxygens sensor is located in the exhaust manifold. The voltage output from this sensor, which varies with the oxygen content in the exhaust gas, is supplied to the ECU. The O_2 sensor is equipped with a heating element that keeps the sensor at the proper operating temperature during all engine operating modes. Maintaining correct sensor temperature at all times allows the system to enter closed loop operation sooner and to remain in closed loop during periods of extended idle. Electrical feed to the O_2 sensor is through the ignition switch.

Knock Sensor

The knock sensor is located on the lower left side of the cylinder block, just above the oil pan. The knock sensor provides and input to the ECU that indicates detonation (knock) during engine operation. When detonation occurs, the ECU retards the ignition timing advance to eliminate the detonation at the applicable cylinder(s).

Speed Sensor

The speed sensor is secured by special shouldered bolts to the flywheel/drive plate housing. It is preset in its mounting at the factory and is non-adjustable in the field. The speed sensor senses TDC and engine speed by detecting the flywheel teeth as they pass during engine operation.

The flylwheel has a large trigger tooth and notch located 12 small teeth before each top dead center (TDC) position. When a small tooth and notch pass the magnet core in the sensor, the concentration and then collapse of the magnetic flux induces a small voltage spike into the sensor pickup coil winding. These small voltage spikes enable the ECU to count the teeth as they pass the sensor.

When a large trigger tooth and notch pass the magnet core in the sensor, the increased concentration/collapse of the magnetic flux induces a higher voltage spike into the pickup coil winding. This higher voltage spike indicates to the ECU that a piston will soon be at the TDC position 12 teeth later. The ignition timing for the cylinder is either advanced or retarded as necessary by the ECU according to the sensor inputs.

214 FUEL SYSTEM

Starter Motor Relay

The engine starter motor relay provides an input to the ECU that indicates the starter motor is engaged.

Throttle Position Sensor (TPS)

The throttle position sensor is mounted on the throttle plate assembly and provides the ECU with an input signal of up to 5 volts to indicate throttle position. At minimum throttle opening (idle speed), a signal input of approximately 1 volt is transmitted to the ECU. As the throttle opening increases, voltage increases to a maximum of approximately 5 volts at the wide open throttle position.

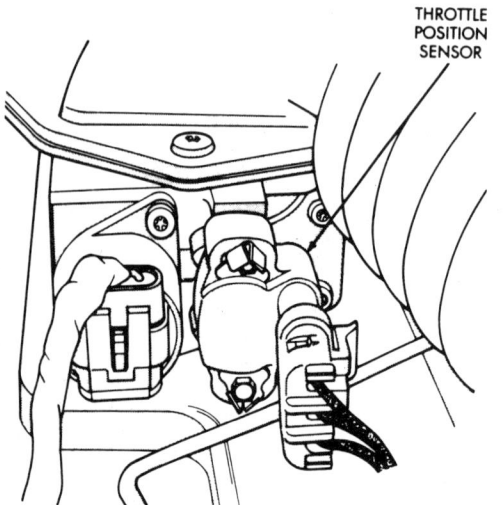

Throttle position sensor with manual transmission and MFI

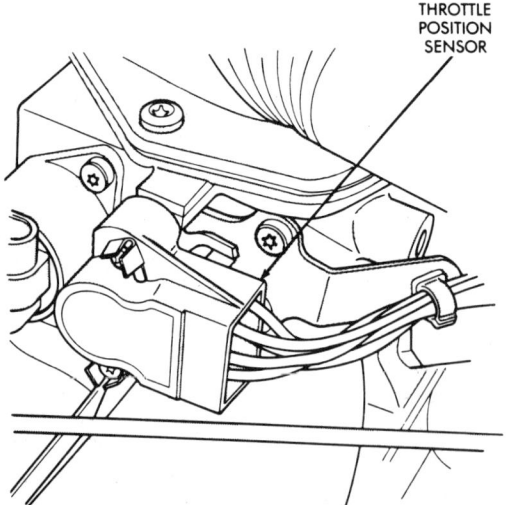

Throttle position sensor with automatic transmission and MFI

A dual TPS is used on models equipped with automatic transmission. This dual TPS not only provides the ECU with input voltages, but also supplies the automatic transmission TCU with an input of throttle position.

Battery Voltage

The battery voltage input to the ECU is monitored so that the injector is energized for the proper amount of time. As the battery voltage input to the ECU varies, as during engine cranking, the ECU varies the injector pulse width to compensate.

In addition to the above inputs, the ECU also receives signals from the Park/Neutral switch on automatic transmission models; an A/C input signal to tell the ECU when the compressor is engaged so it can raise the idle speed to compensate for the load; and a sync pulse (stator) signal generated within the distributor to properly synchronize injector opening with intake valve closing.

ECU OUTPUTS

Oxygen Sensor Heater Relay

The oxygen sensor heater relay is normally closed, supplying voltage to the O_2 sensor heater under warmup and idle conditions. The O_2 heater relay is controlled by the ECU. When the speed sensor and MAP sensor reach a predetermined input, it tells the ECU that the O_2 sensor will stay heated by the exhaust gas under those conditions, and the ECU can open the O_2 sensor heater relay and cut off the voltage supply to the heater.

A/C Clutch Relay

The ECU controls the compressor clutch through the A/C clutch relay. This allows the ECU to receive a request for air conditioning from the A/C temperature control thermostat.

Fuel Pump Relay

The fuel pump relay is located on the right inner fender panel. Battery voltage is supplied to the relay from the ignition switch and is energized when a ground is provided by the ECU. When energized, voltage is supplied to the fuel pump.

EGR Valve Solenoid

The vacuum for the EGR valve operation is controlled by this solenoid. When energized by the ECU, the EGR valve solenoid prevents vacuum from reaching the EGR valve diaphragm. The solenoid is energized during engine warmup, closed throttle (idle), wide open throttle and rapid acceleration/deceleration conditions. If the solenoid wire connector is discon-

FUEL SYSTEM 215

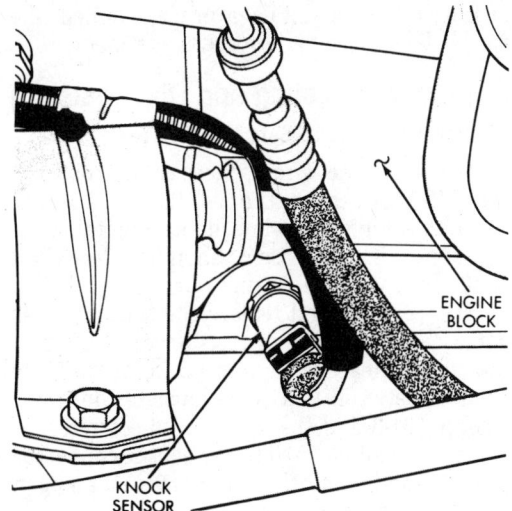

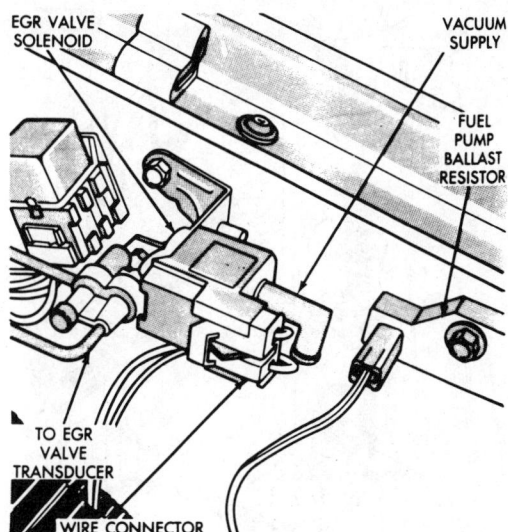

EGR valve solenoid—ECU output, w/MFI

Ignition Control Module

Based on inputs, the ECU triggers the ignition coil to fire via the ignition control module. In this manner, the ECU can control spark timing according to engine operating conditions as reported by the various engine sensors.

Fuel Injectors

The fuel injectors are located in the intake manifold. The injectors are electronically and exclusively controlled by the ECU. The injection time duration, or pulse width, is based on engine operating conditions as reported by the various engine sensors. The ECU controls the injectors by supplying the ground; the longer

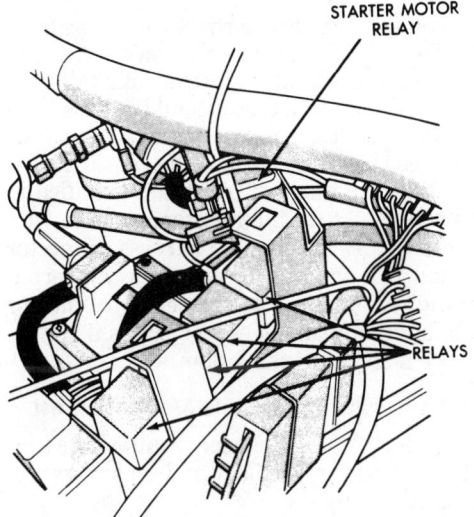

MFI electrical components: knock sensor, fuel pump relay, oxygen sensor heater relay, B+ latch relay, air conditioning clutch relay

nected, the EGR valve will be operative at all times and cause driveability problems.

Upshift Indicator Lamp

The indicator lamp is normally illuminated when the ignition switch is turned to the ON position and goes out when the engine is started. The indicator will be illuminated during engine operation according to engine speed and load conditions. A switch located on the transmission prevents the lamp from being illuminated when the transmission is shifted into its highest gear. The ECU will turn off the upshift indicator if the gear change is not performed within 3-5 seconds.

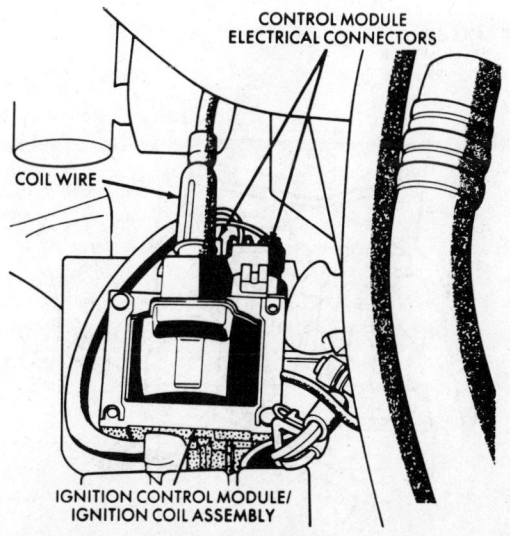

Ignition control module, w/MFI

216 FUEL SYSTEM

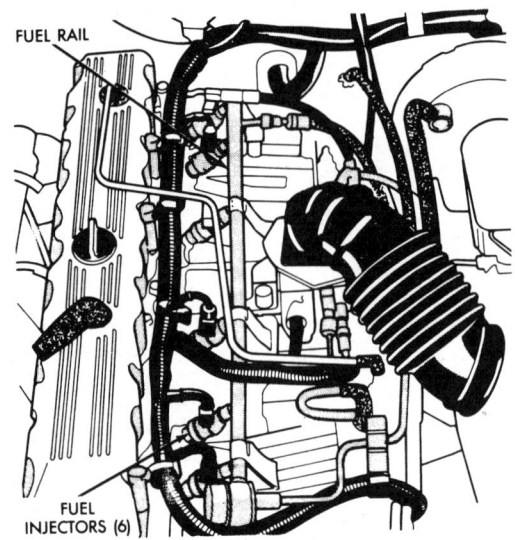

MFI fuel injectors

the ground is supplied, the more fuel delivered to the engine.

Latch Relay

The latch relay is located on the right inner fender panel. This relay is initially energized during engine startup and remains energized until 3-5 seconds after the engine is stopped. This enables the ECU to extend the idle speed stepper motor for the next startup, then cease operation.

Idle Speed Stepper Motor

The idle speed stepper motor is located on the throttle plate assembly. The ECU controls the idle speed by providing the appropriate voltage outputs to mofe the stepper motor pin inward or outward to maintain a predetermined idle speed. There is no idle speed adjustment.

Component Testing and Diagnosis

Coolant Temperature Sensor (CTS) Test

Disconnect the wire harness connector from the CTS and measure the resistance of the sensor with a high input impedence (digital) volt-ohmmeter. The resistance should be less than 1000 ohms with the engine warm. Refer to the resistance chart and replace the sensor if it is not within the range of resistance specified in the chart. Measure the resistance of the wire harness between ECU wire harness connector terminal D-3 and the sensor connector terminal, and terminal C-10 to the sensor connector terminal and repair the wire harness if an open circuit is indicated.

Manifold Air Temperature (MAT) Sensor Test

Disconnect the wire harness connector from the CTS and measure the resistance of the sensor with a high input impedence (digital) volt-ohmmeter. The resistance should be less than 1000 ohms with the engine warm. Refer to the resistance chart and replace the sensor if it is not within the range of resistance specified in the chart. Measure the resistance of the wire harness between ECU wire harness connector terminal D-3 and the sensor connector terminal, and terminal C-8 to the sensor connector terminal and repair the wire harness if the resistance is greater than 1 ohm.

Manifold Absolute Pressure (MAP) Sensor Test

1. Inspect the MAP sensor vacuum hose connection at the throttle body and sensor and repair as necessary.

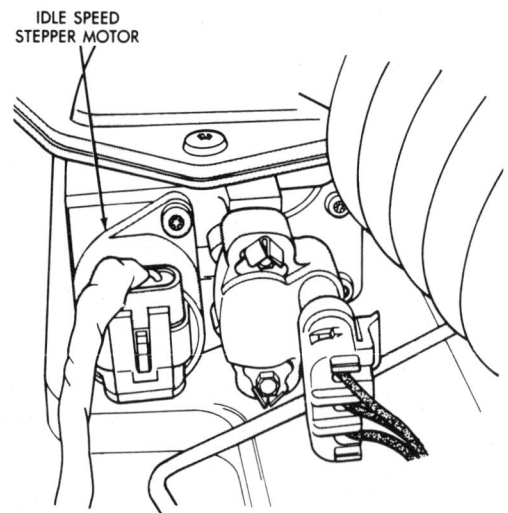

Idle speed stepper motor w/MFI

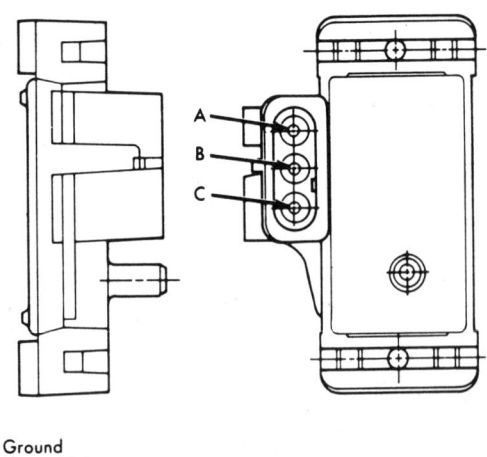

A. Ground
B. Output Voltage
C. 5 Volts

MFI MAP sensor connector terminals

CHILTON'S
FUEL ECONOMY & TUNE-UP TIPS

Tune-up • Spark Plug Diagnosis • Emission Controls
Fuel System • Cooling System • Tires and Wheels
General Maintenance

55 WAYS TO IMPROVE FUEL ECONOMY

CHILTON'S FUEL ECONOMY & TUNE-UP TIPS

Fuel economy is important to everyone, no matter what kind of vehicle you drive. The maintenance-minded motorist can save both money and fuel using these tips and the periodic maintenance and tune-up procedures in this Repair and Tune-Up Guide.

There are more than 130,000,000 cars and trucks registered for private use in the United States. Each travels an average of 10-12,000 miles per year, and, and in total they consume close to 70 billion gallons of fuel each year. This represents nearly ⅔ of the oil imported by the United States each year. The Federal government's goal is to reduce consumption 10% by 1985. A variety of methods are either already in use or under serious consideration, and they all affect you driving and the cars you will drive. In addition to "down-sizing", the auto industry is using or investigating the use of electronic fuel delivery, electronic engine controls and alternative engines for use in smaller and lighter vehicles, among other alternatives to meet the federally mandated Corporate Average Fuel Economy (CAFE) of 27.5 mpg by 1985. The government, for its part, is considering rationing, mandatory driving curtailments and tax increases on motor vehicle fuel in an effort to reduce consumption. The government's goal of a 10% reduction could be realized — and further government regulation avoided — if every private vehicle could use just 1 less gallon of fuel per week.

How Much Can You Save?

Tests have proven that almost anyone can make at least a 10% reduction in fuel consumption through regular maintenance and tune-ups. When a major manufacturer of spark plugs sur-

TUNE-UP

1. Check the cylinder compression to be sure the engine will really benefit from a tune-up and that it is capable of producing good fuel economy. A tune-up will be wasted on an engine in poor mechanical condition.

2. Replace spark plugs regularly. New spark plugs alone can increase fuel economy 3%.

3. Be sure the spark plugs are the correct type (heat range) for your vehicle. See the Tune-Up Specifications.

Heat range refers to the spark plug's ability to conduct heat away from the firing end. It must conduct the heat away in an even pattern to avoid becoming a source of pre-ignition, yet it must also operate hot enough to burn off conductive deposits that could cause misfiring.

The heat range is usually indicated by a number on the spark plug, part of the manufacturer's designation for each individual spark plug. The numbers in bold-face indicate the heat range in each manufacturer's identification system.

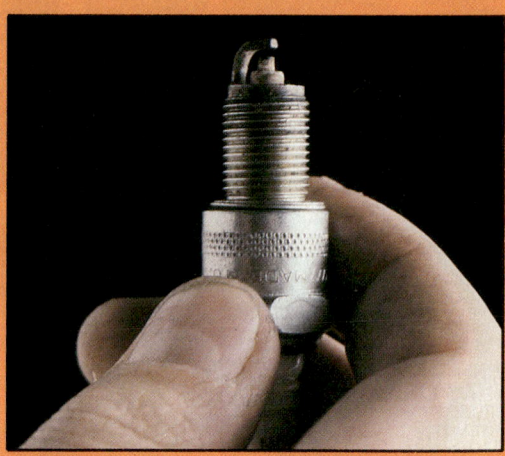

Periodically, check the spark plugs to be sure they are firing efficiently. They are excellent indicators of the internal condition of your engine.

Manufacturer	Typical Designation
AC	R **45** TS
Bosch (old)	WA **145** T30
Bosch (new)	HR **8** Y
Champion	RBL **15** Y
Fram/Autolite	4**15**
Mopar	P-**62** PR
Motorcraft	BRF-**42**
NGK	BP **5** ES-15
Nippondenso	W **16** EP
Prestolite	14GR **5** 2A

On AC, Bosch (new), Champion, Fram/Autolite, Mopar, Motorcraft and Prestolite, a higher number indicates a hotter plug. On Bosch (old), NGK and Nippondenso, a higher number indicates a colder plug.

4. Make sure the spark plugs are properly gapped. See the Tune-Up Specifications in this book.

5. Be sure the spark plugs are firing efficiently. The illustrations on the next 2 pages show you how to "read" the firing end of the spark plug.

6. Check the ignition timing and set it to specifications. Tests show that almost all cars have incorrect ignition timing by more than 2°.

veyed over 6,000 cars nationwide, they found that a tune-up, on cars that needed one, increased fuel economy over 11%. Replacing worn plugs alone, accounted for a 3% increase. The same test also revealed that 8 out of every 10 vehicles will have some maintenance deficiency that will directly affect fuel economy, emissions or performance. Most of this mileage-robbing neglect could be prevented with regular maintenance.

Modern engines require that all of the functioning systems operate properly for maximum efficiency. A malfunction anywhere wastes fuel. You can keep your vehicle running as efficiently and economically as possible, by being aware of your vehicle's operating and performance characteristics. If your vehicle suddenly develops performance or fuel economy problems it could be due to one or more of the following:

PROBLEM	POSSIBLE CAUSE
Engine Idles Rough	Ignition timing, idle mixture, vacuum leak or something amiss in the emission control system.
Hesitates on Acceleration	Dirty carburetor or fuel filter, improper accelerator pump setting, ignition timing or fouled spark plugs.
Starts Hard or Fails to Start	Worn spark plugs, improperly set automatic choke, ice (or water) in fuel system.
Stalls Frequently	Automatic choke improperly adjusted and possible dirty air filter or fuel filter.
Performs Sluggishly	Worn spark plugs, dirty fuel or air filter, ignition timing or automatic choke out of adjustment.

Check spark plug wires on conventional point type ignition for cracks by bending them in a loop around your finger.

Be sure that spark plug wires leading to adjacent cylinders do not run too close together. (Photo courtesy Champion Spark Plug Co.)

7. If your vehicle does not have electronic ignition, check the points, rotor and cap as specified.

8. Check the spark plug wires (used with conventional point-type ignitions) for cracks and burned or broken insulation by bending them in a loop around your finger. Cracked wires decrease fuel efficiency by failing to deliver full voltage to the spark plugs. One misfiring spark plug can cost you as much as 2 mpg.

9. Check the routing of the plug wires. Misfiring can be the result of spark plug leads to adjacent cylinders running parallel to each other and too close together. One wire tends to pick up voltage from the other causing it to fire "out of time".

10. Check all electrical and ignition circuits for voltage drop and resistance.

11. Check the distributor mechanical and/or vacuum advance mechanisms for proper functioning. The vacuum advance can be checked by twisting the distributor plate in the opposite direction of rotation. It should spring back when released.

12. Check and adjust the valve clearance on engines with mechanical lifters. The clearance should be slightly loose rather than too tight.

SPARK PLUG DIAGNOSIS

Normal

APPEARANCE: This plug is typical of one operating normally. The insulator nose varies from a light tan to grayish color with slight electrode wear. The presence of slight deposits is normal on used plugs and will have no adverse effect on engine performance. The spark plug heat range is correct for the engine and the engine is running normally.
CAUSE: Properly running engine.
RECOMMENDATION: Before reinstalling this plug, the electrodes should be cleaned and filed square. Set the gap to specifications. If the plug has been in service for more than 10-12,000 miles, the entire set should probably be replaced with a fresh set of the same heat range.

Oil Deposits

APPEARANCE: The firing end of the plug is covered with a wet, oily coating.
CAUSE: The problem is poor oil control. On high mileage engines, oil is leaking past the rings or valve guides into the combustion chamber. A common cause is also a plugged PCV valve, and a ruptured fuel pump diaphragm can also cause this condition. Oil fouled plugs such as these are often found in new or recently overhauled engines, before normal oil control is achieved, and can be cleaned and reinstalled.
RECOMMENDATION: A hotter spark plug may temporarily relieve the problem, but the engine is probably in need of work.

Incorrect Heat Range

APPEARANCE: The effects of high temperature on a spark plug are indicated by clean white, often blistered insulator. This can also be accompanied by excessive wear of the electrode, and the absence of deposits.
CAUSE: Check for the correct spark plug heat range. A plug which is too hot for the engine can result in overheating. A car operated mostly at high speeds can require a colder plug. Also check ignition timing, cooling system level, fuel mixture and leaking intake manifold.
RECOMMENDATION: If all ignition and engine adjustments are known to be correct, and no other malfunction exists, install spark plugs one heat range colder.

Carbon Deposits

APPEARANCE: Carbon fouling is easily identified by the presence of dry, soft, black, sooty deposits.
CAUSE: Changing the heat range can often lead to carbon fouling, as can prolonged slow, stop-and-start driving. If the heat range is correct, carbon fouling can be attributed to a rich fuel mixture, sticking choke, clogged air cleaner, worn breaker points, retarded timing or low compression. If only one or two plugs are carbon fouled, check for corroded or cracked wires on the affected plugs. Also look for cracks in the distributor cap between the towers of affected cylinders.
RECOMMENDATION: After the problem is corrected, these plugs can be cleaned and reinstalled if not worn severely.

Photos Courtesy Fram Corporation

MMT Fouled

APPEARANCE: Spark plugs fouled by MMT (Methycyclopentadienyl Maganese Tricarbonyl) have reddish, rusty appearance on the insulator and side electrode.
CAUSE: MMT is an anti-knock additive in gasoline used to replace lead. During the combustion process, the MMT leaves a reddish deposit on the insulator and side electrode.
RECOMMENDATION: No engine malfunction is indicated and the deposits will not affect plug performance any more than lead deposits (see Ash Deposits). MMT fouled plugs can be cleaned, regapped and reinstalled.

High Speed Glazing

APPEARANCE: Glazing appears as shiny coating on the plug, either yellow or tan in color.
CAUSE: During hard, fast acceleration, plug temperatures rise suddenly. Deposits from normal combustion have no chance to fluff-off; instead, they melt on the insulator forming an electrically conductive coating which causes misfiring.
RECOMMENDATION: Glazed plugs are not easily cleaned. They should be replaced with a fresh set of plugs of the correct heat range. If the condition recurs, using plugs with a heat range one step colder may cure the problem.

Ash (Lead) Deposits

APPEARANCE: Ash deposits are characterized by light brown or white colored deposits crusted on the side or center electrodes. In some cases it may give the plug a rusty appearance.
CAUSE: Ash deposits are normally derived from oil or fuel additives burned during normal combustion. Normally they are harmless, though excessive amounts can cause misfiring. If deposits are excessive in short mileage, the valve guides may be worn.
RECOMMENDATION: Ash-fouled plugs can be cleaned, gapped and reinstalled.

Detonation

APPEARANCE: Detonation is usually characterized by a broken plug insulator.
CAUSE: A portion of the fuel charge will begin to burn spontaneously, from the increased heat following ignition. The explosion that results applies extreme pressure to engine components, frequently damaging spark plugs and pistons.

Detonation can result by over-advanced ignition timing, inferior gasoline (low octane) lean air/fuel mixture, poor carburetion, engine lugging or an increase in compression ratio due to combustion chamber deposits or engine modification.
RECOMMENDATION: Replace the plugs after correcting the problem.

Photos Courtesy Champion Spark Plug Co.

EMISSION CONTROLS

13. Be aware of the general condition of the emission control system. It contributes to reduced pollution and should be serviced regularly to maintain efficient engine operation.

14. Check all vacuum lines for dried, cracked or brittle conditions. Something as simple as a leaking vacuum hose can cause poor performance and loss of economy.

15. Avoid tampering with the emission control system. Attempting to improve fuel econ-

FUEL SYSTEM

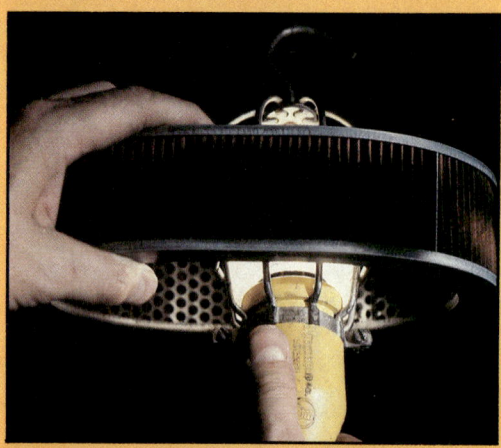

Check the air filter with a light behind it. If you can see light through the filter it can be reused.

Extremely clogged filters should be discarded and replaced with a new one.

18. Replace the air filter regularly. A dirty air filter richens the air/fuel mixture and can increase fuel consumption as much as 10%. Tests show that ⅓ of all vehicles have air filters in need of replacement.

19. Replace the fuel filter at least as often as recommended.

20. Set the idle speed and carburetor mixture to specifications.

21. Check the automatic choke. A sticking or malfunctioning choke wastes gas.

22. During the summer months, adjust the automatic choke for a leaner mixture which will produce faster engine warm-ups.

COOLING SYSTEM

29. Be sure all accessory drive belts are in good condition. Check for cracks or wear.

30. Adjust all accessory drive belts to proper tension.

31. Check all hoses for swollen areas, worn spots, or loose clamps.

32. Check coolant level in the radiator or expansion tank.

33. Be sure the thermostat is operating properly. A stuck thermostat delays engine warm-up and a cold engine uses nearly twice as much fuel as a warm engine.

34. Drain and replace the engine coolant at least as often as recommended. Rust and scale

TIRES & WHEELS

38. Check the tire pressure often with a pencil type gauge. Tests by a major tire manufacturer show that 90% of all vehicles have at least 1 tire improperly inflated. Better mileage can be achieved by over-inflating tires, but never exceed the maximum inflation pressure on the side of the tire.

39. If possible, install radial tires. Radial tires deliver as much as ½ mpg more than bias belted tires.

40. Avoid installing super-wide tires. They only create extra rolling resistance and decrease fuel mileage. Stick to the manufacturer's recommendations.

41. Have the wheels properly balanced.

omy by tampering with emission controls is more likely to worsen fuel economy than improve it. Emission control changes on modern engines are not readily reversible.

16. Clean (or replace) the EGR valve and lines as recommended.

17. Be sure that all vacuum lines and hoses are reconnected properly after working under the hood. An unconnected or misrouted vacuum line can wreak havoc with engine performance.

23. Check for fuel leaks at the carburetor, fuel pump, fuel lines and fuel tank. Be sure all lines and connections are tight.

24. Periodically check the tightness of the carburetor and intake manifold attaching nuts and bolts. These are a common place for vacuum leaks to occur.

25. Clean the carburetor periodically and lubricate the linkage.

26. The condition of the tailpipe can be an excellent indicator of proper engine combustion. After a long drive at highway speeds, the inside of the tailpipe should be a light grey in color. Black or soot on the insides indicates an overly rich mixture.

27. Check the fuel pump pressure. The fuel pump may be supplying more fuel than the engine needs.

28. Use the proper grade of gasoline for your engine. Don't try to compensate for knocking or "pinging" by advancing the ignition timing. This practice will only increase plug temperature and the chances of detonation or pre-ignition with relatively little performance gain.

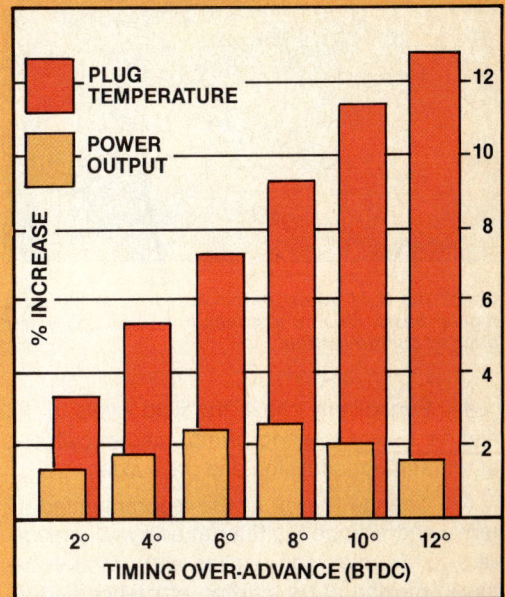

Increasing ignition timing past the specified setting results in a drastic increase in spark plug temperature with increased chance of detonation or preignition. Performance increase is considerably less. (Photo courtesy Champion Spark Plug Co.)

that form in the engine should be flushed out to allow the engine to operate at peak efficiency.

35. Clean the radiator of debris that can decrease cooling efficiency.

36. Install a flex-type or electric cooling fan, if you don't have a clutch type fan. Flex fans use curved plastic blades to push more air at low speeds when more cooling is needed; at high speeds the blades flatten out for less resistance. Electric fans only run when the engine temperature reaches a predetermined level.

37. Check the radiator cap for a worn or cracked gasket. If the cap does not seal properly, the cooling system will not function properly.

42. Be sure the front end is correctly aligned. A misaligned front end actually has wheels going in differed directions. The increased drag can reduce fuel economy by .3 mpg.

43. Correctly adjust the wheel bearings. Wheel bearings that are adjusted too tight increase rolling resistance.

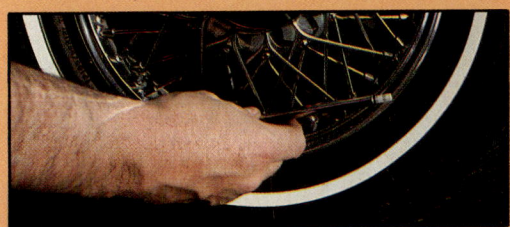

Check tire pressures regularly with a reliable pocket type gauge. Be sure to check the pressure on a cold tire.

GENERAL MAINTENANCE

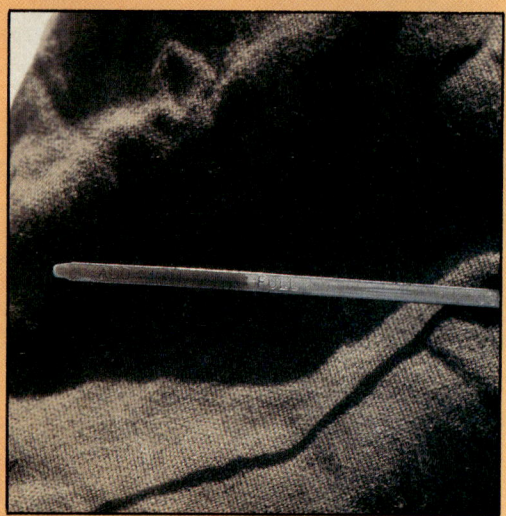

Check the fluid levels (particularly engine oil) on a regular basis. Be sure to check the oil for grit, water or other contamination.

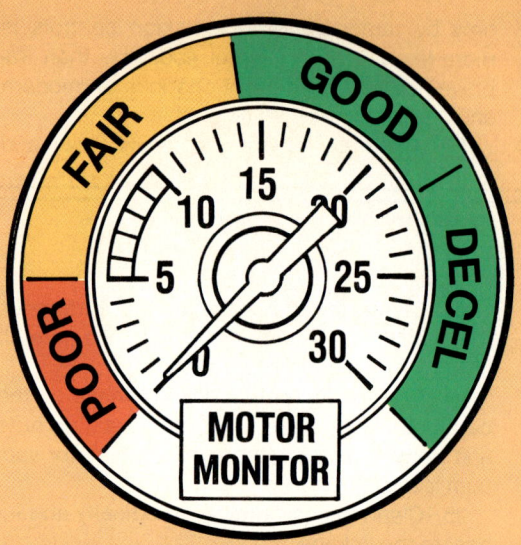

A vacuum gauge is another excellent indicator of internal engine condition and can also be installed in the dash as a mileage indicator.

44. Periodically check the fluid levels in the engine, power steering pump, master cylinder, automatic transmission and drive axle.

45. Change the oil at the recommended interval and change the filter at every oil change. Dirty oil is thick and causes extra friction between moving parts, cutting efficiency and increasing wear. A worn engine requires more frequent tune-ups and gets progressively worse fuel economy. In general, use the lightest viscosity oil for the driving conditions you will encounter.

46. Use the recommended viscosity fluids in the transmission and axle.

47. Be sure the battery is fully charged for fast starts. A slow starting engine wastes fuel.

48. Be sure battery terminals are clean and tight.

49. Check the battery electrolyte level and add distilled water if necessary.

50. Check the exhaust system for crushed pipes, blockages and leaks.

51. Adjust the brakes. Dragging brakes or brakes that are not releasing create increased drag on the engine.

52. Install a vacuum gauge or miles-per-gallon gauge. These gauges visually indicate engine vacuum in the intake manifold. High vacuum = good mileage and low vacuum = poorer mileage. The gauge can also be an excellent indicator of internal engine conditions.

53. Be sure the clutch is properly adjusted. A slipping clutch wastes fuel.

54. Check and periodically lubricate the heat control valve in the exhaust manifold. A sticking or inoperative valve prevents engine warm-up and wastes gas.

55. Keep accurate records to check fuel economy over a period of time. A sudden drop in fuel economy may signal a need for tune-up or other maintenance.

© 1980 Chilton Book Company, Radnor, PA 19089

2. Test the MAP sensor output voltage at the MAP sensor connector terminal B (as marked on the sensor body) with the ignition switch ON and the engine OFF. The output voltage should be 4-5 volts.

NOTE: *The voltage should drop to 0.5-1.5 volts with a hot, neutral idle speed condition.*

3. Test ECU terminal C-6 for the same voltage as in Step 2 to verify the wire harness condition and repair as necessary.
4. Test the MAP sensor supply voltage at the sensor connector terminal C with the ignition ON. The voltage should be 4.5-5.5 volts. The same voltage should be present at terminal C-14 of the ECU wire harness connector. Repair or replace the wire harness as necessary. If the ECU is suspect, use Diagnostic Tester M.S.1700, or equivalent, to test ECU function.
5. Test the MAP sensor ground circuit at the sensor connector terminal A and ECU connector terminal D-3. Repair the wire harness as necessary.
6. Test the MAP sensor ground circuit at the ECU connector between terminal D-3 and terminal B-11 with an ohmmeter. If the ohmmeter indicates an open circuit, check for a defective sensor ground connection located on the right side of the cylinder block. If the ground connection is good, replace the ECU.

NOTE: *If terminal D-3 has a short circuit to 12 volts, correct this condition before replacing the ECU.*

Oxygen Sensor Heating Element Test

Disconnect the O_2 sensor connector and connect ohmmeter test leads to terminals **A** and **B** of the sensor connector. The resistance should be 5-7Ω. Replace the O_2 sensor if the ohmmeter displays an infinity reading. Oxygen sensor operational testing requires the use of a special tester M.S.1700, or equivalent.

Knock Sensor Test

NOTE: *This procedure requires the use of a special tester M.S.1700, or equivalent.*

1. Connect diagnostic tester M.S.1700, or equivalent, to the vehicle according to the manufacturer's instructions.
2. Proceed to state display mode.
3. Start the engine.
4. Observe and note the knock unit value.
5. Using the tip of a screwdriver or a small hammer, gently tap on the cylinder block near the knock sensor and watch the knock value. The knock value should increase while tapping on the block.
6. If the knock value does not increase while tapping on the block, check the sensor connector. If the connection is good, replace the knock sensor.

Speed Sensor Test

Disconnect the speed sensor connector from the ignition control module and connect an ohmmeter between terminals **A** and **B** as marked on the connector. The ohmmeter should read 125-275Ω on a hot engine. Replace the sensor if the readings are not as stated.

Relay Testing

A relay in the de-energized position should have continuity between terminals 87A and 30. Resistance values between terminals 85 and 86 is 70-80 ohms for resistor relays and 81-91 ohms for diode relays. Not all relays have battery voltage connected to terminal 30. Some may have battery voltage connected to terminals 87 or 87A.

Starter Motor Relay Test

1. Disconnect the wire connectors from the **I** and **G** terminals.
2. Measure the resistance between the terminals with an ohmmeter. It should be approximately 22 ohms.
3. Measure the resistance between either terminal and the battery negative post. Reading should be infinite. If defective, replace the relay.
4. Remove the SOL terminal wire connector and connect a voltmeter between the terminal and the battery negative post. With the ignition switch in the START position, the voltmeter should indicate battery voltage (12 volts).
5. If battery voltage is not present, check the related wiring, bulkhead connector and ignition switch adjustment.
6. If battery voltage is present but the relay isn't working, make sure the transmission is in Park or Neutral and connect terminal **I** wire harness connector, then jumper terminal **G** to ground. If the relay doesn't click, replace the relay. If the starter relay does click, repair the ground circuit.

Sync Pulse (Stator) Test

1. Insert the positive (+) lead of a voltmeter into the blue wire at the distributor connector and the negative (−) lead into the gray/white wire at the distributor connector.

NOTE: *Do not disconnect the distributor connector from the distributor. Insert the voltmeter leads into the back side of the connector to make contact with the terminals.*

2. Set the voltmeter on the 15 volt AC scale and turn the ignition switch ON. The voltmeter should read approximately 5 volts. If there is no voltage, check the voltmeter leads for a good connection.
3. If there is still no voltage, remove the ECU and check for voltage at pin C-16 and ground

218　FUEL SYSTEM

with the harness connected. If there is still no voltage present, perform a vehicle test using tester M.S.1700, or equivalent.

4. If voltage is present, check for continuity between the blue wire at the distributor connector and pin C-16 at the ECU. If there is no continuity, repair the wire harness as necessary.

5. Check for continuity between the gray/white wire at the distributor connector and pin C-5 at the ECU. If there is no continuity, repair the wire harness as necessary.

6. Check for continuity between the black wire at the distributor connector and ground. If there is no continuity, repair the wire harness as necessary.

7. Crank the engine while observing the voltmeter; the needle should fluctuate back and forth while the engine is cranking. This verifies that the stator in the distributor is operating properly. If there is no sync pulse, stator replacement is necessary.

EGR Solenoid Test

1. Verify that source vacuum is present at port **C**.
2. Remove vacuum connector at ports **A** and **B** and connect a hand vacuum pump with a gauge at port **B**.
3. Start the engine and read the vacuum level on the gauge. There should be no vacuum at port **B**.
4. Disconnect the electrical connector from the solenoid and again note the reading on the vacuum gauge. There should now be vacuum at port **B**.
5. Reconnect the electrical connector to the solenoid and remove the vacuum gauge. Reconnect all vacuum lines.

Fuel Injector Test

Disconnect the wire connector from the fuel injector and connect an ohmmeter to the injector terminals. The resistance reading should be approximately 16 ohms at 68°F (20°C).

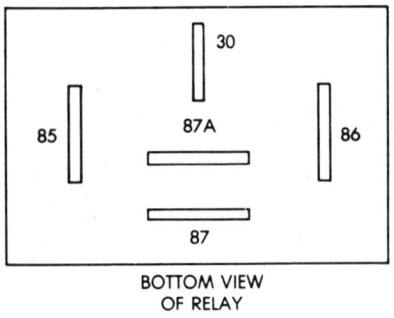

BOTTOM VIEW OF RELAY

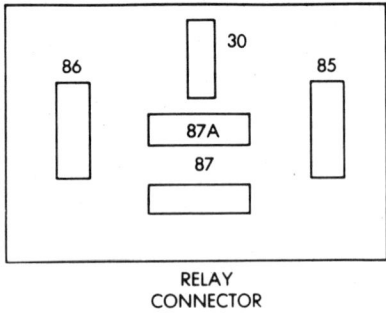

RELAY CONNECTOR

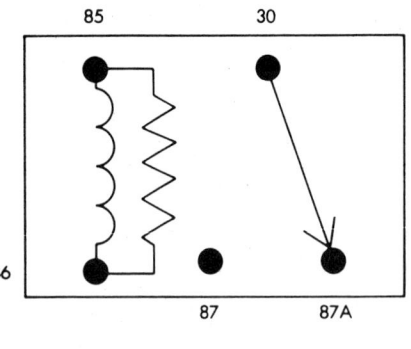

DE-ENERGIZED RELAY

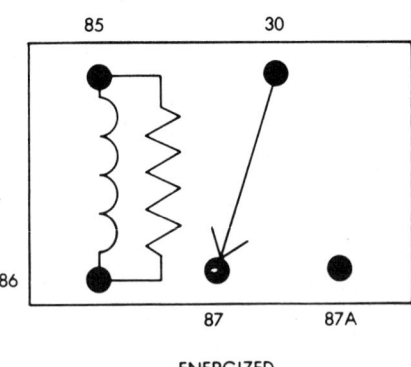

ENERGIZED RELAY

MFI relay terminals

FUEL SYSTEM

Fuel Pressure Test

1. Remove the cap from the pressure test connection on the fuel rail.
2. Connect a fuel pressure gauge (J-34730-1 or equivalent) to the pressure fitting.
3. Start the engine and read the fuel pressure. Normal pressure should be 31 psi with the vacuum hose connected to the pressure regulator and 39 psi with the vacuum hose disconnected from the pressure regulator.
4. If the fuel pressure is not to specifications, check the fuel supply and return lines for kinks or restricting bends. Before replacing the pressure regulator, check the fuel pump flow rate by connecting one end of an old A/C gauge hose to the fuel test port on the fuel rail and inserting the other end into a container of at least 1 liter capacity. A good fuel pump will deliver at least 1 liter of fuel per minute with the return line pinched off. Run the pump by installing a jumper wire into diagnostic connector terminals D1-5 and D1-6.

NOTE: *Be sure to pinch off the return line or most of the fuel will be returned to the fuel tank. The fuel pressure regulator is not adjustable and must be replaced if found to be defective.*

Relieving Fuel System Pressure

CAUTION: *Before opening any part of the fuel system, the pressure in the system must be relieved!*

1. Disconnect the battery ground cable.
2. Remove the fuel tank filler cap.
3. Remove the cap from the pressure test port on the fuel rail in the engine compartment.

CAUTION: *DON'T ALLOW FUEL TO SPRAY OR SPILL ON THE ENGINE OR EXHAUST MANIFOLD! PLACE HEAVY SHOP TOWELS UNDER THE PRESSURE PORT TO ABSORB ANY ESCAPED FUEL!*

4. Using a small pin punch, push the test port valve inward to relieve fuel system pressure.
5. Install the test port cap.

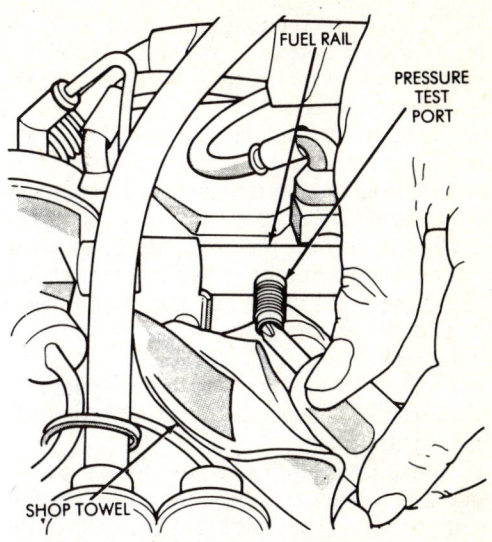
Releasing the fuel pressure with MFI

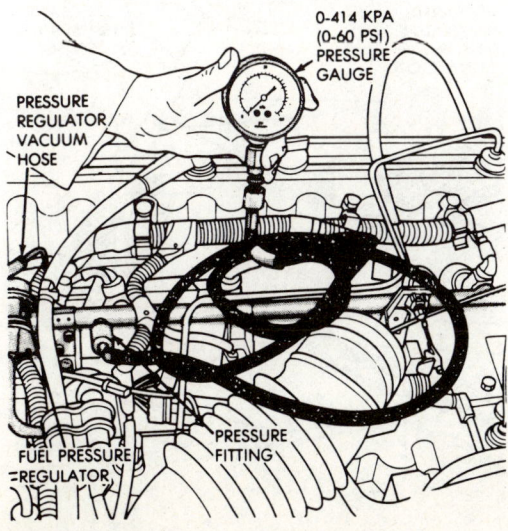
MFI pressure test

Component Service

THROTTLE BODY REPLACEMENT

1. Disconnect the battery ground cable.
2. Disconnect the air inlet tube from the throttle body.
3. Tag and disconnect the wiring and hoses from the throttle body.
4. Disconnect the throttle linkage.
5. Disconnect the automatic transmission line pressure cable.
6. Remove the mounting bolts and remove the throttle body. Discard the gasket.
7. Installation is the reverse of removal. Tighten the mounting bolts to 23 ft. lbs. On thrucks with automatic transmission, the line pressure cable MUST be adjusted! See Chapter 7.

FUEL PUMP
REMOVAL AND INSTALLATION

1. Disconnect the negative battery cable.
2. Remove the fuel tank filler cap.
3. Relieve the fuel system pressure as described above.
4. Drain the fuel from the fuel tank.
5. Raise and support the rear end on jackstands.
6. Remove the fuel inlet and outlet hoses from the sending unit. Be ready to catch any spilled fuel.

FUEL SYSTEM

7. Remove the sending unit wires.
8. Using a brass punch and hammer, remove the sending unit retaining lock ring by tapping it counterclockwise.
9. Remove the sending unit, which incorporates the electric fuel pump, along with the O-ring seal from the fuel tank. Discard the O-ring.
10. Remove and discard the pump inlet filter.
11. Disconnect the fuel pump terminal wires.
12. Remove the pump outlet hose and clamp.
13. Remove the pump top mounting bracket nut and remove the pump.

To install:
14. Install a new inlet filter on the pump.
15. Assemble the pump and bracket. Connect the hose and wiring.
16. Install the unit and new O-ring in the tank. The rubber stopper on the end of the fuel return tube must be inserted into the cup in the fuel tank reservoir.
17. Install the lock ring. Carefully tap it into place until it seats against the stop on the tank.
18. Connect the hoses.
19. Connect the wiring.
20. Lower the truck, fill the tank, run the engine and check for leaks.

COOLANT TEMPERATURE SENSOR (CTS) REPLACEMENT

1. Drain the cooling system.
2. Remove the air cleaner assembly.
3. Disconnect the CTS wire connector.
4. Unscrew the CTS from the engine block.
5. Installation is the reverse of removal. Tighten the sensor to 21 ft. lbs. Refill the cooling system, start the engine and check for leaks.

MANIFOLD AIR TEMPERATURE (MAT) SENSOR REPLACEMENT

The MAT sensor is removed by simply disconnecting the harness connector and removing the sensor from the intake manifold. Tighten the replacement sensor securely and install the connector.

MANIFOLD ABSOLUTE PRESSURE (MAP) SENSOR REPLACEMENT

1. Disconnect the MAP sensor wire harness connector.
2. Remove the MAP sensor vacuum supply hose.
3. Remove the MAP sensor retaining nuts and lift the sensor from the engine compartment.
4. Installation is the reverse of removal.

OXYGEN SENSOR REPLACEMENT

1. Raise the vehicle and support it safely. Allow the exhaust system to cool sufficiently to permit servicing.
2. Disconnect the wire connector from the oxygen sensor.
3. Remove the oxygen sensor from the exhaust manifold.
4. If not already done, coat the threads of the replacement sensor with anti-seize compound. Be careful not to contaminate the oxygen sensor probe with the anti-seize.
5. Install the oxygen sensor into the exhaust manifold and tighten to 35 ft. lbs. (48 Nm). Reconnect the wire connector.

KNOCK SENSOR REPLACEMENT

The knock sensor can be removed from below by raising and supporting the vehicle, discon-

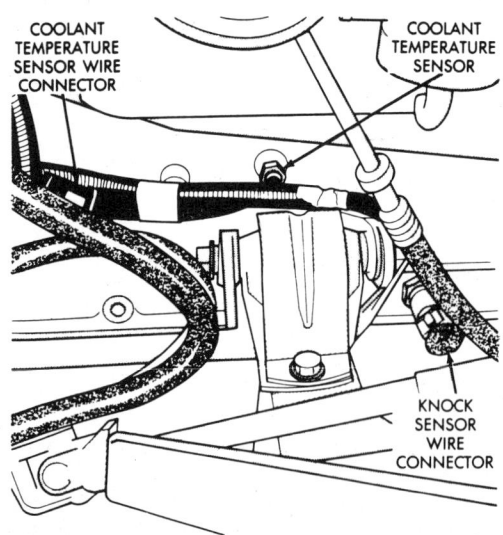

MFI coolant temperature sensor removal

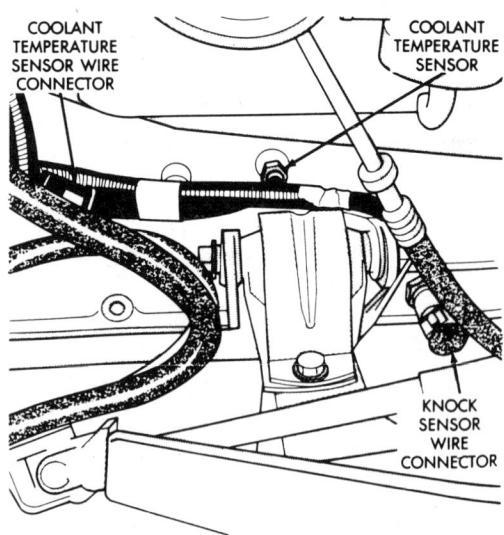

Knock sensor removal

necting the wire harness connector and then removing the knock sensor from the engine block. Install in reverse order.

SPEED SENSOR REPLACEMENT

The speed sensor can be removed by disconnecting the wire connector and removing the two shoulder bolts attaching the sensor to the transmission housing. Install in reverse order. There is no speed sensor adjustment.

THROTTLE POSITION SENSOR (TPS) REPLACEMENT

1. Disconnect the TPS harness connector.
2. Bend back the lock tabs and remove the TPS retaining screws.
3. Remove the TPS from the throttle plate assembly.
4. Position the new TPS onto the throttle plate assembly, then install and snug the mounting bolts. Do not tighten the mounting bolts fully.
5. Connect the harness connector and adjust the TPS as outlined below.

TPS Adjustment

1. Turn the ignition switch to the ON position.
2. Check the sensor input voltage by connecting the negative lead of a voltmeter to sensor terminal **B** and the positive lead to sensor terminal **A**.

NOTE: *Do not disconnect the sensor harness connector. Insert the voltmeter test leads into the back side of the harness connector to make contact with the sensor terminals. On some models, it may also be necessary to remove the throttle body from the intake manifold to gain access to the sensor wire harness connector.*

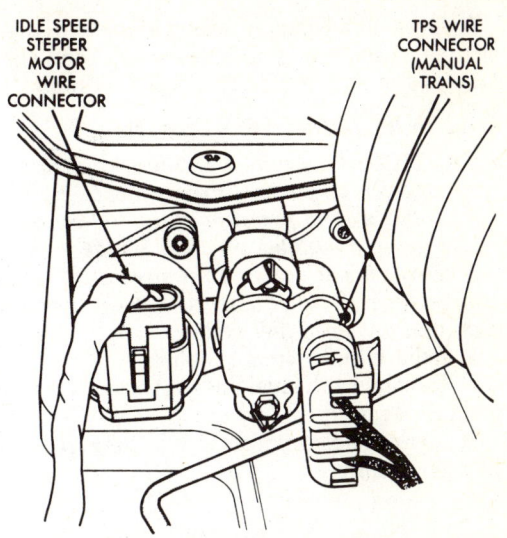

MFI TPS adjustments, w/manual transmission

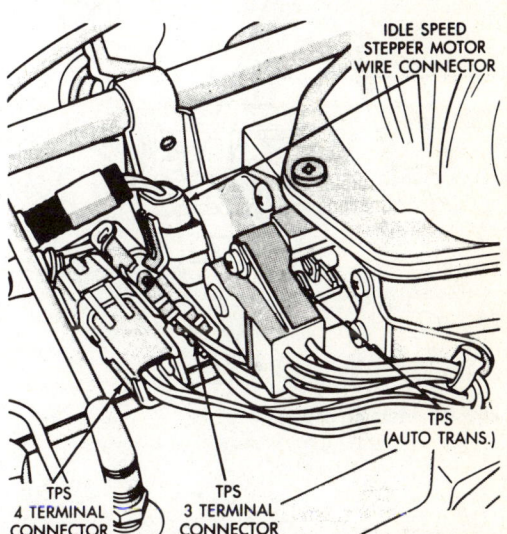

MFI TPS adjustments, w/automatic transmission

3. With the throttle plate in the closed position, adjust the idle stop and note the voltmeter reading. Voltage should be approximately 5 volts.
4. Check the sensor output voltage by disconnecting the voltmeter positive lead from sensor terminal **A** and connecting it to terminal **C**. With the throttle plate in the closed position, output voltage as read on the voltmeter should be approximately 0.8 volts.
5. If the output voltage requires adjustment, loosen the sensor mounting screw **B** and pivot the sensor in the adjustment slot for a coarse adjustment. Loosen the sensor retaining screw **C** and pivot the sensor for a fine adjustment. Adjust the sensor to approximately 16% of the input voltage.

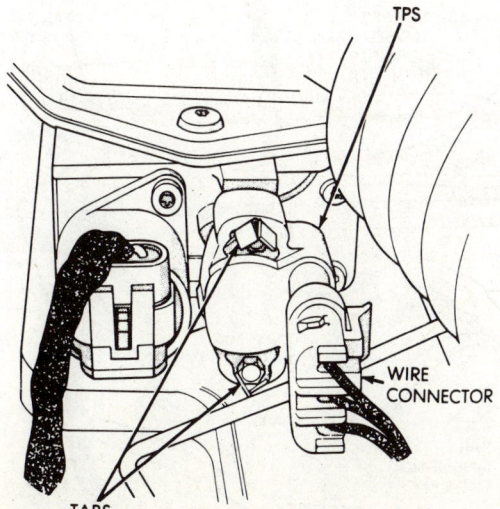

MFI throttle position sensor removal

222 FUEL SYSTEM

6. Once all adjustments are complete, tighten the sensor retaining screws and bend the lock tabs to secure the adjustment screws.

FUEL INJECTORS REPLACEMENT

CAUTION: *Fuel system pressure must be relieved before disconnecting any fuel lines. Release fuel system pressure at the test connection using a suitable pressure gauge with a pressure bleed valve. Take precautions to avoid the risk of fire whenever working on or around any open fuel system.*

1. Relieve fuel system pressure.
2. Disconnect the fuel lines at the ends of the fuel rail assembly.
3. Mark and disconnect the injector wire harness connectors.
4. Remove the fuel rail retaining bolts.
5. Disconnect the vacuum line from the fuel pressure regulator.
6. Remove the fuel rail assembly from the engine.

NOTE: *On models with automatic transmission, it may be necessary to remove the automatic transmission throttle pressure cable and bracke to remove the fuel rail assembly.*

7. Remove the clips that retain the injectors to the fuel rail and remove the injectors. An O-ring kit (part No. PN 8983 503 637) is available which consists of 6 brown seals and 7 black seals. The brown seals fit on the injector tip area and seal the injector to the intake mani-

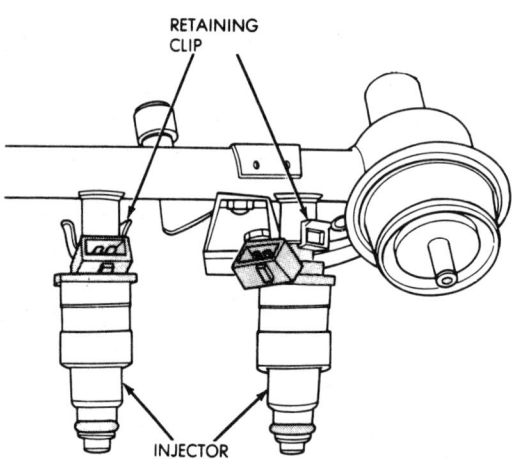

Injector retaining clips

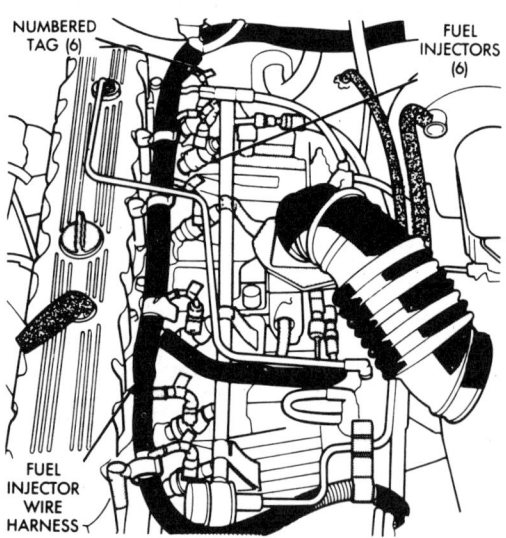

MFI injector harness

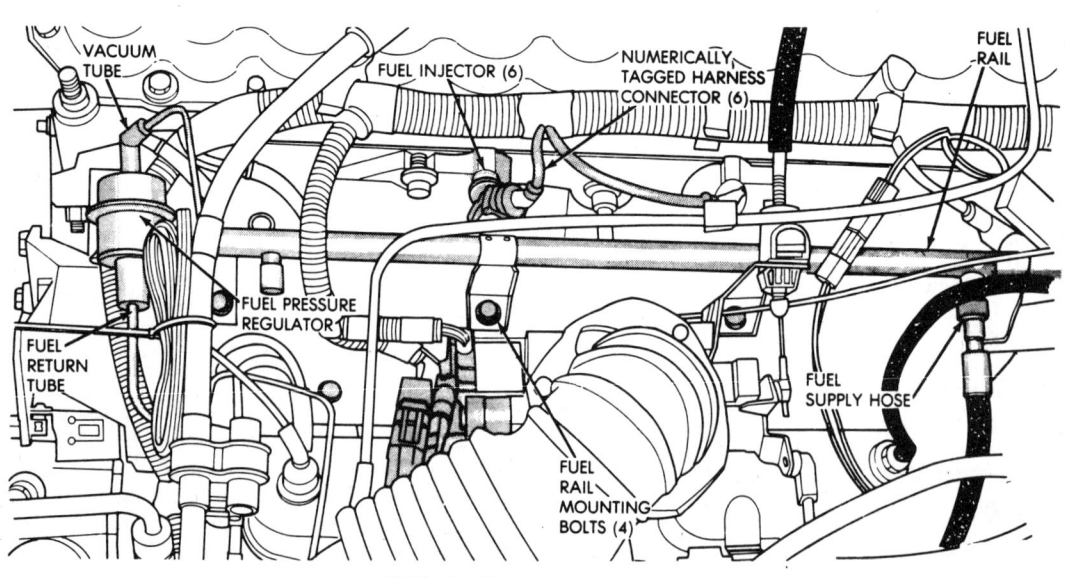

MFI fuel rail assembly removal

FUEL SYSTEM 223

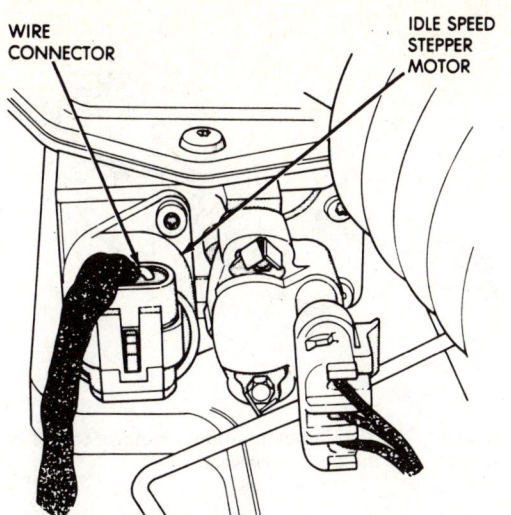

MFI idle speed stepper motor removal

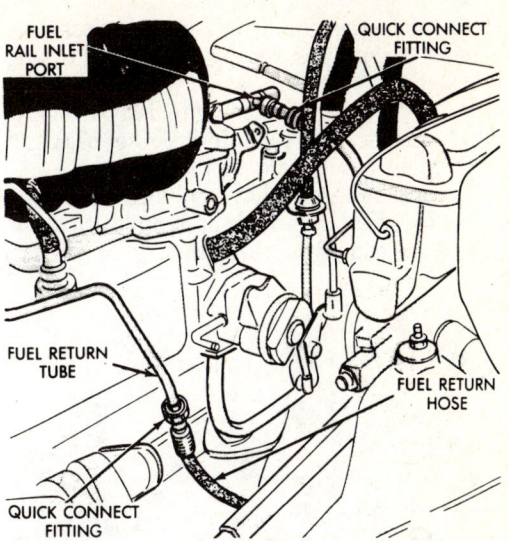

MFI quick-connect fitting location

fold. The black seals fit on the rail end of the injector to to seal the injector when it is installed into the fuel rail. The last black seal is for the fuel pressure regulator to seal the pressure regulator to the fuel rail. These seals cannot be interchanged.

8. Installation is the reverse of removal. Tighten the fuel rail mounting bolts to 20 ft. lbs. (27 Nm).

IDLE SPEED STEPPER MOTOR REPLACEMENT

The idle speed stepper motor is removed by simply disconnecting the harness connector and removing the retaining screws. Install in reverse of removal procedure.

Quick-Connect Fuel Line
O-RING REPLACEMENT

1. Separate the quick-connect fuel line tubes at the inner fender panel by squeezing the two retaining tabs against the fuel line, then pulling the tube and retainer from the fitting.
2. Remove the two O-rings and the spacer from the fitting. This can be accomplished by using a paper clip or piece of heavy wire bent into an L-shape.
3. Remove the retainer from the fuel tube and discard the O-rings, spacer and retainer.
4. Install the new retainer assembly by pushing it into the quick-connect fitting until it clicks.
5. Grasp the disposable plastic plug and remove it from the replacement fitting. By removing only the plastic plug, the O-rings, spacer and retainer will remain in the fitting.
6. Push the fuel line into the fitting until a click is heard and the connection is complete.

Give the fuel line connection a firm tug to verify that it is seated and locked properly.

DIESEL FUEL SYSTEM

The Renault-built diesel engine uses a Bosch VE4/9F injection pump, supplying Bosch KBE 48 57 injectors. A Stanadyne fuel filter cleans the system. Boost is developed by a Garret T-2 turbocharger.

Injection Pump
REMOVAL AND INSTALLATION

NOTE: *Special tools are needed for this job.*
1. Disconnect the negative battery cable.
2. Using heavy clamps, clamp off the coolant inlet and outlet hoses at the cold start capsule. Then, disconnect them.
3. Disconnect the throttle cable and fuel shut-off solenoid wire.
4. If so equipped, disconect the automatic transmission throttle cable, and cruise control cable.
5. Disconnect and plug the fuel delivery and return hoses.
6. Remove the alternator drive belt.
7. Remove the power steering drive belt.
8. Remove the timing belt cover.
9. Rotate the crankshaft clockwise, as viewed from the front, until #1 piston is at TDC compression. Make sure that the camshaft sprocket timing mark is aligned with the center boss on the cylinder head cover. Make sure, also, that the injection pump sprocket timing mark is aligned with the center of the boss on the injection pump.

224 FUEL SYSTEM

10. Rotate the crankshaft counterclockwise, moving the sprocket timing marks by 3 timing belt teeth.
11. Install sprocket holding tool MOT-854. It may be necessary to turn the sprocket back and forth slightly to install the tool.
12. Loosen the sprocket retaining nut on the end of the injection pump shaft, and turn it out just to the end of the threads.

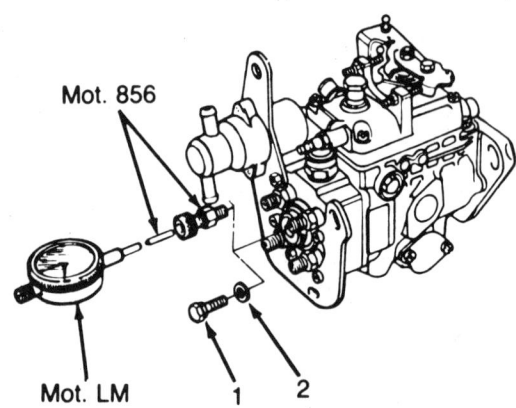

Installing the dial indicator and its support tool. 1 is the bolt; 2 is the copper washer

Diesel timing belt cover

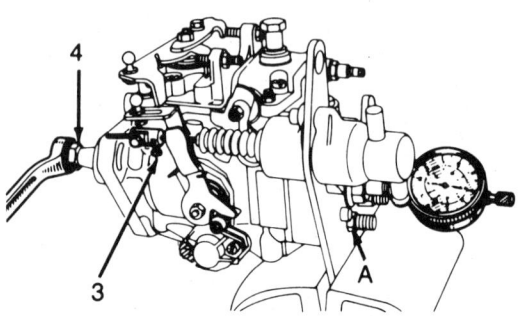

Injection pump adjustment points. 3 is the control cable setscrew; 4 is the injection pump shaft locknut; A is the fuel outlet fitting

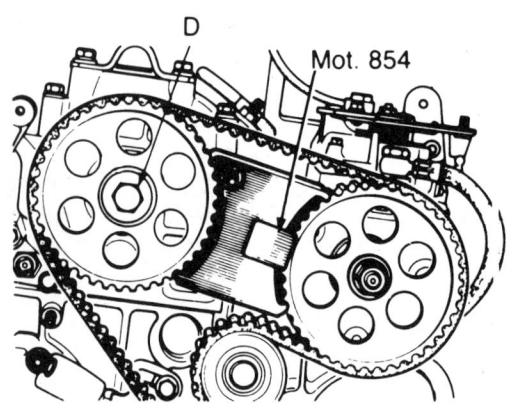

Sprocket holding tool. D is the camshaft sprocket bolt

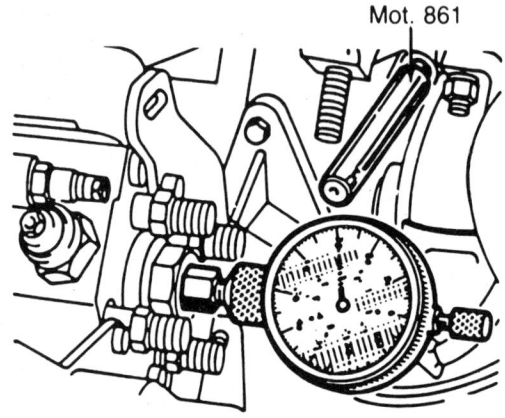

Injection timing procedure using a dial indicator

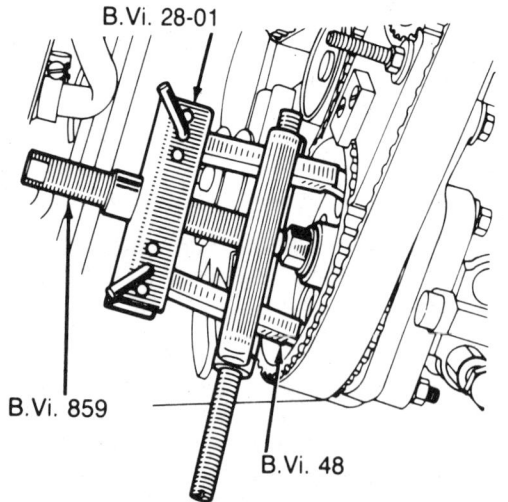

Injection pump sprocket removal tools

13. Assemble the sprocket removal tool jaws, B.Vi.48 and the short screw B.Vi.859, on the sprocket removal tool, B.Vi.28-01.
14. Attach the tool to the injection pump sprocket.
15. Disconnect all the fuel pipe fittings from the injectors. Plug the injectors to prevent dirt from entering the fuel system.
16. Disconnect the fuel pipe fittings from the

fuel injection pump. Plug the fittings to prevent dirt from entering the system.

17. Remove the fuel line fittings from the vehicle. Remove all hoses and connectors from the injection pump assembly.

18. Remove the injection pump rear bracket retaining nuts.

19. Remove the plastic shield from under the injection pump.

20. Remove the three retaining nuts located at the front of the injection pump. The lower nut is hard to get at. It may be necessary to remove the alternator to get a wrench on it.

21. Using the sprocket removal tool, separate the injection pump from the sprocket.

22. Remove the removal tool and the sprocket nut. The sprocket holding tool and the timing belt will hold the sprocket in plate, facilitating injection pump installation.

23. Remove the injection pump from the mounting brackets.

24. Remove the key from the shaft.

25. Remove the screw plug and copper washer located between the four high pressure fuel outlets, at the rear of the pump. Install dial indicator support tool Mot.856 in its place.

26. Install the stem of dial indicator Mot.LM in the support tool.

27. Position a locknut and nut on the end of the injection pump driveshaft.

28. Tighten the locknut against the nut.

29. Loosen the control cable set screw on the clevis, move the levers back slightly and turn the clevis pin ¼ turn to disengage the cold start system.

30. Using the locknut, turn the pump driveshaft in the normal direction of rotation, to position the piston at bottom dead center. The dial indicator pointer will stop moving when the piston is at BDC. Zero the pointer.

31. The pump driveshaft keyway should be located just before the centerline of the number 1 fuel outlet fitting.

32. Remove the nut and locknut.

33. Insert the key in its keyway.

34. Mount the injection pump in the sprocket, aligning the key.

35. Loosely install the washers and retaining nuts on the mounting bracket studs.

36. Install the sprocket washer and retaining nut on the pump driveshaft. Torque the nut to 37 ft. lbs.

37. Remove the sprocket holding tool.

38. Rotate the crankshaft in a clockwise direction at least 2 full revolutions. Check the timing belt tension as follows:

    a. Loosen the timing belt tensioner bolts ½ turn each, maximum.

    b. The belt tensioner should, automatically, place the proper tension on the belt.

    c. Using belt tension gauge Ele.346-04, at the straight, upper run, between the pump and camshaft sprockets, check belt deflection. Deflection should be 3-5mm when the gauge shoulder is flush with the plunger body.

39. Remove the threaded plug from the block, just behind the pump, and insert TDC Rod Mot.861.

40. Slowly rotate the crankshaft clockwise until tool Mot.861 can be inserted into the TDC slot in the crankshaft counterweight.

41. At this point, the dial indicator pointer should indicate a piston travel distance of $0.82mm \pm 0.02mm$.

42. If the indicated travel is not within specifications, adjust it as follows:

    a. Rotate the pump toward, then away from the engine to increase travel, or

    b. Rotate the pump away from the engine to decrease lift.

NOTE: *Adjustment should always be made by rotation away from the engine. That's why rotation toward the engine is necessary in Step 42a.*

43. Tighten the injection pump mounting nuts.

44. Remove the TDC Rod from the counterweight slot.

45. Observe the dial indicator and rotate the crankshaft clockwise 2 full revolutions until the rod can, once again, be installed into the counterweight hole. The dial indicator should return to 0, then move to $0.82mm \pm 0.02mm$. If so, injection pump static timing is correct.

46. Remove the TDC Rod and install the plug.

47. Remove the dial indicator and install the washer and screw plug in the pump.

48. Connect the high pressure lines at the injectors.

49. Compress the timing control lever and install the clevis pin in the first position on the cable clamp.

50. With the lever against the clevis, tighten the setscrew.

51. Install and tighten the pump rear support bracket nuts.

52. Install all other parts in reverse order of removal.

NOTE: *Don't confuse the fuel delivery and return hose banjo bolts. The delivery banjo bolt has two 4mm diameter holes; the return banjo bolt has a calibrated orifice. Never use the banjo bolts from one pump on another!*

Injectors

REMOVAL AND INSTALLATION

NOTE: *A 13mm deep-well socket is necessary for this procedure.*

226 FUEL SYSTEM

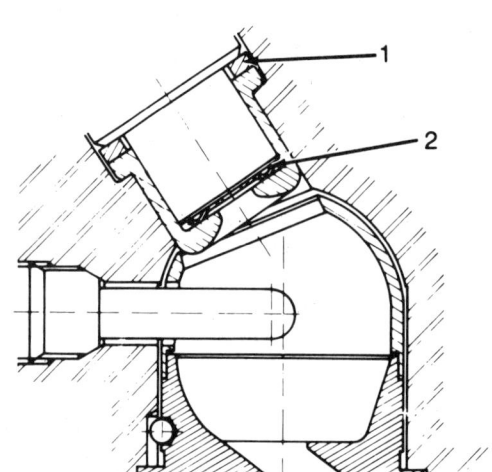

An injector installed. 1 is the copper seal; 2 is the heat shield

1. Disconnect the negative battery cable.
2. Remove the fuel return hoses and fittings from the injectors.
3. Remove the high pressure lines from the injectors.
4. Remove both injector clamp nuts and washers from each injector.
5. Remove the injector clamp.
6. Pull the injector from the head.
7. Remove the copper seal and the heat shield.
8. Clean the injector bore with a brass brush.
9. Install a new heat shield and a new copper seal. Never reuse the old ones!
10. Install the injector, high pressure fuel lines (finger tight at this time), clamps, washers and nuts.
11. Tighten the high pressure fuel lines.
12. Use new washers and install the fuel return lines. Tighten the fittings to 88 in. lbs.

DIESEL INJECTION PUMP STATIC TIMING ADJUSTMENT

NOTE: *Special tools are needed for this job.*
1. Remove the injection pump as described above.
2. Remove the key from the shaft.
3. Remove the screw plug and copper washer located between the four high pressure fuel outlets, at the rear of the pump. Install dial indicator support tool Mot.856 in its place.
4. Install the stem of dial indicator Mot.LM in the support tool.
5. Position a locknut and nut on the end of the injection pump driveshaft.
6. Tighten the locknut against the nut.
7. Loosen the control cable set screw on the clevis, move the levers back slightly and turn the clevis pin ¼ turn to disengage the cold start system.

8. Using the locknut, turn the pump driveshaft in the normal direction of rotation, to position the piston at bottom dead center. The dial indicator pointer will stop moving when the piston is at BDC. Zero the pointer.
9. The pump driveshaft keyway should be located just before the centerline of the number 1 fuel outlet fitting.
10. Remove the nut and locknut.
11. Insert the key in its keyway.
12. Mount the injection pump in the sprocket, aligning the key.
13. Loosely install the washers and retaining nuts on the mounting bracket studs.
14. Install the sprocket washer and retaining nut on the pump driveshaft. Torque the nut to 37 ft. lbs.
15. Remove the sprocket holding tool.
16. Rotate the crankshaft in a clockwise direction at least 2 full revolutions. Check the timing belt tension as follows:
   a. Loosen the timing belt tensioner bolts ½ turn each, maximum.
   b. The belt tensioner should, automatically, place the proper tension on the belt.
   c. Using belt tension gauge Ele.346-04, at the straight, upper run, between the pump and camshaft sprockets, check belt deflection. Deflection should be 3-5mm when the gauge shoulder is flush with the plunger body.
17. Remove the threaded plug from the block, just behind the pump, and insert TDC Rod Mot.861.
18. Slowly rotate the crankshaft clockwise until tool Mot.861 can be inserted into the TDC slot in the crankshaft counterweight.
19. At this point, the dial indicator pointer should indicate a piston travel distance of 0.82mm ± 0.02mm.
20. If the indicated travel is not within specifications, adjust it as follows:
   a. Rotate the pump toward, then away from the engine to increase travel, or
   b. Rotate the pump away from the engine to decrease lift.

NOTE: *Adjustment should always be made by rotation away from the engine. That's why rotation toward the engine is necessary in Step 20a.*

21. Tighten the injection pump mounting nuts.
22. Remove the TDC Rod from the counterweight slot.
23. Observe the dial indicator and rotate the crankshaft clockwise 2 full revolutions until the rod can, once again, be installed into the counterweight hole. The dial indicator should return to 0, then move to 0.82mm ± 0.02mm. If so, injection pump static timing is correct.

FUEL SYSTEM

24. Remove the TDC Rod and install the plug.
25. Remove the dial indicator and install the washer and screw plug in the pump.
26. Connect the high pressure lines at the injectors.
27. Compress the timing control lever and install the clevis pin in the first position on the cable clamp.
28. With the lever against the clevis, tighten the setscrew.
29. Install and tighten the pump rear support bracket nuts.
30. Install all other parts in reverse order of removal.

NOTE: *Don't confuse the fuel delivery and return hose banjo bolts. The delivery banjo bolt has two 4mm diameter holes; the return banjo bolt has a calibrated orifice. Never use the banjo bolts from one pump on another!*

Cold Start Capsule

REMOVAL AND INSTALLATION

NOTE: *Two 6mm x 70mm threaded rods and nuts are necessary for this procedure.*

1. Using heay clamps, clamp off the coolant lines at the cold start capsule.

CAUTION: *Follow this procedure exactly when removing the cold start capsule. There is a great deal of spring tension behind the housings.*

2. Remove one of the capsule retaining bolts and replace it with a 6mm diameter × 70mm long threaded rod.
3. Thread a nut down the rod and tighten it.
4. Remove the other bolt and replace it with a similar rod and nut.
5. Back off the two nuts, alternately and evenly, to release spring tension. Separate the capsule housing from the bracket and cable housing.
6. Remove the threaded rods.

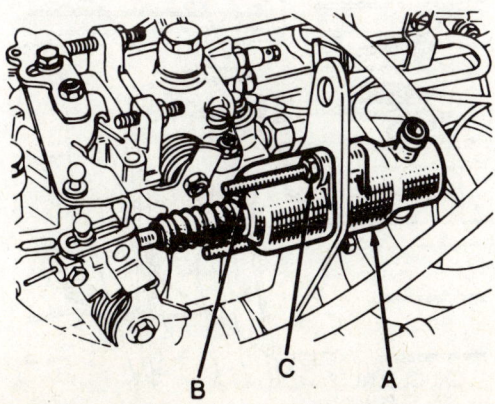

Cold start capsule. A is the capsule; B is the threaded rod; C is the nut

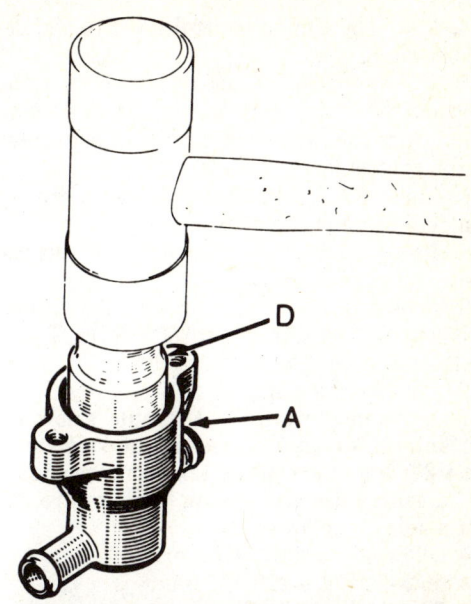

Loosening the slotted nut with a mallet. D is the tubing; A is the capsule housing

7. Insert a 26mm OD section of tubing into the end of the capsule housing and hit the end sharply with a mallet to loosen the slotted retaining nut. Remove the nut, capsule and O-ring.
8. Assembly is the reverse of disassembly. Use the threaded rods to position the capsule housing, tightening them, alternately and evenly, then, replacing them, one at a time, with the bolts. Tighten the bolts securely.

Glow Plugs

REMOVAL AND INSTALLATION

1. Disconnect the battery ground.
2. Disconnect the wire from the glow plug.
3. Unscrew the glow plug from the head.
4. Installation is the reverse of removal. Use a small amount of anti-seize compound on the glow plug threads. Torque the glow plug to 20 ft. lbs.

Cold Start System

ADJUSTMENT

NOTE: *The engine must be cold, shut off for at least 2½ hrs., before starting this procedure. Special tools and shims are necessary for this procedure.*

1. Make sure that the timing control lever is contacting the stop. If not, loosen the setscrew and turn the clevis ¼ turn.
2. Remove the TDC slot access hole plug from the block, just behind the pump.
3. Rotate the crankshaft clockwise 2 full revolutions and insert the TDC Rod Mot.861, into the crankshaft counterweight TDC slot.

FUEL SYSTEM

4. Move the timing control lever to the detent position.

5. Make sure that the clearance between the stop and the timing control lever is now 0.5mm. If not, turn the throttle stop adjustment screw, at the control lever, until it is.

6. Insert a 6.5mm shim between the timing control lever and the stop.

7. Insert a 3.0mm shim between the throttle lever and the idle stop screw.

8. Loosen the pivot ball nut and slide the pivot ball until it contacts the throttle lever. Tighten the nut.

9. Remove the shims.

10. The temperature of the capsule is now important. If the engine has been shut down for at least 2½ hrs., the capsule temperature should be the same as the ambient air temperature. Select a shim as follows:
- below 66°F (19°C): 6.5mm
- 66°F-71°F (19-22°C): 5.9mm
- 72°F-76°F (22-24°C): 5.5mm
- 77°F-85°F (25-29°C): 4.75mm
- 86°F-94°F (30-34°C): 4.0mm
- 95°F-104°F (35-40°C): 3.25mm

11. When the shim thickness has been determined, place the shim between the timing control lever and the stop.

12. Align the clevis and the throttle cable stop so that both screw heads are in the same plane.

13. Tighten the throttle cable and position the clevis and the throttle stop so that they contact the timing control lever.

14. Tighten the throttle cable stop screw.

15. Remove the shim and make sure that the distance between the stop and the timing control lever is the same as the thickness of the shim. Correct it if necessary.

16. Start the engine and run it to normal operating temperature.

17. Make sure that the throttle lever and timing control lever are against their stops and move freely.

18. If necessary, adjust the idle with the idle adjustment screw to obtain an idle of 800 rpm.

19. Insert a 6.5mm shim between the timing control lever and its stop and measure the clearance between the throttle control lever and its stop. The clearance should be 3.0mm. If not, repeat the above adjustments.

FUEL TANK

REMOVAL AND INSTALLATION

Wagoneer and Cherokee

CAUTION: *If the truck is equipped with the 6-243 engine, perform the fuel system pressure release sequence described earlier in this chapter.*

1. Remove the fuel filler cap.
2. Drain the fuel tank.
3. Raise and support the rear end on jackstands.
4. Remove the skid plate.
5. Disconnect all hoses and wires connected to the tank.

CAUTION: *Be prepared to catch any spilled fuel!*

6. Remove the fuel tank shield.
7. Support the tank with a floor jack and remove the strap nuts.
8. Partially lower the tank and disconnect the tank vapor vent hoses.
9. Remove the tank.
10. Installation is the reverse of removal. If 2

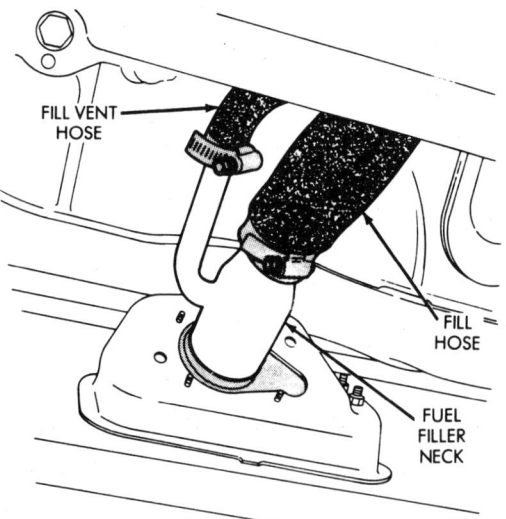

Filler neck hoses

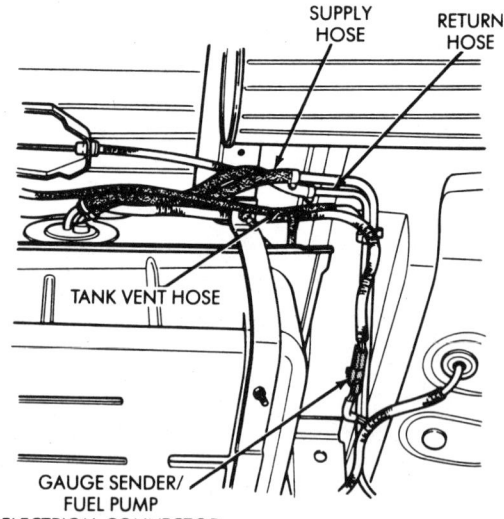

Fuel tank hoses

FUEL SYSTEM

straps are used, torque them to 65 in. lbs. If 3 straps are used, torque the center strap to 43 in. lbs.; the outer straps to 65 in. lbs.

Comanche

CAUTION: *If the truck is equipped with the 6-243 engine, perform the fuel system pressure release sequence described earlier in this chapter.*

1. Disconnect the negative battery cable.
2. Raise and support the vehicle safely.
3. Remove the rear driveshaft.
4. If equipped, remove the skid plate.

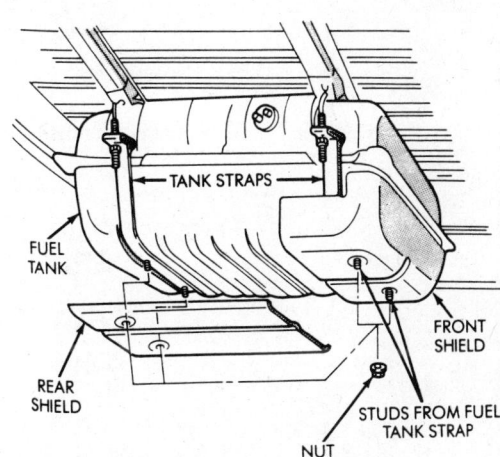

Fuel tank and shield, 2wd and 4wd long bed Comanche

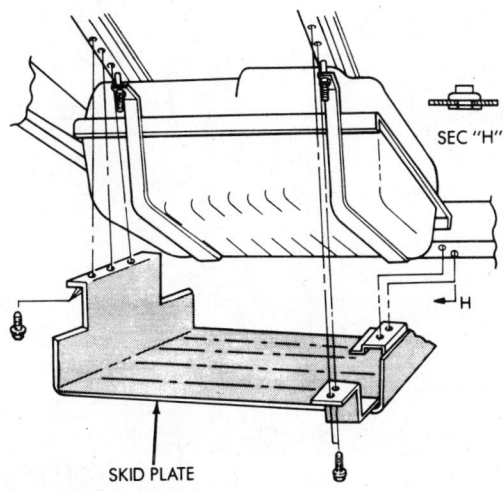

Comanche skid plate

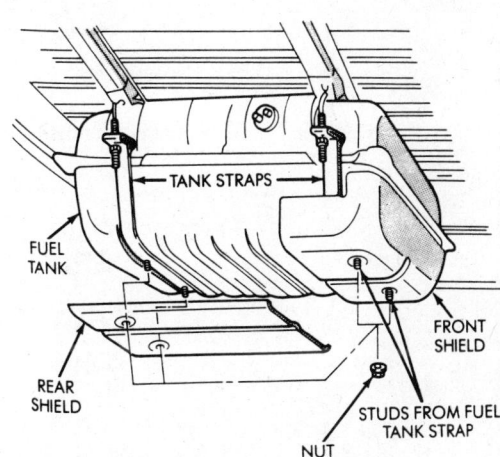

Fuel tank and shield, short bed Comanche

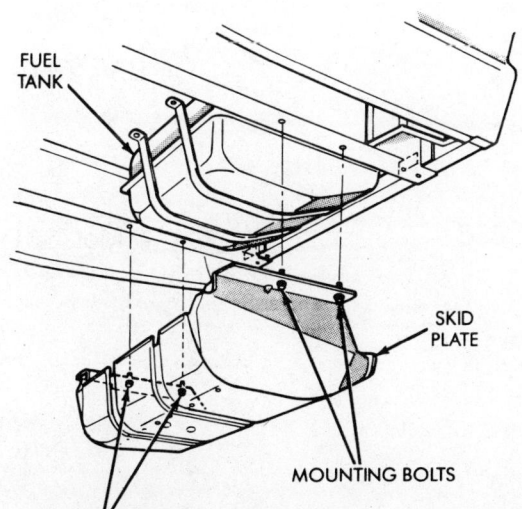

Wagoneer/Cherokee skid plate

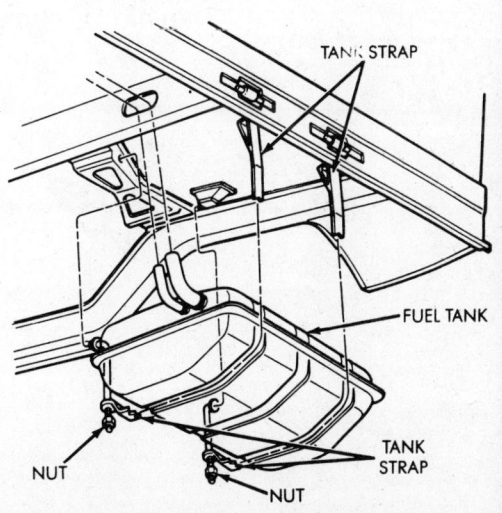

Fuel tank removal, Wagoneer/Cherokee

230 FUEL SYSTEM

CAUTION: *Be prepared to catch any spilled fuel!*

5. Disconnect the fuel inlet and outlet lines at the sending unit.
6. Disconnect the electrical wires from the sending unit.
7. Remove the protective shield.
8. Support the tank with a floor jack.
9. Remove the fuel tank retaining straps.
10. Lower the fuel tank from the vehicle.
11. Installation is the reverse of removal. If 2 straps are used, torque them to 65 in. lbs. If 3 straps are used, torque the center strap to 43 in. lbs.; the outer straps to 65 in. lbs.

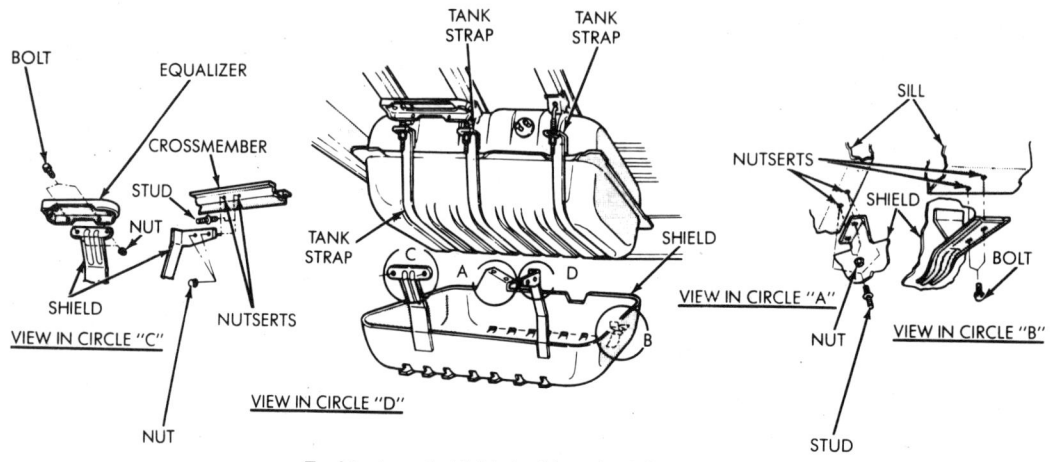

Fuel tank and shield, 4wd long bed Comanche

SPECIAL TOOLS

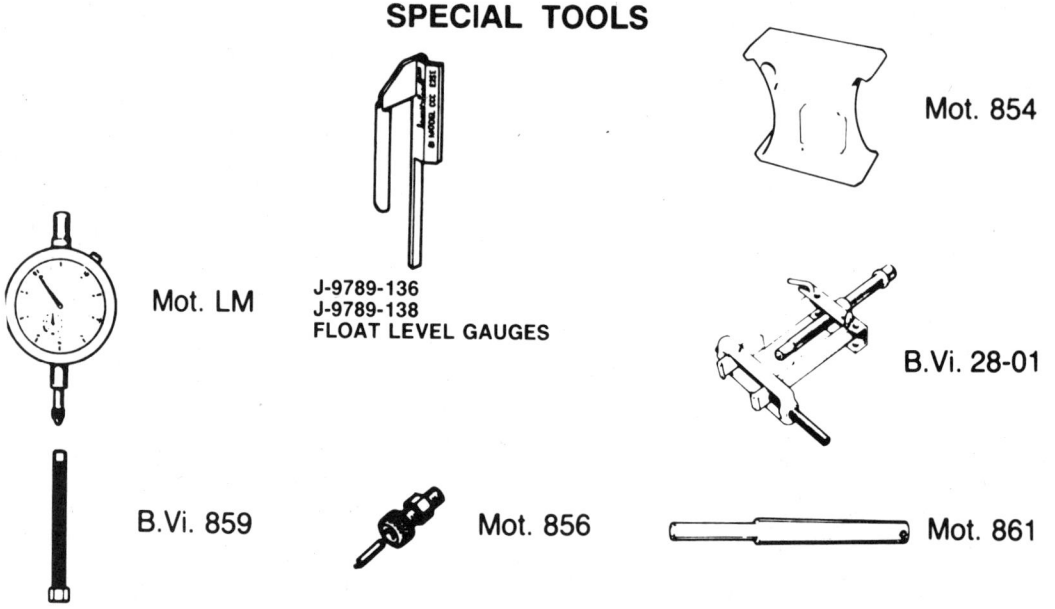

Chassis Electrical

UNDERSTANDING AND TROUBLESHOOTING ELECTRICAL SYSTEMS

With the rate at which both import and domestic manufacturers are incorporating electronic control systems into their production lines, it won't be long before every new vehicle is equipped with one or more on-board computer, like the EEC-IV unit installed on the truck. These electronic components (with no moving parts) should theoretically last the life of the vehicle, provided nothing external happens to damage the circuits or memory chips.

While it is true that electronic components should never wear out, in the real world malfunctions do occur. It is also true that any computer-based system is extremely sensitive to electrical voltages and cannot tolerate careless or haphazard testing or service procedures. An inexperienced individual can literally do major damage looking for a minor problem by using the wrong kind of test equipment or connecting test leads or connectors with the ignition switch ON. When selecting test equipment, make sure the manufacturers instructions state that the tester is compatible with whatever type of electronic control system is being serviced. Read all instructions carefully and double check all test points before installing probes or making any test connections.

The following section outlines basic diagnosis techniques for dealing with computerized automotive control systems. Along with a general explanation of the various types of test equipment available to aid in servicing modern electronic automotive systems, basic repair techniques for wiring harnesses and connectors is given. Read the basic information before attempting any repairs or testing on any computerized system, to provide the background of information necessary to avoid the most common and obvious mistakes that can cost both time and money. Although the replacement and testing procedures are simple in themselves, the systems are not, and unless one has a thorough understanding of all components and their function within a particular computerized control system, the logical test sequence these systems demand cannot be followed. Minor malfunctions can make a big difference, so it is important to know how each component affects the operation of the overall electronic system to find the ultimate cause of a problem without replacing good components unnecessarily. It is not enough to use the correct test equipment; the test equipment must be used correctly.

Safety Precautions

CAUTION: *Whenever working on or around any computer based microprocessor control system, always observe these general precautions to prevent the possibility of personal injury or damage to electronic components.*

• Never install or remove battery cables with the key ON or the engine running. Jumper cables should be connected with the key OFF to avoid power surges that can damage electronic control units. Engines equipped with computer controlled systems should avoid both giving and getting jump starts due to the possibility of serious damage to components from arcing in the engine compartment when connections are made with the ignition ON.

• Always remove the battery cables before charging the battery. Never use a high output charger on an installed battery or attempt to use any type of "hot shot" (24 volt) starting aid.

• Exercise care when inserting test probes into connectors to insure good connections without damaging the connector or spreading the pins. Always probe connectors from the rear (wire) side, NOT the pin side, to avoid acci-

dental shorting of terminals during test procedures.
- Never remove or attach wiring harness connectors with the ignition switch ON, especially to an electronic control unit.
- Do not drop any components during service procedures and never apply 12 volts directly to any component (like a solenoid or relay) unless instructed specifically to do so. Some component electrical windings are designed to safely handle only 4 or 5 volts and can be destroyed in seconds if 12 volts are applied directly to the connector.
- Remove the electronic control unit if the vehicle is to be placed in an environment where temperatures exceed approximately 176°F (80°C), such as a paint spray booth or when arc or gas welding near the control unit location in the car.

ORGANIZED TROUBLESHOOTING

When diagnosing a specific problem, organized troubleshooting is a must. The complexity of a modern automobile demands that you approach any problem in a logical, organized manner. There are certain troubleshooting techniques that are standard:

1. Establish when the problem occurs. Does the problem appear only under certain conditions? Were there any noises, odors, or other unusual symptoms?
2. Isolate the problem area. To do this, make some simple tests and observations; then eliminate the systems that are working properly. Check for obvious problems such as broken wires, dirty connections or split or disconnected vacuum hoses. Always check the obvious before assuming something complicated is the cause.
3. Test for problems systematically to determine the cause once the problem area is isolated. Are all the components functioning properly? Is there power going to electrical switches and motors? Is there vacuum at vacuum switches and/or actuators? Is there a mechanical problem such as bent linkage or loose mounting screws? Doing careful, systematic checks will often turn up most causes on the first inspection without wasting time checking components that have little or no relationship to the problem.
4. Test all repairs after the work is done to make sure that the problem is fixed. Some causes can be traced to more than one component, so a careful verification of repair work is important to pick up additional malfunctions that may cause a problem to reappear or a different problem to arise. A blown fuse, for example, is a simple problem that may require more than another fuse to repair. If you don't look for a problem that caused a fuse to blow, for example, a shorted wire may go undetected.

Experience has shown that most problems tend to be the result of a fairly simple and obvious cause, such as loose or corroded connectors or air leaks in the intake system; making careful inspection of components during testing essential to quick and accurate troubleshooting. Special, hand held computerized testers designed specifically for diagnosing the EEC-IV system are available from a variety of aftermarket sources, as well as from the vehicle manufacturer, but care should be taken that any test equipment being used is designed to diagnose that particular computer controlled system accurately without damaging the control unit (ECU) or components being tested.

NOTE: *Pinpointing the exact cause of trouble in an electrical system can sometimes only be accomplished by the use of special test equipment. The following describes commonly used test equipment and explains how to put it to best use in diagnosis. In addition to the information covered below, the manufacturer's instructions booklet provided with the tester should be read and clearly understood before attempting any test procedures.*

TEST EQUIPMENT

Jumper Wires

Jumper wires are simple, yet extremely valuable, pieces of test equipment. Jumper wires are merely wires that are used to bypass sections of a circuit. The simplest type of jumper wire is merely a length of multistrand wire with an alligator clip at each end. Jumper wires are usually fabricated from lengths of standard automotive wire and whatever type of connector (alligator clip, spade connector or pin connector) that is required for the particular vehicle being tested. The well equipped tool box will have several different styles of jumper wires in several different lengths. Some jumper wires are made with three or more terminals coming from a common splice for special purpose testing. In cramped, hard-to-reach areas it is advisable to have insulated boots over the jumper wire terminals in order to prevent accidental grounding, sparks, and possible fire, especially when testing fuel system components.

Jumper wires are used primarily to locate open electrical circuits, on either the ground (-) side of the circuit or on the hot (+) side. If an electrical component fails to operate, connect the jumper wire between the component and a good ground. If the component operates only with the jumper installed, the ground circuit is open. If the ground circuit is good, but the component does not operate, the circuit between

CHASSIS ELECTRICAL 233

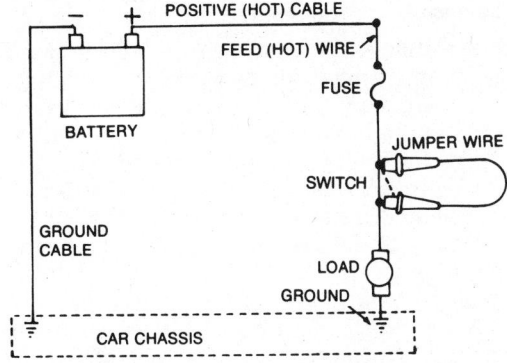

Bypassing a switch with a jumper wire

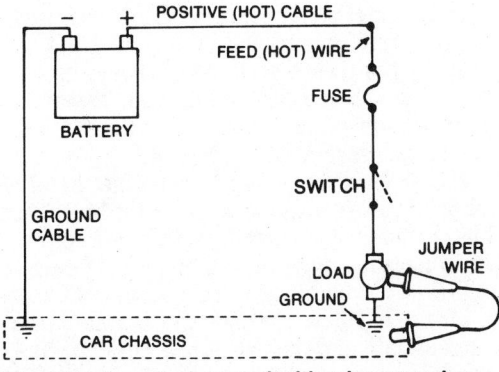

Checking for a bad ground with a jumper wire

the power feed and component is open. You can sometimes connect the jumper wire directly from the battery to the hot terminal of the component, but first make sure the component uses 12 volts in operation. Some electrical components, such as fuel injectors, are designed to operate on about 4 volts and running 12 volts directly to the injector terminals can burn out the wiring. By inserting an inline fuseholder between a set of test leads, a fused jumper wire can be used for bypassing open circuits. Use a 5 amp fuse to provide protection against voltage spikes. When in doubt, use a voltmeter to check the voltage input to the component and measure how much voltage is being applied normally. By moving the jumper wire successively back from the lamp toward the power source, you can isolate the area of the circuit where the open is located. When the component stops functioning, or the power is cut off, the open is in the segment of wire between the jumper and the point previously tested.

CAUTION: *Never use jumpers made from wire that is of lighter gauge than used in the circuit under test. If the jumper wire is of too small gauge, it may overheat and possibly melt. Never use jumpers to bypass high resistance loads (such as motors) in a circuit. Bypassing resistances, in effect, creates a short*

circuit which may, in turn, cause damage and fire. Never use a jumper for anything other than temporary bypassing of components in a circuit.

12 Volt Test Light

The 12 volt test light is used to check circuits and components while electrical current is flowing through them. It is used for voltage and ground tests. Twelve volt test lights come in different styles but all have three main parts; a ground clip, a probe, and a light. The most commonly used 12 volt test lights have pick-type probes. To use a 12 volt test light, connect the ground clip to a good ground and probe wherever necessary with the pick. The pick should be sharp so that it can penetrate wire insulation to make contact with the wire, without making a large hole in the insulation. The wrap-around light is handy in hard to reach areas or where it is difficult to support a wire to push a probe pick into it. To use the wrap around light, hook the wire to probed with the hook and pull the trigger. A small pick will be forced through the wire insulation into the wire core.

CAUTION: *Do not use a test light to probe electronic ignition spark plug or coil wires. Never use a pick-type test light to probe wiring on computer controlled systems unless specifically instructed to do so. Any wire insulation that is pierced by the test light probe should be taped and sealed with silicone after testing.*

Like the jumper wire, the 12 volt test light is used to isolate opens in circuits. But, whereas the jumper wire is used to bypass the open to operate the load, the 12 volt test light is used to locate the presence of voltage in a circuit. If the test light glows, you know that there is power up to that point; if the 12 volt test light does not glow when its probe is inserted into the wire or connector, you know that there is an open circuit (no power). Move the test light in successive steps back toward the power source until the light in the handle does glow. When it does glow, the open is between the probe and point previously probed.

NOTE: *The test light does not detect that 12 volts (or any particular amount of voltage) is present; it only detects that some voltage is present. It is advisable before using the test light to touch its terminals across the battery posts to make sure the light is operating properly.*

Self-Powered Test Light

The self-powered test light usually contains a 1.5 volt penlight battery. One type of self-powered test light is similar in design to the 12 volt test light. This type has both the battery and the light in the handle and pick-type probe tip. The second type has the light toward the open tip, so that the light illuminates the contact point. The self-powered test light is dual purpose piece of test equipment. It can be used to test for either open or short circuits when power is isolated from the circuit (continuity test). A powered test light should not be used on any computer controlled system or component unless specifically instructed to do so. Many engine sensors can be destroyed by even this small amount of voltage applied directly to the terminals.

Open Circuit Testing

To use the self-powered test light to check for open circuits, first isolate the circuit from the vehicle's 12 volt power source by disconnecting the battery or wiring harness connector. Connect the test light ground clip to a good ground and probe sections of the circuit sequentially with the test light. (start from either end of the circuit). If the light is out, the open is between the probe and the circuit ground. If the light is on, the open is between the probe and end of the circuit toward the power source.

Short Circuit Testing

By isolating the circuit both from power and from ground, and using a self-powered test light, you can check for shorts to ground in the circuit. Isolate the circuit from power and ground. Connect the test light ground clip to a good ground and probe any easy-to-reach test point in the circuit. If the light comes on, there is a short somewhere in the circuit. To isolate the short, probe a test point at either end of the isolated circuit (the light should be on). Leave the test light probe connected and open connectors, switches, remove parts, etc., sequentially, until the light goes out. When the light goes out, the short is between the last circuit component opened and the previous circuit opened.

NOTE: *The 1.5 volt battery in the test light does not provide much current. A weak battery may not provide enough power to illuminate the test light even when a complete circuit is made (especially if there are high resistances in the circuit). Always make sure that the test battery is strong. To check the battery, briefly touch the ground clip to the probe; if the light glows brightly the battery is strong enough for testing. Never use a self-powered test light to perform checks for opens or shorts when power is applied to the electrical system under test. The 12 volt vehicle power will quickly burn out the 1.5 volt light bulb in the test light.*

Voltmeter

A voltmeter is used to measure voltage at any point in a circuit, or to measure the voltage drop across any part of a circuit. It can also be used to check continuity in a wire or circuit by indicating current flow from one end to the other. Voltmeters usually have various scales on the meter dial and a selector switch to allow the selection of different voltages. The voltmeter has a positive and a negative lead. To avoid damage to the meter, always connect the negative lead to the negative (-) side of circuit (to ground or nearest the ground side of the circuit) and connect the positive lead to the positive (+) side of the circuit (to the power source or the nearest power source). Note that the negative voltmeter lead will always be black and that the positive voltmeter will always be some color other than black (usually red). Depending on how the voltmeter is connected into the circuit, it has several uses.

A voltmeter can be connected either in parallel or in series with a circuit and it has a very high resistance to current flow. When connected in parallel, only a small amount of current will flow through the voltmeter current path; the rest will flow through the normal circuit current path and the circuit will work normally. When the voltmeter is connected in series with a circuit, only a small amount of current can flow through the circuit. The circuit will not work properly, but the voltmeter reading will show if the circuit is complete or not.

Available Voltage Measurement

Set the voltmeter selector switch to the 20V position and connect the meter negative lead to the negative post of the battery. Connect the positive meter lead to the positive post of the battery and turn the ignition switch ON to provide a load. Read the voltage on the meter or digital display. A well charged battery should register over 12 volts. If the meter reads below 11.5 volts, the battery power may be insufficient to operate the electrical system properly. This test determines voltage available from the battery and should be the first step in any electrical trouble diagnosis procedure. Many electrical problems, especially on computer controlled systems, can be caused by a low state of charge in the battery. Excessive corrosion at the battery cable terminals can cause a poor contact that will prevent proper charging and full battery current flow.

Normal battery voltage is 12 volts when fully charged. When the battery is supplying current to one or more circuits it is said to be "under load". When everything is off the electrical system is under a "no-load" condition. A fully charged battery may show about 12.5 volts at no load; will drop to 12 volts under medium load; and will drop even lower under heavy load. If the battery is partially discharged the voltage decrease under heavy load may be excessive, even though the battery shows 12 volts or more at no load. When allowed to discharge further, the battery's available voltage under load will decrease more severely. For this reason, it is important that the battery be fully charged during all testing procedures to avoid errors in diagnosis and incorrect test results.

Voltage Drop

When current flows through a resistance, the voltage beyond the resistance is reduced (the larger the current, the greater the reduction in voltage). When no current is flowing, there is no voltage drop because there is no current flow. All points in the circuit which are connected to the power source are at the same voltage as the power source. The total voltage drop always equals the total source voltage. In a long circuit with many connectors, a series of small, unwanted voltage drops due to corrosion at the connectors can add up to a total loss of voltage which impairs the operation of the normal loads in the circuit.

INDIRECT COMPUTATION OF VOLTAGE DROPS

1. Set the voltmeter selector switch to the 20 volt position.
2. Connect the meter negative lead to a good ground.
3. Probe all resistances in the circuit with the positive meter lead.
4. Operate the circuit in all modes and observe the voltage readings.

DIRECT MEASUREMENT OF VOLTAGE DROPS

1. Set the voltmeter switch to the 20 volt position.
2. Connect the voltmeter negative lead to the ground side of the resistance load to be measured.
3. Connect the positive lead to the positive side of the resistance or load to be measured.
4. Read the voltage drop directly on the 20 volt scale.

Too high a voltage indicates too high a resistance. If, for example, a blower motor runs too slowly, you can determine if there is too high a resistance in the resistor pack. By taking voltage drop readings in all parts of the circuit, you can isolate the problem. Too low a voltage drop indicates too low a resistance. If, for example, a blower motor runs too fast in the MED and/or LOW position, the problem can be isolated in the resistor pack by taking voltage drop readings in all parts of the circuit to locate a possibly shorted resistor. The maximum allowable voltage drop under load is critical, especially if there is more than one high resistance problem in a circuit because all voltage drops are cumulative. A small drop is normal due to the resistance of the conductors.

HIGH RESISTANCE TESTING

1. Set the voltmeter selector switch to the 4 volt position.
2. Connect the voltmeter positive lead to the positive post of the battery.
3. Turn on the headlights and heater blower to provide a load.
4. Probe various points in the circuit with the negative voltmeter lead.
5. Read the voltage drop on the 4 volt scale. Some average maximum allowable voltage drops are:
FUSE PANEL — 7 volts
IGNITION SWITCH — 5 volts
HEADLIGHT SWITCH — 7 volts
IGNITION COIL (+) — 5 volts
ANY OTHER LOAD — 1.3 volts
NOTE: *Voltage drops are all measured while a load is operating; without current flow, there will be no voltage drop.*

Ohmmeter

The ohmmeter is designed to read resistance (ohms) in a circuit or component. Although there are several different styles of ohmmeters, all will usually have a selector switch which permits the measurement of different ranges of resistance (usually the selector switch allows the multiplication of the meter reading by 10, 100, 1000, and 10,000). A calibration knob allows the meter to be set at zero for accurate measurement. Since all ohmmeters are powered by an internal battery (usually 9 volts), the ohmmeter can be used as a self-powered test light. When the ohmmeter is connected, current from the ohmmeter flows through the circuit or component being tested. Since the ohmmeter's internal resistance and voltage are known values, the amount of current flow through the meter depends on the resistance of the circuit or component being tested.

The ohmmeter can be used to perform continuity test for opens or shorts (either by observation of the meter needle or as a self-powered test light), and to read actual resistance in a circuit. It should be noted that the ohmmeter is used to check the resistance of a component or wire while there is no voltage applied to the circuit. Current flow from an outside voltage source (such as the vehicle battery) can damage the ohmmeter, so the circuit or component should be isolated from the vehicle electrical system before any testing is done. Since the ohmmeter uses its own voltage source, either lead can be connected to any test point.

NOTE: *When checking diodes or other solid state components, the ohmmeter leads can only be connected one way in order to measure current flow in a single direction. Make sure the positive (+) and negative (-) terminal connections are as described in the test procedures to verify the one-way diode operation.*

In using the meter for making continuity checks, do not be concerned with the actual resistance readings. Zero resistance, or any resistance readings, indicate continuity in the circuit. Infinite resistance indicates an open in the circuit. A high resistance reading where there should be none indicates a problem in the circuit. Checks for short circuits are made in the same manner as checks for open circuits except that the circuit must be isolated from both power and normal ground. Infinite resistance indicates no continuity to ground, while zero resistance indicates a dead short to ground.

RESISTANCE MEASUREMENT

The batteries in an ohmmeter will weaken with age and temperature, so the ohmmeter must be calibrated or "zeroed" before taking measurements. To zero the meter, place the selector switch in its lowest range and touch the two ohmmeter leads together. Turn the calibration knob until the meter needle is exactly on zero.

NOTE: *All analog (needle) type ohmmeters must be zeroed before use, but some digital ohmmeter models are automatically calibrated when the switch is turned on. Self-calibrating digital ohmmeters do not have an adjusting knob, but its a good idea to check for a zero readout before use by touching the leads together. All computer controlled systems require the use of a digital ohmmeter with at least 10 meagohms impedance for testing. Before any test procedures are attempted, make sure the ohmmeter used is compatible with the electrical system or damage to the on-board computer could result.*

To measure resistance, first isolate the circuit from the vehicle power source by disconnecting the battery cables or the harness connector. Make sure the key is OFF when disconnecting any components or the battery. Where necessary, also isolate at least one side of the circuit to be checked to avoid reading parallel resistances. Parallel circuit resistances will always give a lower reading than the actual resistance of either of the branches. When measuring the resistance of parallel circuits, the total resistance will always be lower than the smallest resistance in the circuit. Connect the meter leads to both sides of the circuit (wire or component) and read the actual measured ohms on the meter scale. Make sure the selector switch is set to the proper ohm scale for the circuit being tested to avoid misreading the ohmmeter test value.

CAUTION: *Never use an ohmmeter with power applied to the circuit. Like the self-powered test light, the ohmmeter is designed to operate on its own power supply. The normal 12 volt automotive electrical system current could damage the meter.*

Ammeters

An ammeter measures the amount of current flowing through a circuit in units called amperes or amps. Amperes are units of electron flow which indicate how fast the electrons are flowing through the circuit. Since Ohms Law dictates that current flow in a circuit is equal to the circuit voltage divided by the total circuit resistance, increasing voltage also increases the current level (amps). Likewise, any decrease in resistance will increase the amount of amps in a circuit. At normal operating voltage, most circuits have a characteristic amount of amperes, called "current draw" which can be measured using an ammeter. By referring to a specified current draw rating, measuring the amperes, and comparing the two values, one can determine what is happening within the circuit to aid in diagnosis. An open circuit, for example, will not allow any current to flow so the ammeter reading will be zero. More current flows through a heavily loaded circuit or when the charging system is operating.

An ammeter is always connected in series with the circuit being tested. All of the current that normally flows through the circuit must also flow through the ammeter; if there is any other path for the current to follow, the ammeter reading will not be accurate. The ammeter itself has very little resistance to current flow and therefore will not affect the circuit, but it will measure current draw only when the circuit is closed and electricity is flowing. Excessive current draw can blow fuses and drain the battery, while a reduced current draw can cause motors to run slowly, lights to dim and other components to not operate properly. The ammeter can help diagnose these conditions by locating the cause of the high or low reading.

Multimeters

Different combinations of test meters can be built into a single unit designed for specific tests. Some of the more common combination test devices are known as Volt/Amp testers, Tach/Dwell meters, or Digital Multimeters. The Volt/Amp tester is used for charging system, starting system or battery tests and consists of a voltmeter, an ammeter and a variable resistance carbon pile. The voltmeter will usually have at least two ranges for use with 6, 12 and 24 volt systems. The ammeter also has more than one range for testing various levels of battery loads and starter current draw and the carbon pile can be adjusted to offer different amounts of resistance. The Volt/Amp tester has heavy leads to carry large amounts of current and many later models have an inductive ammeter pickup that clamps around the wire to simplify test connections. On some models, the ammeter also has a zero-center scale to allow testing of charging and starting systems without switching leads or polarity. A digital multimeter is a voltmeter, ammeter and ohmmeter combined in an instrument which gives a digital readout. These are often used when testing solid state circuits because of their high input impedance (usually 10 megohms or more).

The tach/dwell meter combines a tachometer and a dwell (cam angle) meter and is a specialized kind of voltmeter. The tachometer scale is marked to show engine speed in rpm and the dwell scale is marked to show degrees of distributor shaft rotation. In most electronic ignition systems, dwell is determined by the control unit, but the dwell meter can also be used to check the duty cycle (operation) of some electronic engine control systems. Some tach/dwell meters are powered by an internal battery, while others take their power from the car battery in use. The battery powered testers usually require calibration much like an ohmmeter before testing.

Special Test Equipment

A variety of diagnostic tools are available to help troubleshoot and repair computerized engine control systems. The most sophisticated of these devices are the console type engine analyzers that usually occupy a garage service bay, but there are several types of aftermarket electronic testers available that will allow quick circuit tests of the engine control system by plugging directly into a special connector located in the engine compartment or under the dashboard. Several tool and equipment manufacturers offer simple, hand held testers that measure various circuit voltage levels on command to check all system components for proper operation. Although these testers usually cost about $300-$500, consider that the average computer control unit (or ECM) can cost just as much and the money saved by not replacing perfectly good sensors or components in an attempt to correct a problem could justify the purchase price of a special diagnostic tester the first time it's used.

These computerized testers can allow quick and easy test measurements while the engine is operating or while the car is being driven. In addition, the on-board computer memory can be read to access any stored trouble codes; in effect allowing the computer to tell you where it hurts and aid trouble diagnosis by pinpointing exactly which circuit or component is malfunctioning. In the same manner, repairs can be tested to make sure the problem has been corrected. The biggest advantage these special testers have is their relatively easy hookups that minimize or eliminate the chances of making the wrong connections and getting false voltage readings or damaging the computer accidentally.

NOTE: *It should be remembered that these testers check voltage levels in circuits; they don't detect mechanical problems or failed components if the circuit voltage falls within the preprogrammed limits stored in the tester PROM unit. Also, most of the hand held testes are designed to work only on one or two systems made by a specific manufacturer.*

A variety of aftermarket testers are available to help diagnose different computerized control systems. Owatonna Tool Company (OTC), for example, markets a device called the OTC Monitor which plugs directly into the assembly line diagnostic link (ALDL). The OTC tester makes diagnosis a simple matter of pressing the correct buttons and, by changing the internal PROM or inserting a different diagnosis cartridge, it will work on any model from full size to subcompact, over a wide range of years. An adapter is supplied with the tester to allow connection to all types of ALDL links, regardless of the number of pin terminals used. By inserting an updated PROM into the OTC tester, it can be easily updated to diagnose any new modifications of computerized control systems.

Wiring Harnesses

The average automobile contains about ½ mile of wiring, with hundreds of individual connections. To protect the many wires from damage and to keep them from becoming a confusing tangle, they are organized into bundles, enclosed in plastic or taped together and called wire harnesses. Different wiring harnesses serve different parts of the vehicle. Individual wires are color coded to help trace them through a harness where sections are hidden from view.

A loose or corroded connection or a replacement wire that is too small for the circuit will add extra resistance and an additional voltage drop to the circuit. A ten percent voltage drop can result in slow or erratic motor operation, for example, even though the circuit is complete. Automotive wiring or circuit conductors can be in any one of three forms:

1. Single strand wire
2. Multistrand wire
3. Printed circuitry

Single strand wire has a solid metal core and is usually used inside such components as alternators, motors, relays and other devices. Multistrand wire has a core made of many small strands of wire twisted together into a single conductor. Most of the wiring in an automotive electrical system is made up of multistrand wire, either as a single conductor or grouped together in a harness. All wiring is color coded on the insulator, either as a solid color or as a colored wire with an identification stripe. A printed circuit is a thin film of copper or other conductor that is printed on an insulator backing. Occasionally, a printed circuit is sandwiched between two sheets of plastic for more protection and flexibility. A complete printed circuit, consisting of conductors, insulating material and connectors for lamps or other components is called a printed circuit board. Printed circuitry is used in place of individual wires or harnesses in places where space is limited, such as behind instrument panels.

Wire Gauge

Since computer controlled automotive electrical systems are very sensitive to changes in resistance, the selection of properly sized wires is critical when systems are repaired. The wire gauge number is an expression of the cross section area of the conductor. The most common system for expressing wire size is the American Wire Gauge (AWG) system.

Wire cross section area is measured in circular mils. A mil is $1/1000''$ (0.001''); a circular mil is the area of a circle one mil in diameter. For example, a conductor ¼'' in diameter is 0.250 in. or 250 mils. The circular mil cross section area of the wire is 250 squared (250^2) or 62,500 circular mils. Imported car models usually use metric wire gauge designations, which is simply the cross section area of the conductor in square millimeters (mm^2).

Gauge numbers are assigned to conductors of various cross section areas. As gauge number increases, area decreases and the conductor becomes smaller. A 5 gauge conductor is smaller than a 1 gauge conductor and a 10 gauge is smaller than a 5 gauge. As the cross section area of a conductor decreases, resistance increases and so does the gauge number. A conductor with a higher gauge number will carry less current than a conductor with a lower gauge number.

NOTE: *Gauge wire size refers to the size of the conductor, not the size of the complete wire. It is possible to have two wires of the same gauge with different diameters because one may have thicker insulation than the other.*

12 volt automotive electrical systems generally use 10, 12, 14, 16 and 18 gauge wire. Main power distribution circuits and larger accessories usually use 10 and 12 gauge wire. Battery cables are usually 4 or 6 gauge, although 1 and 2 gauge wires are occasionally used. Wire length must also be considered when making repairs to a circuit. As conductor length increases, so does resistance. An 18 gauge wire, for example, can carry a 10 amp load for 10 feet without excessive voltage drop; however if a 15 foot wire is required for the same 10 amp load, it must be a 16 gauge wire.

An electrical schematic shows the electrical current paths when a circuit is operating properly. It is essential to understand how a circuit works before trying to figure out why it doesn't. Schematics break the entire electrical system down into individual circuits and show only one particular circuit. In a schematic, no attempt is made to represent wiring and components as they physically appear on the vehicle; switches and other components are shown as simply as possible. Face views of harness connectors show the cavity or terminal locations in all multi-pin connectors to help locate test points.

If you need to backprobe a connector while it is on the component, the order of the terminals must be mentally reversed. The wire color code can help in this situation, as well as a keyway, lock tab or other reference mark.

NOTE: *Wiring diagrams are not included in this book. As trucks have become more complex and available with longer option lists, wiring diagrams have grown in size and complexity. It has become almost impossible to provide a readable reproduction of a wiring diagram in a book this size. Information on ordering wiring diagrams from the vehicle manufacturer can be found in the owner's manual.*

WIRING REPAIR

Soldering is a quick, efficient method of joining metals permanently. Everyone who has the occasion to make wiring repairs should know how to solder. Electrical connections that are soldered are far less likely to come apart and will conduct electricity much better than connections that are only "pig-tailed" together. The most popular (and preferred) method of soldering is with an electrical soldering gun. Soldering irons are available in many sizes and wattage ratings. Irons with higher wattage ratings deliver higher temperatures and recover lost heat faster. A small soldering iron rated for no more than 50 watts is recommended, especially on electrical systems where excess heat can damage the components being soldered.

There are three ingredients necessary for successful soldering; proper flux, good solder and sufficient heat. A soldering flux is necessary to clean the metal of tarnish, prepare it for soldering and to enable the solder to spread into tiny crevices. When soldering, always use a resin flux or resin core solder which is non-corrosive and will not attract moisture once the job is finished. Other types of flux (acid core) will leave a residue that will attract moisture and cause the wires to corrode. Tin is a unique metal with a low melting point. In a molten state, it dissolves and alloys easily with many metals. Solder is made by mixing tin with lead. The most common proportions are 40/60, 50/50 and 60/40, with the percentage of tin listed first. Low priced solders usually contain less tin, making them very difficult for a beginner to use because more heat is required to melt the solder. A common solder is 40/60 which is well suited for all-around general use, but 60/40 melts easier, has more tin for a better joint and is preferred for electrical work.

Soldering Techniques

Successful soldering requires that the metals to be joined be heated to a temperature that will melt the solder—usually 360-460°F (182-238°C). Contrary to popular belief, the purpose of the soldering iron is not to melt the solder itself, but to heat the parts being soldered to a temperature high enough to melt the solder when it is touched to the work. Melting flux-cored solder on the soldering iron will usually destroy the effectiveness of the flux.

NOTE: *Soldering tips are made of copper for good heat conductivity, but must be "tinned" regularly for quick transference of heat to the project and to prevent the solder from sticking to the iron. To "tin" the iron, simply heat it and touch the flux-cored solder to the tip; the solder will flow over the hot tip. Wipe the excess off with a clean rag, but be careful as the iron will be hot.*

After some use, the tip may become pitted. If so, simply dress the tip smooth with a smooth file and "tin" the tip again. An old saying holds that "metals well cleaned are half soldered." Flux-cored solder will remove oxides but rust, bits of insulation and oil or grease must be removed with a wire brush or emery cloth. For maximum strength in soldered parts, the joint must start off clean and tight. Weak joints will result in gaps too wide for the solder to bridge.

If a separate soldering flux is used, it should be brushed or swabbed on only those areas that are to be soldered. Most solders contain a core of flux and separate fluxing is unnecessary. Hold the work to be soldered firmly. It is best to solder on a wooden board, because a metal vise will only rob the piece to be soldered of heat and make it difficult to melt the solder. Hold the soldering tip with the broadest face against the work to be soldered. Apply solder under the tip close to the work, using enough solder to give a heavy film between the iron and the piece being soldered, while moving slowly and making sure the solder melts properly. Keep the work level or the solder will run to the lowest part and favor the thicker parts, because these require more heat to melt the solder. If the soldering tip overheats (the solder coating on the face of the tip burns up), it should be retinned. Once the soldering is completed, let the soldered joint stand until cool. Tape and seal all soldered wire splices after the repair has cooled.

Wire Harness and Connectors

The on-board computer (ECM) wire harness electrically connects the control unit to the various solenoids, switches and sensors used by the control system. Most connectors in the engine compartment or otherwise exposed to the elements are protected against moisture and dirt which could create oxidation and deposits on the terminals. This protection is important because of the very low voltage and current levels used by the computer and sensors. All connectors have a lock which secures the male and female terminals together, with a secondary lock holding the seal and terminal into the connector. Both terminal locks must be released when disconnecting ECM connectors.

These special connectors are weather-proof and all repairs require the use of a special terminal and the tool required to service it. This tool is used to remove the pin and sleeve terminals. If removal is attempted with an ordinary pick, there is a good chance that the terminal will be bent or deformed. Unlike standard blade type terminals, these terminals cannot be straightened once they are bent. Make certain that the connectors are properly seated and all of the sealing rings in place when connecting leads. On some models, a hinge-type flap provides a backup or secondary locking feature for the terminals. Most secondary locks are used to improve the connector reliability by retaining the terminals if the small terminal lock tangs are not positioned properly.

Molded-on connectors require complete replacement of the connection. This means splicing a new connector assembly into the harness. All splices in on-board computer systems should be soldered to insure proper contact. Use care when probing the connections or replacing terminals in them as it is possible to short between opposite terminals. If this hap-

240 CHASSIS ELECTRICAL

pens to the wrong terminal pair, it is possible to damage certain components. Always use jumper wires between connectors for circuit checking and never probe through weatherproof seals.

Open circuits are often difficult to locate by sight because corrosion or terminal misalignment are hidden by the connectors. Merely wiggling a connector on a sensor or in the wiring harness may correct the open circuit condition. This should always be considered when an open circuit or a failed sensor is indicated. Intermittent problems may also be caused by oxidized or loose connections. When using a circuit tester for diagnosis, always probe connections from the wire side. Be careful not to damage sealed connectors with test probes.

All wiring harnesses should be replaced with identical parts, using the same gauge wire and connectors. When signal wires are spliced into a harness, use wire with high temperature insulation only. With the low voltage and current levels found in the system, it is important that the best possible connection at all wire splices be made by soldering the splices together. It is seldom necessary to replace a complete harness. If replacement is necessary, pay close attention to insure proper harness routing. Secure the harness with suitable plastic wire clamps to prevent vibrations from causing the harness to wear in spots or contact any hot components.

NOTE: *Weatherproof connectors cannot be replaced with standard connectors. Instructions are provided with replacement connector and terminal packages. Some wire harnesses have mounting indicators (usually pieces of colored tape) to mark where the harness is to be secured.*

In making wiring repairs, it's important that you always replace damaged wires with wires that are the same gauge as the wire being replaced. The heavier the wire, the smaller the gauge number. Wires are color-coded to aid in identification and whenever possible the same color coded wire should be used for replacement. A wire stripping and crimping tool is necessary to install solderless terminal connectors. Test all crimps by pulling on the wires; it should not be possible to pull the wires out of a good crimp.

Wires which are open, exposed or otherwise damaged are repaired by simple splicing. Where possible, if the wiring harness is accessible and the damaged place in the wire can be located, it is best to open the harness and check for all possible damage. In an inaccessible harness, the wire must be bypassed with a new insert, usually taped to the outside of the old harness.

When replacing fusible links, be sure to use fusible link wire, NOT ordinary automotive wire. Make sure the fusible segment is of the same gauge and construction as the one being replaced and double the stripped end when crimping the terminal connector for a good contact. The melted (open) fusible link segment of the wiring harness should be cut off as close to the harness as possible, then a new segment spliced in as described. In the case of a damaged fusible link that feeds two harness wires, the harness connections should be replaced with two fusible link wires so that each circuit will have its own separate protection.

NOTE: *Most of the problems caused in the wiring harness are due to bad ground connections. Always check all vehicle ground connections for corrosion or looseness before performing any power feed checks to eliminate the chance of a bad ground affecting the circuit.*

Repairing Hard Shell Connectors

Unlike molded connectors, the terminal contacts in hard shell connectors can be replaced. Weatherproof hard-shell connectors with the leads molded into the shell have non-replaceable terminal ends. Replacement usually involves the use of a special terminal removal tool that depress the locking tangs (barbs) on the connector terminal and allow the connector to be removed from the rear of the shell. The connector shell should be replaced if it shows any evidence of burning, melting, cracks, or breaks. Replace individual terminals that are burnt, corroded, distorted or loose.

NOTE: *The insulation crimp must be tight to prevent the insulation from sliding back on the wire when the wire is pulled. The insulation must be visibly compressed under the crimp tabs, and the ends of the crimp should be turned in for a firm grip on the insulation.*

The wire crimp must be made with all wire strands inside the crimp. The terminal must be fully compressed on the wire strands with the ends of the crimp tabs turned in to make a firm grip on the wire. Check all connections with an ohmmeter to insure a good contact. There should be no measurable resistance between the wire and the terminal when connected.

Mechanical Test Equipment

Vacuum Gauge

Most gauges are graduated in inches of mercury (in.Hg), although a device called a manometer reads vacuum in inches of water (in. H_2O). The normal vacuum reading usually varies between 18 and 22 in.Hg at sea level. To test engine vacuum, the vacuum gauge must be connected to a source of manifold vacuum. Many engines have a plug in the intake manifold

CHASSIS ELECTRICAL 241

which can be removed and replaced with an adapter fitting. Connect the vacuum gauge to the fitting with a suitable rubber hose or, if no manifold plug is available, connect the vacuum gauge to any device using manifold vacuum, such as EGR valves, etc. The vacuum gauge can be used to determine if enough vacuum is reaching a component to allow its actuation.

Hand Vacuum Pump

Small, hand-held vacuum pumps come in a variety of designs. Most have a built-in vacuum gauge and allow the component to be tested without removing it from the vehicle. Operate the pump lever or plunger to apply the correct amount of vacuum required for the test specified in the diagnosis routines. The level of vacuum in inches of Mercury (in.Hg) is indicated on the pump gauge. For some testing, an additional vacuum gauge may be necessary.

Intake manifold vacuum is used to operate various systems and devices on late model vehicles. To correctly diagnose and solve problems in vacuum control systems, a vacuum source is necessary for testing. In some cases, vacuum can be taken from the intake manifold when the engine is running, but vacuum is normally provided by a hand vacuum pump. These hand vacuum pumps have a built-in vacuum gauge that allow testing while the device is still attached to the component. For some tests, an additional vacuum gauge may be necessary.

HEATING AND AIR CONDTIONING

Blower Motor

REMOVAL AND INSTALLATION

Except the 6-243

1. Disconnect the electrical connection.
2. Remove the screws that hold the motor in place.
3. Remove the blower motor.
4. Install the blower motor in the reverse order of removal.

6-243

1. Remove the coolant overflow bottle.
2. On trucks with anti-lock brakes, remove the anti-lock brake pump and bracket and position it out of the way.
3. Remove the brake hose retaining bracket screw.
4. Unplug the blower motor wiring connector.
5. Remove the blower motor mounting screws and lift out the motor.
6. Installation is the reverse of removal.

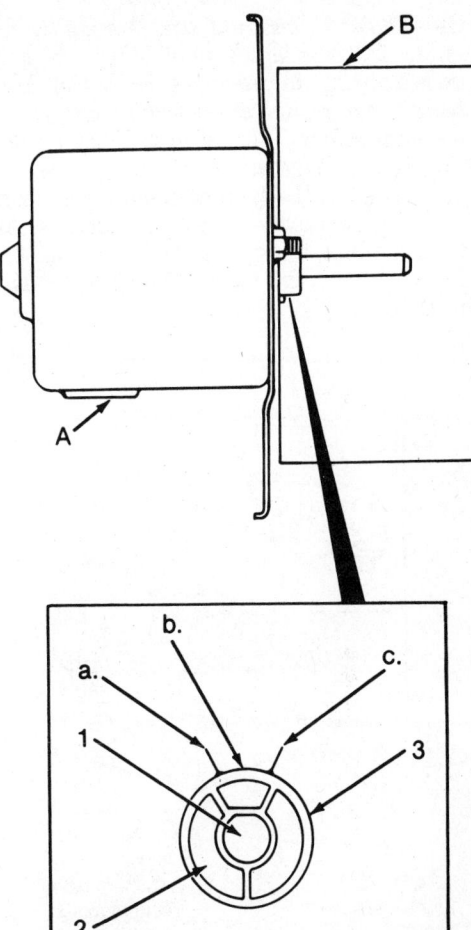

1. Motor shaft
2. Fan hub
3. Retainer clip

NOTE: Ears of retainer clip must be over flat surface on motor shaft (a, b, c).

Blower motor installation

Heater Core

REMOVAL AND INSTALLATION

1. Drain the coolant.

CAUTION: *When draining the coolant, keep in mind that cats and dogs are attracted by the ethylene glycol antifreeze, and are quite likely to drink any that is left in an uncovered container or in puddles on the ground. This will prove fatal in sufficient quantity. Always drain the coolant into a sealable container. Coolant should be reused unless it is contaminated or several years old.*

2. Disconnect the heater hoses at the core tubes.
3. On trucks with air conditioning, discharge the refrigerant.

242 CHASSIS ELECTRICAL

CAUTION: *Unless you are thoroughly familiar with the handling of refrigerant gas, do not attempt to discharge the system. Mishandling of refrigerant gas can cause severe personal injury. Take the system to someone trained in refrigeration.*

4. Disconnect the air conditioning hose from the expansion valve and cap all openings. Always use a back-up wrench on the fitting!
5. Disconnect the blower motor wires and vent tube.

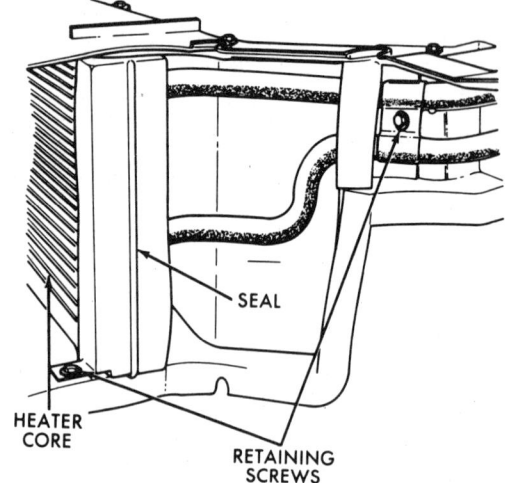

Heater core removal

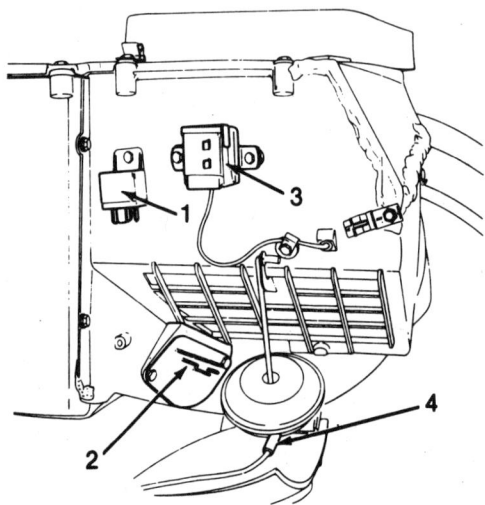

1. A.C. relay
2. A.C. resistor
3. A.C. thermostat
4. Vacuum motor

Evaporator case components

6. Remove the center console, if equipped.
7. Remove the lower half of the instrument panel.
8. Disconnect the wiring at the A/C relay, blower motor resistors and A/C thermostat. Disconnect the vacuum hoses at the vacuum motor.
9. Cut the plastic retaining strap that retains the evaporator housing to the heater core housing.
10. Disconnect and remove the heater control cable.
11. Remove the 3 clips at the rear blower housing flange and remove the retaining screws.
12. Remove the housing attaching nuts from the studs on the engine compartment side of the firewall.
13. Remove the evaporator drain tube.
14. Remove the right kick panel and the instrument panel support bolt.
15. Gently pull out on the right side of the dash and rotate the housing down and toward the rear to disengage the mounting studs from the firewall. Remove the housing.
16. Unbolt and remove the core from the housing.

To install:
17. Install the core in the housing.
18. Position the housing on the mounting studs on the firewall.
19. Install the right kick panel and the instrument panel support bolt.
20. Install the evaporator drain tube.
21. Install the housing attaching nuts from the studs on the engine compartment side of the firewall.
22. Install the 3 clips at the rear blower housing flange and install the retaining screws.
23. Connect the heater control cable.

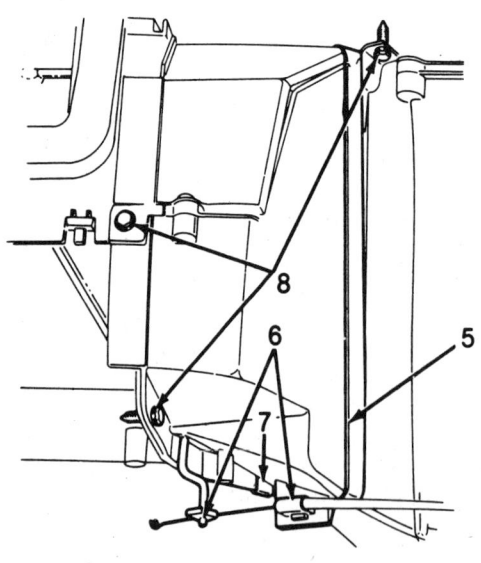

5. Plastic strap
6. Heater cable
7. Clip
8. Screws

Disconnect these points

24. Install a new plastic retaining strap that retains the evaporator housing to the heater core housing.
25. Connect the wiring at the A/C relay, blower motor resistors and A/C thermostat.
26. Connect the vacuum hoses at the vacuum motor.
27. Install the lower half of the instrument panel.
28. Install the center console, if equipped.
29. Connect the blower motor wires and vent tube.
30. Connect the air conditioning hose at the expansion valve. Always use a back-up wrench!
31. Connect the heater hoses at the core tubes.
32. Fill the cooling system.
33. Evacuate, charge and leak test the refrigerant system. See Chapter 1.

Evaporator Core

REMOVAL AND INSTALLATION

1. Drain the coolant.
CAUTION: *When draining the coolant, keep in mind that cats and dogs are attracted by the ethylene glycol antifreeze, and are quite likely to drink any that is left in an uncovered container or in puddles on the ground. This will prove fatal in sufficient quantity. Always drain the coolant into a sealable container. Coolant should be reused unless it is contaminated or several years old.*
2. Disconnect the heater hoses at the core tubes.
3. Discharge the refrigerant.
CAUTION: *Unless you are thoroughly familiar with the handling of refrigerant gas, do not attempt to discharge the system. Mishandling of refrigerant gas can cause severe personal injury. Take the system to someone trained in refrigeration.*
4. Disconnect the air conditioning hose from the expansion valve and cap all openings.
5. Disconnect the blower motor wires and vent tube.
6. Remove the center console, if equipped.
7. Remove the lower half of the instrument panel.
8. Disconnect the wiring at the A/C relay, blower motor resistors and A/C thermostat. Disconnect the vacuum hoses at the vacuum motor.
9. Cut the plastic retaining strap that retains the evaporator housing to the heater core housing.
10. Disconnect and remove the heater control cable.
11. Remove the 3 clips at the rear blower housing flange and remove the retaining screws.
12. Remove the housing attaching nuts from the studs on the engine compartment side of the firewall.
13. Remove the evaporator drain tube.
14. Remove the right kick panel and the instrument panel support bolt.
15. Gently pull out on the right side of the dash and rotate the housing down and toward the rear to disengage the mounting studs from the firewall. Remove the housing.
16. Remove the top housing retaining screws and lift of the top of the housing.
17. Remove the thermostatic switch and capillary tube.
18. Remove the 2 retaining screws and lift the core from the housing.

To install:
NOTE: *If a new core is being installed, add 1 oz. of refrigerant oil to the ne core.*
19. Bolt the core into place in the housing.

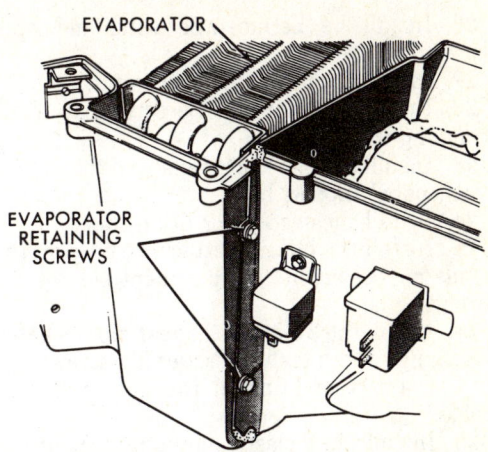
Evaporator removal

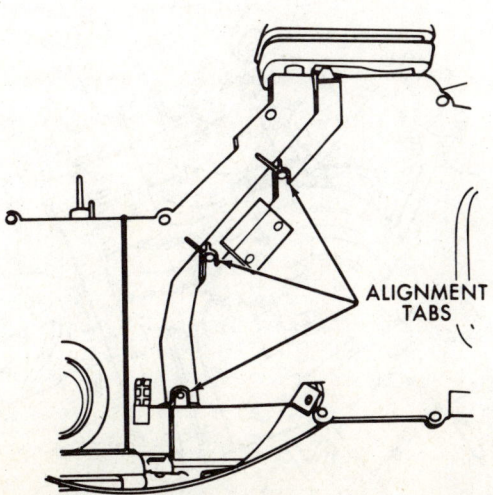
Evaporator housing installation

244 CHASSIS ELECTRICAL

20. Install the thermostatic switch and capillary tube.
21. Install the top of the housing.
22. Install the housing. Be careful to avoid trapping wires.
23. Install the right kick panel and the instrument panel support bolt.
24. Install the evaporator drain tube.
25. Install the housing attaching nuts on the studs on the engine compartment side of the firewall.
26. Install the 3 clips at the rear blower housing flange and install the retaining screws.
27. Connect and Install the heater control cable.
28. Install a new plastic retaining strap on the evaporator housing.
29. Connect the wiring at the A/C relay, blower motor resistors and A/C thermostat. Connect the vacuum hoses at the vacuum motor.
30. Install the lower half of the instrument panel.
31. Install the center console, if equipped.
32. Connect the blower motor wires and vent tube.
33. Connect the air conditioning hose from the expansion valve and cap all openings.
34. Charge the refrigerant.
35. Connect the heater hoses at the core tubes.
36. Fill the cooling system.

Control Panel

REMOVAL AND INSTALLATION

1. Disconnect the battery ground.
2. Remove the lower part of the instrument panel.
3. Remove the instrument panel bezel.
4. Remove the clock.

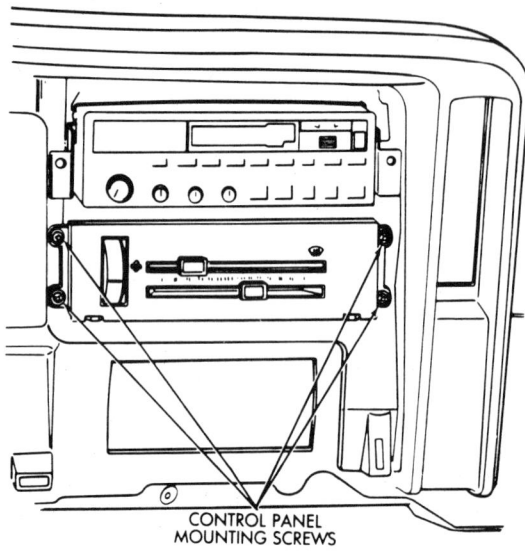
Control panel mounting screw removal

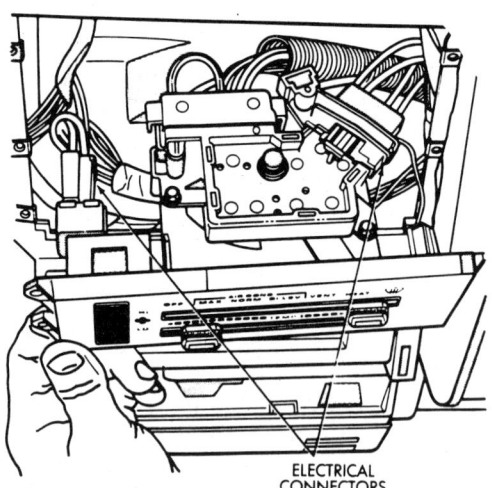
Electrical connectors

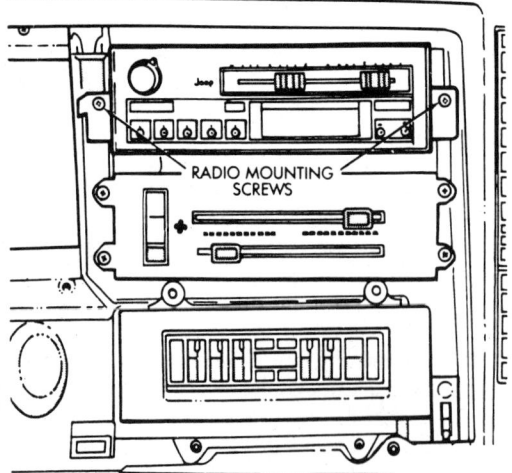
Radio mounting screw removal

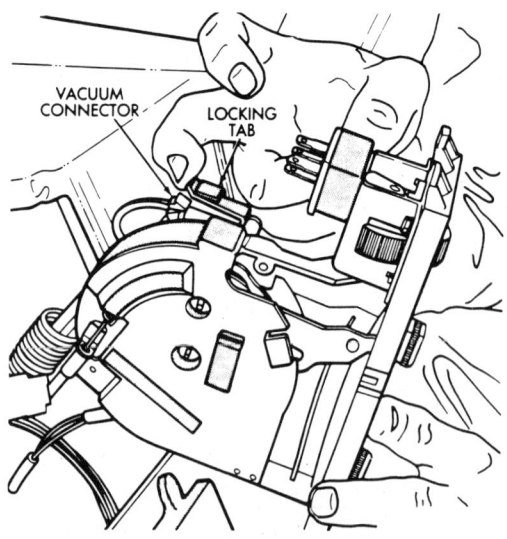
Vacuum harness connector

CHASSIS ELECTRICAL   245

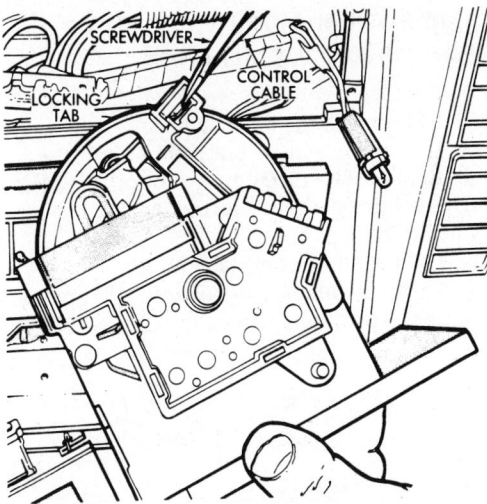
Disconnecting the control cable locking tab

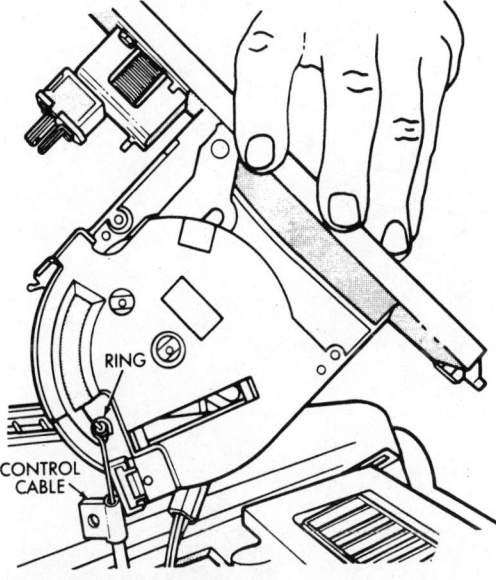
Removing the control cable

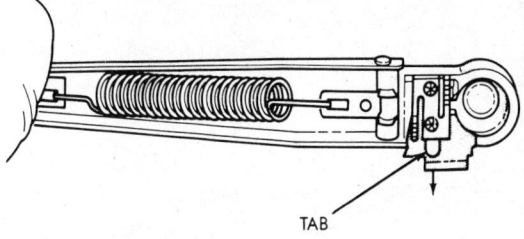
Wiper arm removal

Wiper Arm
REPLACEMENT

1. Raise the blade end of the arm away from the windshield and move the spring tab away from the pivot shaft.
2. Disengage the auxiliary arm retainer clip from the pivot pin and pull the wiper arm from the pivot shaft.
3. Pivot the auxiliary over the pivot pin and engage the retainer clip. Push the wiper arm over the pivot shaft. Be sure that the shaft is in park and the wiper arm is positioned in the down mode.

Windshield Wiper Motor
REMOVAL AND INSTALLATION

1. Remove the wiper arm and blade assemblies.
2. Remove the cowl trim panel.
3. Disconnect the washer hose.
4. Remove the cowl mounting bracket attaching nuts and pivot pin attaching screws.
5. Disconnect the wiring harness and remove the motor.
6. Installation is the reverse of removal. Torque the mounting nuts to 35-50 in. lb.

5. Remove the radio.
6. Remove the control panel screws, pull the panel outward and disconnect and tag the hoses, wires and cable.
7. Installation is the reverse of removal.

WINDSHIELD WIPERS

Wiper Blade
REPLACEMENT

1. Insert a screwdriver into the spring release opening of the blade saddle and depress the spring clip. Pull the blade from the arm.
2. Push the blade saddle onto the mounting clip so that the spring clip engages the pin.

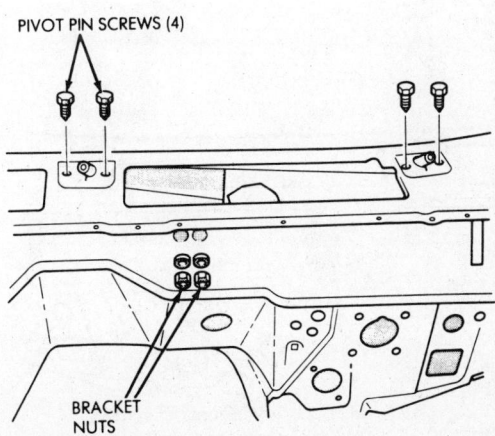
Pivot assembly removal

246 CHASSIS ELECTRICAL

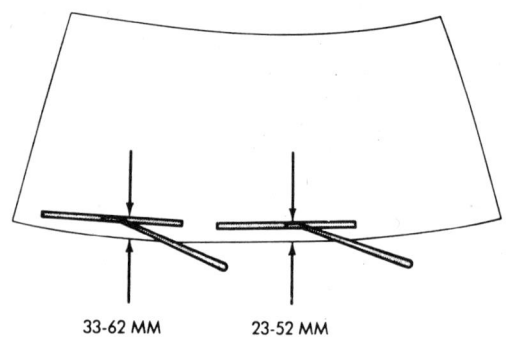
Wiper arm installation

Liftgate Wiper Motor
REMOVAL AND INSTALLATION

1. Remove the wiper arm assembly.
2. Disconnect the washer hose.
3. Remove the pivot pin retaining nut.
4. Remove the liftgate interior trim panel.
5. Disconnect the wiper motor at the wiring harness.
6. Unbolt and remove the motor.
7. Installation is the reverse of removal. Torque the pivot pin attaching nut to 32 in. lbs.

Linkage
REMOVAL AND INSTALLATION

1. Remove the wiper arms and pivot shaft nuts, washers, escutcheons and gaskets.
2. Disconnect the drive arm from the motor crank.
3. Remove individual links where necessary, to remove the pivot shaft bodies without excessive interference.
4. Install in the reverse order of removal.

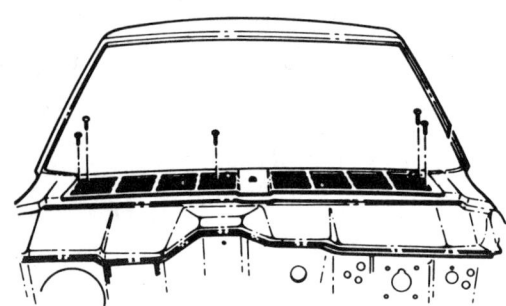
Cowl removal

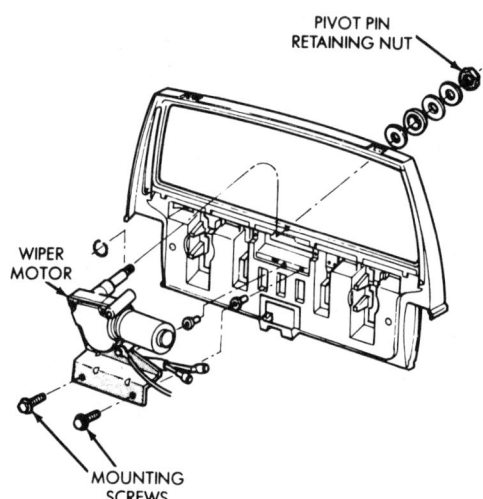
Rear wiper motor removal

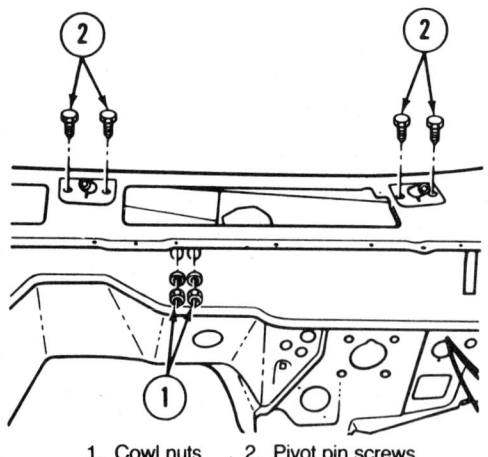
1. Cowl nuts   2. Pivot pin screws
Wiper motor and linkage removal

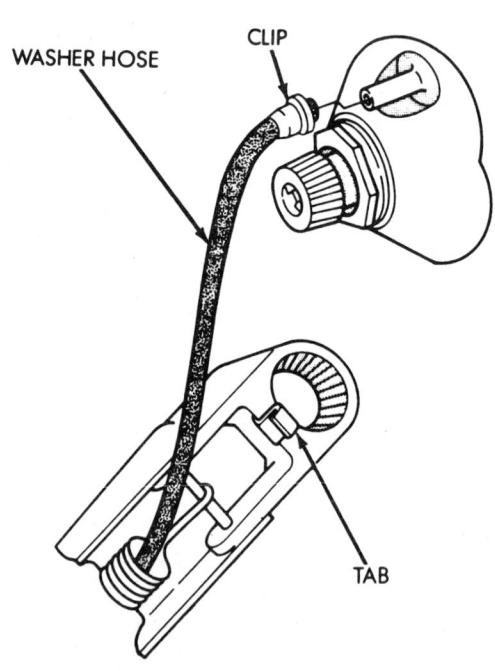
Rear wiper arm removal

PARKED POSITION
25 ± 10 MM
FROM MID-POINT OF
BLADE TO WINDOW SEAL

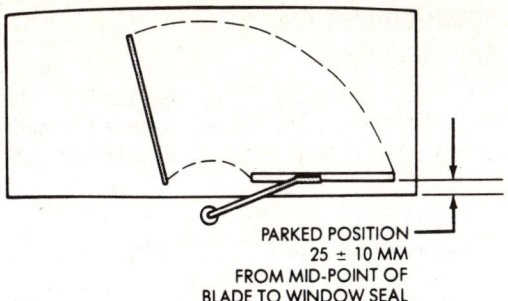

Rear wiper arm positioning

BEZEL
ATTACHING
SCREWS
SNAP FIT
LOCATION
SNAP FIT
LOCATIONS

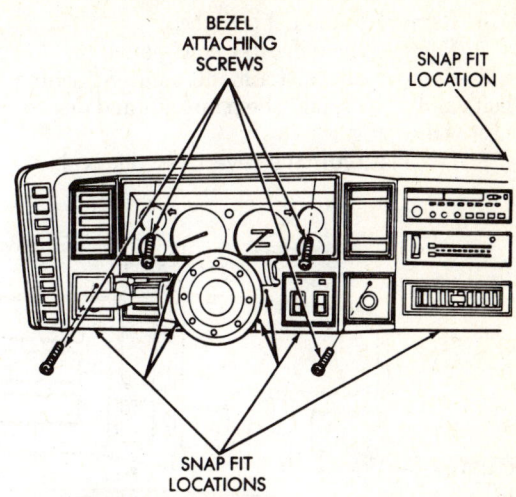

Instrument bezel removal

INSTRUMENTS AND SWITCHES

Instrument Cluster

REMOVAL AND INSTALLATION

1. Disconnect the battery ground.
2. Remove the four instrument panel bezel screws and remove the instrument panel bezel. The bezel is a snap fit a several locations.
3. Remove the lighter housing screws.
4. Remove the rocker switch housing screws.
5. Remove the instrument cluster screws.
6. Disconnect the speedometer cable.
7. Pull the cluster part way out and unplug the connectors.
8. Installation is the reverse of removal.

Instrument Panel

REMOVAL AND INSTALLATION

1. Disconnect the battery ground.
2. Remove the lower instrument panel section.
3. Remove the instrument cluster bezel.
4. Remove the cluster.
5. Remove the radio and heater control panel.

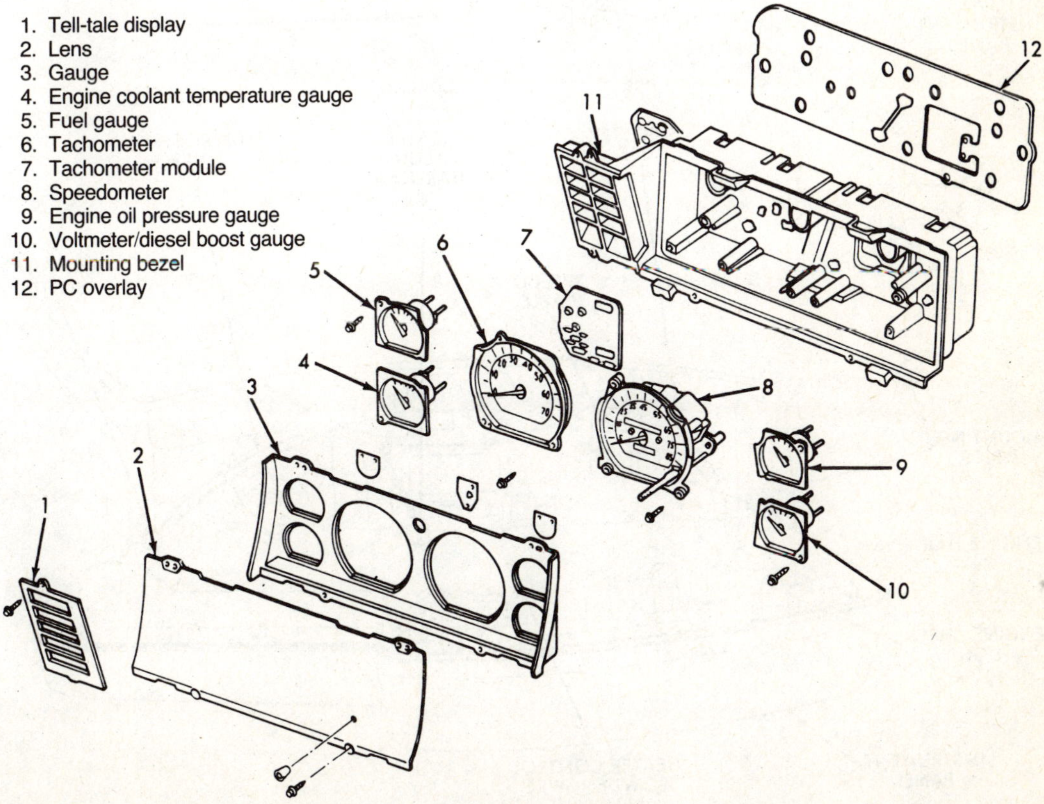

1. Tell-tale display
2. Lens
3. Gauge
4. Engine coolant temperature gauge
5. Fuel gauge
6. Tachometer
7. Tachometer module
8. Speedometer
9. Engine oil pressure gauge
10. Voltmeter/diesel boost gauge
11. Mounting bezel
12. PC overlay

Instrument cluster

CHASSIS ELECTRICAL

6. Remove the panel switches.
7. Remove the defroster cowl panel.
8. Remove the instrument panel attaching bolts and screws, pull the panel out and disconnect the wiring.
9. Installation is the reverse of removal.

Speedometer Cable

REPLACEMENT

1. Reach up behind the speedometer. Depress the spring tab at the point where the cable attaches to the head and pull the cable straight

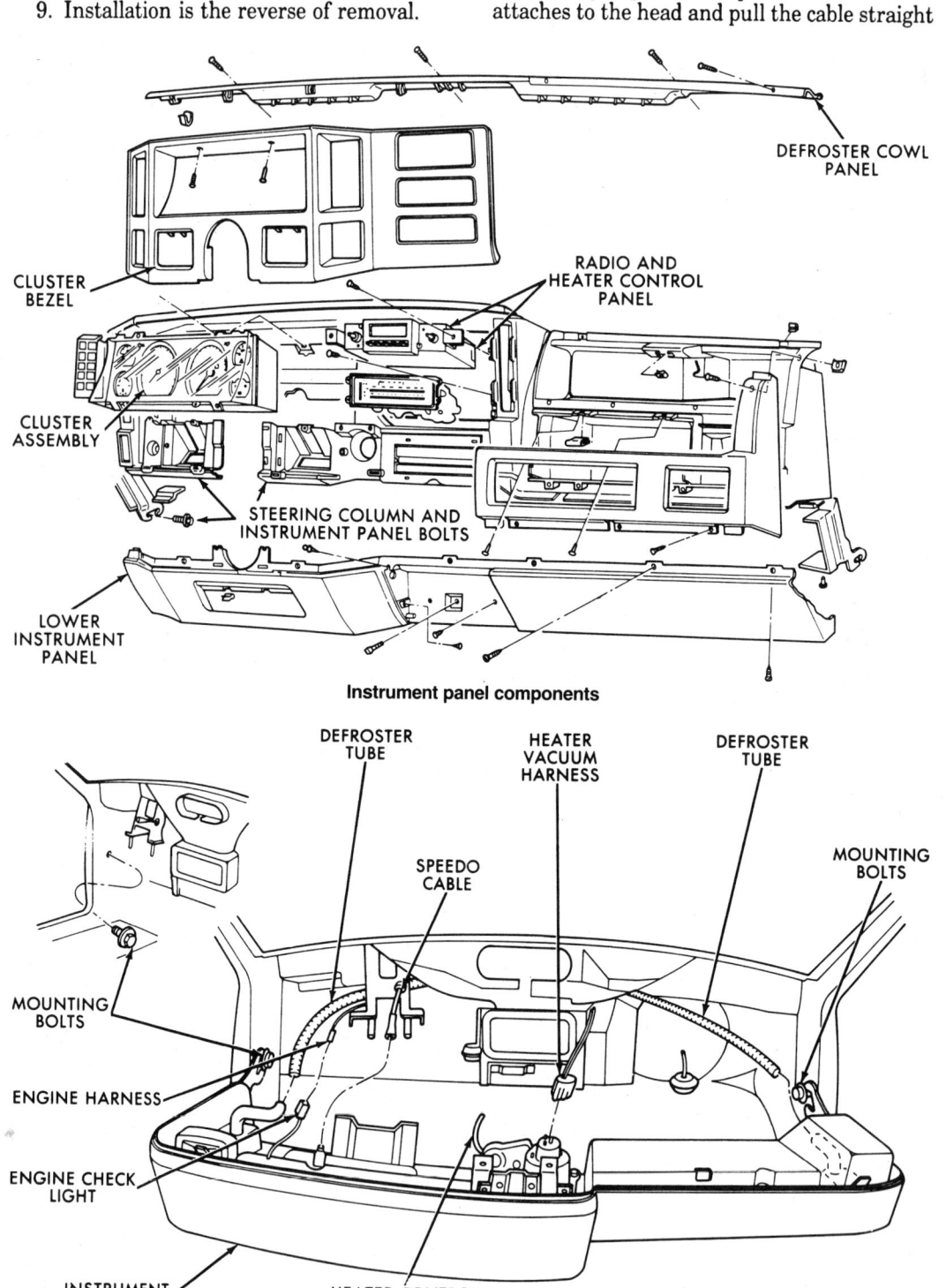

Instrument panel components

Instrument panel installation

CHASSIS ELECTRICAL 249

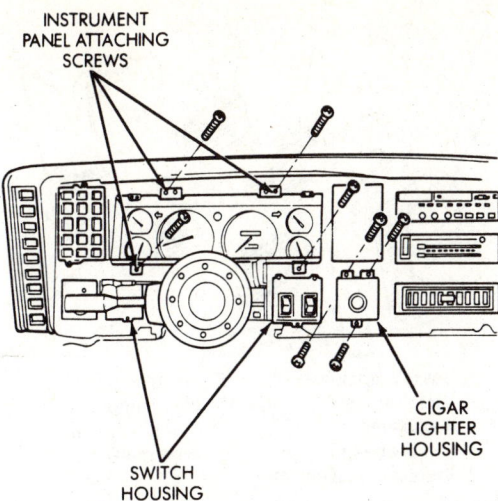

Instrument panel removal

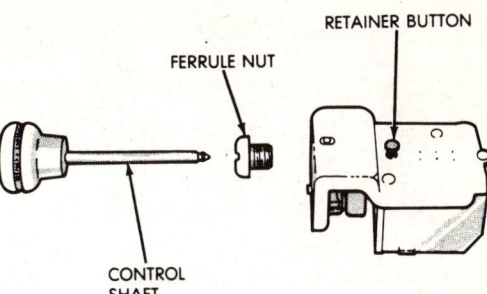

Headlight switch removal

back away from the head. Pull the core from the sheath.

2. If the cable is broken, raise and support the vehicle and remove the cable from the transmission. Pull the broken end from the sheath.

3. When installing the cable, coat it with speedometer cable lubricant before installation.

Headlight Switch

REMOVAL AND INSTALLATION

1. Disconnect the battery ground cable.
2. Pull the switch to the full ON position.
3. Reach up under the panel and depress the switch shaft retainer button while pulling the switch control shaft straight out.
4. Remove the switch ferrule nut from the switch.
5. Disconnect the switch from the harness.
6. Installation is the reverse of removal.

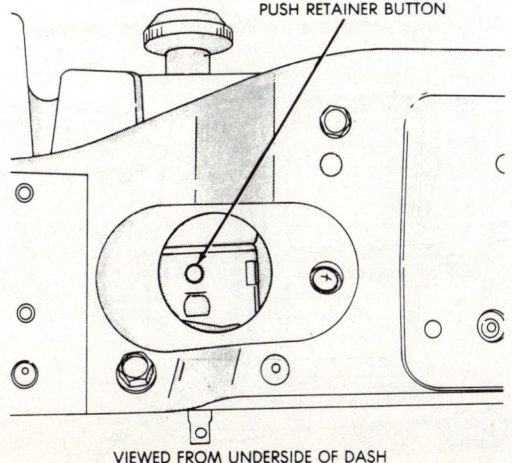

Headlight switch shaft removal

Windshield Wiper Switch

REMOVAL AND INSTALLATION

The wiper switch is part of the multi-function switch. See Chapter 8 for replacement.

Rear Window Wiper Switch

REMOVAL AND INSTALLATION

1. Remove the instrument cluster bezel.
2. Remove the switch housing panel.
3. Unplug the switch connector.
4. Installation is the reverse of removal.

RADIO

REMOVAL AND INSTALLATION

1. Disconnect the battery ground.
2. Remove the instrument panel bezel.
3. Remove the radio attaching screws.
4. Disconnect the radio from the instrument panel wiring harness.
5. Installation is the reverse of removal.

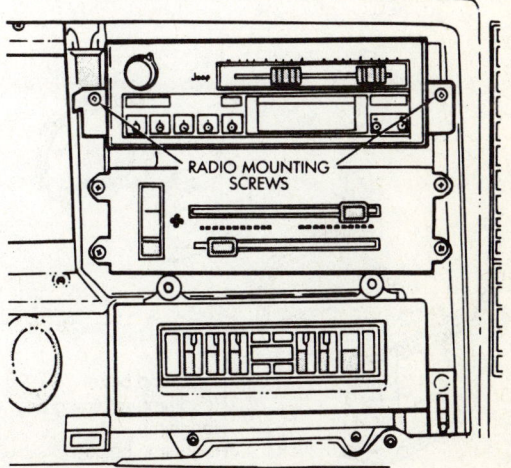

Removing the radio mounting screws

250 CHASSIS ELECTRICAL

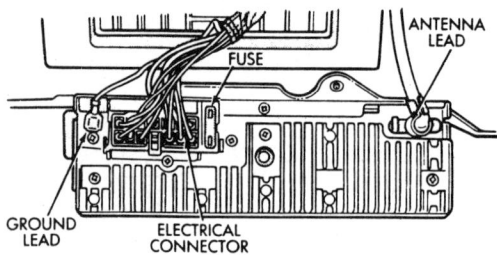

Disconnecting the radio wiring harness

Installing the clip in the underside of the dash

LIGHTING

Headlights

REMOVAL AND INSTALLATION

1. Remove the screws retaining the headlight trim and remove the trim.
2. Remove the screws retaining the retaining ring and remove the ring.
3. Pull the headlight out, disconnect the wire harness and remove the headlight from the vehicle.
4. Install the headlight in the reverse order of removal.

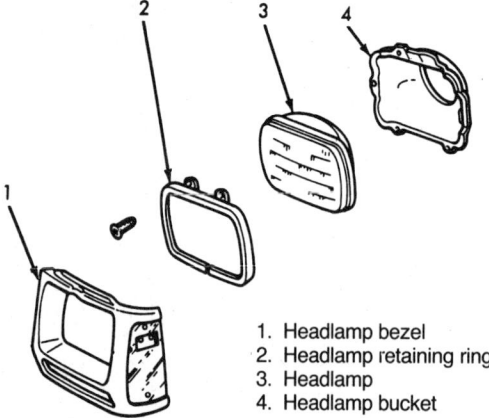

1. Headlamp bezel
2. Headlamp retaining ring
3. Headlamp
4. Headlamp bucket

Single headlight installation

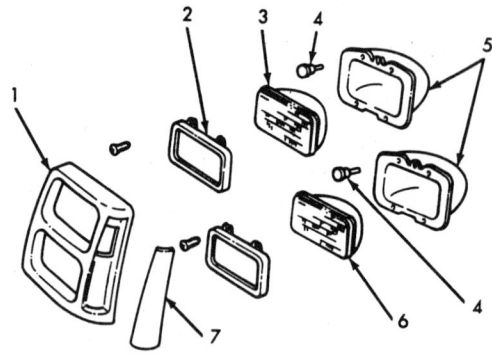

1. Headlamp bezel
2. Retaining ring
3. Headlamp (low beam)
4. Headlamp adjustors
5. Headlamp bracket
6. Headlamp (high beam)
7. Side marker

Dual headlight installation

Front Parking/Turn Signal Lights

REMOVAL AND INSTALLATION

1. Remove the screws from the lens and separate the lens from the headlight bezel.
2. Remove the headlight bezel.
3. Remove the screws from the turn signal housing and pull it out.

Side marker lamps for the Wagoneer and Cherokee

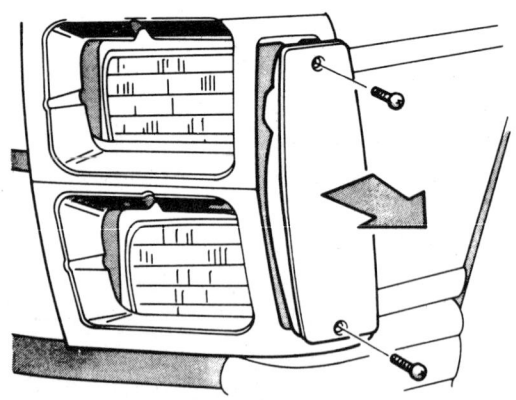

Side marker lamps for the Comanche

CHASSIS ELECTRICAL 251

4. Turn the bulb socket counterclockwise ⅓ turn and remove it.

Side Marker Lights
REMOVAL AND INSTALLATION

1. Remove the screws from the marker lens and separate the lens from the headlight bezel.
2. Pull the bulb from its socket in the back of the lens.
3. Installation is the reverse of removal.

Back-Up/Rear Turn Signal/Tail Lights
REMOVAL AND INSTALLATION

1. Remove the 4 screws and pull out the tail light assembly.
2. The bulbs can be removed by turning them ⅓ turn counterclockwise.

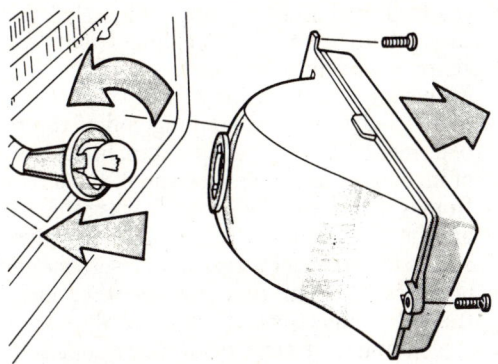
Turn signal assembly removal

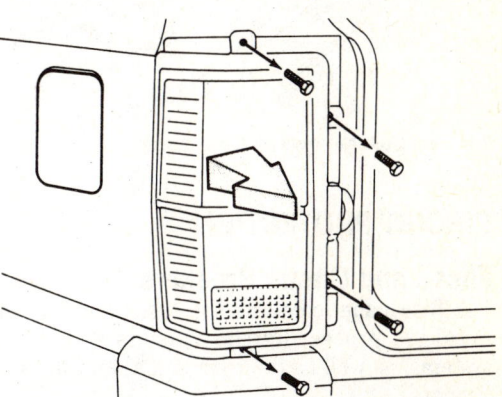
Tail light housing removal on Wagoneer/Cherokee

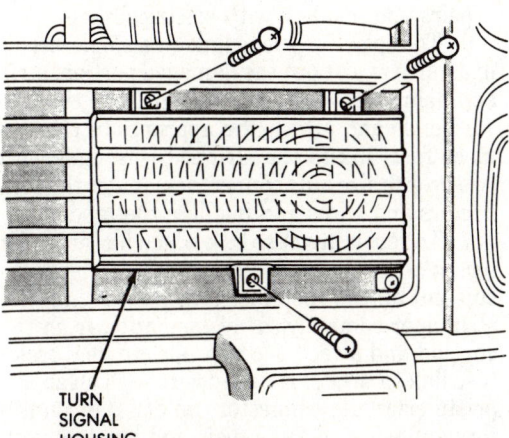
Turn signal housing removal

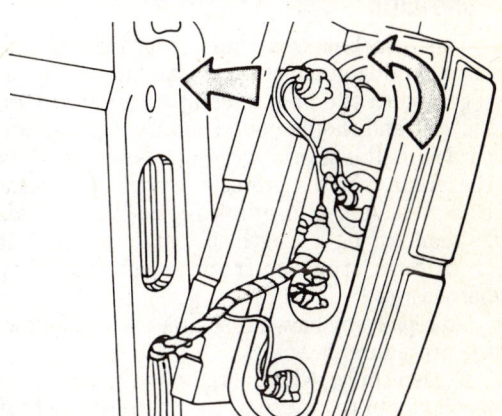
Tail light bulb removal on Wagoneer/Cherokee

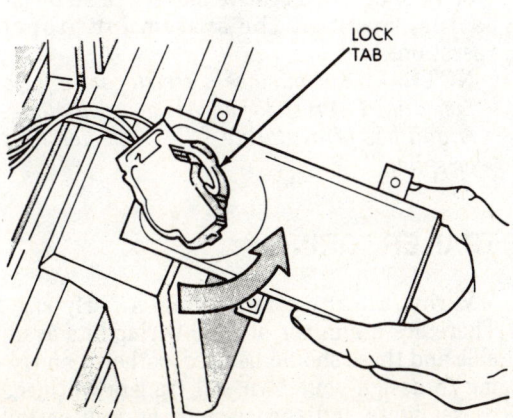
Turn signal bulb removal

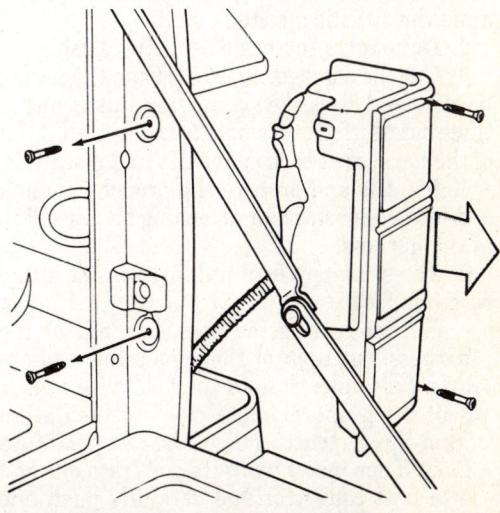
Tail light housing removal on Comanche

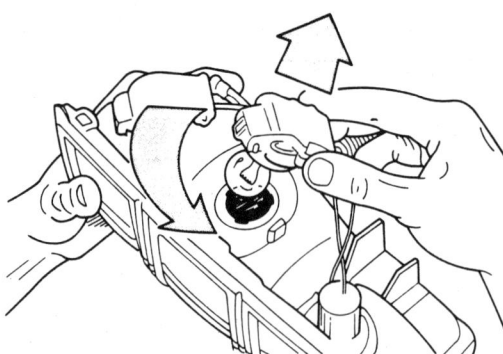

Tail light bulb removal on Comanche

CIRCUIT PROTECTION

Fuses and Circuit Breakers

A fuse panel contains the fuses and circuit breakers protecting the various electrical systems, as well as the turn signal and hazard flashers.

Fuse Link

The fuse link is a short length of special, Hypalon (high temperature) insulated wire, integral with the engine compartment wiring harness and should not be confused with standard wire. It is several wire gauges smaller than the circuit which it protects. Under no circumstances should a fuse link replacement repair be made using a length of standard wire cut from bulk stock or from another wiring harness.

To repair any blown fuse link use the following procedure:

1. Determine which circuit is damaged, its location and the cause of the open fuse link. If the damaged fuse link is one of three fed by a common No. 10 or 12 gauge feed wire, determine the specific affected circuit.
2. Disconnect the negative battery cable.
3. Cut the damaged fuse link from the wiring harness and discard it. If the fuse link is one of three circuits fed by a single feed wire, cut it out of the harness at each splice end and discard it.
4. Identify and procure the proper fuse link and butt connectors for attaching the fuse link to the harness.
5. To repair any fuse link in a 3-link group with one feed:
   a. After cutting the open link out of the harness, cut each of the remaining undamaged fuse links close to the feed wire weld.
   b. Strip approximately ½" of insulation from the detached ends of the two good fuse links. Then insert two wire ends into one end of a butt connector and carefully push one stripped end of the replacement fuse link into the same end of the butt connector and crimp all three firmly together.
   NOTE: *Care must be taken when fitting the three fuse links into the butt connector as the internal diameter is a snug it for three wires. Make sure to use a proper crimping tool. Pliers, side cutters, etc. will not apply the proper crimp to retain the wires and withstand a pull test.*
   c. After crimping the butt connector to the three fuse links, cut the weld portion from the feed wire and strip approximately ½" of insulation from the cut end. Insert the stripped end into the open end of the butt connector and crimp very firmly.
   d. To attach the remaining end of the replacement fuse link, strip approximately ½" of insulation from the wire end of the circuit from which the blown fuse link was removed, and firmly crimp a butt connector or equivalent to the stripped wire. Then, insert the end of the replacement link into the other end of the butt connector and crimp firmly.
   e. Using rosin core solder with a consistency of 60 percent tin and 40 percent lead, solder the connectors and the wires at the repairs and insulate with electrical tape.
6. To replace any fuse link on a single circuit in a harness, cut out the damaged portion, strip approximately ½" of insulation from the two wire ends and attach the appropriate replacement fuse link to the stripped wire ends with two proper size butt connectors. Solder the connectors and wires and insulate the tape.
7. To repair any fuse link which has an eyelet terminal on one end such as the charging circuit, cut off the open fuse link behind the weld, strip approximately ½" of insulation from the cut end and attach the appropriate new eyelet fuse link to the cut stripped wire with an appropriate size butt connector. Solder the connectors and wires at the repair and insulate with tape.
8. Connect the negative battery cable to the battery and test the system for proper operation.

NOTE: *Do not mistake a resistor wire for a fuse link. The resistor wire is generally longer and has print stating, "Resistor: don't cut or splice."*

TRAILER WIRING

Wiring the truck for towing is fairly easy. There are a number of good wiring kits available and these should be used, rather than trying to design your own. All trailers will need brake lights and turn signals as well as tail lights and side marker lights. Most states require extra marker lights for overly wide trailers. Also, most states have recently required back-up lights for trailers, and most trailer manufacturers have been building trailers with back-up lights for several years.

Additionally, some Class I, most Class II and just about all Class III trailers will have electric brakes.

Add to this number an accessories wire, to operate trailer internal equipment or to charge the trailer's battery, and you can have as many as seven wires in the harness.

Determine the equipment on your trailer and buy the wiring kit necessary. The kit will contain all the wires needed, plus a plug adapter set which included the female plug, mounted on the bumper or hitch, and the male plug, wired into, or plugged into the trailer harness.

When installing the kit, follow the manufacturer's instructions. The color coding of the wires is standard throughout the industry.

One point to note, some domestic vehicles, and most imported vehicles, have separate turn signals. On most domestic vehicles, the brake lights and rear turn signals operate with the same bulb. For those vehicles with separate turn signals, you can purchase an isolation unit so that the brake lights won't blink whenever the turn signals are operated, or, you can go to your local electronics supply house and buy four diodes to wire in series with the brake and turn signal bulbs. Diodes will isolate the brake and turn signals. The choice is yours. The isolation units are simple and quick to install, but far more expensive than the diodes. The diodes, however, require more work to install properly, since they require the cutting of each bulb's wire and soldering in place of the diode.

One final point, the best kits are those with a spring loaded cover on the vehicle mounted socket. This cover prevents dirt and moisture from corroding the terminals. Never let the vehicle socket hang loosely. Always mount it securely to the bumper or hitch.

Troubleshooting Basic Windshield Wiper Problems

Problem	Cause	Solution
Electric Wipers		
Wipers do not operate—Wiper motor heats up or hums	• Internal motor defect • Bent or damaged linkage • Arms improperly installed on linking pivots	• Replace motor • Repair or replace linkage • Position linkage in park and reinstall wiper arms
Wipers do not operate—No current to motor	• Fuse or circuit breaker blown • Loose, open or broken wiring • Defective switch • Defective or corroded terminals • No ground circuit for motor or switch	• Replace fuse or circuit breaker • Repair wiring and connections • Replace switch • Replace or clean terminals • Repair ground circuits
Wipers do not operate—Motor runs	• Linkage disconnected or broken	• Connect wiper linkage or replace broken linkage
Vacuum Wipers		
Wipers do not operate	• Control switch or cable inoperative • Loss of engine vacuum to wiper motor (broken hoses, low engine vacuum, defective vacuum/fuel pump) • Linkage broken or disconnected • Defective wiper motor	• Repair or replace switch or cable • Check vacuum lines, engine vacuum and fuel pump • Repair linkage • Replace wiper motor
Wipers stop on engine acceleration	• Leaking vacuum hoses • Dry windshield • Oversize wiper blades • Defective vacuum/fuel pump	• Repair or replace hoses • Wet windshield with washers • Replace with proper size wiper blades • Replace pump

254 CHASSIS ELECTRICAL

Troubleshooting Basic Turn Signal and Flasher Problems

Most problems in the turn signals or flasher system, can be reduced to defective flashers or bulbs, which are easily replaced. Occasionally, problems in the turn signals are traced to the switch in the steering column, which will require professional service.

F = Front   R = Rear   ● = Lights off   o = Lights on

Problem	Solution
Turn signals light, but do not flash	• Replace the flasher
No turn signals light on either side	• Check the fuse. Replace if defective. • Check the flasher by substitution • Check for open circuit, short circuit or poor ground
Both turn signals on one side don't work	• Check for bad bulbs • Check for bad ground in both housings
One turn signal light on one side doesn't work	• Check and/or replace bulb • Check for corrosion in socket. Clean contacts. • Check for poor ground at socket
Turn signal flashes too fast or too slow	• Check any bulb on the side flashing too fast. A heavy-duty bulb is probably installed in place of a regular bulb. • Check the bulb flashing too slow. A standard bulb was probably installed in place of a heavy-duty bulb. • Check for loose connections or corrosion at the bulb socket
Indicator lights don't work in either direction	• Check if the turn signals are working • Check the dash indicator lights • Check the flasher by substitution

One indicator light doesn't light	• On systems with 1 dash indicator: See if the lights work on the same side. Often the filaments have been reversed in systems combining stoplights with taillights and turn signals. Check the flasher by substitution
	• On systems with 2 indicators: Check the bulbs on the same side
	  Check the indicator light bulb
	  Check the flasher by substitution

Troubleshooting Basic Dash Gauge Problems

Problem	Cause	Solution
Coolant Temperature Gauge		
Gauge reads erratically or not at all	• Loose or dirty connections • Defective sending unit • Defective gauge	• Clean/tighten connections • Bi-metal gauge: remove the wire from the sending unit. Ground the wire for an instant. If the gauge registers, replace the sending unit. • Magnetic gauge: disconnect the wire at the sending unit. With ignition ON gauge should register COLD. Ground the wire; gauge should register HOT.
Ammeter Gauge—Turn Headlights ON (do not start engine). Note reaction		
Ammeter shows charge Ammeter shows discharge Ammeter does not move	• Connections reversed on gauge • Ammeter is OK • Loose connections or faulty wiring • Defective gauge	• Reinstall connections • Nothing • Check/correct wiring • Replace gauge
Oil Pressure Gauge		
Gauge does not register or is inaccurate	• On mechanical gauge, Bourdon tube may be bent or kinked • Low oil pressure • Defective gauge • Defective wiring • Defective sending unit	• Check tube for kinks or bends preventing oil from reaching the gauge • Remove sending unit. Idle the engine briefly. If no oil flows from sending unit hole, problem is in engine. • Remove the wire from the sending unit and ground it for an instant with the ignition ON. A good gauge will go to the top of the scale. • Check the wiring to the gauge. If it's OK and the gauge doesn't register when grounded, replace the gauge. • If the wiring is OK and the gauge functions when grounded, replace the sending unit
All Gauges		
All gauges do not operate	• Blown fuse • Defective instrument regulator	• Replace fuse • Replace instrument voltage regulator
All gauges read low or erratically	• Defective or dirty instrument voltage regulator	• Clean contacts or replace
All gauges pegged	• Loss of ground between instrument voltage regulator and car • Defective instrument regulator	• Check ground • Replace regulator
Warning Lights		
Light(s) do not come on when ignition is ON, but engine is not started	• Defective bulb • Defective wire • Defective sending unit	• Replace bulb • Check wire from light to sending unit • Disconnect the wire from the sending unit and ground it. Replace the sending unit if the light comes on with the ignition ON.
Light comes on with engine running	• Problem in individual system • Defective sending unit	• Check system • Check sending unit (see above)

256 CHASSIS ELECTRICAL

Troubleshooting Basic Lighting Problems

Problem	Cause	Solution
Lights		
One or more lights don't work, but others do	• Defective bulb(s) • Blown fuse(s) • Dirty fuse clips or light sockets • Poor ground circuit	• Replace bulb(s) • Replace fuse(s) • Clean connections • Run ground wire from light socket housing to car frame
Lights burn out quickly	• Incorrect voltage regulator setting or defective regulator • Poor battery/alternator connections	• Replace voltage regulator • Check battery/alternator connections
Lights go dim	• Low/discharged battery • Alternator not charging • Corroded sockets or connections • Low voltage output	• Check battery • Check drive belt tension; repair or replace alternator • Clean bulb and socket contacts and connections • Replace voltage regulator
Lights flicker	• Loose connection • Poor ground • Circuit breaker operating (short circuit)	• Tighten all connections • Run ground wire from light housing to car frame • Check connections and look for bare wires
Lights "flare"—Some flare is normal on acceleration—if excessive, see "Lights Burn Out Quickly"	• High voltage setting	• Replace voltage regulator
Lights glare—approaching drivers are blinded	• Lights adjusted too high • Rear springs or shocks sagging • Rear tires soft	• Have headlights aimed • Check rear springs/shocks • Check/correct rear tire pressure
Turn Signals		
Turn signals don't work in either direction	• Blown fuse • Defective flasher • Loose connection	• Replace fuse • Replace flasher • Check/tighten all connections
Right (or left) turn signal only won't work	• Bulb burned out • Right (or left) indicator bulb burned out • Short circuit	• Replace bulb • Check/replace indicator bulb • Check/repair wiring
Flasher rate too slow or too fast	• Incorrect wattage bulb • Incorrect flasher	• Flasher bulb • Replace flasher (use a variable load flasher if you pull a trailer)
Indicator lights do not flash (burn steadily)	• Burned out bulb • Defective flasher	• Replace bulb • Replace flasher
Indicator lights do not light at all	• Burned out indicator bulb • Defective flasher	• Replace indicator bulb • Replace flasher

Troubleshooting the Heater

Problem	Cause	Solution
Blower motor will not turn at any speed	• Blown fuse • Loose connection • Defective ground • Faulty switch • Faulty motor • Faulty resistor	• Replace fuse • Inspect and tighten • Clean and tighten • Replace switch • Replace motor • Replace resistor
Blower motor turns at one speed only	• Faulty switch • Faulty resistor	• Replace switch • Replace resistor
Blower motor turns but does not circulate air	• Intake blocked • Fan not secured to the motor shaft	• Clean intake • Tighten security
Heater will not heat	• Coolant does not reach proper temperature • Heater core blocked internally • Heater core air-bound • Blend-air door not in proper position	• Check and replace thermostat if necessary • Flush or replace core if necessary • Purge air from core • Adjust cable
Heater will not defrost	• Control cable adjustment incorrect • Defroster hose damaged	• Adjust control cable • Replace defroster hose

Drive Train 7

UNDERSTANDING THE MANUAL TRANSMISSION

Because of the way an internal combustion engine breathes, it can produce torque, or twisting force, only within a narrow speed range. Most modern, overhead valve engines must turn at about 2,500 rpm to produce their peak torque. By 4,500 rpm they are producing so little torque that continued increases in engine speed produce no power increases.

The manual transmission and clutch are employed to vary the relationship between engine speed and the speed of the wheels so that adequate engine power can be produced under all circumstances. The clutch allows engine torque to be applied to the transmission input shaft gradually, due to mechanical slippage. The car can, consequently, be started smoothly from a full stop.

The transmission changes the ratio between the rotating speeds of the engine and the wheels by the use of gears. On trucks, three-speed or four-speed transmissions are most common. The lower gears allow full engine power to be applied to the rear wheels during acceleration at low speeds.

The transmission contains a mainshaft which passes all the way through the transmission, from the clutch to the driveshaft. This shaft is separated at one point, so that front and rear portions can turn at different speeds.

Power is transmitted by a countershaft in the lower gears and reverse. The gears of the countershaft mesh with gears on the mainshaft, allowing power to be carried from one to the other. All the countershaft gears are integral with that shaft, while several of the mainshaft gears can either rotate independently of the shaft or be locked to it. Shifting from one gear to the next causes one of the gears to be freed from rotating with the shaft and locks another to it. Gears are locked and unlocked by internal dog clutches which slide between the center of the gear and the shaft. The forward gears usually employ synchronizers; friction members which smoothly bring gear and shaft to the same speed before the toothed dog clutches are engaged.

The clutch is operating properly if:
1. It will stall the engine when released with the vehicle held stationary.
2. The shift lever can be moved freely between 1st and reverse gears when the vehicle is stationary and the clutch disengaged.

MANUAL TRANSMISSION

REMOVAL AND INSTALLATION

2-Wheel Drive

1. Raise the outer gearshift lever boot and remove the upper part of the console.
2. Remove the lower part of the console.
3. Remove the inner boot.
4. Remove the gearshift lever.
5. Raise and support the truck on jackstands.
6. Drain the transmission.
7. Matchmark the driveshaft and yoke for installation alignment.
8. Unbolt and remove the driveshaft.

Manual Transmission Application Chart

Transmission Types	Years
Warner T4 4-speed	1984 w/4-150
Warner T5 5-speed	1984 all
AISIN AX4 4-speed	1984–87 w/4-150
AISIN AX5 5-speed	1984–89 all
BA 10/5 5-speed	1988–89 all

Troubleshooting the Manual Transmission and Transfer Case

Problem	Cause	Solution
Transmission shifts hard	• Clutch adjustment incorrect • Clutch linkage or cable binding • Shift rail binding	• Adjust clutch • Lubricate or repair as necessary • Check for mispositioned selector arm roll pin, loose cover bolts, worn shift rail bores, worn shift rail, distorted oil seal, or extension housing not aligned with case. Repair as necessary.
	• Internal bind in transmission caused by shift forks, selector plates, or synchronizer assemblies • Clutch housing misalignment • Incorrect lubricant • Block rings and/or cone seats worn	• Remove, dissemble and inspect transmission. Replace worn or damaged components as necessary. • Check runout at rear face of clutch housing • Drain and refill transmission • Blocking ring to gear clutch tooth face clearance must be 0.030 inch or greater. If clearance is correct it may still be necessary to inspect blocking rings and cone seats for excessive wear. Repair as necessary.
Gear clash when shifting from one gear to another	• Clutch adjustment incorrect • Clutch linkage or cable binding • Clutch housing misalignment • Lubricant level low or incorrect lubricant • Gearshift components, or synchronizer assemblies worn or damaged	• Adjust clutch • Lubricate or repair as necessary • Check runout at rear of clutch housing • Drain and refill transmission and check for lubricant leaks if level was low. Repair as necessary. • Remove, disassemble and inspect transmission. Replace worn or damaged components as necessary.
Transmission noisy	• Lubricant level low or incorrect lubricant • Clutch housing-to-engine, or transmission-to-clutch housing bolts loose • Dirt, chips, foreign material in transmission • Gearshift mechanism, transmission gears, or bearing components worn or damaged • Clutch housing misalignment	• Drain and refill transmission. If lubricant level was low, check for leaks and repair as necessary. • Check and correct bolt torque as necessary • Drain, flush, and refill transmission • Remove, disassemble and inspect transmission. Replace worn or damaged components as necessary. • Check runout at rear face of clutch housing
Jumps out of gear	• Clutch housing misalignment • Gearshift lever loose • Offset lever nylon insert worn or lever attaching nut loose • Gearshift mechanism, shift forks, selector plates, interlock plate, selector arm, shift rail, detent plugs, springs or shift cover worn or damaged • Clutch shaft or roller bearings worn or damaged	• Check runout at rear face of clutch housing • Check lever for worn fork. Tighten loose attaching bolts. • Remove gearshift lever and check for loose offset lever nut or worn insert. Repair or replace as necessary. • Remove, disassemble and inspect transmission cover assembly. Replace worn or damaged components as necessary. • Replace clutch shaft or roller bearings as necessary

Troubleshooting the Manual Transmission and Transfer Case (cont.)

Problem	Cause	Solution
Jumps out of gear (cont.)	• Gear teeth worn or tapered, synchronizer assemblies worn or damaged, excessive end play caused by worn thrust washers or output shaft gears • Pilot bushing worn	• Remove, disassemble, and inspect transmission. Replace worn or damaged components as necessary. • Replace pilot bushing
Will not shift into one gear	• Gearshift selector plates, interlock plate, or selector arm, worn, damaged, or incorrectly assembled • Shift rail detent plunger worn, spring broken, or plug loose • Gearshift lever worn or damaged • Synchronizer sleeves or hubs, damaged or worn	• Remove, disassemble, and inspect transmission cover assembly. Repair or replace components as necessary. • Tighten plug or replace worn or damaged components as necessary • Replace gearshift lever • Remove, disassemble and inspect transmission. Replace worn or damaged components.
Locked in one gear—cannot be shifted out	• Shift rail(s) worn or broken, shifter fork bent, setscrew loose, center detent plug missing or worn • Broken gear teeth on countershaft gear, clutch shaft, or reverse idler gear • Gearshift lever broken or worn, shift mechanism in cover incorrectly assembled or broken, worn damaged gear train components	• Inspect and replace worn or damaged parts • Inspect and replace damaged part • Disassemble transmission. Replace damaged parts or assemble correctly.
Transfer case difficult to shift or will not shift into desired range	• Vehicle speed too great to permit shifting • If vehicle was operated for extended period in 4H mode on dry paved surface, driveline torque load may cause difficult shifting • Transfer case external shift linkage binding • Insufficient or incorrect lubricant • Internal components binding, worn, or damaged	• Stop vehicle and shift into desired range. Or reduce speed to 3–4 km/h (2–3 mph) before attempting to shift. • Stop vehicle, shift transmission to neutral, shift transfer case to 2H mode and operate vehicle in 2H on dry paved surfaces • Lubricate or repair or replace linkage, or tighten loose components as necessary • Drain and refill to edge of fill hole with SAE 85W-90 gear lubricant only • Disassemble unit and replace worn or damaged components as necessary
Transfer case noisy in all drive modes	• Insufficient or incorrect lubricant	• Drain and refill to edge of fill hole with SAE 85W-90 gear lubricant only. Check for leaks and repair if necessary. Note: If unit is still noisy after drain and refill, disassembly and inspection may be required to locate source of noise.
Noisy in—or jumps out of four wheel drive low range	• Transfer case not completely engaged in 4L position • Shift linkage loose or binding • Shift fork cracked, inserts worn, or fork is binding on shift rail	• Stop vehicle, shift transfer case in Neutral, then shift back into 4L position • Tighten, lubricate, or repair linkage as necessary • Disassemble unit and repair as necessary
Lubricant leaking from output shaft seals or from vent	• Transfer case overfilled • Vent closed or restricted	• Drain to correct level • Clear or replace vent if necessary

Troubleshooting the Manual Transmission and Transfer Case (cont.)

Problem	Cause	Solution
Lubricant leaking from output shaft seals or from vent (cont.)	• Output shaft seals damaged or installed incorrectly	• Replace seals. Be sure seal lip faces interior of case when installed. Also be sure yoke seal surfaces are not scored or nicked. Remove scores, nicks with fine sandpaper or replace yoke(s) if necessary.
Abnormal tire wear	• Extended operation on dry hard surface (paved) roads in 4H range	• Operate in 2H on hard surface (paved) roads

9. Position a floor jack under the transmission and take up the weight slightly.
10. Unbolt and remove the rear crossmember.
11. Disconnect the speedometer cable.
12. Disconnect the back-up light switch.
13. Disconnect all linkage and hoses from the transmission.
14. Chain the transmission to the jack.
15. Unbolt the transmission from the engine and lower the jack while pulling back.

To install:
16. Lightly grease the input shaft splines.
17. Raise the transmission into position.
18. Roll the transmission forward and engage the input shaft and clutch disc spline. You might have to wiggle the output shaft yoke to get the splines to mesh. Once the splines mesh, push the trasmission forward all the way and align the bellhousing-to-engine bolt holes. Install the attaching bolts and torque them to 28 ft. lbs.
19. Connect all linkage and hoses at the transmission.
20. Connect the back-up light switch.
21. Connect the speedometer cable.
22. Install the rear crossmember. Torque the crossmember attaching bolt to 30 ft. lbs.; the transmission to crossmember bolts to 33 ft. lbs.
23. Remove the floor jack.
24. Install the driveshaft. Jeep recommends that new strap bolts be used whenever the driveshaft is disconnected. Torque the nuts to 14 ft. lbs.
25. Fill the transmission.
26. Lower the truck.
27. Install the gearshift lever.
28. Install the inner boot.
29. Install the lower part of the console.
30. Install the upper part of the console.

4-Wheel Drive

1. Raise the outer gearshift lever boot and remove the upper part of the console.
2. Remove the lower part of the console.
3. Remove the inner boot.
4. Remove the gearshift lever.
5. Raise and support the truck on jackstands.
6. Drain the transmission and transfer case.
7. Matchmark the rear driveshaft and yoke for installation alignment.
8. Unbolt and remove the rear driveshaft.
9. Position a floor jack under the transmission and tale up the weight slightly.
10. Unbolt and remove the rear crossmember.
11. Disconnect the speedometer cable.
12. Disconnect the back-up light switch.
13. Disconnect the transfer case vent hose at the case.
14. Disconnect all linkage and hoses from the transfer case and transmission.
15. Matchmark the front driveshaft and yoke.
16. Remove the front driveshaft.
17. Chain the transmission to the jack.
18. Unbolt the transmission/transfer case assembly from the engine and lower the jack while pulling back.

To install:
19. If the transmission and transfer case were separated, torque the bolts to 26 ft. lbs.
20. Lightly grease the input shaft splines.
21. Raise the transmission into position.
22. Roll the transmission forward and engage the input shaft and clutch disc spline. You might have to wiggle the output shaft yoke to get the splines to mesh. Once the splines mesh, push the trasmission forward all the way and align the bellhousing-to-engine bolt holes. Install the attaching bolts and torque them to 28 ft. lbs.
23. Install the front driveshaft. Jeep recommends that new strap bolts be used every time the driveshaft is disconnected. Torque the strap bolt nuts to 14 ft. lbs.; the flange-to-transfer case bolts to 35 ft. lbs.
24. Connect all linkage and hoses at the transfer case and transmission.

262   DRIVE TRAIN

25. Connect the transfer case vent hose at the case.
26. Connect the back-up light switch.
27. Connect the speedometer cable.
28. Install the rear crossmember. Torque the crossmember attaching bolts to 30 ft. lbs.; the transmission-to-crossmember bolts to 33 ft. lbs.
29. Remove the floor jack.
30. Install the rear driveshaft. Use new strap bolts. Torque the strap bolt nuts to 14 ft. lbs.; the flange-to-transfer case bolts to 35 ft. lbs.
31. Fill the transmission and transfer case.
32. Lower the truck.
33. Install the gearshift lever.
34. Install the inner boot.
35. Install the lower part of the console.
36. Install the upper part of the console.

Warner T4 Overhaul

CASE DISASSEMBLY

1. Drain the transmission lubricant. 2WD models are not equipped with a drain plug; the fluid must be siphoned from the transmission.
2. Use a pin punch and hammer to remove the offset lever-to-shift rail roll pin.
3. Remove the extension housing (2WD) or the adapter (4WD). Remove the housing and the offset lever as an assembly.
4. Remove the detent ball and spring from the offset lever. Remove the roll pin from the extension housing or adapter.
5. Remove the countershaft rear thrust bearing and race.
6. Remove the transmission cover and shift fork assembly. Two of the transmission cover bolts are alignment type dowel pins. Mark their location so that they may be reinstalled in their original locations.
7. Remove the reverse lever to reverse lever pivot bolt C-clip.
8. Remove the reverse lever pivot bolt. Remove the reverse lever and fork as an assembly.
9. Mark the position of the front bearing cap to case, then remove the bearing cap bolts and cap.
10. Remove the front bearing race and the shims from the bearing cap. Use a small pry bar and remove the front seal from the bearing cap.
11. Rotate the main drive gear shaft until the flat portion of the gear faces the countershaft, then remove the main drive gear shaft assembly.
12. Remove the thrust bearing and 15 roller bearings from the clutch shaft. Remove the output shaft bearing race. Tap the output shaft with a plastic hammer to loosen it if necessary.
13. Tilt the output shaft assembly upward and remove the assembly from the case.
14. Carefully pull off the countershaft rear bearing with the proper puller after marking the position for reinstallation.
15. Move the countershaft rearward and tilt it upward to remove it from the transmission case. Remove the countershaft bearing spacer.
16. Remove the reverse idler shaft roll pin, then remove the reverse idler shaft and gear.
17. Press off the countershaft front bearing. Use the appropriate pullers and remove the bearing from the main drive gear shaft.
18. Remove the extension housing or adapter oil seal and remove the back-up light switch from the case.

OUTPUT SHAFT DISASSEMBLY

1. Remove the thrust bearing washer from the front of the output shaft.
2. Scribe matchmarks on the hub and sleeve of the 3rd-4th synchronizer so that these parts may be reassembled properly.
3. Remove the 3rd-4th synchronizer blocking ring, sleeve and hub as an assembly.
4. Remove the insert springs and the inserts from the 3rd-4th synchronizer and separate the sleeve from the hub.
5. Remove the 3rd speed gear from the shaft.
6. Remove the 2nd speed gear to output shaft snapring, the tabbed thrust washer and the 2nd speed gear from the shaft.
7. Use an appropriate puller and remove the the output shaft bearing.
8. Remove the 1st gear thrust washer, the roll pin, the 1st speed gear and the blocking ring.
9. Scribe matchmarks on the 1st-2nd synchronizer sleeve and the output shaft.
10. Remove the insert spring and the inserts from the 1st-reverse sliding gear, then remove the gear from the output hub.

OUTPUT SHAFT ASSEMBLY

1. Coat the output shaft and the gear bores with transmission lubricant.
2. Align the matchmarks and install the 1st-2nd synchronizer sleeve on the output shaft hub.
3. Install the three inserts and two springs into the 1st-reverse synchronizer sleeve.
NOTE: *The tanged end of each spring should be positioned on the same insert but the open face of each spring should be opposite each other.*
4. Install the blocking ring and the 2nd speed gear onto the output shaft.
5. Install the tabbed thrust washer and 2nd gear snapring in the output shaft; be sure that the washer is properly seated in the notch.

DRIVE TRAIN 263

6. Install the blocking ring and the 1st speed gear onto the output shaft, then install the 1st gear roll pin.

7. Press the rear bearing onto the shaft.

8. Install the remaining components onto the output shaft: The 1st gear thrust washer. The 3rd speed gear. The 3rd-4th synchronizer hub inserts and the sleeve (the hub offset must face forward). The thrust bearing washer on the rear of the countershaft.

COVER & FORKS DISASSEMBLY

1. Place the selector arm plates and the shift rail centered in the Neutral position.

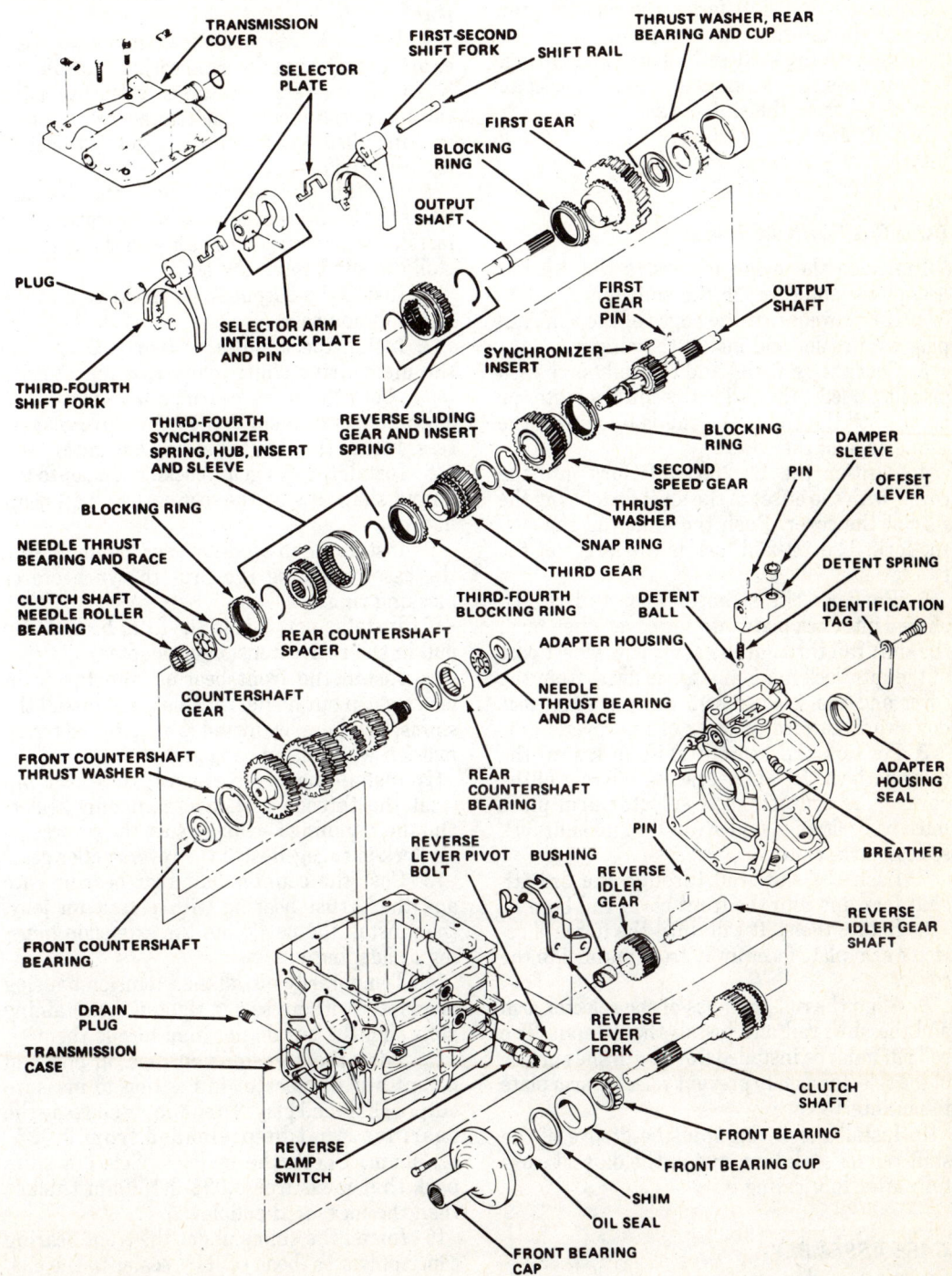

DRIVE TRAIN

2. Rotate the shift rail counterclockwise until the selector arm disengages from the selector arm plates; the selector arm roll pin should now be accessible.
3. Pull the shift rail rearward until the selector contacts the 1st-2nd shift fork.
4. Use a 3/16" pin punch and remove the selector arm roll pin and the shift rail.
5. Remove the shift forks, the selector arm, the roll pin and the interlock plate.
6. Remove the shift rail oil seal and O-ring.
7. Remove the nylon inserts and the selector arm plates from the shift forks.
NOTE: *Mark the position of the parts so that they may be properly installed.*

COVER & FORK ASSEMBLY

1. Attach the nylon inserts to the selector arm plates and through the shift forks.
2. If removed, coat the edges of the shift rail plug with sealer and install the plug.
3. Coat the shift rail and the rail bores with petroleum jelly, then slide the shift rail into the cover until the end of the rail is flush with the inside edge of the cover.
4. Position the 1st-2nd shift fork into the cover; with the offset of the shift fork facing the rear of the cover. Push the shift rail through the fork. The 1st-2nd fork is the larger of the two forks.
5. Position the selector arm and the C-shaped interlock plate into the cover, then push the shift rail through the arm. The widest part of the interlock plate must face away from the cover and the selector arm roll pin must face downward, toward the rear of the cover.
6. Position the 3rd-4th shift fork into the cover with the fork offset facing the rear of the cover. The 3rd-4th shift selector arm plate must be positioned under the 1st-2nd shift fork selector arm plate.
7. Push the shift rail through the 3rd-4th shift fork and into the front cover rail bore.
8. Rotate the shift rail until the forward selector arm plate faces away from parallel to the cover.
9. Align the roll pin holes of the selector arm and the shift rail and install the roll pin. The roll pin must be installed flush with the surface of the selector arm to prevent selector arm plate to pin interference.
10. Install the O-ring into the groove of the shift rail oil seal, then install the oil seal carefully after lubricating it.

CASE ASSEMBLY

1. Apply a coat of Loctite® 601, or equivalent, to the outer cage of the front countershaft bearing, then press the bearing into the bore until it is flush with the case.
2. Apply petroleum jelly to the tabbed countershaft thrust washer and install the washer with the tab engaged in the corresponding case depression.
3. Tip the transmission case on end and install the countershaft into the front bearing bore.
4. Install the rear countershaft bearing spacer and coat the rear bearing with petroleum jelly. Install the rear countershaft bearing using the appropriate tools. The rear bearing is properly installed when 3mm is extended beyond the case surface.
5. Position the reverse idler into the case (the shift lever groove must face rearward) and install the reverse idler shaft into the case. Install the shaft retaining pin.
6. Install the output shaft assembly into the transmission case.
7. Install the main drive gear bearing onto the main drive shaft using the appropriate tools. Coat the roller bearings with petroleum jelly and install them in the main drive gear recess. Install the thrust bearing and race.
8. Install the 4th gear blocking ring onto the output shaft. Install the rear output shaft bearing race.
9. Install the main drive gear assembly into the case, engaging the 3rd-4th synchronizer blocking ring.
10. Install a new seal in the front bearing cap and in the rear extension or adapter.
11. Install the front bearing into the front bearing cap but do not (at this time) install the shims. Temporarily install the cap to the transmission without applying sealer.
12. Install the reverse lever, the pivot pin (coat the threads with non-hardening sealer) and the retaining C-clip. Be sure the reverse lever fork is engaged with the reverse idler gear.
13. Coat the countershaft rear bearing race and the thrust bearing with petroleum jelly, then install the parts into the extension housing or adapter.
14. Temporarily install the extension housing or adapter without sealer, tighten the retaining bolts slightly, but do not final torque them.
15. Turn the transmission case on end and mount a dial indicator in position to measure output shaft end play. To eliminate end play the bearings must be preloaded from 0.025-0.130mm. Check the endplay. Select a shim pack that measures 0.025-0.130mm thicker than the measured endplay.
16. Install the shims under the front bearing cap. Apply a 1/8" bead of RTV sealer to the cap. Align the reference marks and install the cap on the front of the transmission. Torque the

mounting bolts to 15 ft. lbs. Recheck the output shaft end play, none should exist. Adjust if necessary.

17. Remove the extension housing or adapter. Move the shift forks and synchronizer sleeves to their neutral position. Apply a ⅛" bead of RTV sealer to the cover to case mounting surface. Align the forks with their sleeves and carefully lower the cover into position. Center the cover and install the alignment dowels. Install the mounting bolts and tighten to 9 ft. lbs.

NOTE: *The offset lever to shift rail roll pin must be position vertically; if not, repeat Step 17.*

18. Apply a ⅛". bead of RTV sealer to the extension housing or adapter and install over the output shaft.

NOTE: *The shift rail must be positioned so that it just enters the shift cover opening.*

19. Install the detent spring into the offset lever and place the steel ball into the Neutral guide plate detent. Apply pressure to the detent spring and offset lever, then slide the offset lever on the shift rail and seat the extension housing or adapter plate against the transmission case. Install and tighten the mounting bolts to 25 ft. lbs.

20. Install the roll pin into the offset lever and shift rail. Install the damper sleeve in the offset lever. Coat the back up lamp switch threads with sealer and install the switch, tighten to 15 ft. lbs.

Warner T5 Overhaul

CASE DISASSEMBLY

1. Remove drain bolt on transmission case and drain lubricant.
2. Thoroughly clean the exterior of the transmission assembly.
3. Using pin punch and hammer, remove roll pin attaching offset lever to shift rail.
4. Remove extension housing-to-transmission case bolts and remove housing and offset lever as an assembly.

NOTE: *Do not attempt to remove the offset lever while the extension housing is still bolted in place. The lever has a positioning lug engaged in the housing detent plate which prevents moving the lever far enough for removal.*

5. Remove detent ball and spring from offset lever and remove roll pin from extension housing or offset lever.
6. Remove plastic funnel, thrust bearing race and thrust bearing from rear of countershaft.

NOTE: *The countershaft rear thrust bearing, bearing washer and plastic funnel may be found inside the extension housing.*

7. Remove bolts attaching transmission cover and shift fork assembly and remove cover.

NOTE: *Two of the transmission cover attaching bolts are alignment-type dowel bolts. Note the location of these bolts for assembly reference.*

8. Using a punch and hammer, drive the roll pin from the 5th gearshift fork while supporting the end of the shaft with a block of wood.
9. Remove 5th synchronizer gear snapring, shift fork, 5th gear synchronizer sleeve, blocking ring and 5th speed drive gear from rear of countershaft.
10. Remove snapring from 5th speed driven gear.
11. Using a hammer and punch, mark both bearing cap and case for assembly reference.
12. Remove front bearing cap bolts and remove front bearing cap. Remove front bearing race and end play shims from front bearing cap.
13. Rotate drive gear until flat surface faces countershaft and remove drive gear from transmission case.
14. Remove reverse lever C-clip and pivot bolt.
15. Remove mainshaft rear bearing race and then tilt mainshaft assembly upward and remove assembly from transmission case.
16. Unhook overcenter link spring from front of transmission case.
17. Rotate 5th gear-reverse shift rail to disengage rail from reverse lever assembly. Remove shift rail from rear of transmission case.
18. Remove reverse lever and fork assembly from transmission case.
19. Using hammer and punch, drive roll pin from forward end of reverse idler shaft and remove reverse idler shaft, rubber "O" ring and gear from the transmission case.
20. Remove rear countershaft snapring and spacer.
21. Insert a brass drift through drive gear opening in front of transmission case and, using an arbor press, carefully press countershaft rearward to remove rear countershaft bearing.
22. Move countershaft assembly rearward, tilt countershaft upward and remove from case. Remove countershaft front thrust washer and rear bearing spacer.
23. Remove countershaft front bearing from transmission case using an arbor press.

MAINSHAFT DISASSEMBLY

1. Remove thrust bearing washer from front end of mainshaft.
2. Scribe reference mark on 3rd-4th synchronizer hub and sleeve for reassembly.
3. Remove 3rd-4th synchronizer blocking ring, sleeve, hub and 3rd gear as an assembly from mainshaft.

266 DRIVE TRAIN

4. Remove snapring, tabbed thrust washer, and 2nd gear from mainshaft.
5. Remove 5th gear with Tool J-22912-01 or its equal and arbor press. Slide rear bearing off mainshaft.
6. Remove 1st gear thrust washer, roll pin, 1st gear and synchronizer ring from mainshaft.
7. Scribe reference mark on 1st-2nd synchronizer hub and sleeve for reassembly.
8. Remove synchronizer spring and keys

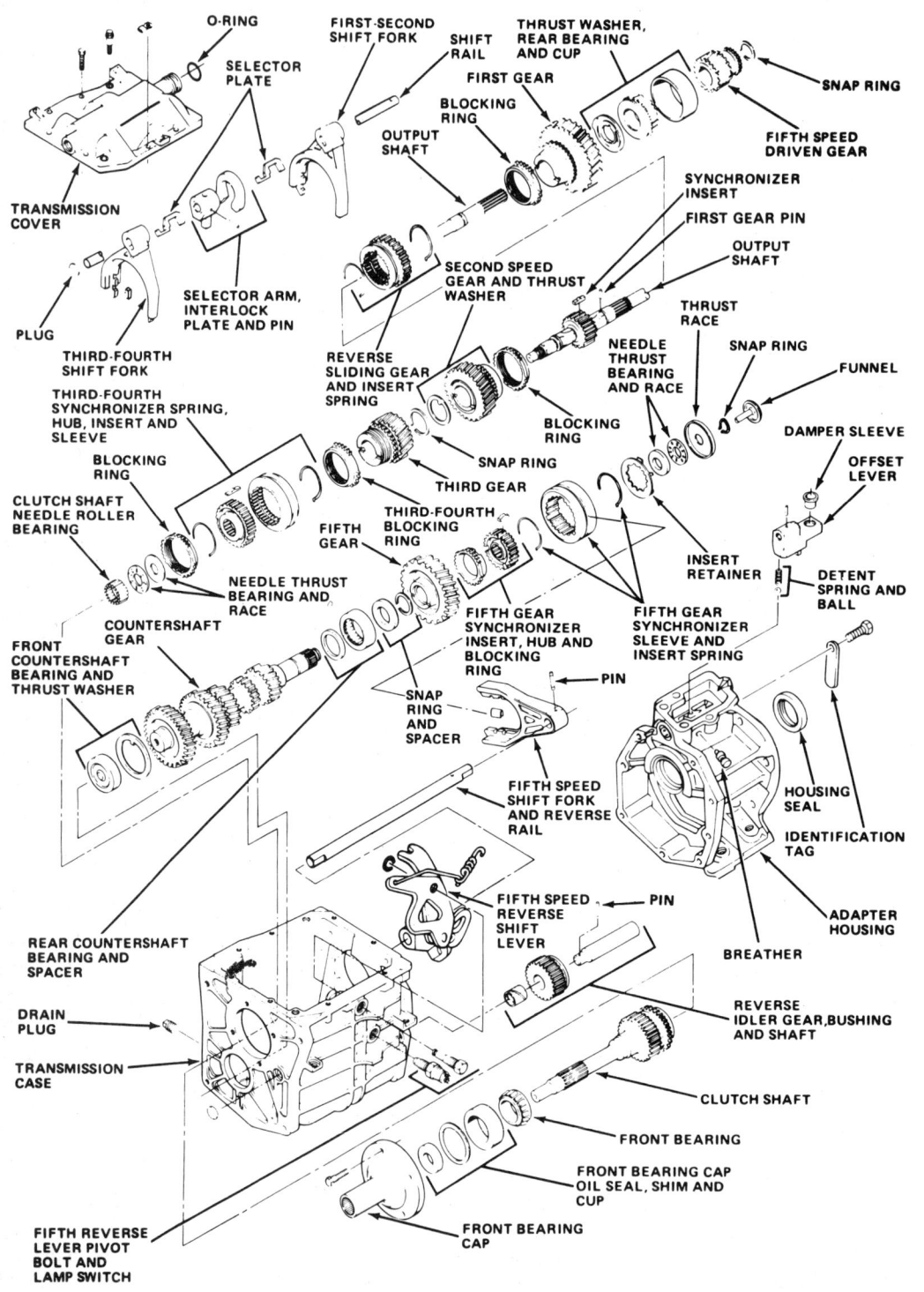

from 1st-reverse sliding gear and remove gear from mainshaft hub. Do not attempt to remove the 1st-2nd-reverse hub from mainshaft. The hub and shaft are assembled and machined as a matched set.

DRIVE GEAR DISASSEMBLY

1. Remove bearing race, thrust bearing, and roller bearings from cavity of drive gear.
2. Using Tool J-22912-01 or its equal and arbor press, remove bearing from drive gear.
3. Wash parts in a cleaning solvent.
4. Inspect gear teeth and drive shaft pilot for wear.

DRIVE GEAR ASSEMBLY

1. Using Tool J-22912-01 or its equal with an arbor press, install bearing on drive gear.
2. Coat roller bearings and drive gear bearing bore with grease. Install roller bearings into bore of drive gear.
3. Install thrust bearing and race in drive gear.

MAINSHAFT ASSEMBLY

1. Coat mainshaft and gear bores with transmission lubricant.
2. Install 1st-2nd synchronizer sleeve on mainshaft hub aligning marks made at disassembly.
3. Install 1st-2nd synchronizer keys and springs. Engage tang end of each spring in same synchronizer key but position open end of springs opposite of each other.
4. Install blocker ring and 2nd gear on mainshaft. Install tabbed thrust washer and 2nd gear retaining snapring on mainshaft. Be sure washer tab is properly seated in mainshaft notch.
5. Install blocker ring and 1st gear on mainshaft. Install 1st gear roll pin and then 1st gear thrust washer.
6. Slide rear bearing on mainshaft.
7. Install 5th speed gear on mainshaft using Tool J-22912-01 and arbor press. Install snapring on mainshaft.
8. Install 3rd gear, 3rd-4th synchronizer assembly and thrust bearing on mainshaft. Synchronizer hub offset must face forward.

CASE ASSEMBLY

1. Coat countershaft front bearing bore with Loctite 601, or equivalent, and install front countershaft bearing flush with facing of case using an arbor press.
2. Coat countershaft tabbed thrust washer with grease and install washer so tab engages depression in case.
3. Tip transmission case on end and install countershaft in front bearing bore.
4. Install countershaft rear bearing spacer. Coat countershaft rear bearing with grease and install bearing using Tool J-29895 and sleeve J-33032, or its equivalent. The bearing when correctly installed will extend beyond the case surface 3mm.
5. Position reverse idler gear in case with shift lever groove facing rear of case and install reverse idler shaft from rear of case. Install roll pin in idler shaft.
6. Install assembled mainshaft in transmission case. Install rear mainshaft bearing race in case.
7. Install drive gear in case, and engage in 3rd-4th synchronizer sleeve and blocker ring.
8. Install front bearing race in front bearing cap. Do not install shims in front bearing cap at this time.
9. Temporarily install front bearing cap.
10. Install 5th speed-reverse lever, pivot bolt and retaining clip. Coat pivot bolt threads with nonhardening sealer. Be sure to engage reverse lever fork in reverse idler gear.
11. Install countershaft rear bearing spacer and retaining snapring.
12. Install 5th speed gear on countershaft.
13. Insert 5th speed-reverse rail in rear of case and install in to reverse 5th speed lever. Rotate rail during installation to simplify engagement with lever. Connect spring to front of case.
14. Position 5th gear shift fork on 5th gear synchronizer assembly and install synchronizer on countershaft and shift fork on shift rail. Make sure roll pin hole in shift fork and shift rail are aligned.
15. Support 5th gear shift rail and fork on a block of wood and install roll pin.
16. Install thrust race against 5th speed synchronizer hub and install snapring. Install thrust bearing against race on countershaft. Coat both bearing and race with petroleum jelly.
17. Install lipped thrust race over needle-type thrust bearing and install plastic funnel into hole in end of countershaft gear.
18. Temporarily install extension housing and attaching bolts. Turn transmission case on end, and mount a dial indicator on extension housing with indicator on the end of mainshaft.
19. Rotate mainshaft and zero dial indicator. Pull upward on mainshaft until end play is removed and record reading. Mainshaft bearings require a preload of 0.025-0.130mm. To set preload, select a shim pack measuring 0.025-0.130mm greater than the dial indicator reading recorded.
20. Remove front bearing cap and front bearing race. Install necessary shims to obtain preload and reinstall bearing race.

268 DRIVE TRAIN

21. Apply a ⅛" bead of RTV sealant, #732 or equivalent, on case mating surface of front bearing cap. Install bearing cap aligning marks made during disassembly and torque bolts to specification.
22. Remove extension housing.
23. Move shift forks on transmission cover and synchronizer sleeves inside transmission to the neutral position.
24. Apply a ⅛" bead of RTV sealant, #732 or equivalent, on cover mating surface of transmission.
25. Lower cover onto case while aligning shift forks and synchronizer sleeves. Center cover and install the 2 dowel bolts. Install remaining bolts and torque to specification. The offset lever to shift rail roll pin hole must be in the vertical position after cover installation.
26. Apply a ⅛" bead of RTV Sealant, #732 or equivalent, on extension housing to transmission case mating surface.
27. Install extension housing over mainshaft and shift rail to a position where shift rail just enters shift cover opening.
28. Install detent spring into offset lever and place steel ball in neutral guide plate detent. Position offset lever on steel ball and apply pressure on offset lever and at the time seat extension housing against transmission case.
29. Install extension housing bolts and torque to specification.
30. Align and install roll pin in offset lever and shift rail.
31. Fill transmission to its proper level with lubricant.

AX4 Overhaul

Model AX4 is a 4-speed manual transmission. The transmission has synchromesh engagement in all forward gears controlled by a floor shift mechanism integrated into the transmission top cover.

NOTE: *The following components and materials must be replaced whenever the transmission is overhauled: Lip-type oil seals. Lock nuts. All roll pins. All snaprings. Loctite Thread®Lock or Loctite®242 Sealer should be used on all fasteners.*

DISASSEMBLY

1. Remove the clutch housing.
2. Remove the straight screw plug, spring and ball using a Torx bit to remove the screw plug, and a magnet to remove spring and ball.
3. Remove five adapter housing bolts and one nut.
4. Remove the shift lever housing set bolt and lock plate.
5. Remove the plug at the rear of the shift fork shaft.
6. Remove the large magnet to pull the shaft out.

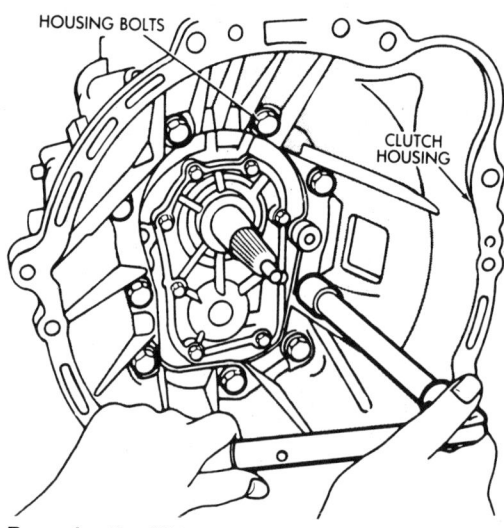

Removing the AX4 or AX5 clutch housing

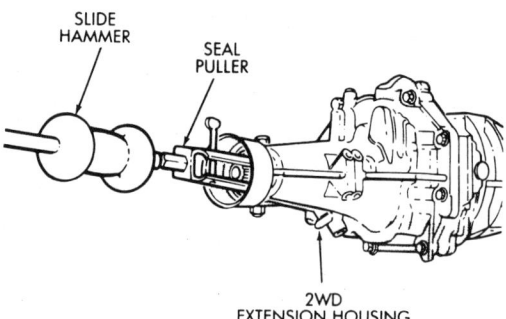

Removing the 2wd extension housing seal from the AX4 or AX5

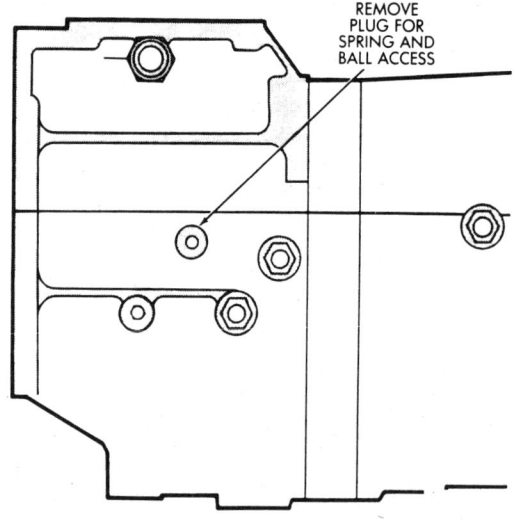

Detent ball plug location on the AX4 or AX5

7. Remove the select lever from the top while rotating.
8. Remove the five adapter housing bolts two studs and one nut.
9. Using a plastic hammer, tap and remove the extension housing. Leave the gasket attached to the intermediate plate.
10. Remove the front bearing retainer and outer snaprings from the two front bearings.
11. Separate the intermediate plate from the transmission case using a small plastic hammer and remove the case.
12. Mount the intermediate plate in a vise. Be careful not to damage the plate.

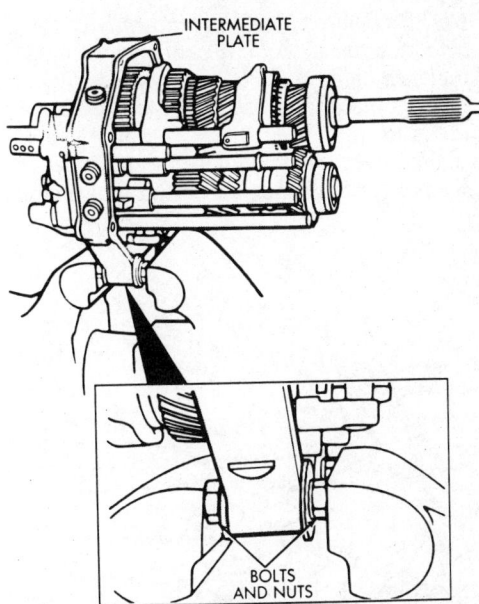

Positioning the intermediate plate in a vise

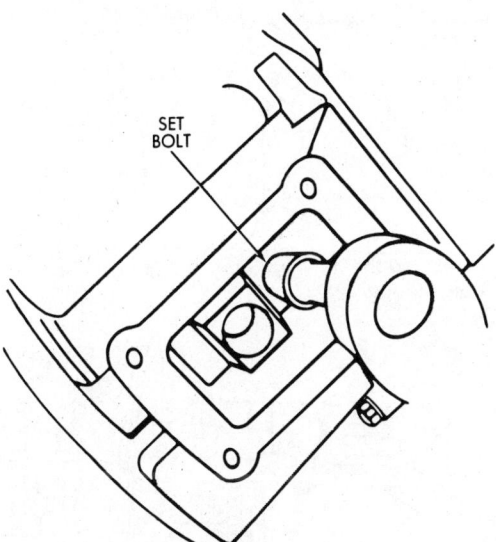

Set bolt removal from the AX4 or AX5

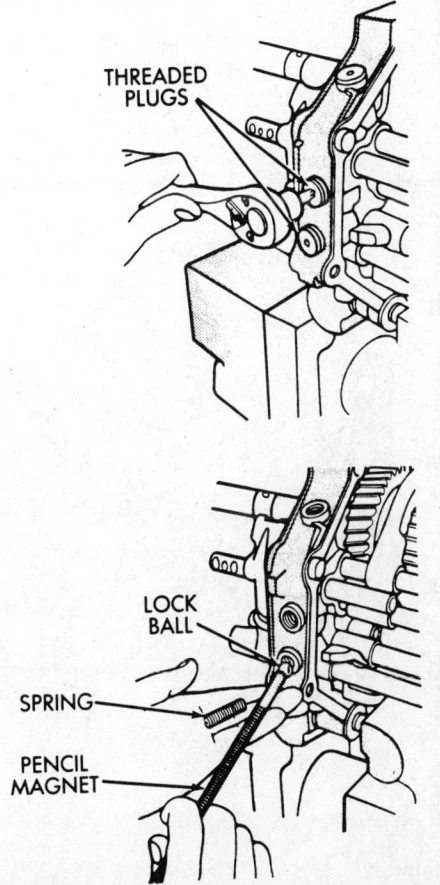

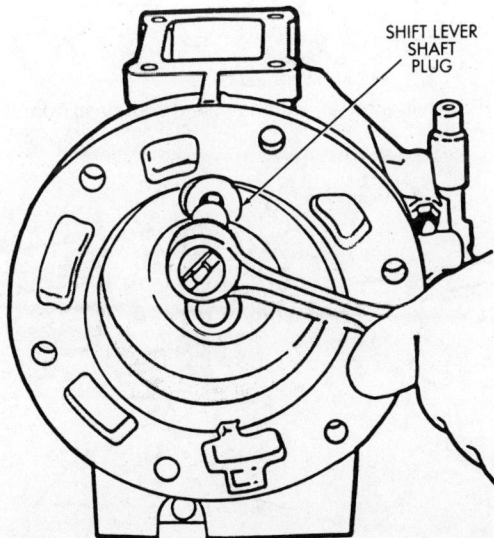

Removing the shift lever shaft plug from the AX4 or AX5

Removing the lock ball and spring from the AX4 or AX5

270 DRIVE TRAIN

NOTE: *Before placing the intermediate plate in a vise, insert bolts, washers, and nuts in the open holes at the bottom of plate. Tighten vise against these bolts to prevent damage to the plate.*

13. Remove the straight screw plug, locking balls and springs using a Torx bit and magnet.

14. Remove the five slotted spring pins using a hammer and punch and then remove the two E-rings from the shift rails.

CAUTION: *The locking ball from the reverse*

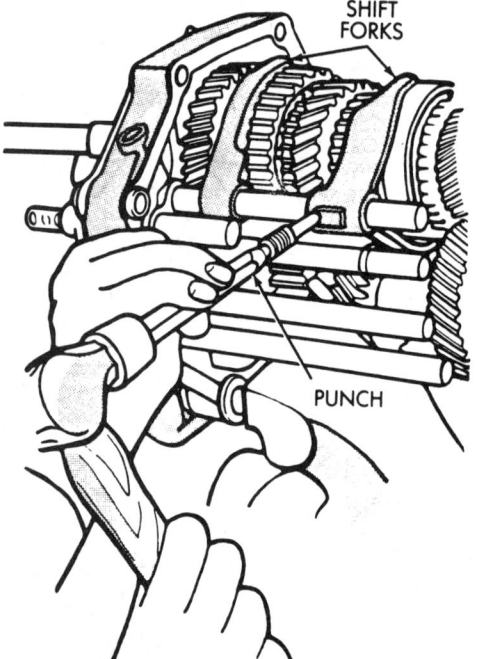

Removing the shift fork pin from the AX4 or AX5

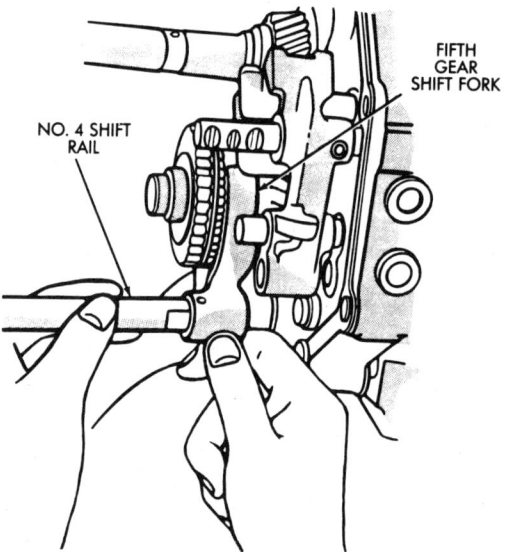

Removing the no. 4 shift rail and 5th gear shift fork from the AX5

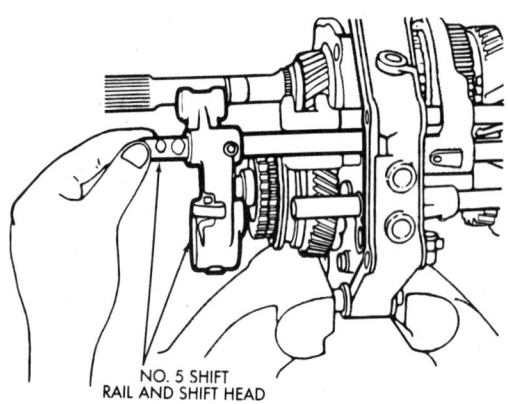

Removing the no. 5 shift rail and shift head from the AX5

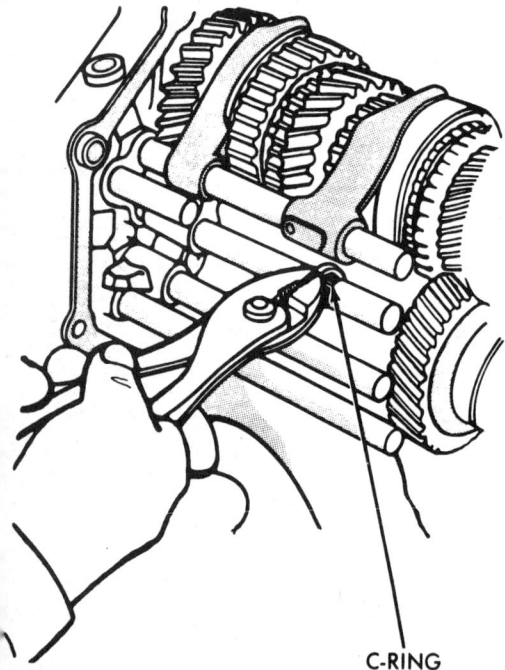

Shift rail C-ring removal from the AX4 or AX5

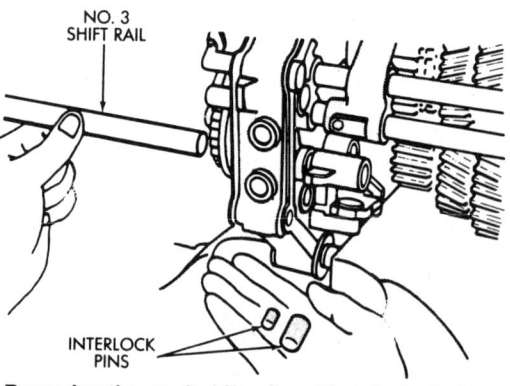

Removing the no. 3 shift rail and interlock pin from the AX4 or AX5

shift head and locking ball and pin from the intermediate housing will fall from the holes so be sure to catch them. If they do not come out, remove them with a magnet.

15. Pull out the shift fork shaft No. 4 from the intermediate plate and catch the locking ball.

16. Remove shift fork shaft No. 4 gear fork.

CAUTION: *The interlock pins will fall from their hole. If they do not come out, remove them with a magnet.*

18. Remove the shift fork shaft No. 3 from the intermediate plate and catch the interlock pins.

CAUTION: *The interlock pin will fall from the hole so be sure to catch it. If it does not come out, remove it with a magnet.*

19. Remove shift fork shaft No. 1 from the intermediate plate being careful not to drop the interlock pin.

20. Remove shift fork shaft No. 2, shift fork No. 2 and shift fork No. 1.

21. Remove the reverse idle gear shaft stopper, reverse idler gear and shaft.

22. Remove the reverse shift arm from the reverse shift arm bracket.

23. Engage two gears to lock the output shaft. Using a hammer and chisel, loosen the staked part of the nut on the countershaft.

24. Remove the lock nut. Disengage the gears.

25. Remove the spacer and use a magnet to remove the ball.

26. Remove the reverse shift arm bracket.

27. Remove the rear bearing retainer bolts with a Torx bit and the snapring using snapring pliers.

28. Remove the output shaft, counter gear and input shaft as a unit from the intermediate plate by pulling on the counter gear and tapping on the intermediate plate with a plastic hammer.

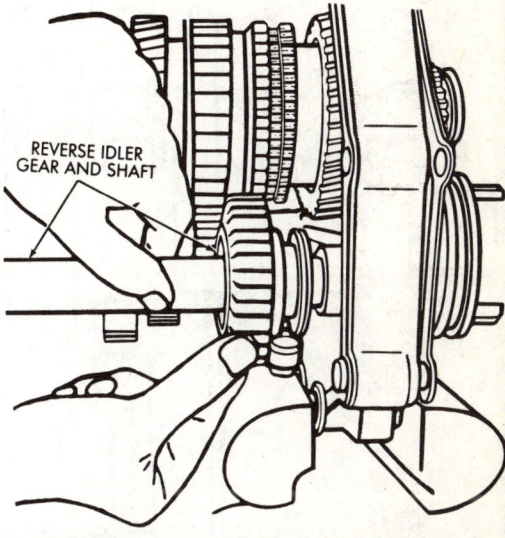

Removing the reverse idler gear and shaft from the AX4 or AX5

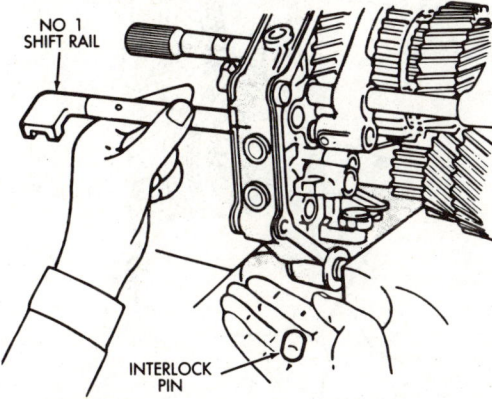

Removing the no. 1 shift rail and interlock pin from the AX4 or AX5

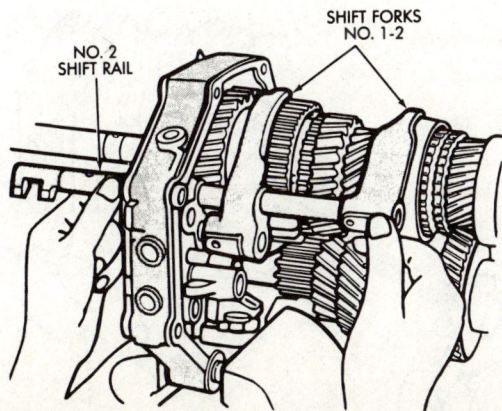

Removing the shift forks and no. 2 shift rail from the AX4 or AX5

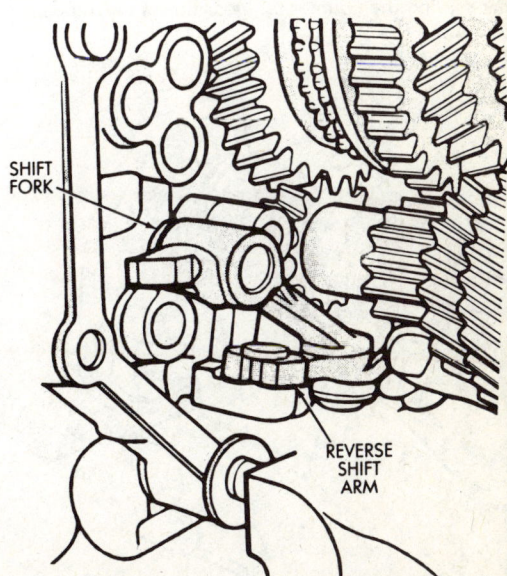

Reverse shift arm removal from the AX4 or AX5

272 DRIVE TRAIN

29. Remove the input shaft with fourteen needle roller bearings from the output shaft.
30. Remove the counter rear bearing from the intermediate plate.
31. Measure the thrust clearance of each gear. Standard Clearance: 0.100-2.540mm.
32. Using two awls and a hammer, tap out the snapring.
33. Using a press, remove the rear bearing, 1st gear and the inner race.
34. Remove the needle roller bearing.
35. Remove the synchronizer ring and locking ball.
36. Using a press, remove hub sleeve No. 1 assembly, synchronizer ring, 2nd gear.
37. Remove the needle roller bearing.
38. Remove the snapring from hub sleeve No. 2.
39. Using a press, remove the hub sleeve, synchronizer ring, and 3rd gear.
40. Remove the needle roller bearing.

COMPONENT INSPECTION

Output Shaft & Inner Race

1. Check the output shaft and inner race for wear or damage.
2. Using calipers, measure the output shaft flange thickness. Minimum thickness is 4.8mm.
3. Using calipers, measure the inner face flange thickness. Minimum thickness is 4.0mm.

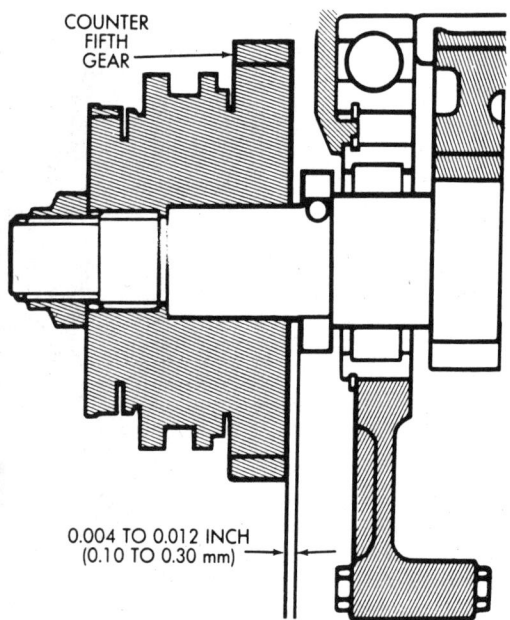

Measuring the counter 5th gear thrust clearance on the AX5

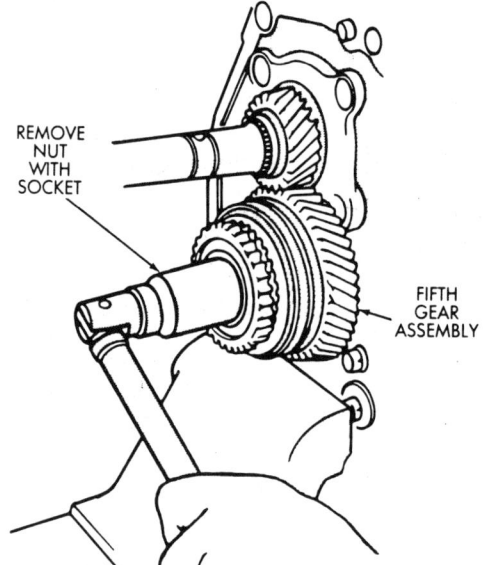

Removing the 5th gear nut from the AX5

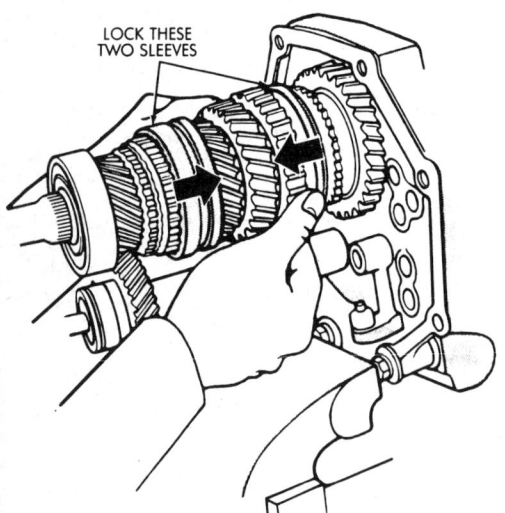

Locking the mainshaft gears on the AX4 or AX5

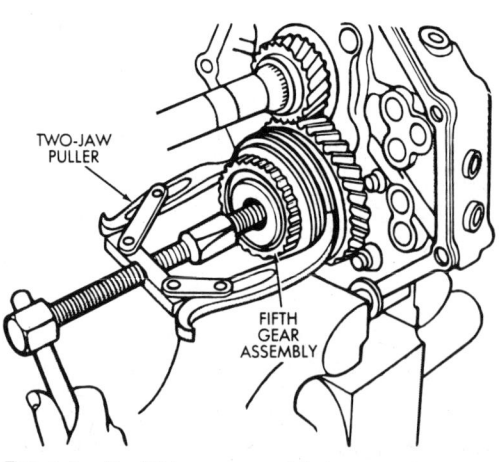

Removing the 5th gear assembly from the AX5

DRIVE TRAIN

4. Using a micrometer, measure the outer diameter of the output shaft journal surface. 2nd Gear minimum is 38mm; 3rd Gear minimum is 35mm.
5. Using a micrometer, measure the outer diameter of the inner race. Minimum diameter is 39mm.
6. Using a dial indicator, measure the shaft runout. Maximum runout is 0.05mm.

1st Gear Oil Clearance

1. Using a dial indicator, measure the oil clearance between the gear and inner race with the needle roller bearing installed. Standard clearance is 0.010-0.033mm.

2. Using a dial indicator, measure the oil clearance between the gear and shaft with the needle roller bearing installed. Standard clearance for 2nd and 3rd gears is 0.010-0.033mm.

Synchronizer Ring Inspection

1. Check for wear or damage. Turn the ring and push it in to check the braking action.
2. Measure the clearance between the synchronizer ring back and the gear spline end.

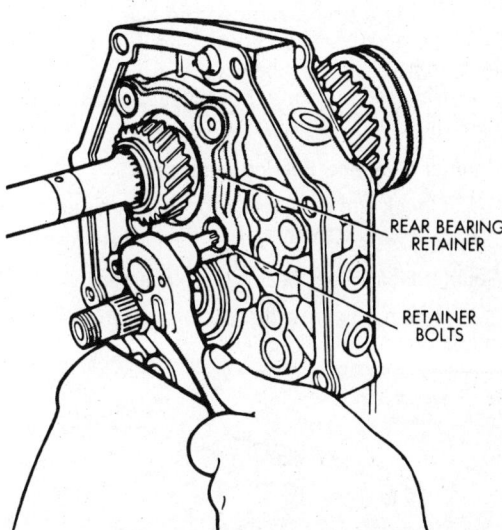

Removing the rear bearing retainer from the AX4 or AX5

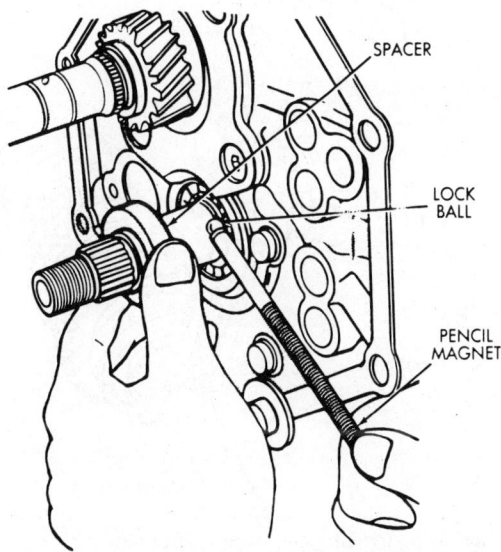

Spacer and lock ball removal from the AX4 or AX5

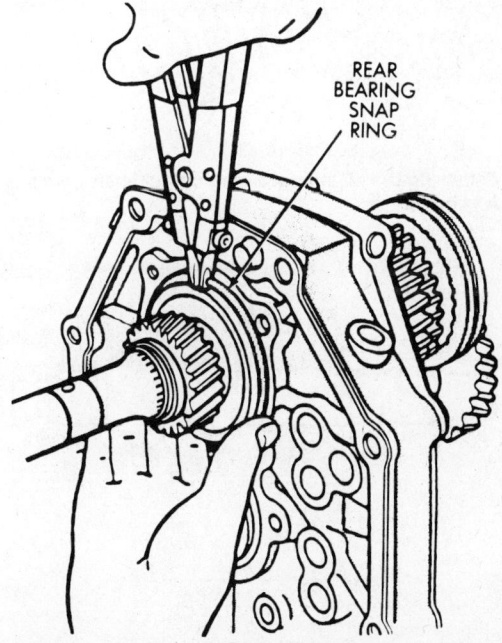

Removing the rear bearing snapring from the AX4 or AX5

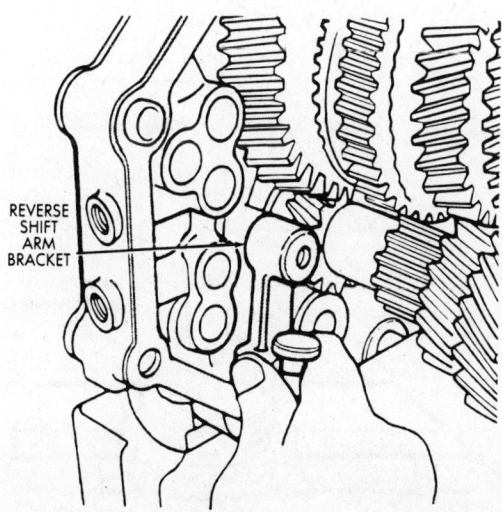

Removing the reverse shift arm bracket from the AX4 or AX5

274 DRIVE TRAIN

Standard clearance is 1.00-2.00mm; minimum clearance is 0.8mm.

Shift Fork and Hub Sleeve Clearance

Using a feeler gauge, measure the clearance between the hub sleeve and shift fork. Maximum Clearance: 1.0mm.

Input Shaft and Bearing Inspection and Removal

1. Check for wear or damage. If necessary, remove the bearing snapring using snapring pliers and remove the bearing.
2. Using a press, remove the bearing.
3. Using a press and tool J-34603 or equivalent, install the new bearing.
4. Select a snapring that will allow minimum axial play and install it on the shaft.

Counter Gear and Bearing Inspection

1. Check the gear teeth for wear or damage.
2. Check the bearing for wear or damage.

Counter Gear Front Bearing Replacement

1. Using snapring pliers, remove the snapring.

2. Press out the bearing using tool J-22912-01 or equivalent.
3. Replace the side race.
4. Using tool J-28406 or equivalent, press in the bearing and inner race.
5. Select a snapring that will allow minimum axial play and install it on the shaft.

Front Bearing Retainer Inspection

1. Check retainer for damage.
2. Check the oil seal lip for wear or damage.

OIL SEAL REPLACEMENT

1. Using a awl, pry the old seal out of the housing.

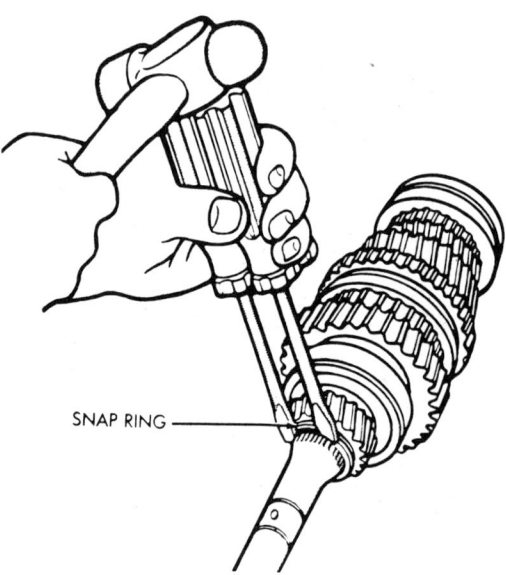

Removing the 5th gear snapring from the AX5

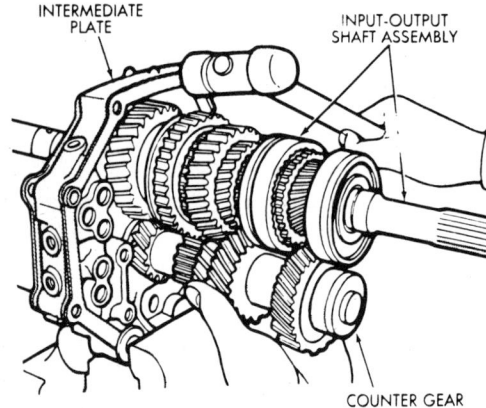

Removing the counter gear and output shaft from the AX4 or AX5

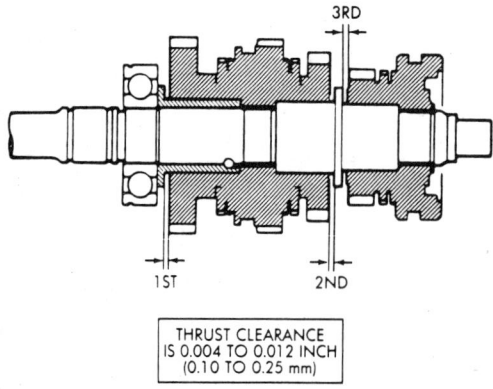

Checking the output shaft gear thrust clearance on the AX4 or AX5

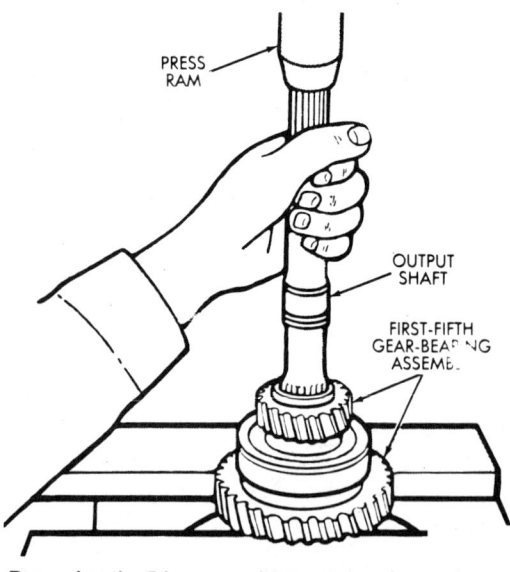

Removing the 5th gear and 1st gear bearing and race from the AX5

2. Press in the new oil seal using tool J-34602 or equivalent.
3. The oil seal depth is 11.20-12.20mm from the housing-to-transmission surface to the top edge of the seal.

REVERSE RESTRICT PIN REPLACEMENT

1. Check for wear or damage.
2. Using a Torx bit, remove the screw plug.
3. Using a hammer and pin punch, drive out the slotted spring pin.
4. Pull off the lever housing and slide out the shaft.
5. Install the lever housing.
6. Using a hammer and pin punch, drive out the slotted spring pin.
7. Using a Torx bit, install and torque the screw plug to 27 ft. lbs. torque.

ADAPTER HOUSING & OIL SEAL INSPECTION & REPLACEMENT

1. Check the adapter housing for wear or damage.
2. Replace the oil seal with tool J-29184 or equivalent.

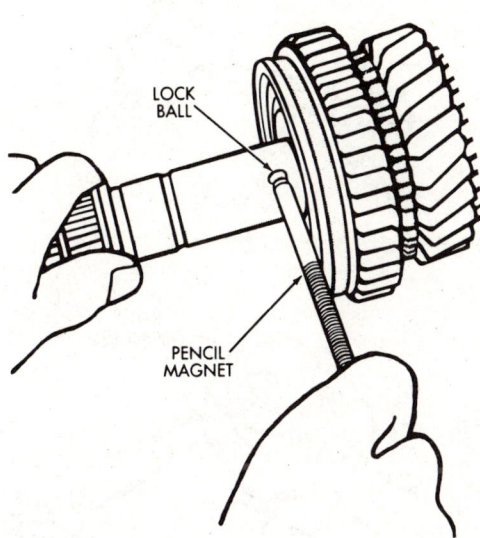

Synchronizer lock ball removal from the AX4 or AX5

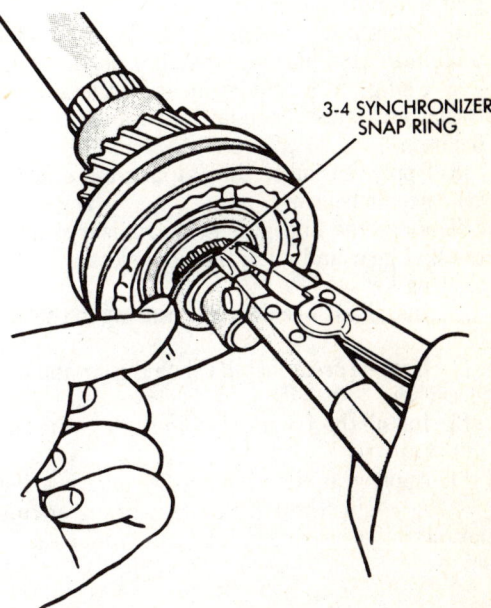

Removing the 3rd-4th synchronizer snapring from the AX4 or AX5

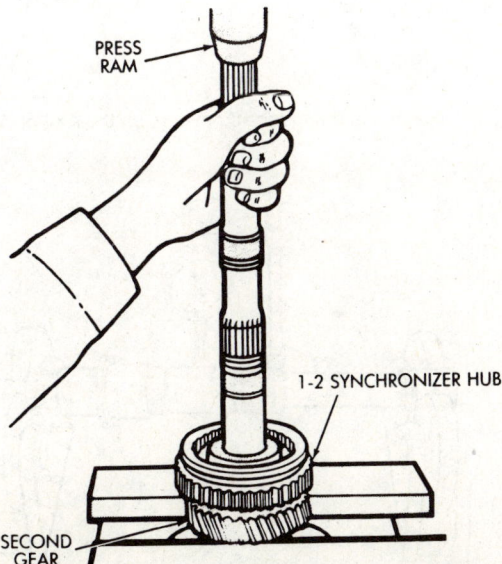

1st-2nd synchronizer/2nd gear removal from the AX4 or AX5

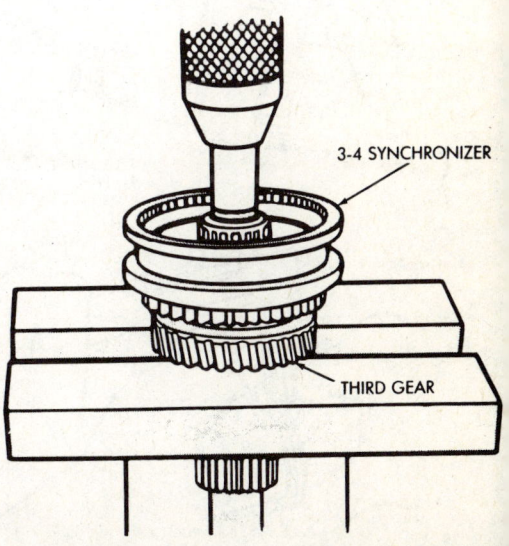

Removing the 3rd-4th synchronizer and 3rd gear from the AX4 or AX5

DRIVE TRAIN

ASSEMBLY

1. Install the clutch hub No. 1 and No. 2 into hub sleeves along with the shifting keys.
   WARNING: *Install the key springs so their gaps are not in line.*
2. Install the shifting springs under the shifting keys.
3. Apply gear oil on the output shaft and 3rd gear needle roller bearing.
4. Place the 3rd gear synchronizer ring on the gear and align the ring slots with the shifting keys.
5. Install the needle roller bearing in the 3rd gear and hub sleeve No. 2.
6. Select a new snapring (2) that will allow minimum axial play and install it on the shaft.
7. Using a feeler gauge, measure the 3rd gear thrust clearance. Standard clearance is 0.10-0.25mm.
8. Apply gear oil on the output shaft and 2nd gear needle bearing.
9. Place the 2nd gear synchronizer ring on the 2nd gear and align the ring slots with the shifting keys.
10. Install the needle roller bearing in the 2nd gear.
11. Using a press install the 2nd gear and hub sleeve No. 1.
13. Install the 1st gear locking ball in the output shaft.
14. Apply gear oil to the needle roller bearing.
15. Assemble the 1st gear, synchronizer ring, needle roller bearing and bearing inner race.
16. Install the assembly on the output shaft, with the synchronizer ring slots aligned with the shifting keys.
17. Turn the inner race to align it with the locking ball.
18. Install the output shaft rear bearing using tool J-34603 or equivalent and a press.

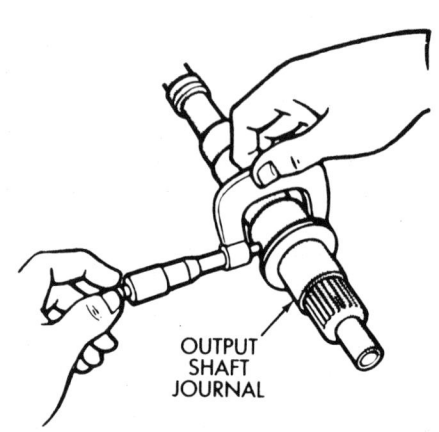

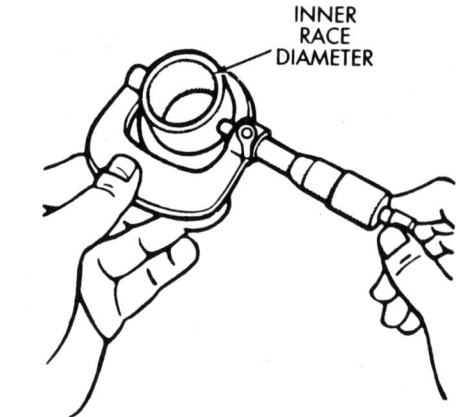

Checking shaft and race diameters on the AX4 or AX5

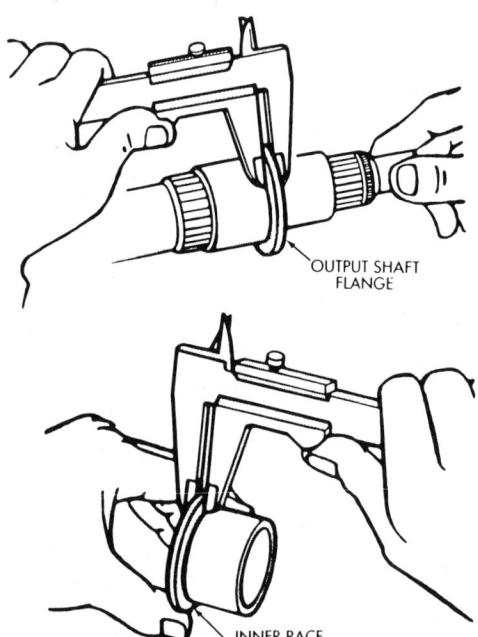

Checking flange thickness on the AX4 or AX5

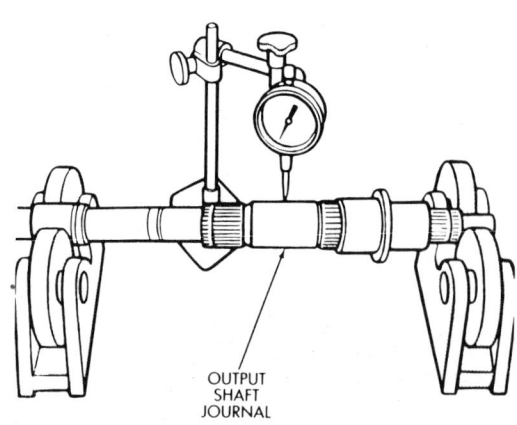

Checking output shaft runout on the AX4 or AX5

DRIVE TRAIN 277

19. Install the bearing on the output shaft with the outer race snapring groove toward the rear.

NOTE: *Hold the 1st gear inner race to prevent it from falling.*

20. Measure the 1st and 2nd gear thrust clearance with a feeler gauge. Standard clearance is 0.10-0.25mm.
21. Select a snapring that will allow minimum axial play.
22. Using a screwdriver and a hammer, tap the snap into position.
23. Apply multi-purpose grease to the fourteen needle roller bearings and install them in the input shaft.
24. Install the output shaft into the intermediate plate by pulling on the output shaft and tapping on the intermediate plate.
25. Install the input shaft to the output shaft with the synchronizer ring slots aligned with the shifting keys.
26. Install the counter gear into the intermediate plate while holding the counter gear, and install the counter rear bearing with a suitable driver.
27. Install the bearing snapring using snapring pliers.

NOTE: *Be sure the snapring is flush with the intermediate plate surface.*

28. Using a Torx bit, install and tighten the screws to 13 ft. lbs. torque.
29. Install the reverse shift arm bracket and tighten the bolts to 13 ft. lbs. torque.
30. Install the ball and spacer.
31. Install shifting key springs under the shifting keys.
32. Install the synchronizer ring on gear spline piece.

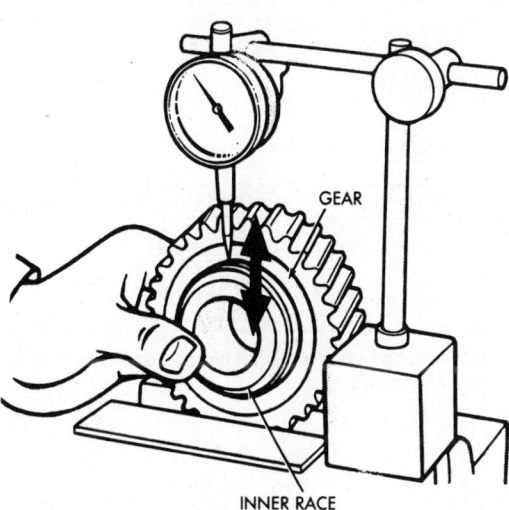

Checking gear-to-race clearance on the AX4 or AX5

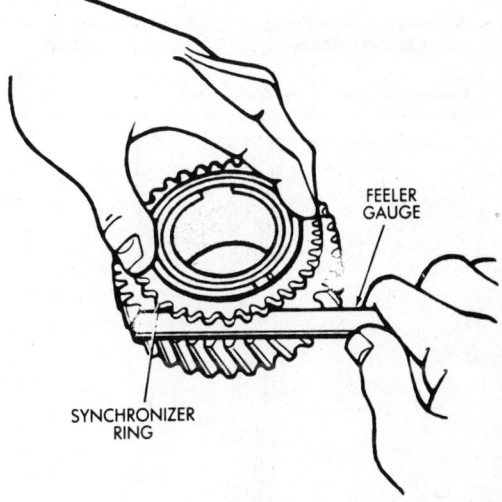

Checking synchronizer ring wear on the AX4 or AX5

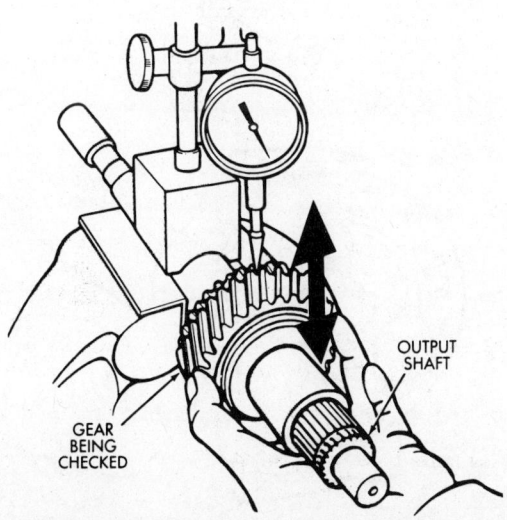

Checking gear-to-shaft clearance on the AX4 or AX5

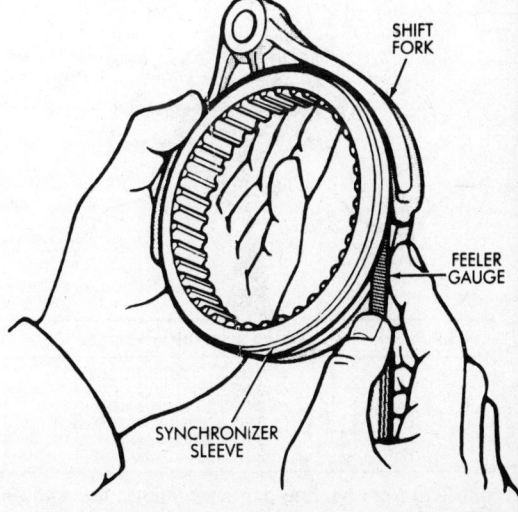

Checking fork-to-hub clearance on the AX4 or AX5

33. Engage two gears to lock the output shaft.
34. Install and tighten the lock nut to 90 ft. lbs. torque on the counter shaft.
35. Stake the lock nut.
36. Disengage the gears.
37. Install the reverse shift arm to the pivot of the reverse shift arm bracket.
38. Install the reverse idler gear on the shaft.
39. Align the reverse shift arm shoe to the reverse idler gear groove and insert the reverse idler gear shift to the intermediate plate.
40. Install the reverse idler gear shaft stopper and tighten the bolt to 13 ft. lbs. torque.
41. Place shift forks No. 1 and No. 2 into groove of hub sleeves No. 1 and No. 2 and install fork shaft No. 2 to the shift forks No. 1 and No. 2 through the intermediate plate.
42. Apply multi-purpose grease to the interlock pins.
43. Using a magnet and screwdriver, install the interlock pin into the intermediate plate.

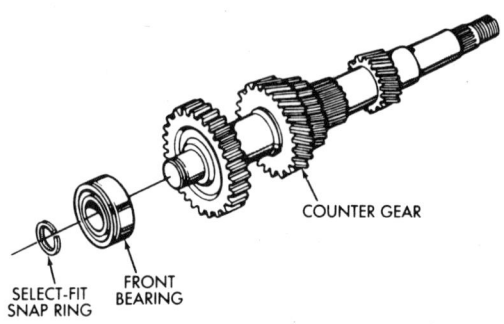

I.D. Mark	Snap Ring Thickness mm (in.)
1	2.05-2.10 (0.0807-0.0827)
2	2.10-2.15 (0.0827-0.0846)
3	2.15-2.20 (0.0846-0.0866)
4	2.20-2.25 (0.0866-0.0886)
5	2.25-2.30 (0.0886-0.0906)
6	2.30-2.35 (0.0906-0.0925)

Installing counter gear front bearing and snapring on the AX4 or AX5

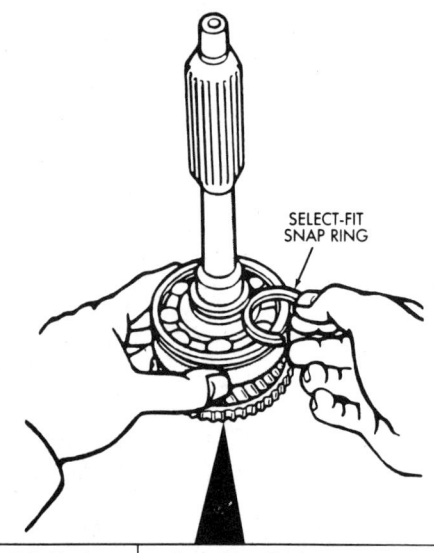

I.D. Mark	Snap Ring Thickness mm (in.)
0	2.05-2.10 (0.0807-0.0827)
1	2.10-2.15 (0.0827-0.0846)
2	2.15-2.20 (0.0846-0.0866)
3	2.20-2.25 (0.0866-0.0886)
4	2.25-2.30 (0.0886-0.0906)
5	2.30-2.35 (0.0906-0.0925)

Installing front bearing and snapring on the AX4 or AX5

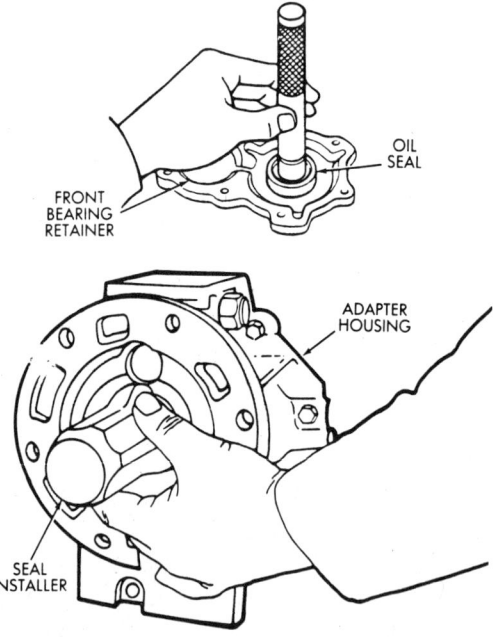

Oil seal installation on the AX4 or AX5

44. Install the interlock pin into the shaft hole.
45. Install fork shaft No. 1 to shift fork No. 1 through the intermediate plate.
46. Using a magnet and screwdriver, install the interlock pin into the intermediate plate.
47. Install the interlock pin into the shaft hole.
48. Install fork shaft No. 3 to the reverse shift arm through the intermediate plate.
49. Using a magnetic finger and screwdriver, install the locking ball into the reverse shift head hole.
50. Place shift fork No. 3 into the groove of hub sleeve No. 3 and install fork shaft No. 4 to shift fork No. 3 and reverse shift arm.
51. Using a magnet and screwdriver, install the locking ball into the intermediate plate and insert fork shaft No. 4 to the intermediate plate.
52. Check the interlock by positioning the shift fork shaft No. 1 to the 1st speed position.
53. Fork shafts No. 2, No. 3 and No. 4 should not move.
54. Using a pin punch and a hammer, drive in new slotted spring pins in each shift fork, reverse shift arm and reverse shift head.
55. Install two fork shaft E-rings.
56. Apply liquid sealer to the screw plugs.
57. Install the locking balls, springs and screw plugs with a Torx bit and tighten to 14 ft. lbs. torque.

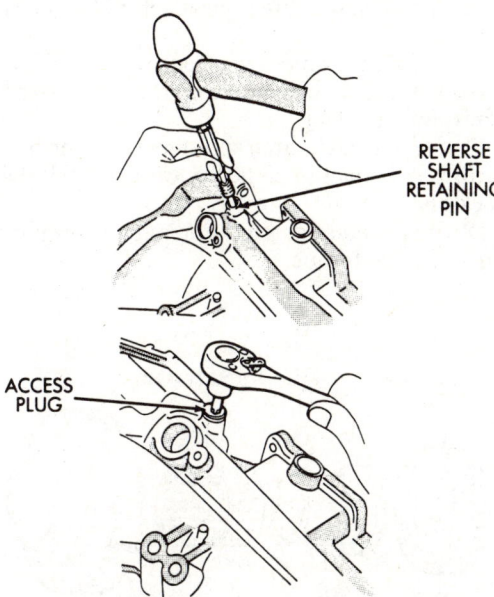

Installing the reverse shaft pin on the AX4 or AX5

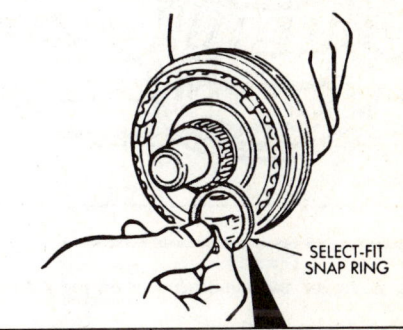

I.D. Mark	Snap Ring Thickness mm (in.)
C-1	1.75-1.80 (0.0689-0.0709)
D	1.80-1.85 (0.0709-0.0728)
D-1	1.85-1.90 (0.0728-0.0748)
E	1.90-1.95 (0.0748-0.0768)
E-1	1.95-2.00 (0.0768-0.0787)
F	2.00-2.05 (0.0788-0.0807)
F-1	2.05-2.10 (0.0807-0.0827)

Installing 3rd gear and 3rd-4th synchronizer on the AX4 or AX5

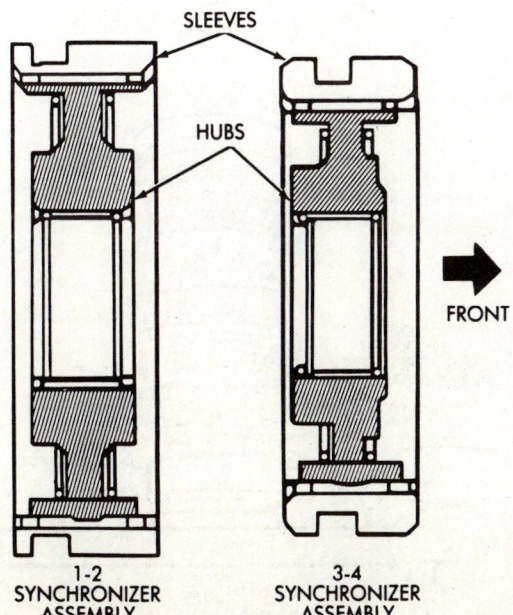

Synchronizer identification on the AX4 or AX5

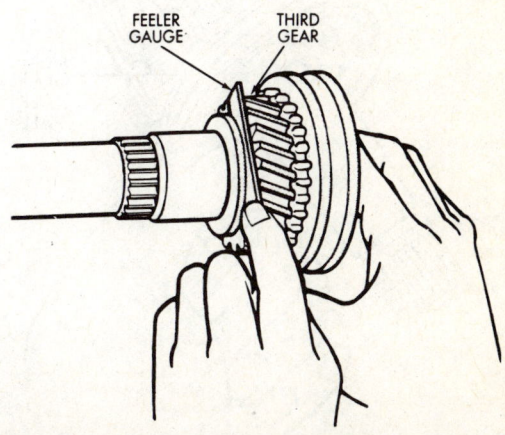

Checking 3rd gear clearance on the AX4 or AX5

280 DRIVE TRAIN

NOTE: *Install the short spring into the tower of the intermediate plate.*

58. Remove the intermediate plate from the vise.

59. Remove the bolts, nuts, washers and gasket.

CASE INSTALLATION

1. Align each bearing outer race, each fork shaft end and reverse idler gear with the holes in the case and install the case on the intermediate plate. If necessary, tap on the case with a plastic hammer.

2. Install two new bearing snaprings.

3. Install front bearing retainer with a new gasket.

4. Apply liquid sealer to the bolts.

5. Install and tighten the bolts to 12 ft. lbs. torque.

6. Install the new gasket to the intermediate plate.

7. Install the adapter housing.

8. Install and tighten the adapter bolts to 27 ft. lbs. torque.

9. Install the shift lever housing.

10. Insert the shift lever into the adapter and shift lever housing.

11. Install and tighten shift lever housing bolt with a lock plate to 28 ft. lbs. torque. Lock the lock plate.

12. Install and tighten the adapter screw plug to 13 ft. lbs. torque.

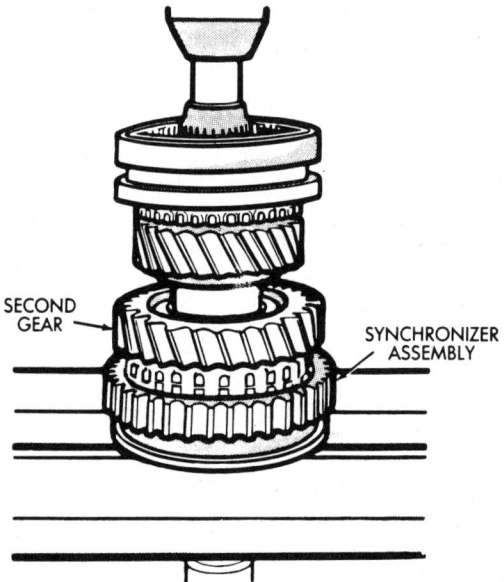

Installing 2nd gear and synchronizer on the AX4 or AX5

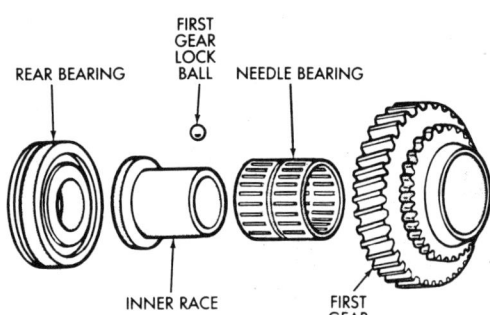

1st gear assembled on the AX4 or AX5

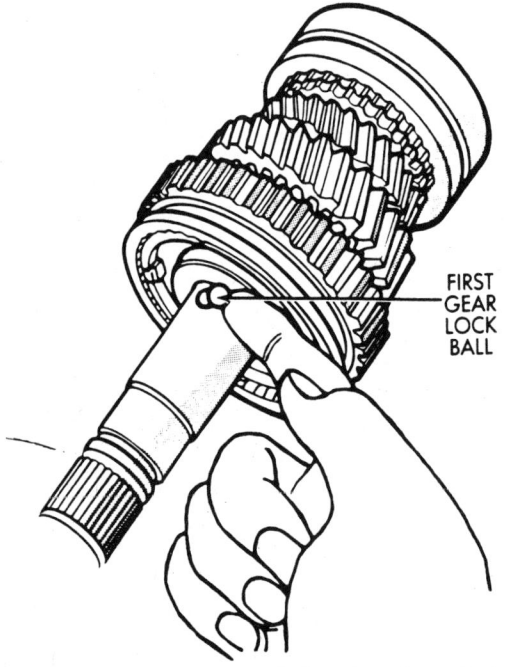

Installing 1st gear and lock ball on the AX4 or AX5

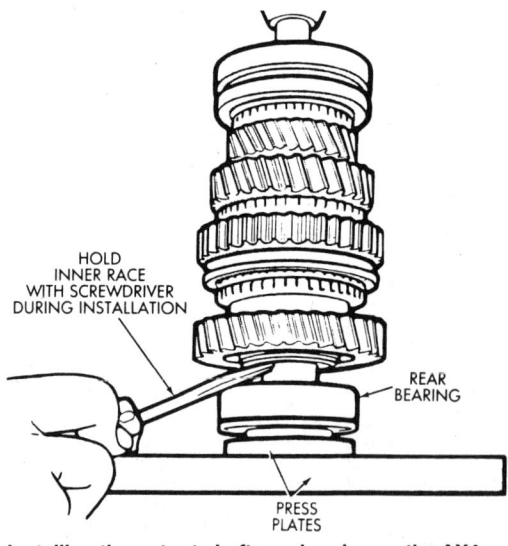

Installing the output shaft rear bearing on the AX4 or AX5

13. Apply liquid sealer to the plug.
14. Install the locking ball, spring and screw plug and tighten the plug to 14 ft. lbs. torque.
15. Check to see that the input shaft and output shafts rotate smoothly.
16. Check to see that shifting can be done smoothly to all positions.
17. Install the black restrict pin on the reverse gear.
18. Install the remaining pin and tighten the pins to 20 ft. lbs. torque.
19. Install the shift lever retainer with a new gasket and tighten the bolts to 13 ft. lbs. torque.
20. Install the back-up light switch and tighten to 27 ft. lbs. torque.
21. Install the clutch housing and tighten the bolts to 27 ft. lbs. torque.

AX 5 Overhaul

Model AX 5 is a 5-speed manual transmission. The transmission has synchromesh engagement in all forward gears controlled by a floor shift mechanism integrated into the transmission top cover.

NOTE: *The following components and materials must be replaced whenever the trans-*

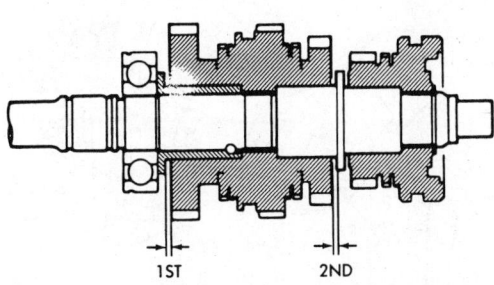

Checking 1st-2nd gear clearance on the AX4 or AX5

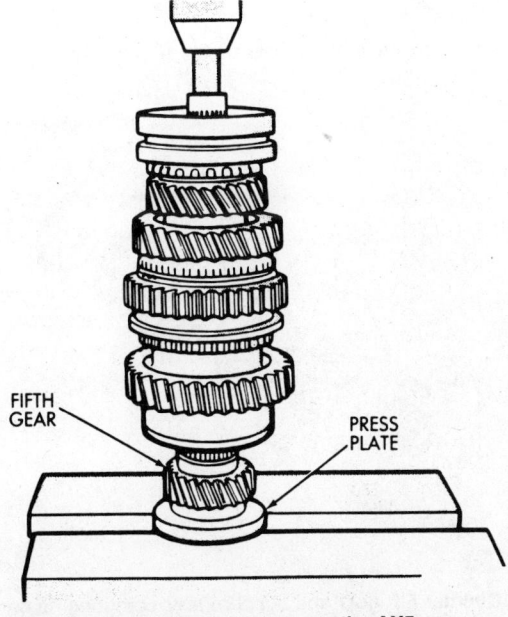

Installing output shaft 5th gear on the AX5

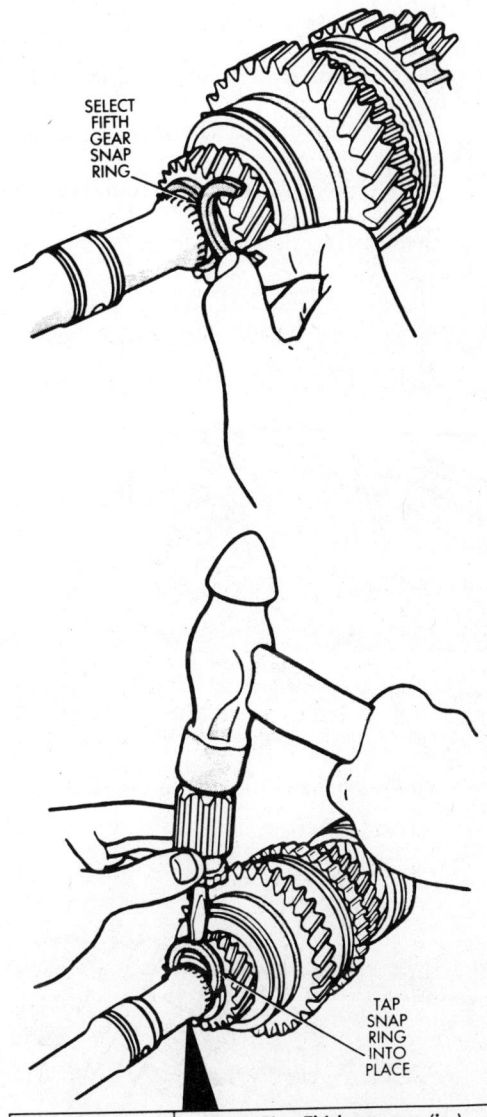

I.D. Mark	Snap Ring Thickness mm (in.)
A	2.67-2.72 (0.1051-0.1071)
B	2.73-2.78 (0.1075-0.1094)
C	2.79-2.84 (0.1098-0.1118)
D	2.85-2.90 (0.1122-0.1142)
E	2.91-2.96 (0.1146-0.1165)
F	2.97-3.02 (0.1169-0.1189)
G	3.03-3.08 (0.1193-0.1213)
H	3.09-3.14 (0.1217-0.1236)
J	3.15-3.20 (0.1240-0.1260)
K	3.21-3.26 (0.1264-0.1283)
L	3.27-3.32 (0.1287-0.1307)

Selecting and installing the 5th gear snapring on the AX5

282 DRIVE TRAIN

mission is overhauled: Lip-type oil seals. Lock nuts. All roll pins. All snaprings. Loctite® Thread Lock or Loctite® 242 Sealer should be used on all fasteners.

DISASSEMBLY

1. Remove the clutch housing.
2. Remove the straight screw plug, spring and ball using a Torx bit to remove the screw plug, and a magnet to remove spring and ball.
3. Remove five adapter housing bolts and one nut.
4. Remove the shift lever housing set bolt and lock plate.
5. Remove the plug at the rear of the shift fork shaft.
6. Remove the large magnet to pull the shaft out.
7. Remove the select lever from the top while rotating.
8. Remove the five adapter housing bolts two studs and one nut.
9. Using a plastic hammer, tap and remove the extension housing. Leave the gasket attached to the intermediate plate.
10. Remove the front bearing retainer and outer snaprings from the two front bearings.
11. Separate the intermediate plate from the transmission case using a small plastic hammer and remove the case.
12. Mount the intermediate plate in a vise. Be careful not to damage the plate.

NOTE: *Before placing the intermediate plate in a vise, insert bolts, washers, and nuts in the open holes at the bottom of plate. Tighten vise against these bolts to prevent damage to the plate.*

13. Remove the straight screw plug, locking

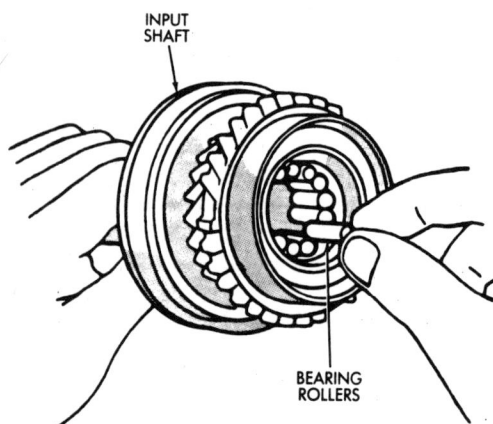

Installing the input shaft bearing rollers on the AX4 or AX5

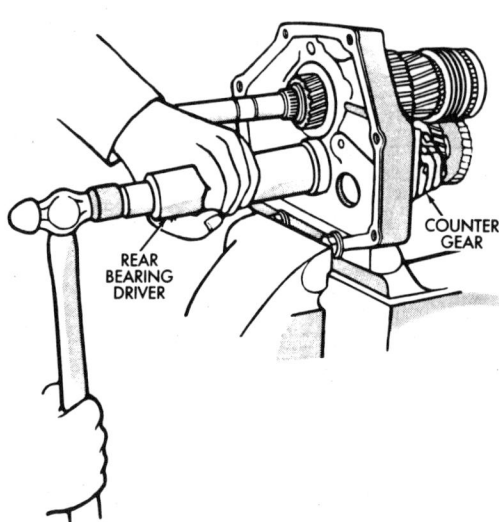

Installing the counter gear on the AX4 or AX5

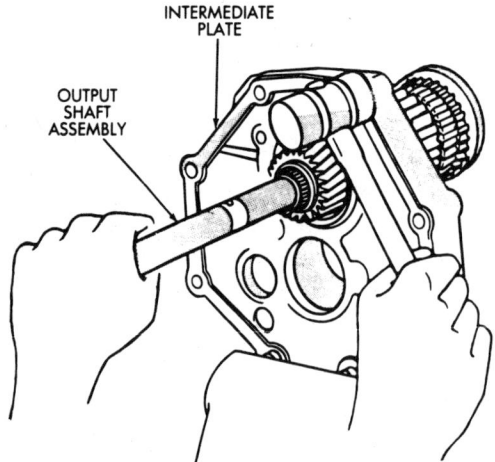

Installing the output shaft in the intermediate plate on the AX4 or AX5

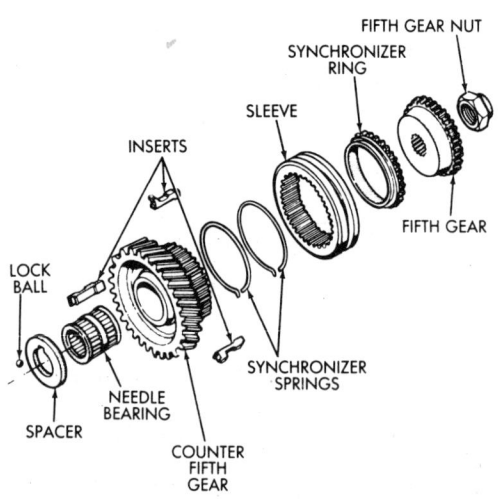

Counter 5th gear and synchronizer components on the AX5

DRIVE TRAIN 283

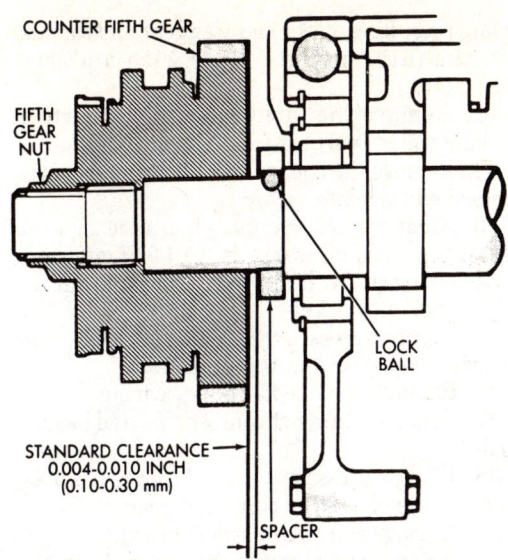

balls and springs using a Torx bit and magnet.

14. Remove the five slotted spring pins using a hammer and punch and then remove the two E-rings from the shift rails.

CAUTION: *The locking ball from the reverse shift head and locking ball and pin from the intermediate housing will fall from the holes so be sure to catch them. If they do not come out, remove them with a magnet.*

15. Pull out the shift fork shaft No. 4 from the intermediate plate and catch the locking ball.
16. Remove shift fork shaft No. 4 and the 5th gear fork.
17. Pull out shift fork shaft No. 5 from the intermediate plate, and remove it with the reverse shift head.

CAUTION: *The interlock pins will fall from their hole. If they do not come out, remove them with a magnet.*

18. Remove the shift fork shaft No. 3 from the

Checking 5th gear thrust clearance on the AX5

1. Reverse fork and shift arm
2. 1–2 shift fork
3. 3–4 shift fork
4. Lock ball, spring and plug
5. Bracket bolt
6. No. 3 shift rail
7. No. 1 shift rail
8. C-ring
9. No. 2 shift rail
10. C-ring
11. Lock ball, spring and plug
12. Shift arm
13. Set bolt and lock plate
14. Shift lever shaft
15. Shaft plug
16. Reverse pin
17. Retaining pin and plug
18. No. 5 shift rail
19. Interlock pin
20. Interlock pin
21. Interlock pin
22. C-ring
23. Interlock pin
24. Fifth-reverse fork
25. Reverse shift head
26. Lock balls
27. No. 4 shift rail
28. Reverse arm bracket

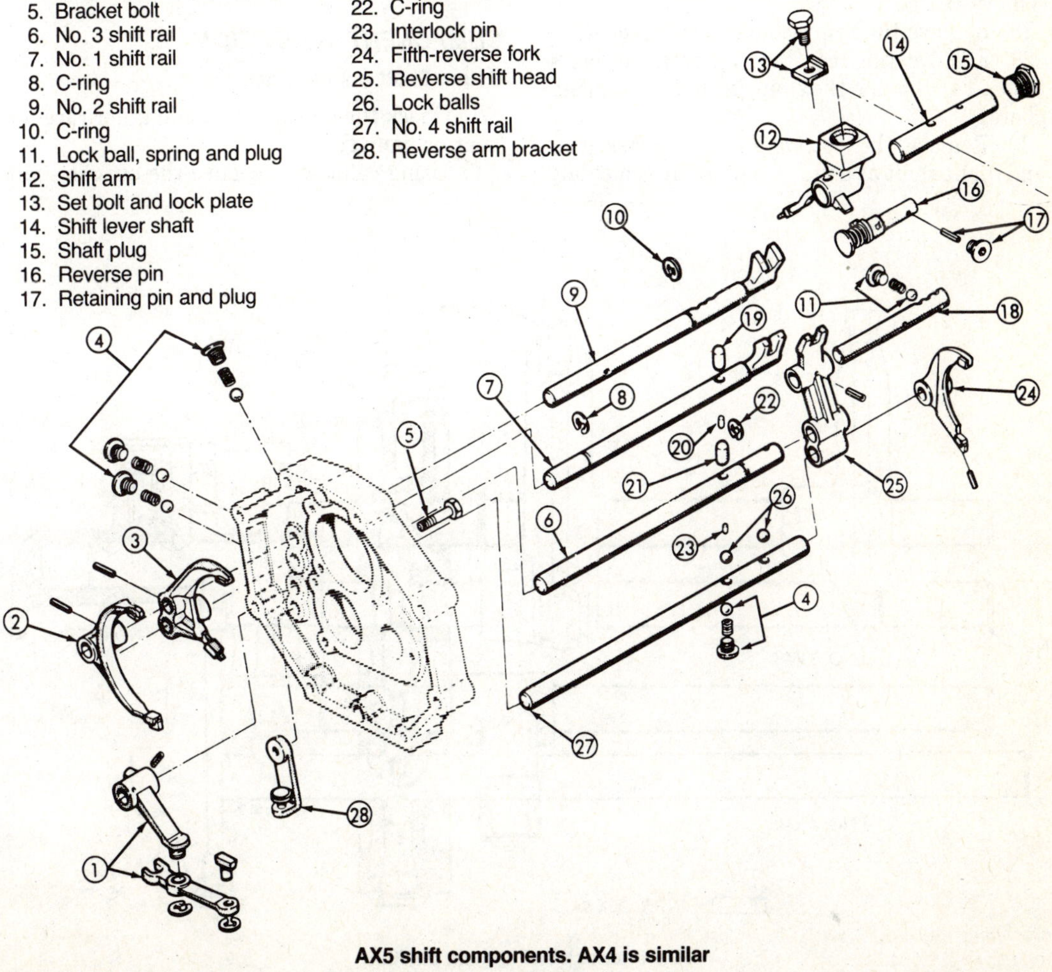

AX5 shift components. AX4 is similar

284   DRIVE TRAIN

intermediate plate and catch the interlock pins.
   CAUTION: *The interlock pin will fall from the hole so be sure to catch it. If it does not come out, remove it with a magnet.*
19. Remove shift fork shaft No. 1 from the intermediate plate being careful not to drop the interlock pin.
20. Remove shift fork shaft No. 2, shift fork No. 2 and shift fork No. 1.
21. Remove the reverse idle gear shaft stopper, reverse idler gear and shaft.
22. Remove the reverse shift arm from the reverse shift arm bracket.
23. Using a feeler gauge, measure the counter 5th gear thrust clearance. Standard Clearance: 0.10-0.30mm.
24. Engage two gears to lock the output shaft. Using a hammer and chisel, loosen the staked part of the nut on the countershaft.
25. Remove the lock nut. Disengage the gears.
26. Remove the gear spline piece No. 5, synchronizer ring, needle roller bearing and counter 5th gear using tool J-22888 or equivalent.
27. Remove the spacer and use a magnet to remove the ball.
28. Remove the reverse shift arm bracket.
29. Remove the rear bearing retainer bolts with a Torx bit and the snapring using snapring pliers.
30. Remove the output shaft, counter gear and input shaft as a unit from the intermediate plate by pulling on the counter gear and tapping on the intermediate plate with a plastic hammer.
31. Remove the input shaft with fourteen needle roller bearings from the output shaft.
32. Remove the counter rear bearing from the intermediate plate.
33. Measure the thrust clearance of each gear. Standard clearance is 0.10-0.25mm.
34. Using two awls and a hammer, tap out the snapring.
35. Using a press, remove the 5th gear, rear bearing, 1st gear and the inner race.
36. Remove the needle roller bearing.
37. Remove the synchronizer ring and locking ball.
38. Using a press, remove hub sleeve No. 1 assembly, synchronizer ring, 2nd gear.
39. Remove the needle roller bearing.
40. Remove the snapring from hub sleeve No. 2.
41. Using a press, remove the hub sleeve, synchronizer ring, and 3rd gear.
42. Remove the needle roller bearing.

COMPONENT INSPECTION
Output Shaft & Inner Race

1. Check the output shaft and inner race for wear or damage.
2. Using calipers, measure the output shaft

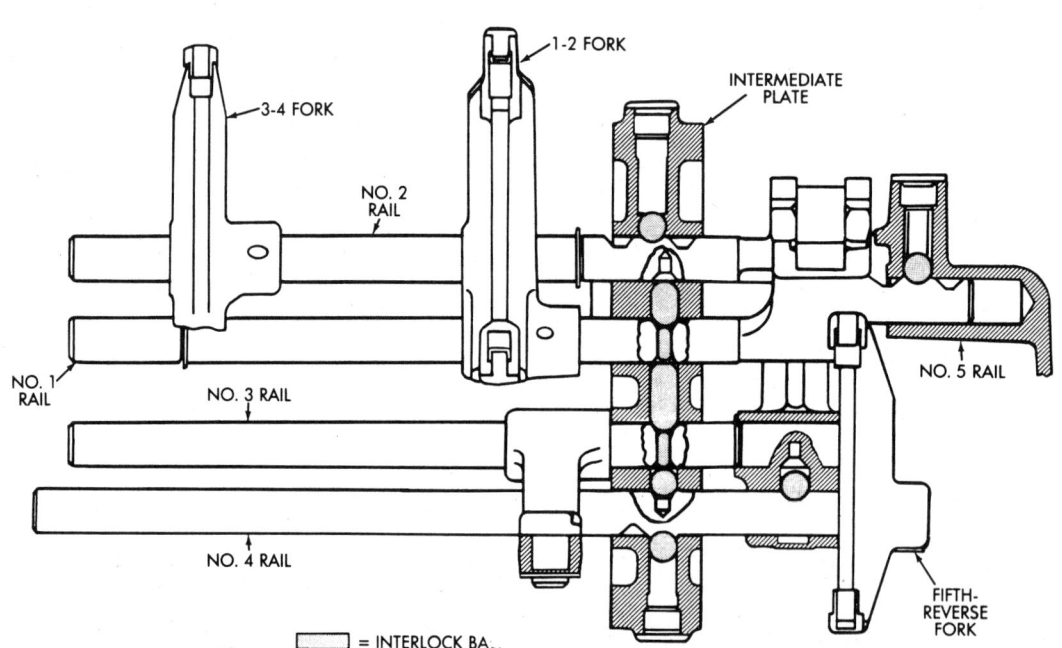

AX5 interlock ball and pin position

flange thickness. Minimum thickness is 4.8mm.

3. Using calipers, measure the inner face flange thickness. Minimum thickness is 4.0mm.

4. Using a micrometer, measure the outer diameter of the output shaft journal surface. 2nd gear minimum is 38mm; 3rd gear minimum is 35mm.

5. Using a micrometer, measure the outer diameter of the inner race. Minimum diameter is 39mm.

6. Using a dial indicator, measure the shaft runout. Maximum Runout: 0.05mm.

1st Gear Oil Clearance

1. Using a dial indicator, measure the oil clearance between the gear and inner race with the needle roller bearing installed. Standard clearance is 0.010-0.033mm.

2. Using a dial indicator, measure the oil clearance between the gear and shaft with the needle roller bearing installed. Standard Clearance: 2nd and 3rd Gears, 0.010-0.033mm; Counter 5th Gear, 0.010-0.033mm.

Synchronizer Ring Inspection

1. Check for wear or damage. Turn the ring and push it in to check the braking action.

2. Measure the clearance between the synchronizer ring back and the gear spline end. Standard clearance is 1.00-1.80mm; minimum clearance: 0.8mm.

Shift Fork and Hub Sleeve Clearance

Using a feeler gauge, measure the clearance between the hub sleeve and shift fork. Maximum clearance is 1.0mm.

Input Shaft and Bearing Inspection and Removal

1. Check for wear or damage. If necessary, remove the bearing snapring using snapring pliers and remove the bearing.

2. Using a press, remove the bearing.

3. Using a press and tool J-34603 or equivalent, install the new bearing.

4. Select a snapring that will allow minimum axial play and install it on the shaft.

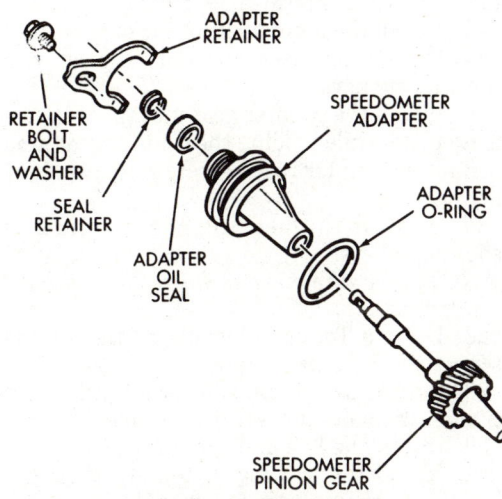

AX4 or AX5 speedometer gear assembly

Counter Gear and Bearing Inspection

1. Check the gear teeth for wear or damage.
2. Check the bearing for wear or damage.

Counter Gear Front Bearing Replacement

1. Using snapring pliers, remove the snapring.

2. Press out the bearing using tool J-22912-01 or equivalent.

3. Replace the side race.

4. Using tool J-28406 or equivalent, press in the bearing and inner race.

5. Select a snapring that will allow minimum axial play and install it on the shaft.

Front Bearing Retainer Inspection

1. Check retainer for damage.
2. Check the oil seal lip for wear or damage.

OIL SEAL REPLACEMENT

1. Using a awl, pry the old seal out of the housing.

2. Press in the new oil seal using tool J-34602 or equivalent.

3. The oil seal depth is 11.20-12.20mm from the housing-to-transmission surface to the top edge of the seal.

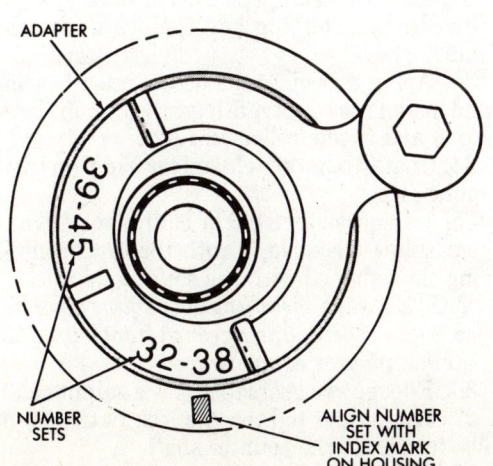

Indexing the speedometer gears on the AX4 or AX5

REVERSE RESTRICT PIN REPLACEMENT

1. Check for wear or damage.
2. Using a Torx bit, remove the screw plug.
3. Using a hammer and pin punch, drive out the slotted spring pin.
4. Pull off the lever housing and slide out the shaft.
5. Install the lever housing.
6. Using a hammer and pin punch, drive out the slotted spring pin.
7. Using a Torx bit, install and torque the screw plug to 27 ft. lbs. torque.

ADAPTER HOUSING & OIL SEAL INSPECTION & REPLACEMENT

1. Check the adapter housing for wear or damage.
2. Replace the oil seal with tool J-29184 or equivalent.

ASSEMBLY

1. Install the clutch hub No. 1 and No. 2 into hub sleeves along with the shifting keys.
CAUTION: *Install the key springs so their gaps are not in line.*
2. Install the shifting springs under the shifting keys.
3. Apply gear oil on the output shaft and 3rd gear needle roller bearing.
4. Place the 3rd gear synchronizer ring on the gear and align the ring slots with the shifting keys.
5. Install the needle roller bearing in the 3rd gear and hub sleeve No. 2.
6. Select a new snapring (2) that will allow minimum axial play and install it on the shaft.
7. Using a feeler gauge, measure the 3rd gear thrust clearance. Standard clearance is 0.10-0.25mm.
8. Apply gear oil on the output shaft and 2nd gear needle bearing.
9. Place the 2nd gear synchronizer ring on the 2nd gear and align the ring slots with the shifting keys.
10. Install the needle roller bearing in the 2nd gear.
11. Using a press install the 2nd gear and hub sleeve No. 1.
12. Install the 1st gear locking ball in the output shaft.
13. Apply gear oil to the needle roller bearing.
14. Assemble the 1st gear, synchronizer ring, needle roller bearing and bearing inner race.
15. Install the assembly on the output shaft, with the synchronizer ring slots aligned with the shifting keys.
16. Turn the inner race to align it with the locking ball.
17. Install the output shaft rear bearing using tool J-34603 or equivalent and a press.
18. Install the bearing on the output shaft with the outer race snapring groove toward the rear.
NOTE: *Hold the 1st gear inner race to prevent it from falling.*
19. Measure the 1st and 2nd gear thrust clearance with a feeler gauge. Standard Clearance: 0.10-0.25mm.
20. Install 5th gear on the output shaft using tool J-34603 or equivalent and a press.
21. Select a snapring that will allow minimum axial play.
22. Using a screwdriver and a hammer, tap the snap into position.
23. Apply multi-purpose grease to the fourteen needle roller bearings and install them in the input shaft.
24. Install the output shaft into the intermediate plate by pulling on the output shaft and tapping on the intermediate plate.
25. Install the input shaft to the output shaft with the synchronizer ring slots aligned with the shifting keys.
26. Install the counter gear into the intermediate plate while holding the counter gear, and install the counter rear bearing with a suitable driver.
27. Install the bearing snapring using snapring pliers.
NOTE: *Be sure the snapring is flush with the intermediate plate surface.*
28. Using a Torx bit, install and tighten the screws to 13 ft. lbs. torque.
29. Install the reverse shift arm bracket and tighten the bolts to 13 ft. lbs. torque.
30. Install the ball and spacer.
31. Install the shifting keys and hub sleeve No. 3 onto the counter 5th gear.
CAUTION: *Install the key springs positioned so the end gaps are not in line.*
32. Install shifting key springs under the shifting keys.
33. Apply gear oil to the needle roller bearing and install the counter 5th gear with hub sleeve No. 3 and needle roller bearings.
34. Install the synchronizer ring on gear spline piece.
35. Using tool J-28406 or equivalent drive in gear spline piece No. 5 with the synchronizer ring slots aligned with the shifting keys.
NOTE: *When installing gear spline piece No. 5, support the counter gear in front with a 3-5 lb. hammer or equivalent.*
36. Engage two gears to lock the output shaft.
37. Install and tighten the lock nut to 90 ft. lbs. torque on the counter shaft.
38. Stake the lock nut.
39. Disengage the gears.

DRIVE TRAIN

40. Measure the counter 5th gear thrust clearance using a feeler gauge. Standard Clearance: 0.10-0.30mm.
41. Install the reverse shift arm to the pivot of the reverse shift arm bracket.
42. Install the reverse idler gear on the shaft.
43. Align the reverse shift arm shoe to the reverse idler gear groove and insert the reverse idler gear shift to the intermediate plate.
44. Install the reverse idler gear shaft stopper and tighten the bolt to 13 ft. lbs. torque.
45. Place shift forks No. 1 and No. 2 into groove of hub sleeves No. 1 and No. 2 and install fork shaft No. 2 to the shift forks No. 1 and No. 2 through the intermediate plate.
46. Apply multi-purpose grease to the interlock pins.
47. Using a magnet and screwdriver, install the interlock pin into the intermediate plate.
48. Install the interlock pin into the shaft hole.
49. Install fork shaft No. 1 to shift fork No. 1 through the intermediate plate.
50. Using a magnet and screwdriver, install the interlock pin into the intermediate plate.
51. Install the interlock pin into the shaft hole.
52. Install fork shaft No. 3 to the reverse shift arm through the intermediate plate.
53. Install the reverse shift head into fork shaft No. 5.
54. Insert fork shaft No. 5 to the intermediate plate and put in the reverse shift head to the shift fork No. 3.
55. Using a magnetic finger and screwdriver, install the locking ball into the reverse shift head hole.
56. Shift hub sleeve No. 3 to the 5th speed position.
57. Place shift fork No. 3 into the groove of hub sleeve No. 3 and install fork shaft No. 4 to shift fork No. 3 and reverse shift arm.
58. Using a magnet and screwdriver, install the locking ball into the intermediate plate and insert fork shaft No. 4 to the intermediate plate.
59. Check the interlock by positioning the shift fork shaft No. 1 to the 1st speed position.
60. Fork shafts No. 2, No. 3, No. 4 and No. 5 should not move.
61. Using a pin punch and a hammer, drive in new slotted spring pins in each shift fork, reverse shift arm and reverse shift head.
62. Install two fork shaft E-rings.
63. Apply liquid sealer to the screw plugs.
64. Install the locking balls, springs and screw plugs with a Torx bit and tighten to 14 ft. lbs. torque.
NOTE: *Install the short spring into the tower of the intermediate plate.*
65. Remove the intermediate plate from the vise.
66. Remove the bolts, nuts, washers and gasket.

CASE INSTALLATION

1. Align each bearing outer race, each fork shaft end and reverse idler gear with the holes in the case and install the case on the intermediate plate. If necessary, tap on the case with a plastic hammer.
2. Install two new bearing snaprings.
3. Install front bearing retainer with a new gasket.
4. Apply liquid sealer to the bolts.
5. Install and tighten the bolts to 12 ft. lbs. torque.
6. Install the new gasket to the intermediate plate.
7. Install the adapter housing.
8. Install and tighten the adapter bolts to 27 ft. lbs. torque.
9. Install the shift lever housing.
10. Insert the shift lever into the adapter and shift lever housing.
11. Install and tighten shift lever housing bolt with a lock plate to 28 ft. lbs. torque. Lock the lock plate.
12. Install and tighten the adapter screw plug to 13 ft. lbs. torque.
13. Apply liquid sealer to the plug.
14. Install the locking ball, spring and screw plug and tighten the plug to 14 ft. lbs. torque.
15. Check to see that the input shaft and output shafts rotate smoothly.
16. Check to see that shifting can be done smoothly to all positions.
17. Install the black restrict pin on the reverse gear/5th gear side.
18. Install the remaining pin and tighten the pins to 20 ft. lbs. torque.
19. Install the shift lever retainer with a new gasket and tighten the bolts to 13 ft. lbs. torque.
20. Install the back-up light switch and tighten to 27 ft. lbs. torque.
21. Install the clutch housing and tighten the bolts to 27 ft. lbs. torque.

BA 10/5 Overhaul

NOTE: *The service tools necessary for overhaul can be found in service tool kit B.Vi.FM.01. The kit is available through a dealer's parts department.*

DISASSEMBLY

1. Mount the transmission in a holding fixture or equivalent and drain the lubricant.
2. Remove the speedometer driven gear socket set screw and remove the driven gear socket from the rear extension housing.

3. Position the transmission in the vertical position with the rear upward. Set the gear selectors in the neutral position. Remove the selection lever return spring.

4. Remove the 5th gear cover plate and its gasket. Remove the extension housing bolts.

5. Place an extractor plate tool or equivalent to the rear housing, using the three bolts of the cover plate. Remove the rear housing from the transmission.

6. Remove the 5th speed gear from the mainshaft with an appropriate puller. The rear bearing will be removed as part of the 5th speed gear.

7. Remove the 5th speed drive gear shim washer, the spacer washer, the 5th gear and its needle bearing from the 5th gear stub shaft.

8. Mark the direction of rotation of the 5th/

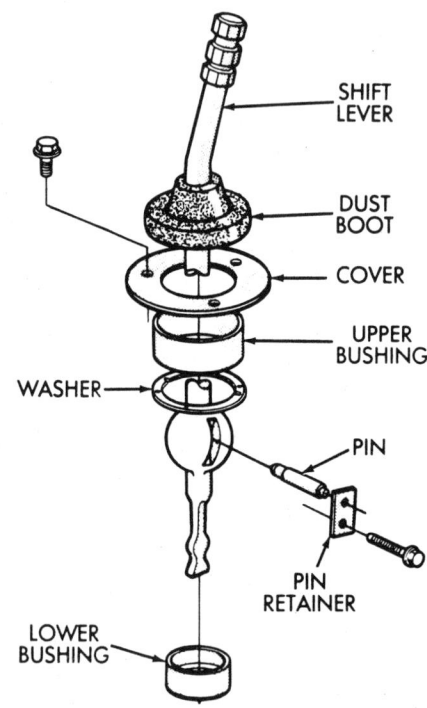

Shift lever removal from the BA 10/5

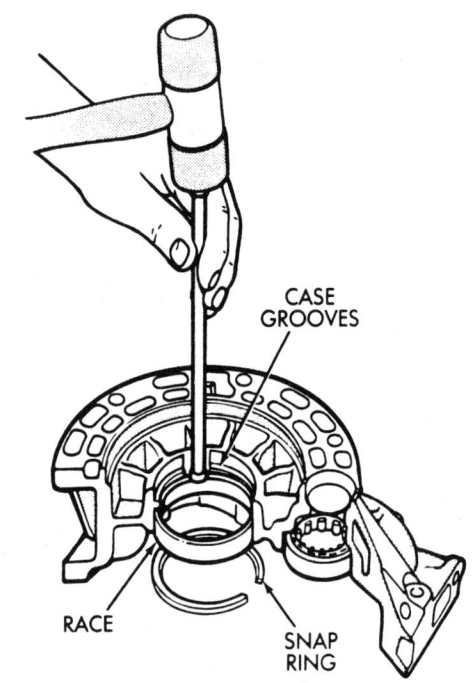

Removing the rear bearing race from the BA 10/5

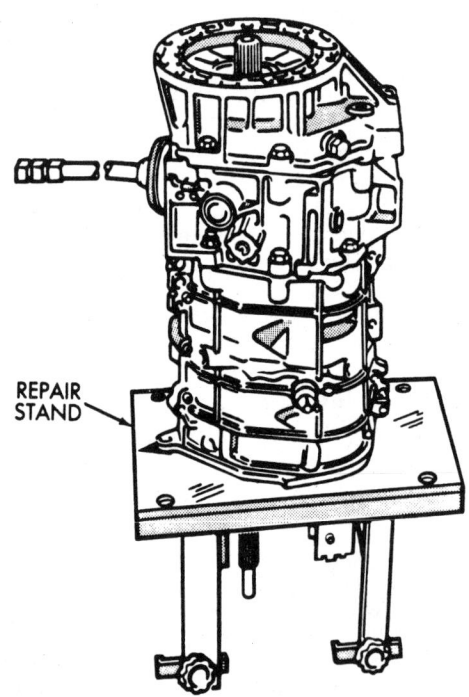

Positioning the BA 10/5 on a stand

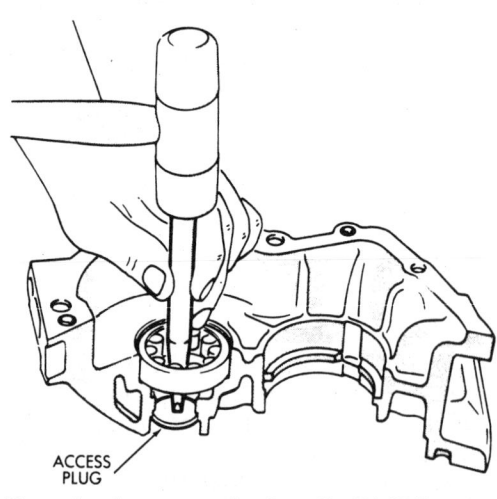

Removing the access plug from the BA 10/5

DRIVE TRAIN

reverse synchronizer and the position of the cage and hub, in relation to each other.

9. Engage the 5th gear and drive the 5th/reverse selector fork roll pin from the fork and rail.

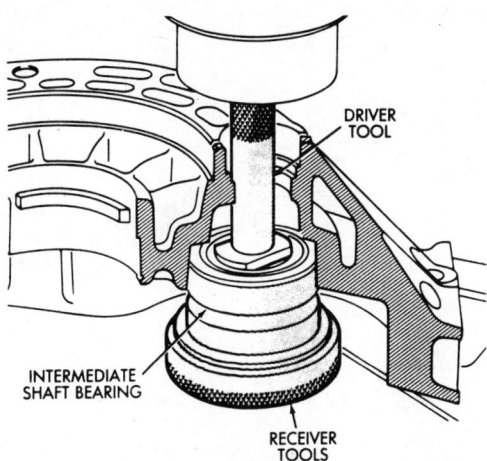
Removing the intermediate shaft bearing from the BA 10/5

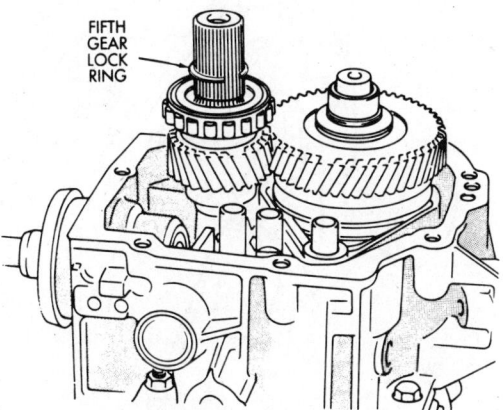
Removing 5th gear lock ring from the BA 10/5

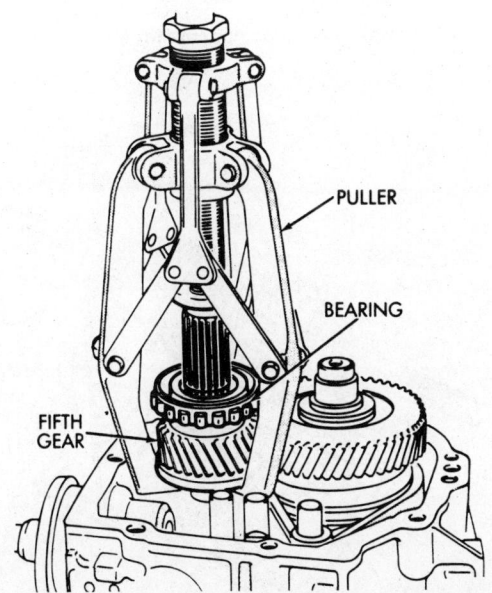
Removing the 5th gear and bearing from the BA 10/5

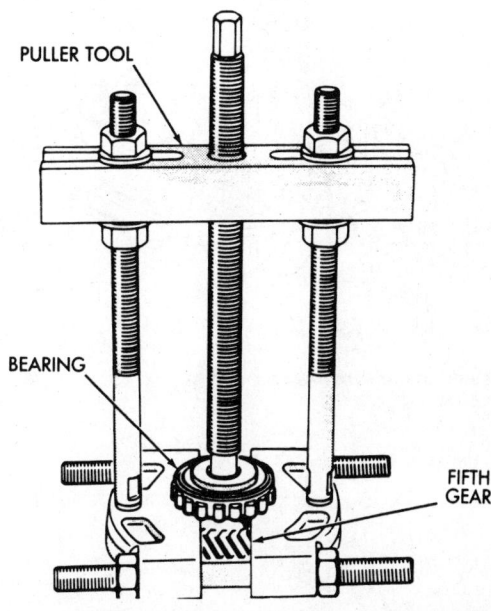
Removing the bearing from the 5th gear from the BA 10/5

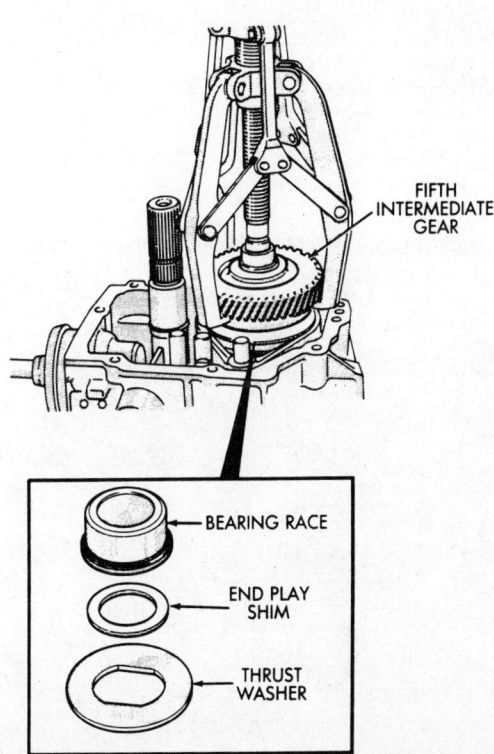
Removing the 5th intermediate gear from the BA 10/5

290 DRIVE TRAIN

WARNING: *Do not damage the mating surface of the housing*

10. Reset the rail to the neutral position and remove the 5th/reverse synchronizer cage and

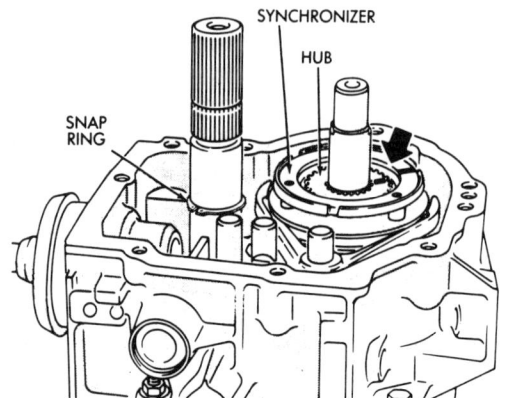

Marking the synchronizer and hub on the BA 10/5

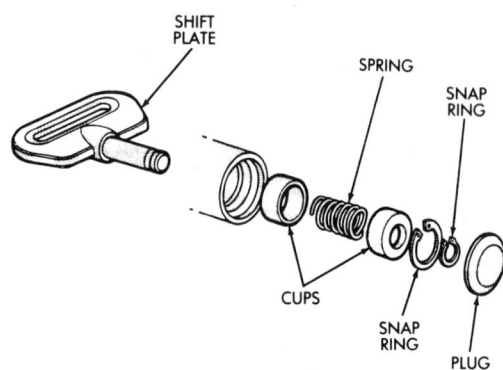

Removing the shift plate from the BA 10/5

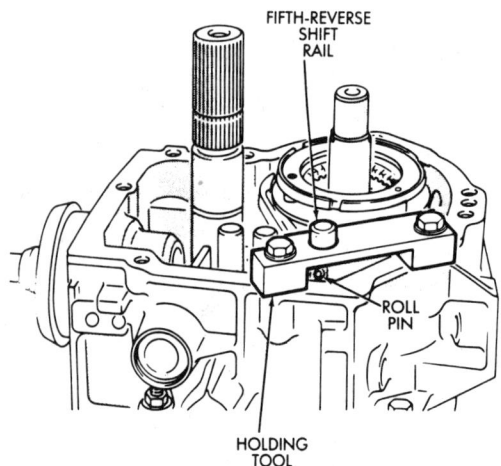

Removing the shift rail roll pin from the BA 10/5

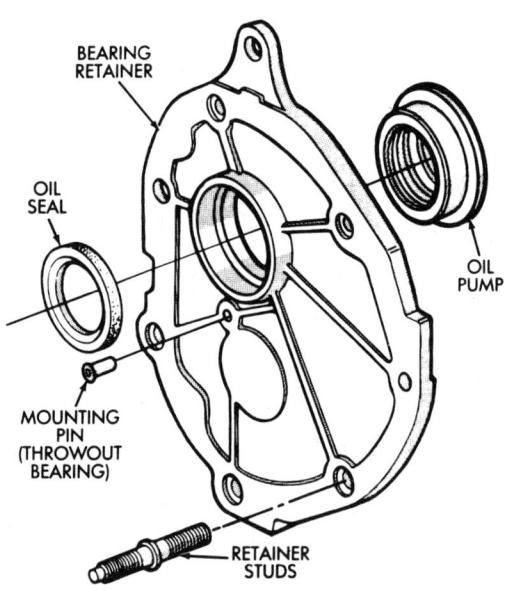

Bearing retainer and components for the BA 10/5

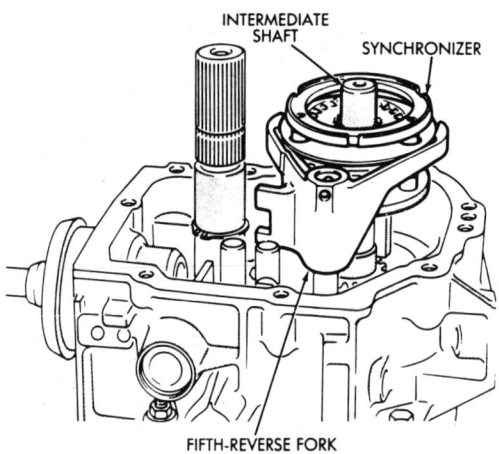

Removing the 5th-reverse fork, synchronizer and intermediate shaft from the BA 10/5

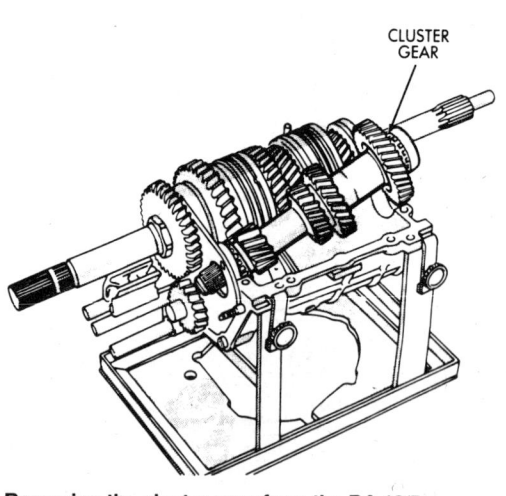

Removing the cluster gear from the BA 10/5

selector fork assembly, the synchronizer hub and the 5th gear subshaft.

11. Disengage the selection lever finger from the selector forks spindles. Remove the intermediate housing and retaining bolts.

12. Place the transmission in a horizontal position with the right side up. Remove the clutch fork and release bearing assembly from the front of the transmission. Remove the clutch housing and bolts.

13. Remove the six Allen headed screws from the rear bearing thrust plate. Remove the right hand housing retaining bolts and the housing.

14. Remove the countershaft from the exposed left hand housing.

NOTE: *Mark and set aside the bearing races, if to be used again.*

15. Lift the input and mainshaft assembly from the case as a unit. Do not separate while removing.

16. Separate the input and the mainshaft when the assembly is on a work bench. Remove the needle bearing from the bore of the input

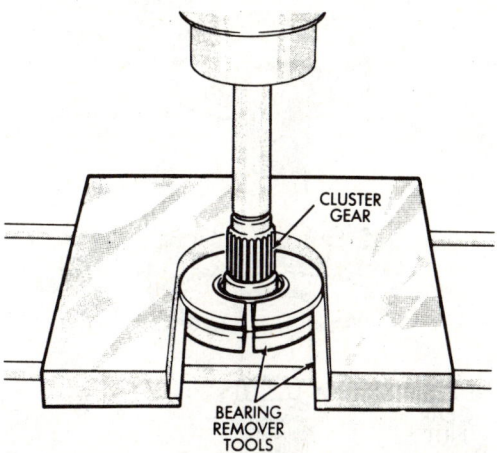
Removing the cluster gear bearings from the BA 10/5

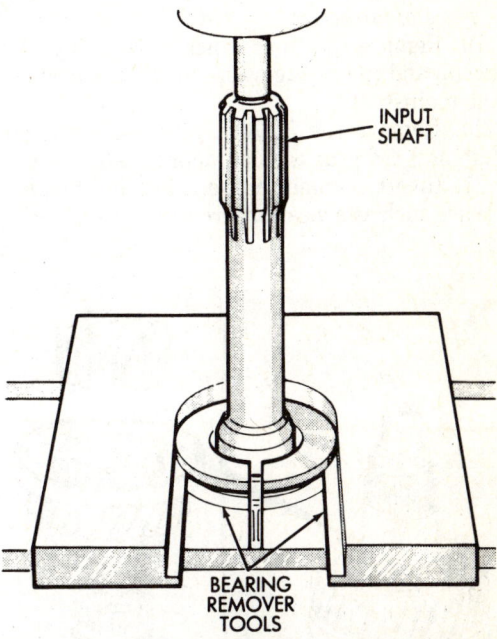
Removing the input shaft bearing from the BA 10/5

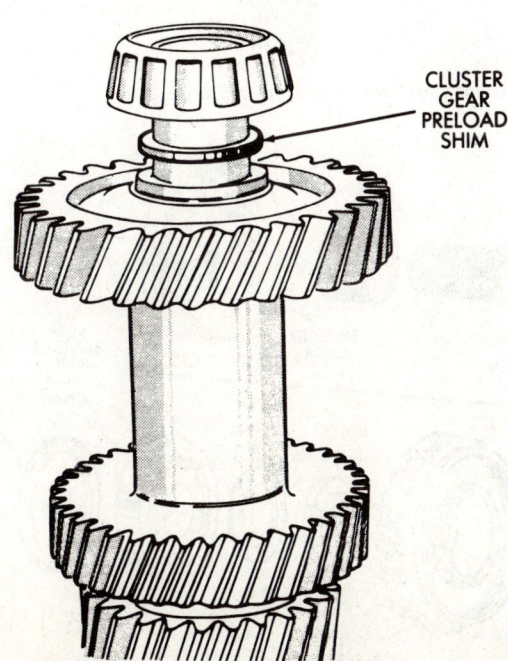
Cluster gear preload shim on the BA 10/5

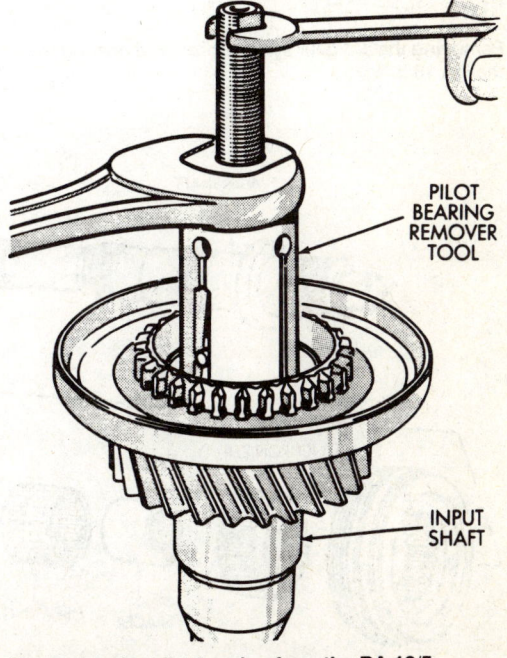
Removing the pilot bearing from the BA 10/5

DRIVE TRAIN

shaft. Hold the mainshaft in the 3rd gear position.

17. To disassemble the input shaft, remove the circlips, the spring washer and press the bearing from the shaft. Do not lose the adjusting shims.

18. To disassemble the mainshaft, mark the direction of rotation of the 3rd/4th synchronizer cage in relation to the synchronizer hub.

NOTE: *Mark the components with a sharp piece of brass welding rod.*

19. Remove the front synchronizer ring, the circlip and the spring washer from the front of the mainshaft.

20. Remove the 3rd/4th gear synchronizer hub and 3rd gear with an appropriate puller.

21. Invert the mainshaft and lock in a holding device such as a vise. Unscrew the reverse driven gear locknut from the mainshaft. Remove the reverse gear from the shaft.

22. Position the mainshaft and the remaining gears on a press bench and press the mainshaft through the rear bearing. Remove the gear components from the mainshaft in the following order:
   a. Rear bearing.
   b. Bearing spacer.
   c. Adjustment shim washer.
   d. 1st speed driven gear.

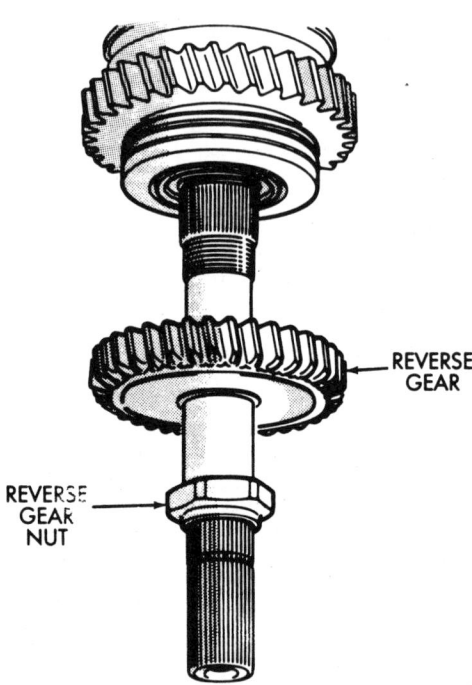

Removing reverse gear from the BA 10/5

Removing the 3rd gear synchronizer and bearing from the BA 10/5

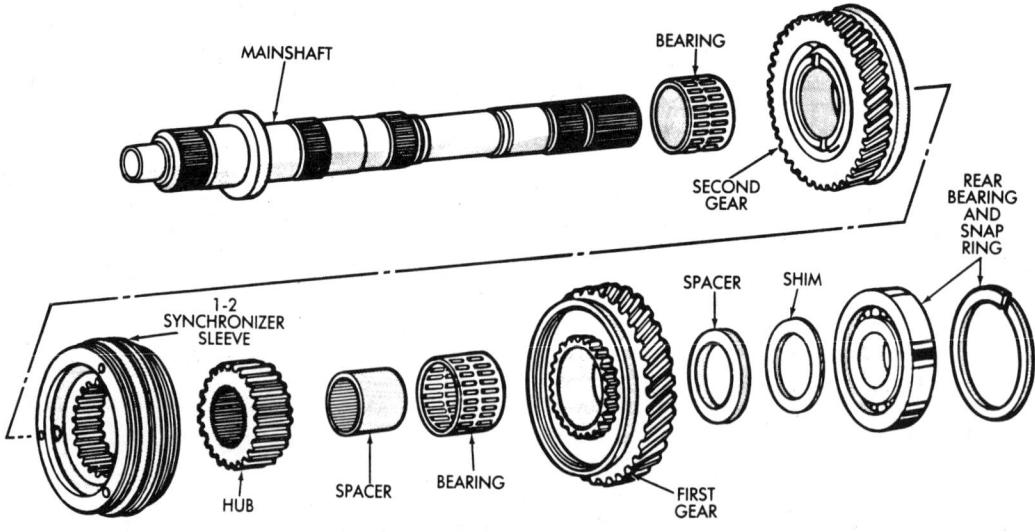

Removing 1st-2nd gears from the BA 10/5

DRIVE TRAIN

e. Needle bearing.
f. 1st gear bushing.
g. 1st/2nd gear synchronizer and hub.
h. 2nd speed driven gear.
i. Needle bearing.

23. Using a press, remove the front bearing and the shim adjusting washers, Remove the rear bearing.

24. To disassemble the rear housing, the ball bearing, the oil seal and the bearing race is pressed from the housing. Locate the shim washer in the race bore.

WARNING: *The press ram should be no bigger than 24mm in diameter.*

Selector Forks and Shift Rail Removal

1. Remove the spring and the 4th speed locking ball from the rear bearing bore of the half case.
2. Move the 4th gear fork and rail to the engaged position and drive the roll pins from the 1st/2nd and 3rd/4th selector forks. Return the 3rd/4th shift rail to the neutral position.
3. Remove the 1st/2nd locking ball plug, spring and ball from the passage on the center of the outer side of the case.
4. Pivot the 3rd/4th selector rail and remove the 1st/2nd rail from the case. Remove the fork.
5. Remove the reverse gear locking ball plug, spring and ball from the opposite side from the 3rd/4th locking ball passage.
6. Disengage the reverse fork and rail assembly and withdraw it from the case.
7. Remove the 3rd/4th shifting rail and remove the fork, interlock pin, the ball and the interlock plunger from the bearing bore.
8. Remove the roll pin from the reverse fork and rail. Push the shifting rail outward. Remove the fork.

Engagement Lever in the Intermediate Cover

Remove the circlip and washer. Remove the engagement lever spindle and recover the

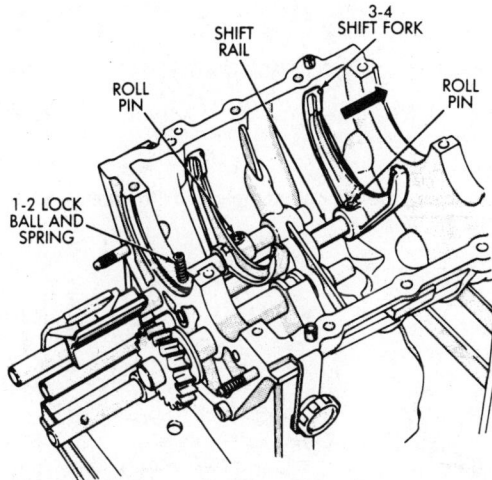

Removing 1st-2nd lock ball and shift fork roll pins from the BA 10/5

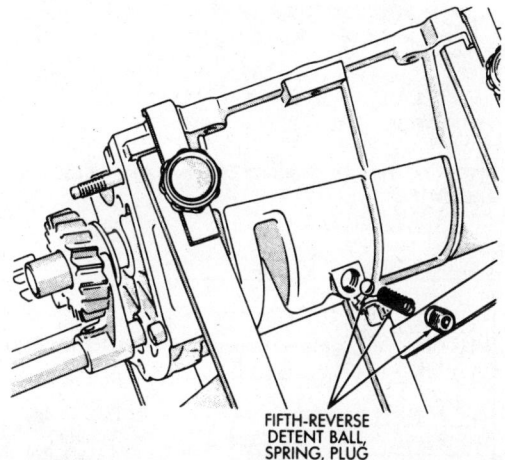

Removing 5th-reverse detent plug, spring and ball from the BA 10/5

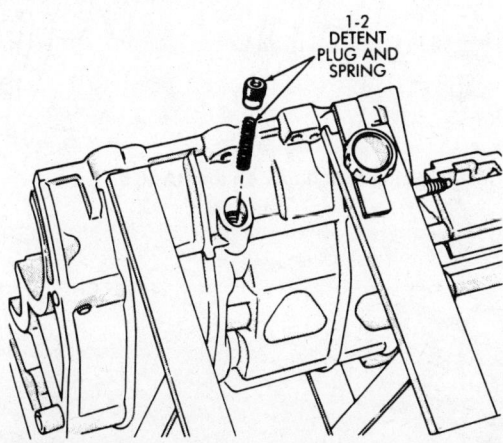

Removing 1st-2nd detent plug and spring from the BA 10/5

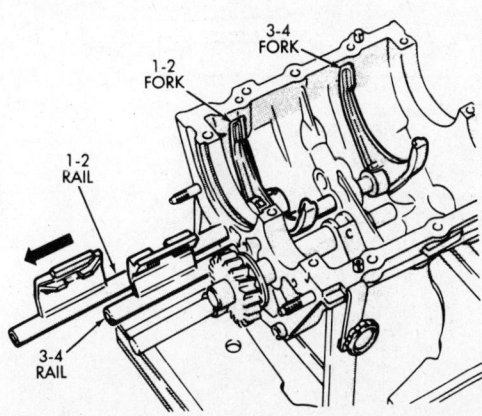

Removing the shift forks and rails from the BA 10/5

294 DRIVE TRAIN

washer, spring, thrust plate and the operating fingers from the inside of the housing.

Clutch Housing

The thrust guide sleeve can be pressed from the housing after the oil seal has been removed.

ASSEMBLY
General

Always replace the following components when overhauling the transmission:

a. Shaft circlips.
b. Spring washers.
c. Roll pins.
d. Mainshaft nut.
e. Output and input seals.
f. O-ring on speedometer driven bushing.
g. Thrust washers.
h. Necessary gaskets.
i. Sealing compound to mating surfaces

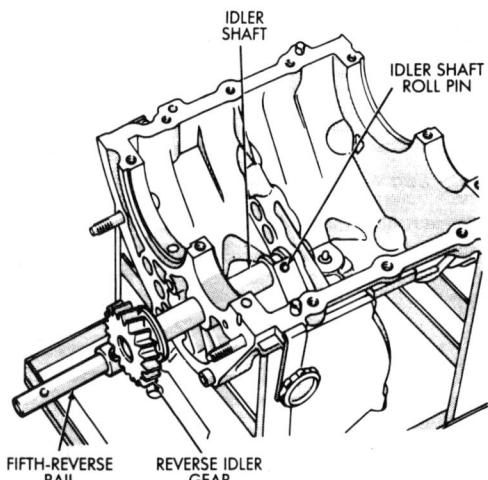

Removing the idler gear and 5th-reverse shift rail from the BA 10/5

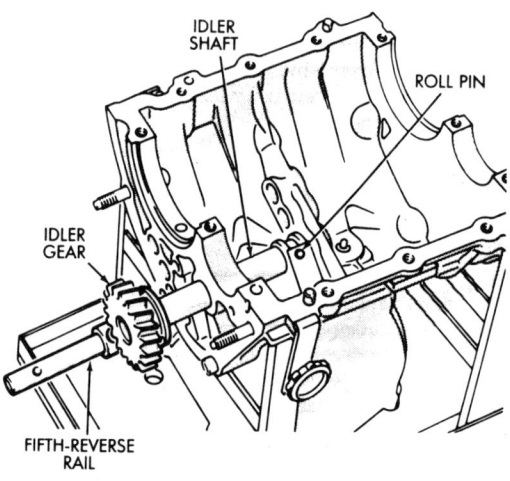

Installing the idler shaft, gear and 5th reverse rail on the BA 10/5

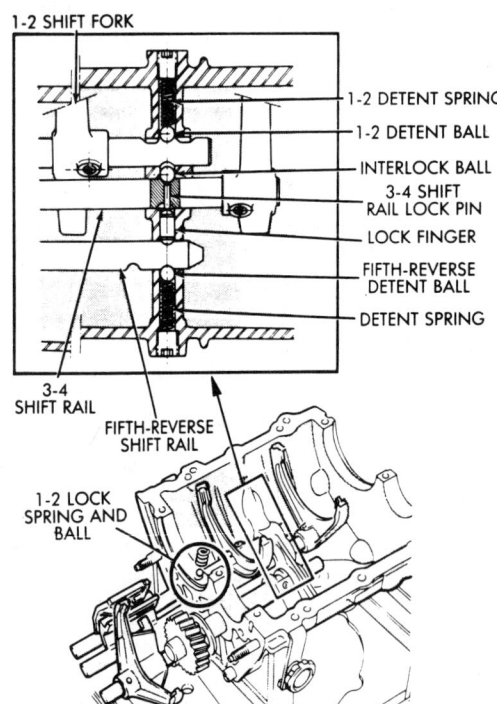

Shift component chart for the BA 10/5

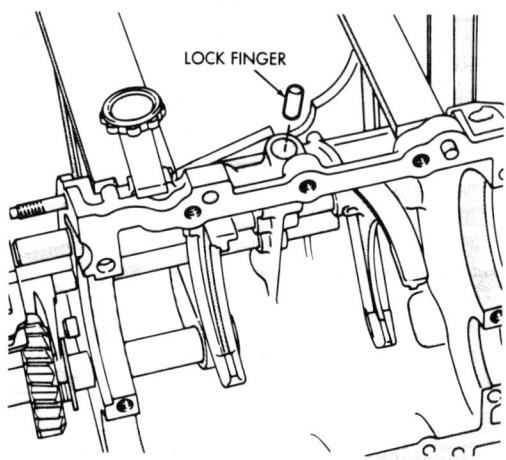

Installing the lock finger on the BA 10/5

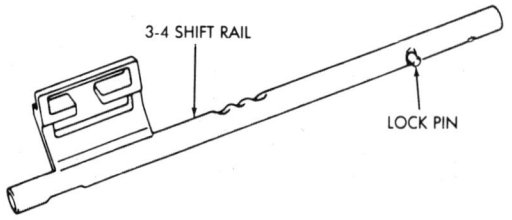

Installing the lock pin in the 3rd-4th shift rail on the BA 10/5

DRIVE TRAIN

Engagement Levers

1. Install the lever spindle while fitting the operating fingers, the spring thrust plate, the spring and the washer.
2. Install the washer and the circlip on the lever spindle, exposed on the side of the intermediate housing.

Forks, Shift Rails and Interlocks

1. Install the reverse gear sliding shift rail into the case and into the bracket. Align the roll pin holes and install a new roll pin.
2. Install the reverse sliding gear with the 5th/reverse fork and shifting rail into the case.
3. Install in the reverse interlock passage on the outside of the case, a ball and spring. Coat the plug with a sealer and install it into the passage. Torque to 114 in. lbs. Move the shift rail to the neutral position.
4. Install the 3rd/4th and 5th/reverse interlock plunger into its passage in the case.
5. Install an interlock pin in the 3rd/4th shift rail and retain with grease. Install the shifting rail into the case. Align the holes in the fork and the rail. Be sure the interlock pin is in the correct position and install a new roll pin.
6. Install an interlock ball in the passage between the 3rd/4th and the 1st/2nd fork rails. Install the 1st/2nd gear fork in the case with the boss towards the front. Install the shifting rail and engage the shifting fork. Align the holes in the fork and the shifting rail and install a new roll pin.
7. Install an interlock ball and spring in the 3rd/4th/2nd/1st interlock passage. Coat the plug with sealer and install it in the passage. Torque to 9.5 ft. lbs.
8. Install the ball and spring in the passage of the rear bearing bore, for the 3rd/4th shifting rail.

Preparing the Input Shaft and Mainshaft for Adjustment

INPUT SHAFT

Press the front bearing on the input shaft with the snapring groove to the front. Do not install any shims.

MAINSHAFT

1. Install the 2nd speed gear and its needle bearing, the 1st/2nd synchronizer hub, the 1st

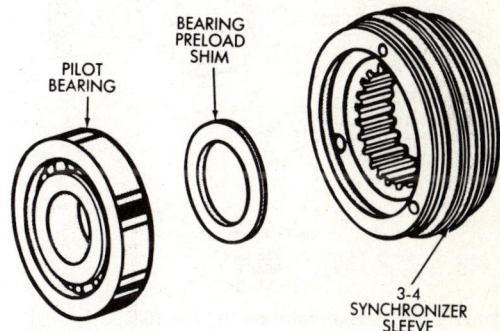

Pilot bearing, shim and 3rd-4th synchronizer sleeve on the BA 10/5

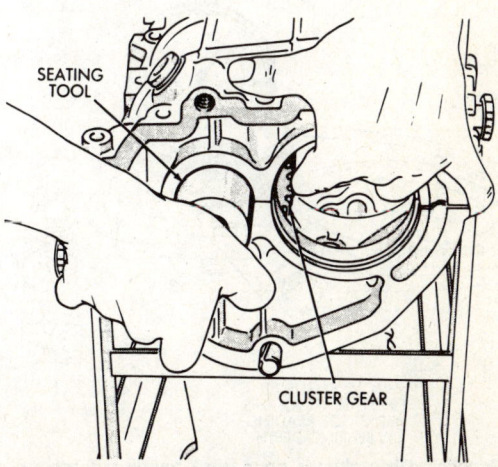

Seating the cluster bearings on the BA 10/5

Setting the lock ring on the BA 10/5

296 DRIVE TRAIN

speed gear spacer and washer. Install the rear bearing along with a new circlip.

NOTE: *The bearing will have to be pressed on the shaft. Do not exceed 3 metric tons pressure after the bearing is seated.*

2. Install the adjustment shim removed during the disassembly, the spacer and a new nut on the shaft following the rear bearing. Tighten the nut to 39 ft. lbs.

COUNTERSHAFT

Press the new bearings onto the countershaft, beginning with the rear bearing and then the front

CLUTCH HOUSING

1. Install the thrust guide sleeve and new circlip in its groove.

NOTE: *Do not install an oil seal in the housing until all adjustments are completed.*

2. Verify the front and rear faces of the clutch housing are parallel with the use of a dial indicator. If out of parallel more than 0.10mm, replace the housing.

Adjustments Prior to Assembly

Five adjustments are necessary, prior to the complete assembly of the transmission. The adjustments are as follows:

1. Position of the 4th gear synchronizer cone (prior to assembly).
2. Positon of the 2nd gear synchronizer cone (prior to assembly).
3. Preload of the countershaft tapered roller bearings (prior to assembly).

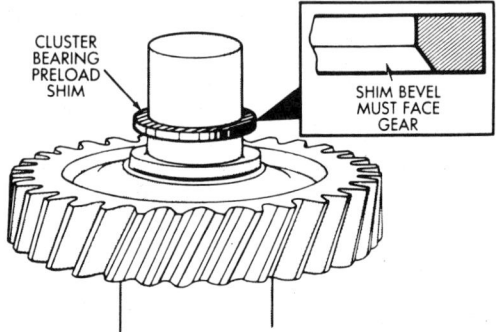

Installing the cluster bearing preload shim on the BA 10/5

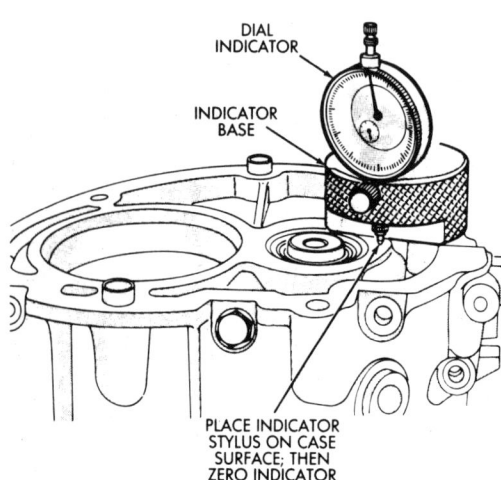

Zeroing the dial indicator on the BA 10/5

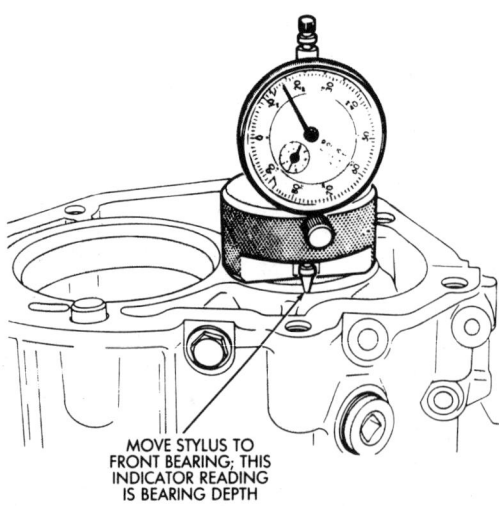

Measuring the cluster gear front bearing depth on the BA 10/5

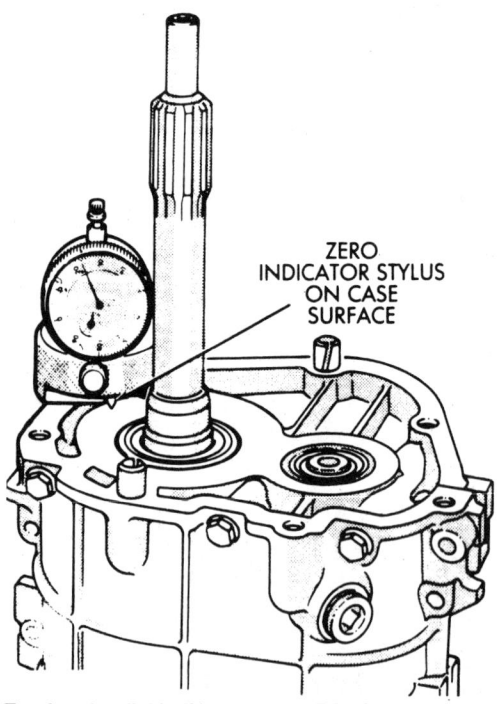

Zeroing the dial indicator on the BA 10/5

DRIVE TRAIN

4. Preload of the mainshaft tapered roller bearings (during assembly).
5. End play of the 5th/reverse sub-shaft (during assembly).

Special tools are available through the manufacturer and other sources for the measurement procedures needed during the adjustment phases. References will be made to the special tools needed.

Position of the 4th Gear Synchronizer Cone

1. Place the clutch housing, front down on a flat surface, and install the input shaft and bearing.
2. Install the right housing onto the clutch housing and secure with two bolts. Tighten to 14 ft. lbs.

WARNING: *Be sure the bearing fits into the bore of the clutch housing and the half housing.*

3. Install the special setting gauge tool, 80314G or equivalent, into the clutch housing, in place of the countershaft front bearing.
4. Place the dial indicator and the special tool base, 80310FZ or equivalent, on the top of the setting tool.
5. Align the dial indicator stem on the edge of the synchronizer cone and rotate the input shaft one complete turn and obtain an average reading. Adjust the indicator to zero at the average reading point on the cone edge.
6. Reposition the dial indicator and base on the setting gauge block and record the measurement.
7. The measurement obtained represents the thickness of shims needed between the input shaft and the front bearing, minus 0.5mm and rounded off to the nearest 0.05mm.

Example:
- Indicator reading 1.12mm
- Minus 0.50mm
- Result 0.62mm
- Rounded off to nearest 0.05mm = 0.60mm

Therefore, a shim pack of 0.60mm is needed between the input shaft and the front bearing to properly position the 4th speed synchronizer cone, in this hypothetical example.

NOTE: *Shims are available in steps of 0.05mm, from 0.15mm to 0.50mm.*

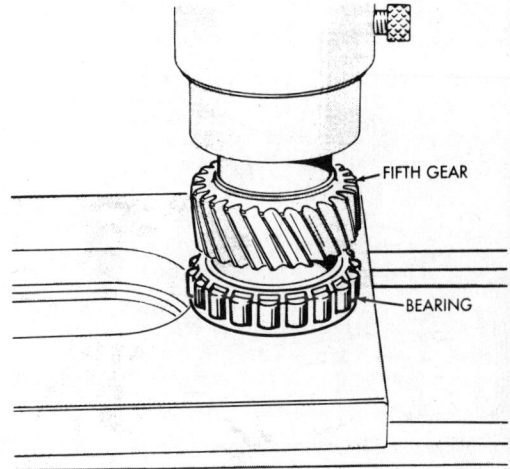

Installing the 5th gear bearing on the BA 10/5

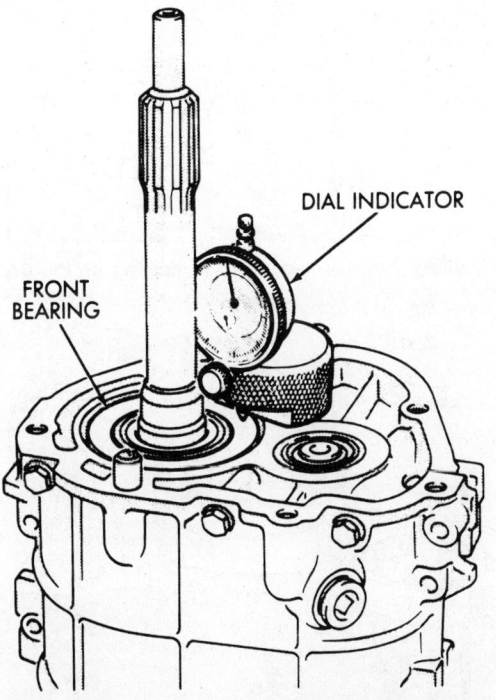

Measuring the input shaft bearing depth on the BA 10/5

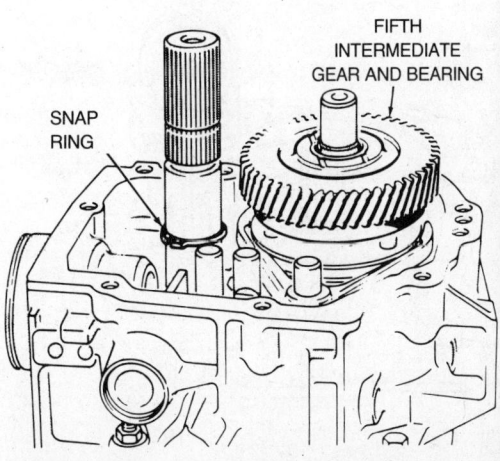

Installing the snapring and 5th intermediate gear on the BA 10/5

Position of the 2nd Gear Synchronizer Cone

1. Install the needle bearing into the bore of the input shaft. Install the mainshaft and prepared components into the input shaft, with the rear bearing seated in its bore on the right hand housing.

NOTE: *Be sure the bearing circlip is installed in the half housing groove.*

2. Install the larger setting tool, 80314K or equivalent, into the countershaft front bearing bore of the clutch housing.
3. Install a longer stem, 80310J or equivalent, onto the indicator. Place the dial indicator and special base on the top of the right hand half housing, in a position to touch both the setting tool and the 2nd synchronizer cone.
4. With the dial indicator set to zero, position the stem on the top of the setting tool.
5. Reposition the indicator stem to the edge of the 2nd synchronizer cone and record the measurement reading. The amount of movement noted, represents the thickness of shims needed between the 1st gear spacer and the rear bearing, plus 0.50mm, rounded off to the nearest 0.05mm.

Example:
- Indicator reading 2.51mm
- Plus 0.50mm
- Result 3.01mm
- Rounded off to nearest 0.05mm = 3.00mm

6. Remove the input and mainshaft assemblies. Separate the clutch housing and the half housing.

Preload of the Countershaft Tapered Roller Bearings

1. Place the left half housing in the support stand or equivalent. Install the countershaft and its bearings into the housing.
2. Place the right housing in place on the left housing, making sure the dowel pins are in position.

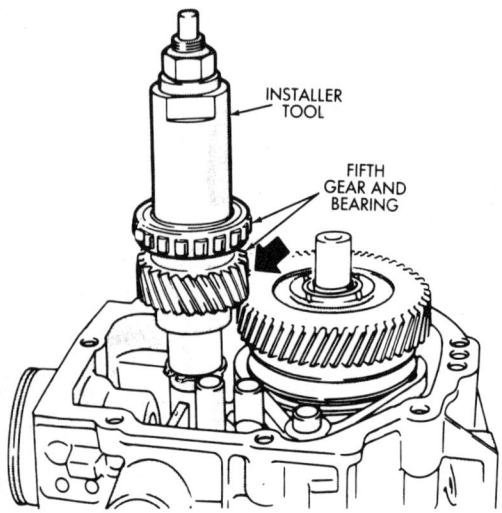
Installing the 5th gear and bearing on the BA 10/5

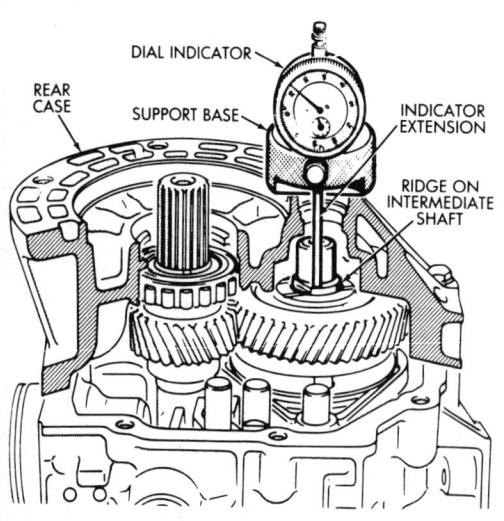
Zero and lock the dial indicator on the BA 10/5

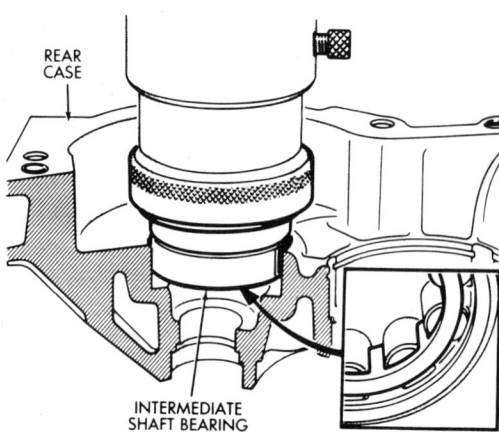
Installing the intermediate shaft bearing on the BA 10/5

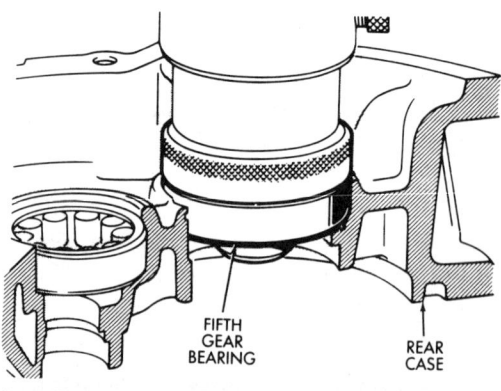
Installing the 5th gear bearing on the BA 10/5

DRIVE TRAIN 299

3. Install two bearings center bolts into the housings and hand tighten the bolts. Install bolts into the rear bearing thrust place and hand tighten the bolts.

4. Position the transmission with the front of the housings upward. Apply a downward pressure to the countershaft front bearing while rotating the countershaft, in order to seat the bearings.

5. Tighten the bearing center bolts and the bearing thrust plate bolts to 7 ft. lb.

6. By placing the dial indicator on the end of the countershaft and rotating it one complete turn with the stem contacting the housings, the run-out between the outer race and the face of the half housings must not exceed 0.03mm.

7. Should the run-out exceed the specifications, the race must be realigned by tapping with a mallet. Should the countershaft be difficult to turn, the bearing center bolts and the bearing thrust plate bolts must be loosened and retightened and the run-out rechecked.

8. If the run-out is within specifications, set the dial indicator with a short stem, to number 2 and zero, with the stem resting on the side of the outer race. Move the indicator until the stem is contacting the face of the housing and record the measurement of the movement. Add 0.10mm to the results for the preload of the bearings and round the results to the nearest 0.05mm.

Example:
- Housing reading 4.27mm
- Bearing reading (preset) 2.00mm
- Result 2.27mm
- Plus preload 0.10mm
- Shim pack needed 2.37mm
- Rounded off to nearest 0.05mm = 2.35mm

NOTE: *Shims are available from 2.15mm to 3.30mm, in increments of 0.05mm.*

9. Remove the countershaft and the front bearing from the countershaft.

10. Install the predeterminded shim with the chamfer facing the gear, between the gear and the bearing.

11. Press the bearing in place.

NOTE: *The 4th and 5th adjustments are made during the assembly of the transmission as noted in the adjustment list.*

FINAL ASSEMBLY

Input Shaft

1. Remove the bearing from the shaft and install the predetermined shim pack between the shaft and the bearing.

2. Reinstall the bearing, with the groove for the large circlip to the front. Press the bearing into position and install the spring washer and circlip on the input shaft. Be sure the circlip engages the groove completely.

Mainshaft

1. Remove the rear bearing and shims from the mainshaft, used in the measurement check.

2. Install in the following order, from the rear to the front of the shaft, the components as listed:

    a. The 2nd gear and its needle bearing (31mm wide).

    b. The synchronizer hub and cage.

    c. The 1st gear and needle bearing (29mm wide).

    d. The spacer and adjusting shim (from measurement check).

    e. The bearing spacer.

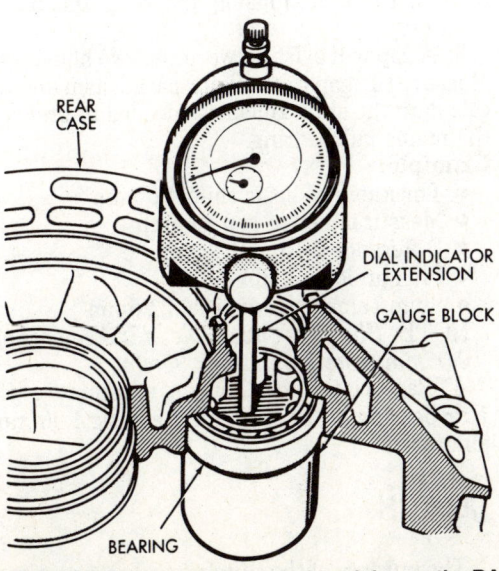

Measuring the intermediate shaft endplay on the BA 10/5

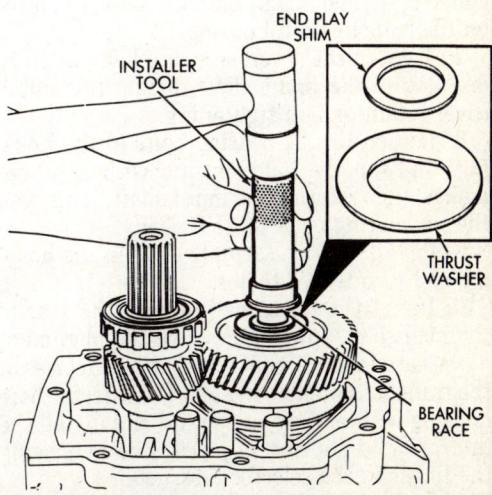

Installing the washer, shim and race on the BA 10/5

DRIVE TRAIN

f. Press the bearing onto the shaft with the circlip to the rear.
g. Install the reverse driven gear with the plain face to the rear.
h. Install a new nut and tighten to 39 ft. lbs. and lock the collar to the shaft.
3. Invert the mainshaft and install the following in order.
   a. 3rd gear along with its needle bearing (31mm wide).
   b. 3rd-4th synchronizer hub.
4. Install a new spring washer and circlip on the end of the mainshaft. Be sure circlip is in the groove.
5. Insert the needle bearing in the bore of the input shaft, fit the 3rd-4th synchronizer cage and assemble the input and mainshaft together. Set the syncrhonizers to neutral positions.

Installing Gear Trains Into Transmission Cases

1. Be sure the reverse synchronizer is in the neutral position and the 3rd-4th gear locking ball and spring is in position in the bearing bore.
2. Install the input and mainshaft assembly into the left half housing, engaging the selector forks with the synchronizer cages.
3. Install the outer races to the countershaft and install the countershaft into the housing. Be sure the teeth of both gear trains mate properly.
4. Be sure the alignment dowel pins are in place. Coat the mating surfaces of the half housings with sealer and position the right hand housing onto the left. Position the rear bearing thrust plate.
5. Install the six bearing bolts and tighten to 3 ft. lbs. Install the two thrust plate bolts and tighten to 7 ft. lbs.
6. Be sure the oil seal is installed in the clutch cover and install the clutch cover in place on the transmission housing.
7. Tighten the seven securing bolts to 19 ft. lbs. Rotate the input shaft during the clutch cover retaining bolt tightening.
8. Loosen the six bearing bolts in the housings and tap the half housing with a rubber mallet while rotating the input shaft. Retighten the six bearing bolts to 11 ft. lbs.
9. Install the six assembly bolts in the housing and torque to 7 ft. lbs.
10. Invert the transmission with the rear of the mainshaft upward. Be sure the alignment dowels are in place, coat the mating surfaces of the transmission housing and the intermediate housing with sealing compound and install the intermediate housing in place, while engaging the finger in the selector fork detents.
11. Tighten the five nuts and two bolts to 13 ft. lbs. Place the 5th/reverse spindle to the 5th gear position.
12. Install the 5th/reverse stub shaft and the 5th/reverse synchronizer hub.
NOTE: *If a new hub is used, the marking groove should be towards the reverse gear.*
13. As a unit, install the 5th/reverse synchronizer cage and the selector fork, bringing together the marks on the synchronizer hub and the cage.
14. Align the holes and install a new roll pin. Set the unit to the neutral position.
15. Install the 5th gear and needle bearing, along with the spacer.

5th Gear Assembly and Preparation for Measurements 4th and 5th

1. Press the bearing on to the gear pinion.
NOTE: *When new parts are used, match the pinion gear to the mainshaft by green or yellow color.*
2. Place the 5th gear pinion with the bearing fitted, on a hot plate and place a small piece of solder on the pinion. When the solder melts, place the pinion gear onto the shaft.
NOTE: *A drift may have to be used to seat the gear.*
3. Remove the alignment dowels from the rear housing and set them aside for later use. Install a shim pack, 4.0mm thick and the bearing race, into the rear housing.

Preload of the Mainshaft Tapered Roller Bearing (Number 4 Measurement)

1. Place the rear housing in position on the transmission case. Fit three bolts to hold housing and hand tighten.
2. Rotate the mainshaft, loosen the three bolts of the rear housing and retighten hand tight only.
3. A gap will exist between the two housings. Measure the gap to check for parallelism and to calculate the shim thickness needed to preload the mainshaft bearing.
Example:
- Thickness of basic shim 4.00mm
- Measurement of gap 1.85mm
- Difference 2.15mm
- Plus preload 0.10mm
- Shim thickness required 2.25mm

NOTE: *Shims are available in increments of 0.05mm from 1.5mm to 2.95mm.*
4. Remove the rear housing and remove the rear bearing outer race and the basic 4.00 mm shim pack.

CLUTCH

The purpose of the clutch is to disconnect and connect engine power at the transmission. A car at rest requires a lot of engine torque to get all that weight moving. An internal combustion engine does not develop a high starting torque (unlike steam engines), so it must be allowed to operate without any load until it builds up enough torque to move the car. Torque increases with engine rpm. The clutch allows the engine to build up torque by physically disconnecting the engine from the transmission, relieving the engine of any load or resistance. The transfer of engine power to the transmission (the load) must be smooth and gradual; if it weren't, drive line components would wear out or break quickly. This gradual power transfer is made possible by gradually releasing the clutch pedal. The clutch disc and pressure plate are the connecting link between the engine and transmission. When the clutch pedal is released, the disc and plate contact each other (clutch engagement), physically joining the engine and transmission. When the pedal is pushed in, the disc and plate separate (the clutch is disengaged), disconnecting the engine from the transmission.

The clutch assembly consists of the flywheel, the clutch disc, the clutch pressure plate, the throwout bearing and fork, the actuating linkage and the pedal. The flywheel and clutch pressure plate (driving members) are connected to the engine crankshaft and rotate with it. The clutch disc is located between the flywheel and pressure plate, and splined to the transmission shaft. A driving member is one that is attached to the engine and transfers engine power to a driven member (clutch disc) on the transmission shaft. A driving member (pressure plate) rotates (drives) a driven member (clutch disc) on contact and, in so doing, turns the transmission shaft. There is a circular diaphragm spring within the pressure plate cover (transmission side). In a relaxed state (when the clutch pedal is fully released), this spring is convex; that is, it is dished outward toward the transmission. Pushing in the clutch pedal actuates an attached linkage rod. Connected to the other end of this rod is the throwout bearing fork. The throwout bearing is attached to the fork. When the clutch pedal is depressed, the clutch linkage pushes the fork and bearing forward to contact the diaphragm spring of the pressure plate. The

Troubleshooting Basic Clutch Problems

Problem	Cause
Excessive clutch noise	Throwout bearing noises are more audible at the lower end of pedal travel. The usual causes are: • Riding the clutch • Too little pedal free-play • Lack of bearing lubrication A bad clutch shaft pilot bearing will make a high pitched squeal, when the clutch is disengaged and the transmission is in gear or within the first 2" of pedal travel. The bearing must be replaced. Noise from the clutch linkage is a clicking or snapping that can be heard or felt as the pedal is moved completely up or down. This usually requires lubrication. Transmitted engine noises are amplified by the clutch housing and heard in the passenger compartment. They are usually the result of insufficient pedal free-play and can be changed by manipulating the clutch pedal.
Clutch slips (the car does not move as it should when the clutch is engaged)	This is usually most noticeable when pulling away from a standing start. A severe test is to start the engine, apply the brakes, shift into high gear and SLOWLY release the clutch pedal. A healthy clutch will stall the engine. If it slips it may be due to: • A worn pressure plate or clutch plate • Oil soaked clutch plate • Insufficient pedal free-play
Clutch drags or fails to release	The clutch disc and some transmission gears spin briefly after clutch disengagement. Under normal conditions in average temperatures, 3 seconds is maximum spin-time. Failure to release properly can be caused by: • Too light transmission lubricant or low lubricant level • Improperly adjusted clutch linkage
Low clutch life	Low clutch life is usually a result of poor driving habits or heavy duty use. Riding the clutch, pulling heavy loads, holding the car on a grade with the clutch instead of the brakes and rapid clutch engagement all contribute to low clutch life.

outer edges of the spring are secured to the pressure plate and are pivoted on rings so that when the center of the spring is compressed by the throwout bearing, the outer edges bow outward and, by so doing, pull the pressure plate in the same direction - away from the clutch disc. This action separates the disc from the plate, disengaging the clutch and allowing the transmission to be shifted into another gear. A coil type clutch return spring attached to the clutch pedal arm permits full release of the pedal. Releasing the pedal pulls the throwout bearing away from the diaphragm spring resulting in a reversal of spring position. As bearing pressure is gradually released from the spring center, the outer edges of the spring bow outward, pushing the pressure plate into closer contact with the clutch disc. As the disc and plate move closer together, friction between the two increases and slippage is reduced until, when full spring pressure is applied (by fully releasing the pedal), The speed of the disc and plate are the same. This stops all slipping, creating a direct connection between the plate and disc which results in the transfer of power from the engine to the transmission. The clutch disc is now rotating with the pressure plate at engine speed and, because it is splined to the transmission shaft, the shaft now turns at the same engine speed. Understanding clutch operation can be rather difficult at first; if you're still confused after reading this, consider the following analogy. The action of the diaphragm spring can be compared to that of an oil can bottom. The bottom of an oil can is shaped very much like the clutch diaphragm spring and pushing in on the can bottom and then releasing it produces a similar effect. As mentioned earlier, the clutch pedal return spring permits full release of the pedal and reduces linkage slack due to wear. As the linkage wears, clutch free-pedal travel will increase and free-travel will decrease as the clutch wears. Free-travel is actually throwout bearing lash.

The diaphragm spring type clutches used are available in two different designs: flat diaphragm springs or bent spring. The bent fingers are bent back to create a centrifugal boost ensuring quick re-engagement at higher engine speeds. This design enables pressure plate load to increase as the clutch disc wears and makes low pedal effort possible even with a heavy-duty clutch. The throwout bearing used with the bent finger design is 1¼" long and is shorter than the bearing used with the flat finger design. These bearings are not interchangeable. If the longer bearing is used with the bent finger clutch, free-pedal travel will not exist. This results in clutch slippage and rapid wear.

The transmission varies the gear ratio between the engine and rear wheels. It can be shifted to change engine speed as driving conditions and loads change. The transmission allows disengaging and reversing power from the engine to the wheels.

REMOVAL AND INSTALLATION

NOTE: *These vehicles use a hydraulic clutch.*

1. Remove the transmission or transmission/transfer case assembly.

CAUTION: *The clutch driven disc contains asbestos, which has been determined to be a cancer causing agent. Never clean clutch sur-*

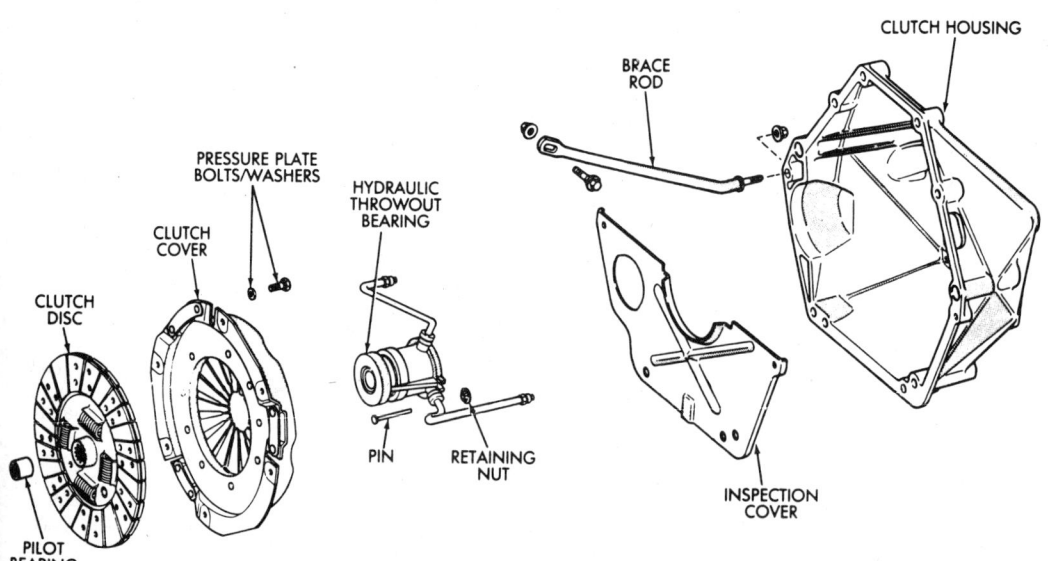

4-cylinder clutch components

DRIVE TRAIN

faces with compressed air! Avoid inhaling any dust from any clutch surface! When cleaning clutch surfaces, use a commercially available brake cleaning fluid.

2. Matchmark the pressure plate and flywheel. Loosen the pressure plate bolts, a little at a time, in rotation, to avoid warpage.

3. Remove the pressure plate and clutch disc.
4. Remove the pilot bushing wick from the bushing bore. Soak the wick in clean engine oil.
5. Installation is the reverse of removal. A clutch aligning tool, either store-bought, or made from an old transmission input shaft, must be used to align the clutch properly for in-

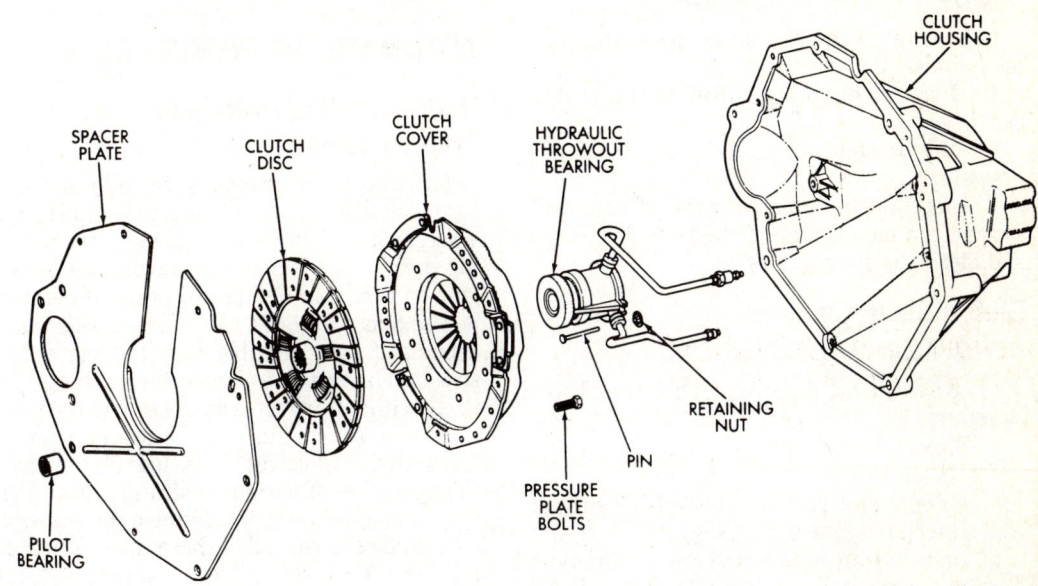

6-cylinder clutch components

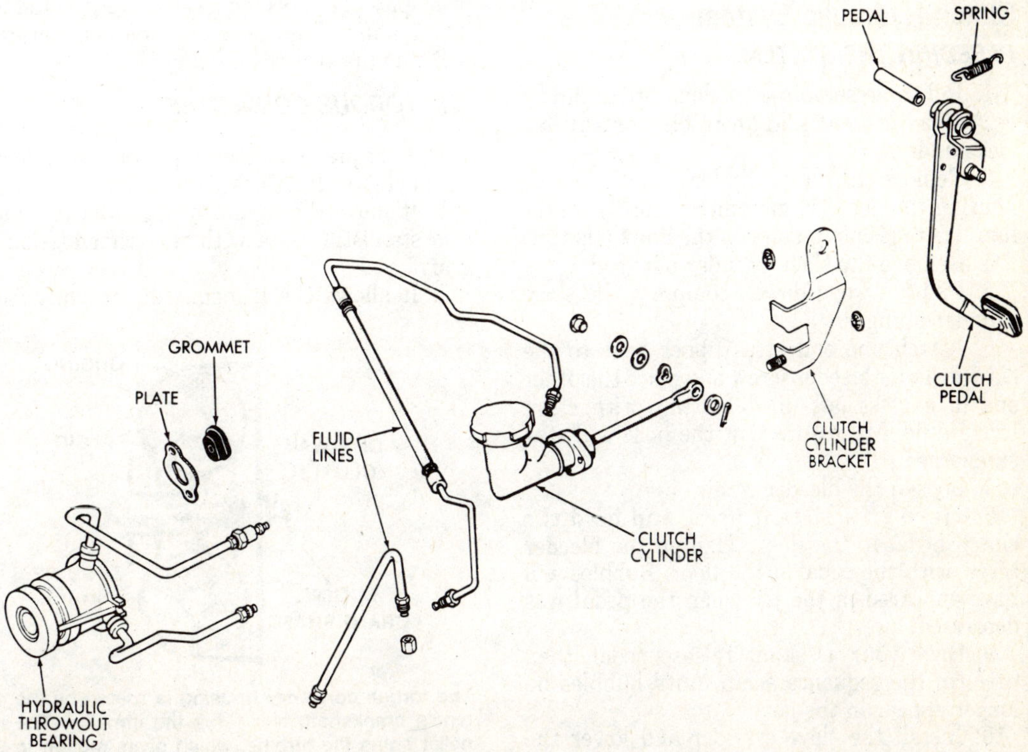

Clutch hydraulic system

DRIVE TRAIN

stallation. The pressure plate bolts must be tightened a little at a time, in rotation, to avoid warpage. Torque the pressure plate bolts to:
- 4-150 and 6-173: 23 ft. lbs.
- 4-126 diesel: 16 ft. lbs.
- 6-243: 40 ft. lbs.

Clutch Master Cylinder

REMOVAL AND INSTALLATION

1. Disconnect the hydraulic line at the master cylinder. Cap the line.
2. Disconnect the pushrod at the clutch pedal.
3. Unbolt the master cylinder from the firewall.
4. Installation is the reverse of removal. Torque the mounting nuts to 19 ft. lbs. Refill and bleed the system.

Clutch Slave Cylinder

REMOVAL AND INSTALLATION

1. Raise and support the truck on jackstands.
2. Disconnect the hydraulic line at the cylinder. Cap the line.
3. Unbolt and remove the slave cylinder from the clutch housing.
4. Installation is the reverse of removal. Torque the mounting bolts to 16 ft. lbs. Refill and bleed the system.

Clutch Hydraulic System

BLEEDING THE SYSTEM

1. Fill the reservoir with clean brake fluid.
2. Raise and support the truck on jackstands.
3. Remove the slave cylinder from the clutch housing, but do not disconnect the hydraulic line. There is enough play in the line to do this.
4. Remove the slave cylinder pushrod.
5. Using a wood dowel, compress the slave cylinder plunger.
6. Attach one end of a rubber hose to the slave cylinder bleeder screw and place the other end in a glass jar, filled halfway with clean brake fluid. Make sure that the hose will stay submerged.
7. Loosen the bleeder screw.
8. Have an assistant press and hold the clutch pedal to the floor. Tighten the bleeder screw with the pedal at the floor. Bubbles will have appeared in the jar when the pedal was depressed.
9. Have your assistant release pedal, then perform the sequence again, until bubbles no longer appear in the jar.
10. Install the slave cylinder and lower the truck. Test the clutch.

Automatic Transmission Application Chart

Transmission	Years
Chrysler 904 3-speed	1984–86
AISIN/Warner AW4 4-speed	1986–89

AUTOMATIC TRANSMISSION

Understanding Automatic Transmissions

The automatic transmission allows engine torque and power to be transmitted to the rear wheels within a narrow range of engine operating speeds. The transmission will allow the engine to turn fast enough to produce plenty of power and torque at very low speeds, while keeping it at a sensible rpm at high vehicle speeds. The transmission performs this job entirely without driver assistance. The transmission uses a light fluid as the medium for the transmission of power. This fluid also works in the operation of various hydraulic control circuits and as a lubricant. Because the transmission fluid performs all of these three functions, trouble within the unit can easily travel from one part to another. For this reason, and because of the complexity and unusual operating principles of the transmission, a very sound understanding of the basic principles of operation will simplify troubleshooting.

THE TORQUE CONVERTER

The torque converter replaces the conventional clutch. It has three functions:
1. It allows the engine to idle with the vehicle at a standstill, even with the transmission in gear.
2. It allows the transmission to shift from

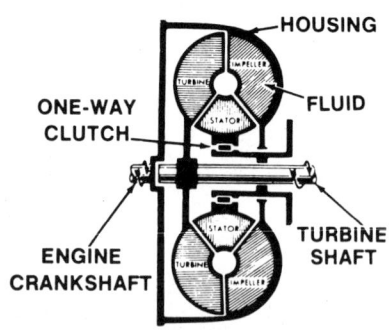

The torque converter housing is roated by the engine's crankshaft, and turns the impeller. The impeller spins the turbine, which gives motion to the turbine shaft, driving the gears

Transmission Fluid Indications

The appearance and odor of the transmission fluid can give valuable clues to the overall condition of the transmission. Always note the appearance of the fluid when you check the fluid level or change the fluid. Rub a small amount of fluid between your fingers to feel for grit and smell the fluid on the dipstick.

If the fluid appears:	It indicates:
Clear and red colored	• Normal operation
Discolored (extremely dark red or brownish) or smells burned	• Band or clutch pack failure, usually caused by an overheated transmission. Hauling very heavy loads with insufficient power or failure to change the fluid, often result in overheating. Do not confuse this appearance with newer fluids that have a darker red color and a strong odor (though not a burned odor).
Foamy or aerated (light in color and full of bubbles)	• The level is too high (gear train is churning oil) • An internal air leak (air is mixing with the fluid). Have the transmission checked professionally.
Solid residue in the fluid	• Defective bands, clutch pack or bearings. Bits of band material or metal abrasives are clinging to the dipstick. Have the transmission checked professionally.
Varnish coating on the dipstick	• The transmission fluid is overheating

Troubleshooting Basic Automatic Transmission Problems

Problem	Cause	Solution
Fluid leakage	• Defective pan gasket	• Replace gasket or tighten pan bolts
	• Loose filler tube	• Tighten tube nut
	• Loose extension housing to transmission case	• Tighten bolts
	• Converter housing area leakage	• Have transmission checked professionally
Fluid flows out the oil filler tube	• High fluid level	• Check and correct fluid level
	• Breather vent clogged	• Open breather vent
	• Clogged oil filter or screen	• Replace filter or clean screen (change fluid also)
	• Internal fluid leakage	• Have transmission checked professionally
Transmission overheats (this is usually accompanied by a strong burned odor to the fluid)	• Low fluid level	• Check and correct fluid level
	• Fluid cooler lines clogged	• Drain and refill transmission. If this doesn't cure the problem, have cooler lines cleared or replaced.
	• Heavy pulling or hauling with insufficient cooling	• Install a transmission oil cooler
	• Faulty oil pump, internal slippage	• Have transmission checked professionally
Buzzing or whining noise	• Low fluid level	• Check and correct fluid level
	• Defective torque converter, scored gears	• Have transmission checked professionally
No forward or reverse gears or slippage in one or more gears	• Low fluid level	• Check and correct fluid level
	• Defective vacuum or linkage controls, internal clutch or band failure	• Have unit checked professionally
Delayed or erratic shift	• Low fluid level	• Check and correct fluid level
	• Broken vacuum lines	• Repair or replace lines
	• Internal malfunction	• Have transmission checked professionally

Lockup Torque Converter Service Diagnosis

Problem	Cause	Solution

No lockup	• Faulty oil pump
	• Sticking governor valve
	• Valve body malfunction
	   (a) Stuck switch valve
	   (b) Stuck lockup valve
	   (c) Stuck fail-safe valve
	• Failed locking clutch
	• Leaking turbine hub seal
	• Faulty input shaft or seal ring
		• Replace oil pump
		• Repair or replace as necessary
		• Repair or replace valve body or its internal components as necessary
		
		• Replace torque converter
		• Replace torque converter
		• Repair or replace as necessary

Will not unlock	• Sticking governor valve
	• Valve body malfunction
	   (a) Stuck switch valve
	   (b) Stuck lockup valve
	   (c) Stuck fail-safe valve
		• Repair or replace as necessary
		• Repair or replace valve body or its internal components as necessary

Stays locked up at too low a speed in direct	• Sticking governor valve
	• Valve body malfunction
	   (a) Stuck switch valve
	   (b) Stuck lockup valve
	   (c) Stuck fail-safe valve
		• Repair or replace as necessary
		• Repair or replace valve body or its internal components as necessary

Locks up or drags in low or second	• Faulty oil pump
	• Valve body malfunction
	   (a) Stuck switch valve
	   (b) Stuck fail-safe valve
		• Replace oil pump
		• Repair or replace valve body or its internal components as necessary

Sluggish or stalls in reverse	• Faulty oil pump
	• Plugged cooler, cooler lines or fittings
	• Valve body malfunction
	   (a) Stuck switch valve
	   (b) Faulty input shaft or seal ring
		• Replace oil pump as necessary
		• Flush or replace cooler and flush lines and fittings
		• Repair or replace valve body or its internal components as necessary

Loud chatter during lockup engagement (cold)	• Faulty torque converter • Failed locking clutch • Leaking turbine hub seal	• Replace torque converter • Replace torque converter • Replace torque converter
Vibration or shudder during lockup engagement	• Faulty oil pump • Valve body malfunction • Faulty torque converter • Engine needs tune-up	• Repair or replace oil pump as necessary • Repair or replace valve body or its internal components as necessary • Replace torque converter • Tune engine
Vibration after lockup engagement	• Faulty torque converter • Exhaust system strikes underbody • Engine needs tune-up • Throttle linkage misadjusted	• Replace torque converter • Align exhaust system • Tune engine • Adjust throttle linkage
Vibration when revved in neutral Overheating: oil blows out of dip stick tube or pump seal	• Torque converter out of balance • Plugged cooler, cooler lines or fittings • Stuck switch valve	• Replace torque converter • Flush or replace cooler and flush lines and fittings • Repair switch valve in valve body or replace valve body
Shudder after lockup engagement	• Faulty oil pump • Plugged cooler, cooler lines or fittings • Valve body malfunction • Faulty torque converter • Fail locking clutch • Exhaust system strikes underbody • Engine needs tune-up • Throttle linkage misadjusted	• Replace oil pump • Flush or replace cooler and flush lines and fittings • Repair or replace valve body or its internal components as necessary • Replace torque converter • Replace torque converter • Align exhaust system • Tune engine • Adjust throttle linkage

range to range smoothly, without requiring that the driver close the throttle during the shift.

3. It multiplies engine torque to an increasing extent as vehicle speed drops and throttle opening is increased. This has the effect of making the transmission more responsive and reduces the amount of shifting required.

The torque converter is a metal case which is shaped lika sphere that has been flattened on opposite sides. It is bolted to the rear end of the engine's crankshaft. Generally, the entire metal case rotates at engine speed and serves as the engine's flywheel.

The case contains three sets of blades. One set is attached directly to the case. This set forms the torus or pump. Another set is directly connected to the output shaft, and forms the turbine. The third set is mounted on a hub which, in turn, is mounted on a stationary shaft through a one-way clutch. This third set is known as the stator.

A pump, which is driven by the covnerter hub at engine speed, keeps the torque converter full of transmission fluid at all times. Fluid flows continuously through the unit to provide cooling.

Under low-speed acceleration, the torque converter functions as follows:

The torus is turning faster than the turbine. It picks up fluid at the center of the converter and, through centrifugal force, slings it outward. Since the outer edge of the converter moves faster than the portions at the center, the fluid picks up speed.

The fluid then enters the outer edge of the turbine blades. It then travels back toward the center of the converter case along the turbine blades. In impinging upon the turbine blades, the fluid loses the energy picked up in the torus.

If the fluid were now to immediately be returned directly into the torus, both halves of the converter would have to turn at approximately the same speed at all times, and torque input and output would both be the same.

In flowing through the torus and turbine, the fluid picks up two types of flow, or flow in two spearate directions. It flows through the turbine blades, and it spins with the engine. The stator, whose blades are stationary when the vehicle is being accelerated at low speeds, converts one type of flow into another. Instead of allowing the fluid to flow straight back into the torus, the stator's curved blades turn the fluid almost 90 degrees toward the direction of rotation of the engine. Thus the fluid does not flow as fast toward the torus, but is already spinning when the torus picks it up. This has the effect of allowing the torus to turn much faster than the turbine. This difference in speed may be compared to the difference in speed between the smaller and larger gears in any gear train. The result is that engine power output is higher, and engine torque is multiplied.

As the speed of the turbine increases, the fluid spins faster and faster in the direction of engine rotation. As a result, the ability of the stator to redirect the fluid flow is reduced. Under cruising conditions, the stator is eventually forced to rotate on its one-way clutch in the direction of engine rotation. Under these conditions, the torque converter begins to behave almost like a solid shaft, with the torus and turbine speeds being almost equal.

THE PLANETARY GEARBOX

The ability of the torque converter to multiply engine torque is limited. Also, the unit tends to be more efficient when the turine is rotating at relatively high speeds. Therefore, a planetary gearbox is used to carry the power output of the turbine to the driveshaft.

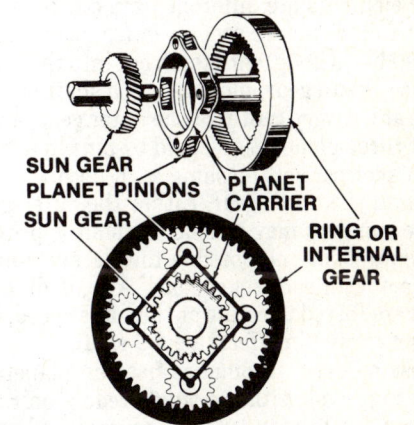

Planetary gears are similar to manual transmission gears but are composed of three parts

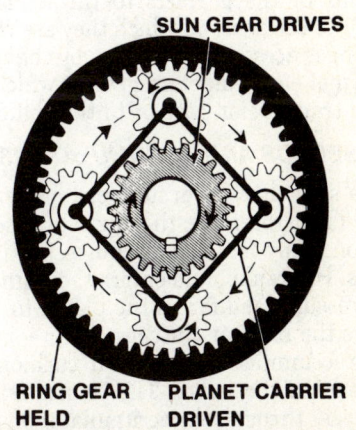

Planetary gears in the maximum reduction (low) range. The ring gear is held and a lower gear ration is obtained

DRIVE TRAIN

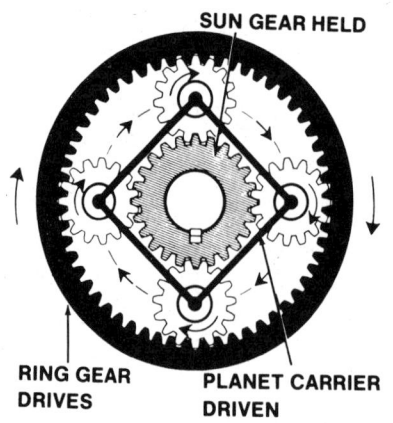

Planetary gears in the minimum reduction (drive) range. The ring gear is allowed to revolve, providing a higher gear ratio

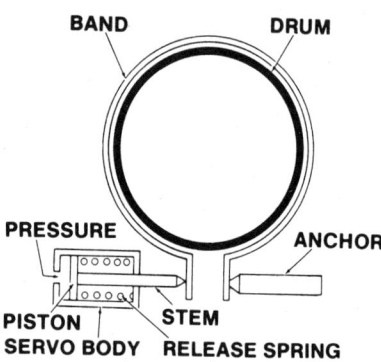

Servos, operated by pressure, are used to apply or release the bands, to either hold the ring gear or allow it to rotate

Planetary gears function very similarly to conventional transmission gears. However, their construction is different in that three elements make up one gear system, and, in that all three elements are different from one another. The three elements are: an outer gear that is shaped like a hoop, with teeth cut into the inner surface; a sun gear, mounted on a shaft and located at the very center of the outer gear; and a set of three planet gears, held by pins in a ring-like planet carrier, meshing with both the sun gear and the outer gear. Either the outer gear or the sun gear may be held stationary, providing more than one possible torque multiplication factor for each set of gears. Also, if all three gears are forced to rotate at the same speed, the gearset forms, in effect, a solid shaft.

Most modern automatics use the planetary gears to provide either a single reduction ratio of about 1.8:1, or two reduction gears: a low of about 2.5:1, and an intermediate of about 1.5:1. Bands and clutches are used to hold various portions of the gearsets to the transmission case or to the shaft on which they are mounted. Shifting is accomplished, then, by changing the portion of each planetary gearset which is held to the tranmission case or to the shaft.

THE SERVOS AND ACCUMULATORS

The servos are hydraulic pistons and cylinders. They resemble the hydraulic actuators used on many familiar machines, such as bulldozers. Hydraulic fluid enters the cylinder, under pressure, and forces the piston to move to engage the band or clutches.

The accumulators are used to cushion the engagement of the servos. The transmission fluid must pass through the accumulator on the way to the servo. The accumulator housing contains a thin piston which is sprung away from the discharge passage of the accumulator. When fluid passes through the accumulator on the way to the servo, it must move the piston against spring pressure, and this action smooths out the action of the servo.

THE HYDRAULIC CONTROL SYSTEM

The hydraulic pressure used to operate the servos comes from the main transmission oil pump. This fluid is channeled to the various servos through the shift valves. There is generally a manual shift valve which is operated by the tranmission selector lever and an automatic shift valvee for each automatic upshift the transmission provides: i.e., two-speed automatics have a low-high shift valve, while three-speeds have a 1-2 valve, and a 2-3 vavle.

There are two pressures which effect the operation of these valves. One is the governor pressure which is affected by vehicle speed. The other is the modulator pressure which is affected by intake manifold vacuum or throttle position. Governor pressure rises with an increase in vehicle speed, and modulator pressure rises as the throttle is opened wider. By responding to these two pressures, the shift valves cause the upshift points to be delayed with increased throttle opening to make the best use of the engine's power output.

Most transmissions also make use of an auxiliary circuit for downshifting. This circuit may be actuated by the throttle linkage or the vacuum line which actuates the modulator, or by a cable or solenoid. It applies pressure to a special downshift surface on the shift valve or valves.

The transmission modulator also governs the line pressure, used to actuate the servos. In this way, the clutches and bands will be actuated with a force matching the torque output of the engine.

Pan Removal and Fluid Change

1. Raise and support the truck on jackstands.

DRIVE TRAIN

2. The pan has no drain plug, so remove the bolts at one corner and loosen the other pan bolts so that the fluid drains neatly from the one, low-hanging corner.

3. Remove the remaining bolts and remove the pan. Discard the gasket.

4. Unbolt and remove the filter from the valve body.

5. Install the new filter and torque the bolts to 35 in. lbs.

6. Coat a new pan gasket with sealer and install the pan. Torque the bolts to 150 in. lbs. (12 ft. lbs.). Fill the transmission.

Auxiliary Oil Cooler

REMOVAL AND INSTALLATION

1. Remove the attaching screws and lift off the grille panel.

2. Using masking tape, mark the cooler lines for installation.

3. Place a drain pan on the ground, under the cooler.

4. Loosen the clamps securing the hoses to the cooler and slide them out of the way.

5. Twist the hoses to free them from the cooler pipes and slide the off. Cap the hose ends

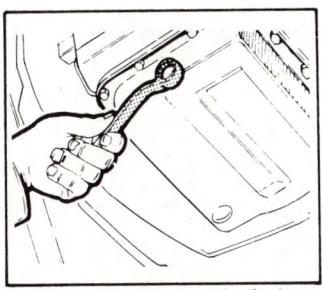

1. Position a catch pan under the transmission. If equipped, remove the drain plug. Be careful; the fluid may be hot.

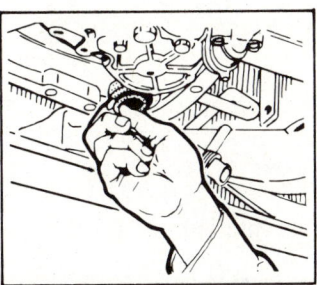

4. Remove the old O-ring from the filter neck and replace with new O-Ring supplied with filter kit.

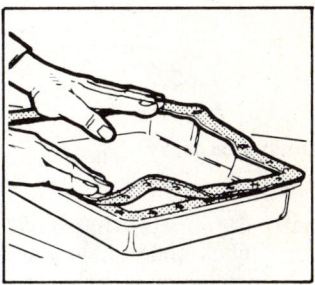

7. Install a new gasket on the pan.

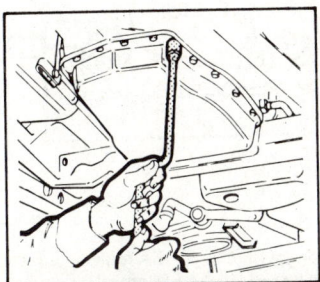

2. Many late-model vehicles have no drain plug. Loosen the pan bolts and allow one corner of the pan to tilt slightly to drain the fluid.

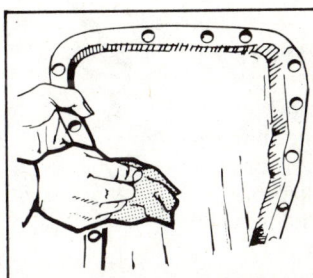

5. Clean the pan thoroughly with gasoline and allow to air dry completely.

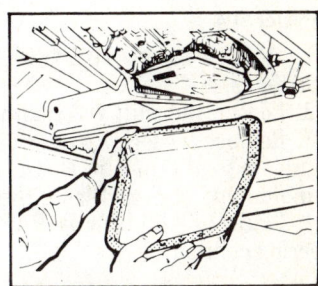

8. Install the new pan and gasket. Do not overtighten the screws.

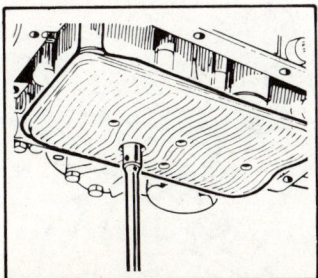

3. The filter or screen is held on by bolts or screws. Remove the filter or screen straight down.

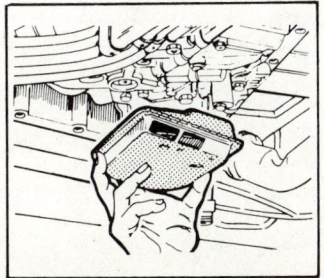

6. Install the new filter. Be sure the intake pipe is seated in the O-ring. Some transmissions use a screen which can be cleaned in gasoline and air dried.

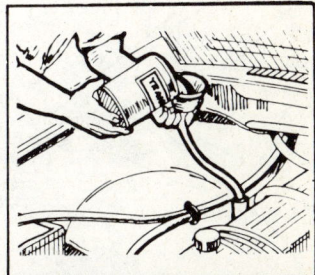

9. Fill the transmission with the required amount of fluid. Do not overfill. Start the engine and shift through all the gears. Check the fluid level and add fluid if necessary.

310 DRIVE TRAIN

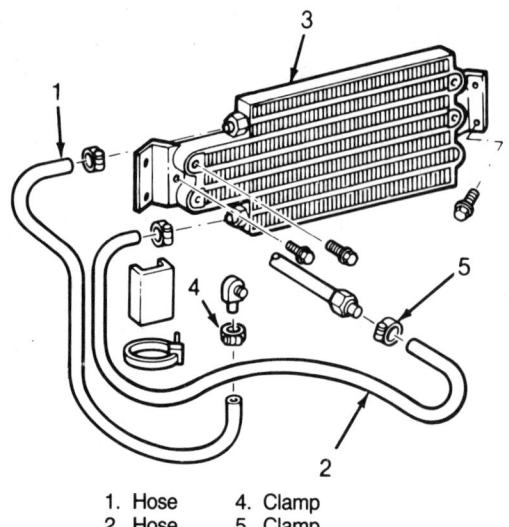

1. Hose
2. Hose
3. Cooler
4. Clamp
5. Clamp

Auxiliary oil cooler

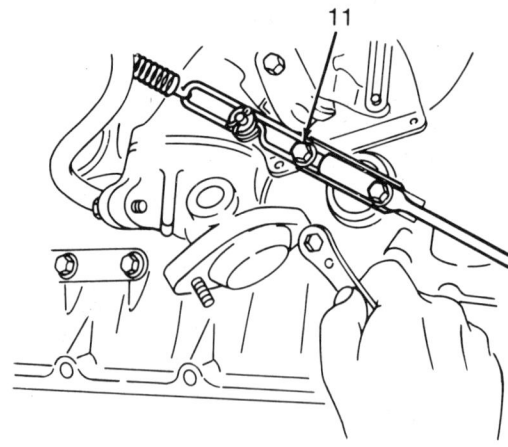

Carbureted 4-150 throttle control adjusting link. 11 is the link bolt

and cooler outlets to prevent dirt from entering.
6. Unbolt and remove the cooler.
7. Installation is the reverse of removal. Add sufficient fluid to refill the system.

Adjustments

SHIFT LINKAGE

Chrysler 904

1. Raise and support the truck on jackstands.
2. Loosen the shift rod trunnion locknuts.
3. Remove the lockpin retaining the shift rod trunnion to the bellcrank and disengage the trunnion and shift rod from the bellcrank.
4. Place the shift lever in PARK and lock the steering column.

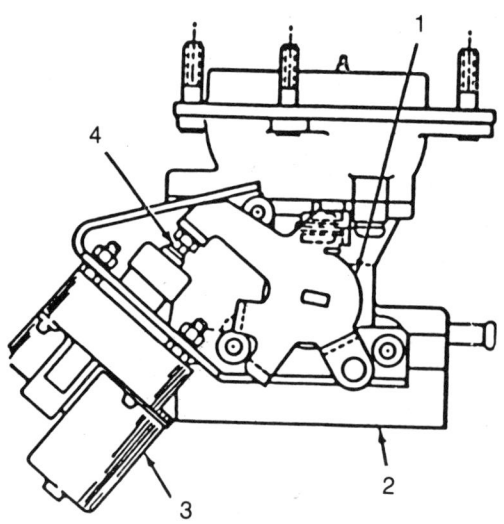

1. Throttle lever
2. Throttle body
3. ISA motor
4. Plunger

ISA motor on the fuel injected 4-150

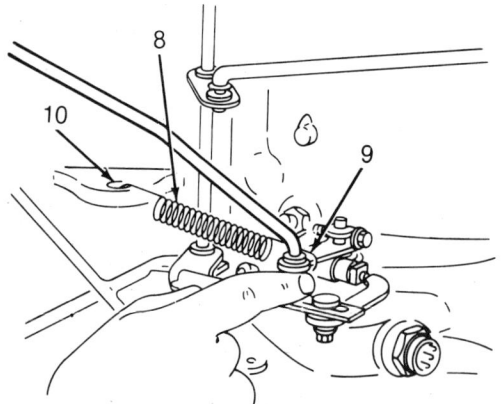

4-150 throttle linkage adjustment. 8 is the spring you supply, 9 is the control lever, 10 is the throttle linkage bellcrank bracket

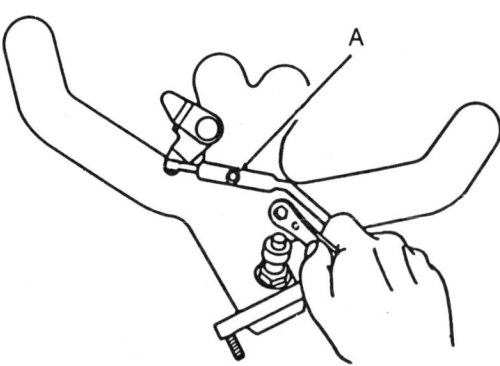

Throttle control adjusting link bolt (A) on the fuel injected 4-150

DRIVE TRAIN 311

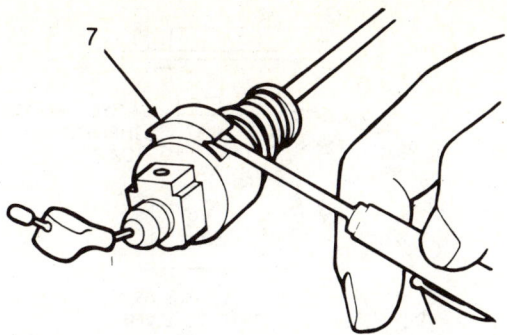

Releasing the T-shaped cable adjuster clamp (7)

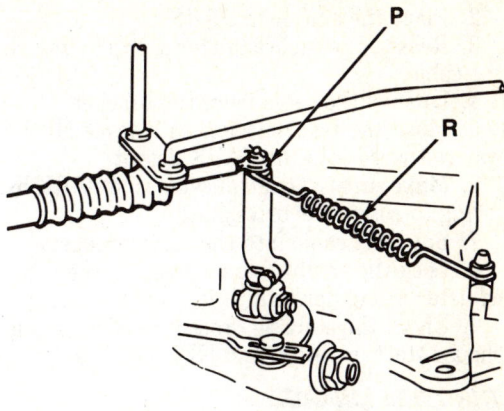

Spring (R), supplied by you, attached to the lever (P)

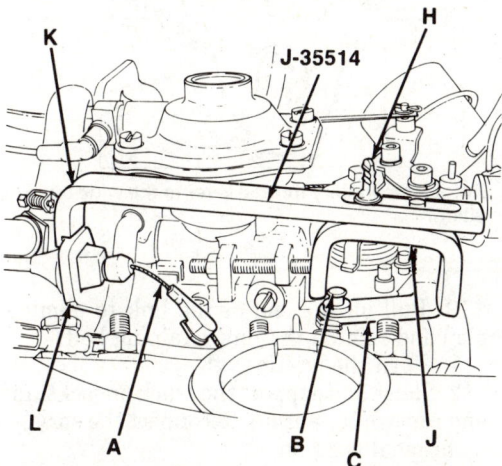

A. Throttle valve cable
B. Cable pin
C. Throttle valve lever
H. Thumbscrew
J. Sliding legs
K. Notched leg
L. Cable bracket

Throttle valve cable and adjusting tool installed

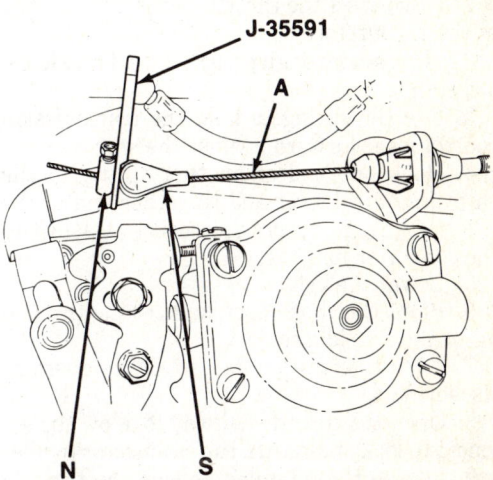

Gauge attached to the cable (A), between the cable stop (N) and the retainer (S)

5. Move the lever on the transmission rearward to the PARK detent. PARK is the last possible rearward position.

6. Check to make sure that PARK is engaged, by trying to rotate the driveshaft by hand.

7. Adjust the shift rod trunnion so that the pin fits freely in the bellcrank arm and tighten the trunnion locknuts. Prevent the shift rod from turning while tightening the locknuts.

NOTE: *All lash in the linkage must be eliminated to provide for proper adjustment. Lash can be eliminated by pulling downward on the shift rod and pressing upward on the bellcrank.*

8. Check that the engine starts in only the PARK and NEUTRAL positions, and that all shift ranges work properly.

9. Lower the truck.

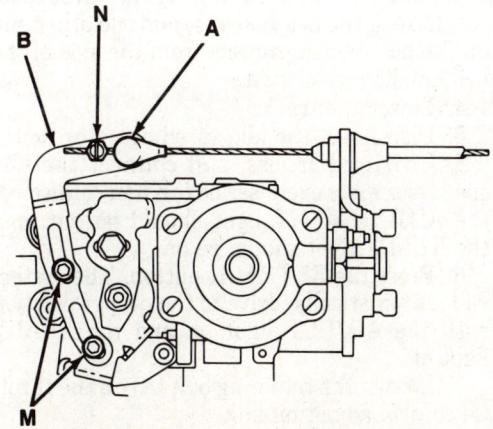

A. Throttle valve cable
B. Lever
M. Adjusting screws
N. Cable stop

Throttle valve cable adjustment points

AW-4

1. Raise and support the front end on jackstands.

312 DRIVE TRAIN

2. Place the shifter in PARK.
3. Release the cable adjuster clamp to unlock the cable.
4. Unsnap the cable from the bracket.
5. Move the transmission shift lever all the way rearward into the PARK detent.
6. Make sure the transmission is in PARK by trying to rotate the driveshaft.
7. Snap the cable into the cable bracket.
8. Lock the shaft cable by pressing the cable adjuster clamp down until it snaps into place.
9. Check the starting procedure. The engine should start in PARK and NEUTRAL only!

THROTTLE LINKAGE

Chrysler 904 With the Carbureted 4-150 Engine

1. Disconnect the throttle control rod spring at the carburetor.
2. Raise and support the truck on jackstands.
3. Use the spring to hold the transmission control lever forward against the stop.
4. Hook one end of another spring to the throttle control lever and the other end to the throttle linkage bellcrank bracket attached to the converter housing.
5. Lower the vehicle.
6. Block the choke open and set the throttle off of the fast idle cam.
7. Turn the ignition lock to ON to energize the solenoid.
8. Open the throttle halfway to allow the solenoid to lock and return the carburetor to idle.
9. Loosen the retaining bolt on the throttle control adjusting link. DO NOT REMOVE THE SPRING CLIP AND NYLON WASHER!

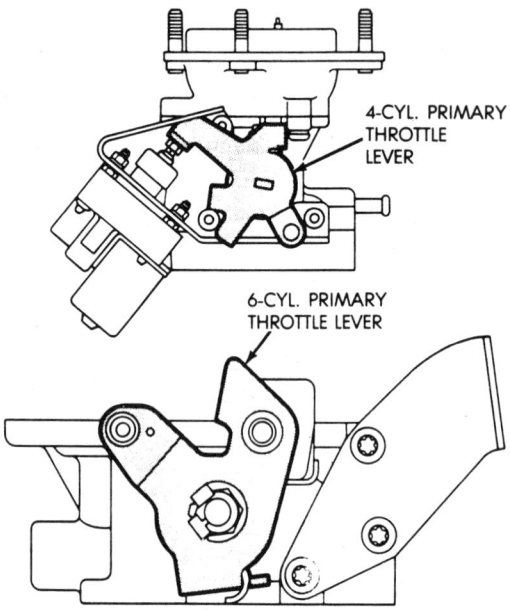

Rotate the primary throttle lever to the wide open position

10. Pull on the end of the link to eliminate play and tighten the link retaining bolt.
11. Turn the ignition off.
12. Raise and support the truck on jackstands and remove the spring. Reconnect the spring in its original position.
13. Lower the truck.

Chrysler 904 with the Fuel Injected 4-150 Engine

1. Place the ignition switch in the OFF position.
2. Raise and support the front end on jackstands.
3. Obtain a small, about 2" long, coil spring. Hook one end of the spring on the throttle lever, next to the bell housing, and the other end on the boss which projects from the side of the bell housing, as shown.
4. Lower the truck.
5. Disconnect the idle speed actuator motor (ISA) wiring harness, and connect the idle speed assembly exerciser box. When connected, the ADJUSTMENT light should go out, and the READY light should go on.
6. Press the RETRACK button. The system will, automatically, drive to the proper position with the ADJUST light on and the READY light off.
7. Loosen the retaining bolt (A) on the throttle control adjusting link.
8. Pull on the end of the link to eliminate all play and tighten the bolt.
9. Press the EXTEND button on the exerciser box until the ISA motor ratchets.

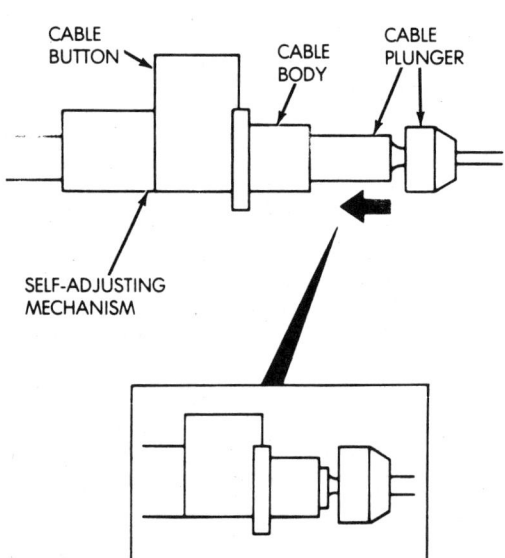

Retract the throttle cable plunger

DRIVE TRAIN 313

10. Disconnect the exerciser box and reconnect the ISA motor harness.
11. Raise the vehicle and remove your spring.
12. Lower the vehicle.

Chrysler 904 With the 6-173 Engine

1. Remove the air cleaner.
2. Raise and support the truck on jackstands.
3. Hold the throttle control lever rearward against its stop, using a spring selected for that purpose.
4. Lower the truck.
5. Block the choke open and set the carburetor linkage completely off of the fast idle cam.
6. Unlock the throttle control cable by releasing the T-shaped cable adjuster clamp. Release the clamp by lifting upward with a small screwdriver.
7. Grasp the cable outer sheath and move the cable and sheath forward to remove any cable load on the throttle bellcrank.
8. Adjust the cable by moving the cable and sheath rearward until there is zero lash between the plastic cable end and the bellcrank ball.
9. Lock the cable end by pressing the T-shaped cable adjuster clamp downward until the clamp snaps into place.
10. Install the air cleaner.
11. Remove the spring.
12. Road test the truck.

THROTTLE CABLE

6-243 with the AW-4

1. Turn the ignition switch to **OFF**.
2. Press the throttle cable button all the way down, then, push the cable plunger inward.
3. Rotate the primary throttle lever to the wide open throttle position.
4. Hold the primary throttle lever in this position and let the cable plunger extend.
5. Release the lever when the plungr is fully extended.
6. The cable is now adjusted.

THROTTLE VALVE LEVER AND CABLE

4-126 Diesel

NOTE: *Special tool J-35514 and gauge J-35591 are necessary for this procedure.*

1. Disconnect the throttle valve cable from the pin on the throttle valve lever.
2. Disconnect the cable from the transmission throttle lever. Remove and discard the cable.
3. Set the injection pump automatic advance lever at the curb idle position (seated against the stop).
4. Loosen the set screw and turn the cable clevis ¼ turn counterclockwise. Tighten the set screw.
5. Install the special tool as shown.
6. Loosen the thumbscrew on the tool and move the sliding legs rearward.
7. Place the notched leg of the tool on the cable bracket. Then, rest the sliding legs on the lever.
8. Move the sliding legs forward until the rear leg lightly touches the cable attaching pin. Tighten the thumbscrew.
9. Move the lever to the wide open throttle position. The cable attaching pin should now lightly touch the forward leg of the sliding legs.
10. If the cable ataching pin does not touch the forward leg, or if the pin tends to move the special tool, hold the lever in the wide open throttle position, loosen the two lever adjusting screws and move the lever to adjust the travel. Tighten the screws to 66 in. lbs. Return the lever to the curb idle position and verify that the pin is, again, lightly touching the rear leg of the sliding legs. If the pin doesn't touch the rear leg at curb idle, loosen the thunbscrew and adjust the tool so that it does, and repeat the adjustment.
11. Install a new throttle valve cable, part number 8953 001 796.
12. The new cable should be supplied with a cable stop, or one can be obtained from a lawn mower shop, motorcycle repair shop or small engines outlet. The throttle stop should have an inside diameter of 1.07mm.
13. The new cable has a factory installed cable stop crimped onto the end of the cable. Cut this off and slide inner cable stop off the cable. Slide the new cable stop into place and hand tighten the set screw.
14. Connect the new cable to the throttle valve lever pin.
15. Obtain a small coil spring and use it to hold the throttle valve lever against its stop.
16. Loosen the cable stop and install gauge J-35591 between the cable stop and the retainer.
17. Remove all slack from the cable.
18. Slide the cable stop rearward against the gauge and retainer. Securely tighten the set screw and remove the gauge. Remove the spring that you used on the throttle lever. Loosen the clevis set screw and turn the clevis screw back ¼ turn.

FRONT BAND

Chrysler 904

1. Raise and support the truck on jackstands. The front band adjusting screw is located on the left side of the case, just above the control levers.
2. Loosen the locknut and back it off about five turns.

314 DRIVE TRAIN

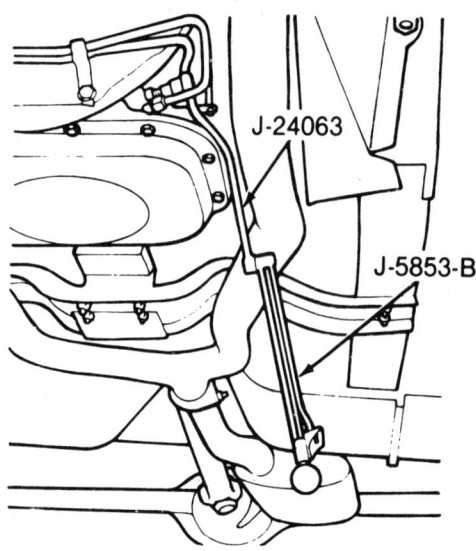

904 front band adjustment

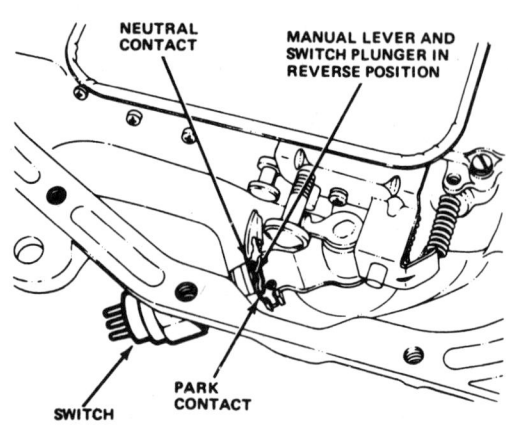

Neutral start switch location on vehicles equipped with Chrysler-built transmissions

3. Make sure that the screw turns freely. Use penetrating oil if it binds.
4. Tighten the screw to 72 in. lbs.
5. Back off the screw 2½ turns.
6. Tighten the locknut to 35 ft. lbs. Hold the screw still while tightening the locknut.
7. Lower the truck.

INTERMEDIATE BAND
Chrysler 904

1. Raise and support the truck on jackstands.
2. Drain the fluid and remove the pan.
3. Remove the adjusting screw locknut.
4. Tighten the adjusting screw to 41 in. lbs.
5. Back off the adjusting screw as follows 7 turns.
6. Hold the adjusting screw still and tighten the locknut to 35 ft. lbs.
7. Replace the pan and fill the unit.

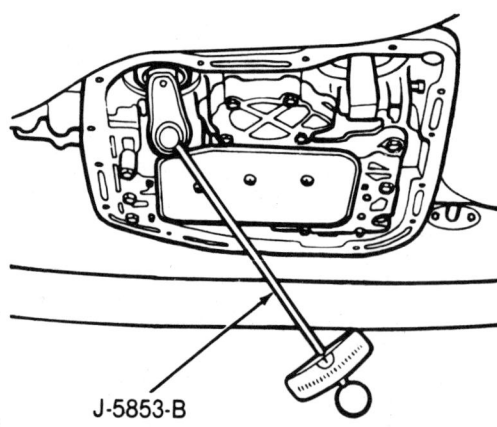

904 intermediate band adjustment

Neutral Start and Back-Up Light Switch

ADJUSTMENT AND REPLACEMENT
Chrysler 904

The neutral start switch on the 904 units is non-adjustable. If the truck starts in any position other than PARK or NEUTRAL, and the linkage adjustment is correct, the switch must be replaced. To replace the switch, simply unbolt it from the transmission, disconnect the wires and install a new switch.

AW-4
REMOVAL

1. Raise and support the front end on jackstands.
2. Disconnect the wiring at the switch.

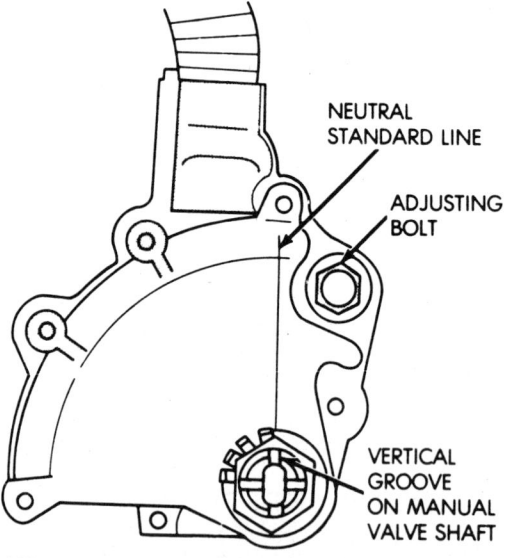

AW-4 neutral start switch adjustment

DRIVE TRAIN

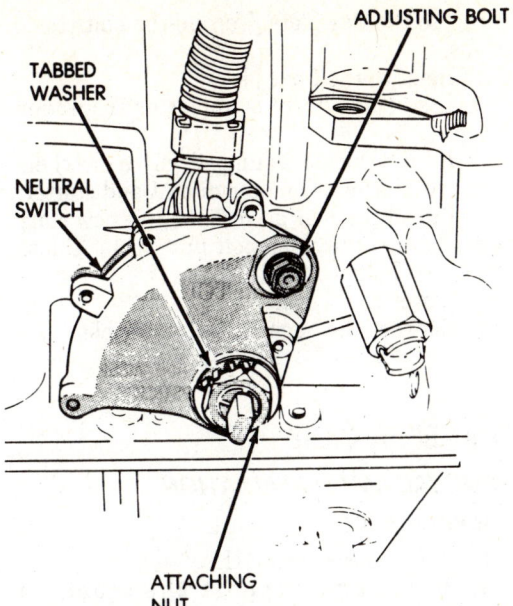

AW-4 neutral start switch removal

3. Pry open the locktabs and remove the switch retaining nut and washer.
4. Remove the switch adjusting bolt.
5. Slide the switch off the manual valve shaft.

INSTALLATION AND ADJUSTMENT

1. Disconnect the shift linkage rod from the shift lever at the transmission.
2. Rotate the shift lever all the way rearward, then forward 2 dentent positions to Neutral.
3. Position the switch on the valve shaft and install the adjusting bolt finger tightly.
4. Install the washer and attaching nut and torque the nut to 60 in. lbs., but don't bend the tabbed washer yet.
5. With the transmission in neutral, rotate the switch to align the neutral standard line with the groove on the valve shaft.
6. Hold the switch in this position and tighten the adjusting bolt to 108 in. lbs.
7. Bend the tabbed washer over the retaining nut.
8. Connect the shift linkage rod.
9. Connect the switch wiring.
10. Check the switch operation. The enfine should start in PARK and NEUTRAL only!

Transmission

REMOVAL AND INSTALLATION

2-Wheel Drive

1. Disconnect the negative battery cable. Raise and support the vehicle on jackstands.

2. Matchmark the rear driveshaft and yoke for reassembly. Disconnect and remove the rear driveshaft.
3. Remove the torque converter inspection cover. Mark the converter drive plate and converter assembly for reassembly.
4. Remove the bolts attaching the torque converter to the flex plate. Support the transmission assembly on a floor jack.
5. Remove the bolts attaching the rear crossmember to the transmission side rail. Disconnect the exhaust pipe at the catalytic converter.
6. Lower the transmission slightly in order to disconnect the fluid cooler lines.
7. Disconnect the backup light switch wire and the speedometer cable. Disconnect the transmission linkage.
8. Remove the bolts attaching the transmission assembly to the engine. Move the transmission assembly and the torque converter rearward to clear the crankshaft.
9. Carefully lower the transmission assembly from the vehicle.

To install:
10. Carefully raise the transmission into position.
11. Install the bolts attaching the transmission assembly to the engine. Torque the bolts to 25 ft. lbs. for the 904 and 999. On the AW-4, torque the 10mm bolts to 25 ft. lbs.; the 12mm bolts to 42 ft. lbs.
12. Connect the backup light switch wire.
13. Connect the speedometer cable.
14. Connect the transmission linkage.
15. Connect the fluid cooler lines.
16. Install the rear crossmember. Torque the crossmember bolts to 30 ft. lbs.; the transmission-to-crossmember bolts to 33 ft. lbs.
17. Connect the exhaust pipe at the catalytic converter.
18. Install the bolts attaching the torque converter to the flex plate. Torque the bolts to 40 ft. lbs.
19. Remove the floor jack.
20. Install the torque converter inspection cover.
21. Install the driveshaft. Jeep recommends that new strap bolts be used everytime the driveshaft is disconnected. Torque the nuts to 14 ft. lbs.
22. Lower the truck.
23. Connect the negative battery cable.

4-Wheel Drive

1. Disconnect the negative battery cable. Raise and support the vehicle safely.
2. Matchmark the rear driveshaft and yoke for reassembly. Disconnect and remove the rear driveshaft.
3. Remove the torque converter inspection

DRIVE TRAIN

cover. Mark the converter drive plate and converter assembly for reassembly.

4. Remove the bolts attaching the torque converter to the flex plate. Support the transmission assembly with a floor jack.

NOTE: *If the vehicle is equipped with a diesel engine, support the engine with a jack ubder the crankshaft damper, and remove the left motor mount and starter in order to gain access to the torque converter drive plate bolts through the starter opening.*

5. Remove the bolts attaching the rear crossmember to the transmission side rail. Disconnect the exhaust pipe at the catalytic converter.

6. Lower the transmission slightly in order to disconnect the fluid cooler lines. Matchmark the front driveshaft assembly for installation. Disconnect the driveshaft at the transfer case and secure the assembly out of the way.

7. Disconnect the backup light switch wire and the speedometer cable. Disconnect the transfer case and the transmission linkage. Disconnect the vacuum lines and the vent hose.

8. Remove the bolts attaching the transmission assembly to the engine. Move the transmission assembly and the torque converter rearward to clear the crankshaft.

9. Carefully lower the transmission assembly from the vehicle. Remove the transfer case retaining bolts from the transmission assembly.

To install:

10. If the transmission and transfer case were separated, torque the bolts to 26 ft. lbs.

11. Carefully raise the transmission into position.

12. Install the bolts attaching the transmission assembly to the engine. Torque the bolts to 25 ft. lbs. for the 904 and 999. On the AW-4, torque the 10mm bolts to 25 ft. lbs.; the 12mm bolts to 42 ft. lbs.

13. Connect the backup light switch wire and the speedometer cable.

14. Connect the transfer case and the transmission linkage.

15. Connect the vacuum lines and the vent hose.

16. Connect the fluid cooler lines.

17. Connect the driveshaft at the transfer case. Jeep recommends that new strap bolt be used whenever the driveshaft is disconnected. Torque the strap bolt nuts to 14 ft. lbs; the flange-to-case bolts to 35 ft. lbs.

18. Install the rear crossmember. Torque the crossmember attaching bolts to 30 ft. lbs.; the transmission-to-crossmember bolts to 33 ft. lbs.

19. Connect the exhaust pipe at the catalytic converter.

20. Install the bolts attaching the torque converter to the flex plate. Torque the bolts to 40 ft. lbs.

21. Remove the floor jack.

22. Install the torque converter inspection cover.

23. If the vehicle is equipped with a diesel engine, install the left motor mount and starter.

24. Install the rear driveshaft. Use new starp bolts. Torque the strap bolt nuts to 14 ft. lbs.; the flange bolts to 35 ft. lbs.

25. Lower the truck.

26. Connect the negative battery cable.

TRANSFER CASE

REMOVAL AND INSTALLATION

New Process 207

1. Shift the case into 4H.
2. Raise and support the truck on jackstands.
3. Drain the case.
4. Matchmark the rear driveshaft and remove it.
5. Disconnect the speedometer cable, vacuum hoses and vent hose from the case.
6. Support the transmission with a floor jack.
7. Remove the crossmember.
8. Matchmark the front driveshaft and remove it.
9. Disconnect the shift lever linkage rod at the case.
10. Remove the shift lever bracket bolts.
11. Support the transfer case with a floor jack or transmission jack and remove the attaching bolts.
12. Pull the case out of the truck.

To install:

13. Raise the transfer case into position. Torque the attaching bolts to 26 ft. lbs.
14. Connect the shift lever linkage rod at the case.
15. Install the shift lever bracket bolts.
16. Install the front driveshaft. Jeep recommends the use of new strap bolts. Torque the

Transfer Case Application Chart

Transfer Case Types	Years
New Process 207	1984–87 all
New Process 228	1985–87 w/auto. trans.
New Process 229	1984 w/auto. trans.
New Process 231	1988–89 all
New Process 242	1988–89 Wagoneer and Cherokee

nuts to 14 ft. lbs. Torque the flange bolts to 35 ft. lbs.
17. Install the crossmember. Torque the bolts to 30 ft. lbs.
18. Remove the floor jack.
19. Connect the speedometer cable, vacuum hoses and vent hose at the case.
20. Install the rear driveshaft. Use new strap bolts, torqued to 14 ft. lbs. Torque the flange bolts to 35 ft. lbs.
21. Fill the case.
22. Lower the truck.

New Process 228

1. Raise and support the truck on jackstands.
2. Drain the case.
3. Disconnect the speedometer cable, vacuum hoses and vent hose from the case.
4. Disconnect the shift lever linkage rod at the case.
5. Support the transmission with a floor jack. Remove the rear crossmember.
6. Matchmark the rear driveshaft and remove it.
7. Matchmark the front driveshaft and remove it.
8. Remove the shift lever bracket bolts.
9. Support the transfer case with a floor jack or transmission jack and remove the attaching bolts.
10. Pull the case rearward out of the truck.
To install:
11. Position the transfer case in the truck. Torque the attaching bolts to 40 ft. lbs.
12. Install the shift lever bracket bolts.
13. Install the front and rear driveshafts. Jeep recommends the use of new strap bolts. Torque the strap bolt nuts to 14 ft. lbs.; the flange nuts to 35 ft. lbs.
14. Install the rear crossmember. Torque the bolts to 30 ft. lbs.
15. Connect the shift lever linkage rod at the case.
16. Connect the speedometer cable, vacuum hoses and vent hose from the case.
17. Fill the case.
18. Lower the truck.

New Process 229

1. Raise and support the truck on jackstands.
2. Drain the case.
3. Disconnect the speedometer cable and vent hose. Disconnect the shift lever link at the operating lever.
4. Support the transmission with a floor jack.
5. Remove the rear crossmember.
6. Matchmark the driveshafts and remove them.
7. Disconnect the shift motor vacuum hoses.
8. Disconnect the shift linkage at the case.
9. Support the transfer case with a floor jack or transmission jack and remove the attaching bolts.
10. Pull the case rearward and remove it.
11. Clean the gasket mating surfaces and use new gasket material for installation.
To install:
12. Raise the transfer case into position. Make certain that the case and transmission are mated without binding, before torquing the attaching bolts. Torque the bolts to 26 ft. lbs.
13. Connect the shift linkage at the case.
14. Connect the shift motor vacuum hoses.
15. Install the driveshafts. Jeep recommends that new strap bolts be used. Torque the nuts to 14 ft. lbs.; torque the flange nuts to 35 ft. lbs.
16. Install the rear crossmember. Torque the bolts to 30 ft. lbs.
17. Remove the transmission floor jack.
18. Connect the speedometer cable and vent hose.
19. Connect the shift lever link at the operating lever.
20. Fill the case.
21. Lower the truck.

New Process 231

1. Shift the case into Neutral.
2. Raise and support the truck on jackstands.
3. Drain the lubricant.
4. Matchmark and remove the front and rear driveshafts.
5. Support the transmission with a jackstand.
6. Remove the rear crossmember.
7. Disconnect the speedometer cable.
8. Disconnect the linkage.
9. Disconnect the vent and vacuum hoses and the indicator wire.
10. Support the transfer case with a transmission jack. Make sure that the case is secured to the jack with chains.
11. Remove the transfer case-to-transmission bolts.
12. Pull the case rearward to disengage it and lower it from the truck.
To install:
13. Raise the transfer case into position. Make certain that the case and transmission are mated without binding, before torquing the attaching bolts. Torque the bolts to 26 ft. lbs.
14. Connect the shift linkage at the case.
15. Connect the vacuum hoses.
16. Install the driveshafts. Jeep recommends

318 DRIVE TRAIN

that new strap bolts be used. Torque the nuts to 14 ft. lbs.; torque the flange nuts to 35 ft. lbs.
17. Install the rear crossmember. Torque the bolts to 30 ft. lbs.
18. Remove the transmission floor jack.
19. Connect the speedometer cable and vent hose.
20. Connect the shift lever link at the operating lever.
21. Fill the case.
22. Lower the truck.

New Process 242

1. Shift the case into Neutral.
2. Raise and support the truck on jackstands.
3. Drain the lubricant.
4. Matchmark and remove the front and rear driveshafts.
5. Support the transmission with a jackstand.
6. Remove the rear crossmember.
7. Disconnect the speedometer cable.
8. Disconnect the linkage.
9. Disconnect the vent and vacuum hoses and the indicator wire.
10. Support the transfer case with a transmission jack. Make sure that the case is secured to the jack with chains.
11. Remove the transfer case-to-transmission bolts.
12. Pull the case rearward to disengage it and lower it from the truck.

To install:
13. Raise the transfer case into position. Make certain that the case and transmission are mated without binding, before torquing the attaching bolts. Torque the bolts to 26 ft. lbs.
14. Connect the shift linkage at the case.
15. Connect the vacuum hoses.
16. Install the driveshafts. Jeep recommends that new strap bolts be used. Torque the nuts to 14 ft. lbs.; torque the flange nuts to 35 ft. lbs.
17. Install the rear crossmember. Torque the bolts to 30 ft. lbs.
18. Remove the transmission floor jack.
19. Connect the speedometer cable and vent hose.
20. Connect the shift lever link at the operating lever.
21. Fill the case.
22. Lower the truck.

Adjustments

RANGE CONTROL LINKAGE ADJUSTMENT
NP-207

1. Place the range control lever in the 2WD position.

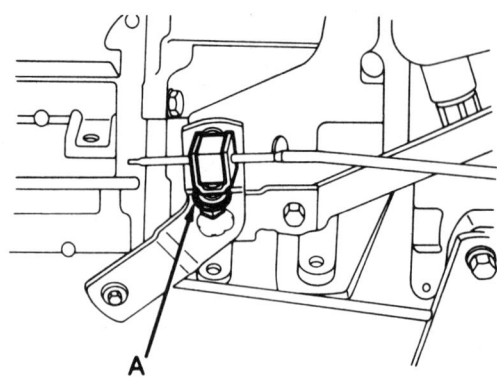

NP-207 range control adjustment; A is the adjustment point.

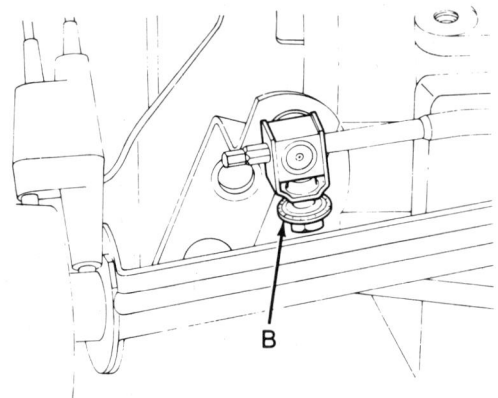

NO-228/229 range control adjustment. B is the adjustment link

2. Insert a 1/8" spacer between the gate and the lever.
3. Hold the lever in this position.
4. Place the transfer case lever in the 2WD position.
5. Adjust the link, at the trunnion, to provide a FREE pin at the case outer lever.

NP-228, 229

1. Place the range control lever in the HIGH position.
2. Insert a 1/8" spacer between the gate and the lever.
3. Hold the lever in this position.
4. Place the transfer case lever in the HIGH position.
5. Adjust the link, at the trunnion, to provide a FREE pin at the case outer lever.

MODE ROD ADJUSTMENT
NP-228, 229

NOTE: *If this adjustment is not properly made, the transfer case may not fully engage*

DRIVE TRAIN

2WD/HIGH and internal damage will result.
1. Fully engage the 2WD/HIGH position.
2. Refer to the accompanying illustration. The range lever (2) and the mode lever (1) must be aligned on the same centerline (3).

NOTE: *To correctly position the mode lever, it is sometimes necessary to rotate the transfer case output shaft. To do this, raise and support the rear end on jackstands and rotate the rear driveshaft, while applying a load on the mode lever. Doing this will help align the spline for full engagement of 2WD/HIGH.*

3. Adjust the length of the mode rod (4) to approximately 6", to eliminate all free play.
4. Make sure all vacuum lines are secure.
5. Drive the vehicle a short distance, shifting between 4WD and 2WD/HIGH.
6. Check the mode lever position. The lever should be aligned as explained in step 2. If not, repeat steps 3 through 5, increasing the length of the mode rod one turn, until proper alignment is achieved.
7. With the transfer case vacuum motor shift rod fully extended and the transfer case in 2WD/HIGH, adjust the mode rod so that the pin (6) moves freely in its hole.

NP-207 Overhaul

CASE DISASSEMBLY

1. Remove fill and drain plugs.
2. Remove front yoke. Discard yoke seal washer and yoke nut.
3. Turn transfer case on end and position front case on wood blocks.
4. Shift transfer case to 4 Lo.
5. Remove extension housing attaching bolts. Using a hammer, tap the shoulder on the extension housing to break sealer loose.

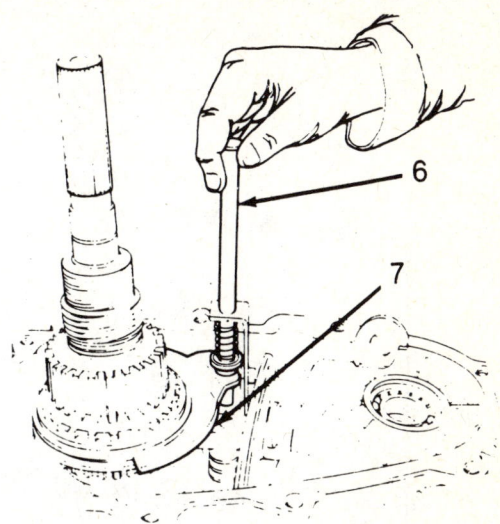

Removing the mode fork rail and mode fork from the NP-207

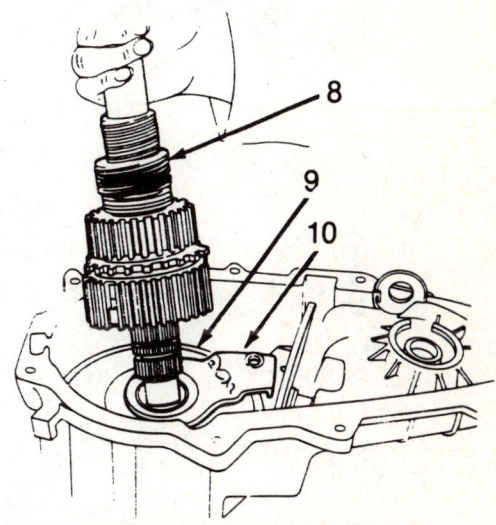

Removing the mainshaft (8) from the NP-207

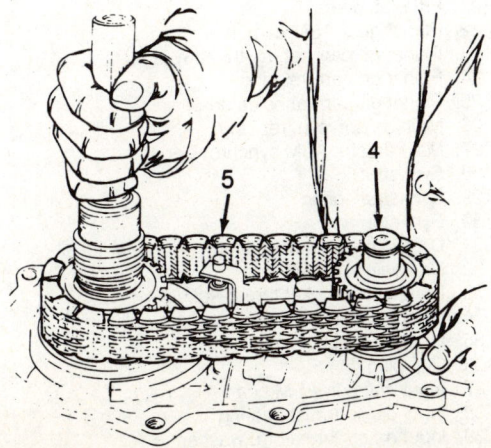

Removing the front output shaft (4) and drive chain (5) from the NP-207

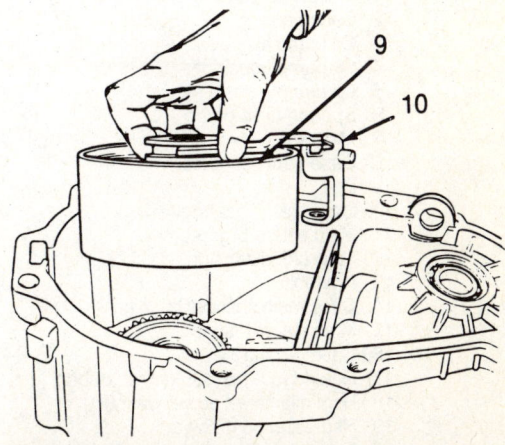

Removing the planetary assembly (9) and range fork (10)

DRIVE TRAIN

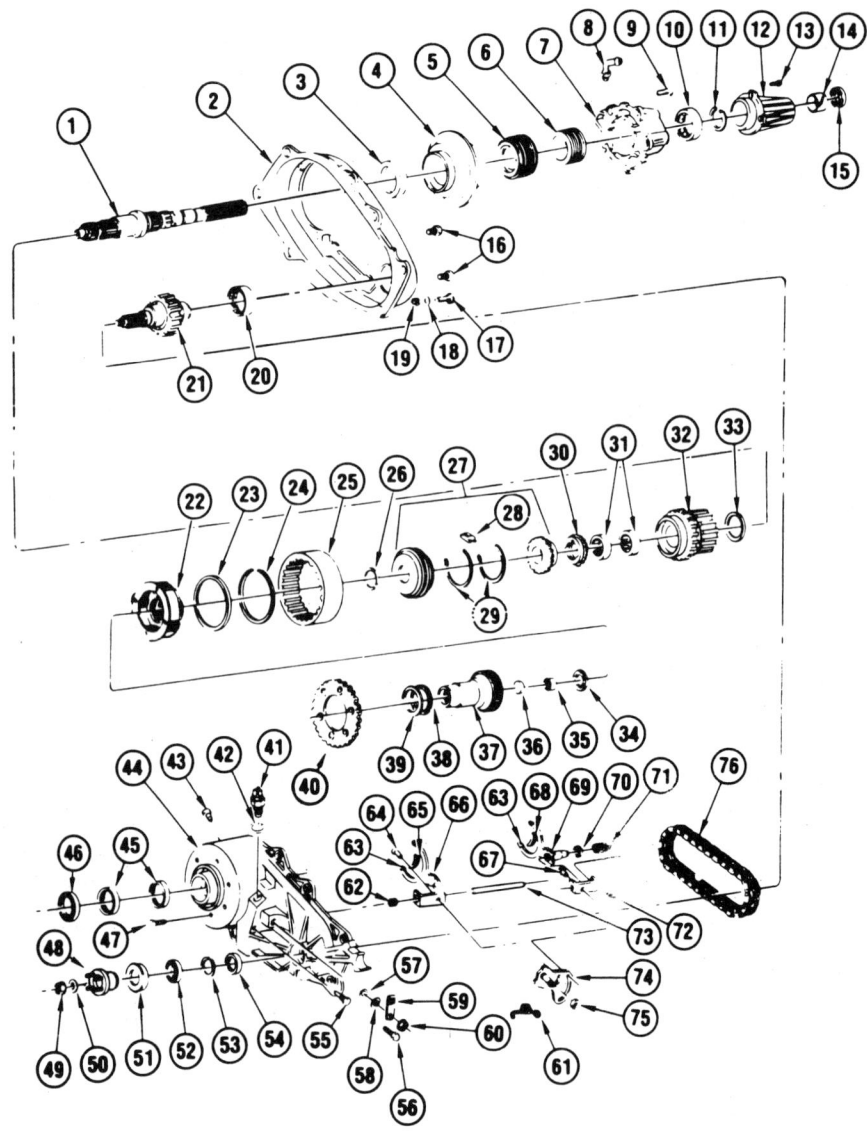

1. Main drive shaft
2. Case housing
3. Oil pump hsg. seal
4. Oil pump housing
5. Oil pump
6. Speedo drive gear
7. Main shf. rr. brg. retainer
8. Case vent connector
9. Bolt
10. Main shf. rr. bearing
11. Main shf. rr. brg. ret. ring
12. Main shf. extension
13. Hex bolt
14. Case main shf. ext. bushing
15. Main shf. ext. seal
16. Case oil plug
17. Hex (M10 × 1.5 × 35) (2 req'd) bolt
18. Hsg. alignment dowel washer
19. Hsg. alignment dowel
20. Frt. otpt. shf. pilot bearing
21. Frt. otpt. shaft
22. Planet gear ASM carrier
23. Planet gr. carr. ret. rg. thrust washer
24. Planet gr. carr. ret. ring
25. Planet gr. carr. annulus gear
26. Main dr. shf. syn. ret. ring
27. Main dr. shf. ASM synchronizer
28. Syn. strut
29. Syn. strut spring
30. Syn. stop ring
31. Dr. chain sprocket bearing
32. Dr. chain sprocket
33. Dr. chain sprocket thrust washer
34. Input main dr. gr. thrust washer
35. Input dr. gr. pilot bearing
36. Cup plug
37. Input main dr. ASM gear
38. Input dr. gr. thrust bearing
39. Input dr. gr. thrust brg. washer
40. Low range lock plate

NP-207 transfer case exploded view

6. Remove the snapring for the rear bearing from the main shaft and discard.
7. Remove the rear retainer attaching bolts. Using a hammer, tap the shoulder on the retainer to break sealer loose.
8. Remove the rear retainer and pump housing from the transfer case.
9. Remove the pump seal from the pump housing and discard.
10. Remove the speedometer drive gear from the main shaft.
11. Remove the pump gear from the main shaft.
12. Remove the bolts attaching the rear case to the front case and remove rear case. To separate the case, insert a prybar into the slots casted in the case ends and pry upward. DO NOT attempt to wedge the case halves apart at any point on the mating surfaces.
13. Remove the front output shaft and drive chain as an assembly. It may be necessary to raise the main shaft slightly for the output shaft to clear the case.
14. Pull up on the mode fork rail until rail clears range fork and rotate mode fork and rail and remove from transfer case.
15. Pull up on the main shaft until it separates from the planetary assembly. Remove the main shaft from the transfer case.
16. Remove the planetary assembly with the range fork from the transfer case.
17. Remove the planetary thrust washer, input gear thrust bearing and front thrust washer from the transfer case.
18. Remove the shift sector detent spring and retaining bolt.
19. Remove the shift sector, shaft and spacer from the transfer case.

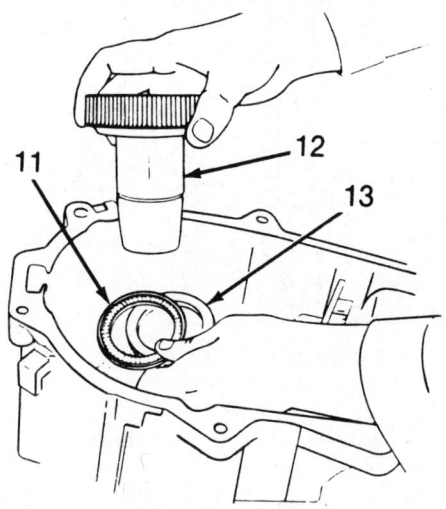

Removing the thrust bearing (11), input gear (12) and thrust washer (13) from the NP-207

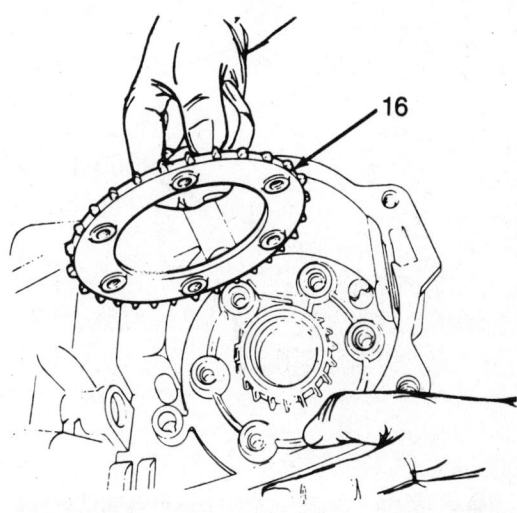

Removing the locking plate (16) from the NP-207 transfer case

41. Vac. four whl. switch
42. Four whl. dr. ind. light switch seal
43. Oil acess hole plug
44. Case (frt. half) housing
45. Input dr. bearing
46. Input dr. gr. seal
47. Hex bolt
48. Frt. otpt. prop. shf. flange yoke
49. Frt. otpt. prop. shf. yoke nut
50. Frt. otpt. prop. shf. yoke (rubber)
51. Frt. otpt. prop. shf. yoke deflector
52. Frt. otpt. shf. seal
53. Frt. otpt. shf. brg. ret. ring
54. Frt. otpt. shf. bearing
55. Shift sector spr. screw
56. Screw
57. Shift sector & shf. oil seal
58. Shift sector & shf. retainer
59. Shifter shf. lever
60. Shift shf. lvr. nut
61. Shift sector ASM spring
62. Range fork bushing
63. Fork end pad
64. Range shift fork pin
65. Range shift fork center
66. Range shift ASM fork
67. Mode shift fork brkt. pin
68. Mode shift fork center pad
69. Mode shift ASM fork
70. Mode shift fork spr. cup
71. Mode shift fork spring
72. Mode shfit fork ASM bracket
73. Shift fork shaft
74. W/shf, shift sector
75. Shift sector shf. spacer
76. Drive chain

NP-207 transfer case exploded view

20. Remove the locking plate retaining bolts and lock plate from the transfer case.
21. Remove the input gear pilot bearing using J-29369-1 or equivalent with a slide hammer.
22. Remove the front output shaft seal, input shaft seal and the rear extension seal using a brass drift.
23. Using J-33841 with J-8092 or equivalent, press the 2 caged roller bearings for the front input shaft gear from the transfer case.
24. Using J-29369-2 with J-33367 or a slide hammer, remove the rear bearing for the front output shaft.
25. Using a hammer and drift, remove the rear main shaft bearing from the rear retainer.
26. Using an awl, remove the snapring retaining the front output shaft bearing. Using a hammer and drift, remove the bearing from the case.
27. Remove the bushing from the extension housing using J-33839 with J-8092 or equivalent. Press bushing from the extension housing.

MAINSHAFT DISASSEMBLY

1. Remove the speedometer gear.
2. Using an awl, pry off the pump gear from the mainshaft.
3. Remove the snapring retaining the synchronizer hub from the mainshaft.
4. Using a brass hammer, tap the synchronizer hub from mainshaft.

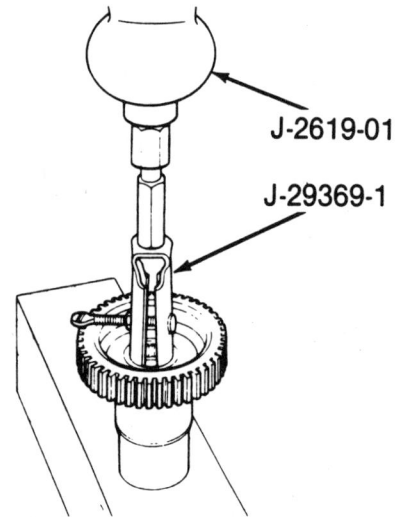

Removing the input gear pilot bearing with the special tool from the NP-207

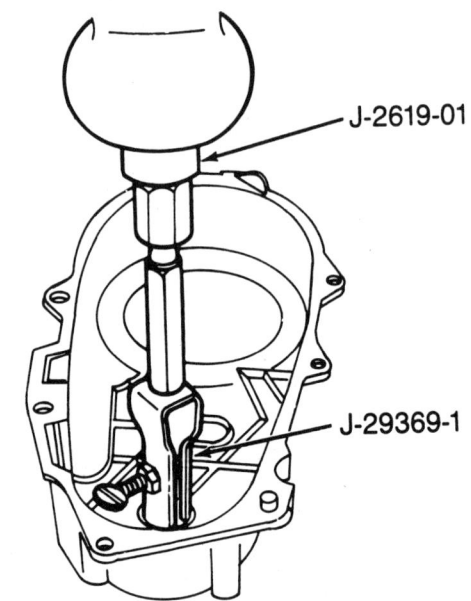

Removing the front output shaft rear bearing from the NP-207

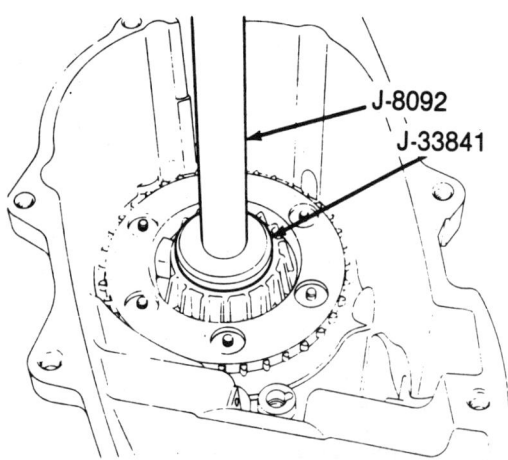

Pressing out the caged roller bearings from the NP-207

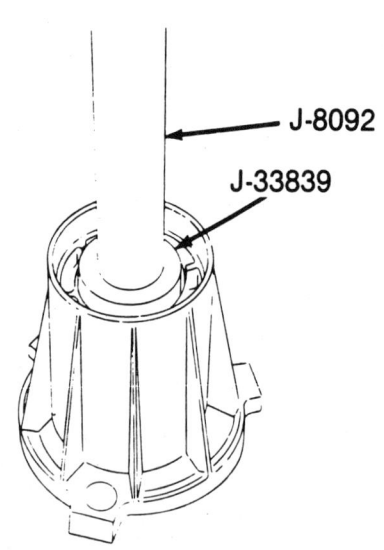

Removing the extension housing bushing from the NP-207

DRIVE TRAIN

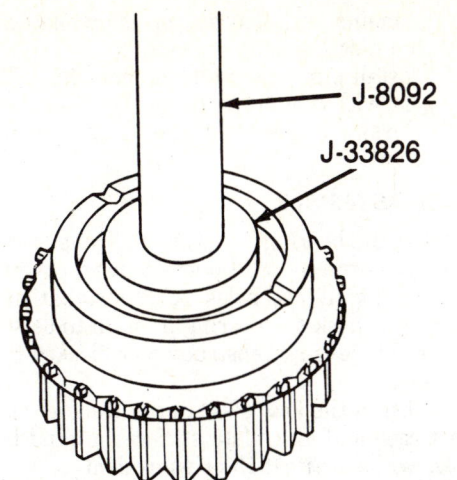

Pressing the caged roller bearings from the drive sprocket from the NP-207

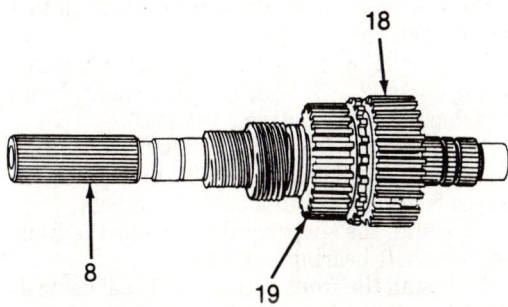

NP-207 mainshaft. (18) is the synchronizer hub; (8) is the mainshaft; (19) is the drive sprocket

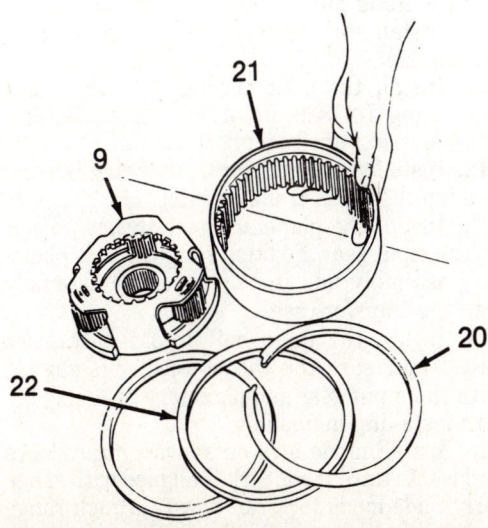

NP-207 planetary gear components. (9) is the planetary gear; (20) is the snapring; (21) is the annulus gear; (22) is the thrust ring

5. Remove the drive sprocket.
6. Using J-33826 and J-8092 or equivalent, press 2 caged roller bearings from the drive sprocket.
7. Remove synchronizer keys and retaining rings from the synchronizer hub.
8. Clean and inspect all parts. Replace any parts if they show evidence of excessive wear, distortion or damage.

PLANETARY GEAR DISASSEMBLY

1. Remove the snapring retaining the planetary gear in the annulus gear.
2. Remove outer thrust ring and discard.
3. Remove planetary assembly from the annulus gear.
4. Remove inner thrust ring from the planetary assembly and discard.
5. Clean and inspect parts. Replace any parts if they show evidence of excessive wear, distortion or damage.

CLEANING & INSPECTION

Wash all parts thoroughly in clean solvent. Be sure all old lubricant, metallic particles, dirt, or foreign material are removed from the surfaces of every part. Apply compressed air to each oil feed port and channel in each case half to remove any obstructions or cleaning solvent residue.

Inspect all gear teeth for signs of excessive wear or damage and check all gear splines for burrs, nicks, wear or damage. Remove minor nicks or scratches with an oil stone. Replace any part exhibiting excessive wear or damage.

Inspect all snaprings and thrust washers for evidence of excessive wear, distortion or damage. Replace any of these parts if they exhibit these conditions.

Inspect the two case halves for cracks, porosity damaged mating surfaces, stripped bolt threads, or distortion. Replace any part that exhibits these conditions. Inspect the low range lock plate in the front case. If the lock plate teeth or the plate hub is cracked, broken, chipped, or excessively worn, replace the lock plate and the lock plate attaching bolts.

Inspect the condition of all needle, roller and thrust bearings in the front and rear case halves and the input gear. Also, check the condition of the bearing bores in both cases and in the input gear, rear output shaft and rear retainer. Replace any part that exhibits signs of excessive wear or damage.

PLANETARY GEAR ASSEMBLY

1. Install the inner thrust ring on planetary assembly.
2. Install the planetary assembly into the annulus gear.

324 DRIVE TRAIN

3. Install the outer thrust ring and then the snapring.

MAINSHAFT ASSEMBLY

1. Using J-33828 and J-8092 or equivalent, install the front drive sprocket bearing. Press bearing until tool bottoms out. Bearing should be flush with front surface. Reverse tool on J-8092 or equivalent and press rear bearing into sprocket until tool bottoms out. The rear bearing should be recessed after installation.
2. Install thrust washer on the mainshaft.
3. Install drive sprocket on the mainshaft.
4. Install blocker ring and synchronizer hub

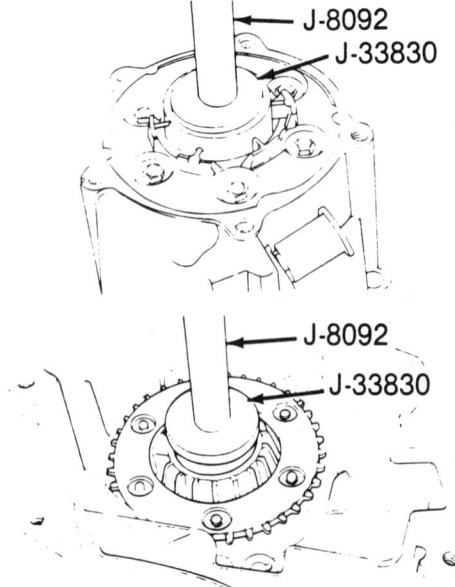

Installing the input shaft roller bearings on the NP-207

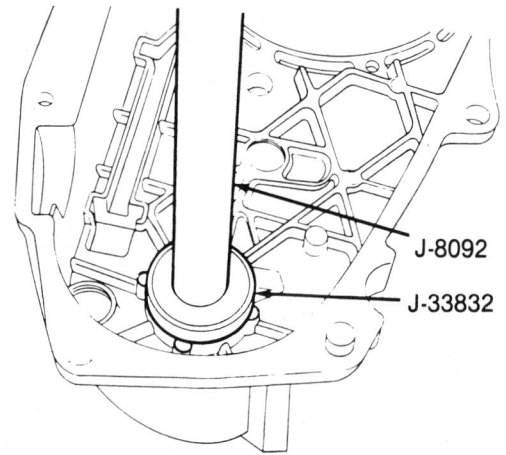

Installing the front output shaft rear bearing on the NP-207

on the mainshaft. Seat hub on main shaft and install a new snapring to retain.
5. Install pump gear on the mainshaft. Tap the gear with a hammer to seat on mainshaft.
6. Install speedometer gear on the mainshaft.

CASE ASSEMBLY

All of the bearings used in the transfer case must be correctly positioned to avoid covering the bearing oil feed holes. After installation of bearings, check the bearing position to be sure the feed hole is not obstructed or blocked by a bearing.

1. Install the lock plate in the transfer case. Coat case and lock plate surfaces around bolt holes with Loctite®515 or equivalent.
2. Position the lock plate to the case and align bolt holes in lock plate with case. Install attaching bolts and torque to specification.
3. Install the roller bearings for the input shaft into the transfer case using J-33830 and J-8092 or equivalent. Press bearings until tool bottoms in bore.
4. Install the front output shaft rear bearing, using J-33832 and J-8092 or equivalent. Press bearing until tool bottoms in case.
5. Install the front output shaft front bearing using J-33833 and J-8092 or equivalent. Press bearing until tool bottoms in bore.
6. Install the snapring that retains the front output shaft bearing in case.
7. Install the front output shaft seal using J-33834 or equivalent.
8. Install the input shaft seal using J-33831 or equivalent.
9. Install spacer on shift sector shaft and install sector in transfer case. Install shift lever and retaining nut. Torque to specification.
10. Install shift sector detent spring and retaining bolt.
11. Install the pilot bearing into the input gear using J-33829 and J-8092 or equivalent. Press bearing until tool bottoms out.
12. Install the input gear front thrust bearing and input gear in transfer case.
13. Install the planetary gear thrust washer on the input gear. Position range fork on planetary assembly and install planetary assembly into the transfer case.
14. Install the mainshaft into the transfer case. Make sure the thrust washer is aligned with the input gear and planetary assembly before installing mainshaft.
15. Install mode fork on synchronizer sleeve and rotate until mode fork is aligned with range fork. Slide mode fork rail down through range fork until rail is seated in bore of transfer case.
16. Position drive chain on front output shaft and install chain on drive sprocket. Install front

output shaft in the transfer case. It may be necessary to slightly raise the main shaft to seat the output shaft in the case.

17. Install the magnet into pocket of transfer case.

18. Apply ⅛" bead of Loctite®515 or equivalent to the mating surface of the front case. Install rear case on the front case aligning dowel pins. Install bolts and torque to 20-25 ft. lbs. Install the two bolts with washers into the dowel pin holes.

19. Install the output bearing into the rear retainer using J-33833 and J-8092 or equivalent. Press bearing until seated in bore.

20. Install pump seal in pump housing using J-33835 or equivalent. Apply petroleum jelly to pump housing tabs and install housing in rear retainer.

21. Apply ⅛" bead of Loctite®515 or equivalent to mating surface of rear retainer. Align retainer to case and install retaining bolts. Torque bolts to specification 15-20 ft. lbs.

22. Using a new snapring, install snapring on mainshaft. Pull up on mainshaft and seat snapring in its groove.

23. Install bushing in extension housing using J-33826 and J-8092 or equivalent. Press bushing until tool bottoms in bore.

24. Install a new seal in the extension housing using J-33843 or equivalent.

25. Apply ⅛" bead of Loctite®515 or equivalent to mating surface of extension housing. Align extension housing to the rear retainer and install attaching bolts. Torque bolts to specification 20-25 ft. lbs.

26. Install front yoke on output shaft. Install a new yoke seal washer with a new nut and torque to specification.

27. Install drain plug and torque to specification. Install fill plug.

NP-228 Overhaul

CASE DISASSEMBLY

1. Drain all the lubricant from the transfer case and remove the front and rear yoke nuts along with their seal washers. Discard the seal washers.

2. Mark the front and rear yokes for easy installation alignment reference and remove the front and rear yokes. It may be necessary to use tool No. J-8614-01 or equivalent to remove the yokes.

3. Place the transfer case on wooden blocks. Cut V-notches in the blocks of wood so there is clearance for the front case mounting studs. Mark the retainer and the rear case for easy assembly reference.

4. Remove the rear retainer bolts and pry off the retainer with a suitable pry bar. Remove the differential shim(s) and speedometer drive gear from the rear output shaft.

5. Remove the bolts that attach the rear transfer case half to the front case half. Be sure to get the washer that are used with the bolts on each end of the transfer case.

NOTE: *Insert two small pry bars into the slots at each end of the rear of the transfer case half to loosen it. Do not attempt to wedge the transfer case halves apart or the case mating surface will be damages.*

6. Remove the rear transfer case half from the front case. Remove the thrust bearing and races from the front output shaft and be to note the order of the bearing and races for easy assembly reference.

7. Remove the oil pump from the rear output shaft, note the position of the pump for easy as-

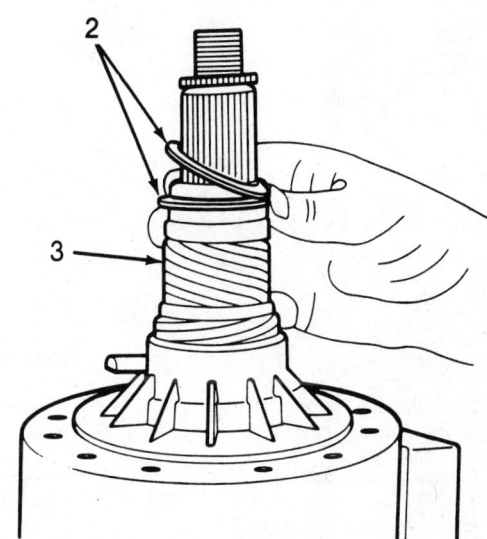

Removing the differential shims (2) and speedometer drive gear (3) from the NP-228

Separating the NP-228 case halves

326　DRIVE TRAIN

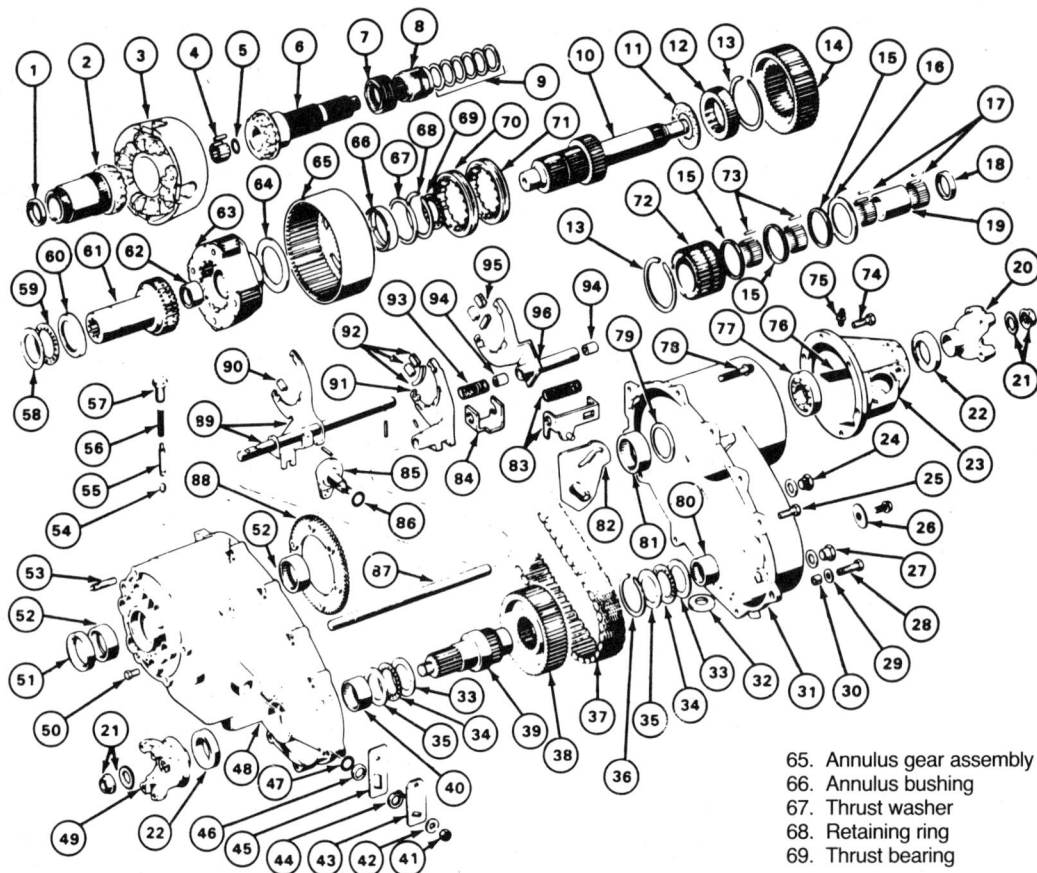

1. Spacer
2. Side gear
3. Differential
4. Pilot bearing rollers (15)
5. O-ring seal
6. Rear output shaft
7. Oil pump
8. Speedometer drive gear
9. Shim kit
10. Mainshaft
11. Mainshaft thrust washer
12. Spline gear
13. Retaining ring
14. Sprocket
15. Spacer
16. Sprocket thrust washer
17. Side gear roller (82)
18. Spacer (short)
19. Spacer (long)
20. Rear yoke
21. Nut and seal washer
22. Seal
23. Rear retainer
24. Plug assembly
25. Bolt
26. Identification tag
27. Plug assembly
28. Dowel bolt
29. Dowel bolt washer
30. Case half dowell
31. Rear half case
32. Magnet
33. Front output shaft bearing assembly race (thick)
34. Front output shaft bearing assembly thrust
35. Front output shaft bearing assembly race (thin)
36. Retaining ring
37. Chain
38. Driven sprocket
39. Front output shaft
40. Front output front bearing
41. Nut
42. Washer
43. Mode lever
44. Snap ring
45. Range lever
46. O-ring retainer
47. O-ring seal
48. Front half case
49. Front output yoke
50. Low range plate bolt
51. Input shaft oil seal
52. Input shaft bearing
53. Stud
54. Ball
55. Plunger
56. Plunger spring
57. Screw
58. Input race
59. Input thrust bearing
60. Input race (thick)
61. Input shaft
62. Input bearing
63. Planetary gear assembly
64. Input gear thrust washer
65. Annulus gear assembly
66. Annulus bushing
67. Thrust washer
68. Retaining ring
69. Thrust bearing
70. High range sliding clutch sleeve
71. Mode sliding clutch sleeve
72. Carrier
73. Carrier rollers (120)
74. Rear retainer bolt
75. Vent
76. Vent seal
77. Output bearing
78. Bolt
79. Seal
80. Front output rear bearing
81. Output shaft inner bearing
82. Range sector
83. Range bracket (outer) and spring
84. Range bracket (inner)
85. Mode sector
86. O-ring seal
87. Range rail
88. Low range lockout plate
89. Mode fork, rail and pin
90. Mode fork pad
91. Range fork
92. Range fork pads
93. Range bracket spring (inner)
94. Locking fork bushing
95. Locking fork pads
96. Locking fork

NP-228 transfer case exploded view

sembly reference. The recessed side of the pump faces the case interior.

8. Remove the rear output shaft from the mainshaft and remove the 15 main needle bearing rollers from the shaft or coupling. Remove the mainshaft O-ring from the end of the shaft. Remove the differential from the mainshaft and side gear.

9. Remove the front output shaft, driven sprocket and drive chain assembly. Lift the front shaft, sprocket and chain upward. Tilt the front shaft toward the mainshaft. Slide the chain off the drive sprocket and remove the assembly.

10. Remove the front output shaft and front thrust bearing assembly from the front case. Remove the drive chain from the output shaft and sprocket.

11. Remove the snapring that retains the riven sprocket on the front output shaft. Mark the sprocket and shaft for assembly reference and remove the sprocket from the shaft.

12. Remove the mainshaft, side gear, drive sprocket and spline gear as an assembly. Place the assembly on a clean shop towel and set it aside until the front case disassembly is completed.

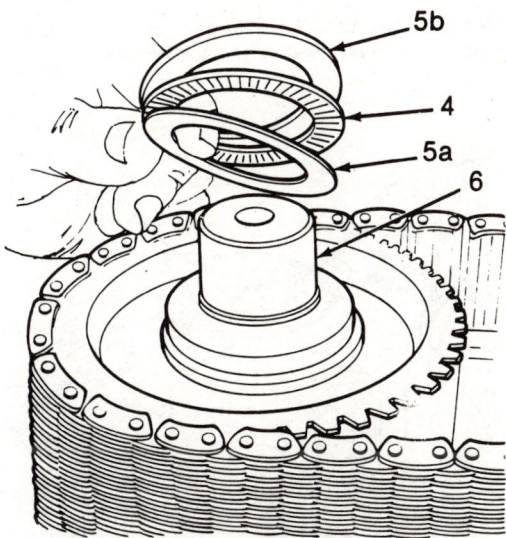

Removing the thrust bearing (4) and races (5a, 5b) from the front output shaft (6) from the NP-228

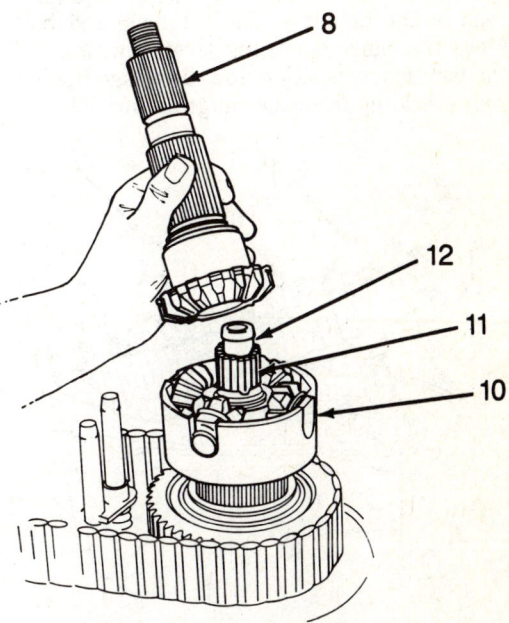

Disassembling the rear output shaft (8), 15 pilot roller (11), and O-ring (12), from the differential (10) from the NP-228

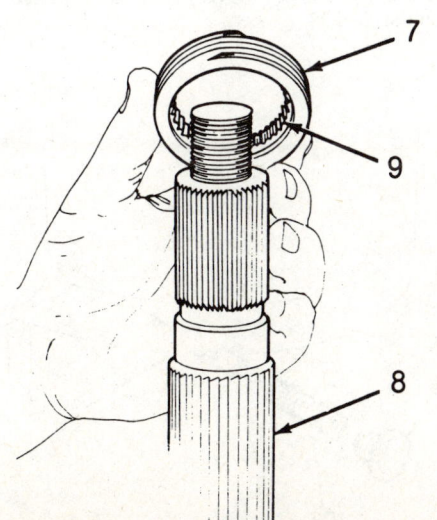

Removing the oil pump (7) from the rear output shaft (8). (9) is the recess in the pump from the NP-228

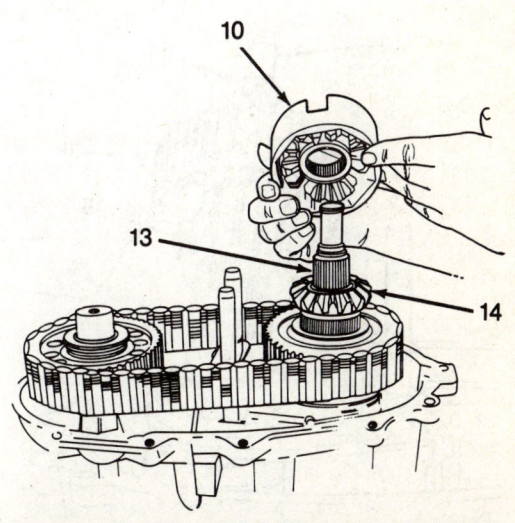

Removing the differential (10) from the mainshaft (13) and side gear (14) from the NP-228

13. Remove the mode fork, shift rail and mode sliding clutch sleeve as an assembly. Mark the sleeve and fork for easy assembly reference and remove the sleeve from the fork.

NOTE: *The mode fork and rail are pinned together so that they will operate as a unit. Remove the pin to separate the two components if necessary.*

14. Remove the locking fork, high range sliding clutch sleeve, fork brackets and fork spring as an assembly. Be sure to take note of the position of these components for an easy assembly reference.

15. Remove the range sector detent screw and remove the detent spring, plunger and ball. Move the range operating lever downward to the last detent position and disengage the low range fork lug from the range sector slot.

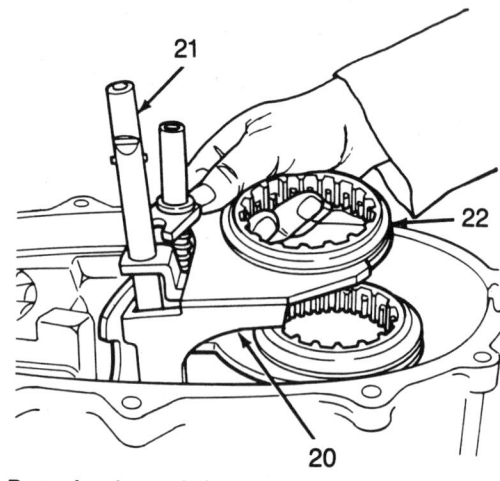

Removing the mode fork (20), shift rail (21) and mode sliding clutch sleeve (22) from the NP-228

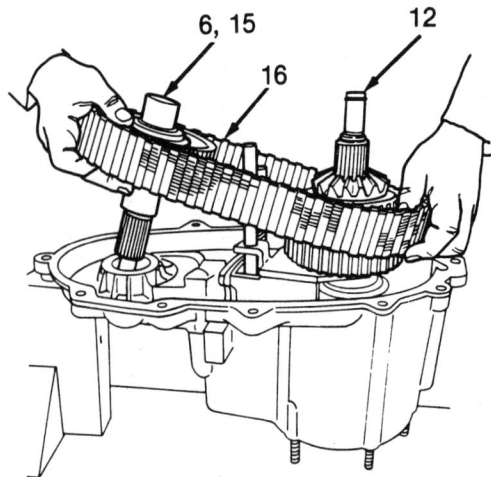

Removing the front output shaft (6), driven sprocket (15) and drive chain (16) from the mainshaft (12) from the NP-228

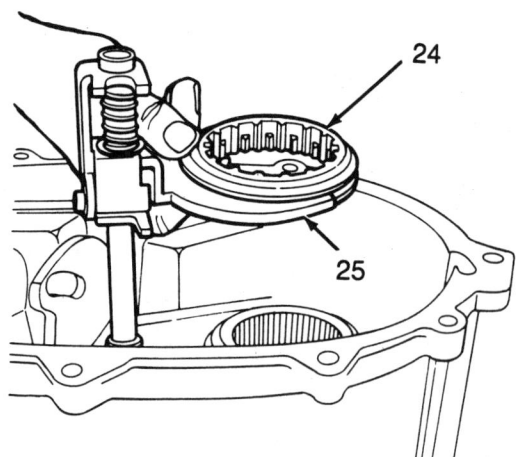

Removing the lock fork (25) and clutch sleeve (24) from the NP-228

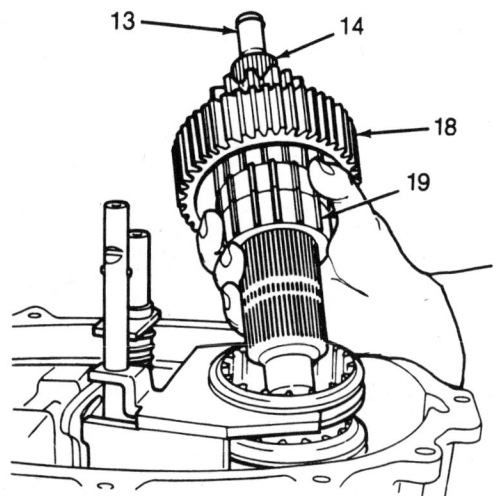

Removing the mainshaft (13), side gear (14), drive sprocket (18) and spline gear (19) from the NP-228

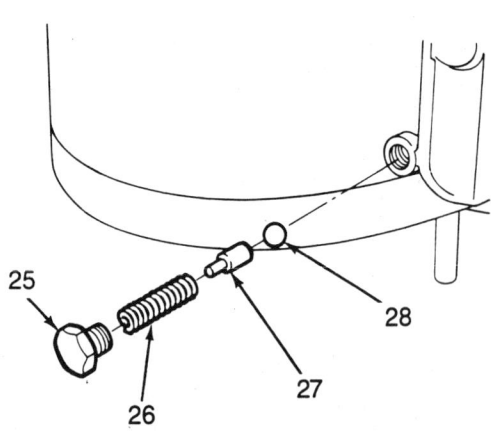

Removing the range sector detent screw, spring, plunger and ball from the NP-228

DRIVE TRAIN

16. Remove the retaining snapring from the annulus gear and remove the thrust washer. Remove the annulus gear, range fork and rail as an assembly and separate the components for cleaning and inspection.
17. Remove the planetary thrust washer from the planetary assembly hub. Remove the planetary assembly, by grasping the planetary hub and lifting the assembly upward.
18. Remove the mainshaft thrust bearing from the input shaft. Remove the input shaft, input shaft thrust bearing and race.
19. Remove the range sector and operating lever attaching nut and lockwasher. Remove the lever.
20. Remove the range sector and shaft from the front case and remove the range sector O-ring and retainer.

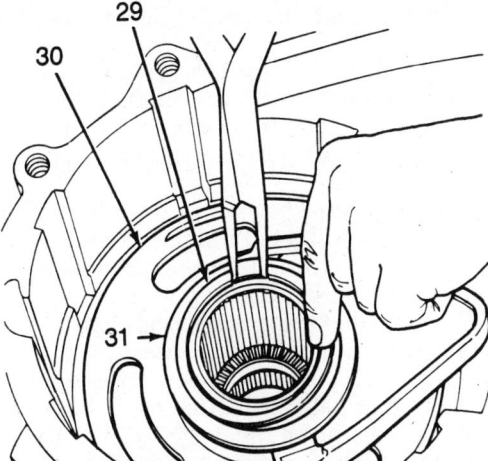

Removing the snapring (29), annulus gear (30) and thrust washer (31) from the NP-228

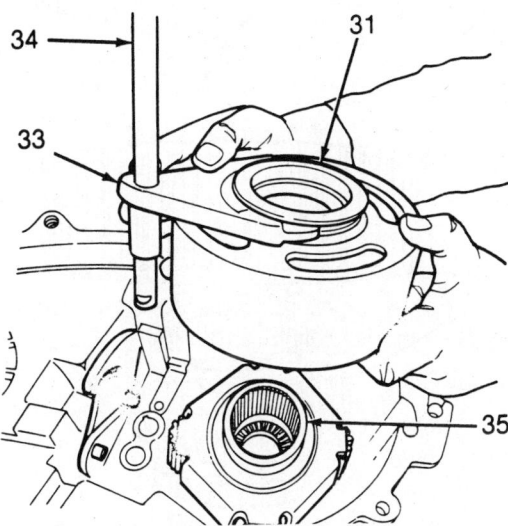

Removing the annulus gear (31), range fork (33) and rail (34) from the NP-228

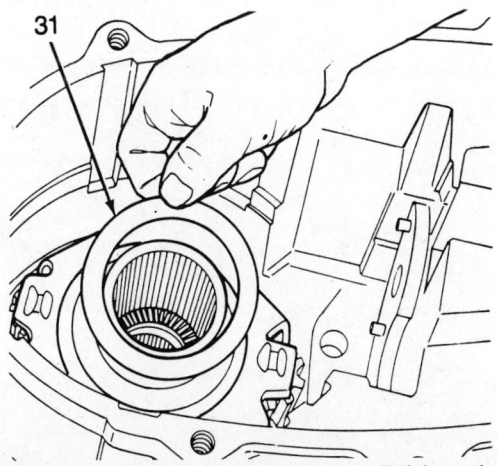

Removing the planetary thrust washer (31) from the NP-228

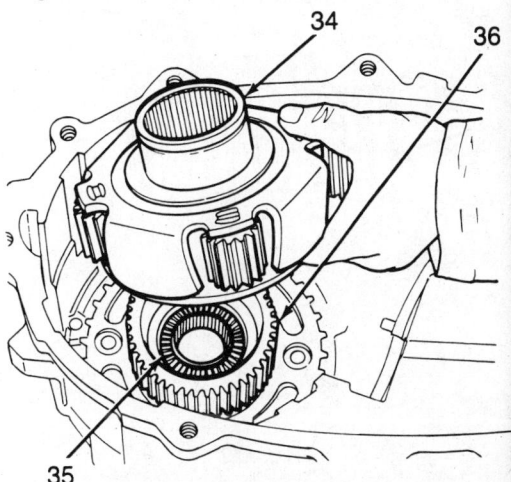

Removing the planetary assembly (34) and the mainshaft thrust bearing (35) from the input shaft from the NP-228

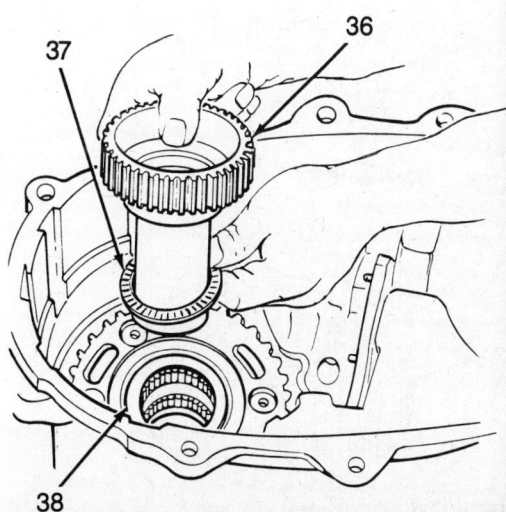

Removing the input shaft (36), input shaft thrust bearing (37) and race (38) from the NP-228

330 DRIVE TRAIN

CASE ASSEMBLY

NOTE: *During the assembly, lubricate all of the transfer case internal components with DEXRON®II transmission fluid or petroleum jelly as indicated in the procedure. Do not use chassis lubricant or similar thick lubricants.*

1. Install a replacement input shaft and rear output shaft bearing oil seals. Set the seals flush with the edge of the seal bore or in the seal groove in the transfer case. Coat the seal lips with petroleum jelly after installation.
2. Install the input shaft thrust bearing race in the transfer case counterbore. Install the input gear thrust bearing on the input shaft and install the shaft and bearing in the transfer case.
3. Install the mainshaft thrust bearing in the bearing recess in the input shaft. Install the planetary assembly on the input shaft. Ensure that the planetary pinion teeth mesh fully with the input shaft.
4. Install the planetary thrust washer on the planetary hub. Install a replacement sector shaft O-ring and install the retainer in the shaft bore in the transfer case.
5. Install the O-ring on the mode sector shaft and insert the mode sector through the range sector. Install the range sector in the front of transfer case half. Install the operating lever and the snapring on the range sector shaft.
6. Install the lever, attaching washer and

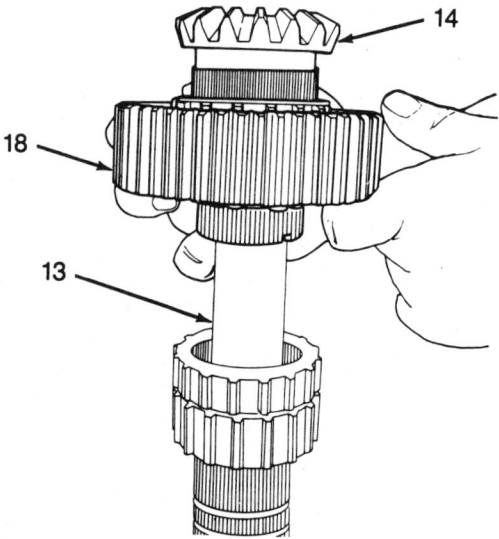

Removing the drive sprocket and side gear from the mainshaft from the NP-228

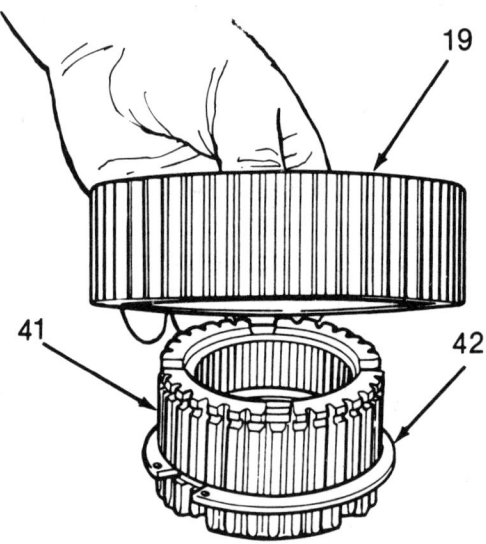

Removing the snapring (42) and drive sprocket (19) from the carrier (41) from the NP-228

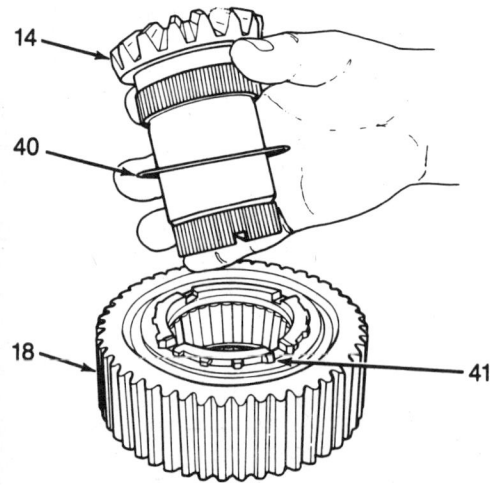

Removing the side gear (14) and thrust washer (40) from the sprocket carrier (41) and drive sprocket (18) from the NP-228

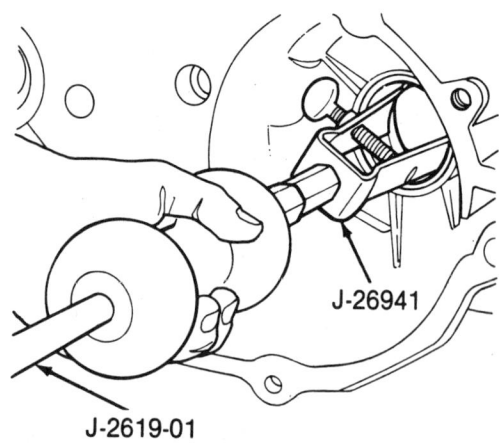

Removing the rear output shaft bearing from the NP-228

lock nut on the mode sector shaft. Torque the lock nut to 17 ft. lbs. Assemble the annulus gear, range fork and rail. Install the assembled fork on and over the planetary assembly.

7. Be sure that the annulus gear is fully meshed with the planetary pinions. Engage the range sector lug into the range sector.

8. Install the annulus thrust washer and the annulus retaining ring onto the annulus gear hub. Install the detent ball, plunger, spring and retaining screw in the front transfer case half detent bore. Torque the retaining screw to 22 ft. lbs.

NOTE: *The locking mode clutch sleeve and the high range clutch sleeve are not interchangeable. The sleeve splines are different.*

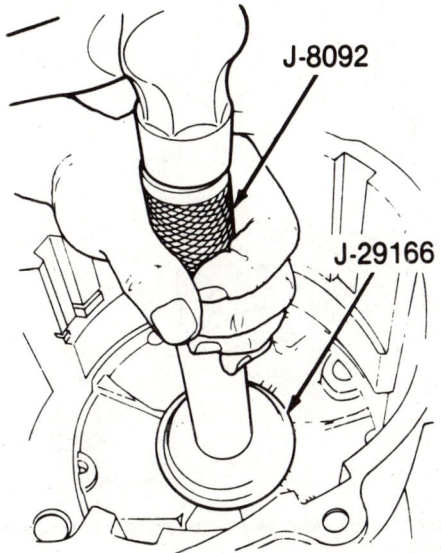

Installing the mainshaft pilot bushing from the NP-228

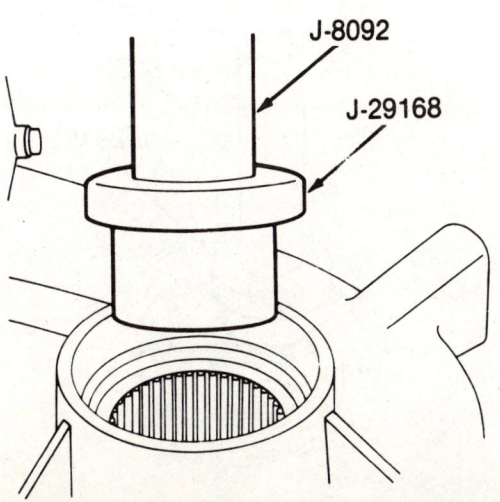

Removing the front output shaft front bearing from the NP-228

So be sure that the correct sleeve is installed in the proper shift fork. Also, the sleeves must be replaced as a set.

9. Assemble and install the locking fork, fork bracket, fork springs and high range clutch sleeves. Be sure that the lug on the fork is seated in the range sector detent slot.

10. Install the range fork lug in the range sector detent notch. Move the range sector to the high range position. Assemble and install the range fork, shift rail and mode clutch sleeve.

NOTE: *Steps 11-16 are to be used if the mainshaft was disassembled, when the transfer case was disassembled.*

11. Install the thrust washer and a replacement O-ring on the mainshaft. Install the needle bearings and bearing spacers on the mainshaft. Coat the shaft bearing surface and all needle bearings with petroleum jelly.

12. Install the first 41 needle bearings and install the long bearing spacer, the remaining 41 needle bearings and the remaining short spacer. Be careful to avoid displacing the bearing when the spacers are installed. Apply additional petroleum jelly to hold the bearing in place if necessary.

13. Install the spline gear on the mainshaft, be careful not to displace the bearing while installing the gear. Install the sprocket carrier in the drive sprocket and install the sprocket carrier snaprings. Make sure that the carrier and sprockets are aligned according to the reference marks made during disassembly.

NOTE: *The sprocket carrier teeth are tapered on one side and the drive sprocket has a deep recess on one side. Be sure that these*

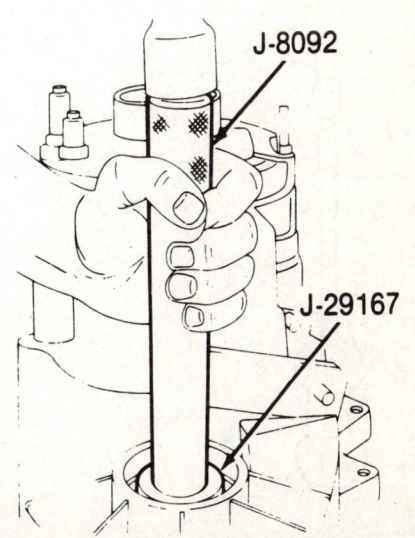

Installing the front output shaft front bearing on the NP-228

components are assembles so that the carrier tapered teeth and sprocket recess are on the same side.

14. Install the sprocket carrier bearings and spacers. Coat the carrier bore and all the 120 carrier needle bearings with petroleum jelly. Install the center spacer.
15. Install the 60 needle bearings in each end of the carrier and install the remaining two spacers, one at each side of the carrier. Apply additional petroleum jelly to hold the bearings in place if necessary.
16. Install the assembled sprocket carrier and drive sprocket on the mainshaft. Do not displace the mainshaft bearing during installation. Be sure that the recessed side of the drive sprocket is facing downward.
17. Install the trust washer in the mainshaft, position the washer on the sprocket carrier. Install the side gear on the mmainshaft and be sure that the side gear is fully seated in the sprocket carrier. Be careful not to displace any of the carrier or mmainshaft needle bearings.
18. Install the mainshaft and gear assembly in the case, making sure that the mainshaft is fully seated in the input gear. Install the driven sprocket on the front output shaft and install the sprocket retaining snapring. Be sure that the sprocket is installed according to the reference marks made during disassembly.
19. Install the front output shaft front thrust bearing assembly in the transfer case front half. Install the thick race in the transfer case and then install the bearing and the thin race.
20. Install the drive chain, front output shaft

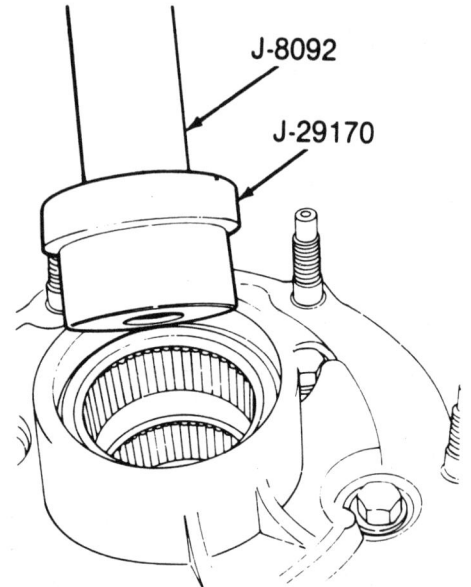

Removing the input gear front and rear bearings from the NP-228

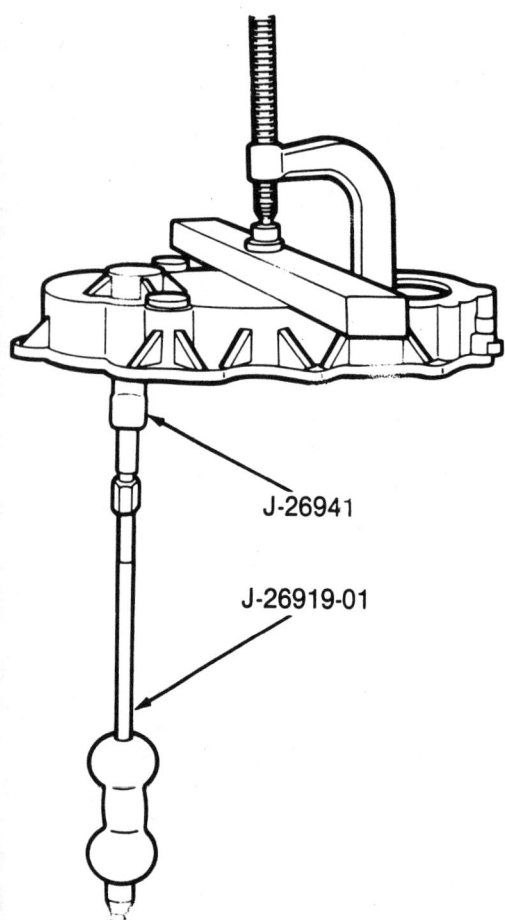

Removing the front output shaft rear bearing from the NP-228

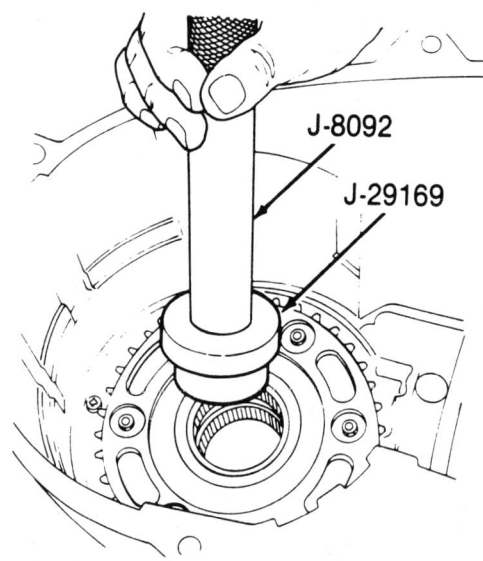

Installing the input gear front and rear bearings on the NP-228

and driven sprocket. Install the chain on the driven sprocket. Raise and tilt the driven sprocket and chain and install the opposite end of the chain on the drive sprocket.

21. Align the front output shaft with the shaft bore in the transfer case front half and install the shaft in the transfer case. Be sure that the front shaft thrust bearing assembly is seated in the transfer case.

22. Install the front output shaft rear thrust bearing assembly on the front output shaft. Install the tin race first, then install the bearing and the thick race. Install the differential on the side gear, making sure that the differential is fully seated.

23. Coat the mainshaft pilot bearing surface and all 15 needle bearings with petroleum jelly and install thew bearing on the shaft. Apply additional petroleum jelly to hold the bearings in place if necessary.

24. Install the rear output shaft on the mainshaft and into the differential, making sure that the shaft is completely seated. If necessary tap the shaft with a plastic mallet or equivalent to seat the shaft. Do not displace the pilot bearing during shaft installation.

25. Install the oil pump and the rear output shaft. Install the oil pump with the recessed side facing down. Install a replacement rear output shaft bearing seal in the rear transfer case half.

26. Apply a bead of Loctite®515 sealant or

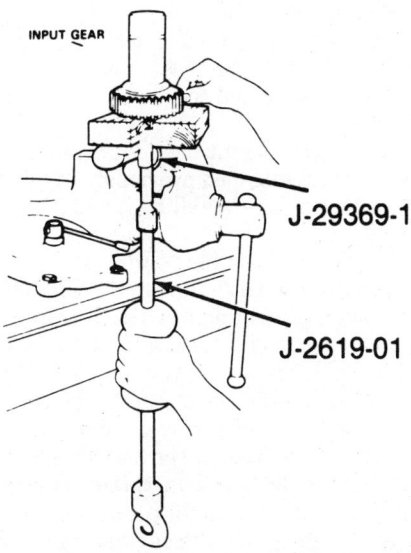

Removing the mainshaft pilot bushing from the NP-228

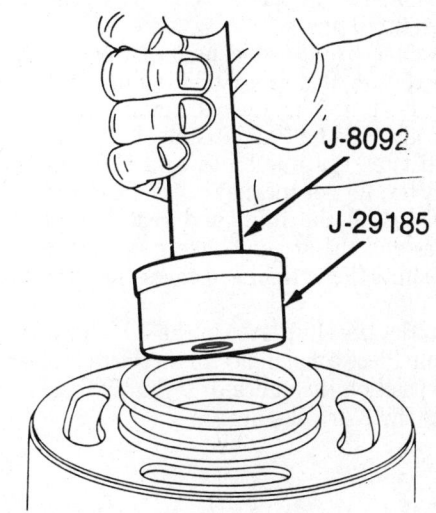

Removing the annulus gear bushing from the NP-228

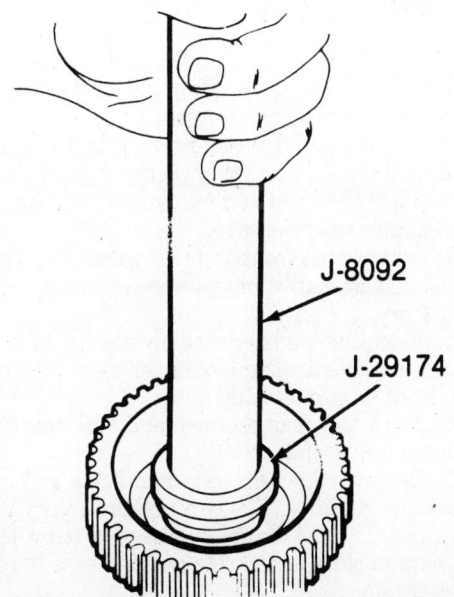

Installing the mainshaft pilot bushing on the NP-288

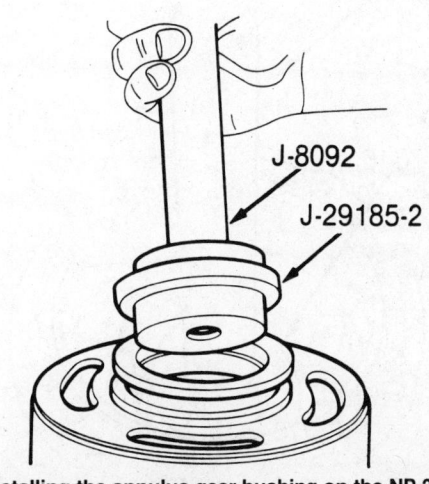

Installing the annulus gear bushing on the NP-228

equivalent, to the mating surface of the rear transfer case half. Install the magnet in the case and attach the rear transfer case half to the front transfer case half. Be sure that the alignment dowels at the front case half ends are aligned with the bolt holes in the rear case half and mate the rear case half with the front case half.

NOTE: *If the rear transfer case half will not mate completely with the front case. Inspect the following; oil in the range fork rail bore, the front output shaft rear thrust bearing assembly is not aligned with the rear case half, the mainshaft is not completely seated or the rear case half is not aligned with the oil pump.*

27. Install the rear case half to the front case half bolts. Torque the bolts to 23 ft. lbs. Be sure that the flat washers are used on the bolts at the case end where the alignment dowels are located. Install the speedometer drive gear on the rear output shaft.

28. Measure the thickness of the shim pack and record. Install a 0.030" shim on the rear output shaft. Align the rear retainer on the rear transfer case half and install the retainer. Install the retainer bolts and tighten them securley, do not torque to specifications.

29. Install the front and rear output shaft yokes and the original yoke nuts. Tighten the yoke nuts finger tight and check the differential end play.

30. Set the shift lever in the 4-high range position. Place a dial indicator on the rear retainer and position the indicator stylus so that it contacts the rear yoke nut.

31. Pull upward on the rear output yoke, note the dial indicator pointer position and record it. Remove the retainer and add or subtract differential shims as necessary to correct the end play. The end play should be between 0.05-0.25mm. The recommended end play is 0.15mm.

32. After adjusting the end play, remove the front and rear yokes. Discard the original yoke nuts. Apply a bead of Loctite®515 sealant or equivalent, to the retainer mating surface and install the retainer. Apply the sealer to the retaining bolts and install the bolts. Torque the bolts to 23 ft. lbs.

33. Position the front and rear yokes and install the replacement yoke seal washers and nuts. Using tool # J-8614-01 or equivalent hold the yokes in place and torque the yoke nuts to 120 ft. lbs.

34. Install the detent ball, spring and bolt if these were not installed previously. Apply sealer to the bolt before installing it and torque the bolt to 23 ft. lbs.

35. Install the drain plug and washer. Fill the transfer case with 7 pints of DEXRON®II transmission fluid or equivalent. Install the fill plug and washer and torque the drain and fill plugs to 18 ft. lbs.

36. Install the plug and washer in the front transfer case half (if removed) and torque the plug to 18 ft. lbs. Install the transfer case into the vehicle as described in this section. Road test the vehicle to check for proper operation of the transfer case, stop the engine and check for leaks.

NP-229 Overhaul

DISASSEMBLY

1. Remove the drain plug and drain the lubricant from the transfer case.
2. Remove the front and rear yoke nuts and seal washers. Discard the washers.
3. Mark the front and rear yokes for installation alignment reference.
4. Remove the front and rear yokes. Use Tool J-8614-01 or equivalent to remove the yokes if necessary.
5. Place the transfer case on wooden blocks. Cut V-notches in the blocks for clearance for the front case mounting studs.
6. Mark the rear retainer and rear case for assembly reference.
7. Remove the rear retainer bolts and remove the retainer. Use two prybars to pry the retainer off the transfer case. Position the prybars in slots in the retainer and case to pry the retainer loose.
8. Remove the differential shim(s) and

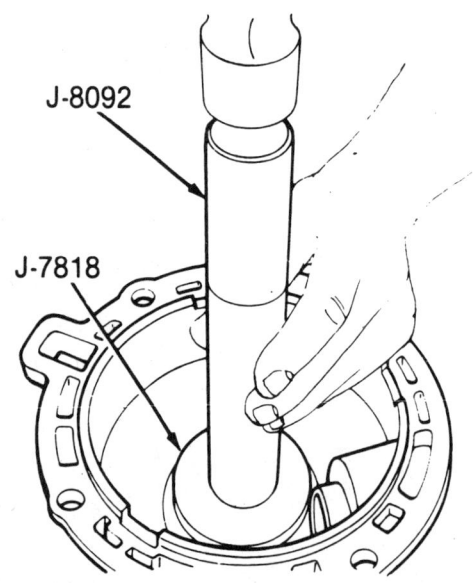

Rear output bearing installation on the NP-228

DRIVE TRAIN

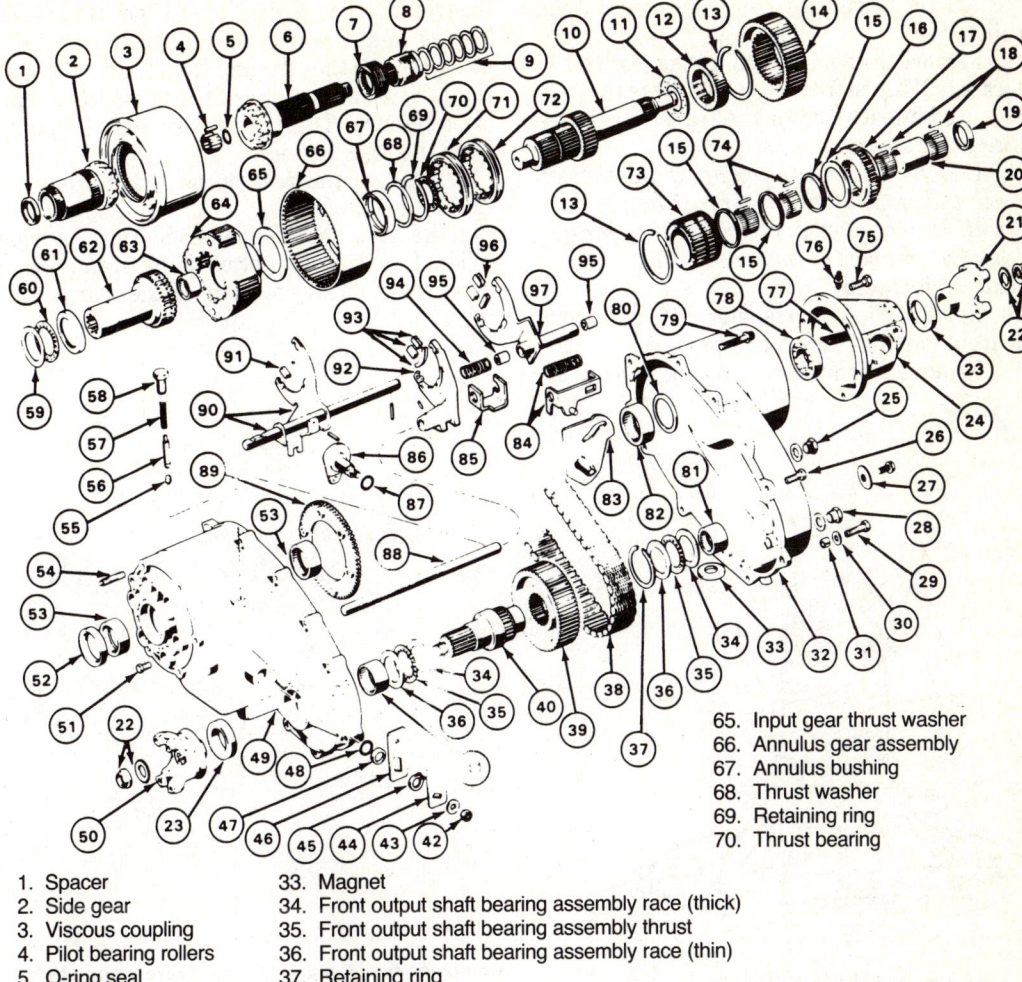

65. Input gear thrust washer
66. Annulus gear assembly
67. Annulus bushing
68. Thrust washer
69. Retaining ring
70. Thrust bearing

1. Spacer
2. Side gear
3. Viscous coupling
4. Pilot bearing rollers
5. O-ring seal
6. Rear output shaft
7. Oil pump
8. Speedometer drive gear
9. Shim kit
10. Mainshaft
11. Mainshaft thrust washer
12. Spline gear
13. Retaining ring
14. Sprocket
15. Spacer
16. Sprocket thrust washer
17. Viscous clutch gear
18. Side gear roller (82)
19. Spacer (short)
20. Spacer (long)
21. Rear yoke
22. Nut and seal washer
23. Seal
24. Rear retainer
25. Plug assembly
26. Bolt
27. Identification tag
28. Plug assembly
29. Dowel bolt
30. Dowel bolt washer
31. Case half dowel
32. Rear half case
33. Magnet
34. Front output shaft bearing assembly race (thick)
35. Front output shaft bearing assembly thrust
36. Front output shaft bearing assembly race (thin)
37. Retaining ring
38. Chain
39. Driven sprocket
40. Front output shaft
41. Front output front bearing
42. Nut
43. Washer
44. Mode lever
45. Snap ring
46. Range lever
47. O-ring retainer
48. O-ring seal
49. Front half case
50. Front output yoke
51. Low range plate bolt
52. Input shaft oil seal
53. Input shaft bearing
54. Stud
55. Ball
56. Plunger
57. Plunger spring
58. Screw
59. Input race
60. Input thrust bearing
61. Input race (thick)
62. Input shaft
63. Input bearing
64. Planetary gear assembly
71. High range sliding clutch sleeve
72. Mode sliding clutch sleeve
73. Carrier
74. Carrier rollers (120)
75. Rear retainer bolt
76. Vent
77. Vent seal
78. Output bearing
79. Botl
80. Seal
81. Front output rear bearing
82. Output shaft inner bearing
83. Range sector
84. Range bracket (outer) and spring
85. Range bracket (inner)
86. Mode sector
87. O-ring seal
88. Range rail
89. Low range lockout plate
90. Mode fork, rail and pin
91. Mode fork pad
92. Range fork
93. Range fork pads
94. Range bracket spring (inner)
95. Locking fork bushing
96. Locking fork pads
97. Locking fork

NP-229 transfer case exploded view

336 DRIVE TRAIN

speedometer drive gear from the rear output shaft.

9. Remove the bolts attaching the rear transfer case half to the front case half. Note that the bolts used at each end of the transfer case require flat washers.

CAUTION: *Insert two prybars in the slots at each end of the rear transfer case half to loosen it. Do not attempt to wedge the transfer case halves apart or the case mating surfaces will be damaged.*

10. Remove the rear transfer case half from the front case half using two prybars.

11. Remove the thrust bearing and races from the front output shaft. Note the position of the bearing and races for assembly reference.

12. Remove the oil pump from the rear output shaft. Note the position of the pump for assembly reference. The recessed side of the pump faces the case interior.

13. Remove the rear output shaft from the viscous coupling.

14. Remove the 15 mainshaft pilot bearing rollers from the shaft or coupling (if the rollers dropped off during removal of the rear output shaft).

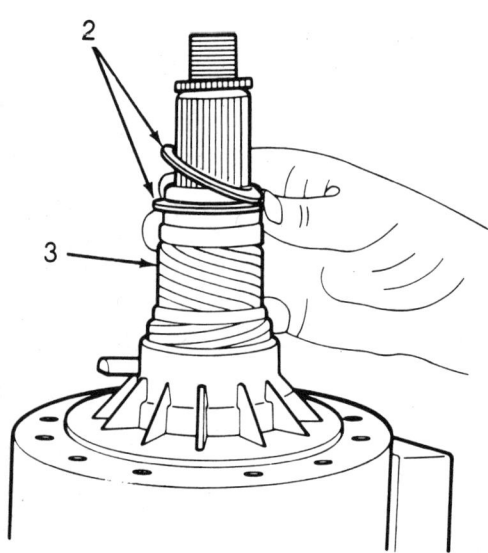

Removing the differential shims (2) and speedometer drive gear (3) from the NP-229

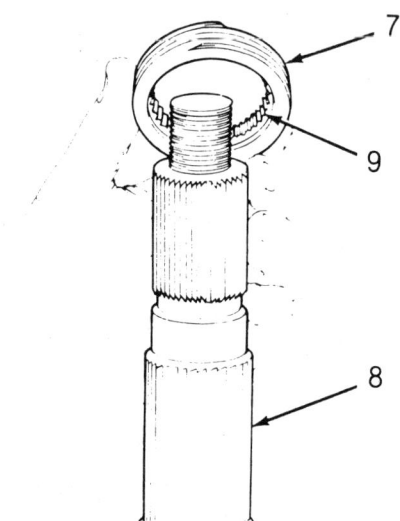

Removing the oil pump (7) from the rear output shaft (8). (9) is the recess in the pump from the NP-229

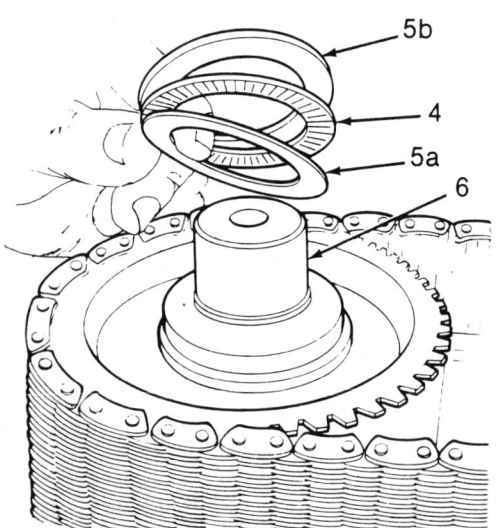

Removing the thrust bearing (4) and races (5a, 5b) from the front output shaft (6) from the NP-229

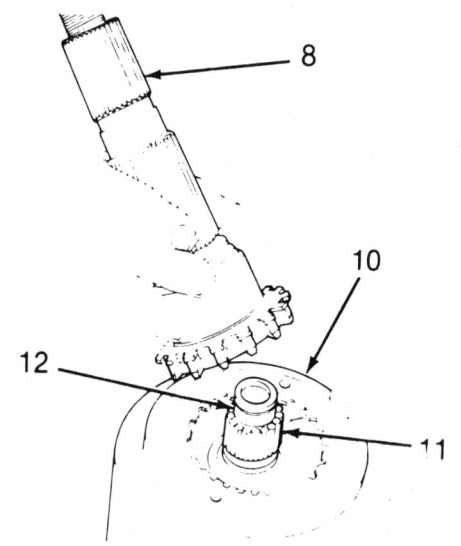

Disassembling the rear output shaft (8), 15 pilot roller (11), and O-ring (12), from the differential (10) from the NP-229

DRIVE TRAIN 337

15. Remove the mainshaft O-ring from the end of the shaft.
16. Remove the viscous coupling from the mainshaft and side gear.
17. Remove the front output shaft, driven sprocket and drive chain assembly. Lift the front shaft, sprocket and chain upward. Tilt the front shaft toward the mainshaft. Slide the chain off the drive sprocket and remove the assembly.
18. Remove the mainshaft, side gear, clutch gear, drive sprocket and spline gear as an assembly. Place the assembly on a clean shop towel and set aside until the front case disassembly is completed.
19. Remove the front output shaft front thrust bearing assembly from the front case, or from the shaft (if the bearing and races remained on the shaft during removal).

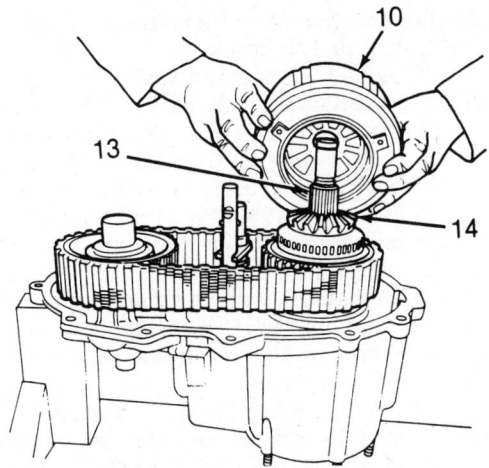

Removing the differential (10) from the mainshaft (13) and side gear (14) from the NP-229

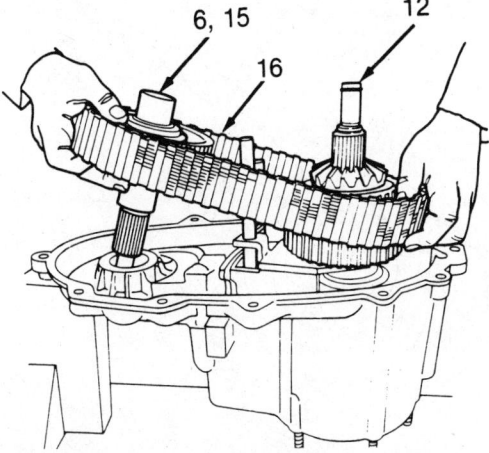

Removing the front output shaft (6), driven sprocket (15) and drive chain (16) from the mainshaft (12) from the NP-229

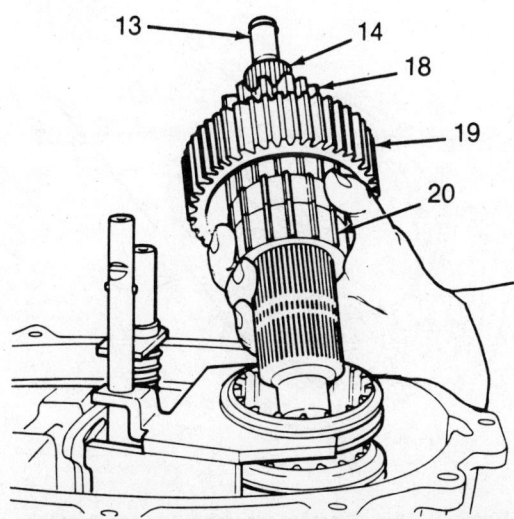

Removing the mainshaft (13), side gear (14), drive sprocket (18) and spline gear (19) from the NP-229

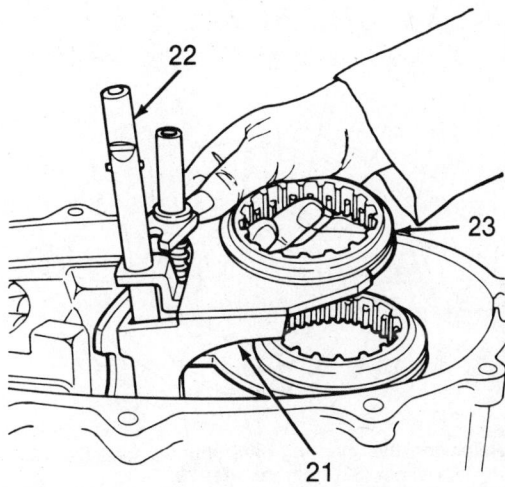

Removing the mode fork (21), shift rail (22) and mode sliding clutch sleeve (23) from the NP-229

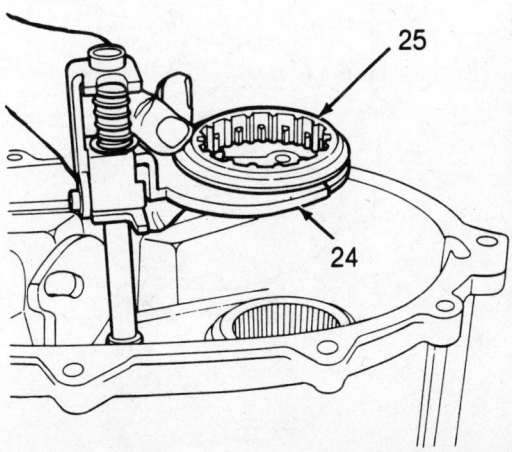

Removing the lock fork (25) and clutch sleeve (24) from the NP-229

338 DRIVE TRAIN

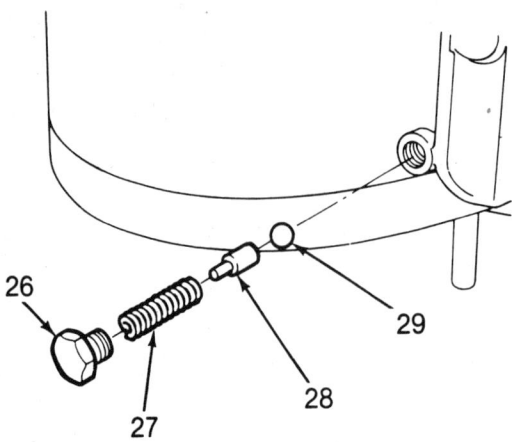

Removing the range sector detent screw, spring, plunger and ball from the NP-229

20. Remove the drive chain from the front output shaft and sprocket.
21. Remove the snapring that retains the driven sprocket on the front output shaft. Mark the sprocket and shaft for assembly reference and remove the sprocket from the shaft.
22. Remove the mode fork, shift rail, and mode sliding clutch sleeve as an assembly. Mark the sleeve and fork for assembly reference and remove the sleeve from the fork.

NOTE: *The mode fork and rail are pinned together so that they will operate as a unit. Remove the pin to separate the two components if necessary.*

23. Remove the locking fork, high range sliding clutch sleeve, fork brackets and fork springs as an assembly. Note the position of the compo-

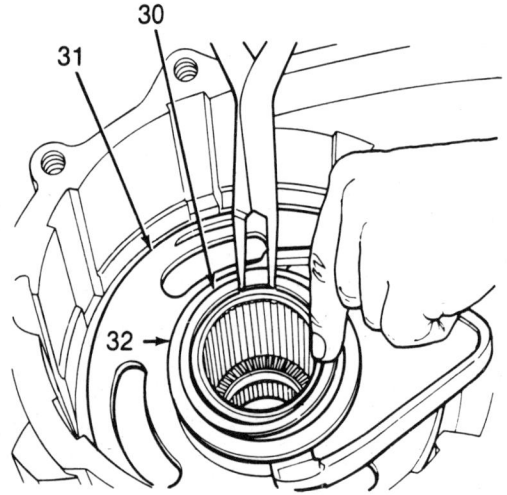

Removing the snapring (30), annulus gear (31) and thrust washer (32) from the NP-229

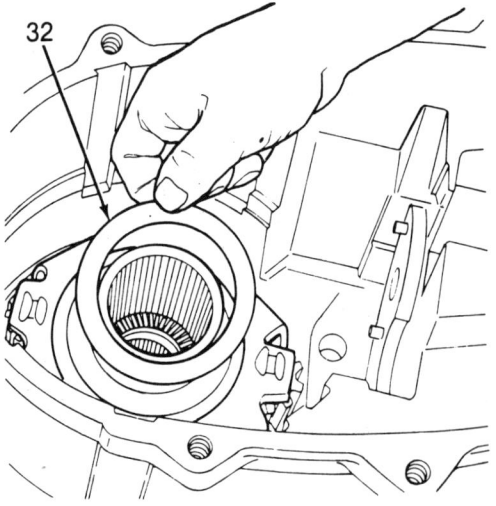

Removing the planetary thrust washer (32) from the NP-229

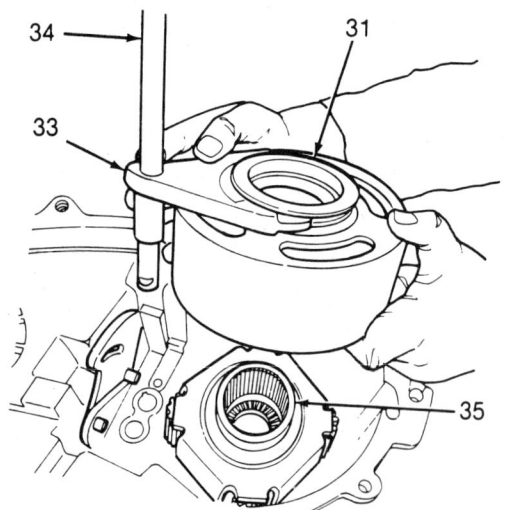

Removing the annulus gear (31), range fork (33) and rail (34) from the NP-229

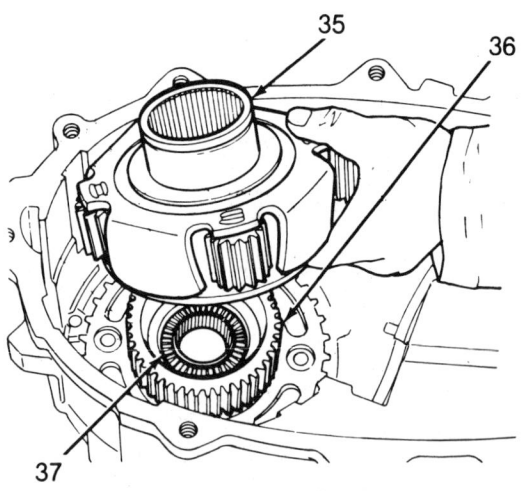

Removing the planetary assembly (35) and the mainshaft thrust bearing (36) from the input shaft from the NP-229

nents for assembly reference and disassemble the components for cleaning and inspection.

24. Remove the range sector detent screw and remove the detent spring, plunger and ball.
25. Move the range operating lever downward to the last detent position.
26. Disengage the low range fork lug from the range sector slot.
27. Remove the retaining snapring from the annulus gear and remove the thrust washer.
28. Remove the annulus gear, range fork and rail as an assembly. Separate the components for cleaning and inspection.
29. Remove the planetary thrust washer from the planetary assembly hub.
30. Remove the planetary assembly. Grasp the planetary hub and lift the assembly upward to remove it.
31. Remove the mainshaft thrust bearing from the input shaft.
32. Remove the input shaft and remove the input shaft thrust bearing and race.
33. Remove the range sector and operating lever attaching nut and lockwasher. Remove the lever.
34. Remove the range sector and shaft from the front case.
35. Remove the range sector O-ring and retainer.

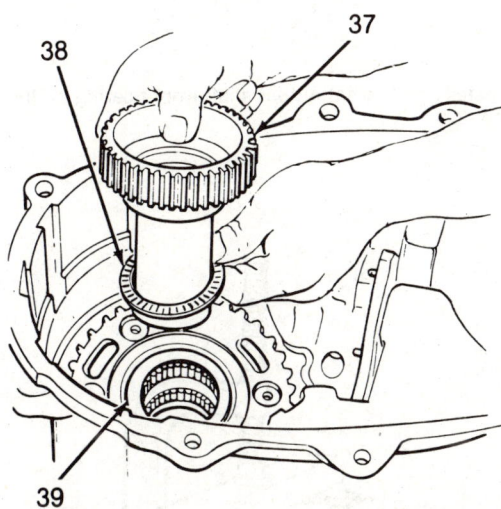

Removing the input shaft (37), input shaft thrust bearing (38) and race (39) from the NP-229

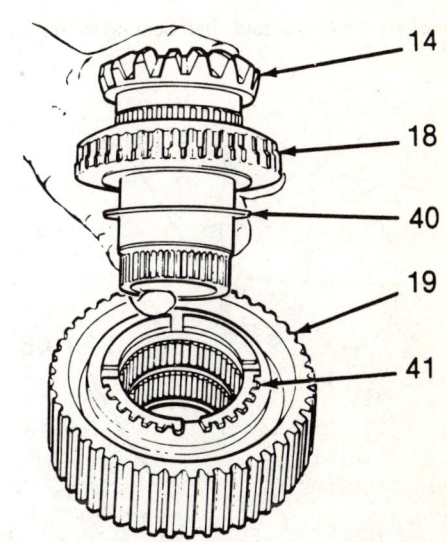

Removing the side gear (14) and thrust washer (40) from the sprocket carrier (41) and drive sprocket (18) from the NP-229

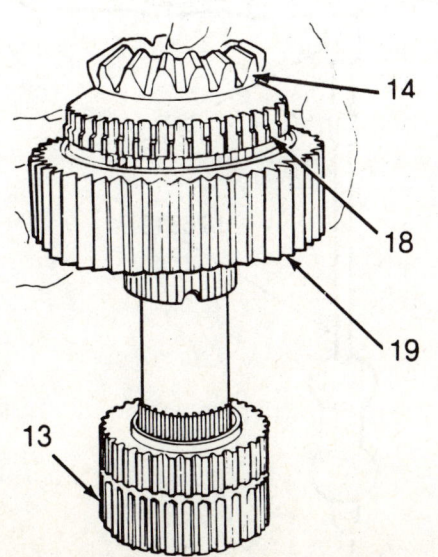

Removing the drive sprocket and side gear from the mainshaft from the NP-229

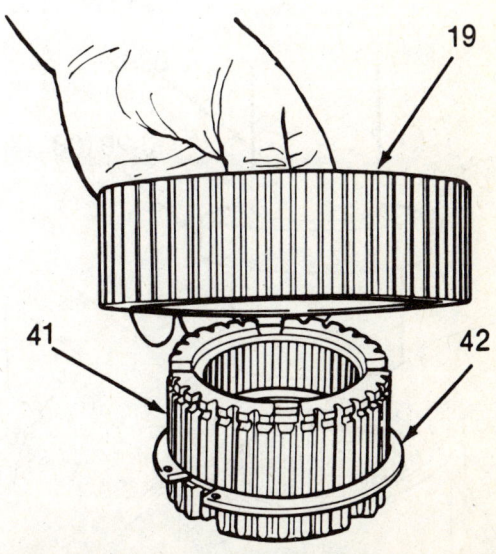

Removing the snapring (42) and drive sprocket (19) from the carrier (41) from the NP-229

340 DRIVE TRAIN

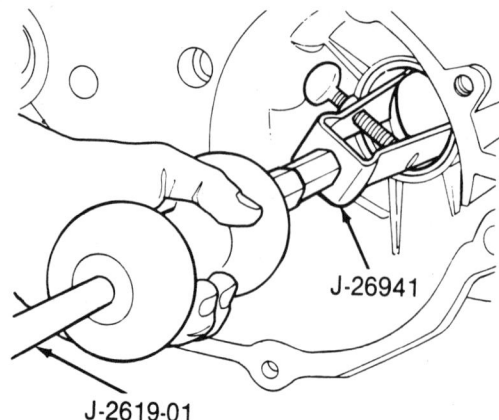

Removing the rear output shaft bearing from the NP-229

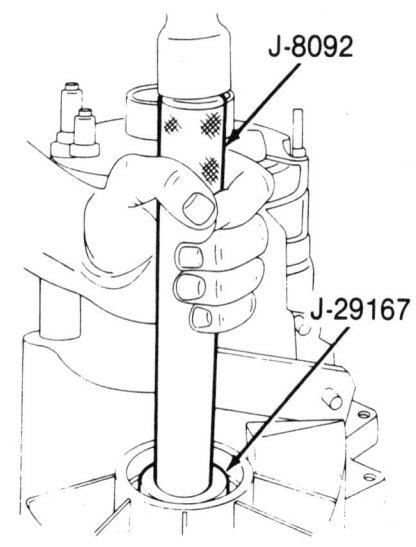

Installing the front output shaft front bearing on the NP-229

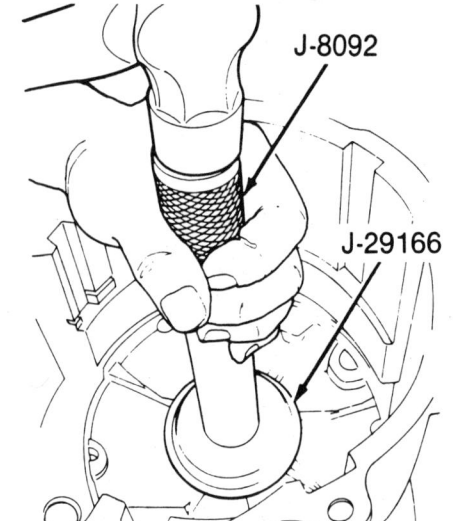

Installing the rear output shaft bearing on the NP-229

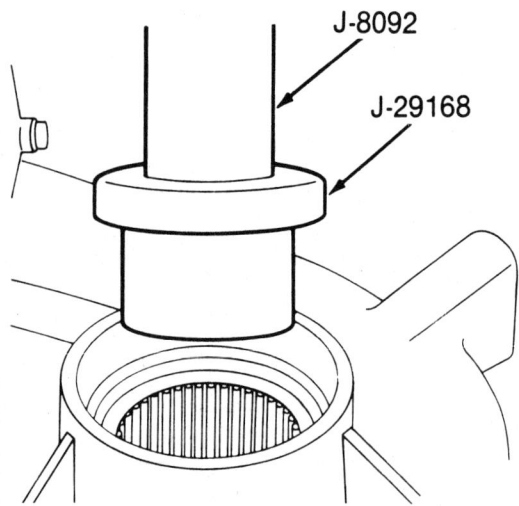

Removing the front output shaft front bearing from the NP-229

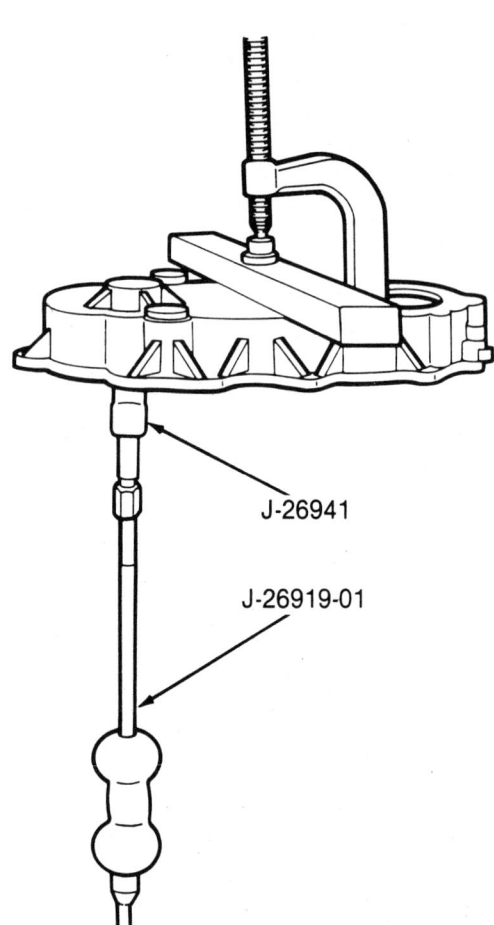

Removing the front output shaft rear bearing from the NP-229

DRIVE TRAIN 341

MAINSHAFT DISASSEMBLY

1. Grasp the drive sprocket and lift the sprocket clutch gear and side gear upward and off the mainshaft.
2. Remove the mainshaft needle bearings and two bearing spacers from the mainshaft; a total of 82 bearings are used; note the spacer position for assembly reference.
3. Remove the spline gear and thrust washer from the mmainshaft.
4. Remove the side gear, clutch gear, and clutch gear thrust washer from the sprocket carrier and sprocket.
5. Remove the clutch gear and thrust washer from the side gear.
6. Remove one sprocket carrier snapring and remove the drive sprocket from the carrier; mark for assembly reference.

CAUTION: *The sprocket carrier and mainshaft needle bearings are different in size. Take care to avoid intermixing them.*

7. Remove the three bearing spacers and all sprocket carrier needle bearings from the carrier; a total of 120 needle bearings are used.

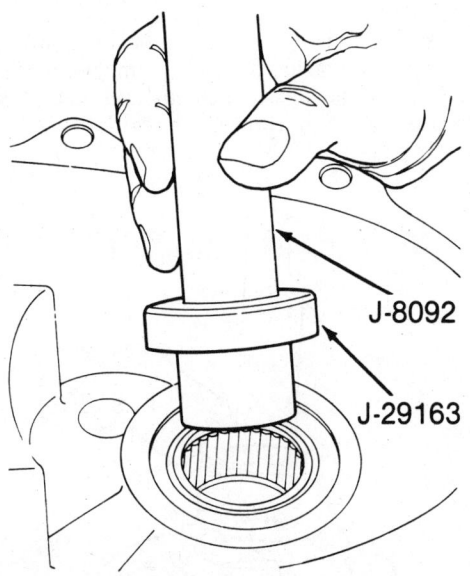

Installing the front output shaft rear bearing on the NP-229

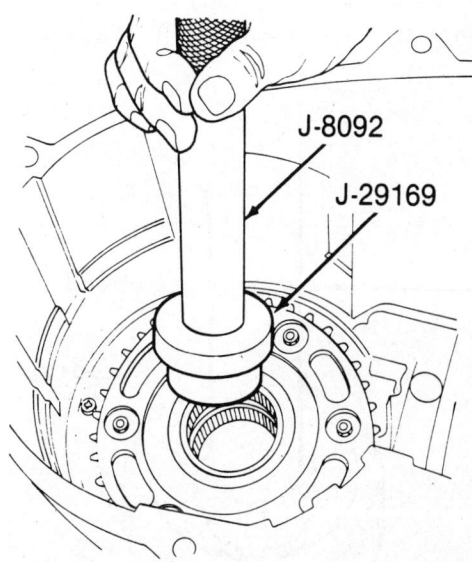

Installing the input gear front and rear bearings on the NP-229

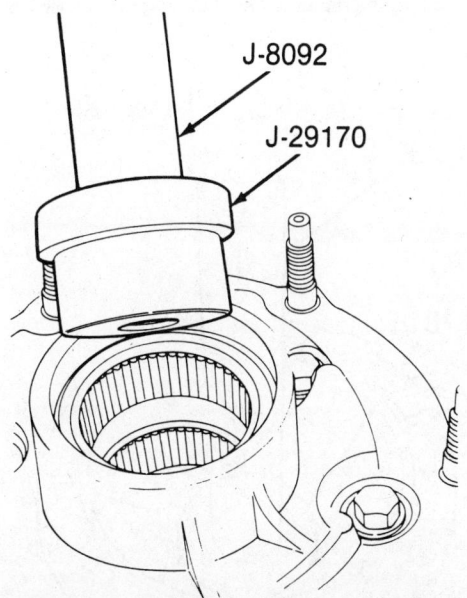

Removing the input gear front and rear bearings from the NP-229

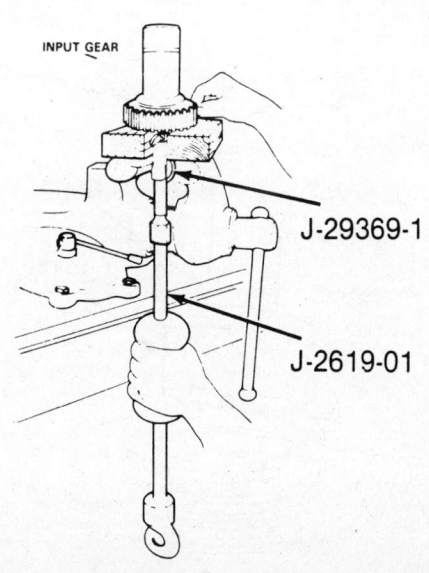

Removing the mainshaft pilot bushing from the NP-229

342 DRIVE TRAIN

8. Remove the rear output bearing and rear yoke seal from the rear retainer; the bearing is shielded on one side; note the bearing position for assembly reference.
9. Remove the input gear and front yoke seals from the front case; use a small prybar to pry the seals out of the case.

CLEANING & INSPECTION

1. Wash all components thoroughly in clean solvent. Ensure that all lubricant, metallic particles, dirt, and foreign material are removed from the surfaces of every component.
2. Apply compressed air to each oil supply port and channel in each transfer case half to remove any obstructions or cleaning solvent residue.
3. Inspect all gear teeth for excessive wear or damage. Inspect all gear splines for burrs, nicks, wear or damage.
4. Remove minor nicks or scratches using an oilstone. Replace any component exhibiting excessive wear or damage.
5. Inspect all snaprings and thrust washers for excessive wear, distortion and damage. Replace any component exhibiting these conditions.
6. Inspect the transfer case halves and rear retainer for cracks, porosity, damaged mating surfaces, stripped bolt threads and distortion. Replace any component exhibiting these conditions.

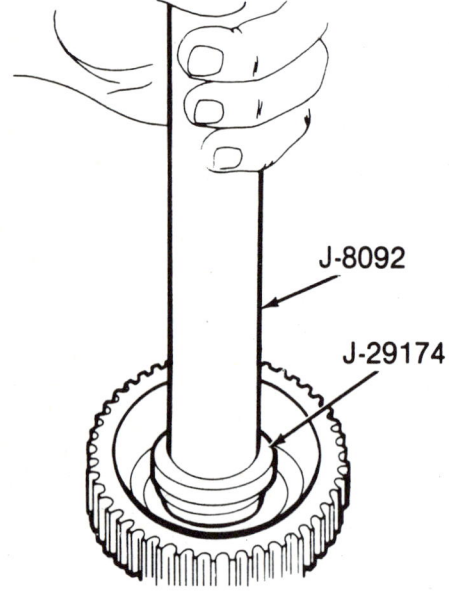

Installing the mainshaft pilot bushing from the NP-229

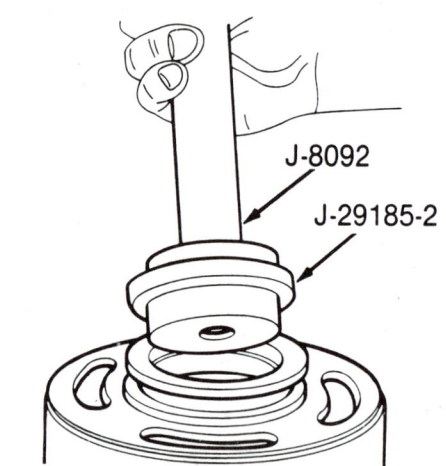

Installing the annulus gear bushing on the NP-229

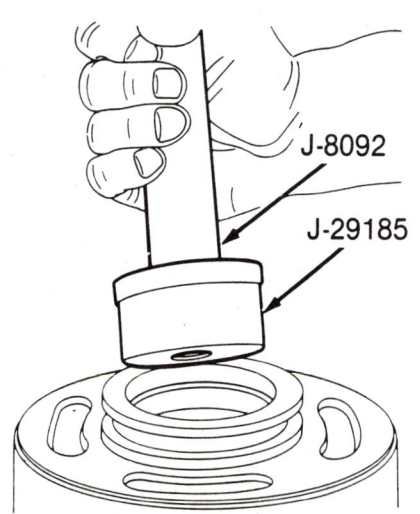

Removing the annulus gear bushing from the NP-229

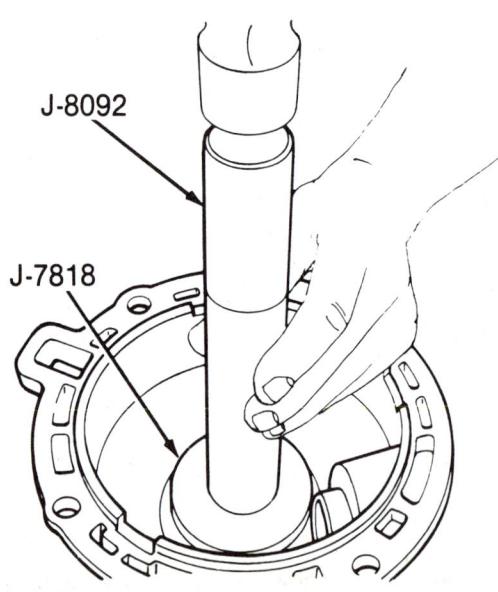

Installing the rear output bearing on the NP-229

DRIVE TRAIN 343

7. Inspect the viscous coupling and differential pinions. If the pinions or carrier are damaged or worn excessively, replace the coupling as an assembly only. If the coupling is cracked, leaking, or damaged, replace the coupling as an assembly only.

8. Inspect the condition of all needle, roller, ball and thrust bearings in the front and rear transfer case halves. Also inspect to determine the condition of the bearing bores in both transfer case halves and in the input gear, rear output shaft, side gear, and rear retainer.

9. Replace any component that is excessively worn or damaged. If any shaft, case half or input gear bearing requires replacement, refer to Bushing/Bearing Replacement.

NOTE: *The front output shaft thrust bearing race surfaces are heat treated during manufacture. Heat treatment causes a brown or blue discoloration of these surfaces. Do not replace a front output shaft because of this type of discoloration.*

BEARINGS & BUSHINGS

CAUTION: *All of the bearings used in the transfer case must be correctly positioned to avoid blocking the bearing oil supply holes. After replacing any bearing, check the bearing position and ensure that the supply hole is not obstructed by the bearing.*

REAR OUTPUT SHAFT BEARING
Removal and Installation

1. Remove the bearing using Remover Tool J-26941 and Slide Hammer J-2619-01 or equivalent. Remove the rear output lip seal using a small awl.

2. Install a replacement lip seal.

3. Install a replacement bearing using Driver Handle J-8092 and Installer Tool J-29166 or equivalent.

4. Remove the tools and inspect the oil supply hole. The bearing must not obstruct the supply hole.

FRONT OUTPUT SHAFT FRONT BEARING
Removal and Installation

1. Remove the bearing using Tools J-8092 and J-29168 or equivalent.

2. Remove the tools and inspect the oil supply hole. The bearing must not obstruct the supply hole.

FRONT OUTPUT SHAFT REAR BEARING
Removal and Installation

1. Remove the bearing using Remover Tool J-26941 and Slide Hammer J-2619-01 or equivalent.

2. Install a replacement bearing using Driver Handle J-8092 and Installer Tool J-29163 or equivalent.

3. Remove the installer tools and inspect the bearing position to ensure the oil supply hole is not obstructed. Also ensure that the bearing is seated flush with the edge of the bore in the case to allow clearance for the thrust bearing assembly.

INPUT GEAR FRONT & REAR BEARINGS
Removal and Installation

1. Remove both bearings simultaneously using Driver Handle J-8092 and Remover Tool J-29170 or equivalent.

2. Install the new bearings one at a time. Install the rear bearing first; then install the front bearing. Use Driver Handle J-8092 and Installer Tool J-29169 or equivalent.

3. Remove the installer tools and inspect the bearing position to ensure the oil supply holes are not obstructed. Also ensure that the bearings are flush with the transfer case bore surfaces.

4. Install a replacement oil seal using seal Installer Tool J-29162 or equivalent.

MAINSHAFT PILOT BUSHING
Removal and Installation

1. Remove the bushing using Slide Hammer J-2619-01 and Remover Tool J-29369-1 or equivalent.

2. Install a replacement bearing using Driver Handle J-8092 and Installer Tool J-29174 or equivalent.

3. Inspect bushing position to ensure that the oil supply hole is not obstructed.

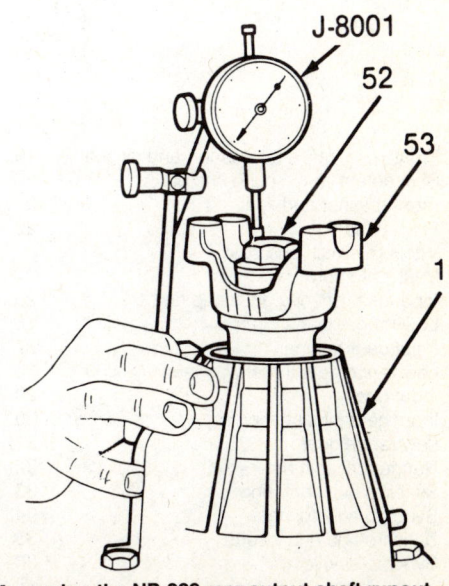

Measuring the NP-229 rear output shaft runout

344 DRIVE TRAIN

ANNULUS GEAR BUSHING
Removal and Installation

1. Remove the bushing using Driver Handle J-8092 and Remover/Installer Tool J-29185 or equivalent.
2. Install a replacement bushing using Tools J-8092 and J-29185-2 or equivalent.
3. Remove any chips generated by the bushing removal and/or installation.

REAR OUTPUT BEARING AND REAR YOKE SEAL
Removal and Installation

1. Remove the bearing using a brass drift and hammer.
2. Remove the seal from the retainer using a brass drift and hammer.

CAUTION: *The rear output bearing is shielded on one side. Ensure that the shielded side faces the transfer case interior after installation.*

3. Install a replacement bearing using Driver Handle J-8092 and Installer Tool J-7818 or equivalent.
4. Install a replacement seal in the retainer using Tool J-29162 or equivalent.

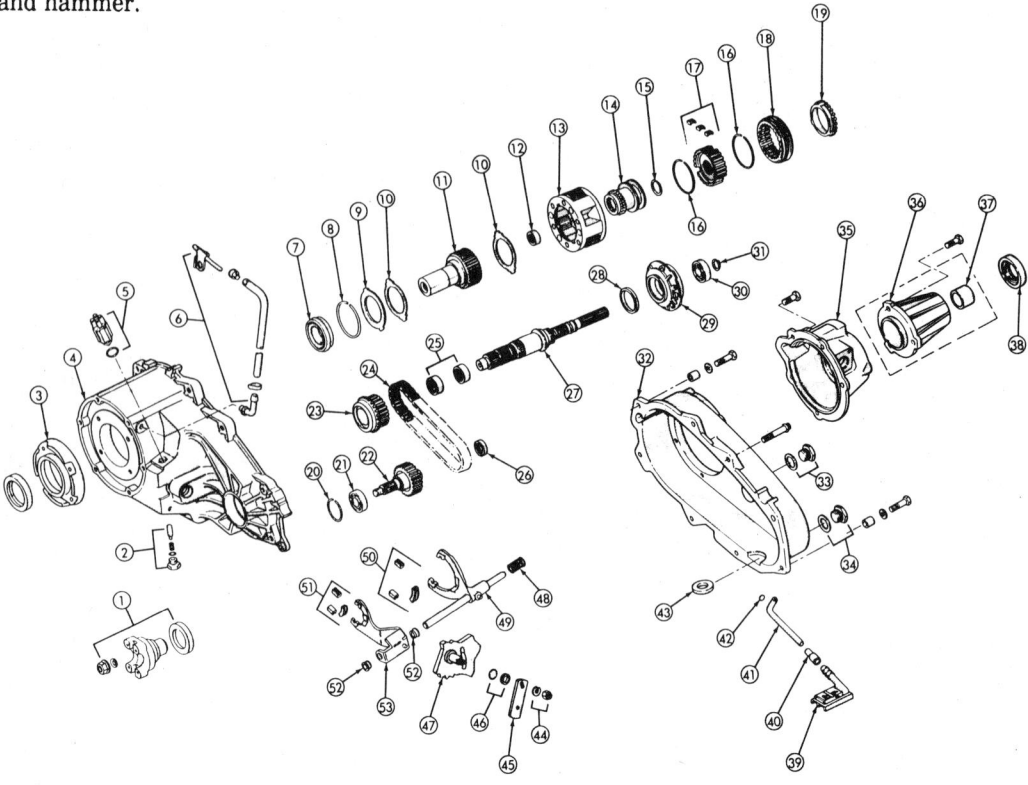

1. Front yoke, nut, seal washer, and oil seal
2. Shift detent plug, spring and pin
3. Front retainer and seal
4. Front case
5. Vacuum switch and seal
6. Vent assembly
7. Input gear bearing and snap ring
8. Low range gear snap ring
9. Input gear retainer
10. Low range gear thrust washers
11. Input gear
12. Input gear pilot bearing
13. Low range gear
14. Range fork shift hub
15. Synchro hub snap ring
16. Synchro hub springs
17. Synchro hub and inserts
18. Synchro sleeve
19. Stop ring
20. Snap ring
21. Output shaft front bearing
22. Output shaft (front)
23. Drive sprocket
24. Drive chain
25. Drive sprocket bearings
26. Output shaft rear bearing
27. Mainshaft
28. Oil seal
29. Oil pump assembly
30. Rear bearing
31. Snap ring
32. Rear case
33. Fill plug and gasket
34. Drain plug and gasket
35. Rear retainer
36. Extension housing
37. Bushing
38. Oil seal
39. Oil pickup screen
40. Tube connector
41. Oil pickup tube
42. Pickup tube O-ring
43. Magnet
44. Range lever nut and washer
45. Range lever
46. O-ring and seal
47. Sector
48. Mode spring
49. Mode fork
50. Mode fork inserts
51. Range fork inserts
52. Range fork bushings
53. Range fork

NP-231 exploded view

DRIVE TRAIN

NP-231 Overhaul

DISASSEMBLY

1. Remove the transfer case from the vehicle as descibed above.
2. Remove the attaching nuts from the front and rear output yokes. Remove the yokes and sealing washers.
3. Remove the bolts and tap the extension housing off of the rear retainer.
4. Remove the snapring from the rear bearing, then, remove the four bolts and separate the rear bearing retainer from the rear case half.
5. Remove the retaining bolts and separate the case halves by inserting a small pry bar in the pry slots on the case.
6. Remove the oil pump, pickup tube and pickup screen from the rear case.

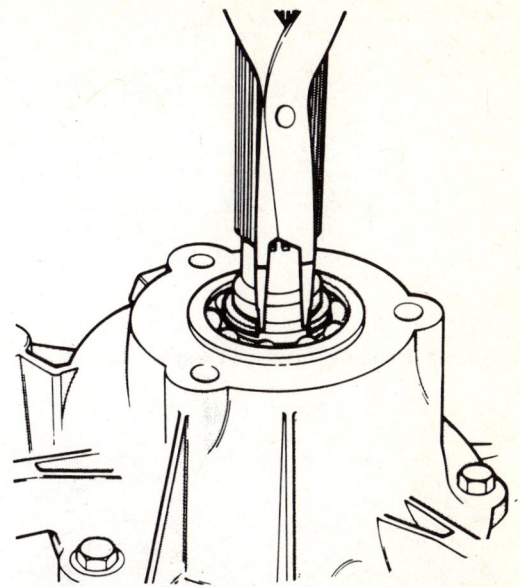

Removing the rear bearing snapring from the NP-231

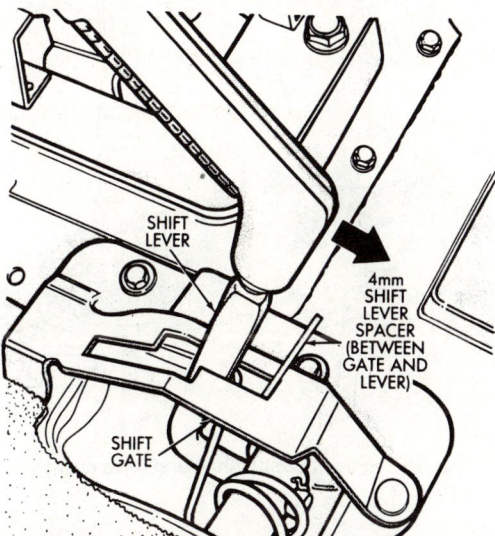

Installing the NP-231 shift lever spacer

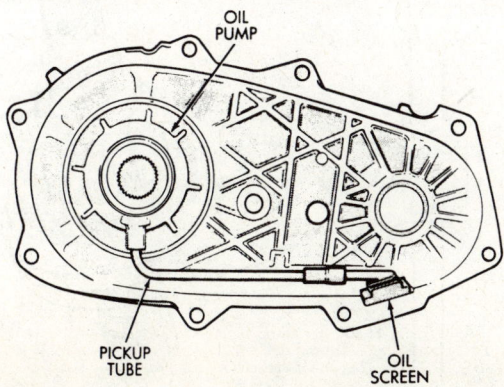

Removing the oil screen and pick-up tube from the NP-231

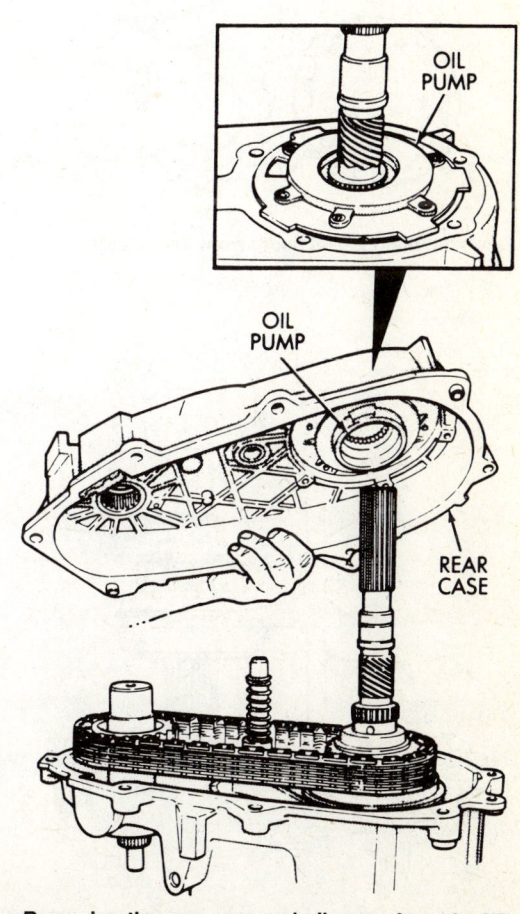

Removing the rear case and oil pump from the NP-231

346 DRIVE TRAIN

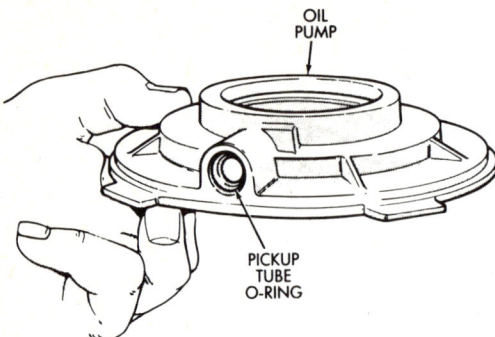

Removing the pick-up tube oil ring from the NP-231

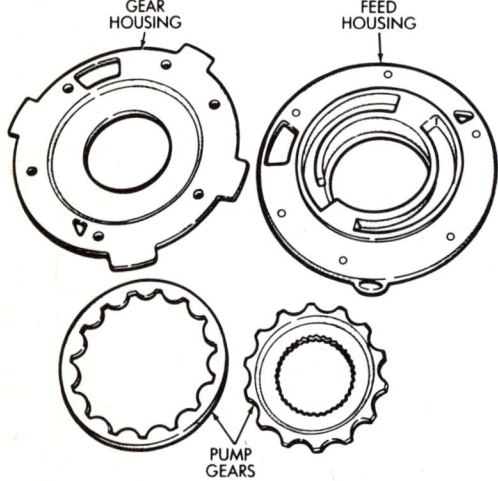

Disassembling the oil pump from the NP-231

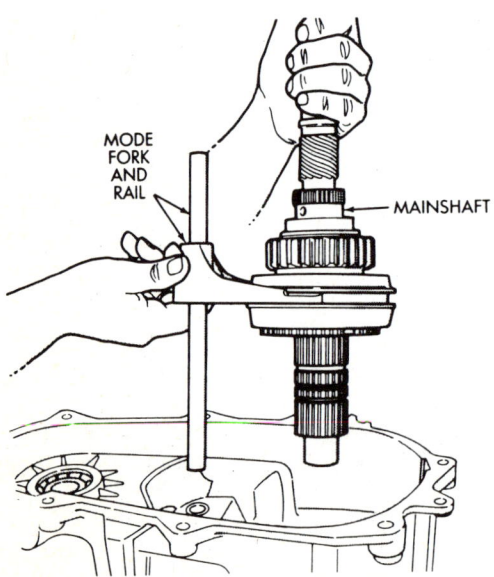

Removing the mainshaft, mode fork and shift rail from the NP-231

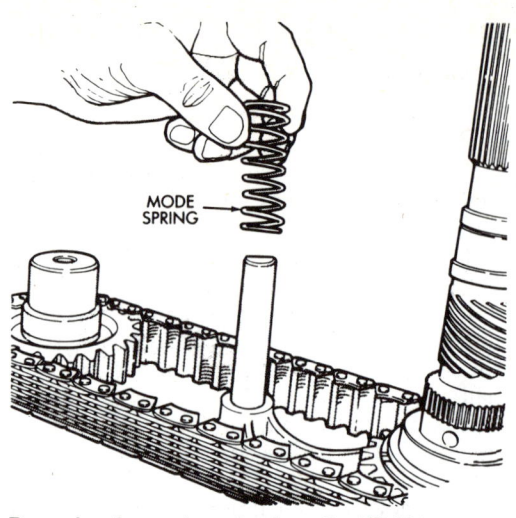

Removing the mode spring from the NP-231

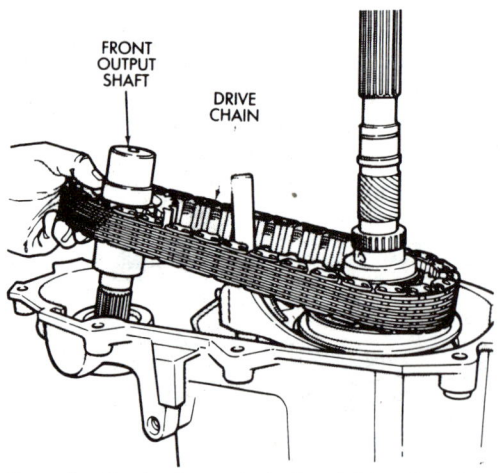

Removing the front ouptut shaft and drive chain from the NP-231

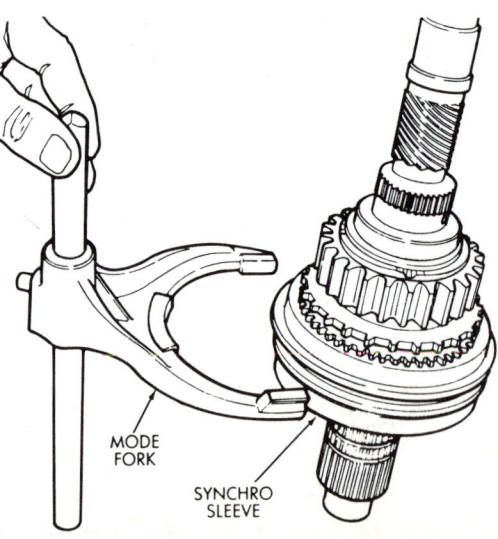

Removing the mode fork from the NP-231

DRIVE TRAIN 347

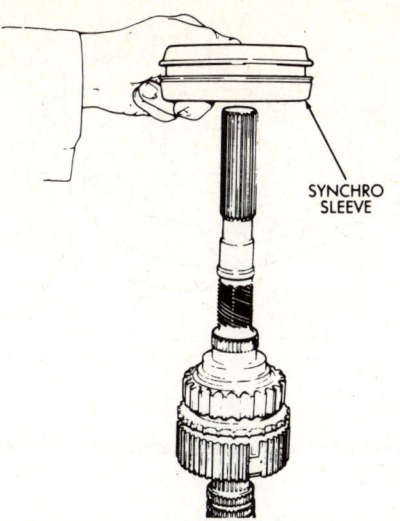

Removing the synchronizer sleeve from the NP-231

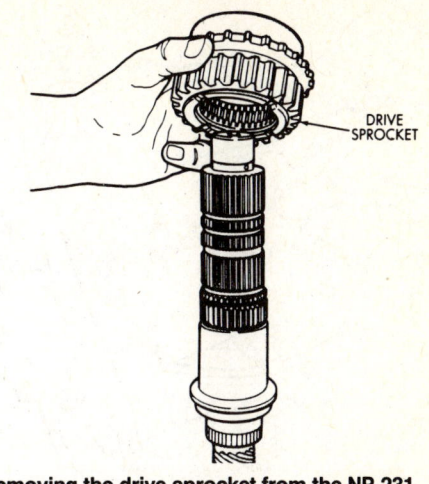

Removing the drive sprocket from the NP-231

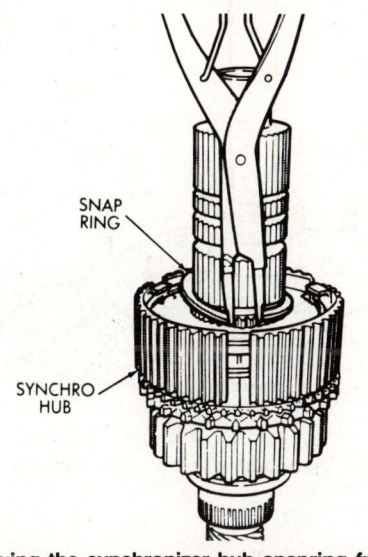

Removing the synchronizer hub snapring from the NP-231

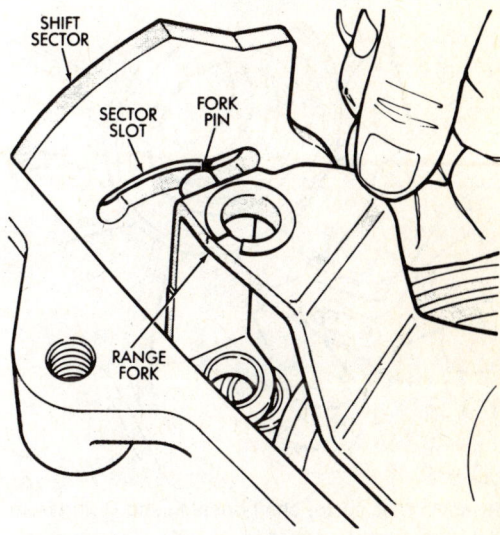

Disengaging the range fork from the NP-231

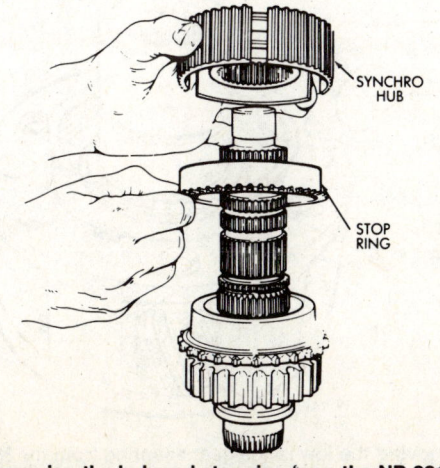

Removing the hub and stop ring from the NP-231

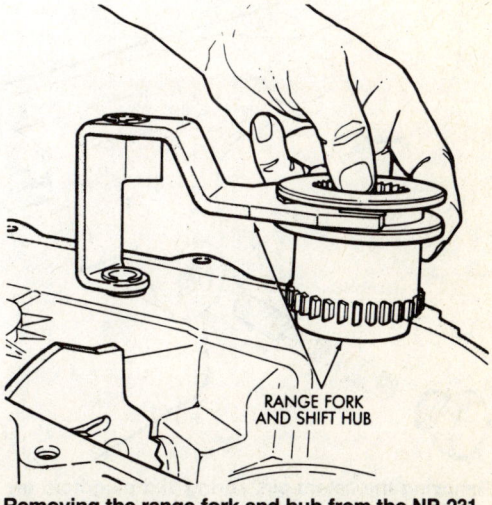

Removing the range fork and hub from the NP-231

348 DRIVE TRAIN

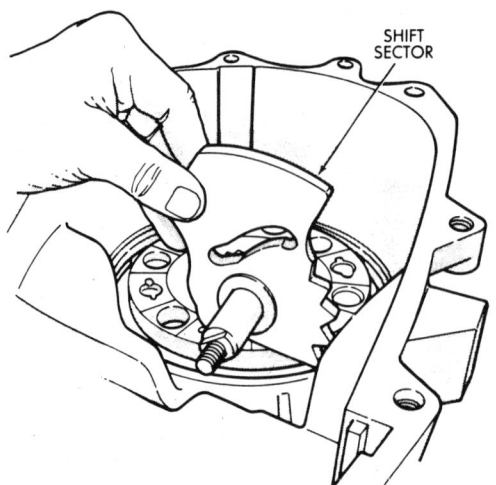

Removing the shift selector from the NP-231

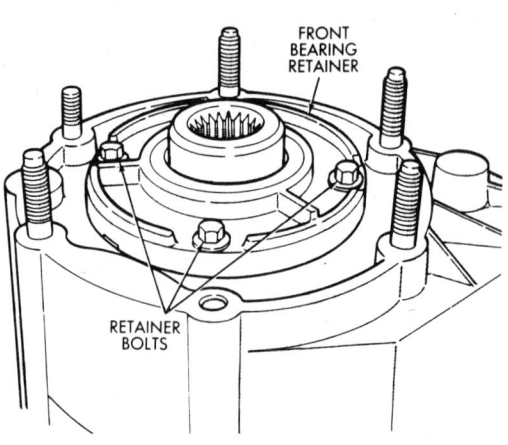

Removing the bearing retainer bolts from the NP-231

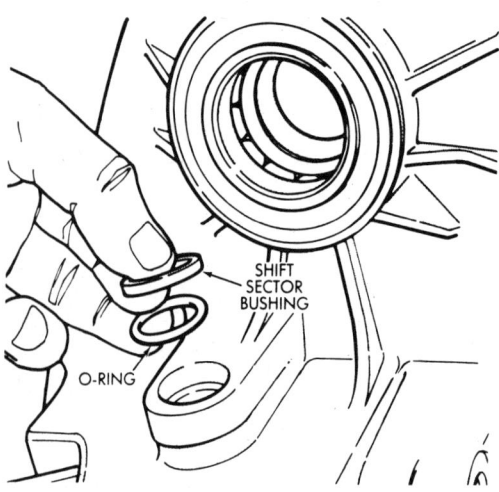

Removing the sector shaft bushing and O-ring from the NP-231

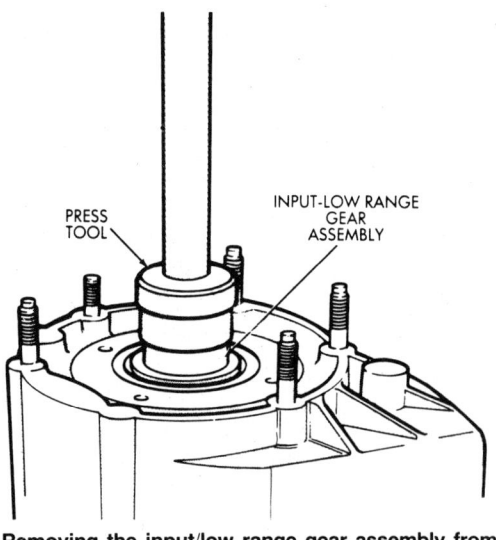

Removing the input/low range gear assembly from the NP-231

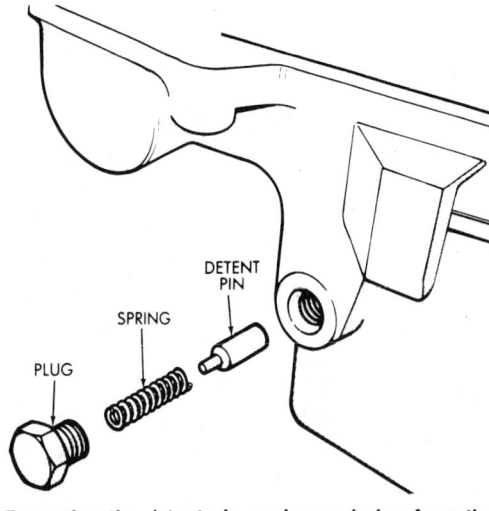

Removing the detent pin, spring and plug from the NP-231

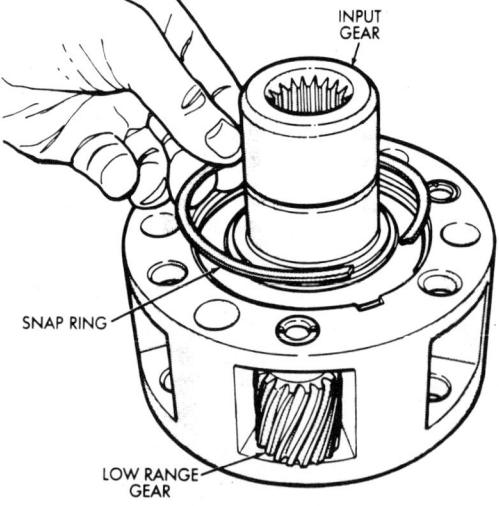

Removing the low range gear snapring from the NP-231

DRIVE TRAIN 349

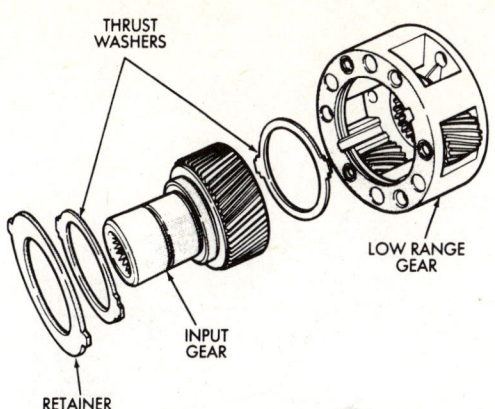

Disassembling the input/low range gear from the NP-231

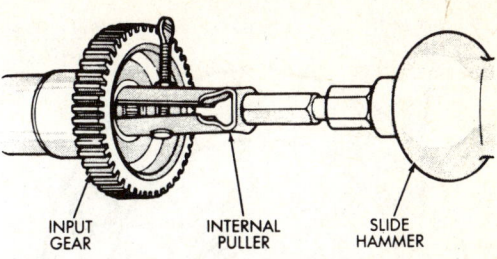

Removing the input gear pilot bearing from the NP-231

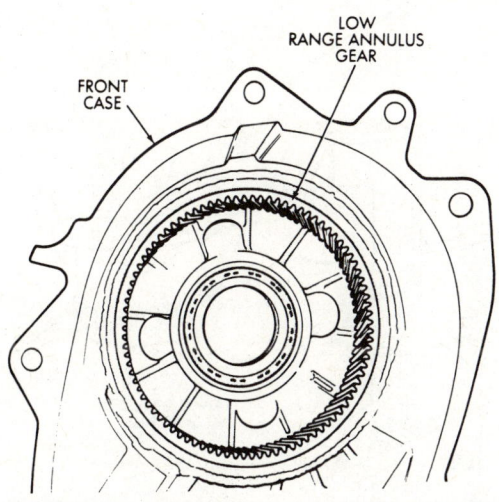

Inspecting the low range annulus gear from the NP-231

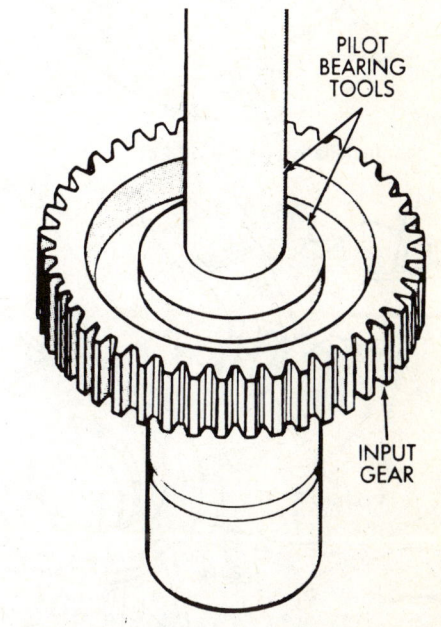

Installing the input gear pilot bearing on the NP-231

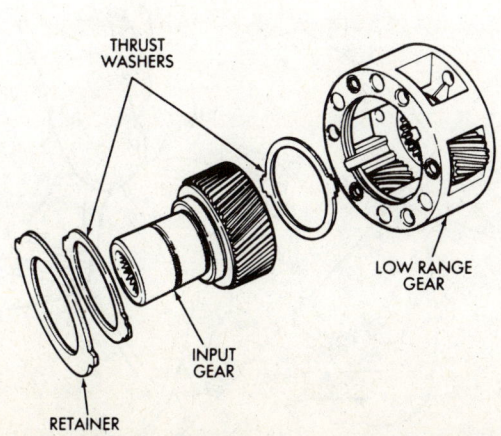

Assembling the input/low range gear on the NP-231

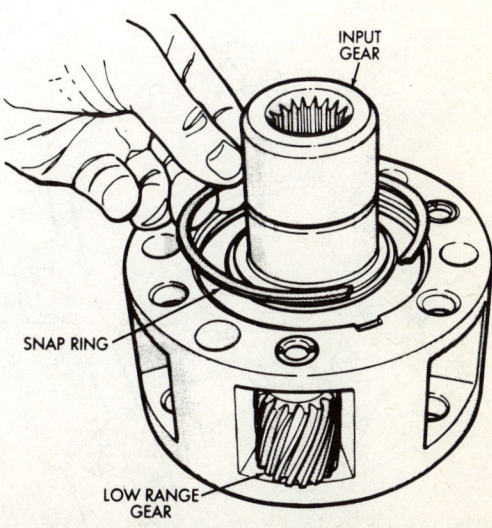

Installing the low range gear snapring on the NP-231

350 DRIVE TRAIN

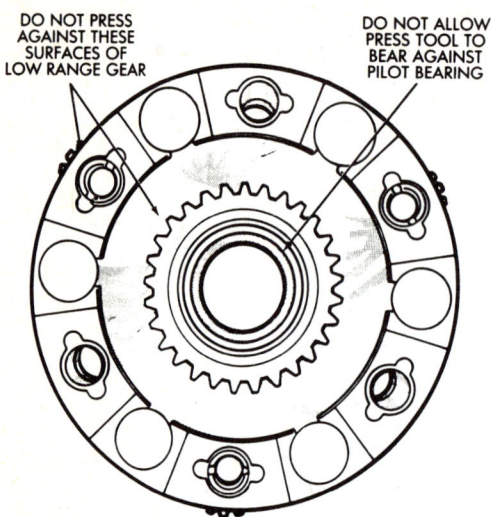

Input gear installation on the NP-231

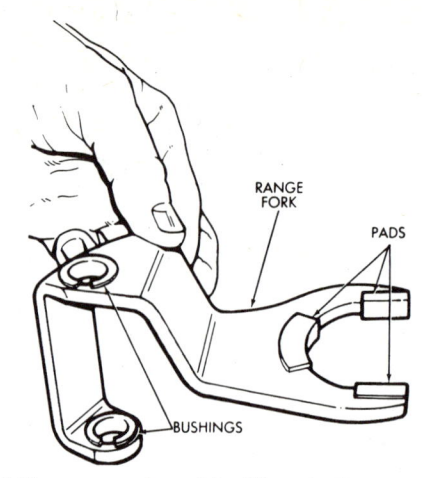

Installing new pads and bushings in the range fork on the NP-231

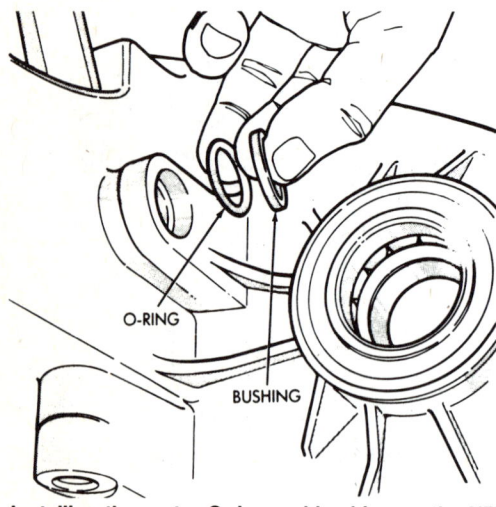

Installing the sector O-ring and bushing on the NP-231

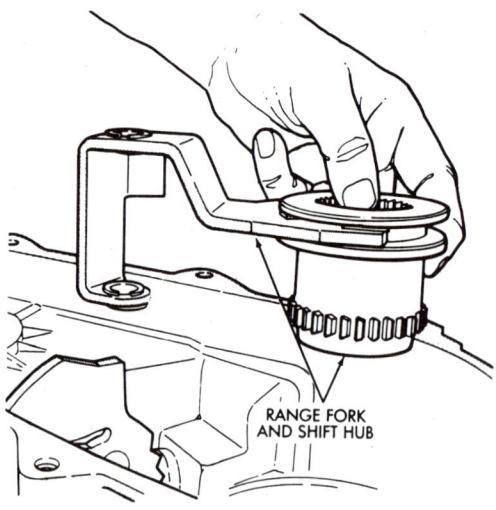

Assembling the range fork and shift hub on the NP-231

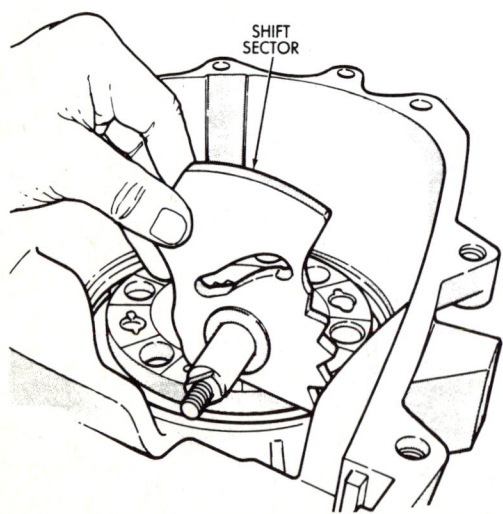

Installing the shift sector on the NP-231

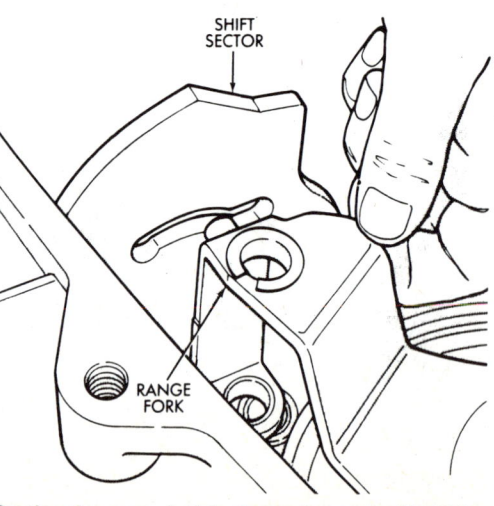

Seating the range fork in the sector on the NP-231

DRIVE TRAIN 351

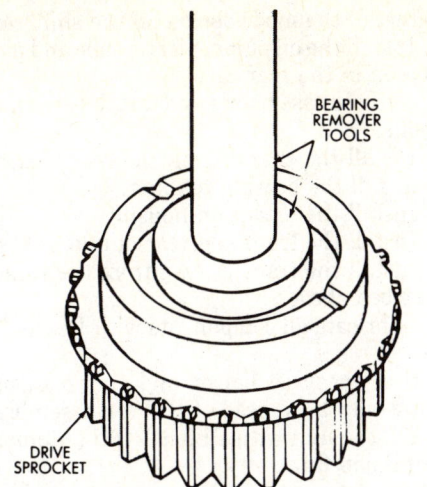

Removing the drive sprocket bearings from the NP-231

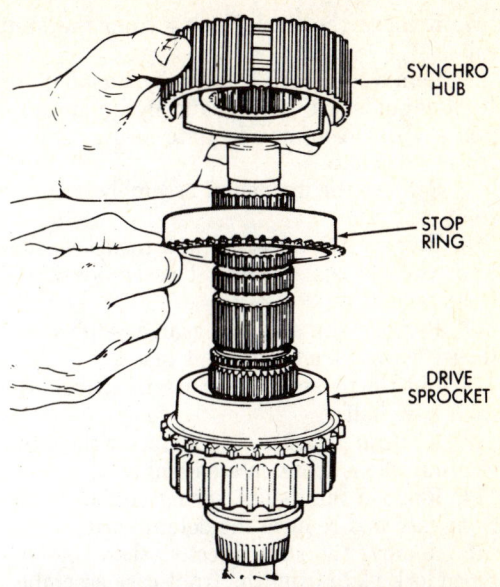

Installing the drive sprocket, stop ring and synchronizer hub on the NP-231

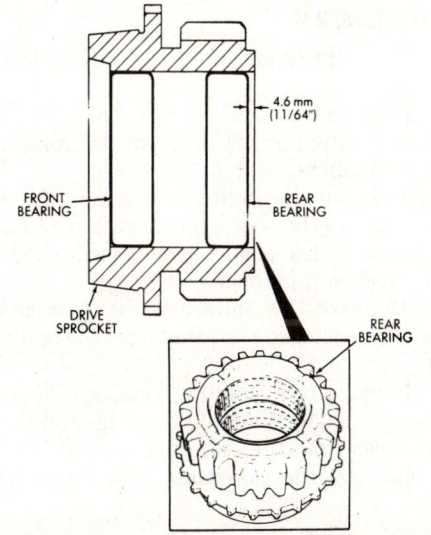

Installing the drive sprocket bearings on the NP-231

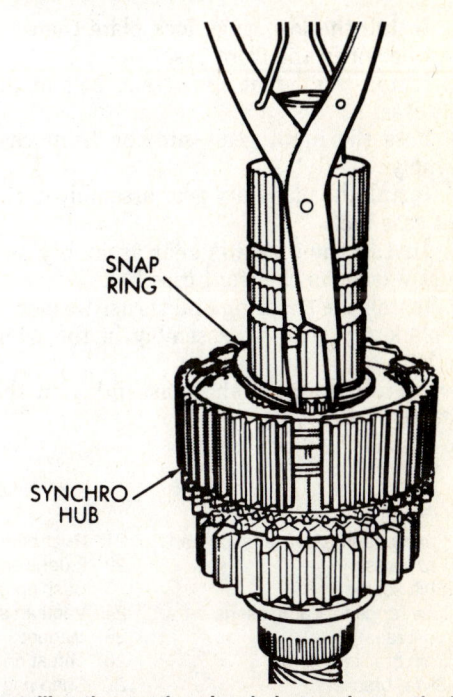

Installing the synchronizer hub snapring on the NP-231

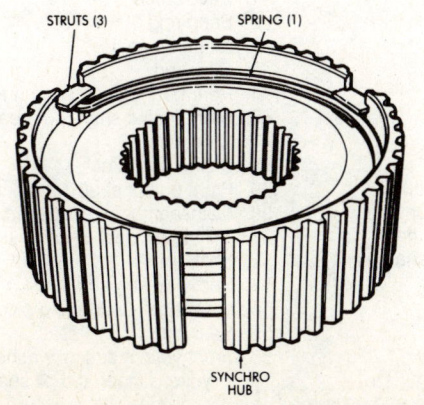

Installing the synchronizer hub spring and struts on the NP-231

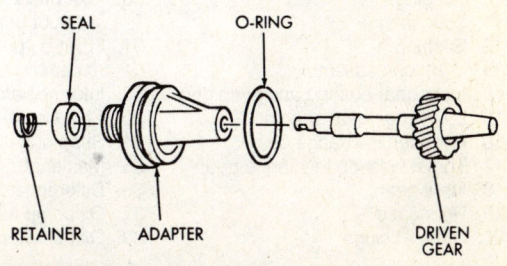

NP-231 speedometer gears

7. Remove the mode spring from the shift rail.
8. Remove the drive chain by pushing the front input shaft inward and by angling the gear slightly to obtain adequate clearance to remove the chain.
9. Remove the mainshaft assembly from the front case half.
10. Remove the snapring and thrust washer from the planetary gear set assembly in the front case half.
11. Remove the annulus gear assembly and thrust washer from the front case half.
12. Lift the planetary gear assembly from the front case half.
13. Using an arbor press ram, press the input gear out of the front case assembly.
14. Remove the detent spring bolt from the front case and remove the detent spring.
15. Remove the shift selector, then the low-range lock plate from the front case assembly.

ASSEMBLY

1. Install the low-range lock plate then the shift selector in the front case assembly.
2. Install the detent spring and bolt in the front case.
3. Pess the input gear into the front case assembly.
4. Install the planetary gear assembly in the front case half.
5. Install the annulus gear assembly and thrust washer in the front case half.
6. Install the snapring and thrust washer in the planetary gear set assembly in the front case half.
7. Install the mainshaft assembly in the front case half.
8. Install the drive chain.
9. Install the mode spring on the shift rail.
10. Install the oil pump, pickup tube and pickup screen in the rear case.
11. Join the case halves and install the retaining bolts.
12. Install the snapring on the rear bearing, then install the bearing retainer.
13. Install the extension housing.
14. Install the front and rear output yokes.
15. Install the transfer case from the vehicle as descibed above.
16. Lubricate all components with Dexron®II ATF.
17. Seal the case halves and the extension housing with a 1/8" bead of RTV on assembly.
18. Fill the unit with DEXRON®II automatic transmission fluid.

NP-242 Overhaul

DISASSEMBLY

1. Drain the fluid from the case if not already drained.
2. Remove the attaching nuts from the front and rear output yokes. Remove the yokes and sealing washers.
3. Remove the indicator switch and seal, then, remove the speedometer switch and seal.
4. Remove the poppet screw, spring and the range selection plunger.
5. Remove the bolts and disconnect the mainshaft extension housing from the rear case half.
6. Remove the retaining ring, speedometer drive gear nylon, oil pump housing, and the oil pump gear from the rear output shaft.
7. Remove the case bolts and separate the

1. Front bearing retainer and seal
2. Front case
3. Shift sector
4. Low range fork and inserts
5. Shift rail
6. Shift bracket
7. Slider bracket
8. Bushing and spring
9. Mode fork and inserts
10. Bushing
11. Fork spring
12. Bushing
13. Vent tube assembly
14. Input gear bearing and snap ring
15. Low range gear snap ring
16. Retainer, low range gear
17. Thrust washer, low range gear
18. Input gear
19. Rear case
20. Drain/fill plugs
21. Rear bearing retainer
22. Extension housing
23. Bushing and oil seal
24. Vacuum switch
25. Magnet
26. Thrust ring
27. Snap ring
28. Shift sleeve
29. Low range gear
30. Pilot bushing (input gear/mainshaft)
31. Front output shaft front bearing and snap ring
32. Intermediate clutch shaft
33. Shift sleeve
34. Snap ring
35. Mainshaft
36. Differential assembly
37. Oil pump tube O-ring
38. Oil pump pickup tube and screen
39. Mainshaft bearing rollers
40. Drive sprocket
41. Drive chain
42. Snap ring
43. Oil pump seal
44. Oil pump
45. Rear bearing and snap ring
46. Front output shaft rear bearing
47. Snap ring
48. Driven sprocket
49. Front output shaft
50. Mainshaft bearing spacers
51. Shift lever washer and nut
52. Shift lever
53. Sector O-ring and seal
54. Detent pin, spring and plug
55. Seal plug
56. Front yoke nut, seal washer, yoke, slinger and oil seal

NP-242 exploded view

DRIVE TRAIN 353

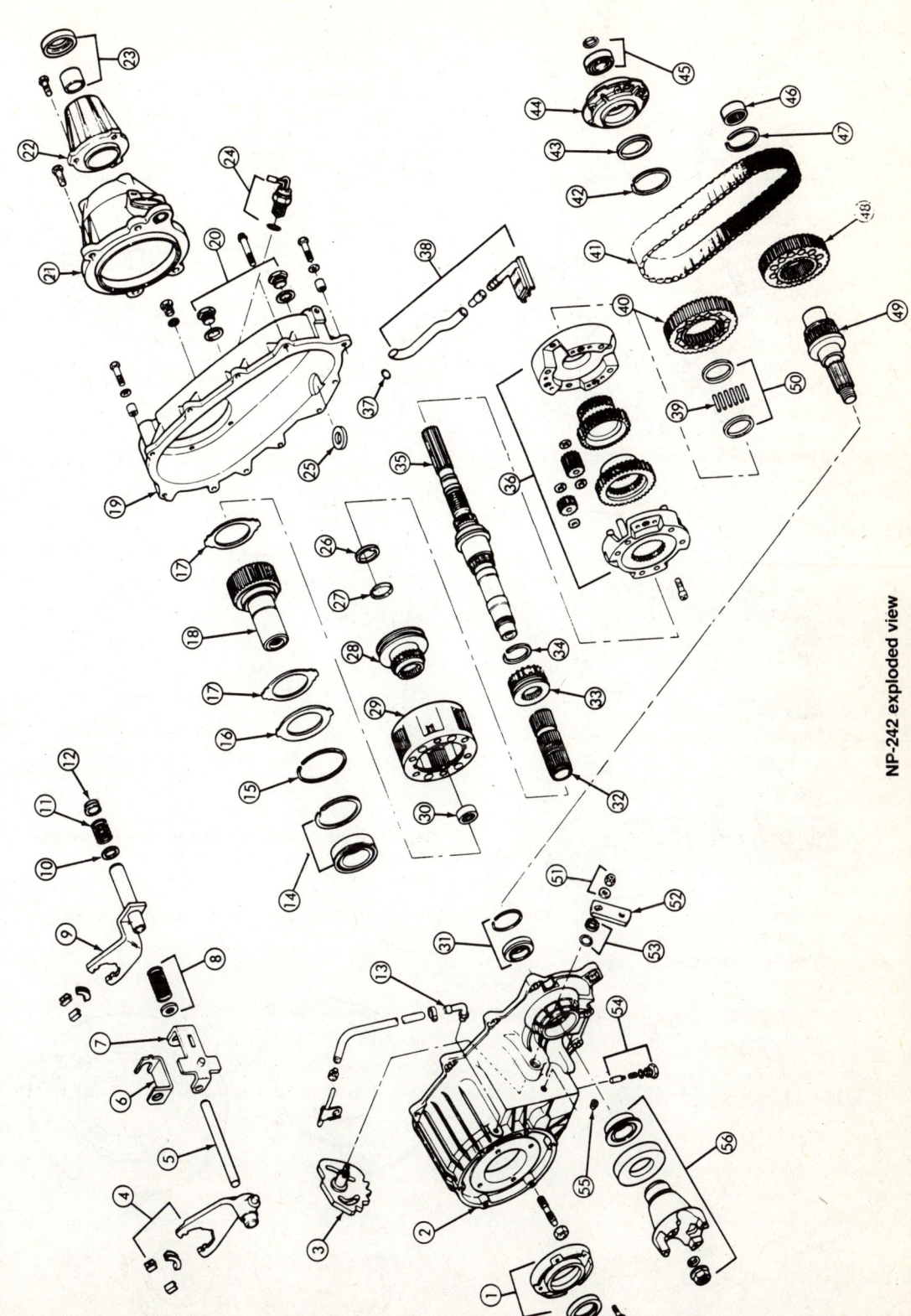

NP-242 exploded view

354 DRIVE TRAIN

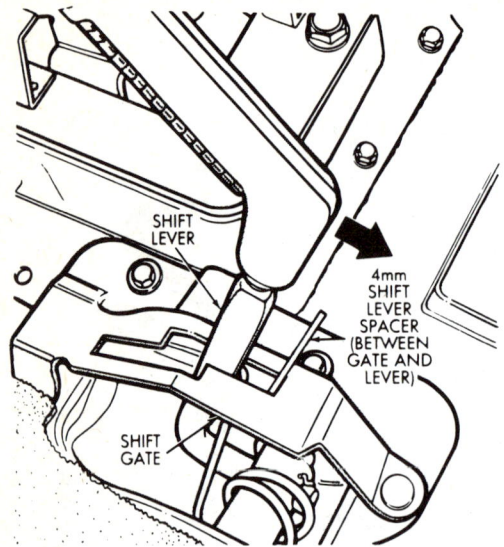

Installing the shift lever spacer on the NP-242

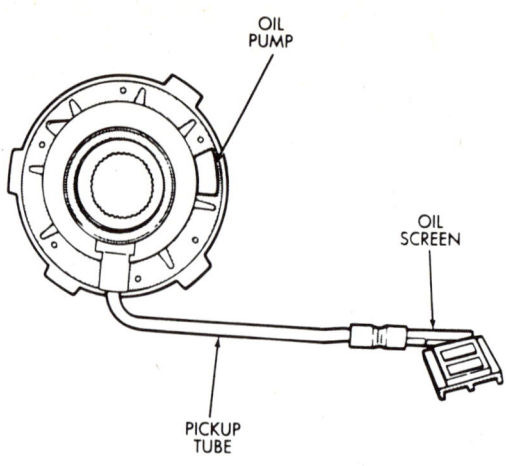

Removing the oil pump, tube and screen from the NP-242

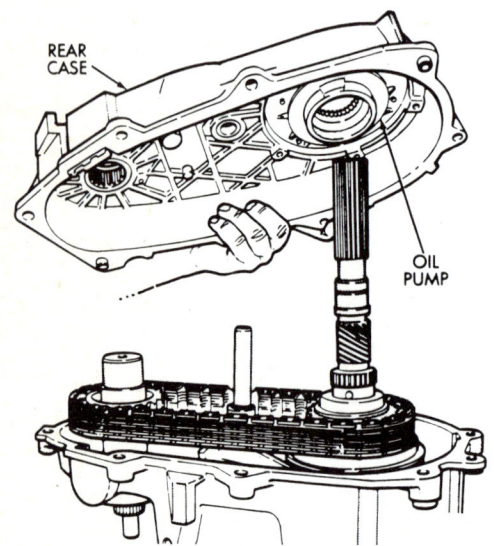

Removing the rear case and oil pump from the NP-242

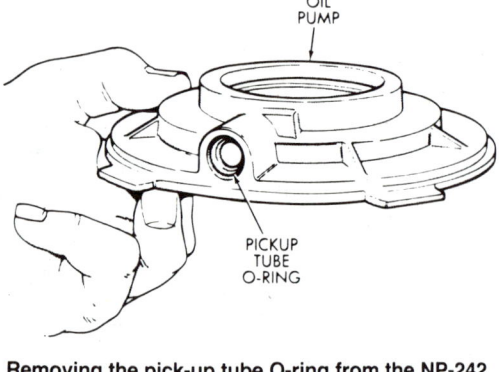

Removing the pick-up tube O-ring from the NP-242

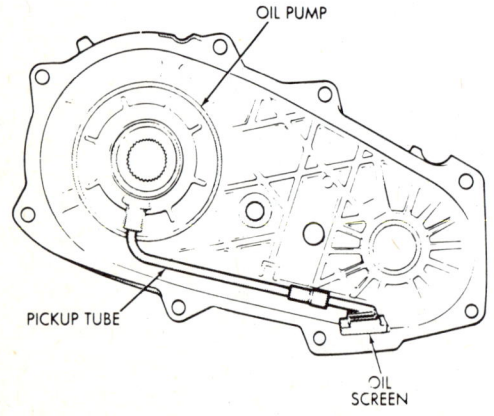

Unseating the oil screen from the NP-242

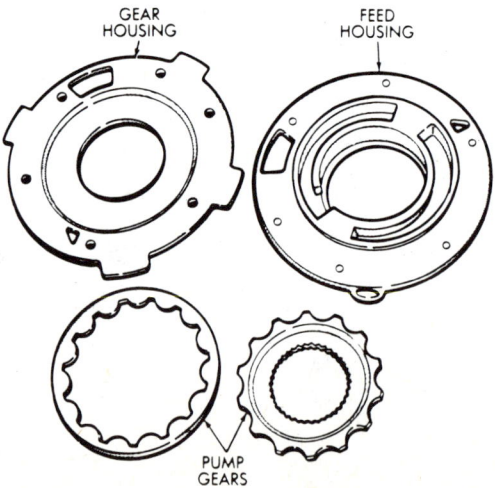

Oil pump components from the NP-242

DRIVE TRAIN

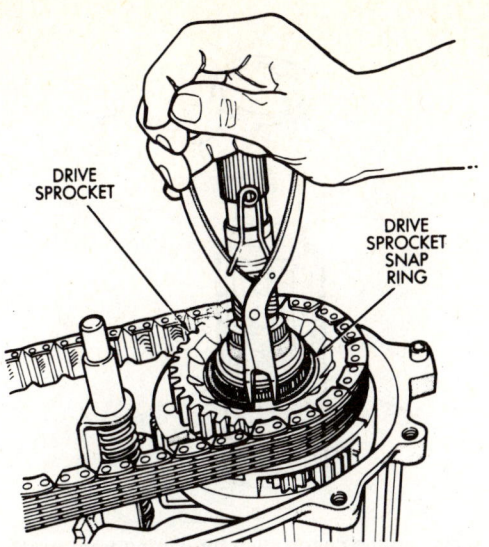

Removing the drive sprocket snapring from the NP-242

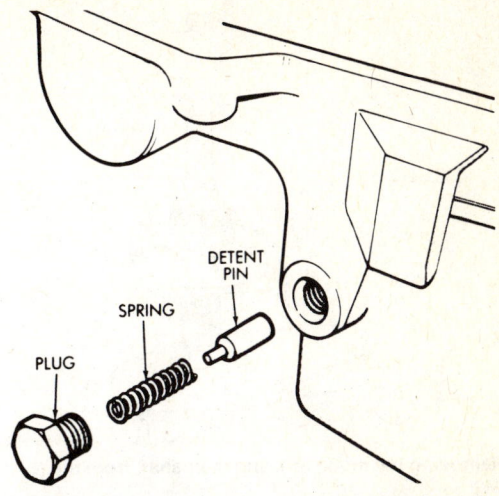

Removing the detent pin, spring and plug from the NP-242

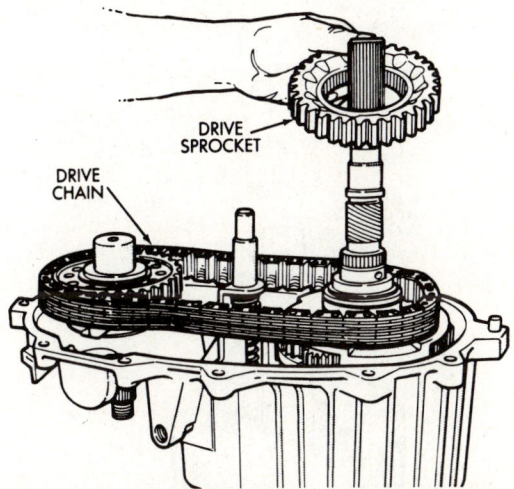

Removing the drive sprocket and chain from the NP-242

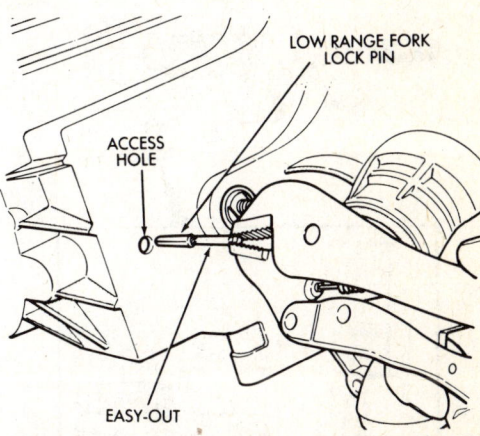

Removing the low range fork lock pin from the NP-242

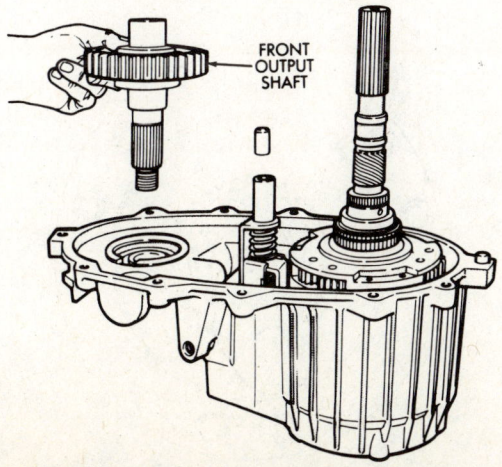

Removing the front ouptut shaft from the NP-242

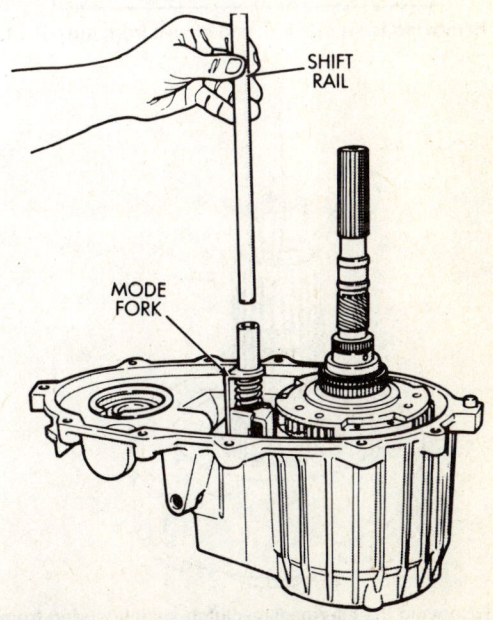

Removing the shfit rail from the NP-242

356 DRIVE TRAIN

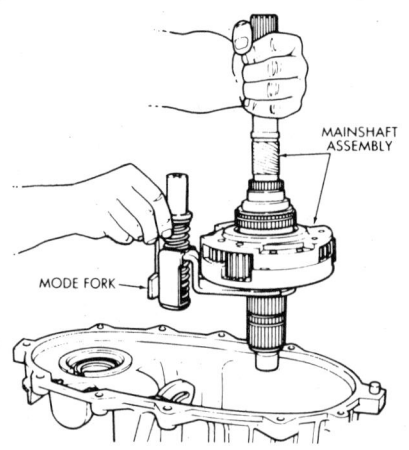

Removing the mode fork and mainshaft from the NP-242

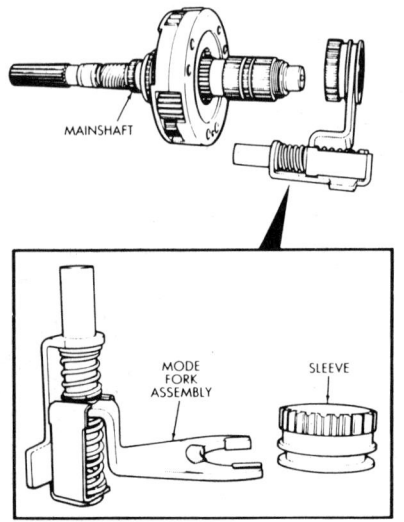

Removing the mode fork and sleeve from the NP-242

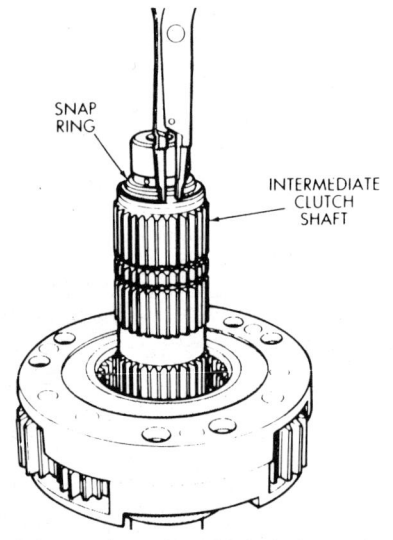

Removing the intermediate clutch shaft snapring from the NP-242

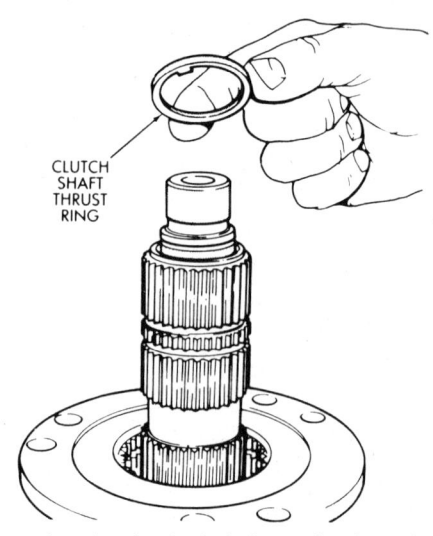

Removing the clutch shaft thrust ring from the NP-242

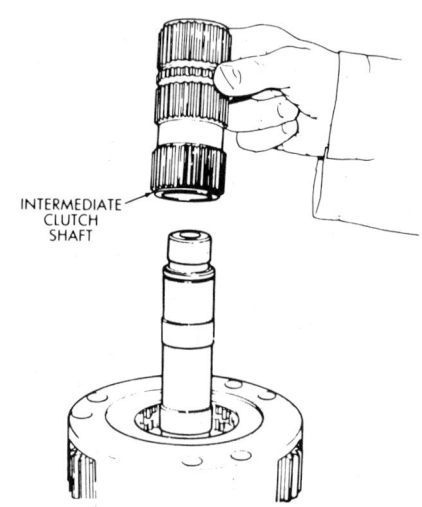

Removing the intermediate clutch shaft from the NP-242

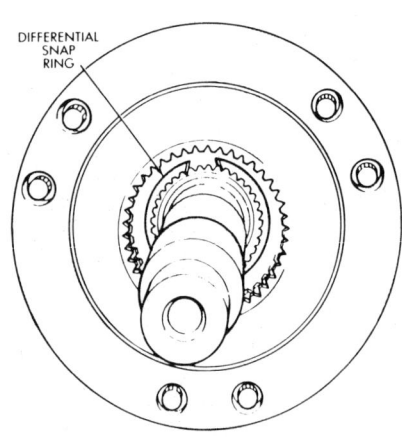

Removing the differential snapring from the NP-242

DRIVE TRAIN 357

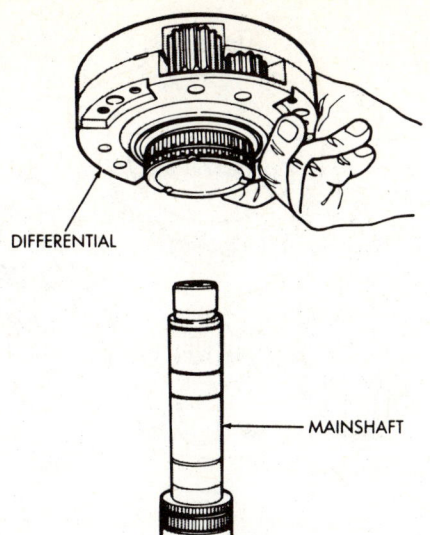

Differential removal from the NP-242

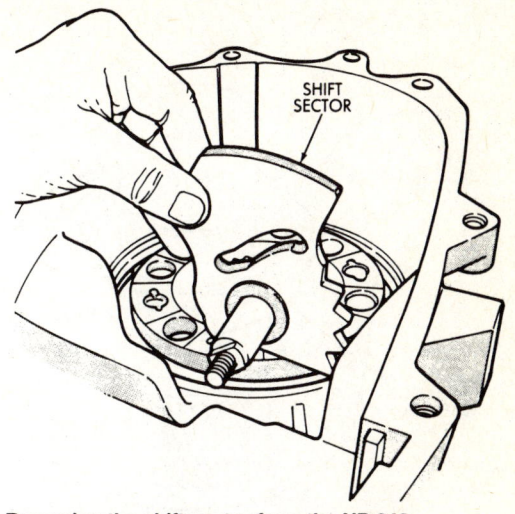

Removing the shift sector from the NP-242

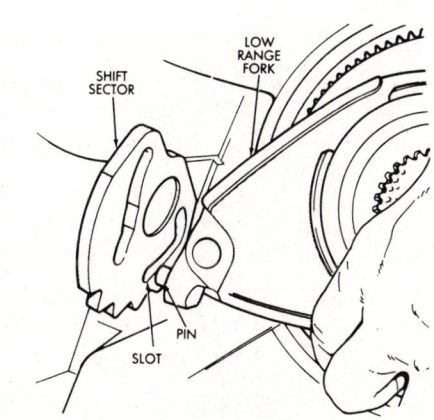

Disengaging the low range fork from the NP-242

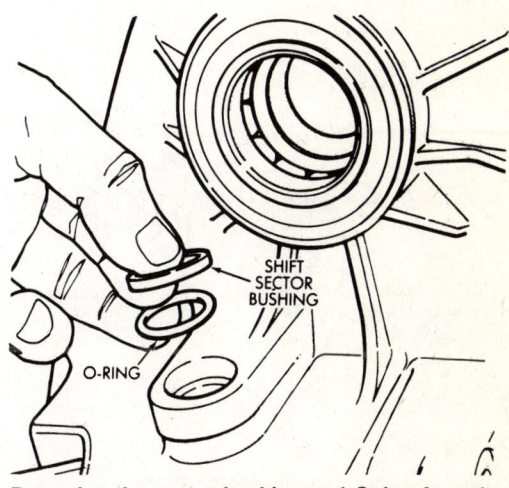

Removing the sector bushing and O-ring from the NP-242

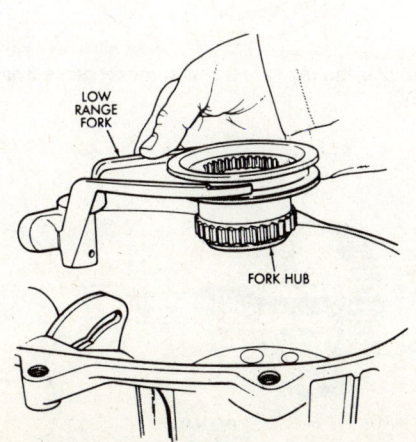

Removing the low range fork and hub from the NP-242

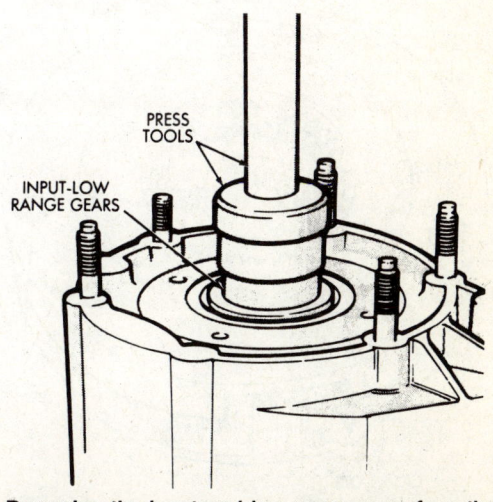

Removing the input and low range gears from the NP-242

358 DRIVE TRAIN

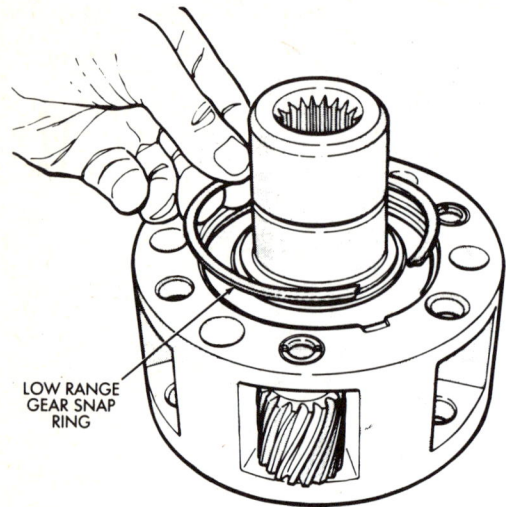

Removing the low range gear snapring from the NP-242

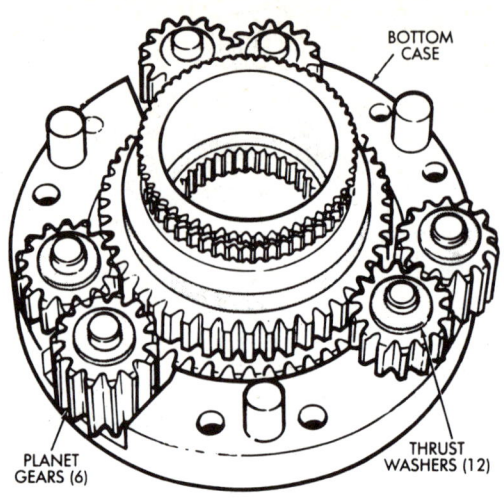

Removing the planet gears and thrust washers from the NP-242

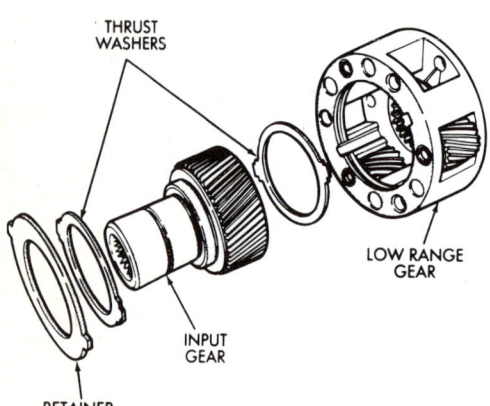

Low range gear components for the NP-242

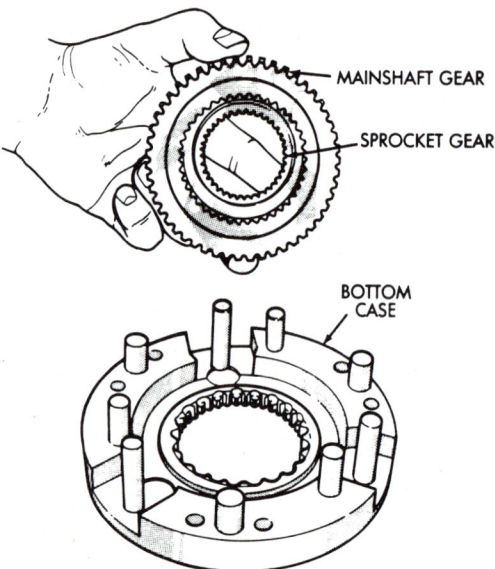

Removing the mainshaft and sprocket gears from the NP-242

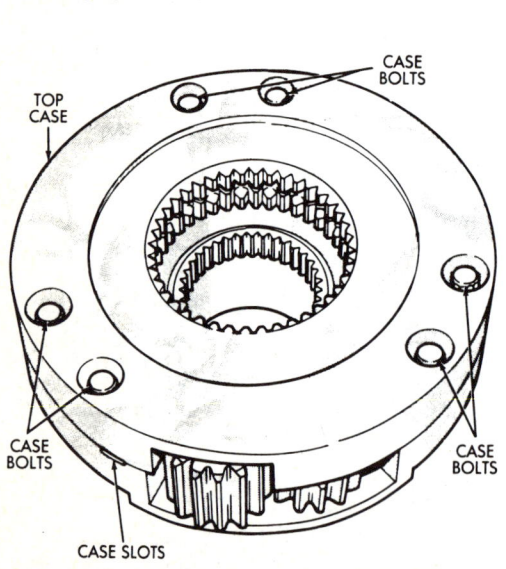

Case bolts securing the NP-242 differential case halves

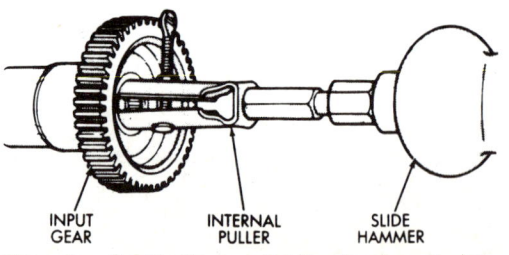

Removing the input gear pilot bearing from the NP-242

DRIVE TRAIN 359

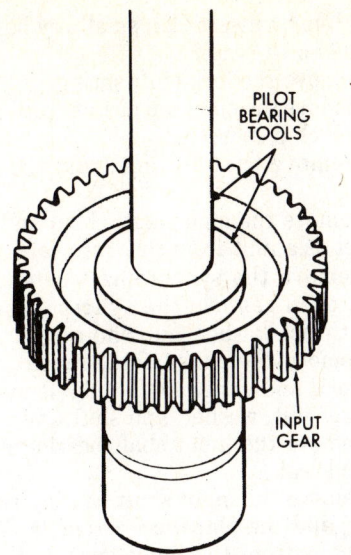

Installing the input gear pilot bearing on the NP-242

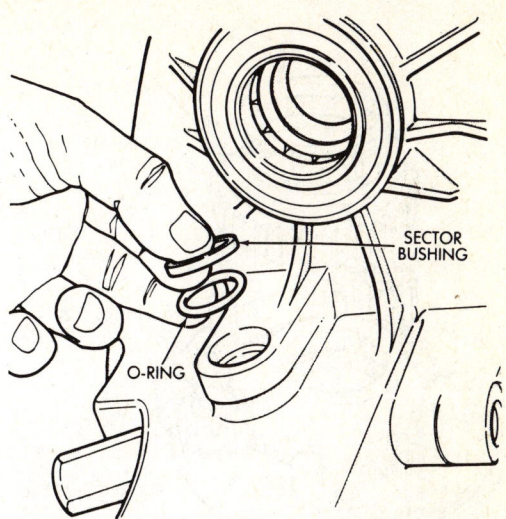

Installing the sector O-ring and bushing on the NP-242

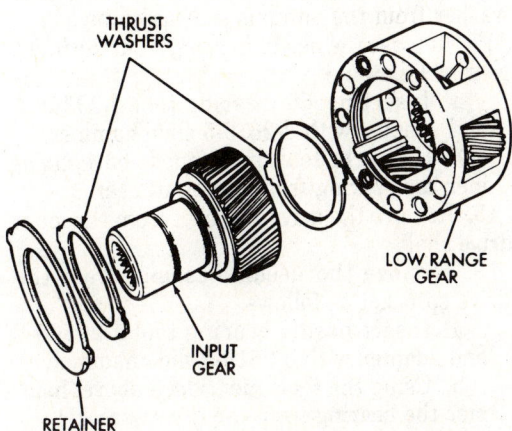

Low range and input gear assembly on the NP-242

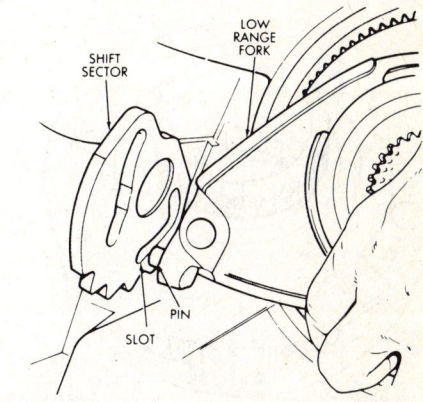

Positioning the low range fork on the NP-242

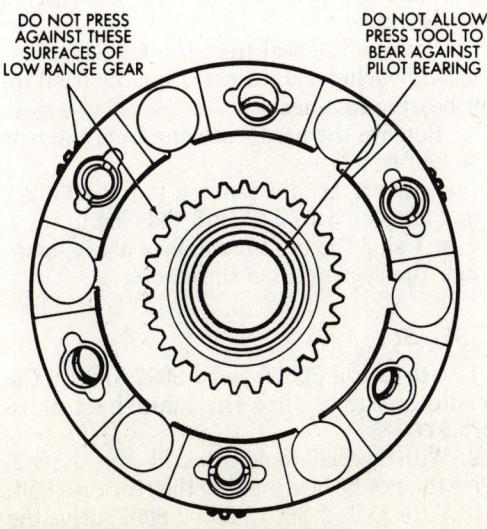

Input gear installation on the NP-242

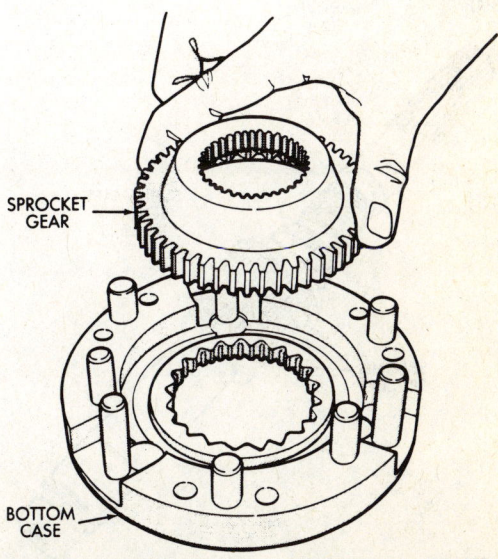

Installing the differential sprocket gear on the NP-242

360 DRIVE TRAIN

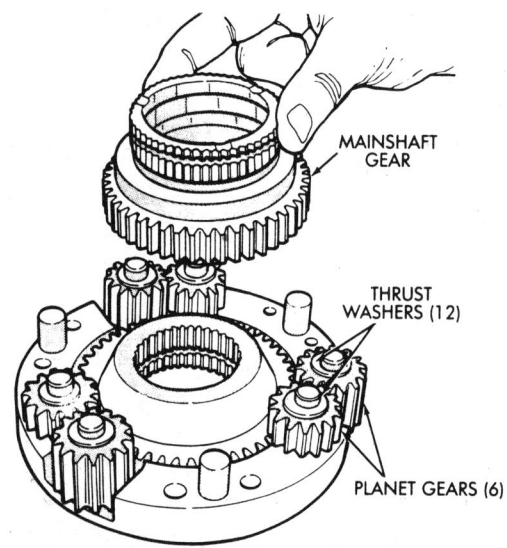

Installing the mainshaft and planet gears on the NP-242

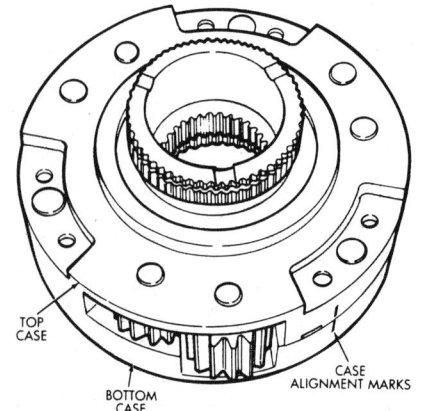

Assembling the differential case halves on the NP-242

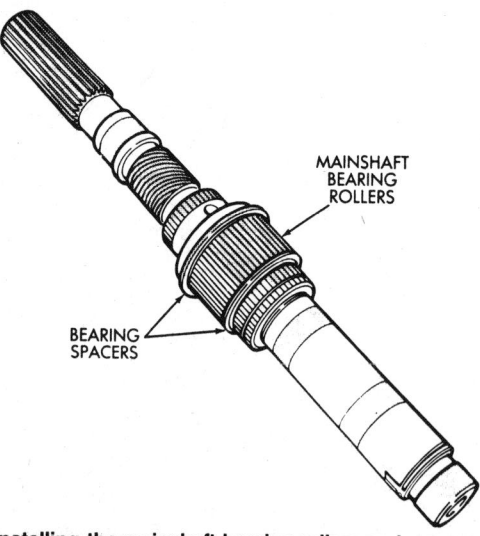

Installing the mainshaft bearing rollers and spacers on the NP-242

case halves by inserting a small pry bar in the pry slots on the case.

8. Remove the fork shift spring.
9. Remove the oil pump pick-up tube and the magnetic chip collector.
10. Remove the retainer from the driven socket.
11. Remove the mainshaft, chain and driven sprocket as a unit from the front case half.
12. Remove the synchronizer assembly retainer, then remove the syncro. assembly, sleeve, thrust washer, hub and ring.
13. Remove the range fork, range selector, mode fork and range shift hub. Remove the shift lever nut, washer, and shift lever.
14. Remove the input shaft bearing retainer plate and seal.
15. Remove the input shaft bearing retainer, bearing, and the planetary assembly. Remove the bearing from the input gear with special tool J-22912-1.
16. Remove the retainer, lock ring and thrust washer from the annulus gear assembly.
17. Remove the needle bearing from the input gear as follows:
    a. Insert needle bearing tool J-29369-1 and adapter with J-2619-5 slide hammer.
    b. Using the tools mentioned above, hammer the bearing from the input gear.
18. Remove the drive sprocket from the main drive shaft.
19. Remove the needle bearings from the drive sprocket as follows:
    a. Insert needle bearing tool J-29369-2 and adapter with J-2619-5 slide hammer.
    b. Using the tools mentioned above, hammer the bearing from the drive sprocket.
20. Remove the retainer and bearing from the front output shaft. Use bearing remover tool J-33832 and driver J-8092 to drive the bearing from the case.
21. Remove the seal from the mainshaft extension housing and the seal from the front input bearing retainer.
22. Remove the needle bearing from the rear case half as follows:
    a. Insert needle bearing tool J-29369-2 and adapter with J-2619-5 slide hammer.
    b. Using the tools mentioned above, hammer the bearing from the case.

ASSEMBLY

1. Use tools J-36370 and J-8092 to drive the needle bearings onto the mainshaft drive sprocket.
2. With special tools J-36372 and J-8092, drive the needle bearing into the rear case half.
3. With tools J-36373 and J-8092, drive the needle bearing into the input gear.

4. Install the bearing into the front case half, using J-36371 and J-36373 to insert the bearing. Install the bearing.
5. Use J-36371 and install the bearing into the oil pump housing.
6. Install the bearing to the input gear, then, install the thrust washer, carrier lock ring and the retainer. Install the bearing to the input gear with tool J-36372.
7. Install the input gear, bearing and planetary assembly into the annulus ring. Use a hammer and a brass drift to seat the bearing.
8. Install the retainer to the input shaft bearing.
9. Install the retainer to the input gear.
10. Install the input shaft bearing retainer, seal and bolts. Tighten the bolts to 14 ft. lbs.
11. Install the range shift hub, mode fork,

Troubleshooting Basic Driveshaft and Rear Axle Problems

When abnormal vibrations or noises are detected in the driveshaft area, this chart can be used to help diagnose possible causes. Remember that other components such as wheels, tires, rear axle and suspension can also produce similar conditions.

BASIC DRIVESHAFT PROBLEMS

Problem	Cause	Solution
Shudder as car accelerates from stop or low speed	• Loose U-joint • Defective center bearing	• Replace U-joint • Replace center bearing
Loud clunk in driveshaft when shifting gears	• Worn U-joints	• Replace U-joints
Roughness or vibration at any speed	• Out-of-balance, bent or dented driveshaft • Worn U-joints • U-joint clamp bolts loose	• Balance or replace driveshaft • Replace U-joints • Tighten U-joint clamp bolts
Squeaking noise at low speeds	• Lack of U-joint lubrication	• Lubricate U-joint; if problem persists, replace U-joint
Knock or clicking noise	• U-joint or driveshaft hitting frame tunnel • Worn CV joint	• Correct overloaded condition • Replace CV joint

BASIC REAR AXLE PROBLEMS

First, determine when the noise is most noticeable.

Drive Noise: Produced under vehicle acceleration.

Coast Noise: Produced while the car coasts with a closed throttle.

Float Noise: Occurs while maintaining constant car speed (just enough to keep speed constant) on a level road.

Road Noise

Brick or rough surfaced concrete roads produce noises that seem to come from the rear axle. Road noise is usually identical in Drive or Coast and driving on a different type of road will tell whether the road is the problem.

Tire Noise

Tire noises are often mistaken for rear axle problems. Snow treads or unevenly worn tires produce vibrations seeming to originate elsewhere. **Temporarily** inflating the tires to 40 lbs will significantly alter tire noise, but will have no effect on rear axle noises (which normally cease below about 30 mph).

Engine/Transmission Noise

Determine at what speed the noise is most pronounced, then stop the car in a quiet place. With the transmission in Neutral, run the engine through speeds corresponding to road speeds where the noise was noticed. Noises produced with the car standing still are coming from the engine or transmission.

Front Wheel Bearings

While holding the car speed steady, lightly apply the footbrake; this will often decease bearing noise, as some of the load is taken from the bearing.

Rear Axle Noises

Eliminating other possible sources can narrow the cause to the rear axle, which normally produces noise from worn gears or bearings. Gear noises tend to peak in a narrow speed range, while bearing noises will usually vary in pitch with engine speeds.

DRIVE TRAIN

NOISE DIAGNOSIS

The Noise Is	Most Probably Produced By
• Identical under Drive or Coast	• Road surface, tires or front wheel bearings
• Different depending on road surface	• Road surface or tires
• Lower as the car speed is lowered	• Tires
• Similar with car standing or moving	• Engine or transmission
• A vibration	• Unbalanced tires, rear wheel bearing, unbalanced driveshaft or worn U-joint
• A knock or click about every 2 tire revolutions	• Rear wheel bearing
• Most pronounced on turns	• Damaged differential gears
• A steady low-pitched whirring or scraping, starting at low speeds	• Damaged or worn pinion bearing
• A chattering vibration on turns	• Wrong differential lubricant or worn clutch plates (limited slip rear axle)
• Noticed only in Drive, Coast or Float conditions	• Worn ring gear and/or pinion gear

range selector and range fork. Install the shift lever, washer and nut and tighten to 20 ft. lbs.

12. Install the drive sprocket and needle bearings to the main drive shaft.

13. Assembly the synchronizer assembly; ring, hub, thrust washer and sleeve, then install the retainer.

14. Install the mainshaft, chain and driven sprocket as a unit into the front case half.

15. Install the retainer to the driven sprocket. Install the shift fork spring.

16. Install the oil pump pick-up, filler and magnetic washer to the rear case half.

17. Apply a bead of Loctite® 515 sealer or equivalent to the case matinng surfaces, then connect the rear and front case halves. Install the bolts and tighten to 23 ft. lbs.

18. Install the speedometer gear retainer, speedometer gear, then the 2nd retainer.

19. Apply a bead of Loctite® 515 sealer or equivalent to the mating surfaces of the pump housing, then connect the housing. Install the bolts and tighten to 30 ft. lbs.

20. Install the bearing retainer to the mainshaft.

21. Apply a bead of Loctite® 515 sealer or equivalent to the mating surfaces of the extension housing, then connect the housing. Install the bolts and tighten to 23 ft. lbs.

22. Install the range selector plunger, spring and poppet screw.

23. Install the speedometer pick-up switch and seal. Tighten the switch to 23 ft. lbs.

24. Install the indicator lamp switch and seal. Tighten the switch to 17 ft. lbs.

25. Install the front output flange, washer and nut. Tighten the nut to 110 ft. lbs.

26. Install the transaxle into the vehicle.

27. Fill the unit with 4.6 pints of DEXRON®II transmission fluid.

DRIVELINE

Front and Rear Driveshaft

REMOVAL AND INSTALLATION

Front Driveshaft on the 4WD 1984 Wagoneer, and Cherokee

1. Matchmark the shaft ends, axle and transfer case.

2. Remove the U-joint strap bolts at the front axle yoke.

3. Remove the double offset joint flange nuts at the transfer case.

4. Installation is the reverse of removal.

Front Driveshaft on the 4WD 1985-89 Wagoneer, Cherokee, Comanche

NOTE: *The vehicles may come equipped with one of two different type front driveshafts. The first type is the same as that used on the 1984 models. This type has a conventional universal joint at the axle, but a double offset joint at the transfer case. The second type has a conventional universal joint at the axle and a double cardan joint at the transfer case.*

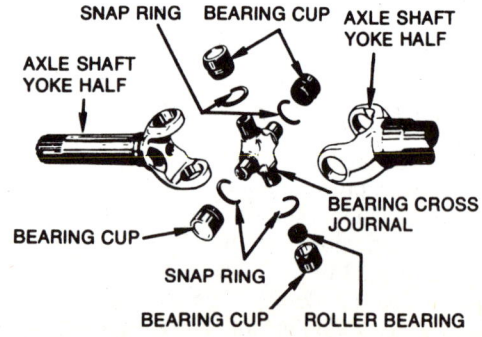

1971 and later Cardan cross-type U-joint

DRIVE TRAIN 363

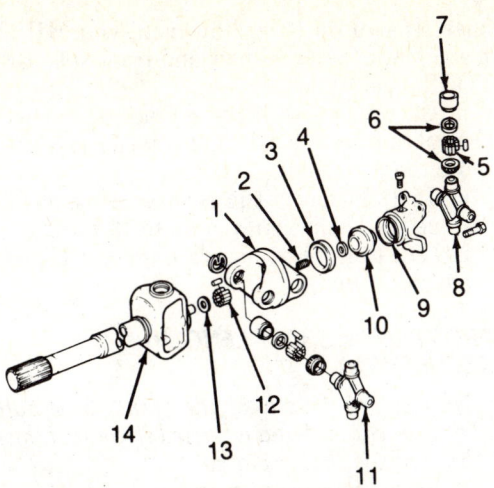

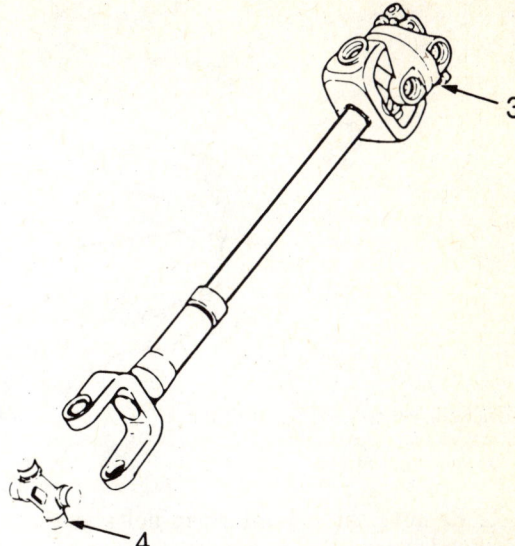

1. Link yoke
2. Socket spring
3. Socket ball retainer
4. Thrust washer
5. Needle bearings
6. Seal
7. Bearing cap
8. Rear spider
9. Socket yoke
10. Socket ball
11. Front spider
12. Socket needle bearings
13. Thrust washer
14. Propeller shaft yoke

Double cardan U-joint

Front driveshaft used in all Comanche models, some 1985–86 Wagoneer/Cherokee models and all 1987–89 Wagoneer/Cherokee models. 3 is the double cardan joint; 4 is the cardan joint

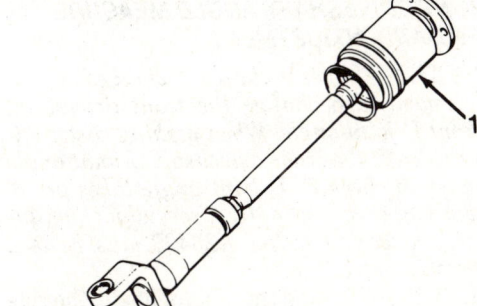

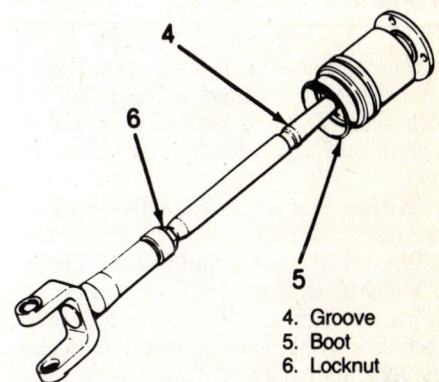

4. Groove
5. Boot
6. Locknut

Double offset joint front driveshaft length adjustment

Double offset joint driveshaft used on all 1984 and some 1985 and later Wagoneer and Cherokee models. 1 is the double offset joint, 2 is the cardan joint

DOUBLE OFFSET JOINT TYPE

1. Matchmark the shaft ends, axle and transfer case.
2. Remove the U-joint strap bolts at the front axle yoke.
3. Remove the double offset joint flange nuts at the transfer case.
4. Installation is the reverse of removal.

DOUBLE CARDAN JOINT TYPE

1. Matchmark the shaft ends, axle and transfer case.

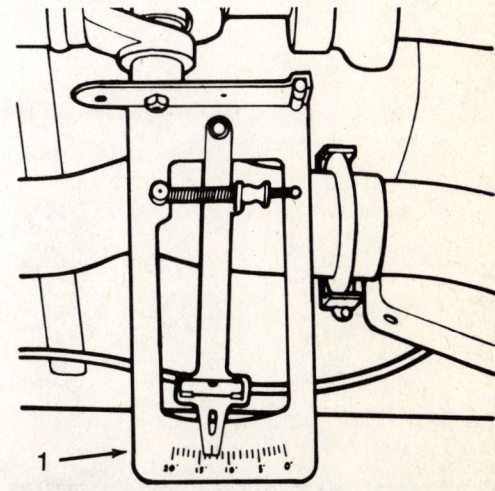

Inclinometer (1) installed for front driveshaft angle adjustment

DRIVE TRAIN

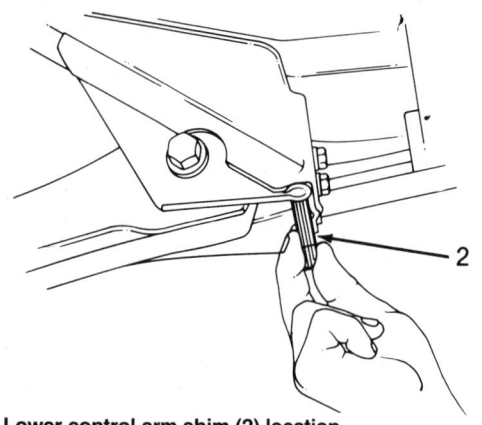

Lower control arm shim (2) location

2. Remove the U-joint strap bolts at the front axle yoke.
3. Remove the double cardan joint flange nuts at the transfer case.
4. Installation is the reverse of removal.

Rear Driveshaft

NOTE: *Two different driveshafts are used on these vehicles. With Command-Trac®, the driveshaft has welded yokes at each end. With Selec-Trac®, a welded yoke is used at the rear and a splined slip yoke is used at the front.*

1. Raise and support the vehicle on jackstands.
2. Place the transmission in NEUTRAL.
3. Matchmark the yokes and flanges.
4. On vehicles with Command-Trac®, the driveshaft may be removed by disconnecting it at the axle and sliding it from the front yoke, leaving the front yoke attached to the transfer case. If you do this, however, you MUST matchmark the driveshaft and front yoke BEFORE separation.
5. On vehicles with Selec-Trac®, disconnect the yokes from the axle and transfer case. Remove the driveshaft.
6. Installation is the reverse of removal. Torque the U-joint strap nuts to 19 ft. lbs.

NOTE: *Jeep recommends that new U-joint straps be used.*

FRONT DRIVESHAFT LENGTH ADJUSTMENT

NOTE: *The length of the front driveshaft must be checked and adjusted if the shaft has been removed or replaced.*

1. Raise the vehicle on ramps.
2. Measure from the rear edge of the groove at the transfer case end of the shaft, to the outer flange of the rubber boot on the double offset joint. The dimension should be 1½-1¾".
3. If not, loosen the slip joint locknut and slide the shaft in or out of the double offset joint to correct the length.
4. Tighten the nut to 55 ft. lbs.

FRONT DRIVESHAFT ANGLE MEASUREMENT AND ADJUSTMENT

NOTE: *Changes in the front wheel caster adjustment also change the front driveshaft, front U-joint angle. When making caster adjustments, the front drivehsaft U-joint angle must be checked. U-joint angle takes precedence over caster angle. A special tool, an inclinometer such as tool J-23498, must be used for this procedure.*

1. Before checking the U-joint angle, the ride height must be checked. Record the measurement from the front and rear axle tubes to the frame sills, directly above the tubes. Front axle measurement should be 157.5-177.8mm; rear axle measurement should be 144.5-165.0mm.

NOTE: *If the vehicle is equipped with P205/75 R15 tires, add 9mm to all dimensions. If the vehicle is equipped with P215/75 R15 tires, add 20mm to all dimensions.*

2. Place the transmission in NEUTRAL.
3. Jack up both the front and rear, and support the truck on jackstands placed under the axle.
4. Install the inclinometer as shown, and make a reading at the axle yoke bearing cap and at the front slip yoke bearing cap.
5. Place the inclinometer magnet on the axle yoke bearing cap and take a reading. Rotate the shaft 90° and take a reading on the driveshaft yoke bearing cap.

NOTE: *The inclinometer must face the same direction on both readings.*

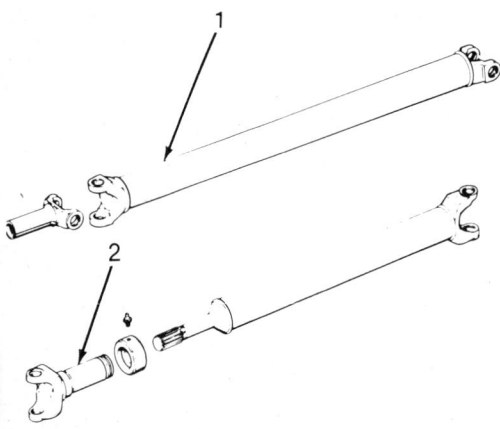

Two types of rear driveshafts used on 1985–89 models. 1 is used with Command-Trac; 2 is used with Selec-Trac

6. The difference between the readings taken at the driveshaft yoke and the axle yoke is the U-joint angle. The U-joint angle should be 0.5°-1.0°. The angle can be adjusted by adding or deleting shims at the rear of the lower control arms.

U-Joints

There are five types of universal joints used: the Cardan cross-type with U-bolts and snaprings; a Cardan cross-type with just snaprings; a double Cardan cross-type; ball and trunnion-type universal joints which serve as a combination slip-joint and universal joint. Some models have a front driveshaft which, at the transfer case end, uses a double offset joint. This unit is not repairable and must be serviced by replacement only.

Universal joints fail for numerous reasons, the primary one being lack of lubrication. Others could be structural damage incurred from hitting something, an unbalanced driveshaft, the entrance of dirt or water due to a rotted rubber seal or just plain wear from excessive mileage.

Rebuilding kits are available for both types of universal joints. The kit for a Cardan cross-type universal joint includes the entire cross assembly, the cross bearing journal, roller bearings, bearing cap with new rubber seal and new snaprings.

The rebuilding kit for the ball and trunnion-type universal joint includes a new grease cover and gasket, universal joint body, two centering buttons and spring washers, two ball and roller bearing assemblies, two thrust washers, dust cover and two dust cover clamps.

OVERHAUL

Cardan Cross-Type with Snaprings

1. Remove the driveshaft from the vehicle.
2. Remove the snaprings by pinching the ends together with a pair of pliers. If the rings do not readily snap out of the groove, tap the end of the bearing lightly to relieve pressure against the rings.
3. After removing the snaprings, press on the end of one bearing until the opposite bearing is pushed from the yoke arm. Turn the joint over and press the first bearing back out of that arm by pressing on the exposed end of the journal shaft. To drive it out, use a soft ground drift with a flat face, about $\frac{1}{32}''$ smaller in diameter than the hole in the yoke; otherwise, there is danger of damaging the bearing.
4. Repeat the procedure for the other two bearings, then lift out the journal assembly by sliding it to one side.
5. Wash all parts in cleaning solvent and inspect the parts after cleaning. Replace the journal assembly if it is worn extensively. Make sure that the grease channel in each journal trunnion is open.
6. Pack all of the bearing caps $\frac{1}{3}$ full of grease and install the rollers (bearings).
7. Press one of the cap/bearing assemblies into one of the yoke arms just far enough so that the cap will remain in position.
8. Place the journal in position in the installed cap, with a cap/bearing assembly placed on the opposite end.
9. Position the free cap so that when it is driven from the opposite end it will be inserted into the opening of the yoke. Repeat this operation for the other two bearings.
10. Install the retaining clips. If the U-joint binds when it is assembled, tap the arms of the yoke slightly to relieve any pressure on the bearings at the end of the journal.

Cardan Cross-Type with U-Bolts and Snaprings

1. Removal of the attaching U-bolt releases one set of bearing races. Slide the driveshaft into the yoke flange to remove that set of bearing races, being careful not to lose the rollers (bearings).
2. After removal of the first set of bearings, release the other set by pinching the ends of the snaprings with pliers and removing them from the sleeve yoke. Should the rings fail to snap readily from the groove, tap the end of the bearing lightly, to relieve the pressure against them.
3. Press on the end of one bearing, until the opposite bearing is pushed out of the yoke arm.
4. Turn the universal joint over and press the first bearing out by pressing on the exposed end of the journal assembly. Use a soft round drift with a flat face about $\frac{1}{32}''$ smaller in diameter than the hole in the yoke arm. Then drive out the bearing.
5. Lift the journal out by sliding it to one side.
6. Install in the reverse order of removal, using the procedures for the snapring U-joints from Step 4 on as a guide.

Double Cardan Type

1. Use a punch to mark the coupling yoke and the adjoining yokes before disassembly, to ensure proper reassembly and driveline balance.
2. It is easiest to remove the bearings from the coupling yoke first.
3. Support the driveshaft horizontally on a press stand, or on the workbench if a vise is being used.
4. If snaprings are used to retain the bearing cups, remove them. Place the rear car of the coupling yoke over a socket large enough to receive the cup. Place a smaller socket, or a cross

DRIVE TRAIN

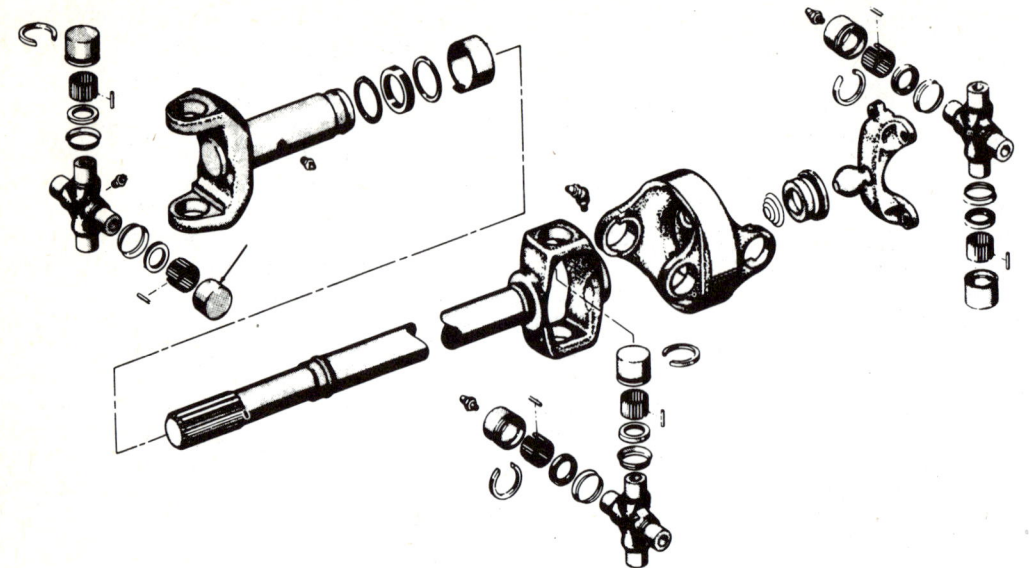

Double cardan U-joint disassembled

press made for the purpose, over the opposite cup. Press the bearing cup out of the coupling yoke ear. If the cup is not completely removed, insert a spacer and complete the operation, or grasp the cup with a pair of slip joint pliers and work it out. If the cups are retained by plastic, this will shear the retainers. Remove any bits of plastic.

5. Rotate the driveshaft and repeat the operation on the opposite cup.

6. Disengage the trunnions of the spider, still attached to the flanged yoke, from the coupling yoke, and pull the flanged yoke and spider from the center ball on the ball support tube yoke.

NOTE: *The joint between the shaft and coupling yoke can be serviced without disassembly of the joint between the coupling yoke and flanged yoke.*

7. Pry the seal from the ball cavity, remove the washers, spring and three seats. Examine the ball stud seat and the ball stud for scores or wear. Worn parts can be replaced with a kit. Clean the ball seat cavity and fill it with grease. Install the spring, washer, ball seats, and spacer (washer) over the ball.

8. To assembly, insert one bearing cup part way into one ear of the ball support tube yoke and turn this cup to the bottom.

9. Insert the spider (cross) into the tube so that the trunnion (arm) seats freely in the cup.

10. Install the opposite cup part way, making sure that both cups are straight.

11. Press the cups into position, making sure that both cups squarely engage the spider. Back off if there is a sudden increase in resistance, indicating that a cup is cocked or a needle bearing is out of place.

12. As soon as one bearing retainer groove clears the yoke, stop and install the retainer (plastic retainer models). On models with snaprings, press the cups into place, then install the snaprings over the cups.

13. If difficulty is encountered installing the plastic retainers or the snaprings, smack the yoke sharply with a hammer to spring the ears slightly.

14. Install one bearing cup part way into the ear of the coupling yoke, Make sure that the alignment marks are matched, then engaged the coupling yoke over the spider and press in the cups, installing the retainers or snaprings as before.

15. Install the cups and spider into the flanged yoke as with the previous yoke.

NOTE: *The flange yoke should snap over center to the right or left and up or down by the pressure of the ball seat spring.*

Ball and Trunnion-Type

1. Remove the driveshaft from the vehicle.

2. Position the tube of the driveshaft near the ball-type universal joint, in a bench vise; clamp tightly.

3. Bend the lugs of the grease cover away from the universal joint body and remove the cover and the gasket.

4. Remove the two clamps from the dust cover. Push the joint body toward the driveshaft tube. Remove the two centering buttons and spring washers, the two ball and roller bearings and the two thrust washers from the trunnion pin.

5. Press the trunnion pin from the ball head with an arbor press.

NOTE: *It is strongly recommended that the trunnion pin be pressed out and in by an arbor press because of the possible damage that could result from other methods such as hammer and drift. This is a critical component in the assembly and any damage could result in a premature failure or even necessitate replacement of the entire driveshaft.*

6. Clean the ball head of the driveshaft with a suitable solvent and dry thoroughly.
7. Secure the larger end of the dust cover to the universal joint body with the larger of the two clamps. Install the smaller clamp at the smaller end of the dust cover, then fit the cover over the ball head shaft.
8. Push the universal joint cover toward the driveshaft tube.
9. With an arbor press, press the trunnion pin into a centered position in the ball head.

NOTE: *The trunnion pin must project an equal distance from each side of the ball head. If it is not centered within 0.15mm, driveshaft vibration may result.*

10. Hold the universal joint body toward the tube of the driveshaft to gain access to the trunnion pin. Install one thrust washer, one ball and roller bearing and one spring washer at one side of the ball head. Compress the centering buttons into the trunnion pin, then move the joint body away from the driveshaft tube, into position to surround the buttons and to hold them in place.
11. Insert the breather between the dust cover and ball head shaft, along the length of the shaft. The breather must extend no more than ½" beyond the dust cover, along the shaft. Tighten the clamp screw to secure the cover to the shaft. Cut away any portion of the dust cover which protrudes from beneath either clamp.
12. Pack the raceways of the universal joint body (inner surfaces which surround the ball and roller bearings) with about 2 oz. of universal joint grease. Divide the grease equally between the raceways. Position the gasket and grease cover on the body of the universal joint and bend the lugs of the cover in place. Move the body inward and outward, toward and away from the driveshaft tube, to distribute the grease in the raceways.
13. Install the driveshaft on the vehicle.

REAR AXLE

Understanding Rear Axles

The rear axle is a special type of transmission that reduces the speed of the drive from the engine and transmission and divides the power to the rear wheels. Power enters the rear axle from the driveshaft via the companion flange. The flange is mounted on the drive pinion shaft. The drive pinion shaft and gear which carry the power into the differential turn at engine speed. The gear on the end of the pinion shaft drives a large ring gear the axis of rotation of which is 90 degrees away from the of the pinion. The pinion and gear reduce the gear ratio of the axle, and change the direction of rotation to turn the axle shafts which drive both wheels. The rear axle gear ratio is found by dividing the number of pinion gear teeth into the number of ring gear teeth.

The ring gear drives the differential case. The case provides the two mounting points for the ends of a pinion shaft on which are mounted two pinion gears. The pinion gears drive the two side gears, one of which is located on the inner end of each axle shaft.

By driving the axle shafts through the arrangement, the differential allows the outer drive wheel to turn faster than the inner drive wheel in a turn.

The main drive pinion and the side bearings, which bear the weight of the differential case, are shimmed to provide proper bearing preload, and to position the pinion and ring gears properly.

NOTE: *The proper adjustment of the relationship of the ring and pinion gears is critical. It should be attempted only by those with extensive equipment and/or experience.*

Limited-slip differentials include clutches which tend to link each axle shaft to the differential case. Clutches may be engaged either by spring action or by pressure produced by the torque on the axles during a turn. During turning on a dry pavement, the effects of the clutches are overcome, and each wheel turns at the required speed. When slippage occurs at either wheel, however, the clutches will transmit some of the power to the wheel which has the greater amount of traction. Because of the presence of clutches, limited-slip units require a special lubricant.

Determining Axle Ratio

The drive axle is said to have a certain axle ratio. This number (usually a whole number and a decimal fraction) is actually a comparison

Rear Drive Axle Application Chart

Axle	Model	Years
AMC 7⁹⁄₁₆ in.	All	1984–86
Dana 35	All	1987–89

DRIVE TRAIN

of the number of gear teeth on the ring gear and the pinion gear. For example, a 4.11 rear means that theoretically, there are 4.11 teeth on the ring gear and one tooth on the pinion gear or, put another way, the driveshaft must turn 4.11 times to turn the wheels once. Actually, on a 4.11 rear, there might be 37 teeth on the ring gear and 9 teeth on the pinion gear. By dividing the number of teeth on the pinion gear into the number of teeth on the ring gear, the numerical axle ratio (4.11) is obtained. This also provides a good method of ascertaining exactly what axle ratio one is dealing with.

Another method of determining gear ratio is to jack up and support the car so that both rear wheels are off the ground. Make a chalk mark on the rear wheel and the driveshaft. Put the transmission in neutral. Turn the rear wheel one complete turn and count the number of turns that the driveshaft makes. The number of turns that the driveshaft makes in one complete revolution of the rear wheel is an approximation of the rear axle ratio.

Axle Shaft

REMOVAL AND INSTALLATION

1. Jack up the vehicle and remove the wheels.
2. Remove the brake drum spring locknuts and remove the drum.
3. Remove the axle shaft flange cup plug by piercing the center with a sharp tool and prying it out.
4. Using the access hole in the axle shaft flange, remove the nuts which attach the backing plate and retainer to the axle tube flange.
5. Remove the axle shaft from the housing with an axle puller.
6. Install in reverse order of removal. Torque the bearing retainer bolts to 50 ft. lbs. in a crisscross pattern

NOTE: *Some axles have and inner oil seal fitted in the axle shaft housing, inboard of the bearing; some do not. If your axle does not have one, don't install one when replacing the bearing! Axles with an inner seal rely on*

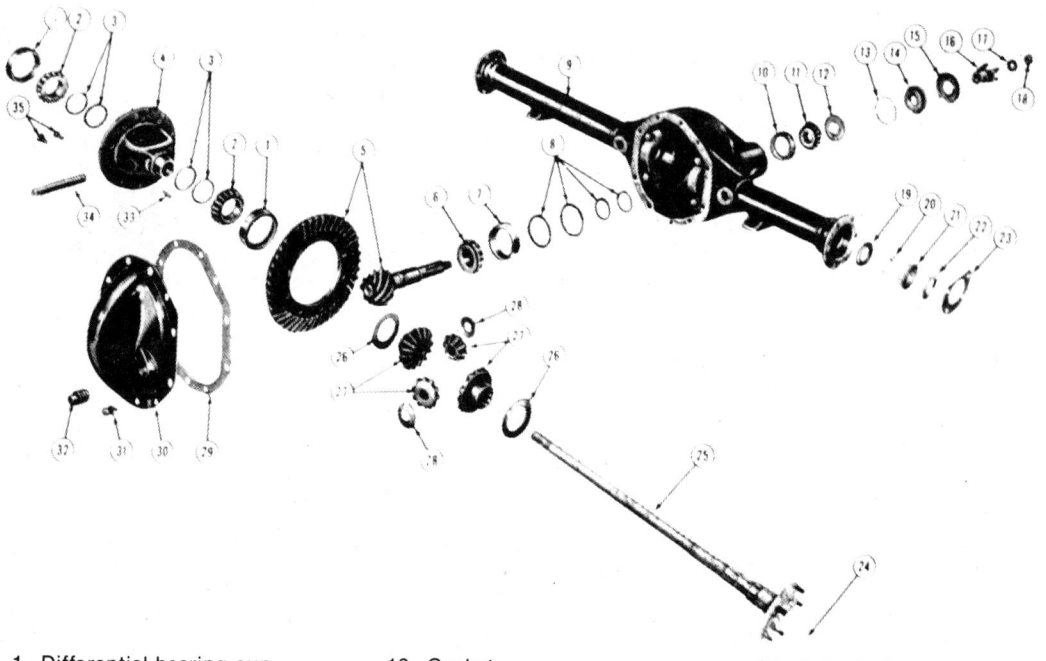

1. Differential bearing cup
2. Differential bearing
3. Shims
4. Differential
5. Ring gear and pinion
6. Pinion inner bearing
7. Pinion inner bearing cup
8. Pinion shims
9. Axle housing
10. Pinion outer bearing cup
11. Pinion outer bearing
12. Oil slinger
13. Gasket
14. Pinion oil seal
15. Dust shield
16. Yoke
17. Flat washer
18. Pinion nut
19. Axle housing oil seal
20. Axle shaft retainer ring
21. Axle shaft bearing
22. Axle shaft oil seal
23. Axle shaft retainer plate
24. Axle shaft cup plug
25. Axle shaft
26. Thrust washer
27. Differential pinion gears
28. Thrust washer
29. Gasket
30. Housing cover
31. Screw and lockwasher
32. Filler plug
33. Lockpin
34. Differential shaft
35. Ring gear screw

Exploded view of the rear axle assembly with a flanged axle shaft

DRIVE TRAIN

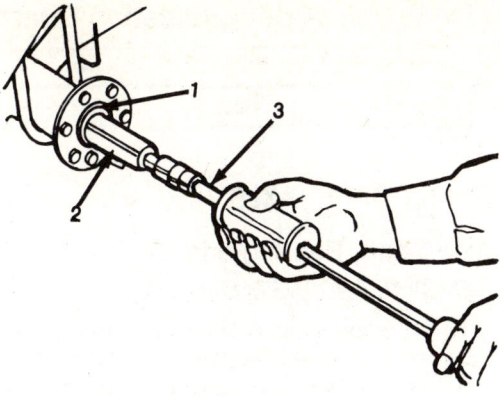

1. Cone and roller
2. Axle
3. Tool

Using a slide hammer-type puller to remove the tapered axle shaft

Splitting the locking ring on the flanged shaft axle

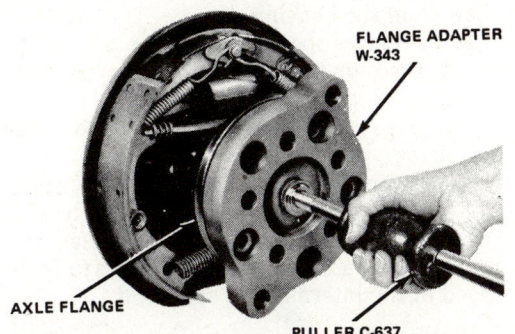

Using a slide hammer-type puller to remove the flanged axle shaft

Arbor press adapter on a flanged shaft bearing

chassis lube for bearing lubrication and must be prelubed prior to installation. Axles without an inner seal rely on differential oil to lubricate the bearing.

Axle Shaft Bearing
REMOVAL AND INSTALLATION

NOTE: *An arbor press is necessary for this procedure.*

1. Position the axle shaft in a vise.
2. Remove the retaining ring by drilling a ¼" hole about ¾ of the way through the ring, then using a cold chisel over the hole, split the ring.
3. Remove the bearing with an arbor press, discard the seal and remove the retainer plate.
4. Installation is the reverse of removal. The new bearing must be pressed on. Make sure it is squarely seated.

Pinion Oil Seal
REMOVAL AND INSTALLATION

1. Raise and support the vehicle.
2. Mark the driveshaft and yoke for refer-

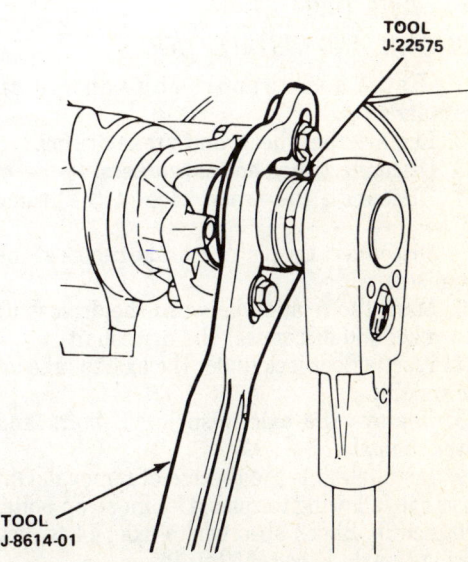

Pinion nut removal on all axles

370 DRIVE TRAIN

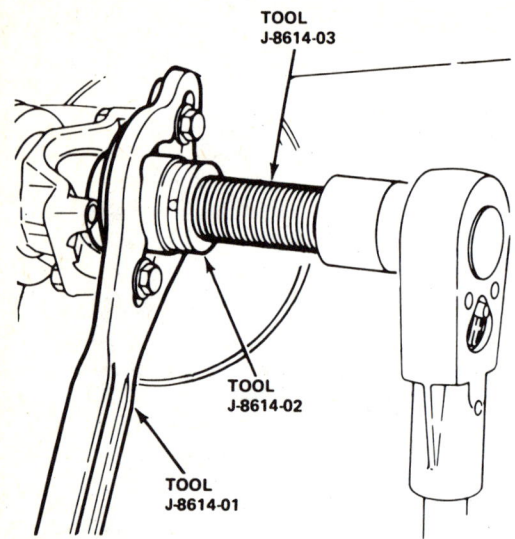

Pinion yoke removal on all axles

ence during assembly and disconnect the driveshaft at the yoke.
3. Remove the pinion shaft nut and washer.
4. Remove the yoke from the pinion shaft, using a puller.
5. Remove the pinion shaft oil seal with tool J-25180 on semi-floating axles, or tool J-25144 on full floating axles.
6. Install the new seal with a suitable driver.
7. Install the pinion shaft washer and nut. Tighten the nut to 210 ft. lbs.
8. Align the index marks on the driveshaft and yoke and install the driveshaft. Tighten the attaching bolts or nuts to 16 ft. lbs.
9. Remove the supports and lower the vehicle.

Rear Axle Unit

REMOVAL AND INSTALLATION

1. Raise and support the vehicle on jackstands.
2. Remove the wheels and brake drums.
3. Disconnect the shock absorbers.
4. Disconnect the brake hose at the frame rail.
5. Disconnect the parking brake cables at the equalizer.
6. Mark the relation between the driveshaft and yoke, and disconnect the driveshaft.
7. Place a floor jack under the axle to take up the weight.
8. Remove the axle-to-spring U-bolts and lower the axle.
9. Installation is the reverse of removal. Observe the following torques: U-joint strap bolts, 170 inch lb. Shock absorber-to-axle, 44 ft. lbs. Spring-to-axle U-bolts, 52 ft. lbs.
10. Bleed the brakes. Road test the truck.

Front Drive Axle Application Chart

Axle	Model	Years
Dana 30	All	1984–89

FRONT DRIVE AXLE

Axle Shaft, Bearing and Seal
REMOVAL AND INSTALLATION

1. Raise and support the vehicle safely.
2. Remove the wheels, calipers and rotors.
3. Remove the cotter pin, locknut and axle hub nut.
4. Remove the hub-to-knuckle attaching bolts.
5. Remove the hub and splash shield from the steering knuckle.
6. To remove the left shaft, remove the axle shaft from the housing.
7. To remove the right shaft:
   a. Disconnect the vacuum harness from the shift motor.
   b. Remove the shift motor from the housing.
   c. Remove the axle shaft from the housing.
8. To install the right axle shaft first be sure that the shift collar is in position on the intermediate shaft and that the axle shaft is fully engaged in the intermediate shaft end.

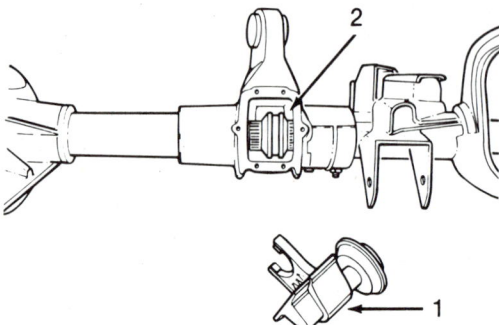

Right side front axle shaft. 1 is the shift motor; 2 is the shift collar

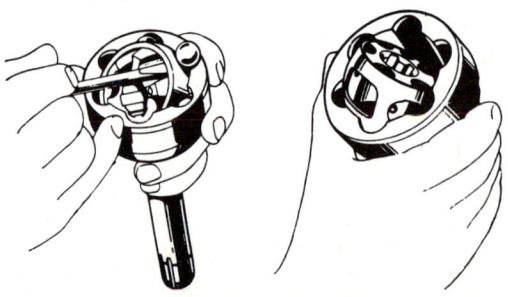

Dismantling the constant velocity joint

DRIVE TRAIN

9. Install the shift motor, making sure that the fork engages with the collar. Tighten the bolts to 8 ft. lbs.
10. On the left side, install the axle shaft in the housing.
11. Partially fill the hub cavity of the knuckle with chassis lube and install the hub and splash shield.
12. Tighten the hub bolts to 75 ft. lbs.
13. Install the hub washer and nut. Torque the nut to 175 ft. lbs. Install the locknut. Install a new cotter pin.
14. Install the rotor, caliper and wheel.

Pinion Shaft Seal
REMOVAL AND INSTALLATION

1. Raise and support the front end on jackstands.
2. Matchamrk and remove the driveshaft.
3. Using a holding tool and socket wrench, remove the pinion yoke nut and washer. Discard the nut.

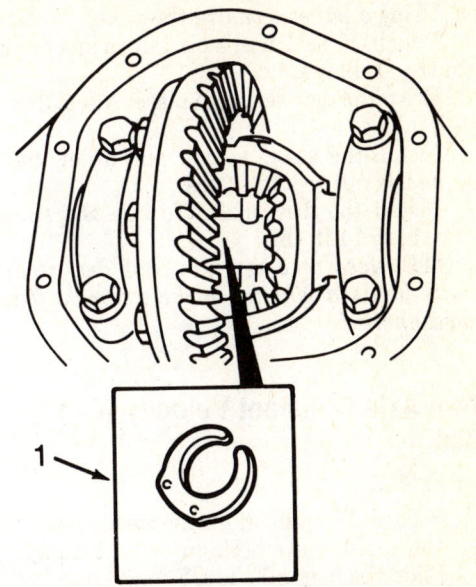

Intermediate shaft retaining clip (1)

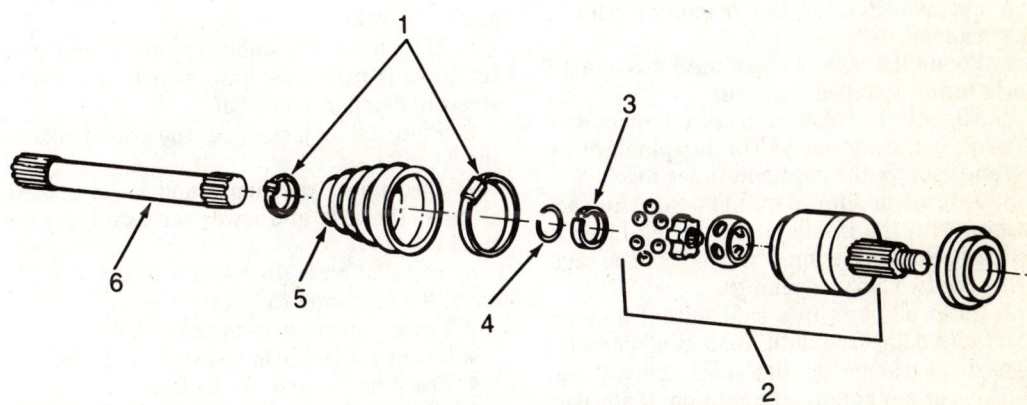

Selec-Trac® outer CV joint exploded view

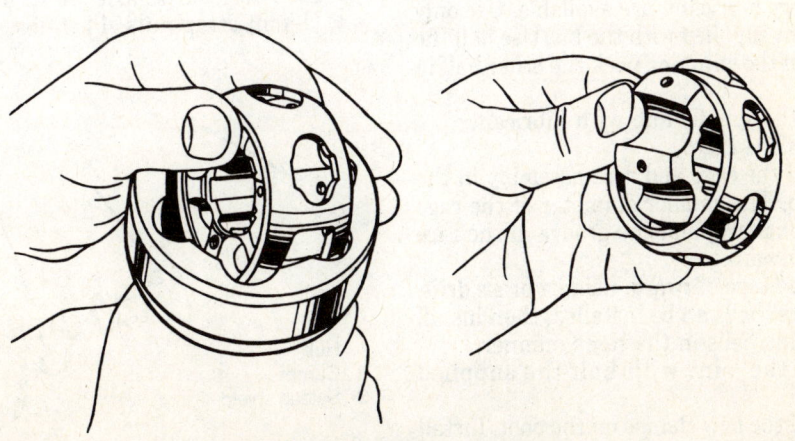

Removing the constant velocity joint

4. Using a puller, remove the yoke.
5. Punch the seal with a pin punch and pry it from the seal bore.
6. Drive the new seal into place. A seal drive is helpful.
7. Install the yoke, washer and a new nut. Torque the nut to 210 ft. lbs.
8. Install the driveshaft. Torque the starp bolt nuts to 14 ft. lbs.
NOTE: *Jeep recommends that new strap bolts be used whenever the driveshaft is disconnected.*

Front Axle Constant Velocity (CV) Joint

OVERHAUL

1. Secure the shaft in a soft-jawed vise.
2. Cut and remove both outer boot clamps.
3. Slide the boot off the CV joint.
4. Using a hardened wood drift, seated on the inner race, tap the joint off the shaft.
5. Using a brass drift, tap the outer CV joint cage until it is tilted out far enough to remove the first ball. Remove the remaining balls in this manner.
6. Rotate the cage outward until it is at a 90° angle to the installed position.
7. Align the two oblong holes in the cage with the slots in the interior wall of the spindle housing and remove the cage and inner race.
8. Align the shoulder, between the race groove, with the inside of the oblong holes in the cage. Rotate the inner race out of the cage, using the two larger openings.
9. Clean all parts in a safe solvent and dry them with a lint-free cloth. Inspect all parts for signs of wear, damage, flat spots, cracks, heat checking or any abnormal condition. If any part is defective, all of the parts should be replaced. These joints should be serviced as assemblies, only. Kits containing all of the parts, as well as the necessary lubricant, are available. Use only the lubricant supplied with the kit. Use half the lubricant on the joint and pack the other half in the boot.
10. Coat the spindle hub with lubricant.
11. Install the cage.
12. Install the cage and race assembly in the spindle hub. The smaller diameter of the cage must face outward, and the groove in the race must face inward.
13. Tilt the cage outward, using a brass drift, until the first ball can be installed, then install the remaining balls in the same manner.
14. Pack the joint with half the supplied lubricant.
15. Install the new clamps on the boot. Install the boot on the shaft.
16. Install the new retaining ring and spacer ring on the shaft.
17. Install the CV joint on the shaft until the inner race contacts the inner snapring.
18. Pack the boot with the remaining lubricant, and slide the boot over the joint. Tighten the clamps.

Intermediate Shaft

REMOVAL AND INSTALLATION

1. Remove the right side axle shaft.
2. Remove the differential cover and drain the lubricant.
3. Remove the intermediate shaft retaining clip in the differential case.
4. Remove the intermediate shaft.
5. Installation is the reverse of removal.

Front Axle Unit

REMOVAL AND INSTALLATION

1. Raise and support the vehicle safely.
2. Remove the wheels, calipers and rotors.
3. Disconnect all vacuum hoses at the axle.
4. Mark the relation between the front driveshaft and yoke.
5. Disconnect the stabilizer bar, rod and center link, front driveshaft, shock absorbers, steering damper, track bar.
6. Place a floor jack under the axle to take up the weight.
7. Disconnect the upper and lower control arms at the axle and lower the axle from the truck.
8. Installation is the reverse of removal. Observe the following torques:
  • Upper control arm-to-axle: 55 ft. lbs.
  • Lower control arm-to-axle: 133 ft. lbs.
  • Track bar-to-axle: 74 ft. lbs.
  • Steering damper-to-axle: 55 ft. lbs.
  • Shock absorber lower bolt: 14 ft. lbs.
  • Center link-to-knuckle: 35 ft. lbs.
  • Stabilizer bar-to-axle: 70 ft. lbs.
  • U-joint strap nuts: 14 ft. lbs.

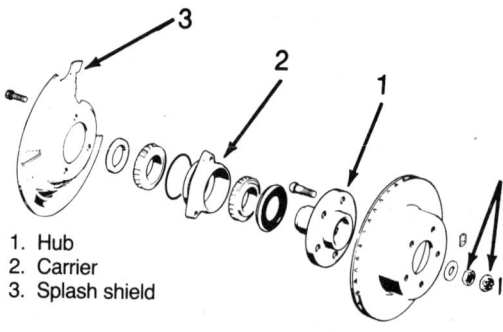

1. Hub
2. Carrier
3. Splash shield

1984–86 Type 1 front wheel bearing

DRIVE TRAIN

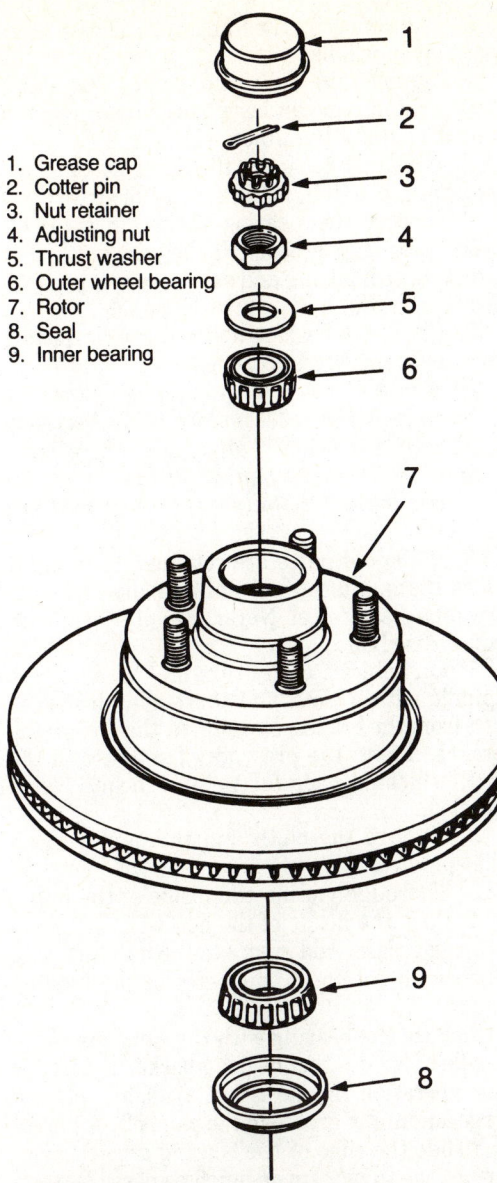

1. Grease cap
2. Cotter pin
3. Nut retainer
4. Adjusting nut
5. Thrust washer
6. Outer wheel bearing
7. Rotor
8. Seal
9. Inner bearing

1984–86 Type 2 front wheel bearing

NOTE: *Discard the U-joint straps. Jeep recommends that new replacement straps must be used whenever the straps are removed.*

2-Wheel Drive Front Wheel Bearings

ADJUSTMENT

NOTE: *Sodium-based grease is not compatible with lithium-based grease. Read the package labels and be careful not to mix the two types. If there is any doubt as to the type of* grease used, completely clean the old grease from the bearing and hub before replacing.

Before handling the bearings, there are a few things that you should remember to do and not to do.

Remember to DO the following:
- Remove all outside dirt from the housing before exposing the bearing.
- Treat a used bearing as gently as you would a new one.
- Work with clean tools in clean surroundings.
- Use clean, dry canvas gloves, or at least clean, dry hands.
- Clean solvents and flushing fluids are a must.
- Use clean paper when laying out the bearings to dry.
- Protect disassembled bearings from rust and dirt. Cover them up.
- Use clean rags to wipe bearings.
- Keep the bearings in oil-proof paper when they are to be stored or are not in use.
- Clean the inside of the housing before replacing the bearing.

Do NOT do the following:
- Don't work in dirty surroundings.
- Don't use dirty, chipped or damaged tools.
- Try not to work on wooden work benches or use wooden mallets.
- Don't handle bearings with dirty or moist hands.
- Do not use gasoline for cleaning; use a safe solvent.
- Do not spin-dry bearings with compressed air. They will be damaged.
- Do not spin dirty bearings.
- Avoid using cotton waste or dirty cloths to wipe bearings.
- Try not to scratch or nick bearing surfaces.
- Do not allow the bearing to come in contact with dirt or rust at any time.

Type One

1. Loosen the lug nuts on the front wheels.
2. Raise and support the front end on jackstands.
3. Remove the front wheels.
4. Remove the calipers, but don't disconnect the brake lines. Suspend the calipers out of the way.
5. Remove the rotor. Be ready to catch the outer bearing.
6. Carefully drive out the inner bearing and seal from the hub, using a wood block.
7. Inspect the bearing races for excessive wear, pitting or grooves. If they are cracked or grooved, or if pitting and excess wear is present, drive them out with a drift or punch.

8. Check the bearing for excess wear, pitting or cracks, or excess looseness.

NOTE: *If it is necessary to replace either the bearing or the race, replace both. Never replace just a bearing or a race. These parts wear in a mating pattern. If just one is replaced, premature failure of the new part will result.*

9. If the old parts are retained, thoroughly clean them in a safe solvent and allow them to dry on a clean towel. Never spin dry them with compressed air.

10. On vehicles with drum brakes, cover the spindle with a cloth and thoroughly brush all dirt from the brakes. Never blow the dirt off the brakes, due to the presence of asbestos in the dirt, which is harmful to your health when inhaled.

11. Remove the cloth and thoroughly clean the spindle.

12. Thoroughly clean the inside of the hub.

13. Pack the inside of the hub with EP wheel bearing grease. Add grease to the hub until it is flush with the inside diameter of the bearing cup.

14. Pack the bearing with the same grease. A needle-shaped wheel bearing packer is best for this operation. If one is not available, place a large amount of grease in the palm of your hand and slide the edge of the bearing cage through the grease to pick up as much as possible, then work the grease in as best you can with your fingers.

15. If a new race is being installed, very carefully drive it into position until it bottoms all around, using a brass drift. Be careful to avoid scratching the surface.

16. Place the inner bearing in the race and install a new grease seal.

17. Position the hub and rotor on the spindle and install the outer bearing.

18. Install the washer and nut.

19. While turning the rotor, torque the nut to 25 ft. lbs. to seat the bearings.

20. Back off the nut ½ turn, and, while turning the rotor, torque the nut to 19 in. lbs.

21. Install the nut cap and a new cotter pin. Install the grease cap.

22. Install the caliper.

23. Install the wheels.

Type 2

1. Raise and support the front end on jackstands.

2. Remove the wheels.

3. Remove the caliper without disconnecting the brake line. Suspend it out of the way.

4. Remove the grease cap, cotter pin, nut cap, nut, and washer from the spindle.

5. Pull slowly on the hub and catch the outer bearing as it falls.

6. Remove the hub and rotor. The inner bearing and seal can be removed by prying out and discarding the inner seal.

7. Carefully drive out the inner bearing and seal from the hub, using a wood block.

8. Inspect the bearing races for excessive wear, pitting or grooves. If they are cracked or grooved, or if pitting and excess wear is present, drive them out with a drift or punch.

9. Check the bearing for excess wear, pitting or cracks, or excess looseness.

NOTE: *If it is necessary to replace either the bearing or the race, replace both. Never replace just a bearing or a race. These parts wear in a mating pattern. If just one is replaced, premature failure of the new part will result.*

10. If the old parts are retained, thoroughly clean them in a safe solvent and allow them to dry on a clean towel. Never spin dry them with compressed air.

11. On vehicles with drum brakes, cover the spindle with a cloth and thoroughly brush all dirt from the brakes. Never blow the dirt off the brakes, due to the presence of asbestos in the dirt, which is harmful to your health when inhaled.

12. Remove the cloth and thoroughly clean the spindle.

13. Thoroughly clean the inside of the hub.

14. Pack the inside of the hub with EP wheel bearing grease. Add grease to the hub until it is flush with the inside diameter of the bearing cup.

15. Pack the bearing with the same grease. A needle-shaped wheel bearing packer is best for this operation. If one is not available, place a large amount of grease in the palm of your hand and slide the edge of the bearing cage through the grease to pick up as much as possible, then work the grease in as best you can with your fingers.

16. If a new race is being installed, very carefully drive it into position until it bottoms all around, using a brass drift. Be careful to avoid scratching the surface.

17. Place the inner bearing in the race and install a new grease seal.

18. Clean and repack the hub and bearings, install the inner bearing and a new seal.

19. Position the hub and rotor on the spindle and install the outer bearing.

20. Install the washer and nut.

21. While turning the rotor, torque the nut to 25 ft. lbs. to seat the bearings.

22. Back off the nut ½ turn, and, while turning the rotor, torque the nut to 19 in. lbs.

23. Install the nut cap and a new cotter pin. Install the grease cap.
24. Install the caliper.
25. Install the wheels.

4-Wheel Drive Front Axle Bearings

WARNING: *The following procedure requires the use of an arbor press. Chrysler Corp. notes that only the special press tools listed below should be used or damage to the internal machined shoulder of the bearing carrier is probable!*

1. Raise and support the front end on jackstands.
2. Remove the wheels.
3. Remove, but do not disconnect, the caliper. Suspend it out of the way.
4. Remove the rotor. See Chapter 9.
5. Remove the cotter pin, nut retainer, axle nut and washer.
6. Remove the 3 bearing carrier bolts.
7. Remove the hub/bearing carrier and the rotor shield.
8. Using an arbor press, press the hub out of the bearing carrier. Special tools 5073 and 5074 are available for this job. Secure the carrier to the press plate with M12 × 1.75mm × 40mm bolts.
9. Cut and remove the plastic cage from the hub inner bearing. Using diagonal pliers or tin snips, cut the bearing cage. Discard the rollers after removing the cage.
10. Remove what remians of the inner bearing by:
  a. Install a bearing separator tool on the inner bearing.
  b. Position the separator tool and hub in an arbor press.
  c. Force the hub out of the inner bearing with press pin tool 5074.
11. Remove the bearing carrier outer seal and discard it.
12. Drive the inner bearing seal out and discard it. If you're using tool 5078, make sure that the word JEEP faces downward.
13. Attach press plate tool 5073 to the rear of the carrier. Secure it in the press using M12 × 1.75mm × 40mm bolts.
14. Position bearing race remover 5076 in the carrier bore between the inner and outer bearing races.
15. Position the press pin tool 5074 on tool 5076.
16. Place the bearing carrier in the press and force the inner bearing race from the carrier bore. Reverse the position of the carrier and tools and force the outer bearing race from the bore.

To assemble and install

17. Thoroughly clean all reusable parts with a safe solvent. Discard any parts that appear worn or damaged.
18. Attach press plate tool 5073 on the bearing carrier. Secure it in the press using M12 × 1.75mm × 40mm bolts.
19. Position the new outer bearing race in the bore.
20. Position bearing race installation tool 5077 on the race. Make sure that the word JEEP faces the downward. Press the race into the bore. The race should be flush with the machined shoulder of the carrier.
21. Position the new inner bearing race in the carrier bore. Reverse the position of the carrier and tools and force the inner race into the bore.
22. Thoroughly pack the new outer bearing with wheel bearing grease. Make sure that the bearing is fully packed.
23. Coat the race with wheel bearing grease and place the bearing in the bore.
24. Place the new outer seal on the bearing and position bearing installation tool 5079 on the seal. Place the carrier in the press and force the seal into the bore. Apply wheel bearing grease to the seal ip.
25. Insert the hub through the seal and outer bearing and into the bearing carrier bore.
26. Install bearing installation tool 5078 into the rear of the bearing carrier bore and place the race installation tool 5077 on the front of the hub. Make sure that the word JEEP on 5077 is facing the hub.
27. Place the assembly in the press and force the hub shaft into the carrier bore.
28. Pack the new inner bearing with wheel bearing grease. Make sure that the bearing is thoroughly packed.
29. Coat the inner seal lip with wheel bearing grease and place it on the inner bearing.
30. Coat the inner bearing race with wheel bearing grease.
31. Place the carrier in a press along with tool 5077. The word JEEP on 5077 must face the hub. Position the bearing and seal in the carrier. Place seal installation tool 5080 on the seal.
32. Force the bearing and seal into the bore and onto the hub shaft.

WARNING: *Use extreme care when forcing the assembly into position! The acrrier must rotate freely after installation of the bearing! Do not attempt to elieminate bearing lash with the press. Final bearing preload is attained by tightening the drive axle nut.*

33. Install the new outer seal on the carrier.
34. Thoroughly clean the axle shaft and apply a thin coating of lithium-based grease to the splines and seal contact surfaces.

DRIVE TRAIN

35. Install the slinger, rotor shield and hub/bearing assembly on the axle shaft.
36. Coat the carrier bolt threads with Loctite®, install them and torque them to 75 ft. lbs.
37. Install the rotor and caliper. See Chapter 9.
38. Install the washer and axle shaft nut. Torque the nut to 175 ft. lbs.
39. Install the nut retainer and cotter pin. NEVER back off the nut to install the cotter pin! ALWAYS advance it!
40. Install the wheel.

SPECIAL TOOLS

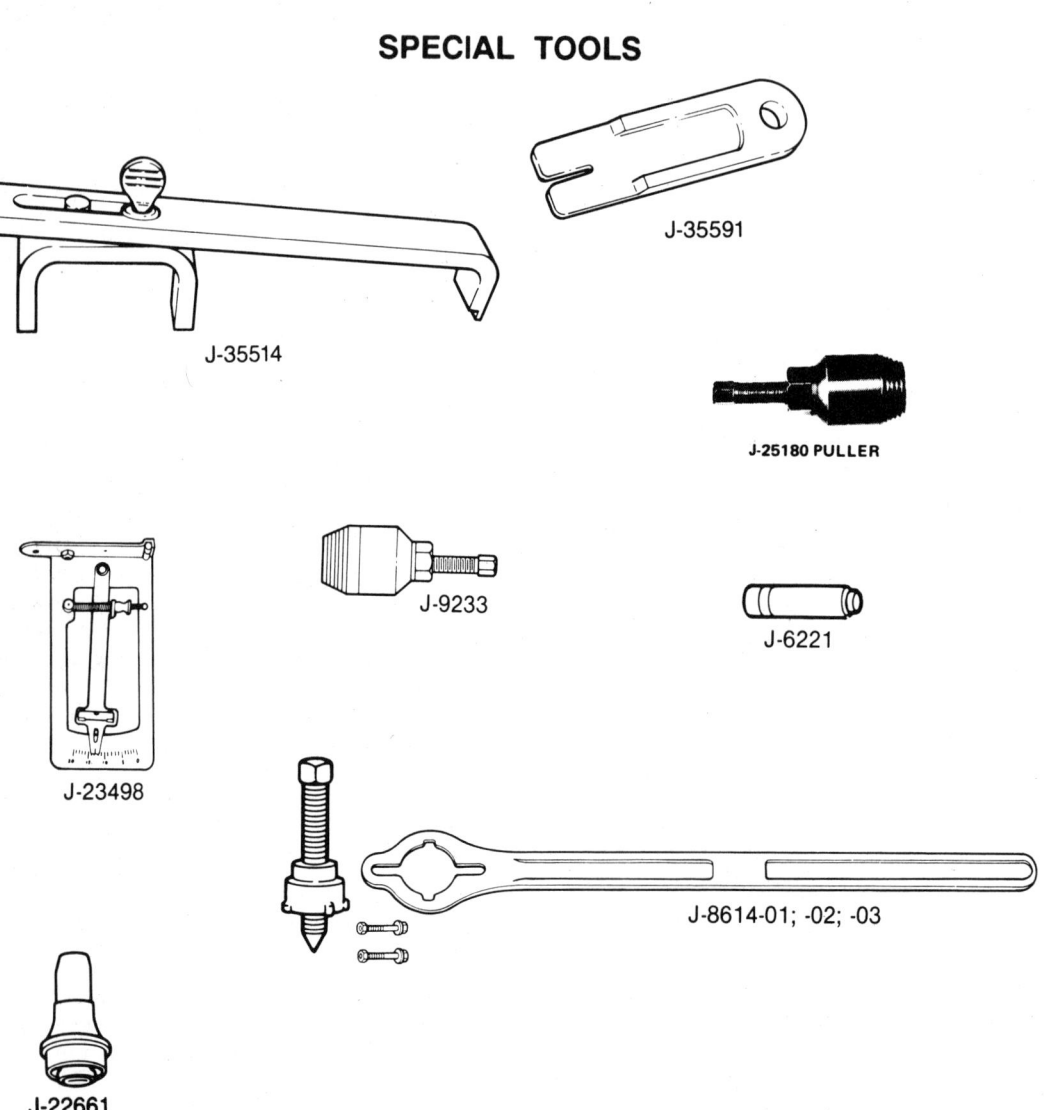

Suspension and Steering

8

FRONT SUSPENSION

Coil Springs

REMOVAL AND INSTALLATION

1. Raise the truck and support it with jackstands under the frame.
2. Support the axle with a floor jack.
3. Remove the wheels.
4. On 4wd trucks, matchmark and disconnect the front driveshaft from the axle.
5. Disconnect the lower control arm at the axle.
6. Disconnect the stabilizer bar links and the shock absorbers at the axle.
7. Disconnect the track bar at the sill bracket.
8. Disconnect the tie rod at the pitman arm.
9. Lower the axle until tension is removed from the spring, then loosen the spring retainer and remove the spring.
10. Installation is the reverse of removal. Observe the following torques:
- control arm-to-axle: 133 ft. lbs.
- shock absorber-to-axle: 14 ft. lbs.
- stabilizer bar-to-axle: 70 ft. lbs.
- U-joint-to-axle: 14 ft. lbs.
- center link-to-pitman arm: 35 ft. lbs.
- track bar-to-frame rail: 35 ft. lbs.

Front Stabilizer Bar

REMOVAL AND INSTALLATION

1. Raise and support the front end on jackstands.
2. Remove the staibilizer bar-to-frame clamps and cushions.
3. Disconnect the stabilizer bar at the connecting links and remove the stabilizer bar. If necessary, disconnect the connecting links from the axle bracket.

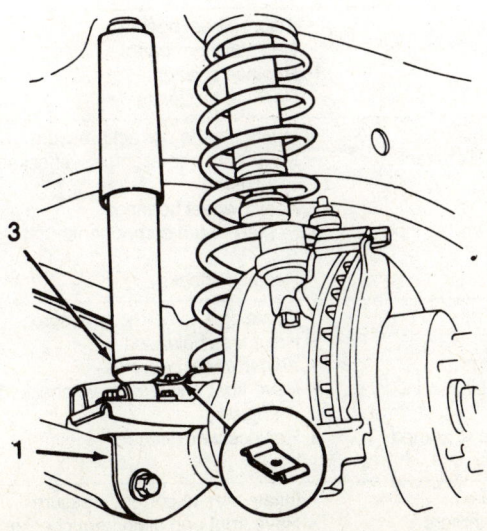

1. Control arm   3. Shock absorber

Front coil spring mounting

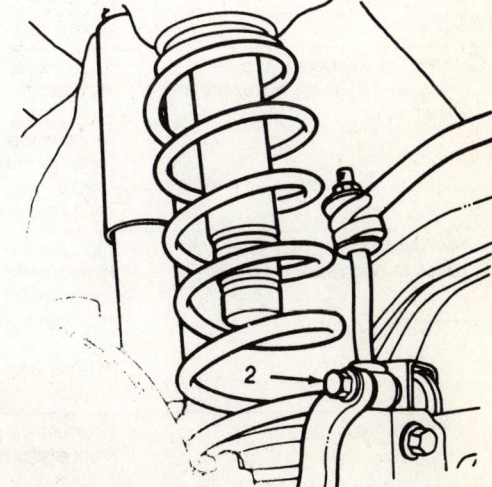

Front stabilizer bar attaching points

SUSPENSION AND STEERING

4. Installation is the reverse of removal. Torque the clamp-to-frame bolts to 55 ft. lbs., the stabilizer bar-to-connecting link nuts to 27 ft. lbs., and, the connecting link-to-axle bolts to 70 ft. lbs.

Track Bar

REMOVAL AND INSTALLATION

1. Raise and support the front end on jackstands.
2. Remove the cotter pin and nut securing the track bar to the frame bracket.
3. Remove the bolt and nut securing the track bar to the axle.
4. Installation is the reverse of removal. Install both ends loosely, then torque the fasteners. Torque the frame-end nut to 35 ft. lbs.; the axle-end bolt to 55 ft. lbs.

Shock Absorbers

REMOVAL AND INSTALLATION

NOTE: *Before installing new shocks, they should be purged of air. To do this, hold the shock upright and fully extend it, then invert and compress it. Do this several times.*

1. Raise and support the front axle on jackstands.
2. Remove the locknuts and washers.

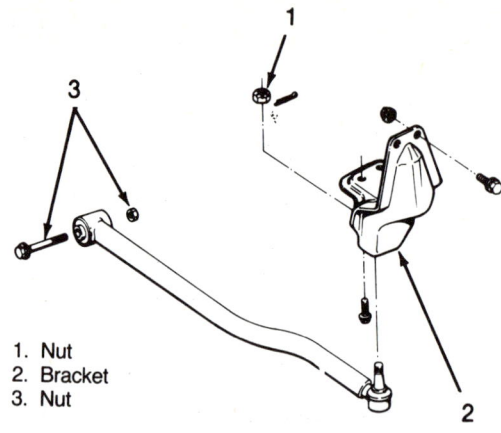

1. Nut
2. Bracket
3. Nut

Track bar

Troubleshooting Basic Steering and Suspension Problems

Problem	Cause	Solution
Hard steering (steering wheel is hard to turn)	• Low or uneven tire pressure • Loose power steering pump drive belt • Low or incorrect power steering fluid • Incorrect front end alignment • Defective power steering pump • Bent or poorly lubricated front end parts	• Inflate tires to correct pressure • Adjust belt • Add fluid as necessary • Have front end alignment checked/adjusted • Check pump • Lubricate and/or replace defective parts
Loose steering (too much play in the steering wheel)	• Loose wheel bearings • Loose or worn steering linkage • Faulty shocks • Worn ball joints	• Adjust wheel bearings • Replace worn parts • Replace shocks • Replace ball joints
Car veers or wanders (car pulls to one side with hands off the steering wheel)	• Incorrect tire pressure • Improper front end alignment • Loose wheel bearings • Loose or bent front end components • Faulty shocks	• Inflate tires to correct pressure • Have front end alignment checked/adjusted • Adjust wheel bearings • Replace worn components • Replace shocks
Wheel oscillation or vibration transmitted through steering wheel	• Improper tire pressures • Tires out of balance • Loose wheel bearings • Improper front end alignment • Worn or bent front end components	• Inflate tires to correct pressure • Have tires balanced • Adjust wheel bearings • Have front end alignment checked/adjusted • Replace worn parts
Uneven tire wear	• Incorrect tire pressure • Front end out of alignment • Tires out of balance	• Inflate tires to correct pressure • Have front end alignment checked/adjusted • Have tires balanced

SUSPENSION AND STEERING

3. Pull the shock absorber eyes and rubber bushings from the mounting pins.
4. Install the shocks in the reverse order of the removal procedure. Observe the following torques:
- Upper end nut: 8 ft.lb.
- Lower end bolts: 14 ft.lb.

NOTE: *Squeaking usually occurs when movement takes place between the rubber bushings and the metal parts. The squeaking may be eliminated by placing the bushings under greater pressure. This is accomplished either by adding additional washers or by tightening the locknuts. Do not use mineral lubricant to stop the squeaking, as it will deteriorate the rubber.*

Upper Control Arm

REMOVAL AND INSTALLATION

1. Raise and support the truck on jackstands under the frame.
2. On trucks with the V6, disconnect the right engine mount and raise the engine so that the rear bolt will clear the exhaust pipe.
3. Remove the wheels.
4. Remove the control arm-to-axle bolt.
5. Remove the control arm-to-frame bolt and remove the arm.
6. Installation is the reverse of removal. Torque the control arm bolts to 55 ft. lbs. at the axle; 66 ft. lbs. at the frame.

Lower Control Arm

REMOVAL AND INSTALLATION

1. Raise and support the truck with jackstands under the frame.

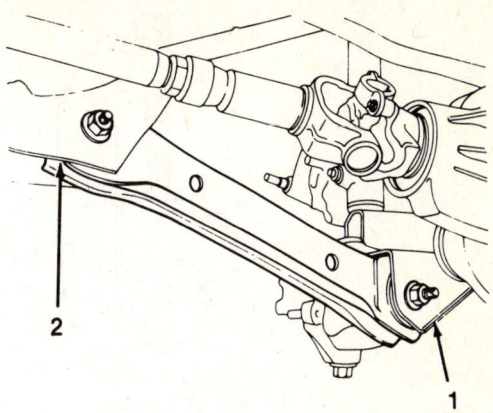
Lower control arm

2. Disconnect the lower control arm at the axle and rear bracket. Remove the arm.
3. Installation is the reverse of removal. Torque the bolts to 133 ft. lbs.

Upper Ball Joint

REMOVAL AND INSTALLATION

NOTE: *This procedure requires the use of a special tool.*

1. Remove the steering knuckle.
2. Position a ball joint removal tool, J-34503-1 and 34503-3, in a C-clamp as shown, and on the upper ball joint.
3. Tighten the clamp screw to remove the joint.
4. Use tools J-34503-5 and J-34503-12, in a

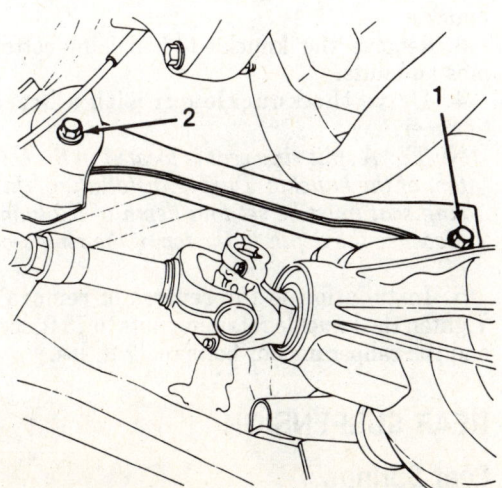
Upper control arm

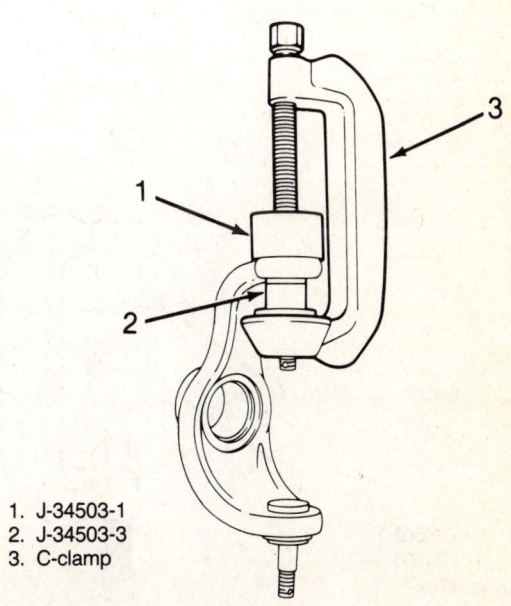
1. J-34503-1
2. J-34503-3
3. C-clamp

Upper ball joint removal

SUSPENSION AND STEERING

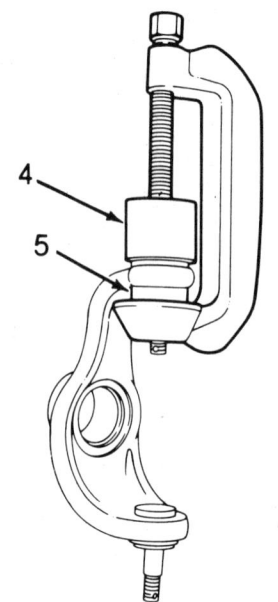

4. J-34503-5
5. J-34503-12

Upper ball joint installation

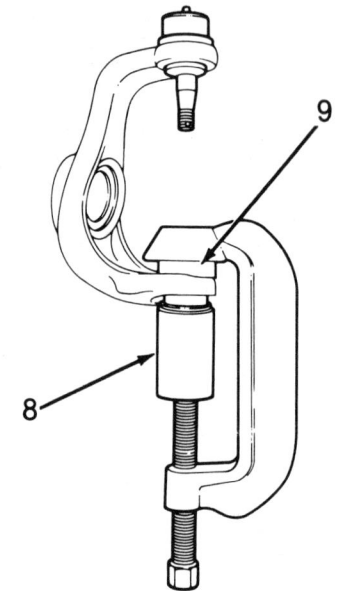

8. J-34503-4
9. J-34503-12

Lower ball joint installation

similar manner, as illustrated, to install the ball joint.
5. Install the knuckle.

Lower Ball Joint

REMOVAL AND INSTALLATION

NOTE: *This procedure requires the use of a special tool.*
1. Remove the steering knuckle.

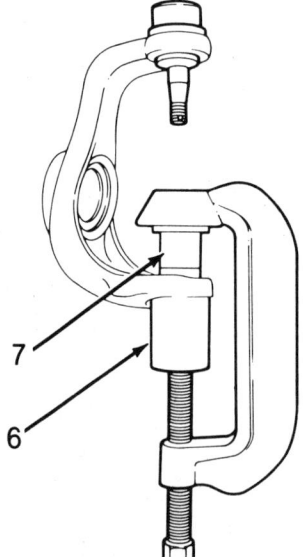

6. J-34503-1
7. J-34503-3

Lower ball joint removal

2. Position a ball joint removal tool, J-34503-1 and J-34503-3, as shown, on the lower ball joint.
3. Tighten the clamp screw to remove the joint.
4. Use tool J-34503-4 and J-34503-12 to install the ball joint by reversing the removal procedure.
5. Install the knuckle.

Steering Knuckle and Pivot-Pins

REMOVAL AND INSTALLATION

1. Remove the outer axle shaft.
2. Remove the caliper anchor plate from the knuckle.
3. Remove the knuckle-to-ball joint cotter pins and nuts.
4. Drive the knuckle out with a brass hammer.
NOTE: *A split ring seat is located in the bottom of the knuckle. During installation, this ring seat must be set to a depth of 5.23mm. Measure the depth to the top of the ring seat (4).*
5. Installation is the reverse of removal. Tighten the knuckle retaining nuts to 75 ft. lbs. and the caliper anchor bolts to 77 ft. lbs.

REAR SUSPENSION

Leaf Springs

Leaf springs should be examined periodically for broken or shifted leaves, loose or missing

SUSPENSION AND STEERING

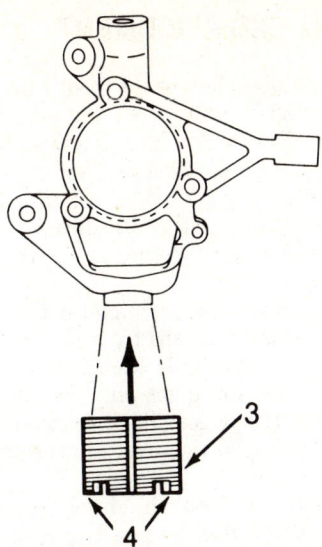

Split ring seat installation details. 3 is the split ring seat; 4 is the top of the seat for measurement purposes

clips, angle of the spring shackles, and position of the springs on the saddles. Springs with shifted leaves do not retain their normal strength. Missing clips may permit the spring leaves to fan out or break on rebound. Broken leaves may make the vehicle hard to handle or permit the axle to shift out of line. Weakened springs may break, causing difficulty in steering. Spring attaching clips or bolts must be tight. It is suggested that they be checked at each vehicle inspection.

REMOVAL AND INSTALLATION

1. Raise and support the truck with jackstands under the frame rails.
2. Take up the weight of the axle with a floor jack.
3. Disconnect the shock absorbers at the axle.
4. Remove the wheels.
5. Disconnect the stabilizer bar links at the spring plate.
6. Remove the U-bolts and spring plates.
7. Remove the rear spring-to-shackle bolt, then the front spring-to-shackle bolt.
8. Lower the axle and remove the spring.
9. Installation is the reverse of removal. Observe the following torques:
- Front and rear shackle bolts: 111 ft. lbs.
- U-bolt nuts: 52 ft. lbs.
- Shock absorber-to-axle nuts: 44 ft. lbs.

Shock Absorbers

REMOVAL AND INSTALLATION

NOTE: *Before installing new shocks, they should be purged of air. To do this, hold the shock upright and fully extend it, then invert and compress it. Do this several times.*

1. Raise and support the rear axle on jackstands.

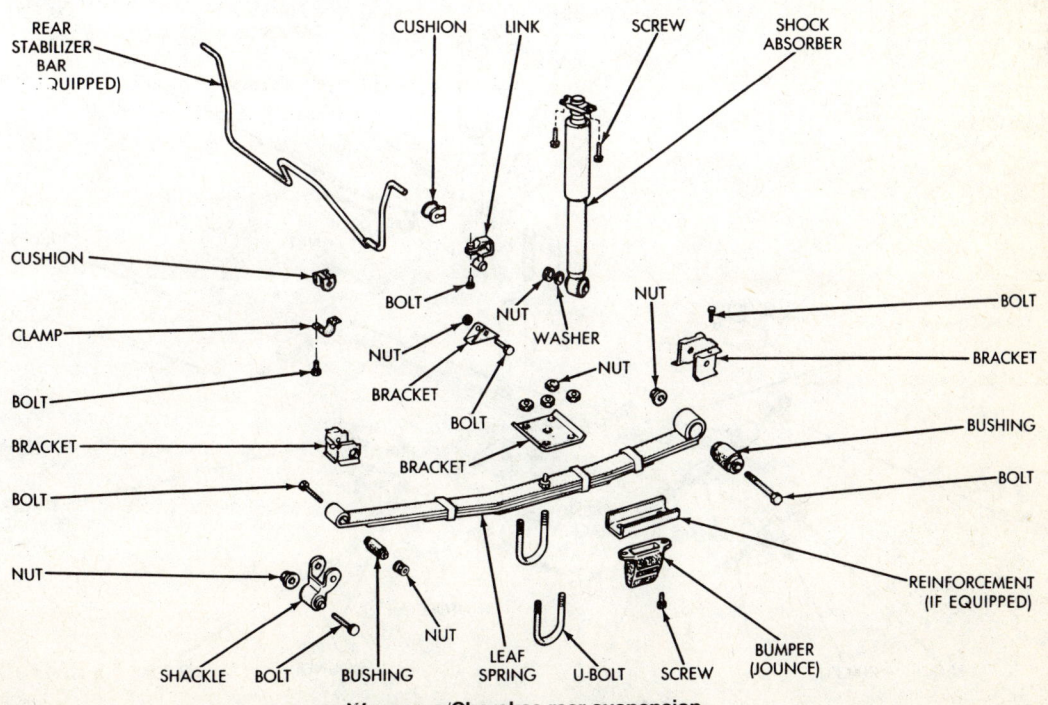

Wagoneer/Cherokee rear suspension

SUSPENSION AND STEERING

2. Remove the locknuts and washers.
3. Pull the shock absorber eyes and rubber bushings from the mounting pins.
4. Install the shocks in the reverse order of the removal procedure. Observe the following torques:
- Upper end bolts: 44 ft.lb.
- Lower end bolts: 44 ft.lb.

NOTE: *Squeaking usually occurs when movement takes place between the rubber bushings and the metal parts. The squeaking may be eliminated by placing the bushings under greater pressure. This is accomplished either by adding additional washers or by tightening the locknuts. Do not use mineral lubricant to stop the squeaking, as it will deteriorate the rubber.*

Rear Stabilizer Bar

REMOVAL AND INSTALLATION

1. Raise and support the rear end on jackstands.
2. Remove the stabilizer bar-to-frame clamps and cushions.
3. Disconnect the stabilizer bar connecting links at the spring tie plates and remove the stabilizer bar.
4. Installation is the reverse of removal. Torque the clamp bolts and the connecting link nuts to 55 ft. lbs.

FRONT END ALIGNMENT

Proper alignment of the front wheels must be maintained in order to ensure ease of steering and satisfactory tire life. The most important factors of front wheel alignment are wheel camber, axle caster, and wheel toe-in.

Wheel toe-in is the distance by which the wheels are closer together at the front than at the rear.

Wheel camber is the amount the top of the wheels incline outward from the vertical.

Front axle caster is the amount in degrees that the steering pivot pins are tilted toward the rear of the vehicle. Positive caster is inclination of the top of the pivot pin toward the rear of the vehicle.

These points should be checked at regular intervals, particularly when the front axle has been subjected to a heavy impact. When checking wheel alignment, it is important that wheel bearings and knuckle bearings be in proper adjustment. Loose bearings will affect instrument readings when checking the camber, pivot pin inclination, and toe-in.

Front wheel camber is preset. Caster can be altered by the use of shims at the rear of the lower control arms.

NOTE: *A change in caster angle also changes the front driveshaft angle. See Front Driveshaft Angle Measurement and Adjust-*

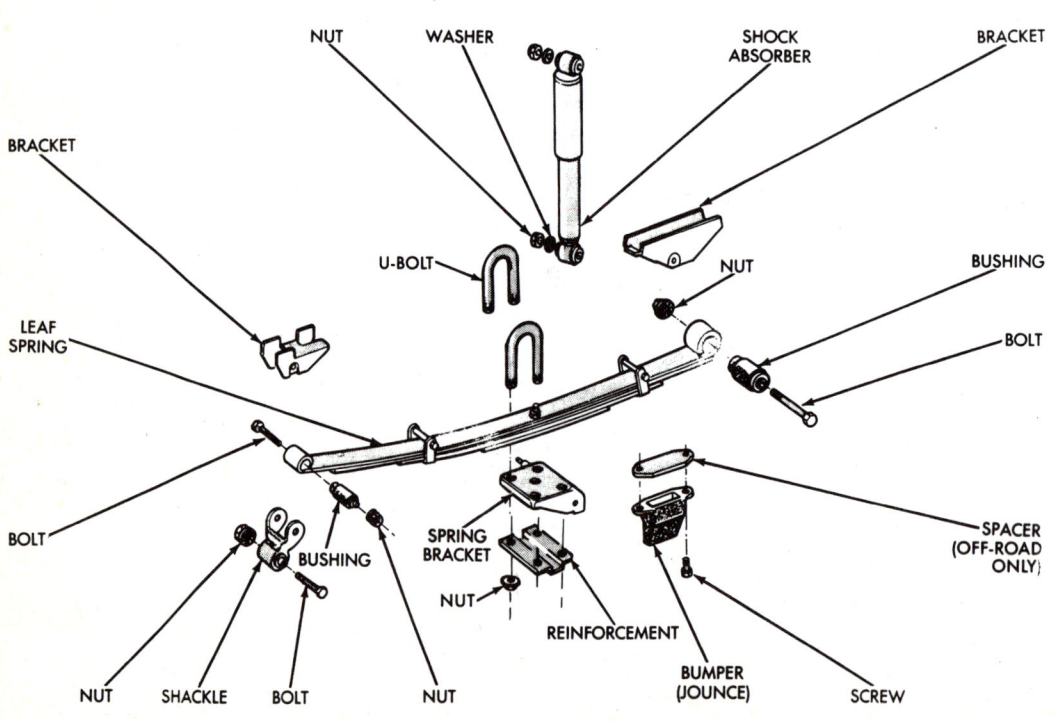

Comanche rear suspension

ment, in Chapter 7. *The driveshaft angle takes precedence.*

Wheel toe-in may be adjusted. To measure wheel toe-in, follow the procedure given later on in this section.

CASTER ADJUSTMENT

Caster angle is established in the axle design by tilting the top of the kingpin toward the rear, and the bottom of the kingpin forward so that an imaginary line through the center of the kingpin would strike the ground at a point ahead of the point of tire contact.

The purpose of caster is to provide steering stability which will keep the front wheels in the straight ahead position and also assist in straightening the wheels when coming out of a turn.

Caster is corrected by adding or installing shims at the rear of the lower control arms.

NOTE: *A change in caster angle also changes the front driveshaft angle. See Front Driveshaft Angle Measurement and Adjustment, in Chapter 7. The driveshaft angle takes precedence.*

If the camber and toe-in are correct and it is known that the axle is not twisted, a satisfactory check may be made by testing the vehicle on the road. Before road testing, make sure all tires are properly inflated, being particularly careful that both front tires are inflated to exactly the same pressure.

If the vehicle turns easily to either side but is hard to straighten out, insufficient caster for easy handling of the vehicle is indicated. If correction is necessary, it can usually be accomplished by installing shims between the springs and axle pads to secure the desired result.

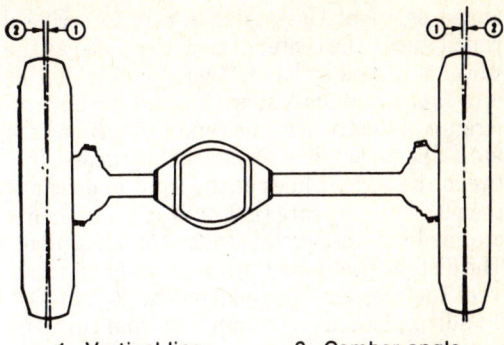

1. Vertical line   2. Camber angle

Wheel camber

CAMBER ADJUSTMENT

The purpose of camber is to more nearly place the weight of the vehicle over the tire contact patch on the road to facilitate ease of steering. The result of excessive camber is irregular wear of the tires on the outside shoulders and is usually caused by bent axle parts.

The result of excessive negative or reverse camber will be hard steering and possibly a wandering condition. Tires will also wear on the inside shoulders. Unequal camber may cause any or a combination of the following conditions: unstable steering, wandering, kickback or road shock, shimmy or excessive tire wear. The cause of unequal camber is usually a bent steering knuckle or axle end.

Correct wheel camber is set in the axle at the time of manufacture and cannot be altered by any adjustment. It is important that the camber be the same on both front wheels. Heating of any parts to facilitate straightening usually destroys the heat treatment given them at the factory. Cold bending may cause a fracture of the steel and is also unsafe. Replacement with new parts is recommended, rather than any straightening of damaged parts.

TOE-IN ADJUSTMENT

First raise the front of the vehicle to free the front wheels. Turn the wheels to the straight

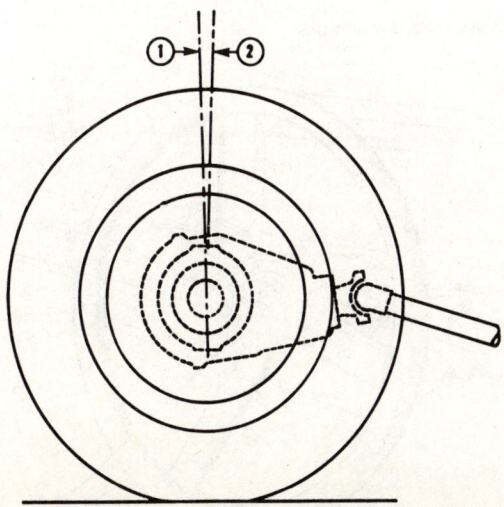

1. Vertical line   2. Caster angle

Axle caster

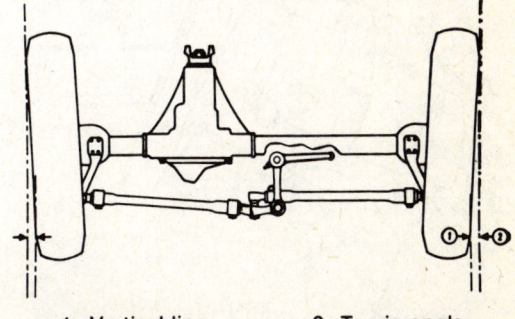

1. Vertical line   2. Toe-in angle

Front wheel toe-in

384 SUSPENSION AND STEERING

ahead position. Use a steady rest to scribe a pencil line in the center of each tire tread as the wheel is turned by hand. A good way to do this is to first run a chalk stripe around the circumference of the tread at the center to form a base for a fine pencil line. Measure the distance between the scribed lines at the front and rear of the wheels using care that both measurements are made at an equal distance from the floor. The distance between the lines should be greater at the rear than at the front by $3/64''$ to $3/32''$. To adjust, loosen the clamp bolts and turn the tie rod with a small pipe wrench. The tie rod is threaded with right and left hand threads to provide equal adjustment at both wheels. Do not overlook retightening the clamp bolts to 15-20 ft. lbs.

It is common practice to measure between the wheel rims. This is satisfactory providing the wheels run true. By scribing a line on the tire tread, measurement is taken between the road contact points, reducing error by wheel runout.

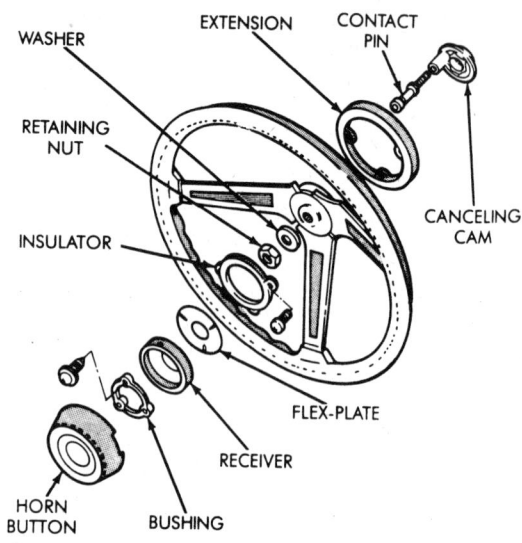
Sport wheel components

STEERING

Steering Wheel

REMOVAL AND INSTALLATION

1. Disconnect the negative battery cable.
2. Set the front tires in a straight ahead position.
3. Pull the horn button from the steering wheel. With sport wheel, remove the button, nut, washer, retainer and horn ring. It is necessary to remove the attaching screws from under the steering wheel spoke to remove the horn cover.

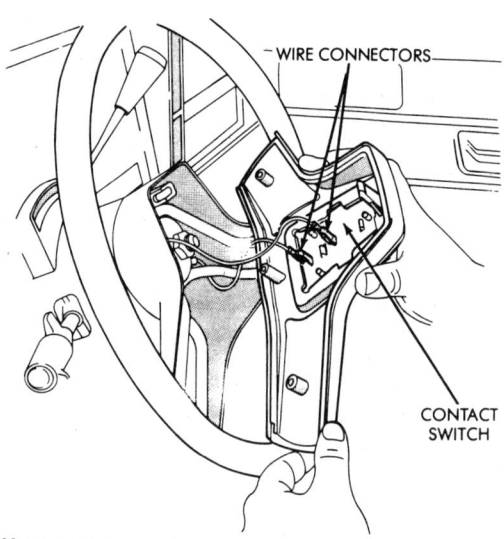
Horn wire connectors

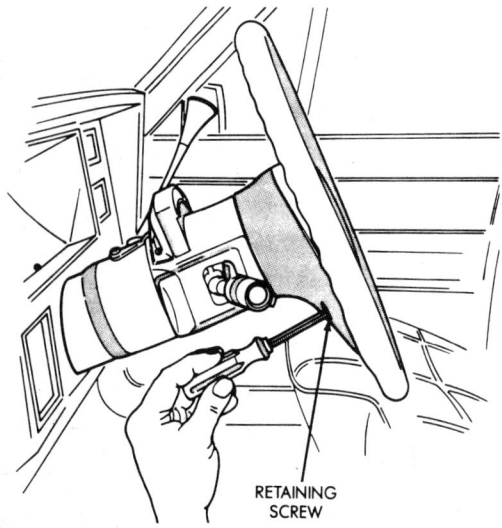
Trim cover removal

Sport wheel horn flex plate

SUSPENSION AND STEERING 385

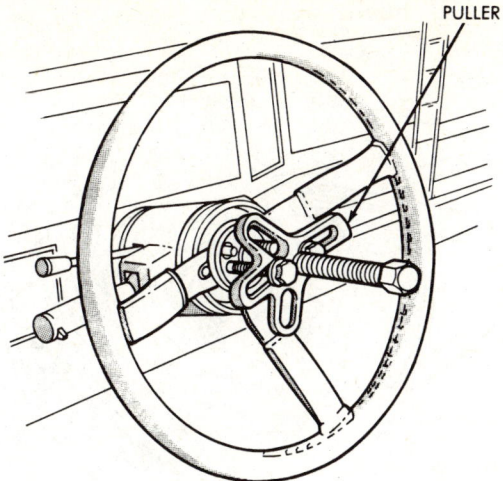

Steering wheel removal

screws and actuator arm, then remove the switch.
10. Installation is the reverse of removal.

Ignition Lock Cylinder
REMOVAL AND INSTALLATION

1. Follow the steps under Turn Signal Switch for removal of the switch.
2. Insert the key in the lock cylinder and turn it to the ON position.
3. Remove the key warning buzzer switch and contacts AS AN ASSEMBLY using needlenosed pliers, or a paper clip with a 90° bend.

4. Remove the steering wheel nut and horn button contact cup.
5. Scribe a line mark on the steering wheel and steering shaft if there is not one already. Release the turn signal assembly from the steering post and install a puller.
6. Remove the steering wheel and spring.
7. To install, align the scribe marks on the steering shaft with the steering wheel and secure the steering wheel spring, steering wheel, and horn button contact cup with the steering wheel nut.
8. Install the horn button.
9. Connect the battery cable and test the horn.

Turn Signal Switch
REPLACEMENT

NOTE: *This procedure requires the use of a special tool.*

1. Remove the steering wheel.
2. Remove the lockplate cover.
3. On tilt columns, remove the tilt lever.
4. Remove the snapring and lockplate using a special compressor tool such as J-23653-A. The spring is under great pressure and the tool can prevent injury. Discard the snapring.
5. Remove the canceling cam, upper bearing preload spring spring seat and thrust washer.
6. Remove the hazard warning switch knob by pressing inward and turning it counterclockwise.
7. Disengage the turn signal/wiper lever by pulling it straight out.
8. Disconnect the turn signal switch wiring harness connector from the bracket at the lower end of the column.
9. Remove the turn signal switch attaching

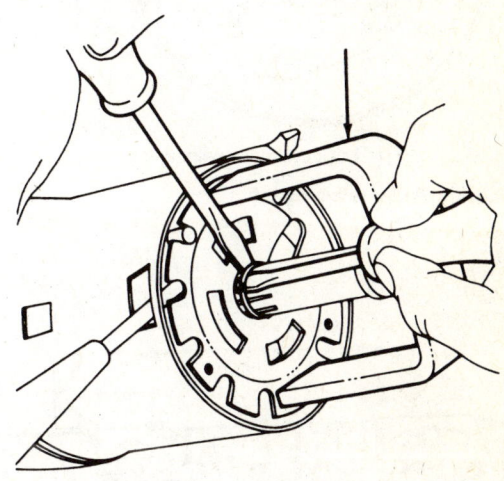

Using lockplate spring compressor

Lockplate components

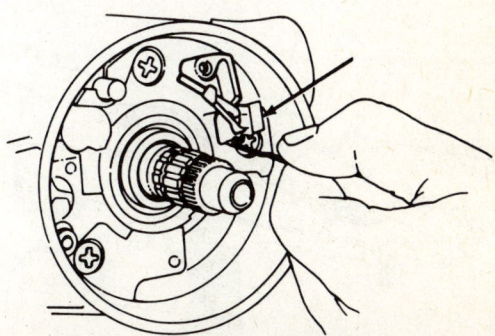

Removing the key warning switch buzzer components

386 SUSPENSION AND STEERING

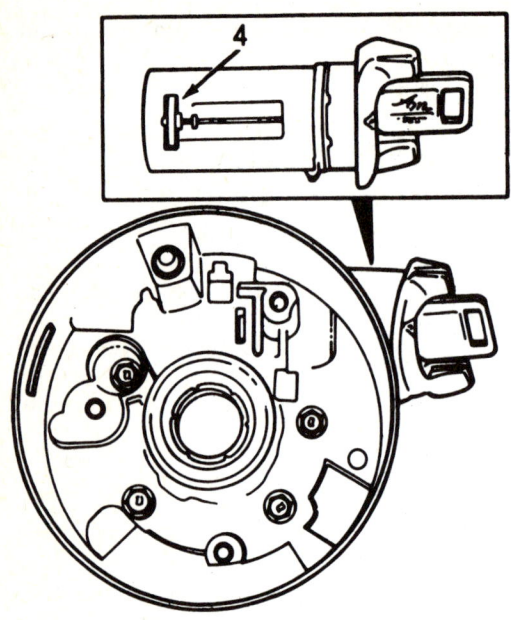

4. Lock cylinder retaining tab

Lock cylinder retaining tab

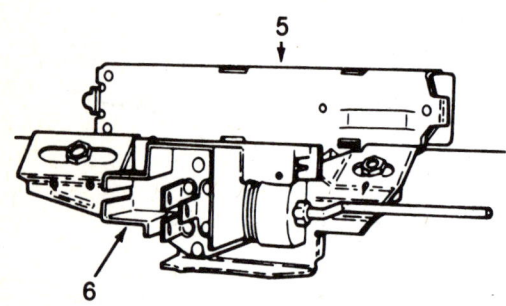

5. Ignition switch   6. Dimmer switch

Ignition switch/dimmer switch assembly

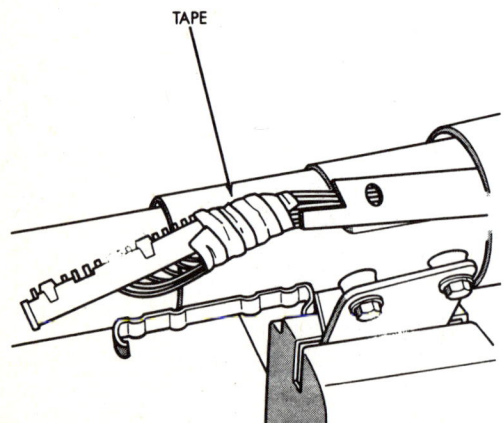

Taped turn signal switch wire harness connector

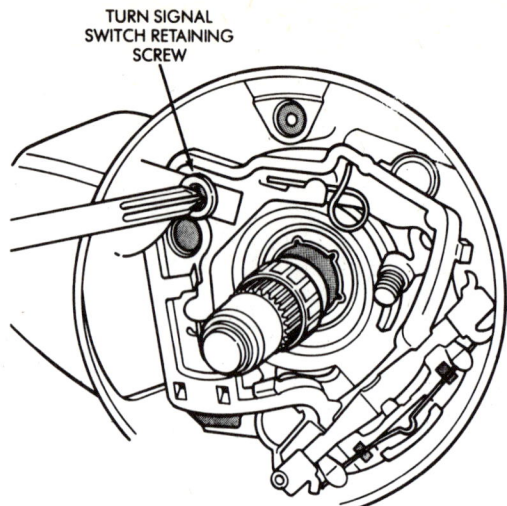

Turn signal switch retaining screw

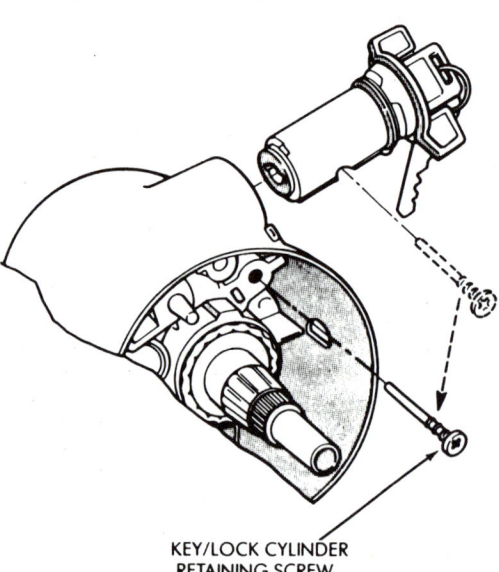

Key/lock cylinder removal

4. Turn the lock cylinder clockwise, two detent positions past OFF-LOCK.
5. Compress the lock cylinder retaining tab using a thin-bladed screwdriver and remove the lock cylinder from the column.
6. Installation is the reverse of removal.

Ignition Switch

REMOVAL AND INSTALLATION

1. Place the ignition lock in the OFF-LOCK position.
2. Remove the two switch mounting screws.
3. Disconnect the switch from the rod.
4. Disconnect the wiring and remove the switch.
5. Installation for non-tilt columns:

SUSPENSION AND STEERING 387

a. With the rod disconnected, move the slider to the extreme left (ACCESSORY) position. Left is the steering wheel end of the switch.

b. Position the rod in the slider hole and position the switch on the column, with the screws loosely installed.

c. Hold the key in the ACCESSORY position and push the switch down the column slightly to remove any slack in the rod. Tighten the screws securely.

d. Connect the white connector, then the black connector.

6. Installation for tilt columns:

a. With the rod disconnected, move the slider to the extreme right (ACCESSORY) position. Right is the end of the switch away from the steering wheel.

b. Position the rod in the slider hole and position the switch on the column, with the screws loosely installed.

c. Hold the key in the ACCESSORY position and lightly push the switch down the column slightly to remove any slack in the rod. Tighten the screws securely.

d. Connect the white connector, then the black connector.

7. Install any removed parts.

Steering Column

REMOVAL AND INSTALLATION

NOTE: *Hammering on, or dropping the column will damage the plastic fasteners that maintain column rigidity.*

1. Disconnect the battery ground.
2. Matchmark the intermediate shaft and steering shaft.
3. Remove the pinch bolt connecting the intermediate shaft and steering shaft.

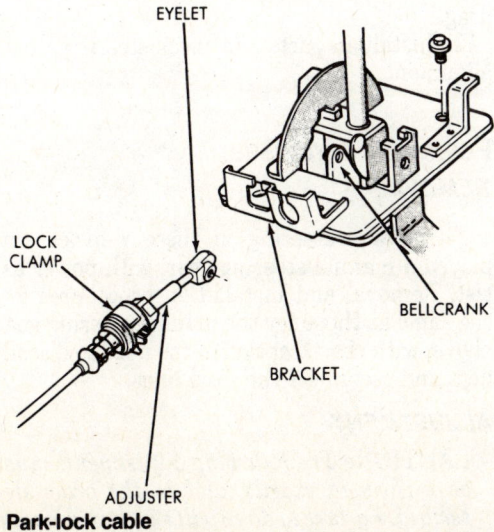

Park-lock cable

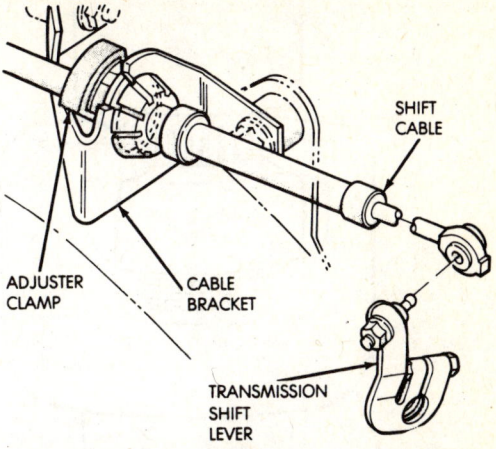

Shift control cable adjustment

4. Remove the lower instrument panel part.
5. Support the column and disconnect it from the instrument panel bracket. Lower the column.
6. Disconnect the ignition switch harness, dimmer switch harness, turn signal switch harness, wiper switch harness, cruise control harness and automatic transmission park/lock cable.
7. Unbolt the column toe plate from the dash panel and pull the column from the truck.

CAUTION: *Use only the specified fasteners when installing the column. If any fastener must be replaced, the replacement part must meet the exact specifications of the original. The use of subgrade or overlength fasteners will cause a failure in the performance of the impact absorbing column.*

8. Installation is the reverse of removal. Install all fasteners finger tight, then, when all the fasteners are installed, tighten them. *Never allow the column to hang unsupported!* Observe the following torques:

• Column mounting bracket-to-instrument panel: 22 ft. lbs.
• Toe plate-to-dash panel: 6 ft. lbs.
• Intermediate shaft-to-steering shaft pinch bolt: 33 ft. lbs.

Manual Steering Gear

REMOVAL AND INSTALLATION

1. Disconnect the steering shaft from the gear.
2. Raise and support the truck on jackstands.
3. Disconnect the center link from the pitman arm.
4. Remove the front stabilizer bar.
5. Remove the pitman arm nut, matchmark the arm and shaft, and remove the arm with a puller.

SUSPENSION AND STEERING

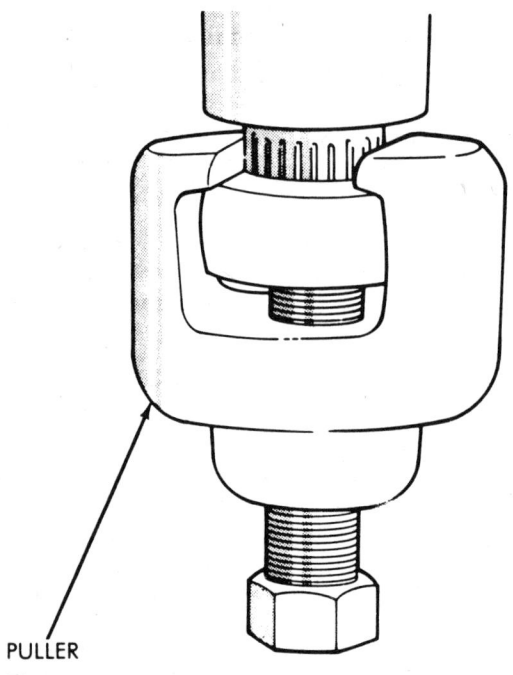

Pitman arm removal

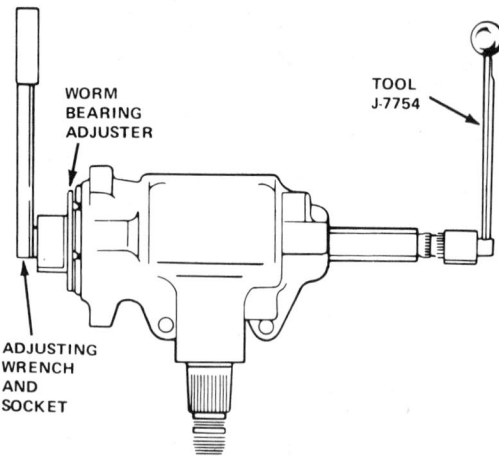

Adjusting worm bearing preload on manual steering gears

6. Unbolt and remove the gear.
7. Installation is the reverse of removal. The pitman arm nut MUST be securely staked. Observe the following torques:
  • Steering gear-to-frame: 65 ft. lbs.
  • Pitman arm-to-shaft: 185 ft. lbs.
  • Stabilizer bar-to-frame: 55 ft. lbs.
  • Stabilizer bar-to-link: 27 ft. lbs.
  • Center link-to-pitman arm: 55 ft. lbs.

ADJUSTMENT

CAUTION: *Follow the adjustment procedures in the order listed below. Failure to follow the procedures exactly will result in gear failure.*

1. Raise and support the truck on jackstands.
2. Check the steering gear mounting bolt torque.
3. Matchmark the pitman arm and shaft, and remove the pitman arm nut. Remove the arm with a puller.
4. Loosen the pitman adjusting screw locknut, then back off the adjusting screw 2-3 turns.
5. Remove the horn button and cover. Slowly turn the steering wheel in one direction as far as it will go, then back ½ turn.
6. Install a socket and inch-pound torque wrench in the steering wheel nut. Measure the worm bearing preload by turning the wheel through a 90° arc (¼ turn) with the wrench. Preload should be 5-8 in. lbs.
7. If preload is not within specifications, turn the adjuster screw clockwise to increase, or counterclockwise to decrease, the preload.
8. When the desired preload is attained, tighten the adjuster locknut to 90 ft. lbs. and recheck the adjustment.
9. Rotate the steering wheel slowly from lock-to-lock, counting the number of turns. Turn the wheel back, ½ the number of turns to center the gear, then turn the wheel ½ turn off of center.
10. Install the inch-pound torque wrench and socket on the steering wheel nut. Measure the torque required to tun the gear through the center point of travel. The drag should equal the worm bearing preload torque plus 4-10 in. lbs., but not exceed a total of 18 in. lbs.
11. If adjustment is required, loosen the pitman shaft screw locknut and turn the adjusting screw to obtain the desired torque. Tighten the locknut to 25 ft. lbs. and recheck the overcenter drag.
12. Install all parts and check steering wheel alignment.

Power Steering Gear

REMOVAL

The power steering in these vehicles employed a manual steering gear, with power assist. Removal and installation procedures are the same as those for the manual steering gear above, with the exception of the need to disconnect and reconnect the fluid lines.

ADJUSTMENT

CAUTION: *The following adjustments must be performed exactly, and in the order described. Failure to do so will result in damage* to the steering gear and a lack of steering response. Always adjust the worm bearing preload first.

Worm Bearing Preload

1. Remove the gear and place in on a clean workbench.
2. Remove the adjuster plug locknut. Seat the adjuster plug firmly by applying about 20 ft. lbs. of torque.
3. Place an index mark on the gear housing, opposite one of the adjuster plug holes.
4. Going counterclockwise, make another mark $3/16$-$1/4''$ from the first mark.
5. Turn the adjuster plug counterclockwise until the hole, which was aligned with the first mark, is now aligned with the second mark.
6. Install the adjuster plug locknut and torque it to 85 ft. lbs., making certain that the adjuster plug does not move.
7. Turn the stub shaft clockwise to its stop, then turn it back $1/4$ turn.
8. Using an inch pound (in. lbs.) torque wrench with a 50 in. lbs. scale and a 12 point deep socket on the stub shaft, take a reading of effort when the beam of the torque wrench passes the vertical point while turning. Torque at this point must be 4-10 in. lbs. If the reading is not correct, the adjuster plug is either not set correctly or moved while tightening the locknut, or, there is internal damage in the gear.

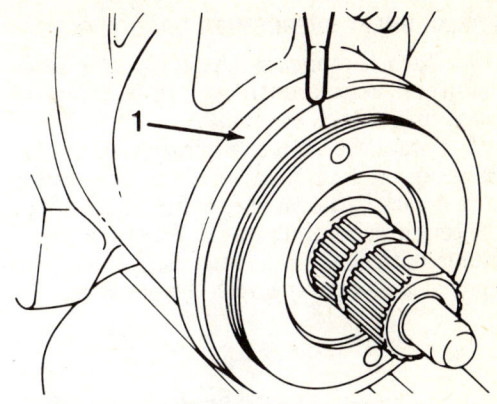

Making the initial mark on the housing

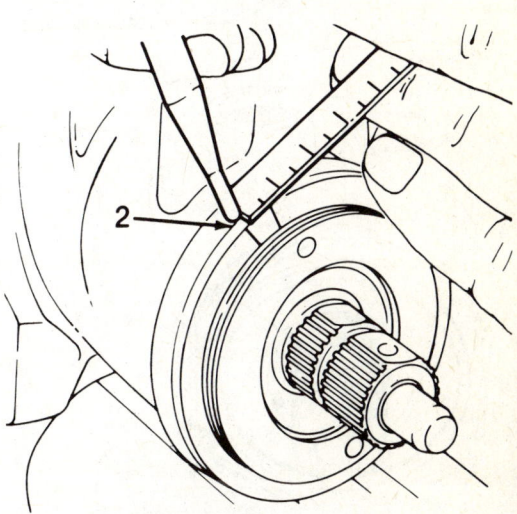

Making the second mark on the housing

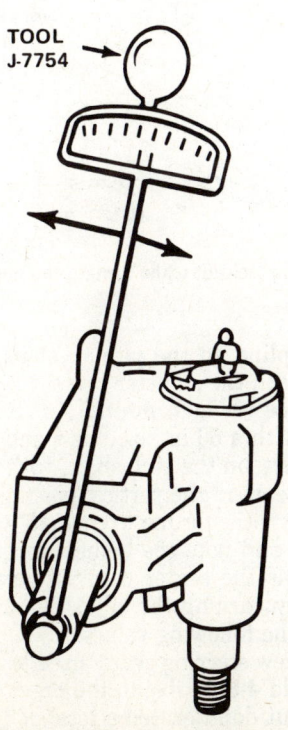

Adjusting pitman shaft overcenter drag

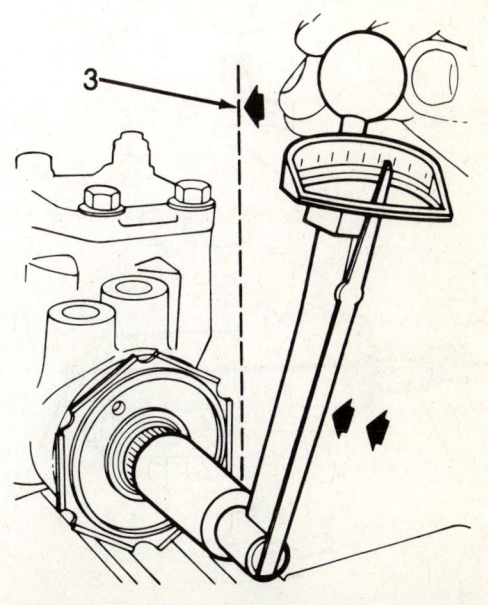

Measuring wormshaft bearing preload. 3 is the imaginary vertical line for reference

SUSPENSION AND STEERING

PITMAN SHAFT OVERCENTER DRAG TORQUE

1. Turn the pitman shaft adjuster screw counterclockwise until it is fully extended, then, turn it back ½ turn.
2. Rotate the stub shaft from stop to stop, counting the total number of full turns, then, turn it back ½ the number of full turns. This is the center point of its travel. When the gear is centered, the flat on the stub shaft should face upward and be parallel with the side cover. The

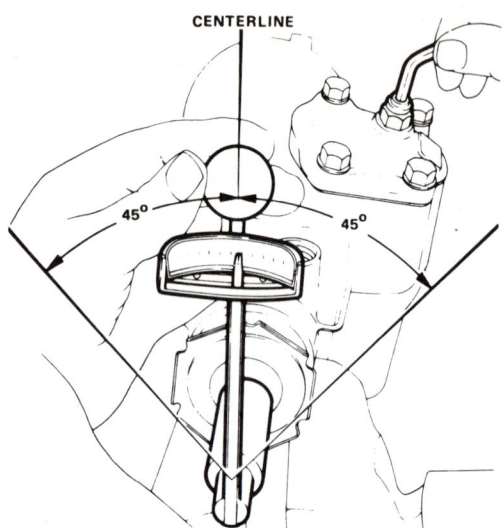

Measuring pitman shaft overcenter drag torque

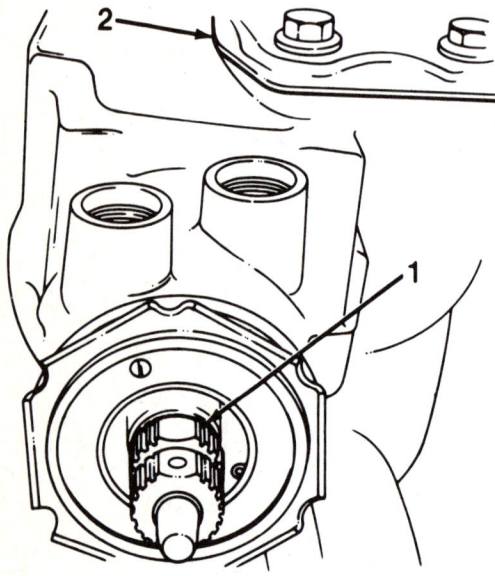

Stubshaft (1) position with gear centered. 2 is the gear housing

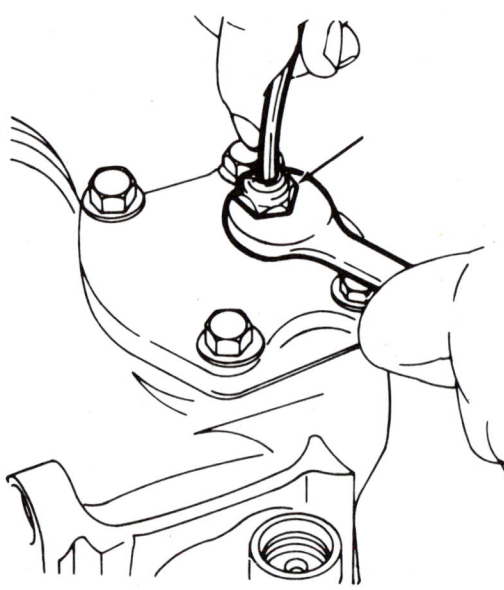

Holding the locknut while turning the adjusting nut

master spline on the pitman shaft should be aligned with the adjuster screw.

3. Place an inch pound (in. lbs.) torque wrench with a 50 in. lbs. scale, and a 12 point deep socket, on the stub shaft, with the torque wrench beam in the vertical position.
4. Rotate the torque wrench 45° to each side of center and note the highest torque reading on or near the center point. Adjust the drag torque, by turning the adjusting screw clockwise, to the following values:

- On new steering gears (used less than 400 miles), add 4-8 in. lbs. to the previously noted torque, but don't exceed a total of 18 in. lbs.
- On used gears (used 400 miles or more),

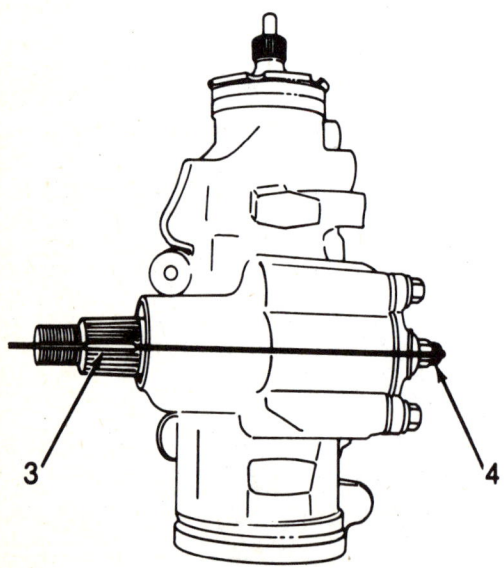

Pitman shaft master spline (3) position with the gear centered. 4 is the adjusting screw

SUSPENSION AND STEERING

add 4-5 in. lbs. to the previously noted torque, but don't exceed a total of 14 in. lbs.
5. When adjustment is complete, tighten the locknut to 20 ft. lbs.
6. Install the gear in the truck.

INSTALLATION

See the procedures for manual steering gear.

Power Steering Pump

REMOVAL AND INSTALLATION

Engines with a Serpentine Drive Belt

NOTE: *A belt tension gauge is needed for this job.*

1. Loosen the alternator adjustment and pivot bolts.
2. Insert the drive lug of a ½" drive ratchet into the adjustment hole in the alternator bracket and move the alternator to relieve tension on the belt.
3. Remove the drive belt.
4. Remove the air cleaner.
5. Disconnect the hoses at the pump and cap the hose ends.
6. Remove the front bracket-to-engine bolts.
7. Support the pump with your hand. Remove the pump-to-rear bracket nuts.
8. Lift out the pump.
9. Installation is the reverse of removal. Torque the pump-to-bracket nuts to 28 ft. lbs.; the bracket-to-engine bolts to 33 ft. lbs. Install the drive belt. Using the ½" drive ratchet, move the alternator to put tension on the belt, tight-

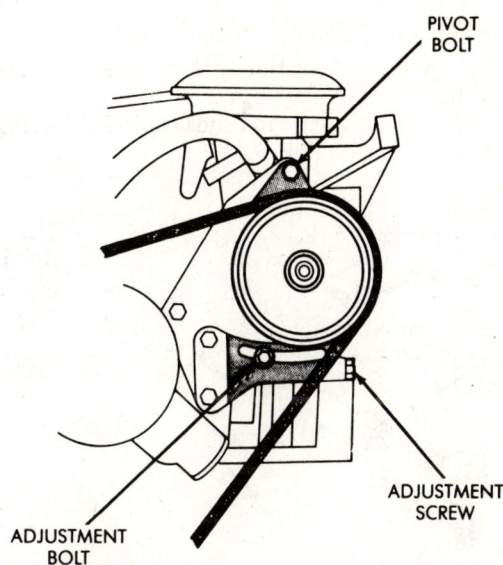

Power steering pump mounting for the 4-150 and 6-243 w/serpentine belt

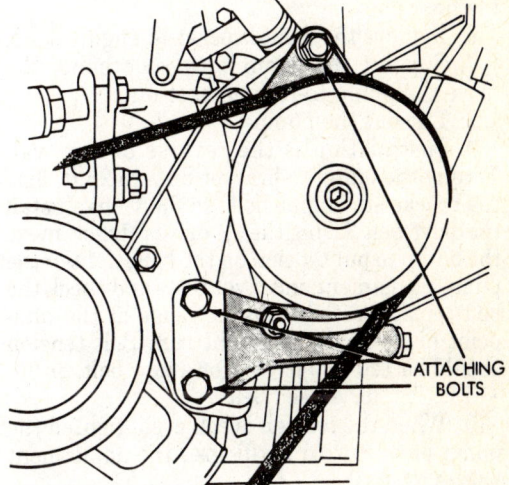

Front bracket bolts

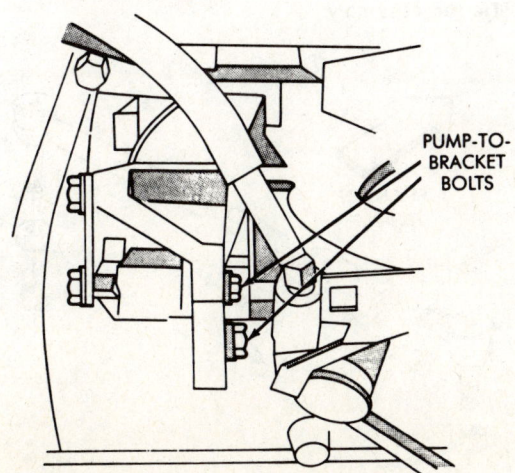

Power steering pump-to-bracket bolts

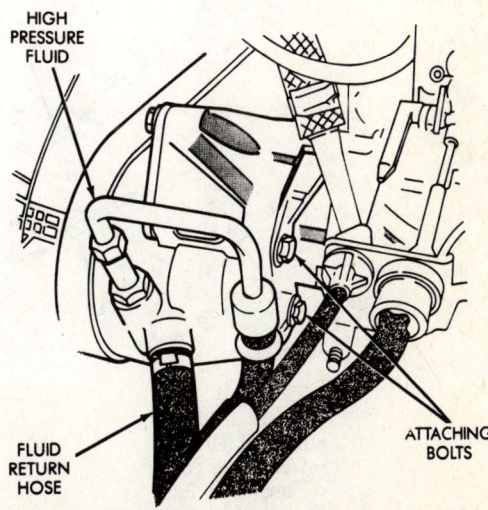

Rear bracket bolts and hose connections

392 SUSPENSION AND STEERING

en the alternator adjustment and pivot bolts and check the belt tension with a tension gauge at the mid-point of its longest straight run. Belt tension should be 180-200 ft. lbs. for a new belt, or 140-160 ft. lbs. for a used belt.

10. When the tension is achieved, tighten the alternator pivot bolt to 28 ft. lbs.; the adjustment bolt to 18 ft. lbs.

Engines with a V-type Drive Belt

1. Loosen the power steering pump adjustment and pivot bolts.
2. Insert the drive lug of a ½" drive ratchet into the adjustment hole in the pump rear bracket and move the pump to relieve tension on the belt.
3. Remove the drive belt.
4. Remove the air cleaner.
5. Disconnect the hoses at the pump and cap the hose ends.
6. Remove the front bracket-to-engine bolts.
7. Support the pump with your hand. Remove the pump-to-rear bracket nuts.
8. Lift out the pump.
9. Installation is the reverse of removal. Torque the pump-to-bracket nuts to 28 ft. lbs.; the bracket-to-engine bolts to 33 ft. lbs. Install the drive belt. Using the ½" drive ratchet, move the pump to put tension on the belt, tighten the pump adjustment and pivot bolts and check the belt tension with a tension gauge at the mid-point of its longest straight run. Belt tension should be 120-160 ft. lbs. for a new belt, or 90-115 ft. lbs. for a used belt.
10. When the tension is achieved, tighten the pump pivot nut to 21 ft. lbs.; the adjustment bolt to 21 ft. lbs.

Pitman Arm (Steering Arm)
REMOVAL AND INSTALLATION

1. Raise and support the vehicle on jackstands.
2. Place the wheels in a straight ahead position.
3. Remove the cotter pin and nut and disconnect the connecting rod from the pitman arm.
4. Matchmark the pitman arm and steering gear housing for installation alignment.
5. Remove the pitman arm nut. Some steering gears have a staked washer securing the nut. The arms of this washer must be bent out of the way to remove the nut.
6. Installation is the reverse of removal. Torque the pitman arm nut to 185 ft. lbs.

Tie Rod End
REMOVAL AND INSTALLATION

1. Remove the cotter pins and retaining nuts at both ends of the tie rod.
2. Remove the tie rod ends from the steering arm and center link.

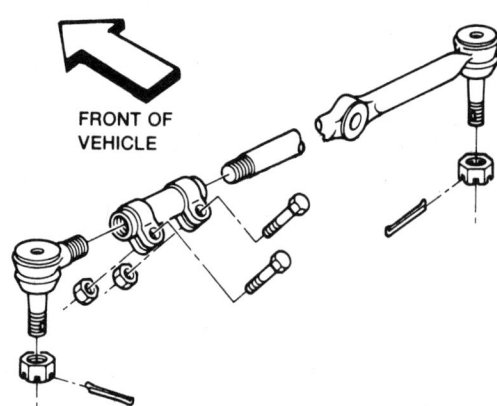

Tie rod assembly

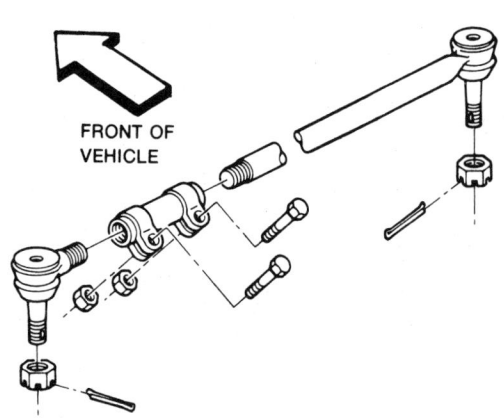

Connecting rod assembly

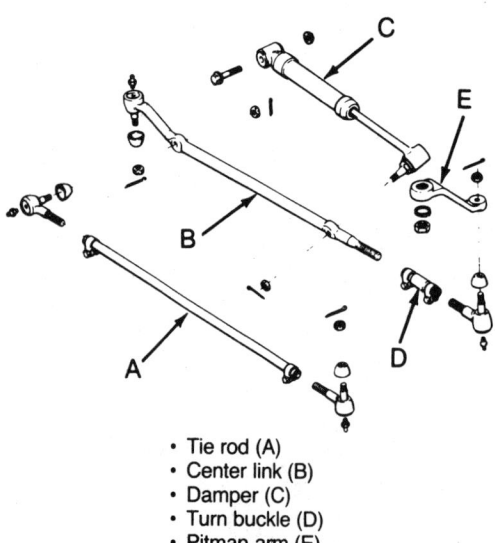

- Tie rod (A)
- Center link (B)
- Damper (C)
- Turn buckle (D)
- Pitman arm (E)

Steering linkage

SUSPENSION AND STEERING

3. Count the number of visible threads on the tie rod and unscrew the tie rod ends.
4. Installation is the reverse of removal. Install the tie rod ends, leaving the same number of threads exposed. Torque the retaining nuts to 35 ft. lbs.

Steering Connecting Rod (Drag Link)
REMOVAL AND INSTALLATION

1. Raise and support the front end on jackstands.
2. Place the wheels in a straight ahead position.
3. Remove the cotter pin and nut and disconnect the steering damper from the connecting rod.
4. Remove the cotter pins and nuts at each end of the rod, and disconnect the connecting rod from the knuckle and the pitman arm.
5. Install the connecting rod, with the wheels straight ahead and the pitman arm parallel with the vehicle centerline. Install the nuts and torque all three nuts to 35 ft. lbs.

Troubleshooting the Steering Column

Problem	Cause	Solution
Will not lock	• Lockbolt spring broken or defective	• Replace lock bolt spring
High effort (required to turn ignition key and lock cylinder)	• Lock cylinder defective • Ignition switch defective • Rack preload spring broken or deformed • Burr on lock sector, lock rack, housing, support or remote rod coupling • Bent sector shaft • Defective lock rack • Remote rod bent, deformed • Ignition switch mounting bracket bent • Distorted coupling slot in lock rack (tilt column)	• Replace lock cylinder • Replace ignition switch • Replace preload spring • Remove burr • Replace shaft • Replace lock rack • Replace rod • Straighten or replace • Replace lock rack
Will stick in "start"	• Remote rod deformed • Ignition switch mounting bracket bent	• Straighten or replace • Straighten or replace
Key cannot be removed in "off-lock"	• Ignition switch is not adjusted correctly • Defective lock cylinder	• Adjust switch • Replace lock cylinder
Lock cylinder can be removed without depressing retainer	• Lock cylinder with defective retainer • Burr over retainer slot in housing cover or on cylinder retainer	• Replace lock cylinder • Remove burr
High effort on lock cylinder between "off" and "off-lock"	• Distorted lock rack • Burr on tang of shift gate (automatic column) • Gearshift linkage not adjusted	• Replace lock rack • Remove burr • Adjust linkage
Noise in column	• One click when in "off-lock" position and the steering wheel is moved (all except automatic column) • Coupling bolts not tightened • Lack of grease on bearings or bearing surfaces • Upper shaft bearing worn or broken • Lower shaft bearing worn or broken • Column not correctly aligned • Coupling pulled apart • Broken coupling lower joint	• Normal—lock bolt is seating • Tighten pinch bolts • Lubricate with chassis grease • Replace bearing assembly • Replace bearing. Check shaft and replace if scored. • Align column • Replace coupling • Repair or replace joint and align column

Troubleshooting the Steering Column (cont.)

Problem	Cause	Solution
Noise in column (cont.)	• Steering shaft snap ring not seated	• Replace ring. Check for proper seating in groove.
	• Shroud loose on shift bowl. Housing loose on jacket—will be noticed with ignition in "off-lock" and when torque is applied to steering wheel.	• Position shroud over lugs on shift bowl. Tighten mounting screws.
High steering shaft effort	• Column misaligned • Defective upper or lower bearing • Tight steering shaft universal joint • Flash on I.D. of shift tube at plastic joint (tilt column only) • Upper or lower bearing seized	• Align column • Replace as required • Repair or replace • Replace shift tube • Replace bearings
Lash in mounted column assembly	• Column mounting bracket bolts loose • Broken weld nuts on column jacket • Column capsule bracket sheared • Column bracket to column jacket mounting bolts loose • Loose lock shoes in housing (tilt column only) • Loose pivot pins (tilt column only) • Loose lock shoe pin (tilt column only) • Loose support screws (tilt column only)	• Tighten bolts • Replace column jacket • Replace bracket assembly • Tighten to specified torque • Replace shoes • Replace pivot pins and support • Replace pin and housing • Tighten screws
Housing loose (tilt column only)	• Excessive clearance between holes in support or housing and pivot pin diameters • Housing support-screws loose	• Replace pivot pins and support • Tighten screws
Steering wheel loose—every other tilt position (tilt column only)	• Loose fit between lock shoe and lock shoe pivot pin	• Replace lock shoes and pivot pin
Steering column not locking in any tilt position (tilt column only)	• Lock shoe seized on pivot pin • Lock shoe grooves have burrs or are filled with foreign material • Lock shoe springs weak or broken	• Replace lock shoes and pin • Clean or replace lock shoes • Replace springs
Noise when tilting column (tilt column only)	• Upper tilt bumpers worn • Tilt spring rubbing in housing	• Replace tilt bumper • Lubricate with chassis grease
One click when in "off-lock" position and the steering wheel is moved	• Seating of lock bolt	• None. Click is normal characteristic sound produced by lock bolt as it seats.
High shift effort (automatic and tilt column only)	• Column not correctly aligned • Lower bearing not aligned correctly • Lack of grease on seal or lower bearing areas	• Align column • Assemble correctly • Lubricate with chassis grease
Improper transmission shifting— automatic and tilt column only	• Sheared shift tube joint • Improper transmission gearshift linkage adjustment • Loose lower shift lever	• Replace shift tube • Adjust linkage • Replace shift tube

SUSPENSION AND STEERING

Troubleshooting the Turn Signal Switch

Problem	Cause	Solution
Turn signal will not cancel	• Loose switch mounting screws • Switch or anchor bosses broken • Broken, missing or out of position detent, or cancelling spring	• Tighten screws • Replace switch • Reposition springs or replace switch as required
Turn signal difficult to operate	• Turn signal lever loose • Switch yoke broken or distorted • Loose or misplaced springs • Foreign parts and/or materials in switch • Switch mounted loosely	• Tighten mounting screws • Replace switch • Reposition springs or replace switch • Remove foreign parts and/or material • Tighten mounting screws
Turn signal will not indicate lane change	• Broken lane change pressure pad or spring hanger • Broken, missing or misplaced lane change spring • Jammed wires	• Replace switch • Replace or reposition as required • Loosen mounting screws, reposition wires and retighten screws
Turn signal will not stay in turn position	• Foreign material or loose parts impeding movement of switch yoke • Defective switch	• Remove material and/or parts • Replace switch
Hazard switch cannot be pulled out	• Foreign material between hazard support cancelling leg and yoke	• Remove foreign material. No foreign material impeding function of hazard switch—replace turn signal switch.
No turn signal lights	• Inoperative turn signal flasher • Defective or blown fuse • Loose chassis to column harness connector • Disconnect column to chassis connector. Connect new switch to chassis and operate switch by hand. If vehicle lights now operate normally, signal switch is inoperative • If vehicle lights do not operate, check chassis wiring for opens, grounds, etc.	• Replace turn signal flasher • Replace fuse • Connect securely • Replace signal switch • Repair chassis wiring as required
Instrument panel turn indicator lights on but not flashing	• Burned out or damaged front or rear turn signal bulb • If vehicle lights do not operate, check light sockets for high resistance connections, the chassis wiring for opens, grounds, etc. • Inoperative flasher • Loose chassis to column harness connection • Inoperative turn signal switch • To determine if turn signal switch is defective, substitute new switch into circuit and operate switch by hand. If the vehicle's lights operate normally, signal switch is inoperative.	• Replace bulb • Repair chassis wiring as required • Replace flasher • Connect securely • Replace turn signal switch • Replace turn signal switch
Stop light not on when turn indicated	• Loose column to chassis connection • Disconnect column to chassis connector. Connect new switch into system without removing old.	• Connect securely • Replace signal switch

Troubleshooting the Turn Signal Switch (cont.)

Problem	Cause	Solution
Stop light not on when turn indicated (cont.)	Operate switch by hand. If brake lights work with switch in the turn position, signal switch is defective. • If brake lights do not work, check connector to stop light sockets for grounds, opens, etc.	• Repair connector to stop light circuits using service manual as guide
Turn indicator panel lights not flashing	• Burned out bulbs • High resistance to ground at bulb socket • Opens, ground in wiring harness from front turn signal bulb socket to indicator lights	• Replace bulbs • Replace socket • Locate and repair as required
Turn signal lights flash very slowly	• High resistance ground at light sockets • Incorrect capacity turn signal flasher or bulb • If flashing rate is still extremely slow, check chassis wiring harness from the connector to light sockets for high resistance • Loose chassis to column harness connection • Disconnect column to chassis connector. Connect new switch into system without removing old. Operate switch by hand. If flashing occurs at normal rate, the signal switch is defective.	• Repair high resistance grounds at light sockets • Replace turn signal flasher or bulb • Locate and repair as required • Connect securely • Replace turn signal switch
Hazard signal lights will not flash—turn signal functions normally	• Blow fuse • Inoperative hazard warning flasher • Loose chassis-to-column harness connection • Disconnect column to chassis connector. Connect new switch into system without removing old. Depress the hazard warning lights. If they now work normally, turn signal switch is defective. • If lights do not flash, check wiring harness "K" lead for open between hazard flasher and connector. If open, fuse block is defective	• Replace fuse • Replace hazard warning flasher in fuse panel • Conect securely • Replace turn signal switch • Repair or replace brown wire or connector as required

Troubleshooting the Ignition Switch

Problem	Cause	Solution
Ignition switch electrically inoperative	• Loose or defective switch connector • Feed wire open (fusible link) • Defective ignition switch	• Tighten or replace connector • Repair or replace • Replace ignition switch
Engine will not crank	• Ignition switch not adjusted properly	• Adjust switch
Ignition switch wil not actuate mechanically	• Defective ignition switch • Defective lock sector • Defective remote rod	• Replace switch • Replace lock sector • Replace remote rod
Ignition switch cannot be adjusted correctly	• Remote rod deformed	• Repair, straighten or replace

SUSPENSION AND STEERING

Troubleshooting the Manual Steering Gear

Problem	Cause	Solution
Hard or erratic steering	• Incorrect tire pressure	• Inflate tires to recommended pressures
	• Insufficient or incorrect lubrication	• Lubricate as required (refer to Maintenance Section)
	• Suspension, or steering linkage parts damaged or misaligned	• Repair or replace parts as necessary
	• Improper front wheel alignment	• Adjust incorrect wheel alignment angles
	• Incorrect steering gear adjustment	• Adjust steering gear
	• Sagging springs	• Replace springs
Play or looseness in steering	• Steering wheel loose	• Inspect shaft spines and repair as necessary. Tighten attaching nut and stake in place.
	• Steering linkage or attaching parts loose or worn	• Tighten, adjust, or replace faulty components
	• Pitman arm loose	• Inspect shaft splines and repair as necessary. Tighten attaching nut and stake in place
	• Steering gear attaching bolts loose	• Tighten bolts
	• Loose or worn wheel bearings	• Adjust or replace bearings
	• Steering gear adjustment incorrect or parts badly worn	• Adjust gear or replace defective parts
Wheel shimmy or tramp	• Improper tire pressure	• Inflate tires to recommended pressures
	• Wheels, tires, or brake rotors out-of-balance or out-of-round	• Inspect and replace or balance parts
	• Inoperative, worn, or loose shock absorbers or mounting parts	• Repair or replace shocks or mountings
	• Loose or worn steering or suspension parts	• Tighten or replace as necessary
	• Loose or worn wheel bearings	• Adjust or replace bearings
	• Incorrect steering gear adjustments	• Adjust steering gear
	• Incorrect front wheel alignment	• Correct front wheel alignment
Tire wear	• Improper tire pressure	• Inflate tires to recommended pressures
	• Failure to rotate tires	• Rotate tires
	• Brakes grabbing	• Adjust or repair brakes
	• Incorrect front wheel alignment	• Align incorrect angles
	• Broken or damaged steering and suspension parts	• Repair or replace defective parts
	• Wheel runout	• Replace faulty wheel
	• Excessive speed on turns	• Make driver aware of conditions
Vehicle leads to one side	• Improper tire pressures	• Inflate tires to recommended pressures
	• Front tires with uneven tread depth, wear pattern, or different cord design (i.e., one bias ply and one belted or radial tire on front wheels)	• Install tires of same cord construction and reasonably even tread depth, design, and wear pattern
	• Incorrect front wheel alignment	• Align incorrect angles
	• Brakes dragging	• Adjust or repair brakes
	• Pulling due to uneven tire construction	• Replace faulty tire

Troubleshooting the Power Steering Gear

Problem	Cause	Solution
Hissing noise in steering gear	• There is some noise in all power steering systems. One of the most common is a hissing sound most evident at standstill parking. There is no relationship between this noise and performance of the steering. Hiss may be expected when steering wheel is at end of travel or when slowly turning at standstill.	• Slight hiss is normal and in no way affects steering. Do not replace valve unless hiss is extremely objectionable. A replacement valve will also exhibit slight noise and is not always a cure. Investigate clearance around flexible coupling rivets. Be sure steering shaft and gear are aligned so flexible coupling rotates in a flat plane and is not distorted as shaft rotates. Any metal-to-metal contacts through flexible coupling will transmit valve hiss into passenger compartment through the steering column.
Rattle or chuckle noise in steering gear	• Gear loose on frame	• Check gear-to-frame mounting screws. Tighten screws to 88 N·m (65 foot pounds) torque.
	• Steering linkage looseness	• Check linkage pivot points for wear. Replace if necessary.
	• Pressure hose touching other parts of car	• Adjust hose position. Do not bend tubing by hand.
	• Loose pitman shaft over center adjustment NOTE: A slight rattle may occur on turns because of increased clearance off the "high point." This is normal and clearance must not be reduced below specified limits to eliminate this slight rattle.	• Adjust to specifications
	• Loose pitman arm	• Tighten pitman arm nut to specifications
Squawk noise in steering gear when turning or recovering from a turn	• Damper O-ring on valve spool cut	• Replace damper O-ring
Poor return of steering wheel to center	• Tires not properly inflated	• Inflate to specified pressure
	• Lack of lubrication in linkage and ball joints	• Lube linkage and ball joints
	• Lower coupling flange rubbing against steering gear adjuster plug	• Loosen pinch bolt and assemble properly
	• Steering gear to column misalignment	• Align steering column
	• Improper front wheel alignment	• Check and adjust as necessary
	• Steering linkage binding	• Replace pivots
	• Ball joints binding	• Replace ball joints
	• Steering wheel rubbing against housing	• Align housing
	• Tight or frozen steering shaft bearings	• Replace bearings
	• Sticking or plugged valve spool	• Remove and clean or replace valve
	• Steering gear adjustments over specifications	• Check adjustment with gear out of car. Adjust as required.
	• Kink in return hose	• Replace hose
Car leads to one side or the other (keep in mind road condition and wind. Test car in both directions on flat road)	• Front end misaligned	• Adjust to specifications
	• Unbalanced steering gear valve NOTE: If this is cause, steering effort will be very light in direction of lead and normal or heavier in opposite direction	• Replace valve

Troubleshooting the Power Steering Gear (cont.)

Problem	Cause	Solution
Momentary increase in effort when turning wheel fast to right or left	• Low oil level • Pump belt slipping • High internal leakage	• Add power steering fluid as required • Tighten or replace belt • Check pump pressure. (See pressure test)
Steering wheel surges or jerks when turning with engine running especially during parking	• Low oil level • Loose pump belt • Steering linkage hitting engine oil pan at full turn • Insufficient pump pressure • Pump flow control valve sticking	• Fill as required • Adjust tension to specification • Correct clearance • Check pump pressure. (See pressure test). Replace relief valve if defective. • Inspect for varnish or damage, replace if necessary
Excessive wheel kickback or loose steering	• Air in system • Steering gear loose on frame • Steering linkage joints worn enough to be loose • Worn poppet valve • Loose thrust bearing preload adjustment • Excessive overcenter lash	• Add oil to pump reservoir and bleed by operating steering. Check hose connectors for proper torque and adjust as required. • Tighten attaching screws to specified torque • Replace loose pivots • Replace poppet valve • Adjust to specification with gear out of vehicle • Adjust to specification with gear out of car
Hard steering or lack of assist	• Loose pump belt • Low oil level NOTE: Low oil level will also result in excessive pump noise • Steering gear to column misalignment • Lower coupling flange rubbing against steering gear adjuster plug • Tires not properly inflated	• Adjust belt tension to specification • Fill to proper level. If excessively low, check all lines and joints for evidence of external leakage. Tighten loose connectors. • Align steering column • Loosen pinch bolt and assemble properly • Inflate to recommended pressure
Foamy milky power steering fluid, low fluid level and possible low pressure	• Air in the fluid, and loss of fluid due to internal pump leakage causing overflow	• Check for leak and correct. Bleed system. Extremely cold temperatures will cause system aeration should the oil level be low. If oil level is correct and pump still foams, remove pump from vehicle and separate reservoir from housing. Check welsh plug and housing for cracks. If plug is loose or housing is cracked, replace housing.
Low pressure due to steering pump	• Flow control valve stuck or inoperative • Pressure plate not flat against cam ring	• Remove burrs or dirt or replace. Flush system. • Correct
Low pressure due to steering gear	• Pressure loss in cylinder due to worn piston ring or badly worn housing bore • Leakage at valve rings, valve body-to-worm seal	• Remove gear from car for disassembly and inspection of ring and housing bore • Remove gear from car for disassembly and replace seals

SUSPENSION AND STEERING

Troubleshooting the Power Steering Pump

Problem	Cause	Solution
Chirp noise in steering pump	• Loose belt	• Adjust belt tension to specification
Belt squeal (particularly noticeable at full wheel travel and stand still parking)	• Loose belt	• Adjust belt tension to specification
Growl noise in steering pump	• Excessive back pressure in hoses or steering gear caused by restriction	• Locate restriction and correct. Replace part if necessary.
Growl noise in steering pump (particularly noticeable at stand still parking)	• Scored pressure plates, thrust plate or rotor • Extreme wear of cam ring	• Replace parts and flush system • Replace parts
Groan noise in steering pump	• Low oil level • Air in the oil. Poor pressure hose connection.	• Fill reservoir to proper level • Tighten connector to specified torque. Bleed system by operating steering from right to left—full turn.
Rattle noise in steering pump	• Vanes not installed properly • Vanes sticking in rotor slots	• Install properly • Free up by removing burrs, varnish, or dirt
Swish noise in steering pump	• Defective flow control valve	• Replace part
Whine noise in steering pump	• Pump shaft bearing scored	• Replace housing and shaft. Flush system.
Hard steering or lack of assist	• Loose pump belt • Low oil level in reservoir NOTE: Low oil level will also result in excessive pump noise • Steering gear to column misalignment • Lower coupling flange rubbing against steering gear adjuster plug • Tires not properly inflated	• Adjust belt tension to specification • Fill to proper level. If excessively low, check all lines and joints for evidence of external leakage. Tighten loose connectors. • Align steering column • Loosen pinch bolt and assemble properly • Inflate to recommended pressure
Foaming milky power steering fluid, low fluid level and possible low pressure	• Air in the fluid, and loss of fluid due to internal pump leakage causing overflow	• Check for leaks and correct. Bleed system. Extremely cold temperatures will cause system aeration should the oil level be low. If oil level is correct and pump still foams, remove pump from vehicle and separate reservoir from body. Check welsh plug and body for cracks. If plug is loose or body is cracked, replace body.
Low pump pressure	• Flow control valve stuck or inoperative • Pressure plate not flat against cam ring	• Remove burrs or dirt or replace. Flush system. • Correct
Momentary increase in effort when turning wheel fast to right or left	• Low oil level in pump • Pump belt slipping • High internal leakage	• Add power steering fluid as required • Tighten or replace belt • Check pump pressure. (See pressure test)
Steering wheel surges or jerks when turning with engine running especially during parking	• Low oil level • Loose pump belt • Steering linkage hitting engine oil pan at full turn • Insufficient pump pressure	• Fill as required • Adjust tension to specification • Correct clearance • Check pump pressure. (See pressure test). Replace flow control valve if defective.

Troubleshooting the Power Steering Pump (cont.)

Problem	Cause	Solution
Steering wheel surges or jerks when turning with engine running especially during parking (cont.)	• Sticking flow control valve	• Inspect for varnish or damage, replace if necessary
Excessive wheel kickback or loose steering	• Air in system	• Add oil to pump reservoir and bleed by operating steering. Check hose connectors for proper torque and adjust as required.
Low pump pressure	• Extreme wear of cam ring • Scored pressure plate, thrust plate, or rotor • Vanes not installed properly • Vanes sticking in rotor slots • Cracked or broken thrust or pressure plate	• Replace parts. Flush system. • Replace parts. Flush system. • Install properly • Freeup by removing burrs, varnish, or dirt • Replace part

Wheel Alignment Specifications

Years	Caster (deg.)		Camber (deg.)		Toe-in (in.)	Outer Wheel Turning Angle (deg.)
	Range	Pref.	Range	Pref.		
1984–86	7P to 8P	7½P	½N to ½P	0	0	32–33
1987–89	7P to 8P	7½P	¾N to ½P	0	0	32–33

Brakes

BRAKE SYSTEMS

Hydraulic System
BASIC OPERATING PRINCIPLES

Except Anti-Lock Braking System

Hydraulic systems are used to actuate the brakes of all modern automobiles. The system transports the power required to force the frictional surfaces of the braking system together from the pedal to the individual brake units at each wheel. A hydraulic system is used for two reasons. First, fluid under pressure can be carried to all parts of an automobile by small hoses-some of which are flexible-without taking up a significant amount of room or posing routing problems. Second, a great mechanical advantage can be given to the brake pedal end of the system, and the foot pressure required to actuate the brakes can be reduced by making the surface area of the master cylinder pistons smaller than that of any of the pistons in the wheel cylinders or calipers.

The master cylinder consists of a fluid reservoir and either a single or double cylinder and piston assembly. Double type master cylinders are designed to separate the front and rear braking systems hydraulically in case of a leak.

Steel lines carry the brake fluid to a point on the vehicle's frame near each of the vehicle's wheels. The fluid is then carried to the wheel cylinders by flexible tubes in order to allow for suspension and steering movements.

Each wheel cylinder contains two pistons, one at either end, which push outward in opposite directions. In disc brake systems, the cylinders are part of the calipers. One or four cylinders are used to force the brake pads against the disc, but all cylinders contain one piston only. All pistons employ some type of seal, usually made of rubber, to minimize fluid leakage. A rubber dust boot seals the outer end of the cylinder against dust and dirt. The boot fits around the outer end of the piston on disc brake calipers, and around the brake actuating rod on wheel cylinders.

The hydraulic system operates as follows: When at rest, the entire system, from the piston(s) in the master cylinder to those in the wheel cylinders or calipers, is full of brake fluid. Upon application of the brake pedal, fluid trapped in front of the master cylinder piston(s) is forced through the lines to the wheel cylinders. Here, it forces the pistons outward, in the case of drum brakes, and inward toward the disc, in the case of disc brakes. The motion of the pistons is opposed by return springs mounted outside the cylinders in drum brakes, and by internal springs or spring seals, in disc brakes.

Upon release of the brake pedal, a spring located inside the master cylinder immediately returns the master cylinder pistons to the normal position. The pistons contain check valves and the master cylinder has compensating ports drilled in it. These are uncovered as the pistons reach their normal position. The piston check valves allow fluid to flow toward the wheel cylinders or calipers as the pistons withdraw. Then, as the return springs force the brake pads or shoes into the released position, the excess fluid reservoir through the compensating ports. It is during the time the pedal is in the released position that any fluid that has leaked out of the system will be replaced through the compensating ports.

Dual circuit master cylinders employ two pistons, located one behind the other, in the same cylinder. The primary piston is actuated directly by mechanical linkage from the brake pedal. The secondary piston is actuated by fluid trapped between the two pistons. If a leak develops in front of the secondary piston, it moves forward until it bottoms against the front of the master cylinder, and the fluid trapped between the pistons will operate the rear brakes. If the rear brakes develop a leak, the primary piston will move forward until direct contact with the secondary piston takes place, and it will force the secondary piston to actuate the front brakes. In either case, the brake pedal moves farther when the brakes are applied, and less braking power is available.

All dual-circuit systems use a switch to warn the driver when only half of the brake system is operational. This switch is located in a valve body which is mounted on the firewall or the frame below the master cylinder. A hydraulic piston receives pressure from both circuits, each circuit's pressure being applied to one end of the piston. When the pressures are in balance, the piston remains stationary. When one circuit has a leak, however, the greater pressure in that circuit during application of the brakes will push the piston to one side, closing the switch and activating the brake warning light.

In disc brake systems, this valve body also contains a metering valve and, in some cases, a proportioning valve. The metering valve keeps pressure from traveling to the disc brakes on the front wheels until the brake shoes on the rear wheels have contacted the drums, ensuring that the front brakes will never be used alone. The proportioning valve controls the pressure to the rear brakes to avoid rear wheel lock-up during very hard braking.

Warning lights may be tested by depressing the brake pedal and holding it while opening one of the wheel cylinder bleeder screws. If this does not cause the light to go on, substitute a new lamp, make continuity checks, and, finally, replace the switch as necessary.

The hydraulic system may be checked for leaks by applying pressure to the pedal gradually and steadily. If the pedal sinks very slowly to the floor, the system has a leak. This is not to be confused with a springy or spongy feel due to the compression of air within the lines. If the system leaks, there will be a gradual change in the position of the pedal with a constant pressure.

Check for leaks along all lines and at wheel cylinders. If no external leaks are apparent, the problem is inside the master cylinder.

Disc Brakes
BASIC OPERATING PRINCIPLES

Instead of the traditional expanding brakes that press outward against a circular drum, disc brake systems utilize a disc (rotor) with brake pads positioned on either side of it. Braking effect is achieved in a manner similar to the way you would squeeze a spinning phonograph record between your fingers. The disc (rotor) is a casting with cooling fins between the two braking surfaces. This enables air to circulate between the braking surfaces making them less sensitive to heat buildup and more resistant to fade. Dirt and water do not affect braking action since contaminants are thrown off by the centrifugal action of the rotor or scraped off the by the pads. Also, the equal clamping action of the two brake pads tends to ensure uniform, straightline stops. Disc brakes are inherently self-adjusting.

There are three general types of disc brake:
1. A fixed caliper.
2. A floating caliper.
3. A sliding caliper.

The fixed caliper design uses two pistons mounted on either side of the rotor (in each side of the caliper). The caliper is mounted rigidly and does not move.

The sliding and floating designs are quite similar. In fact, these two types are often lumped together. In both designs, the pad on the inside of the rotor is moved into contact with the rotor by hydraulic force. The caliper, which is not held in a fixed position, moves slightly, bringing the outside pad into contact with the rotor. There are various methods of attaching floating calipers. Some pivot at the bottom or top, and some slide on mounting bolts. In any event, the end result is the same.

Drum Brakes
BASIC OPERATING PRINCIPLES

Drum brakes employ two brake shoes mounted on a stationary backing plate. These shoes are positioned inside a circular drum which ro-

Brake Specifications
All specifications in inches

Years	Master Cyl. Bore	Brake Disc		Brake Drum		Wheel Cyl. or Caliper Bore	
		Minimum Thickness	Maximum Run-out	Orig. Inside Dia.	Max. Wear Limit	Front	Rear
1984–86	0.937	0.8150	0.005	10.000	10.060	2.598	0.874
1987–89	0.937	0.8150	0.004	10.000	10.060	2.598	0.874

tates with the wheel assembly. The shoes are held in place by springs; this allows them to slide toward the drums (when they are applied) while keeping the linings and drums in alignment. The shoes are actuated by a wheel cylinder which is mounted at the top of the backing plate. When the brakes are applied, hydraulic pressure forces the wheel cylinder's actuating links outward. Since these links bear directly against the top of the brake shoes, the tops of the shoes are then forced against the inner side of the drum. This action forces the bottoms of the two shoes to contact the brake drum by rotating the entire assembly slightly (known as servo action). When pressure within the wheel cylinder is relaxed, return springs pull the shoes back away from the drum.

Most modern drum brakes are designed to self-adjust themselves during application when the vehicle is moving in reverse. This motion causes both shoes to rotate very slightly with the drum, rocking an adjusting lever, thereby causing rotation of the adjusting screw.

Power Boosters

Power brakes operate just as standard brake systems except in the actuation of the master cylinder pistons. A vacuum diaphragm is located on the front of the master cylinder and assists the driver in applying the brakes, reducing both the effort and travel he must put into moving the brake pedal.

The vacuum diaphragm housing is connected to the intake manifold by a vacuum hose. A check valve is placed at the point where the hose enters the diaphragm housing, so that during periods of low manifold vacuum brake assist vacuum will not be lost.

Depressing the brake pedal closes off the vacuum source and allows atmospheric pressure to enter on one side of the diaphragm. This causes the master cylinder pistons to move and apply the brakes. When the brake pedal is released, vacuum is applied to both sides of the diaphragm, and return springs return the diaphragm and master cylinder pistons to the released position. If the vacuum fails, the brake pedal rod will butt against the end of the master cylinder actuating rod, and direct mechanical application will occur as the pedal is depressed.

The hydraulic and mechanical problems that apply to conventional brake systems also apply to power brakes, and should be checked for if the tests below do not reveal the problem.

Test for a system vacuum leak as described below:
1. Operate the engine at idle without touching the brake pedal for at least one minute.
2. Turn off the engine, and wait one minute.
3. Test for the presence of assist vacuum by depressing the brake pedal and releasing it several times. Light application will produce less and less pedal travel, if vacuum was present. If there is no vacuum, air is leaking into the system somewhere.

Test for system operation as follows:
1. Pump the brake pedal (with engine off) until the supply vacuum is entirely gone.
2. Put a light, steady pressure on the pedal.
3. Start the engine, and operate it at idle. If the system is operating, the brake pedal should fall toward the floor if constant pressure is maintained on the pedal.

Power brake systems may be tested for hydraulic leaks just as ordinary systems are tested.

CAUTION: *Brake linings contain asbestos. Asbestos is a known cancer-causing agent. When working on brakes, remember that the dust which accumulates on the brake parts and/or in the drum contains asbestos. Always wear a protective face covering, such as a painter's mask, when working on the brakes. NEVER blow the dust from the brakes or drum! There are solvents made for the purpose of cleaning brake parts. Use them!*

Adjustments

When the brake linings become worn, effective brake pedal travel is reduced. Adjusting the brake shoes will restore the necessary travel for efficient braking.

Before adjusting the brakes, check the spring nuts, brake dust shield-to-axle flange bolts and wheel adjustments. Any looseness in these parts can cause erratic brake operation.

NOTE: *Disc brakes require no manual adjustment, nor are they adjustable. Therefore, the following applies only to drum brakes.*
1. Jack up the vehicle.
2. Remove the access slot cover and using a brake adjusting tool or screwdriver, rotate the

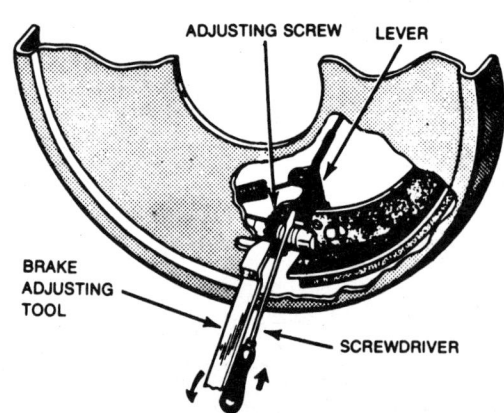

Adjusting drum brakes with starwheel adjusters

starwheel until the wheel is locked and can't be turned by hand. To tighten, rotate the starwheel in the clockwise direction.

3. Back off the starwheel at least 15 to 20 notches. To back off the starwheel on the brake, insert an ice pick or thin screwdriver in the adjusting screw slot to hold the automatic adjusting lever away from the starwheel. Do not attempt to back off on the adjusting screw without holding the adjusting lever away from the starwheel as the adjuster will be damaged.

BRAKE PEDAL FREE PLAY

NOTE: *Pedal free play is measured at the top of the pedal pad.*

Proper free play should be $1/16$-$1/4$". Free play is not adjustable. If free play is not correct, the problem is the result of worn or damaged parts.

Master Cylinder

REMOVAL AND INSTALLATION

Except Anti-Lock Brakes

1. Disconnect and plug the brake lines.
2. Disconnect the wires from the stoplight switch.
3. Remove all attaching bolts and nuts, and lift the assembly from the vehicle.
4. Prior to installation, fill the master cylinder and operate the pushrod until fluid squirts from the ports.
5. Installation is the reverse of removal. Torque the mounting nuts to 15-18 ft. lbs. Bleed the brake system.

OVERHAUL

NOTE: *Do not use any type of mineral oil, gasoline or kerosene to clean any part of any hydraulic brake system. These fluids will cause rubber parts to soften, swell, and distort, resulting in failure. Use only clean brake fluid or alcohol.*

1984-86

1. Remove the cover, drain the cylinder and mount it in a vise.
2. Using a drift or punch, push the primary piston inward and remove the snapring from its groove.
3. Remove the primary and secondary piston assemblies. It may be necessary to apply air pressure through the piston stop hole to free the secondary piston.
4. Inspect all parts after a thorough cleaning. Inspect the tube seats in the outlet ports. Replace the seats only if they are cracked, cocked or loose. To replace a seat:
   a. Drill out the seats with a $13/64$" drill bit.
   b. Place a flat washer on each port and thread a $1/4$-20 × $3/4$" long self tapping screw into the tube seat. Thread in the screw until the seat is loose.
   c. Pry out the seat.
   d. New seats may be pressed in using spare tube fitting nuts.

Rebuilding kits contain all the necessary parts. Replace all parts with those supplied in the kit. Never reuse a rubber part or any part that appears worn or damaged.

Imperfections in the bore may be removed by honing. If any imperfection remains after honing, replace the unit.

5. Prior to assembly, coat all parts with clean brake fluid.
6. Install the secondary piston seals. The seal lip of the rear seal must face the inside of the bore. The front seal lip must face outward when installed.

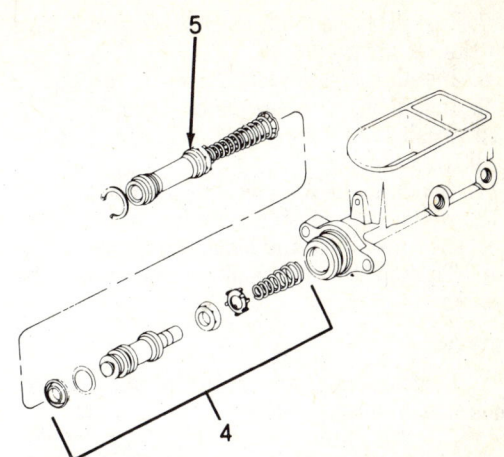
1984–86 master cylinder. 4 is the secondary piston; 5 is the primary piston

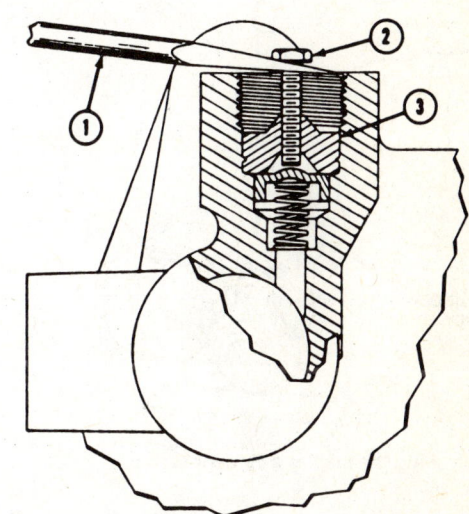
Removing the tube seats from the master cylinder with a screwdriver

7. Install the seal retainer and return spring on the secondary piston.
8. Install the secondary piston in the bore.
9. Install the primary piston assembly.
10. Push the primary piston inward and install the snapring.
11. Bench-bleed the master cylinder
12. Install the master cylinder, loosely connect the brake lines and bleed the master cylinder. Tighten the brake lines and bleed the system.

1987-89

1. Remove the cover, drain the cylinder and mount it in a vise.

2. Using a drift or punch, push the primary piston inward and remove the snapring from its groove.
3. Remove the primary and secondary piston

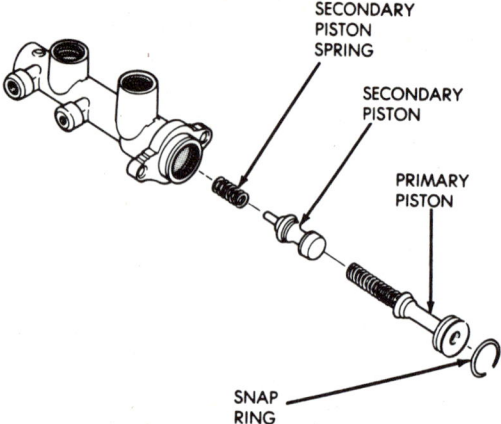
Removing the master cylinder pistons

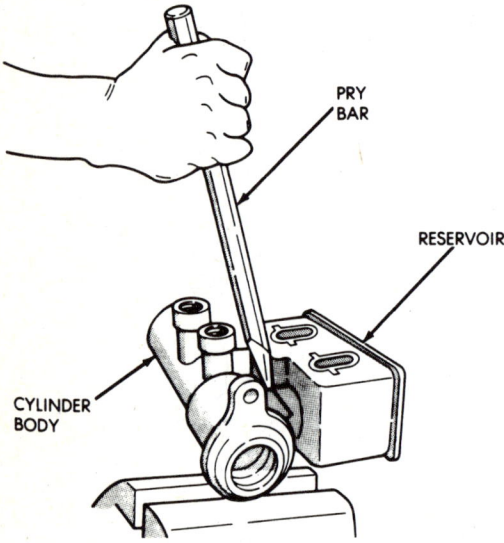
Removing the master cylinder reservoir

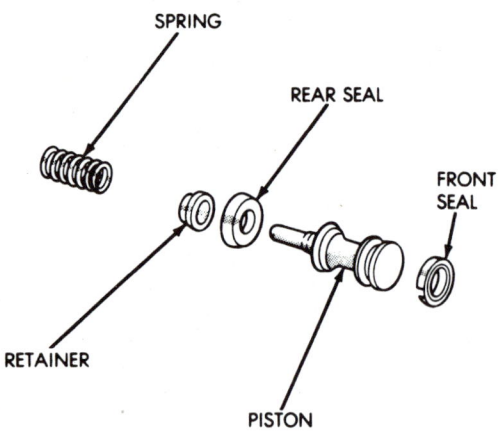
Secondary piston components

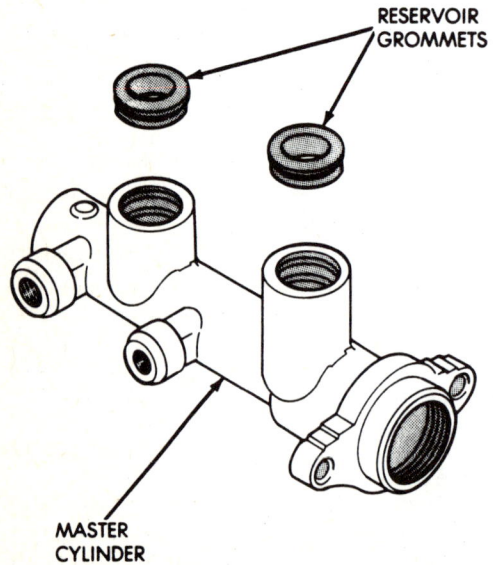
Removing the reservoir grommets

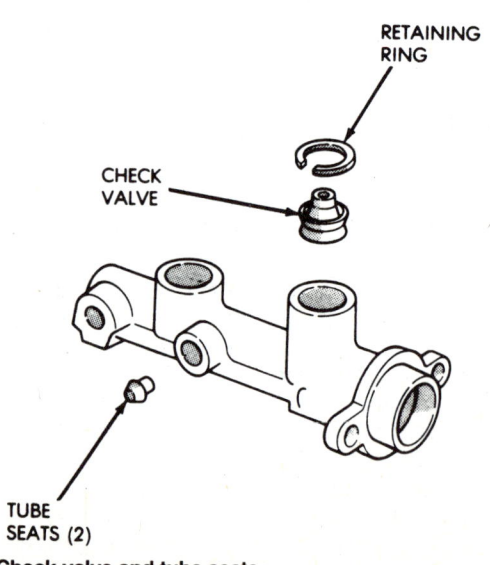
Check valve and tube seats

assemblies. It may be necessary to apply air pressure through the piston stop hole to free the secondary piston.

Rebuilding kits contain all the necessary parts. Replace all parts with those supplied in the kit. Never reuse a rubber part or any part that appears worn or damaged.

Imperfections in the bore may be removed by honing. If any imperfection remains after honing, replace the unit.

4. Prior to assembly, coat all parts with clean brake fluid.

5. Install the secondary piston seals. The seal ip of the rear seal must face the inside of the bore. The front seal lip must face outward when installed.

6. Install the seal retainer and return spring on the secondary piston.

7. Install the secondary piston in the bore.

8. Install the primary piston assembly.

9. Push the primary piston inward and install the snapring.

10. Bench-bleed the master cylinder

11. Install the master cylinder, loosely connect the brake lines and bleed the master cylinder. Tighten the brake lines and bleed the system.

Pressure Differential Valve

These vehicles use a pressure differential valve, mounted immediately below the master cylinder, and a mechanically activated height sensing proportioning valve located above the rear axle.

REMOVAL AND INSTALLATION

1. Disconnect the brake lines at the valve and plug them.
2. Unbolt and remove the valve.
3. Installation is the reverse of removal. Bleed the system.

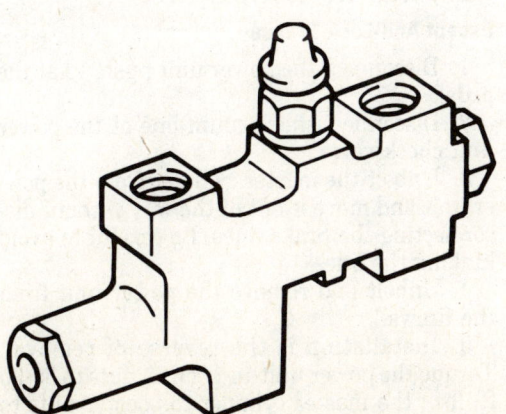

Pressure differential valve

Height Sensing Proportioning Valve

NOTE: *Any time the valve is adjusted, the lever bushing must be replaced. The adjustment must be made with the vehicle level and at curb weight. Special tools are needed for this job.*

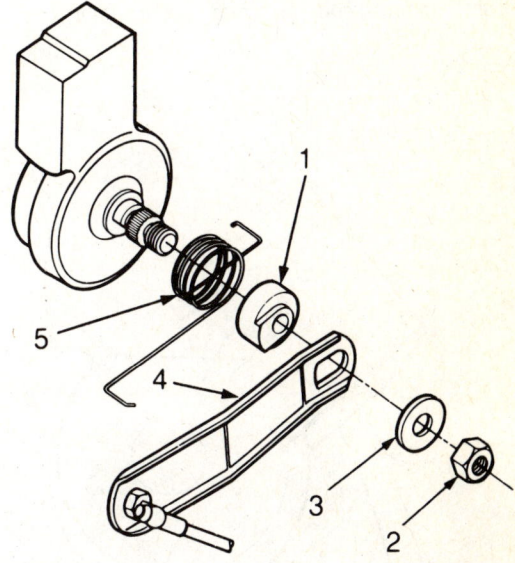

1. Bushing
2. Nut
3. Washer
4. Lever
5. Spring

Height sensing proportioning valve components

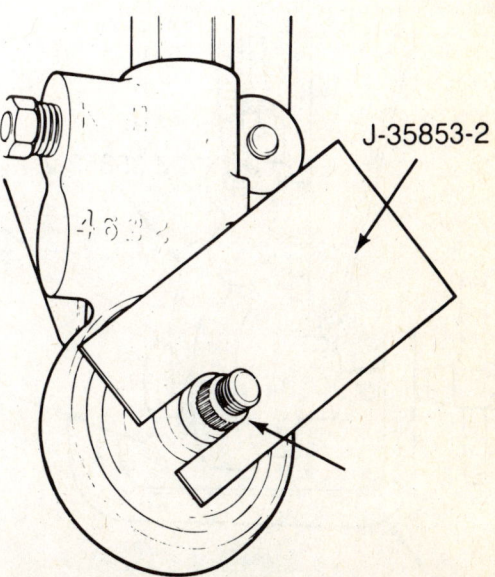

Front view of the height sensing proportioning valve with the adjusting tool installed. The arrow indicates the valve shaft

ADJUSTMENT

1. Remove the valve shaft nut and washer.
2. Disconnect the valve lever and remove the spring.
3. Remove and discard the bushing.
4. Rotate the valve shaft and install adjusting gauge tool J-35853-2.

NOTE: *The gauge must be properly seated on the D shape of the shaft and the valve lower mounting bolt. All linkage components, ex-*

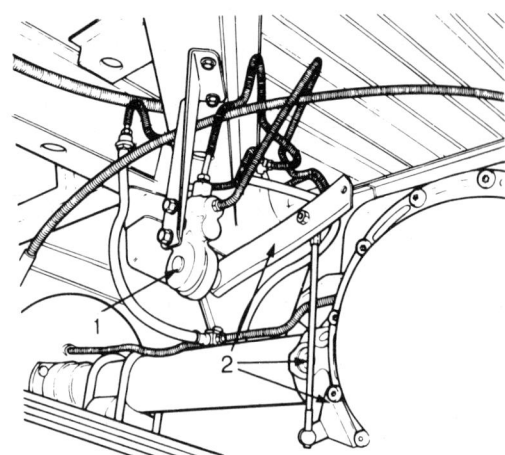

Height sensing proportioning valve. 1 is the valve; 2 indicates the linkage

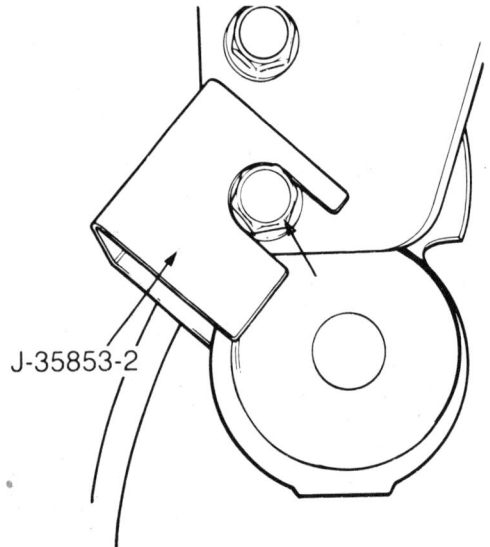

Side view of the height sensing proportioning valve with the adjusting tool installed. The arrow indicates the lower mounting bolt

cept the spring, must be connected before installing the new bushing.

5. Place the bushing in the lever, and, using bushing aligning tool J-35853-1, press the bushing and lever onto the shaft.
6. Remove the lever and adjusting tool J-35853-2 and install the spring.
7. Install the lever, washer and nut. Tighten the nut to 100 in. lbs.
8. Connect the spring.

REMOVAL AND INSTALLATION

1. Disconnect the linkage and spring.
2. Disconnect and cap the brake lines.
3. Unbolt and remove the valve.
4. Installation is the reverse of removal. Torque the Valve bracket-to-frame bolts to 155 in. lbs.; the valve-to-bracket bolts to 118 in. lbs.

Brake Booster

REMOVAL AND INSTALLATION

Except Anti-Lock Brakes

1. Disconnect the power unit pushrod at the pedal.
2. Disconnect the vacuum line at the power unit check valve.
3. Unbolt the master cylinder from the power unit and move it out of the way without disconnecting the brake lines. Be careful to avoid kinking the lines!
4. Unbolt and remove the power unit from the firewall.
5. Installation is the reverse of removal. Torque the power unit-to-firewall nuts to 30-35 ft. lbs.; the master cylinder-to-booster nuts to 15-18 in. lbs. Torque the pushrod nut to 35 ft. lbs.

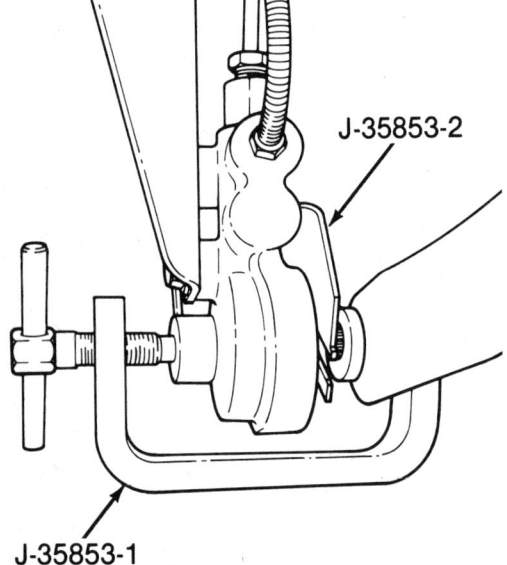

Back view of the height sensing proportioning valve with the adjusting tool and aligning tool installed

BRAKES 409

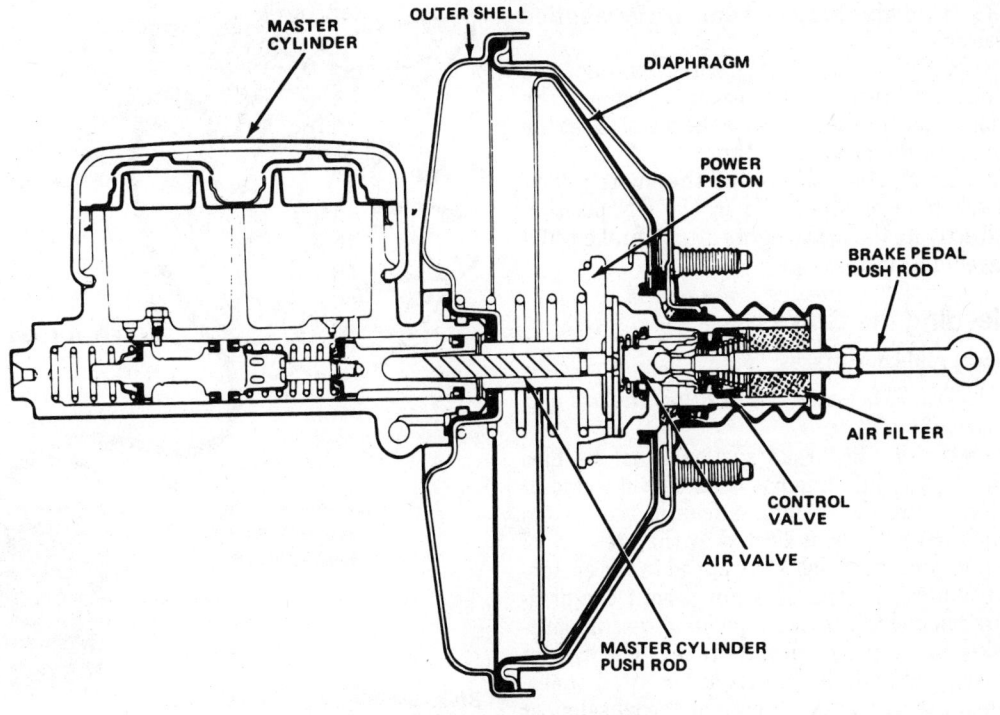

Single diaphragm power booster

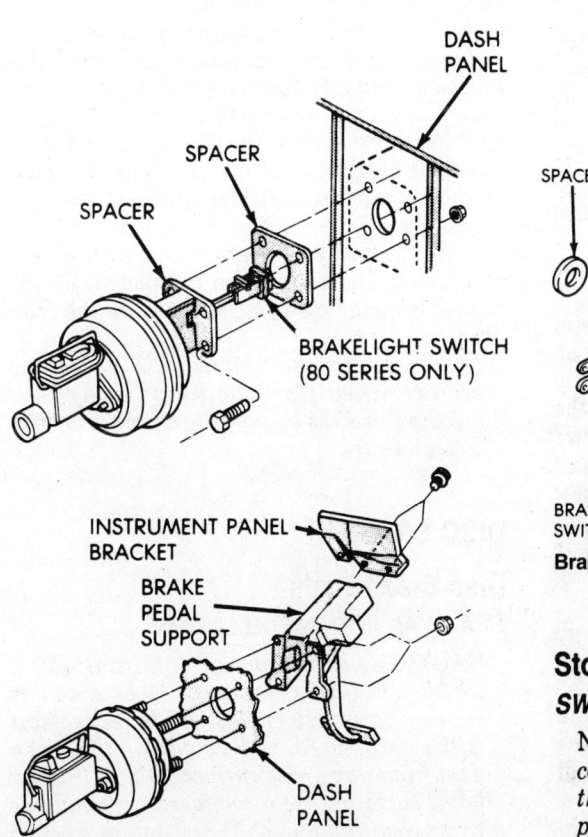

Power brake booster mounting

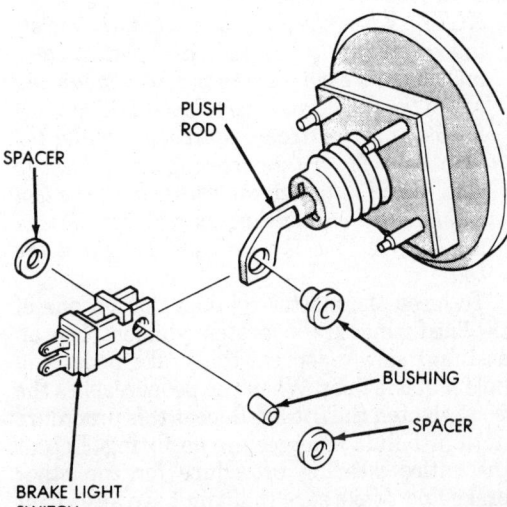

Brakelight switch with cruise control

Stop Light Switch
SWITCH ADJUSTMENT

NOTE: *On some vehicles equipped with air conditioning, remove the screws attaching the evaporator housing to the instrument panel and move the housing away from the panel.*

410 BRAKES

1. Hold the brake pedal in the applied position.
2. Push the stop light switch through the mounting bracket until it stops against the brake pedal bracket. Release the pedal to set the switch in the proper position.
3. Check the position of the switch. The switch plunger should be in the ON position and activate the brake lights after a brake pedal travel of 3/8-5/8".

Bleeding the Brakes
Except Anti-Lock Brakes

NOTE: *This procedure requires the use of a special tool.*

The hydraulic brake system must be bled whenever a fluid line has been disconnected or air gets into the system. A leak in the system may sometimes be indicated by the presence of a spongy brake pedal. Air trapped in the system is compressible and does not permit the pressure applied to the brake pedal to be transmitted solidly through to the brakes. The system must be absolutely free from air at all times. When bleeding brakes, begin at the wheel most distant from the master cylinder first, the next most distant second, and so on. During the bleeding operation, the master cylinder must be kept at least 3/4 full of brake fluid.

NOTE: *When bleeding the brakes, the metering section of the pressure differential valve must be held open. Loosen the front mounting bolt of the valve and insert Tool J-23709, or J-26869, or its fabricated equivalent, under the bolt. Push in on the metering valve stem to open it and retighten the bolt to hold the tool in place. When bleeding is finished, loosen the bolt, remove the tool and retighten the bolt.*

To bleed the master cylinder, loosen one of the line fittings at the master cylinder. Have an assistant slowly depress the brake pedal and hold it at the floor. When the pedal reaches the floor, tighten the fitting. Repeat this procedure until just fluid emerges at the fitting. Repeat the entire bleeding procedure for the other brake line. Make sure that you have absorbant rags under the fittings to catch the fluid. Wear goggles to avoid any fluid spray from hitting your eyes.

To bleed the brakes, first carefully clean all dirt from around the master cylinder filler plug. If a bleeder tank is used, follow the manufacturer's instructions. Remove the filler plug and fill the master cylinder to the lower edge of the filler neck. Clean off the bleeder connections at all of the wheel cylinders or disc brake calipers. Attach the bleeder hose and fixture to the right rear wheel cylinder bleeder screw and place the

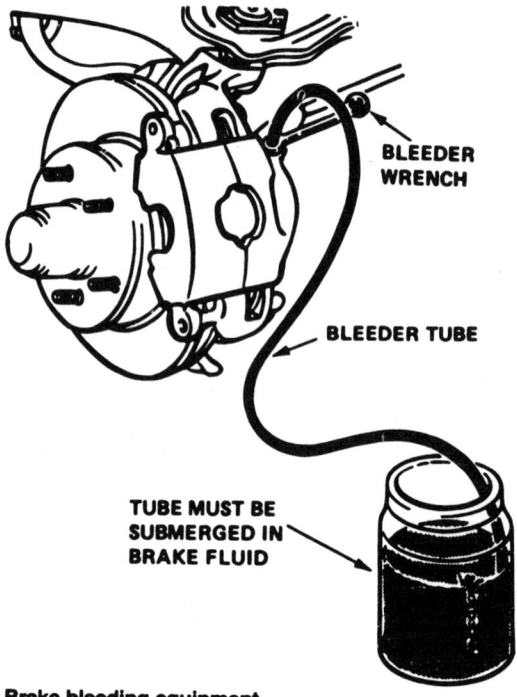

Brake bleeding equipment

end of the tube in a glass jar, submerged in brake fluid. Open the bleeder valve 1/2-3/4 of a turn. Have an assistant depress the brake pedal and allow it to return slowly. Continue this pumping action to force any air out of the system. When bubbles cease to appear at the end of the bleeder hose, close the bleeder valve and remove the hose. Check the level of the brake fluid in the master cylinder and add fluid, if necessary.

After the bleeding operation at each caliper or wheel cylinder has been completed, fill the master cylinder reservoir and replace the filler plug.

NOTE: *Never reuse brake fluid which has been removed from the lines through the bleeding process because it contains air bubbles and dirt.*

DISC BRAKES

Disc Brake Pads
REMOVAL AND INSTALLATION

CAUTION: *Brake shoes contain asbestos, which has been determined to be a cancer causing agent. Never clean the brake surfaces with compressed air! Avoid inhaling any dust from any brake surface! When cleaning brake surfaces, use a commercially available brake cleaning fluid.*

1. Raise and support the vehicle with

BRAKES

jackstands and remove the wheel(s) on the side to be worked on.

2. Drain ⅔ of the brake fluid from the front reservoir. Use the bleeder screw at the front outlet port to drain the fluid.

3. Raise the vehicle so that the wheel to be worked on is off the ground. Support the vehicle with jackstands.

4. Remove the front wheels.

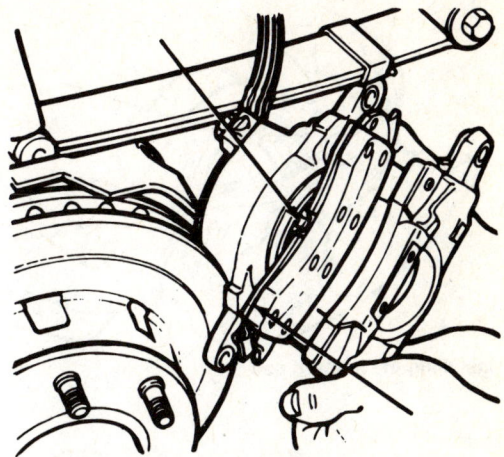
Removing the caliper from the rotor

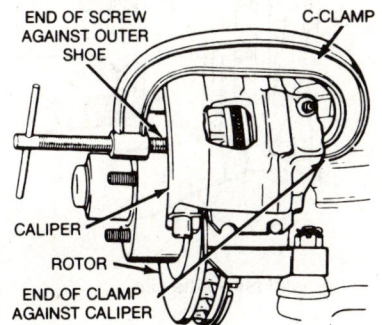
Bottoming the caliper piston

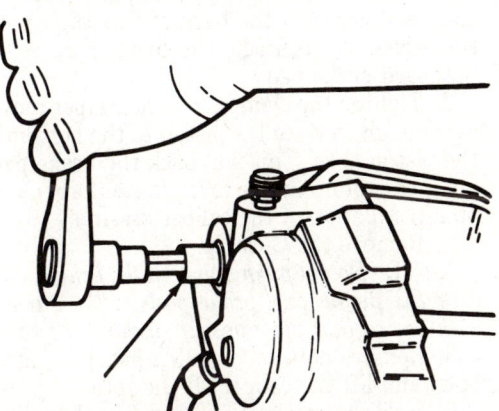
Removing the caliper mounting bolts

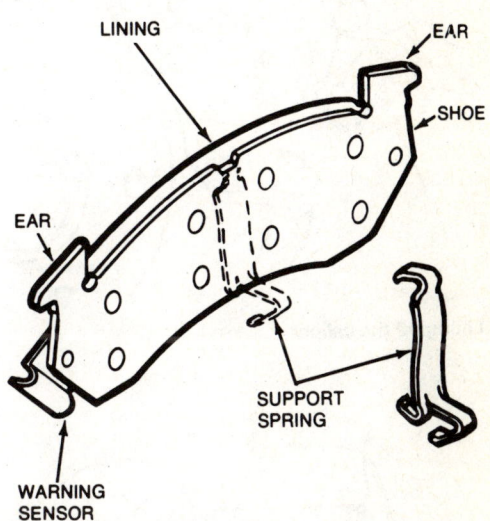
Installing the support spring on the inboard brake pad

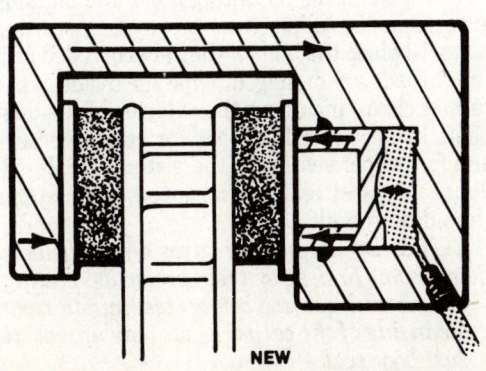 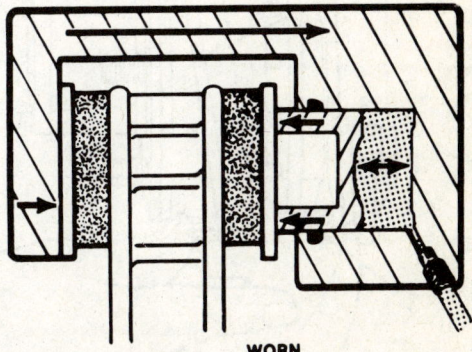
Piston extension on new and worn linings

412 BRAKES

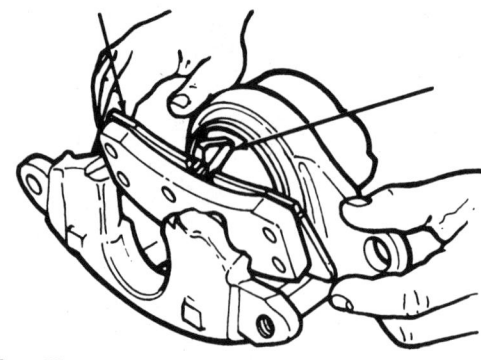

Installing the inboard pad

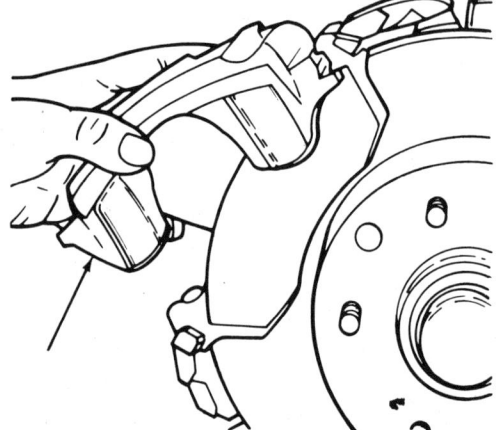

Lifting off the caliper

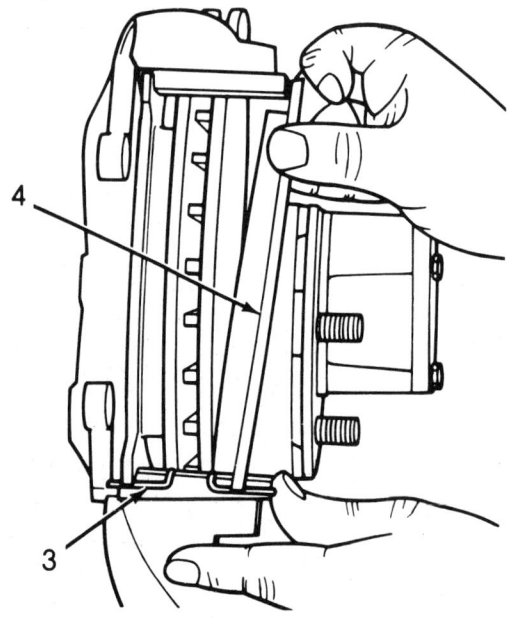

Anti-rattle clip (3) and outboard pad (4)

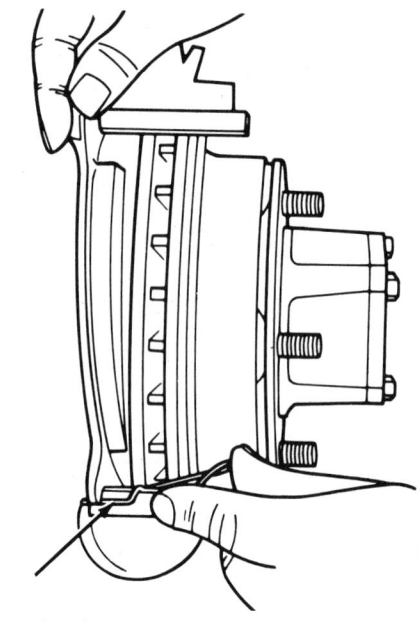

Inboard pad and anti-rattle clip

5. Place a C-clamp on the caliper so that the solid end contacts the back of the caliper and the screw end contacts the metal part of the outboard brake pad.

6. Tighten the clamp until the caliper moves far enough to force the piston to the bottom of the piston bore. This will back the brake pads off of the rotor surface to facilitate the removal and installation of the caliper assembly.

7. Remove the C-clamp.

NOTE: *Do not push down on the brake pedal or the piston and brake pads will return to their original positions up against the rotor.*

8. Remove both of the allen head mounting bolts and lift the caliper off the rotor.

9. Hold the anti-rattle clip against the caliper anchor plate and remove the outboard brake pad.

10. Remove the inboard pad and its anti-rattle clip.

11. Clean all the mounting holes and bushing grooves in the caliper ears. Clean the mounting bolts. Replace the bolts if they are corroded or if the threads are damaged. Wipe the inside of the caliper clean, including the exterior of the dust boot. Inspect the dust boot for cuts or cracks and for proper seating in the piston bore. If evidence of fluid leakage is noted, the caliper should be rebuilt.

NOTE: *Do not use abrasives on the bolts in order not to destroy their protective plating. You should not use compressed air to clean the inside of the caliper, as it may unseat the dust boot seal.*

12. Install the inboard anti-rattle clip on the

trailing end of the anchor plate. The split end of the clip must face away from the rotor.

13. Install the inboard pad in the caliper. The pad must lay flat against the piston.

14. Install the outboard pad in the caliper while holding the anti-rattle clip.

15. With the pads installed, position the caliper over the rotor. Line up the mounting holes in the caliper and the support bracket and insert the mounting bolts. Make sure that the bolts pass under the retaining ears on the inboard shoes. Push the bolts through until they engage the holes of the outboard pad and caliper ears. Thread the bolts into the support bracket and tighten them to 30 ft. lbs.

16. Fill the master cylinder with brake fluid and pump the brake pedal to seat the pads.

17. Install the wheel assembly and lower the vehicle. Check the level of the brake fluid in the master cylinder and fill as necessary. Test the operation of the brakes before taking the vehicle onto the road.

Calipers

REMOVAL AND INSTALLATION

CAUTION: *Brake shoes contain asbestos, which has been determined to be a cancer causing agent. Never clean the brake surfaces with compressed air! Avoid inhaling any dust from any brake surface! When cleaning brake surfaces, use a commercially available brake cleaning fluid.*

1. Drain ⅔ of the brake fluid from the front reservoir. Use the bleeder screw at the front outlet port to drain the fluid.
2. Raise the vehicle so that the wheel to be worked on is off the ground. Support the vehicle with jackstands.
3. Remove the front wheels.
4. Place a C-clamp on the caliper so that the solid end contacts the back of the caliper and the screw end contacts the metal part of the outboard brake pad.
5. Tighten the clamp until the caliper moves far enough to force the piston to the bottom of the piston bore. This will back the brake pads off of the rotor surface to facilitate the removal and installation of the caliper assembly.
6. Remove the C-clamp.

NOTE: *Do not push down on the brake pedal or the piston and brake pads will return to their original positions up against the rotor.*

7. Remove both of the allen head mounting bolts and lift the caliper off the rotor.

NOTE: *If just the brake pads are being replaced, it is not necessary to remove the caliper assembly entirely from the vehicle. Do not remove the brake line. Rest the caliper on the front spring or other suitable support. Do not allow the brake hose to support the weight of the caliper.*

8. If the caliper is being removed in order to be rebuilt, then it is necessary to disconnect the brake fluid hose. Clean the brake fluid hose-to-caliper connection thoroughly. Remove the hose-to-caliper bolt. Cap or tape the open ends to keep dirt out. Discard the copper gaskets; get new ones!

9. Install the caliper in the reverse order of removal. Torque the mounting bolts to 35 ft. lbs.

NOTE: *If the brake fluid hose was disconnected, it will be necessary to bleed the hydraulic system.*

OVERHAUL

1. Remove the caliper assembly and remove the brake pads. If the pads are to be reused, mark their location in the caliper.
2. Clean the caliper exterior with clean brake fluid. Drain any residual fluid from the caliper and place it on a clean work surface.

NOTE: *Removal of the caliper piston re-*

Removing the piston with compressed air

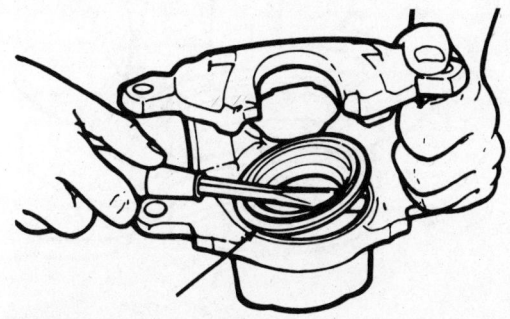

Removing the dust seal

quires the use of compressed air. Do not, under any circumstances, place your fingers in front of the piston in any attempt to catch or protect it when applying compressed air to remove the piston.

3. Pad the interior of the caliper with clean cloths. Use several cloths and pad the interior well to avoid damaging the piston when it comes out of the bore.

4. Insert an air nozzle into the inlet hole in the caliper and gently apply air pressure on the piston to push it out of the bore. Use only enough air pressure to ease the piston out of the bore.

5. Pry the dust boot out of the bore with a screwdriver. Use caution during this operation to prevent scratching the bore. Discard the dust boot.

6. Remove the piston seal from the piston bore and discard the seal. Use only nonscratching implements such as a pencil, wooden stick or a piece of plastic to remove the seal. Do not use a metal tool, as it could very easily scratch the bore.

7. Remove the bleeder screw. Remove and discard the sleeves and rubber bushings from the mounting ears.

8. Clean all the parts with clean brake fluid. Blow out all of the passages in the caliper and bleeder valve. Use only dry and filtered compressed air. Replace the mounting bolts if they are corroded or if the threads are damaged.

NOTE: *Do not attempt to clean the attaching bolts with abrasives, as their protective plating may be removed.*

9. Examine the piston for defects. Replace the piston if it is nicked, scratched, corroded or the protective plating is worn off. Examine the caliper piston bore for the same defects as the piston. The bore is not plated and minor stains or corrosion can be polished with crocus cloth.

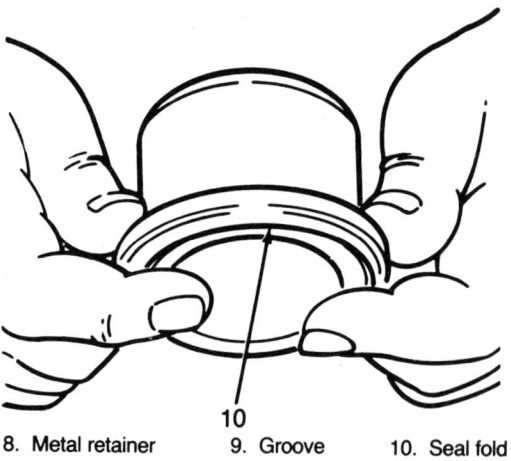

8. Metal retainer   9. Groove   10. Seal fold

Dust seal installation

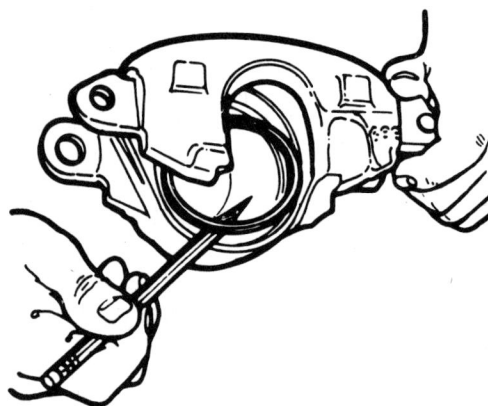

Removing the O-ring

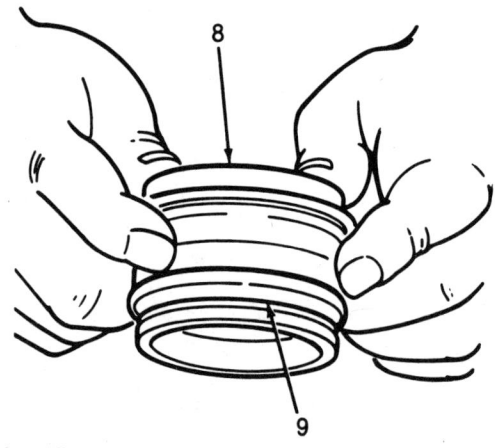

Installing the metal retainer (8) in the groove (9)

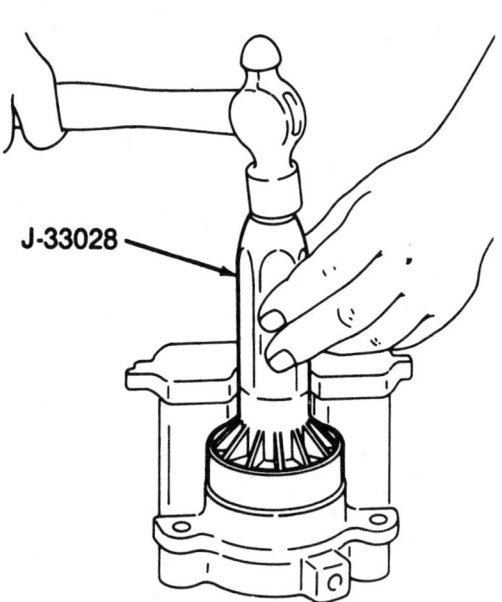

Seating the metal retainer

BRAKES

NOTE: *Do not attempt to refinish the piston in any way. The outside diameter is the sealing surface and is made to very close tolerances. Removal of the nickle-chrome plating will lead to pitting, rusting and eventual cocking of the piston in the piston bore. Do not use emery cloth or similar abrasives on the piston bore. If the bore does not clean up with crocus cloth, replace the caliper. Clean the caliper thoroughly with brake fluid if the bore was polished with crocus cloth.*

10. Lubricate the bore and new seal with brake fluid and install the seal in the groove in the bore.

11. Lubricate the piston with brake fluid and install the new dust boot on the piston. Assemble the dust boot into the piston groove so that the fold in the boot faces the open end of the piston. Slide the metal portion of the dust boot over the open end of the piston and push the retainer toward the back of the piston until the lip on the fold seats in the piston groove. Then push the retainer portion of the boot forward until the boot is flush with the rim at the open end of the piston and snaps into place.

12. Insert the piston in the bore, being careful not to unseat the piston seal. Push the piston to the bottom of the bore. It requires 50-100 lb. of force to bottom the piston.

13. Position the dust boot retainer in the counter bore at the top of the piston bore. Seat the dust boot retainer with a flat-ended punch by tapping the metal ring of the dust boot into place. Be careful not do damage the rubber portion of the dust boot. The metal retainer portion of the boot must be evenly seated in the counterbore, using tool J-33028 or J-22904, and fit below the face of the caliper.

14. Install the bleeder screw. Tighten it to 50-140 in. lbs.

15. Connect the brake line to the caliper using new copper gaskets.

16. Install the brake pads, sleeves and rubber bushings.

17. Install the caliper and tighten the mounting bolts to 35 ft. lbs. Bleed the hydraulic system.

Brake Rotor

REMOVAL AND INSTALLATION

CAUTION: *Brake shoes contain asbestos, which has been determined to be a cancer causing agent. Never clean the brake surfaces with compressed air! Avoid inhaling any dust from any brake surface! When cleaning brake surfaces, use a commercially available brake cleaning fluid.*

NOTE: *Two types of rotors are used on these vehicles.*

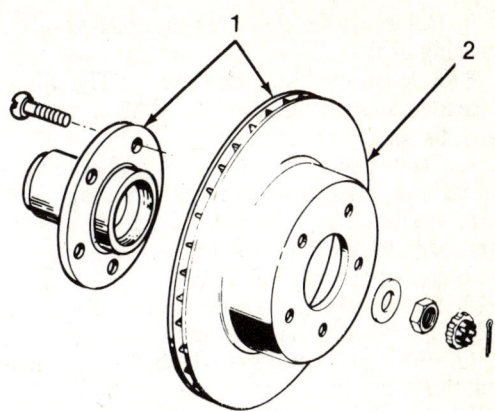

Type 1 rotor used on the 2wd models. 1 is the hub-to-rotor relationship; 2 is the Type 1 rotor

Type One

1. Loosen the lug nuts on the front wheels.
2. Raise and support the front end on jackstands.
3. Remove the front wheels.
4. Remove the calipers, but don't disconnect the brake lines. Suspend the calipers out of the way.
5. Remove the rotor.
6. Installation is the reverse of removal.

Type Two

1. Raise and support the front end on jackstands.
2. Remove the wheels.
3. Remove the caliper without disconnecting the brake line. Suspend it out of the way.
4. Remove the grease cap, cotter pin, nut cap, nut, and washer from the spindle.

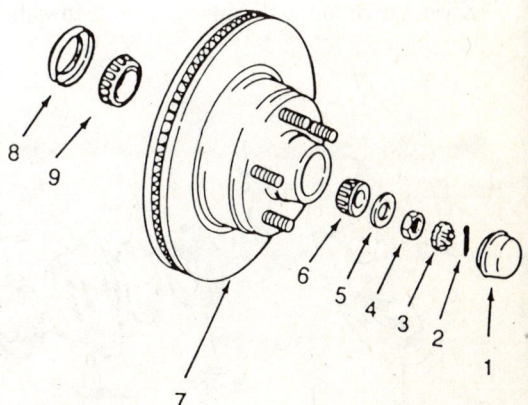

1. Grease cap
2. Cotter pin
3. Nut cap
4. Nut
5. Washer
6. Outer bearing
7. Hub and rotor
8. Inner seal
9. Inner bearing

Type 2 rotor used on 2wd models

416 BRAKES

5. Pull slowly on the hub and catch the outer bearing as it falls.
6. Remove the hub and rotor. The inner bearing and seal can be removed by prying out and discarding the inner seal.
7. Clean and repack the hub and bearings, install the inner bearing and a new seal.
8. Position the hub and rotor on the spindle and install the outer bearing.
9. Install the washer and nut.
10. While turning the rotor, torque the nut to 25 ft. lbs. to seat the bearings.
11. Back off the nut ½ turn, and, while turning the rotor, torque the nut to 19 in. lbs.
12. Install the nut cap and a new cotter pin. Install the grease cap.
13. Install the caliper.
14. Install the wheels.

INSPECTION AND MEASUREMENT

Check the rotor for surface cracks, nicks, broken cooling fins and scoring of both contact surfaces. Some scoring of the surfaces may occur during normal use. Scoring that is 0.015" deep or less is not detrimental to the operation of the brakes.

If the rotor surface is heavily rusted or scaled, clean both surfaces on a disc brake lathe using flat sanding discs before attempting any measurements.

With the hub and rotor assembly mounted on the spindle of the vehicle or a disc brake lathe and all play removed from the wheel bearings, assemble a dial indicator so that the stem contacts the center of the rotor braking surface. Zero the dial indicator before taking any measurements. Lateral runout must not exceed 0.005" with a maximum rate of change not to exceed 0.001" in 30° of rotation.

Excessive runout will cause the rotor to wob-

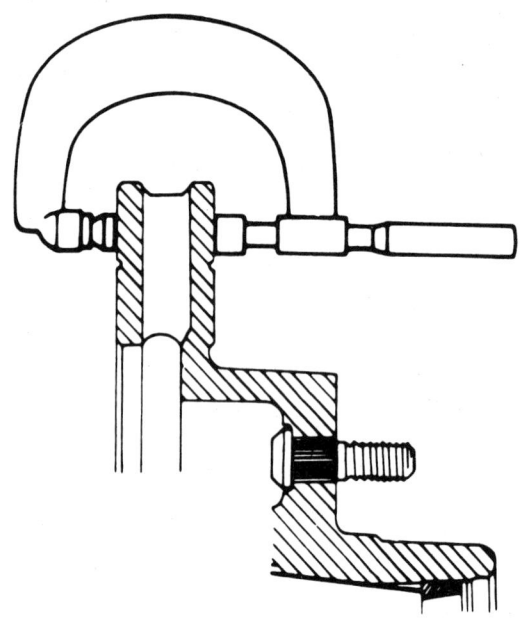

Measuring the rotor thickness with a micrometer

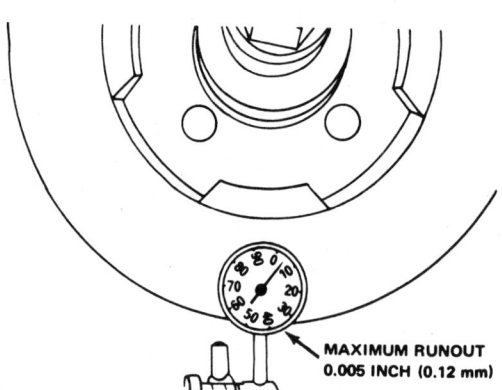

Checking the rotor lateral runout

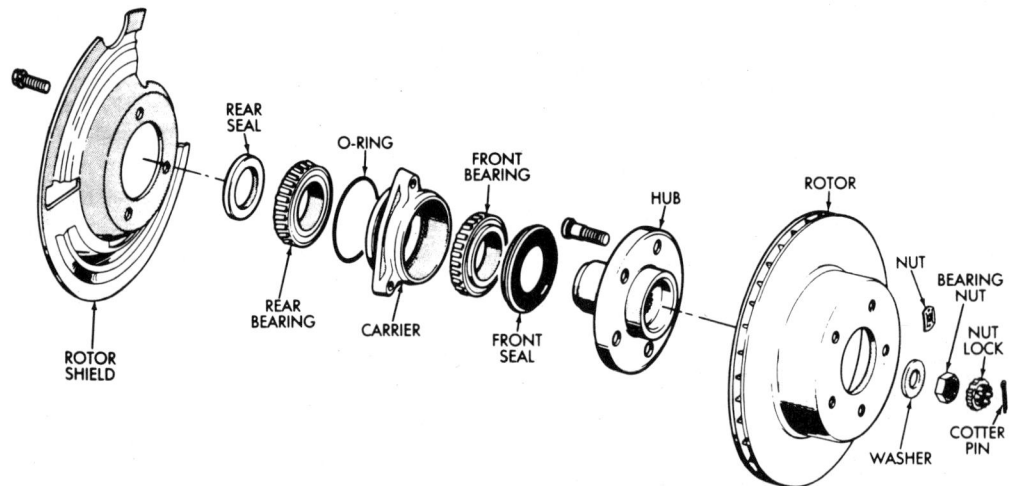

4-wheel drive rotor and hub

ble and knock the piston back into the caliper, causing increased pedal travel, noise and vibration.

Check the Brake Specifications Chart for rotor thickness. Discard the rotor if the thickness is 1.215" or less after finishing.

NOTE: *Remember to adjust the preload on the wheel bearings after the runout measurement has been taken.*

Wheel Bearings

For detailed front wheel bearing service, see Chapter 1.

DRUM BRAKES

Brake Drums

REMOVAL AND INSTALLATION

CAUTION: *Brake shoes contain asbestos, which has been determined to be a cancer causing agent. Never clean the brake surfaces with compressed air! Avoid inhaling any dust from any brake surface! When cleaning brake surfaces, use a commercially available brake cleaning fluid.*

1. Raise and support the rear end on jackstands.
2. Remove the wheel, then the drum from the vehicle.

NOTE: *It may be necessary to back off the brake adjusters to remove the drum.*

3. When placing the drum on the hub, make sure that the contacting surfaces are clean and flat.

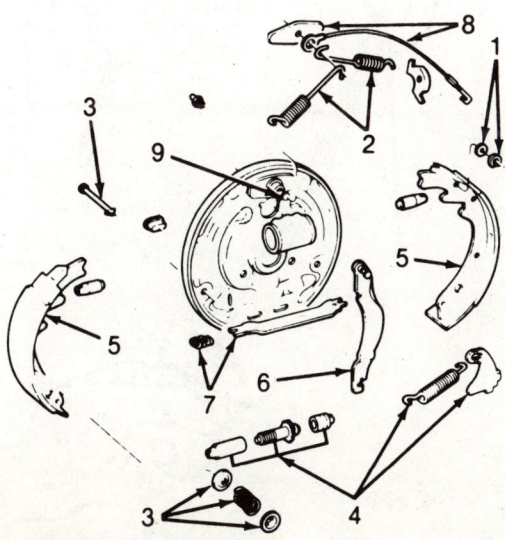

Rear brake components

INSPECTION

Using an inside micrometer, check all drums. Should a brake drum be scored or rough, it may be reconditioned by grinding or turning on a lathe. Do not remove more than 0.030" thickness of metal. If a drum is reconditioned in this manner, it is recommended that either the correct factory supplied, 0.030" oversize lining must be installed, or a shim equal in thickness to the metal removed must be placed between the lining and the brake shoe so that the arc of the lining will be the same as that of the drum.

Brake Shoes

REMOVAL AND INSTALLATION

CAUTION: *Brake shoes contain asbestos, which has been determined to be a cancer causing agent. Never clean the brake surfaces with compressed air! Avoid inhaling any dust from any brake surface! When cleaning brake surfaces, use a commercially available brake cleaning fluid.*

NOTE: *An inexpensive brake spring removal tool, available at most good auto parts stores, will make this procedure much easier.*

1. Jack the vehicle up and support it so that the wheels to be worked on are off the ground.
2. Turn the adjustment starwheel so that the brake shoes are retracted from the brake drum.
3. Remove the wheels and the drums to give access to the brake shoes.
4. Install wheel cylinder clamps to retain the wheel cylinder pistons in place and prevent leakage of brake fluid while replacing the shoes.
5. Remove the return springs with a brake spring remover tool.
6. Remove the adjuster cable, cable guide, adjuster lever and adjuster springs.
7. Remove the holddown washers and springs and remove the brake shoes.
8. Clean the backing plate with a brush or cloth. Place a dab of Lubriplate® on each spot where the brake shoes rub on the backing plate.

NOTE: *Always replace brake linings in axle sets. Never replace linings on one side or just on one wheel.*

9. Thoroughly clean the backing plate.
10. Apply a thin coat of multi-purpose chassis lube to the mounting pads on the backing plate.
11. Transfer the parking brake actuating lever to the new secondary shoe.
12. Position the brake shoes on the backing plate and install the holddown springs. Don't forget to engage the parking brake lever with the cable.
13. Install the parking brake actuating bar and spring between the parking brake lever and primary shoe.

14. Install the self-adjusting cable, cable guide and upper return springs.
15. Thoroughly clean the starwheel and lightly lubricate the threads with lithium based grease.
16. Install the starwheel.
17. Install the self-adjusting cam and lower spring. A big pair of locking pliers is good for this job.
18. Check the surface of the brake shoes for any grease that may have gotten on them.
19. Install the drum and reach through the adjusting opening in the back plate with a brake adjusting tool. Turn the starwheel outward so that the brakes lock the drum, then, holding the adjusting cam with a thin screwdriver, turn the starwheel back so that the drum is free and no drag is felt.
20. Once the wheels are on and the truck is down, Back it up several times, applying the brakes to actuate the self-adjusters.

Wheel Cylinders

OVERHAUL

CAUTION: *Brake shoes contain asbestos, which has been determined to be a cancer causing agent. Never clean the brake surfaces with compressed air! Avoid inhaling any dust from any brake surface! When cleaning brake surfaces, use a commercially available brake cleaning fluid.*

NOTE: *Wheel cylinder rebuilding kits are available for reconditioning wheel cylinders. The kits usually contain new cup springs, cylinder cups and, in some, new boots. The most important factor to keep in mind when rebuilding wheel cylinders is cleanliness. Keep all dirt away from the wheel cylinders when you are reassembling them.*

1. To remove the wheel cylinder, jack up the vehicle and remove the wheel and drum.
2. Disconnect the brake line at the fitting on the brake backing plate.
3. Remove the brake assemblies.
4. Remove the screws or nuts that hold the wheel cylinder to the backing plate and remove the wheel cylinder from the vehicle.
5. Remove the rubber dust covers on the ends of the cylinder. Remove the pistons and piston cups and the spring. Remove the bleeder screw and make sure it is not plugged.
6. Discard all of the parts that the rebuilding kit will replace.
7. Examine the inside of the cylinder. If it is severely rusted, pitted or scratched, then the cylinder must be replaced, as the piston cups won't be able to seal against the walls of the cylinder.
8. Using a wheel cylinder home or emery cloth and crocus cloth, polish the inside of the cylinder. The purpose of this is to put a new surface on the inside of the cylinder. Keep the inside of the cylinder coated with brake fluid while honing.
9. Wash out the cylinder with clean brake fluid after honing.
10. When reassembling the cylinder, dip all of the parts in clean brake fluid. Reassemble in the reverse order of removal.

PARKING BRAKE

ADJUSTMENT

NOTE: *This procedure requires the use of a special tool.*
1. Place the parking brake lever in the fifth notch.
2. Raise and support the truck on jackstands.
3. Using a torque wrench and adjustment adapter J-34651, apply a torque of 45-50 in. lbs.

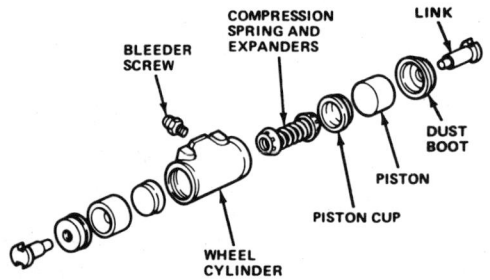

Typical rear wheel cylinder

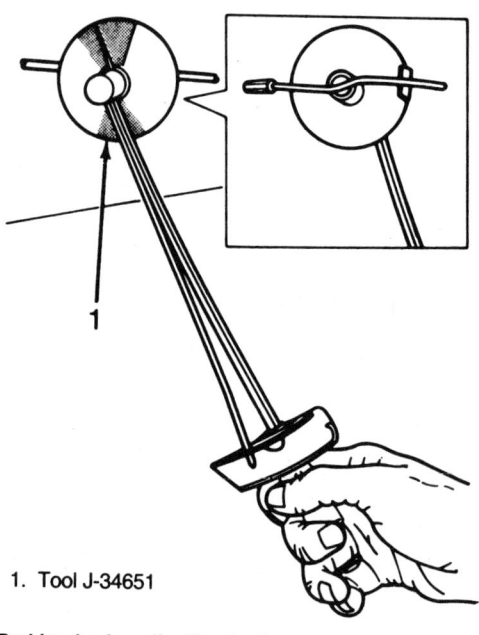

1. Tool J-34651

Parking brake adjusting tool

BRAKES

4. Adjust the equalizer adjusting nut so that the gauge pointer is in the green band on the tool.

5. Apply and release the brake lever fully, five times, and recheck the adjustment.

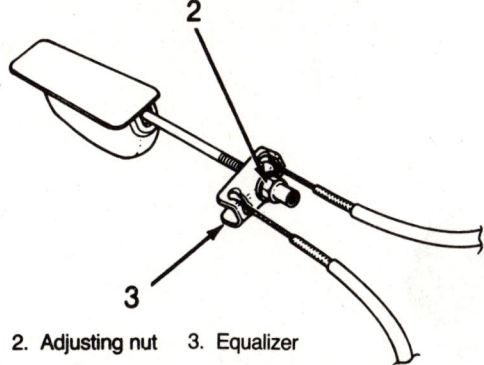

Parking brake adjusting nut and equalizer

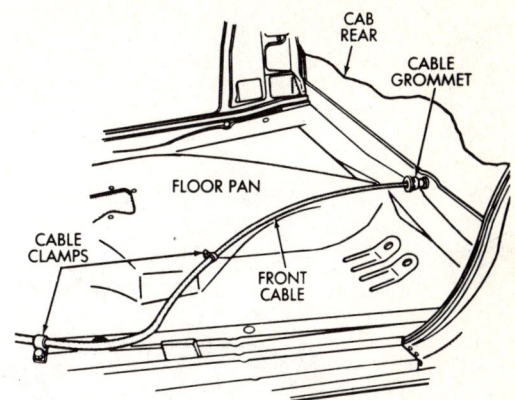

Camanche front cable floorpan attachment

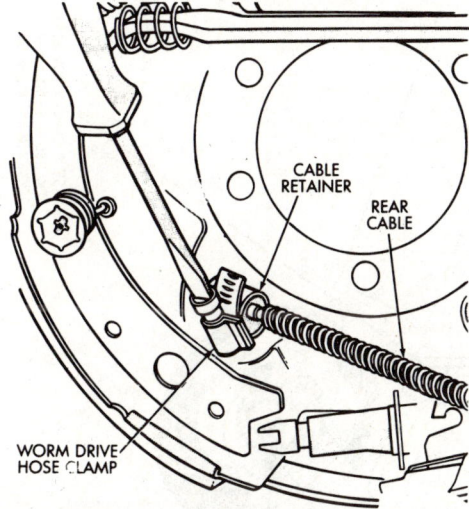

Compressing the cable retainer

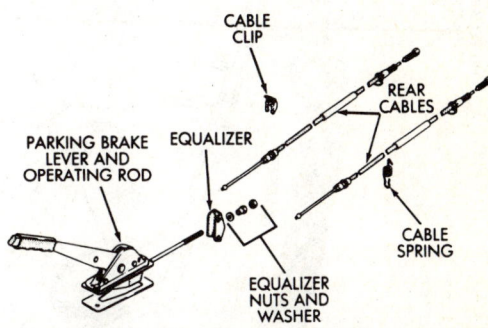

Parking brake cables for the Wagoneer/Cherokee

6. When adjustment is correct, stake the adjusting nut.

REMOVAL AND INSTALLATION

1. Fully release the parking brake.
2. Raise and support the front end on jackstands.
3. Remove the adjusting nut from the operating rod at the equalizer.
4. Disconnect the cable ends at the equalizer.
5. Raise and support the rear end on jackstands.
6. Unclip the cable from the frame bracket and unhook the locating spring from the cable.
7. Remove the rear wheels.
8. Remove the brake drums.
9. Remove the brake shoes.
10. Unhook the cable from the brake shoe actuating lever, compress the lock tabs at the backing plate and pull the cable out.
11. Installation is the reverse of removal.

ANTI-LOCK BRAKE SYSTEM

Operation

This system is available on 1989 Wagoneer and Cherokee models with Selec-Trac 4-wheel drive.

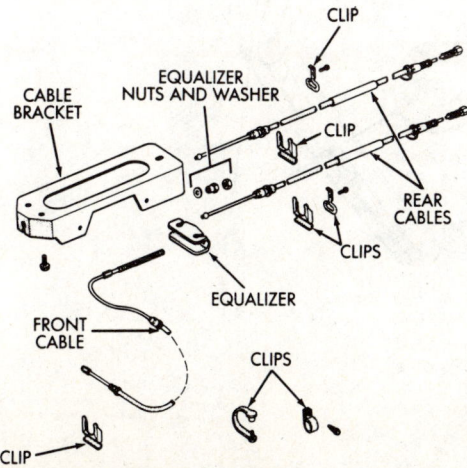

Comanche parking brake cable

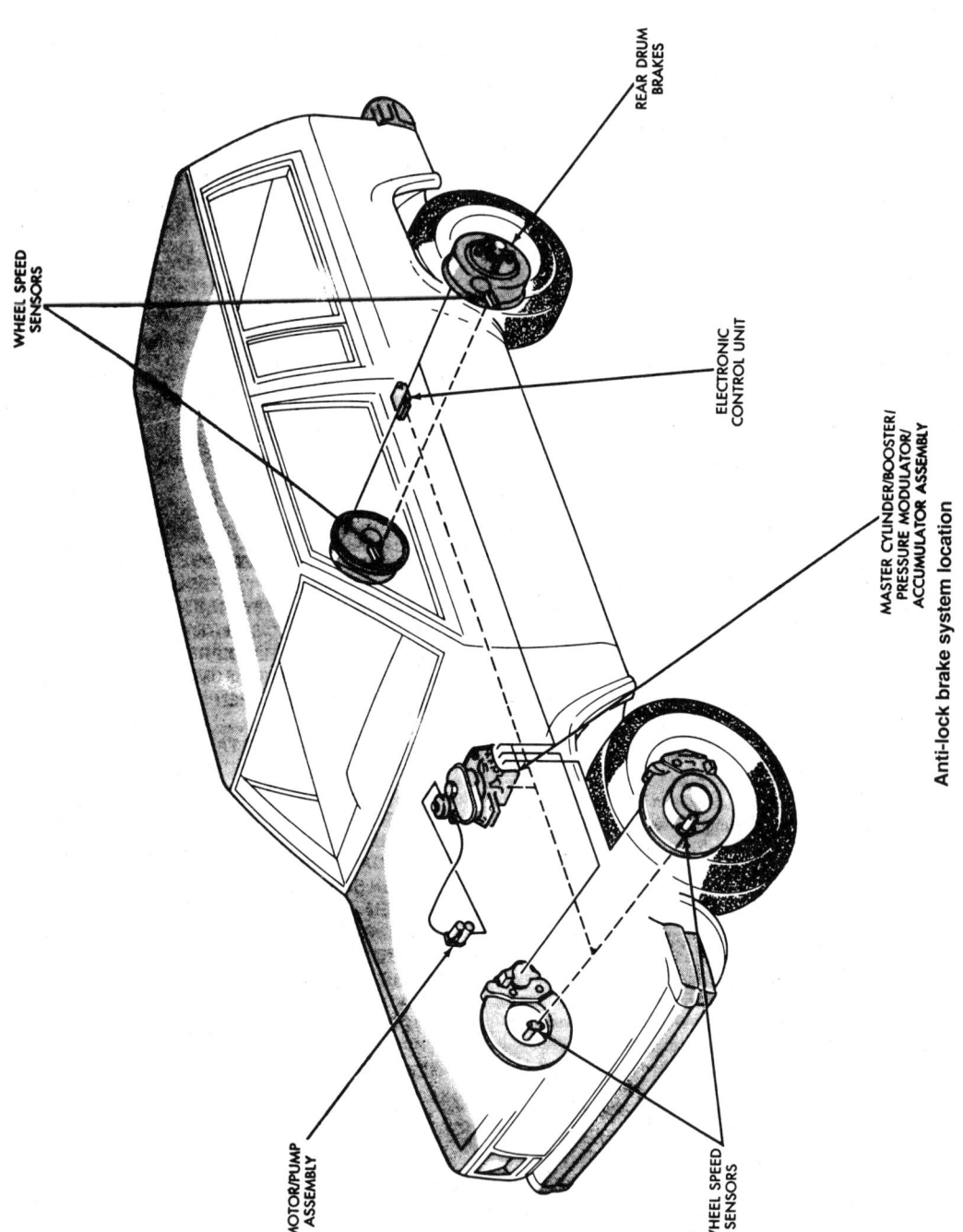

Anti-lock brake system location

BRAKES

The system is designed to retard wheel lock-up during periods of excessive wheeld slipping during braking.

System pressure is modulated according to wheel speed, degree of wheel slip and rate of deceleration. A sensor at each wheel converts wheel speed into electronic signals which are transmitted to the brake system control unit for processing and determination.

Components

Basic system components include:
- wheel sensors
- fluid level and pressure switches
- pressure modulator
- accumulator
- electric booster pump
- master cylinder/boost unit

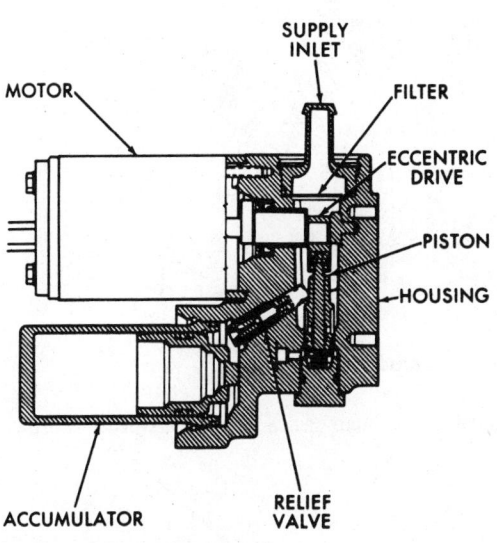
Pump and motor assembly

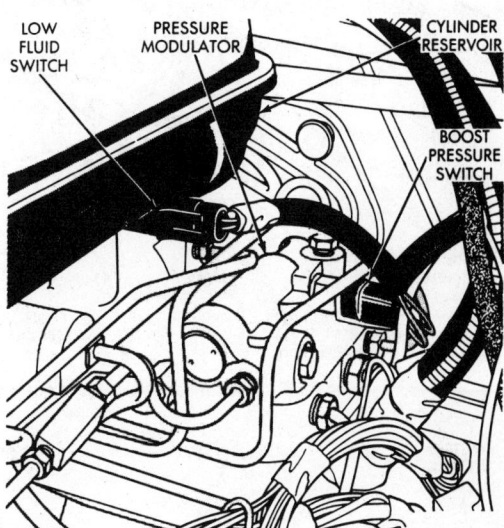
Boost pressure differential and low fluid switch locations

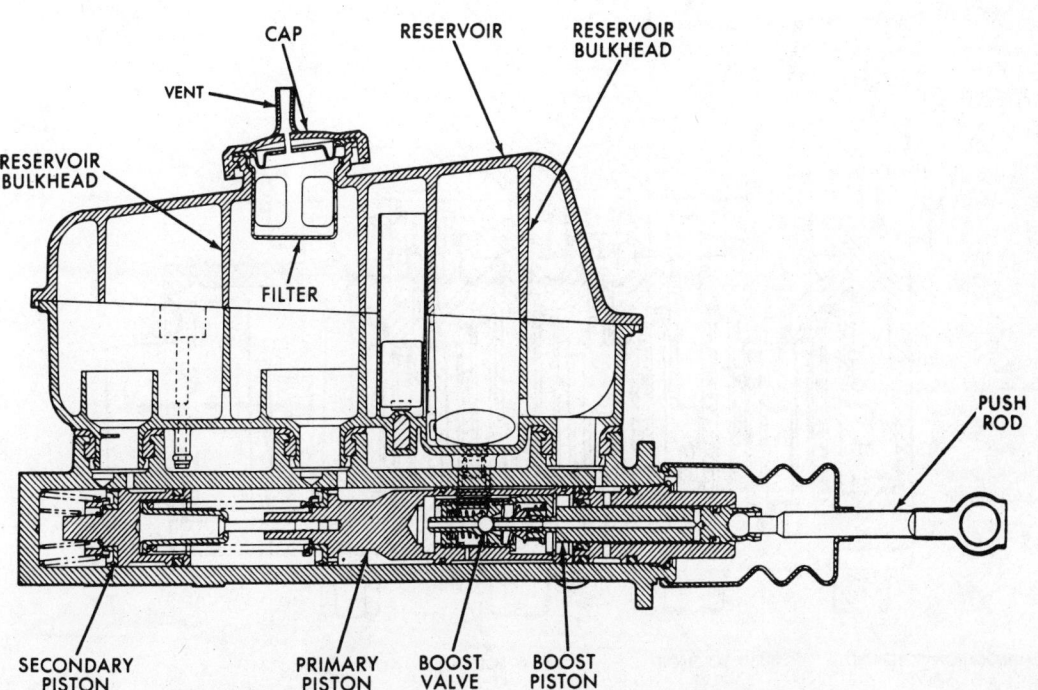
Master cylinder/power boost unit used with anti-lock brakes

422 BRAKES

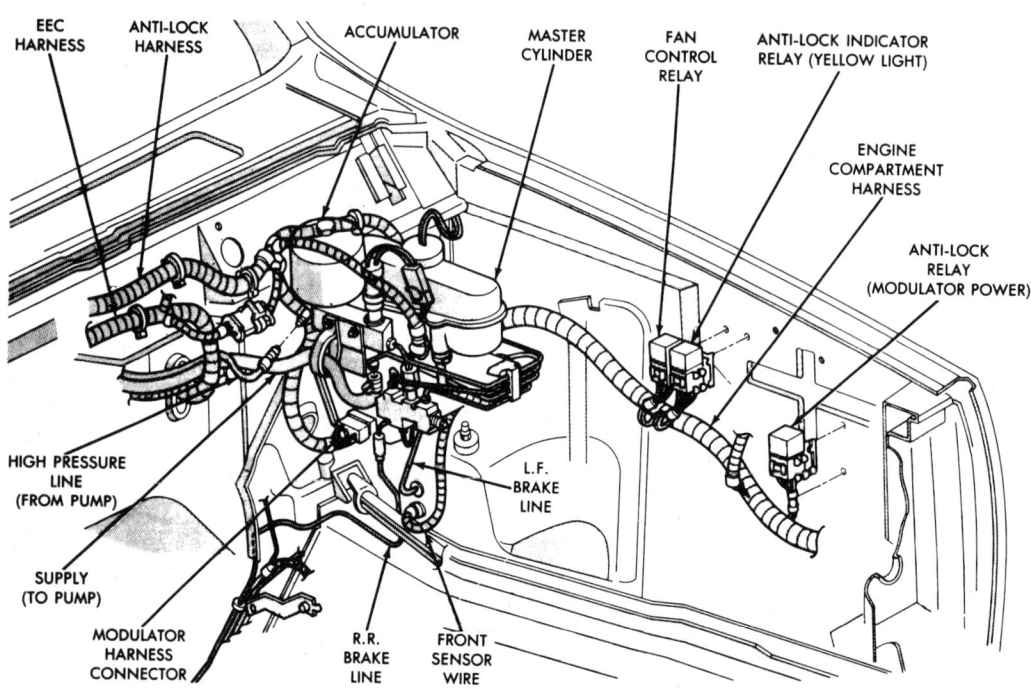

Modulator/indicator light relays and harness locations

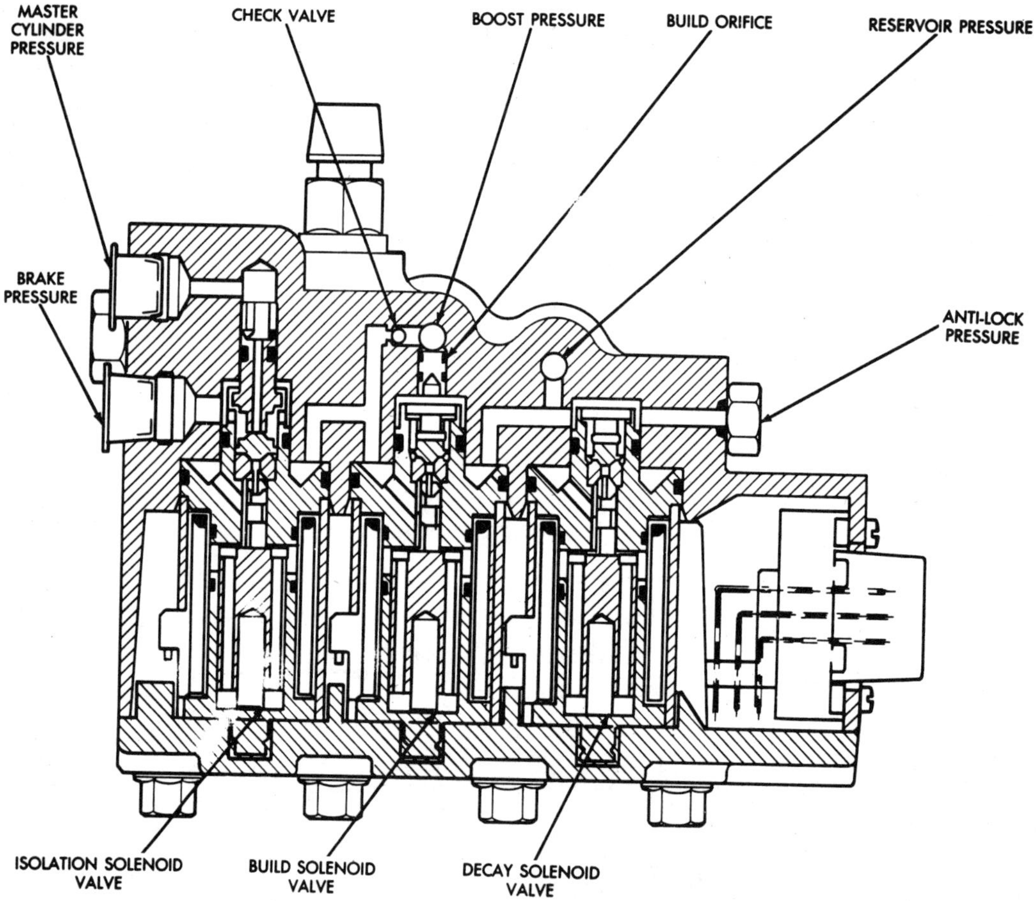

Pressure modulator channel

- electronic control unit
- indicator lights

Safety Precautions

The normal working pressure of teh system is 1,650-2,050 psi! System pressure must be released before any pressure lines are disconnected! Failure to do so will result in serious personal injury!!!

Always wear goggles when disconnecting any pressure line!

The accumulator tank and the small accumulator on the booster pump each contain high pressure gas charges to assist in maintaining booster pressure. NEVER puncture or attempt to disassemble these components!

Keep the system clean! Whenever any part of the system is opened, cap the openings immediately! Before removing the reservoir cap, clean

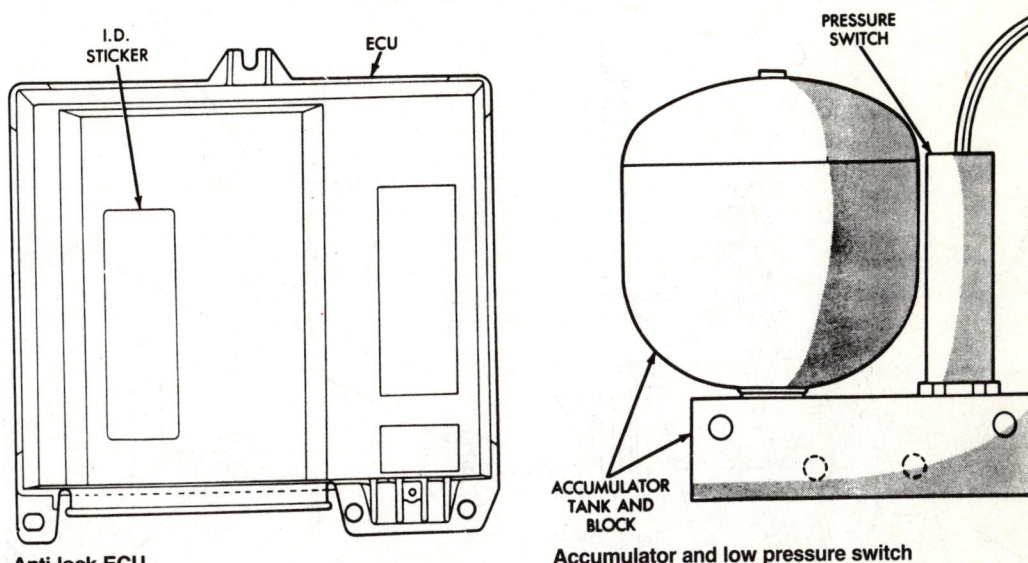

Anti-lock ECU

Accumulator and low pressure switch

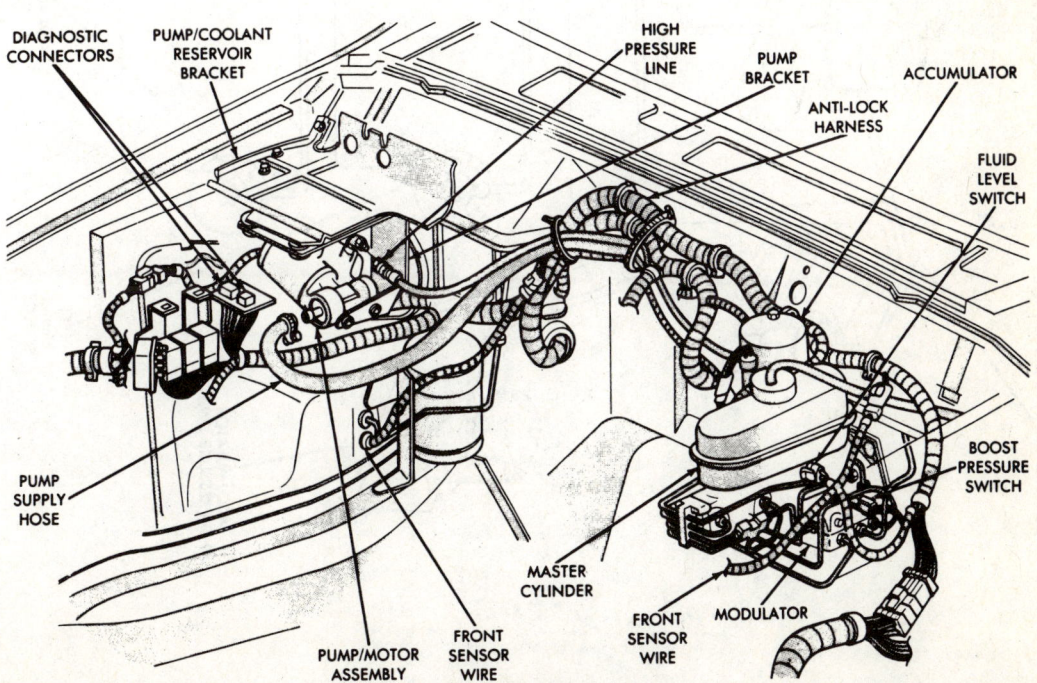

Underhood component locator

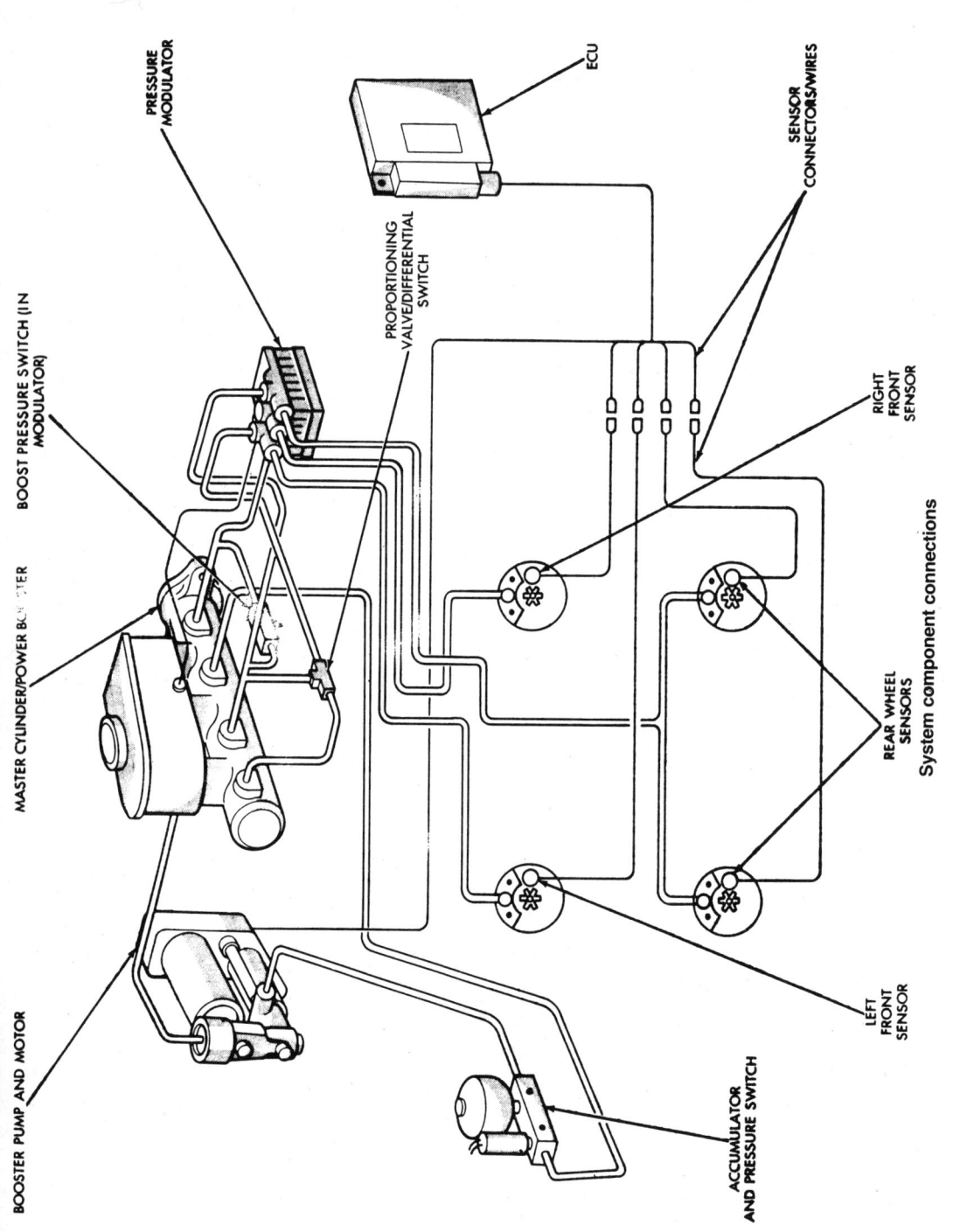

System component connections

BRAKES 425

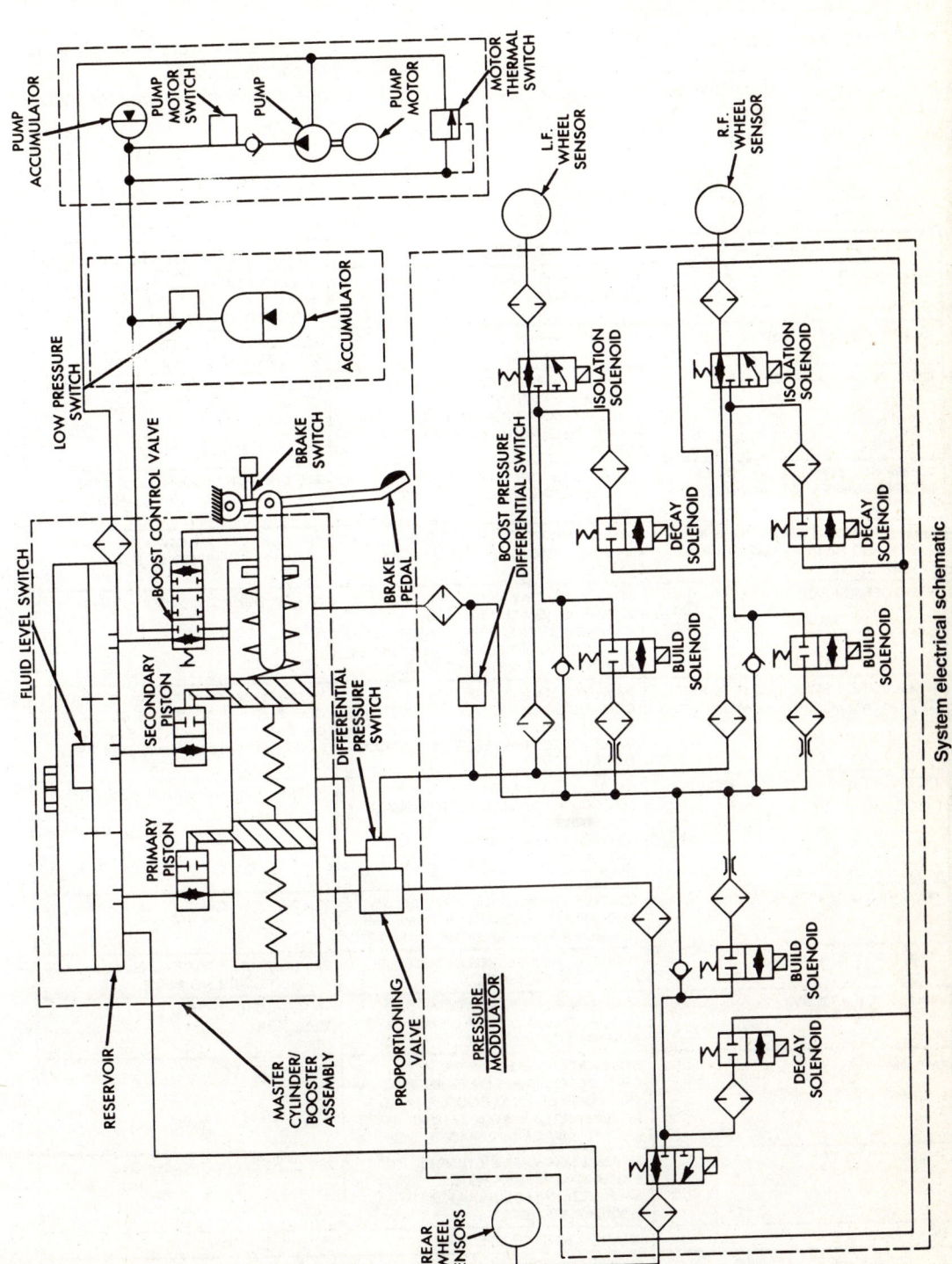

System electrical schematic

426 BRAKES

all dirt from the cap area! Dirt in the system will adversely affect brake performance!

RELIEVING SYSTEM PRESSURE

1. Turn the ignition switch OFF.
2. Apply the brakes 45-50 times, until the pedal is firm, to reduce pressure in the accumulator, booster pump and lines.

Front Wheel Sensor

REMOVAL AND INSTALLATION

1. Raise and support the front end on jackstands.
2. Turn the wheel being worked on outward for easier access to the sensor.
3. Make a note of the wire routing for installation reference.

SYSTEM FAULT	POSSIBLE CAUSE	INDICATOR LIGHT DISPLAY
LOW FLUID	SYSTEM LEAK. ACCUMULATOR CHARGE LOW OR LOST.	RED LIGHT ON. YELLOW LIGHT ON WITHIN 1/2 SECOND WHEN VEHICLE SPEED EXCEEDS 2.5 MPH.
PARKING BRAKES APPLIED	PARKING BRAKES NOT RELEASED BEFORE DRIVING VEHICLE.	RED LIGHT ON. YELLOW LIGHT ON IF VEHICLE SPEED EXCEEDS 2.5 MPH
PRESSURE DROP AT ACCUMULATOR	ACCUMLATOR GAS CHARGE LOST. SYSTEM LEAK. PUMP/MOTOR MALFUNCTION. PROLONGED STOP ON ICY SURFACE WITH TRANSMISSION IN GEAR.	YELLOW LIGHT ON. RED LIGHT WILL ALSO COME ON WITHIN 20 SECONDS.
DIFFERENTIAL PRESSURE SWITCH (IN PROPORTIONING VALVE) ACTUATED	SYSTEM LEAK. MASTER CYLINDER MALFUNCTION (SECONDARY PISTON). AIR IN SYSTEM.	RED LIGHT ON. YELLOW LIGHT COMES ON AT VEHICLE SPEED OF 3 MPH.
PRESSURE DROP AT BOOST PRESSURE SWITCH AND PRESSURE DIFFERENTIAL SWITCH	MASTER CYLINDER MALFUNCTION (PRIMARY PISTON). SYSTEM LEAK. AIR IN SYSTEM.	RED LIGHT ON. YELLOW LIGHT COMES ON AT VEHICLE SPEED OF 3 MPH.
WHEEL SENSOR FAULT (FRONT ONLY)	SENSOR-TO-TONE WHEEL SPACING INCORRECT (SPACE TOO LARGE). DAMAGED SENSOR WIRE, SENSOR, OR TONE WHEEL. SENSOR AND TONE WHEEL MISALIGNED. SENSOR DISCONNECTED.	YELLOW LIGHT ON. (AFTER 15 MPH)
WHEEL SENSOR FAULT (FRONT OR REAR ONE OR TWO MISSING SIGNALS)	DAMAGED SENSOR, WIRE, OR CONNECTOR. SENSOR DISCONNECTED. EXCESSIVE WHEEL SPIN. MISALIGNED OR DAMAGED TONE WHEEL. OPEN SENSOR OR WIRE.	YELLOW LIGHT ON AT 15 MPH IF FAULT OCCURRED BEFORE VEHICLE DRIVE-OFF. OR, ORANGE LIGHT ON AT 8 MPH IF FAULT OCCURRED AFTER VEHICLE DRIVE-OFF.
EXCESSIVE DECAY SOLENOID OPERATION	MODULATOR/SOLENOID FAULT. WHEEL SENSOR FAULT. EXTREMELY LOW AMBIENT TEMPERATURES. VEHICLE ON ICE COVERED SURFACE. TIRES HYDROPLANING ON WATER COVERED ROAD SURFACE.	YELLOW LIGHT ON WITHIN 1-2 SECONDS.
PRESSURE MODULATOR SOLENOID FAULT	SOLENOID SHORTED OR OPEN. DECAY AND BUILD SOLENOID ON AT SAME TIME. OPEN/SHORT IN MODULATOR HARNESS.	YELLOW LIGHT ON.
PUMP/MOTOR RUN-ON	EXCESSIVE RUN TIME. RELAY SHORTED, MOTOR SWITCH SHORTED.	RED LIGHT ON IF PUMP RUNS MORE THAN 4 MINUTES WITH NO BRAKE.
PUMP/MOTOR INOPERATIVE	PUMP RELAY FAULT. NO VOLTAGE TO MOTOR. DAMAGED PUMP OR MOTOR. PUMP GAS CHARGE LOST.	YELLOW LIGHT ON. RED LIGHT ON AFTER 20 SECONDS.
LOW VOLTAGE	SYSTEM VOLTAGE BELOW 9V. SHORT, OPEN IN FEED WIRES OR RELAY. FUSE BAD. POOR GROUND. LOOSE, DISCONNECTED WIRE IN SYSTEM. BATTERY LOW OR DISCHARGED	YELLOW LIGHT ON.
NO BRAKE SIGNAL	SYSTEM LEAK. MASTER CYLINDER MALFUNCTION. PUMP/MOTOR MALFUNCTION. ACCUMULATOR OR MODULATOR FAULT.	RED LIGHT ON DURING BRAKING.
RELAY FAULT	RELAY SHORTED OR OPEN.	YELLOW LIGHT ON.
ECU SELF DIAGNOSTIC FEATURE INOPERATIVE (SOLENOIDS NOT TEST-EXERCISED AT START-UP)	IGNITION SWITCH IN OFF POSITION. PARKING BRAKES ON (NOT RELEASED AT DRIVE-OFF). SYSTEM COMPONENT HAS MALFUNCTIONED. LOW FLUID LEVEL/LEAK IN SYSTEM.	YELLOW LIGHT ON.

Troubleshooting the system

BRAKES

4. Cut the tie straps securing the sensor to the steering knuckle and front brake hose and line.
5. Clean the sensor and surrounding area thoroughly of any dirt or other road splash build-up.
6. Remove the sensor attaching screw and remove the sensor from the knuckle.
7. Unseat the grommet retaining the sensor wire in the wheel housing.
8. In the engine compartment, disconnect the sensor wire connector at the anti-lock harness plug. Remove the sensor and wire.
9. Inspect the new or original sensor and note the condition of the polyethylene spacer strip. If the strip is securely attached to the sen-

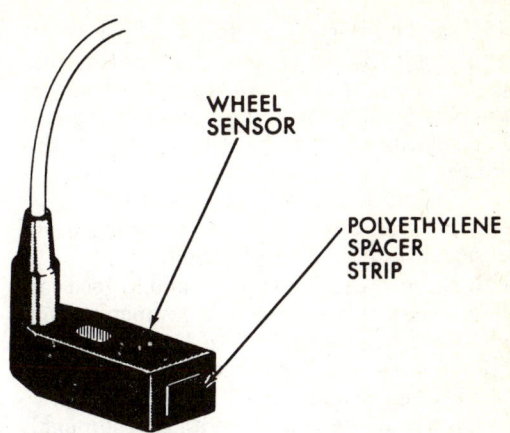
Sensor spacer strip

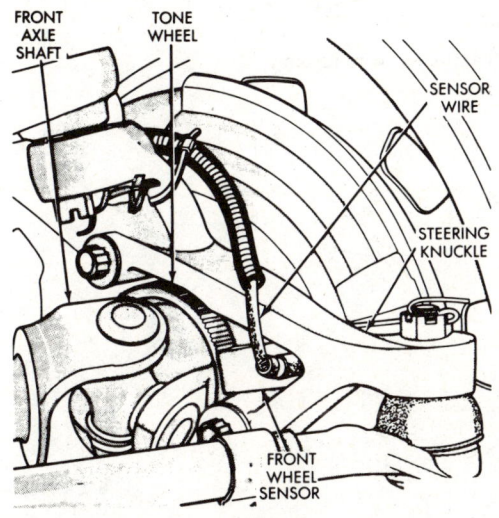
Front wheel sensor and tone wheel

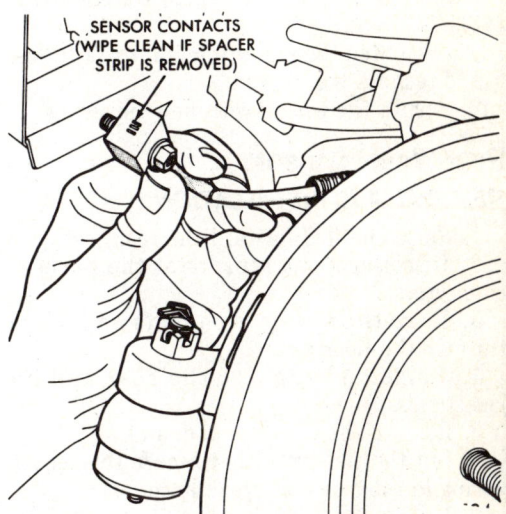
Sensor contacts with the strip removed

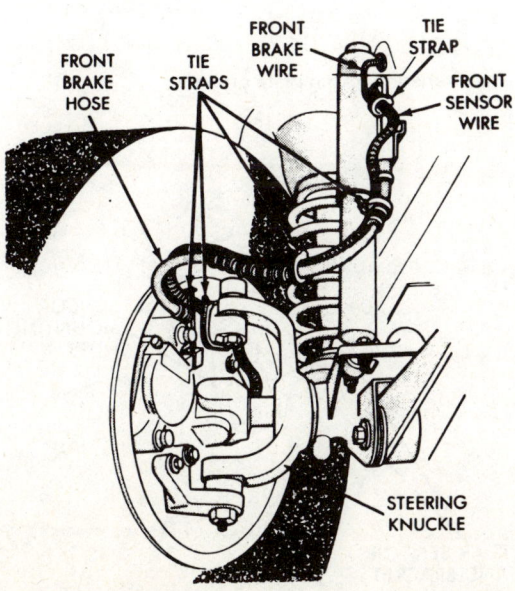
Front sensor wire routing

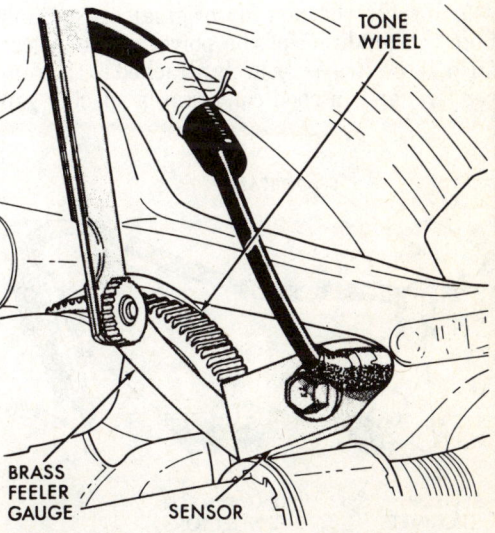
Adjusting the sensor-to-tone wheel air gap

428 BRAKES

sor face, and in good condition, a spacing gap adjustment will not be needed. However, if the strip is loose or damaged, the correct air gap will have to be set, using a brass feeler gauge. The setting will be described later in this procedure.

10. Install the wiring and connect it.
11. Position the sensor on the knuckle and loosely install the mounting bolt.
12. If the spacer strip is tight and in good condition, lightly press the sensor against the tone wheel and tighten the bolt to 11 ft. lbs.
13. If an adjustment is necessary:
    a. Remove and dicard the spacer strip.
    b. Clean the sensor contacts thoroughly with a shop towel.
    c. Using the brass feeler gauge, set the sensor-to-tone wheel gap to 0.013-0.019" (0.33-0.48mm).
    d. Tighten the mounting bolt to 11 ft. lbs. and recheck the air gap.
14. Secure the wiring with new tie straps.

Rear Wheel Sensors

REMOVAL AND INSTALLATION

1. Raise and fold forward the rear seat.
2. Disconnect the sensors at the harness connectors.
3. Push the sensor grommets and wires through the floor pan.
4. Raise and support the rear end on jackstands.
5. Remove the wheels and drums.
6. Cut the tie straps that secure the sensor wiring to the axle and brake hose.
7. Unseat the sensor backing plate grommet.
8. Remove the sensor attaching bolt and remove the sensor by pulling it through the grommet hole in the backing plate.
9. Inspect the new or original sensor and note the condition of the polyethylene spacer strip. If the strip is securely attached to the sensor face, and in good condition, a spacing gap

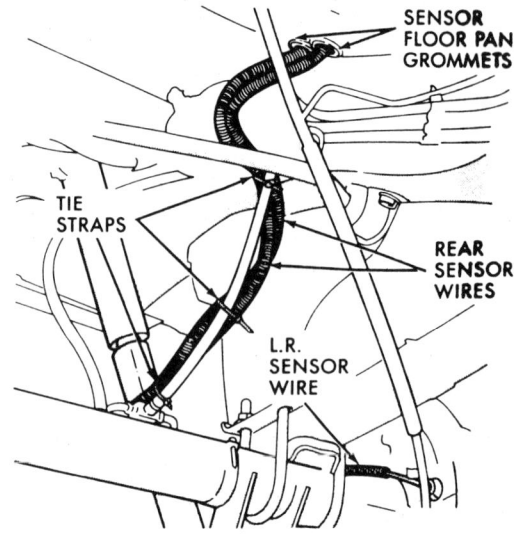

Rear sensor wire routing

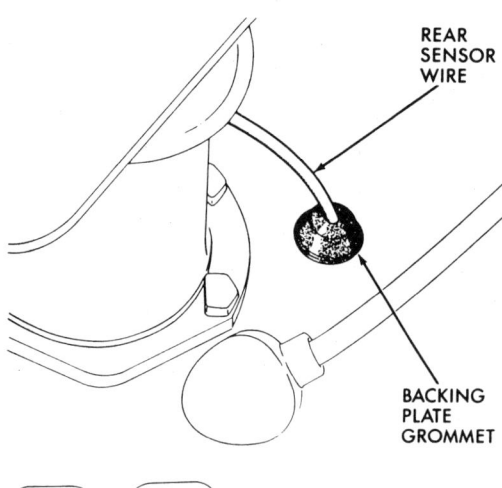

Rear sensor backing plate grommet

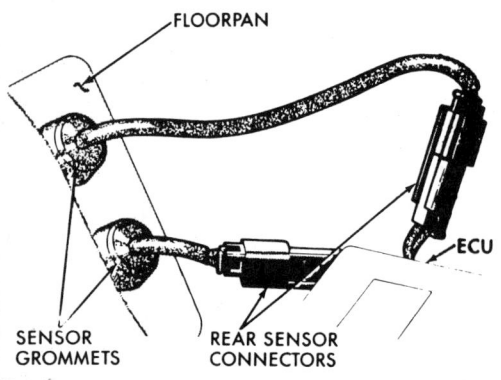

Rear sensor connectors

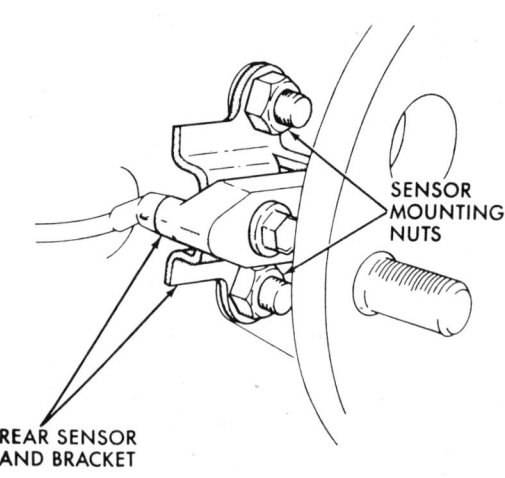

Rear sensor and bracket attachment

BRAKES 429

adjustment will not be needed. However, if the strip is loose or damaged, the correct air gap will have to be set, using a brass feeler gauge. The setting will be described later in this procedure.

10. Install the wiring and connect it.

11. Position the sensor on the bracket and loosely install the mounting bolt.

12. If the spacer strip is tight and in good condition, lightly press the sensor against the tone wheel and tighten the bolt to 11 ft. lbs.

13. If an adjustment is necessary:

  a. Remove and dicard the spacer strip.

  b. Clean the sensor contacts thoroughly with a shop towel.

  c. Using the brass feeler gauge, set the sensor-to-tone wheel gap to 0.030-0.036" (0.76-0.91mm).

  d. Tighten the mounting bolt to 11 ft. lbs. and recheck the air gap.

14. Secure the wiring with new tie straps.

15. Make sure that the wire is clear of any moving components.

16. Install the drum and wheel.

Booster Pump and Motor
REMOVAL AND INSTALLATION

CAUTION: *Relieve the system pressure as described above before opening any fittings! Always wear goggles when opening any fitting!*

1. Once system pressure is relieved, check

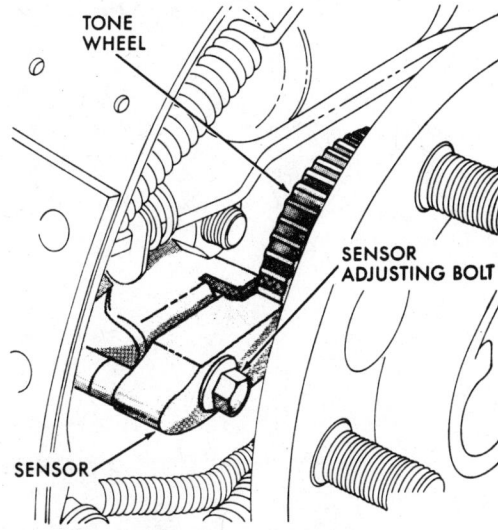

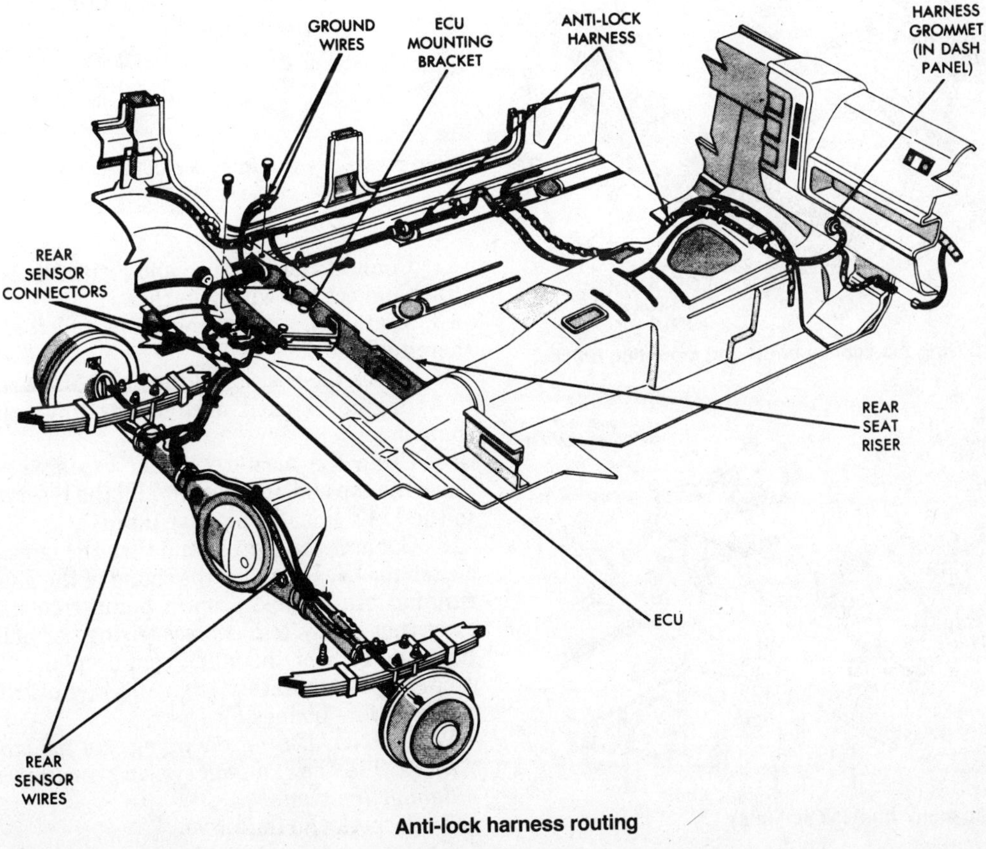

Rear sensor location

Anti-lock harness routing

430 BRAKES

the fluid level in the reservoir. It should have risen above the **MAX** fill line, but not overflowed. If overflowing occured, the system was over-filled to begin with.

2. Disconnect the battery ground cable.
3. Remove the coolant overflow bottle.
4. Remove the pump/motor mounting bracket bolts at the firewall and fender.
5. Rotate the pump/motor assembly to one side for access to the hoses and wires.
6. Unplug the wiring harness connector.
7. **SLOWLY** loosen the pressure line at the pump and allow any residual pressure to bleed off, then, disconnect the line.
8. Position a catch pan under the pump return line, loosen the clamp and disconnect the line. Discard any drined fluid.
9. Remove the pump/motor and bracket as an assembly. After removal, the units can be unbolted from the bracket.

To install:

10. Position the unit in the engine compartment.

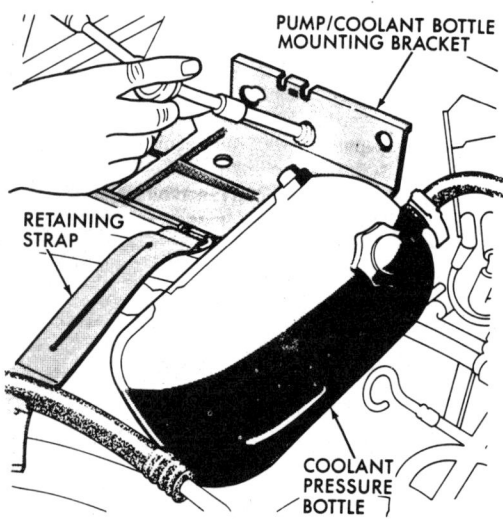

Removing the coolant bottle and mounting bracket

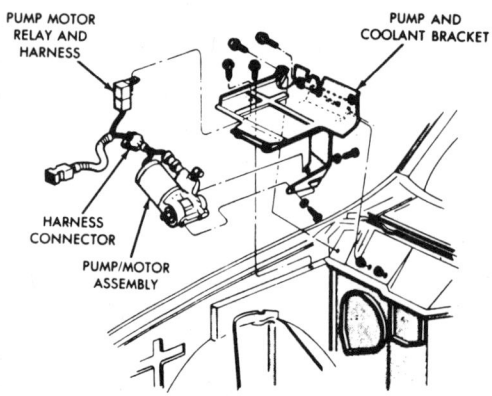

Pump motor harness and relay

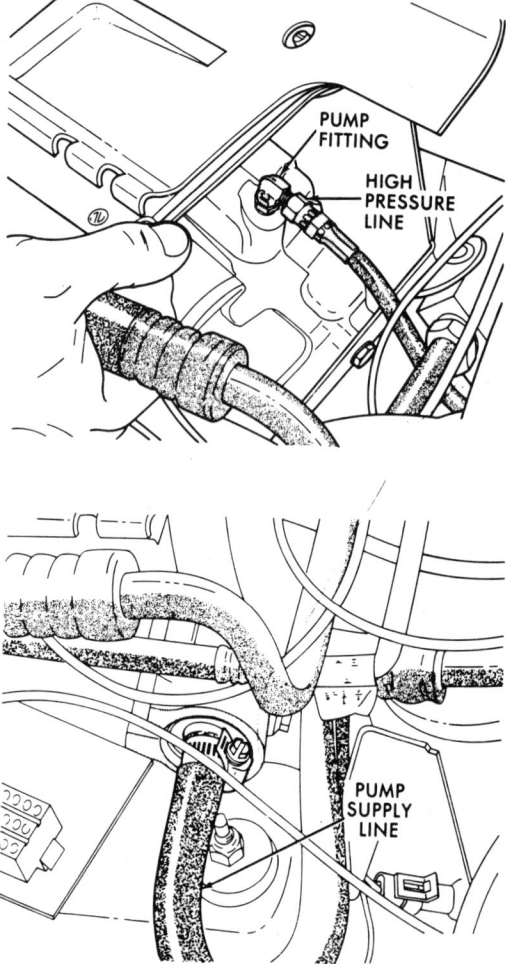

Pump pressure and supply line connections

11. Connect the pressure and return lines.
12. Connect the wiring harness.
13. Install the mounting bolts and torque them to 30 ft. lbs.
14. Check the position of the lines. Make sure they are not kinked or touching any other component.
15. Clean the master cylinder cap area, remove the cap and, if necessary, fill the reservoir to the MAX line. Do not overfill it!
16. Connect the battery and turn the ignition switch to **ON**. Listen for the sound of the pump running. An audible drop in pump rpm indicates that the system is pressurizing normally. If you don't hear the pump rpm drop after 20 seconds, immediately turn the key off and check all line fittings for leaks.

WARNING: *Letting the pump run for more than 20 seconds without system pressure will danage the pump!*

17. Recheck the fluid level.

BRAKES

Master Cylinder/Modulator/Accumulator

REMOVAL AND INSTALLATION

CAUTION: *Relieve the system pressure as described above. Always wear goggles when disconnecting any pressure line!*

1. Disconnect the battery ground cable.
2. Remove the windshield washer bottle.
3. Remove the air cleaner.
4. Disconnect the electronic control unit harness at the pressure modulator.
5. Disconnect the wiring at the proportioning valve.
6. Disconnect the brake line under the proportioning valve at the coupling.
7. Disconnect and cap the pressure line at the accumulator block.
8. Place a drain pan under the supply line and disconnect the supply line at the reservoir. Cap the openings. Discard the drained fluid.
9. Disconnect the low pressure switch wiring.
10. Disconnect the wiring at the modulator boost pressure and fluid level switches.
11. Disconnect the front brake lines at the outboard side of the pressure modulator.
12. Remove the instrument panel lower trim cover.
13. Disconnect the wiring at the brake light switch.
14. Remove the master cylinder pushrod bolt

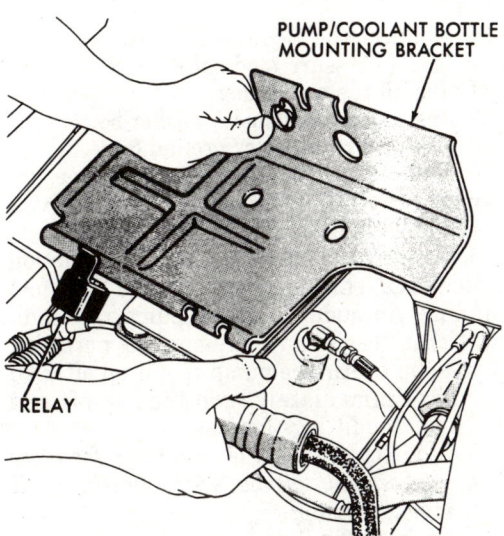

Installing the relay and pump mounting bracket

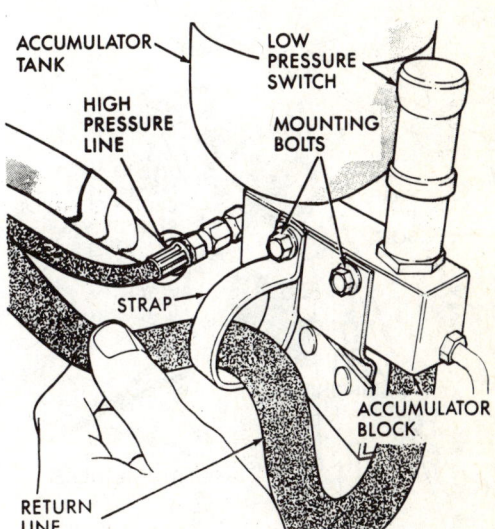

Fluid line connections

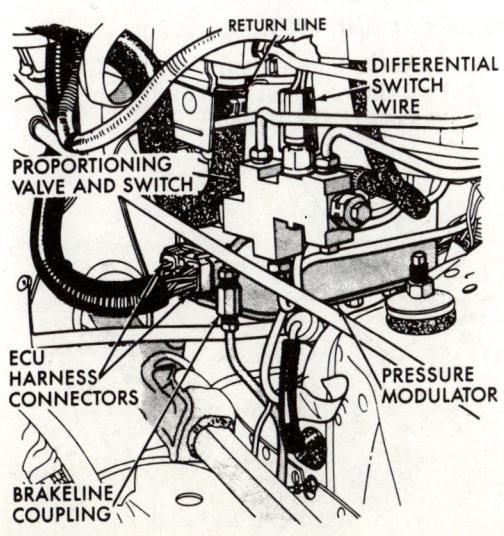

ECU harness and fluid connection

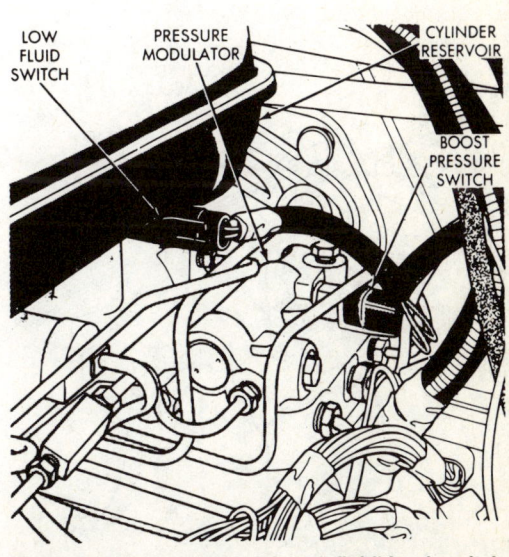

Boost pressure differential and fluid level switch connections

432 BRAKES

and disconnect the pushrod from the brake pedal. Discard the pushrod bolt nuts.
15. Remove the master cylinder mounting stud nuts.
16. In the engine comaprtment, pull the assembly and mounting braket forward until the studs are clear of the firewall.
17. Lift the assembly out of the engine comaprtment.

To install:
18. Position the assembly in the firewall.
19. Install the master cylinder mounting stud nuts. Torque the nuts to 27 ft. lbs.
20. Connect the pushrod at the brake pedal. Torque the new nuts to 25 ft. lbs. for the inner locknut; 75 in. lbs. for the outer jam nut.

NOTE: *The pushrod must be installed with the bolt head on the left side of the pedal.*

21. Connect the wiring at the brake light switch.
22. Install the instrument panel lower trim cover.
23. Connect the front brake lines at the outboard side of the pressure modulator.
24. Connect the wiring at the modulator boost pressure and fluid level switches.
25. Connect the low pressure switch wiring.
26. Connect the supply line at the reservoir.
27. Connect the pressure line at the accumulator block.
28. Connect the brake line under the proportioning valve at the coupling.
29. Connect the wiring at the proportioning valve.
30. Connect the electronic control unit harness at the pressure modulator.
31. Install the air cleaner.
32. Install the windshield washer bottle.
33. Connect the battery ground cable.
34. Clean the master cylinder cap area, remove the cap and, if necessary, fill the reservoir to the MAX line. Do not overfill it!
35. Connect the battery and turn the ignition switch to **ON**. Listen for the sound of the pump running. An audible drop in pump rpm indicates that the system is pressurizing normally. If you don't hear the pump rpm drop after 20 seconds, immediately turn the key off and check all line fittings for leaks.

WARNING: *Letting the pump run for more than 20 seconds without system pressure will danage the pump!*

36. Recheck the fluid level.
37. Bleed the brake system.

Electronic Control Unit
REMOVAL AND INSTALLATION

1. Turn the ignition switch to **OFF**.
2. Fold the rear seat cushion forward.
3. Remove the ECU mouting bracket screws.

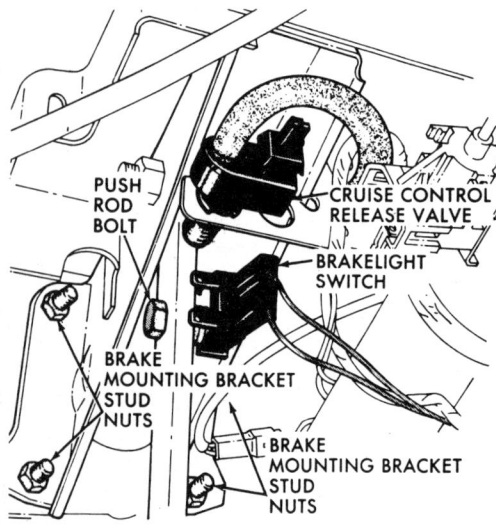

Brake light switch and mounting bracket stud nut location

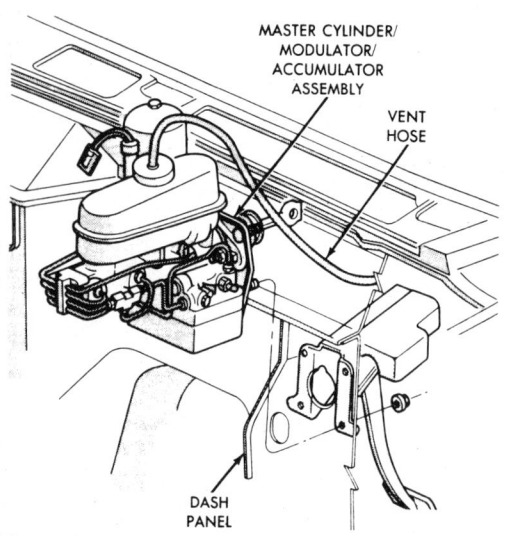

Removing the master cylinder, modulator and accumulator assembly

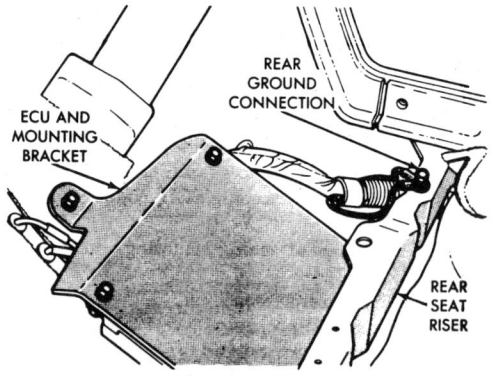

Anti-lock rear ground wires

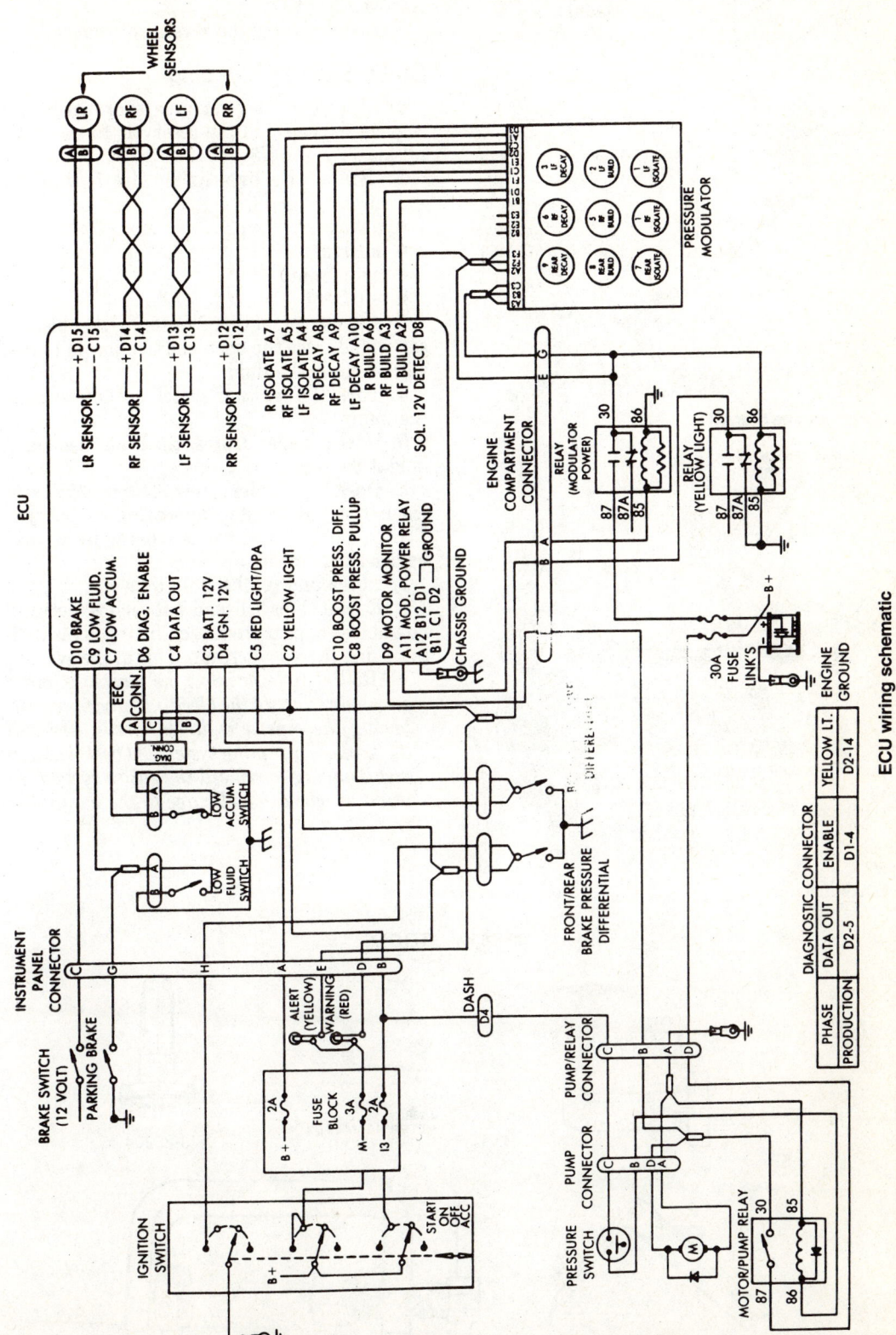

ECU wiring schematic

434 BRAKES

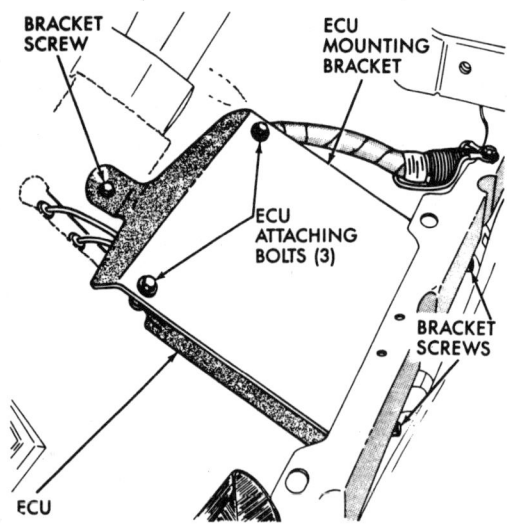

ECU mounting bracket

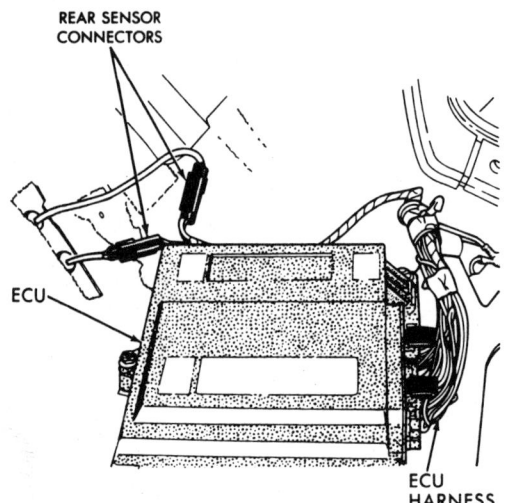

ECU connection

4. Unplug the wiring harness connector and remove the ECU.
5. Installation is the reverse of removal.

Brake System Bleeding

1. Clean the reservoir area thoroughly and remove the cap. Fill the reservoir to the MAX fill line.
2. Bleed the brakes in the following sequence:
- right rear
- left rear
- right front
- left front

3. Attach a length of hose to the bleeder screw and place the open end in a jar half filled with clean brake fluid.
4. Turn the ignition switch to **ON** to cycle the pump.
5. Have a helper depress the brake pedal and hold it depressed.
6. Open the bleeder screw ½ turn and close it when the bubble stop appearing in the jar. THEN, once the screw is closed, have your helper let the pedal up.
7. Check and refill the fluid level.
8. Repeat steps 5, 6, and 7 at each wheel until no bubbles appear from each fitting. This indicates that there is no trapped air in the system.

WARNING: *Never allow the master cylinder to run dry during the bleeding procedure! Allowing the master cylinder to run dry will aloow more air in the system. At best that will mean having to rebleed the entire system. At worst, it will cause danage to the pump!*

SPECIAL TOOLS

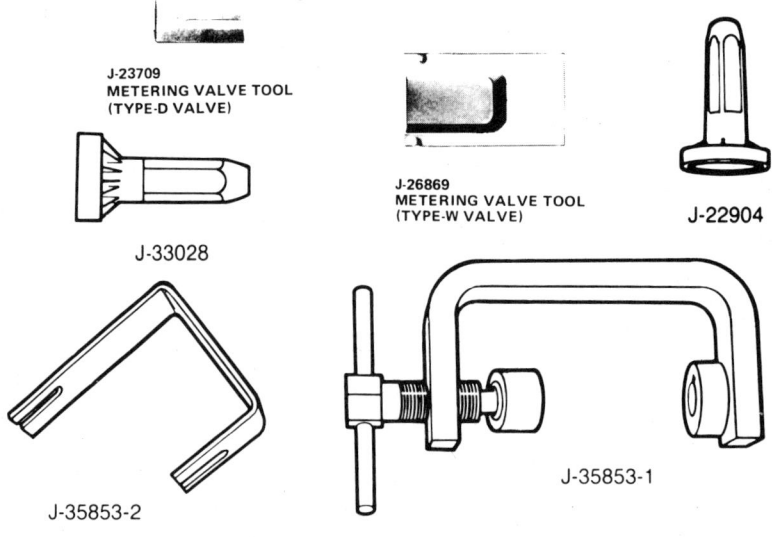

Body 10

EXTERIOR

Hood

REMOVAL AND INSTALLATION

1. If the hood is properly aligned, prior to removal, matchmark the position of the hinges and hood reinforcement.
2. Raise the hood fully.
3. Disconnect the underhood lamp wiring.
4. While your assistant supports the hood, remove the hood-to-hinge bolts and lift off the hood.
5. Installation is the reverse of removal. Torque the bolts to 23 ft. lbs.

ALIGNMENT

NOTE: *Hood hinge mounting holes are oversized to permit movement for hood alignment. If the hood is to be moved to either side, the hood lock striker, hood lever lock and safety hook assembly must first be loosened.*

1. Loosen the hinge mounting bolts slightly on one side and tap the hinge in the direction opposite to that in which the hood is to be moved.
2. Tighten the bolts.
3. Repeat this procedure for the opposite hinge.
4. Check that the lock striker, lever lock and safety hook are properly adjusted to ensure positive locking. Torque the lock bolts to 10-12 ft. lbs.
5. If the rear edge of the hood is not flush with the cowl, add or subtract shims (caster and camber adjusting shims will work) or flat washers between the hinge and the hood at the rear bolt (hood too low) or front bolt (hood too high).
6. Adjust the hood-to-fender height using the front bumpers, located at the left and right front corners of the vehicle.

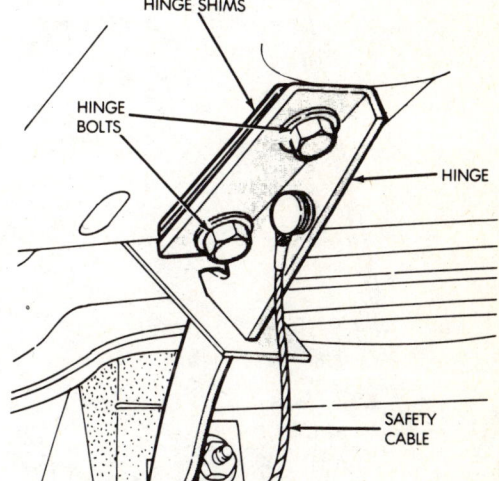
Hood hinge and shim position

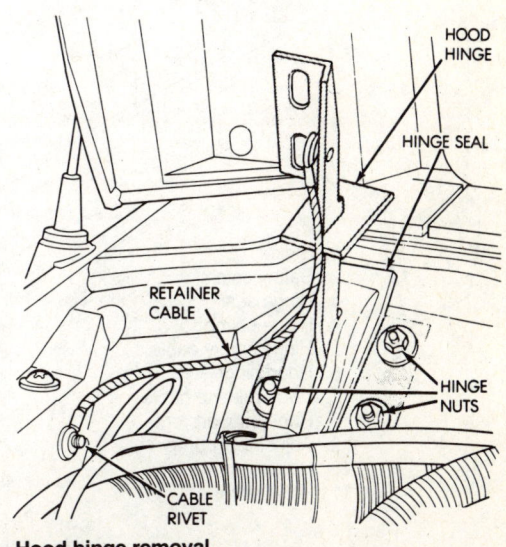
Hood hinge removal

Tailgate

REMOVAL AND INSTALLATION
Comanche

1. Lower the tailgate.
2. Pull each support up at the center and force the upper end forward, then inward, to disengage it from the retaining dowel.
3. Pull the right side of the tailgate rearward to disengage the hinge.
4. Move the tailgate to the right to disengage the left hinge.
5. Installation is the reverse of removal.

ADJUSTMENT

The only adjustment possible to the Commanche's tailgate is the striker adjustment. This is peformed by loosening the striker plate screws and moving the striker to properly position it.

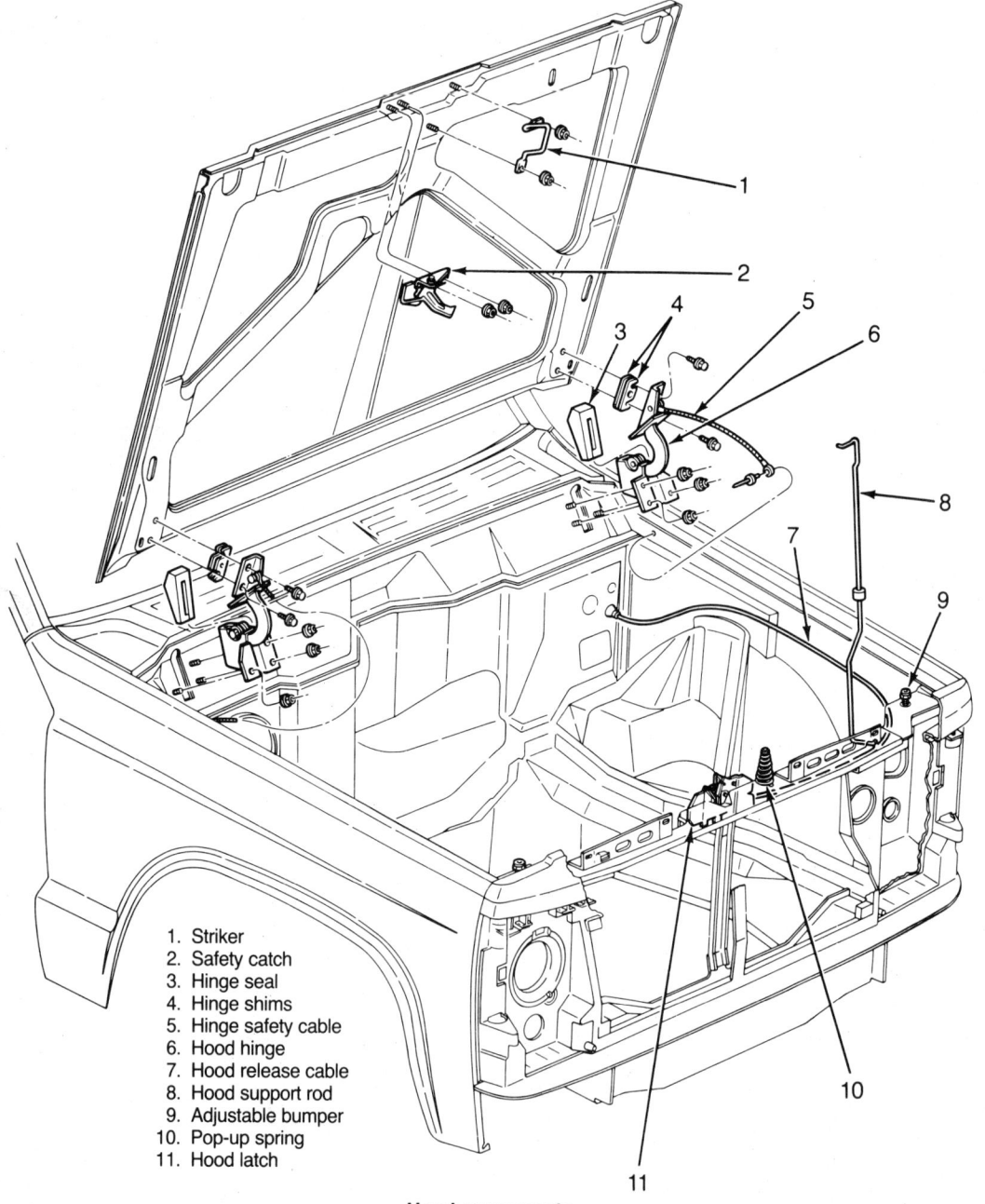

1. Striker
2. Safety catch
3. Hinge seal
4. Hinge shims
5. Hinge safety cable
6. Hood hinge
7. Hood release cable
8. Hood support rod
9. Adjustable bumper
10. Pop-up spring
11. Hood latch

Hood components

BODY 437

Liftgate

REMOVAL AND INSTALLATION

Wagoneer and Cherokee

1. Open the liftgate.
2. Remove the trim panel.

CAUTION: *Never attempt to remove a support cylinder with the liftgate closed. The cylinders contain gas under high pressure. Severe personal injury may occur if the cylinders are disconnect with the liftgate closed!*

3. Remove the retainer clips from the ball studs at the ends of the liftgate support cylinders.
4. Pull the support cylinders off of the ball studs.
5. Disconnect and remove the wiring harness.
6. Have a helper support the liftgate and remove the liftgate hinge bolts.
7. Installation is the reverse of removal. Check alignment.

How to Remove Stains from Fabric Interior

For rest results, spots and stains should be removed as soon as possible. Never use gasoline, lacquer thinner, acetone, nail polish remover or bleach. Use a 3′ x 3″ piece of cheesecloth. Squeeze most of the liquid from the fabric and wipe the stained fabric from the outside of the stain toward the center with a lifting motion. Turn the cheesecloth as soon as one side becomes soiled. When using water to remove a stain, be sure to wash the entire section after the spot has been removed to avoid water stains. Encrusted spots can be broken up with a dull knife and vacuumed before removing the stain.

Type of Stain	How to Remove It
Surface spots	Brush the spots out with a small hand brush or use a commercial preparation such as K2R to lift the stain.
Mildew	Clean around the mildew with warm suds. Rinse in cold water and soak the mildew area in a solution of 1 part table salt and 2 parts water. Wash with upholstery cleaner.
Water stains	Water stains in fabric materials can be removed with a solution made from 1 cup of table salt dissolved in 1 quart of water. Vigorously scrub the solution into the stain and rinse with clear water. Water stains in nylon or other synthetic fabrics should be removed with a commercial type spot remover.
Chewing gum, tar, crayons, shoe polish (greasy stains)	Do not use a cleaner that will soften gum or tar. Harden the deposit with an ice cube and scrape away as much as possible with a dull knife. Moisten the remainder with cleaning fluid and scrub clean.
Ice cream, candy	Most candy has a sugar base and can be removed with a cloth wrung out in warm water. Oily candy, after cleaning with warm water, should be cleaned with upholstery cleaner. Rinse with warm water and clean the remainder with cleaning fluid.
Wine, alcohol, egg, milk, soft drink (non-greasy stains)	Do not use soap. Scrub the stain with a cloth wrung out in warm water. Remove the remainder with cleaning fluid.
Grease, oil, lipstick, butter and related stains	Use a spot remover to avoid leaving a ring. Work from the outisde of the stain to the center and dry with a clean cloth when the spot is gone.
Headliners (cloth)	Mix a solution of warm water and foam upholstery cleaner to give thick suds. Use only foam—liquid may streak or spot. Clean the entire headliner in one operation using a circular motion with a natural sponge.
Headliner (vinyl)	Use a vinyl cleaner with a sponge and wipe clean with a dry cloth.
Seats and door panels	Mix 1 pint upholstery cleaner in 1 gallon of water. Do not soak the fabric around the buttons.
Leather or vinyl fabric	Use a multi-purpose cleaner full strength and a stiff brush. Let stand 2 minutes and scrub thoroughly. Wipe with a clean, soft rag.
Nylon or synthetic fabrics	For normal stains, use the same procedures you would for washing cloth upholstery. If the fabric is extremely dirty, use a multi-purpose cleaner full strength with a stiff scrub brush. Scrub thoroughly in all directions and wipe with a cotton towel or soft rag.

438 BODY

ADJUSTMENT

The hinge-to-body bolt holes are slotted to permit satisfactory alignment.

Windshield

REMOVAL AND INSTALLATION

Thse models use bonded windshields. Windshield installation and the adhesives used are critical in meeting Federal regulations. Therefore, it is recommended that windshield replacement procedures on these vehicles be left to a professional shop.

Rear Window Glass and Rear Quarter Stationary Glass

REMOVAL AND INSTALLATION

NOTE: *This procedure applies to the rear quarter stationary glass in Wagoneers and Cherokees. The rear cab window on the Comanche uses a bonded installation procedure. See the note under Windshields, above.*

1. Remove the interior trim moldings from around the window. Where necessary, remove the spare tire and mounting bracket.

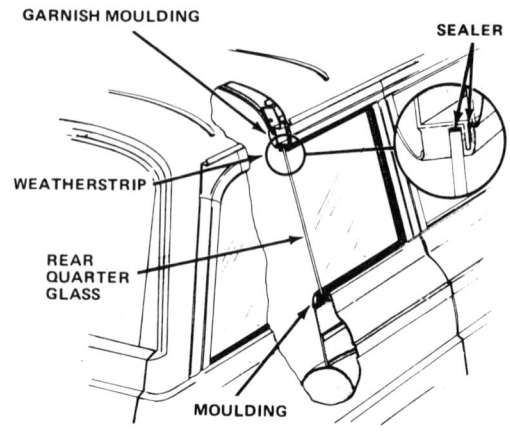

Typical rear quarter stationary glass installation

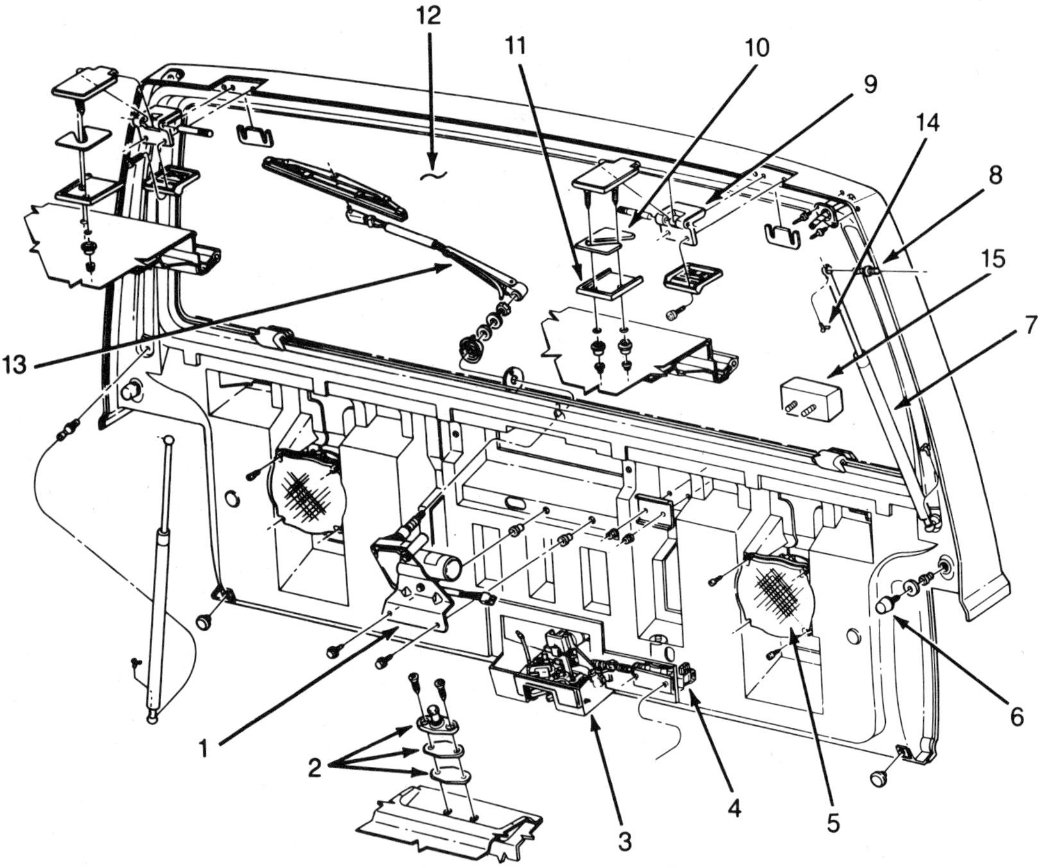

1. Wiper motor assembly
2. Striker and shims
3. Latch assembly
4. Power lock actuator
5. Speaker location
6. Liftgate stop
7. Support cylinder
8. Support cylinder attaching location
9. Liftgate hinge
10. Hinge shim

Liftgate components

BODY 439

2. Break loose the seal between the weatherstripping and the body panels.

3. Have someone outside push inward on the glass while you catch it.

4. Clean all old sealer from the glass and weatherstripping.

5. Fill the glass cavity in the weatherstripping with a $3/16''$ bead of sealer.

6. Fit the glass in the weatherstripping and place a $1/4''$ diameter cord in the frame cavity around the outside diameter of the weatherstripping. Allow the ends of the cord to hang down the outside of the glass from the top center.

7. Place the glass and weatherstripping in the vehicle opening. Pull on the cord ends to

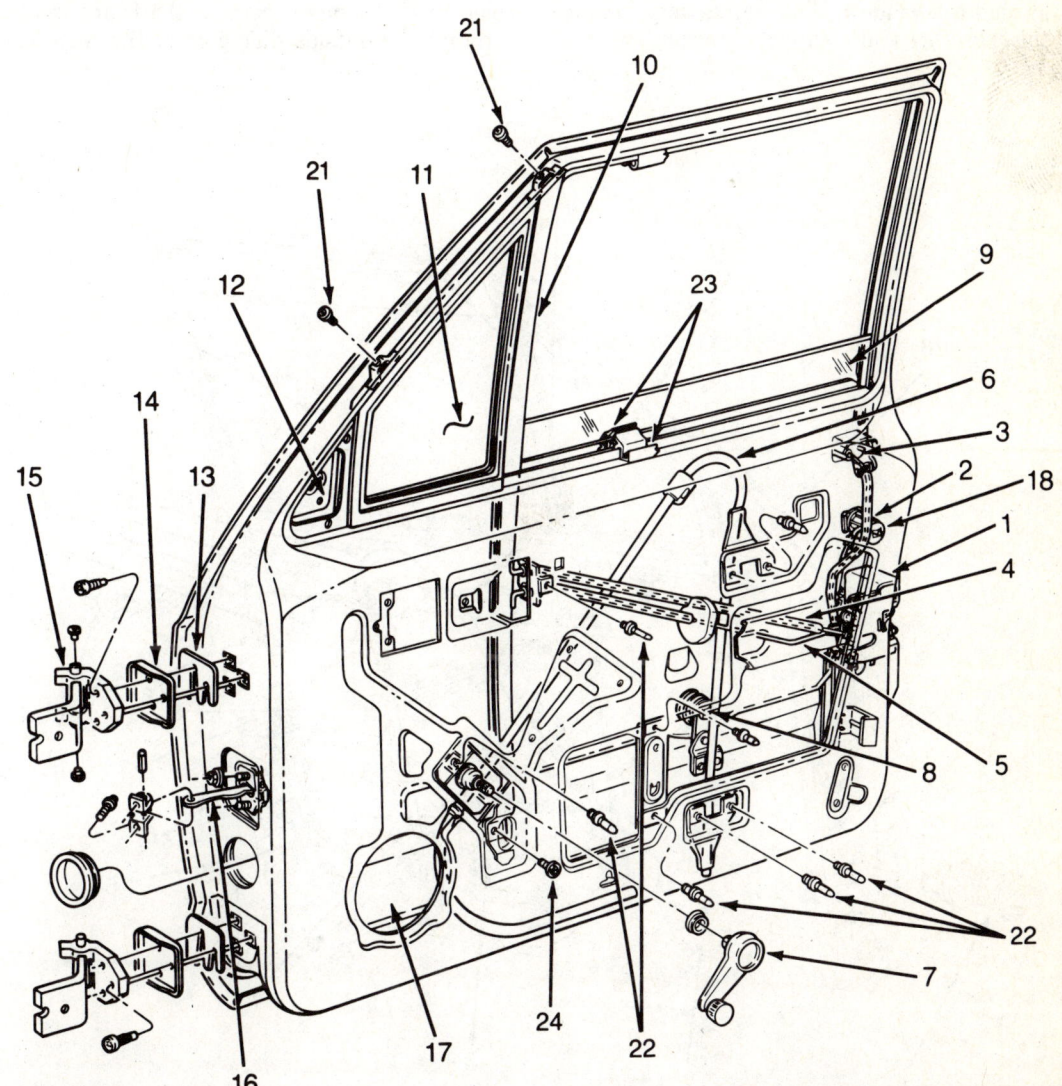

1. Latch assembly
2. Mechanical linkage
3. Exterior door release
4. Internal lock linkage
5. Internal release linkage
6. Window regulator
7. Window regulator handle
8. Window mounting surface
9. Window glass
10. Glass channel
11. Vent window
12. Side view mirror mounting surface
13. Door shims
14. Door shim mounting plate
15. Door hinge
16. Door stop
17. Speaker mounting surface
18. Door lock cylinder
21. Vent window screws
22. Window track rivets and screws
23. Weatherstrip—inner and outer
24. Glass channel screw

Front door with manual window and locks

440 BODY

pull the lip of the weatherstripping over the body panel.

8. Install the trim molding.

Liftgate Window

REMOVAL AND INSTALLATION

Wagoneer and Cherokee

1. Remove the exterior trim moldings from around the window. Where necessary, remove the spare tire and mounting bracket.

2. Break loose the seal between the weatherstripping and the body panel.

3. Have someone inside push outward on the glass while you catch it.

4. Clean all old sealer from the glass and weatherstripping.

5. Fill the glass cavity in the weatherstripping with a $3/16''$ bead of sealer.

6. Fit the glass in the weatherstripping and place a $1/4''$ diameter cord in the frame cavity around the outside diameter of the weather-

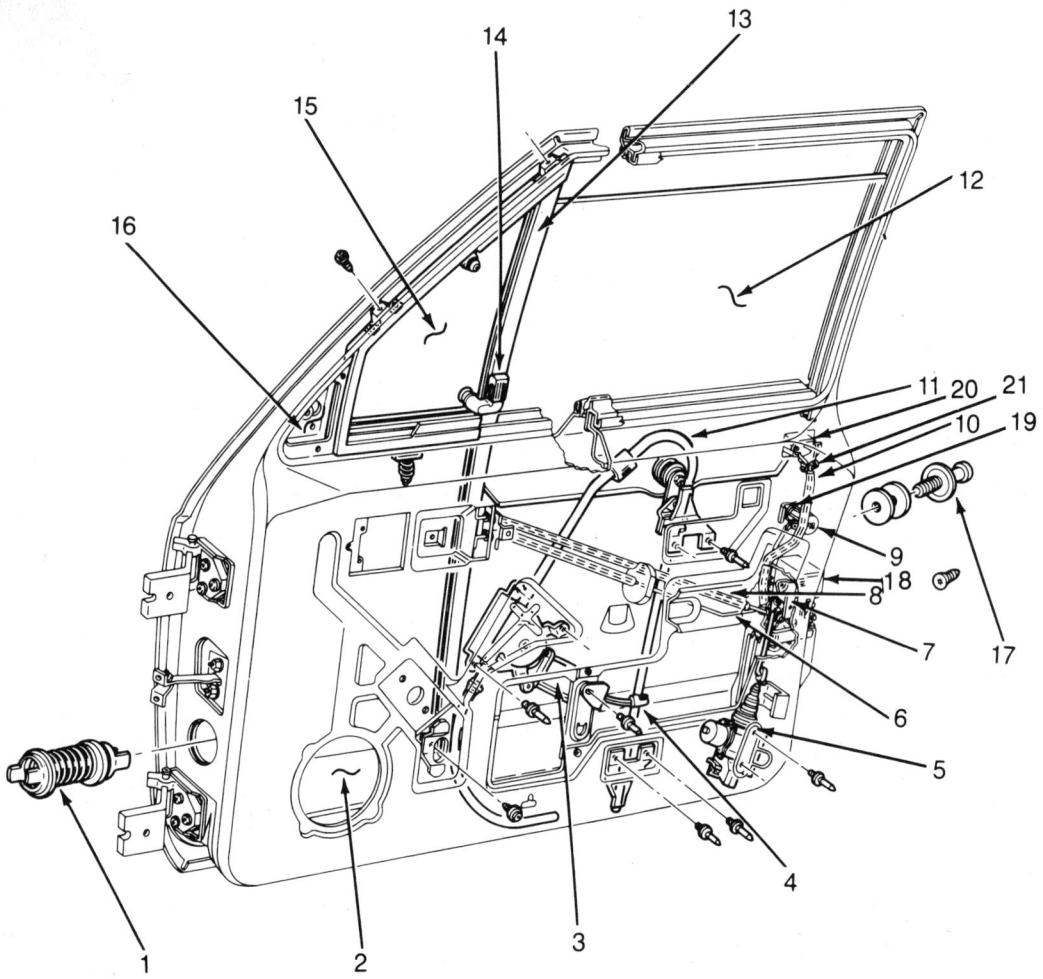

1. Wire harness boot
2. Speaker mounting surface
3. Power window motor
4. Motor wire harness connector
5. Power lock actuator
6. Internal latch release linkage
7. Door latch
8. Internal lock linkage
9. External lock
10. External latch release linkage
11. Window regulator
12. Window glass
13. Window channel
14. Vent window latch
15. Vent window
16. Side view mirror mounting surface
17. Striker
18. Latch assembly
19. External lock cylinder retainer clip
20. External door handle
21. Access plug (external door handle)

Front door with power window and locks

CHILTON'S
AUTO BODY REPAIR TIPS

Tools and Materials • Step-by-Step Illustrated Procedures
How To Repair Dents, Scratches and Rust Holes
Spray Painting and Refinishing Tips

EASY STEP-BY-STEP TIPS FROM PROS

With a little practice, basic body repair procedures can be mastered by any do-it-yourself mechanic. The step-by-step repairs shown here can be applied to almost any type of auto body repair.

TOOLS & MATERIALS

You may already have basic tools, such as hammers and electric drills. Other tools unique to body repair — body hammers, grinding attachments, sanding blocks, dent puller, half-round plastic file and plastic spreaders — are relatively inexpensive and can be obtained wherever auto parts or auto body repair parts are sold. Portable air compressors and paint spray guns can be purchased or rented.

Auto Body Repair Kits

The best and most often used products are available to the do-it-yourselfer in kit form, from major manufacturers of auto body repair products. The same manufacturers also merchandise the individual products for use by pros.

Kits are available to make a wide variety of repairs, including holes, dents and scratches and fiberglass, and offer the advantage of buying the materials you'll need for the job. There is little waste or chance of materials going bad from not being used. Many kits may also contain basic body-working tools such as body files, sanding blocks and spreaders. Check the contents of the kit before buying your tools.

BODY REPAIR TIPS

Safety

Many of the products associated with auto body repair and refinishing contain toxic chemicals. Read all labels before opening containers and store them in a safe place and manner.

• Wear eye protection (safety goggles) when using power tools or when performing any operation that involves the removal of any type of material.

• Wear lung protection (disposable mask or respirator) when grinding, sanding or painting.

Sanding

1 Sand off paint before using a dent puller. When using a non-adhesive sanding disc, cover the back of the disc with an overlapping layer or two of masking tape and trim the edges. The disc will last considerably longer.

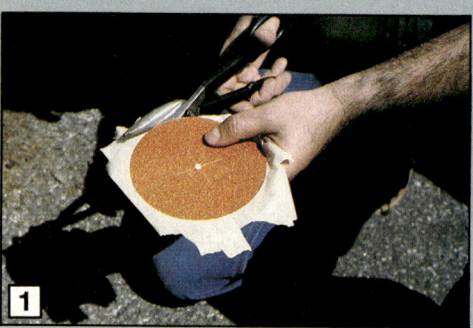

2 Use the circular motion of the sanding disc to grind *into* the edge of the repair. Grinding or sanding away from the jagged edge will only tear the sandpaper.

3 Use the palm of your hand flat on the panel to detect high and low spots. Do not use your fingertips. Slide your hand slowly back and forth.

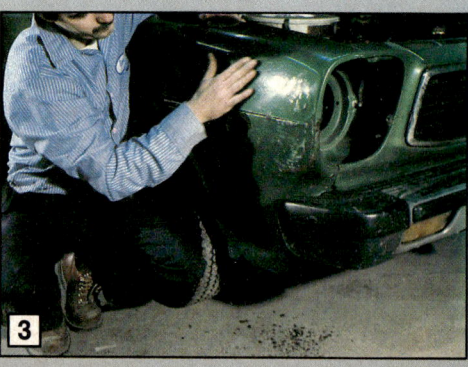

WORKING WITH BODY FILLER

Mixing The Filler

Cleanliness and proper mixing and application are extremely important. Use a clean piece of plastic or glass or a disposable artist's palette to mix body filler.

1 Allow plenty of time and follow directions. No useful purpose will be served by adding more hardener to make it cure (set-up) faster. Less hardener means more curing time, but the mixture dries harder; more hardener means less curing time but a softer mixture.

2 Both the hardener and the filler should be thoroughly kneaded or stirred before mixing. Hardener should be a solid paste and dispense like thin toothpaste. Body filler should be smooth, and free of lumps or thick spots.

Getting the proper amount of hardener in the filler is the trickiest part of preparing the filler. Use the same amount of hardener in cold or warm weather. For contour filler (thick coats), a bead of hardener twice the diameter of the filler is about right. There's about a 15% margin on either side, but, if in doubt use less hardener.

3 Mix the body filler and hardener by wiping across the mixing surface, picking the mixture up and wiping it again. Colder weather requires longer mixing times. Do not mix in a circular motion; this will trap air bubbles which will become holes in the cured filler.

Applying The Filler

1 For best results, filler should not be applied over ¼" thick.

Apply the filler in several coats. Build it up to above the level of the repair surface so that it can be sanded or grated down.

The first coat of filler must be pressed on with a firm wiping motion.

Apply the filler in one direction only. Working the filler back and forth will either pull it off the metal or trap air bubbles.

REPAIRING DENTS

Before you start, take a few minutes to study the damaged area. Try to visualize the shape of the panel before it was damaged. If the damage is on the left fender, look at the right fender and use it as a guide. If there is access to the panel from behind, you can reshape it with a body hammer. If not, you'll have to use a dent puller. Go slowly and work the metal a little at a time. Get the panel as straight as possible before applying filler.

1 This dent is typical of one that can be pulled out or hammered out from behind. Remove the headlight cover, headlight assembly and turn signal housing.

2 Drill a series of holes 1/2 the size of the end of the dent puller along the stress line. Make some trial pulls and assess the results. If necessary, drill more holes and try again. Do not hurry.

3 If possible, use a body hammer and block to shape the metal back to its original contours. Get the metal back as close to its original shape as possible. Don't depend on body filler to fill dents.

4 Using an 80-grit grinding disc on an electric drill, grind the paint from the surrounding area down to bare metal. Use a new grinding pad to prevent heat buildup that will warp metal.

5 The area should look like this when you're finished grinding. Knock the drill holes in and tape over small openings to keep plastic filler out.

6 Mix the body filler (see Body Repair Tips). Spread the body filler evenly over the entire area (see Body Repair Tips). Be sure to cover the area completely.

7 Let the body filler dry until the surface can just be scratched with your fingernail. Knock the high spots from the body filler with a body file ("Cheesegrater"). Check frequently with the palm of your hand for high and low spots.

8 Check to be sure that trim pieces that will be installed later will fit exactly. Sand the area with 40-grit paper.

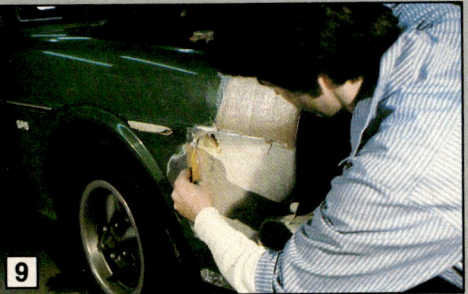

9 If you wind up with low spots, you may have to apply another layer of filler.

10 Knock the high spots off with 40-grit paper. When you are satisfied with the contours of the repair, apply a thin coat of filler to cover pin holes and scratches.

11 Block sand the area with 40-grit paper to a smooth finish. Pay particular attention to body lines and ridges that must be well-defined.

12 Sand the area with 400 paper and then finish with a scuff pad. The finished repair is ready for priming and painting (see Painting Tips).

Materials and photos courtesy of Ritt Jones Auto Body, Prospect Park, PA.

REPAIRING RUST HOLES

There are many ways to repair rust holes. The fiberglass cloth kit shown here is one of the most cost efficient for the owner because it provides a strong repair that resists cracking and moisture and is relatively easy to use. It can be used on large and small holes (with or without backing) and can be applied over contoured areas. Remember, however, that short of replacing an entire panel, no repair is a guarantee that the rust will not return.

1 Remove any trim that will be in the way. Clean away all loose debris. Cut away all the rusted metal. But be sure to leave enough metal to retain the contour or body shape.

2 Grind away all traces of rust with a 24-grit grinding disc. Be sure to grind back 3-4 inches from the edge of the hole down to bare metal and be sure all traces of paint, primer and rust are removed.

3 Block sand the area with 80 or 100 grit sandpaper to get a clear, shiny surface and feathered paint edge. Tap the edges of the hole inward with a ball peen hammer.

4 If you are going to use release film, cut a piece about 2-3" larger than the area you have sanded. Place the film over the repair and mark the sanded area on the film. Avoid any unnecessary wrinkling of the film.

5 Cut 2 pieces of fiberglass matte to match the shape of the repair. One piece should be about 1" smaller than the sanded area and the second piece should be 1" smaller than the first. Mix enough filler and hardener to saturate the fiberglass material (see Body Repair Tips).

6 Lay the release sheet on a flat surface and spread an even layer of filler, large enough to cover the repair. Lay the smaller piece of fiberglass cloth in the center of the sheet and spread another layer of filler over the fiberglass cloth. Repeat the operation for the larger piece of cloth.

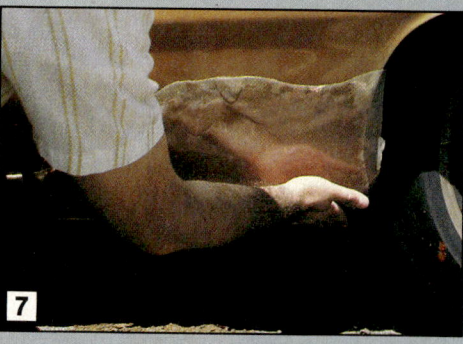

7 Place the repair material over the repair area, with the release film facing outward. Use a spreader and work from the center outward to smooth the material, following the body contours. Be sure to remove all air bubbles.

8 Wait until the repair has dried tack-free and peel off the release sheet. The ideal working temperature is 60°-90° F. Cooler or warmer temperatures or high humidity may require additional curing time. Wait longer, if in doubt.

9 Sand and feather-edge the entire area. The initial sanding can be done with a sanding disc on an electric drill if care is used. Finish the sanding with a block sander. Low spots can be filled with body filler; this may require several applications.

10 When the filler can just be scratched with a fingernail, knock the high spots down with a body file and smooth the entire area with 80-grit. Feather the filled areas into the surrounding areas.

11 When the area is sanded smooth, mix some topcoat and hardener and apply it directly with a spreader. This will give a smooth finish and prevent the glass matte from showing through the paint.

12 Block sand the topcoat smooth with finishing sandpaper (200 grit), and 400 grit. The repair is ready for masking, priming and painting (see Painting Tips).

Materials and photos courtesy Marson Corporation, Chelsea, Massachusetts

PAINTING TIPS

Preparation

1 SANDING — Use a 400 or 600 grit wet or dry sandpaper. Wet-sand the area with a ¼ sheet of sandpaper soaked in clean water. Keep the paper wet while sanding. Sand the area until the repaired area tapers into the original finish.

2 CLEANING — Wash the area to be painted thoroughly with water and a clean rag. Rinse it thoroughly and wipe the surface dry until you're sure it's completely free of dirt, dust, fingerprints, wax, detergent or other foreign matter.

3 MASKING — Protect any areas you don't want to overspray by covering them with masking tape and newspaper. Be careful not get fingerprints on the area to be painted.

4 PRIMING — All exposed metal should be primed before painting. Primer protects the metal and provides an excellent surface for paint adhesion. When the primer is dry, wet-sand the area again with 600 grit wet-sandpaper. Clean the area again after sanding.

Painting Techniques

Paint applied from either a spray gun or a spray can (for small areas) will provide good results. Experiment on an old piece of metal to get the right combination before you begin painting.

SPRAYING VISCOSITY (SPRAY GUN ONLY) — Paint should be thinned to spraying viscosity according to the directions on the can. Use only the recommended thinner or reducer and the same amount of reduction regardless of temperature.

AIR PRESSURE (SPRAY GUN ONLY) — This is extremely important. Be sure you are using the proper recommended pressure.

TEMPERATURE — The surface to be painted should be approximately the same temperature as the surrounding air. Applying warm paint to a cold surface, or vice versa, will completely upset the paint characteristics.

THICKNESS — Spray with smooth strokes. In general, the thicker the coat of paint, the longer the drying time. Apply several thin coats about 30 seconds apart. The paint should remain wet long enough to flow out and no longer; heavier coats will only produce sags or wrinkles. Spray a light (fog) coat, followed by heavier color coats.

DISTANCE — The ideal spraying distance is 8"-12" from the gun or can to the surface. Shorter distances will produce ripples, while greater distances will result in orange peel, dry film and poor color match and loss of material due to overspray.

OVERLAPPING — The gun or can should be kept at right angles to the surface at all times. Work to a wet edge at an even speed, using a 50% overlap and direct the center of the spray at the lower or nearest edge of the previous stroke.

RUBBING OUT (BLENDING) FRESH PAINT — Let the paint dry thoroughly. Runs or imperfections can be sanded out, primed and repainted.

Don't be in too big a hurry to remove the masking. This only produces paint ridges. When the finish has dried for at least a week, apply a small amount of fine grade rubbing compound with a clean, wet cloth. Use lots of water and blend the new paint with the surrounding area.

WRONG

Thin coat. Stroke too fast, not enough overlap, gun too far away.

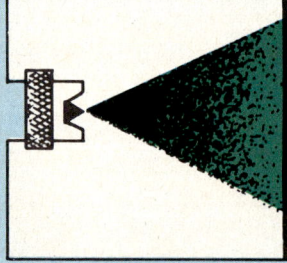

CORRECT

Medium coat. Proper distance, good stroke, proper overlap.

WRONG

Heavy coat. Stroke too slow, too much overlap, gun too close.

BODY

stripping. Allow the ends of the cord to hang down the outside of the glass from the top center.

7. Place the glass and weatherstripping in the vehicle opening. Pull on the cord ends to pull the lip of the weatherstripping over the body panel.

8. Install the trim molding.

Doors

REMOVAL AND INSTALLATION

1. On vehicles with power windows or locks, remove the trim panel and water shield. Disconnect the speaker wiring.
2. Matchmark the hinge-to-door position.
3. Have an assistant support the door.

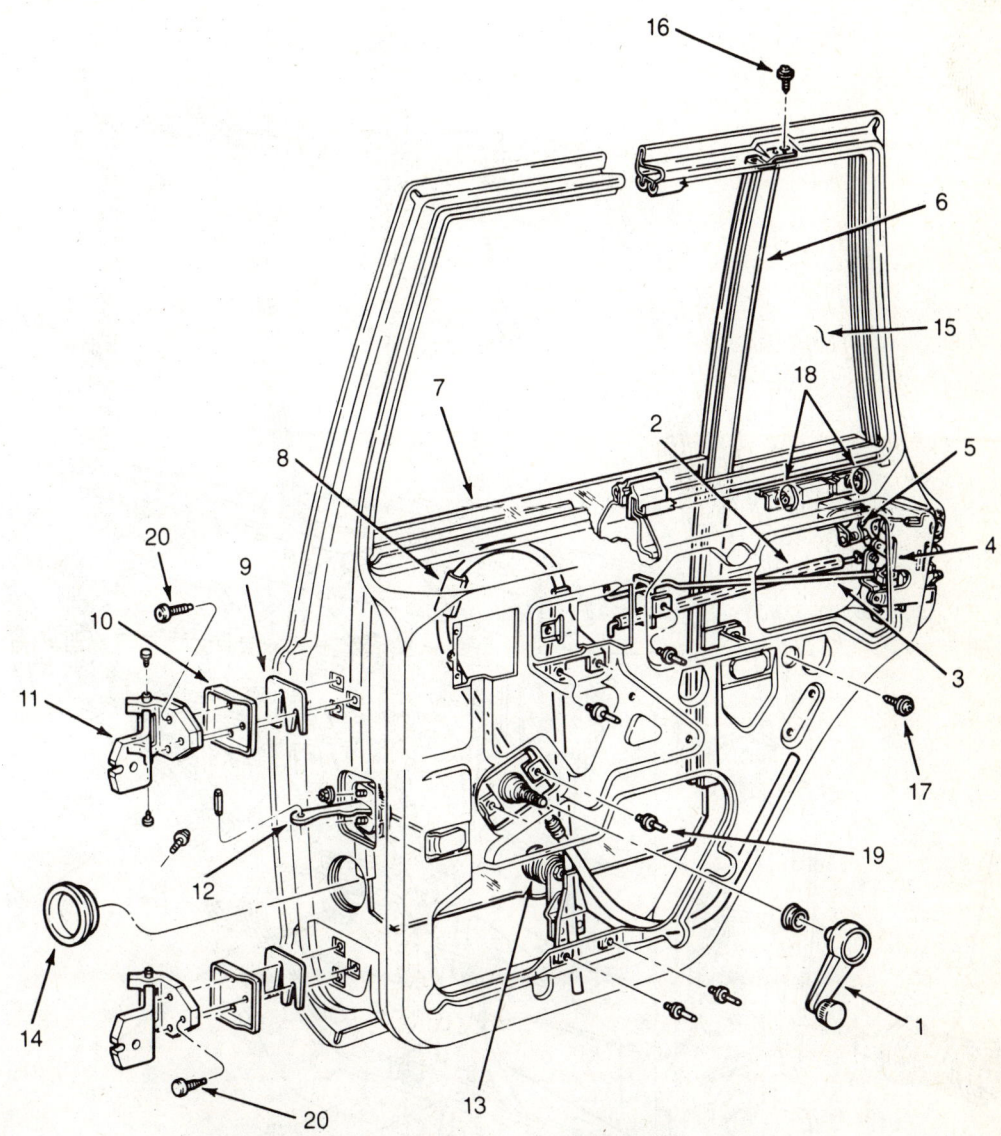

1. Window regulator crank handle
2. Internal latch release linkage
3. Internal lock linkage
4. Latch assembly
5. Exterior door handle
6. Window channel
7. Door glass
8. Window regulator
9. Shims
10. Shim retainer plate
11. Door hinge
12. Door stop
13. Glass attaching surface
14. Access plug
15. Stationary glass
16. Glass channel upper screw
17. Glass channel lower screw
18. Stationary glass frame screws
19. Regulator rivet (typical)
20. Door hinge screw

Rear door with manual window and locks

442 BODY

4. Remove the door stop-to-pillar pin.
5. Remove the hinge-to-door bolts, catch the shims, and lift off the door.
6. Position the door and shims and install, but do not tighten the bolts.
7. Adjust the door, as described below, then, torque the bolts to 26 ft. lbs.

8. Connect the wiring and install the trim panel.

ADJUSTMENT

Door adjustment is made by means of shims located between the door and the hinge. The shims are placed in shim plates. Add or remove

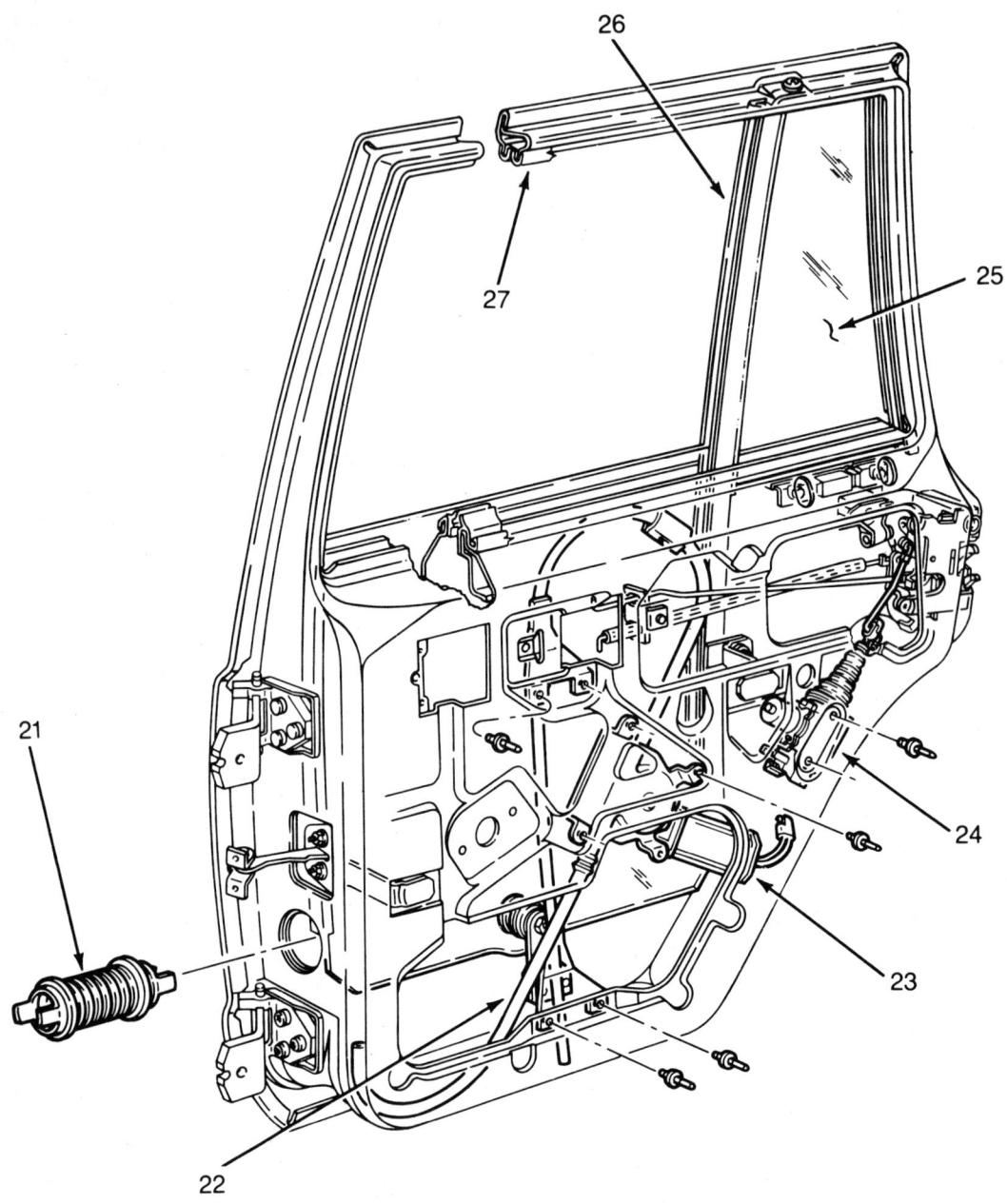

21. Wire harness boot
22. Window regulator
23. Power window motor
24. Power door lock actuator
25. Stationary glass
26. Glass channel
27. Glass slide channel

Rear door with power window and locks

BODY

shims as necessary to obtain proper door fit. When adjustment is complete, torque the mounting bolts to 26 ft. lbs.

Manual Door Locks

REMOVAL AND INSTALLATION

Lock Cylinder

1. Remove the door trim panel and plastic waterproof sheet.
2. Working through an access hole, remove the lock cylinder retaining clip.
3. Disconnect the lock control linkage.
4. Push the lock cylinder from the door.
5. Installation is the reverse of removal.

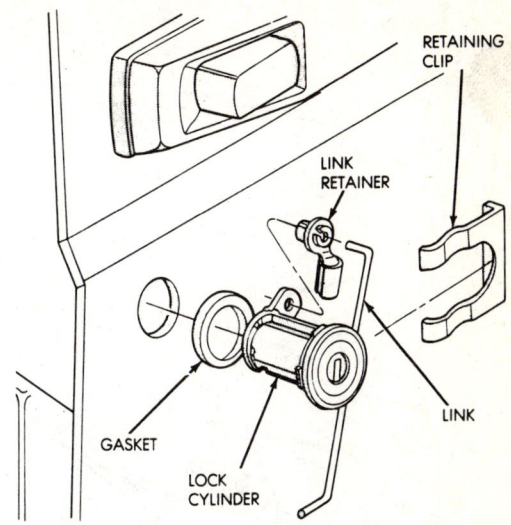

Removing the lock cylinder

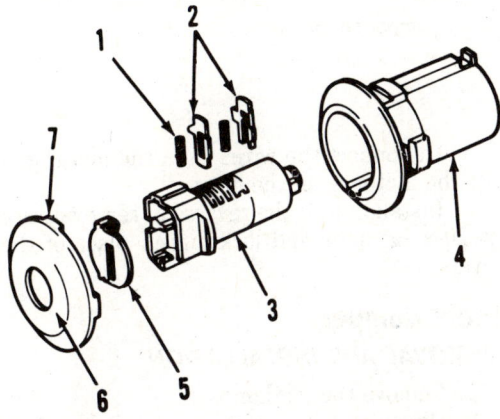

1. Spring
2. Tumblers
3. Cylinder
4. Casing
5. Key door
6. Lock cover
7. Retaining tab

Typical door lock cylinder components

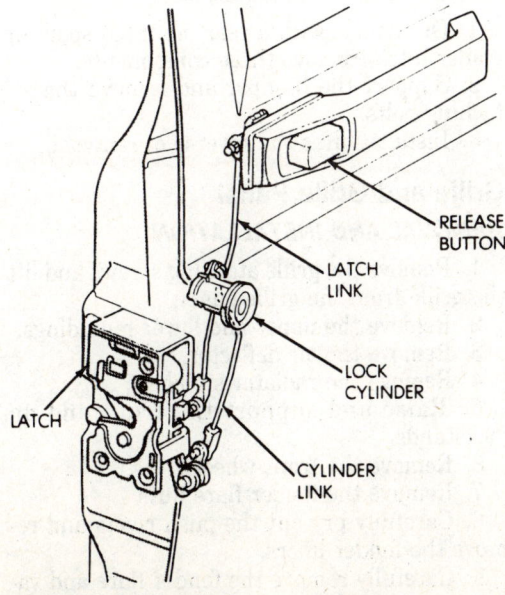

Lock cylinder installed

Latch and Linkage

1. Remove the door trim panel and plastic waterproof sheet.
2. Remove the latch retaining bolts from the rear edge of the door.
3. Disconnect the linkage from the lock cylinder and remove the latch and linkage.

NOTE: *With power locks, it will be necessary to drill out the lock solenoid rivets and remove the solenoid and latch assembly. During installation, the solenoid will have to be attached with pop rivets or bolt/nut assemblies.*

4. Installation is the reverse of removal. Torque the latch retaining bolts to 7 ft. lbs.

Power Door Locks

REMOVAL AND INSTALLATION

Switch

1. Disconnect the battery ground.
2. Remove the door trim panel and watershield.
3. Remove the switch housing from the inner door panel.
4. Disconnect the wiring and pry up the switch retaining clips. Remove the switch.
5. Installation is the reverse of removal.

Actuator Motor

1. Disconnect the battery ground.
2. Remove the door trim panel and watershield.
3. Using a ¼" drill bit, drill out the motor mounting rivets.
4. Disconnect the motor actuator rod from the bellcrank.

444 BODY

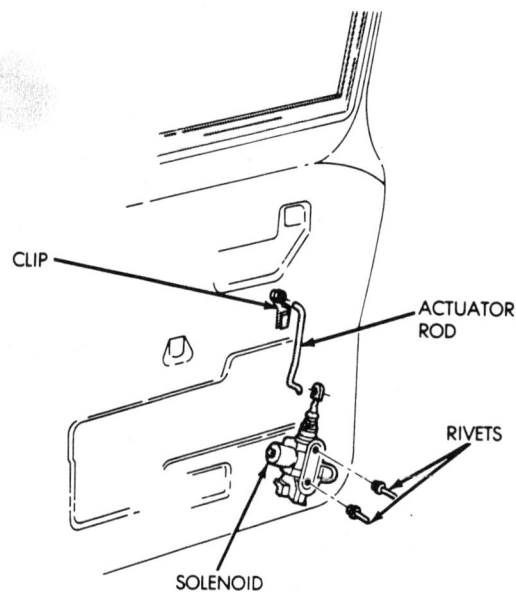

Power door lock solenoid removal

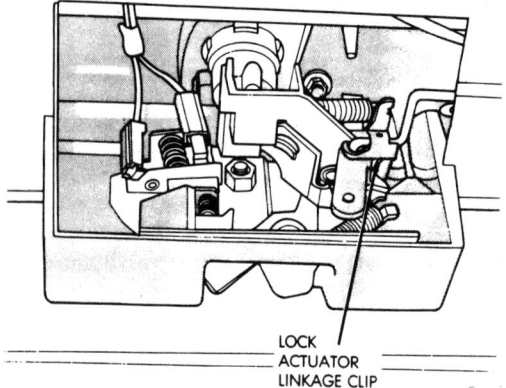

Lock actuator linkage clip

Latch assembly removal

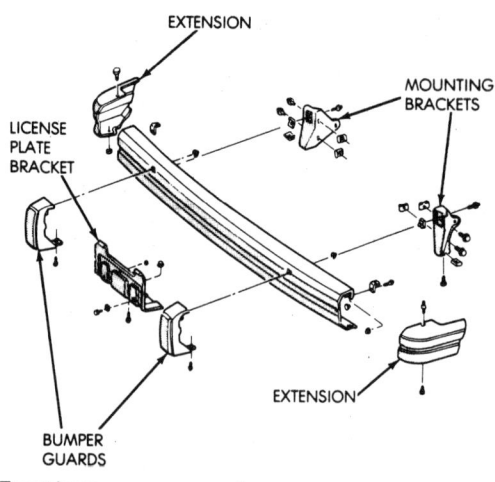

Front bumper components

5. Disconnect the wires from the motor and lift the motor from the door.
6. Installation is the reverse of removal. Use ¼-20 x ½" bolts and locknuts in place of the rivets.

Front Bumper

REMOVAL AND INSTALLATION

1. Remove the fog lamps.
2. Disconnect the vacuum resrvoir harness.
3. Support the bumper and remove the attaching bolts.
4. Installation is the reverse of removal.

Rear Bumper

REMOVAL AND INSTALLATION

1. On models with a rear mounted spare or trailer hitch, remove these components.
2. Support the bumper and remove the attaching bolts.
3. Installation is the reverse of remvoal.

Grille and Grille Panel

REMOVAL AND INSTALLATION

1. Remove the grille ataching screws and lift the grille from the grille panel.
2. Remove the upper and lower mouldings.
3. Remove the air deflector.
4. Remove the radiator supports.
5. Raise and support the front end on jackstands.
6. Remove the front wheels.
7. Remove the fender flare nuts.
8. Carefully pry out the push rivets and remove the fender liners.
9. Carefully remove the fender flare and valance panel push rivets.

BODY 445

10. Remove the fender flare and flare retainers.
11. Remove the nuts at each side of the grille panel through the wheelhouse opening.
12. Remove the nuts at the top of the grille panel.
13. Disconnect the headlamps and turn signal lamps.

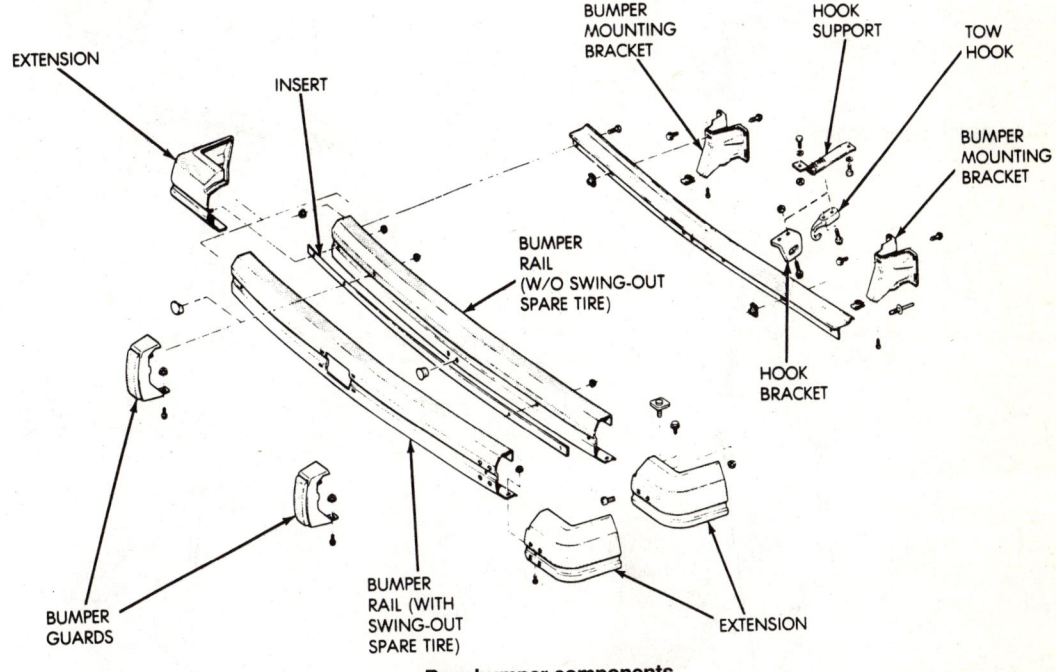
Rear bumper components

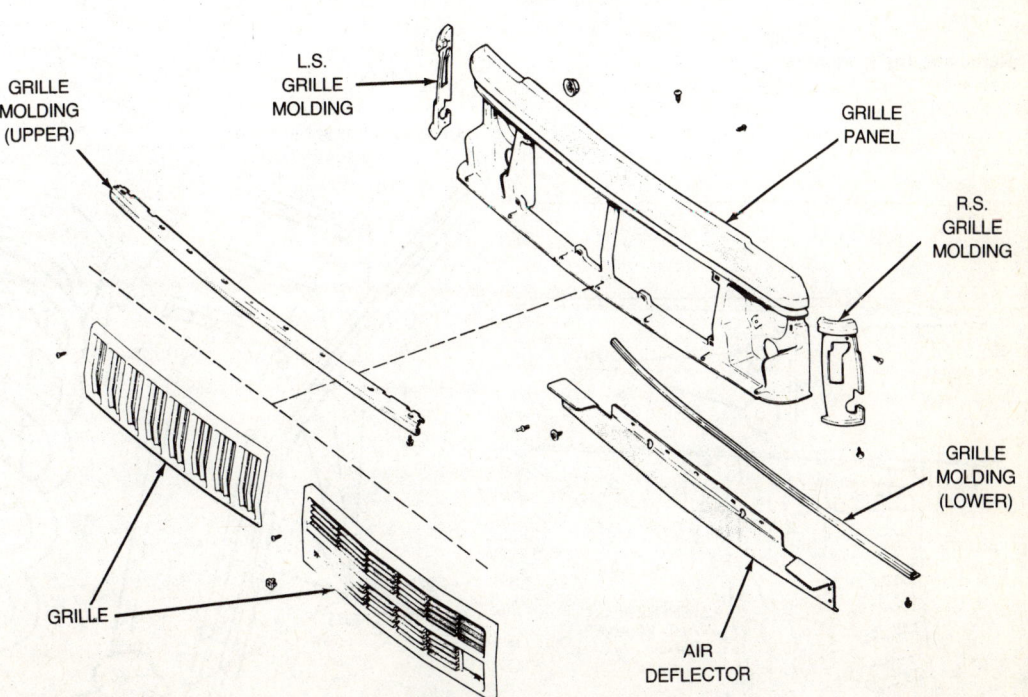
Grille and grille panel components

446 BODY

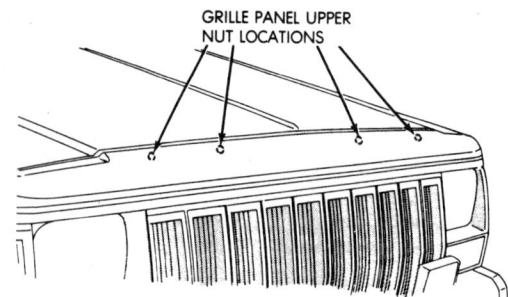

Grille panel upper fasteners

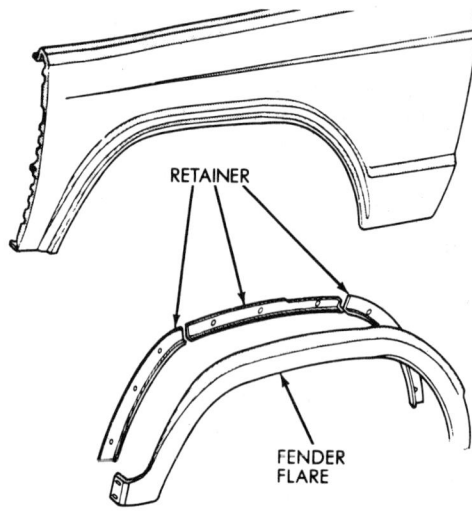

Removing the fender flare and retainer

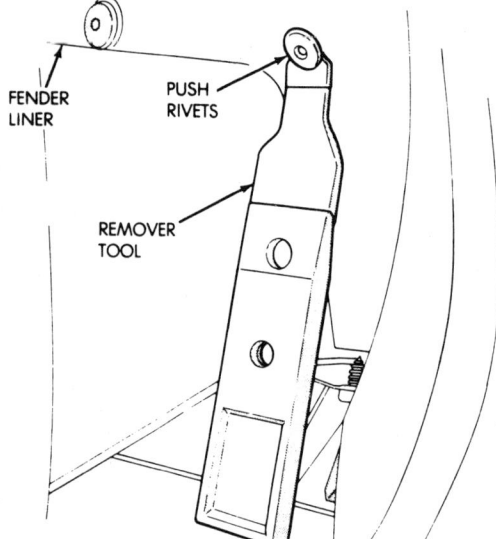

Removing the fender liner

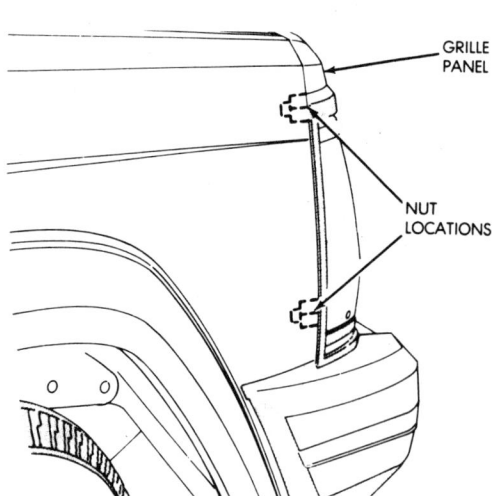

Grille panel side fasteners

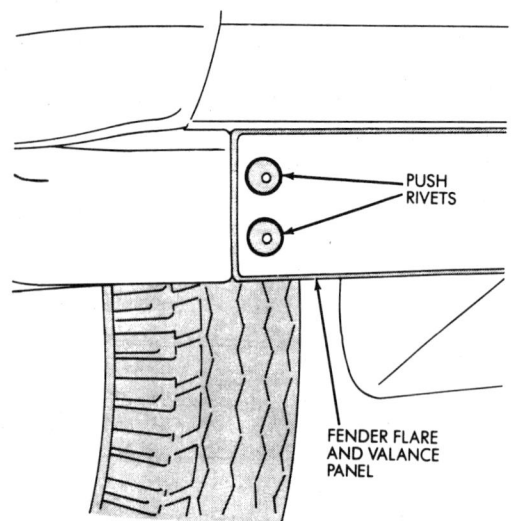

Removing the valence panel-to-fender flare rivets

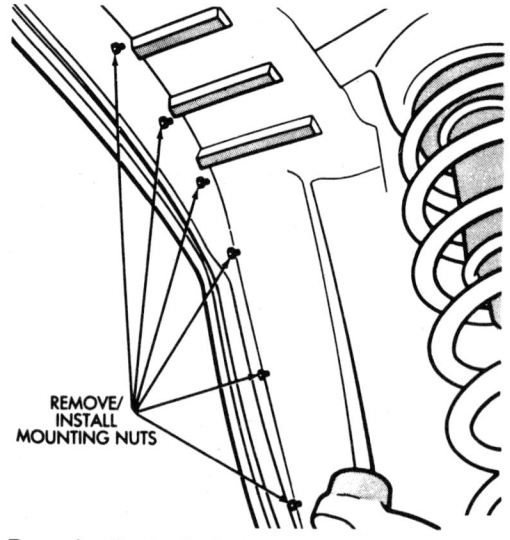

Removing the fender inner splash shield

14. Remove the grille panel.
15. If a new grille panel is being installed, transfer all lighting components.

To install:
16. Install the grille panel.
17. Connect the headlamps and turn signal lamps.
18. Install the nuts at the top of the grille panel.
19. Install the nuts at each side of the grille panel through the wheelhouse opening.
20. Install the fender flare and flare retainers.
21. Carefully install the fender flare and valance panel push rivets.
22. Install the fender liners.
23. Install the fender flare nuts.
24. Install the front wheels.
25. Lower the truck.
26. Install the radiator supports.
27. Install the air deflector.
28. Install the upper and lower mouldings.
29. Install the grille.

Antenna

REMOVAL AND INSTALLATION

1. Remove the fender inner splash shield nuts and move the panel aside far enough to get at the antenna cable and base.
2. Unscrew the antenna mast and nut and remove the antenna pad from the top of the fender.
3. Remove the passenger side kick panel.
4. Disconnect the antenna lead by pull and twisting the metal connectors. NEVER pull on the cable!
5. Pull the rubber grommet out of the kick panel.
6. Remove the antenna assembly from the inside of the wheelhouse.
7. Installation is the reverse of removal.

INTERIOR

Door Panels

REMOVAL AND INSTALLATION

Front Door

1. Unbolt and remove the inside door latch and remove the latch panel retaining screws.
2. Disconnect the door latch control linkage and, if equipped, wiring harness. Remove the control panel.
3. If equipped with manual windows, remove the window crank handles.
4. Remove the armrest lower retaining screws and swing the armrest downward to disengage the upper retaining clip. Pull the armrest straight out from the door panel.
5. Starting at the bottom of the door panel, use a flat tool, such as a wood spatula, pry out the panel-to-door frame retaining pins by levering right up against the pin. If a forked-end tool is available, use one. These pins are easy to rip out of the trim panel.
6. Installation is the reverse of removal. A firm hit with the heel of your palm is usually enough to drive the retainers into the holes in the door panel. Make sure that the retainer is directly over the hole before knocking it in, or it may be damaged.

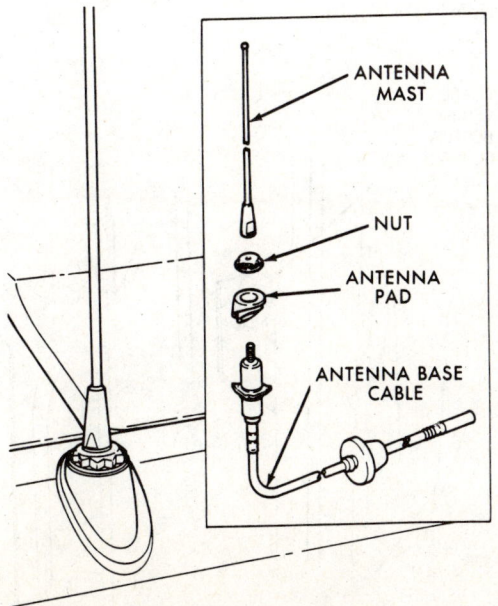

Removing the nut and antenna pad

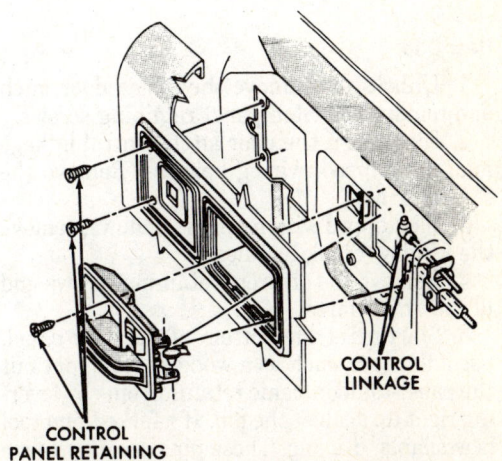

Removing the inside door latch handle

448 BODY

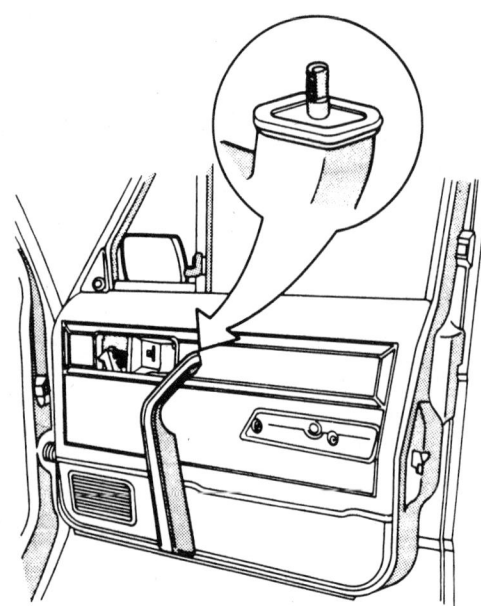

Removing the armrest

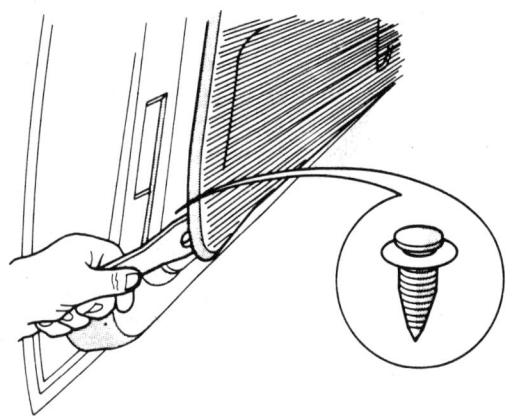

Removing the door trim panel fasteners

Rear Door

1. Unbolt and remove the inside door latch and remove the latch panel retaining screws.
2. Disconnect the door latch control linkage and, if equipped, wiring harness. Remove the control panel.
3. If equipped with manual windows, remove the window crank handles.
4. Remove the armrest retaining screws and lift off the armrest.
5. Starting at the bottom of the door panel, use a flat tool, such as a wood spatula, pry out the panel-to-door frame retaining pins by levering right up against the pin. If a forked-end tool is available, use one. These pins are easy to rip out of the trim panel.
6. Installation is the reverse of removal. A firm hit with the heel of your palm is usually enough to drive the retainers into the holes in the door panel. Make sure that the retainer is directly over the hole before knocking it in, or it may be damaged.

Manual Door Glass and Regulator
REMOVAL AND INSTALLATION
Front Door

1. Remove the trim panel and waterproof plastic sheet.
2. Remove the window frame trim molding.
3. Remove the glass channel bottom screw.
4. Remove the vent window frame screws.
5. Tilt the vent window and glass channel backward and remove it from the door frame.
6. Remove the door glass attaching stud nut and spring washer.
7. If equipped with electric windows, disconnect the wiring harness.
8. Grind the heads off the regulator rivets and knock the rivets out with a hammer and punch.
9. Pull the glass upward and out of the door.
10. Remove the regulator.
11. Installation is the reverse of removal. The regulator must be attached with pop rivets or bolts and nuts. Torque the door glass stud nut to 48 in. lbs.; the vent window bottom screw to 84 in. lbs.; the upper vent window screws to 10 ft. lbs.

Rear Door

1. Remove the trim panel and waterproof plastic sheet.
2. Lower the door glass and remove the weatherstripping.

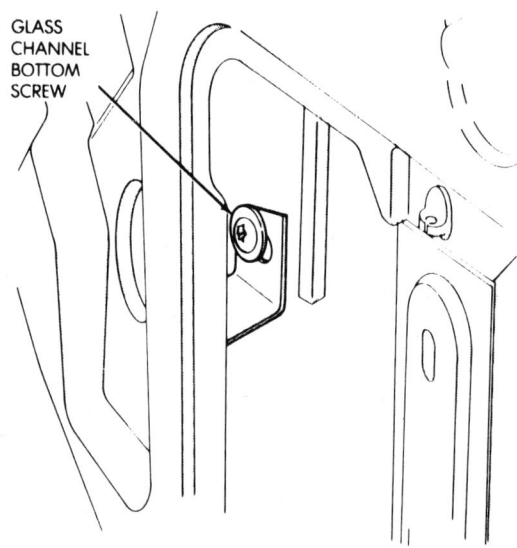

Removing the glass channel bottom screw

BODY

3. Remove the stationary glass frame screws.
4. Remove the glass channel upper screws.
5. Remove the glass channel lower screws.
6. Tilt the stationary glass and its channel forward and remove it.

7. Remove the door glass stud nut and lift the glass from the door.
8. Grind the heads off the regulator rivets and knock the rivets out with a hammer and punch.

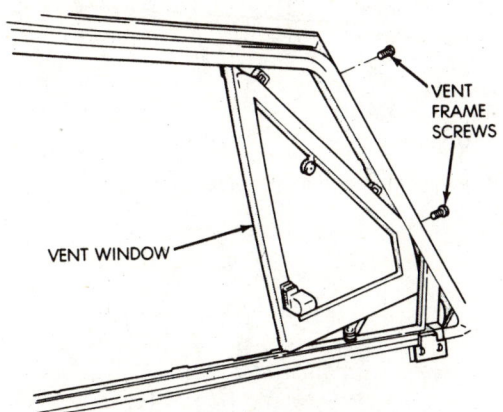

Removing the vent window and channel

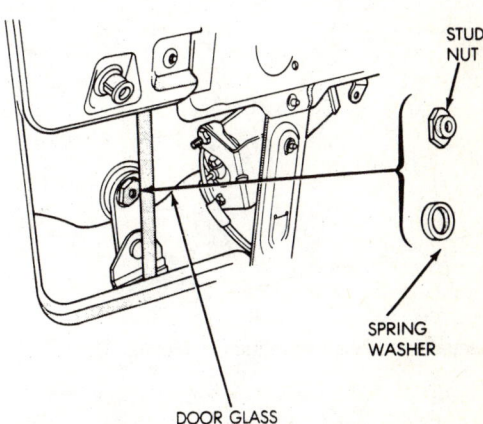

Removing the door glass stud

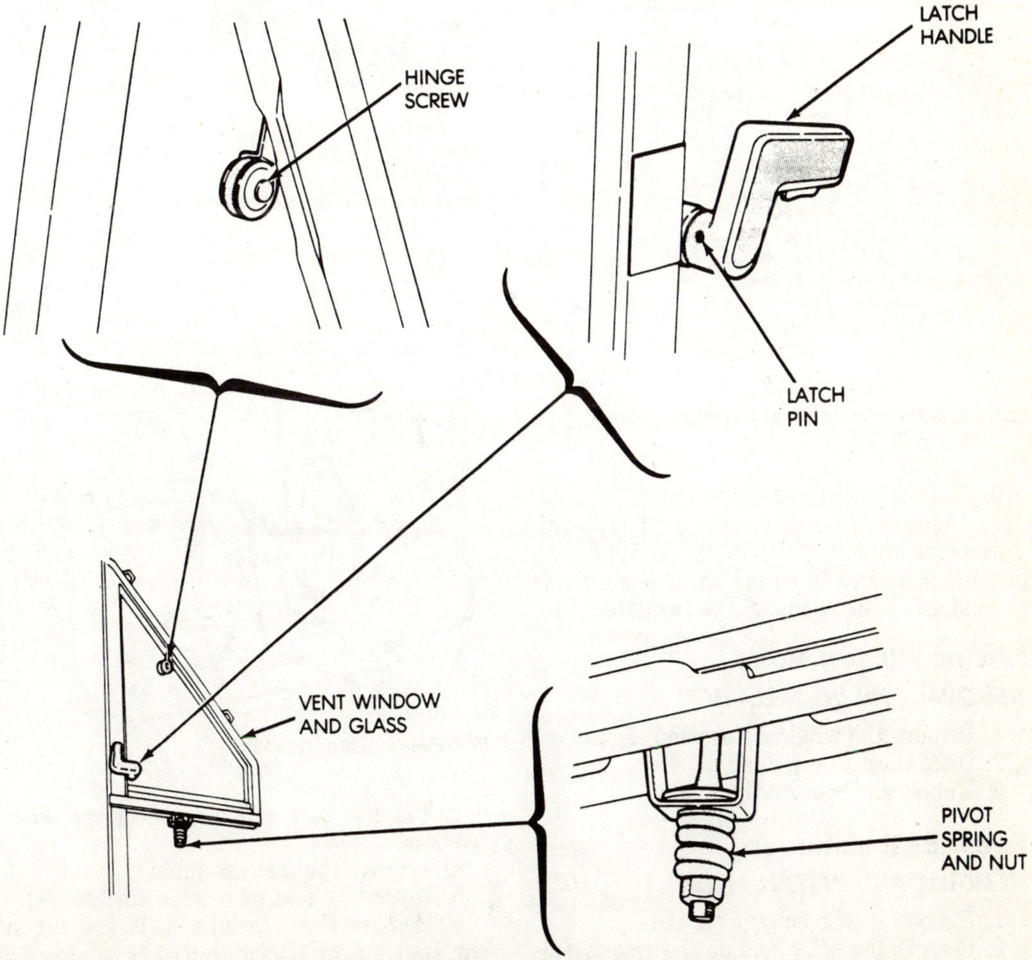

Removing the vent window

450   BODY

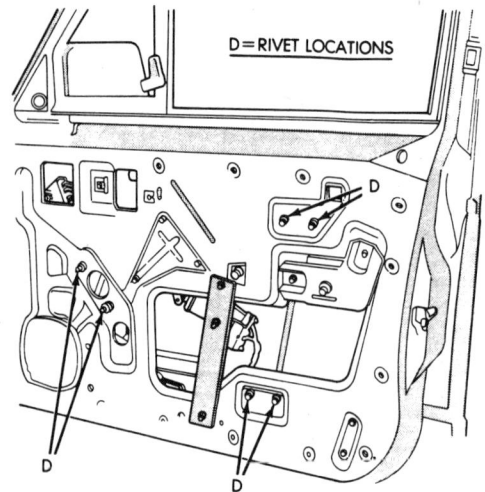

Manual window glass regulator rivet locations

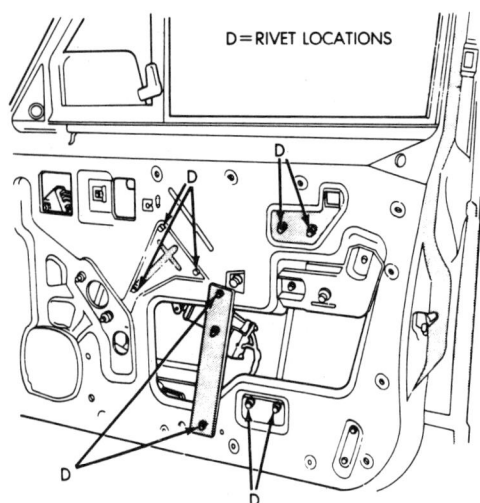

Power window glass regulator rivet locations

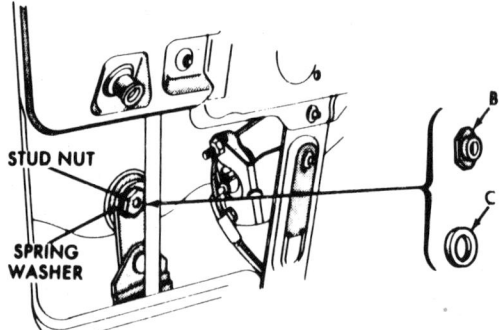

Power window control panel removal

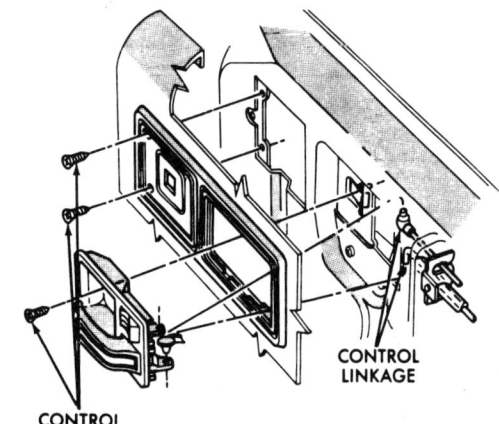

Glass attaching stud nut removal

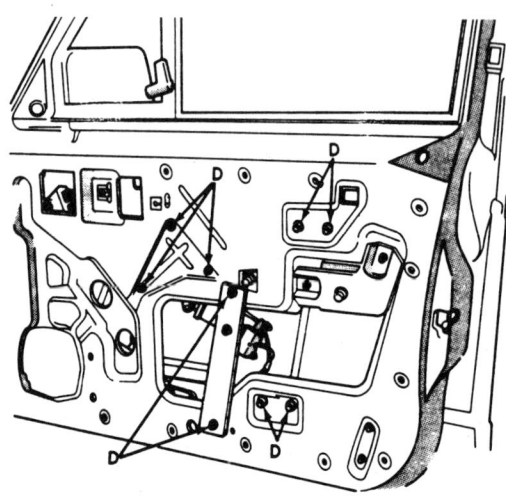

Window regulator removal

9. Pull the glass upward and out of the door.
10. Installation is the reverse of removal. Torque the stud nut to 48 in. lbs. and the glass channel screws to 60-84 in. lbs. Use pop rivets or nuts and bolts to install the regulator.

Electric Window Motor
REMOVAL AND INSTALLATION

1. Remove the window glass and regulator.
2. Disconnect the wiring.
3. Unbolt and remove the motor.

Power Seat Motor
REMOVAL AND INSTALLATION

1. Disconnect the battery ground.
2. Remove the bolts holding the seat assembly to the floor pan.
3. Tilt the seat and disconnect the wiring harness.
4. Remove the seat assembly.
5. Invert the seat on a clean surface.
6. Remove the attaching bolts and lift out the seat motor. Disconnect the wiring and cables.

BODY 451

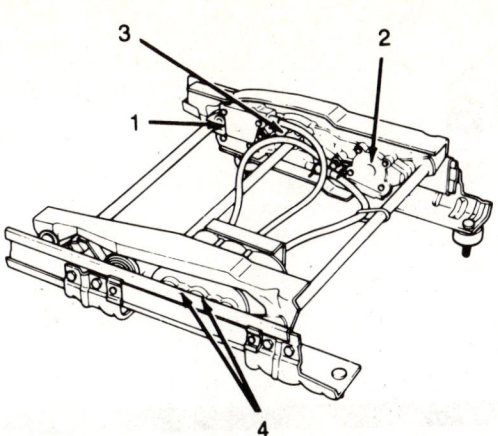

1. Front transmission
2. Rear transmission
3. Horizontal transmission
4. Motor attaching bolts

Typical power seat assembly

7. Installation is the reverse of removal.
NOTE: *If the seat transmission fails, it is not replaceable. The entire seat adjuster assembly will have to be replaced.*

Headliner
REMOVAL AND INSTALLATION

1. Remove the dome lamp(s).
2. Remove the side and rear trim panels.
3. Remove the coat hooks.

NOTE: *The headliner is a one-piece, molded unit, and MUST NOT be bent during removal or installation.*

4. Make sure that all trim clips are removed and pull out the headliner through the tailgate opening on Wagoneer and Cherokee, or through the door on the Comanche.
5. Installation is the reverse of removal.

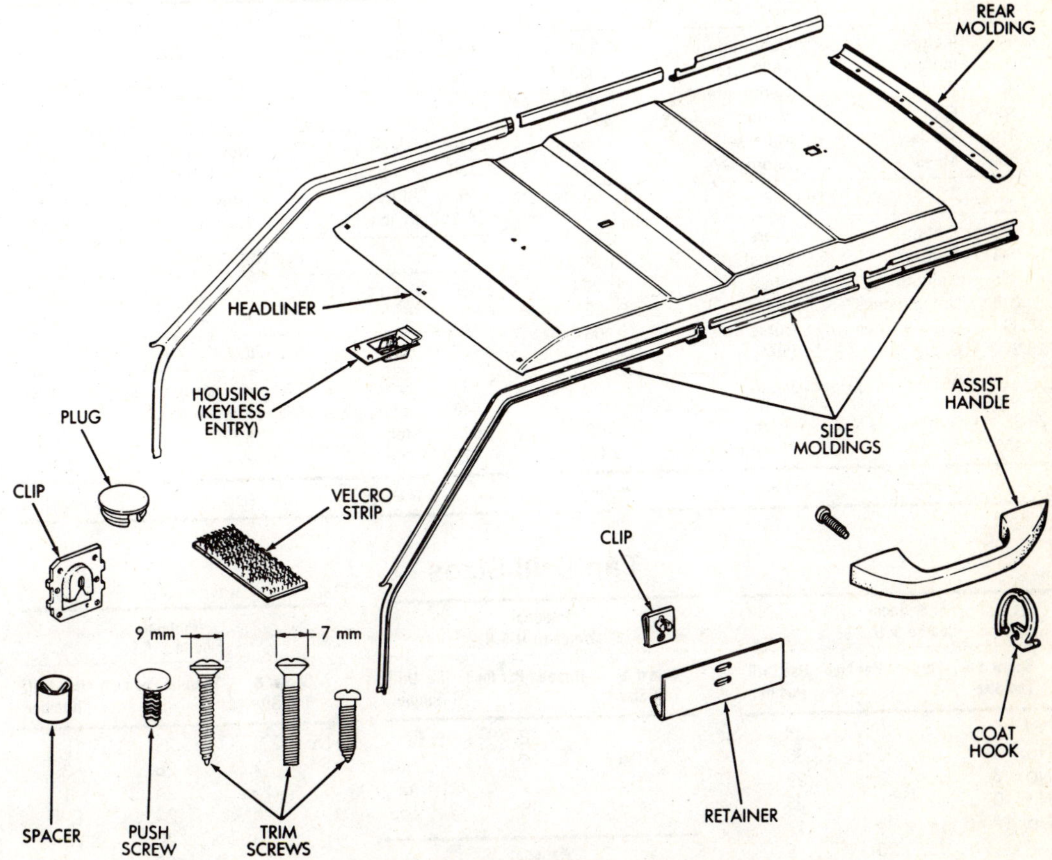

Wagoneer/Cherokee headliner and moldings

Mechanic's Data

General Conversion Table

Multiply By	To Convert	To	
		LENGTH	
2.54	Inches	Centimeters	.3937
25.4	Inches	Millimeters	.03937
30.48	Feet	Centimeters	.0328
.304	Feet	Meters	3.28
.914	Yards	Meters	1.094
1.609	Miles	Kilometers	.621
		VOLUME	
.473	Pints	Liters	2.11
.946	Quarts	Liters	1.06
3.785	Gallons	Liters	.264
.016	Cubic inches	Liters	61.02
16.39	Cubic inches	Cubic cms.	.061
28.3	Cubic feet	Liters	.0353
		MASS (Weight)	
28.35	Ounces	Grams	.035
.4536	Pounds	Kilograms	2.20
—	To obtain	From	Multiply by

Multiply By	To Convert	To	
		AREA	
.645	Square inches	Square cms.	.155
.836	Square yds.	Square meters	1.196
		FORCE	
4.448	Pounds	Newtons	.225
.138	Ft./lbs.	Kilogram/meters	7.23
1.36	Ft./lbs.	Newton-meters	.737
.112	In./lbs.	Newton-meters	8.844
		PRESSURE	
.068	Psi	Atmospheres	14.7
6.89	Psi	Kilopascals	.145
		OTHER	
1.104	Horsepower (DIN)	Horsepower (SAE)	.9861
.746	Horsepower (SAE)	Kilowatts (KW)	1.34
1.60	Mph	Km/h	.625
.425	Mpg	Km/1	2.35
—	To obtain	From	Multiply by

Tap Drill Sizes

National Coarse or U.S.S.

Screw & Tap Size	Threads Per Inch	Use Drill Number
No. 5	40	39
No. 6	32	36
No. 8	32	29
No. 10	24	25
No. 12	24	17
1/4	20	8
5/16	18	F
3/8	16	5/16
7/16	14	U
1/2	13	27/64
9/16	12	31/64
5/8	11	17/32
3/4	10	21/32
7/8	9	49/64

National Coarse or U.S.S.

Screw & Tap Size	Threads Per Inch	Use Drill Number
1	8	7/8
1 1/8	7	63/64
1 1/4	7	1 7/64
1 1/2	6	1 11/32

National Fine or S.A.E.

Screw & Tap Size	Threads Per Inch	Use Drill Number
No. 5	44	37
No. 6	40	33
No. 8	36	29
No. 10	32	21

National Fine or S.A.E.

Screw & Tap Size	Threads Per Inch	Use Drill Number
No. 12	28	15
1/4	28	3
6/16	24	1
3/8	24	Q
7/16	20	W
1/2	20	29/64
9/16	18	33/64
5/8	18	37/64
3/4	16	11/16
7/8	14	13/16
1 1/8	12	1 3/64
1 1/4	12	1 11/64
1 1/2	12	1 27/64

MECHANIC'S DATA

Drill Sizes In Decimal Equivalents

Inch	Decimal	Wire	mm	Inch	Decimal	Wire	mm	Inch	Decimal	Wire & Letter	mm	Inch	Decimal	Letter	mm	Inch	Decimal	mm
1/64	.0156		.39		.0730	49			.1614		4.1		.2717		6.9		.4331	11.0
	.0157		.4		.0748		1.9		.1654		4.2		.2720	I		7/16	.4375	11.11
	.0160	78			.0760	48			.1660	19			.2756		7.0		.4528	11.5
	.0165		.42		.0768		1.95		.1673		4.25		.2770	J		29/64	.4531	11.51
	.0173		.44	5/64	.0781		1.98		.1693		4.3		.2795		7.1	15/32	.4688	11.90
	.0177		.45		.0785	47			.1695	18			.2810	K			.4724	12.0
	.0180	77			.0787		2.0	11/64	.1719		4.36	9/32	.2812		7.14	31/64	.4844	12.30
	.0181		.46		.0807		2.05		.1730	17			.2835		7.2		.4921	12.5
	.0189		.48		.0810	46			.1732		4.4		.2854		7.25	1/2	.5000	12.70
	.0197		.5		.0820	45			.1770	16			.2874		7.3		.5118	13.0
	.0200	76			.0827		2.1		.1772		4.5		.2900	L		33/64	.5156	13.09
	.0210	75			.0846		2.15		.1800	15			.2913		7.4	17/32	.5312	13.49
	.0217		.55		.0860	44			.1811		4.6		.2950	M			.5315	13.5
	.0225	74			.0866		2.2		.1820	14			.2953		7.5	35/64	.5469	13.89
	.0236		.6		.0886		2.25		.1850	13		19/64	.2969		7.54		.5512	14.0
	.0240	73			.0890	43			.1850		4.7		.2992		7.6	9/16	.5625	14.28
	.0250	72			.0906		2.3		.1870		4.75		.3020	N			.5709	14.5
	.0256		.65		.0925		2.35	3/16	.1875		4.76		.3031		7.7	37/64	.5781	14.68
	.0260	71			.0935	42			.1890		4.8		.3051		7.75		.5906	15.0
	.0276		.7	3/32	.0938		2.38		.1890	12			.3071		7.8	19/32	.5938	15.08
	.0280	70			.0945		2.4		.1910	11			.3110		7.9	39/64	.6094	15.47
	.0292	69			.0960	41			.1929		4.9	5/16	.3125		7.93		.6102	15.5
	.0295		.75		.0965		2.45		.1935	10			.3150		8.0	5/8	.6250	15.87
	.0310	68			.0980	40			.1960	9			.3160	O			.6299	16.0
1/32	.0312		.79		.0981		2.5		.1969		5.0		.3189		8.1	41/64	.6406	16.27
	.0315		.8		.0995	39			.1990	8			.3228		8.2		.6496	16.5
	.0320	67			.1015	38			.2008		5.1		.3230	P		21/32	.6562	16.66
	.0330	66			.1024		2.6		.2010	7			.3248		8.25		.6693	17.0
	.0335		.85		.1040	37		13/64	.2031		5.16		.3268		8.3	43/64	.6719	17.06
	.0350	65			.1063		2.7		.2040	6		21/64	.3281		8.33	11/16	.6875	17.46
	.0354		.9		.1065	36			.2047		5.2		.3307		8.4		.6890	17.5
	.0360	64			.1083		2.75		.2055	5			.3320	Q		45/64	.7031	17.85
	.0370	63			.1094		2.77		.2067		5.25		.3346		8.5		.7087	18.0
	.0374		.95	7/64	.1094				.2087		5.3		.3386		8.6	23/32	.7188	18.25
	.0380	62			.1100	35			.2090	4			.3390	R			.7283	18.5
	.0390	61			.1102		2.8		.2126		5.4		.3425		8.7	47/64	.7344	18.65
	.0394		1.0		.1110	34			.2130	3		11/32	.3438		8.73		.7480	19.0
	.0400	60			.1130	33			.2165		5.5		.3445		8.75	3/4	.7500	19.05
	.0410	59			.1142		2.9		.2188		5.55		.3465		8.8	49/64	.7656	19.44
	.0413		1.05		.1160	32		7/32	.2188				.3480	S			.7677	19.5
					.1181		3.0		.2205		5.6							
	.0420	58			.1200	31			.2210	2			.3504		8.9	25/32	.7812	19.84
	.0430	57			.1220		3.1		.2244		5.7		.3543		9.0		.7874	20.0
	.0433		1.1	1/8	.1250		3.17		.2264		5.75		.3580	T		51/64	.7969	20.24
	.0453		1.15		.1260		3.2		.2280	1			.3583		9.1		.8071	20.5
	.0465	56			.1280		3.25		.2283		5.8	23/64	.3594		9.12	13/16	.8125	20.63
3/64	.0469		1.19		.1285	30			.2323		5.9		.3622		9.2		.8268	21.0
	.0472		1.2		.1299		3.3		.2340	A			.3642		9.25	53/64	.8281	21.03
	.0492		1.25		.1339		3.4	15/64	.2344		5.95		.3661		9.3	27/32	.8438	21.43
	.0512		1.3		.1360	29			.2362		6.0		.3680	U			.8465	21.5
	.0520	55			.1378		3.5		.2380	B			.3701		9.4	55/64	.8594	21.82
	.0531		1.35		.1405	28			.2402		6.1		.3740		9.5		.8661	22.0
	.0550	54		9/64	.1406		3.57		.2420	C		3/8	.3750		9.52	7/8	.8750	22.22
	.0551		1.4		.1417		3.6		.2441		6.2		.3770	V			.8858	22.5
	.0571		1.45		.1440	27			.2460	D			.3780		9.6	57/64	.8906	22.62
	.0591		1.5		.1457		3.7		.2461		6.25		.3819		9.7		.9055	23.0
	.0595	53			.1470	26			.2480		6.3		.3839		9.75	29/32	.9062	23.01
	.0610		1.55		.1476		3.75	1/4	.2500	E	6.35		.3858		9.8	59/64	.9219	23.41
1/16	.0625		1.59		.1495	25			.2520		6.		.3860	W			.9252	23.5
	.0630		1.6		.1496		3.8		.2559		6.5		.3898		9.9	15/16	.9375	23.81
	.0635	52			.1520	24			.2570	F		25/64	.3906		9.92		.9449	24.0
	.0650		1.65		.1535		3.9		.2598		6.6		.3937		10.0	61/64	.9531	24.2
	.0669		1.7		.1540	23			.2610	G			.3970	X			.9646	24.5
	.0670	51		5/32	.1562		3.96		.2638		6.7		.4040	Y		31/64	.9688	24.6
	.0689		1.75		.1570	22		17/64	.2656		6.74	13/32	.4062		10.31		.9843	25.0
	.0700	50			.1575		4.0		.2657		6.75		.4130	Z		63/64	.9844	25.0
	.0709		1.8		.1590	21			.2660	H			.4134		10.5	1	1.0000	25.4
	.0728		1.85		.1610	20			.2677		6.8	27/64	.4219		10.71			

GLOSSARY OF TERMS

AIR/FUEL RATIO: The ratio of air to gasoline by weight in the fuel mixture drawn into the engine.

AIR INJECTION: One method of reducing harmful exhaust emissions by injecting air into each of the exhaust ports of an engine. The fresh air entering the hot exhaust manifold causes any remaining fuel to be burned before it can exit the tailpipe.

ALTERNATOR: A device used for converting mechanical energy into electrical energy.

AMMETER: An instrument, calibrated in amperes, used to measure the flow of an electrical current in a circuit. Ammeters are always connected in series with the circuit being tested.

AMPERE: The rate of flow of electrical current present when one volt of electrical pressure is applied against one ohm of electrical resistance.

ANALOG COMPUTER: Any microprocessor that uses similar (analogous) electrical signals to make its calculations.

ARMATURE: A laminated, soft iron core wrapped by a wire that converts electrical energy to mechanical energy as in a motor or relay. When rotated in a magnetic field, it changes mechanical energy into electrical energy as in a generator.

ATMOSPHERIC PRESSURE: The pressure on the Earth's surface caused by the weight of the air in the atmosphere. At sea level, this pressure is 14.7 psi at 32°F (101 kPa at 0°C).

ATOMIZATION: The breaking down of a liquid into a fine mist that can be suspended in air.

AXIAL PLAY: Movement parallel to a shaft or bearing bore.

BACKFIRE: The sudden combustion of gases in the intake or exhaust system that results in a loud explosion.

BACKLASH: The clearance or play between two parts, such as meshed gears.

BACKPRESSURE: Restrictions in the exhaust system that slow the exit of exhaust gases from the combustion chamber.

BAKELITE: A heat resistant, plastic insulator material commonly used in printed circuit boards and transistorized components.

BALL BEARING: A bearing made up of hardened inner and outer races between which hardened steel ball roll.

BALLAST RESISTOR: A resistor in the primary ignition circuit that lowers voltage after the engine is started to reduce wear on ignition components.

BEARING: A friction reducing, supportive device usually located between a stationary part and a moving part.

BIMETAL TEMPERATURE SENSOR: Any sensor or switch made of two dissimilar types of metal that bend when heated or cooled due to the different expansion rates of the alloys. These types of sensors usually function as an on/off switch.

BLOWBY: Combustion gases, composed of water vapor and unburned fuel, that leak past the piston rings into the crankcase during normal engine operation. These gases are removed by the PCV system to prevent the build-up of harmful acids in the crankcase.

BRAKE PAD: A brake shoe and lining assembly used with disc brakes.

BRAKE SHOE: The backing for the brake lining. The term is, however, usually applied to the assembly of the brake backing and lining.

BUSHING: A liner, usually removable, for a bearing; an anti-friction liner used in place of a bearing.

BYPASS: System used to bypass ballast resistor during engine cranking to increase voltage supplied to the coil.

CALIPER: A hydraulically activated device in a disc brake system, which is mounted straddling the brake rotor (disc). The caliper contains at least one piston and two brake pads. Hydraulic pressure on the piston(s) forces the pads against the rotor.

CAMSHAFT: A shaft in the engine on which are the lobes (cams) which operate the valves. The camshaft is driven by the crankshaft, via a belt, chain or gears, at one half the crankshaft speed.

CAPACITOR: A device which stores an electrical charge.

CARBON MONOXIDE (CO): a colorless, odorless gas given off as a normal byproduct of combustion. It is poisonous and extremely dangerous in confined areas, building up slowly to toxic levels without warning if adequate ventilation is not available.

CARBURETOR: A device, usually mounted on the intake manifold of an engine, which mixes the air and fuel in the proper proportion to allow even combustion.

CATALYTIC CONVERTER: A device installed in the exhaust system, like a muffler, that converts harmful byproducts of combustion into carbon dioxide and water vapor by means of a heat-producing chemical reaction.

CENTRIFUGAL ADVANCE: A mechanical method of advancing the spark timing by using flyweights in the distributor that react to centrifugal force generated by the distributor shaft rotation.

CHECK VALVE: Any one-way valve installed to permit the flow of air, fuel or vacuum in one direction only.

CHOKE: A device, usually a moveable valve, placed in the intake path of a carburetor to restrict the flow of air.

CIRCUIT: Any unbroken path through which an electrical current can flow. Also used to describe fuel flow in some instances.

CIRCUIT BREAKER: A switch which protects an electrical circuit from overload by opening the circuit when the current flow exceeds a predetermined level. Some circuit breakers must be reset manually, while other reset automatically

COIL (IGNITION): A transformer in the ignition circuit which steps of the voltage provided to the spark plugs.

COMBINATION MANIFOLD: An assembly which includes both the intake and exhaust manifolds in one casting.

COMBINATION VALVE: A device used in some fuel systems that routes fuel vapors to a charcoal storage canister instead of venting them into the atmosphere. The valve relieves fuel tank pressure and allows fresh air into the tank as fuel level drops to prevent a vapor lock situation.

COMPRESSION RATIO: The comparison of the total volume of the cylinder and combustion chamber with the piston at BDC and the piston at TDC.

CONDENSER: 1. An electrical device which acts to store an electrical charge, preventing voltage surges.
2. A radiator-like device in the air conditioning system in which refrigerant gas condenses into a liquid, giving off heat.

CONDUCTOR: Any material through which an electrical current can be transmitted easily.

CONTINUITY: Continuous or complete circuit. Can be checked with an ohmmeter.

COUNTERSHAFT: An intermediate shaft which is rotated by a mainshaft and transmits, in turn, that rotation to a working part.

CRANKCASE: The lower part of an engine in which the crankshaft and related parts operate.

CRANKSHAFT: The main driving shaft of an engine which receives reciprocating motion from the pistons and converts it to rotary motion.

CYLINDER: In an engine, the round hole in the engine block in which the piston(s) ride.

CYLINDER BLOCK: The main structural member of an engine in which is found the cylinders, crankshaft and other principal parts.

CYLINDER HEAD: The detachable portion of the engine, fastened, usually, to the top of the cylinder block, containing all or most of the combustion chambers. On overhead valve engines, it contains the valves and their operating parts. On overhead cam engines, it contains the camshaft as well.

DEAD CENTER: The extreme top or bottom of the piston stroke.

DETONATION: An unwanted explosion of the air fuel mixture in the combustion chamber caused by excess heat and compression, advanced timing, or an overly lean mixture. Also referred to as "ping".

DIAPHRAGM: A thin, flexible wall separating two cavities, such as in a vacuum advance unit.

DIESELING: A condition in which hot spots in the combustion chamber cause the engine to run on after the key is turned off.

DIFFERENTIAL: A geared assembly which allows the transmission of motion between drive axles, giving one axle the ability to turn faster than the other.

DIODE: An electrical device that will allow current to flow in one direction only.

DISC BRAKE: A hydraulic braking assembly consisting of a brake disc, or rotor, mounted on an axle, and a caliper assembly containing, usually two brake pads which are activated by hydraulic pressure. The pads are forced against the sides of the disc, creating friction which slows the vehicle.

DISTRIBUTOR: A mechanically driven device on an engine which is responsible for electrically firing the spark plug at a predetermined point of the piston stroke.

DOWEL PIN: A pin, inserted in mating holes in two different parts allowing those parts to maintain a fixed relationship.

DRUM BRAKE: A braking system which consists of two brake shoes and one or two wheel cylinders, mounted on a fixed backing plate, and a brake drum, mounted on an axle, which revolves around the assembly. Hydraulic action applied to the wheel cylinders forces the shoes outward against the drum, creating friction and slowing the vehicle.

DWELL: The rate, measured in degrees of shaft rotation, at which an electrical circuit cycles on and off.

ELECTRONIC CONTROL UNIT (ECU): Ignition module, module, amplifier or igniter. See Module for definition.

ELECTRONIC IGNITION: A system in which the timing and firing of the spark plugs is controlled by an electronic control unit, usually called a module. These systems have not points or condenser.

ENDPLAY: The measured amount of axial movement in a shaft.

ENGINE: A device that converts heat into mechanical energy.

EXHAUST MANIFOLD: A set of cast passages or pipes which conduct exhaust gases from the engine.

FEELER GAUGE: A blade, usually metal, of precisely predetermined thickness, used to measure the clearance between two parts. These blades usually are available in sets of assorted thicknesses.

F-Head: An engine configuration in which the intake valves are in the cylinder head, while the camshaft and exhaust valves are located in the cylinder block. The camshaft operates the intake valves via lifters and pushrods, while it operates the exhaust valves directly.

FIRING ORDER: The order in which combustion occurs in the cylinders of an engine. Also the order in which spark is distributed to the plugs by the distributor.

FLATHEAD: An engine configuration in which the camshaft and all the valves are located in the cylinder block.

FLOODING: The presence of too much fuel in the intake manifold and combustion chamber which prevents the air/fuel mixture from firing, thereby causing a no-start situation.

FLYWHEEL: A disc shaped part bolted to the rear end of the crankshaft. Around the outer perimeter is affixed the ring gear. The starter drive engages the ring gear, turning the flywheel, which rotates the crankshaft, imparting the initial starting motion to the engine.

FOOT POUND (ft.lb. or sometimes, ft. lbs.): The amount of energy or work needed to raise an item weighing one pound, a distance of one foot.

FUSE: A protective device in a circuit which prevents circuit overload by breaking the circuit when a specific amperage is present. The device is constructed around a strip or wire of a lower amperage rating than the circuit it is designed to protect. When an amperage higher than that stamped on the fuse is present in the circuit, the strip or wire melts, opening the circuit.

GEAR RATIO: The ratio between the number of teeth on meshing gears.

GENERATOR: A device which converts mechanical energy into electrical energy.

HEAT RANGE: The measure of a spark plug's ability to dissipate heat from its firing end. The higher the heat range, the hotter the plug fires.

HUB: The center part of a wheel or gear.

HYDROCARBON (HC): Any chemical compound made up of hydrogen and carbon. A major pollutant formed by the engine as a byproduct of combustion.

HYDROMETER: An instrument used to measure the specific gravity of a solution.

INCH POUND (in.lb. or sometimes, in. lbs.): One twelfth of a foot pound.

INDUCTION: A means of transferring electrical energy in the form of a magnetic field. Principle used in the ignition coil to increase voltage.

INJECTION PUMP: A device, usually mechanically operated, which meters and delivers fuel under pressure to the fuel injector.

INJECTOR: A device which receives metered fuel under relatively low pressure and is activated to inject the fuel into the engine under relatively high pressure at a predetermined time.

INPUT SHAFT: The shaft to which torque is applied, usually carrying the driving gear or gears.

INTAKE MANIFOLD: A casting of passages or pipes used to conduct air or a fuel/air mixture to the cylinders.

JOURNAL: The bearing surface within which a shaft operates.

KEY: A small block usually fitted in a notch between a shaft and a hub to prevent slippage of the two parts.

MANIFOLD: A casting of passages or set of pipes which connect the cylinders to an inlet or outlet source.

MANIFOLD VACUUM: Low pressure in an engine intake manifold formed just below the throttle plates. Manifold vacuum is highest at idle and drops under acceleration.

MASTER CYLINDER: The primary fluid pressurizing device in a hydraulic system. In automotive use, it is found in brake and hydraulic clutch systems and is pedal activated, either directly or, in a power brake system, through the power booster.

MODULE: Electronic control unit, amplifier or igniter of solid state or integrated design which controls the current flow in the ignition primary circuit based on input from the pickup coil. When the module opens the primary circuit, the high secondary voltage is induced in the coil.

NEEDLE BEARING: A bearing which consists of a number (usually a large number) of long, thin rollers.

OHM: (Ω) The unit used to measure the resistance of conductor to electrical flow. One ohm is the amount of resistance that limits current flow to one ampere in a circuit with one volt of pressure.

OHMMETER: An instrument used for measuring the resistance, in ohms, in an electrical circuit.

OUTPUT SHAFT: The shaft which transmits torque from a device, such as a transmission.

OVERDRIVE: A gear assembly which produces more shaft revolutions than that transmitted to it.

OVERHEAD CAMSHAFT (OHC): An engine configuration in which the camshaft is mounted on top of the cylinder head and operates the valve either directly or by means of rocker arms.

OVERHEAD VALVE (OHV): An engine configuration in which all of the valves are located in the cylinder head and the camshaft is located in the cylinder block. The camshaft operates the valves via lifters and pushrods.

OXIDES OF NITROGEN (NOx): Chemical compounds of nitrogen produced as a byproduct of combustion. They combine with hydrocarbons to produce smog.

OXYGEN SENSOR: Used with the feedback system to sense the presence of oxygen in the exhaust gas and signal the computer which can reference the voltage signal to an air/fuel ratio.

PINION: The smaller of two meshing gears.

GLOSSARY

PISTON RING: An open ended ring which fits into a groove on the outer diameter of the piston. Its chief function is to form a seal between the piston and cylinder wall. Most automotive pistons have three rings: two for compression sealing; one for oil sealing.

PRELOAD: A predetermined load placed on a bearing during assembly or by adjustment.

PRIMARY CIRCUIT: Is the low voltage side of the ignition system which consists of the ignition switch, ballast resistor or resistance wire, bypass, coil, electronic control unit and pick-up coil as well as the connecting wires and harnesses.

PRESS FIT: The mating of two parts under pressure, due to the inner diameter of one being smaller than the outer diameter of the other, or vice versa; an interference fit.

RACE: The surface on the inner or outer ring of a bearing on which the balls, needles or rollers move.

REGULATOR: A device which maintains the amperage and/or voltage levels of a circuit at predetermined values.

RELAY: A switch which automatically opens and/or closes a circuit.

RESISTANCE: The opposition to the flow of current through a circuit or electrical device, and is measured in ohms. Resistance is equal to the voltage divided by the amperage.

RESISTOR: A device, usually made of wire, which offers a preset amount of resistance in an electrical circuit.

RING GEAR: The name given to a ring-shaped gear attached to a differential case, or affixed to a flywheel or as part a planetary gear set.

ROLLER BEARING: A bearing made up of hardened inner and outer races between which hardened steel rollers move.

ROTOR: 1. The disc-shaped part of a disc brake assembly, upon which the brake pads bear; also called, brake disc.
2. The device mounted atop the distributor shaft, which passes current to the distributor cap tower contacts.

SECONDARY CIRCUIT: The high voltage side of the ignition system, usually above 20,000 volts. The secondary includes the ignition coil, coil wire, distributor cap and rotor, spark plug wires and spark plugs.

SENDING UNIT: A mechanical, electrical, hydraulic or electromagnetic device which transmits information to a gauge.

SENSOR: Any device designed to measure engine operating conditions or ambient pressures and temperatures. Usually electronic in nature and designed to send a voltage signal to an on-board computer, some sensors may operate as a simple on/off switch or they may provide a variable voltage signal (like a potentiometer) as conditions or measured parameters change.

SHIM: Spacers of precise, predetermined thickness used between parts to establish a proper working relationship.

SLAVE CYLINDER: In automotive use, a device in the hydraulic clutch system which is activated by hydraulic force, disengaging the clutch.

SOLENOID: A coil used to produce a magnetic field, the effect of which is produce work.

SPARK PLUG: A device screwed into the combustion chamber of a spark ignition engine. The basic construction is a conductive core inside of a ceramic insulator, mounted in an outer conductive base. An electrical charge from the spark plug wire travels along the conductive core and jumps a preset air gap to a grounding point or points at the end of the conductive base. The resultant spark ignites the fuel/air mixture in the combustion chamber.

SPLINES: Ridges machined or cast onto the outer diameter of a shaft or inner diameter of a bore to enable parts to mate without rotation.

TACHOMETER: A device used to measure the rotary speed of an engine, shaft, gear, etc., usually in rotations per minute.

THERMOSTAT: A valve, located in the cooling system of an engine, which is closed when cold and opens gradually in response to engine heating, controlling the temperature of the coolant and rate of coolant flow.

TOP DEAD CENTER (TDC): The point at which the piston reaches the top of its travel on the compression stroke.

TORQUE: The twisting force applied to an object.

TORQUE CONVERTER: A turbine used to transmit power from a driving member to a driven member via hydraulic action, providing changes in drive ratio and torque. In automotive use, it links the driveplate at the rear of the engine to the automatic transmission.

TRANSDUCER: A device used to change a force into an electrical signal.

TRANSISTOR: A semi-conductor component which can be actuated by a small voltage to perform an electrical switching function.

TUNE-UP: A regular maintenance function, usually associated with the replacement and adjustment of parts and components in the electrical and fuel systems of a vehicle for the purpose of attaining optimum performance.

TURBOCHARGER: An exhaust driven pump which compresses intake air and forces it into the combustion chambers at higher than atmospheric pressures. The increased air pressure allows more fuel to be burned and results in increased horsepower being produced.

VACUUM ADVANCE: A device which advances the ignition timing in response to increased engine vacuum.

VACUUM GAUGE: An instrument used to measure the presence of vacuum in a chamber.

VALVE: A device which control the pressure, direction of flow or rate of flow of a liquid or gas.

VALVE CLEARANCE: The measured gap between the end of the valve stem and the rocker arm, cam lobe or follower that activates the valve.

VISCOSITY: The rating of a liquid's internal resistance to flow.

VOLTMETER: An instrument used for measuring electrical force in units called volts. Voltmeters are always connected parallel with the circuit being tested.

WHEEL CYLINDER: Found in the automotive drum brake assembly, it is a device, actuated by hydraulic pressure, which, through internal pistons, pushes the brake shoes outward against the drums.

ABBREVIATIONS AND SYMBOLS

A: Ampere
AC: Alternating current
A/C: Air conditioning
A-h: Ampere hour
AT: Automatic transmission
ATDC: After top dead center
μA: Microampere
bbl: Barrel
BDC: Bottom dead center
bhp: Brake horsepower
BTDC: Before top dead center
BTU: British thermal unit
C: Celsius (Centigrade)
CCA: Cold cranking amps
cd: Candela
cm^2: Square centimeter
cm^3, cc: Cubic centimeter
CO: Carbon monoxide
CO$_2$: Carbon dioxide
cu.in., in^3: Cubic inch
CV: Constant velocity
Cyl.: Cylinder
DC: Direct current
ECM: Electronic control module
EFE: Early fuel evaporation
EFI: Electronic fuel injection
EGR: Exhaust gas recirculation
Exh.: Exhaust
F: Fahrenheit

F: Farad
pF: Picofarad
μF: Microfarad
FI: Fuel injection
ft.lb., ft. lb., ft. lbs.: foot pound(s)
gal: Gallon
g: Gram
HC: Hydrocarbon
HEI: High energy ignition
HO: High output
hp: Horsepower
Hyd.: Hydraulic
Hz: Hertz
ID: Inside diameter
in.lb.; in. lb.; in. lbs: inch pound(s)
Int.: Intake
K: Kelvin
kg: Kilogram
kHz: Kilohertz
km: Kilometer
km/h: Kilometers per hour
kΩ: Kilohm
kPa: Kilopascal
kV: Kilovolt
kW: Kilowatt
l: Liter
l/s: Liters per second
m: Meter
mA: Milliampere

ABBREVIATIONS

mg: Milligram

mHz: Megahertz

mm: Millimeter

mm^2: Square millimeter

m^3: Cubic meter

$M\Omega$: Megohm

m/s: Meters per second

MT: Manual transmission

mV: Millivolt

μm: Micrometer

N: Newton

N-m: Newton meter

NOx: Nitrous oxide

OD: Outside diameter

OHC: Over head camshaft

OHV: Over head valve

Ω: Ohm

PCV: Positive crankcase ventilation

psi: Pounds per square inch

pts: Pints

qts: Quarts

rpm: Rotations per minute

rps: Rotations per second

R-12: A refrigerant gas (Freon)

SAE: Society of Automotive Engineers

SO_2: Sulfur dioxide

T: Ton

t: Megagram

TBI: Throttle Body Injection

TPS: Throttle Position Sensor

V: 1. Volt; 2. Venturi

μV: Microvolt

W: Watt

∞: Infinity

<: Less than

>: Greater than

Index

A

Abbreviations and Symbols, 460
Air cleaner, 10
Air conditioning
  Blower, 241
  Charging, 29
  Compressor, 122
  Condenser, 120
  Control panel, 244
  Discharging, 29
  Evacuating, 29
  Evaporator, 243
  Gauge sets, 25
  General service, 23
  Inspection, 25
  Leak testing, 29
  Operation, 23
  Preventive maintenance, 24
  Safety precautions, 24
  Sight glass check, 25
  System tests, 29
  Troubleshooting, 26-29, 30
Air pump, 165
Alternator
  Alternator precautions, 86
  Operation, 85
  Removal and installation, 87
  Troubleshooting, 86
Alignment, wheel
  Camber, 383
  Caster, 383
  Toe, 383
Antenna, 447
Antifreeze, 44
Automatic transmission
  Adjustments, 310
  Application chart, 304
  Auxiliary oil cooler, 309
  Back-up light switch, 314
  Filter change, 43
  Fluid change, 43
  Linkage adjustments, 312
  Neutral safety switch, 314
  Operation, 304
  Pan removal, 308
  Removal and installation, 315
  Troubleshooting, 305
Axle
  Front, 370
  Rear, 367

B

Back-up light switch, 314
Ball joints, 379, 380
Battery
  Fluid level and maintenance, 13
  Jump starting, 53-54
Bearings
  Axle, 369, 370
  Engine, 146, 150, 151, 156
  Wheel, 47
Belts, 16-21
Boot (CV Joint)
  Replacement, 372
Brakes
  Anti-Lock Brake System
    Accumulator, 431
    Booster pump and motor, 429
    Components, 421
    Electronic control unit, 432
    Front wheel sensor, 426
    Master cylinder, 431
    Modulator, 431
    Operation, 419
    Rear wheel sensor, 428
    Relieving system pressure, 426
    Safety precautions, 423
    System bleeding, 434
    Troubleshooting, 462
  Bleeding, 410
  Brake light switch, 409
  Disc brakes
    Caliper, 413
    Operating principals, 402
    Pads, 410
    Rotor (Disc), 415
  Drum brakes
    Adjustment, 404
    Drum, 417
    Operating principals, 402
    Shoes, 417
    Wheel cylinder, 418
  Fluid level, 45
  Master cylinder, 405
  Operation, 402
  Parking brake
    Adjustment, 418
    Removal and installation, 419
  Power booster
    Operating principals, 403
    Removal and installation, 408
  Proportioning valve, 407
  Specifications, 403
Bulbs, 250
Bumpers, 444

C

Calipers, 413
Camber, 383
Camshaft and bearings, 143
Capacities chart, 58
Carburetor
  Adjustments, 181, 188
  Overhaul, 186, 194
  Removal and installation, 185, 194
  Specifications, 182, 188
Caster, 383
Catalytic converter, 163, 171
Center link/Connecting rod/Drag link, 383

INDEX

Charging system, 85
Chassis electrical system
    Circuit protection, 252
    Heater and air conditioning, 241
    Instrument panel, 247
    Lighting, 250
    Windshield wipers, 245
Chassis lubrication, 46
Circuit breakers, 252
Clutch
    Hydraulic system bleeding, 304
    Master cylinder, 45, 304
    Operation, 300
    Removal and installation, 302
    Slave cylinder, 304
    Troubleshooting, 301
Coil (ignition), 83
Combination switch, 385
Compression testing, 102
Compressor, 122
Condenser, 120
Connecting rods and bearings, 146, 150, 151
Constant velocity (CV) joints, 372
Control arm
    Lower, 379
    Upper, 379
Cooling system, 44
Crankcase ventilation valve, 12, 164
Crankshaft, 156
Crankshaft damper, 133
Cylinder head, 122
Cylinders
    Inspection, 149
    Reboring, 150
    Refinishing, 150

D

Diesel fuel system
    Cold start capsule, 227
    Cold start system, 227
    Glow plugs, 227
    Injection pump, 223
    Injection timing, 226
    Injectors, 225
Disc brakes, 410
Distributor, 83
Door glass, 448
Door locks, 443
Doors, 441
Door trim panel, 447
Drive axle (front)
    Application chart, 370
    Axle shaft, bearing and seal, 370
    CV-joint, 372
    Fluid recommendations, 43
    Front hub and wheel bearings, 375
    Intermediate shaft, 372
    Lubricant level, 44
    Pinion seal and yoke, 371
    Removal and installation, 372
Drive axle (rear)
    Application chart, 367
    Axle shaft, 368
    Axle shaft bearing, 369
    Fluid recommendations, 44
    Identification, 370
    Lubricant level, 44
    Operation, 367
    Pinion oil seal, 369
    Ratios, 367
    Removal and installation, 370
    Troubleshooting, 361
Driveshaft, 362
Drum brakes, 417

E

EGR valve, 170
Electrical
    Chassis
        Battery, 13
        Bulbs, 250
        Circuit breakers, 252
        Fuses, 252
        Fusible links, 252
        Heater and air conditioning, 241
        Understanding the system, 231
    Engine
        Alternator, 85
        Coil, 83
        Distributor, 83
        Electronic engine controls, 63, 171
        Ignition module, 83
        Understanding the system, 81
        Starter, 88
Electronic Ignition, 63
    Air pump, 165
    Catalytic Converter, 171
    Choke Heat By-pass Valve
    Electrically Assisted Choke, 170
    Evaporative canister, 13
    Exhaust Gas Recirculation (EGR) system, 170
    Fuel Tank Vapor Control system, 171
    Oxygen (O_2) sensor, 171, 220
    PCV valve, 164
    Thermostatically controlled air cleaner, 169
Engine
    Application chart, 9
    Camshaft, 143
    Compression testing, 102
    Connecting rods and bearings, 146, 150, 151
    Crankshaft, 156
    Crankshaft damper, 133
    Cylinder head, 122
    Cylinders, 149
    Cylinder sleeves, 151
    Design, 95
    Electronic controls, 63, 171
    Exhaust manifold, 117
    Fluids and lubricants, 37
    Flywheel, 160
    Front (timing) cover, 136
    Front seal, 136
    Identification, 6
    Intake manifold, 114

Engine (*continued*)
  Main bearings, 156
  Oil pan, 133
  Oil pump, 135
  Overhaul tips, 95
  Piston pin, 149
  Pistons, 146, 150, 151
  Rear main seal, 153
  Removal and installation, 103
  Rings, 146, 150, 151
  Rocker cover, 112
  Rocker shafts and studs, 112
  Spark plug wires, 63
  Specifications, 79
  Thermostat, 114
  Timing belt, 139
  Timing chain and gears, 141
  Tools, 2
  Troubleshooting, 96
  Turbocharger, 118
  Valve guides, 132
  Valves, 129
  Valve seats, 132
  Valve springs, 129
  Valve stem oil seals, 132
  Water pump, 120
Evaporative canister, 13
Evaporator, 243
Exhaust pipe, 160
Exhaust system, 160

F

Filters
  Air, 10
  Crankcase, 12, 164
  Fuel, 10
  Oil, 40
Firing orders, 63
Fluids and lubricants
  Automatic transmission, 41
  Battery, 13
  Chassis greasing, 46
  Coolant, 44
  Drive axle, 43
  Engine oil, 37
  Fuel, 37
  Manual transmission, 40
  Master cylinder
    Brake, 45
    Clutch, 45
  Power steering pump, 46
  Steering knuckle, 46
  Transfer case, 41
Flywheel and ring gear, 160
Front bumper, 444
Front drive axle
  Application chart, 370
  Axle shaft, bearing and seal, 370
  Fluid recommendations, 44
  Front hub and wheel bearings, 375
  Lubricant level, 44
  Pinion seal and yoke, 371
  Removal and installation, 372
Front brakes, 410
Front hubs, 375
Front suspension
  Ball joints, 379, 380
  Knuckles, 380
  Lower control arm, 379
  Shock absorbers, 378
  Springs, 377
  Stabilizer bar, 377
  Track bar, 378
  Troubleshooting, 378
  Upper control arm, 379
Front wheel bearings, 47
Fuel injection
  Coolant temperature sensor, 220
  Description, 199, 208
  Diagnosis, 202, 216
  Fuel body, 206
  Fuel pressure regulator, 206
  Fuel pump, 205, 219
  Idle speed actuator motor, 207, 223
  Injectors, 207, 222
  Knock sensor, 220
  MAP sensor, 220
  MAT sensor, 220
  Relieving fuel system pressure, 219
  Testing, 202, 216
  Throttle body, 205, 219
  Throttle position sensor, 207, 221
Fuel filter, 10
Fuel lines, 207, 223
Fuel pump, 181, 205, 219
Fuel system
  Carbureted, 181
  Diesel, 223
  Fuel injection, 199
Fuel tank, 228
Fuses and circuit breakers, 252
Fusible links, 252

G

Gearshift linkage adjustment, 312
Glossary, 454
Grille, 444

H

Headlights, 250
Headliner, 451
Heater
  Blower, 241
  Control panel, 244
  Core, 241
History, 6
Hoisting, 55
Hood, 435
Hoses
  Coolant, 21
  Fuel, 207, 223

INDEX

How to Use This Book, 1
Hubs, 375

I

Identification
    Axle, 10
    Engine, 6, 9
    Model, 6
    Serial number, 6
    Transfer case, 9
    Transmission
        Automatic, 10
        Manual, 9
    Vehicle, 7
Idle speed and mixture adjustment, 75
Ignition
    Coil, 83
    Electronic, 63
    Lock cylinder, 385
    Module, 83
    Switch, 386
    Timing, 72
Injection pump, 223
Injection timing, 226
Injectors, fuel, 202, 222, 225
Instrument cluster, 247
Instrument panel
    Cluster, 247
    Panel removal, 247
    Radio, 249
    Speedometer cable, 248
Intake manifold, 114

J

Jacking points, 55
Jump starting, 53-54

K

Knuckles, 380

L

Lighting
    Headlights, 250
    Signal and marker lights, 250
Liftgate, 437
Liftgate glass, 440
Lower ball joint, 380
Lubrication
    Automatic transmission, 43
    Chassis, 46
    Differential, 44
    Engine, 37
    Manual transmission, 40
    Transfer case, 41

M

Main bearings, 156
Maintenance intervals, 58

Manifolds
    Intake, 114
    Exhaust, 117
Manual steering gear
    Adjustments, 388
    Removal and installation, 387
    Troubleshooting, 397
Manual transmission
    Application chart, 258
    Operation, 258
    Overhaul, 262-300
    Removal and installation, 258
    Troubleshooting, 259
Marker lights, 250
Master cylinder
    Brake, 405
    Clutch, 304
Mechanic's data, 452
Model identification, 6
Module (ignition), 83
Muffler, 163
Multi-function switch, 249

N

Neutral safety switch, 314

O

Oil and fuel recommendations, 37
Oil and filter change (engine), 40
Oil level check
    Engine, 39
    Transfer case, 41
    Transmission
        Manual, 40
Oil pan, 133
Oil pump, 135
Outside vehicle maintenance, 46
Oxygen (O_2) sensor, 171, 200

P

Parking brake, 418
Piston pin, 149
Pistons, 146, 150, 151
Pitman arm, 392
Pivot pins, 380
PCV valve, 12, 164
Power brake booster, 408, 429
Power seat motor, 450
Power steering gear
    Adjustments, 388
    Removal and installation, 388
    Troubleshooting, 398
Power steering pump
    Removal and installation, 391
    Troubleshooting, 400
Power windows, 450
Preventive Maintenance Charts, 58
Pushing, 56

R

Radiator, 119
Radiator cap, 45
Radio, 249
Rear axle
    Axle shaft, 368
    Axle shaft bearing, 369
    Fluid recommendations, 44
    Identification, 370
    Lubricant level, 44
    Operation, 367
    Pinion oil seal, 369
    Ratios, 367
    Removal and installation, 370
Rear brakes, 417
Rear bumper, 444
Rear main oil seal, 153
Rear suspension
    Shock absorbers, 381
    Springs, 380
    Sway bar, 382
    Troubleshooting, 378
Regulator, 88
Rings, 146, 150, 151
Rocker arms or shaft, 112
Rotor (Brake disc), 415
Routine maintenance, 10

S

Safety notice, 4
Serial number location, 6
Shock absorbers, 378, 381
Slave cylinder, 304
Spark plugs, 60
Spark plug wires, 63
Special tools, 2
Specifications Charts
    Brakes, 403
    Camshaft, 79
    Capacities, 58
    Carburetor, 182, 188
    Crankshaft and connecting rod, 79
    Fastener markings and torque standards, 104
    General engine, 80
    Piston and ring, 80
    Preventive maintenance, 58
    Torque, 81
    Tune-up, 60
    Valves, 80
    Wheel alignment, 401
Speedometer cable, 248
Springs, 377, 380
Stain removal, 437
Starter
    Overhaul, 90
    Removal and installation, 89
    Troubleshooting, 88-89
Steering column, 387
Steering gear
    Manual, 387
    Power, 388

Steering knuckles, 380
Steering linkage
    Center link/Connecting rod/Drag link, 393
    Pitman arm, 392
    Tie rod ends, 392
Steering lock, 385
Steering wheel, 384
Stripped threads, 101
Switches
    Back-up light, 314
    Headlight, 249
    Ignition switch, 386
    Rear window wiper, 249
    Windshield wiper, 249

T

Tailgate, 436
Tailpipe, 163
Thermostat, 114
Throttle body, 205, 219
Tie rod ends, 392
Timing (ignition), 72
Timing belt, 139
Timing chain and gears, 141
Timing gear cover, 136
Tires
    Description, 32
    Rotation, 35
    Troubleshooting, 35
    Wear problems, 33
Toe-in, 383
Tools, 2
Torque specifications, 81
Towing, 56
Trailer towing, 56
Transfer Case
    Application chart, 316
    Adjustments, 318
    Overhaul, 319-362
    Removal and installation, 316
Transmission
    Automatic, 304
    Manual, 258
    Routine maintenance, 40
Trouble codes, 177
Troubleshooting Charts
    Air conditioning, 26-30
    Automatic transmission, 305
    Charging system, 86
    Clutch, 301
    Cooling system, 98
    Drive belts, 100
    Driveshaft, 361
    Engine mechanical, 96
    Gauges, 255
    Heater, 257
    Ignition switch, 396
    Lights, 256
    Lockup torque converter, 306
    Manual steering gear, 397
    Manual transmission, 259
    Power steering gear, 398

Power steering pump, 400
Rear axle, 361
Steering and suspension, 378
Steering column, 393
Tires, 35
Transfer case, 259
Transmission fluid indications, 305
Turn signals and flashers, 254
Turn signal switch, 395
Wheels, 35
Windshield wipers, 253
Tune-up
   Distributor, 83
   Idle speed, 75
   Ignition timing, 72
   Procedures, 60
   Spark plugs and wires, 60
   Specifications, 60
Turbocharger, 118
Turn signal switch, 385

U

U-joints, 365
Understanding the manual transmission, 258
Upper ball joint, 379
Upper control arm, 379

V

Vacuum diagrams, 178
Valve guides, 132
Valve lash adjustment, 74
Valve seats, 132
Valve service, 129
Valve specifications, 80
Valve springs, 129
Vehicle identification, 6

W

Water pump, 120
Wheel alignment, 382
Wheel bearings
   Front drive axle, 370
   Front wheel, 47
   Rear wheel, 369
Wheel cylinders, 418
Wheels, 35
Window glass, 438
Window regulator, 438
Windshield, 438
Windshield wipers
   Arm, 245
   Blade, 32
   Linkage, 246
   Motor, 245
   Rear window wiper, 246
   Rear window wiper switch, 249
   Windshield wiper switch, 249
Wiring
   Spark plug, 63
   Trailer, 252

Chilton's Repair & Tune-Up Guides

The Complete line covers domestic cars, imports, trucks, vans, RV's and 4-wheel drive vehicles.

RTUG Title	Part No.
AMC 1975-82	7199
Covers all U.S. and Canadian models	
Aspen/Volare 1976-80	6637
Covers all U.S. and Canadian models	
Audi 1970-73	5902
Covers all U.S. and Canadian models.	
Audi 4000/5000 1978-81	7028
Covers all U.S. and Canadian models including turbocharged and diesel engines	
Barracuda/Challenger 1965-72	5807
Covers all U.S. and Canadian models	
Blazer/Jimmy 1969-82	6931
Covers all U.S. and Canadian 2- and 4-wheel drive models, including diesel engines	
BMW 1970-82	6844
Covers U.S. and Canadian models	
Buick/Olds/Pontiac 1975-85	7308
Covers all U.S. and Canadian full size rear wheel drive models	
Cadillac 1967-84	7462
Covers all U.S. and Canadian rear wheel drive models	
Camaro 1967-81	6735
Covers all U.S. and Canadian models	
Camaro 1982-85	7317
Covers all U.S. and Canadian models	
Capri 1970-77	6695
Covers all U.S. and Canadian models	
Caravan/Voyager 1984-85	7482
Covers all U.S. and Canadian models	
Century/Regal 1975-85	7307
Covers all U.S. and Canadian rear wheel drive models, including turbocharged engines	
Champ/Arrow/Sapporo 1978-83	7041
Covers all U.S. and Canadian models	
Chevette/1000 1976-86	6836
Covers all U.S. and Canadian models	
Chevrolet 1968-85	7135
Covers all U.S. and Canadian models	
Chevrolet 1968-79 Spanish	7082
Chevrolet/GMC Pick-Ups 1970-82 Spanish	7468
Chevrolet/GMC Pick-Ups and Suburban 1970-86	6936
Covers all U.S. and Canadian 1/2, 3/4 and 1 ton models, including 4-wheel drive and diesel engines	
Chevrolet LUV 1972-81	6815
Covers all U.S. and Canadian models	
Chevrolet Mid-Size 1964-86	6840
Covers all U.S. and Canadian models of 1964-77 Chevelle, Malibu and Malibu SS; 1974-77 Laguna; 1978-85 Malibu; 1970-86 Monte Carlo; 1964-84 El Camino, including diesel engines	
Chevrolet Nova 1986	7658
Covers all U.S. and Canadian models	
Chevy/GMC Vans 1967-84	6930
Covers all U.S. and Canadian models of 1/2, 3/4, and 1 ton vans, cutaways, and motor home chassis, including diesel engines	
Chevy S-10 Blazer/GMC S-15 Jimmy 1982-85	7383
Covers all U.S. and Canadian models	
Chevy S-10/GMC S-15 Pick-Ups 1982-85	7310
Covers all U.S. and Canadian models	
Chevy II/Nova 1962-79	6841
Covers all U.S. and Canadian models	
Chrysler K- and E-Car 1981-85	7163
Covers all U.S. and Canadian front wheel drive models	
Colt/Challenger/Vista/Conquest 1971-85	7037
Covers all U.S. and Canadian models	
Corolla/Carina/Tercel/Starlet 1970-85	7036
Covers all U.S. and Canadian models	
Corona/Cressida/Crown/Mk.II/Camry/Van 1970-84	7044
Covers all U.S. and Canadian models	

RTUG Title	Part No.
Corvair 1960-69	6691
Covers all U.S. and Canadian models	
Corvette 1953-62	6576
Covers all U.S. and Canadian models	
Corvette 1963-84	6843
Covers all U.S. and Canadian models	
Cutlass 1970-85	6933
Covers all U.S. and Canadian models	
Dart/Demon 1968-76	6324
Covers all U.S. and Canadian models	
Datsun 1961-72	5790
Covers all U.S. and Canadian models of Nissan Patrol; 1500, 1600 and 2000 sports cars; Pick-Ups; 410, 411, 510, 1200 and 240Z	
Datsun 1973-80 Spanish	7083
Datsun/Nissan F-10, 310, Stanza, Pulsar 1977-86	7196
Covers all U.S. and Canadian models	
Datsun/Nissan Pick-Ups 1970-84	6816
Covers all U.S and Canadian models	
Datsun/Nissan Z & ZX 1970-86	6932
Covers all U.S. and Canadian models	
Datsun/Nissan 1200, 210, Sentra 1973-86	7197
Covers all U.S. and Canadian models	
Datsun/Nissan 200SX, 510, 610, 710, 810, Maxima 1973-84	7170
Covers all U.S. and Canadian models	
Dodge 1968-77	6554
Covers all U.S. and Canadian models	
Dodge Charger 1967-70	6486
Covers all U.S. and Canadian models	
Dodge/Plymouth Trucks 1967-84	7459
Covers all 1/2, 3/4, and 1 ton 2- and 4-wheel drive U.S. and Canadian models, including diesel engines	
Dodge/Plymouth Vans 1967-84	6934
Covers all 1/2, 3/4, and 1 ton U.S. and Canadian models of vans, cutaways and motor home chassis	
D-50/Arrow Pick-Up 1979-81	7032
Covers all U.S. and Canadian models	
Fairlane/Torino 1962-75	6320
Covers all U.S. and Canadian models	
Fairmont/Zephyr 1978-83	6965
Covers all U.S. and Canadian models	
Fiat 1969-81	7042
Covers all U.S. and Canadian models	
Fiesta 1978-80	6846
Covers all U.S. and Canadian models	
Firebird 1967-81	5996
Covers all U.S. and Canadian models	
Firebird 1982-85	7345
Covers all U.S. and Canadian models	
Ford 1968-79 Spanish	7084
Ford Bronco 1966-83	7140
Covers all U.S. and Canadian models	
Ford Bronco II 1984	7408
Covers all U.S. and Canadian models	
Ford Courier 1972-82	6983
Covers all U.S. and Canadian models	
Ford/Mercury Front Wheel Drive 1981-85	7055
Covers all U.S. and Canadian models Escort, EXP, Tempo, Lynx, LN-7 and Topaz	
Ford/Mercury/Lincoln 1968-85	6842
Covers all U.S. and Canadian models of FORD Country Sedan, Country Squire, Crown Victoria, Custom, Custom 500, Galaxie 500, LTD through 1982, Ranch Wagon and XL; MERCURY Colony Park, Commuter, Marquis through 1982, Gran Marquis, Monterey and Park Lane; LINCOLN Continental and Towne Car	
Ford/Mercury/Lincoln Mid-Size 1971-85	6696
Covers all U.S. and Canadian models of FORD Elite, 1983-85 LTD, 1977-79 LTD II, Ranchero, Torino, Gran Torino, 1977-85 Thunderbird; MERCURY 1972-85 Cougar,	

continued on next page

RTUG Title	Part No.
1983-85 Marquis, Montego, 1980-85 XR-7; LINCOLN 1982-85 Continental, 1984-85 Mark VII, 1978-80 Versailles	
Ford Pick-Ups 1965-86 Covers all 1/2, 3/4 and 1 ton, 2- and 4-wheel drive U.S. and Canadian pick-up, chassis cab and camper models, including diesel engines	6913
Ford Pick-Ups 1965-82 Spanish	7469
Ford Ranger 1983-84 Covers all U.S. and Canadian models	7338
Ford Vans 1961-86 Covers all U.S. and Canadian 1/2, 3/4 and 1 ton van and cutaway chassis models, including diesel engines	6849
GM A-Body 1982-85 Covers all front wheel drive U.S. and Canadian models of BUICK Century, CHEVROLET Celebrity, OLDSMOBILE Cutlass Ciera and PONTIAC 6000	7309
GM C-Body 1985 Covers all front wheel drive U.S. and Canadian models of BUICK Electra Park Avenue and Electra T-Type, CADILLAC Fleetwood and deVille, OLDSMOBILE 98 Regency and Regency Brougham	7587
GM J-Car 1982-85 Covers all U.S. and Canadian models of BUICK Skyhawk, CHEVROLET Cavalier, CADILLAC Cimarron, OLDSMOBILE Firenza and PONTIAC 2000 and Sunbird	7059
GM N-Body 1985-86 Covers all U.S. and Canadian models of front wheel drive BUICK Somerset and Skylark, OLDSMOBILE Calais, and PONTIAC Grand Am	7657
GM X-Body 1980-85 Covers all U.S. and Canadian models of BUICK Skylark, CHEVROLET Citation, OLDSMOBILE Omega and PONTIAC Phoenix	7049
GM Subcompact 1971-80 Covers all U.S. and Canadian models of BUICK Skyhawk (1975-80), CHEVROLET Vega and Monza, OLDSMOBILE Starfire, and PONTIAC Astre and 1975-80 Sunbird	6935
Granada/Monarch 1975-82 Covers all U.S. and Canadian models	6937
Honda 1973-84 Covers all U.S. and Canadian models	6980
International Scout 1967-73 Covers all U.S. and Canadian models	5912
Jeep 1945-87 Covers all U.S. and Canadian CJ-2A, CJ-3A, CJ-3B, CJ-5, CJ-6, CJ-7, Scrambler and Wrangler models	6817
Jeep Wagoneer, Commando, Cherokee, Truck 1957-86 Covers all U.S. and Canadian models of Wagoneer, Cherokee, Grand Wagoneer, Jeepster, Jeepster Commando, J-100, J-200, J-300, J-10, J20, FC-150 and FC-170	6739
Laser/Daytona 1984-85 Covers all U.S. and Canadian models	7563
Maverick/Comet 1970-77 Covers all U.S. and Canadian models	6634
Mazda 1971-84 Covers all U.S. and Canadian models of RX-2, RX-3, RX-4, 808, 1300, 1600, Cosmo, GLC and 626	6981
Mazda Pick-Ups 1972-86 Covers all U.S. and Canadian models	7659
Mercedes-Benz 1959-70 Covers all U.S. and Canadian models	6065
Mereceds-Benz 1968-73 Covers all U.S. and Canadian models	5907

RTUG Title	Part No.
Mercedes-Benz 1974-84 Covers all U.S. and Canadian models	6809
Mitsubishi, Cordia, Tredia, Starion, Galant 1983-85 Covers all U.S. and Canadian models	7583
MG 1961-81 Covers all U.S. and Canadian models	6780
Mustang/Capri/Merkur 1979-85 Covers all U.S. and Canadian models	6963
Mustang/Cougar 1965-73 Covers all U.S. and Canadian models	6542
Mustang II 1974-78 Covers all U.S. and Canadian models	6812
Omni/Horizon/Rampage 1978-84 Covers all U.S. and Canadian models of DODGE omni, Miser, 024, Charger 2.2; PLYMOUTH Horizon, Miser, TC3, TC3 Tourismo; Rampage	6845
Opel 1971-75 Covers all U.S. and Canadian models	6575
Peugeot 1970-74 Covers all U.S. and Canadian models	5982
Pinto/Bobcat 1971-80 Covers all U.S. and Canadian models	7027
Plymouth 1968-76 Covers all U.S. and Canadian models	6552
Pontiac Fiero 1984-85 Covers all U.S. and Canadian models	7571
Pontiac Mid-Size 1974-83 Covers all U.S. and Canadian models of Ventura, Grand Am, LeMans, Grand LeMans, GTO, Phoenix, and Grand Prix	7346
Porsche 924/928 1976-81 Covers all U.S. and Canadian models	7048
Renault 1975-85 Covers all U.S. and Canadian models	7165
Roadrunner/Satellite/Belvedere/GTX 1968-73 Covers all U.S. and Canadian models	5821
RX-7 1979-81 Covers all U.S. and Canadian models	7031
SAAB 99 1969-75 Covers all U.S. and Canadian models	5988
SAAB 900 1979-85 Covers all U.S. and Canadian models	7572
Snowmobiles 1976-80 Covers Arctic Cat, John Deere, Kawasaki, Polaris, Ski-Doo and Yamaha	6978
Subaru 1970-84 Covers all U.S. and Canadian models	6982
Tempest/GTO/LeMans 1968-73 Covers all U.S. and Canadian models	5905
Toyota 1966-70 Covers all U.S. and Canadian models of Corona, MkII, Corolla, Crown, Land Cruiser, Stout and Hi-Lux	5795
Toyota 1970-79 Spanish	7467
Toyota Celica/Supra 1971-85 Covers all U.S. and Canadian models	7043
Toyota Trucks 1970-85 Covers all U.S. and Canadian models of pick-ups, Land Cruiser and 4Runner	7035
Valiant/Duster 1968-76 Covers all U.S. and Canadian models	6326
Volvo 1956-69 Covers all U.S. and Canadian models	6529
Volvo 1970-83 Covers all U.S. and Canadian models	7040
VW Front Wheel Drive 1974-85 Covers all U.S. and Canadian models	6962
VW 1949-71 Covers all U.S. and Canadian models	5796
VW 1970-79 Spanish	7081
VW 1970-81 Covers all U.S. and Canadian Beetles, Karmann Ghia, Fastback, Squareback, Vans, 411 and 412	6837

Chilton's Repair & Tune-Up Guides are available at your local retailer or by mailing a check or money order for **$13.95** plus **$3.25** to cover postage and handling to:

Chilton Book Company
Dept. DM
Radnor, PA 19089

NOTE: When ordering be sure to include your name & address, book part No. & title.